TABLE B.2
(*concluded*)
**Percentiles
of the *t*
Distribution.**

				A			
ν	.98	.985	.99	.9925	.995	.9975	.9995
1	15.895	21.205	31.821	42.434	63.657	127.322	636.590
2	4.849	5.643	6.965	8.073	9.925	14.089	31.598
3	3.482	3.896	4.541	5.047	5.841	7.453	12.924
4	2.999	3.298	3.747	4.088	4.604	5.598	8.610
5	2.757	3.003	3.365	3.634	4.032	4.773	6.869
6	2.612	2.829	3.143	3.372	3.707	4.317	5.959
7	2.517	2.715	2.998	3.203	3.499	4.029	5.408
8	2.449	2.634	2.896	3.085	3.355	3.833	5.041
9	2.398	2.574	2.821	2.998	3.250	3.690	4.781
10	2.359	2.527	2.764	2.932	3.169	3.581	4.587
11	2.328	2.491	2.718	2.879	3.106	3.497	4.437
12	2.303	2.461	2.681	2.836	3.055	3.428	4.318
13	2.282	2.436	2.650	2.801	3.012	3.372	4.221
14	2.264	2.415	2.624	2.771	2.977	3.326	4.140
15	2.249	2.397	2.602	2.746	2.947	3.286	4.073
16	2.235	2.382	2.583	2.724	2.921	3.252	4.015
17	2.224	2.368	2.567	2.706	2.898	3.222	3.965
18	2.214	2.356	2.552	2.689	2.878	3.197	3.922
19	2.205	2.346	2.539	2.674	2.861	3.174	3.883
20	2.197	2.336	2.528	2.661	2.845	3.153	3.849
21	2.189	2.328	2.518	2.649	2.831	3.135	3.819
22	2.183	2.320	2.508	2.639	2.819	3.119	3.792
23	2.177	2.313	2.500	2.629	2.807	3.104	3.768
24	2.172	2.307	2.492	2.620	2.797	3.091	3.745
25	2.167	2.301	2.485	2.612	2.787	3.078	3.725
26	2.162	2.296	2.479	2.605	2.779	3.067	3.707
27	2.158	2.291	2.473	2.598	2.771	3.057	3.690
28	2.154	2.286	2.467	2.592	2.763	3.047	3.674
29	2.150	2.282	2.462	2.586	2.756	3.038	3.659
30	2.147	2.278	2.457	2.581	2.750	3.030	3.646
40	2.123	2.250	2.423	2.542	2.704	2.971	3.551
60	2.099	2.223	2.390	2.504	2.660	2.915	3.460
120	2.076	2.196	2.358	2.468	2.617	2.860	3.373
∞	2.054	2.170	2.326	2.432	2.576	2.807	3.291

The McGraw-Hill/Irwin Series: Operations and Decision Sciences

Applied Linear Regression Models

Fourth Edition

Michael H. Kutner
Emory University

Christopher J. Nachtsheim
University of Minnesota

John Neter
University of Georgia

Boston   Burr Ridge, IL   Dubuque, IA   Madison, WI   New York   San Francisco   St. Louis
Bangkok   Bogotá   Caracas   Kuala Lumpur   Lisbon   London   Madrid   Mexico City
Milan   Montreal   New Delhi   Santiago   Seoul   Singapore   Sydney   Taipei   Toronto

The McGraw·Hill Companies

APPLIED LINEAR REGRESSION MODELS
International Edition 2008

10 09 08 07 06 05 04 03 02 01
20 09 08
CTF   BJE

When ordering this title, use ISBN: 978-007-127480-7 or MHID: 007-127480-4

Printed in Singapore

www.mhhe.com

To
Nancy, Michelle, Allison,
Maureen, Abigael, Andrew, Henry G.,
Dorothy, Ron, David

Preface

Linear regression models are widely used today in business administration, economics, engineering, and the social, health, and biological sciences. Successful applications of these models require a sound understanding of both the underlying theory and the practical problems that are encountered in using the models in real-life situations. While *Applied Linear Regression Models,* Fourth Edition, is basically an applied book, it seeks to blend theory and applications effectively, avoiding the extremes of presenting theory in isolation and of giving elements of applications without the needed understanding of the theoretical foundations.

The fourth edition differs from the third in a number of important respects.

1. We have reorganized the chapters for better clarity and flow of topics. Material from the old Chapter 15 on normal correlation models has been integrated throughout the text where appropriate. Much of the material is now found in an expanded Chapter 2, which focuses on inference in regression analysis. Material from the old Chapter 7 pertaining to polynomial and interaction regression models and from old Chapter 11 on qualitative predictors has been integrated into a new Chapter 8 called, "Regression Models for Quantitative and Qualitative Predictors." Material on model validation from old Chapter 10 is now fully integrated with updated material on model selection in a new Chapter 9 entitled, "Building the Regression Model I: Model Selection and Validation."

2. We have added material on important techniques for data mining, including regression trees and neural network models, in Chapters 11 and 13, respectively.

3. We have made extensive revisions to the problem material. Problem data sets are generally larger and more challenging, and we have included a large number of new case data sets in Appendix C. In addition, we have added a new category of chapter exercises, called Case Studies. These are open-ended problems that require students, given an overall objective, to carry out complete analyses of the various case data sets in Appendix C. They are distinct from the material in the Problems and Projects sections, which frequently ask students to simply carry out specific analytical procedures.

4. The chapter on logistic regression (Chapter 14) has been extensively revised and expanded to include a more thorough treatment of logistic, probit, and complementary log-log models, logistic regression residuals, model selection, model assessment, logistic regression diagnostics, and goodness of fit tests. We have also developed new material on polytomous (multicategory) nominal logistic regression models and polytomous ordinal logistic regression models.

5. We have expanded the discussion of model selection methods and criteria. The Akaike information criterion and Schwarz Bayesian criterion have been added, and a greater emphasis is placed on the use of cross-validation for model selection and validation.

6. We have substantially expanded the amount of graphic presentation, including much greater use of scatter plot matrices, three-dimensional rotating plots, three-dimensional response surface and contour plots, and conditional effects plots.

7. Throughout the text, we have made extensive revisions in the exposition on the basis of classroom experience to improve the clarity of the presentation.

We have included in this book not only the more conventional topics in regression, but also topics that are frequently slighted, though important in practice. We devote three chapters (Chapter 9–11) to the model-building process for regression, including computer-assisted selection procedures for identifying good subsets of predictor variables and validation of the chosen regression model. Two chapters (Chapters 8 and 14) are devoted to indicator variables, covering both response and predictor indicator variables. The use of residual analysis and other diagnostics for examining the appropriateness of a regression model is a recurring theme throughout this book. So is the use of remedial measures that may be helpful when the model is not appropriate. In the analysis of the results of a study, we give greater emphasis to the use of estimation procedures than to significance tests, because estimation is often more meaningful in practice. Also, since practical problems seldom are concerned with a single inference, we stress the use of simultaneous inference procedures.

Theoretical ideas are presented to the degree needed for good understanding in making sound applications. Proofs are given in those instances where we feel they serve to demonstrate an important method of approach. Emphasis is placed on a thorough understanding of the regression models, particularly the meaning of the model parameters, since such understanding is basic to proper applications. A wide variety of examples and cases is presented to illustrate the use of the theoretical principles, to show the great diversity of applications of regression models, and to demonstrate how analyses are carried out for different problems.

We use "Comments" sections in each chapter to present additional discussion and matters related to the mainstream of development. In this way, the basic ideas in a chapter are presented concisely and without distraction.

Applications of regression models frequently require extensive computations. We take the position that a computer is available in most applied work and that almost every computer user has access to program packages for regression analysis. Hence, we explain the basic mathematical steps in fitting a regression model but do not dwell on computational details. This approach permits us to avoid many complex formulas and enables us to focus on basic principles. We make extensive use in this text of computer capabilities for performing computations and preparing graphic plots, and we illustrate a variety of computer printouts and plots and explain how they are used for analysis.

A selection of problems is provided at the end of each chapter. Here readers can reinforce their understanding of the methodology and use the concepts learned to analyze data. We have been careful to supply data-analysis problems that typify genuine applications. In most problems the calculations are best handled on a computer. To facilitate data entry, a compact disk is provided with the text that includes the data sets for all examples, problems, exercises, projects, and case studies, as well as for the data sets in Appendix C. The README.TXT file on the compact disk provides information about the identification of the data sets.

We assume that the reader of *Applied Linear Regression Models,* Fourth Edition, has had an introductory course in statistical inference, covering the material outlined in Appendix A. Should some gaps in the reader's background exist, the relevant portions of an introductory text can be studied, or the instructor of the class may use supplemental materials for covering the missing segments. Appendix A is primarily intended as a reference of basic statistical results for continuing use as the reader progresses through the book.

Calculus is not required for reading *Applied Linear Regression Models,* Fourth Edition. In a number of instances, we use calculus to demonstrate how some important results are obtained, but these demonstrations are confined to supplementary comments and can be omitted without any loss of continuity. Readers who do know calculus will find these comments in natural sequence so that the benefits of the mathematical developments are obtained in their immediate context. Some basic elements of matrix algebra are needed for multiple regression. Chapter 5 introduces these elements of matrix algebra in the context of simple regression for easy learning.

Applied Linear Regression Models, Fourth Edition, is intended for use in undergraduate and graduate courses in regression analysis and in second courses in applied statistics. The extent to which material presented in this text is used in a particular course depends upon the amount of time available and the objectives of the course. The basic elements of regression are covered in Chapters 1, 2, 3, 4 (Sections 4.1–4.3), 5, 6, 7, 8, 9, and 10. Chapters 11, 12, 13, and 14 can be covered as time permits and interests dictate.

This book can also be used for self-study by persons engaged in the fields of business administration, economics, engineering, and the social, health, and biological sciences who desire to obtain competence in the application of regression models.

An *Instructor Solutions Manual,* containing detailed solutions to all numerical problems and analytical exercises, is available from the publisher, McGraw-Hill/Irwin, for use by instructors.

A *Student Solutions Manual* is included on the compact disk for use by students. The Student Solutions Manual provides intermediate and final numerical results for easy self-checking of solutions for selected problems. We use an asterisk (*) in front of the problem number to designate the problems for which the solutions appear in the Student Solutions Manual.

Available new for this Fourth Edition is a *SAS and SPSS Program Solution Manual* for examples contained in the text. The manual was prepared by Dr. William Replogle and Dr. William Johnson, both of the University of Mississippi Medical School. The manual uses data files to present solutions, output, and discussion of necessary steps for students to solve examples selected from the book using SAS and SPSS.

The *Student Solutions Manual* and all of the data files on the compact disk can also be downloaded from the book's website at: www.mhhe.com/KutnerALRM4e. A list of errata for the book as well as some useful, related links will also be maintained at this address.

A book such as this cannot be written without substantial assistance from numerous persons. We are indebted to the many contributors who have developed the theory and practice discussed in this book. We also would like to acknowledge appreciation to our students, who helped us in a variety of ways to fashion the method of presentation contained herein. We are grateful to the many users of *Applied Linear Statistical Models* and *Applied Linear Regression Models,* who have provided us with comments and suggestions based on their teaching with these texts. We are also indebted to Professors James E. Holstein, University of Missouri, and David L. Sherry, University of West Florida, for their review of *Applied Linear Statistical Models,* First Edition; to Professors Samuel Kotz, University of Maryland at College Park, Ralph P. Russo, University of Iowa, and Peter F. Thall, The George Washington University, for their review of *Applied Linear Regression Models,* First Edition; to Professors John S. Y Chiu, University of Washington, James A. Calvin, University of Iowa, and Michael F. Driscoll, Arizona State University, for their review of *Applied Linear Statistical Models,* Second Edition; to Professor Richard Anderson-Sprecher, University of Wyoming, for his review of *Applied Linear Regression Models,* Second Edition; and to Professors Alexander von Eye, The Pennsylvania State University, Samuel Kotz, University of

Maryland at College Park, and John B. Willett, Harvard University, for their review of *Applied Linear Statistical Models,* Third Edition; to Professors Jason Abrevaya, University of Chicago, Frank Alt, University of Maryland, Vitoria Chen, Georgia Tech, Rebecca Doerge, Purdue University, Mark Henry, Clemson University, Jim Hobert, University of Florida, Ken Koehler, Iowa State University, Chii-Dean Lin, University of Massachusetts Amherst, Mark Reiser, Arizona State University, Lawrence Ries, University of Missouri Columbia, and Ehsan Soofi, University of Wisconsin Milwaukee, for their reviews of *Applied Linear Regression Models,* Third Edition, or *Applied Linear Statistical Models,* Fourth Edition. These reviews provided many important suggestions, for which we are most grateful.

In addition, valuable assistance was provided by Professors Richard K. Burdick, Arizona State University, R. Dennis Cook, University of Minnesota, W. J. Conover, Texas Tech University, Mark E. Johnson, University of Central Florida, Dick DeVeaux, Williams College, and by Drs. Richard I. Beckman, Los Alamos National Laboratory, Ronald L. Iman, Sandia National Laboratories, and Brad Jones, SAS Institute. We are most appreciative of their willing help. We are also indebted to the 88 participants in a survey concerning *Applied Linear Regression Models,* Second Edition, the 76 participants in a survey concerning *Applied Linear Statistical Models,* Third Edition, and the 73 participants in a survey concerning *Applied Linear Regression Models,* Third Edition, or *Applied Linear Statistical Models,* Fourth Edition. Helpful suggestions were received in these surveys, for which we are thankful.

Weiyong Zhang and Vincent Agboto assisted us in the development of new problem material, and Lexin Li and Yingwen Dong prepared the revised *Instructor Solutions Manual* and *Student Solutions Manual* under considerable time pressure. Amy Hendrickson provided much-needed LaTeX expertise. We are most grateful to these individuals for their invaluable help and assistance. We also wish to thank the various members of the Carlson Executive MBA Program classes of 2003 and 2004, notably Mike Ohmes, Trevor Bynum, Baxter Stephenson, Zakir Salyani, Sanders Marvin, Trent Spurgeon, Nate Ogzawalla, David Mott, Preston McKenzie, Bruce DeJong, and Tim Kensok, for their contributions of interesting and relevant case study data and materials.

Finally, our families bore patiently the pressures caused by our commitment to complete this revision. We are appreciative of their understanding.

Michael H. Kutner

Christopher J. Nachtsheim

John Neter

Contents

Part I

Simple Linear Regression

Chapter 1

Linear Regression with One Predictor Variable

Regression analysis is a statistical methodology that utilizes the relation between two or more quantitative variables so that a response or outcome variable can be predicted from the other, or others. This methodology is widely used in business, the social and behavioral sciences, the biological sciences, and many other disciplines. A few examples of applications are:

1. Sales of a product can be predicted by utilizing the relationship between sales and amount of advertising expenditures.
2. The performance of an employee on a job can be predicted by utilizing the relationship between performance and a battery of aptitude tests.
3. The size of the vocabulary of a child can be predicted by utilizing the relationship between size of vocabulary and age of the child and amount of education of the parents.
4. The length of hospital stay of a surgical patient can be predicted by utilizing the relationship between the time in the hospital and the severity of the operation.

In Part I we take up regression analysis when a single predictor variable is used for predicting the response or outcome variable of interest. In Parts II and III, we consider regression analysis when two or more variables are used for making predictions. In this chapter, we consider the basic ideas of regression analysis and discuss the estimation of the parameters of regression models containing a single predictor variable.

1.1 Relations between Variables

The concept of a relation between two variables, such as between family income and family expenditures for housing, is a familiar one. We distinguish between a *functional relation* and a *statistical relation,* and consider each of these in turn.

Functional Relation between Two Variables

A functional relation between two variables is expressed by a mathematical formula. If X denotes the *independent variable* and Y the *dependent variable,* a functional relation is

FIGURE 1.1
Example of
Functional
Relation.

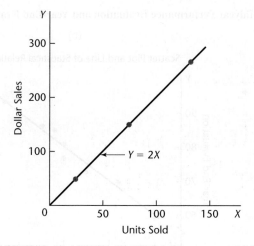

of the form:

$$Y = f(X)$$

Given a particular value of X, the function f indicates the corresponding value of Y.

Example

Consider the relation between dollar sales (Y) of a product sold at a fixed price and number of units sold (X). If the selling price is $2 per unit, the relation is expressed by the equation:

$$Y = 2X$$

This functional relation is shown in Figure 1.1. Number of units sold and dollar sales during three recent periods (while the unit price remained constant at $2) were as follows:

Period	Number of Units Sold	Dollar Sales
1	75	$150
2	25	50
3	130	260

These observations are plotted also in Figure 1.1. Note that all fall directly on the line of functional relationship. This is characteristic of all functional relations.

Statistical Relation between Two Variables

A statistical relation, unlike a functional relation, is not a perfect one. In general, the observations for a statistical relation do not fall directly on the curve of relationship.

Example 1

Performance evaluations for 10 employees were obtained at midyear and at year-end. These data are plotted in Figure 1.2a. Year-end evaluations are taken as the *dependent* or *response variable Y*, and midyear evaluations as the *independent, explanatory,* or *predictor*

FIGURE 1.2   **Statistical Relation between Midyear Performance Evaluation and Year-End Evaluation.**

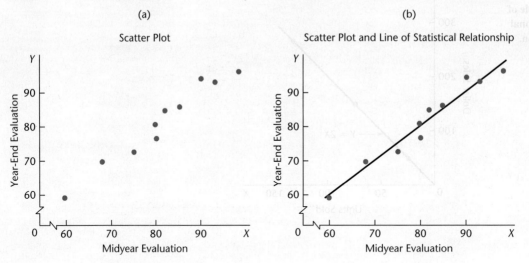

variable X. The plotting is done as before. For instance, the midyear and year-end performance evaluations for the first employee are plotted at $X = 90$, $Y = 94$.

Figure 1.2a clearly suggests that there is a relation between midyear and year-end evaluations, in the sense that the higher the midyear evaluation, the higher tends to be the year-end evaluation. However, the relation is not a perfect one. There is a scattering of points, suggesting that some of the variation in year-end evaluations is not accounted for by midyear performance assessments. For instance, two employees had midyear evaluations of $X = 80$, yet they received somewhat different year-end evaluations. Because of the scattering of points in a statistical relation, Figure 1.2a is called a *scatter diagram* or *scatter plot.* In statistical terminology, each point in the scatter diagram represents a *trial* or a *case.*

In Figure 1.2b, we have plotted a line of relationship that describes the statistical relation between midyear and year-end evaluations. It indicates the general tendency by which year-end evaluations vary with the level of midyear performance evaluation. Note that most of the points do not fall directly on the line of statistical relationship. This scattering of points around the line represents variation in year-end evaluations that is not associated with midyear performance evaluation and that is usually considered to be of a random nature. Statistical relations can be highly useful, even though they do not have the exactitude of a functional relation.

Example 2

Figure 1.3 presents data on age and level of a steroid in plasma for 27 healthy females between 8 and 25 years old. The data strongly suggest that the statistical relationship is *curvilinear* (not linear). The curve of relationship has also been drawn in Figure 1.3. It implies that, as age increases, steroid level increases up to a point and then begins to level off. Note again the scattering of points around the curve of statistical relationship, typical of all statistical relations.

FIGURE 1.3 **Curvilinear Statistical Relation between Age and Steroid Level in Healthy Females Aged 8 to 25.**

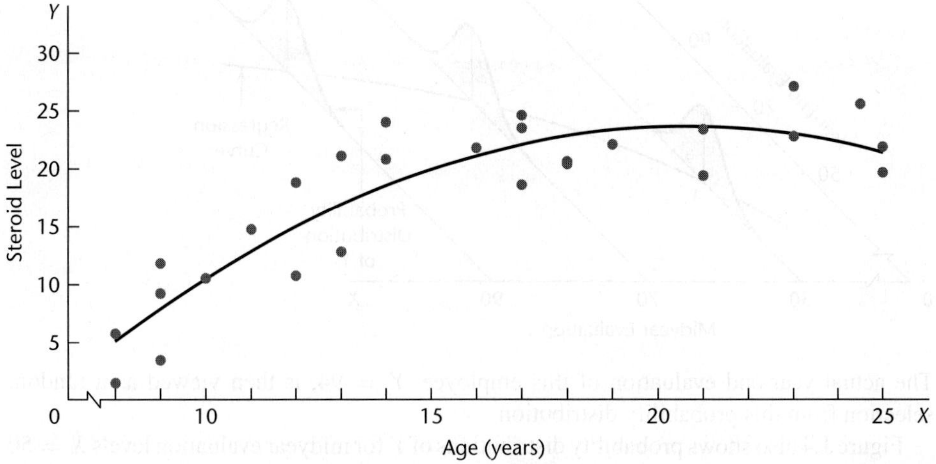

1.2   Regression Models and Their Uses

Historical Origins

Regression analysis was first developed by Sir Francis Galton in the latter part of the 19th century. Galton had studied the relation between heights of parents and children and noted that the heights of children of both tall and short parents appeared to "revert" or "regress" to the mean of the group. He considered this tendency to be a regression to "mediocrity." Galton developed a mathematical description of this regression tendency, the precursor of today's regression models.

The term *regression* persists to this day to describe statistical relations between variables.

Basic Concepts

A regression model is a formal means of expressing the two essential ingredients of a statistical relation:

1. A tendency of the response variable Y to vary with the predictor variable X in a systematic fashion.
2. A scattering of points around the curve of statistical relationship.

These two characteristics are embodied in a regression model by postulating that:

1. There is a probability distribution of Y for each level of X.
2. The means of these probability distributions vary in some systematic fashion with X.

Example

Consider again the performance evaluation example in Figure 1.2. The year-end evaluation Y is treated in a regression model as a random variable. For each level of midyear performance evaluation, there is postulated a probability distribution of Y. Figure 1.4 shows such a probability distribution for $X = 90$, which is the midyear evaluation for the first employee.

FIGURE 1.4
Pictorial
Representation
of Regression
Model.

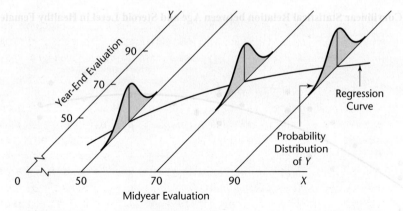

The actual year-end evaluation of this employee, $Y = 94$, is then viewed as a random selection from this probability distribution.

Figure 1.4 also shows probability distributions of Y for midyear evaluation levels $X = 50$ and $X = 70$. Note that the means of the probability distributions have a systematic relation to the level of X. This systematic relationship is called the *regression function of Y on X*. The graph of the regression function is called the *regression curve*. Note that in Figure 1.4 the regression function is slightly curvilinear. This would imply for our example that the increase in the expected (mean) year-end evaluation with an increase in midyear performance evaluation is retarded at higher levels of midyear performance.

Regression models may differ in the form of the regression function (linear, curvilinear), in the shape of the probability distributions of Y (symmetrical, skewed), and in other ways. Whatever the variation, the concept of a probability distribution of Y for any given X is the formal counterpart to the empirical scatter in a statistical relation. Similarly, the regression curve, which describes the relation between the means of the probability distributions of Y and the level of X, is the counterpart to the general tendency of Y to vary with X systematically in a statistical relation.

Regression Models with More than One Predictor Variable.   Regression models may contain more than one predictor variable. Three examples follow.

1. In an efficiency study of 67 branch offices of a consumer finance chain, the response variable was direct operating cost for the year just ended. There were four predictor variables: average size of loan outstanding during the year, average number of loans outstanding, total number of new loan applications processed, and an index of office salaries.

2. In a tractor purchase study, the response variable was volume (in horsepower) of tractor purchases in a sales territory of a farm equipment firm. There were nine predictor variables, including average age of tractors on farms in the territory, number of farms in the territory, and a quantity index of crop production in the territory.

3. In a medical study of short children, the response variable was the peak plasma growth hormone level. There were 14 predictor variables, including age, gender, height, weight, and 10 skinfold measurements.

The model features represented in Figure 1.4 must be extended into further dimensions when there is more than one predictor variable. With two predictor variables X_1 and X_2, for instance, a probability distribution of Y for each (X_1, X_2) combination is assumed by the regression model. The systematic relation between the means of these probability distributions and the predictor variables X_1 and X_2 is then given by a regression surface.

Construction of Regression Models

Selection of Predictor Variables. Since reality must be reduced to manageable proportions whenever we construct models, only a limited number of explanatory or predictor variables can—or should—be included in a regression model for any situation of interest. A central problem in many exploratory studies is therefore that of choosing, for a regression model, a set of predictor variables that is "good" in some sense for the purposes of the analysis. A major consideration in making this choice is the extent to which a chosen variable contributes to reducing the remaining variation in Y after allowance is made for the contributions of other predictor variables that have tentatively been included in the regression model. Other considerations include the importance of the variable as a causal agent in the process under analysis; the degree to which observations on the variable can be obtained more accurately, or quickly, or economically than on competing variables; and the degree to which the variable can be controlled. In Chapter 9, we will discuss procedures and problems in choosing the predictor variables to be included in the regression model.

Functional Form of Regression Relation. The choice of the functional form of the regression relation is tied to the choice of the predictor variables. Sometimes, relevant theory may indicate the appropriate functional form. Learning theory, for instance, may indicate that the regression function relating unit production cost to the number of previous times the item has been produced should have a specified shape with particular asymptotic properties.

More frequently, however, the functional form of the regression relation is not known in advance and must be decided upon empirically once the data have been collected. Linear or quadratic regression functions are often used as satisfactory first approximations to regression functions of unknown nature. Indeed, these simple types of regression functions may be used even when theory provides the relevant functional form, notably when the known form is highly complex but can be reasonably approximated by a linear or quadratic regression function. Figure 1.5a illustrates a case where the complex regression function

FIGURE 1.5 Uses of Linear Regression Functions to Approximate Complex Regression Functions—Bold Line Is the True Regression Function and Dotted Line Is the Regression Approximation.

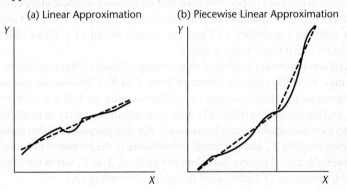

(a) Linear Approximation   (b) Piecewise Linear Approximation

may be reasonably approximated by a linear regression function. Figure 1.5b provides an example where two linear regression functions may be used "piecewise" to approximate a complex regression function.

Scope of Model. In formulating a regression model, we usually need to restrict the coverage of the model to some interval or region of values of the predictor variable(s). The scope is determined either by the design of the investigation or by the range of data at hand. For instance, a company studying the effect of price on sales volume investigated six price levels, ranging from $4.95 to $6.95. Here, the scope of the model is limited to price levels ranging from near $5 to near $7. The shape of the regression function substantially outside this range would be in serious doubt because the investigation provided no evidence as to the nature of the statistical relation below $4.95 or above $6.95.

Uses of Regression Analysis

Regression analysis serves three major purposes: (1) description, (2) control, and (3) prediction. These purposes are illustrated by the three examples cited earlier. The tractor purchase study served a descriptive purpose. In the study of branch office operating costs, the main purpose was administrative control; by developing a usable statistical relation between cost and the predictor variables, management was able to set cost standards for each branch office in the company chain. In the medical study of short children, the purpose was prediction. Clinicians were able to use the statistical relation to predict growth hormone deficiencies in short children by using simple measurements of the children.

The several purposes of regression analysis frequently overlap in practice. The branch office example is a case in point. Knowledge of the relation between operating cost and characteristics of the branch office not only enabled management to set cost standards for each office but management could also predict costs, and at the end of the fiscal year it could compare the actual branch cost against the expected cost.

Regression and Causality

The existence of a statistical relation between the response variable Y and the explanatory or predictor variable X does not imply in any way that Y depends causally on X. No matter how strong is the statistical relation between X and Y, no cause-and-effect pattern is necessarily implied by the regression model. For example, data on size of vocabulary (X) and writing speed (Y) for a sample of young children aged 5–10 will show a positive regression relation. This relation does not imply, however, that an increase in vocabulary causes a faster writing speed. Here, other explanatory variables, such as age of the child and amount of education, affect both the vocabulary (X) and the writing speed (Y). Older children have a larger vocabulary and a faster writing speed.

Even when a strong statistical relationship reflects causal conditions, the causal conditions may act in the opposite direction, from Y to X. Consider, for instance, the calibration of a thermometer. Here, readings of the thermometer are taken at different known temperatures, and the regression relation is studied so that the accuracy of predictions made by using the thermometer readings can be assessed. For this purpose, the thermometer reading is the predictor variable X, and the actual temperature is the response variable Y to be predicted. However, the causal pattern here does not go from X to Y, but in the opposite direction: the actual temperature (Y) affects the thermometer reading (X).

These examples demonstrate the need for care in drawing conclusions about causal relations from regression analysis. Regression analysis by itself provides no information about causal patterns and must be supplemented by additional analyses to obtain insights about causal relations.

Use of Computers

Because regression analysis often entails lengthy and tedious calculations, computers are usually utilized to perform the necessary calculations. Almost every statistics package for computers contains a regression component. While packages differ in many details, their basic regression output tends to be quite similar.

After an initial explanation of required regression calculations, we shall rely on computer calculations for all subsequent examples. We illustrate computer output by presenting output and graphics from BMDP (Ref. 1.1), MINITAB (Ref. 1.2), SAS (Ref. 1.3), SPSS (Ref. 1.4), SYSTAT (Ref. 1.5), JMP (Ref. 1.6), S-Plus (Ref. 1.7), and MATLAB (Ref. 1.8).

1.3 Simple Linear Regression Model with Distribution of Error Terms Unspecified

Formal Statement of Model

In Part I we consider a basic regression model where there is only one predictor variable and the regression function is linear. The model can be stated as follows:

$$Y_i = \beta_0 + \beta_1 X_i + \varepsilon_i \tag{1.1}$$

where:

Y_i is the value of the response variable in the ith trial

β_0 and β_1 are parameters

X_i is a known constant, namely, the value of the predictor variable in the ith trial

ε_i is a random error term with mean $E\{\varepsilon_i\} = 0$ and variance $\sigma^2\{\varepsilon_i\} = \sigma^2$; ε_i and ε_j are uncorrelated so that their covariance is zero (i.e., $\sigma\{\varepsilon_i, \varepsilon_j\} = 0$ for all $i, j; i \neq j$)

$i = 1, \ldots, n$

Regression model (1.1) is said to be *simple, linear in the parameters,* and *linear in the predictor variable.* It is "simple" in that there is only one predictor variable, "linear in the parameters," because no parameter appears as an exponent or is multiplied or divided by another parameter, and "linear in the predictor variable," because this variable appears only in the first power. A model that is linear in the parameters and in the predictor variable is also called a *first-order model.*

Important Features of Model

1. The response Y_i in the ith trial is the sum of two components: (1) the constant term $\beta_0 + \beta_1 X_i$ and (2) the random term ε_i. Hence, Y_i is a random variable.

2. Since $E\{\varepsilon_i\} = 0$, it follows from (A.13c) in Appendix A that:

$$E\{Y_i\} = E\{\beta_0 + \beta_1 X_i + \varepsilon_i\} = \beta_0 + \beta_1 X_i + E\{\varepsilon_i\} = \beta_0 + \beta_1 X_i$$

Note that $\beta_0 + \beta_1 X_i$ plays the role of the constant a in (A.13c).

Thus, the response Y_i, when the level of X in the ith trial is X_i, comes from a probability distribution whose mean is:

$$E\{Y_i\} = \beta_0 + \beta_1 X_i \tag{1.2}$$

We therefore know that the regression function for model (1.1) is:

$$E\{Y\} = \beta_0 + \beta_1 X \tag{1.3}$$

since the regression function relates the means of the probability distributions of Y for given X to the level of X.

3. The response Y_i in the ith trial exceeds or falls short of the value of the regression function by the error term amount ε_i.

4. The error terms ε_i are assumed to have constant variance σ^2. It therefore follows that the responses Y_i have the same constant variance:

$$\sigma^2\{Y_i\} = \sigma^2 \tag{1.4}$$

since, using (A.16a), we have:

$$\sigma^2\{\beta_0 + \beta_1 X_i + \varepsilon_i\} = \sigma^2\{\varepsilon_i\} = \sigma^2$$

Thus, regression model (1.1) assumes that the probability distributions of Y have the same variance σ^2, regardless of the level of the predictor variable X.

5. The error terms are assumed to be uncorrelated. Since the error terms ε_i and ε_j are uncorrelated, so are the responses Y_i and Y_j.

6. In summary, regression model (1.1) implies that the responses Y_i come from probability distributions whose means are $E\{Y_i\} = \beta_0 + \beta_1 X_i$ and whose variances are σ^2, the same for all levels of X. Further, any two responses Y_i and Y_j are uncorrelated.

Example

A consultant for an electrical distributor is studying the relationship between the number of bids requested by construction contractors for basic lighting equipment during a week and the time required to prepare the bids. Suppose that regression model (1.1) is applicable and is as follows:

$$Y_i = 9.5 + 2.1 X_i + \varepsilon_i$$

where X is the number of bids prepared in a week and Y is the number of hours required to prepare the bids. Figure 1.6 contains a presentation of the regression function:

$$E\{Y\} = 9.5 + 2.1 X$$

Suppose that in the ith week, $X_i = 45$ bids are prepared and the actual number of hours required is $Y_i = 108$. In that case, the error term value is $\varepsilon_i = 4$, for we have

$$E\{Y_i\} = 9.5 + 2.1(45) = 104$$

and

$$Y_i = 108 = 104 + 4$$

Figure 1.6 displays the probability distribution of Y when $X = 45$ and indicates from where in this distribution the observation $Y_i = 108$ came. Note again that the error term ε_i is simply the deviation of Y_i from its mean value $E\{Y_i\}$.

FIGURE 1.6
Illustration of
Simple Linear
Regression
Model (1.1).

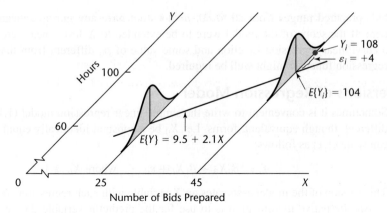

FIGURE 1.7
Meaning of
Parameters of
Simple Linear
Regression
Model (1.1).

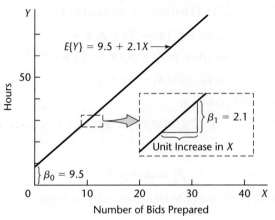

Figure 1.6 also shows the probability distribution of Y when $X = 25$. Note that this distribution exhibits the same variability as the probability distribution when $X = 45$, in conformance with the requirements of regression model (1.1).

Meaning of Regression Parameters

The parameters β_0 and β_1 in regression model (1.1) are called *regression coefficients*. β_1 is the slope of the regression line. It indicates the change in the mean of the probability distribution of Y per unit increase in X. The parameter β_0 is the Y intercept of the regression line. When the scope of the model includes $X = 0$, β_0 gives the mean of the probability distribution of Y at $X = 0$. When the scope of the model does not cover $X = 0$, β_0 does not have any particular meaning as a separate term in the regression model.

Example

Figure 1.7 shows the regression function:

$$E\{Y\} = 9.5 + 2.1X$$

for the electrical distributor example. The slope $\beta_1 = 2.1$ indicates that the preparation of one additional bid in a week leads to an increase in the mean of the probability distribution of Y of 2.1 hours.

The intercept $\beta_0 = 9.5$ indicates the value of the regression function at $X = 0$. However, since the linear regression model was formulated to apply to weeks where the number of bids prepared ranges from 20 to 80, β_0 does not have any intrinsic meaning of its own here. If the scope of the model were to be extended to X levels near zero, a model with a curvilinear regression function and some value of β_0 different from that for the linear regression function might well be required.

Alternative Versions of Regression Model

Sometimes it is convenient to write the simple linear regression model (1.1) in somewhat different, though equivalent, forms. Let X_0 be a constant identically equal to 1. Then, we can write (1.1) as follows:

$$Y_i = \beta_0 X_0 + \beta_1 X_i + \varepsilon_i \qquad \text{where } X_0 \equiv 1 \qquad (1.5)$$

This version of the model associates an X variable with each regression coefficient.

An alternative modification is to use for the predictor variable the deviation $X_i - \bar{X}$ rather than X_i. To leave model (1.1) unchanged, we need to write:

$$\begin{aligned} Y_i &= \beta_0 + \beta_1(X_i - \bar{X}) + \beta_1 \bar{X} + \varepsilon_i \\ &= (\beta_0 + \beta_1 \bar{X}) + \beta_1(X_i - \bar{X}) + \varepsilon_i \\ &= \beta_0^* + \beta_1(X_i - \bar{X}) + \varepsilon_i \end{aligned}$$

Thus, this alternative model version is:

$$Y_i = \beta_0^* + \beta_1(X_i - \bar{X}) + \varepsilon_i \qquad (1.6)$$

where:

$$\beta_0^* = \beta_0 + \beta_1 \bar{X} \qquad (1.6a)$$

We use models (1.1), (1.5), and (1.6) interchangeably as convenience dictates.

1.4   Data for Regression Analysis

Ordinarily, we do not know the values of the regression parameters β_0 and β_1 in regression model (1.1), and we need to estimate them from relevant data. Indeed, as we noted earlier, we frequently do not have adequate *a priori* knowledge of the appropriate predictor variables and of the functional form of the regression relation (e.g., linear or curvilinear), and we need to rely on an analysis of the data for developing a suitable regression model.

Data for regression analysis may be obtained from nonexperimental or experimental studies. We consider each of these in turn.

Observational Data

Observational data are data obtained from nonexperimental studies. Such studies do not control the explanatory or predictor variable(s) of interest. For example, company officials wished to study the relation between age of employee (X) and number of days of illness last year (Y). The needed data for use in the regression analysis were obtained from personnel records. Such data are observational data since the explanatory variable, age, is not controlled.

Regression analyses are frequently based on observational data, since often it is not feasible to conduct controlled experimentation. In the company personnel example just mentioned, for instance, it would not be possible to control age by assigning ages to persons.

A major limitation of observational data is that they often do not provide adequate information about cause-and-effect relationships. For example, a positive relation between age of employee and number of days of illness in the company personnel example may not imply that number of days of illness is the direct result of age. It might be that younger employees of the company primarily work indoors while older employees usually work outdoors, and that work location is more directly responsible for the number of days of illness than age.

Whenever a regression analysis is undertaken for purposes of description based on observational data, one should investigate whether explanatory variables other than those considered in the regression model might more directly explain cause-and-effect relationships.

Experimental Data

Frequently, it is possible to conduct a controlled experiment to provide data from which the regression parameters can be estimated. Consider, for instance, an insurance company that wishes to study the relation between productivity of its analysts in processing claims and length of training. Nine analysts are to be used in the study. Three of them will be selected at random and trained for two weeks, three for three weeks, and three for five weeks. The productivity of the analysts during the next 10 weeks will then be observed. The data so obtained will be experimental data because control is exercised over the explanatory variable, length of training.

When control over the explanatory variable(s) is exercised through random assignments, as in the productivity study example, the resulting experimental data provide much stronger information about cause-and-effect relationships than do observational data. The reason is that randomization tends to balance out the effects of any other variables that might affect the response variable, such as the effect of aptitude of the employee on productivity.

In the terminology of experimental design, the length of training assigned to an analyst in the productivity study example is called a *treatment*. The analysts to be included in the study are called the *experimental units*. Control over the explanatory variable(s) then consists of assigning a treatment to each of the experimental units by means of randomization.

Completely Randomized Design

The most basic type of statistical design for making randomized assignments of treatments to experimental units (or vice versa) is the *completely randomized design*. With this design, the assignments are made completely at random. This complete randomization provides that all combinations of experimental units assigned to the different treatments are equally likely, which implies that every experimental unit has an equal chance to receive any one of the treatments.

A completely randomized design is particularly useful when the experimental units are quite homogeneous. This design is very flexible; it accommodates any number of treatments and permits different sample sizes for different treatments. Its chief disadvantage is that, when the experimental units are heterogeneous, this design is not as efficient as some other statistical designs.

1.5 Overview of Steps in Regression Analysis

The regression models considered in this and subsequent chapters can be utilized either for observational data or for experimental data from a completely randomized design. (Regression analysis can also utilize data from other types of experimental designs, but the regression models presented here will need to be modified.) Whether the data are observational or experimental, it is essential that the conditions of the regression model be appropriate for the data at hand for the model to be applicable.

We begin our discussion of regression analysis by considering inferences about the regression parameters for the simple linear regression model (1.1). For the rare occasion where prior knowledge or theory alone enables us to determine the appropriate regression model, inferences based on the regression model are the first step in the regression analysis. In the usual situation, however, where we do not have adequate knowledge to specify the appropriate regression model in advance, the first step is an exploratory study of the data, as shown in the flowchart in Figure 1.8. On the basis of this initial exploratory analysis, one or more preliminary regression models are developed. These regression models are then examined for their appropriateness for the data at hand and revised, or new models

FIGURE 1.8
Typical Strategy for Regression Analysis.

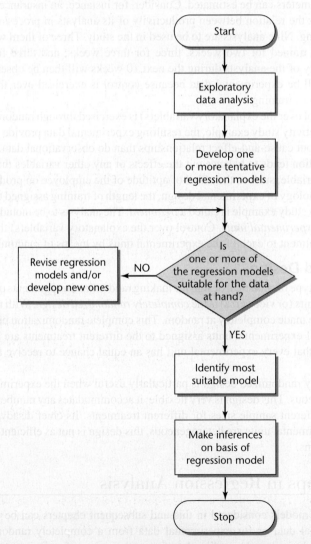

are developed, until the investigator is satisfied with the suitability of a particular regression model. Only then are inferences made on the basis of this regression model, such as inferences about the regression parameters of the model or predictions of new observations.

We begin, for pedagogic reasons, with inferences based on the regression model that is finally considered to be appropriate. One must have an understanding of regression models and how they can be utilized before the issues involved in the development of an appropriate regression model can be fully explained.

1.6   Estimation of Regression Function

The observational or experimental data to be used for estimating the parameters of the regression function consist of observations on the explanatory or predictor variable X and the corresponding observations on the response variable Y. For each trial, there is an X observation and a Y observation. We denote the (X, Y) observations for the first trial as (X_1, Y_1), for the second trial as (X_2, Y_2), and in general for the ith trial as (X_i, Y_i), where $i = 1, \ldots, n$.

Example

In a small-scale study of persistence, an experimenter gave three subjects a very difficult task. Data on the age of the subject (X) and on the number of attempts to accomplish the task before giving up (Y) follow:

Subject i:	1	2	3
Age X_i:	20	55	30
Number of attempts Y_i:	5	12	10

In terms of the notation to be employed, there were $n = 3$ subjects in this study, the observations for the first subject were $(X_1, Y_1) = (20, 5)$, and similarly for the other subjects.

Method of Least Squares

To find "good" estimators of the regression parameters β_0 and β_1, we employ the method of least squares. For the observations (X_i, Y_i) for each case, the method of least squares considers the deviation of Y_i from its expected value:

$$Y_i - (\beta_0 + \beta_1 X_i) \tag{1.7}$$

In particular, the method of least squares requires that we consider the sum of the n squared deviations. This criterion is denoted by Q:

$$Q = \sum_{i=1}^{n} (Y_i - \beta_0 - \beta_1 X_i)^2 \tag{1.8}$$

According to the method of least squares, the estimators of β_0 and β_1 are those values b_0 and b_1, respectively, that minimize the criterion Q for the given sample observations $(X_1, Y_1), (X_2, Y_2), \ldots, (X_n, Y_n)$.

FIGURE 1.9 Illustration of Least Squares Criterion Q for Fit of a Regression Line—Persistence Study Example.

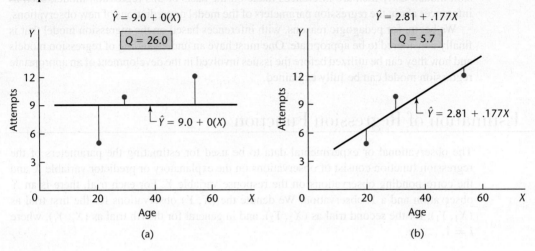

(a)   (b)

Example

Figure 1.9a presents the scatter plot of the data for the persistence study example and the regression line that results when we use the mean of the responses (9.0) as the predictor and ignore X:

$$\hat{Y} = 9.0 + 0(X)$$

Note that this regression line uses estimates $b_0 = 9.0$ and $b_1 = 0$, and that $\hat{Y}$ denotes the ordinate of the estimated regression line. Clearly, this regression line is not a good fit, as evidenced by the large vertical deviations of two of the Y observations from the corresponding ordinates $\hat{Y}$ of the regression line. The deviation for the first subject, for which $(X_1, Y_1) = (20, 5)$, is:

$$Y_1 - (b_0 + b_1 X_1) = 5 - [9.0 + 0(20)] = 5 - 9.0 = -4$$

The sum of the squared deviations for the three cases is:

$$Q = (5 - 9.0)^2 + (12 - 9.0)^2 + (10 - 9.0)^2 = 26.0$$

Figure 1.9b shows the same data with the regression line:

$$\hat{Y} = 2.81 + .177X$$

The fit of this regression line is clearly much better. The vertical deviation for the first case now is:

$$Y_1 - (b_0 + b_1 X_1) = 5 - [2.81 + .177(20)] = 5 - 6.35 = -1.35$$

and the criterion Q is much reduced:

$$Q = (5 - 6.35)^2 + (12 - 12.55)^2 + (10 - 8.12)^2 = 5.7$$

Thus, a better fit of the regression line to the data corresponds to a smaller sum Q.

The objective of the method of least squares is to find estimates b_0 and b_1 for β_0 and β_1, respectively, for which Q is a minimum. In a certain sense, to be discussed shortly, these estimates will provide a "good" fit of the linear regression function. The regression line in Figure 1.9b is, in fact, the least squares regression line.

Least Squares Estimators.   The estimators b_0 and b_1 that satisfy the least squares criterion can be found in two basic ways:

1. Numerical search procedures can be used that evaluate in a systematic fashion the least squares criterion Q for different estimates b_0 and b_1 until the ones that minimize Q are found. This approach was illustrated in Figure 1.9 for the persistence study example.
2. Analytical procedures can often be used to find the values of b_0 and b_1 that minimize Q. The analytical approach is feasible when the regression model is not mathematically complex.

Using the analytical approach, it can be shown for regression model (1.1) that the values b_0 and b_1 that minimize Q for any particular set of sample data are given by the following simultaneous equations:

$$\sum Y_i = nb_0 + b_1 \sum X_i \tag{1.9a}$$

$$\sum X_i Y_i = b_0 \sum X_i + b_1 \sum X_i^2 \tag{1.9b}$$

Equations (1.9a) and (1.9b) are called *normal equations; b_0* and b_1 are called *point estimators* of β_0 and β_1, respectively.

The normal equations (1.9) can be solved simultaneously for b_0 and b_1:

$$b_1 = \frac{\sum (X_i - \bar{X})(Y_i - \bar{Y})}{\sum (X_i - \bar{X})^2} \tag{1.10a}$$

$$b_0 = \frac{1}{n} \left(\sum Y_i - b_1 \sum X_i \right) = \bar{Y} - b_1 \bar{X} \tag{1.10b}$$

where $\bar{X}$ and $\bar{Y}$ are the means of the X_i and the Y_i observations, respectively. Computer calculations generally are based on many digits to obtain accurate values for b_0 and b_1.

Comment

The normal equations (1.9) can be derived by calculus. For given sample observations (X_i, Y_i), the quantity Q in (1.8) is a function of β_0 and β_1. The values of β_0 and β_1 that minimize Q can be derived by differentiating (1.8) with respect to β_0 and β_1. We obtain:

$$\frac{\partial Q}{\partial \beta_0} = -2 \sum (Y_i - \beta_0 - \beta_1 X_i)$$

$$\frac{\partial Q}{\partial \beta_1} = -2 \sum X_i (Y_i - \beta_0 - \beta_1 X_i)$$

We then set these partial derivatives equal to zero, using b_0 and b_1 to denote the particular values of β_0 and β_1 that minimize Q:

$$-2 \sum (Y_i - b_0 - b_1 X_i) = 0$$

$$-2 \sum X_i (Y_i - b_0 - b_1 X_i) = 0$$

Simplifying, we obtain:

$$\sum_{i=1}^{n}(Y_i - b_0 - b_1 X_i) = 0$$

$$\sum_{i=1}^{n} X_i (Y_i - b_0 - b_1 X_i) = 0$$

Expanding, we have:

$$\sum Y_i - n b_0 - b_1 \sum X_i = 0$$

$$\sum X_i Y_i - b_0 \sum X_i - b_1 \sum X_i^2 = 0$$

from which the normal equations (1.9) are obtained by rearranging terms.

A test of the second partial derivatives will show that a minimum is obtained with the least squares estimators b_0 and b_1.   ■

Properties of Least Squares Estimators.   An important theorem, called the *Gauss-Markov theorem*, states:

> Under the conditions of regression model (1.1), the least squares estimators b_0 and b_1 in (1.10) are unbiased and have minimum variance among all unbiased linear estimators.   **(1.11)**

This theorem, proven in the next chapter, states first that b_0 and b_1 are unbiased estimators. Hence:

$$E\{b_0\} = \beta_0 \qquad E\{b_1\} = \beta_1$$

so that neither estimator tends to overestimate or underestimate systematically.

Second, the theorem states that the estimators b_0 and b_1 are more precise (i.e., their sampling distributions are less variable) than any other estimators belonging to the class of unbiased estimators that are linear functions of the observations $Y_1, \ldots, Y_n$. The estimators b_0 and b_1 are such linear functions of the Y_i. Consider, for instance, b_1. We have from (1.10a):

$$b_1 = \frac{\sum(X_i - \bar{X})(Y_i - \bar{Y})}{\sum(X_i - \bar{X})^2}$$

It will be shown in Chapter 2 that this expression is equal to:

$$b_1 = \frac{\sum(X_i - \bar{X}) Y_i}{\sum(X_i - \bar{X})^2} = \sum k_i Y_i$$

where:

$$k_i = \frac{X_i - \bar{X}}{\sum(X_i - \bar{X})^2}$$

Since the k_i are known constants (because the X_i are known constants), b_1 is a linear combination of the Y_i and hence is a linear estimator.

In the same fashion, it can be shown that b_0 is a linear estimator. Among all linear estimators that are unbiased then, b_0 and b_1 have the smallest variability in repeated samples in which the X levels remain unchanged.

Example

The Toluca Company manufactures refrigeration equipment as well as many replacement parts. In the past, one of the replacement parts has been produced periodically in lots of varying sizes. When a cost improvement program was undertaken, company officials wished to determine the optimum lot size for producing this part. The production of this part involves setting up the production process (which must be done no matter what is the lot size) and machining and assembly operations. One key input for the model to ascertain the optimum lot size was the relationship between lot size and labor hours required to produce the lot. To determine this relationship, data on lot size and work hours for 25 recent production runs were utilized. The production conditions were stable during the six-month period in which the 25 runs were made and were expected to continue to be the same during the next three years, the planning period for which the cost improvement program was being conducted.

Table 1.1 contains a portion of the data on lot size and work hours in columns 1 and 2. Note that all lot sizes are multiples of 10, a result of company policy to facilitate the administration of the parts production. Figure 1.10a shows a SYSTAT scatter plot of the data. We see that the lot sizes ranged from 20 to 120 units and that none of the production runs was outlying in the sense of being either unusually small or large. The scatter plot also indicates that the relationship between lot size and work hours is reasonably linear. We also see that no observations on work hours are unusually small or large, with reference to the relationship between lot size and work hours.

To calculate the least squares estimates b_0 and b_1 in (1.10), we require the deviations $X_i - \bar{X}$ and $Y_i - \bar{Y}$. These are given in columns 3 and 4 of Table 1.1. We also require the cross-product terms $(X_i - \bar{X})(Y_i - \bar{Y})$ and the squared deviations $(X_i - \bar{X})^2$; these are shown in columns 5 and 6. The squared deviations $(Y_i - \bar{Y})^2$ in column 7 are for later use.

TABLE 1.1 Data on Lot Size and Work Hours and Needed Calculations for Least Squares Estimates—Toluca Company Example.

Run i	(1) Lot Size X_i	(2) Work Hours Y_i	(3) $X_i - \bar{X}$	(4) $Y_i - \bar{Y}$	(5) $(X_i - \bar{X})(Y_i - \bar{Y})$	(6) $(X_i - \bar{X})^2$	(7) $(Y_i - \bar{Y})^2$
1	80	399	10	86.72	867.2	100	7,520.4
2	30	121	−40	−191.28	7,651.2	1,600	36,588.0
3	50	221	−20	−91.28	1,825.6	400	8,332.0
...	...	...	...	...	...	...	...
23	40	244	−30	−68.28	2,048.4	900	4,662.2
24	80	342	10	29.72	297.2	100	883.3
25	70	323	0	10.72	0.0	0	114.9
Total	1,750	7,807	0	0	70,690	19,800	307,203
Mean	70.0	312.28					

FIGURE 1.10
SYSTAT
Scatter Plot
and Fitted
Regression
Line—Toluca
Company
Example.

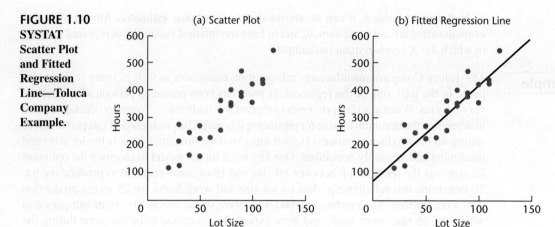

(a) Scatter Plot

(b) Fitted Regression Line

FIGURE 1.11
Portion of
MINITAB
Regression
Output—
Toluca
Company
Example.

```
The regression equation is
Y = 62.4 + 3.57 X

Predictor     Coef      Stdev     t-ratio        p
Constant     62.37      26.18        2.38    0.026
X           3.5702     0.3470       10.29    0.000

s = 48.82     R-sq = 82.2%     R-sq(adj) = 81.4%
```

We see from Table 1.1 that the basic quantities needed to calculate the least squares estimates are as follows:

$$\sum (X_i - \bar{X})(Y_i - \bar{Y}) = 70{,}690$$

$$\sum (X_i - \bar{X})^2 = 19{,}800$$

$$\bar{X} = 70.0$$

$$\bar{Y} = 312.28$$

Using (1.10) we obtain:

$$b_1 = \frac{\sum (X_i - \bar{X})(Y_i - \bar{Y})}{\sum (X_i - \bar{X})^2} = \frac{70{,}690}{19{,}800} = 3.5702$$

$$b_0 = \bar{Y} - b_1 \bar{X} = 312.28 - 3.5702(70.0) = 62.37$$

Thus, we estimate that the mean number of work hours increases by 3.57 hours for each additional unit produced in the lot. This estimate applies to the range of lot sizes in the data from which the estimates were derived, namely to lot sizes ranging from about 20 to about 120.

Figure 1.11 contains a portion of the MINITAB regression output for the Toluca Company example. The estimates b_0 and b_1 are shown in the column labeled Coef, corresponding to the lines Constant and X, respectively. The additional information shown in Figure 1.11 will be explained later.

Point Estimation of Mean Response

Estimated Regression Function.   Given sample estimators b_0 and b_1 of the parameters in the regression function (1.3):

$$E\{Y\} = \beta_0 + \beta_1 X$$

we estimate the regression function as follows:

$$\hat{Y} = b_0 + b_1 X \tag{1.12}$$

where $\hat{Y}$ (read Y hat) is the value of the estimated regression function at the level X of the predictor variable.

We call a *value* of the response variable a *response* and $E\{Y\}$ the *mean response*. Thus, the mean response stands for the mean of the probability distribution of Y corresponding to the level X of the predictor variable. $\hat{Y}$ then is a point estimator of the mean response when the level of the predictor variable is X. It can be shown as an extension of the Gauss-Markov theorem (1.11) that $\hat{Y}$ is an unbiased estimator of $E\{Y\}$, with minimum variance in the class of unbiased linear estimators.

For the cases in the study, we will call $\hat{Y}_i$:

$$\hat{Y}_i = b_0 + b_1 X_i \qquad i = 1, \dots, n \tag{1.13}$$

the *fitted value* for the ith case. Thus, the fitted value $\hat{Y}_i$ is to be viewed in distinction to the *observed value* Y_i.

Example

For the Toluca Company example, we found that the least squares estimates of the regression coefficients are:

$$b_0 = 62.37 \qquad b_1 = 3.5702$$

Hence, the estimated regression function is:

$$\hat{Y} = 62.37 + 3.5702 X$$

This estimated regression function is plotted in Figure 1.10b. It appears to be a good description of the statistical relationship between lot size and work hours.

To estimate the mean response for any level X of the predictor variable, we simply substitute that value of X in the estimated regression function. Suppose that we are interested in the mean number of work hours required when the lot size is $X = 65$; our point estimate is:

$$\hat{Y} = 62.37 + 3.5702(65) = 294.4$$

Thus, we estimate that the mean number of work hours required for production runs of $X = 65$ units is 294.4 hours. We interpret this to mean that if many lots of 65 units are produced under the conditions of the 25 runs on which the estimated regression function is based, the mean labor time for these lots is about 294 hours. Of course, the labor time for any one lot of size 65 is likely to fall above or below the mean response because of inherent variability in the production system, as represented by the error term in the model.

TABLE 1.2
Fitted Values, Residuals, and Squared Residuals— Toluca Company Example.

Run i	(1) Lot Size X_i	(2) Work Hours Y_i	(3) Estimated Mean Response $\hat{Y}_i$	(4) Residual $Y_i - \hat{Y}_i = e_i$	(5) Squared Residual $(Y_i - \hat{Y}_i)^2 = e_i^2$
1	80	399	347.98	51.02	2,603.0
2	30	121	169.47	−48.47	2,349.3
3	50	221	240.88	−19.83	395.2
...	...	...	...	...	...
23	40	244	205.17	38.83	1,507.8
24	80	342	347.98	−5.98	35.8
25	70	323	312.28	10.72	114.9
Total	1,750	7,807	7,807	0	54,825

Fitted values for the sample cases are obtained by substituting the appropriate X values into the estimated regression function. For the first sample case, we have $X_1 = 80$. Hence, the fitted value for the first case is:

$$\hat{Y}_1 = 62.37 + 3.5702(80) = 347.98$$

This compares with the observed work hours of $Y_1 = 399$. Table 1.2 contains the observed and fitted values for a portion of the Toluca Company data in columns 2 and 3, respectively.

Alternative Model (1.6). When the alternative regression model (1.6):

$$Y_i = \beta_0^* + \beta_1(X_i - \bar{X}) + \varepsilon_i$$

is to be utilized, the least squares estimator b_1 of β_1 remains the same as before. The least squares estimator of $\beta_0^* = \beta_0 + \beta_1\bar{X}$ becomes, from (1.10b):

$$b_0^* = b_0 + b_1\bar{X} = (\bar{Y} - b_1\bar{X}) + b_1\bar{X} = \bar{Y} \tag{1.14}$$

Hence, the estimated regression function for alternative model (1.6) is:

$$\hat{Y} = \bar{Y} + b_1(X - \bar{X}) \tag{1.15}$$

In the Toluca Company example, $\bar{Y} = 312.28$ and $\bar{X} = 70.0$ (Table 1.1). Hence, the estimated regression function in alternative form is:

$$\hat{Y} = 312.28 + 3.5702(X - 70.0)$$

For the first lot in our example, $X_1 = 80$; hence, we estimate the mean response to be:

$$\hat{Y}_1 = 312.28 + 3.5702(80 - 70.0) = 347.98$$

which, of course, is identical to our earlier result.

Residuals

The ith *residual* is the difference between the observed value Y_i and the corresponding fitted value $\hat{Y}_i$. This residual is denoted by e_i and is defined in general as follows:

$$e_i = Y_i - \hat{Y}_i \tag{1.16}$$

FIGURE 1.12
Illustration of
Residuals—
Toluca
Company
Example (not
drawn to
scale).

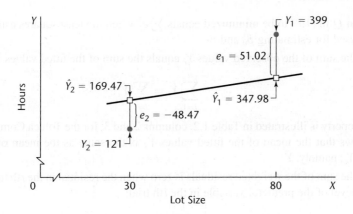

For regression model (1.1), the residual e_i becomes:

$$e_i = Y_i - (b_0 + b_1 X_i) = Y_i - b_0 - b_1 X_i \qquad (1.16a)$$

The calculation of the residuals for the Toluca Company example is shown for a portion of the data in Table 1.2. We see that the residual for the first case is:

$$e_1 = Y_1 - \hat{Y}_1 = 399 - 347.98 = 51.02$$

The residuals for the first two cases are illustrated graphically in Figure 1.12. Note in this figure that the magnitude of a residual is represented by the vertical deviation of the Y_i observation from the corresponding point on the estimated regression function (i.e., from the corresponding fitted value $\hat{Y}_i$).

We need to distinguish between the model error term value $\varepsilon_i = Y_i - E\{Y_i\}$ and the residual $e_i = Y_i - \hat{Y}_i$. The former involves the vertical deviation of Y_i from the unknown true regression line and hence is unknown. On the other hand, the residual is the vertical deviation of Y_i from the fitted value $\hat{Y}_i$ on the estimated regression line, and it is known.

Residuals are highly useful for studying whether a given regression model is appropriate for the data at hand. We discuss this use in Chapter 3.

Properties of Fitted Regression Line

The estimated regression line (1.12) fitted by the method of least squares has a number of properties worth noting. These properties of the least squares estimated regression function do not apply to all regression models, as we shall see in Chapter 4.

1. The sum of the residuals is zero:

$$\sum_{i=1}^{n} e_i = 0 \qquad (1.17)$$

Table 1.2, column 4, illustrates this property for the Toluca Company example. Rounding errors may, of course, be present in any particular case, resulting in a sum of the residuals that does not equal zero exactly.

2. The sum of the squared residuals, $\sum e_i^2$, is a minimum. This was the requirement to be satisfied in deriving the least squares estimators of the regression parameters since the

criterion Q in (1.8) to be minimized equals $\sum e_i^2$ when the least squares estimators b_0 and b_1 are used for estimating β_0 and β_1.

3. The sum of the observed values Y_i equals the sum of the fitted values $\hat{Y}_i$:

$$\sum_{i=1}^{n} Y_i = \sum_{i=1}^{n} \hat{Y}_i \tag{1.18}$$

This property is illustrated in Table 1.2, columns 2 and 3, for the Toluca Company example. It follows that the mean of the fitted values $\hat{Y}_i$ is the same as the mean of the observed values Y_i, namely, $\bar{Y}$.

4. The sum of the weighted residuals is zero when the residual in the ith trial is weighted by the level of the predictor variable in the ith trial:

$$\sum_{i=1}^{n} X_i e_i = 0 \tag{1.19}$$

5. A consequence of properties (1.17) and (1.19) is that the sum of the weighted residuals is zero when the residual in the ith trial is weighted by the fitted value of the response variable for the ith trial:

$$\sum_{i=1}^{n} \hat{Y}_i e_i = 0 \tag{1.20}$$

6. The regression line always goes through the point $(\bar{X}, \bar{Y})$.

Comment

The six properties of the fitted regression line follow directly from the least squares normal equations (1.9). For example, property 1 in (1.17) is proven as follows:

$$\sum e_i = \sum (Y_i - b_0 - b_1 X_i) = \sum Y_i - n b_0 - b_1 \sum X_i$$
$$= 0 \qquad \text{by the first normal equation (1.9a)}$$

Property 6, that the regression line always goes through the point $(\bar{X}, \bar{Y})$, can be demonstrated easily from the alternative form (1.15) of the estimated regression line. When $X = \bar{X}$, we have:

$$\hat{Y} = \bar{Y} + b_1(X - \bar{X}) = \bar{Y} + b_1(\bar{X} - \bar{X}) = \bar{Y} \qquad ∎$$

1.7 Estimation of Error Terms Variance σ^2

The variance σ^2 of the error terms ε_i in regression model (1.1) needs to be estimated to obtain an indication of the variability of the probability distributions of Y. In addition, as we shall see in the next chapter, a variety of inferences concerning the regression function and the prediction of Y require an estimate of σ^2.

Point Estimator of σ^2

To lay the basis for developing an estimator of σ^2 for regression model (1.1), we first consider the simpler problem of sampling from a single population.

Single Population. We know that the variance σ^2 of a single population is estimated by the sample variance s^2. In obtaining the sample variance s^2, we consider the deviation of an observation Y_i from the estimated mean $\bar{Y}$, square it, and then sum all such squared deviations:

$$\sum_{i=1}^{n}(Y_i - \bar{Y})^2$$

Such a sum is called a *sum of squares*. The sum of squares is then divided by the degrees of freedom associated with it. This number is $n - 1$ here, because one degree of freedom is lost by using $\bar{Y}$ as an estimate of the unknown population mean μ. The resulting estimator is the usual sample variance:

$$s^2 = \frac{\sum_{i=1}^{n}(Y_i - \bar{Y})^2}{n-1}$$

which is an unbiased estimator of the variance σ^2 of an infinite population. The sample variance is often called a *mean square,* because a sum of squares has been divided by the appropriate number of degrees of freedom.

Regression Model.   The logic of developing an estimator of σ^2 for the regression model is the same as for sampling from a single population. Recall in this connection from (1.4) that the variance of each observation Y_i for regression model (1.1) is σ^2, the same as that of each error term ε_i. We again need to calculate a sum of squared deviations, but must recognize that the Y_i now come from different probability distributions with different means that depend upon the level X_i. Thus, the deviation of an observation Y_i must be calculated around its own estimated mean $\hat{Y}_i$. Hence, the deviations are the residuals:

$$Y_i - \hat{Y}_i = e_i$$

and the appropriate sum of squares, denoted by *SSE*, is:

$$SSE = \sum_{i=1}^{n}(Y_i - \hat{Y}_i)^2 = \sum_{i=1}^{n} e_i^2 \tag{1.21}$$

where *SSE* stands for *error sum of squares* or *residual sum of squares*.

The sum of squares *SSE* has $n - 2$ degrees of freedom associated with it. Two degrees of freedom are lost because both β_0 and β_1 had to be estimated in obtaining the estimated means $\hat{Y}_i$. Hence, the appropriate mean square, denoted by *MSE* or s^2, is:

$$s^2 = MSE = \frac{SSE}{n-2} = \frac{\sum (Y_i - \hat{Y}_i)^2}{n-2} = \frac{\sum e_i^2}{n-2} \tag{1.22}$$

where *MSE* stands for *error mean square* or *residual mean square*.

It can be shown that *MSE* is an unbiased estimator of σ^2 for regression model (1.1):

$$E\{MSE\} = \sigma^2 \tag{1.23}$$

An estimator of the standard deviation σ is simply $s = \sqrt{MSE}$, the positive square root of *MSE*.

Example

We will calculate *SSE* for the Toluca Company example by (1.21). The residuals were obtained earlier in Table 1.2, column 4. This table also shows the squared residuals in column 5. From these results, we obtain:

$$SSE = 54{,}825$$

Since $25 - 2 = 23$ degrees of freedom are associated with *SSE*, we find:

$$s^2 = MSE = \frac{54{,}825}{23} = 2{,}384$$

Finally, a point estimate of σ, the standard deviation of the probability distribution of Y for any X, is $s = \sqrt{2{,}384} = 48.8$ hours.

Consider again the case where the lot size is $X = 65$ units. We found earlier that the mean of the probability distribution of Y for this lot size is estimated to be 294.4 hours. Now, we have the additional information that the standard deviation of this distribution is estimated to be 48.8 hours. This estimate is shown in the MINITAB output in Figure 1.11, labeled as s. We see that the variation in work hours from lot to lot for lots of 65 units is quite substantial (49 hours) compared to the mean of the distribution (294 hours).

1.8 Normal Error Regression Model

No matter what may be the form of the distribution of the error terms ε_i (and hence of the Y_i), the least squares method provides unbiased point estimators of β_0 and β_1 that have minimum variance among all unbiased linear estimators. To set up interval estimates and make tests, however, we need to make an assumption about the form of the distribution of the ε_i. The standard assumption is that the error terms ε_i are normally distributed, and we will adopt it here. A normal error term greatly simplifies the theory of regression analysis and, as we shall explain shortly, is justifiable in many real-world situations where regression analysis is applied.

Model

The normal error regression model is as follows:

$$Y_i = \beta_0 + \beta_1 X_i + \varepsilon_i \tag{1.24}$$

where:

Y_i is the observed response in the ith trial

X_i is a known constant, the level of the predictor variable in the ith trial

β_0 and β_1 are parameters

ε_i are independent $N(0, \sigma^2)$

$i = 1, \ldots, n$

Comments

1. The symbol $N(0, \sigma^2)$ stands for normally distributed, with mean 0 and variance σ^2.

2. The normal error model (1.24) is the same as regression model (1.1) with unspecified error distribution, except that model (1.24) assumes that the errors ε_i are normally distributed.

3. Because regression model (1.24) assumes that the errors are normally distributed, the assumption of uncorrelatedness of the ε_i in regression model (1.1) becomes one of independence in the normal error model. Hence, the outcome in any one trial has no effect on the error term for any other trial—as to whether it is positive or negative, small or large.

4. Regression model (1.24) implies that the Y_i are independent normal random variables, with mean $E\{Y_i\} = \beta_0 + \beta_1 X_i$ and variance σ^2. Figure 1.6 pictures this normal error model. Each of the probability distributions of Y in Figure 1.6 is normally distributed, with constant variability, and the regression function is linear.

5. The normality assumption for the error terms is justifiable in many situations because the error terms frequently represent the effects of factors omitted from the model that affect the response to some extent and that vary at random without reference to the variable X. For instance, in the Toluca Company example, the effects of such factors as time lapse since the last production run, particular machines used, season of the year, and personnel employed could vary more or less at random from run to run, independent of lot size. Also, there might be random measurement errors in the recording of Y, the hours required. Insofar as these random effects have a degree of mutual independence, the composite error term ε_i representing all these factors would tend to comply with the central limit theorem and the error term distribution would approach normality as the number of factor effects becomes large.

A second reason why the normality assumption of the error terms is frequently justifiable is that the estimation and testing procedures to be discussed in the next chapter are based on the t distribution and are usually only sensitive to large departures from normality. Thus, unless the departures from normality are serious, particularly with respect to skewness, the actual confidence coefficients and risks of errors will be close to the levels for exact normality.   ■

Estimation of Parameters by Method of Maximum Likelihood

When the functional form of the probability distribution of the error terms is specified, estimators of the parameters β_0, β_1, and σ^2 can be obtained by the *method of maximum likelihood*. Essentially, the method of maximum likelihood chooses as estimates those values of the parameters that are most consistent with the sample data. We explain the method of maximum likelihood first for the simple case when a single population with one parameter is sampled. Then we explain this method for regression models.

Single Population.   Consider a normal population whose standard deviation is known to be $\sigma = 10$ and whose mean is unknown. A random sample of $n = 3$ observations is selected from the population and yields the results $Y_1 = 250$, $Y_2 = 265$, $Y_3 = 259$. We now wish to ascertain which value of μ is most consistent with the sample data. Consider $\mu = 230$. Figure 1.13a shows the normal distribution with $\mu = 230$ and $\sigma = 10$; also shown there are the locations of the three sample observations. Note that the sample observations

FIGURE 1.13
Densities for
Sample
Observations
for Two
Possible Values
of μ: $Y_1 = 250$,
$Y_2 = 265$,
$Y_3 = 259$.

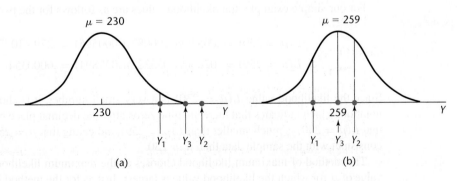

would be in the right tail of the distribution if μ were equal to 230. Since these are unlikely occurrences, $\mu = 230$ is not consistent with the sample data.

Figure 1.13b shows the population and the locations of the sample data if μ were equal to 259. Now the observations would be in the center of the distribution and much more likely. Hence, $\mu = 259$ is more consistent with the sample data than $\mu = 230$.

The method of maximum likelihood uses the density of the probability distribution at Y_i (i.e., the height of the curve at Y_i) as a measure of consistency for the observation Y_i. Consider observation Y_1 in our example. If Y_1 is in the tail, as in Figure 1.13a, the height of the curve will be small. If Y_1 is nearer to the center of the distribution, as in Figure 1.13b, the height will be larger. Using the density function for a normal probability distribution in (A.34) in Appendix A, we find the densities for Y_1, denoted by f_1, for the two cases of μ in Figure 1.13 as follows:

$$\mu = 230: \qquad f_1 = \frac{1}{\sqrt{2\pi}(10)} \exp\left[-\frac{1}{2}\left(\frac{250 - 230}{10}\right)^2\right] = .005399$$

$$\mu = 259: \qquad f_1 = \frac{1}{\sqrt{2\pi}(10)} \exp\left[-\frac{1}{2}\left(\frac{250 - 259}{10}\right)^2\right] = .026609$$

The densities for all three sample observations for the two cases of μ are as follows:

	$\mu = 230$	$\mu = 259$
f_1	.005399	.026609
f_2	.000087	.033322
f_3	.000595	.039894

The method of maximum likelihood uses the product of the densities (i.e., here, the product of the three heights) as the measure of consistency of the parameter value with the sample data. The product is called the *likelihood value* of the parameter value μ and is denoted by $L(\mu)$. If the value of μ is consistent with the sample data, the densities will be relatively large and so will be the product (i.e., the likelihood value). If the value of μ is not consistent with the data, the densities will be small and the product $L(\mu)$ will be small.

For our simple example, the likelihood values are as follows for the two cases of μ:

$$L(\mu = 230) = .005399(.000087)(.000595) = .279 \times 10^{-9}$$

$$L(\mu = 259) = .026609(.033322)(.039894) = .0000354$$

Since the likelihood value $L(\mu = 230)$ is a very small number, it is shown in scientific notation, which indicates that there are nine zeros after the decimal place before 279. Note that $L(\mu = 230)$ is much smaller than $L(\mu = 259)$, indicating that $\mu = 259$ is much more consistent with the sample data than $\mu = 230$.

The method of maximum likelihood chooses as the maximum likelihood estimate that value of μ for which the likelihood value is largest. Just as for the method of least squares, there are two methods of finding maximum likelihood estimates: by a systematic numerical search and by use of an analytical solution. For some problems, analytical solutions for the maximum likelihood estimators are available. For others, a computerized numerical search must be conducted.

For our example, an analytical solution is available. It can be shown that for a normal population the maximum likelihood estimator of μ is the sample mean $\bar{Y}$. In our example, $\bar{Y} = 258$ and the maximum likelihood estimate of μ therefore is 258. The likelihood value of $\mu = 258$ is $L(\mu = 258) = .0000359$, which is slightly larger than the likelihood value of $.0000354$ for $\mu = 259$ that we had calculated earlier.

The product of the densities viewed as a function of the unknown parameters is called the *likelihood function*. For our example, where $\sigma = 10$, the likelihood function is:

$$L(\mu) = \left[\frac{1}{\sqrt{2\pi}(10)}\right]^3 \exp\left[-\frac{1}{2}\left(\frac{250 - \mu}{10}\right)^2\right] \exp\left[-\frac{1}{2}\left(\frac{265 - \mu}{10}\right)^2\right]$$

$$\times \exp\left[-\frac{1}{2}\left(\frac{259 - \mu}{10}\right)^2\right]$$

Figure 1.14 shows a computer plot of the likelihood function for our example. It is based on the calculation of likelihood values $L(\mu)$ for many values of μ. Note that the likelihood values at $\mu = 230$ and $\mu = 259$ correspond to the ones we determined earlier. Also note that the likelihood function reaches a maximum at $\mu = 258$.

The fact that the likelihood function in Figure 1.14 is relatively peaked in the neighborhood of the maximum likelihood estimate $\bar{Y} = 258$ is of particular interest. Note, for instance, that for $\mu = 250$ or $\mu = 266$, the likelihood value is already only a little more than one-half as large as the likelihood value at $\mu = 258$. This indicates that the maximum likelihood estimate here is relatively precise because values of μ not near the maximum likelihood estimate $\bar{Y} = 258$ are much less consistent with the sample data. When the likelihood function is relatively flat in a fairly wide region around the maximum likelihood

FIGURE 1.14
Likelihood Function for Estimation of Mean of Normal Population:
$Y_1 = 250,$
$Y_2 = 265,$
$Y_3 = 259.$

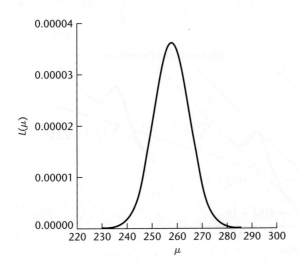

estimate, many values of the parameter are almost as consistent with the sample data as the maximum likelihood estimate, and the maximum likelihood estimate would therefore be relatively imprecise.

Regression Model. The concepts just presented for maximum likelihood estimation of a population mean carry over directly to the estimation of the parameters of normal error regression model (1.24). For this model, each Y_i observation is normally distributed with mean $\beta_0 + \beta_1 X_i$ and standard deviation σ. To illustrate the method of maximum likelihood estimation here, consider the earlier persistence study example on page 15. For simplicity, let us suppose that we know $\sigma = 2.5$. We wish to determine the likelihood value for the parameter values $\beta_0 = 0$ and $\beta_1 = .5$. For subject 1, $X_1 = 20$ and hence the mean of the probability distribution would be $\beta_0 + \beta_1 X_1 = 0 + .5(20) = 10.0$. Figure 1.15a shows the normal distribution with mean 10.0 and standard deviation 2.5. Note that the observed value $Y_1 = 5$ is in the left tail of the distribution and that the density there is relatively small. For the second subject, $X_2 = 55$ and hence $\beta_0 + \beta_1 X_2 = 27.5$. The normal distribution with mean 27.5 is shown in Figure 1.15b. Note that the observed value $Y_2 = 12$ is most unlikely for this case and that the density there is extremely small. Finally, note that the observed value $Y_3 = 10$ is also in the left tail of its distribution if $\beta_0 = 0$ and $\beta_1 = .5$, as shown in Figure 1.15c, and that the density there is also relatively small.

FIGURE 1.15 **Densities for Sample Observations if $\beta_0 = 0$ and $\beta_1 = 5$—Persistence Study Example.**

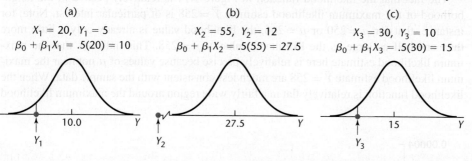

(a)
$X_1 = 20, \ Y_1 = 5$
$\beta_0 + \beta_1 X_1 = .5(20) = 10$

(b)
$X_2 = 55, \ Y_2 = 12$
$\beta_0 + \beta_1 X_2 = .5(55) = 27.5$

(c)
$X_3 = 30, \ Y_3 = 10$
$\beta_0 + \beta_1 X_3 = .5(30) = 15$

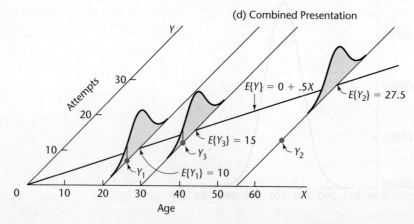

(d) Combined Presentation

Figure 1.15d combines all of this information, showing the regression function $E\{Y\} = 0 + .5X$, the three sample cases, and the three normal distributions. Note how poorly the regression line fits the three sample cases, as was also indicated by the three small density values. Thus, it appears that $\beta_0 = 0$ and $\beta_1 = .5$ are not consistent with the data.

We calculate the densities (i.e., heights of the curve) in the usual way. For $Y_1 = 5$, $X_1 = 20$, the normal density is as follows when $\beta_0 = 0$ and $\beta_1 = .5$:

$$f_1 = \frac{1}{\sqrt{2\pi}(2.5)} \exp\left[-\frac{1}{2}\left(\frac{5 - 10.0}{2.5}\right)^2 \right] = .021596$$

The other densities are $f_2 = .7175 \times 10^{-9}$ and $f_3 = .021596$, and the likelihood value of $\beta_0 = 0$ and $\beta_1 = .5$ therefore is:

$$L(\beta_0 = 0, \beta_1 = .5) = .021596(.7175 \times 10^{-9})(.021596) = .3346 \times 10^{-12}$$

In general, the density of an observation Y_i for the normal error regression model (1.24) is as follows, utilizing the fact that $E\{Y_i\} = \beta_0 + \beta_1 X_i$ and $\sigma^2\{Y_i\} = \sigma^2$:

$$f_i = \frac{1}{\sqrt{2\pi}\sigma} \exp\left[-\frac{1}{2}\left(\frac{Y_i - \beta_0 - \beta_1 X_i}{\sigma}\right)^2 \right] \tag{1.25}$$

The likelihood function for n observations $Y_1, Y_2, \ldots, Y_n$ is the product of the individual densities in (1.25). Since the variance σ^2 of the error terms is usually unknown, the likelihood function is a function of three parameters, β_0, β_1, and σ^2:

$$L(\beta_0, \beta_1, \sigma^2) = \prod_{i=1}^{n} \frac{1}{(2\pi\sigma^2)^{1/2}} \exp\left[-\frac{1}{2\sigma^2}(Y_i - \beta_0 - \beta_1 X_i)^2 \right]$$

$$= \frac{1}{(2\pi\sigma^2)^{n/2}} \exp\left[-\frac{1}{2\sigma^2} \sum_{i=1}^{n}(Y_i - \beta_0 - \beta_1 X_i)^2 \right] \tag{1.26}$$

The values of β_0, β_1, and σ^2 that maximize this likelihood function are the maximum likelihood estimators and are denoted by $\hat{\beta}_0$, $\hat{\beta}_1$, and $\hat{\sigma}^2$, respectively. These estimators can be found analytically, and they are as follows:

Parameter	Maximum Likelihood Estimator	
β_0	$\hat{\beta}_0 = b_0$	same as (1.10b)
β_1	$\hat{\beta}_1 = b_1$	same as (1.10a)
σ^2	$\hat{\sigma}^2 = \dfrac{\sum(Y_i - \hat{Y}_i)^2}{n}$	

$$\tag{1.27}$$

Thus, the maximum likelihood estimators of β_0 and β_1 are the same estimators as those provided by the method of least squares. The maximum likelihood estimator $\hat{\sigma}^2$ is biased, and ordinarily the unbiased estimator *MSE* as given in (1.22) is used. Note that the unbiased estimator *MSE* or s^2 differs but slightly from the maximum likelihood estimator $\hat{\sigma}^2$, especially if n is not small:

$$s^2 = MSE = \frac{n}{n-2}\hat{\sigma}^2 \tag{1.28}$$

Example

For the persistence study example, we know now that the maximum likelihood estimates of β_0 and β_1 are $b_0 = 2.81$ and $b_1 = .177$, the same as the least squares estimates in Figure 1.9b.

Comments

1. Since the maximum likelihood estimators $\hat{\beta}_0$ and $\hat{\beta}_1$ are the same as the least squares estimators b_0 and b_1, they have the properties of all least squares estimators:
   a. They are unbiased.
   b. They have minimum variance among all unbiased linear estimators.
   In addition, the maximum likelihood estimators b_0 and b_1 for the normal error regression model (1.24) have other desirable properties:
   c. They are consistent, as defined in (A.52).
   d. They are sufficient, as defined in (A.53).
   e. They are minimum variance unbiased; that is, they have minimum variance in the class of all unbiased estimators (linear or otherwise).
   Thus, for the normal error model, the estimators b_0 and b_1 have many desirable properties.

2. We find the values of β_0, β_1, and σ^2 that maximize the likelihood function L in (1.26) by taking partial derivatives of L with respect to β_0, β_1, and σ^2, equating each of the partials to zero, and solving the system of equations thus obtained. We can work with $\log_e L$, rather than L, because both L and $\log_e L$ are maximized for the same values of β_0, β_1, and σ^2:

$$\log_e L = -\frac{n}{2}\log_e 2\pi - \frac{n}{2}\log_e \sigma^2 - \frac{1}{2\sigma^2}\sum(Y_i - \beta_0 - \beta_1 X_i)^2 \tag{1.29}$$

Partial differentiation of the logarithm of the likelihood function is much easier; it yields:

$$\frac{\partial(\log_e L)}{\partial\beta_0} = \frac{1}{\sigma^2}\sum(Y_i - \beta_0 - \beta_1 X_i)$$

$$\frac{\partial(\log_e L)}{\partial\beta_1} = \frac{1}{\sigma^2}\sum X_i(Y_i - \beta_0 - \beta_1 X_i)$$

$$\frac{\partial(\log_e L)}{\partial\sigma^2} = -\frac{n}{2\sigma^2} + \frac{1}{2\sigma^4}\sum(Y_i - \beta_0 - \beta_1 X_i)^2$$

We now set these partial derivatives equal to zero, replacing β_0, β_1, and σ^2 by the estimators $\hat{\beta}_0$, $\hat{\beta}_1$, and $\hat{\sigma}^2$. We obtain, after some simplification:

$$\sum(Y_i - \hat{\beta}_0 - \hat{\beta}_1 X_i) = 0 \tag{1.30a}$$

$$\sum X_i(Y_i - \hat{\beta}_0 - \hat{\beta}_1 X_i) = 0 \tag{1.30b}$$

$$\frac{\sum(Y_i - \hat{\beta}_0 - \hat{\beta}_1 X_i)^2}{n} = \hat{\sigma}^2 \tag{1.30c}$$

Formulas (1.30a) and (1.30b) are identical to the earlier least squares normal equations (1.9), and formula (1.30c) is the biased estimator of σ^2 given earlier in (1.27).   ∎

Cited References

1.1. BMDP New System 2.0. Statistical Solutions, Inc.
1.2. MINITAB Release 13. Minitab Inc.
1.3. SAS/STAT Release 8.2. SAS Institute, Inc.
1.4. SPSS 11.5 for Windows. SPSS Inc.
1.5. SYSTAT 10.2. SYSTAT Software, Inc.
1.6. JMP Version 5. SAS Institute, Inc.
1.7. S-Plus 6 for Windows. Insightful Corporation.
1.8. MATLAB 6.5. The MathWorks, Inc.

Problems

1.1. Refer to the sales volume example on page 3. Suppose that the number of units sold is measured accurately, but clerical errors are frequently made in determining the dollar sales. Would the relation between the number of units sold and dollar sales still be a functional one? Discuss.

1.2. The members of a health spa pay annual membership dues of $300 plus a charge of $2 for each visit to the spa. Let Y denote the dollar cost for the year for a member and X the number of visits by the member during the year. Express the relation between X and Y mathematically. Is it a functional relation or a statistical relation?

1.3. Experience with a certain type of plastic indicates that a relation exists between the hardness (measured in Brinell units) of items molded from the plastic (Y) and the elapsed time since termination of the molding process (X). It is proposed to study this relation by means of regression analysis. A participant in the discussion objects, pointing out that the hardening of the plastic "is the result of a natural chemical process that doesn't leave anything to chance, so the relation must be mathematical and regression analysis is not appropriate." Evaluate this objection.

1.4. In Table 1.1, the lot size X is the same in production runs 1 and 24 but the work hours Y differ. What feature of regression model (1.1) is illustrated by this?

1.5. When asked to state the simple linear regression model, a student wrote it as follows: $E\{Y_i\} = \beta_0 + \beta_1 X_i + \varepsilon_i$. Do you agree?

1.6. Consider the normal error regression model (1.24). Suppose that the parameter values are $\beta_0 = 200$, $\beta_1 = 5.0$, and $\sigma = 4$.

 a. Plot this normal error regression model in the fashion of Figure 1.6. Show the distributions of Y for $X = 10, 20,$ and 40.

 b. Explain the meaning of the parameters β_0 and β_1. Assume that the scope of the model includes $X = 0$.

1.7. In a simulation exercise, regression model (1.1) applies with $\beta_0 = 100$, $\beta_1 = 20$, and $\sigma^2 = 25$. An observation on Y will be made for $X = 5$.

 a. Can you state the exact probability that Y will fall between 195 and 205? Explain.

 b. If the normal error regression model (1.24) is applicable, can you now state the exact probability that Y will fall between 195 and 205? If so, state it.

1.8. In Figure 1.6, suppose another Y observation is obtained at $X = 45$. Would $E\{Y\}$ for this new observation still be 104? Would the Y value for this new case again be 108?

1.9. A student in accounting enthusiastically declared: "Regression is a very powerful tool. We can isolate fixed and variable costs by fitting a linear regression model, even when we have no data for small lots." Discuss.

1.10. An analyst in a large corporation studied the relation between current annual salary (Y) and age (X) for the 46 computer programmers presently employed in the company. The analyst concluded that the relation is curvilinear, reaching a maximum at 47 years. Does this imply that the salary for a programmer increases until age 47 and then decreases? Explain.

1.11. The regression function relating production output by an employee after taking a training program (Y) to the production output before the training program (X) is $E\{Y\} = 20 + .95X$, where X ranges from 40 to 100. An observer concludes that the training program does not raise production output on the average because β_1 is not greater than 1.0. Comment.

1.12. In a study of the relationship for senior citizens between physical activity and frequency of colds, participants were asked to monitor their weekly time spent in exercise over a five-year period and the frequency of colds. The study demonstrated that a negative statistical relation exists between time spent in exercise and frequency of colds. The investigator concluded that increasing the time spent in exercise is an effective strategy for reducing the frequency of colds for senior citizens.

   a. Were the data obtained in the study observational or experimental data?

   b. Comment on the validity of the conclusions reached by the investigator.

   c. Identify two or three other explanatory variables that might affect both the time spent in exercise and the frequency of colds for senior citizens simultaneously.

   d. How might the study be changed so that a valid conclusion about causal relationship between amount of exercise and frequency of colds can be reached?

1.13. Computer programmers employed by a software developer were asked to participate in a month-long training seminar. During the seminar, each employee was asked to record the number of hours spent in class preparation each week. After completing the seminar, the productivity level of each participant was measured. A positive linear statistical relationship between participants' productivity levels and time spent in class preparation was found. The seminar leader concluded that increases in employee productivity are caused by increased class preparation time.

   a. Were the data used by the seminar leader observational or experimental data?

   b. Comment on the validity of the conclusion reached by the seminar leader.

   c. Identify two or three alternative variables that might cause both the employee productivity scores and the employee class participation times to increase (decrease) simultaneously.

   d. How might the study be changed so that a valid conclusion about causal relationship between class preparation time and employee productivity can be reached?

1.14. Refer to Problem 1.3. Four different elapsed times since termination of the molding process (treatments) are to be studied to see how they affect the hardness of a plastic. Sixteen batches (experimental units) are available for the study. Each treatment is to be assigned to four experimental units selected at random. Use a table of random digits or a random number generator to make an appropriate randomization of assignments.

1.15. The effects of five dose levels are to be studied in a completely randomized design, and 20 experimental units are available. Each dose level is to be assigned to four experimental units selected at random. Use a table of random digits or a random number generator to make an appropriate randomization of assignments.

1.16. Evaluate the following statement: "For the least squares method to be fully valid, it is required that the distribution of Y be normal."

1.17. A person states that b_0 and b_1 in the fitted regression function (1.13) can be estimated by the method of least squares. Comment.

1.18. According to (1.17), $\sum e_i = 0$ when regression model (1.1) is fitted to a set of n cases by the method of least squares. Is it also true that $\sum \varepsilon_i = 0$? Comment.

1.19. **Grade point average.** The director of admissions of a small college selected 120 students at random from the new freshman class in a study to determine whether a student's grade point average (GPA) at the end of the freshman year (Y) can be predicted from the ACT test score (X). The results of the study follow. Assume that first-order regression model (1.1) is appropriate.

i:	1	2	3	...	118	119	120
X_i:	21	14	28	...	28	16	28
Y_i:	3.897	3.885	3.778	...	3.914	1.860	2.948

a. Obtain the least squares estimates of β_0 and β_1, and state the estimated regression function.

b. Plot the estimated regression function and the data. Does the estimated regression function appear to fit the data well?

c. Obtain a point estimate of the mean freshman GPA for students with ACT test score $X = 30$.

d. What is the point estimate of the change in the mean response when the entrance test score increases by one point?

*1.20. **Copier maintenance.** The Tri-City Office Equipment Corporation sells an imported copier on a franchise basis and performs preventive maintenance and repair service on this copier. The data below have been collected from 45 recent calls on users to perform routine preventive maintenance service; for each call, X is the number of copiers serviced and Y is the total number of minutes spent by the service person. Assume that first-order regression model (1.1) is appropriate.

i:	1	2	3	...	43	44	45
X_i:	2	4	3	...	2	4	5
Y_i:	20	60	46	...	27	61	77

a. Obtain the estimated regression function.

b. Plot the estimated regression function and the data. How well does the estimated regression function fit the data?

c. Interpret b_0 in your estimated regression function. Does b_0 provide any relevant information here? Explain.

d. Obtain a point estimate of the mean service time when $X = 5$ copiers are serviced.

*1.21. **Airfreight breakage.** A substance used in biological and medical research is shipped by airfreight to users in cartons of 1,000 ampules. The data below, involving 10 shipments, were collected on the number of times the carton was transferred from one aircraft to another over the shipment route (X) and the number of ampules found to be broken upon arrival (Y). Assume that first-order regression model (1.1) is appropriate.

i:	1	2	3	4	5	6	7	8	9	10
X_i:	1	0	2	0	3	1	0	1	2	0
Y_i:	16	9	17	12	22	13	8	15	19	11

a. Obtain the estimated regression function. Plot the estimated regression function and the data. Does a linear regression function appear to give a good fit here?

b. Obtain a point estimate of the expected number of broken ampules when $X = 1$ transfer is made.

   c. Estimate the increase in the expected number of ampules broken when there are 2 transfers as compared to 1 transfer.

   d. Verify that your fitted regression line goes through the point $(\bar{X}, \bar{Y})$.

1.22. **Plastic hardness.** Refer to Problems 1.3 and 1.14. Sixteen batches of the plastic were made, and from each batch one test item was molded. Each test item was randomly assigned to one of the four predetermined time levels, and the hardness was measured after the assigned elapsed time. The results are shown below; X is the elapsed time in hours, and Y is hardness in Brinell units. Assume that first-order regression model (1.1) is appropriate.

i:	1	2	3	...	14	15	16
X_i:	16	16	16	...	40	40	40
Y_i:	199	205	196	...	248	253	246

   a. Obtain the estimated regression function. Plot the estimated regression function and the data. Does a linear regression function appear to give a good fit here?

   b. Obtain a point estimate of the mean hardness when $X = 40$ hours.

   c. Obtain a point estimate of the change in mean hardness when X increases by 1 hour.

1.23. Refer to **Grade point average** Problem 1.19.

   a. Obtain the residuals e_i. Do they sum to zero in accord with (1.17)?

   b. Estimate σ^2 and σ. In what units is σ expressed?

*1.24. Refer to **Copier maintenance** Problem 1.20.

   a. Obtain the residuals e_i and the sum of the squared residuals $\sum e_i^2$. What is the relation between the sum of the squared residuals here and the quantity Q in (1.8)?

   b. Obtain point estimates of σ^2 and σ. In what units is σ expressed?

*1.25. Refer to **Airfreight breakage** Problem 1.21.

   a. Obtain the residual for the first case. What is its relation to ε_1?

   b. Compute $\sum e_i^2$ and MSE. What is estimated by MSE?

1.26. Refer to **Plastic hardness** Problem 1.22.

   a. Obtain the residuals e_i. Do they sum to zero in accord with (1.17)?

   b. Estimate σ^2 and σ. In what units is σ expressed?

*1.27. **Muscle mass.** A person's muscle mass is expected to decrease with age. To explore this relationship in women, a nutritionist randomly selected 15 women from each 10-year age group, beginning with age 40 and ending with age 79. The results follow; X is age, and Y is a measure of muscle mass. Assume that first-order regression model (1.1) is appropriate.

i:	1	2	3	...	58	59	60
X_i:	43	41	47	...	76	72	76
Y_i:	106	106	97	...	56	70	74

   a. Obtain the estimated regression function. Plot the estimated regression function and the data. Does a linear regression function appear to give a good fit here? Does your plot support the anticipation that muscle mass decreases with age?

   b. Obtain the following: (1) a point estimate of the difference in the mean muscle mass for women differing in age by one year, (2) a point estimate of the mean muscle mass for women aged $X = 60$ years, (3) the value of the residual for the eighth case, (4) a point estimate of σ^2.

1.28. **Crime rate.** A criminologist studying the relationship between level of education and crime rate in medium-sized U.S. counties collected the following data for a random sample of 84 counties; X is the percentage of individuals in the county having at least a high-school diploma, and Y is the crime rate (crimes reported per 100,000 residents) last year. Assume that first-order regression model (1.1) is appropriate.

i:	1	2	3	...	82	83	84
X_i:	74	82	81	...	88	83	76
Y_i:	8,487	8,179	8,362	...	8,040	6,981	7,582

  a. Obtain the estimated regression function. Plot the estimated regression function and the data. Does the linear regression function appear to give a good fit here? Discuss.

  b. Obtain point estimates of the following: (1) the difference in the mean crime rate for two counties whose high-school graduation rates differ by one percentage point, (2) the mean crime rate last year in counties with high school graduation percentage $X = 80$, (3) ε_{10}, (4) σ^2.

Exercises

1.29. Refer to regression model (1.1). Assume that $X = 0$ is within the scope of the model. What is the implication for the regression function if $\beta_0 = 0$ so that the model is $Y_i = \beta_1 X_i + \varepsilon_i$? How would the regression function plot on a graph?

1.30. Refer to regression model (1.1). What is the implication for the regression function if $\beta_1 = 0$ so that the model is $Y_i = \beta_0 + \varepsilon_i$? How would the regression function plot on a graph?

1.31. Refer to **Plastic hardness** Problem 1.22. Suppose one test item was molded from a single batch of plastic and the hardness of this one item was measured at 16 different points in time. Would the error term in the regression model for this case still reflect the same effects as for the experiment initially described? Would you expect the error terms for the different points in time to be uncorrelated? Discuss.

1.32. Derive the expression for b_1 in (1.10a) from the normal equations in (1.9).

1.33. (Calculus needed.) Refer to the regression model $Y_i = \beta_0 + \varepsilon_i$ in Exercise 1.30. Derive the least squares estimator of β_0 for this model.

1.34. Prove that the least squares estimator of β_0 obtained in Exercise 1.33 is unbiased.

1.35. Prove the result in (1.18) — that the sum of the Y observations is the same as the sum of the fitted values.

1.36. Prove the result in (1.20) — that the sum of the residuals weighted by the fitted values is zero.

1.37. Refer to Table 1.1 for the Toluca Company example. When asked to present a point estimate of the expected work hours for lot sizes of 30 pieces, a person gave the estimate 202 because this is the mean number of work hours in the three runs of size 30 in the study. A critic states that this person's approach "throws away" most of the data in the study because cases with lot sizes other than 30 are ignored. Comment.

1.38. In **Airfreight breakage** Problem 1.21, the least squares estimates are $b_0 = 10.20$ and $b_1 = 4.00$, and $\sum e_i^2 = 17.60$. Evaluate the least squares criterion Q in (1.8) for the estimates (1) $b_0 = 9$, $b_1 = 3$; (2) $b_0 = 11$, $b_1 = 5$. Is the criterion Q larger for these estimates than for the least squares estimates?

1.39. Two observations on Y were obtained at each of three X levels, namely, at $X = 5$, $X = 10$, and $X = 15$.

  a. Show that the least squares regression line fitted to the *three* points $(5, \bar{Y}_1)$, $(10, \bar{Y}_2)$, and $(15, \bar{Y}_3)$, where $\bar{Y}_1$, $\bar{Y}_2$, and $\bar{Y}_3$ denote the means of the Y observations at the three X levels, is identical to the least squares regression line fitted to the original six cases.

b. In this study, could the error term variance σ^2 be estimated without fitting a regression line? Explain.

1.40. In fitting regression model (1.1), it was found that observation Y_i fell directly on the fitted regression line (i.e., $Y_i = \hat{Y}_i$). If this case were deleted, would the least squares regression line fitted to the remaining $n - 1$ cases be changed? [*Hint*: What is the contribution of case i to the least squares criterion Q in (1.8)?]

1.41. (Calculus needed.) Refer to the regression model $Y_i = \beta_1 X_i + \varepsilon_i, i = 1, \ldots, n$, in Exercise 1.29.

a. Find the least squares estimator of β_1.

b. Assume that the error terms ε_i are independent $N(0, \sigma^2)$ and that σ^2 is known. State the likelihood function for the n sample observations on Y and obtain the maximum likelihood estimator of β_1. Is it the same as the least squares estimator?

c. Show that the maximum likelihood estimator of β_1 is unbiased.

1.42. **Typographical errors.** Shown below are the number of galleys for a manuscript (X) and the dollar cost of correcting typographical errors (Y) in a random sample of recent orders handled by a firm specializing in technical manuscripts. Assume that the regression model $Y_i = \beta_1 X_i + \varepsilon_i$ is appropriate, with normally distributed independent error terms whose variance is $\sigma^2 = 16$.

i:	1	2	3	4	5	6
X_i:	7	12	4	14	25	30
Y_i:	128	213	75	250	446	540

a. State the likelihood function for the six Y observations, for $\sigma^2 = 16$.

b. Evaluate the likelihood function for $\beta_1 = 17, 18$, and 19. For which of these β_1 values is the likelihood function largest?

c. The maximum likelihood estimator is $b_1 = \sum X_i Y_i / \sum X_i^2$. Find the maximum likelihood estimate. Are your results in part (b) consistent with this estimate?

d. Using a computer graphics or statistics package, evaluate the likelihood function for values of β_1 between $\beta_1 = 17$ and $\beta_1 = 19$ and plot the function. Does the point at which the likelihood function is maximized correspond to the maximum likelihood estimate found in part (c)?

Projects

1.43. Refer to the **CDI** data set in Appendix C.2. The number of active physicians in a CDI (Y) is expected to be related to total population, number of hospital beds, and total personal income. Assume that first-order regression model (1.1) is appropriate for each of the three predictor variables.

a. Regress the number of active physicians in turn on each of the three predictor variables. State the estimated regression functions.

b. Plot the three estimated regression functions and data on separate graphs. Does a linear regression relation appear to provide a good fit for each of the three predictor variables?

c. Calculate *MSE* for each of the three predictor variables. Which predictor variable leads to the smallest variability around the fitted regression line?

1.44. Refer to the **CDI** data set in Appendix C.2.

a. For each geographic region, regress per capita income in a CDI (Y) against the percentage of individuals in a county having at least a bachelor's degree (X). Assume that first-order regression model (1.1) is appropriate for each region. State the estimated regression functions.

b. Are the estimated regression functions similar for the four regions? Discuss.

c. Calculate *MSE* for each region. Is the variability around the fitted regression line approximately the same for the four regions? Discuss.

1.45. Refer to the **SENIC** data set in Appendix C.1. The average length of stay in a hospital (Y) is anticipated to be related to infection risk, available facilities and services, and routine chest X-ray ratio. Assume that first-order regression model (1.1) is appropriate for each of the three predictor variables.

a. Regress average length of stay on each of the three predictor variables. State the estimated regression functions.

b. Plot the three estimated regression functions and data on separate graphs. Does a linear relation appear to provide a good fit for each of the three predictor variables?

c. Calculate *MSE* for each of the three predictor variables. Which predictor variable leads to the smallest variability around the fitted regression line?

1.46. Refer to the **SENIC** data set in Appendix C.1.

a. For each geographic region, regress average length of stay in hospital (Y) against infection risk (X). Assume that first-order regression model (1.1) is appropriate for each region. State the estimated regression functions.

b. Are the estimated regression functions similar for the four regions? Discuss.

c. Calculate *MSE* for each region. Is the variability around the fitted regression line approximately the same for the four regions? Discuss.

1.47. Refer to **Typographical errors** Problem 1.42. Assume that first-order regression model (1.1) is appropriate, with normally distributed independent error terms whose variance is $\sigma^2 = 16$.

a. State the likelihood function for the six observations, for $\sigma^2 = 16$.

b. Obtain the maximum likelihood estimates of β_0 and β_1, using (1.27).

c. Using a computer graphics or statistics package, obtain a three-dimensional plot of the likelihood function for values of β_0 between $\beta_0 = -10$ and $\beta_0 = 10$ and for values of β_1 between $\beta_1 = 17$ and $\beta_1 = 19$. Does the likelihood appear to be maximized by the maximum likelihood estimates found in part (b)?

Chapter 2

Inferences in Regression and Correlation Analysis

In this chapter, we first take up inferences concerning the regression parameters β_0 and β_1, considering both interval estimation of these parameters and tests about them. We then discuss interval estimation of the mean $E\{Y\}$ of the probability distribution of Y, for given X, prediction intervals for a new observation Y, confidence bands for the regression line, the analysis of variance approach to regression analysis, the general linear test approach, and descriptive measures of association. Finally, we take up the correlation coefficient, a measure of association between X and Y when both X and Y are random variables.

Throughout this chapter (excluding Section 2.11), and in the remainder of Part I unless otherwise stated, we assume that the normal error regression model (1.24) is applicable. This model is:

$$Y_i = \beta_0 + \beta_1 X_i + \varepsilon_i \qquad (2.1)$$

where:

β_0 and β_1 are parameters

X_i are known constants

ε_i are independent $N(0, \sigma^2)$

2.1 Inferences Concerning β_1

Frequently, we are interested in drawing inferences about β_1, the slope of the regression line in model (2.1). For instance, a market research analyst studying the relation between sales (Y) and advertising expenditures (X) may wish to obtain an interval estimate of β_1 because it will provide information as to how many additional sales dollars, on the average, are generated by an additional dollar of advertising expenditure.

At times, tests concerning β_1 are of interest, particularly one of the form:

$$H_0: \beta_1 = 0$$
$$H_a: \beta_1 \neq 0$$

FIGURE 2.1
Regression
Model (2.1)
when $\beta_1 = 0$.

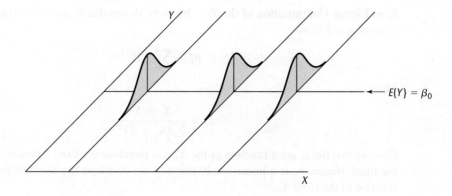

The reason for interest in testing whether or not $\beta_1 = 0$ is that, when $\beta_1 = 0$, there is no linear association between Y and X. Figure 2.1 illustrates the case when $\beta_1 = 0$. Note that the regression line is horizontal and that the means of the probability distributions of Y are therefore all equal, namely:

$$E\{Y\} = \beta_0 + (0)X = \beta_0$$

For normal error regression model (2.1), the condition $\beta_1 = 0$ implies even more than no linear association between Y and X. Since for this model all probability distributions of Y are normal with constant variance, and since the means are equal when $\beta_1 = 0$, it follows that the probability distributions of Y are identical when $\beta_1 = 0$. This is shown in Figure 2.1. Thus, $\beta_1 = 0$ for the normal error regression model (2.1) implies not only that there is no linear association between Y and X but also that there is no relation of any type between Y and X, since the probability distributions of Y are then identical at all levels of X.

Before discussing inferences concerning β_1 further, we need to consider the sampling distribution of b_1, the point estimator of β_1.

Sampling Distribution of b_1

The point estimator b_1 was given in (1.10a) as follows:

$$b_1 = \frac{\sum(X_i - \bar{X})(Y_i - \bar{Y})}{\sum(X_i - \bar{X})^2} \tag{2.2}$$

The sampling distribution of b_1 refers to the different values of b_1 that would be obtained with repeated sampling when the levels of the predictor variable X are held constant from sample to sample.

For normal error regression model (2.1), the sampling distribution of b_1 is normal, with mean and variance: **(2.3)**

$$E\{b_1\} = \beta_1 \tag{2.3a}$$

$$\sigma^2\{b_1\} = \frac{\sigma^2}{\sum(X_i - \bar{X})^2} \tag{2.3b}$$

To show this, we need to recognize that b_1 is a linear combination of the observations Y_i.

b_1 as Linear Combination of the Y_i. It can be shown that b_1, as defined in (2.2), can be expressed as follows:

$$b_1 = \sum k_i Y_i \tag{2.4}$$

where:

$$k_i = \frac{X_i - \bar{X}}{\sum (X_i - \bar{X})^2} \tag{2.4a}$$

Observe that the k_i are a function of the X_i and therefore are fixed quantities since the X_i are fixed. Hence, b_1 is a linear combination of the Y_i where the coefficients are solely a function of the fixed X_i.

The coefficients k_i have a number of interesting properties that will be used later:

$$\sum k_i = 0 \tag{2.5}$$

$$\sum k_i X_i = 1 \tag{2.6}$$

$$\sum k_i^2 = \frac{1}{\sum (X_i - \bar{X})^2} \tag{2.7}$$

Comments

1. To show that b_1 is a linear combination of the Y_i with coefficients k_i, we first prove:

$$\sum (X_i - \bar{X})(Y_i - \bar{Y}) = \sum (X_i - \bar{X}) Y_i \tag{2.8}$$

This follows since:

$$\sum (X_i - \bar{X})(Y_i - \bar{Y}) = \sum (X_i - \bar{X}) Y_i - \sum (X_i - \bar{X}) \bar{Y}$$

But $\sum (X_i - \bar{X}) \bar{Y} = \bar{Y} \sum (X_i - \bar{X}) = 0$ since $\sum (X_i - \bar{X}) = 0$, Hence, (2.8) holds.

We now express b_1 using (2.8) and (2.4a):

$$b_1 = \frac{\sum (X_i - \bar{X})(Y_i - \bar{Y})}{\sum (X_i - \bar{X})^2} = \frac{\sum (X_i - \bar{X}) Y_i}{\sum (X_i - \bar{X})^2} = \sum k_i Y_i$$

2. The proofs of the properties of the k_i are direct. For example, property (2.5) follows because:

$$\sum k_i = \sum \left[\frac{X_i - \bar{X}}{\sum (X_i - \bar{X})^2} \right] = \frac{1}{\sum (X_i - \bar{X})^2} \sum (X_i - \bar{X}) = \frac{0}{\sum (X_i - \bar{X})^2} = 0$$

Similarly, property (2.7) follows because:

$$\sum k_i^2 = \sum \left[\frac{X_i - \bar{X}}{\sum (X_i - \bar{X})^2} \right]^2 = \frac{1}{\left[\sum (X_i - \bar{X})^2 \right]^2} \sum (X_i - \bar{X})^2 = \frac{1}{\sum (X_i - \bar{X})^2}$$

■

Normality. We return now to the sampling distribution of b_1 for the normal error regression model (2.1). The normality of the sampling distribution of b_1 follows at once from the fact that b_1 is a linear combination of the Y_i. The Y_i are independently, normally distributed according to model (2.1), and (A.40) in Appendix A states that a linear combination of independent normal random variables is normally distributed.

Mean.   The unbiasedness of the point estimator b_1, stated earlier in the Gauss-Markov theorem (1.11), is easy to show:

$$E\{b_1\} = E\left\{\sum k_i Y_i\right\} = \sum k_i E\{Y_i\} = \sum k_i (\beta_0 + \beta_1 X_i)$$

$$= \beta_0 \sum k_i + \beta_1 \sum k_i X_i$$

By (2.5) and (2.6), we then obtain $E\{b_1\} = \beta_1$.

Variance.   The variance of b_1 can be derived readily. We need only remember that the Y_i are independent random variables, each with variance σ^2, and that the k_i are constants. Hence, we obtain by (A.31):

$$\sigma^2\{b_1\} = \sigma^2\left\{\sum k_i Y_i\right\} = \sum k_i^2 \sigma^2\{Y_i\}$$

$$= \sum k_i^2 \sigma^2 = \sigma^2 \sum k_i^2$$

$$= \sigma^2 \frac{1}{\sum (X_i - \bar{X})^2}$$

The last step follows from (2.7).

Estimated Variance.   We can estimate the variance of the sampling distribution of b_1:

$$\sigma^2\{b_1\} = \frac{\sigma^2}{\sum (X_i - \bar{X})^2}$$

by replacing the parameter σ^2 with *MSE*, the unbiased estimator of σ^2:

$$s^2\{b_1\} = \frac{MSE}{\sum (X_i - \bar{X})^2} \tag{2.9}$$

The point estimator $s^2\{b_1\}$ is an unbiased estimator of $\sigma^2\{b_1\}$. Taking the positive square root, we obtain $s\{b_1\}$, the point estimator of $\sigma\{b_1\}$.

Comment

We stated in theorem (1.11) that b_1 has minimum variance among all unbiased linear estimators of the form:

$$\hat{\beta}_1 = \sum c_i Y_i$$

where the c_i are arbitrary constants. We now prove this. Since $\hat{\beta}_1$ is required to be unbiased, the following must hold:

$$E\{\hat{\beta}_1\} = E\left\{\sum c_i Y_i\right\} = \sum c_i E\{Y_i\} = \beta_1$$

Now $E\{Y_i\} = \beta_0 + \beta_1 X_i$ by (1.2), so the above condition becomes:

$$E\{\hat{\beta}_1\} = \sum c_i (\beta_0 + \beta_1 X_i) = \beta_0 \sum c_i + \beta_1 \sum c_i X_i = \beta_1$$

For the unbiasedness condition to hold, the c_i must follow the restrictions:

$$\sum c_i = 0 \qquad \sum c_i X_i = 1$$

Now the variance of $\hat{\beta}_1$ is, by (A.31):

$$\sigma^2\{\hat{\beta}_1\} = \sum c_i^2 \sigma^2\{Y_i\} = \sigma^2 \sum c_i^2$$

Let us define $c_i = k_i + d_i$, where the k_i are the least squares constants in (2.4a) and the d_i are arbitrary constants. We can then write:

$$\sigma^2\{\hat{\beta}_1\} = \sigma^2 \sum c_i^2 = \sigma^2 \sum (k_i + d_i)^2 = \sigma^2 \left(\sum k_i^2 + \sum d_i^2 + 2 \sum k_i d_i \right)$$

We know that $\sigma^2 \sum k_i^2 = \sigma^2\{b_1\}$ from our proof above. Further, $\sum k_i d_i = 0$ because of the restrictions on the k_i and c_i above:

$$\sum k_i d_i = \sum k_i (c_i - k_i)$$

$$= \sum c_i k_i - \sum k_i^2$$

$$= \sum c_i \left[\frac{X_i - \bar{X}}{\sum (X_i - \bar{X})^2} \right] - \frac{1}{\sum (X_i - \bar{X})^2}$$

$$= \frac{\sum c_i X_i - \bar{X} \sum c_i}{\sum (X_i - \bar{X})^2} - \frac{1}{\sum (X_i - \bar{X})^2} = 0$$

Hence, we have:

$$\sigma^2\{\hat{\beta}_1\} = \sigma^2\{b_1\} + \sigma^2 \sum d_i^2$$

Note that the smallest value of $\sum d_i^2$ is zero. Hence, the variance of $\hat{\beta}_1$ is at a minimum when $\sum d_i^2 = 0$. But this can only occur if all $d_i = 0$, which implies $c_i \equiv k_i$. Thus, the least squares estimator b_1 has minimum variance among all unbiased linear estimators. ∎

Sampling Distribution of $(b_1 - \beta_1)/s\{b_1\}$

Since b_1 is normally distributed, we know that the standardized statistic $(b_1 - \beta_1)/\sigma\{b_1\}$ is a standard normal variable. Ordinarily, of course, we need to estimate $\sigma\{b_1\}$ by $s\{b_1\}$, and hence are interested in the distribution of the statistic $(b_1 - \beta_1)/s\{b_1\}$. When a statistic is standardized but the denominator is an estimated standard deviation rather than the true standard deviation, it is called a *studentized statistic*. An important theorem in statistics states the following about the studentized statistic $(b_1 - \beta_1)/s\{b_1\}$:

$$\frac{b_1 - \beta_1}{s\{b_1\}} \text{ is distributed as } t(n-2) \text{ for regression model (2.1)} \qquad \textbf{(2.10)}$$

Intuitively, this result should not be unexpected. We know that if the observations Y_i come from the same normal population, $(\bar{Y} - \mu)/s\{\bar{Y}\}$ follows the t distribution with $n-1$ degrees of freedom. The estimator b_1, like $\bar{Y}$, is a linear combination of the observations Y_i. The reason for the difference in the degrees of freedom is that two parameters (β_0 and β_1) need to be estimated for the regression model; hence, two degrees of freedom are lost here.

Comment

We can show that the studentized statistic $(b_1 - \beta_1)/s\{b_1\}$ is distributed as t with $n - 2$ degrees of freedom by relying on the following theorem:

> For regression model (2.1), SSE/σ^2 is distributed as χ^2 with $n - 2$ degrees of freedom and is independent of b_0 and b_1. **(2.11)**

First, let us rewrite $(b_1 - \beta_1)/s\{b_1\}$ as follows:

$$\frac{b_1 - \beta_1}{\sigma\{b_1\}} \div \frac{s\{b_1\}}{\sigma\{b_1\}}$$

The numerator is a standard normal variable z. The nature of the denominator can be seen by first considering:

$$\frac{s^2\{b_1\}}{\sigma^2\{b_1\}} = \frac{\dfrac{MSE}{\sum(X_i - \bar{X})^2}}{\dfrac{\sigma^2}{\sum(X_i - \bar{X})^2}} = \frac{MSE}{\sigma^2} = \frac{\dfrac{SSE}{n-2}}{\sigma^2}$$

$$= \frac{SSE}{\sigma^2(n-2)} \sim \frac{\chi^2(n-2)}{n-2}$$

where the symbol $\sim$ stands for "is distributed as." The last step follows from (2.11). Hence, we have:

$$\frac{b_1 - \beta_1}{s\{b_1\}} \sim \frac{z}{\sqrt{\dfrac{\chi^2(n-2)}{n-2}}}$$

But by theorem (2.11), z and χ^2 are independent since z is a function of b_1 and b_1 is independent of $SSE/\sigma^2 \sim \chi^2$. Hence, by (A.44), it follows that:

$$\frac{b_1 - \beta_1}{s\{b_1\}} \sim t(n-2)$$

This result places us in a position to readily make inferences concerning β_1. ∎

Confidence Interval for β_1

Since $(b_1 - \beta_1)/s\{b_1\}$ follows a t distribution, we can make the following probability statement:

$$P\{t(\alpha/2; n-2) \le (b_1 - \beta_1)/s\{b_1\} \le t(1 - \alpha/2; n-2)\} = 1 - \alpha \quad \textbf{(2.12)}$$

Here, $t(\alpha/2; n-2)$ denotes the $(\alpha/2)100$ percentile of the t distribution with $n - 2$ degrees of freedom. Because of the symmetry of the t distribution around its mean 0, it follows that:

$$t(\alpha/2; n-2) = -t(1 - \alpha/2; n-2) \quad \textbf{(2.13)}$$

Rearranging the inequalities in (2.12) and using (2.13), we obtain:

$$P\{b_1 - t(1 - \alpha/2; n-2)s\{b_1\} \le \beta_1 \le b_1 + t(1 - \alpha/2; n-2)s\{b_1\}\} = 1 - \alpha$$

$$\textbf{(2.14)}$$

Since (2.14) holds for all possible values of β_1, the $1 - \alpha$ confidence limits for β_1 are:

$$b_1 \pm t(1 - \alpha/2; n-2)s\{b_1\} \quad \textbf{(2.15)}$$

Example

Consider the Toluca Company example of Chapter 1. Management wishes an estimate of β_1 with 95 percent confidence coefficient. We summarize in Table 2.1 the needed results obtained earlier. First, we need to obtain $s\{b_1\}$:

$$s^2\{b_1\} = \frac{MSE}{\sum(X_i - \bar{X})^2} = \frac{2,384}{19,800} = .12040$$

$$s\{b_1\} = .3470$$

This estimated standard deviation is shown in the MINITAB output in Figure 2.2 in the column labeled Stdev corresponding to the row labeled X. Figure 2.2 repeats the MINITAB output presented earlier in Chapter 1 and contains some additional results that we will utilize shortly.

For a 95 percent confidence coefficient, we require $t(.975; 23)$. From Table B.2 in Appendix B, we find $t(.975; 23) = 2.069$. The 95 percent confidence interval, by (2.15), then is:

$$3.5702 - 2.069(.3470) \le \beta_1 \le 3.5702 + 2.069(.3470)$$

$$2.85 \le \beta_1 \le 4.29$$

Thus, with confidence coefficient .95, we estimate that the mean number of work hours increases by somewhere between 2.85 and 4.29 hours for each additional unit in the lot.

Comment

In Chapter 1, we noted that the scope of a regression model is restricted ordinarily to some range of values of the predictor variable. This is particularly important to keep in mind in using estimates of the slope β_1. In our Toluca Company example, a linear regression model appeared appropriate for lot sizes between 20 and 120, the range of the predictor variable in the recent past. It may not be

TABLE 2.1
Results for
Toluca
Company
Example
Obtained in
Chapter 1.

$$n = 25 \qquad\qquad \bar{X} = 70.00$$
$$b_0 = 62.37 \qquad\qquad b_1 = 3.5702$$
$$\hat{Y} = 62.37 + 3.5702X \qquad SSE = 54,825$$
$$\sum(X_i - \bar{X})^2 = 19,800 \qquad MSE = 2,384$$
$$\sum(Y_i - \bar{Y})^2 = 307,203$$

FIGURE 2.2
Portion of
MINITAB
Regression
Output—
Toluca
Company
Example.

```
The regression equation is
Y = 62.4 + 3.57 X

Predictor      Coef      Stdev     t-ratio        p
Constant      62.37      26.18        2.38    0.026
X            3.5702     0.3470       10.29    0.000

s = 48.82      R-sq = 82.2%      R-sq(adj) = 81.4%

Analysis of Variance

SOURCE        DF          SS          MS        F        p
Regression     1      252378      252378   105.88    0.000
Error         23       54825        2384
Total         24      307203
```

reasonable to use the estimate of the slope to infer the effect of lot size on number of work hours far outside this range since the regression relation may not be linear there. ∎

Tests Concerning β_1

Since $(b_1 - \beta_1)/s\{b_1\}$ is distributed as t with $n - 2$ degrees of freedom, tests concerning β_1 can be set up in ordinary fashion using the t distribution.

Example 1

Two-Sided Test A cost analyst in the Toluca Company is interested in testing, using regression model (2.1), whether or not there is a linear association between work hours and lot size, i.e., whether or not $\beta_1 = 0$. The two alternatives then are:

$$H_0: \beta_1 = 0$$
$$H_a: \beta_1 \neq 0 \tag{2.16}$$

The analyst wishes to control the risk of a Type I error at $\alpha = .05$. The conclusion H_a could be reached at once by referring to the 95 percent confidence interval for β_1 constructed earlier, since this interval does not include 0.

An explicit test of the alternatives (2.16) is based on the test statistic:

$$t^* = \frac{b_1}{s\{b_1\}} \tag{2.17}$$

The decision rule with this test statistic for controlling the level of significance at α is:

$$\text{If } |t^*| \leq t(1 - \alpha/2; n - 2), \text{ conclude } H_0$$
$$\text{If } |t^*| > t(1 - \alpha/2; n - 2), \text{ conclude } H_a \tag{2.18}$$

For the Toluca Company example, where $\alpha = .05$, $b_1 = 3.5702$, and $s\{b_1\} = .3470$, we require $t(.975; 23) = 2.069$. Thus, the decision rule for testing alternatives (2.16) is:

$$\text{If } |t^*| \leq 2.069, \text{ conclude } H_0$$
$$\text{If } |t^*| > 2.069, \text{ conclude } H_a$$

Since $|t^*| = |3.5702/.3470| = 10.29 > 2.069$, we conclude H_a, that $\beta_1 \neq 0$ or that there is a linear association between work hours and lot size. The value of the test statistic, $t^* = 10.29$, is shown in the MINITAB output in Figure 2.2 in the column labeled t-ratio and the row labeled X.

The two-sided P-value for the sample outcome is obtained by first finding the one-sided P-value, $P\{t(23) > t^* = 10.29\}$. We see from Table B.2 that this probability is less than .0005. Many statistical calculators and computer packages will provide the actual probability; it is almost 0, denoted by 0+. Thus, the two-sided P-value is $2(0+) = 0+$. Since the two-sided P-value is less than the specified level of significance $\alpha = .05$, we could conclude H_a directly. The MINITAB output in Figure 2.2 shows the P-value in the column labeled p, corresponding to the row labeled X. It is shown as 0.000.

Comment

When the test of whether or not $\beta_1 = 0$ leads to the conclusion that $\beta_1 \neq 0$, the association between Y and X is sometimes described to be a linear statistical association. ∎

Example 2

One-Sided Test Suppose the analyst had wished to test whether or not β_1 is positive, controlling the level of significance at $\alpha = .05$. The alternatives then would be:

$$H_0: \beta_1 \leq 0$$
$$H_a: \beta_1 > 0$$

and the decision rule based on test statistic (2.17) would be:

$$\text{If } t^* \leq t(1 - \alpha; n - 2), \text{ conclude } H_0$$
$$\text{If } t^* > t(1 - \alpha; n - 2), \text{ conclude } H_a$$

For $\alpha = .05$, we require $t(.95; 23) = 1.714$. Since $t^* = 10.29 > 1.714$, we would conclude H_a, that β_1 is positive.

This same conclusion could be reached directly from the one-sided P-value, which was noted in Example 1 to be 0+. Since this P-value is less than .05, we would conclude H_a.

Comments

1. The P-value is sometimes called the observed level of significance.

2. Many scientific publications commonly report the P-value together with the value of the test statistic. In this way, one can conduct a test at any desired level of significance α by comparing the P-value with the specified level α.

3. Users of statistical calculators and computer packages need to be careful to ascertain whether one-sided or two-sided P-values are reported. Many commonly used labels, such as PROB or P, do not reveal whether the P-value is one- or two-sided.

4. Occasionally, it is desired to test whether or not β_1 equals some specified nonzero value β_{10}, which may be a historical norm, the value for a comparable process, or an engineering specification. The alternatives now are:

$$H_0: \beta_1 = \beta_{10}$$
$$H_a: \beta_1 \neq \beta_{10} \tag{2.19}$$

and the appropriate test statistic is:

$$t^* = \frac{b_1 - \beta_{10}}{s\{b_1\}} \tag{2.20}$$

The decision rule to be employed here still is (2.18), but it is now based on t^* defined in (2.20).

Note that test statistic (2.20) simplifies to test statistic (2.17) when the test involves $H_0: \beta_1 = \beta_{10} = 0$. ∎

2.2 Inferences Concerning β_0

As noted in Chapter 1, there are only infrequent occasions when we wish to make inferences concerning β_0, the intercept of the regression line. These occur when the scope of the model includes $X = 0$.

Sampling Distribution of b_0

The point estimator b_0 was given in (1.10b) as follows:

$$b_0 = \bar{Y} - b_1 \bar{X} \tag{2.21}$$

The sampling distribution of b_0 refers to the different values of b_0 that would be obtained with repeated sampling when the levels of the predictor variable X are held constant from sample to sample.

For regression model (2.1), the sampling distribution of b_0 is normal, with mean and variance: **(2.22)**

$$E\{b_0\} = \beta_0 \tag{2.22a}$$

$$\sigma^2\{b_0\} = \sigma^2 \left[\frac{1}{n} + \frac{\bar{X}^2}{\sum(X_i - \bar{X})^2} \right] \tag{2.22b}$$

The normality of the sampling distribution of b_0 follows because b_0, like b_1, is a linear combination of the observations Y_i. The results for the mean and variance of the sampling distribution of b_0 can be obtained in similar fashion as those for b_1.

An estimator of $\sigma^2\{b_0\}$ is obtained by replacing σ^2 by its point estimator *MSE*:

$$s^2\{b_0\} = MSE \left[\frac{1}{n} + \frac{\bar{X}^2}{\sum(X_i - \bar{X})^2} \right] \tag{2.23}$$

The positive square root, $s\{b_0\}$, is an estimator of $\sigma\{b_0\}$.

Sampling Distribution of $(b_0 - \beta_0)/s\{b_0\}$

Analogous to theorem (2.10) for b_1, a theorem for b_0 states:

$$\frac{b_0 - \beta_0}{s\{b_0\}} \text{ is distributed as } t(n-2) \text{ for regression model (2.1)} \tag{2.24}$$

Hence, confidence intervals for β_0 and tests concerning β_0 can be set up in ordinary fashion, using the t distribution.

Confidence Interval for β_0

The $1 - \alpha$ confidence limits for β_0 are obtained in the same manner as those for β_1 derived earlier. They are:

$$b_0 \pm t(1 - \alpha/2; n - 2)s\{b_0\} \tag{2.25}$$

Example

As noted earlier, the scope of the model for the Toluca Company example does not extend to lot sizes of $X = 0$. Hence, the regression parameter β_0 may not have intrinsic meaning here. If, nevertheless, a 90 percent confidence interval for β_0 were desired, we would proceed by finding $t(.95; 23)$ and $s\{b_0\}$. From Table B.2, we find $t(.95; 23) = 1.714$. Using the earlier results summarized in Table 2.1, we obtain by (2.23):

$$s^2\{b_0\} = MSE \left[\frac{1}{n} + \frac{\bar{X}^2}{\sum(X_i - \bar{X})^2} \right] = 2,384 \left[\frac{1}{25} + \frac{(70.00)^2}{19,800} \right] = 685.34$$

or:

$$s\{b_0\} = 26.18$$

The MINITAB output in Figure 2.2 shows this estimated standard deviation in the column labeled Stdev and the row labeled Constant.

The 90 percent confidence interval for β_0 is:

$$62.37 - 1.714(26.18) \le \beta_0 \le 62.37 + 1.714(26.18)$$
$$17.5 \le \beta_0 \le 107.2$$

We caution again that this confidence interval does not necessarily provide meaningful information. For instance, it does not necessarily provide information about the "setup" cost (the cost incurred in setting up the production process for the part) since we are not certain whether a linear regression model is appropriate when the scope of the model is extended to $X = 0$.

2.3 Some Considerations on Making Inferences Concerning β_0 and β_1

Effects of Departures from Normality

If the probability distributions of Y are not exactly normal but do not depart seriously, the sampling distributions of b_0 and b_1 will be approximately normal, and the use of the t distribution will provide approximately the specified confidence coefficient or level of significance. Even if the distributions of Y are far from normal, the estimators b_0 and b_1 generally have the property of *asymptotic normality*—their distributions approach normality under very general conditions as the sample size increases. Thus, with sufficiently large samples, the confidence intervals and decision rules given earlier still apply even if the probability distributions of Y depart far from normality. For large samples, the t value is, of course, replaced by the z value for the standard normal distribution.

Interpretation of Confidence Coefficient and Risks of Errors

Since regression model (2.1) assumes that the X_i are known constants, the confidence coefficient and risks of errors are interpreted with respect to taking repeated samples in which the X observations are kept at the same levels as in the observed sample. For instance, we constructed a confidence interval for β_1 with confidence coefficient .95 in the Toluca Company example. This coefficient is interpreted to mean that if many independent samples are taken where the levels of X (the lot sizes) are the same as in the data set and a 95 percent confidence interval is constructed for each sample, 95 percent of the intervals will contain the true value of β_1.

Spacing of the X Levels

Inspection of formulas (2.3b) and (2.22b) for the variances of b_1 and b_0, respectively, indicates that for given n and σ^2 these variances are affected by the spacing of the X levels in the observed data. For example, the greater is the spread in the X levels, the larger is the quantity $\sum(X_i - \bar{X})^2$ and the smaller is the variance of b_1. We discuss in Chapter 4 how the X observations should be spaced in experiments where spacing can be controlled.

Power of Tests

The power of tests on β_0 and β_1 can be obtained from Appendix Table B.5. Consider, for example, the general test concerning β_1 in (2.19):

$$H_0: \beta_1 = \beta_{10}$$
$$H_a: \beta_1 \neq \beta_{10}$$

for which test statistic (2.20) is employed:

$$t^* = \frac{b_1 - \beta_{10}}{s\{b_1\}}$$

and the decision rule for level of significance α is given in (2.18):

If $|t^*| \le t(1 - \alpha/2; n - 2)$, conclude H_0

If $|t^*| > t(1 - \alpha/2; n - 2)$, conclude H_a

The power of this test is the probability that the decision rule will lead to conclusion H_a when H_a in fact holds. Specifically, the power is given by:

$$\text{Power} = P\{|t^*| > t(1 - \alpha/2; n - 2) \mid \delta\} \tag{2.26}$$

where δ is the *noncentrality measure*—i.e., a measure of how far the true value of β_1 is from β_{10}:

$$\delta = \frac{|\beta_1 - \beta_{10}|}{\sigma\{b_1\}} \tag{2.27}$$

Table B.5 presents the power of the two-sided t test for $\alpha = .05$ and $\alpha = .01$, for various degrees of freedom df. To illustrate the use of this table, let us return to the Toluca Company example where we tested:

$$H_0: \beta_1 = \beta_{10} = 0$$

$$H_a: \beta_1 \ne \beta_{10} = 0$$

Suppose we wish to know the power of the test when $\beta_1 = 1.5$. To ascertain this, we need to know σ^2, the variance of the error terms. Assume, based on prior information or pilot data, that a reasonable planning value for the unknown variance is $\sigma^2 = 2,500$, so $\sigma^2\{b_1\}$ for our example would be:

$$\sigma^2\{b_1\} = \frac{\sigma^2}{\sum(X_i - \bar{X})^2} = \frac{2,500}{19,800} = .1263$$

or $\sigma\{b_1\} = .3553$. Then $\delta = |1.5 - 0| \div .3553 = 4.22$. We enter Table B.5 for $\alpha = .05$ (the level of significance used in the test) and 23 degrees of freedom and interpolate linearly between $\delta = 4.00$ and $\delta = 5.00$. We obtain:

$$.97 + \frac{4.22 - 4.00}{5.00 - 4.00}(1.00 - .97) = .9766$$

Thus, if $\beta_1 = 1.5$, the probability would be about .98 that we would be led to conclude H_a ($\beta_1 \ne 0$). In other words, if $\beta_1 = 1.5$, we would be almost certain to conclude that there is a linear relation between work hours and lot size.

The power of tests concerning β_0 can be obtained from Table B.5 in completely analogous fashion. For one-sided tests, Table B.5 should be entered so that one-half the level of significance shown there is the level of significance of the one-sided test.

2.4 Interval Estimation of $E\{Y_h\}$

A common objective in regression analysis is to estimate the mean for one or more probability distributions of Y. Consider, for example, a study of the relation between level of piecework pay (X) and worker productivity (Y). The mean productivity at high and medium levels of piecework pay may be of particular interest for purposes of analyzing the benefits obtained from an increase in the pay. As another example, the Toluca Company was interested in the mean response (mean number of work hours) for a range of lot sizes for purposes of finding the optimum lot size.

Let X_h denote the level of X for which we wish to estimate the mean response. X_h may be a value which occurred in the sample, or it may be some other value of the predictor variable within the scope of the model. The mean response when $X = X_h$ is denoted by $E\{Y_h\}$. Formula (1.12) gives us the point estimator $\hat{Y}_h$ of $E\{Y_h\}$:

$$\hat{Y}_h = b_0 + b_1 X_h \tag{2.28}$$

We consider now the sampling distribution of $\hat{Y}_h$.

Sampling Distribution of $\hat{Y}_h$

The sampling distribution of $\hat{Y}_h$, like the earlier sampling distributions discussed, refers to the different values of $\hat{Y}_h$ that would be obtained if repeated samples were selected, each holding the levels of the predictor variable X constant, and calculating $\hat{Y}_h$ for each sample.

> For normal error regression model (2.1), the sampling distribution of $\hat{Y}_h$ is normal, with mean and variance: $\qquad$ (2.29)

$$E\{\hat{Y}_h\} = E\{Y_h\} \tag{2.29a}$$

$$\sigma^2\{\hat{Y}_h\} = \sigma^2 \left[\frac{1}{n} + \frac{(X_h - \bar{X})^2}{\sum(X_i - \bar{X})^2} \right] \tag{2.29b}$$

Normality. The normality of the sampling distribution of $\hat{Y}_h$ follows directly from the fact that $\hat{Y}_h$, like b_0 and b_1, is a linear combination of the observations Y_i.

Mean. Note from (2.29a) that $\hat{Y}_h$ is an unbiased estimator of $E\{Y_h\}$. To prove this, we proceed as follows:

$$E\{\hat{Y}_h\} = E\{b_0 + b_1 X_h\} = E\{b_0\} + X_h E\{b_1\} = \beta_0 + \beta_1 X_h$$

by (2.3a) and (2.22a).

Variance. Note from (2.29b) that the variability of the sampling distribution of $\hat{Y}_h$ is affected by how far X_h is from $\bar{X}$, through the term $(X_h - \bar{X})^2$. The further from $\bar{X}$ is X_h, the greater is the quantity $(X_h - \bar{X})^2$ and the larger is the variance of $\hat{Y}_h$. An intuitive explanation of this effect is found in Figure 2.3. Shown there are two sample regression lines, based on two samples for the same set of X values. The two regression lines are assumed to go through the same $(\bar{X}, \bar{Y})$ point to isolate the effect of interest, namely, the effect of variation in the estimated slope b_1 from sample to sample. Note that at X_1, near $\bar{X}$, the fitted values $\hat{Y}_1$ for the two sample regression lines are close to each other. At X_2, which is far from $\bar{X}$, the situation is different. Here, the fitted values $\hat{Y}_2$ differ substantially.

FIGURE 2.3
Effect on $\hat{Y}_h$ of Variation in b_1 from Sample to Sample in Two Samples with Same Means $\bar{Y}$ and $\bar{X}$.

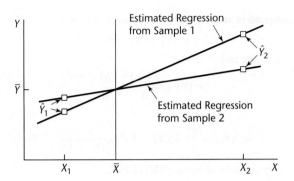

Thus, variation in the slope b_1 from sample to sample has a much more pronounced effect on $\hat{Y}_h$ for X levels far from the mean $\bar{X}$ than for X levels near $\bar{X}$. Hence, the variation in the $\hat{Y}_h$ values from sample to sample will be greater when X_h is far from the mean than when X_h is near the mean.

When *MSE* is substituted for σ^2 in (2.29b), we obtain $s^2\{\hat{Y}_h\}$, the estimated variance of $\hat{Y}_h$:

$$s^2\{\hat{Y}_h\} = MSE\left[\frac{1}{n} + \frac{(X_h - \bar{X})^2}{\sum(X_i - \bar{X})^2}\right] \qquad (2.30)$$

The estimated standard deviation of $\hat{Y}_h$ is then $s\{\hat{Y}_h\}$, the positive square root of $s^2\{\hat{Y}_h\}$.

Comments

1. When $X_h = 0$, the variance of $\hat{Y}_h$ in (2.29b) reduces to the variance of b_0 in (2.22b). Similarly, $s^2\{\hat{Y}_h\}$ in (2.30) reduces to $s^2\{b_0\}$ in (2.23). The reason is that $\hat{Y}_h = b_0$ when $X_h = 0$ since $\hat{Y}_h = b_0 + b_1 X_h$.

2. To derive $\sigma^2\{\hat{Y}_h\}$, we first show that b_1 and $\bar{Y}$ are uncorrelated and, hence, for regression model (2.1), independent:

$$\sigma\{\bar{Y}, b_1\} = 0 \qquad (2.31)$$

where $\sigma\{\bar{Y}, b_1\}$ denotes the covariance between $\bar{Y}$ and b_1. We begin with the definitions:

$$\bar{Y} = \sum\left(\frac{1}{n}\right)Y_i \qquad b_1 = \sum k_i Y_i$$

where k_i is as defined in (2.4a). We now use (A.32), with $a_i = 1/n$ and $c_i = k_i$; remember that the Y_i are independent random variables:

$$\sigma\{\bar{Y}, b_1\} = \sum\left(\frac{1}{n}\right)k_i\sigma^2\{Y_i\} = \frac{\sigma^2}{n}\sum k_i$$

But we know from (2.5) that $\sum k_i = 0$. Hence, the covariance is 0.

Now we are ready to find the variance of $\hat{Y}_h$. We shall use the estimator in the alternative form (1.15):

$$\sigma^2\{\hat{Y}_h\} = \sigma^2\{\bar{Y} + b_1(X_h - \bar{X})\}$$

Since $\bar{Y}$ and b_1 are independent and X_h and $\bar{X}$ are constants, we obtain:

$$\sigma^2\{\hat{Y}_h\} = \sigma^2\{\bar{Y}\} + (X_h - \bar{X})^2\sigma^2\{b_1\}$$

Now $\sigma^2\{b_1\}$ is given in (2.3b), and:

$$\sigma^2\{\bar{Y}\} = \frac{\sigma^2\{Y_i\}}{n} = \frac{\sigma^2}{n}$$

Hence:

$$\sigma^2\{\hat{Y}_h\} = \frac{\sigma^2}{n} + (X_h - \bar{X})^2\frac{\sigma^2}{\sum(X_i - \bar{X})^2}$$

which, upon a slight rearrangement of terms, yields (2.29b).   ∎

Sampling Distribution of $(\hat{Y}_h - E\{Y_h\})/s\{\hat{Y}_h\}$

Since we have encountered the t distribution in each type of inference for regression model (2.1) up to this point, it should not be surprising that:

$$\frac{\hat{Y}_h - E\{Y_h\}}{s\{\hat{Y}_h\}} \text{ is distributed as } t(n-2) \text{ for regression model (2.1)} \qquad \textbf{(2.32)}$$

Hence, all inferences concerning $E\{Y_h\}$ are carried out in the usual fashion with the t distribution. We illustrate the construction of confidence intervals, since in practice these are used more frequently than tests.

Confidence Interval for $E\{Y_h\}$

A confidence interval for $E\{Y_h\}$ is constructed in the standard fashion, making use of the t distribution as indicated by theorem (2.32). The $1 - \alpha$ confidence limits are:

$$\hat{Y}_h \pm t(1 - \alpha/2; n - 2)s\{\hat{Y}_h\} \qquad \textbf{(2.33)}$$

Example 1

Returning to the Toluca Company example, let us find a 90 percent confidence interval for $E\{Y_h\}$ when the lot size is $X_h = 65$ units. Using the earlier results in Table 2.1, we find the point estimate $\hat{Y}_h$:

$$\hat{Y}_h = 62.37 + 3.5702(65) = 294.4$$

Next, we need to find the estimated standard deviation $s\{\hat{Y}_h\}$. We obtain, using (2.30):

$$s^2\{\hat{Y}_h\} = 2,384\left[\frac{1}{25} + \frac{(65 - 70.00)^2}{19,800}\right] = 98.37$$

$$s\{\hat{Y}_h\} = 9.918$$

For a 90 percent confidence coefficient, we require $t(.95; 23) = 1.714$. Hence, our confidence interval with confidence coefficient .90 is by (2.33):

$$294.4 - 1.714(9.918) \le E\{Y_h\} \le 294.4 + 1.714(9.918)$$

$$277.4 \le E\{Y_h\} \le 311.4$$

We conclude with confidence coefficient .90 that the mean number of work hours required when lots of 65 units are produced is somewhere between 277.4 and 311.4 hours. We see that our estimate of the mean number of work hours is moderately precise.

Example 2   Suppose the Toluca Company wishes to estimate $E\{Y_h\}$ for lots with $X_h = 100$ units with a 90 percent confidence interval. We require:

$$\hat{Y}_h = 62.37 + 3.5702(100) = 419.4$$

$$s^2\{\hat{Y}_h\} = 2{,}384 \left[\frac{1}{25} + \frac{(100 - 70.00)^2}{19{,}800} \right] = 203.72$$

$$s\{\hat{Y}_h\} = 14.27$$

$$t(.95; 23) = 1.714$$

Hence, the 90 percent confidence interval is:

$$419.4 - 1.714(14.27) \leq E\{Y_h\} \leq 419.4 + 1.714(14.27)$$

$$394.9 \leq E\{Y_h\} \leq 443.9$$

Note that this confidence interval is somewhat wider than that for Example 1, since the X_h level here ($X_h = 100$) is substantially farther from the mean $\bar{X} = 70.0$ than the X_h level for Example 1 ($X_h = 65$).

Comments

1. Since the X_i are known constants in regression model (2.1), the interpretation of confidence intervals and risks of errors in inferences on the mean response is in terms of taking repeated samples in which the X observations are at the same levels as in the actual study. We noted this same point in connection with inferences on β_0 and β_1.
2. We see from formula (2.29b) that, for given sample results, the variance of $\hat{Y}_h$ is smallest when $X_h = \bar{X}$. Thus, in an experiment to estimate the mean response at a particular level X_h of the predictor variable, the precision of the estimate will be greatest if (everything else remaining equal) the observations on X are spaced so that $\bar{X} = X_h$.
3. The usual relationship between confidence intervals and tests applies in inferences concerning the mean response. Thus, the two-sided confidence limits (2.33) can be utilized for two-sided tests concerning the mean response at X_h. Alternatively, a regular decision rule can be set up.
4. The confidence limits (2.33) for a mean response $E\{Y_h\}$ are not sensitive to moderate departures from the assumption that the error terms are normally distributed. Indeed, the limits are not sensitive to substantial departures from normality if the sample size is large. This robustness in estimating the mean response is related to the robustness of the confidence limits for β_0 and β_1, noted earlier.
5. Confidence limits (2.33) apply when a single mean response is to be estimated from the study. We discuss in Chapter 4 how to proceed when several mean responses are to be estimated from the same data.   ∎

2.5   Prediction of New Observation

We consider now the prediction of a new observation Y corresponding to a given level X of the predictor variable. Three illustrations where prediction of a new observation is needed follow.

1. In the Toluca Company example, the next lot to be produced consists of 100 units and management wishes to predict the number of work hours for this particular lot.

2. An economist has estimated the regression relation between company sales and number of persons 16 or more years old from data for the past 10 years. Using a reliable demographic projection of the number of persons 16 or more years old for next year, the economist wishes to predict next year's company sales.

3. An admissions officer at a university has estimated the regression relation between the high school grade point average (GPA) of admitted students and the first-year college GPA. The officer wishes to predict the first-year college GPA for an applicant whose high school GPA is 3.5 as part of the information on which an admissions decision will be based.

The new observation on Y to be predicted is viewed as the result of a new trial, independent of the trials on which the regression analysis is based. We denote the level of X for the new trial as X_h and the new observation on Y as $Y_{h(new)}$. Of course, we assume that the underlying regression model applicable for the basic sample data continues to be appropriate for the new observation.

The distinction between estimation of the mean response $E\{Y_h\}$, discussed in the preceding section, and prediction of a new response $Y_{h(new)}$, discussed now, is basic. In the former case, we estimate the *mean* of the distribution of Y. In the present case, we predict an *individual outcome* drawn from the distribution of Y. Of course, the great majority of individual outcomes deviate from the mean response, and this must be taken into account by the procedure for predicting $Y_{h(new)}$.

Prediction Interval for $y_{h(new)}$ when Parameters Known

To illustrate the nature of a *prediction interval* for a new observation $Y_{h(new)}$ in as simple a fashion as possible, we shall first assume that all regression parameters are known. Later we drop this assumption and make appropriate modifications.

Suppose that in the college admissions example the relevant parameters of the regression model are known to be:

$$\beta_0 = .10 \qquad \beta_1 = .95$$
$$E\{Y\} = .10 + .95X$$
$$\sigma = .12$$

The admissions officer is considering an applicant whose high school GPA is $X_h = 3.5$. The mean college GPA for students whose high school average is 3.5 is:

$$E\{Y_h\} = .10 + .95(3.5) = 3.425$$

Figure 2.4 shows the probability distribution of Y for $X_h = 3.5$. Its mean is $E\{Y_h\} = 3.425$, and its standard deviation is $\sigma = .12$. Further, the distribution is normal in accord with regression model (2.1).

Suppose we were to predict that the college GPA of the applicant whose high school GPA is $X_h = 3.5$ will be between:

$$E\{Y_h\} \pm 3\sigma$$
$$3.425 \pm 3(.12)$$

so that the prediction interval would be:

$$3.065 \le Y_{h(new)} \le 3.785$$

FIGURE 2.4
Prediction of
$Y_{h(\text{new})}$ **when**
Parameters
Known.

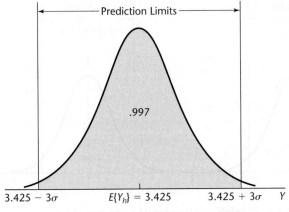

Probability Distribution of Y when $X_h = 3.5$

Since 99.7 percent of the area in a normal probability distribution falls within three standard deviations from the mean, the probability is .997 that this prediction interval will give a correct prediction for the applicant with high school GPA of 3.5. While the prediction limits here are rather wide, so that the prediction is not too precise, the prediction interval does indicate to the admissions officer that the applicant is expected to attain at least a 3.0 GPA in the first year of college.

The basic idea of a prediction interval is thus to choose a range in the distribution of Y wherein most of the observations will fall, and then to declare that the next observation will fall in this range. The usefulness of the prediction interval depends, as always, on the width of the interval and the needs for precision by the user.

In general, when the regression parameters of normal error regression model (2.1) are known, the $1 - \alpha$ prediction limits for $Y_{h(\text{new})}$ are:

$$E\{Y_h\} \pm z(1 - \alpha/2)\sigma \tag{2.34}$$

In centering the limits around $E\{Y_h\}$, we obtain the narrowest interval consistent with the specified probability of a correct prediction.

Prediction Interval for $Y_{h(\text{new})}$ when Parameters Unknown

When the regression parameters are unknown, they must be estimated. The mean of the distribution of Y is estimated by $\hat{Y}_h$, as usual, and the variance of the distribution of Y is estimated by *MSE*. We cannot, however, simply use the prediction limits (2.34) with the parameters replaced by the corresponding point estimators. The reason is illustrated intuitively in Figure 2.5. Shown there are two probability distributions of Y, corresponding to the upper and lower limits of a confidence interval for $E\{Y_h\}$. In other words, the distribution of Y could be located as far left as the one shown, as far right as the other one shown, or anywhere in between. Since we do not know the mean $E\{Y_h\}$ and only estimate it by a confidence interval, we cannot be certain of the location of the distribution of Y.

Figure 2.5 also shows the prediction limits for each of the two probability distributions of Y presented there. Since we cannot be certain of the location of the distribution

FIGURE 2.5
Prediction of
$Y_{h(\text{new})}$ **when**
Parameters
Unknown.

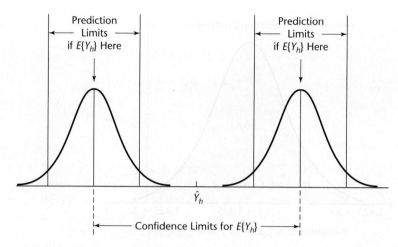

of Y, prediction limits for $Y_{h(\text{new})}$ clearly must take account of two elements, as shown in Figure 2.5:

1. Variation in possible location of the distribution of Y.
2. Variation within the probability distribution of Y.

Prediction limits for a new observation $Y_{h(\text{new})}$ at a given level X_h are obtained by means of the following theorem:

$$\frac{Y_{h(\text{new})} - \hat{Y}_h}{s\{\text{pred}\}} \text{ is distributed as } t(n-2) \text{ for normal error regression model (2.1)} \quad \textbf{(2.35)}$$

Note that the studentized statistic (2.35) uses the point estimator $\hat{Y}_h$ in the numerator rather than the true mean $E\{Y_h\}$ because the true mean is unknown and cannot be used in making a prediction. The estimated standard deviation of the prediction, $s\{\text{pred}\}$, in the denominator of the studentized statistic will be defined shortly.

From theorem (2.35), it follows in the usual fashion that the $1 - \alpha$ prediction limits for a new observation $Y_{h(\text{new})}$ are (for instance, compare (2.35) to (2.10) and relate $\hat{Y}_h$ to b_1 and $Y_{h(\text{new})}$ to β_1):

$$\hat{Y}_h \pm t(1 - \alpha/2; n - 2)s\{\text{pred}\} \quad \textbf{(2.36)}$$

Note that the numerator of the studentized statistic (2.35) represents how far the new observation $Y_{h(\text{new})}$ will deviate from the estimated mean $\hat{Y}_h$ based on the original n cases in the study. This difference may be viewed as the prediction error, with $\hat{Y}_h$ serving as the best point estimate of the value of the new observation $Y_{h(\text{new})}$. The variance of this prediction error can be readily obtained by utilizing the independence of the new observation $Y_{h(\text{new})}$ and the original n sample cases on which $\hat{Y}_h$ is based. We denote the variance of the prediction error by $\sigma^2\{\text{pred}\}$, and we obtain by (A.31b):

$$\sigma^2\{\text{pred}\} = \sigma^2\{Y_{h(\text{new})} - \hat{Y}_h\} = \sigma^2\{Y_{h(\text{new})}\} + \sigma^2\{\hat{Y}_h\} = \sigma^2 + \sigma^2\{\hat{Y}_h\} \quad \textbf{(2.37)}$$

Note that $\sigma^2\{\text{pred}\}$ has two components:

1. The variance of the distribution of Y at $X = X_h$, namely σ^2.
2. The variance of the sampling distribution of $\hat{Y}_h$, namely $\sigma^2\{\hat{Y}_h\}$.

An unbiased estimator of $\sigma^2\{\text{pred}\}$ is:

$$s^2\{\text{pred}\} = MSE + s^2\{\hat{Y}_h\} \tag{2.38}$$

which can be expressed as follows, using (2.30):

$$s^2\{\text{pred}\} = MSE\left[1 + \frac{1}{n} + \frac{(X_h - \bar{X})^2}{\sum(X_i - \bar{X})^2}\right] \tag{2.38a}$$

Example

The Toluca Company studied the relationship between lot size and work hours primarily to obtain information on the mean work hours required for different lot sizes for use in determining the optimum lot size. The company was also interested, however, to see whether the regression relationship is useful for predicting the required work hours for individual lots. Suppose that the next lot to be produced consists of $X_h = 100$ units and that a 90 percent prediction interval is desired. We require $t(.95; 23) = 1.714$. From earlier work, we have:

$$\hat{Y}_h = 419.4 \qquad s^2\{\hat{Y}_h\} = 203.72 \qquad MSE = 2,384$$

Using (2.38), we obtain:

$$s^2\{\text{pred}\} = 2,384 + 203.72 = 2,587.72$$
$$s\{\text{pred}\} = 50.87$$

Hence, the 90 percent prediction interval for $Y_{h(\text{new})}$ is by (2.36):

$$419.4 - 1.714(50.87) \le Y_{h(\text{new})} \le 419.4 + 1.714(50.87)$$
$$332.2 \le Y_{h(\text{new})} \le 506.6$$

With confidence coefficient .90, we predict that the number of work hours for the next production run of 100 units will be somewhere between 332 and 507 hours.

This prediction interval is rather wide and may not be too useful for planning worker requirements for the next lot. The interval can still be useful for control purposes, though. For instance, suppose that the actual work hours on the next lot of 100 units were 550 hours. Since the actual work hours fall outside the prediction limits, management would have an indication that a change in the production process may have occurred and would be alerted to the possible need for remedial action.

Note that the primary reason for the wide prediction interval is the large lot-to-lot variability in work hours for any given lot size; $MSE = 2,384$ accounts for 92 percent of the estimated prediction variance $s^2\{\text{pred}\} = 2,587.72$. It may be that the large lot-to-lot variability reflects other factors that affect the required number of work hours besides lot size, such as the amount of experience of employees assigned to the lot production. If so, a multiple regression model incorporating these other factors might lead to much more precise predictions. Alternatively, a designed experiment could be conducted to determine the main factors leading to the large lot-to-lot variation. A quality improvement program would then use these findings to achieve more uniform performance, for example, by additional training of employees if inadequate training accounted for much of the variability.

Comments

1. The 90 percent prediction interval for $Y_{h(\text{new})}$ obtained in the Toluca Company example is wider than the 90 percent confidence interval for $E\{Y_h\}$ obtained in Example 2 on page 55. The reason is that when predicting the work hours required for a new lot, we encounter both the variability in $\hat{Y}_h$ from sample to sample as well as the lot-to-lot variation within the probability distribution of Y.

2. Formula (2.38a) indicates that the prediction interval is wider the further X_h is from $\bar{X}$. The reason for this is that the estimate of the mean $\hat{Y}_h$, as noted earlier, is less precise as X_h is located farther away from $\bar{X}$.

3. The prediction limits (2.36), unlike the confidence limits (2.33) for a mean response $E\{Y_h\}$, are sensitive to departures from normality of the error terms distribution. In Chapter 3, we discuss diagnostic procedures for examining the nature of the probability distribution of the error terms, and we describe remedial measures if the departure from normality is serious.

4. The confidence coefficient for the prediction limits (2.36) refers to the taking of repeated samples based on the same set of X values, and calculating prediction limits for $Y_{h(\text{new})}$ for each sample.

5. Prediction limits (2.36) apply for a single prediction based on the sample data. Next, we discuss how to predict the mean of several new observations at a given X_h, and in Chapter 4 we take up how to make several predictions at different X_h levels.

6. Prediction intervals resemble confidence intervals. However, they differ conceptually. A confidence interval represents an inference on a parameter and is an interval that is intended to cover the value of the parameter. A prediction interval, on the other hand, is a statement about the value to be taken by a random variable, the new observation $Y_{h(\text{new})}$. ∎

Prediction of Mean of *m* New Observations for Given X_h

Occasionally, one would like to predict the mean of m new observations on Y for a given level of the predictor variable. Suppose the Toluca Company has been asked to bid on a contract that calls for $m = 3$ production runs of $X_h = 100$ units during the next few months. Management would like to predict the mean work hours per lot for these three runs and then convert this into a prediction of the total work hours required to fill the contract.

We denote the mean of the new Y observations to be predicted as $\bar{Y}_{h(\text{new})}$. It can be shown that the appropriate $1 - \alpha$ prediction limits are, assuming that the new Y observations are independent:

$$\hat{Y}_h \pm t(1 - \alpha/2; n - 2)s\{\text{predmean}\} \qquad (2.39)$$

where:

$$s^2\{\text{predmean}\} = \frac{MSE}{m} + s^2\{\hat{Y}_h\} \qquad (2.39a)$$

or equivalently:

$$s^2\{\text{predmean}\} = MSE\left[\frac{1}{m} + \frac{1}{n} + \frac{(X_h - \bar{X})^2}{\sum(X_i - \bar{X})^2}\right] \qquad (2.39b)$$

Note from (2.39a) that the variance $s^2\{\text{predmean}\}$ has two components:

1. The variance of the mean of m observations from the probability distribution of Y at $X = X_h$.

2. The variance of the sampling distribution of $\hat{Y}_h$.

Example

In the Toluca Company example, let us find the 90 percent prediction interval for the mean number of work hours $\bar{Y}_{h(\text{new})}$ in three new production runs, each for $X_h = 100$ units. From previous work, we have:

$$\hat{Y}_h = 419.4 \qquad s^2\{\hat{Y}_h\} = 203.72$$

$$MSE = 2{,}384 \qquad t(.95; 23) = 1.714$$

Hence, we obtain:

$$s^2\{\text{predmean}\} = \frac{2{,}384}{3} + 203.72 = 998.4$$

$$s\{\text{predmean}\} = 31.60$$

The prediction interval for the mean work hours per lot then is:

$$419.4 - 1.714(31.60) \le \bar{Y}_{h(\text{new})} \le 419.4 + 1.714(31.60)$$

$$365.2 \le \bar{Y}_{h(\text{new})} \le 473.6$$

Note that these prediction limits are narrower than those for predicting the work hours for a single lot of 100 units because they involve a prediction of the mean work hours for three lots.

We obtain the prediction interval for the total number of work hours for the three lots by multiplying the prediction limits for $\bar{Y}_{h(\text{new})}$ by 3:

$$1{,}095.6 = 3(365.2) \le \text{Total work hours} \le 3(473.6) = 1{,}420.8$$

Thus, it can be predicted with 90 percent confidence that between 1,096 and 1,421 work hours will be needed to fill the contract for three lots of 100 units each.

Comment

The 90 percent prediction interval for $\bar{Y}_{h(\text{new})}$, obtained for the Toluca Company example above, is narrower than that obtained for $Y_{h(\text{new})}$ on page 59, as expected. Furthermore, both of the prediction intervals are wider than the 90 percent confidence interval for $E\{Y_h\}$ obtained in Example 2 on page 55— also as expected. ∎

2.6 Confidence Band for Regression Line

At times we would like to obtain a confidence band for the entire regression line $E\{Y\} = \beta_0 + \beta_1 X$. This band enables us to see the region in which the entire regression line lies. It is particularly useful for determining the appropriateness of a fitted regression function, as we explain in Chapter 3.

The Working-Hotelling $1 - \alpha$ confidence band for the regression line for regression model (2.1) has the following two boundary values at any level X_h:

$$\hat{Y}_h \pm Ws\{\hat{Y}_h\} \tag{2.40}$$

where:

$$W^2 = 2F(1 - \alpha; 2, n - 2) \tag{2.40a}$$

and $\hat{Y}_h$ and $s\{\hat{Y}_h\}$ are defined in (2.28) and (2.30), respectively. Note that the formula for the boundary values is of exactly the same form as formula (2.33) for the confidence limits for the mean response at X_h, except that the t multiple has been replaced by the W

multiple. Consequently, the boundary points of the confidence band for the regression line are wider apart the further X_h is from the mean $\bar{X}$ of the X observations. The W multiple will be larger than the t multiple in (2.33) because the confidence band must encompass the entire regression line, whereas the confidence limits for $E\{Y_h\}$ at X_h apply only at the single level X_h.

Example

We wish to determine how precisely we have been able to estimate the regression function for the Toluca Company example by obtaining the 90 percent confidence band for the regression line. We illustrate the calculations of the boundary values of the confidence band when $X_h = 100$. We found earlier for this case:

$$\hat{Y}_h = 419.4 \qquad s\{\hat{Y}_h\} = 14.27$$

We now require:

$$W^2 = 2F(1 - \alpha; 2, n - 2) = 2F(.90; 2, 23) = 2(2.549) = 5.098$$

$$W = 2.258$$

Hence, the boundary values of the confidence band for the regression line at $X_h = 100$ are $419.4 \pm 2.258(14.27)$, and the confidence band there is:

$$387.2 \leq \beta_0 + \beta_1 X_h \leq 451.6 \qquad \text{for } X_h = 100$$

In similar fashion, we can calculate the boundary values for other values of X_h by obtaining $\hat{Y}_h$ and $s\{\hat{Y}_h\}$ for each X_h level from (2.28) and (2.30) and then finding the boundary values by means of (2.40). Figure 2.6 contains a plot of the confidence band for the regression line. Note that at $X_h = 100$, the boundary values are 387.2 and 451.6, as we calculated earlier.

We see from Figure 2.6 that the regression line for the Toluca Company example has been estimated fairly precisely. The slope of the regression line is clearly positive, and the levels of the regression line at different levels of X are estimated fairly precisely except for small and large lot sizes.

FIGURE 2.6
Confidence Band for Regression Line—Toluca Company Example.

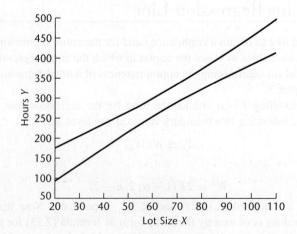

Comments

1. The boundary values of the confidence band for the regression line in (2.40) define a hyperbola, as may be seen by replacing $\hat{Y}_h$ and $s\{\hat{Y}_h\}$ by their definitions in (2.28) and (2.30), respectively:

$$b_0 + b_1 X \pm W \sqrt{MSE} \left[\frac{1}{n} + \frac{(X - \bar{X})^2}{\sum (X_i - \bar{X})^2} \right]^{1/2} \tag{2.41}$$

2. The boundary values of the confidence band for the regression line at any value X_h often are not substantially wider than the confidence limits for the mean response at that single X_h level. In the Toluca Company example, the t multiple for estimating the mean response at $X_h = 100$ with a 90 percent confidence interval was $t(.95; 23) = 1.714$. This compares with the W multiple for the 90 percent confidence band for the entire regression line of $W = 2.258$. With the somewhat wider limits for the entire regression line, one is able to draw conclusions about any and all mean responses for the entire regression line and not just about the mean response at a given X level. Some uses of this broader base for inference will be explained in the next two chapters.

3. The confidence band (2.40) applies to the entire regression line over all real-numbered values of X from $-\infty$ to ∞. The confidence coefficient indicates the proportion of time that the estimating procedure will yield a band that covers the entire line, in a long series of samples in which the X observations are kept at the same level as in the actual study.

In applications, the confidence band is ignored for that part of the regression line which is not of interest in the problem at hand. In the Toluca Company example, for instance, negative lot sizes would be ignored. The confidence coefficient for a limited segment of the band of interest is somewhat higher than $1 - \alpha$, so $1 - \alpha$ serves then as a lower bound to the confidence coefficient.

4. Some alternative procedures for developing confidence bands for the regression line have been developed. The simplicity of the Working-Hotelling confidence band (2.40) arises from the fact that it is a direct extension of the confidence limits for a single mean response in (2.33). ∎

2.7   Analysis of Variance Approach to Regression Analysis

We now have developed the basic regression model and demonstrated its major uses. At this point, we consider the regression analysis from the perspective of analysis of variance. This new perspective will not enable us to do anything new, but the analysis of variance approach will come into its own when we take up multiple regression models and other types of linear statistical models.

Partitioning of Total Sum of Squares

Basic Notions.   The analysis of variance approach is based on the partitioning of sums of squares and degrees of freedom associated with the response variable Y. To explain the motivation of this approach, consider again the Toluca Company example. Figure 2.7a shows the observations Y_i for the first two production runs presented in Table 1.1. Disregarding the lot sizes, we see that there is variation in the number of work hours Y_i, as in all statistical data. This variation is conventionally measured in terms of the deviations of the Y_i around their mean $\bar{Y}$:

$$Y_i - \bar{Y} \tag{2.42}$$

FIGURE 2.7 Illustration of Partitioning of Total Deviations $Y_i - \bar{Y}$—Toluca Company Example (not drawn to scale; only observations Y_1 and Y_2 are shown).

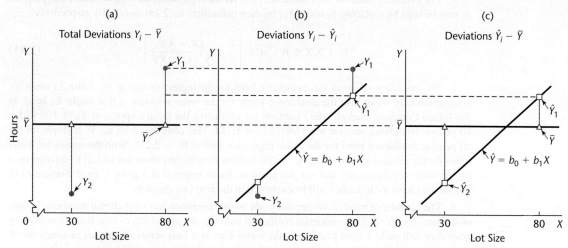

These deviations are shown by the vertical lines in Figure 2.7a. The measure of total variation, denoted by *SSTO*, is the sum of the squared deviations (2.42):

$$SSTO = \sum(Y_i - \bar{Y})^2 \qquad (2.43)$$

Here *SSTO* stands for *total sum of squares*. If all Y_i observations are the same, $SSTO = 0$. The greater the variation among the Y_i observations, the larger is *SSTO*. Thus, *SSTO* for our example is a measure of the uncertainty pertaining to the work hours required for a lot, when the lot size is not taken into account.

When we utilize the predictor variable X, the variation reflecting the uncertainty concerning the variable Y is that of the Y_i observations around the fitted regression line:

$$Y_i - \hat{Y}_i \qquad (2.44)$$

These deviations are shown by the vertical lines in Figure 2.7b. The measure of variation in the Y_i observations that is present when the predictor variable X is taken into account is the sum of the squared deviations (2.44), which is the familiar *SSE* of (1.21):

$$SSE = \sum(Y_i - \hat{Y}_i)^2 \qquad (2.45)$$

Again, *SSE* denotes *error sum of squares*. If all Y_i observations fall on the fitted regression line, $SSE = 0$. The greater the variation of the Y_i observations around the fitted regression line, the larger is *SSE*.

For the Toluca Company example, we know from earlier work (Table 2.1) that:

$$SSTO = 307,203 \qquad SSE = 54,825$$

What accounts for the substantial difference between these two sums of squares? The difference, as we show shortly, is another sum of squares:

$$SSR = \sum(\hat{Y}_i - \bar{Y})^2 \qquad (2.46)$$

where *SSR* stands for *regression sum of squares*. Note that *SSR* is a sum of squared deviations, the deviations being:

$$\hat{Y}_i - \bar{Y} \tag{2.47}$$

These deviations are shown by the vertical lines in Figure 2.7c. Each deviation is simply the difference between the fitted value on the regression line and the mean of the fitted values $\bar{Y}$. (Recall from (1.18) that the mean of the fitted values $\hat{Y}_i$ is $\bar{Y}$.) If the regression line is horizontal so that $\hat{Y}_i - \bar{Y} \equiv 0$, then $SSR = 0$. Otherwise, *SSR* is positive.

SSR may be considered a measure of that part of the variability of the Y_i which is associated with the regression line. The larger *SSR* is in relation to *SSTO*, the greater is the effect of the regression relation in accounting for the total variation in the Y_i observations.

For the Toluca Company example, we have:

$$SSR = SSTO - SSE = 307{,}203 - 54{,}825 = 252{,}378$$

which indicates that most of the total variability in work hours is accounted for by the relation between lot size and work hours.

Formal Development of Partitioning.   The total deviation $Y_i - \bar{Y}$, used in the measure of the total variation of the observations Y_i without taking the predictor variable into account, can be decomposed into two components:

$$\underbrace{Y_i - \bar{Y}}_{\substack{\text{Total} \\ \text{deviation}}} = \underbrace{\hat{Y}_i - \bar{Y}}_{\substack{\text{Deviation} \\ \text{of fitted} \\ \text{regression} \\ \text{value} \\ \text{around mean}}} + \underbrace{Y_i - \hat{Y}_i}_{\substack{\text{Deviation} \\ \text{around} \\ \text{fitted} \\ \text{regression} \\ \text{line}}} \tag{2.48}$$

The two components are:

1. The deviation of the fitted value $\hat{Y}_i$ around the mean $\bar{Y}$.
2. The deviation of the observation Y_i around the fitted regression line.

Figure 2.7 shows this decomposition for observation Y_1 by the broken lines.

It is a remarkable property that the sums of these squared deviations have the same relationship:

$$\sum (Y_i - \bar{Y})^2 = \sum (\hat{Y}_i - \bar{Y})^2 + \sum (Y_i - \hat{Y}_i)^2 \tag{2.49}$$

or, using the notation in (2.43), (2.45), and (2.46):

$$SSTO = SSR + SSE \tag{2.50}$$

To prove this basic result in the analysis of variance, we proceed as follows:

$$\sum (Y_i - \bar{Y})^2 = \sum [(\hat{Y}_i - \bar{Y}) + (Y_i - \hat{Y}_i)]^2$$
$$= \sum [(\hat{Y}_i - \bar{Y})^2 + (Y_i - \hat{Y}_i)^2 + 2(\hat{Y}_i - \bar{Y})(Y_i - \hat{Y}_i)]$$
$$= \sum (\hat{Y}_i - \bar{Y})^2 + \sum (Y_i - \hat{Y}_i)^2 + 2 \sum (\hat{Y}_i - \bar{Y})(Y_i - \hat{Y}_i)$$

The last term on the right equals zero, as we can see by expanding it:

$$2 \sum (\hat{Y}_i - \bar{Y})(Y_i - \hat{Y}_i) = 2 \sum \hat{Y}_i(Y_i - \hat{Y}_i) - 2\bar{Y} \sum (Y_i - \hat{Y}_i)$$

The first summation on the right equals zero by (1.20), and the second equals zero by (1.17). Hence, (2.49) follows.

Comment

The formulas for *SSTO*, *SSR*, and *SSE* given in (2.43), (2.45), and (2.46) are best for computational accuracy. Alternative formulas that are algebraically equivalent are available. One that is useful for deriving analytical results is:

$$SSR = b_1^2 \sum (X_i - \bar{X})^2 \tag{2.51}$$

■

Breakdown of Degrees of Freedom

Corresponding to the partitioning of the total sum of squares *SSTO*, there is a partitioning of the associated degrees of freedom (abbreviated *df*). We have $n - 1$ degrees of freedom associated with *SSTO*. One degree of freedom is lost because the deviations $Y_i - \bar{Y}$ are subject to one constraint: they must sum to zero. Equivalently, one degree of freedom is lost because the sample mean $\bar{Y}$ is used to estimate the population mean.

SSE, as noted earlier, has $n - 2$ degrees of freedom associated with it. Two degrees of freedom are lost because the two parameters β_0 and β_1 are estimated in obtaining the fitted values $\hat{Y}_i$.

SSR has one degree of freedom associated with it. Although there are n deviations $\hat{Y}_i - \bar{Y}$, all fitted values $\hat{Y}_i$ are calculated from the same estimated regression line. Two degrees of freedom are associated with a regression line, corresponding to the intercept and the slope of the line. One of the two degrees of freedom is lost because the deviations $\hat{Y}_i - \bar{Y}$ are subject to a constraint: they must sum to zero.

Note that the degrees of freedom are additive:

$$n - 1 = 1 + (n - 2)$$

For the Toluca Company example, these degrees of freedom are:

$$24 = 1 + 23$$

Mean Squares

A sum of squares divided by its associated degrees of freedom is called a *mean square* (abbreviated *MS*). For instance, an ordinary sample variance is a mean square since a sum of squares, $\sum (Y_i - \bar{Y})^2$, is divided by its associated degrees of freedom, $n - 1$. We are interested here in the *regression mean square*, denoted by *MSR*:

$$MSR = \frac{SSR}{1} = SSR \tag{2.52}$$

and in the *error mean square*, *MSE*, defined earlier in (1.22):

$$MSE = \frac{SSE}{n - 2} \tag{2.53}$$

For the Toluca Company example, we have $SSR = 252{,}378$ and $SSE = 54{,}825$. Hence:

$$MSR = \frac{252{,}378}{1} = 252{,}378$$

Also, we obtained earlier:

$$MSE = \frac{54{,}825}{23} = 2{,}384$$

Comment

The two mean squares MSR and MSE do not add to

$$\frac{SSTO}{(n-1)} = \frac{307{,}203}{24} = 12{,}800$$

Thus, mean squares are not additive. ∎

Analysis of Variance Table

Basic Table. The breakdowns of the total sum of squares and associated degrees of freedom are displayed in the form of an analysis of variance table (ANOVA table) in Table 2.2. Mean squares of interest also are shown. In addition, the ANOVA table contains a column of expected mean squares that will be utilized shortly. The ANOVA table for the Toluca Company example is shown in Figure 2.2. The columns for degrees of freedom and sums of squares are reversed in the MINITAB output.

Modified Table. Sometimes an ANOVA table showing one additional element of decomposition is utilized. This modified table is based on the fact that the total sum of squares can be decomposed into two parts, as follows:

$$SSTO = \sum (Y_i - \bar{Y})^2 = \sum Y_i^2 - n\bar{Y}^2$$

In the modified ANOVA table, the *total uncorrected sum of squares,* denoted by $SSTOU$, is defined as:

$$SSTOU = \sum Y_i^2 \qquad (2.54)$$

and the *correction for the mean sum of squares,* denoted by SS(correction for mean), is defined as:

$$SS\text{(correction for mean)} = n\bar{Y}^2 \qquad (2.55)$$

Table 2.3 shows the general format of this modified ANOVA table. While both types of ANOVA tables are widely used, we shall usually utilize the basic type of table.

TABLE 2.2
ANOVA Table for Simple Linear Regression.

Source of Variation	SS	df	MS	E{MS}
Regression	$SSR = \sum (\hat{Y}_i - \bar{Y})^2$	1	$MSR = \dfrac{SSR}{1}$	$\sigma^2 + \beta_1^2 \sum (X_i - \bar{X})^2$
Error	$SSE = \sum (Y_i - \hat{Y}_i)^2$	$n-2$	$MSE = \dfrac{SSE}{n-2}$	σ^2
Total	$SSTO = \sum (Y_i - \bar{Y})^2$	$n-1$		

TABLE 2.3
Modified
ANOVA Table
for Simple
Linear
Regression.

Source of Variation	SS	df	MS
Regression	$SSR = \sum(\hat{Y}_i - \bar{Y})^2$	1	$MSR = \dfrac{SSR}{1}$
Error	$SSE = \sum(Y_i - \hat{Y}_i)^2$	$n - 2$	$MSE = \dfrac{SSE}{n - 2}$
Total	$SSTO = \sum(Y_i - \bar{Y})^2$	$n - 1$	
Correction for mean	$SS(\text{correction for mean}) = n\bar{Y}^2$	1	
Total, uncorrected	$SSTOU = \sum Y_i^2$	n	

Expected Mean Squares

In order to make inferences based on the analysis of variance approach, we need to know the expected value of each of the mean squares. The expected value of a mean square is the mean of its sampling distribution and tells us what is being estimated by the mean square. Statistical theory provides the following results:

$$E\{MSE\} = \sigma^2 \qquad (2.56)$$

$$E\{MSR\} = \sigma^2 + \beta_1^2 \sum(X_i - \bar{X})^2 \qquad (2.57)$$

The expected mean squares in (2.56) and (2.57) are shown in the analysis of variance table in Table 2.2. Note that result (2.56) is in accord with our earlier statement that MSE is an unbiased estimator of σ^2.

Two important implications of the expected mean squares in (2.56) and (2.57) are the following:

1. The mean of the sampling distribution of MSE is σ^2 whether or not X and Y are linearly related, i.e., whether or not $\beta_1 = 0$.
2. The mean of the sampling distribution of MSR is also σ^2 when $\beta_1 = 0$. Hence, when $\beta_1 = 0$, the sampling distributions of MSR and MSE are located identically and MSR and MSE will tend to be of the same order of magnitude.

   On the other hand, when $\beta_1 \neq 0$, the mean of the sampling distribution of MSR is greater than σ^2 since the term $\beta_1^2 \sum(X_i - \bar{X})^2$ in (2.57) then must be positive. Thus, when $\beta_1 \neq 0$, the mean of the sampling distribution of MSR is located to the right of that of MSE and, hence, MSR will tend to be larger than MSE.

This suggests that a comparison of MSR and MSE is useful for testing whether or not $\beta_1 = 0$. If MSR and MSE are of the same order of magnitude, this would suggest that $\beta_1 = 0$. On the other hand, if MSR is substantially greater than MSE, this would suggest that $\beta_1 \neq 0$. This indeed is the basic idea underlying the analysis of variance test to be discussed next.

Comment

The derivation of (2.56) follows from theorem (2.11), which states that $SSE/\sigma^2 \sim \chi^2(n - 2)$ for regression model (2.1). Hence, it follows from property (A.42) of the chi-square distribution that:

$$E\left\{\frac{SSE}{\sigma^2}\right\} = n - 2$$

or that:

$$E\left\{\frac{SSE}{n-2}\right\} = E\{MSE\} = \sigma^2$$

To find the expected value of *MSR*, we begin with (2.51):

$$SSR = b_1^2 \sum (X_i - \bar{X})^2$$

Now by (A.15a), we have:

$$\sigma^2\{b_1\} = E\{b_1^2\} - (E\{b_1\})^2 \tag{2.58}$$

We know from (2.3a) that $E\{b_1\} = \beta_1$ and from (2.3b) that:

$$\sigma^2\{b_1\} = \frac{\sigma^2}{\sum (X_i - \bar{X})^2}$$

Hence, substituting into (2.58), we obtain:

$$E\{b_1^2\} = \frac{\sigma^2}{\sum (X_i - \bar{X})^2} + \beta_1^2$$

It now follows that:

$$E\{SSR\} = E\{b_1^2\} \sum (X_i - \bar{X})^2 = \sigma^2 + \beta_1^2 \sum (X_i - \bar{X})^2$$

Finally, $E\{MSR\}$ is:

$$E\{MSR\} = E\left\{\frac{SSR}{1}\right\} = \sigma^2 + \beta_1^2 \sum (X_i - \bar{X})^2$$

∎

F Test of $\beta_1 = 0$ versus $\beta_1 \neq 0$

The analysis of variance approach provides us with a battery of highly useful tests for regression models (and other linear statistical models). For the simple linear regression case considered here, the analysis of variance provides us with a test for:

$$\begin{aligned} H_0&: \beta_1 = 0 \\ H_a&: \beta_1 \neq 0 \end{aligned} \tag{2.59}$$

Test Statistic.   The test statistic for the analysis of variance approach is denoted by F^*. As just mentioned, it compares *MSR* and *MSE* in the following fashion:

$$F^* = \frac{MSR}{MSE} \tag{2.60}$$

The earlier motivation, based on the expected mean squares in Table 2.2, suggests that large values of F^* support H_a and values of F^* near 1 support H_0. In other words, the appropriate test is an upper-tail one.

Sampling Distribution of F^*.   In order to be able to construct a statistical decision rule and examine its properties, we need to know the sampling distribution of F^*. We begin by considering the sampling distribution of F^* when H_0 ($\beta_1 = 0$) holds. *Cochran's theorem* will be most helpful in this connection. For our purposes, this theorem can be stated as follows:

> If all n observations Y_i come from the same normal distribution with mean μ and variance σ^2, and $SSTO$ is decomposed into k sums of squares SS_r, each with degrees of freedom df_r, then the SS_r/σ^2 terms are independent χ^2 variables with df_r degrees of freedom if: $\qquad$ (2.61)

$$\sum_{r=1}^{k} df_r = n - 1$$

Note from Table 2.2 that we have decomposed $SSTO$ into the two sums of squares SSR and SSE and that their degrees of freedom are additive. Hence:

> If $\beta_1 = 0$ so that all Y_i have the same mean $\mu = \beta_0$ and the same variance σ^2, SSE/σ^2 and SSR/σ^2 are independent χ^2 variables.

Now consider test statistic F^*, which we can write as follows:

$$F^* = \frac{\dfrac{SSR}{\sigma^2}}{1} \div \frac{\dfrac{SSE}{\sigma^2}}{n-2} = \frac{MSR}{MSE}$$

But by Cochran's theorem, we have when H_0 holds:

$$F^* \sim \frac{\chi^2(1)}{1} \div \frac{\chi^2(n-2)}{n-2} \qquad \text{when } H_0 \text{ holds}$$

where the χ^2 variables are independent. Thus, when H_0 holds, F^* is the ratio of two independent χ^2 variables, each divided by its degrees of freedom. But this is the definition of an F random variable in (A.47).

We have thus established that if H_0 holds, F^* follows the F distribution, specifically the $F(1, n - 2)$ distribution.

When H_a holds, it can be shown that F^* follows the noncentral F distribution, a complex distribution that we need not consider further at this time.

Comment

Even if $\beta_1 \neq 0$, SSR and SSE are independent and $SSE/\sigma^2 \sim \chi^2$. However, the condition that both SSR/σ^2 and SSE/σ^2 are χ^2 random variables requires $\beta_1 = 0$. ∎

Construction of Decision Rule. Since the test is upper-tail and F^* is distributed as $F(1, n - 2)$ when H_0 holds, the decision rule is as follows when the risk of a Type I error is to be controlled at α:

$$\text{If } F^* \leq F(1 - \alpha; 1, n - 2), \text{ conclude } H_0$$
$$\text{If } F^* > F(1 - \alpha; 1, n - 2), \text{ conclude } H_a \qquad (2.62)$$

where $F(1 - \alpha; 1, n - 2)$ is the $(1 - \alpha)100$ percentile of the appropriate F distribution.

Example

For the Toluca Company example, we shall repeat the earlier test on β_1, this time using the F test. The alternative conclusions are:

$$H_0: \beta_1 = 0$$
$$H_a: \beta_1 \neq 0$$

As before, let $\alpha = .05$. Since $n = 25$, we require $F(.95; 1, 23) = 4.28$. The decision rule is:

If $F^* \leq 4.28$, conclude H_0

If $F^* > 4.28$, conclude H_a

We have from earlier that $MSR = 252{,}378$ and $MSE = 2{,}384$. Hence, F^* is:

$$F^* = \frac{252{,}378}{2{,}384} = 105.9$$

Since $F^* = 105.9 > 4.28$, we conclude H_a, that $\beta_1 \neq 0$, or that there is a linear association between work hours and lot size. This is the same result as when the t test was employed, as it must be according to our discussion below.

The MINITAB output in Figure 2.2 on page 46 shows the F^* statistic in the column labeled F. Next to it is shown the P-value, $P\{F(1, 23) > 105.9\}$, namely, $0+$, indicating that the data are not consistent with $\beta_1 = 0$.

Equivalence of F Test and t Test.   For a given α level, the F test of $\beta_1 = 0$ versus $\beta_1 \neq 0$ is equivalent algebraically to the two-tailed t test. To see this, recall from (2.51) that:

$$SSR = b_1^2 \sum (X_i - \bar{X})^2$$

Thus, we can write:

$$F^* = \frac{SSR \div 1}{SSE \div (n-2)} = \frac{b_1^2 \sum (X_i - \bar{X})^2}{MSE}$$

But since $s^2\{b_1\} = MSE / \sum (X_i - \bar{X})^2$, we obtain:

$$F^* = \frac{b_1^2}{s^2\{b_1\}} = \left(\frac{b_1}{s\{b_1\}} \right)^2 = (t^*)^2 \qquad \textbf{(2.63)}$$

The last step follows because the t^* statistic for testing whether or not $\beta_1 = 0$ is by (2.17):

$$t^* = \frac{b_1}{s\{b_1\}}$$

In the Toluca Company example, we just calculated that $F^* = 105.9$. From earlier work, we have $t^* = 10.29$ (see Figure 2.2). We thus see that $(10.29)^2 = 105.9$.

Corresponding to the relation between t^* and F^*, we have the following relation between the required percentiles of the t and F distributions for the tests: $[t(1 - \alpha/2; n - 2)]^2 = F(1 - \alpha; 1, n - 2)$. In our tests on β_1, these percentiles were $[t(.975; 23)]^2 = (2.069)^2 = 4.28 = F(.95; 1, 23)$. Remember that the t test is two-tailed whereas the F test is one-tailed.

Thus, at any given α level, we can use either the t test or the F test for testing $\beta_1 = 0$ versus $\beta_1 \neq 0$. Whenever one test leads to H_0, so will the other, and correspondingly for H_a. The t test, however, is more flexible since it can be used for one-sided alternatives involving $\beta_1(\leq \geq) 0$ versus $\beta_1(> <) 0$, while the F test cannot.

2.8 General Linear Test Approach

The analysis of variance test of $\beta_1 = 0$ versus $\beta_1 \neq 0$ is an example of the general test for a linear statistical model. We now explain this general test approach in terms of the simple linear regression model. We do so at this time because of the generality of the approach and the wide use we shall make of it, and because of the simplicity of understanding the approach in terms of simple linear regression.

The general linear test approach involves three basic steps, which we now describe in turn.

Full Model

We begin with the model considered to be appropriate for the data, which in this context is called the *full* or *unrestricted model*. For the simple linear regression case, the full model is the normal error regression model (2.1):

$$Y_i = \beta_0 + \beta_1 X_i + \varepsilon_i \qquad \text{Full model} \qquad (2.64)$$

We fit this full model, either by the method of least squares or by the method of maximum likelihood, and obtain the error sum of squares. The error sum of squares is the sum of the squared deviations of each observation Y_i around its estimated expected value. In this context, we shall denote this sum of squares by $SSE(F)$ to indicate that it is the error sum of squares for the full model. Here, we have:

$$SSE(F) = \sum [Y_i - (b_0 + b_1 X_i)]^2 = \sum (Y_i - \hat{Y}_i)^2 = SSE \qquad (2.65)$$

Thus, for the full model (2.64), the error sum of squares is simply SSE, which measures the variability of the Y_i observations around the fitted regression line.

Reduced Model

Next, we consider H_0. In this instance, we have:

$$H_0: \beta_1 = 0$$
$$H_a: \beta_1 \neq 0 \qquad (2.66)$$

The model when H_0 holds is called the *reduced* or *restricted model*. When $\beta_1 = 0$, model (2.64) reduces to:

$$Y_i = \beta_0 + \varepsilon_i \qquad \text{Reduced model} \qquad (2.67)$$

We fit this reduced model, by either the method of least squares or the method of maximum likelihood, and obtain the error sum of squares for this reduced model, denoted by $SSE(R)$. When we fit the particular reduced model (2.67), it can be shown that the least squares and maximum likelihood estimator of β_0 is $\bar{Y}$. Hence, the estimated expected value for each observation is $b_0 = \bar{Y}$, and the error sum of squares for this reduced model is:

$$SSE(R) = \sum (Y_i - b_0)^2 = \sum (Y_i - \bar{Y})^2 = SSTO \qquad (2.68)$$

Test Statistic

The logic now is to compare the two error sums of squares $SSE(F)$ and $SSE(R)$. It can be shown that $SSE(F)$ never is greater than $SSE(R)$:

$$SSE(F) \leq SSE(R) \tag{2.69}$$

The reason is that the more parameters are in the model, the better one can fit the data and the smaller are the deviations around the fitted regression function. When $SSE(F)$ is not much less than $SSE(R)$, using the full model does not account for much more of the variability of the Y_i than does the reduced model, in which case the data suggest that the reduced model is adequate (i.e., that H_0 holds). To put this another way, when $SSE(F)$ is close to $SSE(R)$, the variation of the observations around the fitted regression function for the full model is almost as great as the variation around the fitted regression function for the reduced model. In this case, the added parameters in the full model really do not help to reduce the variation in the Y_i about the fitted regression function. Thus, a small difference $SSE(R) - SSE(F)$ suggests that H_0 holds. On the other hand, a large difference suggests that H_a holds because the additional parameters in the model do help to reduce substantially the variation of the observations Y_i around the fitted regression function.

The actual test statistic is a function of $SSE(R) - SSE(F)$, namely:

$$F^* = \frac{SSE(R) - SSE(F)}{df_R - df_F} \div \frac{SSE(F)}{df_F} \tag{2.70}$$

which follows the F distribution when H_0 holds. The degrees of freedom df_R and df_F are those associated with the reduced and full model error sums of squares, respectively. Large values of F^* lead to H_a because a large difference $SSE(R) - SSE(F)$ suggests that H_a holds. The decision rule therefore is:

$$\begin{array}{l} \text{If } F^* \leq F(1 - \alpha; df_R - df_F, \ df_F), \text{ conclude } H_0 \\ \text{If } F^* > F(1 - \alpha; df_R - df_F, \ df_F), \text{ conclude } H_a \end{array} \tag{2.71}$$

For testing whether or not $\beta_1 = 0$, we therefore have:

$$\begin{array}{cc} SSE(R) = SSTO & SSE(F) = SSE \\ df_R = n - 1 & df_F = n - 2 \end{array}$$

so that we obtain when substituting into (2.70):

$$F^* = \frac{SSTO - SSE}{(n-1) - (n-2)} \div \frac{SSE}{n-2} = \frac{SSR}{1} \div \frac{SSE}{n-2} = \frac{MSR}{MSE}$$

which is identical to the analysis of variance test statistic (2.60).

Summary

The general linear test approach can be used for highly complex tests of linear statistical models, as well as for simple tests. The basic steps in summary form are:

1. Fit the full model and obtain the error sum of squares $SSE(F)$.
2. Fit the reduced model under H_0 and obtain the error sum of squares $SSE(R)$.
3. Use test statistic (2.70) and decision rule (2.71).

2.9   Descriptive Measures of Linear Association between X and Y

We have discussed the major uses of regression analysis—estimation of parameters and means and prediction of new observations—without mentioning the "degree of linear association" between X and Y, or similar terms. The reason is that the usefulness of estimates or predictions depends upon the width of the interval and the user's needs for precision, which vary from one application to another. Hence, no single descriptive measure of the "degree of linear association" can capture the essential information as to whether a given regression relation is useful in any particular application.

Nevertheless, there are times when the degree of linear association is of interest in its own right. We shall now briefly discuss two descriptive measures that are frequently used in practice to describe the degree of linear association between X and Y.

Coefficient of Determination

We saw earlier that *SSTO* measures the variation in the observations Y_i, or the uncertainty in predicting Y, when no account of the predictor variable X is taken. Thus, *SSTO* is a measure of the uncertainty in predicting Y when X is not considered. Similarly, *SSE* measures the variation in the Y_i when a regression model utilizing the predictor variable X is employed. A natural measure of the effect of X in reducing the variation in Y, i.e., in reducing the uncertainty in predicting Y, is to express the reduction in variation ($SSTO - SSE = SSR$) as a proportion of the total variation:

$$R^2 = \frac{SSR}{SSTO} = 1 - \frac{SSE}{SSTO} \tag{2.72}$$

The measure R^2 is called the *coefficient of determination*. Since $0 \le SSE \le SSTO$, it follows that:

$$0 \le R^2 \le 1 \tag{2.72a}$$

We may interpret R^2 as the proportionate reduction of total variation associated with the use of the predictor variable X. Thus, the larger R^2 is, the more the total variation of Y is reduced by introducing the predictor variable X. The limiting values of R^2 occur as follows:

1. When all observations fall on the fitted regression line, then $SSE = 0$ and $R^2 = 1$. This case is shown in Figure 2.8a. Here, the predictor variable X accounts for all variation in the observations Y_i.

2. When the fitted regression line is horizontal so that $b_1 = 0$ and $\hat{Y}_i \equiv \bar{Y}$, then $SSE = SSTO$ and $R^2 = 0$. This case is shown in Figure 2.8b. Here, there is no linear association between X and Y in the sample data, and the predictor variable X is of no help in reducing the variation in the observations Y_i with linear regression.

In practice, R^2 is not likely to be 0 or 1 but somewhere between these limits. The closer it is to 1, the greater is said to be the degree of linear association between X and Y.

FIGURE 2.8
Scatter Plots
when $R^2 = 1$
and $R^2 = 0$.

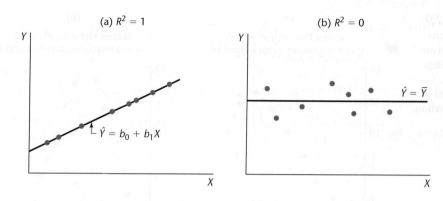

(a) $R^2 = 1$

$\hat{Y} = b_0 + b_1 X$

(b) $R^2 = 0$

$\hat{Y} = \bar{Y}$

Example

For the Toluca Company example, we obtained $SSTO = 307{,}203$ and $SSR = 252{,}378$. Hence:

$$R^2 = \frac{252{,}378}{307{,}203} = .822$$

Thus, the variation in work hours is reduced by 82.2 percent when lot size is considered.

The MINITAB output in Figure 2.2 shows the coefficient of determination R^2 labeled as R–sq in percent form. The output also shows the coefficient R–sq(adj), which will be explained in Chapter 6.

Limitations of R^2

We noted that no single measure will be adequate for describing the usefulness of a regression model for different applications. Still, the coefficient of determination is widely used. Unfortunately, it is subject to serious misunderstandings. We consider now three common misunderstandings:

Misunderstanding 1. A high coefficient of determination indicates that useful predictions can be made. This is not necessarily correct. In the Toluca Company example, we saw that the coefficient of determination was high ($R^2 = .82$). Yet the 90 percent prediction interval for the next lot, consisting of 100 units, was wide (332 to 507 hours) and not precise enough to permit management to schedule workers effectively.

Misunderstanding 2. A high coefficient of determination indicates that the estimated regression line is a good fit. Again, this is not necessarily correct. Figure 2.9a shows a scatter plot where the coefficient of determination is high ($R^2 = .69$). Yet a linear regression function would not be a good fit since the regression relation is curvilinear.

Misunderstanding 3. A coefficient of determination near zero indicates that X and Y are not related. This also is not necessarily correct. Figure 2.9b shows a scatter plot where the coefficient of determination between X and Y is $R^2 = .02$. Yet X and Y are strongly related; however, the relationship between the two variables is curvilinear.

FIGURE 2.9
Illustrations
of Two Misun-
derstandings
about
Coefficient of
Determination.

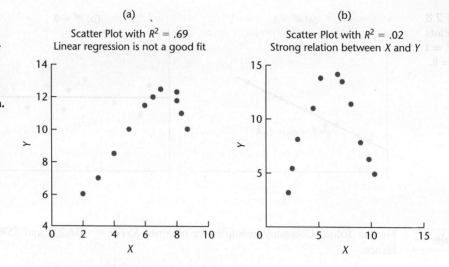

(a)
Scatter Plot with $R^2 = .69$
Linear regression is not a good fit

(b)
Scatter Plot with $R^2 = .02$
Strong relation between X and Y

Misunderstanding 1 arises because R^2 measures only a relative reduction from *SSTO* and provides no information about absolute precision for estimating a mean response or predicting a new observation. Misunderstandings 2 and 3 arise because R^2 measures the degree of *linear* association between X and Y, whereas the actual regression relation may be curvilinear.

Coefficient of Correlation

A measure of linear association between Y and X when both Y and X are random is the *coefficient of correlation*. This measure is the signed square root of R^2:

$$r = \pm\sqrt{R^2} \tag{2.73}$$

A plus or minus sign is attached to this measure according to whether the slope of the fitted regression line is positive or negative. Thus, the range of r is: $-1 \leq r \leq 1$.

Example

For the Toluca Company example, we obtained $R^2 = .822$. Treating X as a random variable, the correlation coefficient here is:

$$r = +\sqrt{.822} = .907$$

The plus sign is affixed since b_1 is positive. We take up the topic of correlation analysis in more detail in Section 2.11.

Comments

1. The value taken by R^2 in a given sample tends to be affected by the spacing of the X observations. This is implied in (2.72). *SSE* is not affected systematically by the spacing of the X_i since, for regression model (2.1), $\sigma^2\{Y_i\} = \sigma^2$ at all X levels. However, the wider the spacing of the X_i in the sample when $b_1 \neq 0$, the greater will tend to be the spread of the observed Y_i around $\bar{Y}$ and hence the greater *SSTO* will be. Consequently, the wider the X_i are spaced, the higher R^2 will tend to be.

2. The regression sum of squares *SSR* is often called the "explained variation" in Y, and the residual sum of squares *SSE* is called the "unexplained variation." The coefficient R^2 then is interpreted in terms of the proportion of the total variation in Y (*SSTO*) which has been "explained" by X. Unfortunately,

this terminology frequently is taken literally and, hence, misunderstood. Remember that in a regression model there is no implication that Y necessarily depends on X in a causal or explanatory sense.

3. Regression models do not contain a parameter to be estimated by R^2 or r. These are simply descriptive measures of the degree of linear association between X and Y in the sample observations that may, or may not, be useful in any instance.   ∎

2.10   Considerations in Applying Regression Analysis

We have now discussed the major uses of regression analysis—to make inferences about the regression parameters, to estimate the mean response for a given X, and to predict a new observation Y for a given X. It remains to make a few cautionary remarks about implementing applications of regression analysis.

1. Frequently, regression analysis is used to make inferences for the future. For instance, for planning staffing requirements, a school board may wish to predict future enrollments by using a regression model containing several demographic variables as predictor variables. In applications of this type, it is important to remember that the validity of the regression application depends upon whether basic causal conditions in the period ahead will be similar to those in existence during the period upon which the regression analysis is based. This caution applies whether mean responses are to be estimated, new observations predicted, or regression parameters estimated.

2. In predicting new observations on Y, the predictor variable X itself often has to be predicted. For instance, we mentioned earlier the prediction of company sales for next year from the demographic projection of the number of persons 16 years of age or older next year. A prediction of company sales under these circumstances is a conditional prediction, dependent upon the correctness of the population projection. It is easy to forget the conditional nature of this type of prediction.

3. Another caution deals with inferences pertaining to levels of the predictor variable that fall outside the range of observations. Unfortunately, this situation frequently occurs in practice. A company that predicts its sales from a regression relation of company sales to disposable personal income will often find the level of disposable personal income of interest (e.g., for the year ahead) to fall beyond the range of past data. If the X level does not fall far beyond this range, one may have reasonable confidence in the application of the regression analysis. On the other hand, if the X level falls far beyond the range of past data, extreme caution should be exercised since one cannot be sure that the regression function that fits the past data is appropriate over the wider range of the predictor variable.

4. A statistical test that leads to the conclusion that $\beta_1 \neq 0$ does not establish a cause-and-effect relation between the predictor and response variables. As we noted in Chapter 1, with nonexperimental data both the X and Y variables may be simultaneously influenced by other variables not in the regression model. On the other hand, the existence of a regression relation in controlled experiments is often good evidence of a cause-and-effect relation.

5. We should note again that frequently we wish to estimate several mean responses or predict several new observations for different levels of the predictor variable, and that special problems arise in this case. The confidence coefficients for the limits (2.33) for estimating a mean response and for the prediction limits (2.36) for a new observation apply

only for a single level of X for a given sample. In Chapter 4, we discuss how to make multiple inferences from a given sample.

6. Finally, when observations on the predictor variable X are subject to measurement errors, the resulting parameter estimates are generally no longer unbiased. In Chapter 4, we discuss several ways to handle this situation.

2.11 Normal Correlation Models

Distinction between Regression and Correlation Model

The normal error regression model (2.1), which has been used throughout this chapter and which will continue to be used, assumes that the X values are known constants. As a consequence of this, the confidence coefficients and risks of errors refer to repeated sampling when the X values are kept the same from sample to sample.

Frequently, it may not be appropriate to consider the X values as known constants. For instance, consider regressing daily bathing suit sales by a department store on mean daily temperature. Surely, the department store cannot control daily temperatures, so it would not be meaningful to think of repeated sampling where the temperature levels are the same from sample to sample. As a second example, an analyst may use a correlation model for the two variables "height of person" and "weight of person" in a study of a sample of persons, each variable being taken as random. The analyst might wish to study the relation between the two variables or might be interested in making inferences about weight of a person on the basis of the person's height, in making inferences about height on the basis of weight, or in both.

Other examples where a correlation model, rather than a regression model, may be appropriate are:

1. To study the relation between service station sales of gasoline, and sales of auxiliary products.
2. To study the relation between company net income determined by generally accepted accounting principles and net income according to tax regulations.
3. To study the relation between blood pressure and age in human subjects.

The correlation model most widely employed is the normal correlation model. We discuss it here for the case of two variables.

Bivariate Normal Distribution

The normal correlation model for the case of two variables is based on the *bivariate normal distribution*. Let us denote the two variables as Y_1 and Y_2. (We do not use the notation X and Y here because both variables play a symmetrical role in correlation analysis.) We say that Y_1 and Y_2 are *jointly normally distributed* if the density function of their joint distribution is that of the bivariate normal distribution.

FIGURE 2.10
Example of
Bivariate
Normal
Distribution.

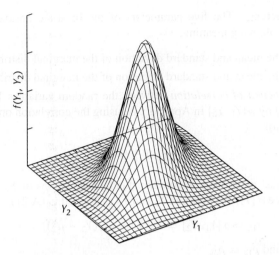

Density Function.   The density function of the bivariate normal distribution is as follows:

$$f(Y_1, Y_2) = \frac{1}{2\pi \sigma_1 \sigma_2 \sqrt{1 - \rho_{12}^2}} \exp\left\{-\frac{1}{2(1 - \rho_{12}^2)}\left[\left(\frac{Y_1 - \mu_1}{\sigma_1}\right)^2\right.\right.$$
$$\left.\left. - 2\rho_{12}\left(\frac{Y_1 - \mu_1}{\sigma_1}\right)\left(\frac{Y_2 - \mu_2}{\sigma_2}\right) + \left(\frac{Y_2 - \mu_2}{\sigma_2}\right)^2\right]\right\} \qquad \textbf{(2.74)}$$

Note that this density function involves five parameters: $\mu_1, \mu_2, \sigma_1, \sigma_2, \rho_{12}$. We shall explain the meaning of these parameters shortly. First, let us consider a graphic representation of the bivariate normal distribution.

Figure 2.10 contains a SYSTAT three-dimensional plot of a bivariate normal probability distribution. The probability distribution is a surface in three-dimensional space. For every pair of (Y_1, Y_2) values, the density $f(Y_1, Y_2)$ represents the height of the surface at that point. The surface is continuous, and probability corresponds to volume under the surface.

Marginal Distributions.   If Y_1 and Y_2 are jointly normally distributed, it can be shown that their marginal distributions have the following characteristics:

The marginal distribution of Y_1 is normal with mean μ_1
and standard deviation σ_1:   **(2.75a)**

$$f_1(Y_1) = \frac{1}{\sqrt{2\pi}\sigma_1} \exp\left[-\frac{1}{2}\left(\frac{Y_1 - \mu_1}{\sigma_1}\right)^2\right]$$

The marginal distribution of Y_2 is normal with mean μ_2
and standard deviation σ_2:   **(2.75b)**

$$f_2(Y_2) = \frac{1}{\sqrt{2\pi}\sigma_2} \exp\left[-\frac{1}{2}\left(\frac{Y_2 - \mu_2}{\sigma_2}\right)^2\right]$$

Thus, when Y_1 and Y_2 are jointly normally distributed, each of the two variables by itself is normally distributed. The converse, however, is not generally true; if Y_1 and Y_2 are each normally distributed, they need not be jointly normally distributed in accord with (2.74).

Meaning of Parameters. The five parameters of the bivariate normal density function (2.74) have the following meaning:

1. μ_1 and σ_1 are the mean and standard deviation of the marginal distribution of Y_1.
2. μ_2 and σ_2 are the mean and standard deviation of the marginal distribution of Y_2.
3. ρ_{12} is the *coefficient of correlation* between the random variables Y_1 and Y_2. This coefficient is denoted by $\rho\{Y_1, Y_2\}$ in Appendix A, using the correlation operator notation, and defined in (A.25a):

$$\rho_{12} = \rho\{Y_1, Y_2\} = \frac{\sigma_{12}}{\sigma_1 \sigma_2} \tag{2.76}$$

Here, σ_1 and σ_2, as just mentioned, denote the standard deviations of Y_1 and Y_2, and σ_{12} denotes the covariance $\sigma\{Y_1, Y_2\}$ between Y_1 and Y_2 as defined in (A.21):

$$\sigma_{12} = \sigma\{Y_1, Y_2\} = E\{(Y_1 - \mu_1)(Y_2 - \mu_2)\} \tag{2.77}$$

Note that $\sigma_{12} \equiv \sigma_{21}$ and $\rho_{12} \equiv \rho_{21}$.

If Y_1 and Y_2 are independent, $\sigma_{12} = 0$ according to (A.28) so that $\rho_{12} = 0$. If Y_1 and Y_2 are positively related—that is, Y_1 tends to be large when Y_2 is large, or small when Y_2 is small—σ_{12} is positive and so is ρ_{12}. On the other hand, if Y_1 and Y_2 are negatively related—that is, Y_1 tends to be large when Y_2 is small, or vice versa—σ_{12} is negative and so is ρ_{12}. The coefficient of correlation ρ_{12} can take on any value between -1 and 1 inclusive. It assumes 1 if the linear relation between Y_1 and Y_2 is perfectly positive (direct) and -1 if it is perfectly negative (inverse).

Conditional Inferences

As noted, one principal use of a bivariate correlation model is to make conditional inferences regarding one variable, given the other variable. Suppose Y_1 represents a service station's gasoline sales and Y_2 its sales of auxiliary products. We may then wish to predict a service station's sales of auxiliary products Y_2, given that its gasoline sales are $Y_1 = \$5,500$.

Such conditional inferences require the use of conditional probability distributions, which we discuss next.

Conditional Probability Distribution of Y_1. The density function of the conditional probability distribution of Y_1 for any given value of Y_2 is denoted by $f(Y_1|Y_2)$ and defined as follows:

$$f(Y_1|Y_2) = \frac{f(Y_1, Y_2)}{f_2(Y_2)} \tag{2.78}$$

where $f(Y_1, Y_2)$ is the joint density function of Y_1 and Y_2, and $f_2(Y_2)$ is the marginal density function of Y_2. When Y_1 and Y_2 are jointly normally distributed according to (2.74) so that the marginal density function $f_2(Y_2)$ is given by (2.75b), it can be shown that:

The conditional probability distribution of Y_1 for any given value of Y_2 is normal with mean $\alpha_{1|2} + \beta_{12}Y_2$ and standard deviation $\sigma_{1|2}$ and its density function is: (2.79)

$$f(Y_1|Y_2) = \frac{1}{\sqrt{2\pi}\sigma_{1|2}} \exp\left[-\frac{1}{2}\left(\frac{Y_1 - \alpha_{1|2} - \beta_{12}Y_2}{\sigma_{1|2}}\right)^2\right]$$

The parameters $\alpha_{1|2}$, β_{12}, and $\sigma_{1|2}$ of the conditional probability distributions of Y_1 are functions of the parameters of the joint probability distribution (2.74), as follows:

$$\alpha_{1|2} = \mu_1 - \mu_2 \rho_{12} \frac{\sigma_1}{\sigma_2} \tag{2.80a}$$

$$\beta_{12} = \rho_{12} \frac{\sigma_1}{\sigma_2} \tag{2.80b}$$

$$\sigma_{1|2}^2 = \sigma_1^2 (1 - \rho_{12}^2) \tag{2.80c}$$

The parameter $\alpha_{1|2}$ is the intercept of the line of regression of Y_1 on Y_2, and the parameter β_{12} is the slope of this line. Thus we find that the conditional distribution of Y_1, given Y_2, is equivalent to the normal error regression model (1.24).

Conditional Probability Distributions of Y_2. The random variables Y_1 and Y_2 play symmetrical roles in the bivariate normal probability distribution (2.74). Hence, it follows:

> The conditional probability distribution of Y_2 for any given
> value of Y_1 is normal with mean $\alpha_{2|1} + \beta_{21} Y_1$ and standard
> deviation $\sigma_{2|1}$ and its density function is: $\qquad$ **(2.81)**
>
> $$f(Y_2|Y_1) = \frac{1}{\sqrt{2\pi}\,\sigma_{2|1}} \exp\left[-\frac{1}{2} \left(\frac{Y_2 - \alpha_{2|1} - \beta_{21} Y_1}{\sigma_{2|1}} \right)^2 \right]$$

The parameters $\alpha_{2|1}$, β_{21}, and $\sigma_{2|1}$ of the conditional probability distributions of Y_2 are functions of the parameters of the joint probability distribution (2.74), as follows:

$$\alpha_{2|1} = \mu_2 - \mu_1 \rho_{12} \frac{\sigma_2}{\sigma_1} \tag{2.82a}$$

$$\beta_{21} = \rho_{12} \frac{\sigma_2}{\sigma_1} \tag{2.82b}$$

$$\sigma_{2|1}^2 = \sigma_2^2 (1 - \rho_{12}^2) \tag{2.82c}$$

Important Characteristics of Conditional Distributions. Three important characteristics of the conditional probability distributions of Y_1 are normality, linear regression, and constant variance. We take up each of these in turn.

1. The conditional probability distribution of Y_1 for any given value of Y_2 is normal. Imagine that we slice a bivariate normal distribution vertically at a given value of Y_2, say, at Y_{h2}. That is, we slice it parallel to the Y_1 axis. This slicing is shown in Figure 2.11. The exposed cross section has the shape of a normal distribution, and after being scaled so that its area is 1, it portrays the conditional probability distribution of Y_1, given that $Y_2 = Y_{h2}$.

   This property of normality holds no matter what the value Y_{h2} is. Thus, whenever we slice the bivariate normal distribution parallel to the Y_1 axis, we obtain (after proper scaling) a normal conditional probability distribution.

2. The means of the conditional probability distributions of Y_1 fall on a straight line, and hence are a linear function of Y_2:

$$E\{Y_1|Y_2\} = \alpha_{1|2} + \beta_{12} Y_2 \tag{2.83}$$

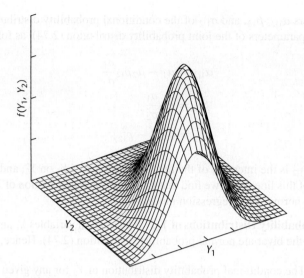

Here, $\alpha_{1|2}$ is the intercept parameter and β_{12} the slope parameter. Thus, the relation between the conditional means and Y_2 is given by a linear regression function.

3. All conditional probability distributions of Y_1 have the same standard deviation $\sigma_{1|2}$. Thus, no matter where we slice the bivariate normal distribution parallel to the Y_1 axis, the resulting conditional probability distribution (after scaling to have an area of 1) has the same standard deviation. Hence, constant variances characterize the conditional probability distributions of Y_1.

Equivalence to Normal Error Regression Model. Suppose that we select a random sample of observations (Y_1, Y_2) from a bivariate normal population and wish to make conditional inferences about Y_1, given Y_2. The preceding discussion makes it clear that the normal error regression model (1.24) is entirely applicable because:

1. The Y_1 observations are independent.
2. The Y_1 observations when Y_2 is considered given or fixed are normally distributed with mean $E\{Y_1|Y_2\} = \alpha_{1|2} + \beta_{12}Y_2$ and constant variance $\sigma_{1|2}^2$.

Use of Regression Analysis. In view of the equivalence of each of the conditional bivariate normal correlation models (2.81) and (2.79) with the normal error regression model (1.24), all conditional inferences with these correlation models can be made by means of the usual regression methods. For instance, if a researcher has data that can be appropriately described as having been generated from a bivariate normal distribution and wishes to make inferences about Y_2, given a particular value of Y_1, the ordinary regression techniques will be applicable. Thus, the regression function of Y_2 on Y_1 can be estimated by means of (1.12), the slope of the regression line can be estimated by means of the interval estimate (2.15), a new observation Y_2, given the value of Y_1, can be predicted by means of (2.36), and so on. Computer regression packages can be used in the usual manner. To avoid notational problems, it may be helpful to relabel the variables according to regression usage: $Y = Y_2$, $X = Y_1$. Of course, if conditional inferences on Y_1 for given values of Y_2 are desired, the notation correspondences would be: $Y = Y_1$, $X = Y_2$.

Can we still use regression model (2.1) if Y_1 and Y_2 are not bivariate normal? It can be shown that all results on estimation, testing, and prediction obtained from regression model (2.1) apply if $Y_1 = Y$ and $Y_2 = X$ are random variables, and if the following conditions hold:

1. The conditional distributions of the Y_i, given X_i, are normal and independent, with conditional means $\beta_0 + \beta_1 X_i$ and conditional variance σ^2.
2. The X_i are independent random variables whose probability distribution $g(X_i)$ does not involve the parameters β_0, β_1, σ^2.

These conditions require only that regression model (2.1) is appropriate for each *conditional* distribution of Y_i, and that the probability distribution of the X_i does not involve the regression parameters. If these conditions are met, all earlier results on estimation, testing, and prediction still hold even though the X_i are now random variables. The major modification occurs in the interpretation of confidence coefficients and specified risks of error. When X is random, these refer to repeated sampling of pairs of (X_i, Y_i) values, where the X_i values as well as the Y_i values change from sample to sample. Thus, in our bathing suit sales illustration, a confidence coefficient would refer to the proportion of correct interval estimates if repeated samples of n days' sales and temperatures were obtained and the confidence interval calculated for each sample. Another modification occurs in the test's power, which is different when X is a random variable.

Comments

1. The notation for the parameters of the conditional correlation models departs somewhat from our previous notation for regression models. The symbol α is now used to denote the regression intercept. The subscript $1|2$ to α indicates that Y_1 is regressed on Y_2. Similarly, the subscript $2|1$ to α indicates that Y_2 is regressed on Y_1. The symbol β_{12} indicates that it is the slope in the regression of Y_1 on Y_2, while β_{21} is the slope in the regression of Y_2 on Y_1. Finally, $\sigma_{2|1}$ is the standard deviation of the conditional probability distributions of Y_2 for any given Y_1, while $\sigma_{1|2}$ is the standard deviation of the conditional probability distributions of Y_1 for any given Y_2.

2. Two distinct regressions are involved in a bivariate normal model, that of Y_1 on Y_2 when Y_2 is fixed and that of Y_2 on Y_1 when Y_1 is fixed. In general, the two regression lines are not the same. For instance, the two slopes β_{12} and β_{21} are the same only if $\sigma_1 = \sigma_2$, as can be seen from (2.80b) and (2.82b).

3. When interval estimates for the conditional correlation models are obtained, the confidence coefficient refers to repeated samples where pairs of observations (Y_1, Y_2) are obtained from the bivariate normal distribution. ∎

Inferences on Correlation Coefficients

A principal use of the bivariate normal correlation model is to study the relationship between two variables. In a bivariate normal model, the parameter ρ_{12} provides information about the degree of the linear relationship between the two variables Y_1 and Y_2.

Point Estimator of ρ_{12}. The maximum likelihood estimator of ρ_{12}, denoted by r_{12}, is given by:

$$r_{12} = \frac{\sum (Y_{i1} - \bar{Y}_1)(Y_{i2} - \bar{Y}_2)}{\left[\sum (Y_{i1} - \bar{Y}_1)^2 \sum (Y_{i2} - \bar{Y}_2)^2 \right]^{1/2}} \tag{2.84}$$

This estimator is often called the *Pearson product-moment correlation coefficient.* It is a biased estimator of ρ_{12} (unless $\rho_{12} = 0$ or 1), but the bias is small when n is large.

It can be shown that the range of r_{12} is:

$$-1 \leq r_{12} \leq 1 \tag{2.85}$$

Generally, values of r_{12} near 1 indicate a strong positive (direct) linear association between Y_1 and Y_2 whereas values of r_{12} near -1 indicate a strong negative (indirect) linear association. Values of r_{12} near 0 indicate little or no linear association between Y_1 and Y_2.

Test whether $\rho_{12} = 0$.   When the population is bivariate normal, it is frequently desired to test whether the coefficient of correlation is zero:

$$H_0: \rho_{12} = 0$$
$$H_a: \rho_{12} \neq 0 \tag{2.86}$$

The reason for interest in this test is that in the case where Y_1 and Y_2 are jointly normally distributed, $\rho_{12} = 0$ implies that Y_1 and Y_2 are independent.

We can use regression procedures for the test since (2.80b) implies that the following alternatives are equivalent to those in (2.86):

$$H_0: \beta_{12} = 0$$
$$H_a: \beta_{12} \neq 0 \tag{2.86a}$$

and (2.82b) implies that the following alternatives are also equivalent to the ones in (2.86):

$$H_0: \beta_{21} = 0$$
$$H_a: \beta_{21} \neq 0 \tag{2.86b}$$

It can be shown that the test statistics for testing either (2.86a) or (2.86b) are the same and can be expressed directly in terms of r_{12}:

$$t^* = \frac{r_{12}\sqrt{n-2}}{\sqrt{1 - r_{12}^2}} \tag{2.87}$$

If H_0 holds, t^* follows the $t(n-2)$ distribution. The appropriate decision rule to control the Type I error at α is:

$$\text{If } |t^*| \leq t(1 - \alpha/2; n - 2), \text{ conclude } H_0$$
$$\text{If } |t^*| > t(1 - \alpha/2; n - 2), \text{ conclude } H_a \tag{2.88}$$

Test statistic (2.87) is identical to the regression t^* test statistic (2.17).

Example

A national oil company was interested in the relationship between its service station gasoline sales and its sales of auxiliary products. A company analyst obtained a random sample of 23 of its service stations and obtained average monthly sales data on gasoline sales (Y_1) and comparable sales of its auxiliary products and services (Y_2). These data (not shown) resulted in an estimated correlation coefficient $r_{12} = .52$. Suppose the analyst wished to test whether or not the association was positive, controlling the level of significance at $\alpha = .05$. The alternatives would then be:

$$H_0: \rho_{12} \leq 0$$
$$H_a: \rho_{12} > 0$$

and the decision rule based on test statistic (2.87) would be:

$$\text{If } t^* \leq t(1 - \alpha; n - 2), \text{ conclude } H_0$$
$$\text{If } t^* > t(1 - \alpha; n - 2), \text{ conclude } H_a$$

For $\alpha = .05$, we require $t(.95; 21) = 1.721$. Since:

$$t^* = \frac{.52\sqrt{21}}{\sqrt{1 - (.52)^2}} = 2.79$$

is greater than 1.721, we would conclude H_a, that $\rho_{12} > 0$. The *P*-value for this test is .006.

Interval Estimation of ρ_{12} Using the z' Transformation. Because the sampling distribution of r_{12} is complicated when $\rho_{12} \neq 0$, interval estimation of ρ_{12} is usually carried out by means of an approximate procedure based on a transformation. This transformation, known as the *Fisher z transformation*, is as follows:

$$z' = \frac{1}{2} \log_e \left(\frac{1 + r_{12}}{1 - r_{12}} \right) \tag{2.89}$$

When n is large (25 or more is a useful rule of thumb), the distribution of z' is approximately normal with approximate mean and variance:

$$E\{z'\} = \zeta = \frac{1}{2} \log_e \left(\frac{1 + \rho_{12}}{1 - \rho_{12}} \right) \tag{2.90}$$

$$\sigma^2\{z'\} = \frac{1}{n - 3} \tag{2.91}$$

Note that the transformation from r_{12} to z' in (2.89) is the same as the relation in (2.90) between ρ_{12} and $E\{z'\} = \zeta$. Also note that the approximate variance of z' is a known constant, depending only on the sample size n.

Table B.8 gives paired values for the left and right sides of (2.89) and (2.90), thus eliminating the need for calculations. For instance, if r_{12} or ρ_{12} equals .25, Table B.8 indicates that z' or ζ equals .2554, and vice versa. The values on the two sides of the transformation always have the same sign. Thus, if r_{12} or ρ_{12} is negative, a minus sign is attached to the value in Table B.8. For instance, if $r_{12} = -.25$, $z' = -.2554$.

Interval Estimate. When the sample size is large ($n \geq 25$), the standardized statistic:

$$\frac{z' - \zeta}{\sigma\{z'\}} \tag{2.92}$$

is approximately a standard normal variable. Therefore, approximate $1 - \alpha$ confidence limits for ζ are:

$$z' \pm z(1 - \alpha/2)\sigma\{z'\} \tag{2.93}$$

where $z(1 - \alpha/2)$ is the $(1 - \alpha/2)100$ percentile of the standard normal distribution. The $1 - \alpha$ confidence limits for ρ_{12} are then obtained by transforming the limits on ζ by means of (2.90).

Example

An economist investigated food purchasing patterns by households in a midwestern city. Two hundred households with family incomes between \$40,000 and \$60,000 were selected to ascertain, among other things, the proportions of the food budget expended for beef and poultry, respectively. The economist expected these to be negatively related, and wished to estimate the coefficient of correlation with a 95 percent confidence interval. Some supporting evidence suggested that the joint distribution of the two variables does not depart markedly from a bivariate normal one.

The point estimate of ρ_{12} was $r_{12} = -.61$ (data and calculations not shown). To obtain an approximate 95 percent confidence interval estimate, we require:

$$z' = -.7089 \quad \text{when } r_{12} = -.61 \qquad \text{(from Table B.8)}$$

$$\sigma\{z'\} = \frac{1}{\sqrt{200 - 3}} = .07125$$

$$z(.975) = 1.960$$

Hence, the confidence limits for ζ, by (2.93), are $-.7089 \pm 1.960(.07125)$, and the approximate 95 percent confidence interval is:

$$-.849 \leq \zeta \leq -.569$$

Using Table B.8 to transform back to ρ_{12}, we obtain:

$$-.69 \leq \rho_{12} \leq -.51$$

This confidence interval was sufficiently precise to be useful to the economist, confirming the negative relation and indicating that the degree of linear association is moderately high.

Comments

1. As usual, a confidence interval for ρ_{12} can be employed to test whether or not ρ_{12} has a specified value—say, .5—by noting whether or not the specified value falls within the confidence limits.

2. It can be shown that the square of the coefficient of correlation, namely ρ_{12}^2, measures the relative reduction in the variability of Y_2 associated with the use of variable Y_1. To see this, we noted earlier in (2.80c) and (2.82c) that:

$$\sigma_{1|2}^2 = \sigma_1^2 \left(1 - \rho_{12}^2\right) \tag{2.94a}$$

$$\sigma_{2|1}^2 = \sigma_2^2 \left(1 - \rho_{12}^2\right) \tag{2.94b}$$

We can rewrite these expressions as follows:

$$\rho_{12}^2 = \frac{\sigma_1^2 - \sigma_{1|2}^2}{\sigma_1^2} \tag{2.95a}$$

$$\rho_{12}^2 = \frac{\sigma_2^2 - \sigma_{2|1}^2}{\sigma_2^2} \tag{2.95b}$$

The meaning of ρ_{12}^2 is now clear. Consider first (2.95a). ρ_{12}^2 measures how much smaller relatively is the variability in the conditional distributions of Y_1, for any given level of Y_2, than is the variability in the marginal distribution of Y_1. Thus, ρ_{12}^2 measures the relative reduction in the variability of Y_1 associated with the use of variable Y_2. Correspondingly, (2.95b) shows that ρ_{12}^2 also measures the relative reduction in the variability of Y_2 associated with the use of variable Y_1.

It can be shown that:

$$0 \le \rho_{12}^2 \le 1 \tag{2.96}$$

The limiting value $\rho_{12}^2 = 0$ occurs when Y_1 and Y_2 are independent, so that the variances of each variable in the conditional probability distributions are then no smaller than the variance in the marginal distribution. The limiting value $\rho_{12}^2 = 1$ occurs when there is no variability in the conditional probability distributions for each variable, so perfect predictions of either variable can be made from the other.

3. The interpretation of ρ_{12}^2 as measuring the relative reduction in the conditional variances as compared with the marginal variance is valid for the case of a bivariate normal population, but not for many other bivariate populations. Of course, the interpretation implies nothing in a causal sense.

4. Confidence limits for ρ_{12}^2 can be obtained by squaring the respective confidence limits for ρ_{12}, provided the latter limits do not differ in sign.   ∎

Spearman Rank Correlation Coefficient

At times the joint distribution of two random variables Y_1 and Y_2 differs considerably from the bivariate normal distribution (2.74). In those cases, transformations of the variables Y_1 and Y_2 may be sought to make the joint distribution of the transformed variables approximately bivariate normal and thus permit the use of the inference procedures about ρ_{12} described earlier.

When no appropriate transformations can be found, a nonparametric *rank correlation* procedure may be useful for making inferences about the association between Y_1 and Y_2. The *Spearman rank correlation coefficient* is widely used for this purpose. First, the observations on Y_1 (i.e., $Y_{11}, \ldots, Y_{n1}$) are expressed in ranks from 1 to n. We denote the rank of Y_{i1} by R_{i1}. Similarly, the observations on Y_2 (i.e., $Y_{12}, \ldots, Y_{n2}$) are ranked, with the rank of Y_{i2} denoted by R_{i2}. The Spearman rank correlation coefficient, to be denoted by r_S, is then defined as the ordinary Pearson product-moment correlation coefficient in (2.84) based on the rank data:

$$r_S = \frac{\sum (R_{i1} - \bar{R}_1)(R_{i2} - \bar{R}_2)}{\left[\sum (R_{i1} - \bar{R}_1)^2 \sum (R_{i2} - \bar{R}_2)^2 \right]^{1/2}} \tag{2.97}$$

Here $\bar{R}_1$ is the mean of the ranks R_{i1} and $\bar{R}_2$ is the mean of the ranks R_{i2}. Of course, since the ranks R_{i1} and R_{i2} are the integers $1, \ldots, n$, it follows that $\bar{R}_1 = \bar{R}_2 = (n + 1)/2$.

Like an ordinary correlation coefficient, the Spearman rank correlation coefficient takes on values between -1 and 1 inclusive:

$$-1 \le r_S \le 1 \tag{2.98}$$

The coefficient r_S equals 1 when the ranks for Y_1 are identical to those for Y_2, that is, when the case with rank 1 for Y_1 also has rank 1 for Y_2, and so on. In that case, there is perfect association between the ranks for the two variables. The coefficient r_S equals -1 when the case with rank 1 for Y_1 has rank n for Y_2, the case with rank 2 for Y_1 has rank $n - 1$ for Y_2, and so on. In that event, there is perfect inverse association between the ranks for the two variables. When there is little, if any, association between the ranks of Y_1 and Y_2, the Spearman rank correlation coefficient tends to have a value near zero.

The Spearman rank correlation coefficient can be used to test the alternatives:

$$H_0: \text{There is no association between } Y_1 \text{ and } Y_2$$
$$H_a: \text{There is an association between } Y_1 \text{ and } Y_2 \qquad \textbf{(2.99)}$$

A two-sided test is conducted here since H_a includes either positive or negative association. When the alternative H_a is:

$$H_a: \text{There is positive (negative) association between } Y_1 \text{ and } Y_2 \qquad \textbf{(2.100)}$$

an upper-tail (lower-tail) one-sided test is conducted.

The probability distribution of r_S under H_0 is not difficult to obtain. It is based on the condition that, for any ranking of Y_1, all rankings of Y_2 are equally likely when there is no association between Y_1 and Y_2. Tables have been prepared and are presented in specialized texts such as Reference 2.1. Computer packages generally do not present the probability distribution of r_S under H_0 but give only the two-sided P-value. When the sample size n exceeds 10, the test can be carried out approximately by using test statistic (2.87):

$$t^* = \frac{r_S \sqrt{n-2}}{\sqrt{1-r_S^2}} \qquad \textbf{(2.101)}$$

based on the t distribution with $n - 2$ degrees of freedom.

Example

A market researcher wished to examine whether an association exists between population size (Y_1) and per capita expenditures for a new food product (Y_2). The data for a random sample of 12 test markets are given in Table 2.4, columns 1 and 2. Because the distributions of the variables do not appear to be approximately normal, a nonparametric test of association is desired. The ranks for the variables are given in Table 2.4, columns 3 and 4. A computer package found that the coefficient of simple correlation between the ranked data in columns 3 and 4 is $r_S = .895$. The alternatives of interest are the two-sided ones in (2.99). Since n

TABLE 2.4
Data on Population and Expenditures and Their Ranks—Sales Marketing Example.

Test Market i	(1) Population (in thousands) Y_{i1}	(2) Per Capita Expenditure (dollars) Y_{i2}	(3) R_{i1}	(4) R_{i2}
1	29	127	1	2
2	435	214	8	11
3	86	133	3	4
4	1,090	208	11	10
5	219	153	7	6
6	503	184	9	8
7	47	130	2	3
8	3,524	217	12	12
9	185	141	6	5
10	98	154	5	7
11	952	194	10	9
12	89	103	4	1

exceeds 10 here, we use test statistic (2.101):

$$t^* = \frac{.895\sqrt{12 - 2}}{\sqrt{1 - (.895)^2}} = 6.34$$

For $\alpha = .01$, we require $t(.995; 10) = 3.169$. Since $|t^*| = 6.34 > 3.169$, we conclude H_a, that there is an association between population size and per capita expenditures for the food product. The two-sided P-value of the test is .00008.

Comments

1. In case of ties among some data values, each of the tied values is given the average of the ranks involved.

2. It is interesting to note that had the data in Table 2.4 been analyzed by assuming the bivariate normal distribution assumption (2.74) and test statistic (2.87), then the strength of the association would have been somewhat weaker. In particular, the Pearson product-moment correlation coefficient is $r_{12} = .674$, with $t^* = .674\sqrt{10}/\sqrt{1 - (.674)^2} = 2.885$. Our conclusion would have been to conclude H_0, that there is no association between population size and per capita expenditures for the food product. The two-sided P-value of the test is .016.

3. Another nonparametric rank procedure similar to Spearman's r_S is *Kendall's* τ. This statistic also measures how far the rankings of Y_1 and Y_2 differ from each other, but in a somewhat different way than the Spearman rank correlation coefficient. A discussion of Kendall's τ may be found in Reference 2.2. ∎

Cited References

2.1. Gibbons, J. D. *Nonparametric Methods for Quantitative Analysis.* 2nd ed. Columbus, Ohio: American Sciences Press, 1985.

2.2. Kendall, M. G., and J. D. Gibbons. *Rank Correlation Methods.* 5th ed. London: Oxford University Press, 1990.

Problems

2.1. A student working on a summer internship in the economic research department of a large corporation studied the relation between sales of a product (Y, in million dollars) and population (X, in million persons) in the firm's 50 marketing districts. The normal error regression model (2.1) was employed. The student first wished to test whether or not a linear association between Y and X existed. The student accessed a simple linear regression program and obtained the following information on the regression coefficients:

Parameter	Estimated Value	95 Percent Confidence Limits	
Intercept	7.43119	−1.18518	16.0476
Slope	.755048	.452886	1.05721

a. The student concluded from these results that there is a linear association between Y and X. Is the conclusion warranted? What is the implied level of significance?

b. Someone questioned the negative lower confidence limit for the intercept, pointing out that dollar sales cannot be negative even if the population in a district is zero. Discuss.

2.2. In a test of the alternatives $H_0: \beta_1 \leq 0$ versus $H_a: \beta_1 > 0$, an analyst concluded H_0. Does this conclusion imply that there is no linear association between X and Y? Explain.

2.3. A member of a student team playing an interactive marketing game received the following computer output when studying the relation between advertising expenditures (X) and sales (Y) for one of the team's products:

$$\text{Estimated regression equation: } \hat{Y} = 350.7 - .18X$$
$$\text{Two-sided } P\text{-value for estimated slope: } .91$$

The student stated: "The message I get here is that the more we spend on advertising this product, the fewer units we sell!" Comment.

2.4. Refer to **Grade point average** Problem 1.19.

a. Obtain a 99 percent confidence interval for β_1. Interpret your confidence interval. Does it include zero? Why might the director of admissions be interested in whether the confidence interval includes zero?

b. Test, using the test statistic t^*, whether or not a linear association exists between student's ACT score (X) and GPA at the end of the freshman year (Y). Use a level of significance of .01. State the alternatives, decision rule, and conclusion.

c. What is the P-value of your test in part (b)? How does it support the conclusion reached in part (b)?

*2.5. Refer to **Copier maintenance** Problem 1.20.

a. Estimate the change in the mean service time when the number of copiers serviced increases by one. Use a 90 percent confidence interval. Interpret your confidence interval.

b. Conduct a t test to determine whether or not there is a linear association between X and Y here; control the α risk at .10. State the alternatives, decision rule, and conclusion. What is the P-value of your test?

c. Are your results in parts (a) and (b) consistent? Explain.

d. The manufacturer has suggested that the mean required time should not increase by more than 14 minutes for each additional copier that is serviced on a service call. Conduct a test to decide whether this standard is being satisfied by Tri-City. Control the risk of a Type I error at .05. State the alternatives, decision rule, and conclusion. What is the P-value of the test?

e. Does b_0 give any relevant information here about the "start-up" time on calls—i.e., about the time required before service work is begun on the copiers at a customer location?

*2.6. Refer to **Airfreight breakage** Problem 1.21.

a. Estimate β_1 with a 95 percent confidence interval. Interpret your interval estimate.

b. Conduct a t test to decide whether or not there is a linear association between number of times a carton is transferred (X) and number of broken ampules (Y). Use a level of significance of .05. State the alternatives, decision rule, and conclusion. What is the P-value of the test?

c. β_0 represents here the mean number of ampules broken when no transfers of the shipment are made—i.e., when $X = 0$. Obtain a 95 percent confidence interval for β_0 and interpret it.

d. A consultant has suggested, on the basis of previous experience, that the mean number of broken ampules should not exceed 9.0 when no transfers are made. Conduct an appropriate test, using $\alpha = .025$. State the alternatives, decision rule, and conclusion. What is the P-value of the test?

e. Obtain the power of your test in part (b) if actually $\beta_1 = 2.0$. Assume $\sigma\{b_1\} = .50$. Also obtain the power of your test in part (d) if actually $\beta_0 = 11$. Assume $\sigma\{b_0\} = .75$.

2.7. Refer to **Plastic hardness** Problem 1.22.

a. Estimate the change in the mean hardness when the elapsed time increases by one hour. Use a 99 percent confidence interval. Interpret your interval estimate.

b. The plastic manufacturer has stated that the mean hardness should increase by 2 Brinell units per hour. Conduct a two-sided test to decide whether this standard is being satisfied; use $\alpha = .01$. State the alternatives, decision rule, and conclusion. What is the P-value of the test?

c. Obtain the power of your test in part (b) if the standard actually is being exceeded by .3 Brinell units per hour. Assume $\sigma\{b_1\} = .1$.

2.8. Refer to Figure 2.2 for the Toluca Company example. A consultant has advised that an increase of one unit in lot size should require an increase of 3.0 in the expected number of work hours for the given production item.

a. Conduct a test to decide whether or not the increase in the expected number of work hours in the Toluca Company equals this standard. Use $\alpha = .05$. State the alternatives, decision rule, and conclusion.

b. Obtain the power of your test in part (a) if the consultant's standard actually is being exceeded by .5 hour. Assume $\sigma\{b_1\} = .35$.

c. Why is $F^* = 105.88$, given in the printout, not relevant for the test in part (a)?

2.9. Refer to Figure 2.2. A student, noting that $s\{b_1\}$ is furnished in the printout, asks why $s\{\hat{Y}_h\}$ is not also given. Discuss.

2.10. For each of the following questions, explain whether a confidence interval for a mean response or a prediction interval for a new observation is appropriate.

a. What will be the humidity level in this greenhouse tomorrow when we set the temperature level at 31°C?

b. How much do families whose disposable income is $23,500 spend, on the average, for meals away from home?

c. How many kilowatt-hours of electricity will be consumed next month by commercial and industrial users in the Twin Cities service area, given that the index of business activity for the area remains at its present level?

2.11. A person asks if there is a difference between the "mean response at $X = X_h$" and the "mean of m new observations at $X = X_h$." Reply.

2.12. Can $\sigma^2\{\text{pred}\}$ in (2.37) be brought increasingly close to 0 as n becomes large? Is this also the case for $\sigma^2\{\hat{Y}_h\}$ in (2.29b)? What is the implication of this difference?

2.13. Refer to **Grade point average** Problem 1.19.

a. Obtain a 95 percent interval estimate of the mean freshman GPA for students whose ACT test score is 28. Interpret your confidence interval.

b. Mary Jones obtained a score of 28 on the entrance test. Predict her freshman GPA using a 95 percent prediction interval. Interpret your prediction interval.

c. Is the prediction interval in part (b) wider than the confidence interval in part (a)? Should it be?

d. Determine the boundary values of the 95 percent confidence band for the regression line when $X_h = 28$. Is your confidence band wider at this point than the confidence interval in part (a)? Should it be?

*2.14. Refer to **Copier maintenance** Problem 1.20.

a. Obtain a 90 percent confidence interval for the mean service time on calls in which six copiers are serviced. Interpret your confidence interval.

b. Obtain a 90 percent prediction interval for the service time on the next call in which six copiers are serviced. Is your prediction interval wider than the corresponding confidence interval in part (a)? Should it be?

c. Management wishes to estimate the expected service time *per copier* on calls in which six copiers are serviced. Obtain an appropriate 90 percent confidence interval by converting the interval obtained in part (a). Interpret the converted confidence interval.

d. Determine the boundary values of the 90 percent confidence band for the regression line when $X_h = 6$. Is your confidence band wider at this point than the confidence interval in part (a)? Should it be?

*2.15. Refer to **Airfreight breakage** Problem 1.21.

a. Because of changes in airline routes, shipments may have to be transferred more frequently than in the past. Estimate the mean breakage for the following numbers of transfers: $X = 2$, 4. Use separate 99 percent confidence intervals. Interpret your results.

b. The next shipment will entail two transfers. Obtain a 99 percent prediction interval for the number of broken ampules for this shipment. Interpret your prediction interval.

c. In the next several days, three independent shipments will be made, each entailing two transfers. Obtain a 99 percent prediction interval for the mean number of ampules broken in the three shipments. Convert this interval into a 99 percent prediction interval for the total number of ampules broken in the three shipments.

d. Determine the boundary values of the 99 percent confidence band for the regression line when $X_h = 2$ and when $X_h = 4$. Is your confidence band wider at these two points than the corresponding confidence intervals in part (a)? Should it be?

2.16. Refer to **Plastic hardness** Problem 1.22.

a. Obtain a 98 percent confidence interval for the mean hardness of molded items with an elapsed time of 30 hours. Interpret your confidence interval.

b. Obtain a 98 percent prediction interval for the hardness of a newly molded test item with an elapsed time of 30 hours.

c. Obtain a 98 percent prediction interval for the mean hardness of 10 newly molded test items, each with an elapsed time of 30 hours.

d. Is the prediction interval in part (c) narrower than the one in part (b)? Should it be?

e. Determine the boundary values of the 98 percent confidence band for the regression line when $X_h = 30$. Is your confidence band wider at this point than the confidence interval in part (a)? Should it be?

2.17. An analyst fitted normal error regression model (2.1) and conducted an F test of $\beta_1 = 0$ versus $\beta_1 \neq 0$. The P-value of the test was .033, and the analyst concluded H_a: $\beta_1 \neq 0$. Was the α level used by the analyst greater than or smaller than .033? If the α level had been .01, what would have been the appropriate conclusion?

2.18. For conducting statistical tests concerning the parameter β_1, why is the t test more versatile than the F test?

2.19. When testing whether or not $\beta_1 = 0$, why is the F test a one-sided test even though H_a includes both $\beta_1 < 0$ and $\beta_1 > 0$? [*Hint*: Refer to (2.57).]

2.20. A student asks whether R^2 is a point estimator of any parameter in the normal error regression model (2.1). Respond.

2.21. A value of R^2 near 1 is sometimes interpreted to imply that the relation between Y and X is sufficiently close so that suitably precise predictions of Y can be made from knowledge of X. Is this implication a necessary consequence of the definition of R^2?

2.22. Using the normal error regression model (2.1) in an engineering safety experiment, a researcher found for the first 10 cases that R^2 was zero. Is it possible that for the complete set of 30 cases R^2 will not be zero? Could R^2 not be zero for the first 10 cases, yet equal zero for all 30 cases? Explain.

2.23. Refer to **Grade point average** Problem 1.19.

    a. Set up the ANOVA table.

    b. What is estimated by *MSR* in your ANOVA table? by *MSE*? Under what condition do *MSR* and *MSE* estimate the same quantity?

    c. Conduct an *F* test of whether or not $\beta_1 = 0$. Control the α risk at .01. State the alternatives, decision rule, and conclusion.

    d. What is the absolute magnitude of the reduction in the variation of Y when X is introduced into the regression model? What is the relative reduction? What is the name of the latter measure?

    e. Obtain r and attach the appropriate sign.

    f. Which measure, R^2 or r, has the more clear-cut operational interpretation? Explain.

*2.24. Refer to **Copier maintenance** Problem 1.20.

    a. Set up the basic ANOVA table in the format of Table 2.2. Which elements of your table are additive? Also set up the ANOVA table in the format of Table 2.3. How do the two tables differ?

    b. Conduct an *F* test to determine whether or not there is a linear association between time spent and number of copiers serviced; use $\alpha = .10$. State the alternatives, decision rule, and conclusion.

    c. By how much, relatively, is the total variation in number of minutes spent on a call reduced when the number of copiers serviced is introduced into the analysis? Is this a relatively small or large reduction? What is the name of this measure?

    d. Calculate r and attach the appropriate sign.

    e. Which measure, r or R^2, has the more clear-cut operational interpretation?

*2.25. Refer to **Airfreight breakage** Problem 1.21.

    a. Set up the ANOVA table. Which elements are additive?

    b. Conduct an *F* test to decide whether or not there is a linear association between the number of times a carton is transferred and the number of broken ampules; control the α risk at .05. State the alternatives, decision rule, and conclusion.

    c. Obtain the t^* statistic for the test in part (b) and demonstrate numerically its equivalence to the F^* statistic obtained in part (b).

    d. Calculate R^2 and r. What proportion of the variation in Y is accounted for by introducing X into the regression model?

2.26. Refer to **Plastic hardness** Problem 1.22.

    a. Set up the ANOVA table.

    b. Test by means of an *F* test whether or not there is a linear association between the hardness of the plastic and the elapsed time. Use $\alpha = .01$. State the alternatives, decision rule, and conclusion.

    c. Plot the deviations $Y_i - \hat{Y}_i$ against X_i on a graph. Plot the deviations $\hat{Y}_i - \bar{Y}$ against X_i on another graph, using the same scales as for the first graph. From your two graphs, does *SSE* or *SSR* appear to be the larger component of *SSTO*? What does this imply about the magnitude of R^2?

    d. Calculate R^2 and r.

*2.27. Refer to **Muscle mass** Problem 1.27.

    a. Conduct a test to decide whether or not there is a negative linear association between amount of muscle mass and age. Control the risk of Type I error at .05. State the alternatives, decision rule, and conclusion. What is the P-value of the test?

b. The two-sided *P*-value for the test whether $\beta_0 = 0$ is 0+. Can it now be concluded that b_0 provides relevant information on the amount of muscle mass at birth for a female child?

c. Estimate with a 95 percent confidence interval the difference in expected muscle mass for women whose ages differ by one year. Why is it not necessary to know the specific ages to make this estimate?

*2.28. Refer to **Muscle mass** Problem 1.27.

a. Obtain a 95 percent confidence interval for the mean muscle mass for women of age 60. Interpret your confidence interval.

b. Obtain a 95 percent prediction interval for the muscle mass of a woman whose age is 60. Is the prediction interval relatively precise?

c. Determine the boundary values of the 95 percent confidence band for the regression line when $X_h = 60$. Is your confidence band wider at this point than the confidence interval in part (a)? Should it be?

*2.29. Refer to **Muscle mass** Problem 1.27.

a. Plot the deviations $Y_i - \hat{Y}_i$ against X_i on one graph. Plot the deviations $\hat{Y}_i - \bar{Y}$ against X_i on another graph, using the same scales as in the first graph. From your two graphs, does *SSE* or *SSR* appear to be the larger component of *SSTO*? What does this imply about the magnitude of R^2?

b. Set up the ANOVA table.

c. Test whether or not $\beta_1 = 0$ using an *F* test with $\alpha = .05$. State the alternatives, decision rule, and conclusion.

d. What proportion of the total variation in muscle mass remains "unexplained" when age is introduced into the analysis? Is this proportion relatively small or large?

e. Obtain R^2 and r.

2.30. Refer to **Crime rate** Problem 1.28.

a. Test whether or not there is a linear association between crime rate and percentage of high school graduates, using a *t* test with $\alpha = .01$. State the alternatives, decision rule, and conclusion. What is the *P*-value of the test?

b. Estimate β_1 with a 99 percent confidence interval. Interpret your interval estimate.

2.31. Refer to **Crime rate** Problem 1.28

a. Set up the ANOVA table.

b. Carry out the test in Problem 2.30a by means of the *F* test. Show the numerical equivalence of the two test statistics and decision rules. Is the *P*-value for the *F* test the same as that for the *t* test?

c. By how much is the total variation in crime rate reduced when percentage of high school graduates is introduced into the analysis? Is this a relatively large or small reduction?

d. Obtain r.

2.32. Refer to **Crime rate** Problems 1.28 and 2.30. Suppose that the test in Problem 2.30a is to be carried out by means of a general linear test.

a. State the full and reduced models.

b. Obtain (1) $SSE(F)$, (2) $SSE(R)$, (3) df_F, (4) df_R, (5) test statistic F^* for the general linear test, (6) decision rule.

c. Are the test statistic F^* and the decision rule for the general linear test numerically equivalent to those in Problem 2.30a?

2.33. In developing empirically a cost function from observed data on a complex chemical experiment, an analyst employed normal error regression model (2.1). β_0 was interpreted here as the cost of setting up the experiment. The analyst hypothesized that this cost should be $7.5 thousand and wished to test the hypothesis by means of a general linear test.

   a. Indicate the alternative conclusions for the test.

   b. Specify the full and reduced models.

   c. Without additional information, can you tell what the quantity $df_R - df_F$ in test statistic (2.70) will equal in the analyst's test? Explain.

2.34. Refer to **Grade point average** Problem 1.19.

   a. Would it be more reasonable to consider the X_i as known constants or as random variables here? Explain.

   b. If the X_i were considered to be random variables, would this have any effect on prediction intervals for new applicants? Explain.

2.35. Refer to **Copier maintenance** Problems 1.20 and 2.5. How would the meaning of the confidence coefficient in Problem 2.5a change if the predictor variable were considered a random variable and the conditions on page 83 were applicable?

2.36. A management trainee in a production department wished to study the relation between weight of rough casting and machining time to produce the finished block. The trainee selected castings so that the weights would be spaced equally apart in the sample and then observed the corresponding machining times. Would you recommend that a regression or a correlation model be used? Explain.

2.37. A social scientist stated: "The conditions for the bivariate normal distribution are so rarely met in my experience that I feel much safer using a regression model." Comment.

2.38. A student was investigating from a large sample whether variables Y_1 and Y_2 follow a bivariate normal distribution. The student obtained the residuals when regressing Y_1 on Y_2, and also obtained the residuals when regressing Y_2 on Y_1, and then prepared a normal probability plot for each set of residuals. Do these two normal probability plots provide sufficient information for determining whether the two variables follow a bivariate normal distribution? Explain.

2.39. For the bivariate normal distribution with parameters $\mu_1 = 50$, $\mu_2 = 100$, $\sigma_1 = 3$, $\sigma_2 = 4$, and $\rho_{12} = .80$.

   a. State the characteristics of the marginal distribution of Y_1.

   b. State the characteristics of the conditional distribution of Y_2 when $Y_1 = 55$.

   c. State the characteristics of the conditional distribution of Y_1 when $Y_2 = 95$.

2.40. Explain whether any of the following would be affected if the bivariate normal model (2.74) were employed instead of the normal error regression model (2.1) with fixed levels of the predictor variable: (1) point estimates of the regression coefficients, (2) confidence limits for the regression coefficients, (3) interpretation of the confidence coefficient.

2.41. Refer to **Plastic hardness** Problem 1.22. A student was analyzing these data and received the following standard query from the interactive regression and correlation computer package: CALCULATE CONFIDENCE INTERVAL FOR POPULATION CORRELATION COEFFICIENT RHO? ANSWER Y OR N. Would a "yes" response lead to meaningful information here? Explain.

*2.42. **Property assessments.** The data that follow show assessed value for property tax purposes (Y_1, in thousand dollars) and sales price (Y_2, in thousand dollars) for a sample of 15 parcels of land for industrial development sold recently in "arm's length" transactions in a tax district. Assume that bivariate normal model (2.74) is appropriate here.

i:	1	2	3	...	13	14	15
Y_{i1}:	13.9	16.0	10.3	...	14.9	12.9	15.8
Y_{i2}:	28.6	34.7	21.0	...	35.1	30.0	36.2

a. Plot the data in a scatter diagram. Does the bivariate normal model appear to be appropriate here? Discuss.

b. Calculate r_{12}. What parameter is estimated by r_{12}? What is the interpretation of this parameter?

c. Test whether or not Y_1 and Y_2 are statistically independent in the population, using test statistic (2.87) and level of significance .01. State the alternatives, decision rule, and conclusion.

d. To test $\rho_{12} = .6$ versus $\rho_{12} \neq .6$, would it be appropriate to use test statistic (2.87)?

2.43. **Contract profitability.** A cost analyst for a drilling and blasting contractor examined 84 contracts handled in the last two years and found that the coefficient of correlation between value of contract (Y_1) and profit contribution generated by the contract (Y_2) is $r_{12} = .61$. Assume that bivariate normal model (2.74) applies.

a. Test whether or not Y_1 and Y_2 are statistically independent in the population; use $\alpha = .05$. State the alternatives, decision rule, and conclusion.

b. Estimate ρ_{12} with a 95 percent confidence interval.

c. Convert the confidence interval in part (b) to a 95 percent confidence interval for ρ_{12}^2. Interpret this interval estimate.

*2.44. **Bid preparation.** A building construction consultant studied the relationship between cost of bid preparation (Y_1) and amount of bid (Y_2) for the consulting firm's clients. In a sample of 103 bids prepared by clients, $r_{12} = .87$. Assume that bivariate normal model (2.74) applies.

a. Test whether or not $\rho_{12} = 0$; control the risk of Type I error at .10. State the alternatives, decision rule, and conclusion. What would be the implication if $\rho_{12} = 0$?

b. Obtain a 90 percent confidence interval for ρ_{12}. Interpret this interval estimate.

c. Convert the confidence interval in part (b) to a 90 percent confidence interval for ρ_{12}^2.

2.45. **Water flow.** An engineer, desiring to estimate the coefficient of correlation ρ_{12} between rate of water flow at point A in a stream (Y_1) and concurrent rate of flow at point B (Y_2), obtained $r_{12} = .83$ in a sample of 147 cases. Assume that bivariate normal model (2.74) is appropriate.

a. Obtain a 99 percent confidence interval for ρ_{12}.

b. Convert the confidence interval in part (a) to a 99 percent confidence interval for ρ_{12}^2.

2.46. Refer to **Property assessments** Problem 2.42. There is some question as to whether or not bivariate model (2.74) is appropriate.

a. Obtain the Spearman rank correlation coefficient r_S.

b. Test by means of the Spearman rank correlation coefficient whether an association exists between property assessments and sales prices using test statistic (2.101) with $\alpha = .01$. State the alternatives, decision rule, and conclusion.

c. How do your estimates and conclusions in parts (a) and (b) compare to those obtained in Problem 2.42?

*2.47. Refer to **Muscle mass** Problem 1.27. Assume that the normal bivariate model (2.74) is appropriate.

a. Compute the Pearson product-moment correlation coefficient r_{12}.

b. Test whether muscle mass and age are statistically independent in the population; use $\alpha = .05$. State the alternatives, decision rule, and conclusion.

c. The bivariate normal model (2.74) assumption is possibly inappropriate here. Compute the Spearman rank correlation coefficient, r_S.

d. Repeat part (b), this time basing the test of independence on the Spearman rank correlation computed in part (c) and test statistic (2.101). Use $\alpha = .05$. State the alternatives, decision rule, and conclusion.

e. How do your estimates and conclusions in parts (a) and (b) compare to those obtained in parts (c) and (d)?

2.48. Refer to **Crime rate** Problems 1.28, 2.30, and 2.31. Assume that the normal bivariate model (2.74) is appropriate.

a. Compute the Pearson product-moment correlation coefficient r_{12}.

b. Test whether crime rate and percentage of high school graduates are statistically independent in the population; use $\alpha = .01$. State the alternatives, decision rule, and conclusion.

c. How do your estimates and conclusions in parts (a) and (b) compare to those obtained in 2.31b and 2.30a, respectively?

2.49. Refer to **Crime rate** Problems 1.28 and 2.48. The bivariate normal model (2.74) assumption is possibly inappropriate here.

a. Compute the Spearman rank correlation coefficient r_S.

b. Test by means of the Spearman rank correlation coefficient whether an association exists between crime rate and percentage of high school graduates using test statistic (2.101) and a level of significance .01. State the alternatives, decision rule, and conclusion.

c. How do your estimates and conclusions in parts (a) and (b) compare to those obtained in Problems 2.48a and 2.48b, respectively?

Exercises

2.50. Derive the property in (2.6) for the k_i.

2.51. Show that b_0 as defined in (2.21) is an unbiased estimator of β_0.

2.52. Derive the expression in (2.22b) for the variance of b_0, making use of (2.31). Also explain how variance (2.22b) is a special case of variance (2.29b).

2.53. (Calculus needed.)

a. Obtain the likelihood function for the sample observations $Y_1, \ldots, Y_n$ given $X_1, \ldots, X_n$, if the conditions on page 83 apply.

b. Obtain the maximum likelihood estimators of β_0, β_1, and σ^2. Are the estimators of β_0 and β_1 the same as those in (1.27) when the X_i are fixed?

2.54. Suppose that normal error regression model (2.1) is applicable except that the error variance is not constant; rather the variance is larger, the larger is X. Does $\beta_1 = 0$ still imply that there is no linear association between X and Y? That there is no association between X and Y? Explain.

2.55. Derive the expression for *SSR* in (2.51).

2.56. In a small-scale regression study, five observations on Y were obtained corresponding to $X = 1$, 4, 10, 11, and 14. Assume that $\sigma = .6$, $\beta_0 = 5$, and $\beta_1 = 3$.

a. What are the expected values of *MSR* and *MSE* here?

b. For determining whether or not a regression relation exists, would it have been better or worse to have made the five observations at $X = 6, 7, 8, 9,$ and 10? Why? Would the same answer apply if the principal purpose were to estimate the mean response for $X = 8$? Discuss.

2.57. The normal error regression model (2.1) is assumed to be applicable.

a. When testing H_0: $\beta_1 = 5$ versus H_a: $\beta_1 \neq 5$ by means of a general linear test, what is the reduced model? What are the degrees of freedom df_R?

b. When testing H_0: $\beta_0 = 2$, $\beta_1 = 5$ versus H_a: not both $\beta_0 = 2$ and $\beta_1 = 5$ by means of a general linear test, what is the reduced model? What are the degrees of freedom df_R?

2.58. The random variables Y_1 and Y_2 follow the bivariate normal distribution in (2.74). Show that if $\rho_{12} = 0$, Y_1 and Y_2 are independent random variables.

2.59. (Calculus needed.)

a. Obtain the maximum likelihood estimators of the parameters of the bivariate normal distribution in (2.74).

b. Using the results in part (a), obtain the maximum likelihood estimators of the parameters of the conditional probability distribution of Y_1 for any value of Y_2 in (2.80).

c. Show that the maximum likelihood estimators of $\alpha_{1|2}$ and β_{12} obtained in part (b) are the same as the least squares estimators (1.10) for the regression coefficients in the simple linear regression model.

2.60. Show that test statistics (2.17) and (2.87) are equivalent.

2.61. Show that the ratio $SSR/SSTO$ is the same whether Y_1 is regressed on Y_2 or Y_2 is regressed on Y_1. [*Hint*: Use (1.10a) and (2.51).]

Projects

2.62. Refer to the **CDI** data set in Appendix C.2 and Project 1.43. Using R^2 as the criterion, which predictor variable accounts for the largest reduction in the variability in the number of active physicians?

2.63. Refer to the **CDI** data set in Appendix C.2 and Project 1.44. Obtain a separate interval estimate of β_1 for each region. Use a 90 percent confidence coefficient in each case. Do the regression lines for the different regions appear to have similar slopes?

2.64. Refer to the **SENIC** data set in Appendix C.1 and Project 1.45. Using R^2 as the criterion, which predictor variable accounts for the largest reduction in the variability of the average length of stay?

2.65. Refer to the **SENIC** data set in Appendix C.1 and Project 1.46. Obtain a separate interval estimate of β_1 for each region. Use a 95 percent confidence coefficient in each case. Do the regression lines for the different regions appear to have similar slopes?

2.66. Five observations on Y are to be taken when $X = 4, 8, 12, 16,$ and 20, respectively. The true regression function is $E\{Y\} = 20 + 4X$, and the ε_i are independent $N(0, 25)$.

a. Generate five normal random numbers, with mean 0 and variance 25. Consider these random numbers as the error terms for the five Y observations at $X = 4, 8, 12, 16,$ and 20 and calculate $Y_1, Y_2, Y_3, Y_4,$ and Y_5. Obtain the least squares estimates b_0 and b_1 when fitting a straight line to the five cases. Also calculate $\hat{Y}_h$ when $X_h = 10$ and obtain a 95 percent confidence interval for $E\{Y_h\}$ when $X_h = 10$.

b. Repeat part (a) 200 times, generating new random numbers each time.

c. Make a frequency distribution of the 200 estimates b_1. Calculate the mean and standard deviation of the 200 estimates b_1. Are the results consistent with theoretical expectations?

d. What proportion of the 200 confidence intervals for $E\{Y_h\}$ when $X_h = 10$ include $E\{Y_h\}$? Is this result consistent with theoretical expectations?

2.67. Refer to **Grade point average** Problem 1.19.

    a. Plot the data, with the least squares regression line for ACT scores between 20 and 30 superimposed.

    b. On the plot in part (a), superimpose a plot of the 95 percent confidence band for the true regression line for ACT scores between 20 and 30. Does the confidence band suggest that the true regression relation has been precisely estimated? Discuss.

2.68. Refer to **Copier maintenance** Problem 1.20.

    a. Plot the data, with the least squares regression line for numbers of copiers serviced between 1 and 8 superimposed.

    b. On the plot in part (a), superimpose a plot of the 90 percent confidence band for the true regression line for numbers of copiers serviced between 1 and 8. Does the confidence band suggest that the true regression relation has been precisely estimated? Discuss.

Chapter 3

Diagnostics and Remedial Measures

When a regression model, such as the simple linear regression model (2.1), is considered for an application, we can usually not be certain in advance that the model is appropriate for that application. Any one, or several, of the features of the model, such as linearity of the regression function or normality of the error terms, may not be appropriate for the particular data at hand. Hence, it is important to examine the aptness of the model for the data before inferences based on that model are undertaken. In this chapter, we discuss some simple graphic methods for studying the appropriateness of a model, as well as some formal statistical tests for doing so. We also consider some remedial techniques that can be helpful when the data are not in accordance with the conditions of regression model (2.1). We conclude the chapter with a case example that brings together the concepts and methods presented in this and the earlier chapters.

While the discussion in this chapter is in terms of the appropriateness of the simple linear regression model (2.1), the basic principles apply to all statistical models discussed in this book. In later chapters, additional methods useful for examining the appropriateness of statistical models and other remedial measures will be presented, as well as methods for validating the statistical model.

3.1 Diagnostics for Predictor Variable

We begin by considering some graphic diagnostics for the predictor variable. We need diagnostic information about the predictor variable to see if there are any outlying X values that could influence the appropriateness of the fitted regression function. We discuss the role of influential cases in detail in Chapter 10. Diagnostic information about the range and concentration of the X levels in the study is also useful for ascertaining the range of validity for the regression analysis.

Figure 3.1a contains a simple *dot plot* for the lot sizes in the Toluca Company example in Figure 1.10. A dot plot is helpful when the number of observations in the data set is not large. The dot plot in Figure 3.1a shows that the minimum and maximum lot sizes are 20 and 120, respectively, that the lot size levels are spread throughout this interval, and that

FIGURE 3.1   **MINITAB and SYGRAPH Diagnostic Plots for Predictor Variable—Toluca Company Example.**

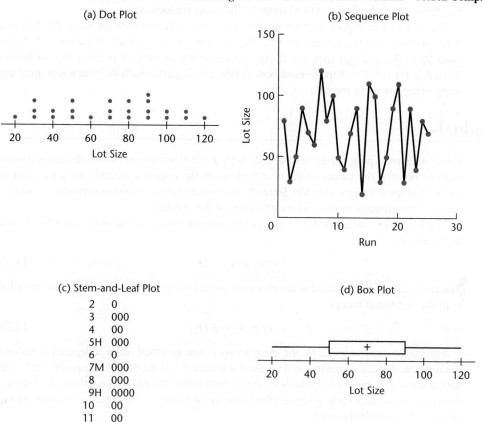

(a) Dot Plot

(b) Sequence Plot

(c) Stem-and-Leaf Plot

```
 2    0
 3    000
 4    00
 5H   000
 6    0
 7M   000
 8    000
 9H   0000
10    00
11    00
12    0
```

(d) Box Plot

there are no lot sizes that are far outlying. The dot plot also shows that in a number of cases several runs were made for the same lot size.

A second useful diagnostic for the predictor variable is a *sequence plot*. Figure 3.1b contains a time sequence plot of the lot sizes for the Toluca Company example. Lot size is here plotted against production run (i.e., against time sequence). The points in the plot are connected to show more effectively the time sequence. Sequence plots should be utilized whenever data are obtained in a sequence, such as over time or for adjacent geographic areas. The sequence plot in Figure 3.1b contains no special pattern. If, say, the plot had shown that smaller lot sizes had been utilized early on and larger lot sizes later on, this information could be very helpful for subsequent diagnostic studies of the aptness of the fitted regression model.

Figures 3.1c and 3.1d contain two other diagnostic plots that present information similar to the dot plot in Figure 3.1a. The *stem-and-leaf plot* in Figure 3.1c provides information similar to a frequency histogram. By displaying the last digits, this plot also indicates here that all lot sizes in the Toluca Company example were multiples of 10. The letter M in the

SYGRAPH output denotes the stem where the median is located, and the letter H denotes the stems where the first and third quartiles (hinges) are located.

The *box plot* in Figure 3.1d shows the minimum and maximum lot sizes, the first and third quartiles, and the median lot size. We see that the middle half of the lot sizes range from 50 to 90, and that they are fairly symmetrically distributed because the median is located in the middle of the central box. A box plot is particularly helpful when there are many observations in the data set.

3.2   Residuals

Direct diagnostic plots for the response variable Y are ordinarily not too useful in regression analysis because the values of the observations on the response variable are a function of the level of the predictor variable. Instead, diagnostics for the response variable are usually carried out indirectly through an examination of the residuals.

The residual e_i, as defined in (1.16), is the difference between the observed value Y_i and the fitted value $\hat{Y}_i$:

$$e_i = Y_i - \hat{Y}_i \tag{3.1}$$

The residual may be regarded as the observed error, in distinction to the unknown true error ε_i in the regression model:

$$\varepsilon_i = Y_i - E\{Y_i\} \tag{3.2}$$

For regression model (2.1), the error terms ε_i are assumed to be independent normal random variables, with mean 0 and constant variance σ^2. If the model is appropriate for the data at hand, the observed residuals e_i should then reflect the properties assumed for the ε_i. This is the basic idea underlying *residual analysis,* a highly useful means of examining the aptness of a statistical model.

Properties of Residuals

Mean.   The mean of the n residuals e_i for the simple linear regression model (2.1) is, by (1.17):

$$\bar{e} = \frac{\sum e_i}{n} = 0 \tag{3.3}$$

where $\bar{e}$ denotes the mean of the residuals. Thus, since $\bar{e}$ is always 0, it provides no information as to whether the true errors ε_i have expected value $E\{\varepsilon_i\} = 0$.

Variance.   The variance of the n residuals e_i is defined as follows for regression model (2.1):

$$s^2 = \frac{\sum(e_i - \bar{e})^2}{n-2} = \frac{\sum e_i^2}{n-2} = \frac{SSE}{n-2} = MSE \tag{3.4}$$

If the model is appropriate, *MSE* is, as noted earlier, an unbiased estimator of the variance of the error terms σ^2.

Nonindependence.   The residuals e_i are not independent random variables because they involve the fitted values $\hat{Y}_i$ which are based on the same fitted regression function. As a result, the residuals for regression model (2.1) are subject to two constraints. These are constraint (1.17)—that the sum of the e_i must be 0—and constraint (1.19)—that the products $X_i e_i$ must sum to 0.

When the sample size is large in comparison to the number of parameters in the regression model, the dependency effect among the residuals e_i is relatively unimportant and can be ignored for most purposes.

Semistudentized Residuals

At times, it is helpful to standardize the residuals for residual analysis. Since the standard deviation of the error terms ε_i is σ, which is estimated by $\sqrt{MSE}$, it is natural to consider the following form of standardization:

$$e_i^* = \frac{e_i - \bar{e}}{\sqrt{MSE}} = \frac{e_i}{\sqrt{MSE}} \tag{3.5}$$

If $\sqrt{MSE}$ were an estimate of the standard deviation of the residual e_i, we would call e_i^* a studentized residual. However, the standard deviation of e_i is complex and varies for the different residuals e_i, and $\sqrt{MSE}$ is only an approximation of the standard deviation of e_i. Hence, we call the statistic e_i^* in (3.5) a *semistudentized residual*. We shall take up studentized residuals in Chapter 10. Both semistudentized residuals and studentized residuals can be very helpful in identifying outlying observations.

Departures from Model to Be Studied by Residuals

We shall consider the use of residuals for examining six important types of departures from the simple linear regression model (2.1) with normal errors:

1. The regression function is not linear.
2. The error terms do not have constant variance.
3. The error terms are not independent.
4. The model fits all but one or a few outlier observations.
5. The error terms are not normally distributed.
6. One or several important predictor variables have been omitted from the model.

3.3   Diagnostics for Residuals

We take up now some informal diagnostic plots of residuals to provide information on whether any of the six types of departures from the simple linear regression model (2.1) just mentioned are present. The following plots of residuals (or semistudentized residuals) will be utilized here for this purpose:

1. Plot of residuals against predictor variable.
2. Plot of absolute or squared residuals against predictor variable.
3. Plot of residuals against fitted values.
4. Plot of residuals against time or other sequence.
5. Plots of residuals against omitted predictor variables.
6. Box plot of residuals.
7. Normal probability plot of residuals.

FIGURE 3.2 **MINITAB and SYGRAPH Diagnostic Residual Plots—Toluca Company Example.**

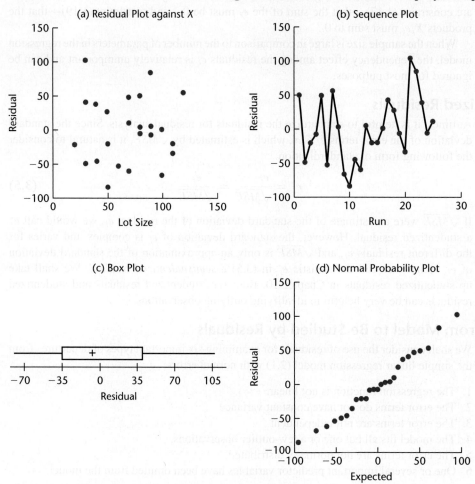

Figure 3.2 contains, for the Toluca Company example, MINITAB and SYGRAPH plots of the residuals in Table 1.2 against the predictor variable and against time, a box plot, and a normal probability plot. All of these plots, as we shall see, support the appropriateness of regression model (2.1) for the data.

We turn now to consider how residual analysis can be helpful in studying each of the six departures from regression model (2.1).

Nonlinearity of Regression Function

Whether a linear regression function is appropriate for the data being analyzed can be studied from a *residual plot against the predictor variable* or, equivalently, from a *residual plot against the fitted values*. Nonlinearity of the regression function can also be studied from a *scatter plot*, but this plot is not always as effective as a residual plot. Figure 3.3a

FIGURE 3.3
Scatter Plot and Residual Plot Illustrating Nonlinear Regression Function— Transit Example.

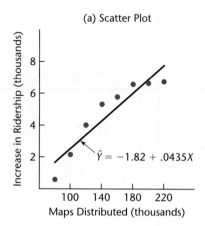

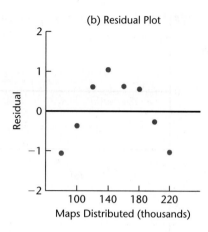

TABLE 3.1
Number of Maps Distributed and Increase in Ridership— Transit Example.

City i	(1) Increase in Ridership (thousands) Y_i	(2) Maps Distributed (thousands) X_i	(3) Fitted Value $\hat{Y}_i$	(4) Residual $Y_i - \hat{Y}_i = e_i$
1	.60	80	1.66	−1.06
2	6.70	220	7.75	−1.05
3	5.30	140	4.27	1.03
4	4.00	120	3.40	.60
5	6.55	180	6.01	.54
6	2.15	100	2.53	−.38
7	6.60	200	6.88	−.28
8	5.75	160	5.14	.61

$$\hat{Y} = -1.82 + .0435X$$

contains a scatter plot of the data and the fitted regression line for a study of the relation between maps distributed and bus ridership in eight test cities. Here, X is the number of bus transit maps distributed free to residents of the city at the beginning of the test period and Y is the increase during the test period in average daily bus ridership during nonpeak hours. The original data and fitted values are given in Table 3.1, columns 1, 2, and 3. The plot suggests strongly that a linear regression function is not appropriate.

Figure 3.3b presents a plot of the residuals, shown in Table 3.1, column 4, against the predictor variable X. The lack of fit of the linear regression function is even more strongly suggested by the residual plot against X in Figure 3.3b than by the scatter plot. Note that the residuals depart from 0 in a systematic fashion; they are negative for smaller X values, positive for medium-size X values, and negative again for large X values.

In this case, both Figures 3.3a and 3.3b point out the lack of linearity of the regression function. In general, however, the residual plot is to be preferred, because it has some important advantages over the scatter plot. First, the residual plot can easily be used for examining other facets of the aptness of the model. Second, there are occasions when the

FIGURE 3.4
Prototype
Residual Plots.

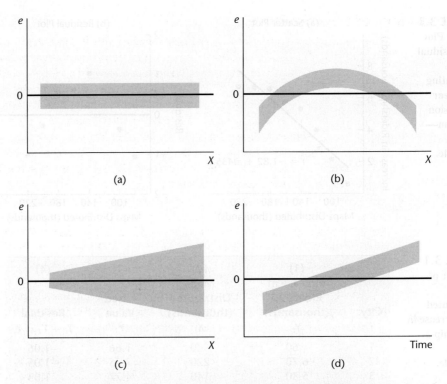

(a)

(b)

(c)

(d)

scaling of the scatter plot places the Y_i observations close to the fitted values $\hat{Y}_i$, for instance, when there is a steep slope. It then becomes more difficult to study the appropriateness of a linear regression function from the scatter plot. A residual plot, on the other hand, can clearly show any systematic pattern in the deviations around the fitted regression line under these conditions.

Figure 3.4a shows a prototype situation of the residual plot against X when a linear regression model is appropriate. The residuals then fall within a horizontal band centered around 0, displaying no systematic tendencies to be positive and negative. This is the case in Figure 3.2a for the Toluca Company example.

Figure 3.4b shows a prototype situation of a departure from the linear regression model that indicates the need for a curvilinear regression function. Here the residuals tend to vary in a systematic fashion between being positive and negative. This is the case in Figure 3.3b for the transit example. A different type of departure from linearity would, of course, lead to a picture different from the prototype pattern in Figure 3.4b.

Comment

A plot of residuals against the fitted values $\hat{Y}$ provides equivalent information as a plot of residuals against X for the simple linear regression model, and thus is not needed in addition to the residual plot against X. The two plots provide the same information because the fitted values $\hat{Y}_i$ are a linear function of the values X_i for the predictor variable. Thus, only the X scale values, not the basic pattern of the plotted points, are affected by whether the residual plot is against the X_i or the $\hat{Y}_i$. For curvilinear regression and multiple regression, on the other hand, separate plots of the residuals against the fitted values and against the predictor variable(s) are usually helpful. ∎

Nonconstancy of Error Variance

Plots of the residuals against the predictor variable or against the fitted values are not only helpful to study whether a linear regression function is appropriate but also to examine whether the variance of the error terms is constant. Figure 3.5a shows a residual plot against age for a study of the relation between diastolic blood pressure of healthy, adult women (Y) and their age (X). The plot suggests that the older the woman is, the more spread out the residuals are. Since the relation between blood pressure and age is positive, this suggests that the error variance is larger for older women than for younger ones.

The prototype plot in Figure 3.4a exemplifies residual plots when the error term variance is constant. The residual plot in Figure 3.2a for the Toluca Company example is of this type, suggesting that the error terms have constant variance here.

Figure 3.4c shows a prototype picture of residual plots when the error variance increases with X. In many business, social science, and biological science applications, departures from constancy of the error variance tend to be of the "megaphone" type shown in Figure 3.4c, as in the blood pressure example in Figure 3.5a. One can also encounter error variances decreasing with increasing levels of the predictor variable and occasionally varying in some more complex fashion.

Plots of the absolute values of the residuals or of the squared residuals against the predictor variable X or against the fitted values $\hat{Y}$ are also useful for diagnosing nonconstancy of the error variance since the signs of the residuals are not meaningful for examining the constancy of the error variance. These plots are especially useful when there are not many cases in the data set because plotting of either the absolute or squared residuals places all of the information on changing magnitudes of the residuals above the horizontal zero line so that one can more readily see whether the magnitude of the residuals (irrespective of sign) is changing with the level of X or $\hat{Y}$.

Figure 3.5b contains a plot of the absolute residuals against age for the blood pressure example. This plot shows more clearly that the residuals tend to be larger in absolute magnitude for older-aged women.

FIGURE 3.5
Residual Plots Illustrating Nonconstant Error Variance.

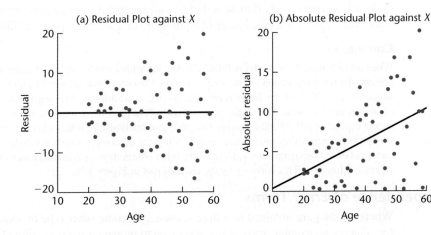

(a) Residual Plot against X

(b) Absolute Residual Plot against X

FIGURE 3.6
Residual Plot
with Outlier.

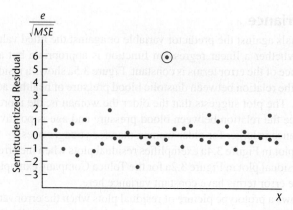

Presence of Outliers

Outliers are extreme observations. Residual outliers can be identified from *residual plots against X or $\hat{Y}$*, as well as from *box plots, stem-and-leaf plots,* and *dot plots* of the residuals. Plotting of semistudentized residuals is particularly helpful for distinguishing outlying observations, since it then becomes easy to identify residuals that lie many standard deviations from zero. A rough rule of thumb when the number of cases is large is to consider semistudentized residuals with absolute value of four or more to be outliers. We shall take up more refined procedures for identifying outliers in Chapter 10.

The residual plot in Figure 3.6 presents semistudentized residuals and contains one outlier, which is circled. Note that this residual represents an observation almost six standard deviations from the fitted value.

Outliers can create great difficulty. When we encounter one, our first suspicion is that the observation resulted from a mistake or other extraneous effect, and hence should be discarded. A major reason for discarding it is that under the least squares method, a fitted line may be pulled disproportionately toward an outlying observation because the sum of the *squared* deviations is minimized. This could cause a misleading fit if indeed the outlying observation resulted from a mistake or other extraneous cause. On the other hand, outliers may convey significant information, as when an outlier occurs because of an interaction with another predictor variable omitted from the model. A safe rule frequently suggested is to discard an outlier only if there is direct evidence that it represents an error in recording, a miscalculation, a malfunctioning of equipment, or a similar type of circumstance.

Comment

When a linear regression model is fitted to a data set with a small number of cases and an outlier is present, the fitted regression can be so distorted by the outlier that the residual plot may improperly suggest a lack of fit of the linear regression model, in addition to flagging the outlier. Figure 3.7 illustrates this situation. The scatter plot in Figure 3.7a presents a situation where all observations except the outlier fall around a straight-line statistical relationship. When a linear regression function is fitted to these data, the outlier causes such a shift in the fitted regression line as to lead to a systematic pattern of deviations from the fitted line for the other observations, suggesting a lack of fit of the linear regression function. This is shown by the residual plot in Figure 3.7b. ■

Nonindependence of Error Terms

Whenever data are obtained in a time sequence or some other type of sequence, such as for adjacent geographic areas, it is a good idea to prepare a *sequence plot of the residuals*.

FIGURE 3.7
Distorting
Effect on
Residuals
Caused by an
Outlier When
Remaining
Data Follow
Linear
Regression.

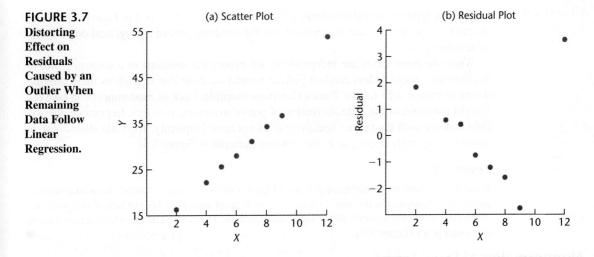

(a) Scatter Plot

(b) Residual Plot

FIGURE 3.8   Residual Time Sequence Plots Illustrating Nonindependence of Error Terms.

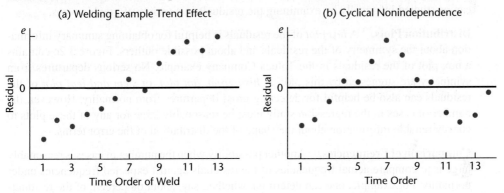

(a) Welding Example Trend Effect

(b) Cyclical Nonindependence

The purpose of plotting the residuals against time or in some other type of sequence is to see if there is any correlation between error terms that are near each other in the sequence. Figure 3.8a contains a time sequence plot of the residuals in an experiment to study the relation between the diameter of a weld (X) and the shear strength of the weld (Y). An evident correlation between the error terms stands out. Negative residuals are associated mainly with the early trials, and positive residuals with the later trials. Apparently, some effect connected with time was present, such as learning by the welder or a gradual change in the welding equipment, so the shear strength tended to be greater in the later welds because of this effect.

A prototype residual plot showing a time-related trend effect is presented in Figure 3.4d, which portrays a linear time-related trend effect, as in the welding example. It is sometimes useful to view the problem of nonindependence of the error terms as one in which an important variable (in this case, time) has been omitted from the model. We shall discuss this type of problem shortly.

Another type of nonindependence of the error terms is illustrated in Figure 3.8b. Here the adjacent error terms are also related, but the resulting pattern is a cyclical one with no trend effect present.

When the error terms are independent, we expect the residuals in a sequence plot to fluctuate in a more or less random pattern around the base line 0, such as the scattering shown in Figure 3.2b for the Toluca Company example. Lack of randomness can take the form of too much or too little alternation of points around the zero line. In practice, there is little concern with the former because it does not arise frequently. Too little alternation, in contrast, frequently occurs, as in the welding example in Figure 3.8a.

Comment

When the residuals are plotted against X, as in Figure 3.3b for the transit example, the scatter may not appear to be random. For this plot, however, the basic problem is probably not lack of independence of the error terms but a poorly fitting regression function. This, indeed, is the situation portrayed in the scatter plot in Figure 3.3a.   ∎

Nonnormality of Error Terms

As we noted earlier, small departures from normality do not create any serious problems. Major departures, on the other hand, should be of concern. The normality of the error terms can be studied informally by examining the residuals in a variety of graphic ways.

Distribution Plots.   A *box plot* of the residuals is helpful for obtaining summary information about the symmetry of the residuals and about possible outliers. Figure 3.2c contains a box plot of the residuals in the Toluca Company example. No serious departures from symmetry are suggested by this plot. A *histogram, dot plot,* or *stem-and-leaf plot* of the residuals can also be helpful for detecting gross departures from normality. However, the number of cases in the regression study must be reasonably large for any of these plots to convey reliable information about the shape of the distribution of the error terms.

Comparison of Frequencies.   Another possibility when the number of cases is reasonably large is to compare actual frequencies of the residuals against expected frequencies under normality. For example, one can determine whether, say, about 68 percent of the residuals e_i fall between $\pm\sqrt{MSE}$ or about 90 percent fall between $\pm 1.645\sqrt{MSE}$. When the sample size is moderately large, corresponding t values may be used for the comparison.

To illustrate this procedure, we again consider the Toluca Company example of Chapter 1. Table 3.2, column 1, repeats the residuals from Table 1.2. We see from Figure 2.2 that $\sqrt{MSE} = 48.82$. Using the t distribution, we expect under normality about 90 percent of the residuals to fall between $\pm t(.95; 23)\sqrt{MSE} = \pm 1.714(48.82)$, or between -83.68 and 83.68. Actually, 22 residuals, or 88 percent, fall within these limits. Similarly, under normality, we expect about 60 percent of the residuals to fall between -41.89 and 41.89. The actual percentage here is 52 percent. Thus, the actual frequencies here are reasonably consistent with those expected under normality.

Normal Probability Plot.   Still another possibility is to prepare a *normal probability plot of the residuals*. Here each residual is plotted against its expected value under normality. A plot that is nearly linear suggests agreement with normality, whereas a plot that departs substantially from linearity suggests that the error distribution is not normal.

Table 3.2, column 1, contains the residuals for the Toluca Company example. To find the expected values of the ordered residuals under normality, we utilize the facts that (1)

TABLE 3.2
Residuals and Expected Values under Normality— Toluca Company Example.

Run i	(1) Residual e_i	(2) Rank k	(3) Expected Value under Normality
1	51.02	22	51.95
2	−48.47	5	−44.10
3	−19.88	10	−14.76
...	...	...	...
23	38.83	19	31.05
24	−5.98	13	0
25	10.72	17	19.93

the expected value of the error terms for regression model (2.1) is zero and (2) the standard deviation of the error terms is estimated by $\sqrt{MSE}$. Statistical theory has shown that for a normal random variable with mean 0 and estimated standard deviation $\sqrt{MSE}$, a good approximation of the expected value of the kth smallest observation in a random sample of n is:

$$\sqrt{MSE}\left[z\left(\frac{k - .375}{n + .25}\right)\right] \tag{3.6}$$

where $z(A)$ as usual denotes the $(A)100$ percentile of the standard normal distribution.

Using this approximation, let us calculate the expected values of the residuals under normality for the Toluca Company example. Column 2 of Table 3.2 shows the ranks of the residuals, with the smallest residual being assigned rank 1. We see that the rank of the residual for run 1, $e_1 = 51.02$, is 22, which indicates that this residual is the 22nd smallest among the 25 residuals. Hence, for this residual $k = 22$. We found earlier (Table 2.1) that $MSE = 2,384$. Hence:

$$\frac{k - .375}{n + .25} = \frac{22 - .375}{25 + .25} = \frac{21.625}{25.25} = .8564$$

so that the expected value of this residual under normality is:

$$\sqrt{2,384}[z(.8564)] = \sqrt{2,384}(1.064) = 51.95$$

Similarly, the expected value of the residual for run 2, $e_2 = -48.47$, is obtained by noting that the rank of this residual is $k = 5$; in other words, this residual is the fifth smallest one among the 25 residuals. Hence, we require $(k - .375)/(n + .25) = (5 - .375)/(25 + .25) = .1832$, so that the expected value of this residual under normality is:

$$\sqrt{2,384}[z(.1832)] = \sqrt{2,384}(-.9032) = -44.10$$

Table 3.2, column 3, contains the expected values under the assumption of normality for a portion of the 25 residuals. Figure 3.2d presents a plot of the residuals against their expected values under normality. Note that the points in Figure 3.2d fall reasonably close to a straight line, suggesting that the distribution of the error terms does not depart substantially from a normal distribution.

Figure 3.9 shows three normal probability plots when the distribution of the error terms departs substantially from normality. Figure 3.9a shows a normal probability plot when the error term distribution is highly skewed to the right. Note the concave-upward shape

FIGURE 3.9   **Normal Probability Plots when Error Term Distribution Is Not Normal.**

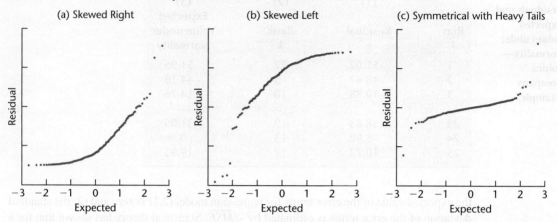

of the plot. Figure 3.9b shows a normal probability plot when the error term distribution is highly skewed to the left. Here, the pattern is concave downward. Finally, Figure 3.9c shows a normal probability plot when the distribution of the error terms is symmetrical but has heavy tails; in other words, the distribution has higher probabilities in the tails than a normal distribution. Note the concave-downward curvature in the plot at the left end, corresponding to the plot for a left-skewed distribution, and the concave-upward plot at the right end, corresponding to a right-skewed distribution.

Comments

1. Many computer packages will prepare normal probability plots, either automatically or at the option of the user. Some of these plots utilize semistudentized residuals, others omit the factor $\sqrt{MSE}$ in (3.6), but neither of these variations affect the nature of the plot.

2. For continuous data, ties among the residuals should occur only rarely. If two residuals do have the same value, a simple procedure is to use the average rank for the tied residuals for calculating the corresponding expected values.   ∎

Difficulties in Assessing Normality.   The analysis for model departures with respect to normality is, in many respects, more difficult than that for other types of departures. In the first place, random variation can be particularly mischievous when studying the nature of a probability distribution unless the sample size is quite large. Even worse, other types of departures can and do affect the distribution of the residuals. For instance, residuals may appear to be not normally distributed because an inappropriate regression function is used or because the error variance is not constant. Hence, it is usually a good strategy to investigate these other types of departures first, before concerning oneself with the normality of the error terms.

Omission of Important Predictor Variables

Residuals should also be plotted against variables omitted from the model that might have important effects on the response. The time variable cited earlier in the welding example is

FIGURE 3.10
Residual Plots
for Possible
Omission of
Important
Predictor
Variable—
Productivity
Example.

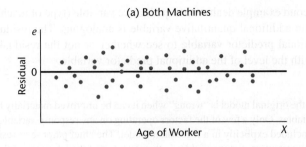

(a) Both Machines

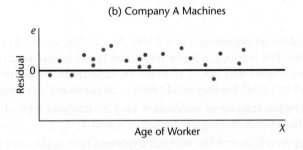

(b) Company A Machines

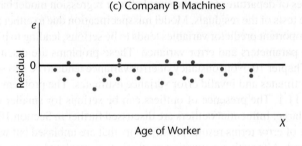

(c) Company B Machines

an illustration. The purpose of this additional analysis is to determine whether there are any other key variables that could provide important additional descriptive and predictive power to the model.

As another example, in a study to predict output by piece-rate workers in an assembling operation, the relation between output (Y) and age (X) of worker was studied for a sample of employees. The plot of the residuals against X, shown in Figure 3.10a, indicates no ground for suspecting the appropriateness of the linearity of the regression function or the constancy of the error variance. Since machines produced by two companies (A and B) are used in the assembling operation and could have an effect on output, residual plots against X by type of machine were undertaken and are shown in Figures 3.10b and 3.10c. Note that the residuals for Company A machines tend to be positive, while those for Company B machines tend to be negative. Thus, type of machine appears to have a definite effect on productivity, and output predictions may turn out to be far superior when this variable is added to the model.

While this second example dealt with a qualitative variable (type of machine), the residual analysis for an additional quantitative variable is analogous. The residuals are plotted against the additional predictor variable to see whether or not the residuals tend to vary systematically with the level of the additional predictor variable.

Comment

We do not say that the original model is "wrong" when it can be improved materially by adding one or more predictor variables. Only a few of the factors operating on any response variable Y in real-world situations can be included explicitly in a regression model. The chief purpose of residual analysis in identifying other important predictor variables is therefore to test the adequacy of the model and see whether it could be improved materially by adding one or more predictor variables. ∎

Some Final Comments

1. We discussed model departures one at a time. In actuality, several types of departures may occur together. For instance, a linear regression function may be a poor fit and the variance of the error terms may not be constant. In these cases, the prototype patterns of Figure 3.4 can still be useful, but they would need to be combined into composite patterns.

2. Although graphic analysis of residuals is only an informal method of analysis, in many cases it suffices for examining the aptness of a model.

3. The basic approach to residual analysis explained here applies not only to simple linear regression but also to more complex regression and other types of statistical models.

4. Several types of departures from the simple linear regression model have been identified by diagnostic tests of the residuals. Model misspecification due to either nonlinearity or the omission of important predictor variables tends to be serious, leading to biased estimates of the regression parameters and error variance. These problems are discussed further in Section 3.9 and Chapter 10. Nonconstancy of error variance tends to be less serious, leading to less efficient estimates and invalid error variance estimates. The problem is discussed in depth in Section 11.1. The presence of outliers can be serious for smaller data sets when their influence is large. Influential outliers are discussed further in Section 10.4. Finally, the nonindependence of error terms results in estimators that are unbiased but whose variances are seriously biased. Alternative estimation methods for correlated errors are discussed in Chapter 12.

3.4 Overview of Tests Involving Residuals

Graphic analysis of residuals is inherently subjective. Nevertheless, subjective analysis of a variety of interrelated residual plots will frequently reveal difficulties with the model more clearly than particular formal tests. There are occasions, however, when one wishes to put specific questions to a test. We now briefly review some of the relevant tests.

Most statistical tests require independent observations. As we have seen, however, the residuals are dependent. Fortunately, the dependencies become quite small for large samples, so that one can usually then ignore them.

Tests for Randomness

A runs test is frequently used to test for lack of randomness in the residuals arranged in time order. Another test, specifically designed for lack of randomness in least squares residuals, is the Durbin-Watson test. This test is discussed in Chapter 12.

Tests for Constancy of Variance

When a residual plot gives the impression that the variance may be increasing or decreasing in a systematic manner related to X or $E\{Y\}$, a simple test is based on the rank correlation between the absolute values of the residuals and the corresponding values of the predictor variable. Two other simple tests for constancy of the error variance—the Brown-Forsythe test and the Breusch-Pagan test—are discussed in Section 3.6.

Tests for Outliers

A simple test for identifying an outlier observation involves fitting a new regression line to the other $n - 1$ observations. The suspect observation, which was not used in fitting the new line, can now be regarded as a new observation. One can calculate the probability that in n observations, a deviation from the fitted line as great as that of the outlier will be obtained by chance. If this probability is sufficiently small, the outlier can be rejected as not having come from the same population as the other $n - 1$ observations. Otherwise, the outlier is retained. We discuss this approach in detail in Chapter 10.

Many other tests to aid in evaluating outliers have been developed. These are discussed in specialized references, such as Reference 3.1.

Tests for Normality

Goodness of fit tests can be used for examining the normality of the error terms. For instance, the chi-square test or the Kolmogorov-Smirnov test and its modification, the Lilliefors test, can be employed for testing the normality of the error terms by analyzing the residuals. A simple test based on the normal probability plot of the residuals will be taken up in Section 3.5.

Comment

The runs test, rank correlation, and goodness of fit tests are commonly used statistical procedures and are discussed in many basic statistics texts. ∎

3.5 Correlation Test for Normality

In addition to visually assessing the approximate linearity of the points plotted in a normal probability plot, a formal test for normality of the error terms can be conducted by calculating the coefficient of correlation (2.74) between the residuals e_i and their expected values under normality. A high value of the correlation coefficient is indicative of normality. Table B.6, prepared by Looney and Gulledge (Ref. 3.2), contains critical values (percentiles) for various sample sizes for the distribution of the coefficient of correlation between the ordered residuals and their expected values under normality when the error terms are normally distributed. If the observed coefficient of correlation is at least as large as the tabled value, for a given α level, one can conclude that the error terms are reasonably normally distributed.

Example

For the Toluca Company example in Table 3.2, the coefficient of correlation between the ordered residuals and their expected values under normality is .991. Controlling the α risk at .05, we find from Table B.6 that the critical value for $n = 25$ is .959. Since the observed coefficient exceeds this level, we have support for our earlier conclusion that the distribution of the error terms does not depart substantially from a normal distribution.

Comment

The correlation test for normality presented here is simpler than the Shapiro-Wilk test (Ref. 3.3), which can be viewed as being based approximately also on the coefficient of correlation between the ordered residuals and their expected values under normality. ∎

3.6 Tests for Constancy of Error Variance

We present two formal tests for ascertaining whether the error terms have constant variance: the Brown-Forsythe test and the Breusch-Pagan test.

Brown-Forsythe Test

The Brown-Forsythe test, a modification of the Levene test (Ref. 3.4), does not depend on normality of the error terms. Indeed, this test is robust against serious departures from normality, in the sense that the nominal significance level remains approximately correct when the error terms have equal variances even if the distribution of the error terms is far from normal. Yet the test is still relatively efficient when the error terms are normally distributed. The Brown-Forsythe test as described is applicable to simple linear regression when the variance of the error terms either increases or decreases with X, as illustrated in the prototype megaphone plot in Figure 3.4c. The sample size needs to be large enough so that the dependencies among the residuals can be ignored.

The test is based on the variability of the residuals. The larger the error variance, the larger the variability of the residuals will tend to be. To conduct the Brown-Forsythe test, we divide the data set into two groups, according to the level of X, so that one group consists of cases where the X level is comparatively low and the other group consists of cases where the X level is comparatively high. If the error variance is either increasing or decreasing with X, the residuals in one group will tend to be more variable than those in the other group. Equivalently, the absolute deviations of the residuals around their group mean will tend to be larger for one group than for the other group. In order to make the test more robust, we utilize the absolute deviations of the residuals around the median for the group (Ref. 3.5). The Brown-Forsythe test then consists simply of the two-sample t test based on test statistic (A.67) to determine whether the mean of the absolute deviations for one group differs significantly from the mean absolute deviation for the second group.

Although the distribution of the absolute deviations of the residuals is usually not normal, it has been shown that the t^* test statistic still follows approximately the t distribution when the variance of the error terms is constant and the sample sizes of the two groups are not extremely small.

We shall now use e_{i1} to denote the ith residual for group 1 and e_{i2} to denote the ith residual for group 2. Also we shall use n_1 and n_2 to denote the sample sizes of the two groups, where:

$$n = n_1 + n_2 \tag{3.7}$$

Further, we shall use $\tilde{e}_1$ and $\tilde{e}_2$ to denote the medians of the residuals in the two groups. The Brown-Forsythe test uses the absolute deviations of the residuals around their group median, to be denoted by d_{i1} and d_{i2}:

$$d_{i1} = |e_{i1} - \tilde{e}_1| \qquad d_{i2} = |e_{i2} - \tilde{e}_2| \tag{3.8}$$

With this notation, the two-sample t test statistic (A.67) becomes:

$$t^*_{BF} = \frac{\bar{d}_1 - \bar{d}_2}{s\sqrt{\frac{1}{n_1} + \frac{1}{n_2}}} \tag{3.9}$$

where $\bar{d}_1$ and $\bar{d}_2$ are the sample means of the d_{i1} and d_{i2}, respectively, and the pooled variance s^2 in (A.63) becomes:

$$s^2 = \frac{\sum(d_{i1} - \bar{d}_1)^2 + \sum(d_{i2} - \bar{d}_2)^2}{n - 2} \tag{3.9a}$$

We denote the test statistic for the Brown-Forsythe test by t^*_{BF}.

If the error terms have constant variance and n_1 and n_2 are not extremely small, t^*_{BF} follows approximately the t distribution with $n - 2$ degrees of freedom. Large absolute values of t^*_{BF} indicate that the error terms do not have constant variance.

Example

We wish to use the Brown-Forsythe test for the Toluca Company example to determine whether or not the error term variance varies with the level of X. Since the X levels are spread fairly uniformly (see Figure 3.1a), we divide the 25 cases into two groups with approximately equal X ranges. The first group consists of the 13 runs with lot sizes from 20 to 70. The second group consists of the 12 runs with lot sizes from 80 to 120. Table 3.3

TABLE 3.3
Calculations for Brown-Forsythe Test for Constancy of Error Variance— Toluca Company Example.

			Group 1		
		(1)	(2)	(3)	(4)
		Lot	Residual		
i	Run	Size	e_{i1}	d_{i1}	$(d_{i1} - \bar{d}_1)^2$
1	14	20	−20.77	.89	1,929.41
2	2	30	−48.47	28.59	263.25
...	...	...	...	...	...
12	12	70	−60.28	40.40	19.49
13	25	70	10.72	30.60	202.07
	Total			582.60	12,566.6

$$\tilde{e}_1 = -19.88 \qquad \bar{d}_1 = 44.815$$

			Group 2		
		(1)	(2)	(3)	(4)
		Lot	Residual		
i	Run	Size	e_{i2}	d_{i2}	$(d_{i2} - \bar{d}_2)^2$
1	1	80	51.02	53.70	637.56
2	8	80	4.02	6.70	473.06
...	...	...	...	...	...
11	20	110	−34.09	31.41	8.76
12	7	120	55.21	57.89	866.71
	Total			341.40	9,610.2

$$\tilde{e}_2 = -2.68 \qquad \bar{d}_2 = 28.450$$

presents a portion of the data for each group. In columns 1 and 2 are repeated the lot sizes and residuals from Table 1.2. We see from Table 3.3 that the median residual is $\tilde{e}_1 = -19.88$ for group 1 and $\tilde{e}_2 = -2.68$ for group 2. Column 3 contains the absolute deviations of the residuals around their respective group medians. For instance, we obtain:

$$d_{11} = |e_{11} - \tilde{e}_1| = |-20.77 - (-19.88)| = .89$$
$$d_{12} = |e_{12} - \tilde{e}_2| = |51.02 - (-2.68)| = 53.70$$

The means of the absolute deviations are obtained in the usual fashion:

$$\bar{d}_1 = \frac{582.60}{13} = 44.815 \qquad \bar{d}_2 = \frac{341.40}{12} = 28.450$$

Finally, column 4 contains the squares of the deviations of the d_{i1} and d_{i2} around their respective group means. For instance, we have:

$$(d_{11} - \bar{d}_1)^2 = (.89 - 44.815)^2 = 1,929.41$$
$$(d_{12} - \bar{d}_2)^2 = (53.70 - 28.450)^2 = 637.56$$

We are now ready to calculate test statistic (3.9):

$$s^2 = \frac{12,566.6 + 9,610.2}{25 - 2} = 964.21$$

$$s = 31.05$$

$$t^*_{BF} = \frac{44.815 - 28.450}{31.05\sqrt{\frac{1}{13} + \frac{1}{12}}} = 1.32$$

To control the α risk at .05, we require $t(.975; 23) = 2.069$. The decision rule therefore is:

If $|t^*_{BF}| \leq 2.069$, conclude the error variance is constant

If $|t^*_{BF}| > 2.069$, conclude the error variance is not constant

Since $|t^*_{BF}| = 1.32 \leq 2.069$, we conclude that the error variance is constant and does not vary with the level of X. The two-sided P-value of this test is .20.

Comments

1. If the data set contains many cases, the two-sample t test for constancy of error variance can be conducted after dividing the cases into three or four groups, according to the level of X, and using the two extreme groups.

2. A robust test for constancy of the error variance is desirable because nonnormality and lack of constant variance often go hand in hand. For example, the distribution of the error terms may become increasingly skewed and hence more variable with increasing levels of X. ∎

Breusch-Pagan Test

A second test for the constancy of the error variance is the Breusch-Pagan test (Ref. 3.6). This test, a large-sample test, assumes that the error terms are independent and normally distributed and that the variance of the error term ε_i, denoted by σ_i^2, is related to the level of X in the following way:

$$\log_e \sigma_i^2 = \gamma_0 + \gamma_1 X_i \tag{3.10}$$

Note that (3.10) implies that σ_i^2 either increases or decreases with the level of X, depending on the sign of γ_1. Constancy of error variance corresponds to $\gamma_1 = 0$. The test of H_0: $\gamma_1 = 0$ versus H_a: $\gamma_1 \neq 0$ is carried out by means of regressing the squared residuals e_i^2 against X_i in the usual manner and obtaining the regression sum of squares, to be denoted by SSR^*. The test statistic X_{BP}^2 is as follows:

$$X_{BP}^2 = \frac{SSR^*}{2} \div \left(\frac{SSE}{n} \right)^2 \tag{3.11}$$

where SSR^* is the regression sum of squares when regressing e^2 on X and SSE is the error sum of squares when regressing Y on X. If H_0: $\gamma_1 = 0$ holds and n is reasonably large, X_{BP}^2 follows approximately the chi-square distribution with one degree of freedom. Large values of X_{BP}^2 lead to conclusion H_a, that the error variance is not constant.

Example

To conduct the Breusch-Pagan test for the Toluca Company example, we regress the squared residuals in Table 1.2, column 5, against X and obtain $SSR^* = 7{,}896{,}128$. We know from Figure 2.2 that $SSE = 54{,}825$. Hence, test statistic (3.11) is:

$$X_{BP}^2 = \frac{7{,}896{,}128}{2} \div \left(\frac{54{,}825}{25} \right)^2 = .821$$

To control the α risk at .05, we require $\chi^2(.95; 1) = 3.84$. Since $X_{BP}^2 = .821 \leq 3.84$, we conclude H_0, that the error variance is constant. The P-value of this test is .64 so that the data are quite consistent with constancy of the error variance.

Comments

1. The Breusch-Pagan test can be modified to allow for different relationships between the error variance and the level of X than the one in (3.10).
2. Test statistic (3.11) was developed independently by Cook and Weisberg (Ref. 3.7), and the test is sometimes referred to as the Cook-Weisberg test. ∎

3.7 *F* Test for Lack of Fit

We next take up a formal test for determining whether a specific type of regression function adequately fits the data. We illustrate this test for ascertaining whether a linear regression function is a good fit for the data.

Assumptions

The lack of fit test assumes that the observations Y for given X are (1) independent and (2) normally distributed, and that (3) the distributions of Y have the same variance σ^2.

The lack of fit test requires repeat observations at one or more X levels. In nonexperimental data, these may occur fortuitously, as when in a productivity study relating workers' output and age, several workers of the same age happen to be included in the study. In an experiment, one can assure by design that there are repeat observations. For instance, in an experiment on the effect of size of salesperson bonus on sales, three salespersons can be offered a particular size of bonus, for each of six bonus sizes, and their sales then observed.

Repeat trials for the same level of the predictor variable, of the type described, are called *replications*. The resulting observations are called *replicates*.

Example

In an experiment involving 12 similar but scattered suburban branch offices of a commercial bank, holders of checking accounts at the offices were offered gifts for setting up money market accounts. Minimum initial deposits in the new money market account were specified to qualify for the gift. The value of the gift was directly proportional to the specified minimum deposit. Various levels of minimum deposit and related gift values were used in the experiment in order to ascertain the relation between the specified minimum deposit and gift value, on the one hand, and number of accounts opened at the office, on the other. Altogether, six levels of minimum deposit and proportional gift value were used, with two of the branch offices assigned at random to each level. One branch office had a fire during the period and was dropped from the study. Table 3.4a contains the results, where X is the amount of minimum deposit and Y is the number of new money market accounts that were opened and qualified for the gift during the test period.

A linear regression function was fitted in the usual fashion; it is:

$$\hat{Y} = 50.72251 + .48670X$$

The analysis of variance table also was obtained and is shown in Table 3.4b. A scatter plot, together with the fitted regression line, is shown in Figure 3.11. The indications are strong that a linear regression function is inappropriate. To test this formally, we shall use the general linear test approach described in Section 2.8.

TABLE 3.4
Data and Analysis of Variance Table—Bank Example.

		(a) Data				
Branch i	Size of Minimum Deposit (dollars) X_i	Number of New Accounts Y_i		Branch i	Size of Minimum Deposit (dollars) X_i	Number of New Accounts Y_i
1	125	160		7	75	42
2	100	112		8	175	124
3	200	124		9	125	150
4	75	28		10	200	104
5	150	152		11	100	136
6	175	156				

(b) ANOVA Table			
Source of Variation	SS	df	MS
Regression	5,141.3	1	5,141.3
Error	14,741.6	9	1,638.0
Total	19,882.9	10	

FIGURE 3.11
Scatter Plot
and Fitted
Regression
Line—Bank
Example.

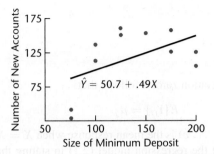

TABLE 3.5
Data Arranged
by Replicate
Number and
Minimum
Deposit—Bank
Example.

	Size of Minimum Deposit (dollars)					
	$j = 1$	$j = 2$	$j = 3$	$j = 4$	$j = 5$	$j = 6$
Replicate	$X_1 = 75$	$X_2 = 100$	$X_3 = 125$	$X_4 = 150$	$X_5 = 175$	$X_6 = 200$
$i = 1$	28	112	160	152	156	124
$i = 2$	42	136	150		124	104
Mean $\bar{Y}_j$	35	124	155	152	140	114

Notation

First, we need to modify our notation to recognize the existence of replications at some levels of X. Table 3.5 presents the same data as Table 3.4a, but in an arrangement that recognizes the replicates. We shall denote the different X levels in the study, whether or not replicated observations are present, as $X_1, \ldots, X_c$. For the bank example, $c = 6$ since there are six minimum deposit size levels in the study, for five of which there are two observations and for one there is a single observation. We shall let $X_1 = 75$ (the smallest minimum deposit level), $X_2 = 100, \ldots, X_6 = 200$. Further, we shall denote the number of replicates for the jth level of X as n_j; for our example, $n_1 = n_2 = n_3 = n_5 = n_6 = 2$ and $n_4 = 1$. Thus, the total number of observations n is given by:

$$n = \sum_{j=1}^{c} n_j \tag{3.12}$$

We shall denote the observed value of the response variable for the ith replicate for the jth level of X by Y_{ij}, where $i = 1, \ldots, n_j$, $j = 1, \ldots, c$. For the bank example (Table 3.5), $Y_{11} = 28$, $Y_{21} = 42$, $Y_{12} = 112$, and so on. Finally, we shall denote the mean of the Y observations at the level $X = X_j$ by $\bar{Y}_j$. Thus, $\bar{Y}_1 = (28 + 42)/2 = 35$ and $\bar{Y}_4 = 152/1 = 152$.

Full Model

The general linear test approach begins with the specification of the full model. The full model used for the lack of fit test makes the same assumptions as the simple linear regression model (2.1) except for assuming a linear regression relation, the subject of the test. This full model is:

$$Y_{ij} = \mu_j + \varepsilon_{ij} \qquad \text{Full model} \tag{3.13}$$

where:

μ_j are parameters $j = 1, \ldots, c$

ε_{ij} are independent $N(0, \sigma^2)$

Since the error terms have expectation zero, it follows that:

$$E\{Y_{ij}\} = \mu_j \qquad \text{(3.14)}$$

Thus, the parameter μ_j $(j = 1, \ldots, c)$ is the mean response when $X = X_j$.

The full model (3.13) is like the regression model (2.1) in stating that each response Y is made up of two components: the mean response when $X = X_j$ and a random error term. The difference between the two models is that in the full model (3.13) there are no restrictions on the means μ_j, whereas in the regression model (2.1) the mean responses are linearly related to X (i.e., $E\{Y\} = \beta_0 + \beta_1 X$).

To fit the full model to the data, we require the least squares or maximum likelihood estimators for the parameters μ_j. It can be shown that these estimators of μ_j are simply the sample means $\bar{Y}_j$:

$$\hat{\mu}_j = \bar{Y}_j \qquad \text{(3.15)}$$

Thus, the estimated expected value for observation Y_{ij} is $\bar{Y}_j$, and the error sum of squares for the full model therefore is:

$$SSE(F) = \sum_j \sum_i (Y_{ij} - \bar{Y}_j)^2 = SSPE \qquad \text{(3.16)}$$

In the context of the test for lack of fit, the full model error sum of squares (3.16) is called the *pure error sum of squares* and is denoted by *SSPE*.

Note that *SSPE* is made up of the sums of squared deviations at each X level. At level $X = X_j$, this sum of squared deviations is:

$$\sum_i (Y_{ij} - \bar{Y}_j)^2 \qquad \text{(3.17)}$$

These sums of squares are then added over all of the X levels $(j = 1, \ldots, c)$. For the bank example, we have:

$$\begin{aligned} SSPE = &(28 - 35)^2 + (42 - 35)^2 + (112 - 124)^2 + (136 - 124)^2 + (160 - 155)^2 \\ &+ (150 - 155)^2 + (152 - 152)^2 + (156 - 140)^2 + (124 - 140)^2 \\ &+ (124 - 114)^2 + (104 - 114)^2 \\ = &\, 1{,}148 \end{aligned}$$

Note that any X level with no replications makes no contribution to *SSPE* because $\bar{Y}_j = Y_{1j}$ then. Thus, $(152 - 152)^2 = 0$ for $j = 4$ in the bank example.

The degrees of freedom associated with *SSPE* can be obtained by recognizing that the sum of squared deviations (3.17) at a given level of X is like an ordinary total sum of squares based on n observations, which has $n - 1$ degrees of freedom associated with it. Here, there are n_j observations when $X = X_j$; hence the degrees of freedom are $n_j - 1$. Just as *SSPE* is the sum of the sums of squares (3.17), so the number of degrees of freedom associated with *SSPE* is the sum of the component degrees of freedom:

$$df_F = \sum_j (n_j - 1) = \sum_j n_j - c = n - c \tag{3.18}$$

For the bank example, we have $df_F = 11 - 6 = 5$. Note that any X level with no replications makes no contribution to df_F because $n_j - 1 = 1 - 1 = 0$ then, just as such an X level makes no contribution to *SSPE*.

Reduced Model

The general linear test approach next requires consideration of the reduced model under H_0. For testing the appropriateness of a linear regression relation, the alternatives are:

$$H_0: E\{Y\} = \beta_0 + \beta_1 X$$
$$H_a: E\{Y\} \neq \beta_0 + \beta_1 X \tag{3.19}$$

Thus, H_0 postulates that μ_j in the full model (3.13) is linearly related to X_j:

$$\mu_j = \beta_0 + \beta_1 X_j$$

The reduced model under H_0 therefore is:

$$Y_{ij} = \beta_0 + \beta_1 X_j + \varepsilon_{ij} \qquad \text{Reduced model} \tag{3.20}$$

Note that the reduced model is the ordinary simple linear regression model (2.1), with the subscripts modified to recognize the existence of replications. We know that the estimated expected value for observation Y_{ij} with regression model (2.1) is the fitted value $\hat{Y}_{ij}$:

$$\hat{Y}_{ij} = b_0 + b_1 X_j \tag{3.21}$$

Hence, the error sum of squares for the reduced model is the usual error sum of squares *SSE*:

$$SSE(R) = \sum \sum [Y_{ij} - (b_0 + b_1 X_j)]^2$$
$$= \sum \sum (Y_{ij} - \hat{Y}_{ij})^2 = SSE \tag{3.22}$$

We also know that the degrees of freedom associated with $SSE(R)$ are:

$$df_R = n - 2$$

For the bank example, we have from Table 3.4b:

$$SSE(R) = SSE = 14{,}741.6$$
$$df_R = 9$$

Test Statistic

The general linear test statistic (2.70):

$$F^* = \frac{SSE(R) - SSE(F)}{df_R - df_F} \div \frac{SSE(F)}{df_F}$$

here becomes:

$$F^* = \frac{SSE - SSPE}{(n-2) - (n-c)} \div \frac{SSPE}{n-c} \tag{3.23}$$

The difference between the two error sums of squares is called the *lack of fit sum of squares* here and is denoted by *SSLF*:

$$SSLF = SSE - SSPE \tag{3.24}$$

We can then express the test statistic as follows:

$$F^* = \frac{SSLF}{c - 2} \div \frac{SSPE}{n - c}$$

$$= \frac{MSLF}{MSPE} \tag{3.25}$$

where *MSLF* denotes the *lack of fit mean square* and *MSPE* denotes the *pure error mean square*.

We know that large values of F^* lead to conclusion H_a in the general linear test. Decision rule (2.71) here becomes:

$$\begin{array}{c} \text{If } F^* \leq F(1 - \alpha; c - 2, n - c), \text{ conclude } H_0 \\ \text{If } F^* > F(1 - \alpha; c - 2, n - c), \text{ conclude } H_a \end{array} \tag{3.26}$$

For the bank example, the test statistic can be constructed easily from our earlier results:

$$SSPE = 1,148.0 \qquad\qquad\qquad n - c = 11 - 6 = 5$$

$$SSE = 14,741.6$$

$$SSLF = 14,741.6 - 1,148.0 = 13,593.6 \qquad c - 2 = 6 - 2 = 4$$

$$F^* = \frac{13,593.6}{4} \div \frac{1,148.0}{5}$$

$$= \frac{3,398.4}{229.6} = 14.80$$

If the level of significance is to be $\alpha = .01$, we require $F(.99; 4, 5) = 11.4$. Since $F^* = 14.80 > 11.4$, we conclude H_a, that the regression function is not linear. This, of course, accords with our visual impression from Figure 3.11. The *P*-value for the test is .006.

ANOVA Table

The definition of the lack of fit sum of squares *SSLF* in (3.24) indicates that we have, in fact, decomposed the error sum of squares *SSE* into two components:

$$SSE = SSPE + SSLF \tag{3.27}$$

This decomposition follows from the identity:

$$\underbrace{Y_{ij} - \hat{Y}_{ij}}_{\substack{\text{Error} \\ \text{deviation}}} = \underbrace{Y_{ij} - \bar{Y}_j}_{\substack{\text{Pure error} \\ \text{deviation}}} + \underbrace{\bar{Y}_j - \hat{Y}_{ij}}_{\substack{\text{Lack of fit} \\ \text{deviation}}} \tag{3.28}$$

This identity shows that the error deviations in *SSE* are made up of a pure error component and a lack of fit component. Figure 3.12 illustrates this partitioning for the case $Y_{13} = 160$, $X_3 = 125$ in the bank example.

FIGURE 3.12
Illustration of
Decomposition
of Error
Deviation
$Y_{ij} - \hat{Y}_{ij}$—
Bank
Example.

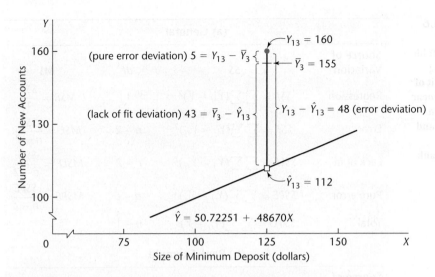

When (3.28) is squared and summed over all observations, we obtain (3.27) since the cross-product sum equals zero:

$$\sum\sum(Y_{ij} - \hat{Y}_{ij})^2 = \sum\sum(Y_{ij} - \bar{Y}_j)^2 + \sum\sum(\bar{Y}_j - \hat{Y}_{ij})^2 \tag{3.29}$$
$$SSE=SSPE+SSLF$$

Note from (3.29) that we can define the lack of fit sum of squares directly as follows:

$$SSLF = \sum\sum(\bar{Y}_j - \hat{Y}_{ij})^2 \tag{3.30}$$

Since all Y_{ij} observations at the level X_j have the same fitted value, which we can denote by $\hat{Y}_j$, we can express (3.30) equivalently as:

$$SSLF = \sum_j n_j(\bar{Y}_j - \hat{Y}_j)^2 \tag{3.30a}$$

Formula (3.30a) indicates clearly why *SSLF* measures lack of fit. If the linear regression function is appropriate, then the means $\bar{Y}_j$ will be near the fitted values $\hat{Y}_j$ calculated from the estimated linear regression function and *SSLF* will be small. On the other hand, if the linear regression function is not appropriate, the means $\bar{Y}_j$ will not be near the fitted values calculated from the estimated linear regression function, as in Figure 3.11 for the bank example, and *SSLF* will be large.

Formula (3.30a) also indicates why $c - 2$ degrees of freedom are associated with *SSLF*. There are c means $\bar{Y}_j$ in the sum of squares, and two degrees of freedom are lost in estimating the parameters β_0 and β_1 of the linear regression function to obtain the fitted values $\hat{Y}_j$.

An ANOVA table can be constructed for the decomposition of *SSE*. Table 3.6a contains the general ANOVA table, including the decomposition of *SSE* just explained and the mean squares of interest, and Table 3.6b contains the ANOVA decomposition for the bank example.

TABLE 3.6
General ANOVA Table for Testing Lack of Fit of Simple Linear Regression Function and ANOVA Table—Bank Example.

(a) General			
Source of Variation	SS	df	MS
Regression	$SSR = \sum\sum(\hat{Y}_{ij} - \bar{Y})^2$	1	$MSR = \dfrac{SSR}{1}$
Error	$SSE = \sum\sum(Y_{ij} - \hat{Y}_{ij})^2$	$n - 2$	$MSE = \dfrac{SSE}{n-2}$
Lack of fit	$SSLF = \sum\sum(\bar{Y}_j - \hat{Y}_{ij})^2$	$c - 2$	$MSLF = \dfrac{SSLF}{c-2}$
Pure error	$SSPE = \sum\sum(Y_{ij} - \bar{Y}_j)^2$	$n - c$	$MSPE = \dfrac{SSPE}{n-c}$
Total	$SSTO = \sum\sum(Y_{ij} - \bar{Y})^2$	$n - 1$	

(b) Bank Example			
Source of Variation	SS	df	MS
Regression	5,141.3	1	5,141.3
Error	14,741.6	9	1,638.0
Lack of fit	13,593.6	4	3,398.4
Pure error	1,148.0	5	229.6
Total	19,882.9	10	

Comments

1. As shown by the bank example, not all levels of X need have repeat observations for the F test for lack of fit to be applicable. Repeat observations at only one or some levels of X are sufficient.

2. It can be shown that the mean squares $MSPE$ and $MSLF$ have the following expectations when testing whether the regression function is linear:

$$E\{MSPE\} = \sigma^2 \tag{3.31}$$

$$E\{MSLF\} = \sigma^2 + \frac{\sum n_j[\mu_j - (\beta_0 + \beta_1 X_j)]^2}{c-2} \tag{3.32}$$

The reason for the term "pure error" is that $MSPE$ is always an unbiased estimator of the error term variance σ^2, no matter what is the true regression function. The expected value of $MSLF$ also is σ^2 if the regression function is linear, because $\mu_j = \beta_0 + \beta_1 X_j$ then and the second term in (3.32) becomes zero. On the other hand, if the regression function is not linear, $\mu_j \neq \beta_0 + \beta_1 X_j$ and $E\{MSLF\}$ will be greater than σ^2. Hence, a value of F^* near 1 accords with a linear regression function; large values of F^* indicate that the regression function is not linear.

3. The terminology "error sum of squares" and "error mean square" is not precise when the regression function under test in H_0 is not the true function since the error sum of squares and error mean square then reflect the effects of both the lack of fit and the variability of the error terms. We continue to use the terminology for consistency and now use the term "pure error" to identify the variability associated with the error term only.

4. Suppose that prior to any analysis of the appropriateness of the model, we had fitted a linear regression model and wished to test whether or not $\beta_1 = 0$ for the bank example (Table 3.4b). Test statistic (2.60) would be:

$$F^* = \frac{MSR}{MSE} = \frac{5,141.3}{1,638.0} = 3.14$$

For $\alpha = .10$, $F(.90; 1, 9) = 3.36$, and we would conclude H_0, that $\beta_1 = 0$ or that there is no *linear association* between minimum deposit size (and value of gift) and number of new accounts. A conclusion that there is no *relation* between these variables would be improper, however. Such an inference requires that regression model (2.1) be appropriate. Here, there is a definite relationship, but the regression function is not linear. This illustrates the importance of always examining the appropriateness of a model before any inferences are drawn.

5. The general linear test approach just explained can be used to test the appropriateness of other regression functions. Only the degrees of freedom for *SSLF* will need be modified. In general, $c - p$ degrees of freedom are associated with *SSLF*, where p is the number of parameters in the regression function. For the test of a simple linear regression function, $p = 2$ because there are two parameters, β_0 and β_1, in the regression function.

6. The alternative H_a in (3.19) includes all regression functions other than a linear one. For instance, it includes a quadratic regression function or a logarithmic one. If H_a is concluded, a study of residuals can be helpful in identifying an appropriate function.

7. When we conclude that the employed model in H_0 is appropriate, the usual practice is to use the error mean square *MSE* as an estimator of σ^2 in preference to the pure error mean square *MSPE*, since the former contains more degrees of freedom.

8. Observations at the same level of X are genuine repeats only if they involve independent trials with respect to the error term. Suppose that in a regression analysis of the relation between hardness (Y) and amount of carbon (X) in specimens of an alloy, the error term in the model covers, among other things, random errors in the measurement of hardness by the analyst and effects of uncontrolled production factors, which vary at random from specimen to specimen and affect hardness. If the analyst takes two readings on the hardness of a specimen, this will not provide a genuine replication because the effects of random variation in the production factors are fixed in any given specimen. For genuine replications, different specimens with the same carbon content (X) would have to be measured by the analyst so that *all* the effects covered in the error term could vary at random from one repeated observation to the next.

9. When no replications are present in a data set, an approximate test for lack of fit can be conducted if there are some cases at adjacent X levels for which the mean responses are quite close to each other. Such adjacent cases are grouped together and treated as pseudoreplicates, and the test for lack of fit is then carried out using these groupings of adjacent cases. A useful summary of this and related procedures for conducting a test for lack of fit when no replicates are present may be found in Reference 3.8. ■

3.8 Overview of Remedial Measures

If the simple linear regression model (2.1) is not appropriate for a data set, there are two basic choices:

1. Abandon regression model (2.1) and develop and use a more appropriate model.
2. Employ some transformation on the data so that regression model (2.1) is appropriate for the transformed data.

Each approach has advantages and disadvantages. The first approach may entail a more complex model that could yield better insights, but may also lead to more complex procedures for estimating the parameters. Successful use of transformations, on the other hand, leads to relatively simple methods of estimation and may involve fewer parameters than a complex model, an advantage when the sample size is small. Yet transformations may obscure the fundamental interconnections between the variables, though at other times they may illuminate them.

We consider the use of transformations in this chapter and the use of more complex models in later chapters. First, we provide a brief overview of remedial measures.

Nonlinearity of Regression Function

When the regression function is not linear, a direct approach is to modify regression model (2.1) by altering the nature of the regression function. For instance, a quadratic regression function might be used:

$$E\{Y\} = \beta_0 + \beta_1 X + \beta_2 X^2$$

or an exponential regression function:

$$E\{Y\} = \beta_0 \beta_1^X$$

In Chapter 7, we discuss polynomial regression functions, and in Part III we take up nonlinear regression functions, such as an exponential regression function.

The transformation approach employs a transformation to linearize, at least approximately, a nonlinear regression function. We discuss the use of transformations to linearize regression functions in Section 3.9.

When the nature of the regression function is not known, exploratory analysis that does not require specifying a particular type of function is often useful. We discuss exploratory regression analysis in Section 3.10.

Nonconstancy of Error Variance

When the error variance is not constant but varies in a systematic fashion, a direct approach is to modify the model to allow for this and use the method of *weighted least squares* to obtain the estimators of the parameters. We discuss the use of weighted least squares for this purpose in Chapter 11.

Transformations can also be effective in stabilizing the variance. Some of these are discussed in Section 3.9.

Nonindependence of Error Terms

When the error terms are correlated, a direct remedial measure is to work with a model that calls for correlated error terms. We discuss such a model in Chapter 12. A simple remedial transformation that is often helpful is to work with first differences, a topic also discussed in Chapter 12.

Nonnormality of Error Terms

Lack of normality and nonconstant error variances frequently go hand in hand. Fortunately, it is often the case that the same transformation that helps stabilize the variance is also helpful in approximately normalizing the error terms. It is therefore desirable that the transformation for stabilizing the error variance be utilized first, and then the residuals studied to see if serious departures from normality are still present. We discuss transformations to achieve approximate normality in Section 3.9.

Omission of Important Predictor Variables

When residual analysis indicates that an important predictor variable has been omitted from the model, the solution is to modify the model. In Chapter 6 and later chapters, we discuss multiple regression analysis in which two or more predictor variables are utilized.

Outlying Observations

When outlying observations are present, as in Figure 3.7a, use of the least squares and maximum likelihood estimators (1.10) for regression model (2.1) may lead to serious distortions in the estimated regression function. When the outlying observations do not represent recording errors and should not be discarded, it may be desirable to use an estimation procedure that places less emphasis on such outlying observations. We discuss one such robust estimation procedure in Chapter 11.

3.9 Transformations

We now consider in more detail the use of transformations of one or both of the original variables before carrying out the regression analysis. Simple transformations of either the response variable Y or the predictor variable X, or of both, are often sufficient to make the simple linear regression model appropriate for the transformed data.

Transformations for Nonlinear Relation Only

We first consider transformations for linearizing a nonlinear regression relation when the distribution of the error terms is reasonably close to a normal distribution and the error terms have approximately constant variance. In this situation, transformations on X should be attempted. The reason why transformations on Y may not be desirable here is that a transformation on Y, such as $Y' = \sqrt{Y}$, may materially change the shape of the distribution of the error terms from the normal distribution and may also lead to substantially differing error term variances.

Figure 3.13 contains some prototype nonlinear regression relations with constant error variance and also presents some simple transformations on X that may be helpful to linearize the regression relationship without affecting the distributions of Y. Several alternative transformations may be tried. Scatter plots and residual plots based on each transformation should then be prepared and analyzed to decide which transformation is most effective.

Example

Data from an experiment on the effect of number of days of training received (X) on performance (Y) in a battery of simulated sales situations are presented in Table 3.7, columns 1 and 2, for the 10 participants in the study. A scatter plot of these data is shown in Figure 3.14a. Clearly the regression relation appears to be curvilinear, so the simple linear regression model (2.1) does not seem to be appropriate. Since the variability at the different X levels appears to be fairly constant, we shall consider a transformation on X. Based on the prototype plot in Figure 3.13a, we shall consider initially the square root transformation $X' = \sqrt{X}$. The transformed values are shown in column 3 of Table 3.7.

FIGURE 3.13
Prototype
Nonlinear
Regression
Patterns with
Constant Error
Variance and
Simple Trans-
formations
of *X*.

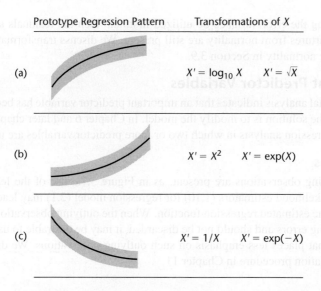

	Prototype Regression Pattern	Transformations of *X*
(a)		$X' = \log_{10} X \quad X' = \sqrt{X}$
(b)		$X' = X^2 \quad X' = \exp(X)$
(c)		$X' = 1/X \quad X' = \exp(-X)$

TABLE 3.7
Use of Square
Root Transfor-
mation of *X* **to**
Linearize
Regression
Relation—
Sales Training
Example.

	(1)	(2)	(3)
Sales Trainee *i*	Days of Training X_i	Performance Score Y_i	$X'_i = \sqrt{X_i}$
1	.5	42.5	.70711
2	.5	50.6	.70711
3	1.0	68.5	1.00000
4	1.0	80.7	1.00000
5	1.5	89.0	1.22474
6	1.5	99.6	1.22474
7	2.0	105.3	1.41421
8	2.0	111.8	1.41421
9	2.5	112.3	1.58114
10	2.5	125.7	1.58114

In Figure 3.14b, the same data are plotted with the predictor variable transformed to $X' = \sqrt{X}$. Note that the scatter plot now shows a reasonably linear relation. The variability of the scatter at the different X levels is the same as before, since we did not make a transformation on Y.

To examine further whether the simple linear regression model (2.1) is appropriate now, we fit it to the transformed X data. The regression calculations with the transformed X data are carried out in the usual fashion, except that the predictor variable now is X'. We obtain the following fitted regression function:

$$\hat{Y} = -10.33 + 83.45X'$$

Figure 3.14c contains a plot of the residuals against X'. There is no evidence of lack of fit or of strongly unequal error variances. Figure 3.14d contains a normal probability plot of

FIGURE 3.14   Scatter Plots and Residual Plots—Sales Training Example.

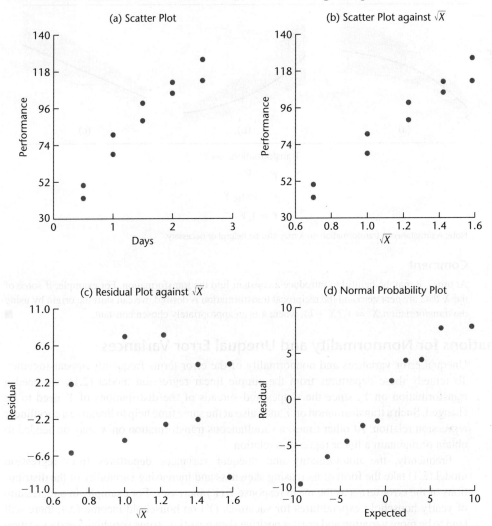

the residuals. No strong indications of substantial departures from normality are indicated by this plot. This conclusion is supported by the high coefficient of correlation between the ordered residuals and their expected values under normality, .979. For $\alpha = .01$, Table B.6 shows that the critical value is .879, so the observed coefficient is substantially larger and supports the reasonableness of normal error terms. Thus, the simple linear regression model (2.1) appears to be appropriate here for the transformed data.

The fitted regression function in the original units of X can easily be obtained, if desired:

$$\hat{Y} = -10.33 + 83.45\sqrt{X}$$

FIGURE 3.15
Prototype
Regression
Patterns with
Unequal Error
Variances and
Simple Trans-
formations
of Y.

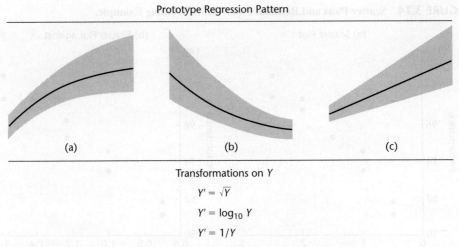

Prototype Regression Pattern

(a)   (b)   (c)

Transformations on Y

$$Y' = \sqrt{Y}$$

$$Y' = \log_{10} Y$$

$$Y' = 1/Y$$

Note: A simultaneous transformation on X may also be helpful or necessary.

Comment

At times, it may be helpful to introduce a constant into the transformation. For example, if some of the X data are near zero and the reciprocal transformation is desired, we can shift the origin by using the transformation $X' = 1/(X + k)$, where k is an appropriately chosen constant.   ∎

Transformations for Nonnormality and Unequal Error Variances

Unequal error variances and nonnormality of the error terms frequently appear together. To remedy these departures from the simple linear regression model (2.1), we need a transformation on Y, since the shapes and spreads of the distributions of Y need to be changed. Such a transformation on Y may also at the same time help to linearize a curvilinear regression relation. At other times, a simultaneous transformation on X may be needed to obtain or maintain a linear regression relation.

Frequently, the nonnormality and unequal variances departures from regression model (2.1) take the form of increasing skewness and increasing variability of the distributions of the error terms as the mean response $E\{Y\}$ increases. For example, in a regression of yearly household expenditures for vacations (Y) on household income (X), there will tend to be more variation and greater positive skewness (i.e., some very high yearly vacation expenditures) for high-income households than for low-income households, who tend to consistently spend much less for vacations. Figure 3.15 contains some prototype regression relations where the skewness and the error variance increase with the mean response $E\{Y\}$. This figure also presents some simple transformations on Y that may be helpful for these cases. Several alternative transformations on Y may be tried, as well as some simultaneous transformations on X. Scatter plots and residual plots should be prepared to determine the most effective transformation(s).

Example

Data on age (X) and plasma level of a polyamine (Y) for a portion of the 25 healthy children in a study are presented in columns 1 and 2 of Table 3.8. These data are plotted in Figure 3.16a as a scatter plot. Note the distinct curvilinear regression relationship, as well as the greater variability for younger children than for older ones.

TABLE 3.8
Use of
Logarithmic
Transforma-
tion of Y to
Linearize
Regression
Relation and
Stabilize Error
Variance—
Plasma Levels
Example.

Child i	(1) Age X_i		(2) Plasma Level Y_i	(3) $Y_i' = \log_{10} Y_i$
1	0	(newborn)	13.44	1.1284
2	0	(newborn)	12.84	1.1086
3	0	(newborn)	11.91	1.0759
4	0	(newborn)	20.09	1.3030
5	0	(newborn)	15.60	1.1931
6	1.0		10.11	1.0048
7	1.0		11.38	1.0561
...	...		...	...
19	3.0		6.90	.8388
20	3.0		6.77	.8306
21	4.0		4.86	.6866
22	4.0		5.10	.7076
23	4.0		5.67	.7536
24	4.0		5.75	.7597
25	4.0		6.23	.7945

On the basis of the prototype regression pattern in Figure 3.15b, we shall first try the logarithmic transformation $Y' = \log_{10} Y$. The transformed Y values are shown in column 3 of Table 3.8. Figure 3.16b contains the scatter plot with this transformation. Note that the transformation not only has led to a reasonably linear regression relation, but the variability at the different levels of X also has become reasonably constant.

To further examine the reasonableness of the transformation $Y' = \log_{10} Y$, we fitted the simple linear regression model (2.1) to the transformed Y data and obtained:

$$\hat{Y}' = 1.135 - .1023X$$

A plot of the residuals against X is shown in Figure 3.16c, and a normal probability plot of the residuals is shown in Figure 3.16d. The coefficient of correlation between the ordered residuals and their expected values under normality is .981. For $\alpha = .05$, Table B.6 indicates that the critical value is .959 so that the observed coefficient supports the assumption of normality of the error terms. All of this evidence supports the appropriateness of regression model (2.1) for the transformed Y data.

Comments

1. At times it may be desirable to introduce a constant into a transformation of Y, such as when Y may be negative. For instance, the logarithmic transformation to shift the origin in Y and make all Y observations positive would be $Y' = \log_{10}(Y + k)$, where k is an appropriately chosen constant.

2. When unequal error variances are present but the regression relation is linear, a transformation on Y may not be sufficient. While such a transformation may stabilize the error variance, it will also change the linear relationship to a curvilinear one. A transformation on X may therefore also be required. This case can also be handled by using weighted least squares, a procedure explained in Chapter 11.   ∎

FIGURE 3.16 **Scatter Plots and Residual Plots—Plasma Levels Example.**

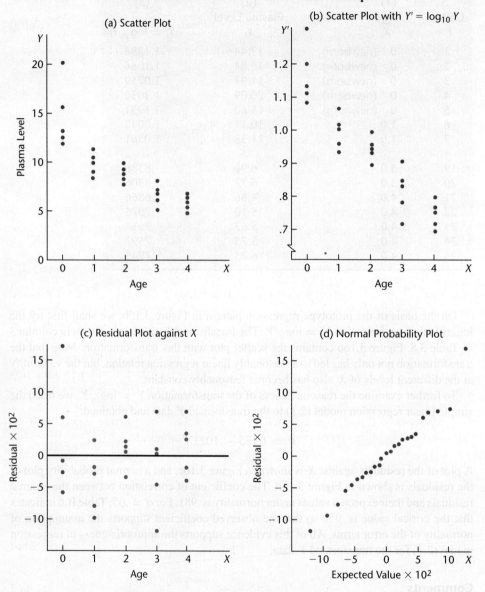

(a) Scatter Plot

(b) Scatter Plot with $Y' = \log_{10} Y$

(c) Residual Plot against X

(d) Normal Probability Plot

Box-Cox Transformations

It is often difficult to determine from diagnostic plots, such as the one in Figure 3.16a for the plasma levels example, which transformation of Y is most appropriate for correcting skewness of the distributions of error terms, unequal error variances, and nonlinearity of the regression function. The Box-Cox procedure (Ref. 3.9) automatically identifies a transformation from the family of power transformations on Y. The family of power transformations is of the form:

$$Y' = Y^\lambda \tag{3.33}$$

where λ is a parameter to be determined from the data. Note that this family encompasses the following simple transformations:

$$
\begin{array}{lll}
\lambda = 2 & Y' = Y^2 & \\
\lambda = .5 & Y' = \sqrt{Y} & \\
\lambda = 0 & Y' = \log_e Y & \text{(by definition)} \\
\lambda = -.5 & Y' = \dfrac{1}{\sqrt{Y}} & \\
\lambda = -1.0 & Y' = \dfrac{1}{Y} &
\end{array}
\tag{3.34}
$$

The normal error regression model with the response variable a member of the family of power transformations in (3.33) becomes:

$$Y_i^\lambda = \beta_0 + \beta_1 X_i + \varepsilon_i \tag{3.35}$$

Note that regression model (3.35) includes an additional parameter, λ, which needs to be estimated. The Box-Cox procedure uses the method of maximum likelihood to estimate λ, as well as the other parameters β_0, β_1, and σ^2. In this way, the Box-Cox procedure identifies $\hat{\lambda}$, the maximum likelihood estimate of λ to use in the power transformation.

Since some statistical software packages do not automatically provide the Box-Cox maximum likelihood estimate $\hat{\lambda}$ for the power transformation, a simple procedure for obtaining $\hat{\lambda}$ using standard regression software can be employed instead. This procedure involves a numerical search in a range of potential λ values; for example, $\lambda = -2$, $\lambda = -1.75$, ..., $\lambda = 1.75$, $\lambda = 2$. For each λ value, the Y_i^λ observations are first standardized so that the magnitude of the error sum of squares does not depend on the value of λ:

$$
W_i = \begin{cases} K_1\left(Y_i^\lambda - 1\right) & \lambda \neq 0 \\ K_2(\log_e Y_i) & \lambda = 0 \end{cases}
\tag{3.36}
$$

where:

$$K_2 = \left(\prod_{i=1}^{n} Y_i \right)^{1/n} \tag{3.36a}$$

$$K_1 = \frac{1}{\lambda K_2^{\lambda-1}} \tag{3.36b}$$

Note that K_2 is the geometric mean of the Y_i observations.

Once the standardized observations W_i have been obtained for a given λ value, they are regressed on the predictor variable X and the error sum of squares SSE is obtained. It can be shown that the maximum likelihood estimate $\hat{\lambda}$ is that value of λ for which SSE is a minimum.

If desired, a finer search can be conducted in the neighborhood of the λ value that minimizes SSE. However, the Box-Cox procedure ordinarily is used only to provide a guide for selecting a transformation, so overly precise results are not needed. In any case, scatter and residual plots should be utilized to examine the appropriateness of the transformation identified by the Box-Cox procedure.

Example

Table 3.9 contains the Box-Cox results for the plasma levels example. Selected values of λ, ranging from -1.0 to 1.0, were chosen, and for each chosen λ the transformation (3.36) was made and the linear regression of W on X was fitted. For instance, for $\lambda = .5$, the transformation $W_i = K_1(\sqrt{Y_i} - 1)$ was made and the linear regression of W on X was fitted. For this fitted linear regression, the error sum of squares is $SSE = 48.4$. The transformation that leads to the smallest value of SSE corresponds to $\lambda = -.5$, for which $SSE = 30.6$.

Figure 3.17 contains the SAS-JMP Box-Cox results for this example. It consists of a plot of SSE as a function of λ. From the plot, it is clear that a power value near $\lambda = -.50$ is indicated. However, SSE as a function of λ is fairly stable in the range from near 0 to -1.0, so the earlier choice of the logarithmic transformation $Y' = \log_{10} Y$ for the plasma levels example, corresponding to $\lambda = 0$, is not unreasonable according to the Box-Cox approach. One reason the logarithmic transformation was chosen here is because of the ease of interpreting it. The use of logarithms to base 10 rather than natural logarithms does not, of course, affect the appropriateness of the logarithmic transformation.

Comments

1. At times, theoretical or a priori considerations can be utilized to help in choosing an appropriate transformation. For example, when the shape of the scatter in a study of the relation between price of a commodity (X) and quantity demanded (Y) is that in Figure 3.15b, economists may prefer logarithmic transformations of both Y and X because the slope of the regression line for the transformed variables then measures the price elasticity of demand. The slope is then commonly interpreted as showing the percent change in quantity demanded per 1 percent change in price, where it is understood that the changes are in opposite directions.

TABLE 3.9
Box-Cox
Results—
Plasma Levels
Example.

λ	SSE	λ	SSE
1.0	78.0	$-.1$	33.1
.9	70.4	$-.3$	31.2
.7	57.8	$-.4$	30.7
.5	48.4	$-.5$	30.6
.3	41.4	$-.6$	30.7
.1	36.4	$-.7$	31.1
0	34.5	$-.9$	32.7
		-1.0	33.9

FIGURE 3.17
SAS-JMP
Box-Cox
Results—
Plasma Levels
Example.

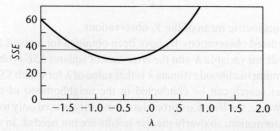

Similarly, scientists may prefer logarithmic transformations of both Y and X when studying the relation between radioactive decay (Y) of a substance and time (X) for a curvilinear relation of the type illustrated in Figure 3.15b because the slope of the regression line for the transformed variables then measures the decay rate.

2. After a transformation has been tentatively selected, residual plots and other analyses described earlier need to be employed to ascertain that the simple linear regression model (2.1) is appropriate for the transformed data.

3. When transformed models are employed, the estimators b_0 and b_1 obtained by least squares have the least squares properties with respect to the transformed observations, not the original ones.

4. The maximum likelihood estimate of λ with the Box-Cox procedure is subject to sampling variability. In addition, the error sum of squares SSE is often fairly stable in a neighborhood around the estimate. It is therefore often reasonable to use a nearby λ value for which the power transformation is easy to understand. For example, use of $\lambda = 0$ instead of the maximum likelihood estimate $\hat{\lambda} = .13$ or use of $\lambda = -.5$ instead of $\hat{\lambda} = -.79$ may facilitate understanding without sacrificing much in terms of the effectiveness of the transformation. To determine the reasonableness of using an easier-to-understand value of λ, one should examine the flatness of the likelihood function in the neighborhood of $\hat{\lambda}$, as we did in the plasma levels example. Alternatively, one may construct an approximate confidence interval for λ; the procedure for constructing such an interval is discussed in Reference 3.10.

5. When the Box-Cox procedure leads to a λ value near 1, no transformation of Y may be needed.

■

3.10   Exploration of Shape of Regression Function

Scatter plots often indicate readily the nature of the regression function. For instance, Figure 1.3 clearly shows the curvilinear nature of the regression relationship between steroid level and age. At other times, however, the scatter plot is complex and it becomes difficult to see the nature of the regression relationship, if any, from the plot. In these cases, it is helpful to explore the nature of the regression relationship by fitting a smoothed curve without any constraints on the regression function. These smoothed curves are also called *nonparametric regression curves*. They are useful not only for exploring regression relationships but also for confirming the nature of the regression function when the scatter plot visually suggests the nature of the regression relationship.

Many smoothing methods have been developed for obtaining smoothed curves for time series data, where the X_i denote time periods that are equally spaced apart. The *method of moving averages* uses the mean of the Y observations for adjacent time periods to obtain smoothed values. For example, the mean of the Y values for the first three time periods in the time series might constitute the first smoothed value corresponding to the middle of the three time periods, in other words, corresponding to time period 2. Then the mean of the Y values for the second, third, and fourth time periods would constitute the second smoothed value, corresponding to the middle of these three time periods, in other words, corresponding to time period 3, and so on. Special procedures are required for obtaining smoothed values at the two ends of the time series. The larger the successive neighborhoods used for obtaining the smoothed values, the smoother the curve will be.

The *method of running medians* is similar to the method of moving averages, except that the median is used as the average measure in order to reduce the influence of outlying observations. With this method, as well as with the moving average method, successive smoothing of the smoothed values and other refinements may be undertaken to provide a suitable smoothed curve for the time series. Reference 3.11 provides a good introduction to the running median smoothing method.

Many smoothing methods have also been developed for regression data when the X values are not equally spaced apart. A simple smoothing method, *band regression,* divides the data set into a number of groups or "bands" consisting of adjacent cases according to their X levels. For each band, the median X value and the median Y value are calculated, and the points defined by the pairs of these median values are then connected by straight lines. For example, consider the following simple data set divided into three groups:

X	Y	Median X	Median Y
2.0	13.1		
3.4	15.7	2.7	14.4
3.7	14.9		
4.5	16.8	4.5	16.8
5.0	17.1		
5.2	16.9		
5.9	17.8	5.55	17.35

The three pairs of medians are then plotted on the scatter plot of the data and connected by straight lines as a simple smoothed nonparametric regression curve.

Lowess Method

The *lowess method,* developed by Cleveland (Ref. 3.12), is a more refined nonparametric method than band regression. It obtains a smoothed curve by fitting successive linear regression functions in local neighborhoods. The name lowess stands for *locally weighted regression scatter plot smoothing.* The method is similar to the moving average and running median methods in that it uses a neighborhood around each X value to obtain a smoothed Y value corresponding to that X value. It obtains the smoothed Y value at a given X by fitting a linear regression to the data in the neighborhood of the X value and then using the fitted value at X as the smoothed value. To illustrate this concretely, let (X_1, Y_1) denote the sample case with the smallest X value, (X_2, Y_2) denote the sample case with the second smallest X value, and so on. If neighborhoods of three X values are used with the lowess method, then a linear regression would be fitted to the data:

$$(X_1, Y_1) \quad (X_2, Y_2) \quad (X_3, Y_3)$$

The fitted value at X_2 would constitute the smoothed value corresponding to X_2. Another linear regression would be fitted to the data:

$$(X_2, Y_2) \quad (X_3, Y_3) \quad (X_4, Y_4)$$

and the fitted value at X_3 would constitute the smoothed value corresponding to X_3. Smoothed values at each end of the X range are also obtained by the lowess procedure.

The lowess method uses a number of refinements in obtaining the final smoothed values to improve the smoothing and to make the procedure robust to outlying observations.

1. The linear regression is weighted to give cases further from the middle X level in each neighborhood smaller weights.

2. To make the procedure robust to outlying observations, the linear regression fitting is repeated, with the weights revised so that cases that had large residuals in the first fitting receive smaller weights in the second fitting.

3. To improve the robustness of the procedure further, step 2 is repeated one or more times by revising the weights according to the size of the residuals in the latest fitting.

To implement the lowess procedure, one must choose the size of the successive neighborhoods to be used when fitting each linear regression. One must also choose the weight function that gives less weight to neighborhood cases with X values far from each center X level and another weight function that gives less weight to cases with large residuals. Finally, the number of iterations to make the procedure robust must be chosen.

In practice, two iterations appear to be sufficient to provide robustness. Also, the weight functions suggested by Cleveland appear to be adequate for many circumstances. Hence, the primary choice to be made for a particular application is the size of the successive neighborhoods. The larger the size, the smoother the function but the greater the danger that the smoothing will lose essential features of the regression relationship. It may require some experimentation with different neighborhood sizes in order to find the size that best brings out the regression relationship. We explain the lowess method in detail in Chapter 11 in the context of multiple regression. Specific choices of weight functions and neighborhood sizes are discussed there.

Example Figure 3.18a contains a scatter plot based on a study of research quality at 24 research laboratories. The response variable is a measure of the quality of the research done at the laboratory, and the explanatory variable is a measure of the volume of research performed at the laboratory. Note that it is very difficult to tell from this scatter plot whether or not a relationship exists between research quality and quantity. Figure 3.18b repeats the scatter plot and also shows the lowess smoothed curve. The curve suggests that there might be somewhat higher research quality for medium-sized laboratories. However, the scatter is great so that this suggested relationship should be considered only as a possibility. Also, because any particular measures of research quality and quantity are so limited, other measures should be considered to see if these corroborate the relationship suggested in Figure 3.18b.

Use of Smoothed Curves to Confirm Fitted Regression Function

Smoothed curves are useful not only in the exploratory stages when a regression model is selected but they are also helpful in confirming the regression function chosen. The procedure for confirmation is simple: The smoothed curve is plotted together with the confidence band for the fitted regression function. If the smoothed curve falls within the confidence band, we have supporting evidence of the appropriateness of the fitted regression function.

FIGURE 3.18
MINITAB
Scatter Plot
and Lowess
Smoothed
Curve—
Research
Laboratories
Example.

FIGURE 3.19
MINITAB
Lowess Curve
and Confidence
Band for
Regression
Line—Toluca
Company
Example.

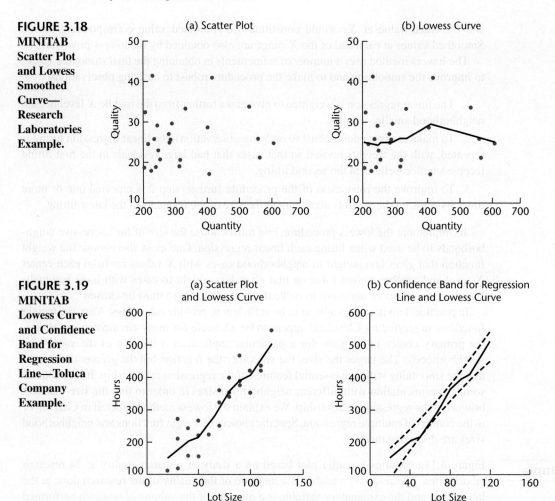

Example

Figure 3.19a repeats the scatter plot for the Toluca Company example from Figure 1.10a and shows the lowess smoothed curve. It appears that the regression relation is linear or possibly slightly curved. Figure 3.19b repeats the confidence band for the regression line from Figure 2.6 and shows the lowess smoothed curve. We see that the smoothed curve falls within the confidence band for the regression line and thereby supports the appropriateness of a linear regression function.

Comments

1. Smoothed curves, such as the lowess curve, do not provide an analytical expression for the functional form of the regression relationship. They only suggest the shape of the regression curve.

2. The lowess procedure is not restricted to fitting linear regression functions in each neighborhood. Higher-degree polynomials can also be utilized with this method.

3. Smoothed curves are also useful when examining residual plots to ascertain whether the residuals (or the absolute or squared residuals) follow some relationship with X or $\hat{Y}$.

4. References 3.13 and 3.14 provide good introductions to other nonparametric methods in regression analysis.   ∎

3.11   Case Example—Plutonium Measurement

Some environmental cleanup work requires that nuclear materials, such as plutonium 238, be located and completely removed from a restoration site. When plutonium has become mixed with other materials in very small amounts, detecting its presence can be a difficult task. Even very small amounts can be traced, however, because plutonium emits subatomic particles—alpha particles—that can be detected. Devices that are used to detect plutonium record the intensity of alpha particle strikes in counts per second (#/sec). The regression relationship between alpha counts per second (the response variable) and plutonium activity (the explanatory variable) is then used to estimate the activity of plutonium in the material under study. This use of a regression relationship involves inverse prediction [i.e., predicting plutonium activity (X) from the observed alpha count (Y)], a procedure discussed in Chapter 4.

The task here is to estimate the regression relationship between alpha counts per second and plutonium activity. This relationship varies for each measurement device and must be established precisely each time a different measurement device is used. It is reasonable to assume here that the level of alpha counts increases with plutonium activity, but the exact nature of the relationship is generally unknown.

In a study to establish the regression relationship for a particular measurement device, four plutonium *standards* were used. These standards are aluminum/plutonium rods containing a fixed, known level of plutonium activity. The levels of plutonium activity in the four standards were 0.0, 5.0, 10.0, and 20.0 picocuries per gram (pCi/g). Each standard was exposed to the detection device from 4 to 10 times, and the rate of alpha strikes, measured as counts per second, was observed for each replication. A portion of the data is shown in Table 3.10, and the data are plotted as a scatter plot in Figure 3.20a. Notice that, as expected, the strike rate tends to increase with the activity level of plutonium. Notice also that nonzero strike rates are recorded for the standard containing no plutonium. This results from background radiation and indicates that a regression model with an intercept term is required here.

TABLE 3.10
Basic Data—
Plutonium
Measurement
Example.

Case	Plutonium Activity (pCi/g)	Alpha Count Rate (#/sec)
1	20	.150
2	0	.004
3	10	.069
...	...	...
22	0	.002
23	5	.049
24	0	.106

FIGURE 3.20
SAS-JMP
Scatter Plot
and Lowess
Smoothed
Curve—
Plutonium
Measurement
Example.

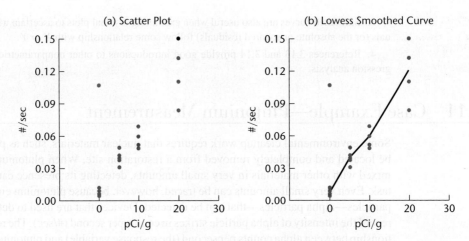

(a) Scatter Plot

(b) Lowess Smoothed Curve

As an initial step to examine the nature of the regression relationship, a lowess smoothed curve was obtained; this curve is shown in Figure 3.20b. We see that the regression relationship may be linear or slightly curvilinear in the range of the plutonium activity levels included in the study. We also see that one of the readings taken at 0.0 pCi/g (case 24) does not appear to fit with the rest of the observations. An examination of laboratory records revealed that the experimental conditions were not properly maintained for the last case, and it was therefore decided that case 24 should be discarded. Note, incidentally, how robust the lowess smoothing process was here by assigning very little weight to the outlying observation.

A linear regression function was fitted next, based on the remaining 23 cases. The SAS-JMP regression output is shown in Figure 3.21a, a plot of the residuals against the fitted values is shown in Figure 3.21b, and a normal probability plot is shown in Figure 3.21c. The JMP output uses the label Model to denote the regression component of the analysis of variance; the label C Total stands for corrected total. We see from the regression output that the slope of the regression line is not zero ($F^* = 228.9984$, P-value $= .0000$) so that a regression relationship exists. We also see from the flared, megaphone shape of the residual plot that the error variance appears to be increasing with the level of plutonium activity. The normal probability plot suggests nonnormality (heavy tails), but the nonlinearity of the plot is likely to be related (at least in part) to the unequal error variances. The existence of nonconstant variance is confirmed by the Breusch-Pagan test statistic (3.11):

$$X_{BP}^2 = 23.29 > \chi^2(.95; 1) = 3.84$$

The presence of nonconstant variance clearly requires remediation. A number of approaches could be followed, including the use of weighted least squares discussed in Chapter 11. Often with count data, the error variance can be stabilized through the use of a square root transformation of the response variable. Since this is just one in a range of power transformations that might be useful, we shall use the Box-Cox procedure to suggest an appropriate power transformation. Using the standardized variable (3.36), we find the maximum likelihood estimate of λ to be $\hat{\lambda} = .65$. Because the likelihood function is fairly flat in the neighborhood of $\hat{\lambda} = .65$, the Box-Cox procedure supports the use of the square root transformation (i.e., use of $\lambda = .5$). The results of fitting a linear regression function when the response variable is $Y' = \sqrt{Y}$ are shown in Figure 3.22a.

FIGURE 3.21 **SAS-JMP Regression Output and Diagnostic Plots for Untransformed Data—Plutonium Measurement Example.**

(a) Regression Output

Term	Estimate	Std Error	t Ratio	Prob>|t|
Intercept	0.0070331	0.0036	1.95	0.0641
Plutonium	0.005537	0.00037	15.13	0.0000

Source	DF	Sum of Squares	Mean Square	F Ratio
Model	1	0.03619042	0.036190	228.9984
Error	21	0.00331880	0.000158	Prob>F
C Total	22	0.03950922		0.0000

Source	DF	Sum of Squares	Mean Square	F Ratio
Lack of Fit	2	0.00016811	0.000084	0.5069
Pure Error	19	0.00315069	0.000166	Prob>F
Total Error	21	0.00331880		0.6103

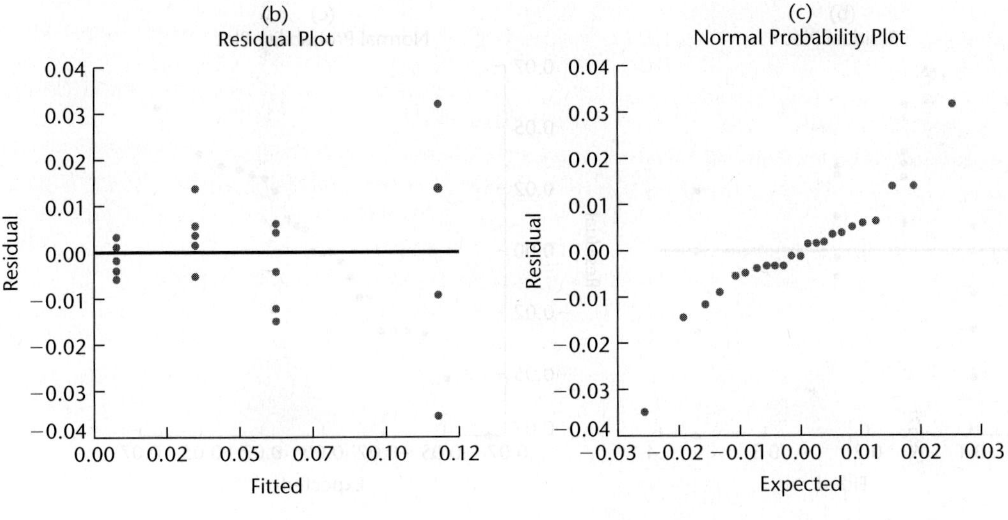

(b)
Residual Plot

(c)
Normal Probability Plot

At this point a new problem has arisen. Although the residual plot in Figure 3.22b shows that the error variance appears to be more stable and the points in the normal probability plot in Figure 3.22c fall roughly on a straight line, the residual plot now suggests that Y' is nonlinearly related to X. This concern is confirmed by the lack of fit test statistic (3.25) ($F^* = 10.1364$, P-value $= .0010$). Of course, this result is not completely unexpected, since Y was linearly related to X.

To restore a linear relation with the transformed Y variable, we shall see if a square root transformation of X will lead to a satisfactory linear fit. The regression results when regressing $Y' = \sqrt{Y}$ on $X' = \sqrt{X}$ are presented in Figure 3.23. Notice from the residual plot in Figure 3.23b that the square root transformation of the predictor variable has eliminated the lack of fit. Also, the normal probability plot of the residuals in Figure 3.23c appears to be satisfactory, and the correlation test ($r = .986$) supports the assumption of normally distributed error terms (the interpolated critical value in Table B.6 for $\alpha = .05$ and $n = 23$ is .9555). However, the residual plot suggests that some nonconstancy of the error variance

FIGURE 3.22 **SAS-JMP Regression Output and Diagnostic Plots for Transformed Response Variable—Plutonium Measurement Example.**

(a) Regression Output

Term	Estimate	Std Error	t Ratio	Prob>|t|
Intercept	0.0947596	0.00957	9.91	0.0000
Plutonium	0.0133648	0.00097	13.74	0.0000

Source	DF	Sum of Squares	Mean Square	F Ratio
Model	1	0.21084655	0.210847	188.7960
Error	21	0.02345271	0.001117	Prob>F
C Total	22	0.23429926		0.0000

Source	DF	Sum of Squares	Mean Square	F Ratio
Lack of Fit	2	0.01210640	0.006053	10.1364
Pure Error	19	0.01134631	0.000597	Prob>F
Total Error	21	0.02345271		0.0010

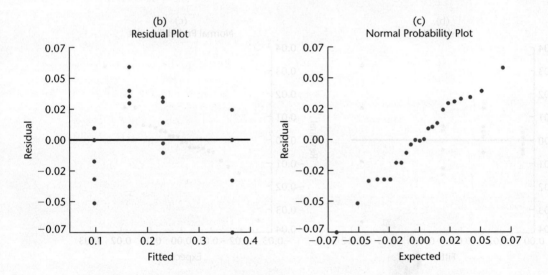

(b) Residual Plot

(c) Normal Probability Plot

may still remain; but if so, it does not appear to be substantial. The Breusch-Pagan test statistic (3.11) is $X_{BP}^2 = 3.85$, which corresponds to a P-value of .05, supporting the conclusion from the residual plot that the nonconstancy of the error variance is not substantial.

Figure 3.23d contains a SYSTAT plot of the confidence band (2.40) for the fitted regression line:

$$\hat{Y}' = .0730 + .0573X'.$$

We see that the regression line has been estimated fairly precisely. Also plotted in this figure is the lowess smoothed curve. This smoothed curve falls entirely within the confidence band, supporting the reasonableness of a linear regression relation between Y' and X'. The lack of fit test statistic (3.25) now is $F^* = 1.2868$ (P-value = .2992), also supporting the linearity of the regression relating $Y' = \sqrt{Y}$ to $X' = \sqrt{X}$.

FIGURE 3.23 SAS-JMP Regression Output and Diagnostic Plots for Transformed Response and Predictor Variables—Plutonium Measurement Example.

(a) Regression Output

Term	Estimate	Std Error	t Ratio	Prob>|t|
Intercept	0.0730056	0.00783	9.32	0.0000
Sqrt Plutonium	0.0573055	0.00302	19.00	0.0000

Source	DF	Sum of Squares	Mean Square	F Ratio
Model	1	0.22141612	0.221416	360.9166
Error	21	0.01288314	0.000613	Prob>F
C Total	22	0.23429926		0.0000

Source	DF	Sum of Squares	Mean Square	F Ratio
Lack of Fit	2	0.00153683	0.000768	1.2868
Pure Error	19	0.01134631	0.000597	Prob>F
Total Error	21	0.01288314		0.2992

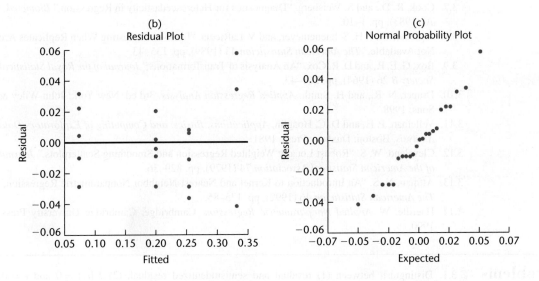

(b)
Residual Plot

(c)
Normal Probability Plot

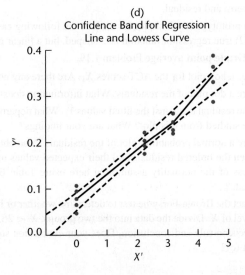

(d)
Confidence Band for Regression
Line and Lowess Curve

Cited References

3.1. Barnett, V., and T. Lewis. *Outliers in Statistical Data*. 3rd ed. New York: John Wiley & Sons, 1994.

3.2. Looney, S. W., and T. R. Gulledge, Jr. "Use of the Correlation Coefficient with Normal Probability Plots," *The American Statistician* 39 (1985), pp. 75–79.

3.3. Shapiro, S. S., and M. B. Wilk. "An Analysis of Variance Test for Normality (Complete Samples)," *Biometrika* 52 (1965), pp. 591–611.

3.4. Levene, H. "Robust Tests for Equality of Variances," in *Contributions to Probability and Statistics,* ed. I. Olkin. Palo Alto, Calif.: Stanford University Press, 1960, pp. 278–92.

3.5. Brown, M. B., and A. B. Forsythe. "Robust Tests for Equality of Variances," *Journal of the American Statistical Association* 69 (1974), pp. 364–67.

3.6. Breusch, T. S., and A. R. Pagan. "A Simple Test for Heteroscedasticity and Random Coefficient Variation," *Econometrica* 47 (1979), pp. 1287–94.

3.7. Cook, R. D., and S. Weisberg. "Diagnostics for Heteroscedasticity in Regression," *Biometrika* 70 (1983), pp. 1–10.

3.8. Joglekar, G., J. H. Schuenemeyer, and V. LaRiccia. "Lack-of-Fit Testing When Replicates Are Not Available," *The American Statistician* 43 (1989), pp. 135–43.

3.9. Box, G. E. P., and D. R. Cox. "An Analysis of Transformations," *Journal of the Royal Statistical Society B* 26 (1964), pp. 211–43.

3.10. Draper, N. R., and H. Smith. *Applied Regression Analysis*. 3rd ed. New York: John Wiley & Sons, 1998.

3.11. Velleman, P. F., and D. C. Hoaglin. *Applications, Basics, and Computing of Exploratory Data Analysis*. Boston: Duxbury Press, 1981.

3.12. Cleveland, W. S. "Robust Locally Weighted Regression and Smoothing Scatterplots," *Journal of the American Statistical Association* 74 (1979), pp. 829–36.

3.13. Altman, N. S. "An Introduction to Kernel and Nearest-Neighbor Nonparametric Regression," *The American Statistician* 46 (1992), pp. 175–85.

3.14. Haerdle, W. *Applied Nonparametric Regression*. Cambridge: Cambridge University Press, 1990.

Problems

3.1. Distinguish between (1) residual and semistudentized residual, (2) $E\{\varepsilon_i\} = 0$ and $\bar{e} = 0$, (3) error term and residual.

3.2. Prepare a prototype residual plot for each of the following cases: (1) error variance decreases with X; (2) true regression function is $\cup$ shaped, but a linear regression function is fitted.

3.3. Refer to **Grade point average** Problem 1.19.

   a. Prepare a box plot for the ACT scores X_i. Are there any noteworthy features in this plot?

   b. Prepare a dot plot of the residuals. What information does this plot provide?

   c. Plot the residual e_i against the fitted values $\hat{Y}_i$. What departures from regression model (2.1) can be studied from this plot? What are your findings?

   d. Prepare a normal probability plot of the residuals. Also obtain the coefficient of correlation between the ordered residuals and their expected values under normality. Test the reasonableness of the normality assumption here using Table B.6 and $\alpha = .05$. What do you conclude?

   e. Conduct the Brown-Forsythe test to determine whether or not the error variance varies with the level of X. Divide the data into the two groups, $X < 26$, $X \geq 26$, and use $\alpha = .01$. State the decision rule and conclusion. Does your conclusion support your preliminary findings in part (c)?

f. Information is given below for each student on two variables not included in the model, namely, intelligence test score (X_2) and high school class rank percentile (X_3). (Note that larger class rank percentiles indicate higher standing in the class, e.g., 1% is near the bottom of the class and 99% is near the top of the class.) Plot the residuals against X_2 and X_3 on separate graphs to ascertain whether the model can be improved by including either of these variables. What do you conclude?

i:	1	2	3	...	118	119	120
X_2:	122	132	119	...	140	111	110
X_3:	99	71	75	...	97	65	85

*3.4. Refer to **Copier maintenance** Problem 1.20.

a. Prepare a dot plot for the number of copiers serviced X_i. What information is provided by this plot? Are there any outlying cases with respect to this variable?

b. The cases are given in time order. Prepare a time plot for the number of copiers serviced. What does your plot show?

c. Prepare a stem-and-leaf plot of the residuals. Are there any noteworthy features in this plot?

d. Prepare residual plots of e_i versus $\hat{Y}_i$ and e_i versus X_i on separate graphs. Do these plots provide the same information? What departures from regression model (2.1) can be studied from these plots? State your findings.

e. Prepare a normal probability plot of the residuals. Also obtain the coefficient of correlation between the ordered residuals and their expected values under normality. Does the normality assumption appear to be tenable here? Use Table B.6 and $\alpha = .10$.

f. Prepare a time plot of the residuals to ascertain whether the error terms are correlated over time. What is your conclusion?

g. Assume that (3.10) is applicable and conduct the Breusch-Pagan test to determine whether or not the error variance varies with the level of X. Use $\alpha = .05$. State the alternatives, decision rule, and conclusion.

h. Information is given below on two variables not included in the regression model, namely, mean operational age of copiers serviced on the call (X_2, in months) and years of experience of the service person making the call (X_3). Plot the residuals against X_2 and X_3 on separate graphs to ascertain whether the model can be improved by including either or both of these variables. What do you conclude?

i:	1	2	3	...	43	44	45
X_2:	20	19	27	...	28	26	33
X_3:	4	5	4	...	3	3	6

*3.5. Refer to **Airfreight breakage** Problem 1.21.

a. Prepare a dot plot for the number of transfers X_i. Does the distribution of number of transfers appear to be asymmetrical?

b. The cases are given in time order. Prepare a time plot for the number of transfers. Is any systematic pattern evident in your plot? Discuss.

c. Obtain the residuals e_i and prepare a stem-and-leaf plot of the residuals. What information is provided by your plot?

d. Plot the residuals e_i against X_i to ascertain whether any departures from regression model (2.1) are evident. What is your conclusion?

e. Prepare a normal probability plot of the residuals. Also obtain the coefficient of correlation between the ordered residuals and their expected values under normality to ascertain whether the normality assumption is reasonable here. Use Table B.6 and $\alpha = .01$. What do you conclude?

f. Prepare a time plot of the residuals. What information is provided by your plot?

g. Assume that (3.10) is applicable and conduct the Breusch-Pagan test to determine whether or not the error variance varies with the level of X. Use $\alpha = .10$. State the alternatives, decision rule, and conclusion. Does your conclusion support your preliminary findings in part (d)?

3.6. Refer to **Plastic hardness** Problem 1.22.

a. Obtain the residuals e_i and prepare a box plot of the residuals. What information is provided by your plot?

b. Plot the residuals e_i against the fitted values $\hat{Y}_i$ to ascertain whether any departures from regression model (2.1) are evident. State your findings.

c. Prepare a normal probability plot of the residuals. Also obtain the coefficient of correlation between the ordered residuals and their expected values under normality. Does the normality assumption appear to be reasonable here? Use Table B.6 and $\alpha = .05$.

d. Compare the frequencies of the residuals against the expected frequencies under normality, using the 25th, 50th, and 75th percentiles of the relevant t distribution. Is the information provided by these comparisons consistent with the findings from the normal probability plot in part (c)?

e. Use the Brown-Forsythe test to determine whether or not the error variance varies with the level of X. Divide the data into the two groups, $X \leq 24$, $X > 24$, and use $\alpha = .05$. State the decision rule and conclusion. Does your conclusion support your preliminary findings in part (b)?

*3.7. Refer to **Muscle mass** Problem 1.27.

a. Prepare a stem-and-leaf plot for the ages X_i. Is this plot consistent with the random selection of women from each 10-year age group? Explain.

b. Obtain the residuals e_i and prepare a dot plot of the residuals. What does your plot show?

c. Plot the residuals e_i against $\hat{Y}_i$ and also against X_i on separate graphs to ascertain whether any departures from regression model (2.1) are evident. Do the two plots provide the same information? State your conclusions.

d. Prepare a normal probability plot of the residuals. Also obtain the coefficient of correlation between the ordered residuals and their expected values under normality to ascertain whether the normality assumption is tenable here. Use Table B.6 and $\alpha = .10$. What do you conclude?

e. Assume that (3.10) is applicable and conduct the Breusch-Pagan test to determine whether or not the error variance varies with the level of X. Use $\alpha = .01$. State the alternatives, decision rule, and conclusion. Is your conclusion consistent with your preliminary findings in part (c)?

3.8. Refer to **Crime rate** Problem 1.28.

a. Prepare a stem-and-leaf plot for the percentage of individuals in the county having at least a high school diploma X_i. What information does your plot provide?

b. Obtain the residuals e_i and prepare a box plot of the residuals. Does the distribution of the residuals appear to be symmetrical?

c. Make a residual plot of e_i versus $\hat{Y}_i$. What does the plot show?

d. Prepare a normal probability plot of the residuals. Also obtain the coefficient of correlation between the ordered residuals and their expected values under normality. Test the reasonableness of the normality assumption using Table B.6 and $\alpha = .05$. What do you conclude?

e. Conduct the Brown-Forsythe test to determine whether or not the error variance varies with the level of X. Divide the data into the two groups, $X \leq 69$, $X > 69$, and use $\alpha = .05$. State the decision rule and conclusion. Does your conclusion support your preliminary findings in part (c)?

3.9. **Electricity consumption.** An economist studying the relation between household electricity consumption (Y) and number of rooms in the home (X) employed linear regression model (2.1) and obtained the following residuals:

i:	1	2	3	4	5	6	7	8	9	10
X_i:	2	3	4	5	6	7	8	9	10	11
e_i:	3.2	2.9	−1.7	−2.0	−2.3	−1.2	−.9	.8	.7	.5

Plot the residuals e_i against X_i. What problem appears to be present here? Might a transformation alleviate this problem?

3.10. **Per capita earnings.** A sociologist employed linear regression model (2.1) to relate per capita earnings (Y) to average number of years of schooling (X) for 12 cities. The fitted values $\hat{Y}_i$ and the semistudentized residuals e_i^* follow.

i:	1	2	3	...	10	11	12
$\hat{Y}_i$:	9.9	9.3	10.2	...	15.6	11.2	13.1
e_i^*:	−1.12	.81	−.76	...	−3.78	.74	.32

a. Plot the semistudentized residuals against the fitted values. What does the plot suggest?

b. How many semistudentized residuals are outside ± 1 standard deviation? Approximately how many would you expect to see if the normal error model is appropriate?

3.11. **Drug concentration.** A pharmacologist employed linear regression model (2.1) to study the relation between the concentration of a drug in plasma (Y) and the log-dose of the drug (X). The residuals and log-dose levels follow.

i:	1	2	3	4	5	6	7	8	9
X_i:	−1	0	1	−1	0	1	−1	0	1
e_i:	.5	2.1	−3.4	.3	−1.7	4.2	−.6	2.6	−4.0

a. Plot the residuals e_i against X_i. What conclusions do you draw from the plot?

b. Assume that (3.10) is applicable and conduct the Breusch-Pagan test to determine whether or not the error variance varies with log-dose of the drug (X). Use $\alpha = .05$. State the alternatives, decision rule, and conclusion. Does your conclusion support your preliminary findings in part (a)?

3.12. A student does not understand why the sum of squares defined in (3.16) is called a pure error sum of squares "since the formula looks like one for an ordinary sum of squares." Explain.

*3.13. Refer to **Copier maintenance** Problem 1.20.

    a. What are the alternative conclusions when testing for lack of fit of a linear regression function?

    b. Perform the test indicated in part (a). Control the risk of Type I error at .05. State the decision rule and conclusion.

    c. Does the test in part (b) detect other departures from regression model (2.1), such as lack of constant variance or lack of normality in the error terms? Could the results of the test of lack of fit be affected by such departures? Discuss.

3.14. Refer to **Plastic hardness** Problem 1.22.

    a. Perform the F test to determine whether or not there is lack of fit of a linear regression function; use $\alpha = .01$. State the alternatives, decision rule, and conclusion.

    b. Is there any advantage of having an equal number of replications at each of the X levels? Is there any disadvantage?

    c. Does the test in part (a) indicate what regression function is appropriate when it leads to the conclusion that the regression function is not linear? How would you proceed?

3.15. **Solution concentration.** A chemist studied the concentration of a solution (Y) over time (X). Fifteen identical solutions were prepared. The 15 solutions were randomly divided into five sets of three, and the five sets were measured, respectively, after 1, 3, 5, 7, and 9 hours. The results follow.

i:	1	2	3	$\ldots$	13	14	15
X_i:	9	9	9	$\ldots$	1	1	1
Y_i:	.07	.09	.08	$\ldots$	2.84	2.57	3.10

    a. Fit a linear regression function.

    b. Perform the F test to determine whether or not there is lack of fit of a linear regression function; use $\alpha = .025$. State the alternatives, decision rule, and conclusion.

    c. Does the test in part (b) indicate what regression function is appropriate when it leads to the conclusion that lack of fit of a linear regression function exists? Explain.

3.16. Refer to **Solution concentration** Problem 3.15.

    a. Prepare a scatter plot of the data. What transformation of Y might you try, using the prototype patterns in Figure 3.15 to achieve constant variance and linearity?

    b. Use the Box-Cox procedure and standardization (3.36) to find an appropriate power transformation. Evaluate SSE for $\lambda = -.2, -.1, 0, .1, .2$. What transformation of Y is suggested?

    c. Use the transformation $Y' = \log_{10} Y$ and obtain the estimated linear regression function for the transformed data.

    d. Plot the estimated regression line and the transformed data. Does the regression line appear to be a good fit to the transformed data?

    e. Obtain the residuals and plot them against the fitted values. Also prepare a normal probability plot. What do your plots show?

    f. Express the estimated regression function in the original units.

*3.17. **Sales growth.** A marketing researcher studied annual sales of a product that had been introduced 10 years ago. The data are as follows, where X is the year (coded) and Y is sales in thousands of units:

i:	1	2	3	4	5	6	7	8	9	10
X_i:	0	1	2	3	4	5	6	7	8	9
Y_i:	98	135	162	178	221	232	283	300	374	395

a. Prepare a scatter plot of the data. Does a linear relation appear adequate here?

b. Use the Box-Cox procedure and standardization (3.36) to find an appropriate power transformation of Y. Evaluate SSE for $\lambda = .3, .4, .5, .6, .7$. What transformation of Y is suggested?

c. Use the transformation $Y' = \sqrt{Y}$ and obtain the estimated linear regression function for the transformed data.

d. Plot the estimated regression line and the transformed data. Does the regression line appear to be a good fit to the transformed data?

e. Obtain the residuals and plot them against the fitted values. Also prepare a normal probability plot. What do your plots show?

f. Express the estimated regression function in the original units.

3.18. **Production time.** In a manufacturing study, the production times for 111 recent production runs were obtained. The table below lists for each run the production time in hours (Y) and the production lot size (X).

i:	1	2	3	...	109	110	111
X_i:	15	9	7	...	12	9	15
Y_i:	14.28	8.80	12.49	...	16.37	11.45	15.78

a. Prepare a scatter plot of the data. Does a linear relation appear adequate here? Would a transformation on X or Y be more appropriate here? Why?

b. Use the transformation $X' = \sqrt{X}$ and obtain the estimated linear regression function for the transformed data.

c. Plot the estimated regression line and the transformed data. Does the regression line appear to be a good fit to the transformed data?

d. Obtain the residuals and plot them against the fitted values. Also prepare a normal probability plot. What do your plots show?

e. Express the estimated regression function in the original units.

Exercises

3.19. A student fitted a linear regression function for a class assignment. The student plotted the residuals e_i against Y_i and found a positive relation. When the residuals were plotted against the fitted values $\hat{Y}_i$, the student found no relation. How could this difference arise? Which is the more meaningful plot?

3.20. If the error terms in a regression model are independent $N(0, \sigma^2)$, what can be said about the error terms after transformation $X' = 1/X$ is used? Is the situation the same after transformation $Y' = 1/Y$ is used?

3.21. Derive the result in (3.29).

3.22. Using (A.70), (A.41), and (A.42), show that $E\{MSPE\} = \sigma^2$ for normal error regression model (2.1).

3.23. A linear regression model with intercept $\beta_0 = 0$ is under consideration. Data have been obtained that contain replications. State the full and reduced models for testing the appropriateness of the regression function under consideration. What are the degrees of freedom associated with the full and reduced models if $n = 20$ and $c = 10$?

Projects

3.24. **Blood pressure.** The following data were obtained in a study of the relation between diastolic blood pressure (Y) and age (X) for boys 5 to 13 years old.

i:	1	2	3	4	5	6	7	8
X_i:	5	8	11	7	13	12	12	6
Y_i:	63	67	74	64	75	69	90	60

a. Assuming normal error regression model (2.1) is appropriate, obtain the estimated regression function and plot the residuals e_i against X_i. What does your residual plot show?

b. Omit case 7 from the data and obtain the estimated regression function based on the remaining seven cases. Compare this estimated regression function to that obtained in part (a). What can you conclude about the effect of case 7?

c. Using your fitted regression function in part (b), obtain a 99 percent prediction interval for a new Y observation at $X = 12$. Does observation Y_7 fall outside this prediction interval? What is the significance of this?

3.25. Refer to the **CDI** data set in Appendix C.2 and Project 1.43. For each of the three fitted regression models, obtain the residuals and prepare a residual plot against X and a normal probability plot. Summarize your conclusions. Is linear regression model (2.1) more appropriate in one case than in the others?

3.26. Refer to the **CDI** data set in Appendix C.2 and Project 1.44. For each geographic region, obtain the residuals and prepare a residual plot against X and a normal probability plot. Do the four regions appear to have similar error variances? What other conclusions do you draw from your plots?

3.27. Refer to the **SENIC** data set in Appendix C.1 and Project 1.45.

a. For each of the three fitted regression models, obtain the residuals and prepare a residual plot against X and a normal probability plot. Summarize your conclusions. Is linear regression model (2.1) more apt in one case than in the others?

b. Obtain the fitted regression function for the relation between length of stay and infection risk after deleting cases 47 ($X_{47} = 6.5$, $Y_{47} = 19.56$) and 112 ($X_{112} = 5.9$, $Y_{112} = 17.94$). From this fitted regression function obtain separate 95 percent prediction intervals for new Y observations at $X = 6.5$ and $X = 5.9$, respectively. Do observations Y_{47} and Y_{112} fall outside these prediction intervals? Discuss the significance of this.

3.28. Refer to the **SENIC** data set in Appendix C.1 and Project 1.46. For each geographic region, obtain the residuals and prepare a residual plot against X and a normal probability plot. Do the four regions appear to have similar error variances? What other conclusions do you draw from your plots?

3.29. Refer to **Copier maintenance** Problem 1.20.

a. Divide the data into four bands according to the number of copiers serviced (X). Band 1 ranges from $X = .5$ to $X = 2.5$; band 2 ranges from $X = 2.5$ to $X = 4.5$; and so forth. Determine the median value of X and the median value of Y in each of the bands and develop the band smooth by connecting the four pairs of medians by straight lines on a scatter plot of the data. Does the band smooth suggest that the regression relation is linear? Discuss.

b. Obtain the 90 percent confidence band for the true regression line and plot it on the scatter plot prepared in part (a). Does the band smooth fall entirely inside the confidence band? What does this tell you about the appropriateness of the linear regression function?

c. Create a series of six overlapping neighborhoods of width 3.0 beginning at $X = .5$. The first neighborhood will range from $X = .5$ to $X = 3.5$; the second neighborhood will range from $X = 1.5$ to $X = 4.5$; and so on. For each of the six overlapping neighborhoods, fit a linear regression function and obtain the fitted value $\hat{Y}_c$ at the center X_c of the neighborhood. Develop a simplified version of the lowess smooth by connecting the six $(X_c, \hat{Y}_c)$ pairs by straight lines on a scatter plot of the data. In what ways does your simplified lowess smooth differ from the band smooth obtained in part (a)?

3.30. Refer to **Sales growth** Problem 3.17.

a. Divide the range of the predictor variable (coded years) into five bands of width 2.0, as follows: Band 1 ranges from $X = -.5$ to $X = 1.5$; band 2 ranges from $X = 1.5$ to $X = 3.5$; and so on. Determine the median value of X and the median value of Y in each band and develop the band smooth by connecting the five pairs of medians by straight lines on a scatter plot of the data. Does the band smooth suggest that the regression relation is linear? Discuss.

b. Create a series of seven overlapping neighborhoods of width 3.0 beginning at $X = -.5$. The first neighborhood will range from $X = -.5$ to $X = 2.5$; the second neighborhood will range from $X = .5$ to $X = 3.5$; and so on. For each of the seven overlapping neighborhoods, fit a linear regression function and obtain the fitted value $\hat{Y}_c$ at the center X_c of the neighborhood. Develop a simplified version of the lowess smooth by connecting the seven $(X_c, \hat{Y}_c)$ pairs by straight lines on a scatter plot of the data.

c. Obtain the 95 percent confidence band for the true regression line and plot it on the plot prepared in part (b). Does the simplified lowess smooth fall entirely within the confidence band for the regression line? What does this tell you about the appropriateness of the linear regression function?

Case Studies

3.31. Refer to the **Real estate sales** data set in Appendix C.7. Obtain a random sample of 200 cases from the 522 cases in this data set. Using the random sample, build a regression model to predict sales price (Y) as a function of finished square feet (X). The analysis should include an assessment of the degree to which the key regression assumptions are satisfied. If the regression assumptions are not met, include and justify appropriate remedial measures. Use the final model to predict sales price for two houses that are about to come on the market: the first has $X = 1100$ finished square feet and the second has $X = 4900$ finished square feet. Assess the strengths and weaknesses of the final model.

3.32. Refer to the **Prostate cancer** data set in Appendix C.5. Build a regression model to predict PSA level (Y) as a function of cancer volume (X). The analysis should include an assessment of the degree to which the key regression assumptions are satisfied. If the regression assumptions are not met, include and justify appropriate remedial measures. Use the final model to estimate mean PSA level for a patient whose cancer volume is 20 cc. Assess the strengths and weaknesses of the final model.

Chapter 4

Simultaneous Inferences and Other Topics in Regression Analysis

In this chapter, we take up a variety of topics in simple linear regression analysis. Several of the topics pertain to how to make simultaneous inferences from the same set of sample observations.

4.1 Joint Estimation of β_0 and β_1

Need for Joint Estimation

A market research analyst conducted a study of the relation between level of advertising expenditures (X) and sales (Y). The study included six different levels of advertising expenditures, one of which was no advertising ($X = 0$). The scatter plot suggested a linear relationship in the range of the advertising expenditures levels studied. The analyst now wishes to draw inferences with confidence coefficient .95 about both the intercept β_0 and the slope β_1. The analyst could use the methods of Chapter 2 to construct separate 95 percent confidence intervals for β_0 and β_1. The difficulty is that these would not provide 95 percent confidence that the conclusions for *both* β_0 and β_1 are correct. If the inferences were independent, the probability of both being correct would be $(.95)^2$, or only .9025. The inferences are not, however, independent, coming as they do from the same set of sample data, which makes the determination of the probability of both inferences being correct much more difficult.

Analysis of data frequently requires a series of estimates (or tests) where the analyst would like to have an assurance about the correctness of the entire set of estimates (or tests). We shall call the set of estimates (or tests) of interest the *family* of estimates (or tests). In our illustration, the family consists of two estimates, for β_0 and β_1. We then distinguish between a statement confidence coefficient and a family confidence coefficient. A *statement confidence coefficient* is the familiar type of confidence coefficient discussed earlier, which indicates the proportion of correct estimates that are obtained when repeated samples are selected and the specified confidence interval is calculated for each sample. A *family confidence coefficient*, on the other hand, indicates the proportion of families of estimates that are entirely correct when repeated samples are selected and the specified confidence intervals for the entire family are calculated for each sample. Thus, a family confidence coefficient corresponds to the probability, in advance of sampling, that the entire family of statements will be correct.

To illustrate the meaning of a family confidence coefficient further, consider again the joint estimation of β_0 and β_1. A family confidence coefficient of, say, .95 would indicate here that if repeated samples are selected and interval estimates for both β_0 and β_1 are calculated for each sample by specified procedures, 95 percent of the samples would lead to a family of estimates where *both* confidence intervals are correct. For 5 percent of the samples, either one or both of the interval estimates would be incorrect.

A procedure that provides a family confidence coefficient when estimating both β_0 and β_1 is often highly desirable since it permits the analyst to weave the two separate results together into an integrated set of conclusions, with an assurance that the entire set of estimates is correct. We now discuss one procedure for constructing simultaneous confidence intervals for β_0 and β_1 with a specified family confidence coefficient—the Bonferroni procedure.

Bonferroni Joint Confidence Intervals

The Bonferroni procedure for developing joint confidence intervals for β_0 and β_1 with a specified family confidence coefficient is very simple: each statement confidence coefficient is adjusted to be higher than $1 - \alpha$ so that the family confidence coefficient is at least $1 - \alpha$. The procedure is a general one that can be applied in many cases, as we shall see, not just for the joint estimation of β_0 and β_1.

We start with ordinary confidence limits for β_0 and β_1 with statement confidence coefficients $1 - \alpha$ each. These limits are:

$$b_0 \pm t(1 - \alpha/2; n - 2)s\{b_0\}$$
$$b_1 \pm t(1 - \alpha/2; n - 2)s\{b_1\}$$

We first ask what is the probability that one or both of these intervals are incorrect. Let A_1 denote the event that the first confidence interval does not cover β_0, and let A_2 denote the event that the second confidence interval does not cover β_1. We know:

$$P(A_1) = \alpha \qquad P(A_2) = \alpha$$

Probability theorem (A.6) gives the desired probability:

$$P(A_1 \cup A_2) = P(A_1) + P(A_2) - P(A_1 \cap A_2)$$

Next, we use complementation property (A.9) to obtain the probability that both intervals are correct, denoted by $P(\bar{A}_1 \cap \bar{A}_2)$:

$$P(\bar{A}_1 \cap \bar{A}_2) = 1 - P(A_1 \cup A_2) = 1 - P(A_1) - P(A_2) + P(A_1 \cap A_2) \qquad \textbf{(4.1)}$$

Note from probability properties (A.9) and (A.10) that $\bar{A}_1 \cap \bar{A}_2$ and $A_1 \cup A_2$ are complementary events:

$$1 - P(A_1 \cup A_2) = P(\overline{A_1 \cup A_2}) = P(\bar{A}_1 \cap \bar{A}_2)$$

Finally, we use the fact that $P(A_1 \cap A_2) \geq 0$ to obtain from (4.1) the *Bonferroni inequality:*

$$P(\bar{A}_1 \cap \bar{A}_2) \geq 1 - P(A_1) - P(A_2) \qquad \textbf{(4.2)}$$

which for our situation is:

$$P(\bar{A}_1 \cap \bar{A}_2) \geq 1 - \alpha - \alpha = 1 - 2\alpha \qquad \text{(4.2a)}$$

Thus, if β_0 and β_1 are separately estimated with, say, 95 percent confidence intervals, the Bonferroni inequality guarantees us a family confidence coefficient of at least 90 percent that both intervals based on the same sample are correct.

We can easily use the Bonferroni inequality (4.2a) to obtain a family confidence coefficient of at least $1 - \alpha$ for estimating β_0 and β_1. We do this by estimating β_0 and β_1 separately with statement confidence coefficients of $1 - \alpha/2$ each. This yields the Bonferroni bound $1 - \alpha/2 - \alpha/2 = 1 - \alpha$. Thus, the $1 - \alpha$ family confidence limits for β_0 and β_1 for regression model (2.1) by the Bonferroni procedure are:

$$b_0 \pm Bs\{b_0\} \qquad b_1 \pm Bs\{b_1\} \qquad \text{(4.3)}$$

where:

$$B = t(1 - \alpha/4; n - 2) \qquad \text{(4.3a)}$$

and b_0, b_1, $s\{b_0\}$, and $s\{b_1\}$ are defined in (1.10), (2.9), and (2.23). Note that a statement confidence coefficient of $1 - \alpha/2$ requires the $(1 - \alpha/4)100$ percentile of the t distribution for a two-sided confidence interval.

Example

For the Toluca Company example, 90 percent family confidence intervals for β_0 and β_1 require $B = t(1 - .10/4; 23) = t(.975; 23) = 2.069$. We have from Chapter 2:

$$b_0 = 62.37 \qquad s\{b_0\} = 26.18$$
$$b_1 = 3.5702 \qquad s\{b_1\} = .3470$$

Hence, the respective confidence limits for β_0 and β_1 are $62.37 \pm 2.069(26.18)$ and $3.5702 \pm 2.069(.3470)$, and the joint confidence intervals are:

$$8.20 \leq \beta_0 \leq 116.5$$
$$2.85 \leq \beta_1 \leq 4.29$$

Thus, we conclude that β_0 is between 8.20 and 116.5 *and* β_1 is between 2.85 and 4.29. The family confidence coefficient is at least .90 that the procedure leads to correct pairs of interval estimates.

Comments

1. We reiterate that the Bonferroni $1 - \alpha$ family confidence coefficient is actually a lower bound on the true (but often unknown) family confidence coefficient. To the extent that incorrect interval estimates of β_0 and β_1 tend to pair up in the family, the families of statements will tend to be correct more than $(1 - \alpha)100$ percent of the time. Because of this conservative nature of the Bonferroni procedure, family confidence coefficients are frequently specified at lower levels (e.g., 90 percent) than when a single estimate is made.

2. The Bonferroni inequality (4.2a) can easily be extended to g simultaneous confidence intervals with family confidence coefficient $1 - \alpha$:

$$P\left(\bigcap_{i=1}^{g} \bar{A}_i\right) \geq 1 - g\alpha \qquad \text{(4.4)}$$

Thus, if g interval estimates are desired with family confidence coefficient $1 - \alpha$, constructing each interval estimate with statement confidence coefficient $1 - \alpha/g$ will suffice.

3. For a given family confidence coefficient, the larger the number of confidence intervals in the family, the greater becomes the multiple B, which may make some or all of the confidence intervals too wide to be helpful. The Bonferroni technique is ordinarily most useful when the number of simultaneous estimates is not too large.

4. It is not necessary with the Bonferroni procedure that the confidence intervals have the same statement confidence coefficient. Different statement confidence coefficients, depending on the importance of each estimate, can be used. For instance, in our earlier illustration β_0 might be estimated with a 92 percent confidence interval and β_1 with a 98 percent confidence interval. The family confidence coefficient by (4.2) will still be at least 90 percent.

5. Joint confidence intervals can be used directly for testing. To illustrate this use, an industrial engineer working for the Toluca Company theorized that the regression function should have an intercept of 30.0 and a slope of 2.50. Although 30.0 falls in the confidence interval for β_0, 2.50 does not fall in the confidence interval for β_1. Thus, the engineer's theoretical expectations are not correct at the $\alpha = .10$ family level of significance.

6. The estimators b_0 and b_1 are usually correlated, but the Bonferroni simultaneous confidence limits in (4.3) only recognize this correlation by means of the bound on the family confidence coefficient. It can be shown that the covariance between b_0 and b_1 is:

$$\sigma\{b_0, b_1\} = -\bar{X}\sigma^2\{b_1\} \tag{4.5}$$

Note that if $\bar{X}$ is positive, b_0 and b_1 are negatively correlated, implying that if the estimate b_1 is too high, the estimate b_0 is likely to be too low, and vice versa.

In the Toluca Company example, $\bar{X} = 70.00$; hence the covariance between b_0 and b_1 is negative. This implies that the estimators b_0 and b_1 here tend to err in opposite directions. We expect this intuitively. Since the observed points (X_i, Y_i) fall in the first quadrant (see Figure 1.10a), we anticipate that if the slope of the fitted regression line is too steep (b_1 overestimates β_1), the intercept is most likely to be too low (b_0 underestimates β_0), and vice versa.

When the independent variable is $X_i - \bar{X}$, as in the alternative model (1.6), b_0^* and b_1 are uncorrelated according to (4.5) because the mean of the $X_i - \bar{X}$ observations is zero. ∎

4.2 Simultaneous Estimation of Mean Responses

Often the mean responses at a number of X levels need to be estimated from the same sample data. The Toluca Company, for instance, needed to estimate the mean number of work hours for lots of 30, 65, and 100 units in its search for the optimum lot size. We already know how to estimate the mean response for any one level of X with given statement confidence coefficient. Now we shall discuss two procedures for simultaneous estimation of a number of different mean responses with a family confidence coefficient, so that there is a known assurance of all of the estimates of mean responses being correct. These are the Working-Hotelling and the Bonferroni procedures.

The reason why a family confidence coefficient is needed for estimating several mean responses even though all estimates are based on the same fitted regression line is that the separate interval estimates of $E\{Y_h\}$ at the different X_h levels need not all be correct or all be incorrect. The combination of sampling errors in b_0 and b_1 may be such that the interval estimates of $E\{Y_h\}$ will be correct over some range of X levels and incorrect elsewhere.

Working-Hotelling Procedure

The Working-Hotelling procedure is based on the confidence band for the regression line discussed in Section 2.6. The confidence band in (2.40) contains the entire regression line and therefore contains the mean responses at all X levels. Hence, we can use the boundary values of the confidence band at selected X levels as simultaneous estimates of the mean responses at these X levels. The family confidence coefficient for these simultaneous estimates will be at least $1 - \alpha$ because the confidence coefficient that the entire confidence band for the regression line is correct is $1 - \alpha$.

The Working-Hotelling procedure for obtaining simultaneous confidence intervals for the mean responses at selected X levels is therefore simply to use the boundary values in (2.40) for the X levels of interest. The simultaneous confidence limits for g mean responses $E\{Y_h\}$ for regression model (2.1) with the Working-Hotelling procedure therefore are:

$$\hat{Y}_h \pm Ws\{\hat{Y}_h\} \tag{4.6}$$

where:

$$W^2 = 2F(1 - \alpha; 2, n - 2) \tag{4.6a}$$

and $\hat{Y}_h$ and $s\{\hat{Y}_h\}$ are defined in (2.28) and (2.30), respectively.

Example

For the Toluca Company example, we require a family of estimates of the mean number of work hours at the following lot size levels: $X_h = 30, 65, 100$. The family confidence coefficient is to be .90. In Chapter 2 we obtained $\hat{Y}_h$ and $s\{\hat{Y}_h\}$ for $X_h = 65$ and 100. In similar fashion, we can obtain the needed results for lot size $X_h = 30$. We summarize the results here:

X_h	$\hat{Y}_h$	$s\{\hat{Y}_h\}$
30	169.5	16.97
65	294.4	9.918
100	419.4	14.27

For a family confidence coefficient of .90, we require $F(.90; 2, 23) = 2.549$. Hence:

$$W^2 = 2(2.549) = 5.098 \qquad W = 2.258$$

We can now obtain the confidence intervals for the mean number of work hours at $X_h = 30$, 65, and 100:

$$131.2 = 169.5 - 2.258(16.97) \leq E\{Y_h\} \leq 169.5 + 2.258(16.97) = 207.8$$

$$272.0 = 294.4 - 2.258(9.918) \leq E\{Y_h\} \leq 294.4 + 2.258(9.918) = 316.8$$

$$387.2 = 419.4 - 2.258(14.27) \leq E\{Y_h\} \leq 419.4 + 2.258(14.27) = 451.6$$

With family confidence coefficient .90, we conclude that the mean number of work hours required is between 131.2 and 207.8 for lots of 30 parts, between 272.0 and 316.8 for lots of 65 parts, and between 387.2 and 451.6 for lots of 100 parts. The family confidence coefficient .90 provides assurance that the procedure leads to all correct estimates in the family of estimates.

Bonferroni Procedure

The Bonferroni procedure, discussed earlier for simultaneous estimation of β_0 and β_1, is a completely general procedure. To construct a family of confidence intervals for mean responses at different X levels with this procedure, we calculate in each instance the usual confidence limits for a single mean response $E\{Y_h\}$ in (2.33), adjusting the statement confidence coefficient to yield the specified family confidence coefficient.

When $E\{Y_h\}$ is to be estimated for g levels X_h with family confidence coefficient $1 - \alpha$, the Bonferroni confidence limits for regression model (2.1) are:

$$\hat{Y}_h \pm Bs\{\hat{Y}_h\} \tag{4.7}$$

where:

$$B = t(1 - \alpha/2g; n - 2) \tag{4.7a}$$

and g is the number of confidence intervals in the family.

Example

For the Toluca Company example, the Bonferroni simultaneous estimates of the mean number of work hours for lot sizes $X_h = 30, 65$, and 100 with family confidence coefficient .90 require the same data as with the Working-Hotelling procedure. In addition, we require $B = t[1 - .10/2(3); 23] = t(.9833; 23) = 2.263$.

We thus obtain the following confidence intervals, with 90 percent family confidence coefficient, for the mean number of work hours for lot sizes $X_h = 30, 65$, and 100:

$$131.1 = 169.5 - 2.263(16.97) \leq E\{Y_h\} \leq 169.5 + 2.263(16.97) = 207.9$$
$$272.0 = 294.4 - 2.263(9.918) \leq E\{Y_h\} \leq 294.4 + 2.263(9.918) = 316.8$$
$$387.1 = 419.4 - 2.263(14.27) \leq E\{Y_h\} \leq 419.4 + 2.263(14.27) = 451.7$$

Comments

1. In this instance the Working-Hotelling confidence limits are slightly tighter than, or the same as, the Bonferroni limits. In other cases where the number of statements is small, the Bonferroni limits may be tighter. For larger families, the Working-Hotelling confidence limits will always be the tighter, since W in (4.6a) stays the same for any number of statements in the family whereas B in (4.7a) becomes larger as the number of statements increases. In practice, once the family confidence coefficient has been decided upon, one can calculate the W and B multiples to determine which procedure leads to tighter confidence limits.

2. Both the Working-Hotelling and Bonferroni procedures provide lower bounds to the actual family confidence coefficient.

3. The levels of the predictor variable for which the mean response is to be estimated are sometimes not known in advance. Instead, the levels of interest are determined as the analysis proceeds. This was the case in the Toluca Company example, where the lot size levels of interest were determined after analyses relating to other factors affecting the optimum lot size were completed. In such cases, it is better to use the Working-Hotelling procedure because the family for this procedure encompasses all possible levels of X. ∎

4.3 Simultaneous Prediction Intervals for New Observations

Now we consider the simultaneous predictions of g new observations on Y in g independent trials at g different levels of X. Simultaneous prediction intervals are frequently of interest. For instance, a company may wish to predict sales in each of its sales regions from a regression relation between region sales and population size in the region.

Two procedures for making simultaneous predictions will be considered here: the Scheffé and Bonferroni procedures. Both utilize the same type of limits as those for predicting a single observation in (2.36), and only the multiple of the estimated standard deviation is changed. The Scheffé procedure uses the F distribution, whereas the Bonferroni procedure uses the t distribution. The simultaneous prediction limits for g predictions with the Scheffé procedure with family confidence coefficient $1 - \alpha$ are:

$$\hat{Y}_h \pm S s\{\text{pred}\} \tag{4.8}$$

where:

$$S^2 = g F(1 - \alpha; g, n - 2) \tag{4.8a}$$

and $s\{\text{pred}\}$ is defined in (2.38). With the Bonferroni procedure, the $1 - \alpha$ simultaneous prediction limits are:

$$\hat{Y}_h \pm B s\{\text{pred}\} \tag{4.9}$$

where:

$$B = t(1 - \alpha/2g; n - 2) \tag{4.9a}$$

The S and B multiples can be evaluated in advance to see which procedure provides tighter prediction limits.

Example

The Toluca Company wishes to predict the work hours required for each of the next two lots, which will consist of 80 and 100 units. The family confidence coefficient is to be 95 percent. To determine which procedure will give tighter prediction limits, we obtain the S and B multiples:

$$S^2 = 2F(.95; 2, 23) = 2(3.422) = 6.844 \qquad S = 2.616$$
$$B = t[1 - .05/2(2); 23] = t(.9875; 23) = 2.398$$

We see that the Bonferroni procedure will yield somewhat tighter prediction limits. The needed estimates, based on earlier results, are (calculations not shown):

X_h	$\hat{Y}_h$	$s\{\text{pred}\}$	$B s\{\text{pred}\}$
80	348.0	49.91	119.7
100	419.4	50.87	122.0

The simultaneous prediction limits for the next two lots, with family confidence coefficient .95, when $X_h = 80$ and 100 then are:

$$228.3 = 348.0 - 119.7 \le Y_{h(\text{new})} \le 348.0 + 119.7 = 467.7$$
$$297.4 = 419.4 - 122.0 \le Y_{h(\text{new})} \le 419.4 + 122.0 = 541.4$$

With family confidence coefficient at least .95, we can predict that the work hours for the next two production runs will be within the above pair of limits. As we noted in Chapter 2, the prediction limits are very wide and may not be too useful for planning worker requirements.

Comments

1. Simultaneous prediction intervals for g new observations on Y at g different levels of X with a $1 - \alpha$ family confidence coefficient are wider than the corresponding single prediction intervals of (2.36). When the number of simultaneous predictions is not large, however, the difference in the width is only moderate. For instance, a single 95 percent prediction interval for the Toluca Company example would utilize a t multiple of $t(.975; 23) = 2.069$, which is only moderately smaller than the multiple $B = 2.398$ for two simultaneous predictions.

2. Note that both the B and S multiples for simultaneous predictions become larger as g increases. This contrasts with simultaneous estimation of mean responses where the B multiple becomes larger but not the W multiple. When g is large, both the B and S multiples for simultaneous predictions may become so large that the prediction intervals will be too wide to be useful. Other simultaneous estimation techniques might then be considered, as discussed in Reference 4.1.   ∎

4.4   Regression through Origin

Sometimes the regression function is known to be linear and to go through the origin at $(0, 0)$. This may occur, for instance, when X is units of output and Y is variable cost, so Y is zero by definition when X is zero. Another example is where X is the number of brands of beer stocked in a supermarket in an experiment (including some supermarkets with no brands stocked) and Y is the volume of beer sales in the supermarket.

Model

The normal error model for these cases is the same as regression model (2.1) except that $\beta_0 = 0$:

$$Y_i = \beta_1 X_i + \varepsilon_i \tag{4.10}$$

where:

β_1 is a parameter

X_i are known constants

ε_i are independent $N(0, \sigma^2)$

The regression function for model (4.10) is:

$$E\{Y\} = \beta_1 X \tag{4.11}$$

which is a straight line through the origin, with slope β_1.

Inferences

The least squares estimator of β_1 in regression model (4.10) is obtained by minimizing:

$$Q = \sum (Y_i - \beta_1 X_i)^2 \tag{4.12}$$

with respect to β_1. The resulting normal equation is:

$$\sum X_i(Y_i - b_1 X_i) = 0 \qquad \textbf{(4.13)}$$

leading to the point estimator:

$$b_1 = \frac{\sum X_i Y_i}{\sum X_i^2} \qquad \textbf{(4.14)}$$

The estimator b_1 in (4.14) is also the maximum likelihood estimator for the normal error regression model (4.10).

The fitted value $\hat{Y}_i$ for the ith case is:

$$\hat{Y}_i = b_1 X_i \qquad \textbf{(4.15)}$$

and the ith residual is defined, as usual, as the difference between the observed and fitted values:

$$e_i = Y_i - \hat{Y}_i = Y_i - b_1 X_i \qquad \textbf{(4.16)}$$

An unbiased estimator of the error variance σ^2 for regression model (4.10) is:

$$s^2 = MSE = \frac{\sum(Y_i - \hat{Y}_i)^2}{n-1} = \frac{\sum e_i^2}{n-1} \qquad \textbf{(4.17)}$$

The reason for the denominator $n-1$ is that only one degree of freedom is lost in estimating the single parameter in the regression function (4.11).

Confidence limits for β_1, $E\{Y_h\}$, and a new observation $Y_{h(\text{new})}$ for regression model (4.10) are shown in Table 4.1. Note that the t multiple has $n-1$ degrees of freedom here, the degrees of freedom associated with *MSE*. The results in Table 4.1 are derived in analogous fashion to the earlier results for regression model (2.1). Whereas for model (2.1) with an intercept we encounter terms $(X_i - \bar{X})^2$ or $(X_h - \bar{X})^2$, here we find X_i^2 and X_h^2 because of the regression through the origin.

Example

The Charles Plumbing Supplies Company operates 12 warehouses. In an attempt to tighten procedures for planning and control, a consultant studied the relation between number of work units performed (X) and total variable labor cost (Y) in the warehouses during a test period. A portion of the data is given in Table 4.2, columns 1 and 2, and the observations are shown as a scatter plot in Figure 4.1.

TABLE 4.1
Confidence Limits for Regression through Origin.

Estimate of	Estimated Variance	Confidence Limits	
β_1	$s^2\{b_1\} = \dfrac{MSE}{\sum X_i^2}$	$b_1 \pm ts\{b_1\}$	**(4.18)**
$E\{Y_h\}$	$s^2\{\hat{Y}_h\} = \dfrac{X_h^2 MSE}{\sum X_i^2}$	$\hat{Y}_h \pm ts\{\hat{Y}_h\}$	**(4.19)**
$Y_{h(\text{new})}$	$s^2\{\text{pred}\} = MSE\left(1 + \dfrac{X_h^2}{\sum X_i^2}\right)$	$\hat{Y}_h \pm ts\{\text{pred}\}$	**(4.20)**
		where: $t = t(1 - \alpha/2; n-1)$	

TABLE 4.2
Regression
through
Origin—
Warehouse
Example.

Warehouse i	(1) Work Units Performed X_i	(2) Variable Labor Cost (dollars) Y_i	(3) X_iY_i	(4) X_i^2	(5) $\hat{Y}_i$	(6) e_i
1	20	114	2,280	400	93.71	20.29
2	196	921	180,516	38,416	918.31	2.69
3	115	560	64,400	13,225	538.81	21.19
...	...	...	...	...	...	...
10	147	670	98,490	21,609	688.74	−18.74
11	182	828	150,696	33,124	852.72	−24.72
12	160	762	121,920	25,600	749.64	12.36
Total	1,359	6,390	894,714	190,963	6,367.28	22.72

FIGURE 4.1
Scatter Plot
and Fitted
Regression
through
Origin—
Warehouse
Example.

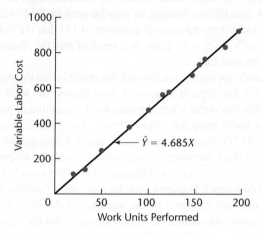

Model (4.10) for regression through the origin was employed since Y involves variable costs only and the other conditions of the model appeared to be satisfied as well. From Table 4.2, columns 3 and 4, we have $\sum X_iY_i = 894,714$ and $\sum X_i^2 = 190,963$. Hence:

$$b_1 = \frac{\sum X_iY_i}{\sum X_i^2} = \frac{894,714}{190,963} = 4.68527$$

and the estimated regression function is:

$$\hat{Y} = 4.68527X$$

In Table 4.2, the fitted values are shown in column 5, the residuals in column 6. The fitted regression line is plotted in Figure 4.1 and it appears to be a good fit.

An interval estimate of β_1 is desired with a 95 percent confidence coefficient. By squaring the residuals in Table 4.2, column 6, and then summing them, we obtain (calculations not shown):

$$s^2 = MSE = \frac{\sum e_i^2}{n-1} = \frac{2,457.6}{11} = 223.42$$

From Table 4.2, column 4, we have $\sum X_i^2 = 190{,}963$. Hence:

$$s^2\{b_1\} = \frac{MSE}{\sum X_i^2} = \frac{223.42}{190{,}963} = .0011700 \qquad s\{b_1\} = .034205$$

For a 95 percent confidence coefficient, we require $t(.975; 11) = 2.201$. The confidence limits, by (4.18) in Table 4.1, are $4.68527 \pm 2.201(.034205)$. The 95 percent confidence interval for β_1 therefore is:

$$4.61 \leq \beta_1 \leq 4.76$$

Thus, with 95 percent confidence, it is estimated that the mean variable labor cost increases by somewhere between \$4.61 and \$4.76 for each additional work unit performed.

Important Cautions for Using Regression through Origin

In using regression-through-the-origin model (4.10), the residuals must be interpreted with care because they do not sum to zero usually, as may be seen in Table 4.2, column 6, for the warehouse example. Note from the normal equation (4.13) that the only constraint on the residuals is of the form $\sum X_i e_i = 0$. Thus, in a residual plot the residuals will usually not be balanced around the zero line.

Another important caution for regression through the origin is that the sum of the squared residuals $SSE = \sum e_i^2$ for this type of regression may exceed the total sum of squares $SSTO = \sum (Y_i - \bar{Y})^2$. This can occur when the data form a curvilinear pattern or a linear pattern with an intercept away from the origin. Hence, the coefficient of determination in (2.72), $R^2 = 1 - SSE/SSTO$, may turn out to be negative. Consequently, the coefficient of determination R^2 has no clear meaning for regression through the origin.

Like any other statistical model, regression-through-the-origin model (4.10) needs to be evaluated for aptness. Even when it is known that the regression function must go through the origin, the function may not be linear or the variance of the error terms may not be constant. In many other cases, one cannot be sure in advance that the regression line goes through the origin. Hence, it is generally a safe practice not to use regression-through-the-origin model (4.10) and instead use the intercept regression model (2.1). If the regression line does go through the origin, b_0 with the intercept model will differ from 0 only by a small sampling error, and unless the sample size is very small use of the intercept regression model (2.1) has no disadvantages of any consequence. If the regression line does not go through the origin, use of the intercept regression model (2.1) will avoid potentially serious difficulties resulting from forcing the regression line through the origin when this is not appropriate.

Comments

1. In interval estimation of $E\{Y_h\}$ or prediction of $Y_{h(\text{new})}$ with regression through the origin, note that the intervals (4.19) and (4.20) in Table 4.1 widen the further X_h is from the origin. The reason is that the value of the true regression function is known precisely at the origin, so the effect of the sampling error in the slope b_1 becomes increasingly important the farther X_h is from the origin.

2. Since with regression through the origin only one parameter, β_1, must be estimated for regression function (4.11), simultaneous estimation methods are not required to make a family of statements about several mean responses. For a given confidence coefficient $1 - \alpha$, formula (4.19) in Table 4.1

can be used repeatedly with the given sample results for different levels of X to generate a family of statements for which the family confidence coefficient is still $1 - \alpha$.

3. Some statistical packages calculate R^2 for regression through the origin according to (2.72) and hence will sometimes show a negative value for R^2. Other statistical packages calculate R^2 using the total uncorrected sum of squares $SSTOU$ in (2.54). This procedure avoids obtaining a negative coefficient but lacks any meaningful interpretation.

4. The ANOVA tables for regression through the origin shown in the output for many statistical packages are based on $SSTOU = \sum Y_i^2$, $SSRU = \sum \hat{Y}_i^2 = b_1^2 \sum X_i^2$, and $SSE = \sum (Y_i - b_1 X_i)^2$, where $SSRU$ stands for the uncorrected regression sum of squares. It can be shown that these sums of squares are additive: $SSTOU = SSRU + SSE$. ∎

4.5 Effects of Measurement Errors

In our discussion of regression models up to this point, we have not explicitly considered the presence of measurement errors in the observations on either the response variable Y or the predictor variable X. We now examine briefly the effects of measurement errors in the observations on the response and predictor variables.

Measurement Errors in *Y*

When random measurement errors are present in the observations on the response variable Y, no new problems are created when these errors are uncorrelated and not biased (positive and negative measurement errors tend to cancel out). Consider, for example, a study of the relation between the time required to complete a task (Y) and the complexity of the task (X). The time to complete the task may not be measured accurately because the person operating the stopwatch may not do so at the precise instants called for. As long as such measurement errors are of a random nature, uncorrelated, and not biased, these measurement errors are simply absorbed in the model error term ε. The model error term always reflects the composite effects of a large number of factors not considered in the model, one of which now would be the random variation due to inaccuracy in the process of measuring Y.

Measurement Errors in *X*

Unfortunately, a different situation holds when the observations on the predictor variable X are subject to measurement errors. Frequently, to be sure, the observations on X are accurate, with no measurement errors, as when the predictor variable is the price of a product in different stores, the number of variables in different optimization problems, or the wage rate for different classes of employees. At other times, however, measurement errors may enter the value observed for the predictor variable, for instance, when the predictor variable is pressure in a tank, temperature in an oven, speed of a production line, or reported age of a person.

We shall use the last illustration in our development of the nature of the problem. Suppose we are interested in the relation between employees' piecework earnings and their ages. Let X_i denote the true age of the ith employee and X_i^* the age reported by the employee on the employment record. Needless to say, the two are not always the same. We define the measurement error δ_i as follows:

$$\delta_i = X_i^* - X_i \qquad (4.21)$$

The regression model we would like to study is:

$$Y_i = \beta_0 + \beta_1 X_i + \varepsilon_i \qquad (4.22)$$

However, we observe only X_i^*, so we must replace the true age X_i in (4.22) by the reported age X_i^*, using (4.21):

$$Y_i = \beta_0 + \beta_1(X_i^* - \delta_i) + \varepsilon_i \qquad (4.23)$$

We can now rewrite (4.23) as follows:

$$Y_i = \beta_0 + \beta_1 X_i^* + (\varepsilon_i - \beta_1 \delta_i) \qquad (4.24)$$

Model (4.24) may appear like an ordinary regression model, with predictor variable X^* and error term $\varepsilon - \beta_1\delta$, but it is not. The predictor variable observation X_i^* is a random variable, which, as we shall see, is correlated with the error term $\varepsilon_i - \beta_1\delta_i$.

Intuitively, we know that $\varepsilon_i - \beta_1\delta_i$ is not independent of X_i^* since (4.21) constrains $X_i^* - \delta_i$ to equal X_i. To determine the dependence formally, let us assume the following simple conditions:

$$E\{\delta_i\} = 0 \qquad (4.25a)$$

$$E\{\varepsilon_i\} = 0 \qquad (4.25b)$$

$$E\{\delta_i\varepsilon_i\} = 0 \qquad (4.25c)$$

Note that condition (4.25a) implies that $E\{X_i^*\} = E\{X_i + \delta_i\} = X_i$, so that in our example the reported ages would be unbiased estimates of the true ages. Condition (4.25b) is the usual requirement that the model error terms ε_i have expectation 0, balancing around the regression line. Finally, condition (4.25c) requires that the measurement error δ_i not be correlated with the model error ε_i; this follows because, by (A.21a), $\sigma\{\delta_i, \varepsilon_i\} = E\{\delta_i\varepsilon_i\}$ since $E\{\delta_i\} = E\{\varepsilon_i\} = 0$ by (4.25a) and (4.25b).

We now wish to find the covariance between the observations X_i^* and the random terms $\varepsilon_i - \beta_1\delta_i$ in model (4.24) under the conditions in (4.25), which imply that $E\{X_i^*\} = X_i$ and $E\{\varepsilon_i - \beta_1\delta_i\} = 0$:

$$\sigma\{X_i^*, \varepsilon_i - \beta_1\delta_i\} = E\{[X_i^* - E\{X_i^*\}][(\varepsilon_i - \beta_1\delta_i) - E\{\varepsilon_i - \beta_1\delta_i\}]\}$$
$$= E\{(X_i^* - X_i)(\varepsilon_i - \beta_1\delta_i)\}$$
$$= E\{\delta_i(\varepsilon_i - \beta_1\delta_i)\}$$
$$= E\left\{\delta_i\varepsilon_i - \beta_1\delta_i^2\right\}$$

Now $E\{\delta_i\varepsilon_i\} = 0$ by (4.25c), and $E\{\delta_i^2\} = \sigma^2\{\delta_i\}$ by (A.15a) because $E\{\delta_i\} = 0$ by (4.25a). We therefore obtain:

$$\sigma\{X_i^*, \varepsilon_i - \beta_1\delta_i\} = -\beta_1\sigma^2\{\delta_i\} \qquad (4.26)$$

This covariance is not zero whenever there is a linear regression relation between X and Y.

If we assume that the response Y and the random predictor variable X^* follow a bivariate normal distribution, then the conditional distribution of the $Y_i, i = 1, \ldots n$, given X_i^*,

$i = 1, \ldots n$, are normal and independent, with conditional mean $E\{Y_i|X_i^*\} = \beta_0^* + \beta_1^* X_i^*$ and conditional variance $\sigma_{Y|X^*}^2$. Furthermore, it can be shown that $\beta_1^* = \beta_1[\sigma_X^2/(\sigma_X^2 + \sigma_Y^2)]$, where σ_X^2 is the variance of X and σ_Y^2 is the variance of Y. Hence, the least squares slope estimate from fitting Y on X^* is not an estimate of β_1, but is an estimate of $\beta_1^* \leq \beta_1$. The resulting estimated regression coefficient of β_1^* will be too small on average, with the magnitude of the bias dependent upon the relative sizes of σ_X^2 and σ_Y^2. If σ_Y^2 is small relative to σ_X^2, then the bias would be small; otherwise the bias may be substantial. Discussion of possible approaches to estimating β_1^* that are obtained by estimating these unknown variances σ_X^2 and σ_Y^2 will be found in specialized texts such as Reference 4.2.

Another approach is to use additional variables that are known to be related to the true value of X but not to the errors of measurement δ. Such variables are called *instrumental variables* because they are used as an instrument in studying the relation between X and Y. Instrumental variables make it possible to obtain consistent estimators of the regression parameters. Again, the reader is referred to Reference 4.2.

Comment

What, it may be asked, is the distinction between the case when X is a random variable, considered in Chapter 2, and the case when X is subject to random measurement errors, and why are there special problems with the latter? When X is a random variable, the observations on X are not under the control of the analyst and will vary at random from trial to trial, as when X is the number of persons entering a store in a day. If this random variable X is not subject to measurement errors, however, it can be accurately ascertained for a given trial. Thus, if there are no measurement errors in counting the number of persons entering a store in a day, the analyst has accurate information to study the relation between number of persons entering the store and sales, even though the levels of number of persons entering the store that actually occur cannot be controlled. If, on the other hand, measurement errors are present in the observed number of persons entering the store, a distorted picture of the relation between number of persons and sales will occur because the sales observations will frequently be matched against an incorrect number of persons. ∎

Berkson Model

There is one situation where measurement errors in X are no problem. This case was first noted by Berkson (Ref. 4.3). Frequently, in an experiment the predictor variable is set at a target value. For instance, in an experiment on the effect of room temperature on word processor productivity, the temperature may be set at target levels of $68°$ F, $70°$ F, and $72°$ F, according to the temperature control on the thermostat. The observed temperature X_i^* is fixed here, whereas the actual temperature X_i is a random variable since the thermostat may not be completely accurate. Similar situations exist when water pressure is set according to a gauge, or employees of specified ages according to their employment records are selected for a study.

In all of these cases, the observation X_i^* is a fixed quantity, whereas the unobserved true value X_i is a random variable. The measurement error is, as before:

$$\delta_i = X_i^* - X_i \tag{4.27}$$

Here, however, there is no constraint on the relation between X_i^* and δ_i, since X_i^* is a fixed quantity. Again, we assume that $E\{\delta_i\} = 0$.

Model (4.24), which we obtained when replacing X_i by $X_i^* - \delta_i$, is still applicable for the Berkson case:

$$Y_i = \beta_0 + \beta_1 X_i^* + (\varepsilon_i - \beta_1 \delta_i) \tag{4.28}$$

The expected value of the error term, $E\{\varepsilon_i - \beta_1 \delta_i\}$, is zero as before under conditions (4.25a) and (4.25b), since $E\{\varepsilon_i\} = 0$ and $E\{\delta_i\} = 0$. However, $\varepsilon_i - \beta_1 \delta_i$ is now uncorrelated with X_i^*, since X_i^* is a constant for the Berkson case. Hence, the following conditions of an ordinary regression model are met:

1. The error terms have expectation zero.
2. The predictor variable is a constant, and hence the error terms are not correlated with it.

Thus, least squares procedures can be applied for the Berkson case without modification, and the estimators b_0 and b_1 will be unbiased. If we can make the standard normality and constant variance assumptions for the errors $\varepsilon_i - \beta_1 \delta_i$, the usual tests and interval estimates can be utilized.

4.6   Inverse Predictions

At times, a regression model of Y on X is used to make a prediction of the value of X which gave rise to a new observation Y. This is known as an *inverse prediction*. We illustrate inverse predictions by two examples:

1. A trade association analyst has regressed the selling price of a product (Y) on its cost (X) for the 15 member firms of the association. The selling price $Y_{h(\text{new})}$ for another firm not belonging to the trade association is known, and it is desired to estimate the cost $X_{h(\text{new})}$ for this firm.

2. A regression analysis of the amount of decrease in cholesterol level (Y) achieved with a given dosage of a new drug (X) has been conducted, based on observations for 50 patients. A physician is treating a new patient for whom the cholesterol level should decrease by the amount $Y_{h(\text{new})}$. It is desired to estimate the appropriate dosage level $X_{h(\text{new})}$ to be administered to bring about the needed cholesterol decrease $Y_{h(\text{new})}$.

In inverse predictions, regression model (2.1) is assumed as before:

$$Y_i = \beta_0 + \beta_1 X_i + \varepsilon_i \tag{4.29}$$

The estimated regression function based on n observations is obtained as usual:

$$\hat{Y} = b_0 + b_1 X \tag{4.30}$$

A new observation $Y_{h(\text{new})}$ becomes available, and it is desired to estimate the level $X_{h(\text{new})}$ that gave rise to this new observation. A natural point estimator is obtained by solving (4.30) for X, given $Y_{h(\text{new})}$:

$$\hat{X}_{h(\text{new})} = \frac{Y_{h(\text{new})} - b_0}{b_1} \qquad b_1 \neq 0 \tag{4.31}$$

where $\hat{X}_{h(\text{new})}$ denotes the point estimator of the new level $X_{h(\text{new})}$. Figure 4.2 contains a representation of this point estimator for an example to be discussed shortly. It can be shown that the estimator $\hat{X}_{h(\text{new})}$ is the maximum likelihood estimator of $X_{h(\text{new})}$ for normal error regression model (2.1).

Approximate $1 - \alpha$ confidence limits for $X_{h(\text{new})}$ are:

$$\hat{X}_{h(\text{new})} \pm t(1 - \alpha/2;\, n - 2)s\{\text{pred}X\} \tag{4.32}$$

where:

$$s^2\{\text{pred}X\} = \frac{MSE}{b_1^2}\left[1 + \frac{1}{n} + \frac{(\hat{X}_{h(\text{new})} - \bar{X})^2}{\sum(X_i - \bar{X})^2}\right] \tag{4.32a}$$

Example

A medical researcher studied a new, quick method for measuring low concentration of galactose (sugar) in the blood. Twelve samples were used in the study containing known concentrations (X), with three samples at each of four different levels. The measured concentration (Y) was then observed for each sample. Linear regression model (2.1) was fitted with the following results:

$$n = 12 \qquad b_0 = -.100 \qquad b_1 = 1.017 \qquad MSE = .0272$$

$$s\{b_1\} = .0142 \qquad \bar{X} = 5.500 \qquad \bar{Y} = 5.492 \qquad \sum(X_i - \bar{X})^2 = 135$$

$$\hat{Y} = -.100 + 1.017X$$

The data and the estimated regression line are plotted in Figure 4.2.

The researcher first wished to make sure that there is a linear association between the two variables. A test of $H_0: \beta_1 = 0$ versus $H_a: \beta_1 \neq 0$, utilizing test statistic $t^* = b_1/s\{b_1\} = 1.017/.0142 = 71.6$, was conducted for $\alpha = .05$. Since $t(.975; 10) = 2.228$ and $|t^*| = 71.6 > 2.228$, it was concluded that $\beta_1 \neq 0$, or that a linear association exists between the measured concentration and the actual concentration.

The researcher now wishes to use the regression relation to ascertain the actual concentration $X_{h(\text{new})}$ for a new patient for whom the quick procedure yielded a measured concentration of $Y_{h(\text{new})} = 6.52$. It is desired to estimate $X_{h(\text{new})}$ by means of a 95 percent

FIGURE 4.2
Scatter Plot and Fitted Regression Line— Calibration Example.

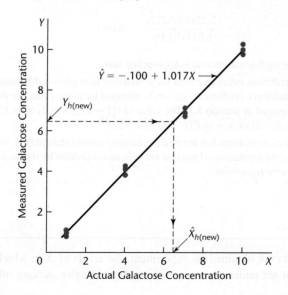

confidence interval. Using (4.31) and (4.32a), we obtain:

$$\hat{X}_{h(new)} = \frac{6.52 - (-.100)}{1.017} = 6.509$$

$$s^2\{predX\} = \frac{.0272}{(1.017)^2}\left[1 + \frac{1}{12} + \frac{(6.509 - 5.500)^2}{135}\right] = .0287$$

so that $s\{predX\} = .1694$. We require $t(.975; 10) = 2.228$, and using (4.32) we obtain the confidence limits $6.509 \pm 2.228(.1694)$. Hence, the 95 percent confidence interval is:

$$6.13 \le X_{h(new)} \le 6.89$$

Thus, it can be concluded with 95 percent confidence that the actual galactose concentration for the patient is between 6.13 and 6.89. This is approximately a ± 6 percent error, which is considered reasonable by the researcher.

Comments

1. The inverse prediction problem is also known as a *calibration problem* since it is applicable when inexpensive, quick, and approximate measurements (Y) are related to precise, often expensive, and time-consuming measurements (X) based on n observations. The resulting regression model is then used to estimate the precise measurement $X_{h(new)}$ for a new approximate measurement $Y_{h(new)}$. We illustrated this use in the calibration example.

2. The approximate confidence interval (4.32) is appropriate if the quantity:

$$\frac{[t(1 - \alpha/2; n - 2)]^2 MSE}{b_1^2 \sum(X_i - \bar{X})^2} \tag{4.33}$$

is small, say less than .1. For the calibration example, this quantity is:

$$\frac{(2.228)^2(.0272)}{(1.017)^2(135)} = .00097$$

so that the approximate confidence interval is appropriate here.

3. Simultaneous prediction intervals based on g different new observed measurements $Y_{h(new)}$, with a $1 - \alpha$ family confidence coefficient, are easily obtained by using either the Bonferroni or the Scheffé procedures discussed in Section 4.3. The value of $t(1 - \alpha/2; n - 2)$ in (4.32) is replaced by either $B = t(1 - \alpha/2g; n - 2)$ or $S = [g F(1 - \alpha; g, n - 2)]^{1/2}$.

4. The inverse prediction problem has aroused controversy among statisticians. Some statisticians have suggested that inverse predictions should be made in direct fashion by regressing X on Y. This regression is called *inverse regression*. ∎

4.7 Choice of X Levels

When regression data are obtained by experiment, the levels of X at which observations on Y are to be taken are under the control of the experimenter. Among other things, the experimenter will have to consider:

1. How many levels of X should be investigated?
2. What shall the two extreme levels be?
3. How shall the other levels of X, if any, be spaced?
4. How many observations should be taken at each level of X?

There is no single answer to these questions, since different purposes of the regression analysis lead to different answers. The possible objectives in regression analysis are varied, as we have noted earlier. The main objective may be to estimate the slope of the regression line or, in some cases, to estimate the intercept. In many cases, the main objective is to predict one or more new observations or to estimate one or more mean responses. When the regression function is curvilinear, the main objective may be to locate the maximum or minimum mean response. At still other times, the main purpose is to determine the nature of the regression function.

To illustrate how the purpose affects the design, consider the variances of b_0, b_1, $\hat{Y}_h$, and for predicting $Y_{h(\text{new})}$, which were developed earlier for regression model (2.1):

$$\sigma^2\{b_0\} = \sigma^2 \left[\frac{1}{n} + \frac{\bar{X}^2}{\sum(X_i - \bar{X})^2} \right] \tag{4.34}$$

$$\sigma^2\{b_1\} = \frac{\sigma^2}{\sum(X_i - \bar{X})^2} \tag{4.35}$$

$$\sigma^2\{\hat{Y}_h\} = \sigma^2 \left[\frac{1}{n} + \frac{(X_h - \bar{X})^2}{\sum(X_i - \bar{X})^2} \right] \tag{4.36}$$

$$\sigma^2\{\text{pred}\} = \sigma^2 \left[1 + \frac{1}{n} + \frac{(X_h - \bar{X})^2}{\sum(X_i - \bar{X})^2} \right] \tag{4.37}$$

If the main purpose of the regression analysis is to estimate the slope β_1, the variance of b_1 is minimized if $\sum(X_i - \bar{X})^2$ is maximized. This is accomplished by using two levels of X, at the two extremes for the scope of the model, and placing half of the observations at each of the two levels. Of course, if one were not sure of the linearity of the regression function, one would be hesitant to use only two levels since they would provide no information about possible departures from linearity. If the main purpose is to estimate the intercept β_0, the number and placement of levels does not affect the variance of b_0 as long as $\bar{X} = 0$. On the other hand, to estimate the mean response or to predict a new observation at the level X_h, the relevant variance is minimized by using X levels so that $\bar{X} = X_h$.

Although the number and spacing of X levels depends very much on the major purpose of the regression analysis, the general advice given by D. R. Cox is still relevant:

Use two levels when the object is primarily to examine whether or not . . . (the predictor variable) . . . has an effect and in which direction that effect is. Use three levels whenever a description of the response curve by its slope and curvature is likely to be adequate; this should cover most cases. Use four levels if further examination of the shape of the response curve is important. Use more than four levels when it is required to estimate the detailed shape of the response curve, or when the curve is expected to rise to an asymptotic value, or in general to show features not adequately described by slope and curvature. Except in these last cases it is generally satisfactory to use equally spaced levels with equal numbers of observations per level (Ref. 4.4).

Cited References

4.1. Miller, R. G., Jr. *Simultaneous Statistical Inference*. 2nd ed. New York: Springer-Verlag, 1991.

4.2. Fuller, W. A. *Measurement Error Models*. New York: John Wiley & Sons, 1987.

4.3. Berkson, J. "Are There Two Regressions?" *Journal of the American Statistical Association* 45 (1950), pp. 164–80.

4.4. Cox, D. R. *Planning of Experiments*. New York: John Wiley & Sons, 1958, pp. 141–42.

Problems

4.1. When joint confidence intervals for β_0 and β_1 are developed by the Bonferroni method with a family confidence coefficient of 90 percent, does this imply that 10 percent of the time the confidence interval for β_0 will be incorrect? That 5 percent of the time the confidence interval for β_0 will be incorrect and 5 percent of the time that for β_1 will be incorrect? Discuss.

4.2. Refer to Problem 2.1. Suppose the student combines the two confidence intervals into a confidence set. What can you say about the family confidence coefficient for this set?

*4.3. Refer to **Copier maintenance** Problem 1.20.

   a. Will b_0 and b_1 tend to err in the same direction or in opposite directions here? Explain.

   b. Obtain Bonferroni joint confidence intervals for β_0 and β_1, using a 95 percent family confidence coefficient.

   c. A consultant has suggested that β_0 should be 0 and β_1 should equal 14.0. Do your joint confidence intervals in part (b) support this view?

*4.4. Refer to **Airfreight breakage** Problem 1.21.

   a. Will b_0 and b_1 tend to err in the same direction or in opposite directions here? Explain.

   b. Obtain Bonferroni joint confidence intervals for β_0 and β_1, using a 99 percent family confidence coefficient. Interpret your confidence intervals.

4.5. Refer to **Plastic hardness** Problem 1.22.

   a. Obtain Bonferroni joint confidence intervals for β_0 and β_1, using a 90 percent family confidence coefficient. Interpret your confidence intervals.

   b. Are b_0 and b_1 positively or negatively correlated here? Is this reflected in your joint confidence intervals in part (a)?

   c. What is the meaning of the family confidence coefficient in part (a)?

*4.6. Refer to **Muscle mass** Problem 1.27.

   a. Obtain Bonferroni joint confidence intervals for β_0 and β_1, using a 99 percent family confidence coefficient. Interpret your confidence intervals.

   b. Will b_0 and b_1 tend to err in the same direction or in opposite directions here? Explain.

   c. A researcher has suggested that β_0 should equal approximately 160 and that β_1 should be between -1.9 and -1.5. Do the joint confidence intervals in part (a) support this expectation?

*4.7. Refer to **Copier maintenance** Problem 1.20.

   a. Estimate the expected number of minutes spent when there are 3, 5, and 7 copiers to be serviced, respectively. Use interval estimates with a 90 percent family confidence coefficient based on the Working-Hotelling procedure.

   b. Two service calls for preventive maintenance are scheduled in which the numbers of copiers to be serviced are 4 and 7, respectively. A family of prediction intervals for the times to be spent on these calls is desired with a 90 percent family confidence coefficient. Which procedure, Scheffé or Bonferroni, will provide tighter prediction limits here?

   c. Obtain the family of prediction intervals required in part (b), using the more efficient procedure.

*4.8. Refer to **Airfreight breakage** Problem 1.21.

    a. It is desired to obtain interval estimates of the mean number of broken ampules when there are 0, 1, and 2 transfers for a shipment, using a 95 percent family confidence coefficient. Obtain the desired confidence intervals, using the Working-Hotelling procedure.

    b. Are the confidence intervals obtained in part (a) more efficient than Bonferroni intervals here? Explain.

    c. The next three shipments will make 0, 1, and 2 transfers, respectively. Obtain prediction intervals for the number of broken ampules for each of these three shipments, using the Scheffé procedure and a 95 percent family confidence coefficient.

    d. Would the Bonferroni procedure have been more efficient in developing the prediction intervals in part (c)? Explain.

4.9. Refer to **Plastic hardness** Problem 1.22.

    a. Management wishes to obtain interval estimates of the mean hardness when the elapsed time is 20, 30, and 40 hours, respectively. Calculate the desired confidence intervals, using the Bonferroni procedure and a 90 percent family confidence coefficient. What is the meaning of the family confidence coefficient here?

    b. Is the Bonferroni procedure employed in part (a) the most efficient one that could be employed here? Explain.

    c. The next two test items will be measured after 30 and 40 hours of elapsed time, respectively. Predict the hardness for each of these two items, using the most efficient procedure and a 90 percent family confidence coefficient.

*4.10. Refer to **Muscle mass** Problem 1.27.

    a. The nutritionist is particularly interested in the mean muscle mass for women aged 45, 55, and 65. Obtain joint confidence intervals for the means of interest using the Working-Hotelling procedure and a 95 percent family confidence coefficient.

    b. Is the Working-Hotelling procedure the most efficient one to be employed in part (a)? Explain.

    c. Three additional women aged 48, 59, and 74 have contacted the nutritionist. Predict the muscle mass for each of these three women using the Bonferroni procedure and a 95 percent family confidence coefficient.

    d. Subsequently, the nutritionist wishes to predict the muscle mass for a fourth woman aged 64, with a family confidence coefficient of 95 percent for the four predictions. Will the three prediction intervals in part (c) have to be recalculated? Would this also be true if the Scheffé procedure had been used in constructing the prediction intervals?

4.11. A behavioral scientist said, "I am never sure whether the regression line goes through the origin. Hence, I will not use such a model." Comment.

4.12. **Typographical errors.** Shown below are the number of galleys for a manuscript (X) and the total dollar cost of correcting typographical errors (Y) in a random sample of recent orders handled by a firm specializing in technical manuscripts. Since Y involves variable costs only, an analyst wished to determine whether regression-through-the-origin model (4.10) is appropriate for studying the relation between the two variables.

i:	1	2	3	4	5	6	7	8	9	10	11	12
X_i:	7	12	10	10	14	25	30	25	18	10	4	6
Y_i:	128	213	191	178	250	446	540	457	324	177	75	107

    a. Fit regression model (4.10) and state the estimated regression function.

b. Plot the estimated regression function and the data. Does a linear regression function through the origin appear to provide a good fit here? Comment.

c. In estimating costs of handling prospective orders, management has used a standard of $17.50 per galley for the cost of correcting typographical errors. Test whether or not this standard should be revised; use $\alpha = .02$. State the alternatives, decision rule, and conclusion.

d. Obtain a prediction interval for the correction cost on a forthcoming job involving 10 galleys. Use a confidence coefficient of 98 percent.

4.13. Refer to **Typographical errors** Problem 4.12.

a. Obtain the residuals e_i. Do they sum to zero? Plot the residuals against the fitted values $\hat{Y}_i$. What conclusions can be drawn from your plot?

b. Conduct a formal test for lack of fit of linear regression through the origin; use $\alpha = .01$. State the alternatives, decision rule, and conclusion. What is the P-value of the test?

4.14. Refer to **Grade point average** Problem 1.19. Assume that linear regression through the origin model (4.10) is appropriate.

a. Fit regression model (4.10) and state the estimated regression function.

b. Estimate β_1 with a 95 percent confidence interval. Interpret your interval estimate.

c. Estimate the mean freshman GPA for students whose ACT test score is 30. Use a 95 percent confidence interval.

4.15. Refer to **Grade point average** Problem 4.14.

a. Plot the fitted regression line and the data. Does the linear regression function through the origin appear to be a good fit here?

b. Obtain the residuals e_i. Do they sum to zero? Plot the residuals against the fitted values $\hat{Y}_i$. What conclusions can be drawn from your plot?

c. Conduct a formal test for lack of fit of linear regression through the origin; use $\alpha = .005$. State the alternatives, decision rule, and conclusion. What is the P-value of the test?

*4.16. Refer to **Copier maintenance** Problem 1.20. Assume that linear regression through the origin model (4.10) is appropriate.

a. Obtain the estimated regression function.

b. Estimate β_1 with a 90 percent confidence interval. Interpret your interval estimate.

c. Predict the service time on a new call in which six copiers are to be serviced. Use a 90 percent prediction interval.

*4.17. Refer to **Copier maintenance** Problem 4.16.

a. Plot the fitted regression line and the data. Does the linear regression function through the origin appear to be a good fit here?

b. Obtain the residuals e_i. Do they sum to zero? Plot the residuals against the fitted values $\hat{Y}_i$. What conclusions can be drawn from your plot?

c. Conduct a formal test for lack of fit of linear regression through the origin; use $\alpha = .01$. State the alternatives, decision rule, and conclusion. What is the P-value of the test?

4.18. Refer to **Plastic hardness** Problem 1.22. Suppose that errors arise in X because the laboratory technician is instructed to measure the hardness of the ith specimen (Y_i) at a prerecorded elapsed time (X_i), but the timing is imperfect so the true elapsed time varies at random from the prerecorded elapsed time. Will ordinary least squares estimates be biased here? Discuss.

4.19. Refer to **Grade point average** Problem 1.19. A new student earned a grade point average of 3.4 in the freshman year.

a. Obtain a 90 percent confidence interval for the student's ACT test score. Interpret your confidence interval.

b. Is criterion (4.33) as to the appropriateness of the approximate confidence interval met here?

4.20. Refer to **Plastic hardness** Problem 1.22. The measurement of a new test item showed 238 Brinell units of hardness.

a. Obtain a 99 percent confidence interval for the elapsed time before the hardness was measured. Interpret your confidence interval.

b. Is criterion (4.33) as to the appropriateness of the approximate confidence interval met here?

Exercises

4.21. When the predictor variable is so coded that $\bar{X} = 0$ and the normal error regression model (2.1) applies, are b_0 and b_1 independent? Are the joint confidence intervals for β_0 and β_1 then independent?

4.22. Derive an extension of the Bonferroni inequality (4.2a) for the case of three statements, each with statement confidence coefficient $1 - \alpha$.

4.23. Show that for the fitted least squares regression line through the origin (4.15), $\sum X_i e_i = 0$.

4.24. Show that $\hat{Y}$ as defined in (4.15) for linear regression through the origin is an unbiased estimator of $E\{Y\}$.

4.25. Derive the formula for $s^2\{\hat{Y}_h\}$ given in Table 4.1 for linear regression through the origin.

Projects

4.26. Refer to the **CDI** data set in Appendix C.2 and Project 1.43. Consider the regression relation of number of active physicians to total population.

a. Obtain Bonferroni joint confidence intervals for β_0 and β_1, using a 95 percent family confidence coefficient.

b. An investigator has suggested that β_0 should be -100 and β_1 should be .0028. Do the joint confidence intervals in part (a) support this view? Discuss.

c. It is desired to estimate the expected number of active physicians for counties with total population of $X = 500$, 1,000, 5,000 thousands with family confidence coefficient .90. Which procedure, the Working-Hotelling or the Bonferroni, is more efficient here?

d. Obtain the family of interval estimates required in part (c), using the more efficient procedure. Interpret your confidence intervals.

4.27. Refer to the **SENIC** data set in Appendix C.1 and Project 1.45. Consider the regression relation of average length of stay to infection risk.

a. Obtain Bonferroni joint confidence intervals for β_0 and β_1, using a 90 percent family confidence coefficient.

b. A researcher suggested that β_0 should be approximately 7 and β_1 should be approximately 1. Do the joint intervals in part (a) support this expectation? Discuss.

c. It is desired to estimate the expected hospital stay for persons with infection risks $X = 2, 3, 4, 5$ with family confidence coefficient .95. Which procedure, the Working-Hotelling or the Bonferroni, is more efficient here?

d. Obtain the family of interval estimates required in part (c), using the more efficient procedure. Interpret your confidence intervals.

Chapter 5

Matrix Approach to Simple Linear Regression Analysis

Matrix algebra is widely used for mathematical and statistical analysis. The matrix approach is practically a necessity in multiple regression analysis, since it permits extensive systems of equations and large arrays of data to be denoted compactly and operated upon efficiently.

In this chapter, we first take up a brief introduction to matrix algebra. (A more comprehensive treatment of matrix algebra may be found in specialized texts such as Reference 5.1.) Then we apply matrix methods to the simple linear regression model discussed in previous chapters. Although matrix algebra is not really required for simple linear regression, the application of matrix methods to this case will provide a useful transition to multiple regression, which will be taken up in Parts II and III.

Readers familiar with matrix algebra may wish to scan the introductory parts of this chapter and focus upon the later parts dealing with the use of matrix methods in regression analysis.

5.1 Matrices

Definition of Matrix

A matrix is a rectangular array of elements arranged in rows and columns. An example of a matrix is:

$$
\begin{array}{c}
 \\
\text{Row 1} \\
\text{Row 2} \\
\text{Row 3}
\end{array}
\begin{array}{cc}
\text{Column} & \text{Column} \\
1 & 2 \\
\left[\begin{array}{cc}
16{,}000 & 23 \\
33{,}000 & 47 \\
21{,}000 & 35
\end{array}\right]
\end{array}
$$

The *elements* of this particular matrix are numbers representing income (column 1) and age (column 2) of three persons. The elements are arranged by row (person) and column (characteristic of person). Thus, the element in the first row and first column (16,000) represents the income of the first person. The element in the first row and second column (23) represents the age of the first person. The *dimension* of the matrix is 3×2, i.e., 3 rows by

2 columns. If we wanted to present income and age for 1,000 persons in a matrix with the same format as the one earlier, we would require a $1,000 \times 2$ matrix.

Other examples of matrices are:

$$\begin{bmatrix} 1 & 0 \\ 5 & 10 \end{bmatrix} \quad \begin{bmatrix} 4 & 7 & 12 & 16 \\ 3 & 15 & 9 & 8 \end{bmatrix}$$

These two matrices have dimensions of 2×2 and 2×4, respectively. Note that in giving the dimension of a matrix, we always specify the number of rows first and then the number of columns. As in ordinary algebra, we may use symbols to identify the elements of a matrix:

$$\begin{array}{c} \quad\quad j = 1 \quad j = 2 \quad j = 3 \\ \begin{array}{c} i = 1 \\ i = 2 \end{array} \begin{bmatrix} a_{11} & a_{12} & a_{13} \\ a_{21} & a_{22} & a_{23} \end{bmatrix} \end{array}$$

Note that the first subscript identifies the row number and the second the column number. We shall use the general notation a_{ij} for the element in the ith row and the jth column. In our above example, $i = 1, 2$ and $j = 1, 2, 3$.

A matrix may be denoted by a symbol such as **A**, **X**, or **Z**. The symbol is in **boldface** to identify that it refers to a matrix. Thus, we might define for the above matrix:

$$\mathbf{A} = \begin{bmatrix} a_{11} & a_{12} & a_{13} \\ a_{21} & a_{22} & a_{23} \end{bmatrix}$$

Reference to the matrix **A** then implies reference to the 2×3 array just given.

Another notation for the matrix **A** just given is:

$$\mathbf{A} = [a_{ij}] \quad\quad i = 1, 2; j = 1, 2, 3$$

This notation avoids the need for writing out all elements of the matrix by stating only the general element. It can only be used, of course, when the elements of a matrix are symbols.

To summarize, a matrix with r rows and c columns will be represented either in full:

$$\mathbf{A} = \begin{bmatrix} a_{11} & a_{12} & \cdots & a_{1j} & \cdots & a_{1c} \\ a_{21} & a_{22} & \cdots & a_{2j} & \cdots & a_{2c} \\ \vdots & \vdots & & \vdots & & \vdots \\ a_{i1} & a_{i2} & \cdots & a_{ij} & \cdots & a_{ic} \\ \vdots & \vdots & & \vdots & & \vdots \\ a_{r1} & a_{r2} & \cdots & a_{rj} & \cdots & a_{rc} \end{bmatrix} \quad\quad (5.1)$$

or in abbreviated form:

$$\mathbf{A} = [a_{ij}] \quad\quad i = 1, \ldots, r; j = 1, \ldots, c$$

or simply by a boldface symbol, such as **A**.

Comments

1. Do not think of a matrix as a number. It is a set of elements arranged in an array. Only when the matrix has dimension 1×1 is there a single number in a matrix, in which case one *can* think of it interchangeably as either a matrix or a number.

2. The following is *not* a matrix:

$$\begin{bmatrix} & 14 & \\ & 8 & \\ 10 & & 15 \\ 9 & & 16 \end{bmatrix}$$

since the numbers are not arranged in columns and rows. ■

Square Matrix

A matrix is said to be square if the number of rows equals the number of columns. Two examples are:

$$\begin{bmatrix} 4 & 7 \\ 3 & 9 \end{bmatrix} \qquad \begin{bmatrix} a_{11} & a_{12} & a_{13} \\ a_{21} & a_{22} & a_{23} \\ a_{31} & a_{32} & a_{33} \end{bmatrix}$$

Vector

A matrix containing only one column is called a *column vector* or simply a *vector*. Two examples are:

$$\mathbf{A} = \begin{bmatrix} 4 \\ 7 \\ 10 \end{bmatrix} \qquad \mathbf{C} = \begin{bmatrix} c_1 \\ c_2 \\ c_3 \\ c_4 \\ c_5 \end{bmatrix}$$

The vector $\mathbf{A}$ is a 3×1 matrix, and the vector $\mathbf{C}$ is a 5×1 matrix.

A matrix containing only one row is called a *row vector*. Two examples are:

$$\mathbf{B}' = [15 \quad 25 \quad 50] \qquad \mathbf{F}' = [f_1 \quad f_2]$$

We use the prime symbol for row vectors for reasons to be seen shortly. Note that the row vector $\mathbf{B}'$ is a 1×3 matrix and the row vector $\mathbf{F}'$ is a 1×2 matrix.

A single subscript suffices to identify the elements of a vector.

Transpose

The transpose of a matrix $\mathbf{A}$ is another matrix, denoted by $\mathbf{A}'$, that is obtained by interchanging corresponding columns and rows of the matrix $\mathbf{A}$.

For example, if:

$$\underset{3\times2}{\mathbf{A}} = \begin{bmatrix} 2 & 5 \\ 7 & 10 \\ 3 & 4 \end{bmatrix}$$

then the transpose $\mathbf{A}'$ is:

$$\underset{2\times3}{\mathbf{A}'} = \begin{bmatrix} 2 & 7 & 3 \\ 5 & 10 & 4 \end{bmatrix}$$

Note that the first column of $\mathbf{A}$ is the first row of $\mathbf{A}'$, and similarly the second column of $\mathbf{A}$ is the second row of $\mathbf{A}'$. Correspondingly, the first row of $\mathbf{A}$ has become the first column of $\mathbf{A}'$, and so on. Note that the dimension of $\mathbf{A}$, indicated under the symbol $\mathbf{A}$, becomes reversed for the dimension of $\mathbf{A}'$.

As another example, consider:

$$\mathbf{C}_{3 \times 1} = \begin{bmatrix} 4 \\ 7 \\ 10 \end{bmatrix} \qquad \mathbf{C}'_{1 \times 3} = [4 \quad 7 \quad 10]$$

Thus, the transpose of a column vector is a row vector, and vice versa. This is the reason why we used the symbol $\mathbf{B}'$ earlier to identify a row vector, since it may be thought of as the transpose of a column vector $\mathbf{B}$.

In general, we have:

$$\mathbf{A}_{r \times c} = \begin{bmatrix} a_{11} & \cdots & a_{1c} \\ \vdots & & \vdots \\ a_{r1} & \cdots & a_{rc} \end{bmatrix} = [a_{ij}] \qquad i = 1, \ldots, r; j = 1, \ldots, c \qquad \text{(5.2)}$$

$$\underset{\substack{\text{Row} \quad \text{Column} \\ \text{index} \quad \text{index}}}{[a_{ij}]}$$

$$\mathbf{A}'_{c \times r} = \begin{bmatrix} a_{11} & \cdots & a_{r1} \\ \vdots & & \vdots \\ a_{1c} & \cdots & a_{rc} \end{bmatrix} = [a_{ji}] \qquad j = 1, \ldots, c; i = 1, \ldots, r \qquad \text{(5.3)}$$

$$\underset{\substack{\text{Row} \quad \text{Column} \\ \text{index} \quad \text{index}}}{[a_{ji}]}$$

Thus, the element in the ith row and the jth column in $\mathbf{A}$ is found in the jth row and ith column in $\mathbf{A}'$.

Equality of Matrices

Two matrices $\mathbf{A}$ and $\mathbf{B}$ are said to be equal if they have the same dimension and if all corresponding elements are equal. Conversely, if two matrices are equal, their corresponding elements are equal. For example, if:

$$\mathbf{A}_{3 \times 1} = \begin{bmatrix} a_1 \\ a_2 \\ a_3 \end{bmatrix} \qquad \mathbf{B}_{3 \times 1} = \begin{bmatrix} 4 \\ 7 \\ 3 \end{bmatrix}$$

then $\mathbf{A} = \mathbf{B}$ implies:

$$a_1 = 4 \qquad a_2 = 7 \qquad a_3 = 3$$

Similarly, if:

$$\mathbf{A}_{3 \times 2} = \begin{bmatrix} a_{11} & a_{12} \\ a_{21} & a_{22} \\ a_{31} & a_{32} \end{bmatrix} \qquad \mathbf{B}_{3 \times 2} = \begin{bmatrix} 17 & 2 \\ 14 & 5 \\ 13 & 9 \end{bmatrix}$$

then $\mathbf{A} = \mathbf{B}$ implies:

$$
\begin{array}{ll}
a_{11} = 17 & a_{12} = 2 \\
a_{21} = 14 & a_{22} = 5 \\
a_{31} = 13 & a_{32} = 9
\end{array}
$$

Regression Examples

In regression analysis, one basic matrix is the vector $\mathbf{Y}$, consisting of the n observations on the response variable:

$$
\underset{n \times 1}{\mathbf{Y}} = \begin{bmatrix} Y_1 \\ Y_2 \\ \vdots \\ Y_n \end{bmatrix} \tag{5.4}
$$

Note that the transpose $\mathbf{Y}'$ is the row vector:

$$
\underset{1 \times n}{\mathbf{Y}'} = [Y_1 \ Y_2 \ \cdots \ Y_n] \tag{5.5}
$$

Another basic matrix in regression analysis is the $\mathbf{X}$ matrix, which is defined as follows for simple linear regression analysis:

$$
\underset{n \times 2}{\mathbf{X}} = \begin{bmatrix} 1 & X_1 \\ 1 & X_2 \\ \vdots & \vdots \\ 1 & X_n \end{bmatrix} \tag{5.6}
$$

The matrix $\mathbf{X}$ consists of a column of 1s and a column containing the n observations on the predictor variable X. Note that the transpose of $\mathbf{X}$ is:

$$
\underset{2 \times n}{\mathbf{X}'} = \begin{bmatrix} 1 & 1 & \cdots & 1 \\ X_1 & X_2 & \cdots & X_n \end{bmatrix} \tag{5.7}
$$

The $\mathbf{X}$ matrix is often referred to as the *design matrix*.

5.2 Matrix Addition and Subtraction

Adding or subtracting two matrices requires that they have the same dimension. The sum, or difference, of two matrices is another matrix whose elements each consist of the sum, or difference, of the corresponding elements of the two matrices. Suppose:

$$
\underset{3 \times 2}{\mathbf{A}} = \begin{bmatrix} 1 & 4 \\ 2 & 5 \\ 3 & 6 \end{bmatrix} \qquad \underset{3 \times 2}{\mathbf{B}} = \begin{bmatrix} 1 & 2 \\ 2 & 3 \\ 3 & 4 \end{bmatrix}
$$

then:

$$
\underset{3 \times 2}{\mathbf{A} + \mathbf{B}} = \begin{bmatrix} 1+1 & 4+2 \\ 2+2 & 5+3 \\ 3+3 & 6+4 \end{bmatrix} = \begin{bmatrix} 2 & 6 \\ 4 & 8 \\ 6 & 10 \end{bmatrix}
$$

Similarly:

$$\mathbf{A} - \mathbf{B} = \begin{bmatrix} 1-1 & 4-2 \\ 2-2 & 5-3 \\ 3-3 & 6-4 \end{bmatrix} = \begin{bmatrix} 0 & 2 \\ 0 & 2 \\ 0 & 2 \end{bmatrix}$$

In general, if:

$$\underset{r \times c}{\mathbf{A}} = [a_{ij}] \qquad \underset{r \times c}{\mathbf{B}} = [b_{ij}] \qquad i = 1, \ldots, r; j = 1, \ldots, c$$

then:

$$\underset{r \times c}{\mathbf{A} + \mathbf{B}} = [a_{ij} + b_{ij}] \qquad \text{and} \qquad \underset{r \times c}{\mathbf{A} - \mathbf{B}} = [a_{ij} - b_{ij}] \tag{5.8}$$

Formula (5.8) generalizes in an obvious way to addition and subtraction of more than two matrices. Note also that $\mathbf{A} + \mathbf{B} = \mathbf{B} + \mathbf{A}$, as in ordinary algebra.

Regression Example

The regression model:

$$Y_i = E\{Y_i\} + \varepsilon_i \qquad i = 1, \ldots, n$$

can be written compactly in matrix notation. First, let us define the vector of the mean responses:

$$\underset{n \times 1}{\mathbf{E}\{\mathbf{Y}\}} = \begin{bmatrix} E\{Y_1\} \\ E\{Y_2\} \\ \vdots \\ E\{Y_n\} \end{bmatrix} \tag{5.9}$$

and the vector of the error terms:

$$\underset{n \times 1}{\boldsymbol{\varepsilon}} = \begin{bmatrix} \varepsilon_1 \\ \varepsilon_2 \\ \vdots \\ \varepsilon_n \end{bmatrix} \tag{5.10}$$

Recalling the definition of the observations vector $\mathbf{Y}$ in (5.4), we can write the regression model as follows:

$$\underset{n \times 1}{\mathbf{Y}} = \underset{n \times 1}{\mathbf{E}\{\mathbf{Y}\}} + \underset{n \times 1}{\boldsymbol{\varepsilon}}$$

because:

$$\begin{bmatrix} Y_1 \\ Y_2 \\ \vdots \\ Y_n \end{bmatrix} = \begin{bmatrix} E\{Y_1\} \\ E\{Y_2\} \\ \vdots \\ E\{Y_n\} \end{bmatrix} + \begin{bmatrix} \varepsilon_1 \\ \varepsilon_2 \\ \vdots \\ \varepsilon_n \end{bmatrix} = \begin{bmatrix} E\{Y_1\} + \varepsilon_1 \\ E\{Y_2\} + \varepsilon_2 \\ \vdots \\ E\{Y_n\} + \varepsilon_n \end{bmatrix}$$

Thus, the observations vector $\mathbf{Y}$ equals the sum of two vectors, a vector containing the expected values and another containing the error terms.

5.3 Matrix Multiplication

Multiplication of a Matrix by a Scalar

A *scalar* is an ordinary number or a symbol representing a number. In multiplication of a matrix by a scalar, every element of the matrix is multiplied by the scalar. For example, suppose the matrix **A** is given by:

$$\mathbf{A} = \begin{bmatrix} 2 & 7 \\ 9 & 3 \end{bmatrix}$$

Then 4**A**, where 4 is the scalar, equals:

$$4\mathbf{A} = 4 \begin{bmatrix} 2 & 7 \\ 9 & 3 \end{bmatrix} = \begin{bmatrix} 8 & 28 \\ 36 & 12 \end{bmatrix}$$

Similarly, $k\mathbf{A}$ equals:

$$k\mathbf{A} = k \begin{bmatrix} 2 & 7 \\ 9 & 3 \end{bmatrix} = \begin{bmatrix} 2k & 7k \\ 9k & 3k \end{bmatrix}$$

where k denotes a scalar.

If every element of a matrix has a common factor, this factor can be taken outside the matrix and treated as a scalar. For example:

$$\begin{bmatrix} 9 & 27 \\ 15 & 18 \end{bmatrix} = 3 \begin{bmatrix} 3 & 9 \\ 5 & 6 \end{bmatrix}$$

Similarly:

$$\begin{bmatrix} \dfrac{5}{k} & \dfrac{2}{k} \\ \dfrac{3}{k} & \dfrac{8}{k} \end{bmatrix} = \frac{1}{k} \begin{bmatrix} 5 & 2 \\ 3 & 8 \end{bmatrix}$$

In general, if $\mathbf{A} = [a_{ij}]$ and k is a scalar, we have:

$$k\mathbf{A} = \mathbf{A}k = [ka_{ij}] \tag{5.11}$$

Multiplication of a Matrix by a Matrix

Multiplication of a matrix by a matrix may appear somewhat complicated at first, but a little practice will make it a routine operation.

Consider the two matrices:

$$\mathbf{A}_{2\times2} = \begin{bmatrix} 2 & 5 \\ 4 & 1 \end{bmatrix} \qquad \mathbf{B}_{2\times2} = \begin{bmatrix} 4 & 6 \\ 5 & 8 \end{bmatrix}$$

The product **AB** will be a 2×2 matrix whose elements are obtained by finding the cross products of rows of **A** with columns of **B** and summing the cross products. For instance, to find the element in the first row and the first column of the product **AB**, we work with the first row of **A** and the first column of **B**, as follows:

$$
\begin{array}{c} \\ \text{Row 1} \\ \text{Row 2} \end{array}
\begin{array}{c} \mathbf{A} \\ \begin{bmatrix} \boxed{2 \quad 5} \\ 4 \quad 1 \end{bmatrix} \end{array}
\qquad
\begin{array}{c} \mathbf{B} \\ \begin{bmatrix} \boxed{4} \quad 6 \\ \boxed{5} \quad 8 \end{bmatrix} \\ \text{Col. 1 Col. 2} \end{array}
\qquad
\begin{array}{c} \mathbf{AB} \\ \text{Row 1} \begin{bmatrix} 33 \\ \; \end{bmatrix} \\ \text{Col. 1} \end{array}
$$

We take the cross products and sum:

$$2(4) + 5(5) = 33$$

The number 33 is the element in the first row and first column of the matrix **AB**.

To find the element in the first row and second column of **AB**, we work with the first row of **A** and the second column of **B**:

$$
\begin{array}{c} \\ \text{Row 1} \\ \text{Row 2} \end{array}
\begin{array}{c} \mathbf{A} \\ \begin{bmatrix} \boxed{2 \quad 5} \\ 4 \quad 1 \end{bmatrix} \end{array}
\qquad
\begin{array}{c} \mathbf{B} \\ \begin{bmatrix} 4 \quad \boxed{6} \\ 5 \quad \boxed{8} \end{bmatrix} \\ \text{Col. 1 Col. 2} \end{array}
\qquad
\begin{array}{c} \mathbf{AB} \\ \text{Row 1} \begin{bmatrix} 33 \quad 52 \\ \; \end{bmatrix} \\ \text{Col. 1 Col. 2} \end{array}
$$

The sum of the cross products is:

$$2(6) + 5(8) = 52$$

Continuing this process, we find the product **AB** to be:

$$\mathbf{AB}_{2\times 2} = \begin{bmatrix} 2 & 5 \\ 4 & 1 \end{bmatrix} \begin{bmatrix} 4 & 6 \\ 5 & 8 \end{bmatrix} = \begin{bmatrix} 33 & 52 \\ 21 & 32 \end{bmatrix}$$

Let us consider another example:

$$\mathbf{A}_{2\times 3} = \begin{bmatrix} 1 & 3 & 4 \\ 0 & 5 & 8 \end{bmatrix} \qquad \mathbf{B}_{3\times 1} = \begin{bmatrix} 3 \\ 5 \\ 2 \end{bmatrix}$$

$$\mathbf{AB}_{2\times 1} = \begin{bmatrix} 1 & 3 & 4 \\ 0 & 5 & 8 \end{bmatrix} \begin{bmatrix} 3 \\ 5 \\ 2 \end{bmatrix} = \begin{bmatrix} 26 \\ 41 \end{bmatrix}$$

When obtaining the product **AB**, we say that **A** is *postmultiplied* by **B** or **B** is *premultiplied* by **A**. The reason for this precise terminology is that multiplication rules for ordinary algebra do not apply to matrix algebra. In ordinary algebra, $xy = yx$. In matrix algebra, $\mathbf{AB} \neq \mathbf{BA}$ usually. In fact, even though the product **AB** may be defined, the product **BA** may not be defined at all.

In general, the product **AB** is defined only when the number of columns in **A** equals the number of rows in **B** so that there will be corresponding terms in the cross products. Thus, in our previous two examples, we had:

$$
\begin{array}{ccc}
& \text{Equal} & \\
\mathbf{A} & \searrow \mathbf{B} & = \mathbf{AB} \\
2 \times 2 & 2 \times 2 & 2 \times 2 \\
& \nearrow & \\
& \text{Dimension} & \\
& \text{of product} &
\end{array}
\qquad
\begin{array}{ccc}
& \text{Equal} & \\
\mathbf{A} & \searrow \mathbf{B} & = \mathbf{AB} \\
2 \times 3 & 3 \times 1 & 2 \times 1 \\
& \nearrow & \\
& \text{Dimension} & \\
& \text{of product} &
\end{array}
$$

Note that the dimension of the product **AB** is given by the number of rows in **A** and the number of columns in **B**. Note also that in the second case the product **BA** would not be defined since the number of columns in **B** is not equal to the number of rows in **A**:

$$\underset{\substack{\textbf{B} \\ 3 \times 1}}{\overset{\displaystyle \swarrow}{}} \overset{\text{Unequal}}{\underset{\substack{\textbf{A} \\ 2 \times 3}}{\overset{\displaystyle \searrow}{}}}$$

Here is another example of matrix multiplication:

$$\mathbf{AB} = \begin{bmatrix} a_{11} & a_{12} & a_{13} \\ a_{21} & a_{22} & a_{23} \end{bmatrix} \begin{bmatrix} b_{11} & b_{12} \\ b_{21} & b_{22} \\ b_{31} & b_{32} \end{bmatrix}$$

$$= \begin{bmatrix} a_{11}b_{11} + a_{12}b_{21} + a_{13}b_{31} & a_{11}b_{12} + a_{12}b_{22} + a_{13}b_{32} \\ a_{21}b_{11} + a_{22}b_{21} + a_{23}b_{31} & a_{21}b_{12} + a_{22}b_{22} + a_{23}b_{32} \end{bmatrix}$$

In general, if **A** has dimension $r \times c$ and **B** has dimension $c \times s$, the product **AB** is a matrix of dimension $r \times s$ whose element in the ith row and jth column is:

$$\sum_{k=1}^{c} a_{ik}b_{kj}$$

so that:

$$\mathbf{AB}_{r \times s} = \left[\sum_{k=1}^{c} a_{ik}b_{kj} \right] \qquad i = 1, \dots, r; \, j = 1, \dots, s \qquad (5.12)$$

Thus, in the foregoing example, the element in the first row and second column of the product **AB** is:

$$\sum_{k=1}^{3} a_{1k}b_{k2} = a_{11}b_{12} + a_{12}b_{22} + a_{13}b_{32}$$

as indeed we found by taking the cross products of the elements in the first row of **A** and second column of **B** and summing.

Additional Examples

1. $$\begin{bmatrix} 4 & 2 \\ 5 & 8 \end{bmatrix} \begin{bmatrix} a_1 \\ a_2 \end{bmatrix} = \begin{bmatrix} 4a_1 + 2a_2 \\ 5a_1 + 8a_2 \end{bmatrix}$$

2. $$\begin{bmatrix} 2 & 3 & 5 \end{bmatrix} \begin{bmatrix} 2 \\ 3 \\ 5 \end{bmatrix} = [2^2 + 3^2 + 5^2] = [38]$$

Here, the product is a 1×1 matrix, which is equivalent to a scalar. Thus, the matrix product here equals the number 38.

3. $$\begin{bmatrix} 1 & X_1 \\ 1 & X_2 \\ 1 & X_3 \end{bmatrix} \begin{bmatrix} \beta_0 \\ \beta_1 \end{bmatrix} = \begin{bmatrix} \beta_0 + \beta_1 X_1 \\ \beta_0 + \beta_1 X_2 \\ \beta_0 + \beta_1 X_3 \end{bmatrix}$$

Regression Examples

A product frequently needed is $\mathbf{Y}'\mathbf{Y}$, where $\mathbf{Y}$ is the vector of observations on the response variable as defined in (5.4):

$$
\mathbf{Y}'\mathbf{Y}_{1 \times 1} = [Y_1 \quad Y_2 \quad \cdots \quad Y_n] \begin{bmatrix} Y_1 \\ Y_2 \\ \vdots \\ Y_n \end{bmatrix} = [Y_1^2 + Y_2^2 + \cdots + Y_n^2] = \left[\sum Y_i^2 \right] \quad \textbf{(5.13)}
$$

Note that $\mathbf{Y}'\mathbf{Y}$ is a 1×1 matrix, or a scalar. We thus have a compact way of writing a sum of squared terms: $\mathbf{Y}'\mathbf{Y} = \sum Y_i^2$.

We also will need $\mathbf{X}'\mathbf{X}$, which is a 2×2 matrix, where $\mathbf{X}$ is defined in (5.6):

$$
\mathbf{X}'\mathbf{X}_{2 \times 2} = \begin{bmatrix} 1 & 1 & \cdots & 1 \\ X_1 & X_2 & \cdots & X_n \end{bmatrix} \begin{bmatrix} 1 & X_1 \\ 1 & X_2 \\ \vdots & \vdots \\ 1 & X_n \end{bmatrix} = \begin{bmatrix} n & \sum X_i \\ \sum X_i & \sum X_i^2 \end{bmatrix} \quad \textbf{(5.14)}
$$

and $\mathbf{X}'\mathbf{Y}$, which is a 2×1 matrix:

$$
\mathbf{X}'\mathbf{Y}_{2 \times 1} = \begin{bmatrix} 1 & 1 & \cdots & 1 \\ X_1 & X_2 & \cdots & X_n \end{bmatrix} \begin{bmatrix} Y_1 \\ Y_2 \\ \vdots \\ Y_n \end{bmatrix} = \begin{bmatrix} \sum Y_i \\ \sum X_i Y_i \end{bmatrix} \quad \textbf{(5.15)}
$$

5.4 Special Types of Matrices

Certain special types of matrices arise regularly in regression analysis. We consider the most important of these.

Symmetric Matrix

If $\mathbf{A} = \mathbf{A}'$, $\mathbf{A}$ is said to be symmetric. Thus, $\mathbf{A}$ below is symmetric:

$$
\mathbf{A}_{3 \times 3} = \begin{bmatrix} 1 & 4 & 6 \\ 4 & 2 & 5 \\ 6 & 5 & 3 \end{bmatrix} \qquad \mathbf{A}'_{3 \times 3} = \begin{bmatrix} 1 & 4 & 6 \\ 4 & 2 & 5 \\ 6 & 5 & 3 \end{bmatrix}
$$

A symmetric matrix necessarily is square. Symmetric matrices arise typically in regression analysis when we premultiply a matrix, say, $\mathbf{X}$, by its transpose, $\mathbf{X}'$. The resulting matrix, $\mathbf{X}'\mathbf{X}$, is symmetric, as can readily be seen from (5.14).

Diagonal Matrix

A diagonal matrix is a square matrix whose off-diagonal elements are all zeros, such as:

$$
\mathbf{A}_{3 \times 3} = \begin{bmatrix} a_1 & 0 & 0 \\ 0 & a_2 & 0 \\ 0 & 0 & a_3 \end{bmatrix} \qquad \mathbf{B}_{4 \times 4} = \begin{bmatrix} 4 & 0 & 0 & 0 \\ 0 & 1 & 0 & 0 \\ 0 & 0 & 10 & 0 \\ 0 & 0 & 0 & 5 \end{bmatrix}
$$

We will often not show all zeros for a diagonal matrix, presenting it in the form:

$$
\underset{3\times 3}{\mathbf{A}} =
\begin{bmatrix}
a_1 & & 0 \\
& a_2 & \\
0 & & a_3
\end{bmatrix}
\qquad
\underset{4\times 4}{\mathbf{B}} =
\begin{bmatrix}
4 & & & 0 \\
& 1 & & \\
& & 10 & \\
0 & & & 5
\end{bmatrix}
$$

Two important types of diagonal matrices are the identity matrix and the scalar matrix.

Identity Matrix. The identity matrix or unit matrix is denoted by $\mathbf{I}$. It is a diagonal matrix whose elements on the main diagonal are all 1s. Premultiplying or postmultiplying any $r \times r$ matrix $\mathbf{A}$ by the $r \times r$ identity matrix $\mathbf{I}$ leaves $\mathbf{A}$ unchanged. For example:

$$
\mathbf{IA} =
\begin{bmatrix}
1 & 0 & 0 \\
0 & 1 & 0 \\
0 & 0 & 1
\end{bmatrix}
\begin{bmatrix}
a_{11} & a_{12} & a_{13} \\
a_{21} & a_{22} & a_{23} \\
a_{31} & a_{32} & a_{33}
\end{bmatrix}
=
\begin{bmatrix}
a_{11} & a_{12} & a_{13} \\
a_{21} & a_{22} & a_{23} \\
a_{31} & a_{32} & a_{33}
\end{bmatrix}
$$

Similarly, we have:

$$
\mathbf{AI} =
\begin{bmatrix}
a_{11} & a_{12} & a_{13} \\
a_{21} & a_{22} & a_{23} \\
a_{31} & a_{32} & a_{33}
\end{bmatrix}
\begin{bmatrix}
1 & 0 & 0 \\
0 & 1 & 0 \\
0 & 0 & 1
\end{bmatrix}
=
\begin{bmatrix}
a_{11} & a_{12} & a_{13} \\
a_{21} & a_{22} & a_{23} \\
a_{31} & a_{32} & a_{33}
\end{bmatrix}
$$

Note that the identity matrix $\mathbf{I}$ therefore corresponds to the number 1 in ordinary algebra, since we have there that $1 \cdot x = x \cdot 1 = x$.

In general, we have for any $r \times r$ matrix $\mathbf{A}$:

$$
\mathbf{AI} = \mathbf{IA} = \mathbf{A} \tag{5.16}
$$

Thus, the identity matrix can be inserted or dropped from a matrix expression whenever it is convenient to do so.

Scalar Matrix. A scalar matrix is a diagonal matrix whose main-diagonal elements are the same. Two examples of scalar matrices are:

$$
\begin{bmatrix}
2 & 0 \\
0 & 2
\end{bmatrix}
\qquad
\begin{bmatrix}
k & 0 & 0 \\
0 & k & 0 \\
0 & 0 & k
\end{bmatrix}
$$

A scalar matrix can be expressed as $k\mathbf{I}$, where k is the scalar. For instance:

$$
\begin{bmatrix}
2 & 0 \\
0 & 2
\end{bmatrix}
= 2
\begin{bmatrix}
1 & 0 \\
0 & 1
\end{bmatrix}
= 2\mathbf{I}
$$

$$
\begin{bmatrix}
k & 0 & 0 \\
0 & k & 0 \\
0 & 0 & k
\end{bmatrix}
= k
\begin{bmatrix}
1 & 0 & 0 \\
0 & 1 & 0 \\
0 & 0 & 1
\end{bmatrix}
= k\mathbf{I}
$$

Multiplying an $r \times r$ matrix $\mathbf{A}$ by the $r \times r$ scalar matrix $k\mathbf{I}$ is equivalent to multiplying $\mathbf{A}$ by the scalar k.

Vector and Matrix with All Elements Unity

A column vector with all elements 1 will be denoted by **1**:

$$\mathbf{1}_{r \times 1} = \begin{bmatrix} 1 \\ 1 \\ \vdots \\ 1 \end{bmatrix} \tag{5.17}$$

and a square matrix with all elements 1 will be denoted by **J**:

$$\mathbf{J}_{r \times r} = \begin{bmatrix} 1 & \cdots & 1 \\ \vdots & & \vdots \\ 1 & \cdots & 1 \end{bmatrix} \tag{5.18}$$

For instance, we have:

$$\mathbf{1}_{3 \times 1} = \begin{bmatrix} 1 \\ 1 \\ 1 \end{bmatrix} \qquad \mathbf{J}_{3 \times 3} = \begin{bmatrix} 1 & 1 & 1 \\ 1 & 1 & 1 \\ 1 & 1 & 1 \end{bmatrix}$$

Note that for an $n \times 1$ vector **1** we obtain:

$$\mathbf{1}'\mathbf{1}_{1 \times 1} = \begin{bmatrix} 1 & \cdots & 1 \end{bmatrix} \begin{bmatrix} 1 \\ \vdots \\ 1 \end{bmatrix} = [n] = n$$

and:

$$\mathbf{1}\mathbf{1}'_{n \times n} = \begin{bmatrix} 1 \\ \vdots \\ 1 \end{bmatrix} \begin{bmatrix} 1 & \cdots & 1 \end{bmatrix} = \begin{bmatrix} 1 & \cdots & 1 \\ \vdots & & \vdots \\ 1 & \cdots & 1 \end{bmatrix} = \mathbf{J}_{n \times n}$$

Zero Vector

A zero vector is a vector containing only zeros. The zero column vector will be denoted by **0**:

$$\mathbf{0}_{r \times 1} = \begin{bmatrix} 0 \\ 0 \\ \vdots \\ 0 \end{bmatrix} \tag{5.19}$$

For example, we have:

$$\mathbf{0}_{3 \times 1} = \begin{bmatrix} 0 \\ 0 \\ 0 \end{bmatrix}$$

5.5 Linear Dependence and Rank of Matrix

Linear Dependence

Consider the following matrix:

$$A = \begin{bmatrix} 1 & 2 & 5 & 1 \\ 2 & 2 & 10 & 6 \\ 3 & 4 & 15 & 1 \end{bmatrix}$$

Let us think now of the columns of this matrix as vectors. Thus, we view A as being made up of four column vectors. It happens here that the columns are interrelated in a special manner. Note that the third column vector is a multiple of the first column vector:

$$\begin{bmatrix} 5 \\ 10 \\ 15 \end{bmatrix} = 5 \begin{bmatrix} 1 \\ 2 \\ 3 \end{bmatrix}$$

We say that the columns of A are linearly dependent. They contain redundant information, so to speak, since one column can be obtained as a linear combination of the others.

We define the set of c column vectors $C_1, \ldots, C_c$ in an $r \times c$ matrix to be linearly dependent if one vector can be expressed as a linear combination of the others. If no vector in the set can be so expressed, we define the set of vectors to be linearly independent. A more general, though equivalent, definition is:

When c scalars $k_1, \ldots, k_c$, not all zero, can be found such that:

$$k_1 C_1 + k_2 C_2 + \cdots + k_c C_c = 0$$

where 0 denotes the zero column vector, the c column vectors are *linearly* **(5.20)** *dependent*. If the only set of scalars for which the equality holds is $k_1 = 0, \ldots, k_c = 0$, the set of c column vectors is *linearly independent*.

To illustrate for our example, $k_1 = 5$, $k_2 = 0$, $k_3 = -1$, $k_4 = 0$ leads to:

$$5 \begin{bmatrix} 1 \\ 2 \\ 3 \end{bmatrix} + 0 \begin{bmatrix} 2 \\ 2 \\ 4 \end{bmatrix} - 1 \begin{bmatrix} 5 \\ 10 \\ 15 \end{bmatrix} + 0 \begin{bmatrix} 1 \\ 6 \\ 1 \end{bmatrix} = \begin{bmatrix} 0 \\ 0 \\ 0 \end{bmatrix}$$

Hence, the column vectors are linearly dependent. Note that some of the k_j equal zero here. For linear dependence, it is only required that not all k_j be zero.

Rank of Matrix

The rank of a matrix is defined to be the maximum number of linearly independent columns in the matrix. We know that the rank of A in our earlier example cannot be 4, since the four columns are linearly dependent. We can, however, find three columns (1, 2, and 4) which are linearly independent. There are no scalars k_1, k_2, k_4 such that $k_1 C_1 + k_2 C_2 + k_4 C_4 = 0$ other than $k_1 = k_2 = k_4 = 0$. Thus, the rank of A in our example is 3.

The rank of a matrix is unique and can equivalently be defined as the maximum number of linearly independent rows. It follows that the rank of an $r \times c$ matrix cannot exceed $\min(r, c)$, the minimum of the two values r and c.

When a matrix is the product of two matrices, its rank cannot exceed the smaller of the two ranks for the matrices being multiplied. Thus, if $\mathbf{C} = \mathbf{AB}$, the rank of $\mathbf{C}$ cannot exceed $\min(\text{rank } \mathbf{A}, \text{rank } \mathbf{B})$.

5.6 Inverse of a Matrix

In ordinary algebra, the inverse of a number is its reciprocal. Thus, the inverse of 6 is $\frac{1}{6}$. A number multiplied by its inverse always equals 1:

$$6 \cdot \frac{1}{6} = \frac{1}{6} \cdot 6 = 1$$

$$x \cdot \frac{1}{x} = x \cdot x^{-1} = x^{-1} \cdot x = 1$$

In matrix algebra, the inverse of a matrix $\mathbf{A}$ is another matrix, denoted by $\mathbf{A}^{-1}$, such that:

$$\mathbf{A}^{-1}\mathbf{A} = \mathbf{A}\mathbf{A}^{-1} = \mathbf{I} \tag{5.21}$$

where $\mathbf{I}$ is the identity matrix. Thus, again, the identity matrix $\mathbf{I}$ plays the same role as the number 1 in ordinary algebra. An inverse of a matrix is defined only for square matrices. Even so, many square matrices do not have inverses. If a square matrix does have an inverse, the inverse is unique.

Examples

1. The inverse of the matrix:

$$\underset{2\times2}{\mathbf{A}} = \begin{bmatrix} 2 & 4 \\ 3 & 1 \end{bmatrix}$$

is:

$$\underset{2\times2}{\mathbf{A}^{-1}} = \begin{bmatrix} -.1 & .4 \\ .3 & -.2 \end{bmatrix}$$

since:

$$\mathbf{A}^{-1}\mathbf{A} = \begin{bmatrix} -.1 & .4 \\ .3 & -.2 \end{bmatrix} \begin{bmatrix} 2 & 4 \\ 3 & 1 \end{bmatrix} = \begin{bmatrix} 1 & 0 \\ 0 & 1 \end{bmatrix} = \mathbf{I}$$

or:

$$\mathbf{A}\mathbf{A}^{-1} = \begin{bmatrix} 2 & 4 \\ 3 & 1 \end{bmatrix} \begin{bmatrix} -.1 & .4 \\ .3 & -.2 \end{bmatrix} = \begin{bmatrix} 1 & 0 \\ 0 & 1 \end{bmatrix} = \mathbf{I}$$

2. The inverse of the matrix:

$$\underset{3\times3}{\mathbf{A}} = \begin{bmatrix} 3 & 0 & 0 \\ 0 & 4 & 0 \\ 0 & 0 & 2 \end{bmatrix}$$

is:

$$\underset{3\times3}{\mathbf{A}^{-1}} = \begin{bmatrix} \frac{1}{3} & 0 & 0 \\ 0 & \frac{1}{4} & 0 \\ 0 & 0 & \frac{1}{2} \end{bmatrix}$$

since:

$$\mathbf{A}^{-1}\mathbf{A} = \begin{bmatrix} \dfrac{1}{3} & 0 & 0 \\ 0 & \dfrac{1}{4} & 0 \\ 0 & 0 & \dfrac{1}{2} \end{bmatrix} \begin{bmatrix} 3 & 0 & 0 \\ 0 & 4 & 0 \\ 0 & 0 & 2 \end{bmatrix} = \begin{bmatrix} 1 & 0 & 0 \\ 0 & 1 & 0 \\ 0 & 0 & 1 \end{bmatrix} = \mathbf{I}$$

Note that the inverse of a diagonal matrix is a diagonal matrix consisting simply of the reciprocals of the elements on the diagonal.

Finding the Inverse

Up to this point, the inverse of a matrix $\mathbf{A}$ has been given, and we have only checked to make sure it is the inverse by seeing whether or not $\mathbf{A}^{-1}\mathbf{A} = \mathbf{I}$. But how does one find the inverse, and when does it exist?

An inverse of a square $r \times r$ matrix exists if the rank of the matrix is r. Such a matrix is said to be *nonsingular* or of *full rank*. An $r \times r$ matrix with rank less than r is said to be *singular* or *not of full rank,* and does not have an inverse. The inverse of an $r \times r$ matrix of full rank also has rank r.

Finding the inverse of a matrix can often require a large amount of computing. We shall take the approach in this book that the inverse of a 2×2 matrix and a 3×3 matrix can be calculated by hand. For any larger matrix, one ordinarily uses a computer to find the inverse, unless the matrix is of a special form such as a diagonal matrix. It can be shown that the inverses for 2×2 and 3×3 matrices are as follows:

1. If:

$$\underset{2\times2}{\mathbf{A}} = \begin{bmatrix} a & b \\ c & d \end{bmatrix}$$

then:

$$\underset{2\times2}{\mathbf{A}^{-1}} = \begin{bmatrix} a & b \\ c & d \end{bmatrix}^{-1} = \begin{bmatrix} \dfrac{d}{D} & \dfrac{-b}{D} \\ \dfrac{-c}{D} & \dfrac{a}{D} \end{bmatrix} \tag{5.22}$$

where:

$$D = ad - bc \tag{5.22a}$$

D is called the *determinant* of the matrix $\mathbf{A}$. If $\mathbf{A}$ were singular, its determinant would equal zero and no inverse of $\mathbf{A}$ would exist.

2. If:

$$\underset{3\times3}{\mathbf{B}} = \begin{bmatrix} a & b & c \\ d & e & f \\ g & h & k \end{bmatrix}$$

then:

$$\underset{3\times3}{\mathbf{B}^{-1}} = \begin{bmatrix} a & b & c \\ d & e & f \\ g & h & k \end{bmatrix}^{-1} = \begin{bmatrix} A & B & C \\ D & E & F \\ G & H & K \end{bmatrix} \tag{5.23}$$

where:

$$A = (ek - fh)/Z \qquad B = -(bk - ch)/Z \qquad C = (bf - ce)/Z$$

$$D = -(dk - fg)/Z \qquad E = (ak - cg)/Z \qquad F = -(af - cd)/Z \qquad \textbf{(5.23a)}$$

$$G = (dh - eg)/Z \qquad H = -(ah - bg)/Z \qquad K = (ae - bd)/Z$$

and:

$$Z = a(ek - fh) - b(dk - fg) + c(dh - eg) \qquad \textbf{(5.23b)}$$

Z is called the determinant of the matrix **B**.

Let us use (5.22) to find the inverse of:

$$\mathbf{A} = \begin{bmatrix} 2 & 4 \\ 3 & 1 \end{bmatrix}$$

We have:

$$\begin{array}{cc} a = 2 & b = 4 \\ c = 3 & d = 1 \end{array}$$

$$D = ad - bc = 2(1) - 4(3) = -10$$

Hence:

$$\mathbf{A}^{-1} = \begin{bmatrix} \dfrac{1}{-10} & \dfrac{-4}{-10} \\ \dfrac{-3}{-10} & \dfrac{2}{-10} \end{bmatrix} = \begin{bmatrix} -.1 & .4 \\ .3 & -.2 \end{bmatrix}$$

as was given in an earlier example.

When an inverse $\mathbf{A}^{-1}$ has been obtained by hand calculations or from a computer program for which the accuracy of inverting a matrix is not known, it may be wise to compute $\mathbf{A}^{-1}\mathbf{A}$ to check whether the product equals the identity matrix, allowing for minor rounding departures from 0 and 1.

Regression Example

The principal inverse matrix encountered in regression analysis is the inverse of the matrix $\mathbf{X'X}$ in (5.14):

$$\underset{2 \times 2}{\mathbf{X'X}} = \begin{bmatrix} n & \sum X_i \\ \sum X_i & \sum X_i^2 \end{bmatrix}$$

Using rule (5.22), we have:

$$\begin{array}{cc} a = n & b = \sum X_i \\ c = \sum X_i & d = \sum X_i^2 \end{array}$$

so that:

$$D = n \sum X_i^2 - \left(\sum X_i\right)\left(\sum X_i\right) = n\left[\sum X_i^2 - \frac{\left(\sum X_i\right)^2}{n}\right] = n \sum (X_i - \bar{X})^2$$

Hence:

$$(\mathbf{X'X})^{-1}_{2\times2} = \begin{bmatrix} \dfrac{\sum X_i^2}{n\sum(X_i - \bar{X})^2} & \dfrac{-\sum X_i}{n\sum(X_i - \bar{X})^2} \\[4mm] \dfrac{-\sum X_i}{n\sum(X_i - \bar{X})^2} & \dfrac{n}{n\sum(X_i - \bar{X})^2} \end{bmatrix} \tag{5.24}$$

Since $\sum X_i = n\bar{X}$ and $\sum(X_i - \bar{X})^2 = \sum X_i^2 - n\bar{X}^2$, we can simplify (5.24):

$$(\mathbf{X'X})^{-1}_{2\times2} = \begin{bmatrix} \dfrac{1}{n} + \dfrac{\bar{X}^2}{\sum(X_i - \bar{X})^2} & \dfrac{-\bar{X}}{\sum(X_i - \bar{X})^2} \\[4mm] \dfrac{-\bar{X}}{\sum(X_i - \bar{X})^2} & \dfrac{1}{\sum(X_i - \bar{X})^2} \end{bmatrix} \tag{5.24a}$$

Uses of Inverse Matrix

In ordinary algebra, we solve an equation of the type:

$$5y = 20$$

by multiplying both sides of the equation by the inverse of 5, namely:

$$\frac{1}{5}(5y) = \frac{1}{5}(20)$$

and we obtain the solution:

$$y = \frac{1}{5}(20) = 4$$

In matrix algebra, if we have an equation:

$$\mathbf{AY} = \mathbf{C}$$

we correspondingly premultiply both sides by $\mathbf{A}^{-1}$, assuming $\mathbf{A}$ has an inverse:

$$\mathbf{A}^{-1}\mathbf{AY} = \mathbf{A}^{-1}\mathbf{C}$$

Since $\mathbf{A}^{-1}\mathbf{AY} = \mathbf{IY} = \mathbf{Y}$, we obtain the solution:

$$\mathbf{Y} = \mathbf{A}^{-1}\mathbf{C}$$

To illustrate this use, suppose we have two simultaneous equations:

$$2y_1 + 4y_2 = 20$$
$$3y_1 + y_2 = 10$$

which can be written as follows in matrix notation:

$$\begin{bmatrix} 2 & 4 \\ 3 & 1 \end{bmatrix} \begin{bmatrix} y_1 \\ y_2 \end{bmatrix} = \begin{bmatrix} 20 \\ 10 \end{bmatrix}$$

The solution of these equations then is:

$$\begin{bmatrix} y_1 \\ y_2 \end{bmatrix} = \begin{bmatrix} 2 & 4 \\ 3 & 1 \end{bmatrix}^{-1} \begin{bmatrix} 20 \\ 10 \end{bmatrix}$$

Earlier we found the required inverse, so we obtain:

$$\begin{bmatrix} y_1 \\ y_2 \end{bmatrix} = \begin{bmatrix} -.1 & .4 \\ .3 & -.2 \end{bmatrix} \begin{bmatrix} 20 \\ 10 \end{bmatrix} = \begin{bmatrix} 2 \\ 4 \end{bmatrix}$$

Hence, $y_1 = 2$ and $y_2 = 4$ satisfy these two equations.

5.7   Some Basic Results for Matrices

We list here, without proof, some basic results for matrices which we will utilize in later work.

$$\mathbf{A} + \mathbf{B} = \mathbf{B} + \mathbf{A} \tag{5.25}$$

$$(\mathbf{A} + \mathbf{B}) + \mathbf{C} = \mathbf{A} + (\mathbf{B} + \mathbf{C}) \tag{5.26}$$

$$(\mathbf{AB})\mathbf{C} = \mathbf{A}(\mathbf{BC}) \tag{5.27}$$

$$\mathbf{C}(\mathbf{A} + \mathbf{B}) = \mathbf{CA} + \mathbf{CB} \tag{5.28}$$

$$k(\mathbf{A} + \mathbf{B}) = k\mathbf{A} + k\mathbf{B} \tag{5.29}$$

$$(\mathbf{A}')' = \mathbf{A} \tag{5.30}$$

$$(\mathbf{A} + \mathbf{B})' = \mathbf{A}' + \mathbf{B}' \tag{5.31}$$

$$(\mathbf{AB})' = \mathbf{B}'\mathbf{A}' \tag{5.32}$$

$$(\mathbf{ABC})' = \mathbf{C}'\mathbf{B}'\mathbf{A}' \tag{5.33}$$

$$(\mathbf{AB})^{-1} = \mathbf{B}^{-1}\mathbf{A}^{-1} \tag{5.34}$$

$$(\mathbf{ABC})^{-1} = \mathbf{C}^{-1}\mathbf{B}^{-1}\mathbf{A}^{-1} \tag{5.35}$$

$$(\mathbf{A}^{-1})^{-1} = \mathbf{A} \tag{5.36}$$

$$(\mathbf{A}')^{-1} = (\mathbf{A}^{-1})' \tag{5.37}$$

5.8   Random Vectors and Matrices

A random vector or a random matrix contains elements that are random variables. Thus, the observations vector $\mathbf{Y}$ in (5.4) is a random vector since the Y_i elements are random variables.

Expectation of Random Vector or Matrix

Suppose we have $n = 3$ observations in the observations vector $\mathbf{Y}$:

$$\mathbf{Y}_{3 \times 1} = \begin{bmatrix} Y_1 \\ Y_2 \\ Y_3 \end{bmatrix}$$

The expected value of $\mathbf{Y}$ is a vector, denoted by $\mathbf{E}\{\mathbf{Y}\}$, that is defined as follows:

$$\mathbf{E}\{\mathbf{Y}\}_{3 \times 1} = \begin{bmatrix} E\{Y_1\} \\ E\{Y_2\} \\ E\{Y_3\} \end{bmatrix}$$

Thus, the expected value of a random vector is a vector whose elements are the expected values of the random variables that are the elements of the random vector. Similarly, the expectation of a random matrix is a matrix whose elements are the expected values of the corresponding random variables in the original matrix. We encountered a vector of expected values earlier in (5.9).

In general, for a random vector $\mathbf{Y}$ the expectation is:

$$\underset{n \times 1}{\mathbf{E}\{\mathbf{Y}\}} = [E\{Y_i\}] \qquad i = 1, \ldots, n \tag{5.38}$$

and for a random matrix $\mathbf{Y}$ with dimension $n \times p$, the expectation is:

$$\underset{n \times p}{\mathbf{E}\{\mathbf{Y}\}} = [E\{Y_{ij}\}] \qquad i = 1, \ldots, n; j = 1, \ldots, p \tag{5.39}$$

Regression Example

Suppose the number of cases in a regression application is $n = 3$. The three error terms ε_1, ε_2, ε_3 each have expectation zero. For the error terms vector:

$$\underset{3 \times 1}{\boldsymbol{\varepsilon}} = \begin{bmatrix} \varepsilon_1 \\ \varepsilon_2 \\ \varepsilon_3 \end{bmatrix}$$

we have:

$$\underset{3 \times 1}{\mathbf{E}\{\boldsymbol{\varepsilon}\}} = \underset{3 \times 1}{\mathbf{0}}$$

since:

$$\begin{bmatrix} E\{\varepsilon_1\} \\ E\{\varepsilon_2\} \\ E\{\varepsilon_3\} \end{bmatrix} = \begin{bmatrix} 0 \\ 0 \\ 0 \end{bmatrix}$$

Variance-Covariance Matrix of Random Vector

Consider again the random vector $\mathbf{Y}$ consisting of three observations Y_1, Y_2, Y_3. The variances of the three random variables, $\sigma^2\{Y_i\}$, and the covariances between any two of the random variables, $\sigma\{Y_i, Y_j\}$, are assembled in the *variance-covariance matrix of* $\mathbf{Y}$, denoted by $\sigma^2\{\mathbf{Y}\}$, in the following form:

$$\sigma^2\{\mathbf{Y}\} = \begin{bmatrix} \sigma^2\{Y_1\} & \sigma\{Y_1, Y_2\} & \sigma\{Y_1, Y_3\} \\ \sigma\{Y_2, Y_1\} & \sigma^2\{Y_2\} & \sigma\{Y_2, Y_3\} \\ \sigma\{Y_3, Y_1\} & \sigma\{Y_3, Y_2\} & \sigma^2\{Y_3\} \end{bmatrix} \tag{5.40}$$

Note that the variances are on the main diagonal, and the covariance $\sigma\{Y_i, Y_j\}$ is found in the ith row and jth column of the matrix. Thus, $\sigma\{Y_2, Y_1\}$ is found in the second row, first column, and $\sigma\{Y_1, Y_2\}$ is found in the first row, second column. Remember, of course, that $\sigma\{Y_2, Y_1\} = \sigma\{Y_1, Y_2\}$. Since $\sigma\{Y_i, Y_j\} = \sigma\{Y_j, Y_i\}$ for all $i \neq j$, $\sigma^2\{\mathbf{Y}\}$ is a symmetric matrix.

It follows readily that:

$$\sigma^2\{\mathbf{Y}\} = \mathbf{E}\{[\mathbf{Y} - \mathbf{E}\{\mathbf{Y}\}][\mathbf{Y} - \mathbf{E}\{\mathbf{Y}\}]'\} \tag{5.41}$$

For our illustration, we have:

$$\sigma^2\{\mathbf{Y}\} = \mathbf{E}\left\{\begin{bmatrix} Y_1 - E\{Y_1\} \\ Y_2 - E\{Y_2\} \\ Y_3 - E\{Y_3\} \end{bmatrix} [Y_1 - E\{Y_1\} \quad Y_2 - E\{Y_2\} \quad Y_3 - E\{Y_3\}]\right\}$$

Multiplying the two matrices and then taking expectations, we obtain:

Location in Product	Term	Expected Value
Row 1, column 1	$(Y_1 - E\{Y_1\})^2$	$\sigma^2\{Y_1\}$
Row 1, column 2	$(Y_1 - E\{Y_1\})(Y_2 - E\{Y_2\})$	$\sigma\{Y_1, Y_2\}$
Row 1, column 3	$(Y_1 - E\{Y_1\})(Y_3 - E\{Y_3\})$	$\sigma\{Y_1, Y_3\}$
Row 2, column 1	$(Y_2 - E\{Y_2\})(Y_1 - E\{Y_1\})$	$\sigma\{Y_2, Y_1\}$
etc.	etc.	etc.

This, of course, leads to the variance-covariance matrix in (5.40). Remember the definitions of variance and covariance in (A.15) and (A.21), respectively, when taking expectations.

To generalize, the variance-covariance matrix for an $n \times 1$ random vector $\mathbf{Y}$ is:

$$\underset{n \times n}{\sigma^2\{\mathbf{Y}\}} = \begin{bmatrix} \sigma^2\{Y_1\} & \sigma\{Y_1, Y_2\} & \cdots & \sigma\{Y_1, Y_n\} \\ \sigma\{Y_2, Y_1\} & \sigma^2\{Y_2\} & \cdots & \sigma\{Y_2, Y_n\} \\ \vdots & \vdots & & \vdots \\ \sigma\{Y_n, Y_1\} & \sigma\{Y_n, Y_2\} & \cdots & \sigma^2\{Y_n\} \end{bmatrix} \tag{5.42}$$

Note again that $\sigma^2\{\mathbf{Y}\}$ is a symmetric matrix.

Regression Example

Let us return to the example based on $n = 3$ cases. Suppose that the three error terms have constant variance, $\sigma^2\{\varepsilon_i\} = \sigma^2$, and are uncorrelated so that $\sigma\{\varepsilon_i, \varepsilon_j\} = 0$ for $i \neq j$. The variance-covariance matrix for the random vector $\boldsymbol{\varepsilon}$ of the previous example is therefore as follows:

$$\underset{3 \times 3}{\sigma^2\{\boldsymbol{\varepsilon}\}} = \begin{bmatrix} \sigma^2 & 0 & 0 \\ 0 & \sigma^2 & 0 \\ 0 & 0 & \sigma^2 \end{bmatrix}$$

Note that all variances are σ^2 and all covariances are zero. Note also that this variance-covariance matrix is a scalar matrix, with the common variance σ^2 the scalar. Hence, we can express the variance-covariance matrix in the following simple fashion:

$$\underset{3 \times 3}{\sigma^2\{\boldsymbol{\varepsilon\}}} = \underset{3 \times 3}{\sigma^2 \mathbf{I}}$$

since:

$$\sigma^2 \mathbf{I} = \sigma^2 \begin{bmatrix} 1 & 0 & 0 \\ 0 & 1 & 0 \\ 0 & 0 & 1 \end{bmatrix} = \begin{bmatrix} \sigma^2 & 0 & 0 \\ 0 & \sigma^2 & 0 \\ 0 & 0 & \sigma^2 \end{bmatrix}$$

Some Basic Results

Frequently, we shall encounter a random vector $\mathbf{W}$ that is obtained by premultiplying the random vector $\mathbf{Y}$ by a constant matrix $\mathbf{A}$ (a matrix whose elements are fixed):

$$\mathbf{W} = \mathbf{AY} \tag{5.43}$$

Some basic results for this case are:

$$E\{\mathbf{A}\} = \mathbf{A} \tag{5.44}$$

$$E\{\mathbf{W}\} = E\{\mathbf{AY}\} = \mathbf{A}E\{\mathbf{Y}\} \tag{5.45}$$

$$\sigma^2\{\mathbf{W}\} = \sigma^2\{\mathbf{AY}\} = \mathbf{A}\sigma^2\{\mathbf{Y}\}\mathbf{A}' \tag{5.46}$$

where $\sigma^2\{\mathbf{Y}\}$ is the variance-covariance matrix of $\mathbf{Y}$.

Example

As a simple illustration of the use of these results, consider:

$$\underset{2\times 1}{\begin{bmatrix} W_1 \\ W_2 \end{bmatrix}} = \underset{2\times 2}{\begin{bmatrix} 1 & -1 \\ 1 & 1 \end{bmatrix}} \underset{2\times 1}{\begin{bmatrix} Y_1 \\ Y_2 \end{bmatrix}} = \begin{bmatrix} Y_1 - Y_2 \\ Y_1 + Y_2 \end{bmatrix}$$

$$\quad\quad \underset{2\times1}{\mathbf{W}} \quad\quad \underset{2\times2}{\mathbf{A}} \quad\quad \underset{2\times1}{\mathbf{Y}}$$

We then have by (5.45):

$$\underset{2\times1}{E\{\mathbf{W}\}} = \begin{bmatrix} 1 & -1 \\ 1 & 1 \end{bmatrix} \begin{bmatrix} E\{Y_1\} \\ E\{Y_2\} \end{bmatrix} = \begin{bmatrix} E\{Y_1\} - E\{Y_2\} \\ E\{Y_1\} + E\{Y_2\} \end{bmatrix}$$

and by (5.46):

$$\underset{2\times2}{\sigma^2\{\mathbf{W}\}} = \begin{bmatrix} 1 & -1 \\ 1 & 1 \end{bmatrix} \begin{bmatrix} \sigma^2\{Y_1\} & \sigma\{Y_1, Y_2\} \\ \sigma\{Y_2, Y_1\} & \sigma^2\{Y_2\} \end{bmatrix} \begin{bmatrix} 1 & 1 \\ -1 & 1 \end{bmatrix}$$

$$= \begin{bmatrix} \sigma^2\{Y_1\} + \sigma^2\{Y_2\} - 2\sigma\{Y_1, Y_2\} & \sigma^2\{Y_1\} - \sigma^2\{Y_2\} \\ \sigma^2\{Y_1\} - \sigma^2\{Y_2\} & \sigma^2\{Y_1\} + \sigma^2\{Y_2\} + 2\sigma\{Y_1, Y_2\} \end{bmatrix}$$

Thus:

$$\sigma^2\{W_1\} = \sigma^2\{Y_1 - Y_2\} = \sigma^2\{Y_1\} + \sigma^2\{Y_2\} - 2\sigma\{Y_1, Y_2\}$$

$$\sigma^2\{W_2\} = \sigma^2\{Y_1 + Y_2\} = \sigma^2\{Y_1\} + \sigma^2\{Y_2\} + 2\sigma\{Y_1, Y_2\}$$

$$\sigma\{W_1, W_2\} = \sigma\{Y_1 - Y_2, Y_1 + Y_2\} = \sigma^2\{Y_1\} - \sigma^2\{Y_2\}$$

Multivariate Normal Distribution

Density Function. The density function for the multivariate normal distribution is best given in matrix form. We first need to define some vectors and matrices. The observations vector **Y** containing an observation on each of the p Y variables is defined as usual:

$$\underset{p \times 1}{\mathbf{Y}} = \begin{bmatrix} Y_1 \\ Y_2 \\ \vdots \\ Y_p \end{bmatrix} \tag{5.47}$$

The mean vector $E\{\mathbf{Y}\}$, denoted by $\boldsymbol{\mu}$, contains the expected values for each of the p Y variables:

$$\underset{p \times 1}{\boldsymbol{\mu}} = \begin{bmatrix} \mu_1 \\ \mu_2 \\ \vdots \\ \mu_p \end{bmatrix} \tag{5.48}$$

Finally, the variance-covariance matrix $\sigma^2\{\mathbf{Y}\}$ is denoted by $\boldsymbol{\Sigma}$ and contains as always the variances and covariances of the p Y variables:

$$\underset{p \times p}{\boldsymbol{\Sigma}} = \begin{bmatrix} \sigma_1^2 & \sigma_{12} & \cdots & \sigma_{1p} \\ \sigma_{21} & \sigma_2^2 & \cdots & \sigma_{2p} \\ \vdots & \vdots & & \vdots \\ \sigma_{p1} & \sigma_{p2} & \cdots & \sigma_p^2 \end{bmatrix} \tag{5.49}$$

Here, σ_1^2 denotes the variance of Y_1, σ_{12} denotes the covariance of Y_1 and Y_2, and the like. The density function of the multivariate normal distribution can now be stated as follows:

$$f(\mathbf{Y}) = \frac{1}{(2\pi)^{p/2}|\boldsymbol{\Sigma}|^{1/2}} \exp\left[-\frac{1}{2}(\mathbf{Y} - \boldsymbol{\mu})'\boldsymbol{\Sigma}^{-1}(\mathbf{Y} - \boldsymbol{\mu})\right] \tag{5.50}$$

Here, $|\boldsymbol{\Sigma}|$ is the determinant of the variance-covariance matrix $\boldsymbol{\Sigma}$. When there are $p = 2$ variables, the multivariate normal density function (5.50) simplifies to the bivariate normal density function (2.74).

The multivariate normal density function has properties that correspond to the ones described for the bivariate normal distribution. For instance, if $Y_1, \ldots, Y_p$ are jointly normally distributed (i.e., they follow the multivariate normal distribution), the marginal probability distribution of each variable Y_k is normal, with mean μ_k and standard deviation σ_k.

5.9 Simple Linear Regression Model in Matrix Terms

We are now ready to develop simple linear regression in matrix terms. Remember again that we will not present any new results, but shall only state in matrix terms the results obtained earlier. We begin with the normal error regression model (2.1):

$$Y_i = \beta_0 + \beta_1 X_i + \varepsilon_i \qquad i = 1, \ldots, n \tag{5.51}$$

This implies:

$$Y_1 = \beta_0 + \beta_1 X_1 + \varepsilon_1$$

$$Y_2 = \beta_0 + \beta_1 X_2 + \varepsilon_2$$ (5.51a)

$$\vdots$$

$$Y_n = \beta_0 + \beta_1 X_n + \varepsilon_n$$

We defined earlier the observations vector $\mathbf{Y}$ in (5.4), the $\mathbf{X}$ matrix in (5.6), and the $\boldsymbol{\varepsilon}$ vector in (5.10). Let us repeat these definitions and also define the $\boldsymbol{\beta}$ vector of the regression coefficients:

$$\underset{n\times 1}{\mathbf{Y}} = \begin{bmatrix} Y_1 \\ Y_2 \\ \vdots \\ Y_n \end{bmatrix} \qquad \underset{n\times 2}{\mathbf{X}} = \begin{bmatrix} 1 & X_1 \\ 1 & X_2 \\ \vdots & \vdots \\ 1 & X_n \end{bmatrix} \qquad \underset{2\times 1}{\boldsymbol{\beta}} = \begin{bmatrix} \beta_0 \\ \beta_1 \end{bmatrix} \qquad \underset{n\times 1}{\boldsymbol{\varepsilon}} = \begin{bmatrix} \varepsilon_1 \\ \varepsilon_2 \\ \vdots \\ \varepsilon_n \end{bmatrix}$$ (5.52)

Now we can write (5.51a) in matrix terms compactly as follows:

$$\underset{n\times 1}{\mathbf{Y}} = \underset{n\times 2}{\mathbf{X}} \underset{2\times 1}{\boldsymbol{\beta}} + \underset{n\times 1}{\boldsymbol{\varepsilon}}$$ (5.53)

since:

$$\begin{bmatrix} Y_1 \\ Y_2 \\ \vdots \\ Y_n \end{bmatrix} = \begin{bmatrix} 1 & X_1 \\ 1 & X_2 \\ \vdots & \vdots \\ 1 & X_n \end{bmatrix} \begin{bmatrix} \beta_0 \\ \beta_1 \end{bmatrix} + \begin{bmatrix} \varepsilon_1 \\ \varepsilon_2 \\ \vdots \\ \varepsilon_n \end{bmatrix}$$

$$= \begin{bmatrix} \beta_0 + \beta_1 X_1 \\ \beta_0 + \beta_1 X_2 \\ \vdots \\ \beta_0 + \beta_1 X_n \end{bmatrix} + \begin{bmatrix} \varepsilon_1 \\ \varepsilon_2 \\ \vdots \\ \varepsilon_n \end{bmatrix} = \begin{bmatrix} \beta_0 + \beta_1 X_1 + \varepsilon_1 \\ \beta_0 + \beta_1 X_2 + \varepsilon_2 \\ \vdots \\ \beta_0 + \beta_1 X_n + \varepsilon_n \end{bmatrix}$$

Note that $\mathbf{X}\boldsymbol{\beta}$ is the vector of the expected values of the Y_i observations since $E\{Y_i\} = \beta_0 + \beta_1 X_i$; hence:

$$\underset{n\times 1}{E\{\mathbf{Y}\}} = \underset{n\times 1}{\mathbf{X}\boldsymbol{\beta}}$$ (5.54)

where $E\{\mathbf{Y}\}$ is defined in (5.9).

The column of 1s in the $\mathbf{X}$ matrix may be viewed as consisting of the constant $X_0 \equiv 1$ in the alternative regression model (1.5):

$$Y_i = \beta_0 X_0 + \beta_1 X_i + \varepsilon_i \qquad \text{where } X_0 \equiv 1$$

Thus, the $\mathbf{X}$ matrix may be considered to contain a column vector consisting of 1s and another column vector consisting of the predictor variable observations X_i.

With respect to the error terms, regression model (2.1) assumes that $E\{\varepsilon_i\} = 0, \sigma^2\{\varepsilon_i\} = \sigma^2$, and that the ε_i are independent normal random variables. The condition $E\{\varepsilon_i\} = 0$ in matrix terms is:

$$E\{\boldsymbol{\varepsilon}\} = \mathbf{0}$$
$$\underset{n\times 1}{} \quad \underset{n\times 1}{}$$

(5.55)

since (5.55) states:

$$\begin{bmatrix} E\{\varepsilon_1\} \\ E\{\varepsilon_2\} \\ \vdots \\ E\{\varepsilon_n\} \end{bmatrix} = \begin{bmatrix} 0 \\ 0 \\ \vdots \\ 0 \end{bmatrix}$$

The condition that the error terms have constant variance σ^2 and that all covariances $\sigma\{\varepsilon_i, \varepsilon_j\}$ for $i \neq j$ are zero (since the ε_i are independent) is expressed in matrix terms through the variance-covariance matrix of the error terms:

$$\underset{n\times n}{\sigma^2\{\boldsymbol{\varepsilon}\}} = \begin{bmatrix} \sigma^2 & 0 & 0 & \cdots & 0 \\ 0 & \sigma^2 & 0 & \cdots & 0 \\ \vdots & \vdots & \vdots & & \vdots \\ 0 & 0 & 0 & \cdots & \sigma^2 \end{bmatrix}$$

(5.56)

Since this is a scalar matrix, we know from the earlier example that it can be expressed in the following simple fashion:

$$\underset{n\times n}{\sigma^2\{\boldsymbol{\varepsilon}\}} = \underset{n\times n}{\sigma^2 \mathbf{I}}$$

(5.56a)

Thus, the normal error regression model (2.1) in matrix terms is:

$$\mathbf{Y} = \mathbf{X}\boldsymbol{\beta} + \boldsymbol{\varepsilon}$$

(5.57)

where:

    $\boldsymbol{\varepsilon}$ is a vector of independent normal random variables with $E\{\boldsymbol{\varepsilon}\} = \mathbf{0}$ and $\sigma^2\{\boldsymbol{\varepsilon}\} = \sigma^2 \mathbf{I}$

5.10 Least Squares Estimation of Regression Parameters

Normal Equations

The normal equations (1.9):

$$\begin{aligned} nb_0 + b_1 \sum X_i &= \sum Y_i \\ b_0 \sum X_i + b_1 \sum X_i^2 &= \sum X_i Y_i \end{aligned}$$

(5.58)

in matrix terms are:

$$\underset{2\times 2}{\mathbf{X}'\mathbf{X}} \underset{2\times 1}{\mathbf{b}} = \underset{2\times 1}{\mathbf{X}'\mathbf{Y}}$$

(5.59)

where **b** is the vector of the least squares regression coefficients:

$$\underset{2\times 1}{\mathbf{b}} = \begin{bmatrix} b_0 \\ b_1 \end{bmatrix}$$

(5.59a)

To see this, recall that we obtained $\mathbf{X'X}$ in (5.14) and $\mathbf{X'Y}$ in (5.15). Equation (5.59) thus states:

$$
\begin{bmatrix} n & \sum X_i \\ \sum X_i & \sum X_i^2 \end{bmatrix} \begin{bmatrix} b_0 \\ b_1 \end{bmatrix} = \begin{bmatrix} \sum Y_i \\ \sum X_i Y_i \end{bmatrix}
$$

or:

$$
\begin{bmatrix} nb_0 + b_1 \sum X_i \\ b_0 \sum X_i + b_1 \sum X_i^2 \end{bmatrix} = \begin{bmatrix} \sum Y_i \\ \sum X_i Y_i \end{bmatrix}
$$

These are precisely the normal equations in (5.58).

Estimated Regression Coefficients

To obtain the estimated regression coefficients from the normal equations (5.59) by matrix methods, we premultiply both sides by the inverse of $\mathbf{X'X}$ (we assume this exists):

$$
(\mathbf{X'X})^{-1}\mathbf{X'Xb} = (\mathbf{X'X})^{-1}\mathbf{X'Y}
$$

We then find, since $(\mathbf{X'X})^{-1}\mathbf{X'X} = \mathbf{I}$ and $\mathbf{Ib} = \mathbf{b}$:

$$
\underset{2\times1}{\mathbf{b}} = \underset{2\times2}{(\mathbf{X'X})^{-1}} \underset{2\times1}{\mathbf{X'Y}} \tag{5.60}
$$

The estimators b_0 and b_1 in $\mathbf{b}$ are the same as those given earlier in (1.10a) and (1.10b). We shall demonstrate this by an example.

Example

We shall use matrix methods to obtain the estimated regression coefficients for the Toluca Company example. The data on the Y and X variables were given in Table 1.1. Using these data, we define the $\mathbf{Y}$ observations vector and the $\mathbf{X}$ matrix as follows:

$$
\textbf{(5.61a)} \quad \mathbf{Y} = \begin{bmatrix} 399 \\ 121 \\ \vdots \\ 323 \end{bmatrix} \qquad \textbf{(5.61b)} \quad \mathbf{X} = \begin{bmatrix} 1 & 80 \\ 1 & 30 \\ \vdots & \vdots \\ 1 & 70 \end{bmatrix} \tag{5.61}
$$

We now require the following matrix products:

$$
\mathbf{X'X} = \begin{bmatrix} 1 & 1 & \cdots & 1 \\ 80 & 30 & \cdots & 70 \end{bmatrix} \begin{bmatrix} 1 & 80 \\ 1 & 30 \\ \vdots & \vdots \\ 1 & 70 \end{bmatrix} = \begin{bmatrix} 25 & 1{,}750 \\ 1{,}750 & 142{,}300 \end{bmatrix} \tag{5.62}
$$

$$
\mathbf{X'Y} = \begin{bmatrix} 1 & 1 & \cdots & 1 \\ 80 & 30 & \cdots & 70 \end{bmatrix} \begin{bmatrix} 399 \\ 121 \\ \vdots \\ 323 \end{bmatrix} = \begin{bmatrix} 7{,}807 \\ 617{,}180 \end{bmatrix} \tag{5.63}
$$

Using (5.22), we find the inverse of $\mathbf{X}'\mathbf{X}$:

$$(\mathbf{X}'\mathbf{X})^{-1} = \begin{bmatrix} .287475 & -.003535 \\ -.003535 & .00005051 \end{bmatrix} \qquad (5.64)$$

In subsequent matrix calculations utilizing this inverse matrix and other matrix results, we shall actually utilize more digits for the matrix elements than are shown.

Finally, we employ (5.60) to obtain:

$$\mathbf{b} = \begin{bmatrix} b_0 \\ b_1 \end{bmatrix} = (\mathbf{X}'\mathbf{X})^{-1}\mathbf{X}'\mathbf{Y} = \begin{bmatrix} .287475 & -.003535 \\ -.003535 & .00005051 \end{bmatrix} \begin{bmatrix} 7,807 \\ 617,180 \end{bmatrix}$$

$$= \begin{bmatrix} 62.37 \\ 3.5702 \end{bmatrix} \qquad (5.65)$$

or $b_0 = 62.37$ and $b_1 = 3.5702$. These results agree with the ones in Chapter 1. Any differences would have been due to rounding effects.

Comments

1. To derive the normal equations by the method of least squares, we minimize the quantity:

$$Q = \sum [Y_i - (\beta_0 + \beta_1 X_i)]^2$$

In matrix notation:

$$Q = (\mathbf{Y} - \mathbf{X}\boldsymbol{\beta})'(\mathbf{Y} - \mathbf{X}\boldsymbol{\beta}) \qquad (5.66)$$

Expanding, we obtain:

$$Q = \mathbf{Y}'\mathbf{Y} - \boldsymbol{\beta}'\mathbf{X}'\mathbf{Y} - \mathbf{Y}'\mathbf{X}\boldsymbol{\beta} + \boldsymbol{\beta}'\mathbf{X}'\mathbf{X}\boldsymbol{\beta}$$

since $(\mathbf{X}\boldsymbol{\beta})' = \boldsymbol{\beta}'\mathbf{X}'$ by (5.32). Note now that $\mathbf{Y}'\mathbf{X}\boldsymbol{\beta}$ is 1×1, hence is equal to its transpose, which according to (5.33) is $\boldsymbol{\beta}'\mathbf{X}'\mathbf{Y}$. Thus, we find:

$$Q = \mathbf{Y}'\mathbf{Y} - 2\boldsymbol{\beta}'\mathbf{X}'\mathbf{Y} + \boldsymbol{\beta}'\mathbf{X}'\mathbf{X}\boldsymbol{\beta} \qquad (5.67)$$

To find the value of $\boldsymbol{\beta}$ that minimizes Q, we differentiate with respect to β_0 and β_1. Let:

$$\frac{\partial}{\partial \boldsymbol{\beta}}(Q) = \begin{bmatrix} \dfrac{\partial Q}{\partial \beta_0} \\[2mm] \dfrac{\partial Q}{\partial \beta_1} \end{bmatrix} \qquad (5.68)$$

Then it follows that:

$$\frac{\partial}{\partial \boldsymbol{\beta}}(Q) = -2\mathbf{X}'\mathbf{Y} + 2\mathbf{X}'\mathbf{X}\boldsymbol{\beta} \qquad (5.69)$$

Equating to the zero vector, dividing by 2, and substituting $\mathbf{b}$ for $\boldsymbol{\beta}$ gives the matrix form of the least squares normal equations in (5.59).

2. A comparison of the normal equations and $\mathbf{X}'\mathbf{X}$ shows that whenever the columns of $\mathbf{X}'\mathbf{X}$ are linearly dependent, the normal equations will be linearly dependent also. No unique solutions can then be obtained for b_0 and b_1. Fortunately, in most regression applications, the columns of $\mathbf{X}'\mathbf{X}$ are linearly independent, leading to unique solutions for b_0 and b_1. ∎

5.11 Fitted Values and Residuals

Fitted Values

Let the vector of the fitted values $\hat{Y}_i$ be denoted by $\hat{\mathbf{Y}}$:

$$\underset{n \times 1}{\hat{\mathbf{Y}}} = \begin{bmatrix} \hat{Y}_1 \\ \hat{Y}_2 \\ \vdots \\ \hat{Y}_n \end{bmatrix} \tag{5.70}$$

In matrix notation, we then have:

$$\underset{n \times 1}{\hat{\mathbf{Y}}} = \underset{n \times 2}{\mathbf{X}} \; \underset{2 \times 1}{\mathbf{b}} \tag{5.71}$$

because:

$$\begin{bmatrix} \hat{Y}_1 \\ \hat{Y}_2 \\ \vdots \\ \hat{Y}_n \end{bmatrix} = \begin{bmatrix} 1 & X_1 \\ 1 & X_2 \\ \vdots & \vdots \\ 1 & X_n \end{bmatrix} \begin{bmatrix} b_0 \\ b_1 \end{bmatrix} = \begin{bmatrix} b_0 + b_1 X_1 \\ b_0 + b_1 X_2 \\ \vdots \\ b_0 + b_1 X_n \end{bmatrix}$$

Example

For the Toluca Company example, we obtain the vector of fitted values using the matrices in (5.61b) and (5.65):

$$\hat{\mathbf{Y}} = \mathbf{Xb} = \begin{bmatrix} 1 & 80 \\ 1 & 30 \\ \vdots & \vdots \\ 1 & 70 \end{bmatrix} \begin{bmatrix} 62.37 \\ 3.5702 \end{bmatrix} = \begin{bmatrix} 347.98 \\ 169.47 \\ \vdots \\ 312.28 \end{bmatrix} \tag{5.72}$$

The fitted values are the same, of course, as in Table 1.2.

Hat Matrix. We can express the matrix result for $\hat{\mathbf{Y}}$ in (5.71) as follows by using the expression for **b** in (5.60):

$$\hat{\mathbf{Y}} = \mathbf{X}(\mathbf{X}'\mathbf{X})^{-1}\mathbf{X}'\mathbf{Y}$$

or, equivalently:

$$\underset{n \times 1}{\hat{\mathbf{Y}}} = \underset{n \times n}{\mathbf{H}} \; \underset{n \times 1}{\mathbf{Y}} \tag{5.73}$$

where:

$$\underset{n \times n}{\mathbf{H}} = \mathbf{X}(\mathbf{X}'\mathbf{X})^{-1}\mathbf{X}' \tag{5.73a}$$

We see from (5.73) that the fitted values $\hat{Y}_i$ can be expressed as linear combinations of the response variable observations Y_i, with the coefficients being elements of the matrix **H**. The **H** matrix involves only the observations on the predictor variable X, as is evident from (5.73a).

The square $n \times n$ matrix **H** is called the *hat matrix*. It plays an important role in diagnostics for regression analysis, as we shall see in Chapter 10 when we consider whether regression results are unduly influenced by one or a few observations. The matrix **H** is symmetric and has the special property (called idempotency):

$$\mathbf{HH} = \mathbf{H} \tag{5.74}$$

In general, a matrix **M** is said to be *idempotent* if $\mathbf{MM} = \mathbf{M}$.

Residuals

Let the vector of the residuals $e_i = Y_i - \hat{Y}_i$ be denoted by **e**:

$$\underset{n \times 1}{\mathbf{e}} = \begin{bmatrix} e_1 \\ e_2 \\ \vdots \\ e_n \end{bmatrix} \tag{5.75}$$

In matrix notation, we then have:

$$\underset{n \times 1}{\mathbf{e}} = \underset{n \times 1}{\mathbf{Y}} - \underset{n \times 1}{\hat{\mathbf{Y}}} = \underset{n \times 1}{\mathbf{Y}} - \underset{n \times 1}{\mathbf{Xb}} \tag{5.76}$$

Example

For the Toluca Company example, we obtain the vector of the residuals by using the results in (5.61a) and (5.72):

$$\mathbf{e} = \begin{bmatrix} 399 \\ 121 \\ \vdots \\ 323 \end{bmatrix} - \begin{bmatrix} 347.98 \\ 169.47 \\ \vdots \\ 312.28 \end{bmatrix} = \begin{bmatrix} 51.02 \\ -48.47 \\ \vdots \\ 10.72 \end{bmatrix} \tag{5.77}$$

The residuals are the same as in Table 1.2.

Variance-Covariance Matrix of Residuals. The residuals e_i, like the fitted values $\hat{Y}_i$, can be expressed as linear combinations of the response variable observations Y_i, using the result in (5.73) for $\hat{\mathbf{Y}}$:

$$\mathbf{e} = \mathbf{Y} - \hat{\mathbf{Y}} = \mathbf{Y} - \mathbf{HY} = (\mathbf{I} - \mathbf{H})\mathbf{Y}$$

We thus have the important result:

$$\underset{n \times 1}{\mathbf{e}} = \underset{n \times n}{(\mathbf{I} - \mathbf{H})} \underset{n \times 1}{\mathbf{Y}} \tag{5.78}$$

where **H** is the hat matrix defined in (5.53a). The matrix $\mathbf{I} - \mathbf{H}$, like the matrix **H**, is symmetric and idempotent.

The variance-covariance matrix of the vector of residuals **e** involves the matrix $\mathbf{I} - \mathbf{H}$:

$$\underset{n \times n}{\sigma^2\{\mathbf{e}\}} = \sigma^2(\mathbf{I} - \mathbf{H}) \tag{5.79}$$

and is estimated by:

$$\underset{n \times n}{s^2\{\mathbf{e}\}} = MSE(\mathbf{I} - \mathbf{H}) \tag{5.80}$$

Comment

The variance-covariance matrix of $\mathbf{e}$ in (5.79) can be derived by means of (5.46). Since $\mathbf{e} = (\mathbf{I} - \mathbf{H})\mathbf{Y}$, we obtain:

$$\sigma^2\{\mathbf{e}\} = (\mathbf{I} - \mathbf{H})\sigma^2\{\mathbf{Y}\}(\mathbf{I} - \mathbf{H})'$$

Now $\sigma^2\{\mathbf{Y}\} = \sigma^2\{\boldsymbol{\varepsilon}\} = \sigma^2\mathbf{I}$ for the normal error model according to (5.56a). Also, $(\mathbf{I} - \mathbf{H})' = \mathbf{I} - \mathbf{H}$ because of the symmetry of the matrix. Hence:

$$\sigma^2\{\mathbf{e}\} = \sigma^2(\mathbf{I} - \mathbf{H})\mathbf{I}(\mathbf{I} - \mathbf{H})$$

$$= \sigma^2(\mathbf{I} - \mathbf{H})(\mathbf{I} - \mathbf{H})$$

In view of the fact that the matrix $\mathbf{I} - \mathbf{H}$ is idempotent, we know that $(\mathbf{I} - \mathbf{H})(\mathbf{I} - \mathbf{H}) = \mathbf{I} - \mathbf{H}$ and we obtain formula (5.79). ∎

5.12 Analysis of Variance Results

Sums of Squares

To see how the sums of squares are expressed in matrix notation, we begin with the total sum of squares *SSTO*, defined in (2.43). It will be convenient to use an algebraically equivalent expression:

$$SSTO = \sum (Y_i - \bar{Y})^2 = \sum Y_i^2 - \frac{(\sum Y_i)^2}{n} \tag{5.81}$$

We know from (5.13) that:

$$\mathbf{Y}'\mathbf{Y} = \sum Y_i^2$$

The subtraction term $(\sum Y_i)^2/n$ in matrix form uses $\mathbf{J}$, the matrix of 1s defined in (5.18), as follows:

$$\frac{(\sum Y_i)^2}{n} = \left(\frac{1}{n}\right)\mathbf{Y}'\mathbf{J}\mathbf{Y} \tag{5.82}$$

For instance, if $n = 2$, we have:

$$\left(\frac{1}{2}\right)[Y_1 \quad Y_2]\begin{bmatrix} 1 & 1 \\ 1 & 1 \end{bmatrix}\begin{bmatrix} Y_1 \\ Y_2 \end{bmatrix} = \frac{(Y_1 + Y_2)(Y_1 + Y_2)}{2}$$

Hence, it follows that:

$$SSTO = \mathbf{Y}'\mathbf{Y} - \left(\frac{1}{n}\right)\mathbf{Y}'\mathbf{J}\mathbf{Y} \tag{5.83}$$

Just as $\sum Y_i^2$ is represented by $\mathbf{Y}'\mathbf{Y}$ in matrix terms, so $SSE = \sum e_i^2 = \sum (Y_i - \hat{Y}_i)^2$ can be represented as follows:

$$SSE = \mathbf{e}'\mathbf{e} = (\mathbf{Y} - \mathbf{Xb})'(\mathbf{Y} - \mathbf{Xb}) \tag{5.84}$$

which can be shown to equal:

$$SSE = \mathbf{Y}'\mathbf{Y} - \mathbf{b}'\mathbf{X}'\mathbf{Y} \tag{5.84a}$$

Finally, it can be shown that:

$$SSR = \mathbf{b'X'Y} - \left(\frac{1}{n}\right)\mathbf{Y'JY} \tag{5.85}$$

Example

Let us find *SSE* for the Toluca Company example by matrix methods, using (5.84a). Using (5.61a), we obtain:

$$\mathbf{Y'Y} = [399 \quad 121 \quad \cdots \quad 323]\begin{bmatrix} 399 \\ 121 \\ \vdots \\ 323 \end{bmatrix} = 2{,}745{,}173$$

and using (5.65) and (5.63), we find:

$$\mathbf{b'X'Y} = [62.37 \quad 3.5702]\begin{bmatrix} 7{,}807 \\ 617{,}180 \end{bmatrix} = 2{,}690{,}348$$

Hence:

$$SSE = \mathbf{Y'Y} - \mathbf{b'X'Y} = 2{,}745{,}173 - 2{,}690{,}348 = 54{,}825$$

which is the same result as that obtained in Chapter 1. Any difference would have been due to rounding effects.

Comment

To illustrate the derivation of the sums of squares expressions in matrix notation, consider *SSE*:

$$SSE = \mathbf{e'e} = (\mathbf{Y - Xb})'(\mathbf{Y - Xb}) = \mathbf{Y'Y} - 2\mathbf{b'X'Y} + \mathbf{b'X'Xb}$$

In substituting for the rightmost **b** we obtain by (5.60):

$$SSE = \mathbf{Y'Y} - 2\mathbf{b'X'Y} + \mathbf{b'X'X(X'X)^{-1}X'Y}$$
$$= \mathbf{Y'Y} - 2\mathbf{b'X'Y} + \mathbf{b'IX'Y}$$

In dropping **I** and subtracting, we obtain the result in (5.84a). ∎

Sums of Squares as Quadratic Forms

The ANOVA sums of squares can be shown to be *quadratic forms*. An example of a quadratic form of the observations Y_i when $n = 2$ is:

$$5Y_1^2 + 6Y_1Y_2 + 4Y_2^2 \tag{5.86}$$

Note that this expression is a second-degree polynomial containing terms involving the squares of the observations and the cross product. We can express (5.86) in matrix terms as follows:

$$[Y_1 \quad Y_2]\begin{bmatrix} 5 & 3 \\ 3 & 4 \end{bmatrix}\begin{bmatrix} Y_1 \\ Y_2 \end{bmatrix} = \mathbf{Y'AY} \tag{5.86a}$$

where **A** is a symmetric matrix.

In general, a quadratic form is defined as:

$$\underset{1\times 1}{\mathbf{Y}'\mathbf{A}\mathbf{Y}} = \sum_{i=1}^{n}\sum_{j=1}^{n} a_{ij}Y_iY_j \qquad \text{where } a_{ij} = a_{ji} \qquad (5.87)$$

$\mathbf{A}$ is a symmetric $n \times n$ matrix and is called the *matrix of the quadratic form*.

The ANOVA sums of squares *SSTO*, *SSE*, and *SSR* are all quadratic forms, as can be seen by reexpressing $\mathbf{b}'\mathbf{X}'$. From (5.71), we know, using (5.32), that:

$$\mathbf{b}'\mathbf{X}' = (\mathbf{X}\mathbf{b})' = \hat{\mathbf{Y}}'$$

We now use the result in (5.73) to obtain:

$$\mathbf{b}'\mathbf{X}' = (\mathbf{H}\mathbf{Y})'$$

Since $\mathbf{H}$ is a symmetric matrix so that $\mathbf{H}' = \mathbf{H}$, we finally obtain, using (5.32):

$$\mathbf{b}'\mathbf{X}' = \mathbf{Y}'\mathbf{H} \qquad (5.88)$$

This result enables us to express the ANOVA sums of squares as follows:

$$SSTO = \mathbf{Y}'\left[\mathbf{I} - \left(\frac{1}{n}\right)\mathbf{J}\right]\mathbf{Y} \qquad (5.89a)$$

$$SSE = \mathbf{Y}'(\mathbf{I} - \mathbf{H})\mathbf{Y} \qquad (5.89b)$$

$$SSR = \mathbf{Y}'\left[\mathbf{H} - \left(\frac{1}{n}\right)\mathbf{J}\right]\mathbf{Y} \qquad (5.89c)$$

Each of these sums of squares can now be seen to be of the form $\mathbf{Y}'\mathbf{A}\mathbf{Y}$, where the three $\mathbf{A}$ matrices are:

$$\mathbf{I} - \left(\frac{1}{n}\right)\mathbf{J} \qquad (5.90a)$$

$$\mathbf{I} - \mathbf{H} \qquad (5.90b)$$

$$\mathbf{H} - \left(\frac{1}{n}\right)\mathbf{J} \qquad (5.90c)$$

Since each of these $\mathbf{A}$ matrices is symmetric, *SSTO*, *SSE*, and *SSR* are quadratic forms, with the matrices of the quadratic forms given in (5.90). Quadratic forms play an important role in statistics because all sums of squares in the analysis of variance for linear statistical models can be expressed as quadratic forms.

5.13   Inferences in Regression Analysis

As we saw in earlier chapters, all interval estimates are of the following form: point estimator plus and minus a certain number of estimated standard deviations of the point estimator. Similarly, all tests require the point estimator and the estimated standard deviation of the point estimator or, in the case of analysis of variance tests, various sums of squares. Matrix algebra is of principal help in inference making when obtaining the estimated standard deviations and sums of squares. We have already given the matrix equivalents of the sums of squares for the analysis of variance. We focus here chiefly on the matrix expressions for the estimated variances of point estimators of interest.

Regression Coefficients

The variance-covariance matrix of **b**:

$$\sigma^2\{\mathbf{b}\} = \begin{bmatrix} \sigma^2\{b_0\} & \sigma\{b_0, b_1\} \\ \sigma\{b_1, b_0\} & \sigma^2\{b_1\} \end{bmatrix} \qquad (5.91)$$
$$\underset{2\times 2}{}$$

is:

$$\sigma^2\{\mathbf{b}\} = \sigma^2(\mathbf{X'X})^{-1} \qquad (5.92)$$
$$\underset{2\times 2}{}$$

or, from (5.24a):

$$\sigma^2\{\mathbf{b}\} = \begin{bmatrix} \dfrac{\sigma^2}{n} + \dfrac{\sigma^2 \bar{X}^2}{\sum(X_i - \bar{X})^2} & \dfrac{-\bar{X}\sigma^2}{\sum(X_i - \bar{X})^2} \\ \dfrac{-\bar{X}\sigma^2}{\sum(X_i - \bar{X})^2} & \dfrac{\sigma^2}{\sum(X_i - \bar{X})^2} \end{bmatrix} \qquad (5.92a)$$
$$\underset{2\times 2}{}$$

When *MSE* is substituted for σ^2 in (5.92a), we obtain the estimated variance-covariance matrix of **b**, denoted by $\mathbf{s}^2\{\mathbf{b}\}$:

$$\mathbf{s}^2\{\mathbf{b}\} = MSE(\mathbf{X'X})^{-1} = \begin{bmatrix} \dfrac{MSE}{n} + \dfrac{\bar{X}^2 MSE}{\sum(X_i - \bar{X})^2} & \dfrac{-\bar{X} MSE}{\sum(X_i - \bar{X})^2} \\ \dfrac{-\bar{X} MSE}{\sum(X_i - \bar{X})^2} & \dfrac{MSE}{\sum(X_i - \bar{X})^2} \end{bmatrix} \qquad (5.93)$$
$$\underset{2\times 2}{}$$

In (5.92a), you will recognize the variances of b_0 in (2.22b) and of b_1 in (2.3b) and the covariance of b_0 and b_1 in (4.5). Likewise, the estimated variances in (5.93) are familiar from earlier chapters.

Example

We wish to find $s^2\{b_0\}$ and $s^2\{b_1\}$ for the Toluca Company example by matrix methods. Using the results in Figure 2.2 and in (5.64), we obtain:

$$\mathbf{s}^2\{\mathbf{b}\} = MSE(\mathbf{X'X})^{-1} = 2{,}384 \begin{bmatrix} .287475 & -.003535 \\ -.003535 & .00005051 \end{bmatrix}$$

$$= \begin{bmatrix} 685.34 & -8.428 \\ -8.428 & .12040 \end{bmatrix} \qquad (5.94)$$

Thus, $s^2\{b_0\} = 685.34$ and $s^2\{b_1\} = .12040$. These are the same as the results obtained in Chapter 2.

Comment

To derive the variance-covariance matrix of **b**, recall that:

$$\mathbf{b} = (\mathbf{X'X})^{-1}\mathbf{X'Y} = \mathbf{AY}$$

where **A** is a constant matrix:

$$\mathbf{A} = (\mathbf{X'X})^{-1}\mathbf{X'}$$

Hence, by (5.46) we have:

$$\sigma^2\{\mathbf{b}\} = \mathbf{A}\sigma^2\{\mathbf{Y}\}\mathbf{A'}$$

Now $\sigma^2\{\mathbf{Y}\} = \sigma^2\mathbf{I}$. Further, it follows from (5.32) and the fact that $(\mathbf{X'X})^{-1}$ is symmetric that:

$$\mathbf{A'} = \mathbf{X(X'X)}^{-1}$$

We find therefore:

$$\sigma^2\{\mathbf{b}\} = (\mathbf{X'X})^{-1}\mathbf{X'}\sigma^2\mathbf{IX(X'X)}^{-1}$$
$$= \sigma^2(\mathbf{X'X})^{-1}\mathbf{X'X(X'X)}^{-1}$$
$$= \sigma^2(\mathbf{X'X})^{-1}\mathbf{I}$$
$$= \sigma^2(\mathbf{X'X})^{-1}$$

■

Mean Response

To estimate the mean response at X_h, let us define the vector:

$$\underset{2\times 1}{\mathbf{X}_h} = \begin{bmatrix} 1 \\ X_h \end{bmatrix} \qquad \text{or} \qquad \underset{1\times 2}{\mathbf{X}'_h} = [1 \quad X_h] \tag{5.95}$$

The fitted value in matrix notation then is:

$$\hat{Y}_h = \mathbf{X}'_h\mathbf{b} \tag{5.96}$$

since:

$$\mathbf{X}'_h\mathbf{b} = [1 \quad X_h]\begin{bmatrix} b_0 \\ b_1 \end{bmatrix} = [b_0 + b_1 X_h] = [\hat{Y}_h] = \hat{Y}_h$$

Note that $\mathbf{X}'_h\mathbf{b}$ is a 1×1 matrix; hence, we can write the final result as a scalar.

The variance of $\hat{Y}_h$, given earlier in (2.29b), in matrix notation is:

$$\sigma^2\{\hat{Y}_h\} = \sigma^2\mathbf{X}'_h(\mathbf{X'X})^{-1}\mathbf{X}_h \tag{5.97}$$

The variance of $\hat{Y}_h$ in (5.93) can be expressed as a function of $\sigma^2\{\mathbf{b}\}$, the variance-covariance matrix of the estimated regression coefficients, by making use of the result in (5.92):

$$\sigma^2\{\hat{Y}_h\} = \mathbf{X}'_h\sigma^2\{\mathbf{b}\}\mathbf{X}_h \tag{5.97a}$$

The estimated variance of $\hat{Y}_h$, given earlier in (2.30), in matrix notation is:

$$s^2\{\hat{Y}_h\} = MSE(\mathbf{X}'_h(\mathbf{X'X})^{-1}\mathbf{X}_h) \tag{5.98}$$

Example

We wish to find $s^2\{\hat{Y}_h\}$ for the Toluca Company example when $X_h = 65$. We define:

$$\mathbf{X}'_h = [1 \quad 65]$$

and use the result in (5.94) to obtain:

$$s^2\{\hat{Y}_h\} = \mathbf{X}'_h s^2\{\mathbf{b}\}\mathbf{X}_h$$

$$= [1 \quad 65]\begin{bmatrix} 685.34 & -8.428 \\ -8.428 & .12040 \end{bmatrix}\begin{bmatrix} 1 \\ 65 \end{bmatrix} = 98.37$$

This is the same result as that obtained in Chapter 2.

Comment

The result in (5.97a) can be derived directly by using (5.46), since $\hat{Y}_h = \mathbf{X}'_h \mathbf{b}$:

$$\sigma^2\{\hat{Y}_h\} = \mathbf{X}'_h \sigma^2\{\mathbf{b}\} \mathbf{X}_h$$

Hence:

$$\sigma^2\{\hat{Y}_h\} = [1 \quad X_h] \begin{bmatrix} \sigma^2\{b_0\} & \sigma\{b_0, b_1\} \\ \sigma\{b_1, b_0\} & \sigma^2\{b_1\} \end{bmatrix} \begin{bmatrix} 1 \\ X_h \end{bmatrix}$$

or:

$$\sigma^2\{\hat{Y}_h\} = \sigma^2\{b_0\} + 2X_h \sigma\{b_0, b_1\} + X_h^2 \sigma^2\{b_1\} \tag{5.99}$$

Using the results from (5.92a), we obtain:

$$\sigma^2\{\hat{Y}_h\} = \frac{\sigma^2}{n} + \frac{\sigma^2 \bar{X}^2}{\sum(X_i - \bar{X})^2} + \frac{2X_h(-\bar{X})\sigma^2}{\sum(X_i - \bar{X})^2} + \frac{X_h^2 \sigma^2}{\sum(X_i - \bar{X})^2}$$

which reduces to the familiar expression:

$$\sigma^2\{\hat{Y}_h\} = \sigma^2 \left[\frac{1}{n} + \frac{(X_h - \bar{X})^2}{\sum(X_i - \bar{X})^2} \right] \tag{5.99a}$$

Thus, we see explicitly that the variance expression in (5.99a) contains contributions from $\sigma^2\{b_0\}$, $\sigma^2\{b_1\}$, and $\sigma\{b_0, b_1\}$, which it must according to (A.30b) since $\hat{Y}_h = b_0 + b_1 X_h$ is a linear combination of b_0 and b_1. ∎

Prediction of New Observation

The estimated variance $s^2\{\text{pred}\}$, given earlier in (2.38), in matrix notation is:

$$s^2\{\text{pred}\} = MSE(1 + \mathbf{X}'_h (\mathbf{X}'\mathbf{X})^{-1} \mathbf{X}_h) \tag{5.100}$$

Cited Reference

5.1. Graybill, F. A. *Matrices with Applications in Statistics*. 2nd ed. Belmont, Calif.: Wadsworth, 2002.

Problems

5.1. For the matrices below, obtain (1) $\mathbf{A} + \mathbf{B}$, (2) $\mathbf{A} - \mathbf{B}$, (3) $\mathbf{AC}$, (4) $\mathbf{AB}'$, (5) $\mathbf{B}'\mathbf{A}$.

$$\mathbf{A} = \begin{bmatrix} 1 & 4 \\ 2 & 6 \\ 3 & 8 \end{bmatrix} \quad \mathbf{B} = \begin{bmatrix} 1 & 3 \\ 1 & 4 \\ 2 & 5 \end{bmatrix} \quad \mathbf{C} = \begin{bmatrix} 3 & 8 & 1 \\ 5 & 4 & 0 \end{bmatrix}$$

State the dimension of each resulting matrix.

5.2. For the matrices below, obtain (1) $\mathbf{A} + \mathbf{C}$, (2) $\mathbf{A} - \mathbf{C}$, (3) $\mathbf{B}'\mathbf{A}$, (4) $\mathbf{AC}'$, (5) $\mathbf{C}'\mathbf{A}$.

$$\mathbf{A} = \begin{bmatrix} 2 & 1 \\ 3 & 5 \\ 5 & 7 \\ 4 & 8 \end{bmatrix} \quad \mathbf{B} = \begin{bmatrix} 6 \\ 9 \\ 3 \\ 1 \end{bmatrix} \quad \mathbf{C} = \begin{bmatrix} 3 & 8 \\ 8 & 6 \\ 5 & 1 \\ 2 & 4 \end{bmatrix}$$

State the dimension of each resulting matrix.

5.3. Show how the following expressions are written in terms of matrices: (1) $Y_i - \hat{Y}_i = e_i$, (2) $\sum X_i e_i = 0$. Assume $i = 1, \dots, 4$.

*5.4. **Flavor deterioration.** The results shown below were obtained in a small-scale experiment to study the relation between $°F$ of storage temperature (X) and number of weeks before flavor deterioration of a food product begins to occur (Y).

i:	1	2	3	4	5
X_i:	8	4	0	−4	−8
Y_i:	7.8	9.0	10.2	11.0	11.7

Assume that first-order regression model (2.1) is applicable. Using matrix methods, find (1) $\mathbf{Y'Y}$, (2) $\mathbf{X'X}$, (3) $\mathbf{X'Y}$.

5.5. **Consumer finance.** The data below show, for a consumer finance company operating in six cities, the number of competing loan companies operating in the city (X) and the number per thousand of the company's loans made in that city that are currently delinquent (Y):

i:	1	2	3	4	5	6
X_i:	4	1	2	3	3	4
Y_i:	16	5	10	15	13	22

Assume that first-order regression model (2.1) is applicable. Using matrix methods, find (1) $\mathbf{Y'Y}$, (2) $\mathbf{X'X}$, (3) $\mathbf{X'Y}$.

*5.6. Refer to **Airfreight breakage** Problem 1.21. Using matrix methods, find (1) $\mathbf{Y'Y}$, (2) $\mathbf{X'X}$, (3) $\mathbf{X'Y}$.

5.7. Refer to **Plastic hardness** Problem 1.22. Using matrix methods, find (1) $\mathbf{Y'Y}$, (2) $\mathbf{X'X}$, (3) $\mathbf{X'Y}$.

5.8. Let **B** be defined as follows:

$$\mathbf{B} = \begin{bmatrix} 1 & 5 & 0 \\ 1 & 0 & 5 \\ 1 & 0 & 5 \end{bmatrix}$$

a. Are the column vectors of **B** linearly dependent?

b. What is the rank of **B**?

c. What must be the determinant of **B**?

5.9. Let **A** be defined as follows:

$$\mathbf{A} = \begin{bmatrix} 0 & 1 & 8 \\ 0 & 3 & 1 \\ 0 & 5 & 5 \end{bmatrix}$$

a. Are the column vectors of **A** linearly dependent?

b. Restate definition (5.20) in terms of row vectors. Are the row vectors of **A** linearly dependent?

c. What is the rank of **A**?

d. Calculate the determinant of **A**.

5.10. Find the inverse of each of the following matrices:

$$\mathbf{A} = \begin{bmatrix} 2 & 4 \\ 3 & 1 \end{bmatrix} \qquad \mathbf{B} = \begin{bmatrix} 4 & 3 & 2 \\ 6 & 5 & 10 \\ 10 & 1 & 6 \end{bmatrix}$$

Check in each case that the resulting matrix is indeed the inverse.

5.11. Find the inverse of the following matrix:

$$\mathbf{A} = \begin{bmatrix} 5 & 1 & 3 \\ 4 & 0 & 5 \\ 1 & 9 & 6 \end{bmatrix}$$

Check that the resulting matrix is indeed the inverse.

*5.12. Refer to **Flavor deterioration** Problem 5.4. Find $(\mathbf{X}'\mathbf{X})^{-1}$.

5.13. Refer to **Consumer finance** Problem 5.5. Find $(\mathbf{X}'\mathbf{X})^{-1}$.

*5.14. Consider the simultaneous equations:

$$4y_1 + 7y_2 = 25$$
$$2y_1 + 3y_2 = 12$$

a. Write these equations in matrix notation.

b. Using matrix methods, find the solutions for y_1 and y_2.

5.15. Consider the simultaneous equations:

$$5y_1 + 2y_2 = 8$$
$$23y_1 + 7y_2 = 28$$

a. Write these equations in matrix notation.

b. Using matrix methods, find the solutions for y_1 and y_2.

5.16. Consider the estimated linear regression function in the form of (1.15). Write expressions in this form for the fitted values $\hat{Y}_i$ in matrix terms for $i = 1, \ldots, 5$.

5.17. Consider the following functions of the random variables Y_1, Y_2, and Y_3:

$$W_1 = Y_1 + Y_2 + Y_3$$
$$W_2 = Y_1 - Y_2$$
$$W_3 = Y_1 - Y_2 - Y_3$$

a. State the above in matrix notation.

b. Find the expectation of the random vector $\mathbf{W}$.

c. Find the variance-covariance matrix of $\mathbf{W}$.

*5.18. Consider the following functions of the random variables Y_1, Y_2, Y_3, and Y_4:

$$W_1 = \frac{1}{4}(Y_1 + Y_2 + Y_3 + Y_4)$$
$$W_2 = \frac{1}{2}(Y_1 + Y_2) - \frac{1}{2}(Y_3 + Y_4)$$

a. State the above in matrix notation.

b. Find the expectation of the random vector $\mathbf{W}$.

c. Find the variance-covariance matrix of $\mathbf{W}$.

*5.19. Find the matrix $\mathbf{A}$ of the quadratic form:

$$3Y_1^2 + 10Y_1Y_2 + 17Y_2^2$$

5.20. Find the matrix $\mathbf{A}$ of the quadratic form:

$$7Y_1^2 - 8Y_1Y_2 + 8Y_2^2$$

*5.21. For the matrix:

$$A = \begin{bmatrix} 5 & 2 \\ 2 & 1 \end{bmatrix}$$

find the quadratic form of the observations Y_1 and Y_2.

5.22. For the matrix:

$$A = \begin{bmatrix} 1 & 0 & 4 \\ 0 & 3 & 0 \\ 4 & 0 & 9 \end{bmatrix}$$

find the quadratic form of the observations Y_1, Y_2, and Y_3.

*5.23. Refer to **Flavor deterioration** Problems 5.4 and 5.12.

a. Using matrix methods, obtain the following: (1) vector of estimated regression coefficients, (2) vector of residuals, (3) SSR, (4) SSE, (5) estimated variance-covariance matrix of **b**, (6) point estimate of $E\{Y_h\}$ when $X_h = -6$, (7) estimated variance of $\hat{Y}_h$ when $X_h = -6$.

b. What simplifications arose from the spacing of the X levels in the experiment?

c. Find the hat matrix **H**.

d. Find $s^2\{e\}$.

5.24. Refer to **Consumer finance** Problems 5.5 and 5.13.

a. Using matrix methods, obtain the following: (1) vector of estimated regression coefficients, (2) vector of residuals, (3) SSR, (4) SSE, (5) estimated variance-covariance matrix of **b**, (6) point estimate of $E\{Y_h\}$ when $X_h = 4$, (7) $s^2\{\text{pred}\}$ when $X_h = 4$.

b. From your estimated variance-covariance matrix in part (a5), obtain the following: (1) $s\{b_0, b_1\}$; (2) $s^2\{b_0\}$; (3) $s\{b_1\}$.

c. Find the hat matrix **H**.

d. Find $s^2\{e\}$.

*5.25. Refer to **Airfreight breakage** Problems 1.21 and 5.6.

a. Using matrix methods, obtain the following: (1) $(\mathbf{X'X})^{-1}$, (2) **b**, (3) **e**, (4) **H**, (5) SSE, (6) $s^2\{\mathbf{b}\}$, (7) $\hat{Y}_h$ when $X_h = 2$, (8) $s^2\{\hat{Y}_h\}$ when $X_h = 2$.

b. From part (a6), obtain the following: (1) $s^2\{b_1\}$; (2) $s\{b_0, b_1\}$; (3) $s\{b_0\}$.

c. Find the matrix of the quadratic form for SSR.

5.26. Refer to **Plastic hardness** Problems 1.22 and 5.7.

a. Using matrix methods, obtain the following: (1) $(\mathbf{X'X})^{-1}$, (2) **b**, (3) $\hat{\mathbf{Y}}$, (4) **H**, (5) SSE, (6) $s^2\{\mathbf{b}\}$, (7) $s^2\{\text{pred}\}$ when $X_h = 30$.

b. From part (a6), obtain the following: (1) $s^2\{b_0\}$; (2) $s\{b_0, b_1\}$; (3) $s\{b_1\}$.

c. Obtain the matrix of the quadratic form for SSE.

Exercises

5.27. Refer to regression-through-the-origin model (4.10). Set up the expectation vector for **ε**. Assume that $i = 1, \ldots, 4$.

5.28. Consider model (4.10) for regression through the origin and the estimator b_1 given in (4.14). Obtain (4.14) by utilizing (5.60) with **X** suitably defined.

5.29. Consider the least squares estimator **b** given in (5.60). Using matrix methods, show that **b** is an unbiased estimator.

5.30. Show that $\hat{Y}_h$ in (5.96) can be expressed in matrix terms as $\mathbf{b'X}_h$.

5.31. Obtain an expression for the variance-covariance matrix of the fitted values $\hat{Y}_i$, $i = 1, \ldots, n$, in terms of the hat matrix.

Part **II**

Multiple Linear Regression

Chapter 6

Multiple Regression I

Multiple regression analysis is one of the most widely used of all statistical methods. In this chapter, we first discuss a variety of multiple regression models. Then we present the basic statistical results for multiple regression in matrix form. Since the matrix expressions for multiple regression are the same as for simple linear regression, we state the results without much discussion. We conclude the chapter with an example, illustrating a variety of inferences and residual analyses in multiple regression analysis.

6.1 Multiple Regression Models

Need for Several Predictor Variables

When we first introduced regression analysis in Chapter 1, we spoke of regression models containing a number of predictor variables. We mentioned a regression model where the response variable was direct operating cost for a branch office of a consumer finance chain, and four predictor variables were considered, including average number of loans outstanding at the branch and total number of new loan applications processed by the branch. We also mentioned a tractor purchase study where the response variable was volume of tractor purchases in a sales territory, and the nine predictor variables included number of farms in the territory and quantity of crop production in the territory. In addition, we mentioned a study of short children where the response variable was the peak plasma growth hormone level, and the 14 predictor variables included gender, age, and various body measurements. In all these examples, a single predictor variable in the model would have provided an inadequate description since a number of key variables affect the response variable in important and distinctive ways. Furthermore, in situations of this type, we frequently find that predictions of the response variable based on a model containing only a single predictor variable are too imprecise to be useful. We noted the imprecise predictions with a single predictor variable in the Toluca Company example in Chapter 2. A more complex model, containing additional predictor variables, typically is more helpful in providing sufficiently precise predictions of the response variable.

In each of the examples just mentioned, the analysis was based on observational data because the predictor variables were not controlled, usually because they were not susceptible to direct control. Multiple regression analysis is also highly useful in experimental situations where the experimenter can control the predictor variables. An experimenter typically will wish to investigate a number of predictor variables simultaneously because almost always more than one key predictor variable influences the response. For example, in a study of productivity of work crews, the experimenter may wish to control both the size of the crew and the level of bonus pay. Similarly, in a study of responsiveness to a drug, the experimenter may wish to control both the dose of the drug and the method of administration.

The multiple regression models which we now describe can be utilized for either observational data or for experimental data from a completely randomized design.

First-Order Model with Two Predictor Variables

When there are two predictor variables X_1 and X_2, the regression model:

$$Y_i = \beta_0 + \beta_1 X_{i1} + \beta_2 X_{i2} + \varepsilon_i \tag{6.1}$$

is called a first-order model with two predictor variables. A first-order model, as we noted in Chapter 1, is linear in the predictor variables. Y_i denotes as usual the response in the ith trial, and X_{i1} and X_{i2} are the values of the two predictor variables in the ith trial. The parameters of the model are β_0, β_1, and β_2, and the error term is ε_i.

Assuming that $E\{\varepsilon_i\} = 0$, the regression function for model (6.1) is:

$$E\{Y\} = \beta_0 + \beta_1 X_1 + \beta_2 X_2 \tag{6.2}$$

Analogous to simple linear regression, where the regression function $E\{Y\} = \beta_0 + \beta_1 X$ is a line, regression function (6.2) is a plane. Figure 6.1 contains a representation of a portion of the response plane:

$$E\{Y\} = 10 + 2X_1 + 5X_2 \tag{6.3}$$

Note that any point on the response plane (6.3) corresponds to the mean response $E\{Y\}$ at the given combination of levels of X_1 and X_2.

Figure 6.1 also shows an observation Y_i corresponding to the levels (X_{i1}, X_{i2}) of the two predictor variables. Note that the vertical rule in Figure 6.1 between Y_i and the response plane represents the difference between Y_i and the mean $E\{Y_i\}$ of the probability distribution of Y for the given (X_{i1}, X_{i2}) combination. Hence, the vertical distance from Y_i to the response plane represents the error term $\varepsilon_i = Y_i - E\{Y_i\}$.

FIGURE 6.1
Response Function is a Plane—Sales Promotion Example.

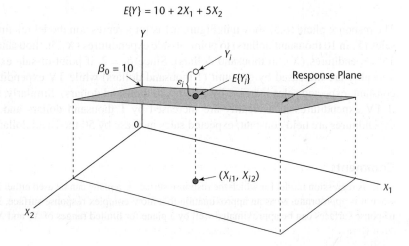

$E\{Y\} = 10 + 2X_1 + 5X_2$

Frequently the regression function in multiple regression is called a *regression surface* or a *response surface*. In Figure 6.1, the response surface is a plane, but in other cases the response surface may be more complex in nature.

Meaning of Regression Coefficients.   Let us now consider the meaning of the regression coefficients in the multiple regression function (6.3). The parameter $\beta_0 = 10$ is the Y intercept of the regression plane. If the scope of the model includes $X_1 = 0$, $X_2 = 0$, then $\beta_0 = 10$ represents the mean response $E\{Y\}$ at $X_1 = 0$, $X_2 = 0$. Otherwise, β_0 does not have any particular meaning as a separate term in the regression model.

The parameter β_1 indicates the change in the mean response $E\{Y\}$ per unit increase in X_1 when X_2 is held constant. Likewise, β_2 indicates the change in the mean response per unit increase in X_2 when X_1 is held constant. To see this for our example, suppose X_2 is held at the level $X_2 = 2$. The regression function (6.3) now is:

$$E\{Y\} = 10 + 2X_1 + 5(2) = 20 + 2X_1 \qquad X_2 = 2 \qquad \textbf{(6.4)}$$

Note that this response function is a straight line with slope $\beta_1 = 2$. The same is true for any other value of X_2; only the intercept of the response function will differ. Hence, $\beta_1 = 2$ indicates that the mean response $E\{Y\}$ increases by 2 with a unit increase in X_1 when X_2 is constant, no matter what the level of X_2. We confirm therefore that β_1 indicates the change in $E\{Y\}$ with a unit increase in X_1 when X_2 is held constant.

Similarly, $\beta_2 = 5$ in regression function (6.3) indicates that the mean response $E\{Y\}$ increases by 5 with a unit increase in X_2 when X_1 is held constant.

When the effect of X_1 on the mean response does not depend on the level of X_2, and correspondingly the effect of X_2 does not depend on the level of X_1, the two predictor variables are said to have *additive effects* or *not to interact*. Thus, the first-order regression model (6.1) is designed for predictor variables whose effects on the mean response are additive or do not interact.

The parameters β_1 and β_2 are sometimes called *partial regression coefficients* because they reflect the partial effect of one predictor variable when the other predictor variable is included in the model and is held constant.

Example

The response plane (6.3) shown in Figure 6.1 is for a regression model relating test market sales (Y, in 10 thousand dollars) to point-of-sale expenditures (X_1, in thousand dollars) and TV expenditures (X_2, in thousand dollars). Since $\beta_1 = 2$, if point-of-sale expenditures in a locality are increased by one unit (1 thousand dollars) while TV expenditures are held constant, expected sales increase by 2 units (20 thousand dollars). Similarly, since $\beta_2 = 5$, if TV expenditures in a locality are increased by 1 thousand dollars and point-of-sale expenditures are held constant, expected sales increase by 50 thousand dollars.

Comments

1. A regression model for which the response surface is a plane can be used either in its own right when it is appropriate, or as an approximation to a more complex response surface. Many complex response surfaces can be approximated well by a plane for limited ranges of X_1 and X_2.

2. We can readily establish the meaning of β_1 and β_2 by calculus, taking partial derivatives of the response surface (6.2) with respect to X_1 and X_2 in turn:

$$\frac{\partial E\{Y\}}{\partial X_1} = \beta_1 \qquad \frac{\partial E\{Y\}}{\partial X_2} = \beta_2$$

The partial derivatives measure the rate of change in $E\{Y\}$ with respect to one predictor variable when the other is held constant. ∎

First-Order Model with More than Two Predictor Variables

We consider now the case where there are $p - 1$ predictor variables $X_1, \ldots, X_{p-1}$. The regression model:

$$Y_i = \beta_0 + \beta_1 X_{i1} + \beta_2 X_{i2} + \cdots + \beta_{p-1} X_{i,p-1} + \varepsilon_i \tag{6.5}$$

is called a first-order model with $p - 1$ predictor variables. It can also be written:

$$Y_i = \beta_0 + \sum_{k=1}^{p-1} \beta_k X_{ik} + \varepsilon_i \tag{6.5a}$$

or, if we let $X_{i0} \equiv 1$, it can be written as:

$$Y_i = \sum_{k=0}^{p-1} \beta_k X_{ik} + \varepsilon_i \qquad \text{where } X_{i0} \equiv 1 \tag{6.5b}$$

Assuming that $E\{\varepsilon_i\} = 0$, the response function for regression model (6.5) is:

$$E\{Y\} = \beta_0 + \beta_1 X_1 + \beta_2 X_2 + \cdots + \beta_{p-1} X_{p-1} \tag{6.6}$$

This response function is a *hyperplane,* which is a plane in more than two dimensions. It is no longer possible to picture this response surface, as we were able to do in Figure 6.1 for the case of two predictor variables. Nevertheless, the meaning of the parameters is analogous to the case of two predictor variables. The parameter β_k indicates the change in the mean response $E\{Y\}$ with a unit increase in the predictor variable X_k, when all other predictor variables in the regression model are held constant. Note again that the effect of any predictor variable on the mean response is the same for regression model (6.5) no matter what are the levels at which the other predictor variables are held. Hence, first-order regression model (6.5) is designed for predictor variables whose effects on the mean response are additive and therefore do not interact.

Comment

When $p - 1 = 1$, regression model (6.5) reduces to:

$$Y_i = \beta_0 + \beta_1 X_{i1} + \varepsilon_i$$

which is the simple linear regression model considered in earlier chapters. ∎

General Linear Regression Model

In general, the variables $X_1, \ldots, X_{p-1}$ in a regression model do not need to represent different predictor variables, as we shall shortly see. We therefore define the general linear regression model, with normal error terms, simply in terms of X variables:

$$Y_i = \beta_0 + \beta_1 X_{i1} + \beta_2 X_{i2} + \cdots + \beta_{p-1} X_{i,p-1} + \varepsilon_i \qquad \textbf{(6.7)}$$

where:

$\beta_0, \beta_1, \ldots, \beta_{p-1}$ are parameters

$X_{i1}, \ldots, X_{i,p-1}$ are known constants

ε_i are independent $N(0, \sigma^2)$

$i = 1, \ldots, n$

If we let $X_{i0} \equiv 1$, regression model (6.7) can be written as follows:

$$Y_i = \beta_0 X_{i0} + \beta_1 X_{i1} + \beta_2 X_{i2} + \cdots + \beta_{p-1} X_{i,p-1} + \varepsilon_i \qquad \textbf{(6.7a)}$$

where $X_{i0} \equiv 1$, or:

$$Y_i = \sum_{k=0}^{p-1} \beta_k X_{ik} + \varepsilon_i \qquad \text{where } X_{i0} \equiv 1 \qquad \textbf{(6.7b)}$$

The response function for regression model (6.7) is, since $E\{\varepsilon_i\} = 0$:

$$E\{Y\} = \beta_0 + \beta_1 X_1 + \beta_2 X_2 + \cdots + \beta_{p-1} X_{p-1} \qquad \textbf{(6.8)}$$

Thus, the general linear regression model with normal error terms implies that the observations Y_i are independent normal variables, with mean $E\{Y_i\}$ as given by (6.8) and with constant variance σ^2.

This general linear model encompasses a vast variety of situations. We consider a few of these now.

$p - 1$ Predictor Variables. When $X_1, \ldots, X_{p-1}$ represent $p - 1$ different predictor variables, general linear regression model (6.7) is, as we have seen, a first-order model in which there are no interaction effects between the predictor variables. The example in Figure 6.1 involves a first-order model with two predictor variables.

Qualitative Predictor Variables. The general linear regression model (6.7) encompasses not only quantitative predictor variables but also qualitative ones, such as gender (male, female) or disability status (not disabled, partially disabled, fully disabled). We use indicator variables that take on the values 0 and 1 to identify the classes of a qualitative variable.

Consider a regression analysis to predict the length of hospital stay (Y) based on the age (X_1) and gender (X_2) of the patient. We define X_2 as follows:

$$X_2 = \begin{cases} 1 & \text{if patient female} \\ 0 & \text{if patient male} \end{cases}$$

The first-order regression model then is as follows:

$$Y_i = \beta_0 + \beta_1 X_{i1} + \beta_2 X_{i2} + \varepsilon_i \qquad \textbf{(6.9)}$$

where:

$X_{i1} = \text{patient's age}$

$$X_{i2} = \begin{cases} 1 & \text{if patient female} \\ 0 & \text{if patient male} \end{cases}$$

The response function for regression model (6.9) is:

$$E\{Y\} = \beta_0 + \beta_1 X_1 + \beta_2 X_2 \qquad \textbf{(6.10)}$$

For male patients, $X_2 = 0$ and response function (6.10) becomes:

$$E\{Y\} = \beta_0 + \beta_1 X_1 \qquad \text{Male patients} \qquad \textbf{(6.10a)}$$

For female patients, $X_2 = 1$ and response function (6.10) becomes:

$$E\{Y\} = (\beta_0 + \beta_2) + \beta_1 X_1 \qquad \text{Female patients} \qquad \textbf{(6.10b)}$$

These two response functions represent parallel straight lines with different intercepts.

In general, we represent a qualitative variable with c classes by means of $c - 1$ indicator variables. For instance, if in the hospital stay example the qualitative variable disability status is to be added as another predictor variable, it can be represented as follows by the two indicator variables X_3 and X_4:

$$X_3 = \begin{cases} 1 & \text{if patient not disabled} \\ 0 & \text{otherwise} \end{cases}$$

$$X_4 = \begin{cases} 1 & \text{if patient partially disabled} \\ 0 & \text{otherwise} \end{cases}$$

The first-order model with age, gender, and disability status as predictor variables then is:

$$Y_i = \beta_0 + \beta_1 X_{i1} + \beta_2 X_{i2} + \beta_3 X_{i3} + \beta_4 X_{i4} + \varepsilon_i \qquad \textbf{(6.11)}$$

where:

$$X_{i1} = \text{patient's age}$$

$$X_{i2} = \begin{cases} 1 & \text{if patient female} \\ 0 & \text{if patient male} \end{cases}$$

$$X_{i3} = \begin{cases} 1 & \text{if patient not disabled} \\ 0 & \text{otherwise} \end{cases}$$

$$X_{i4} = \begin{cases} 1 & \text{if patient partially disabled} \\ 0 & \text{otherwise} \end{cases}$$

In Chapter 8 we present a comprehensive discussion of how to model qualitative predictor variables and how to interpret regression models containing qualitative predictor variables.

Polynomial Regression. Polynomial regression models are special cases of the general linear regression model. They contain squared and higher-order terms of the predictor variable(s), making the response function curvilinear. The following is a polynomial regression model with one predictor variable:

$$Y_i = \beta_0 + \beta_1 X_i + \beta_2 X_i^2 + \varepsilon_i \qquad \textbf{(6.12)}$$

Figure 1.3 on page 5 shows an example of a polynomial regression function with one predictor variable.

Despite the curvilinear nature of the response function for regression model (6.12), it is a special case of general linear regression model (6.7). If we let $X_{i1} = X_i$ and $X_{i2} = X_i^2$, we can write (6.12) as follows:

$$Y_i = \beta_0 + \beta_1 X_{i1} + \beta_2 X_{i2} + \varepsilon_i$$

which is in the form of general linear regression model (6.7). While (6.12) illustrates a curvilinear regression model where the response function is quadratic, models with higher-degree polynomial response functions are also particular cases of the general linear regression model. We shall discuss polynomial regression models in more detail in Chapter 8.

Transformed Variables. Models with transformed variables involve complex, curvilinear response functions, yet still are special cases of the general linear regression model. Consider the following model with a transformed Y variable:

$$\log Y_i = \beta_0 + \beta_1 X_{i1} + \beta_2 X_{i2} + \beta_3 X_{i3} + \varepsilon_i \tag{6.13}$$

Here, the response surface is complex, yet model (6.13) can still be treated as a general linear regression model. If we let $Y_i' = \log Y_i$, we can write regression model (6.13) as follows:

$$Y_i' = \beta_0 + \beta_1 X_{i1} + \beta_2 X_{i2} + \beta_3 X_{i3} + \varepsilon_i$$

which is in the form of general linear regression model (6.7). The response variable just happens to be the logarithm of Y.

Many models can be transformed into the general linear regression model. For instance, the model:

$$Y_i = \frac{1}{\beta_0 + \beta_1 X_{i1} + \beta_2 X_{i2} + \varepsilon_i} \tag{6.14}$$

can be transformed to the general linear regression model by letting $Y_i' = 1/Y_i$. We then have:

$$Y_i' = \beta_0 + \beta_1 X_{i1} + \beta_2 X_{i2} + \varepsilon_i$$

Interaction Effects. When the effects of the predictor variables on the response variable are not additive, the effect of one predictor variable depends on the levels of the other predictor variables. The general linear regression model (6.7) encompasses regression models with nonadditive or interacting effects. An example of a nonadditive regression model with two predictor variables X_1 and X_2 is the following:

$$Y_i = \beta_0 + \beta_1 X_{i1} + \beta_2 X_{i2} + \beta_3 X_{i1} X_{i2} + \varepsilon_i \tag{6.15}$$

Here, the response function is complex because of the interaction term $\beta_3 X_{i1} X_{i2}$. Yet regression model (6.15) is a special case of the general linear regression model. Let $X_{i3} = X_{i1} X_{i2}$ and then write (6.15) as follows:

$$Y_i = \beta_0 + \beta_1 X_{i1} + \beta_2 X_{i2} + \beta_3 X_{i3} + \varepsilon_i$$

We see that this model is in the form of general linear regression model (6.7). We shall discuss regression models with interaction effects in more detail in Chapter 8.

Combination of Cases. A regression model may combine several of the elements we have just noted and still be treated as a general linear regression model. Consider the following regression model containing linear and quadratic terms for each of two predictor variables and an interaction term represented by the cross-product term:

$$Y_i = \beta_0 + \beta_1 X_{i1} + \beta_2 X_{i1}^2 + \beta_3 X_{i2} + \beta_4 X_{i2}^2 + \beta_5 X_{i1} X_{i2} + \varepsilon_i \tag{6.16}$$

FIGURE 6.2 **Additional Examples of Response Functions.**

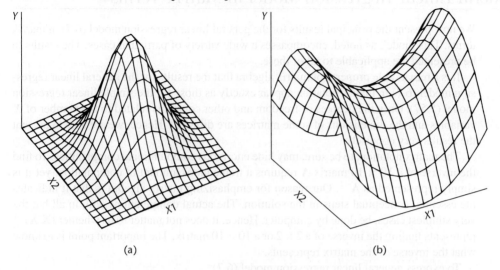

(a)   (b)

Let us define:

$$Z_{i1} = X_{i1} \qquad Z_{i2} = X_{i1}^2 \qquad Z_{i3} = X_{i2} \qquad Z_{i4} = X_{i2}^2 \qquad Z_{i5} = X_{i1}X_{i2}$$

We can then write regression model (6.16) as follows:

$$Y_i = \beta_0 + \beta_1 Z_{i1} + \beta_2 Z_{i2} + \beta_3 Z_{i3} + \beta_4 Z_{i4} + \beta_5 Z_{i5} + \varepsilon_i$$

which is in the form of general linear regression model (6.7).

The general linear regression model (6.7) includes many complex models, some of which may be highly complex. Figure 6.2 illustrates two complex response surfaces when there are two predictor variables, that can be represented by general linear regression model (6.7).

Meaning of Linear in General Linear Regression Model. It should be clear from the various examples that general linear regression model (6.7) is not restricted to linear response surfaces. The term *linear model* refers to the fact that model (6.7) is linear in the parameters; it does not refer to the shape of the response surface.

We say that a regression model is linear in the parameters when it can be written in the form:

$$Y_i = c_{i0}\beta_0 + c_{i1}\beta_1 + c_{i2}\beta_2 + \cdots + c_{i,p-1}\beta_{p-1} + \varepsilon_i \tag{6.17}$$

where the terms c_{i0}, c_{i1}, etc., are coefficients involving the predictor variables. For example, first-order model (6.1) in two predictor variables:

$$Y_i = \beta_0 + \beta_1 X_{i1} + \beta_2 X_{i2} + \varepsilon_i$$

is linear in the parameters, with $c_{i0} = 1$, $c_{i1} = X_{i1}$, and $c_{i2} = X_{i2}$.

An example of a nonlinear regression model is the following:

$$Y_i = \beta_0 \exp(\beta_1 X_i) + \varepsilon_i$$

This is a nonlinear regression model because it cannot be expressed in the form of (6.17). We shall discuss nonlinear regression models in Part III.

6.2 General Linear Regression Model in Matrix Terms

We now present the principal results for the general linear regression model (6.7) in matrix terms. This model, as noted, encompasses a wide variety of particular cases. The results to be presented are applicable to all of these.

It is a remarkable property of matrix algebra that the results for the general linear regression model (6.7) in matrix notation appear exactly as those for the simple linear regression model (5.57). Only the degrees of freedom and other constants related to the number of X variables and the dimensions of some matrices are different. Hence, we are able to present the results very concisely.

The matrix notation, to be sure, may hide enormous computational complexities. To find the inverse of a 10×10 matrix $\mathbf{A}$ requires a tremendous amount of computation, yet it is simply represented as $\mathbf{A}^{-1}$. Our reason for emphasizing matrix algebra is that it indicates the essential conceptual steps in the solution. The actual computations will, in all but the very simplest cases, be done by computer. Hence, it does not matter to us whether $(\mathbf{X'X})^{-1}$ represents finding the inverse of a 2×2 or a 10×10 matrix. The important point is to know what the inverse of the matrix represents.

To express general linear regression model (6.7):

$$Y_i = \beta_0 + \beta_1 X_{i1} + \beta_2 X_{i2} + \cdots + \beta_{p-1} X_{i,p-1} + \varepsilon_i$$

in matrix terms, we need to define the following matrices:

(6.18a) **(6.18b)**

$$\underset{n\times 1}{\mathbf{Y}} = \begin{bmatrix} Y_1 \\ Y_2 \\ \vdots \\ Y_n \end{bmatrix} \qquad \underset{n\times p}{\mathbf{X}} = \begin{bmatrix} 1 & X_{11} & X_{12} & \cdots & X_{1,p-1} \\ 1 & X_{21} & X_{22} & \cdots & X_{2,p-1} \\ \vdots & \vdots & \vdots & & \vdots \\ 1 & X_{n1} & X_{n2} & \cdots & X_{n,p-1} \end{bmatrix}$$

(6.18)

(6.18c) **(6.18d)**

$$\underset{p\times 1}{\boldsymbol{\beta}} = \begin{bmatrix} \beta_0 \\ \beta_1 \\ \vdots \\ \beta_{p-1} \end{bmatrix} \qquad \underset{n\times 1}{\boldsymbol{\varepsilon}} = \begin{bmatrix} \varepsilon_1 \\ \varepsilon_2 \\ \vdots \\ \varepsilon_n \end{bmatrix}$$

Note that the $\mathbf{Y}$ and $\boldsymbol{\varepsilon}$ vectors are the same as for simple linear regression. The $\boldsymbol{\beta}$ vector contains additional regression parameters, and the $\mathbf{X}$ matrix contains a column of 1s as well as a column of the n observations for each of the $p-1$ X variables in the regression model. The row subscript for each element X_{ik} in the $\mathbf{X}$ matrix identifies the trial or case, and the column subscript identifies the $\mathbf{X}$ variable.

In matrix terms, the general linear regression model (6.7) is:

$$\underset{n\times 1}{\mathbf{Y}} = \underset{n\times p}{\mathbf{X}} \underset{p\times p}{\boldsymbol{\beta}} + \underset{n\times 1}{\boldsymbol{\varepsilon}} \qquad \text{(6.19)}$$

where:

Y is a vector of responses

β is a vector of parameters

X is a matrix of constants

ε is a vector of independent normal random variables with expectation

$E\{\boldsymbol{\varepsilon}\} = \mathbf{0}$ and variance-covariance matrix:

$$\underset{n \times n}{\sigma^2\{\boldsymbol{\varepsilon}\}} = \begin{bmatrix} \sigma^2 & 0 & \cdots & 0 \\ 0 & \sigma^2 & \cdots & 0 \\ \vdots & \vdots & & \vdots \\ 0 & 0 & \cdots & \sigma^2 \end{bmatrix} = \sigma^2 \mathbf{I}$$

Consequently, the random vector **Y** has expectation:

$$\underset{n \times 1}{E\{\mathbf{Y}\}} = \mathbf{X}\boldsymbol{\beta} \tag{6.20}$$

and the variance-covariance matrix of **Y** is the same as that of **ε**:

$$\underset{n \times n}{\sigma^2\{\mathbf{Y}\}} = \sigma^2 \mathbf{I} \tag{6.21}$$

6.3 Estimation of Regression Coefficients

The least squares criterion (1.8) is generalized as follows for general linear regression model (6.7):

$$Q = \sum_{i=1}^{n} (Y_i - \beta_0 - \beta_1 X_{i1} - \cdots - \beta_{p-1} X_{i,p-1})^2 \tag{6.22}$$

The least squares estimators are those values of $\beta_0, \beta_1, \ldots, \beta_{p-1}$ that minimize Q. Let us denote the vector of the least squares estimated regression coefficients $b_0, b_1, \ldots, b_{p-1}$ as **b**:

$$\underset{p \times 1}{\mathbf{b}} = \begin{bmatrix} b_0 \\ b_1 \\ \vdots \\ b_{p-1} \end{bmatrix} \tag{6.23}$$

The least squares normal equations for the general linear regression model (6.19) are:

$$\mathbf{X}'\mathbf{X}\mathbf{b} = \mathbf{X}'\mathbf{Y} \tag{6.24}$$

and the least squares estimators are:

$$\underset{2 \times 1}{\mathbf{b}} = \underset{2 \times 2}{(\mathbf{X}'\mathbf{X})^{-1}} \underset{2 \times 1}{(\mathbf{X}'\mathbf{X})} \mathbf{Y} \tag{6.25}$$

The method of maximum likelihood leads to the same estimators for normal error regression model (6.19) as those obtained by the method of least squares in (6.25). The likelihood function in (1.26) generalizes directly for multiple regression as follows:

$$L(\boldsymbol{\beta}, \sigma^2) = \frac{1}{(2\pi\sigma^2)^{n/2}} \exp\left[-\frac{1}{2\sigma^2} \sum_{i=1}^{n} (Y_i - \beta_0 - \beta_1 X_{i1} - \cdots - \beta_{p-1} X_{i,p-1})^2\right] \quad (6.26)$$

Maximizing this likelihood function with respect to $\beta_0, \beta_1, \ldots, \beta_{p-1}$ leads to the estimators in (6.25). These estimators are least squares and maximum likelihood estimators and have all the properties mentioned in Chapter 1: they are minimum variance unbiased, consistent, and sufficient.

6.4 Fitted Values and Residuals

Let the vector of the fitted values $\hat{Y}_i$ be denoted by $\hat{\mathbf{Y}}$ and the vector of the residual terms $e_i = Y_i - \hat{Y}_i$ be denoted by $\mathbf{e}$:

$$(6.27a) \quad \underset{n \times 1}{\hat{\mathbf{Y}}} = \begin{bmatrix} \hat{Y}_1 \\ \hat{Y}_2 \\ \vdots \\ \hat{Y}_n \end{bmatrix} \qquad (6.27b) \quad \underset{n \times 1}{\mathbf{e}} = \begin{bmatrix} e_1 \\ e_2 \\ \vdots \\ e_n \end{bmatrix} \quad (6.27)$$

The fitted values are represented by:

$$\underset{n \times 1}{\hat{\mathbf{Y}}} = \mathbf{Xb} \quad (6.28)$$

and the residual terms by:

$$\underset{n \times 1}{\mathbf{e}} = \mathbf{Y} - \hat{\mathbf{Y}} = \mathbf{Y} - \mathbf{Xb} \quad (6.29)$$

The vector of the fitted values $\hat{\mathbf{Y}}$ can be expressed in terms of the hat matrix $\mathbf{H}$ as follows:

$$\underset{n \times 1}{\hat{\mathbf{Y}}} = \mathbf{HY} \quad (6.30)$$

where:

$$\underset{n \times n}{\mathbf{H}} = \mathbf{X}(\mathbf{X'X})^{-1}\mathbf{X'} \quad (6.30a)$$

Similarly, the vector of residuals can be expressed as follows:

$$\underset{n \times 1}{\mathbf{e}} = (\mathbf{I} - \mathbf{H})\mathbf{Y} \quad (6.31)$$

The variance-covariance matrix of the residuals is:

$$\underset{n \times n}{\sigma^2\{\mathbf{e}\}} = \sigma^2(\mathbf{I} - \mathbf{H}) \quad (6.32)$$

which is estimated by:

$$\mathbf{s}^2\{\mathbf{e}\} = MSE(\mathbf{I} - \underset{n\times n}{\mathbf{H}}) \tag{6.33}$$

6.5 Analysis of Variance Results

Sums of Squares and Mean Squares

The sums of squares for the analysis of variance in matrix terms are, from (5.89):

$$SSTO = \mathbf{Y'Y} - \left(\frac{1}{n}\right)\mathbf{Y'JY} = \mathbf{Y'}\left[\mathbf{I} - \left(\frac{1}{n}\right)\mathbf{J}\right]\mathbf{Y} \tag{6.34}$$

$$SSE = \mathbf{e'e} = (\mathbf{Y} - \mathbf{Xb})'(\mathbf{Y} - \mathbf{Xb}) = \mathbf{Y'Y} - \mathbf{b'X'Y} = \mathbf{Y'(I - H)Y} \tag{6.35}$$

$$SSR = \mathbf{b'X'Y} - \left(\frac{1}{n}\right)\mathbf{Y'JY} = \mathbf{Y'}\left[\mathbf{H} - \left(\frac{1}{n}\right)\mathbf{J}\right]\mathbf{Y} \tag{6.36}$$

where $\mathbf{J}$ is an $n \times n$ matrix of 1s defined in (5.18) and $\mathbf{H}$ is the hat matrix defined in (6.30a).

SSTO, as usual, has $n - 1$ degrees of freedom associated with it. *SSE* has $n - p$ degrees of freedom associated with it since p parameters need to be estimated in the regression function for model (6.19). Finally, *SSR* has $p - 1$ degrees of freedom associated with it, representing the number of X variables $X_1, \ldots, X_{p-1}$.

Table 6.1 shows these analysis of variance results, as well as the mean squares *MSR* and *MSE*:

$$MSR = \frac{SSR}{p - 1} \tag{6.37}$$

$$MSE = \frac{SSE}{n - p} \tag{6.38}$$

The expectation of *MSE* is σ^2, as for simple linear regression. The expectation of *MSR* is σ^2 plus a quantity that is nonnegative. For instance, when $p - 1 = 2$, we have:

$$E\{MSR\} = \sigma^2 + \frac{1}{2}\left[\beta_1^2 \sum(X_{i1} - \bar{X}_1)^2 + \beta_2^2 \sum(X_{i2} - \bar{X}_2)^2 \right.$$
$$\left. + 2\beta_1\beta_2 \sum(X_{i1} - \bar{X}_1)(X_{i2} - \bar{X}_2)\right]$$

Note that if both β_1 and β_2 equal zero, $E\{MSR\} = \sigma^2$. Otherwise $E\{MSR\} > \sigma^2$.

TABLE 6.1
ANOVA Table for General Linear Regression Model (6.19).

Source of Variation	SS	df	MS
Regression	$SSR = \mathbf{b'X'Y} - \left(\frac{1}{n}\right)\mathbf{Y'JY}$	$p - 1$	$MSR = \frac{SSR}{p - 1}$
Error	$SSE = \mathbf{Y'Y} - \mathbf{b'X'Y}$	$n - p$	$MSE = \frac{SSE}{n - p}$
Total	$SSTO = \mathbf{Y'Y} - \left(\frac{1}{n}\right)\mathbf{Y'JY}$	$n - 1$	

F Test for Regression Relation

To test whether there is a regression relation between the response variable Y and the set of X variables $X_1, \ldots, X_{p-1}$, i.e., to choose between the alternatives:

$$H_0: \beta_1 = \beta_2 = \cdots = \beta_{p-1} = 0$$
$$H_a: \text{not all } \beta_k \ (k = 1, \ldots, p-1) \text{ equal zero} \tag{6.39a}$$

we use the test statistic:

$$F^* = \frac{MSR}{MSE} \tag{6.39b}$$

The decision rule to control the Type I error at α is:

$$\text{If } F^* \leq F(1-\alpha; p-1, n-p), \text{ conclude } H_0$$
$$\text{If } F^* > F(1-\alpha; p-1, n-p), \text{ conclude } H_a \tag{6.39c}$$

The existence of a regression relation by itself does not, of course, ensure that useful predictions can be made by using it.

Note that when $p - 1 = 1$, this test reduces to the F test in (2.60) for testing in simple linear regression whether or not $\beta_1 = 0$.

Coefficient of Multiple Determination

The coefficient of multiple determination, denoted by R^2, is defined as follows:

$$R^2 = \frac{SSR}{SSTO} = 1 - \frac{SSE}{SSTO} \tag{6.40}$$

It measures the proportionate reduction of total variation in Y associated with the use of the set of X variables $X_1, \ldots, X_{p-1}$. The coefficient of multiple determination R^2 reduces to the coefficient of simple determination in (2.72) for simple linear regression when $p - 1 = 1$, i.e., when one X variable is in regression model (6.19). Just as before, we have:

$$0 \leq R^2 \leq 1 \tag{6.41}$$

where R^2 assumes the value 0 when all $b_k = 0$ $(k = 1, \ldots, p-1)$, and the value 1 when all Y observations fall directly on the fitted regression surface, i.e., when $Y_i = \hat{Y}_i$ for all i.

Adding more X variables to the regression model can only increase R^2 and never reduce it, because SSE can never become larger with more X variables and $SSTO$ is always the same for a given set of responses. Since R^2 usually can be made larger by including a larger number of predictor variables, it is sometimes suggested that a modified measure be used that adjusts for the number of X variables in the model. The *adjusted coefficient of multiple determination*, denoted by R_a^2, adjusts R^2 by dividing each sum of squares by its associated degrees of freedom:

$$R_a^2 = 1 - \frac{\dfrac{SSE}{n-p}}{\dfrac{SSTO}{n-1}} = 1 - \left(\frac{n-1}{n-p}\right)\frac{SSE}{SSTO} \tag{6.42}$$

This adjusted coefficient of multiple determination may actually become smaller when another X variable is introduced into the model, because any decrease in SSE may be more than offset by the loss of a degree of freedom in the denominator $n - p$.

Comments

1. To distinguish between the coefficients of determination for simple and multiple regression, we shall from now on refer to the former as the coefficient of simple determination.

2. It can be shown that the coefficient of multiple determination R^2 can be viewed as a coefficient of simple determination between the responses Y_i and the fitted values $\hat{Y}_i$.

3. A large value of R^2 does not necessarily imply that the fitted model is a useful one. For instance, observations may have been taken at only a few levels of the predictor variables. Despite a high R^2 in this case, the fitted model may not be useful if most predictions require extrapolations outside the region of observations. Again, even though R^2 is large, *MSE* may still be too large for inferences to be useful when high precision is required. ∎

Coefficient of Multiple Correlation

The coefficient of multiple correlation R is the positive square root of R^2:

$$R = \sqrt{R^2} \tag{6.43}$$

When there is one X variable in regression model (6.19), i.e., when $p-1 = 1$, the coefficient of multiple correlation R equals in absolute value the correlation coefficient r in (2.73) for simple correlation.

6.6 Inferences about Regression Parameters

The least squares and maximum likelihood estimators in $\mathbf{b}$ are unbiased:

$$E\{\mathbf{b}\} = \boldsymbol{\beta} \tag{6.44}$$

The variance-covariance matrix $\sigma^2\{\mathbf{b}\}$:

$$\underset{p\times p}{\sigma^2\{\mathbf{b}\}} = \begin{bmatrix} \sigma^2\{b_0\} & \sigma\{b_0, b_1\} & \cdots & \sigma\{b_0, b_{p-1}\} \\ \sigma\{b_1, b_0\} & \sigma^2\{b_1\} & \cdots & \sigma\{b_1, b_{p-1}\} \\ \vdots & \vdots & & \vdots \\ \sigma\{b_{p-1}, b_0\} & \sigma\{b_{p-1}, b_1\} & \cdots & \sigma^2\{b_{p-1}\} \end{bmatrix} \tag{6.45}$$

is given by:

$$\underset{p\times p}{\sigma^2\{\mathbf{b}\}} = \sigma^2(\mathbf{X'X})^{-1} \tag{6.46}$$

The estimated variance-covariance matrix $s^2\{\mathbf{b}\}$:

$$\underset{p\times p}{s^2\{\mathbf{b}\}} = \begin{bmatrix} s^2\{b_0\} & s\{b_0, b_1\} & \cdots & s\{b_0, b_{p-1}\} \\ s\{b_1, b_0\} & s^2\{b_1\} & \cdots & s\{b_1, b_{p-1}\} \\ \vdots & \vdots & & \vdots \\ s\{b_{p-1}, b_0\} & s\{b_{p-1}, b_1\} & \cdots & s^2\{b_{p-1}\} \end{bmatrix} \tag{6.47}$$

is given by:

$$\underset{p\times p}{s^2\{\mathbf{b}\}} = MSE(\mathbf{X'X})^{-1} \tag{6.48}$$

From $\mathbf{s}^2\{\mathbf{b}\}$, one can obtain $s^2\{b_0\}$, $s^2\{b_1\}$, or whatever other variance is needed, or any needed covariances.

Interval Estimation of β_k

For the normal error regression model (6.19), we have:

$$\frac{b_k - \beta_k}{s\{b_k\}} \sim t(n - p) \qquad k = 0, 1, \ldots, p - 1 \tag{6.49}$$

Hence, the confidence limits for β_k with $1 - \alpha$ confidence coefficient are:

$$b_k \pm t(1 - \alpha/2; n - p)s\{b_k\} \tag{6.50}$$

Tests for β_k

Tests for β_k are set up in the usual fashion. To test:

$$H_0: \beta_k = 0 \tag{6.51a}$$
$$H_a: \beta_k \neq 0$$

we may use the test statistic:

$$t^* = \frac{b_k}{s\{b_k\}} \tag{6.51b}$$

and the decision rule:

$$\text{If } |t^*| \leq t(1 - \alpha/2; n - p), \text{ conclude } H_0 \tag{6.51c}$$
$$\text{Otherwise conclude } H_a$$

The power of the t test can be obtained as explained in Chapter 2, with the degrees of freedom modified to $n - p$.

As with simple linear regression, an F test can also be conducted to determine whether or not $\beta_k = 0$ in multiple regression models. We discuss this test in Chapter 7.

Joint Inferences

The Bonferroni joint confidence intervals can be used to estimate several regression coefficients simultaneously. If g parameters are to be estimated jointly (where $g \leq p$), the confidence limits with family confidence coefficient $1 - \alpha$ are:

$$b_k \pm Bs\{b_k\} \tag{6.52}$$

where:

$$B = t(1 - \alpha/2g; n - p) \tag{6.52a}$$

In Chapter 7, we discuss tests concerning subsets of the regression parameters.

6.7 Estimation of Mean Response and Prediction of New Observation

Interval Estimation of $E\{Y_h\}$

For given values of $X_1, \ldots, X_{p-1}$, denoted by $X_{h1}, \ldots, X_{h,p-1}$, the mean response is denoted by $E\{Y_h\}$. We define the vector $\mathbf{X}_h$:

$$\underset{p \times 1}{\mathbf{X}_h} = \begin{bmatrix} 1 \\ X_{h1} \\ \vdots \\ X_{h,p-1} \end{bmatrix} \tag{6.53}$$

so that the mean response to be estimated is:

$$E\{Y_h\} = \mathbf{X}_h'\boldsymbol{\beta} \tag{6.54}$$

The estimated mean response corresponding to $\mathbf{X}_h$, denoted by $\hat{Y}_h$, is:

$$\hat{Y}_h = \mathbf{X}_h'\mathbf{b} \tag{6.55}$$

This estimator is unbiased:

$$E\{\hat{Y}_h\} = \mathbf{X}_h'\boldsymbol{\beta} = E\{Y_h\} \tag{6.56}$$

and its variance is:

$$\sigma^2\{\hat{Y}_h\} = \sigma^2 \mathbf{X}_h'(\mathbf{X}'\mathbf{X})^{-1}\mathbf{X}_h \tag{6.57}$$

This variance can be expressed as a function of the variance-covariance matrix of the estimated regression coefficients:

$$\sigma^2\{\hat{Y}_h\} = \mathbf{X}_h'\sigma^2\{\mathbf{b}\}\mathbf{X}_h \tag{6.57a}$$

Note from (6.57a) that the variance $\sigma^2\{\hat{Y}_h\}$ is a function of the variances $\sigma^2\{b_k\}$ of the regression coefficients and of the covariances $\sigma\{b_k, b_{k'}\}$ between pairs of regression coefficients, just as in simple linear regression. The estimated variance $s^2\{\hat{Y}_h\}$ is given by:

$$s^2\{\hat{Y}_h\} = MSE(\mathbf{X}_h'(\mathbf{X}'\mathbf{X})^{-1}\mathbf{X}_h) = \mathbf{X}_h's^2\{\mathbf{b}\}\mathbf{X}_h \tag{6.58}$$

The $1 - \alpha$ confidence limits for $E\{Y_h\}$ are:

$$\hat{Y}_h \pm t(1 - \alpha/2; n - p)s\{\hat{Y}_h\} \tag{6.59}$$

Confidence Region for Regression Surface

The $1 - \alpha$ confidence region for the entire regression surface is an extension of the Working-Hotelling confidence band (2.40) for the regression line when there is one predictor variable. Boundary points of the confidence region at $\mathbf{X}_h$ are obtained from:

$$\hat{Y}_h \pm Ws\{\hat{Y}_h\} \tag{6.60}$$

where:

$$W^2 = pF(1 - \alpha; p, n - p) \quad\quad\quad (6.60a)$$

The confidence coefficient $1 - \alpha$ provides assurance that the region contains the entire regression surface over all combinations of values of the X variables.

Simultaneous Confidence Intervals for Several Mean Responses

To estimate a number of mean responses $E\{Y_h\}$ corresponding to different $\mathbf{X}_h$ vectors with family confidence coefficient $1 - \alpha$, we can employ two basic approaches:

1. Use the Working-Hotelling confidence region bounds (6.60) for the several $\mathbf{X}_h$ vectors of interest:

$$\hat{Y}_h \pm W s\{\hat{Y}_h\} \quad\quad\quad (6.61)$$

where $\hat{Y}_h$, W, and $s\{\hat{Y}_h\}$ are defined in (6.55), (6.60a), and (6.58), respectively. Since the Working-Hotelling confidence region covers the mean responses for all possible $\mathbf{X}_h$ vectors with confidence coefficient $1 - \alpha$, the selected boundary values will cover the mean responses for the $\mathbf{X}_h$ vectors of interest with family confidence coefficient greater than $1 - \alpha$.

2. Use Bonferroni simultaneous confidence intervals. When g interval estimates are to be made, the Bonferroni confidence limits are:

$$\hat{Y}_h \pm B s\{\hat{Y}_h\} \quad\quad\quad (6.62)$$

where:

$$B = t(1 - \alpha/2g; n - p) \quad\quad\quad (6.62a)$$

For any particular application, we can compare the W and B multiples to see which procedure will lead to narrower confidence intervals. If the $\mathbf{X}_h$ levels are not specified in advance but are determined as the analysis proceeds, it is better to use the Working-Hotelling limits (6.61) since the family for this procedure includes all possible $\mathbf{X}_h$ levels.

Prediction of New Observation $Y_{h(new)}$

The $1 - \alpha$ prediction limits for a new observation $Y_{h(new)}$ corresponding to $\mathbf{X}_h$, the specified values of the X variables, are:

$$\hat{Y}_h \pm t(1 - \alpha/2; n - p)s\{\text{pred}\} \qu\quad\quad (6.63)$$

where:

$$s^2\{\text{pred}\} = MSE + s^2\{\hat{Y}_h\} = MSE(1 + \mathbf{X}_h'(\mathbf{X}'\mathbf{X})^{-1}\mathbf{X}_h) \quad\quad\quad (6.63a)$$

and $s^2\{\hat{Y}_h\}$ is given by (6.58).

Prediction of Mean of m New Observations at X_h

When m new observations are to be selected at the same levels $\mathbf{X}_h$ and their mean $\bar{Y}_{h(new)}$ is to be predicted, the $1 - \alpha$ prediction limits are:

$$\hat{Y}_h \pm t(1 - \alpha/2; n - p)s\{\text{predmean}\} \quad\quad\quad (6.64)$$

where:

$$s^2\{\text{predmean}\} = \frac{MSE}{m} + s^2\{\hat{Y}_h\} = MSE\left(\frac{1}{m} + \mathbf{X}_h'(\mathbf{X}'\mathbf{X})^{-1}\mathbf{X}_h\right) \qquad \textbf{(6.64a)}$$

Predictions of *g* New Observations

Simultaneous Scheffé prediction limits for *g* new observations at *g* different levels $\mathbf{X}_h$ with family confidence coefficient $1 - \alpha$ are given by:

$$\hat{Y}_h \pm Ss\{\text{pred}\} \qquad \textbf{(6.65)}$$

where:

$$S^2 = gF(1 - \alpha; g, n - p) \qquad \textbf{(6.65a)}$$

and $s^2\{\text{pred}\}$ is given by (6.63a).

Alternatively, Bonferroni simultaneous prediction limits can be used. For *g* predictions with family confidence coefficient $1 - \alpha$, they are:

$$\hat{Y}_h \pm Bs\{\text{pred}\} \qquad \textbf{(6.66)}$$

where:

$$B = t(1 - \alpha/2g; n - p) \qquad \textbf{(6.66a)}$$

A comparison of *S* and *B* in advance of any particular use will indicate which procedure will lead to narrower prediction intervals.

Caution about Hidden Extrapolations

When estimating a mean response or predicting a new observation in multiple regression, one needs to be particularly careful that the estimate or prediction does not fall outside the scope of the model. The danger, of course, is that the model may not be appropriate when it is extended outside the region of the observations. In multiple regression, it is particularly easy to lose track of this region since the levels of $X_1, \ldots, X_{p-1}$ *jointly* define the region. Thus, one cannot merely look at the ranges of each predictor variable. Consider Figure 6.3,

FIGURE 6.3
Region of Observations on X_1 and X_2 Jointly, Compared with Ranges of X_1 and X_2 Individually.

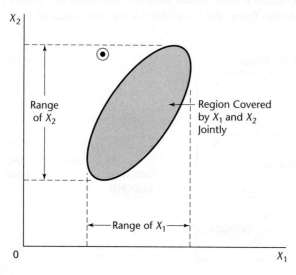

where the shaded region is the region of observations for a multiple regression application with two predictor variables and the circled dot represents the values (X_{h1}, X_{h2}) for which a prediction is to be made. The circled dot is within the ranges of the predictor variables X_1 and X_2 individually, yet is well outside the joint region of observations. It is easy to spot this extrapolation when there are only two predictor variables, but it becomes much more difficult when the number of predictor variables is large. We discuss in Chapter 10 a procedure for identifying hidden extrapolations when there are more than two predictor variables.

6.8 Diagnostics and Remedial Measures

Diagnostics play an important role in the development and evaluation of multiple regression models. Most of the diagnostic procedures for simple linear regression that we described in Chapter 3 carry over directly to multiple regression. We review these diagnostic procedures now, as well as the remedial measures for simple linear regression that carry over directly to multiple regression.

Many specialized diagnostics and remedial procedures for multiple regression have also been developed. Some important ones will be discussed in Chapters 10 and 11.

Scatter Plot Matrix

Box plots, sequence plots, stem-and-leaf plots, and dot plots for each of the predictor variables and for the response variable can provide helpful, preliminary univariate information about these variables. Scatter plots of the response variable against each predictor variable can aid in determining the nature and strength of the bivariate relationships between each of the predictor variables and the response variable and in identifying gaps in the data points as well as outlying data points. Scatter plots of each predictor variable against each of the other predictor variables are helpful for studying the bivariate relationships among the predictor variables and for finding gaps and detecting outliers.

Analysis is facilitated if these scatter plots are assembled in a *scatter plot matrix*, such as in Figure 6.4. In this figure, the Y variable for any one scatter plot is the name found in

FIGURE 6.4
SYGRAPH
Scatter Plot
Matrix and
Correlation
Matrix—
Dwaine Studios
Example.

(a) Scatter Plot Matrix

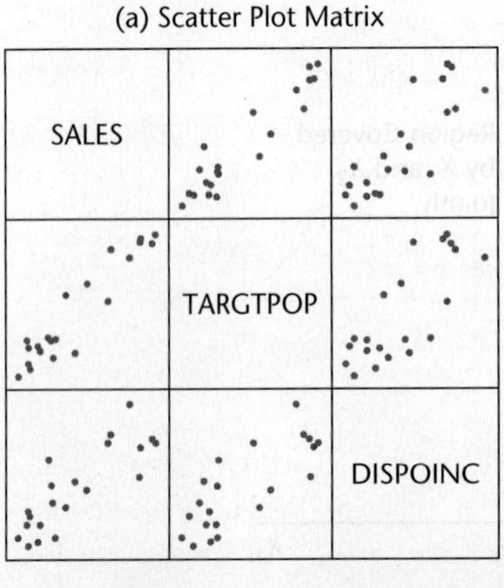

(b) Correlation Matrix

	SALES	TARGTPOP	DISPOINC
SALES	1.000	.945	.836
TARGTPOP		1.000	.781
DISPOINC			1.000

its row, and the X variable is the name found in its column. Thus, the scatter plot matrix in Figure 6.4 shows in the first row the plots of Y (SALES) against X_1 (TARGETPOP) and X_2 (DISPOINC), of X_1 against Y and X_2 in the second row, and of X_2 against Y and X_1 in the third row. These variables are described on page 236. Alternatively, by viewing the first column, one can compare the plots of X_1 and X_2 each against Y, and similarly for the other two columns. A scatter plot matrix facilitates the study of the relationships among the variables by comparing the scatter plots within a row or a column. Examples in this and subsequent chapters will illustrate the usefulness of scatter plot matrices.

A complement to the scatter plot matrix that may be useful at times is the correlation matrix. This matrix contains the coefficients of simple correlation $r_{Y1}, r_{Y2}, \ldots, r_{Y,p-1}$ between Y and each of the predictor variables, as well as all of the coefficients of simple correlation among the predictor variables—r_{12} between X_1 and X_2, r_{13} between X_1 and X_3, etc. The format of the correlation matrix follows that of the scatter plot matrix:

$$
\begin{bmatrix}
1 & r_{Y1} & r_{Y2} & \cdots & r_{Y,p-1} \\
r_{Y1} & 1 & r_{12} & \cdots & r_{1,p-1} \\
\vdots & \vdots & \vdots & & \vdots \\
r_{Y,p-1} & r_{1,p-1} & r_{2,p-1} & \cdots & 1
\end{bmatrix}
\tag{6.67}
$$

Note that the correlation matrix is symmetric and that its main diagonal contains 1s because the coefficient of correlation between a variable and itself is 1. Many statistics packages provide the correlation matrix as an option. Since this matrix is symmetric, the lower (or upper) triangular block of elements is frequently omitted in the output.

Some interactive statistics packages enable the user to employ *brushing* with scatter plot matrices. When a point in a scatter plot is brushed, it is given a distinctive appearance on the computer screen in each scatter plot in the matrix. The case corresponding to the brushed point may also be identified. Brushing is helpful to see whether a case that is outlying in one scatter plot is also outlying in some or all of the other plots. Brushing may also be applied to a group of points to see, for instance, whether a group of cases that does not fit the relationship for the remaining cases in one scatter plot also follows a distinct pattern in any of the other scatter plots.

Three-Dimensional Scatter Plots

Some interactive statistics packages provide *three-dimensional scatter plots* or *point clouds*, and permit spinning of these plots to enable the viewer to see the point cloud from different perspectives. This can be very helpful for identifying patterns that are only apparent from certain perspectives. Figure 6.6 on page 238 illustrates a three-dimensional scatter plot and the use of spinning.

Residual Plots

A plot of the residuals against the fitted values is useful for assessing the appropriateness of the multiple regression function and the constancy of the variance of the error terms, as well as for providing information about outliers, just as for simple linear regression. Similarly, a plot of the residuals against time or against some other sequence can provide diagnostic information about possible correlations between the error terms in multiple regression. Box plots and normal probability plots of the residuals are useful for examining whether the error terms are reasonably normally distributed.

In addition, residuals should be plotted against each of the predictor variables. Each of these plots can provide further information about the adequacy of the regression function with respect to that predictor variable (e.g., whether a curvature effect is required for that variable) and about possible variation in the magnitude of the error variance in relation to that predictor variable.

Residuals should also be plotted against important predictor variables that were omitted from the model, to see if the omitted variables have substantial additional effects on the response variable that have not yet been recognized in the regression model. Also, residuals should be plotted against interaction terms for potential interaction effects not included in the regression model, such as against $X_1 X_2$, $X_1 X_3$, and $X_2 X_3$, to see whether some or all of these interaction terms are required in the model.

A plot of the absolute residuals or the squared residuals against the fitted values is useful for examining the constancy of the variance of the error terms. If nonconstancy is detected, a plot of the absolute residuals or the squared residuals against each of the predictor variables may identify one or several of the predictor variables to which the magnitude of the error variability is related.

Correlation Test for Normality

The correlation test for normality described in Chapter 3 carries forward directly to multiple regression. The expected values of the ordered residuals under normality are calculated according to (3.6), and the coefficient of correlation between the residuals and the expected values under normality is then obtained. Table B.6 is employed to assess whether or not the magnitude of the correlation coefficient supports the reasonableness of the normality assumption.

Brown-Forsythe Test for Constancy of Error Variance

The Brown-Forsythe test statistic (3.9) for assessing the constancy of the error variance can be used readily in multiple regression when the error variance increases or decreases with one of the predictor variables. To conduct the Brown-Forsythe test, we divide the data set into two groups, as for simple linear regression, where one group consists of cases where the level of the predictor variable is relatively low and the other group consists of cases where the level of the predictor variable is relatively high. The Brown-Forsythe test then proceeds as for simple linear regression.

Breusch-Pagan Test for Constancy of Error Variance

The Breusch-Pagan test (3.11) for constancy of the error variance in multiple regression is carried out exactly the same as for simple linear regression when the error variance increases or decreases with one of the predictor variables. The squared residuals are simply regressed against the predictor variable to obtain the regression sum of squares SSR^*, and the test proceeds as before, using the error sum of squares SSE for the full multiple regression model.

When the error variance is a function of more than one predictor variable, a multiple regression of the squared residuals against these predictor variables is conducted and the regression sum of squares SSR^* is obtained. The test statistic again uses SSE for the full multiple regression model, but now the chi-square distribution involves q degrees of freedom, where q is the number of predictor variables against which the squared residuals are regressed.

F Test for Lack of Fit

The lack of fit F test described in Chapter 3 for simple linear regression can be carried over to test whether the multiple regression response function:

$$E\{Y\} = \beta_0 + \beta_1 X_1 + \cdots + \beta_{p-1} X_{p-1}$$

is an appropriate response surface. Repeat observations in multiple regression are replicate observations on Y corresponding to levels of each of the X variables that are constant from trial to trial. Thus, with two predictor variables, repeat observations require that X_1 and X_2 each remain at given levels from trial to trial.

Once the ANOVA table, shown in Table 6.1, has been obtained, SSE is decomposed into pure error and lack of fit components. The pure error sum of squares $SSPE$ is obtained by first calculating for each replicate group the sum of squared deviations of the Y observations around the group mean, where a replicate group has the same values for each of the X variables. Let c denote the number of groups with distinct sets of levels for the X variables, and let the mean of the Y observations for the jth group be denoted by $\bar{Y}_j$. Then the sum of squares for the jth group is given by (3.17), and the pure error sum of squares is the sum of these sums of squares, as given by (3.16). The lack of fit sum of squares $SSLF$ equals the difference $SSE - SSPE$, as indicated by (3.24).

The number of degrees of freedom associated with $SSPE$ is $n - c$, and the number of degrees of freedom associated with $SSLF$ is $(n - p) - (n - c) = c - p$. Thus, for testing the alternatives:

$$
\begin{aligned}
H_0&: E\{Y\} = \beta_0 + \beta_1 X_1 + \cdots + \beta_{p-1} X_{p-1} \\
H_a&: E\{Y\} \neq \beta_0 + \beta_1 X_1 + \cdots + \beta_{p-1} X_{p-1}
\end{aligned}
\tag{6.68a}
$$

the appropriate test statistic is:

$$F^* = \frac{SSLF}{c - p} \div \frac{SSPE}{n - c} = \frac{MSLF}{MSPE} \tag{6.68b}$$

where $SSLF$ and $SSPE$ are given by (3.24) and (3.16), respectively, and the appropriate decision rule is:

$$
\begin{aligned}
&\text{If } F^* \leq F(1 - \alpha; c - p, n - c), \text{ conclude } H_0 \\
&\text{If } F^* > F(1 - \alpha; c - p, n - c), \text{ conclude } H_a
\end{aligned}
\tag{6.68c}
$$

Comment

When replicate observations are not available, an approximate lack of fit test can be conducted if there are cases that have similar $\mathbf{X}_h$ vectors. These cases are grouped together and treated as pseudoreplicates, and the test for lack of fit is then carried out using these groupings of similar cases. ∎

Remedial Measures

The remedial measures described in Chapter 3 are also applicable to multiple regression. When a more complex model is required to recognize curvature or interaction effects, the multiple regression model can be expanded to include these effects. For example, X_2^2 might be added as a variable to take into account a curvature effect of X_2, or $X_1 X_3$ might be added as a variable to recognize an interaction effect between X_1 and X_3 on the response variable. Alternatively, transformations on the response and/or the predictor variables can be made, following the principles discussed in Chapter 3, to remedy model deficiencies. Transformations on the response variable Y may be helpful when the distributions of the error terms are quite skewed and the variance of the error terms is not constant. Transformations of some of the predictor variables may be helpful when the effects of these variables are curvilinear. In addition, transformations on Y and/or the predictor variables may be helpful in eliminating or substantially reducing interaction effects.

As with simple linear regression, the usefulness of potential transformations needs to be examined by means of residual plots and other diagnostic tools to determine whether the multiple regression model for the transformed data is appropriate.

Box-Cox Transformations. The Box-Cox procedure for determining an appropriate power transformation on Y for simple linear regression models described in Chapter 3 is also applicable to multiple regression models. The standardized variable W in (3.36) is again obtained for different values of the parameter λ and is now regressed against the set of X variables in the multiple regression model to find that value of λ that minimizes the error sum of squares *SSE*.

Box and Tidwell (Ref. 6.1) have also developed an iterative approach for ascertaining appropriate power transformations for each predictor variable in a multiple regression model when transformations on the predictor variables may be required.

6.9   An Example—Multiple Regression with Two Predictor Variables

In this section, we shall develop a multiple regression application with two predictor variables. We shall illustrate several diagnostic procedures and several types of inferences that might be made for this application. We shall set up the necessary calculations in matrix format but, for ease of viewing, show fewer significant digits for the elements of the matrices than are used in the actual calculations.

Setting

Dwaine Studios, Inc., operates portrait studios in 21 cities of medium size. These studios specialize in portraits of children. The company is considering an expansion into other cities of medium size and wishes to investigate whether sales (Y) in a community can be predicted from the number of persons aged 16 or younger in the community (X_1) and the per capita disposable personal income in the community (X_2). Data on these variables for the most recent year for the 21 cities in which Dwaine Studios is now operating are shown in Figure 6.5b. Sales are expressed in thousands of dollars and are labeled Y or SALES; the number of persons aged 16 or younger is expressed in thousands of persons and is

FIGURE 6.5
SYSTAT
Multiple
Regression
Output and
Basic
Data—Dwaine
Studios
Example.

(a) Multiple Regression Output

```
DEP VAR: SALES N: 21 MULTIPLE R: 0.957 SQUARED MULTIPLE R:
                                                    0.917
ADJUSTED SQUARED MULTIPLE R: .907 STANDARD ERROR OF ESTIMATE:
                                                  11.0074



VARIABLE    COEFFICIENT    STD ERROR    STD COEF   TOLERANCE        T      P(2 TAIL)

CONSTANT     -68.8571       60.0170       0.0000        .        -1.1473     0.2663
TARGTPOP       1.4546        0.2118       0.7484     0.3896       6.8682     0.0000
DISPOINC       9.3655        4.0640       0.2511     0.3896       2.3045     0.0333




                    ANALYSIS OF VARIANCE

SOURCE          SUM-OF-SQUARES    DF      MEAN-SQUARE    F-RATIO      P

REGRESSION        24015.2821      2       12007.6411    99.1035    0.0000
RESIDUAL           2180.9274     18         121.1626



INVERSE (X'X)

                     1          2          3

             1   29.7289
             2    0.0722     0.00037
             3   -1.9926    -0.0056     0.1363
```

(b) Basic Data

CASE	X1	X2	Y	FITTED	RESIDUAL
1	68.5	16.7	174.4	187.184	-12.7841
2	45.2	16.8	164.4	154.229	10.1706
3	91.3	18.2	244.2	234.396	9.8037
4	47.8	16.3	154.6	153.329	1.2715
5	46.9	17.3	181.6	161.385	20.2151
6	66.1	18.2	207.5	197.741	9.7586
7	49.5	15.9	152.8	152.055	0.7449
8	52.0	17.2	163.2	167.867	-4.6666
9	48.9	16.6	145.4	157.738	-12.3382
10	38.4	16.0	137.2	136.846	0.3540
11	87.9	18.3	241.9	230.387	11.5126
12	72.8	17.1	191.1	197.185	-6.0849
13	88.4	17.4	232.0	222.686	9.3143
14	42.9	15.8	145.3	141.518	3.7816
15	52.5	17.8	161.1	174.213	-13.1132
16	85.7	18.4	209.7	228.124	-18.4239
17	41.3	16.5	146.4	145.747	0.6530
18	51.7	16.3	144.0	159.001	-15.0013
19	89.6	18.1	232.6	230.987	1.6130
20	82.7	19.1	224.1	230.316	-6.2160
21	52.3	16.0	166.5	157.064	9.4356

labeled X_1 or TARGTPOP for target population; and per capita disposable personal income is expressed in thousands of dollars and labeled X_2 or DISPOINC for disposable income.

The first-order regression model:

$$Y_i = \beta_0 + \beta_1 X_{i1} + \beta_2 X_{i2} + \varepsilon_i \tag{6.69}$$

with normal error terms is expected to be appropriate, on the basis of the SYGRAPH scatter plot matrix in Figure 6.4a. Note the linear relation between target population and sales and between disposable income and sales. Also note that there is more scatter in the latter relationship. Finally note that there is also some linear relationship between the two predictor variables. The correlation matrix in Figure 6.4b bears out these visual impressions from the scatter plot matrix.

A SYGRAPH plot of the point cloud is shown in Figure 6.6a. By spinning the axes, we obtain the perspective in Figure 6.6b which supports the tentative conclusion that a response plane may be a reasonable regression function to utilize here.

Basic Calculations

The **X** and **Y** matrices for the Dwaine Studios example are as follows:

$$\mathbf{X} = \begin{bmatrix} 1 & 68.5 & 16.7 \\ 1 & 45.2 & 16.8 \\ \vdots & \vdots & \vdots \\ 1 & 52.3 & 16.0 \end{bmatrix} \quad \mathbf{Y} = \begin{bmatrix} 174.4 \\ 164.4 \\ \vdots \\ 166.5 \end{bmatrix} \tag{6.70}$$

FIGURE 6.6 **SYGRAPH Plot of Point Cloud before and after Spinning—Dwaine Studios Example.**

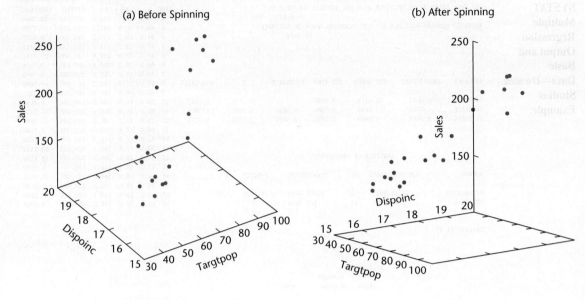

(a) Before Spinning   (b) After Spinning

We require:

1.

$$X'X = \begin{bmatrix} 1 & 1 & \cdots & 1 \\ 68.5 & 45.2 & \cdots & 52.3 \\ 16.7 & 16.8 & \cdots & 16.0 \end{bmatrix} \begin{bmatrix} 1 & 68.5 & 16.7 \\ 1 & 45.2 & 16.8 \\ \vdots & \vdots & \vdots \\ 1 & 52.3 & 16.0 \end{bmatrix}$$

which yields:

$$X'X = \begin{bmatrix} 21.0 & 1{,}302.4 & 360.0 \\ 1{,}302.4 & 87{,}707.9 & 22{,}609.2 \\ 360.0 & 22{,}609.2 & 6{,}190.3 \end{bmatrix} \tag{6.71}$$

2.

$$X'Y = \begin{bmatrix} 1 & 1 & \cdots & 1 \\ 68.5 & 45.2 & \cdots & 52.3 \\ 16.7 & 16.8 & \cdots & 16.0 \end{bmatrix} \begin{bmatrix} 174.4 \\ 164.4 \\ \vdots \\ 166.5 \end{bmatrix}$$

which yields:

$$X'Y = \begin{bmatrix} 3{,}820 \\ 249{,}643 \\ 66{,}073 \end{bmatrix} \tag{6.72}$$

3.

$$(\mathbf{X'X})^{-1} = \begin{bmatrix} 21.0 & 1{,}302.4 & 360.0 \\ 1{,}302.4 & 87{,}707.9 & 22{,}609.2 \\ 360.0 & 22{,}609.2 & 6{,}190.3 \end{bmatrix}^{-1}$$

Using (5.23), we obtain:

$$(\mathbf{X'X})^{-1} = \begin{bmatrix} 29.7289 & .0722 & -1.9926 \\ .0722 & .00037 & -.0056 \\ -1.9926 & -.0056 & .1363 \end{bmatrix} \tag{6.73}$$

Algebraic Equivalents.   Note that $\mathbf{X'X}$ for the first-order regression model (6.69) with two predictor variables is:

$$\mathbf{X'X} = \begin{bmatrix} 1 & 1 & \cdots & 1 \\ X_{11} & X_{21} & \cdots & X_{n1} \\ X_{12} & X_{22} & \cdots & X_{n2} \end{bmatrix} \begin{bmatrix} 1 & X_{11} & X_{12} \\ 1 & X_{21} & X_{22} \\ \vdots & \vdots & \vdots \\ 1 & X_{n1} & X_{n2} \end{bmatrix}$$

or:

$$\mathbf{X'X} = \begin{bmatrix} n & \sum X_{i1} & \sum X_{i2} \\ \sum X_{i1} & \sum X_{i1}^2 & \sum X_{i1}X_{i2} \\ \sum X_{i2} & \sum X_{i2}X_{i1} & \sum X_{i2}^2 \end{bmatrix} \tag{6.74}$$

For the Dwaine Studios example, we have:

$$n = 21$$

$$\sum X_{i1} = 68.5 + 45.2 + \cdots = 1{,}302.4$$

$$\sum X_{i1}X_{i2} = 68.5(16.7) + 45.2(16.8) + \cdots = 22{,}609.2$$

etc.

These elements are found in (6.71).

Also note that $\mathbf{X'Y}$ for the first-order regression model (6.69) with two predictor variables is:

$$\mathbf{X'Y} = \begin{bmatrix} 1 & 1 & \cdots & 1 \\ X_{11} & X_{21} & \cdots & X_{n1} \\ X_{12} & X_{22} & \cdots & X_{n2} \end{bmatrix} \begin{bmatrix} Y_1 \\ Y_2 \\ \vdots \\ Y_n \end{bmatrix} = \begin{bmatrix} \sum Y_i \\ \sum X_{i1}Y_i \\ \sum X_{i2}Y_i \end{bmatrix} \tag{6.75}$$

For the Dwaine Studios example, we have:

$$\sum Y_i = 174.4 + 164.4 + \cdots = 3{,}820$$

$$\sum X_{i1}Y_i = 68.5(174.4) + 45.2(164.4) + \cdots = 249{,}643$$

$$\sum X_{i2}Y_i = 16.7(174.4) + 16.8(164.4) + \cdots = 66{,}073$$

These are the elements found in (6.72).

Estimated Regression Function

The least squares estimates **b** are readily obtained by (6.25), using our basic calculations in (6.72) and (6.73):

$$\mathbf{b} = (\mathbf{X}'\mathbf{X})^{-1}\mathbf{X}'\mathbf{Y} = \begin{bmatrix} 29.7289 & .0722 & -1.9926 \\ .0722 & .00037 & -.0056 \\ -1.9926 & -.0056 & .1363 \end{bmatrix} \begin{bmatrix} 3,820 \\ 249,643 \\ 66,073 \end{bmatrix}$$

which yields:

$$\mathbf{b} = \begin{bmatrix} b_0 \\ b_1 \\ b_2 \end{bmatrix} = \begin{bmatrix} -68.857 \\ 1.455 \\ 9.366 \end{bmatrix} \tag{6.76}$$

and the estimated regression function is:

$$\hat{Y} = -68.857 + 1.455X_1 + 9.366X_2$$

A three-dimensional plot of the estimated regression function, with the responses super-imposed, is shown in Figure 6.7. The residuals are represented by the small vertical lines connecting the responses to the estimated regression surface.

This estimated regression function indicates that mean sales are expected to increase by 1.455 thousand dollars when the target population increases by 1 thousand persons aged 16 years or younger, holding per capita disposable personal income constant, and that mean sales are expected to increase by 9.366 thousand dollars when per capita income increases by 1 thousand dollars, holding the target population constant.

Figure 6.5a contains SYSTAT multiple regression output for the Dwaine Studios example. The estimated regression coefficients are shown in the column labeled COEFFICIENT; the output shows one more decimal place than we have given in the text.

The SYSTAT output also contains the inverse of the $\mathbf{X}'\mathbf{X}$ matrix that we calculated earlier; only the lower portion of the symmetric matrix is shown. The results are the same as in (6.73).

FIGURE 6.7
S-Plus Plot of Estimated Regression Surface— Dwaine Studios Example.

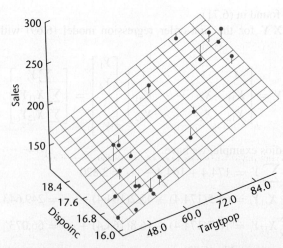

Algebraic Version of Normal Equations. The normal equations in algebraic form for the case of two predictor variables can be obtained readily from (6.74) and (6.75). We have:

$$(\mathbf{X'X})\mathbf{b} = \mathbf{X'Y}$$

$$\begin{bmatrix} n & \sum X_{i1} & \sum X_{i2} \\ \sum X_{i1} & \sum X_{i1}^2 & \sum X_{i1}X_{i2} \\ \sum X_{i2} & \sum X_{i2}X_{i1} & \sum X_{i2}^2 \end{bmatrix} \begin{bmatrix} b_0 \\ b_1 \\ b_2 \end{bmatrix} = \begin{bmatrix} \sum Y_i \\ \sum X_{i1}Y_i \\ \sum X_{i2}Y_i \end{bmatrix}$$

from which we obtain the normal equations:

$$\sum Y_i = nb_0 + b_1 \sum X_{i1} + b_2 \sum X_{i2}$$

$$\sum X_{i1}Y_i = b_0 \sum X_{i1} + b_1 \sum X_{i1}^2 + b_2 \sum X_{i1}X_{i2} \qquad \textbf{(6.77)}$$

$$\sum X_{i2}Y_i = b_0 \sum X_{i2} + b_1 \sum X_{i1}X_{i2} + b_2 \sum X_{i2}^2$$

Fitted Values and Residuals

To examine the appropriateness of regression model (6.69) for the data at hand, we require the fitted values $\hat{Y}_i$ and the residuals $e_i = Y_i - \hat{Y}_i$. We obtain by (6.28):

$$\hat{\mathbf{Y}} = \mathbf{Xb}$$

$$\begin{bmatrix} \hat{Y}_1 \\ \hat{Y}_2 \\ \vdots \\ \hat{Y}_{21} \end{bmatrix} = \begin{bmatrix} 1 & 68.5 & 16.7 \\ 1 & 45.2 & 16.8 \\ \vdots & \vdots & \vdots \\ 1 & 52.3 & 16.0 \end{bmatrix} \begin{bmatrix} -68.857 \\ 1.455 \\ 9.366 \end{bmatrix} = \begin{bmatrix} 187.2 \\ 154.2 \\ \vdots \\ 157.1 \end{bmatrix}$$

Further, by (6.29) we find:

$$\mathbf{e} = \mathbf{Y} - \hat{\mathbf{Y}}$$

$$\begin{bmatrix} e_1 \\ e_2 \\ \vdots \\ e_{21} \end{bmatrix} = \begin{bmatrix} 174.4 \\ 164.4 \\ \vdots \\ 166.5 \end{bmatrix} - \begin{bmatrix} 187.2 \\ 154.2 \\ \vdots \\ 157.1 \end{bmatrix} = \begin{bmatrix} -12.8 \\ 10.2 \\ \vdots \\ 9.4 \end{bmatrix}$$

Figure 6.5b shows the computer output for the fitted values and residuals to more decimal places than we have presented.

Analysis of Appropriateness of Model

We begin our analysis of the appropriateness of regression model (6.69) for the Dwaine Studios example by considering the plot of the residuals e against the fitted values $\hat{Y}$ in Figure 6.8a. This plot does not suggest any systematic deviations from the response plane,

FIGURE 6.8
SYGRAPH
Diagnostic
Plots—Dwaine
Studios
Example.

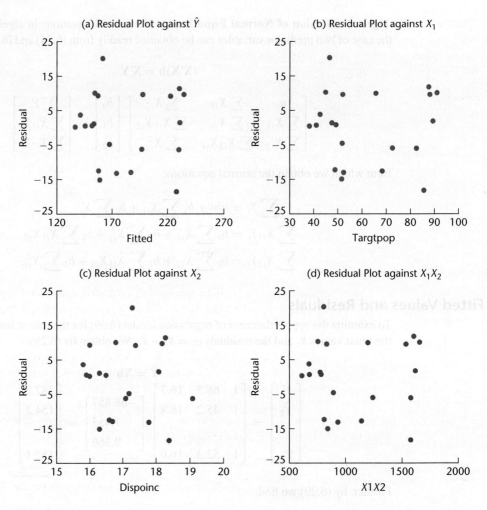

(a) Residual Plot against $\hat{Y}$

(b) Residual Plot against X_1

(c) Residual Plot against X_2

(d) Residual Plot against $X_1 X_2$

nor that the variance of the error terms varies with the level of $\hat{Y}$. Plots of the residuals e against X_1 and X_2 in Figures 6.8b and 6.8c, respectively, are entirely consistent with the conclusions of good fit by the response function and constant variance of the error terms.

In multiple regression applications, there is frequently the possibility of interaction effects being present. To examine this for the Dwaine Studios example, we plotted the residuals e against the interaction term $X_1 X_2$ in Figure 6.8d. A systematic pattern in this plot would suggest that an interaction effect may be present, so that a response function of the type:

$$E\{Y\} = \beta_0 + \beta_1 X_1 + \beta_2 X_2 + \beta_3 X_1 X_2$$

might be more appropriate. Figure 6.8d does not exhibit any systematic pattern; hence, no interaction effects reflected by the model term $\beta_3 X_1 X_2$ appear to be present.

FIGURE 6.9
Additional
Diagnostic
Plots—Dwaine
Studios
Example.

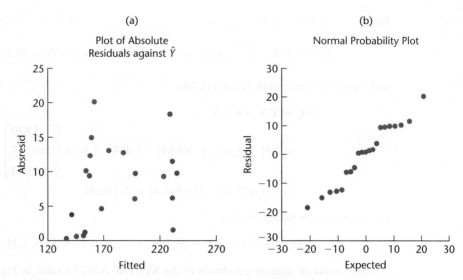

(a)

Plot of Absolute
Residuals against $\hat{Y}$

(b)

Normal Probability Plot

Figure 6.9 contains two additional diagnostic plots. Figure 6.9a presents a plot of the absolute residuals against the fitted values. There is no indication of nonconstancy of the error variance. Figure 6.9b contains a normal probability plot of the residuals. The pattern is moderately linear. The coefficient of correlation between the ordered residuals and their expected values under normality is .980. This high value (the interpolated critical value in Table B.6 for $n = 21$ and $\alpha = .05$ is .9525) helps to confirm the reasonableness of the conclusion that the error terms are fairly normally distributed.

Since the Dwaine Studios data are cross-sectional and do not involve a time sequence, a time sequence plot is not relevant here. Thus, all of the diagnostics support the use of regression model (6.69) for the Dwaine Studios example.

Analysis of Variance

To test whether sales are related to target population and per capita disposable income, we require the ANOVA table. The basic quantities needed are:

$$\mathbf{Y'Y} = [174.4 \quad 164.4 \quad \cdots \quad 166.5] \begin{bmatrix} 174.4 \\ 164.4 \\ \vdots \\ 166.5 \end{bmatrix}$$

$$= 721{,}072.40$$

$$\left(\frac{1}{n}\right) \mathbf{Y'JY} = \frac{1}{21}[174.4 \quad 164.4 \quad \cdots \quad 166.5] \begin{bmatrix} 1 & 1 & \cdots & 1 \\ 1 & 1 & \cdots & 1 \\ \vdots & \vdots & & \vdots \\ 1 & 1 & \cdots & 1 \end{bmatrix} \begin{bmatrix} 174.4 \\ 164.4 \\ \vdots \\ 166.5 \end{bmatrix}$$

$$= \frac{(3{,}820.0)^2}{21} = 694{,}876.19$$

Thus:

$$SSTO = \mathbf{Y'Y} - \left(\frac{1}{n}\right)\mathbf{Y'JY} = 721,072.40 - 694,876.19 = 26,196.21$$

and, from our results in (6.72) and (6.76):

$$SSE = \mathbf{Y'Y} - \mathbf{b'X'Y}$$

$$= 721,072.40 - [-68.857 \quad 1.455 \quad 9.366] \begin{bmatrix} 3,820 \\ 249,643 \\ 66,073 \end{bmatrix}$$

$$= 721,072.40 - 718,891.47 = 2,180.93$$

Finally, we obtain by subtraction:

$$SSR = SSTO - SSE = 26,196.21 - 2,180.93 = 24,015.28$$

These sums of squares are shown in the SYSTAT ANOVA table in Figure 6.5a. Also shown in the ANOVA table are degrees of freedom and mean squares. Note that three regression parameters had to be estimated; hence, $21 - 3 = 18$ degrees of freedom are associated with SSE. Also, the number of degrees of freedom associated with SSR is 2—the number of X variables in the model.

Test of Regression Relation. To test whether sales are related to target population and per capita disposable income:

$$H_0: \beta_1 = 0 \text{ and } \beta_2 = 0$$
$$H_a: \text{not both } \beta_1 \text{ and } \beta_2 \text{ equal zero}$$

we use test statistic (6.39b):

$$F^* = \frac{MSR}{MSE} = \frac{12,007.64}{121.1626} = 99.1$$

This test statistic is labeled F-RATIO in the SYSTAT output. For $\alpha = .05$, we require $F(.95; 2, 18) = 3.55$. Since $F^* = 99.1 > 3.55$, we conclude H_a, that sales are related to target population and per capita disposable income. The P-value for this test is .0000, as shown in the SYSTAT output labeled P.

Whether the regression relation is useful for making predictions of sales or estimates of mean sales still remains to be seen.

Coefficient of Multiple Determination. For our example, we have by (6.40):

$$R^2 = \frac{SSR}{SSTO} = \frac{24,015.28}{26,196.21} = .917$$

Thus, when the two predictor variables, target population and per capita disposable income, are considered, the variation in sales is reduced by 91.7 percent. The coefficient of multiple determination is shown in the SYSTAT output labeled SQUARED MULTIPLE R. Also shown in the output is the coefficient of multiple correlation $R = .957$ and the adjusted coefficient of multiple determination (6.42), $R_a^2 = .907$, which is labeled in the output

ADJUSTED SQUARED MULTIPLE R. Note that adjusting for the number of predictor variables in the model had only a small effect here on R^2.

Estimation of Regression Parameters

Dwaine Studios is not interested in the parameter β_0 since it falls far outside the scope of the model. It is desired to estimate β_1 and β_2 jointly with family confidence coefficient .90. We shall use the simultaneous Bonferroni confidence limits (6.52).

First, we need the estimated variance-covariance matrix $s^2\{\mathbf{b}\}$:

$$s^2\{\mathbf{b}\} = MSE(\mathbf{X'X})^{-1}$$

MSE is given in Figure 6.5a, and $(\mathbf{X'X})^{-1}$ was obtained in (6.73). Hence:

$$s^2\{\mathbf{b}\} = 121.1626 \begin{bmatrix} 29.7289 & .0722 & -1.9926 \\ .0722 & .00037 & -.0056 \\ -1.9926 & -.0056 & .1363 \end{bmatrix}$$

$$= \begin{bmatrix} 3{,}602.0 & 8.748 & -241.43 \\ 8.748 & .0448 & -.679 \\ -241.43 & -.679 & 16.514 \end{bmatrix}$$

(6.78)

The two estimated variances we require are:

$$s^2\{b_1\} = .0448 \quad \text{or} \quad s\{b_1\} = .212$$
$$s^2\{b_2\} = 16.514 \quad \text{or} \quad s\{b_2\} = 4.06$$

These estimated standard deviations are shown in the SYSTAT output in Figure 6.5a, labeled STD ERROR, to four decimal places.

Next, we require for $g = 2$ simultaneous estimates:

$$B = t[1 - .10/2(2); 18] = t(.975; 18) = 2.101$$

The two pairs of simultaneous confidence limits therefore are $1.455 \pm 2.101(.212)$ and $9.366 \pm 2.101(4.06)$, which yield the confidence intervals:

$$1.01 \leq \beta_1 \leq 1.90$$
$$.84 \leq \beta_2 \leq 17.9$$

With family confidence coefficient .90, we conclude that β_1 falls between 1.01 and 1.90 and that β_2 falls between .84 and 17.9.

Note that the simultaneous confidence intervals suggest that both β_1 and β_2 are positive, which is in accord with theoretical expectations that sales should increase with higher target population and higher per capita disposable income, the other variable being held constant.

Estimation of Mean Response

Dwaine Studios would like to estimate expected (mean) sales in cities with target population $X_{h1} = 65.4$ thousand persons aged 16 years or younger and per capita disposable income

$X_{h2} = 17.6$ thousand dollars with a 95 percent confidence interval. We define:

$$\mathbf{X}_h = \begin{bmatrix} 1 \\ 65.4 \\ 17.6 \end{bmatrix}$$

The point estimate of mean sales is by (6.55):

$$\hat{Y}_h = \mathbf{X}'_h \mathbf{b} = \begin{bmatrix} 1 & 65.4 & 17.6 \end{bmatrix} \begin{bmatrix} -68.857 \\ 1.455 \\ 9.366 \end{bmatrix} = 191.10$$

The estimated variance by (6.58), using the results in (6.78), is:

$$s^2\{\hat{Y}_h\} = \mathbf{X}'_h s^2\{\mathbf{b}\}\mathbf{X}_h$$

$$= \begin{bmatrix} 1 & 65.4 & 17.6 \end{bmatrix} \begin{bmatrix} 3{,}602.0 & 8.748 & -241.43 \\ 8.748 & .0448 & -.679 \\ -241.43 & -.679 & 16.514 \end{bmatrix} \begin{bmatrix} 1 \\ 65.4 \\ 17.6 \end{bmatrix}$$

$$= 7.656$$

or:

$$s\{\hat{Y}_h\} = 2.77$$

For confidence coefficient .95, we need $t(.975; 18) = 2.101$, and we obtain by (6.59) the confidence limits $191.10 \pm 2.101(2.77)$. The confidence interval for $E\{Y_h\}$ therefore is:

$$185.3 \le E\{Y_h\} \le 196.9$$

Thus, with confidence coefficient .95, we estimate that mean sales in cities with target population of 65.4 thousand persons aged 16 years or younger and per capita disposable income of 17.6 thousand dollars are somewhere between 185.3 and 196.9 thousand dollars. Dwaine Studios considers this confidence interval to provide information about expected (average) sales in communities of this size and income level that is precise enough for planning purposes.

Algebraic Version of Estimated Variance $s^2\{\hat{Y}_h\}$. Since by (6.58):

$$s^2\{\hat{Y}_h\} = \mathbf{X}'_h s^2\{\mathbf{b}\}\mathbf{X}_h$$

it follows for the case of two predictor variables in a first-order model:

$$s^2\{\hat{Y}_h\} = s^2\{b_0\} + X_{h1}^2 s^2\{b_1\} + X_{h2}^2 s^2\{b_2\} + 2X_{h1}s\{b_0, b_1\}$$

$$+ 2X_{h2}s\{b_0, b_2\} + 2X_{h1}X_{h2}s\{b_1, b_2\} \tag{6.79}$$

Prediction Limits for New Observations

Dwaine Studios as part of a possible expansion program would like to predict sales for two new cities, with the following characteristics:

	City A	City B
X_{h1}	65.4	53.1
X_{h2}	17.6	17.7

Prediction intervals with a 90 percent family confidence coefficient are desired. Note that the two new cities have characteristics that fall well within the pattern of the 21 cities on which the regression analysis is based.

To determine which simultaneous prediction intervals are best here, we find S as given in (6.65a) and B as given in (6.66a) for $g = 2$ and $1 - \alpha = .90$:

$$S^2 = 2F(.90; 2, 18) = 2(2.62) = 5.24 \qquad S = 2.29$$

and:

$$B = t[1 - .10/2(2); 18] = t(.975; 18) = 2.101$$

Hence, the Bonferroni limits are more efficient here.

For city A, we use the results obtained when estimating mean sales, since the levels of the predictor variables are the same here. We have from before:

$$\hat{Y}_h = 191.10 \qquad s^2\{\hat{Y}_h\} = 7.656 \qquad MSE = 121.1626$$

Hence, by (6.63a):

$$s^2\{\text{pred}\} = MSE + s^2\{\hat{Y}_h\} = 121.1626 + 7.656 = 128.82$$

or:

$$s\{\text{pred}\} = 11.35$$

In similar fashion, we obtain for city B (calculations not shown):

$$\hat{Y}_h = 174.15 \qquad s\{\text{pred}\} = 11.93$$

We previously found that the Bonferroni multiple is $B = 2.101$. Hence, by (6.66) the simultaneous Bonferroni prediction limits with family confidence coefficient .90 are $191.10 \pm 2.101(11.35)$ and $174.15 \pm 2.101(11.93)$, leading to the simultaneous prediction intervals:

$$\text{City A: } 167.3 \le Y_{h(\text{new})} \le 214.9$$
$$\text{City B: } 149.1 \le Y_{h(\text{new})} \le 199.2$$

With family confidence coefficient .90, we predict that sales in the two cities will be within the indicated limits. Dwaine Studios considers these prediction limits to be somewhat useful for planning purposes, but would prefer tighter intervals for predicting sales for a particular city. A consulting firm has been engaged to see if additional or alternative predictor variables can be found that will lead to tighter prediction intervals.

Note incidentally that even though the coefficient of multiple determination, $R^2 = .917$, is high, the prediction limits here are not fully satisfactory. This serves as another reminder that a high value of R^2 does not necessarily indicate that precise predictions can be made.

Cited Reference	6.1. Box, G. E. P., and P. W. Tidwell. "Transformations of the Independent Variables," *Technometrics* 4 (1962), pp. 531–50.

Problems

6.1. Set up the **X** matrix and $\boldsymbol{\beta}$ vector for each of the following regression models (assume $i = 1, \ldots, 4$):

   a. $Y_i = \beta_0 + \beta_1 X_{i1} + \beta_2 X_{i1} X_{i2} + \varepsilon_i$

   b. $\log Y_i = \beta_0 + \beta_1 X_{i1} + \beta_2 X_{i2} + \varepsilon_i$

6.2. Set up the **X** matrix and $\boldsymbol{\beta}$ vector for each of the following regression models (assume $i = 1, \ldots, 5$):

   a. $Y_i = \beta_1 X_{i1} + \beta_2 X_{i2} + \beta_3 X_{i1}^2 + \varepsilon_i$

   b. $\sqrt{Y_i} = \beta_0 + \beta_1 X_{i1} + \beta_2 \log_{10} X_{i2} + \varepsilon_i$

6.3. A student stated: "Adding predictor variables to a regression model can never reduce R^2, so we should include all available predictor variables in the model." Comment.

6.4. Why is it not meaningful to attach a sign to the coefficient of multiple correlation R, although we do so for the coefficient of simple correlation r_{12}?

6.5. **Brand preference.** In a small-scale experimental study of the relation between degree of brand liking (Y) and moisture content (X_1) and sweetness (X_2) of the product, the following results were obtained from the experiment based on a completely randomized design (data are coded):

i:	1	2	3	$\ldots$	14	15	16
X_{i1}:	4	4	4	$\ldots$	10	10	10
X_{i2}:	2	4	2	$\ldots$	4	2	4
Y_i:	64	73	61	$\ldots$	95	94	100

   a. Obtain the scatter plot matrix and the correlation matrix. What information do these diagnostic aids provide here?

   b. Fit regression model (6.1) to the data. State the estimated regression function. How is b_1 interpreted here?

   c. Obtain the residuals and prepare a box plot of the residuals. What information does this plot provide?

   d. Plot the residuals against $\hat{Y}$, X_1, X_2, and $X_1 X_2$ on separate graphs. Also prepare a normal probability plot. Interpret the plots and summarize your findings.

   e. Conduct the Breusch-Pagan test for constancy of the error variance, assuming $\log \sigma_i^2 = \gamma_0 + \gamma_1 X_{i1} + \gamma_2 X_{i2}$; use $\alpha = .01$. State the alternatives, decision rule, and conclusion.

   f. Conduct a formal test for lack of fit of the first-order regression function; use $\alpha = .01$. State the alternatives, decision rule, and conclusion.

6.6. Refer to **Brand preference** Problem 6.5. Assume that regression model (6.1) with independent normal error terms is appropriate.

   a. Test whether there is a regression relation, using $\alpha = .01$. State the alternatives, decision rule, and conclusion. What does your test imply about β_1 and β_2?

b. What is the *P*-value of the test in part (a)?

c. Estimate β_1 and β_2 jointly by the Bonferroni procedure, using a 99 percent family confidence coefficient. Interpret your results.

6.7. Refer to **Brand preference** Problem 6.5.

a. Calculate the coefficient of multiple determination R^2. How is it interpreted here?

b. Calculate the coefficient of simple determination R^2 between Y_i and $\hat{Y}_i$. Does it equal the coefficient of multiple determination in part (a)?

6.8. Refer to **Brand preference** Problem 6.5. Assume that regression model (6.1) with independent normal error terms is appropriate.

a. Obtain an interval estimate of $E\{Y_h\}$ when $X_{h1} = 5$ and $X_{h2} = 4$. Use a 99 percent confidence coefficient. Interpret your interval estimate.

b. Obtain a prediction interval for a new observation $Y_{h(new)}$ when $X_{h1} = 5$ and $X_{h2} = 4$. Use a 99 percent confidence coefficient.

*6.9. **Grocery retailer.** A large, national grocery retailer tracks productivity and costs of its facilities closely. Data below were obtained from a single distribution center for a one-year period. Each data point for each variable represents one week of activity. The variables included are the number of cases shipped (X_1), the indirect costs of the total labor hours as a percentage (X_2), a qualitative predictor called holiday that is coded 1 if the week has a holiday and 0 otherwise (X_3), and the total labor hours (Y).

i:	1	2	3	...	50	51	52
X_{i1}:	305,657	328,476	317,164	...	290,455	411,750	292,087
X_{i2}:	7.17	6.20	4.61	...	7.99	7.83	7.77
X_{i3}:	0	0	0	...	0	0	0
Y_i:	4264	4496	4317	...	4499	4186	4342

a. Prepare separate stem-and-leaf plots for the number of cases shipped X_{i1} and the indirect cost of the total hours X_{i2}. Are there any outlying cases present? Are there any gaps in the data?

b. The cases are given in consecutive weeks. Prepare a time plot for each predictor variable. What do the plots show?

c. Obtain the scatter plot matrix and the correlation matrix. What information do these diagnostic aids provide here?

*6.10. Refer to **Grocery retailer** Problem 6.9.

a. Fit regression model (6.5) to the data for three predictor variables. State the estimated regression function. How are b_1, b_2, and b_3 interpreted here?

b. Obtain the residuals and prepare a box plot of the residuals. What information does this plot provide?

c. Plot the residuals against $\hat{Y}$, X_1, X_2, X_3, and X_1X_2 on separate graphs. Also prepare a normal probability plot. Interpret the plots and summarize your findings.

d. Prepare a time plot of the residuals. Is there any indication that the error terms are correlated? Discuss.

e. Divide the 52 cases into two groups, placing the 26 cases with the smallest fitted values $\hat{Y}_i$ into group 1 and the other 26 cases into group 2. Conduct the Brown-Forsythe test for constancy of the error variance, using $\alpha = .01$. State the decision rule and conclusion.

*6.11. Refer to **Grocery retailer** Problem 6.9. Assume that regression model (6.5) for three predictor variables with independent normal error terms is appropriate.

    a. Test whether there is a regression relation, using level of significance .05. State the alternatives, decision rule, and conclusion. What does your test result imply about β_1, β_2, and β_3? What is the P-value of the test?

    b. Estimate β_1 and β_3 jointly by the Bonferroni procedure, using a 95 percent family confidence coefficient. Interpret your results.

    c. Calculate the coefficient of multiple determination R^2. How is this measure interpreted here?

*6.12. Refer to **Grocery retailer** Problem 6.9. Assume that regression model (6.5) for three predictor variables with independent normal error terms is appropriate.

    a. Management desires simultaneous interval estimates of the total labor hours for the following five typical weekly shipments:

	1	2	3	4	5
X_1:	302,000	245,000	280,000	350,000	295,000
X_2:	7.20	7.40	6.90	7.00	6.70
X_3:	0	0	0	0	1

Obtain the family of estimates using a 95 percent family confidence coefficient. Employ the Working-Hotelling or the Bonferroni procedure, whichever is more efficient.

    b. For the data in Problem 6.9 on which the regression fit is based, would you consider a shipment of 400,000 cases with an indirect percentage of 7.20 on a nonholiday week to be within the scope of the model? What about a shipment of 400,000 cases with an indirect percentage of 9.9 on a nonholiday week? Support your answers by preparing a relevant plot.

*6.13. Refer to **Grocery retailer** Problem 6.9. Assume that regression model (6.5) for three predictor variables with independent normal error terms is appropriate. Four separate shipments with the following characteristics must be processed next month:

	1	2	3	4
X_1:	230,000	250,000	280,000	340,000
X_2:	7.50	7.30	7.10	6.90
X_3:	0	0	0	0

Management desires predictions of the handling times for these shipments so that the actual handling times can be compared with the predicted times to determine whether any are out of line. Develop the needed predictions, using the most efficient approach and a family confidence coefficient of 95 percent.

*6.14. Refer to **Grocery retailer** Problem 6.9. Assume that regression model (6.5) for three predictor variables with independent normal error terms is appropriate. Three new shipments are to be received, each with $X_{h1} = 282,000$, $X_{h2} = 7.10$, and $X_{h3} = 0$.

    a. Obtain a 95 percent prediction interval for the mean handling time for these shipments.

    b. Convert the interval obtained in part (a) into a 95 percent prediction interval for the total labor hours for the three shipments.

*6.15. **Patient satisfaction.** A hospital administrator wished to study the relation between patient satisfaction (Y) and patient's age (X_1, in years), severity of illness (X_2, an index), and anxiety level (X_3, an index). The administrator randomly selected 46 patients and collected the data presented below, where larger values of Y, X_2, and X_3 are, respectively, associated with more satisfaction, increased severity of illness, and more anxiety.

i:	1	2	3	...	44	45	46
X_{i1}:	50	36	40	...	45	37	28
X_{i2}:	51	46	48	...	51	53	46
X_{i3}:	2.3	2.3	2.2	...	2.2	2.1	1.8
Y_i:	48	57	66	...	68	59	92

a. Prepare a stem-and-leaf plot for each of the predictor variables. Are any noteworthy features revealed by these plots?

b. Obtain the scatter plot matrix and the correlation matrix. Interpret these and state your principal findings.

c. Fit regression model (6.5) for three predictor variables to the data and state the estimated regression function. How is b_2 interpreted here?

d. Obtain the residuals and prepare a box plot of the residuals. Do there appear to be any outliers?

e. Plot the residuals against $\hat{Y}$, each of the predictor variables, and each two-factor interaction term on separate graphs. Also prepare a normal probability plot. Interpret your plots and summarize your findings.

f. Can you conduct a formal test for lack of fit here?

g. Conduct the Breusch-Pagan test for constancy of the error variance, assuming $\log \sigma_i^2 = \gamma_0 + \gamma_1 X_{i1} + \gamma_2 X_{i2} + \gamma_3 X_{i3}$; use $\alpha = .01$. State the alternatives, decision rule, and conclusion.

*6.16. Refer to **Patient satisfaction** Problem 6.15. Assume that regression model (6.5) for three predictor variables with independent normal error terms is appropriate.

a. Test whether there is a regression relation; use $\alpha = .10$. State the alternatives, decision rule, and conclusion. What does your test imply about β_1, β_2, and β_3? What is the P-value of the test?

b. Obtain joint interval estimates of β_1, β_2, and β_3, using a 90 percent family confidence coefficient. Interpret your results.

c. Calculate the coefficient of multiple determination. What does it indicate here?

*6.17. Refer to **Patient satisfaction** Problem 6.15. Assume that regression model (6.5) for three predictor variables with independent normal error terms is appropriate.

a. Obtain an interval estimate of the mean satisfaction when $X_{h1} = 35$, $X_{h2} = 45$, and $X_{h3} = 2.2$. Use a 90 percent confidence coefficient. Interpret your confidence interval.

b. Obtain a prediction interval for a new patient's satisfaction when $X_{h1} = 35$, $X_{h2} = 45$, and $X_{h3} = 2.2$. Use a 90 percent confidence coefficient. Interpret your prediction interval.

6.18. **Commercial properties.** A commercial real estate company evaluates vacancy rates, square footage, rental rates, and operating expenses for commercial properties in a large metropolitan area in order to provide clients with quantitative information upon which to make rental decisions. The data below are taken from 81 suburban commercial properties that are the newest, best located, most attractive, and expensive for five specific geographic areas. Shown here are the age (X_1), operating expenses and taxes (X_2), vacancy rates (X_3), total square footage (X_4), and rental rates (Y).

i:	1	2	3	...	79	80	81
X_{i1}:	1	14	16	...	15	11	14
X_{i2}:	5.02	8.19	3.00	...	11.97	11.27	12.68
X_{i3}:	0.14	0.27	0	...	0.14	0.03	0.03
X_{i4}:	123,000	104,079	39,998	...	254,700	434,746	201,930
Y_i:	13.50	12.00	10.50	...	15.00	15.25	14.50

a. Prepare a stem-and-leaf plot for each predictor variable. What information do these plots provide?

b. Obtain the scatter plot matrix and the correlation matrix. Interpret these and state your principal findings.

c. Fit regression model (6.5) for four predictor variables to the data. State the estimated regression function.

d. Obtain the residuals and prepare a box plot of the residuals. Does the distribution appear to be fairly symmetrical?

e. Plot the residuals against $\hat{Y}$, each predictor variable, and each two-factor interaction term on separate graphs. Also prepare a normal probability plot. Analyze your plots and summarize your findings.

f. Can you conduct a formal test for lack of fit here?

g. Divide the 81 cases into two groups, placing the 40 cases with the smallest fitted values $\hat{Y}_i$ into group 1 and the remaining cases into group 2. Conduct the Brown-Forsythe test for constancy of the error variance, using $\alpha = .05$. State the decision rule and conclusion.

6.19. Refer to **Commercial properties** Problem 6.18. Assume that regression model (6.5) for four predictor variables with independent normal error terms is appropriate.

a. Test whether there is a regression relation; use $\alpha = .05$. State the alternatives, decision rule, and conclusion. What does your test imply about β_1, β_2, β_3, and β_4? What is the P-value of the test?

b. Estimate β_1, β_2, β_3, and β_4 jointly by the Bonferroni procedure, using a 95 percent family confidence coefficient. Interpret your results.

c. Calculate R^2 and interpret this measure.

6.20. Refer to **Commercial properties** Problem 6.18. Assume that regression model (6.5) for four predictor variables with independent normal error terms is appropriate. The researcher wishes to obtain simultaneous interval estimates of the mean rental rates for four typical properties specified as follows:

	1	2	3	4
X_1:	5.0	6.0	14.0	12.0
X_2:	8.25	8.50	11.50	10.25
X_3:	0	0.23	0.11	0
X_4:	250,000	270,000	300,000	310,000

Obtain the family of estimates using a 95 percent family confidence coefficient. Employ the most efficient procedure.

6.21. Refer to **Commercial properties** Problem 6.18. Assume that regression model (6.5) for four predictor variables with independent normal error terms is appropriate. Three properties with the following characteristics did not have any rental information available.

	1	2	3
X_1:	4.0	6.0	12.0
X_2:	10.0	11.5	12.5
X_3:	0.10	0	0.32
X_4:	80,000	120,000	340,000

Develop separate prediction intervals for the rental rates of these properties, using a 95 percent statement confidence coefficient in each case. Can the rental rates of these three properties be predicted fairly precisely? What is the family confidence level for the set of three predictions?

Exercises

6.22. For each of the following regression models, indicate whether it is a general linear regression model. If it is not, state whether it can be expressed in the form of (6.7) by a suitable transformation:

a. $Y_i = \beta_0 + \beta_1 X_{i1} + \beta_2 \log_{10} X_{i2} + \beta_3 X_{i1}^2 + \varepsilon_i$

b. $Y_i = \varepsilon_i \exp(\beta_0 + \beta_1 X_{i1} + \beta_2 X_{i2}^2)$

c. $Y_i = \log_{10}(\beta_1 X_{i1}) + \beta_2 X_{i2} + \varepsilon_i$

d. $Y_i = \beta_0 \exp(\beta_1 X_{i1}) + \varepsilon_i$

e. $Y_i = [1 + \exp(\beta_0 + \beta_1 X_{i1} + \varepsilon_i)]^{-1}$

6.23. (Calculus needed.) Consider the multiple regression model:

$$Y_i = \beta_1 X_{i1} + \beta_2 X_{i2} + \varepsilon_i \qquad i = 1, \ldots, n$$

where the ε_i are uncorrelated, with $E\{\varepsilon_i\} = 0$ and $\sigma^2\{\varepsilon_i\} = \sigma^2$.

a. State the least squares criterion and derive the least squares estimators of β_1 and β_2.

b. Assuming that the ε_i are independent normal random variables, state the likelihood function and obtain the maximum likelihood estimators of β_1 and β_2. Are these the same as the least squares estimators?

6.24. (Calculus needed.) Consider the multiple regression model:

$$Y_i = \beta_0 + \beta_1 X_{i1} + \beta_2 X_{i1}^2 + \beta_3 X_{i2} + \varepsilon_i \qquad i = 1, \ldots, n$$

where the ε_i are independent $N(0, \sigma^2)$.

a. State the least squares criterion and derive the least squares normal equations.

b. State the likelihood function and explain why the maximum likelihood estimators will be the same as the least squares estimators.

6.25. An analyst wanted to fit the regression model $Y_i = \beta_0 + \beta_1 X_{i1} + \beta_2 X_{i2} + \beta_3 X_{i3} + \varepsilon_i$, $i = 1, \ldots, n$, by the method of least squares when it is known that $\beta_2 = 4$. How can the analyst obtain the desired fit by using a multiple regression computer program?

6.26. For regression model (6.1), show that the coefficient of simple determination between Y_i and $\hat{Y}_i$ equals the coefficient of multiple determination R^2.

6.27. In a small-scale regression study, the following data were obtained:

i:	1	2	3	4	5	6
X_{i1}:	7	4	16	3	21	8
X_{i2}:	33	41	7	49	5	31
Y_i:	42	33	75	28	91	55

Assume that regression model (6.1) with independent normal error terms is appropriate. Using matrix methods, obtain (a) $\mathbf{b}$; (b) $\mathbf{e}$; (c) $\mathbf{H}$; (d) SSR; (e) $s^2\{\mathbf{b}\}$; (f) $\hat{Y}_h$ when $X_{h1} = 10$, $X_{h2} = 30$; (g) $s^2\{\hat{Y}_h\}$ when $X_{h1} = 10$, $X_{h2} = 30$.

Projects

6.28. Refer to the **CDI** data set in Appendix C.2. You have been asked to evaluate two alternative models for predicting the number of active physicians (Y) in a CDI. Proposed model I includes as predictor variables total population (X_1), land area (X_2), and total personal income (X_3). Proposed model II includes as predictor variables population density (X_1, total population divided by land area), percent of population greater than 64 years old (X_2), and total personal income (X_3).

 a. Prepare a stem-and-leaf plot for each of the predictor variables. What noteworthy information is provided by your plots?

 b. Obtain the scatter plot matrix and the correlation matrix for each proposed model. Summarize the information provided.

 c. For each proposed model, fit the first-order regression model (6.5) with three predictor variables.

 d. Calculate R^2 for each model. Is one model clearly preferable in terms of this measure?

 e. For each model, obtain the residuals and plot them against $\hat{Y}$, each of the three predictor variables, and each of the two-factor interaction terms. Also prepare a normal probability plot for each of the two fitted models. Interpret your plots and state your findings. Is one model clearly preferable in terms of appropriateness?

6.29. Refer to the **CDI** data set in Appendix C.2.

 a. For each geographic region, regress the number of serious crimes in a CDI (Y) against population density (X_1, total population divided by land area), per capita personal income (X_2), and percent high school graduates (X_3). Use first-order regression model (6.5) with three predictor variables. State the estimated regression functions.

 b. Are the estimated regression functions similar for the four regions? Discuss.

 c. Calculate MSE and R^2 for each region. Are these measures similar for the four regions? Discuss.

 d. Obtain the residuals for each fitted model and prepare a box plot of the residuals for each fitted model. Interpret your plots and state your findings.

6.30. Refer to the **SENIC** data set in Appendix C.1. Two models have been proposed for predicting the average length of patient stay in a hospital (Y). Model I utilizes as predictor variables age (X_1), infection risk (X_2), and available facilities and services (X_3). Model II uses as predictor variables number of beds (X_1), infection risk (X_2), and available facilities and services (X_3).

 a. Prepare a stem-and-leaf plot for each of the predictor variables. What information do these plots provide?

 b. Obtain the scatter plot matrix and the correlation matrix for each proposed model. Interpret these and state your principal findings.

c. For each of the two proposed models, fit first-order regression model (6.5) with three predictor variables.

d. Calculate R^2 for each model. Is one model clearly preferable in terms of this measure?

e. For each model, obtain the residuals and plot them against $\hat{Y}$, each of the three predictor variables, and each of the two-factor interaction terms. Also prepare a normal probability plot of the residuals for each of the two fitted models. Interpret your plots and state your findings. Is one model clearly more appropriate than the other?

6.31. Refer to the **SENIC** data set in Appendix C.1.

a. For each geographic region, regress infection risk (Y) against the predictor variables age (X_1), routine culturing ratio (X_2), average daily census (X_3), and available facilities and services (X_4). Use first-order regression model (6.5) with four predictor variables. State the estimated regression functions.

b. Are the estimated regression functions similar for the four regions? Discuss.

c. Calculate *MSE* and R^2 for each region. Are these measures similar for the four regions? Discuss.

d. Obtain the residuals for each fitted model and prepare a box plot of the residuals for each fitted model. Interpret the plots and state your findings.

Chapter 7

Multiple Regression II

In this chapter, we take up some specialized topics that are unique to multiple regression. These include extra sums of squares, which are useful for conducting a variety of tests about the regression coefficients, the standardized version of the multiple regression model, and multicollinearity, a condition where the predictor variables are highly correlated.

7.1 Extra Sums of Squares

Basic Ideas

An extra sum of squares measures the marginal reduction in the error sum of squares when one or several predictor variables are added to the regression model, given that other predictor variables are already in the model. Equivalently, one can view an extra sum of squares as measuring the marginal increase in the regression sum of squares when one or several predictor variables are added to the regression model.

We first utilize an example to illustrate these ideas, and then we present definitions of extra sums of squares and discuss a variety of uses of extra sums of squares in tests about regression coefficients.

Example

Table 7.1 contains a portion of the data for a study of the relation of amount of body fat (Y) to several possible predictor variables, based on a sample of 20 healthy females 25–34 years old. The possible predictor variables are triceps skinfold thickness (X_1), thigh circumference (X_2), and midarm circumference (X_3). The amount of body fat in Table 7.1 for each of the 20 persons was obtained by a cumbersome and expensive procedure requiring the immersion of the person in water. It would therefore be very helpful if a regression model with some or all of these predictor variables could provide reliable estimates of the amount of body fat since the measurements needed for the predictor variables are easy to obtain.

Table 7.2 contains some of the main regression results when body fat (Y) is regressed (1) on triceps skinfold thickness (X_1) alone, (2) on thigh circumference (X_2) alone, (3) on X_1 and X_2 only, and (4) on all three predictor variables. To keep track of the regression model that is fitted, we shall modify our notation slightly. The regression sum of squares when X_1 only is in the model is, according to Table 7.2a, 352.27. This sum of squares will be denoted by $SSR(X_1)$. The error sum of squares for this model will be denoted by $SSE(X_1)$; according to Table 7.2a it is $SSE(X_1) = 143.12$.

Similarly, Table 7.2c indicates that when X_1 and X_2 are in the regression model, the regression sum of squares is $SSR(X_1, X_2) = 385.44$ and the error sum of squares is $SSE(X_1, X_2) = 109.95$.

Notice that the error sum of squares when X_1 and X_2 are in the model, $SSE(X_1, X_2) = 109.95$, is smaller than when the model contains only X_1, $SSE(X_1) = 143.12$. The difference is called an *extra sum of squares* and will be denoted by $SSR(X_2|X_1)$:

$$SSR(X_2|X_1) = SSE(X_1) - SSE(X_1, X_2)$$
$$= 143.12 - 109.95 = 33.17$$

TABLE 7.1
Basic Data—Body Fat Example.

Subject i	Triceps Skinfold Thickness X_{i1}	Thigh Circumference X_{i2}	Midarm Circumference X_{i3}	Body Fat Y_i
1	19.5	43.1	29.1	11.9
2	24.7	49.8	28.2	22.8
3	30.7	51.9	37.0	18.7
...	...	...	...	...
18	30.2	58.6	24.6	25.4
19	22.7	48.2	27.1	14.8
20	25.2	51.0	27.5	21.1

TABLE 7.2
Regression Results for Several Fitted Models—Body Fat Example.

(a) Regression of Y on X_1
$\hat{Y} = -1.496 + .8572X_1$

Source of Variation	SS	df	MS
Regression	352.27	1	352.27
Error	143.12	18	7.95
Total	495.39	19	

Variable	Estimated Regression Coefficient	Estimated Standard Deviation	t^*
X_1	$b_1 = .8572$	$s\{b_1\} = .1288$	6.66

(b) Regression of Y on X_2
$\hat{Y} = -23.634 + .8565X_2$

Source of Variation	SS	df	MS
Regression	381.97	1	381.97
Error	113.42	18	6.30
Total	495.39	19	

Variable	Estimated Regression Coefficient	Estimated Standard Deviation	t^*
X_2	$b_2 = .8565$	$s\{b_2\} = .1100$	7.79

(continued)

TABLE 7.2
(Continued).

(c) Regression of Y on X_1 and X_2 $\hat{Y} = -19.174 + .2224X_1 + .6594X_2$			
Source of Variation	SS	df	MS
Regression	385.44	2	192.72
Error	109.95	17	6.47
Total	495.39	19	
Variable	Estimated Regression Coefficient	Estimated Standard Deviation	t^*
X_1	$b_1 = .2224$	$s\{b_1\} = .3034$	.73
X_2	$b_2 = .6594$	$s\{b_2\} = .2912$	2.26
(d) Regression of Y on X_1, X_2, and X_3 $\hat{Y} = 117.08 + 4.334X_1 - 2.857X_2 - 2.186X_3$			
Source of Variation	SS	df	MS
Regression	396.98	3	132.33
Error	98.41	16	6.15
Total	495.39	19	
Variable	Estimated Regression Coefficient	Estimated Standard Deviation	t^*
X_1	$b_1 = 4.334$	$s\{b_1\} = 3.016$	1.44
X_2	$b_2 = -2.857$	$s\{b_2\} = 2.582$	-1.11
X_3	$b_3 = -2.186$	$s\{b_3\} = 1.596$	-1.37

This reduction in the error sum of squares is the result of adding X_2 to the regression model when X_1 is already included in the model. Thus, the extra sum of squares $SSR(X_2|X_1)$ measures the marginal effect of adding X_2 to the regression model when X_1 is already in the model. The notation $SSR(X_2|X_1)$ reflects this additional or extra reduction in the error sum of squares associated with X_2, given that X_1 is already included in the model.

The extra sum of squares $SSR(X_2|X_1)$ equivalently can be viewed as the marginal increase in the regression sum of squares:

$$SSR(X_2|X_1) = SSR(X_1, X_2) - SSR(X_1)$$
$$= 385.44 - 352.27 = 33.17$$

The reason for the equivalence of the marginal reduction in the error sum of squares and the marginal increase in the regression sum of squares is the basic analysis of variance identity (2.50):

$$SSTO = SSR + SSE$$

Since $SSTO$ measures the variability of the Y_i observations and hence does not depend on the regression model fitted, any reduction in SSE implies an identical increase in SSR.

We can consider other extra sums of squares, such as the marginal effect of adding X_3 to the regression model when X_1 and X_2 are already in the model. We find from Tables 7.2c and 7.2d that:

$$SSR(X_3|X_1, X_2) = SSE(X_1, X_2) - SSE(X_1, X_2, X_3)$$
$$= 109.95 - 98.41 = 11.54$$

or, equivalently:

$$SSR(X_3|X_1, X_2) = SSR(X_1, X_2, X_3) - SSR(X_1, X_2)$$
$$= 396.98 - 385.44 = 11.54$$

We can even consider the marginal effect of adding several variables, such as adding both X_2 and X_3 to the regression model already containing X_1 (see Tables 7.2a and 7.2d):

$$SSR(X_2, X_3|X_1) = SSE(X_1) - SSE(X_1, X_2, X_3)$$
$$= 143.12 - 98.41 = 44.71$$

or, equivalently:

$$SSR(X_2, X_3|X_1) = SSR(X_1, X_2, X_3) - SSR(X_1)$$
$$= 396.98 - 352.27 = 44.71$$

Definitions

We assemble now our earlier definitions of extra sums of squares and provide some additional ones. As we noted earlier, an extra sum of squares always involves the difference between the error sum of squares for the regression model containing the X variable(s) already in the model and the error sum of squares for the regression model containing both the original X variable(s) and the new X variable(s). Equivalently, an extra sum of squares involves the difference between the two corresponding regression sums of squares.

Thus, we define:

$$SSR(X_1|X_2) = SSE(X_2) - SSE(X_1, X_2) \tag{7.1a}$$

or, equivalently:

$$SSR(X_1|X_2) = SSR(X_1, X_2) - SSR(X_2) \tag{7.1b}$$

If X_2 is the extra variable, we define:

$$SSR(X_2|X_1) = SSE(X_1) - SSE(X_1, X_2) \tag{7.2a}$$

or, equivalently:

$$SSR(X_2|X_1) = SSR(X_1, X_2) - SSR(X_1) \tag{7.2b}$$

Extensions for three or more variables are straightforward. For example, we define:

$$SSR(X_3|X_1, X_2) = SSE(X_1, X_2) - SSE(X_1, X_2, X_3) \tag{7.3a}$$

or:

$$SSR(X_3|X_1, X_2) = SSR(X_1, X_2, X_3) - SSR(X_1, X_2) \tag{7.3b}$$

and:

$$SSR(X_2, X_3|X_1) = SSE(X_1) - SSE(X_1, X_2, X_3) \tag{7.4a}$$

or:

$$SSR(X_2, X_3|X_1) = SSR(X_1, X_2, X_3) - SSR(X_1) \tag{7.4b}$$

Decomposition of *SSR* into Extra Sums of Squares

In multiple regression, unlike simple linear regression, we can obtain a variety of decompositions of the regression sum of squares *SSR* into extra sums of squares. Let us consider the case of two X variables. We begin with the identity (2.50) for variable X_1:

$$SSTO = SSR(X_1) + SSE(X_1) \tag{7.5}$$

where the notation now shows explicitly that X_1 is the X variable in the model. Replacing $SSE(X_1)$ by its equivalent in (7.2a), we obtain:

$$SSTO = SSR(X_1) + SSR(X_2|X_1) + SSE(X_1, X_2) \tag{7.6}$$

We now make use of the same identity for multiple regression with two X variables as in (7.5) for a single X variable, namely:

$$SSTO = SSR(X_1, X_2) + SSE(X_1, X_2) \tag{7.7}$$

Solving (7.7) for $SSE(X_1, X_2)$ and using this expression in (7.6) lead to:

$$SSR(X_1, X_2) = SSR(X_1) + SSR(X_2|X_1) \tag{7.8}$$

Thus, we have decomposed the regression sum of squares $SSR(X_1, X_2)$ into two marginal components: (1) $SSR(X_1)$, measuring the contribution by including X_1 alone in the model, and (2) $SSR(X_2|X_1)$, measuring the additional contribution when X_2 is included, given that X_1 is already in the model.

Of course, the order of the X variables is arbitrary. Here, we can also obtain the decomposition:

$$SSR(X_1, X_2) = SSR(X_2) + SSR(X_1|X_2) \tag{7.9}$$

We show in Figure 7.1 schematic representations of the two decompositions of $SSR(X_1, X_2)$ for the body fat example. The total bar on the left represents *SSTO* and presents decomposition (7.9). The unshaded component of this bar is $SSR(X_2)$, and the combined shaded area represents $SSE(X_2)$. The latter area in turn is the combination of the extra sum of squares $SSR(X_1|X_2)$ and the error sum of squares $SSE(X_1, X_2)$ when both X_1 and X_2 are included in the model. Similarly, the bar on the right in Figure 7.1 shows decomposition (7.8). Note in both cases how the extra sum of squares can be viewed either as a reduction in the error sum of squares or as an increase in the regression sum of squares when the second predictor variable is added to the regression model.

When the regression model contains three X variables, a variety of decompositions of $SSR(X_1, X_2, X_3)$ can be obtained. We illustrate three of these:

$$SSR(X_1, X_2, X_3) = SSR(X_1) + SSR(X_2|X_1) + SSR(X_3|X_1, X_2) \tag{7.10a}$$

$$SSR(X_1, X_2, X_3) = SSR(X_2) + SSR(X_3|X_2) + SSR(X_1|X_2, X_3) \tag{7.10b}$$

$$SSR(X_1, X_2, X_3) = SSR(X_1) + SSR(X_2, X_3|X_1) \tag{7.10c}$$

FIGURE 7.1   Schematic Representation of Extra Sums of Squares—Body Fat Example.

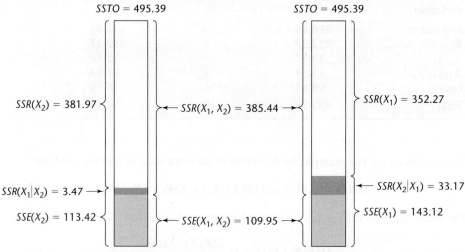

TABLE 7.3
Example of
ANOVA Table
with
Decomposition
of *SSR* for
Three *X*
Variables.

Source of Variation	SS	df	MS
Regression	$SSR(X_1, X_2, X_3)$	3	$MSR(X_1, X_2, X_3)$
X_1	$SSR(X_1)$	1	$MSR(X_1)$
$X_2 \mid X_1$	$SSR(X_2 \mid X_1)$	1	$MSR(X_2 \mid X_1)$
$X_3 \mid X_1, X_2$	$SSR(X_3 \mid X_1, X_2)$	1	$MSR(X_3 \mid X_1, X_2)$
Error	$SSE(X_1, X_2, X_3)$	$n - 4$	$MSE(X_1, X_2, X_3)$
Total	$SSTO$	$n - 1$	

It is obvious that the number of possible decompositions becomes vast as the number of X variables in the regression model increases.

ANOVA Table Containing Decomposition of *SSR*

ANOVA tables can be constructed containing decompositions of the regression sum of squares into extra sums of squares. Table 7.3 contains the ANOVA table decomposition for the case of three X variables often used in regression packages, and Table 7.4 contains this same decomposition for the body fat example. The decomposition involves single extra X variables.

Note that each extra sum of squares involving a single extra X variable has associated with it one degree of freedom. The resulting mean squares are constructed as usual. For example, $MSR(X_2 \mid X_1)$ in Table 7.3 is obtained as follows:

$$MSR(X_2 \mid X_1) = \frac{SSR(X_2 \mid X_1)}{1}$$

Extra sums of squares involving two extra X variables, such as $SSR(X_2, X_3 \mid X_1)$, have two degrees of freedom associated with them. This follows because we can express such an extra sum of squares as a sum of two extra sums of squares, each associated with one

TABLE 7.4	Source of Variation	SS	df	MS
ANOVA Table with Decomposition of *SSR*—Body Fat Example with Three Predictor Variables.	Regression	396.98	3	132.33
	X_1	352.27	1	352.27
	$X_2\|X_1$	33.17	1	33.17
	$X_3\|X_1, X_2$	11.54	1	11.54
	Error	98.41	16	6.15
	Total	495.39	19	

degree of freedom. For example, by definition of the extra sums of squares, we have:

$$SSR(X_2, X_3|X_1) = SSR(X_2|X_1) + SSR(X_3|X_1, X_2) \qquad (7.11)$$

The mean square $MSR(X_2, X_3|X_1)$ is therefore obtained as follows:

$$MSR(X_2, X_3|X_1) = \frac{SSR(X_2, X_3|X_1)}{2}$$

Many computer regression packages provide decompositions of *SSR* into single-degree-of-freedom extra sums of squares, usually in the order in which the X variables are entered into the model. Thus, if the X variables are entered in the order X_1, X_2, X_3, the extra sums of squares given in the output are:

$$SSR(X_1)$$
$$SSR(X_2|X_1)$$
$$SSR(X_3|X_1, X_2)$$

If an extra sum of squares involving several extra X variables is desired, it can be obtained by summing appropriate single-degree-of-freedom extra sums of squares. For instance, to obtain $SSR(X_2, X_3|X_1)$ in our earlier illustration, we would utilize (7.11) and simply add $SSR(X_2|X_1)$ and $SSR(X_3|X_1, X_2)$.

If the extra sum of squares $SSR(X_1, X_3|X_2)$ were desired with a computer package that provides single-degree-of-freedom extra sums of squares in the order in which the X variables are entered, the X variables would need to be entered in the order X_2, X_1, X_3 or X_2, X_3, X_1. The first ordering would give:

$$SSR(X_2)$$
$$SSR(X_1|X_2)$$
$$SSR(X_3|X_1, X_2)$$

The sum of the last two extra sums of squares will yield $SSR(X_1, X_3|X_2)$.

The reason why extra sums of squares are of interest is that they occur in a variety of tests about regression coefficients where the question of concern is whether certain X variables can be dropped from the regression model. We turn next to this use of extra sums of squares.

7.2 Uses of Extra Sums of Squares in Tests for Regression Coefficients

Test whether a Single $\beta_k = 0$

When we wish to test whether the term $\beta_k X_k$ can be dropped from a multiple regression model, we are interested in the alternatives:

$$H_0: \beta_k = 0$$
$$H_a: \beta_k \neq 0$$

We already know that test statistic (6.51b):

$$t^* = \frac{b_k}{s\{b_k\}}$$

is appropriate for this test.

Equivalently, we can use the general linear test approach described in Section 2.8. We now show that this approach involves an extra sum of squares. Let us consider the first-order regression model with three predictor variables:

$$Y_i = \beta_0 + \beta_1 X_{i1} + \beta_2 X_{i2} + \beta_3 X_{i3} + \varepsilon_i \qquad \text{Full model} \qquad \textbf{(7.12)}$$

To test the alternatives:

$$H_0: \beta_3 = 0$$
$$H_a: \beta_3 \neq 0 \qquad \textbf{(7.13)}$$

we fit the full model and obtain the error sum of squares $SSE(F)$. We now explicitly show the variables in the full model, as follows:

$$SSE(F) = SSE(X_1, X_2, X_3)$$

The degrees of freedom associated with $SSE(F)$ are $df_F = n - 4$ since there are four parameters in the regression function for the full model (7.12).

The reduced model when H_0 in (7.13) holds is:

$$Y_i = \beta_0 + \beta_1 X_{i1} + \beta_2 X_{i2} + \varepsilon_i \qquad \text{Reduced model} \qquad \textbf{(7.14)}$$

We next fit this reduced model and obtain:

$$SSE(R) = SSE(X_1, X_2)$$

There are $df_R = n - 3$ degrees of freedom associated with the reduced model.

The general linear test statistic (2.70):

$$F^* = \frac{SSE(R) - SSE(F)}{df_R - df_F} \div \frac{SSE(F)}{df_F}$$

here becomes:

$$F^* = \frac{SSE(X_1, X_2) - SSE(X_1, X_2, X_3)}{(n - 3) - (n - 4)} \div \frac{SSE(X_1, X_2, X_3)}{n - 4}$$

Note that the difference between the two error sums of squares in the numerator term is the extra sum of squares (7.3a):

$$SSE(X_1, X_2) - SSE(X_1, X_2, X_3) = SSR(X_3|X_1, X_2)$$

Hence the general linear test statistic here is:

$$F^* = \frac{SSR(X_3|X_1, X_2)}{1} \div \frac{SSE(X_1, X_2, X_3)}{n-4} = \frac{MSR(X_3|X_1, X_2)}{MSE(X_1, X_2, X_3)} \quad \text{(7.15)}$$

We thus see that the test whether or not $\beta_3 = 0$ is a marginal test, given that X_1 and X_2 are already in the model. We also note that the extra sum of squares $SSR(X_3|X_1, X_2)$ has one degree of freedom associated with it, just as we noted earlier.

Test statistic (7.15) shows that we do not need to fit both the full model and the reduced model to use the general linear test approach here. A single computer run can provide a fit of the full model and the appropriate extra sum of squares.

Example

In the body fat example, we wish to test for the model with all three predictor variables whether midarm circumference (X_3) can be dropped from the model. The test alternatives are those of (7.13). Table 7.4 contains the ANOVA results from a computer fit of the full regression model (7.12), including the extra sums of squares when the predictor variables are entered in the order X_1, X_2, X_3. Hence, test statistic (7.15) here is:

$$F^* = \frac{SSR(X_3|X_1, X_2)}{1} \div \frac{SSE(X_1, X_2, X_3)}{n-4}$$

$$= \frac{11.54}{1} \div \frac{98.41}{16} = 1.88$$

For $\alpha = .01$, we require $F(.99; 1, 16) = 8.53$. Since $F^* = 1.88 \leq 8.53$, we conclude H_0, that X_3 can be dropped from the regression model that already contains X_1 and X_2.

Note from Table 7.2d that the t^* test statistic here is:

$$t^* = \frac{b_3}{s\{b_3\}} = \frac{-2.186}{1.596} = -1.37$$

Since $(t^*)^2 = (-1.37)^2 = 1.88 = F^*$, we see that the two test statistics are equivalent, just as for simple linear regression.

Comment

The F^* test statistic (7.15) to test whether or not $\beta_3 = 0$ is called a *partial F test* statistic to distinguish it from the F^* statistic in (6.39b) for testing whether *all* $\beta_k = 0$, i.e., whether or not there is a regression relation between Y and the set of X variables. The latter test is called the *overall F test*. ∎

Test whether Several $\beta_k = 0$

In multiple regression we are frequently interested in whether several terms in the regression model can be dropped. For example, we may wish to know whether both $\beta_2 X_2$ and $\beta_3 X_3$ can be dropped from the full model (7.12). The alternatives here are:

$$H_0: \beta_2 = \beta_3 = 0$$
$$H_a: \text{not both } \beta_2 \text{ and } \beta_3 \text{ equal zero} \quad \text{(7.16)}$$

With the general linear test approach, the reduced model under H_0 is:

$$Y_i = \beta_0 + \beta_1 X_{i1} + \varepsilon_i \qquad \text{Reduced model} \qquad (7.17)$$

and the error sum of squares for the reduced model is:

$$SSE(R) = SSE(X_1)$$

This error sum of squares has $df_R = n - 2$ degrees of freedom associated with it. The general linear test statistic (2.70) thus becomes here:

$$F^* = \frac{SSE(X_1) - SSE(X_1, X_2, X_3)}{(n-2) - (n-4)} \div \frac{SSE(X_1, X_2, X_3)}{n-4}$$

Again the difference between the two error sums of squares in the numerator term is an extra sum of squares, namely:

$$SSE(X_1) - SSE(X_1, X_2, X_3) = SSR(X_2, X_3 | X_1)$$

Hence, the test statistic becomes:

$$F^* = \frac{SSR(X_2, X_3 | X_1)}{2} \div \frac{SSE(X_1, X_2, X_3)}{n-4} = \frac{MSR(X_2, X_3 | X_1)}{MSE(X_1, X_2, X_3)} \qquad (7.18)$$

Note that $SSR(X_2, X_3 | X_1)$ has two degrees of freedom associated with it, as we pointed out earlier.

Example

We wish to test in the body fat example for the model with all three predictor variables whether both thigh circumference (X_2) and midarm circumference (X_3) can be dropped from the full regression model (7.12). The alternatives are those in (7.16). The appropriate extra sum of squares can be obtained from Table 7.4, using (7.11):

$$SSR(X_2, X_3 | X_1) = SSR(X_2 | X_1) + SSR(X_3 | X_1, X_2)$$

$$= 33.17 + 11.54 = 44.71$$

Test statistic (7.18) therefore is:

$$F^* = \frac{SSR(X_2, X_3 | X_1)}{2} \div MSE(X_1, X_2, X_3)$$

$$= \frac{44.71}{2} \div 6.15 = 3.63$$

For $\alpha = .05$, we require $F(.95; 2, 16) = 3.63$. Since $F^* = 3.63$ is at the boundary of the decision rule (the P-value of the test statistic is .05), we may wish to make further analyses before deciding whether X_2 and X_3 should be dropped from the regression model that already contains X_1.

Comments

1. For testing whether a single β_k equals zero, two equivalent test statistics are available: the t^* test statistic and the F^* general linear test statistic. When testing whether several β_k equal zero, only the general linear test statistic F^* is available.

2. General linear test statistic (2.70) for testing whether several X variables can be dropped from the general linear regression model (6.7) can be expressed in terms of the coefficients of

multiple determination for the full and reduced models. Denoting these by R_F^2 and R_R^2, respectively, we have:

$$F^* = \frac{R_F^2 - R_R^2}{df_R - df_F} \div \frac{1 - R_F^2}{df_F} \qquad (7.19)$$

Specifically for testing the alternatives in (7.16) for the body fat example, test statistic (7.19) becomes:

$$F^* = \frac{R_{Y|123}^2 - R_{Y|1}^2}{(n-2)-(n-4)} \div \frac{1 - R_{Y|123}^2}{n-4} \qquad (7.20)$$

where $R_{Y|123}^2$ denotes the coefficient of multiple determination when Y is regressed on X_1, X_2, and X_3, and $R_{Y|1}^2$ denotes the coefficient when Y is regressed on X_1 alone.

We see from Table 7.4 that $R_{Y|123}^2 = 396.98/495.39 = .80135$ and $R_{Y|1}^2 = 352.27/495.39 = .71110$. Hence, we obtain by substituting in (7.20):

$$F^* = \frac{.80135 - .71110}{(20-2)-(20-4)} \div \frac{1 - .80135}{16} = 3.63$$

This is the same result as before. Note that $R_{Y|1}^2$ corresponds to the coefficient of simple determination R^2 between Y and X_1.

Test statistic (7.19) is not appropriate when the full and reduced regression models do not contain the intercept term β_0. In that case, the general linear test statistic in the form (2.70) must be used. ∎

7.3   Summary of Tests Concerning Regression Coefficients

We have already discussed how to conduct several types of tests concerning regression coefficients in a multiple regression model. For completeness, we summarize here these tests as well as some additional types of tests.

Test whether All $\beta_k = 0$

This is the *overall F test* (6.39) of whether or not there is a regression relation between the response variable Y and the set of X variables. The alternatives are:

$$H_0: \beta_1 = \beta_2 = \cdots = \beta_{p-1} = 0$$
$$H_a: \text{not all } \beta_k \ (k = 1, \ldots, p-1) \text{ equal zero} \qquad (7.21)$$

and the test statistic is:

$$F^* = \frac{SSR(X_1, \ldots, X_{p-1})}{p-1} \div \frac{SSE(X_1, \ldots, X_{p-1})}{n-p}$$
$$= \frac{MSR}{MSE} \qquad (7.22)$$

If H_0 holds, $F^* \sim F(p-1, n-p)$. Large values of F^* lead to conclusion H_a.

Test whether a Single $\beta_k = 0$

This is a *partial F test* of whether a particular regression coefficient β_k equals zero. The alternatives are:

$$H_0: \beta_k = 0$$
$$H_a: \beta_k \neq 0 \tag{7.23}$$

and the test statistic is:

$$F^* = \frac{SSR(X_k|X_1, \ldots, X_{k-1}, X_{k+1}, \ldots, X_{p-1})}{1} \div \frac{SSE(X_1, \ldots, X_{p-1})}{n-p}$$

$$= \frac{MSR(X_k|X_1, \ldots, X_{k-1}, X_{k+1}, \ldots, X_{p-1})}{MSE} \tag{7.24}$$

If H_0 holds, $F^* \sim F(1, n-p)$. Large values of F^* lead to conclusion H_a. Statistics packages that provide extra sums of squares permit use of this test without having to fit the reduced model.

An equivalent test statistic is (6.51b):

$$t^* = \frac{b_k}{s\{b_k\}} \tag{7.25}$$

If H_0 holds, $t^* \sim t(n-p)$. Large values of $|t^*|$ lead to conclusion H_a.

Since the two tests are equivalent, the choice is usually made in terms of available information provided by the regression package output.

Test whether Some $\beta_k = 0$

This is another *partial F test*. Here, the alternatives are:

$$H_0: \beta_q = \beta_{q+1} = \cdots = \beta_{p-1} = 0$$
$$H_a: \text{ not all of the } \beta_k \text{ in } H_0 \text{ equal zero} \tag{7.26}$$

where for convenience, we arrange the model so that the last $p - q$ coefficients are the ones to be tested. The test statistic is:

$$F^* = \frac{SSR(X_q, \ldots, X_{p-1}|X_1, \ldots, X_{q-1})}{p-q} \div \frac{SSE(X_1, \ldots, X_{p-1})}{n-p}$$

$$= \frac{MSR(X_q, \ldots, X_{p-1}|X_1, \ldots, X_{q-1})}{MSE} \tag{7.27}$$

If H_0 holds, $F^* \sim F(p-q, n-p)$. Large values of F^* lead to conclusion H_a.

Note that test statistic (7.27) actually encompasses the two earlier cases. If $q = 1$, the test is whether all regression coefficients equal zero. If $q = p - 1$, the test is whether a single regression coefficient equals zero. Also note that test statistic (7.27) can be calculated without having to fit the reduced model if the regression package provides the needed extra sums of squares:

$$SSR(X_q, \ldots, X_{p-1}|X_1, \ldots, X_{q-1})$$
$$= SSR(X_q|X_1, \ldots, X_{q-1}) + \cdots + SSR(X_{p-1}|X_1, \ldots, X_{p-2}) \tag{7.28}$$

Test statistic (7.27) can be stated equivalently in terms of the coefficients of multiple determination for the full and reduced models when these models contain the intercept term β_0, as follows:

$$F^* = \frac{R^2_{Y|1\cdots p-1} - R^2_{Y|1\cdots q-1}}{p - q} \div \frac{1 - R^2_{Y|1\cdots p-1}}{n - p} \tag{7.29}$$

where $R^2_{Y|1\cdots p-1}$ denotes the coefficient of multiple determination when Y is regressed on all X variables, and $R^2_{Y|1\cdots q-1}$ denotes the coefficient when Y is regressed on $X_1, \ldots, X_{q-1}$ only.

Other Tests

When tests about regression coefficients are desired that do not involve testing whether one or several β_k equal zero, extra sums of squares cannot be used and the general linear test approach requires separate fittings of the full and reduced models. For instance, for the full model containing three X variables:

$$Y_i = \beta_0 + \beta_1 X_{i1} + \beta_2 X_{i2} + \beta_3 X_{i3} + \varepsilon_i \qquad \text{Full model} \tag{7.30}$$

we might wish to test:

$$\begin{aligned} H_0&: \beta_1 = \beta_2 \\ H_a&: \beta_1 \neq \beta_2 \end{aligned} \tag{7.31}$$

The procedure would be to fit the full model (7.30), and then the reduced model:

$$Y_i = \beta_0 + \beta_c(X_{i1} + X_{i2}) + \beta_3 X_{i3} + \varepsilon_i \qquad \text{Reduced model} \tag{7.32}$$

where β_c denotes the common coefficient for β_1 and β_2 under H_0 and $X_{i1} + X_{i2}$ is the corresponding new X variable. We then use the general F^* test statistic (2.70) with 1 and $n - 4$ degrees of freedom.

Another example where extra sums of squares cannot be used is in the following test for regression model (7.30):

$$\begin{aligned} H_0&: \beta_1 = 3, \beta_3 = 5 \\ H_a&: \text{not both equalities in } H_0 \text{ hold} \end{aligned} \tag{7.33}$$

Here, the reduced model would be:

$$Y_i - 3X_{i1} - 5X_{i3} = \beta_0 + \beta_2 X_{i2} + \varepsilon_i \qquad \text{Reduced model} \tag{7.34}$$

Note the new response variable $Y - 3X_1 - 5X_3$ in the reduced model, since $\beta_1 X_1$ and $\beta_3 X_3$ are known constants under H_0. We then use the general linear test statistic F^* in (2.70) with 2 and $n - 4$ degrees of freedom.

7.4   Coefficients of Partial Determination

Extra sums of squares are not only useful for tests on the regression coefficients of a multiple regression model, but they are also encountered in descriptive measures of relationship called coefficients of partial determination. Recall that the coefficient of multiple determination, R^2, measures the proportionate reduction in the variation of Y achieved by the introduction of the entire set of X variables considered in the model. A *coefficient of partial determination,* in contrast, measures the marginal contribution of one X variable when all others are already included in the model.

Two Predictor Variables

We first consider a first-order multiple regression model with two predictor variables, as given in (6.1):

$$Y_i = \beta_0 + \beta_1 X_{i1} + \beta_2 X_{i2} + \varepsilon_i$$

$SSE(X_2)$ measures the variation in Y when X_2 is included in the model. $SSE(X_1, X_2)$ measures the variation in Y when both X_1 and X_2 are included in the model. Hence, the relative marginal reduction in the variation in Y associated with X_1 when X_2 is already in the model is:

$$\frac{SSE(X_2) - SSE(X_1, X_2)}{SSE(X_2)} = \frac{SSR(X_1|X_2)}{SSE(X_2)}$$

This measure is the coefficient of partial determination between Y and X_1, given that X_2 is in the model. We denote this measure by $R^2_{Y1|2}$:

$$R^2_{Y1|2} = \frac{SSE(X_2) - SSE(X_1, X_2)}{SSE(X_2)} = \frac{SSR(X_1|X_2)}{SSE(X_2)} \tag{7.35}$$

Thus, $R^2_{Y1|2}$ measures the proportionate reduction in the variation in Y remaining after X_2 is included in the model that is gained by also including X_1 in the model.

The coefficient of partial determination between Y and X_2, given that X_1 is in the model, is defined correspondingly:

$$R^2_{Y2|1} = \frac{SSR(X_2|X_1)}{SSE(X_1)} \tag{7.36}$$

General Case

The generalization of coefficients of partial determination to three or more X variables in the model is immediate. For instance:

$$R^2_{Y1|23} = \frac{SSR(X_1|X_2, X_3)}{SSE(X_2, X_3)} \tag{7.37}$$

$$R^2_{Y2|13} = \frac{SSR(X_2|X_1, X_3)}{SSE(X_1, X_3)} \tag{7.38}$$

$$R^2_{Y3|12} = \frac{SSR(X_3|X_1, X_2)}{SSE(X_1, X_2)} \tag{7.39}$$

$$R^2_{Y4|123} = \frac{SSR(X_4|X_1, X_2, X_3)}{SSE(X_1, X_2, X_3)} \tag{7.40}$$

Note that in the subscripts to R^2, the entries to the left of the vertical bar show in turn the variable taken as the response and the X variable being added. The entries to the right of the vertical bar show the X variables already in the model.

Example

For the body fat example, we can obtain a variety of coefficients of partial determination. Here are three (Tables 7.2 and 7.4):

$$R^2_{Y2|1} = \frac{SSR(X_2|X_1)}{SSE(X_1)} = \frac{33.17}{143.12} = .232$$

$$R^2_{Y3|12} = \frac{SSR(X_3|X_1, X_2)}{SSE(X_1, X_2)} = \frac{11.54}{109.95} = .105$$

$$R^2_{Y1|2} = \frac{SSR(X_1|X_2)}{SSE(X_2)} = \frac{3.47}{113.42} = .031$$

We see that when X_2 is added to the regression model containing X_1 here, the error sum of squares $SSE(X_1)$ is reduced by 23.2 percent. The error sum of squares for the model containing both X_1 and X_2 is only reduced by another 10.5 percent when X_3 is added to the model. Finally, if the regression model already contains X_2, adding X_1 reduces $SSE(X_2)$ by only 3.1 percent.

Comments

1. The coefficients of partial determination can take on values between 0 and 1, as the definitions readily indicate.

2. A coefficient of partial determination can be interpreted as a coefficient of simple determination. Consider a multiple regression model with two X variables. Suppose we regress Y on X_2 and obtain the residuals:

$$e_i(Y|X_2) = Y_i - \hat{Y}_i(X_2)$$

where $\hat{Y}_i(X_2)$ denotes the fitted values of Y when X_2 is in the model. Suppose we further regress X_1 on X_2 and obtain the residuals:

$$e_i(X_1|X_2) = X_{i1} - \hat{X}_{i1}(X_2)$$

where $\hat{X}_{i1}(X_2)$ denotes the fitted values of X_1 in the regression of X_1 on X_2. The coefficient of simple determination R^2 between these two sets of residuals equals the coefficient of partial determination $R^2_{Y1|2}$. Thus, this coefficient measures the relation between Y and X_1 when both of these variables have been adjusted for their linear relationships to X_2.

3. The plot of the residuals $e_i(Y|X_2)$ against $e_i(X_1|X_2)$ provides a graphical representation of the strength of the relationship between Y and X_1, adjusted for X_2. Such plots of residuals, called *added variable plots* or *partial regression plots*, are discussed in Section 10.1. ∎

Coefficients of Partial Correlation

The square root of a coefficient of partial determination is called a *coefficient of partial correlation*. It is given the same sign as that of the corresponding regression coefficient in the fitted regression function. Coefficients of partial correlation are frequently used in practice, although they do not have as clear a meaning as coefficients of partial determination. One use of partial correlation coefficients is in computer routines for finding the best predictor variable to be selected next for inclusion in the regression model. We discuss this use in Chapter 9.

Example

For the body fat example, we have:

$$r_{Y2|1} = \sqrt{.232} = .482$$
$$r_{Y3|12} = -\sqrt{.105} = -.324$$
$$r_{Y1|2} = \sqrt{.031} = .176$$

Note that the coefficients $r_{Y2|1}$ and $r_{Y1|2}$ are positive because we see from Table 7.2c that $b_2 = .6594$ and $b_1 = .2224$ are positive. Similarly, $r_{Y3|12}$ is negative because we see from Table 7.2d that $b_3 = -2.186$ is negative.

Comment

Coefficients of partial determination can be expressed in terms of simple or other partial correlation coefficients. For example:

$$R^2_{Y2|1} = [r_{Y2|1}]^2 = \frac{(r_{Y2} - r_{12}r_{Y1})^2}{(1 - r_{12}^2)(1 - r_{Y1}^2)} \tag{7.41}$$

$$R^2_{Y2|13} = [r_{Y2|13}]^2 = \frac{(r_{Y2|3} - r_{12|3}r_{Y1|3})^2}{(1 - r_{12|3}^2)(1 - r_{Y1|3}^2)} \tag{7.42}$$

where r_{Y1} denotes the coefficient of simple correlation between Y and X_1, r_{12} denotes the coefficient of simple correlation between X_1 and X_2, and so on. Extensions are straightforward. ∎

7.5 Standardized Multiple Regression Model

A standardized form of the general multiple regression model (6.7) is employed to control roundoff errors in normal equations calculations and to permit comparisons of the estimated regression coefficients in common units.

Roundoff Errors in Normal Equations Calculations

The results from normal equations calculations can be sensitive to rounding of data in intermediate stages of calculations. When the number of X variables is small—say, three or less—roundoff effects can be controlled by carrying a sufficient number of digits in intermediate calculations. Indeed, most computer regression programs use double-precision arithmetic in all computations to control roundoff effects. Still, with a large number of X variables, serious roundoff effects can arise despite the use of many digits in intermediate calculations.

Roundoff errors tend to enter normal equations calculations primarily when the inverse of $\mathbf{X'X}$ is taken. Of course, any errors in $(\mathbf{X'X})^{-1}$ may be magnified in calculating $\mathbf{b}$ and other subsequent statistics. The danger of serious roundoff errors in $(\mathbf{X'X})^{-1}$ is particularly great when (1) $\mathbf{X'X}$ has a determinant that is close to zero and/or (2) the elements of $\mathbf{X'X}$ differ substantially in order of magnitude. The first condition arises when some or all of the X variables are highly intercorrelated. We shall discuss this situation in Section 7.6.

The second condition arises when the X variables have substantially different magnitudes so that the entries in the $\mathbf{X'X}$ matrix cover a wide range, say, from 15 to 49,000,000. A solution for this condition is to transform the variables and thereby reparameterize the regression model into the standardized regression model.

The transformation to obtain the standardized regression model, called the *correlation transformation,* makes all entries in the $\mathbf{X'X}$ matrix for the transformed variables fall between -1 and 1 inclusive, so that the calculation of the inverse matrix becomes much less subject to roundoff errors due to dissimilar orders of magnitudes than with the original variables.

Comment

In order to avoid the computational difficulties inherent in inverting the $\mathbf{X'X}$ matrix, many statistical packages use an entirely different computational approach that involves decomposing the $\mathbf{X}$ matrix into a product of several matrices with special properties. The $\mathbf{X}$ matrix is often first modified by centering each of the variables (i.e., using the deviations around the mean) to further improve computational accuracy. Information on decomposition strategies may be found in texts on statistical computing, such as Reference 7.1. ∎

Lack of Comparability in Regression Coefficients

A second difficulty with the nonstandardized multiple regression model (6.7) is that ordinarily regression coefficients cannot be compared because of differences in the units involved. We cite two examples.

1. When considering the fitted response function:

$$\hat{Y} = 200 + 20,000X_1 + .2X_2$$

one may be tempted to conclude that X_1 is the only important predictor variable, and that X_2 has little effect on the response variable Y. A little reflection should make one wary of this conclusion. The reason is that we do not know the units involved. Suppose the units are:

Y in dollars
X_1 in thousand dollars
X_2 in cents

In that event, the effect on the mean response of a \$1,000 increase in X_1 (i.e., a 1-unit increase) when X_2 is constant would be an increase of \$20,000. This is exactly the same as the effect of a \$1,000 increase in X_2 (i.e., a 100,000-unit increase) when X_1 is constant, despite the difference in the regression coefficients.

2. In the Dwaine Studios example of Figure 6.5, we cannot make any comparison between b_1 and b_2 because X_1 is in units of thousand persons aged 16 or younger, whereas X_2 is in units of thousand dollars of per capita disposable income.

Correlation Transformation

Use of the correlation transformation helps with controlling roundoff errors and, by expressing the regression coefficients in the same units, may be of help when these coefficients are compared. We shall first describe the correlation transformation and then the resulting standardized regression model.

The correlation transformation is a simple modification of the usual standardization of a variable. Standardizing a variable, as in (A.37), involves centering and scaling the variable. *Centering* involves taking the difference between each observation and the mean of all observations for the variable; *scaling* involves expressing the centered observations in units of the standard deviation of the observations for the variable. Thus, the usual standardizations of the response variable Y and the predictor variables $X_1, \ldots, X_{p-1}$ are as follows:

$$\frac{Y_i - \bar{Y}}{s_Y} \tag{7.43a}$$

$$\frac{X_{ik} - \bar{X}_k}{s_k} \qquad (k = 1, \ldots, p-1) \tag{7.43b}$$

where $\bar{Y}$ and $\bar{X}_k$ are the respective means of the Y and the X_k observations, and s_Y and s_k are the respective standard deviations defined as follows:

$$s_Y = \sqrt{\frac{\sum_i (Y_i - \bar{Y})^2}{n-1}} \tag{7.43c}$$

$$s_k = \sqrt{\frac{\sum_i (X_{ik} - \bar{X}_k)^2}{n-1}} \qquad (k = 1, \ldots, p-1) \tag{7.43d}$$

The correlation transformation is a simple function of the standardized variables in (7.43a, b):

$$Y_i^* = \frac{1}{\sqrt{n-1}} \left(\frac{Y_i - \bar{Y}}{s_Y} \right) \tag{7.44a}$$

$$X_{ik}^* = \frac{1}{\sqrt{n-1}} \left(\frac{X_{ik} - \bar{X}_k}{s_k} \right) \qquad (k = 1, \ldots, p-1) \tag{7.44b}$$

Standardized Regression Model

The regression model with the transformed variables Y^* and X_k^* as defined by the correlation transformation in (7.44) is called a *standardized regression model* and is as follows:

$$Y_i^* = \beta_1^* X_{i1}^* + \cdots + \beta_{p-1}^* X_{i,p-1}^* + \varepsilon_i^* \tag{7.45}$$

The reason why there is no intercept parameter in the standardized regression model (7.45) is that the least squares or maximum likelihood calculations always would lead to an estimated intercept term of zero if an intercept parameter were present in the model.

It is easy to show that the parameters $\beta_1^*, \ldots, \beta_{p-1}^*$ in the standardized regression model and the original parameters $\beta_0, \beta_1, \ldots, \beta_{p-1}$ in the ordinary multiple regression model (6.7) are related as follows:

$$\beta_k = \left(\frac{s_Y}{s_k} \right) \beta_k^* \qquad (k = 1, \ldots, p-1) \tag{7.46a}$$

$$\beta_0 = \bar{Y} - \beta_1 \bar{X}_1 - \cdots - \beta_{p-1} \bar{X}_{p-1} \tag{7.46b}$$

We see that the standardized regression coefficients β_k^* and the original regression coefficients β_k $(k = 1, \ldots, p-1)$ are related by simple scaling factors involving ratios of standard deviations.

X'X Matrix for Transformed Variables

In order to be able to study the special nature of the $\mathbf{X'X}$ matrix and the least squares normal equations when the variables have been transformed by the correlation transformation, we need to decompose the correlation matrix in (6.67) containing all pairwise correlation coefficients among the response and predictor variables $Y, X_1, X_2, \ldots, X_{p-1}$ into two matrices.

1. The first matrix, denoted by $\mathbf{r}_{XX}$, is called the *correlation matrix of the X variables*. It has as its elements the coefficients of simple correlation between all pairs of the X variables. This matrix is defined as follows:

$$\underset{(p-1)\times(p-1)}{\mathbf{r}_{XX}} = \begin{bmatrix} 1 & r_{12} & \cdots & r_{1,p-1} \\ r_{21} & 1 & \cdots & r_{2,p-1} \\ \vdots & \vdots & & \vdots \\ r_{p-1,1} & r_{p-1,2} & \cdots & 1 \end{bmatrix} \tag{7.47}$$

Here, r_{12} again denotes the coefficient of simple correlation between X_1 and X_2, and so on. Note that the main diagonal consists of 1s because the coefficient of simple correlation between a variable and itself is 1. The correlation matrix $\mathbf{r}_{XX}$ is symmetric; remember that $r_{kk'} = r_{k'k}$. Because of the symmetry of this matrix, computer printouts frequently omit the lower or upper triangular block of elements.

2. The second matrix, denoted by $\mathbf{r}_{YX}$, is a vector containing the coefficients of simple correlation between the response variable Y and each of the X variables, denoted again by r_{Y1}, r_{Y2}, etc.:

$$\underset{(p-1)\times 1}{\mathbf{r}_{YX}} = \begin{bmatrix} r_{Y1} \\ r_{Y2} \\ \vdots \\ r_{Y,p-1} \end{bmatrix} \tag{7.48}$$

Now we are ready to consider the $\mathbf{X'X}$ matrix for the transformed variables in the standardized regression model (7.45). The $\mathbf{X}$ matrix here is:

$$\underset{n\times(p-1)}{\mathbf{X}} = \begin{bmatrix} X_{11}^* & \cdots & X_{1,p-1}^* \\ X_{21}^* & \cdots & X_{2,p-1}^* \\ \vdots & & \vdots \\ X_{n1}^* & \cdots & X_{n,p-1}^* \end{bmatrix} \tag{7.49}$$

Remember that the standardized regression model (7.45) does not contain an intercept term; hence, there is no column of 1s in the $\mathbf{X}$ matrix. It can be shown that the $\mathbf{X'X}$ matrix for the transformed variables is simply the correlation matrix of the X variables defined in (7.47):

$$\underset{(p-1)\times(p-1)}{\mathbf{X'X}} = \mathbf{r}_{XX} \tag{7.50}$$

Since the $\mathbf{X'X}$ matrix for the transformed variables consists of coefficients of correlation between the X variables, all of its elements are between -1 and 1 and thus are of the same order of magnitude. As we pointed out earlier, this can be of great help in controlling roundoff errors when inverting the $\mathbf{X'X}$ matrix.

Comment

We illustrate that the $\mathbf{X'X}$ matrix for the transformed variables is the correlation matrix of the X variables by considering two entries in the matrix:

1. In the upper left corner of $\mathbf{X'X}$ we have:

$$\sum (X_{i1}^*)^2 = \sum \left(\frac{X_{i1} - \bar{X}_1}{\sqrt{n-1}\, s_1} \right)^2 = \frac{\sum (X_{i1} - \bar{X}_1)^2}{n-1} \div s_1^2 = 1$$

2. In the first row, second column of $\mathbf{X'X}$, we have:

$$\sum X_{i1}^* X_{i2}^* = \sum \left(\frac{X_{i1} - \bar{X}_1}{\sqrt{n-1}\, s_1} \right) \left(\frac{X_{i2} - \bar{X}_2}{\sqrt{n-1}\, s_2} \right)$$

$$= \frac{1}{n-1} \frac{\sum (X_{i1} - \bar{X}_1)(X_{i2} - \bar{X}_2)}{s_1 s_2}$$

$$= \frac{\sum (X_{i1} - \bar{X}_1)(X_{i2} - \bar{X}_2)}{\left[\sum (X_{i1} - \bar{X}_1)^2 \sum (X_{i2} - \bar{X}_2)^2 \right]^{1/2}}$$

But this equals r_{12}, the coefficient of correlation between X_1 and X_2, by (2.84). ∎

Estimated Standardized Regression Coefficients

The least squares normal equations (6.24) for the ordinary multiple regression model:

$$\mathbf{X'Xb} = \mathbf{X'Y}$$

and the least squares estimators (6.25):

$$\mathbf{b} = (\mathbf{X'X})^{-1} \mathbf{X'Y}$$

can be expressed simply for the transformed variables. It can be shown that for the transformed variables, $\mathbf{X'Y}$ becomes:

$$\underset{(p-1)\times 1}{\mathbf{X'Y}} = \mathbf{r}_{YX} \tag{7.51}$$

where $\mathbf{r}_{YX}$ is defined in (7.48) as the vector of the coefficients of simple correlation between Y and each X variable. It now follows from (7.50) and (7.51) that the least squares normal equations and estimators of the regression coefficients of the standardized regression model (7.45) are as follows:

$$\mathbf{r}_{XX} \mathbf{b} = \mathbf{r}_{YX} \tag{7.52a}$$

$$\mathbf{b} = \mathbf{r}_{XX}^{-1} \mathbf{r}_{YX} \tag{7.52b}$$

where:

$$\underset{(p-1)\times 1}{\mathbf{b}} = \begin{bmatrix} b_1^* \\ b_2^* \\ \vdots \\ b_{p-1}^* \end{bmatrix} \tag{7.52c}$$

The regression coefficients $b_1^*, \ldots, b_{p-1}^*$ are often called *standardized regression coefficients*.

The return to the estimated regression coefficients for regression model (6.7) in the original variables is accomplished by employing the relations:

$$b_k = \left(\frac{s_Y}{s_k}\right) b_k^* \qquad (k = 1, \ldots, p - 1) \tag{7.53a}$$

$$b_0 = \bar{Y} - b_1 \bar{X}_1 - \cdots - b_{p-1} \bar{X}_{p-1} \tag{7.53b}$$

Comment

When there are two X variables in the regression model, i.e., when $p - 1 = 2$, we can readily see the algebraic form of the standardized regression coefficients. We have:

$$\mathbf{r}_{XX} = \begin{bmatrix} 1 & r_{12} \\ r_{12} & 1 \end{bmatrix} \tag{7.54a}$$

$$\mathbf{r}_{YX} = \begin{bmatrix} r_{Y1} \\ r_{Y2} \end{bmatrix} \tag{7.54b}$$

$$\mathbf{r}_{XX}^{-1} = \frac{1}{1 - r_{12}^2} \begin{bmatrix} 1 & -r_{12} \\ -r_{12} & 1 \end{bmatrix} \tag{7.54c}$$

Hence, by (7.52b) we obtain:

$$\mathbf{b} = \frac{1}{1 - r_{12}^2} \begin{bmatrix} 1 & -r_{12} \\ -r_{12} & 1 \end{bmatrix} \begin{bmatrix} r_{Y1} \\ r_{Y2} \end{bmatrix} = \frac{1}{1 - r_{12}^2} \begin{bmatrix} r_{Y1} - r_{12}r_{Y2} \\ r_{Y2} - r_{12}r_{Y1} \end{bmatrix} \tag{7.55}$$

Thus:

$$b_1^* = \frac{r_{Y1} - r_{12}r_{Y2}}{1 - r_{12}^2} \tag{7.55a}$$

$$b_2^* = \frac{r_{Y2} - r_{12}r_{Y1}}{1 - r_{12}^2} \tag{7.55b}$$

∎

Example

Table 7.5a repeats a portion of the original data for the Dwaine Studios example in Figure 6.5b, and Table 7.5b contains the data transformed according to the correlation transformation (7.44). We illustrate the calculation of the transformed data for the first case, using the means and standard deviations in Table 7.5a (differences in the last digit of the transformed data are due to rounding effects):

$$Y_1^* = \frac{1}{\sqrt{n-1}} \left(\frac{Y_1 - \bar{Y}}{s_Y}\right) \qquad\qquad X_{11}^* = \frac{1}{\sqrt{n-1}} \left(\frac{X_{11} - \bar{X}_1}{s_1}\right)$$

$$= \frac{1}{\sqrt{21-1}} \left(\frac{174.4 - 181.90}{36.191}\right) \qquad\qquad = \frac{1}{\sqrt{21-1}} \left(\frac{68.5 - 62.019}{18.620}\right)$$

$$= -.04634 \qquad\qquad\qquad\qquad = .07783$$

$$X_{12}^* = \frac{1}{\sqrt{n-1}} \left(\frac{X_{12} - \bar{X}_2}{s_2}\right) = \frac{1}{\sqrt{21-1}} \left(\frac{16.7 - 17.143}{.97035}\right) = -.10208$$

TABLE 7.5
Correlation Transformation and Fitted Standardized Regression Model— Dwaine Studios Example.

(a) Original Data			
Case i	Sales Y_i	Target Population X_{i1}	Per Capita Disposable Income X_{i2}
1	174.4	68.5	16.7
2	164.4	45.2	16.8
...	...	...	...
20	224.1	82.7	19.1
21	166.5	52.3	16.0
	$\bar{Y} = 181.90$	$\bar{X}_1 = 62.019$	$\bar{X}_2 = 17.143$
	$s_Y = 36.191$	$s_1 = 18.620$	$s_2 = .97035$

(b) Transformed Data			
i	Y_i^*	X_{i1}^*	X_{i2}^*
1	−.04637	.07783	−.10205
2	−.10815	−.20198	−.07901
...	...	...	...
20	.26070	.24835	.45100
21	−.09518	−.11671	−.26336

(c) Fitted Standardized Model

$$\hat{Y}^* = .7484\,X_1^* + .2511\,X_2^*$$

When fitting the standardized regression model (7.45) to the transformed data, we obtain the fitted model in Table 7.5c:

$$\hat{Y}^* = .7484X_1^* + .2511X_2^*$$

The standardized regression coefficients $b_1^* = .7484$ and $b_2^* = .2511$ are shown in the SYSTAT regression output in Figure 6.5a on page 237, labeled STD COEF. We see from the standardized regression coefficients that an increase of one standard deviation of X_1 (target population) when X_2 (per capita disposable income) is fixed leads to a much larger increase in expected sales (in units of standard deviations of Y) than does an increase of one standard deviation of X_2 when X_1 is fixed.

To shift from the standardized regression coefficients b_1^* and b_2^* back to the regression coefficients for the model with the original variables, we employ (7.53). Using the data in Table 7.5, we obtain:

$$b_1 = \left(\frac{s_Y}{s_1}\right)b_1^* = \frac{36.191}{18.620}(.7484) = 1.4546$$

$$b_2 = \left(\frac{s_Y}{s_2}\right)b_2^* = \frac{36.191}{.97035}(.2511) = 9.3652$$

$$b_0 = \bar{Y} - b_1\bar{X}_1 - b_2\bar{X}_2 = 181.90 - 1.4546(62.019) - 9.3652(17.143) = -68.860$$

The estimated regression function for the multiple regression model in the original variables therefore is:

$$\hat{Y} = -68.860 + 1.455X_1 + 9.365X_2$$

This is the same fitted regression function we obtained in Chapter 6, except for slight rounding effect differences. Here, b_1 and b_2 cannot be compared directly because X_1 is in units of thousands of persons and X_2 is in units of thousands of dollars.

Sometimes the standardized regression coefficients $b_1^* = .7484$ and $b_2^* = .2511$ are interpreted as showing that target population (X_1) has a much greater impact on sales than per capita disposable income (X_2) because b_1^* is much larger than b_2^*. However, as we will see in the next section, one must be cautious about interpreting any regression coefficient, whether standardized or not. The reason is that when the predictor variables are correlated among themselves, as here, the regression coefficients are affected by the other predictor variables in the model. For the Dwaine Studios data, the correlation between X_1 and X_2 is $r_{12} = .781$, as shown in the correlation matrix in Figure 6.4b on page 232.

The magnitudes of the standardized regression coefficients are affected not only by the presence of correlations among the predictor variables but also by the spacings of the observations on each of these variables. Sometimes these spacings may be quite arbitrary. Hence, it is ordinarily not wise to interpret the magnitudes of standardized regression coefficients as reflecting the comparative importance of the predictor variables.

Comments

1. Some computer packages present both the regression coefficients b_k for the model in the original variables as well as the standardized coefficients b_k^*, as in the SYSTAT output in Figure 6.5a. The standardized coefficients are sometimes labeled *beta coefficients* in printouts.

2. Some computer printouts show the magnitude of the determinant of the correlation matrix of the X variables. A near-zero value for this determinant implies both a high degree of linear association among the X variables and a high potential for roundoff errors. For two X variables, this determinant is seen from (7.54) to be $1 - r_{12}^2$, which approaches 0 as r_{12}^2 approaches 1.

3. It is possible to use the correlation transformation with a computer package that does not permit regression through the origin, because the intercept coefficient b_0^* will always be zero for data so transformed. The other regression coefficients will also be correct.

4. Use of the standardized variables (7.43) without the correlation transformation modification in (7.44) will lead to the same standardized regression coefficients as those in (7.52b) for the correlation-transformed variables. However, the elements of the $\mathbf{X'X}$ matrix will not then be bounded between -1 and 1.   ∎

7.6   Multicollinearity and Its Effects

In multiple regression analysis, the nature and significance of the relations between the predictor or explanatory variables and the response variable are often of particular interest. Some questions frequently asked are:

1. What is the relative importance of the effects of the different predictor variables?
2. What is the magnitude of the effect of a given predictor variable on the response variable?
3. Can any predictor variable be dropped from the model because it has little or no effect on the response variable?

4. Should any predictor variables not yet included in the model be considered for possible inclusion?

If the predictor variables included in the model are (1) uncorrelated among themselves and (2) uncorrelated with any other predictor variables that are related to the response variable but are omitted from the model, relatively simple answers can be given to these questions. Unfortunately, in many nonexperimental situations in business, economics, and the social and biological sciences, the predictor or explanatory variables tend to be correlated among themselves and with other variables that are related to the response variable but are not included in the model. For example, in a regression of family food expenditures on the explanatory variables family income, family savings, and age of head of household, the explanatory variables will be correlated among themselves. Further, they will also be correlated with other socioeconomic variables not included in the model that do affect family food expenditures, such as family size.

When the predictor variables are correlated among themselves, *intercorrelation* or *multicollinearity* among them is said to exist. (Sometimes the latter term is reserved for those instances when the correlation among the predictor variables is very high.) We shall explore a variety of interrelated problems created by multicollinearity among the predictor variables. First, however, we examine the situation when the predictor variables are not correlated.

Uncorrelated Predictor Variables

Table 7.6 contains data for a small-scale experiment on the effect of work crew size (X_1) and level of bonus pay (X_2) on crew productivity (Y). The predictor variables X_1 and X_2 are uncorrelated here, i.e., $r_{12}^2 = 0$, where r_{12}^2 denotes the coefficient of simple determination between X_1 and X_2. Table 7.7a contains the fitted regression function and the analysis of variance table when both X_1 and X_2 are included in the model. Table 7.7b contains the same information when only X_1 is included in the model, and Table 7.7c contains this information when only X_2 is in the model.

An important feature to note in Table 7.7 is that the regression coefficient for X_1, $b_1 = 5.375$, is the same whether only X_1 is included in the model or both predictor variables are included. The same holds for $b_2 = 9.250$. This is the result of the two predictor variables being uncorrelated.

		Bonus Pay	
Case	**Crew Size**	**(dollars)**	**Crew Productivity**
i	X_{i1}	X_{i2}	Y_i
1	4	2	42
2	4	2	39
3	4	3	48
4	4	3	51
5	6	2	49
6	6	2	53
7	6	3	61
8	6	3	60

TABLE 7.6 Uncorrelated Predictor Variables— Work Crew Productivity Example.

TABLE 7.7
Regression
Results when
Predictor
Variables Are
Uncorrelated—
Work Crew
Productivity
Example.

(a) Regression of Y on X_1 and X_2
$$\hat{Y} = .375 + 5.375X_1 + 9.250X_2$$

Source of Variation	SS	df	MS
Regression	402.250	2	201.125
Error	17.625	5	3.525
Total	419.875	7	

(b) Regression of Y on X_1
$$\hat{Y} = 23.500 + 5.375X_1$$

Source of Variation	SS	df	MS
Regression	231.125	1	231.125
Error	188.750	6	31.458
Total	419.875	7	

(c) Regression of Y on X_2
$$\hat{Y} = 27.250 + 9.250X_2$$

Source of Variation	SS	df	MS
Regression	171.125	1	171.125
Error	248.750	6	41.458
Total	419.875	7	

Thus, when the predictor variables are uncorrelated, the effects ascribed to them by a first-order regression model are the same no matter which other of these predictor variables are included in the model. This is a strong argument for controlled experiments whenever possible, since experimental control permits choosing the levels of the predictor variables so as to make these variables uncorrelated.

Another important feature of Table 7.7 is related to the error sums of squares. Note from Table 7.7 that the extra sum of squares $SSR(X_1|X_2)$ equals the regression sum of squares $SSR(X_1)$ when only X_1 is in the regression model:

$$SSR(X_1|X_2) = SSE(X_2) - SSE(X_1, X_2)$$
$$= 248.750 - 17.625 = 231.125$$
$$SSR(X_1) = 231.125$$

Similarly, the extra sum of squares $SSR(X_2|X_1)$ equals $SSR(X_2)$, the regression sum of squares when only X_2 is in the regression model:

$$SSR(X_2|X_1) = SSE(X_1) - SSE(X_1, X_2)$$
$$= 188.750 - 17.625 = 171.125$$
$$SSR(X_2) = 171.125$$

In general, when two or more predictor variables are uncorrelated, the marginal contribution of one predictor variable in reducing the error sum of squares when the other predictor variables are in the model is exactly the same as when this predictor variable is in the model alone.

Comment

To show that the regression coefficient of X_1 is unchanged when X_2 is added to the regression model in the case where X_1 and X_2 are uncorrelated, consider the following algebraic expression for b_1 in the first-order multiple regression model with two predictor variables:

$$b_1 = \frac{\dfrac{\sum(X_{i1} - \bar{X}_1)(Y_i - \bar{Y})}{\sum(X_{i1} - \bar{X}_1)^2} - \left[\dfrac{\sum(Y_i - \bar{Y})^2}{\sum(X_{i1} - \bar{X}_1)^2}\right]^{1/2} r_{Y2} r_{12}}{1 - r_{12}^2} \tag{7.56}$$

where, as before, r_{Y2} denotes the coefficient of simple correlation between Y and X_2, and r_{12} denotes the coefficient of simple correlation between X_1 and X_2.

If X_1 and X_2 are uncorrelated, $r_{12} = 0$, and (7.56) reduces to:

$$b_1 = \frac{\sum(X_{i1} - \bar{X}_1)(Y_i - \bar{Y})}{\sum(X_{i1} - \bar{X}_1)^2} \qquad \text{when } r_{12} = 0 \tag{7.56a}$$

But (7.56a) is the estimator of the slope for the simple linear regression of Y on X_1, per (1.10a).

Hence, when X_1 and X_2 are uncorrelated, adding X_2 to the regression model does not change the regression coefficient for X_1; correspondingly, adding X_1 to the regression model does not change the regression coefficient for X_2. ∎

Nature of Problem when Predictor Variables Are Perfectly Correlated

To see the essential nature of the problem of multicollinearity, we shall employ a simple example where the two predictor variables are perfectly correlated. The data in Table 7.8 refer to four sample observations on a response variable and two predictor variables. Mr. A was asked to fit the first-order multiple regression function:

$$E\{Y\} = \beta_0 + \beta_1 X_1 + \beta_2 X_2 \tag{7.57}$$

TABLE 7.8
Example of Perfectly Correlated Predictor Variables.

Case i	X_{i1}	X_{i2}	Y_i	Fitted Values for Regression Function (7.58)	(7.59)
1	2	6	23	23	23
2	8	9	83	83	83
3	6	8	63	63	63
4	10	10	103	103	103

Response Functions:
$\hat{Y} = -87 + X_1 + 18X_2$ (7.58)
$\hat{Y} = -7 + 9X_1 + 2X_2$ (7.59)

FIGURE 7.2
Two Response Planes That Intersect when $X_2 = 5 + .5X_1$.

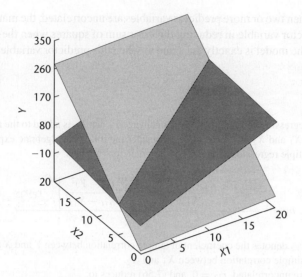

He returned in a short time with the fitted response function:

$$\hat{Y} = -87 + X_1 + 18X_2 \tag{7.58}$$

He was proud because the response function fits the data perfectly. The fitted values are shown in Table 7.8.

It so happened that Ms. B also was asked to fit the response function (7.57) to the same data, and she proudly obtained:

$$\hat{Y} = -7 + 9X_1 + 2X_2 \tag{7.59}$$

Her response function also fits the data perfectly, as shown in Table 7.8.

Indeed, it can be shown that infinitely many response functions will fit the data in Table 7.8 perfectly. The reason is that the predictor variables X_1 and X_2 are perfectly related, according to the relation:

$$X_2 = 5 + .5X_1 \tag{7.60}$$

Note that the fitted response functions (7.58) and (7.59) are entirely different response surfaces, as may be seen in Figure 7.2. The two response surfaces have the same fitted values only when they intersect. This occurs when X_1 and X_2 follow relation (7.60), i.e., when $X_2 = 5 + .5X_1$.

Thus, when X_1 and X_2 are perfectly related and, as in our example, the data do not contain any random error component, many different response functions will lead to the same perfectly fitted values for the observations and to the same fitted values for any other (X_1, X_2) combinations following the relation between X_1 and X_2. Yet these response functions are not the same and will lead to different fitted values for (X_1, X_2) combinations that do not follow the relation between X_1 and X_2.

Two key implications of this example are:

1. The perfect relation between X_1 and X_2 did not inhibit our ability to obtain a good fit to the data.

2. Since many different response functions provide the same good fit, we cannot interpret any one set of regression coefficients as reflecting the effects of the different predictor variables. Thus, in response function (7.58), $b_1 = 1$ and $b_2 = 18$ do not imply that X_2 is the key predictor variable and X_1 plays little role, because response function (7.59) provides an equally good fit and its regression coefficients have opposite comparative magnitudes.

Effects of Multicollinearity

In practice, we seldom find predictor variables that are perfectly related or data that do not contain some random error component. Nevertheless, the implications just noted for our idealized example still have relevance.

1. The fact that some or all predictor variables are correlated among themselves does not, in general, inhibit our ability to obtain a good fit nor does it tend to affect inferences about mean responses or predictions of new observations, provided these inferences are made within the region of observations. (Figure 6.3 on p. 231 illustrates the concept of the region of observations for the case of two predictor variables.)

2. The counterpart in real life to the many different regression functions providing equally good fits to the data in our idealized example is that the estimated regression coefficients tend to have large sampling variability when the predictor variables are highly correlated. Thus, the estimated regression coefficients tend to vary widely from one sample to the next when the predictor variables are highly correlated. As a result, only imprecise information may be available about the individual true regression coefficients. Indeed, many of the estimated regression coefficients individually may be statistically not significant even though a definite statistical relation exists between the response variable and the set of predictor variables.

3. The common interpretation of a regression coefficient as measuring the change in the expected value of the response variable when the given predictor variable is increased by one unit while all other predictor variables are held constant is not fully applicable when multicollinearity exists. It may be conceptually feasible to think of varying one predictor variable and holding the others constant, but it may not be possible in practice to do so for predictor variables that are highly correlated. For example, in a regression model for predicting crop yield from amount of rainfall and hours of sunshine, the relation between the two predictor variables makes it unrealistic to consider varying one while holding the other constant. Therefore, the simple interpretation of the regression coefficients as measuring marginal effects is often unwarranted with highly correlated predictor variables.

We illustrate these effects of multicollinearity by returning to the body fat example. A portion of the basic data was given in Table 7.1, and regression results for different fitted models were presented in Table 7.2. Figure 7.3 contains the scatter plot matrix and the correlation matrix of the predictor variables. It is evident from the scatter plot matrix that predictor variables X_1 and X_2 are highly correlated; the correlation matrix of the X variables shows that the coefficient of simple correlation is $r_{12} = .924$. On the other hand, X_3 is not so highly related to X_1 and X_2 individually; the correlation matrix shows that the correlation coefficients are $r_{13} = .458$ and $r_{23} = .085$. (But X_3 is highly correlated with X_1 and X_2 together; the coefficient of multiple determination when X_3 is regressed on X_1 and X_2 is .998.)

FIGURE 7.3
Scatter Plot Matrix and Correlation Matrix of the Predictor Variables— Body Fat Example.

(a) Scatter Plot Matrix of *X* Variables

(b) Correlation Matrix of *X* Variables

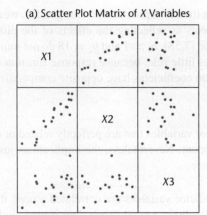

$$r_{XX} = \begin{bmatrix} 1.0 & .924 & .458 \\ .924 & 1.0 & .085 \\ .458 & .085 & 1.0 \end{bmatrix}$$

Effects on Regression Coefficients. Note from Table 7.2 that the regression coefficient for X_1, triceps skinfold thickness, varies markedly depending on which other variables are included in the model:

Variables in Model	b_1	b_2
X_1	.8572	—
X_2	—	.8565
X_1, X_2	.2224	.6594
X_1, X_2, X_3	4.334	−2.857

The story is the same for the regression coefficient for X_2. Indeed, the regression coefficient b_2 even changes sign when X_3 is added to the model that includes X_1 and X_2.

The important conclusion we must draw is: When predictor variables are correlated, the regression coefficient of any one variable depends on which other predictor variables are included in the model and which ones are left out. Thus, a regression coefficient does not reflect any inherent effect of the particular predictor variable on the response variable but only a marginal or partial effect, given whatever other correlated predictor variables are included in the model.

Comment

Another illustration of how intercorrelated predictor variables that are omitted from the regression model can influence the regression coefficients in the regression model is provided by an analyst who was perplexed about the sign of a regression coefficient in the fitted regression model. The analyst had found in a regression of territory company sales on territory population size, per capita income, and some other predictor variables that the regression coefficient for population size was negative, and this conclusion was supported by a confidence interval for the regression coefficient. A consultant noted that the analyst did not include the major competitor's market penetration as a predictor variable in the model. The competitor was most active and effective in territories with large populations, thereby keeping company sales down in these territories. The result of the omission of this predictor variable from the model was a negative coefficient for the population size variable. ∎

Effects on Extra Sums of Squares. When predictor variables are correlated, the marginal contribution of any one predictor variable in reducing the error sum of squares varies, depending on which other variables are already in the regression model, just as for regression coefficients. For example, Table 7.2 provides the following extra sums of squares for X_1:

$$SSR(X_1) = 352.27$$

$$SSR(X_1|X_2) = 3.47$$

The reason why $SSR(X_1|X_2)$ is so small compared with $SSR(X_1)$ is that X_1 and X_2 are highly correlated with each other and with the response variable. Thus, when X_2 is already in the regression model, the marginal contribution of X_1 in reducing the error sum of squares is comparatively small because X_2 contains much of the same information as X_1.

The same story is found in Table 7.2 for X_2. Here $SSR(X_2|X_1) = 33.17$, which is much smaller than $SSR(X_2) = 381.97$. The important conclusion is this: When predictor variables are correlated, there is no unique sum of squares that can be ascribed to any one predictor variable as reflecting its effect in reducing the total variation in Y. The reduction in the total variation ascribed to a predictor variable must be viewed in the context of the other correlated predictor variables already included in the model.

Comments

1. Multicollinearity also affects the coefficients of partial determination through its effects on the extra sums of squares. Note from Table 7.2 for the body fat example, for instance, that X_1 is highly correlated with Y:

$$R_{Y1}^2 = \frac{SSR(X_1)}{SSTO} = \frac{352.27}{495.39} = .71$$

However, the coefficient of partial determination between Y and X_1, when X_2 is already in the regression model, is much smaller:

$$R_{Y1|2}^2 = \frac{SSR(X_1|X_2)}{SSE(X_2)} = \frac{3.47}{113.42} = .03$$

The reason for the small coefficient of partial determination here is, as we have seen, that X_1 and X_2 are highly correlated with each other and with the response variable. Hence, X_1 provides only relatively limited additional information beyond that furnished by X_2.

2. The extra sum of squares for a predictor variable after other correlated predictor variables are in the model need not necessarily be smaller than before these other variables are in the model, as we found in the body fat example. In special cases, it can be larger. Consider the following special data set and its correlation matrix:

Y	X_1	X_2		Y	X_1	X_2
20	5	25	Y	1.0	.026	.976
20	10	30	X_1		1.0	.243
0	5	5	X_2			1.0
1	10	10				

Here, Y and X_2 are highly positively correlated, but Y and X_1 are practically uncorrelated. In addition, X_1 and X_2 are moderately positively correlated. The extra sum of squares for X_1 when it is the only variable in the model for this data set is $SSR(X_1) = .25$, but when X_2 already is in the model the extra sum of squares is $SSR(X_1|X_2) = 18.01$. Similarly, we have for these data:

$$SSR(X_2) = 362.49 \qquad SSR(X_2|X_1) = 380.25$$

The increase in the extra sums of squares with the addition of the other predictor variable in the model is related to the special situation here that X_1 is practically uncorrelated with Y but moderately correlated with X_2, which in turn is highly correlated with Y. The general point even here still holds—the extra sum of squares is affected by the other correlated predictor variables already in the model.

When $SSR(X_1|X_2) > SSR(X_1)$, as in the example just cited, the variable X_2 is sometimes called a *suppressor variable*. Since $SSR(X_2|X_1) > SSR(X_2)$ in the example, the variable X_1 would also be called a suppressor variable. ∎

Effects on $s\{b_k\}$. Note from Table 7.2 for the body fat example how much more imprecise the estimated regression coefficients b_1 and b_2 become as more predictor variables are added to the regression model:

Variables in Model	$s\{b_1\}$	$s\{b_2\}$
X_1	.1288	—
X_2	—	.1100
X_1, X_2	.3034	.2912
X_1, X_2, X_3	3.016	2.582

Again, the high degree of multicollinearity among the predictor variables is responsible for the inflated variability of the estimated regression coefficients.

Effects on Fitted Values and Predictions. Notice in Table 7.2 for the body fat example that the high multicollinearity among the predictor variables does not prevent the mean square error, measuring the variability of the error terms, from being steadily reduced as additional variables are added to the regression model:

Variables in Model	MSE
X_1	7.95
X_1, X_2	6.47
X_1, X_2, X_3	6.15

Furthermore, the precision of fitted values within the range of the observations on the predictor variables is not eroded with the addition of correlated predictor variables into the regression model. Consider the estimation of mean body fat when the only predictor variable in the model is triceps skinfold thickness (X_1) for $X_{h1} = 25.0$. The fitted value and its estimated standard deviation are (calculations not shown):

$$\hat{Y}_h = 19.93 \qquad s\{\hat{Y}_h\} = .632$$

When the highly correlated predictor variable thigh circumference (X_2) is also included in the model, the estimated mean body fat and its estimated standard deviation are as follows for $X_{h1} = 25.0$ and $X_{h2} = 50.0$:

$$\hat{Y}_h = 19.36 \qquad s\{\hat{Y}_h\} = .624$$

Thus, the precision of the estimated mean response is equally good as before, despite the addition of the second predictor variable that is highly correlated with the first one. This stability in the precision of the estimated mean response occurred despite the fact that the estimated standard deviation of b_1 became substantially larger when X_2 was added to the model (Table 7.2). The essential reason for the stability is that the covariance between b_1 and b_2 is negative, which plays a strong counteracting influence to the increase in $s^2\{b_1\}$ in determining the value of $s^2\{\hat{Y}_h\}$ as given in (6.79).

When all three predictor variables are included in the model, the estimated mean body fat and its estimated standard deviation are as follows for $X_{h1} = 25.0$, $X_{h2} = 50.0$, and $X_{h3} = 29.0$:

$$\hat{Y}_h = 19.19 \qquad s\{\hat{Y}_h\} = .621$$

Thus, the addition of the third predictor variable, which is highly correlated with the first two predictor variables together, also does not materially affect the precision of the estimated mean response.

Effects on Simultaneous Tests of β_k. A not infrequent abuse in the analysis of multiple regression models is to examine the t^* statistic in (6.51b):

$$t^* = \frac{b_k}{s\{b_k\}}$$

for each regression coefficient in turn to decide whether $\beta_k = 0$ for $k = 1, \ldots, p-1$. Even if a simultaneous inference procedure is used, and often it is not, problems still exist when the predictor variables are highly correlated.

Suppose we wish to test whether $\beta_1 = 0$ and $\beta_2 = 0$ in the body fat example regression model with two predictor variables of Table 7.2c. Controlling the family level of significance at .05, we require with the Bonferroni method that each of the two t tests be conducted with level of significance .025. Hence, we need $t(.9875; 17) = 2.46$. Since both t^* statistics in Table 7.2c have absolute values that do not exceed 2.46, we would conclude from the two separate tests that $\beta_1 = 0$ and that $\beta_2 = 0$. Yet the proper F test for $H_0: \beta_1 = \beta_2 = 0$ would lead to the conclusion H_a, that not both coefficients equal zero. This can be seen from Table 7.2c, where we find $F^* = MSR/MSE = 192.72/6.47 = 29.8$, which far exceeds $F(.95; 2, 17) = 3.59$.

The reason for this apparently paradoxical result is that each t^* test is a marginal test, as we have seen in (7.15) from the perspective of the general linear test approach. Thus, a small $SSR(X_1|X_2)$ here indicates that X_1 does not provide much additional information beyond X_2, which already is in the model; hence, we are led to the conclusion that $\beta_1 = 0$. Similarly, we are led to conclude $\beta_2 = 0$ here because $SSR(X_2|X_1)$ is small, indicating that X_2 does not provide much more additional information when X_1 is already in the model. But the two tests of the marginal effects of X_1 and X_2 together are not equivalent to testing whether there is a regression relation between Y and the two predictor variables. The reason is that the reduced model for each of the separate tests contains the other predictor variable, whereas the reduced model for testing whether both $\beta_1 = 0$ and $\beta_2 = 0$ would contain neither predictor variable. The proper F test shows that there is a definite regression relation here between Y and X_1 and X_2.

The same paradox would be encountered in Table 7.2d for the regression model with three predictor variables if three simultaneous tests on the regression coefficients were conducted at family level of significance .05.

Comments

1. It was noted in Section 7.5 that a near-zero determinant of $\mathbf{X'X}$ is a potential source of serious roundoff errors in normal equations calculations. Severe multicollinearity has the effect of making this determinant come close to zero. Thus, under severe multicollinearity, the regression coefficients may be subject to large roundoff errors as well as large sampling variances. Hence, it is particularly advisable to employ the correlation transformation (7.44) in normal equations calculations when multicollinearity is present.

2. Just as high intercorrelations among the predictor variables tend to make the estimated regression coefficients imprecise (i.e., erratic from sample to sample), so do the coefficients of partial correlation between the response variable and each predictor variable tend to become erratic from sample to sample when the predictor variables are highly correlated.

3. The effect of intercorrelations among the predictor variables on the standard deviations of the estimated regression coefficients can be seen readily when the variables in the model are transformed by means of the correlation transformation (7.44). Consider the first-order model with two predictor variables:

$$Y_i = \beta_0 + \beta_1 X_{i1} + \beta_2 X_{i2} + \varepsilon_i \tag{7.61}$$

This model in the variables transformed by (7.44) becomes:

$$Y_i^* = \beta_1^* X_{i1}^* + \beta_2^* X_{i2}^* + \varepsilon_i^* \tag{7.62}$$

The $(\mathbf{X'X})^{-1}$ matrix for this standardized model is given by (7.50) and (7.54c):

$$(\mathbf{X'X})^{-1} = \mathbf{r}_{XX}^{-1} = \frac{1}{1 - r_{12}^2} \begin{bmatrix} 1 & -r_{12} \\ -r_{12} & 1 \end{bmatrix} \tag{7.63}$$

Hence, the variance-covariance matrix of the estimated regression coefficients is by (6.46) and (7.63):

$$\sigma^2\{\mathbf{b}\} = (\sigma^*)^2 \mathbf{r}_{XX}^{-1} = (\sigma^*)^2 \frac{1}{1 - r_{12}^2} \begin{bmatrix} 1 & -r_{12} \\ -r_{12} & 1 \end{bmatrix} \tag{7.64}$$

where $(\sigma^*)^2$ is the error term variance for the standardized model (7.62). We see that the estimated regression coefficients b_1^* and b_2^* have the same variance here:

$$\sigma^2\{b_1^*\} = \sigma^2\{b_2^*\} = \frac{(\sigma^*)^2}{1 - r_{12}^2} \tag{7.65}$$

and that each of these variances become larger as the correlation between X_1 and X_2 increases. Indeed, as X_1 and X_2 approach perfect correlation (i.e., as r_{12}^2 approaches 1), the variances of b_1^* and b_2^* become larger without limit.

4. We noted in our discussion of simultaneous tests of the regression coefficients that it is possible that a set of predictor variables is related to the response variable, yet all of the individual tests on the regression coefficients will lead to the conclusion that they equal zero because of the multicollinearity among the predictor variables. This apparently paradoxical result is also possible under special circumstances when there is no multicollinearity among the predictor variables. The special circumstances are not likely to be found in practice, however. ∎

Need for More Powerful Diagnostics for Multicollinearity

As we have seen, multicollinearity among the predictor variables can have important consequences for interpreting and using a fitted regression model. The diagnostic tool considered here for identifying multicollinearity—namely, the pairwise coefficients of simple correlation between the predictor variables—is frequently helpful. Often, however, serious multicollinearity exists without being disclosed by the pairwise correlation coefficients. In Chapter 10, we present a more powerful tool for identifying the existence of serious multicollinearity. Some remedial measures for lessening the effects of multicollinearity will be considered in Chapter 11.

Cited Reference

7.1. Kennedy, W. J., Jr., and J. E. Gentle. *Statistical Computing*. New York: Marcel Dekker, 1980.

Problems

7.1. State the number of degrees of freedom that are associated with each of the following extra sums of squares: (1) $SSR(X_1|X_2)$; (2) $SSR(X_2|X_1, X_3)$; (3) $SSR(X_1, X_2|X_3, X_4)$; (4) $SSR(X_1, X_2, X_3|X_4, X_5)$.

7.2. Explain in what sense the regression sum of squares $SSR(X_1)$ is an extra sum of squares.

7.3. Refer to **Brand preference** Problem 6.5.

   a. Obtain the analysis of variance table that decomposes the regression sum of squares into extra sums of squares associated with X_1 and with X_2, given X_1.

   b. Test whether X_2 can be dropped from the regression model given that X_1 is retained. Use the F^* test statistic and level of significance .01. State the alternatives, decision rule, and conclusion. What is the P-value of the test?

*7.4. Refer to **Grocery retailer** Problem 6.9.

   a. Obtain the analysis of variance table that decomposes the regression sum of squares into extra sums of squares associated with X_1; with X_3, given X_1; and with X_2, given X_1 and X_3.

   b. Test whether X_2 can be dropped from the regression model given that X_1 and X_3 are retained. Use the F^* test statistic and $\alpha = .05$. State the alternatives, decision rule, and conclusion. What is the P-value of the test?

   c. Does $SSR(X_1) + SSR(X_2|X_1)$ equal $SSR(X_2) + SSR(X_1|X_2)$ here? Must this always be the case?

*7.5. Refer to **Patient satisfaction** Problem 6.15.

   a. Obtain the analysis of variance table that decomposes the regression sum of squares into extra sums of squares associated with X_2; with X_1, given X_2; and with X_3, given X_2 and X_1.

   b. Test whether X_3 can be dropped from the regression model given that X_1 and X_2 are retained. Use the F^* test statistic and level of significance .025. State the alternatives, decision rule, and conclusion. What is the P-value of the test?

*7.6. Refer to **Patient satisfaction** Problem 6.15. Test whether both X_2 and X_3 can be dropped from the regression model given that X_1 is retained. Use $\alpha = .025$. State the alternatives, decision rule, and conclusion. What is the P-value of the test?

7.7. Refer to **Commercial properties** Problem 6.18.

   a. Obtain the analysis of variance table that decomposes the regression sum of squares into extra sums of squares associated with X_4; with X_1, given X_4; with X_2, given X_1 and X_4; and with X_3, given X_1, X_2 and X_4.

b. Test whether X_3 can be dropped from the regression model given that X_1, X_2 and X_4 are retained. Use the F^* test statistic and level of significance .01. State the alternatives, decision rule, and conclusion. What is the P-value of the test?

7.8. Refer to **Commercial properties** Problems 6.18 and 7.7. Test whether both X_2 and X_3 can be dropped from the regression model given that X_1 and X_4 are retained; use $\alpha = .01$. State the alternatives, decision rule, and conclusion. What is the P-value of the test?

*7.9. Refer to **Patient satisfaction** Problem 6.15. Test whether $\beta_1 = -1.0$ and $\beta_2 = 0$; use $\alpha = .025$. State the alternatives, full and reduced models, decision rule, and conclusion.

7.10. Refer to **Commercial properties** Problem 6.18. Test whether $\beta_1 = -.1$ and $\beta_2 = .4$; use $\alpha = .01$. State the alternatives, full and reduced models, decision rule, and conclusion.

7.11. Refer to the work crew productivity example in Table 7.6.

a. Calculate R^2_{Y1}, R^2_{Y2}, R^2_{12}, $R^2_{Y1|2}$, $R^2_{Y2|1}$, and R^2. Explain what each coefficient measures and interpret your results.

b. Are any of the results obtained in part (a) special because the two predictor variables are uncorrelated?

7.12. Refer to **Brand preference** Problem 6.5. Calculate R^2_{Y1}, R^2_{Y2}, R^2_{12}, $R^2_{Y1|2}$, $R^2_{Y2|1}$, and R^2. Explain what each coefficient measures and interpret your results.

*7.13. Refer to **Grocery retailer** Problem 6.9. Calculate R^2_{Y1}, R^2_{Y2}, R^2_{12}, $R^2_{Y1|2}$, $R^2_{Y2|1}$, $R^2_{Y2|13}$, and R^2. Explain what each coefficient measures and interpret your results.

*7.14. Refer to **Patient satisfaction** Problem 6.15.

a. Calculate R^2_{Y1}, $R^2_{Y1|2}$, and $R^2_{Y1|23}$. How is the degree of marginal linear association between Y and X_1 affected, when adjusted for X_2? When adjusted for both X_2 and X_3?

b. Make a similar analysis to that in part (a) for the degree of marginal linear association between Y and X_2. Are your findings similar to those in part (a) for Y and X_1?

7.15. Refer to **Commercial properties** Problems 6.18 and 7.7. Calculate R^2_{Y4}, R^2_{Y1}, $R^2_{Y1|4}$, R^2_{14}, $R^2_{Y2|14}$, $R^2_{Y3|124}$, and R^2. Explain what each coefficient measures and interpret your results. How is the degree of marginal linear association between Y and X_1 affected, when adjusted for X_4?

7.16. Refer to **Brand preference** Problem 6.5.

a. Transform the variables by means of the correlation transformation (7.44) and fit the standardized regression model (7.45).

b. Interpret the standardized regression coefficient b^*_1.

c. Transform the estimated standardized regression coefficients by means of (7.53) back to the ones for the fitted regression model in the original variables. Verify that they are the same as the ones obtained in Problem 6.5b.

*7.17. Refer to **Grocery retailer** Problem 6.9.

a. Transform the variables by means of the correlation transformation (7.44) and fit the standardized regression model (7.45).

b. Calculate the coefficients of determination between all pairs of predictor variables. Is it meaningful here to consider the standardized regression coefficients to reflect the effect of one predictor variable when the others are held constant?

c. Transform the estimated standardized regression coefficients by means of (7.53) back to the ones for the fitted regression model in the original variables. Verify that they are the same as the ones obtained in Problem 6.10a.

*7.18. Refer to **Patient satisfaction** Problem 6.15.

a. Transform the variables by means of the correlation transformation (7.44) and fit the standardized regression model (7.45).

b. Calculate the coefficients of determination between all pairs of predictor variables. Do these indicate that it is meaningful here to consider the standardized regression coefficients as indicating the effect of one predictor variable when the others are held constant?

c. Transform the estimated standardized regression coefficients by means of (7.53) back to the ones for the fitted regression model in the original variables. Verify that they are the same as the ones obtained in Problem 6.15c.

7.19. Refer to **Commercial properties** Problem 6.18.

a. Transform the variables by means of the correlation transformation (7.44) and fit the standardized regression model (7.45).

b. Interpret the standardized regression coefficient b_2^*.

c. Transform the estimated standardized regression coefficients by means of (7.53) back to the ones for the fitted regression model in the original variables. Verify that they are the same as the ones obtained in Problem 6.18c.

7.20. A speaker stated in a workshop on applied regression analysis: "In business and the social sciences, some degree of multicollinearity in survey data is practically inevitable." Does this statement apply equally to experimental data?

7.21. Refer to the example of perfectly correlated predictor variables in Table 7.8.

a. Develop another response function, like response functions (7.58) and (7.59), that fits the data perfectly.

b. What is the intersection of the infinitely many response surfaces that fit the data perfectly?

7.22. The progress report of a research analyst to the supervisor stated: "All the estimated regression coefficients in our model with three predictor variables to predict sales are statistically significant. Our new preliminary model with seven predictor variables, which includes the three variables of our smaller model, is less satisfactory because only two of the seven regression coefficients are statistically significant. Yet in some initial trials the expanded model is giving more precise sales predictions than the smaller model. The reasons for this anomaly are now being investigated." Comment.

7.23. Two authors wrote as follows: "Our research utilized a multiple regression model. Two of the predictor variables important in our theory turned out to be highly correlated in our data set. This made it difficult to assess the individual effects of each of these variables separately. We retained both variables in our model, however, because the high coefficient of multiple determination makes this difficulty unimportant." Comment.

7.24. Refer to **Brand preference** Problem 6.5.

a. Fit first-order simple linear regression model (2.1) for relating brand liking (Y) to moisture content (X_1). State the fitted regression function.

b. Compare the estimated regression coefficient for moisture content obtained in part (a) with the corresponding coefficient obtained in Problem 6.5b. What do you find?

c. Does $SSR(X_1)$ equal $SSR(X_1|X_2)$ here? If not, is the difference substantial?

d. Refer to the correlation matrix obtained in Problem 6.5a. What bearing does this have on your findings in parts (b) and (c)?

*7.25. Refer to **Grocery retailer** Problem 6.9.

a. Fit first-order simple linear regression model (2.1) for relating total hours required to handle shipment (Y) to total number of cases shipped (X_1). State the fitted regression function.

b. Compare the estimated regression coefficient for total cases shipped obtained in part (a) with the corresponding coefficient obtained in Problem 6.10a. What do you find?

c. Does $SSR(X_1)$ equal $SSR(X_1|X_2)$ here? If not, is the difference substantial?

d. Refer to the correlation matrix obtained in Problem 6.9c. What bearing does this have on your findings in parts (b) and (c)?

*7.26. Refer to **Patient satisfaction** Problem 6.15.

a. Fit first-order linear regression model (6.1) for relating patient satisfaction (Y) to patient's age (X_1) and severity of illness (X_2). State the fitted regression function.

b. Compare the estimated regression coefficients for patient's age and severity of illness obtained in part (a) with the corresponding coefficients obtained in Problem 6.15c. What do you find?

c. Does $SSR(X_1)$ equal $SSR(X_1|X_3)$ here? Does $SSR(X_2)$ equal $SSR(X_2|X_3)$?

d. Refer to the correlation matrix obtained in Problem 6.15b. What bearing does it have on your findings in parts (b) and (c)?

7.27. Refer to **Commercial properties** Problem 6.18.

a. Fit first-order linear regression model (6.1) for relating rental rates (Y) to property age (X_1) and size (X_4). State the fitted regression function.

b. Compare the estimated regression coefficients for property age and size with the corresponding coefficients obtained in Problem 6.18c. What do you find?

c. Does $SSR(X_4)$ equal $SSR(X_4|X_3)$ here? Does $SSR(X_1)$ equal $SSR(X_1|X_3)$?

d. Refer to the correlation matrix obtained in Problem 6.18b. What bearing does this have on your findings in parts (b) and (c)?

Exercises

7.28. a. Define each of the following extra sums of squares: (1) $SSR(X_5|X_1)$; (2) $SSR(X_3, X_4|X_1)$; (3) $SSR(X_4|X_1, X_2, X_3)$.

b. For a multiple regression model with five X variables, what is the relevant extra sum of squares for testing whether or not $\beta_5 = 0$? whether or not $\beta_2 = \beta_4 = 0$?

7.29. Show that:

a. $SSR(X_1, X_2, X_3, X_4) = SSR(X_1) + SSR(X_2, X_3|X_1) + SSR(X_4|X_1, X_2, X_3)$.

b. $SSR(X_1, X_2, X_3, X_4) = SSR(X_2, X_3) + SSR(X_1|X_2, X_3) + SSR(X_4|X_1, X_2, X_3)$.

7.30. Refer to **Brand preference** Problem 6.5.

a. Regress Y on X_2 using simple linear regression model (2.1) and obtain the residuals.

b. Regress X_1 on X_2 using simple linear regression model (2.1) and obtain the residuals.

c. Calculate the coefficient of simple correlation between the two sets of residuals and show that it equals $r_{Y1|2}$.

7.31. The following regression model is being considered in a water resources study:

$$Y_i = \beta_0 + \beta_1 X_{i1} + \beta_2 X_{i2} + \beta_3 X_{i1} X_{i2} + \beta_4 \sqrt{X_{i3}} + \varepsilon_i$$

State the reduced models for testing whether or not: (1) $\beta_3 = \beta_4 = 0$, (2) $\beta_3 = 0$, (3) $\beta_1 = \beta_2 = 5$, (4) $\beta_4 = 7$.

7.32. The following regression model is being considered in a market research study:

$$Y_i = \beta_0 + \beta_1 X_{i1} + \beta_2 X_{i2} + \beta_3 X_{i1}^2 + \varepsilon_i$$

State the reduced models for testing whether or not: (1) $\beta_1 = \beta_3 = 0$, (2) $\beta_0 = 0$, (3) $\beta_3 = 5$, (4) $\beta_0 = 10$, (5) $\beta_1 = \beta_2$.

7.33. Show the equivalence of the expressions in (7.36) and (7.41) for $R^2_{Y2|1}$.

7.34. Refer to the work crew productivity example in Table 7.6.

    a. For the variables transformed according to (7.44), obtain: (1) $\mathbf{X'X}$, (2) $\mathbf{X'Y}$, (3) $\mathbf{b}$, (4) $s^2\{\mathbf{b}\}$.

    b. Show that the standardized regression coefficients obtained in part (a3) are related to the regression coefficients for the regression model in the original variables according to (7.53).

7.35. Derive the relations between the β_k and β_k^* in (7.46a) for $p - 1 = 2$.

7.36. Derive the expression for $\mathbf{X'Y}$ in (7.51) for standardized regression model (7.30.) for $p - 1 = 2$.

Projects

7.37. Refer to the **CDI** data set in Appendix C.2. For predicting the number of active physicians (Y) in a county, it has been decided to include total population (X_1) and total personal income (X_2) as predictor variables. The question now is whether an additional predictor variable would be helpful in the model and, if so, which variable would be most helpful. Assume that a first-order multiple regression model is appropriate.

    a. For each of the following variables, calculate the coefficient of partial determination given that X_1 and X_2 are included in the model: land area (X_3), percent of population 65 or older (X_4), number of hospital beds (X_5), and total serious crimes (X_6).

    b. On the basis of the results in part (a), which of the four additional predictor variables is best? Is the extra sum of squares associated with this variable larger than those for the other three variables?

    c. Using the F^* test statistic, test whether or not the variable determined to be best in part (b) is helpful in the regression model when X_1 and X_2 are included in the model; use $\alpha = .01$. State the alternatives, decision rule, and conclusion. Would the F^* test statistics for the other three potential predictor variables be as large as the one here? Discuss.

7.38. Refer to the **SENIC** data set in Appendix C.1. For predicting the average length of stay of patients in a hospital (Y), it has been decided to include age (X_1) and infection risk (X_2) as predictor variables. The question now is whether an additional predictor variable would be helpful in the model and, if so, which variable would be most helpful. Assume that a first-order multiple regression model is appropriate.

    a. For each of the following variables, calculate the coefficient of partial determination given that X_1 and X_2 are included in the model: routine culturing ratio (X_3), average daily census (X_4), number of nurses (X_5), and available facilities and services (X_6).

    b. On the basis of the results in part (a), which of the four additional predictor variables is best? Is the extra sum of squares associated with this variable larger than those for the other three variables?

    c. Using the F^* test statistic, test whether or not the variable determined to be best in part (b) is helpful in the regression model when X_1 and X_2 are included in the model; use $\alpha = .05$. State the alternatives, decision rule, and conclusion. Would the F^* test statistics for the other three potential predictor variables be as large as the one here? Discuss.

Chapter

8

Regression Models for Quantitative and Qualitative Predictors

In this chapter, we consider in greater detail standard modeling techniques for quantitative predictors, for qualitative predictors, and for regression models containing both quantitative and qualitative predictors. These techniques include the use of interaction and polynomial terms for quantitative predictors, and the use of indicator variables for qualitative predictors.

8.1 Polynomial Regression Models

We first consider polynomial regression models for quantitative predictor variables. They are among the most frequently used curvilinear response models in practice because they are handled easily as a special case of the general linear regression model (6.7). Next, we discuss several commonly used polynomial regression models. Then we present a case to illustrate some of the major issues encountered with polynomial regression models.

Uses of Polynomial Models

Polynomial regression models have two basic types of uses:

1. When the true curvilinear response function is indeed a polynomial function.
2. When the true curvilinear response function is unknown (or complex) but a polynomial function is a good approximation to the true function.

The second type of use, where the polynomial function is employed as an approximation when the shape of the true curvilinear response function is unknown, is very common. It may be viewed as a nonparametric approach to obtaining information about the shape of the response function.

A main danger in using polynomial regression models, as we shall see, is that extrapolations may be hazardous with these models, especially those with higher-order terms. Polynomial regression models may provide good fits for the data at hand, but may turn in unexpected directions when extrapolated beyond the range of the data.

One Predictor Variable—Second Order

Polynomial regression models may contain one, two, or more than two predictor variables. Further, each predictor variable may be present in various powers. We begin by considering a polynomial regression model with one predictor variable raised to the first and second powers:

$$Y_i = \beta_0 + \beta_1 x_i + \beta_2 x_i^2 + \varepsilon_i \qquad (8.1)$$

where:

$$x_i = X_i - \bar{X}$$

This polynomial model is called a *second-order model with one predictor variable* because the single predictor variable is expressed in the model to the first and second powers. Note that the predictor variable is centered—in other words, expressed as a deviation around its mean $\bar{X}$—and that the ith centered observation is denoted by x_i. The reason for using a centered predictor variable in the polynomial regression model is that X and X^2 often will be highly correlated. This, as we noted in Section 7.5, can cause serious computational difficulties when the $\mathbf{X'X}$ matrix is inverted for estimating the regression coefficients in the normal equations calculations. Centering the predictor variable often reduces the multicollinearity substantially, as we shall illustrate in an example, and tends to avoid computational difficulties.

The regression coefficients in polynomial regression are frequently written in a slightly different fashion, to reflect the pattern of the exponents:

$$Y_i = \beta_0 + \beta_1 x_i + \beta_{11} x_i^2 + \varepsilon_i \qquad (8.2)$$

We shall employ this latter notation in this section.

The response function for regression model (8.2) is:

$$E\{Y\} = \beta_0 + \beta_1 x + \beta_{11} x^2 \qquad (8.3)$$

This response function is a parabola and is frequently called a *quadratic response function*. Figure 8.1 contains two examples of second-order polynomial response functions.

FIGURE 8.1
Examples of Second-Order Polynomial Response Functions.

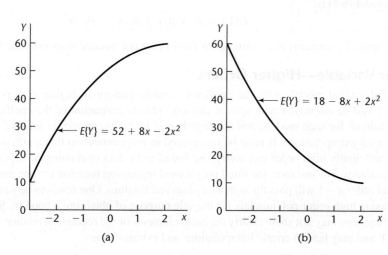

(a)   (b)

The regression coefficient β_0 represents the mean response of Y when $x = 0$, i.e., when $X = \bar{X}$. The regression coefficient β_1 is often called the *linear effect coefficient*, and β_{11} is called the *quadratic effect coefficient*.

Comments

1. The danger of extrapolating a polynomial response function is illustrated by the response function in Figure 8.1a. If this function is extrapolated beyond $x = 2$, it actually turns downward, which might not be appropriate in a given case.
2. The algebraic version of the least squares normal equations:

$$\mathbf{X'Xb = X'Y}$$

for the second-order polynomial regression model (8.2) can be readily obtained from (6.77) by replacing X_{i1} by x_i and X_{i2} by x_i^2. Since $\sum x_i = 0$, this yields the normal equations:

$$\sum Y_i = nb_0 + b_{11} \sum x_i^2$$

$$\sum x_i Y_i = b_1 \sum x_i^2 + b_{11} \sum x_i^3 \qquad (8.4)$$

$$\sum x_i^2 Y_i = b_0 \sum x_i^2 + b_1 \sum x_i^3 + b_{11} \sum x_i^4$$

∎

One Predictor Variable—Third Order

The regression model:

$$Y_i = \beta_0 + \beta_1 x_i + \beta_{11} x_i^2 + \beta_{111} x_i^3 + \varepsilon_i \qquad (8.5)$$

where:

$$x_i = X_i - \bar{X}$$

is a *third-order model with one predictor variable*. The response function for regression model (8.5) is:

$$E\{Y\} = \beta_0 + \beta_1 x + \beta_{11} x^2 + \beta_{111} x^3 \qquad (8.6)$$

Figure 8.2 contains two examples of third-order polynomial response functions.

One Predictor Variable—Higher Orders

Polynomial models with the predictor variable present in higher powers than the third should be employed with special caution. The interpretation of the coefficients becomes difficult for such models, and the models may be highly erratic for interpolations and even small extrapolations. It must be recognized in this connection that a polynomial model of sufficiently high order can always be found to fit data containing no repeat observations perfectly. For instance, the fitted polynomial regression function for one predictor variable of order $n - 1$ will pass through all n observed Y values. One needs to be wary, therefore, of using high-order polynomials for the sole purpose of obtaining a good fit. Such regression functions may not show clearly the basic elements of the regression relation between X and Y and may lead to erratic interpolations and extrapolations.

FIGURE 8.2
Examples of
Third-Order
Polynomial
Response
Functions.

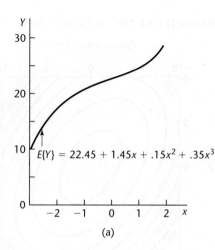

$E\{Y\} = 22.45 + 1.45x + .15x^2 + .35x^3$

(a)

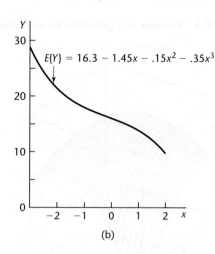

$E\{Y\} = 16.3 - 1.45x - .15x^2 - .35x^3$

(b)

Two Predictor Variables—Second Order

The regression model:

$$Y_i = \beta_0 + \beta_1 x_{i1} + \beta_2 x_{i2} + \beta_{11} x_{i1}^2 + \beta_{22} x_{i2}^2 + \beta_{12} x_{i1} x_{i2} + \varepsilon_i \tag{8.7}$$

where:

$$x_{i1} = X_{i1} - \bar{X}_1$$
$$x_{i2} = X_{i2} - \bar{X}_2$$

is a *second-order model with two predictor variables*. The response function is:

$$E\{Y\} = \beta_0 + \beta_1 x_1 + \beta_2 x_2 + \beta_{11} x_1^2 + \beta_{22} x_2^2 + \beta_{12} x_1 x_2 \tag{8.8}$$

which is the equation of a conic section. Note that regression model (8.7) contains separate linear and quadratic components for each of the two predictor variables and a cross-product term. The latter represents the interaction effect between x_1 and x_2, as we noted in Chapter 6. The coefficient β_{12} is often called the *interaction effect coefficient*.

Figure 8.3 contains a representation of the response surface and the contour curves for a second-order response function with two predictor variables:

$$E\{Y\} = 1,740 - 4x_1^2 - 3x_2^2 - 3x_1 x_2$$

The contour curves correspond to different response levels and show the various combinations of levels of the two predictor variables that yield the same level of response. Note that the response surface in Figure 8.3a has a maximum at $x_1 = 0$ and $x_2 = 0$. Figure 6.2b presents another type of second-order polynomial response function with two predictor variables, this one containing a saddle point.

Comment

The cross-product term $\beta_{12} x_1 x_2$ in (8.8) is considered to be a second-order term, the same as $\beta_{11} x_1^2$ or $\beta_{22} x_2^2$. The reason can be seen by writing the latter terms as $\beta_{11} x_1 x_1$ and $\beta_{22} x_2 x_2$, respectively. ∎

FIGURE 8.3   **Example of a Quadratic Response Surface—$E\{Y\} = 1,740 - 4x_1^2 - 3x_2^2 - 3x_1x_2$.**

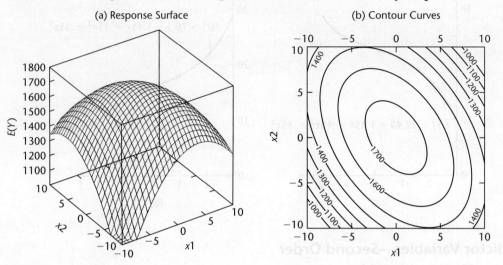

(a) Response Surface

(b) Contour Curves

Three Predictor Variables—Second Order

The *second-order regression model with three predictor variables* is:

$$Y_i = \beta_0 + \beta_1 x_{i1} + \beta_2 x_{i2} + \beta_3 x_{i3} + \beta_{11} x_{i1}^2 + \beta_{22} x_{i2}^2 + \beta_{33} x_{i3}^2$$
$$+ \beta_{12} x_{i1} x_{i2} + \beta_{13} x_{i1} x_{i3} + \beta_{23} x_{i2} x_{i3} + \varepsilon_i \tag{8.9}$$

where:

$$x_{i1} = X_{i1} - \bar{X}_1$$
$$x_{i2} = X_{i2} - \bar{X}_2$$
$$x_{i3} = X_{i3} - \bar{X}_3$$

The response function for this regression model is:

$$E\{Y\} = \beta_0 + \beta_1 x_1 + \beta_2 x_2 + \beta_3 x_3 + \beta_{11} x_1^2 + \beta_{22} x_2^2 + \beta_{33} x_3^2$$
$$+ \beta_{12} x_1 x_2 + \beta_{13} x_1 x_3 + \beta_{23} x_2 x_3 \tag{8.10}$$

The coefficients β_{12}, β_{13}, and β_{23} are interaction effect coefficients for interactions between pairs of predictor variables.

Implementation of Polynomial Regression Models

Fitting of Polynomial Models.   Fitting of polynomial regression models presents no new problems since, as we have seen in Chapter 6, they are special cases of the general linear regression model (6.7). Hence, all earlier results on fitting apply, as do the earlier results on making inferences.

Hierarchical Approach to Fitting.   When using a polynomial regression model as an approximation to the true regression function, statisticians will often fit a second-order or third-order model and then explore whether a lower-order model is adequate. For instance, with one predictor variable, the model:

$$Y_i = \beta_0 + \beta_1 x_i + \beta_{11} x_i^2 + \beta_{111} x_i^3 + \varepsilon_i$$

may be fitted with the hope that the cubic term and perhaps even the quadratic term can be dropped. Thus, one would wish to test whether or not $\beta_{111} = 0$, or whether or not both $\beta_{11} = 0$ and $\beta_{111} = 0$. The decomposition of *SSR* into extra sums of squares therefore proceeds as follows:

$$SSR(x)$$
$$SSR(x^2|x)$$
$$SSR(x^3|x, x^2)$$

To test whether $\beta_{111} = 0$, the appropriate extra sum of squares is $SSR(x^3|x, x^2)$. If, instead, one wishes to test whether a linear term is adequate, i.e., whether $\beta_{11} = \beta_{111} = 0$, the appropriate extra sum of squares is $SSR(x^2, x^3|x) = SSR(x^2|x) + SSR(x^3|x, x^2)$.

With the hierarchical approach, if a polynomial term of a given order is retained, then all related terms of lower order are also retained in the model. Thus, one would not drop the quadratic term of a predictor variable but retain the cubic term in the model. Since the quadratic term is of lower order, it is viewed as providing more basic information about the shape of the response function; the cubic term is of higher order and is viewed as providing refinements in the specification of the shape of the response function. The hierarchical approach to testing operates similarly for polynomial regression models with two or more predictor variables. Here, for instance, an interaction term (second power) would not be retained without also retaining the terms for the predictor variables to the first power.

Regression Function in Terms of X.   After a polynomial regression model has been developed, we often wish to express the final model in terms of the original variables rather than keeping it in terms of the centered variables. This can be done readily. For example, the fitted second-order model for one predictor variable that is expressed in terms of centered values $x = X - \bar{X}$:

$$\hat{Y} = b_0 + b_1 x + b_{11} x^2 \tag{8.11}$$

becomes in terms of the original X variable:

$$\hat{Y} = b_0' + b_1' X + b_{11}' X^2 \tag{8.12}$$

where:

$$b_0' = b_0 - b_1 \bar{X} + b_{11} \bar{X}^2 \tag{8.12a}$$

$$b_1' = b_1 - 2b_{11} \bar{X} \tag{8.12b}$$

$$b_{11}' = b_{11} \tag{8.12c}$$

The fitted values and residuals for the regression function in terms of X are exactly the same as for the regression function in terms of the centered values x. The reason, as we noted earlier, for utilizing a model that is expressed in terms of centered observations is to reduce potential calculational difficulties due to multicollinearity among X, X^2, X^3, etc., inherent in polynomial regression.

Comment

The estimated standard deviations of the regression coefficients in terms of the centered variables x in (8.11) do not apply to the regression coefficients in terms of the original variables X in (8.12). If the estimated standard deviations for the regression coefficients in terms of X are desired, they may be obtained by using (5.46), where the transformation matrix $\mathbf{A}$ is developed from (8.12a–c). ∎

Case Example

Setting. A researcher studied the effects of the charge rate and temperature on the life of a new type of power cell in a preliminary small-scale experiment. The charge rate (X_1) was controlled at three levels (.6, 1.0, and 1.4 amperes) and the ambient temperature (X_2) was controlled at three levels (10, 20, 30°C). Factors pertaining to the discharge of the power cell were held at fixed levels. The life of the power cell (Y) was measured in terms of the number of discharge-charge cycles that a power cell underwent before it failed. The data obtained in the study are contained in Table 8.1, columns 1–3.

The researcher was not sure about the nature of the response function in the range of the factors studied. Hence, the researcher decided to fit the second-order polynomial regression model (8.7):

$$Y_i = \beta_0 + \beta_1 x_{i1} + \beta_2 x_{i2} + \beta_{11} x_{i1}^2 + \beta_{22} x_{i2}^2 + \beta_{12} x_{i1} x_{i2} + \varepsilon_i \tag{8.13}$$

for which the response function is:

$$E\{Y\} = \beta_0 + \beta_1 x_1 + \beta_2 x_2 + \beta_{11} x_1^2 + \beta_{22} x_2^2 + \beta_{12} x_1 x_2 \tag{8.14}$$

TABLE 8.1 **Data—Power Cells Example.**

Cell i	(1) Number of Cycles Y_i	(2) Charge Rate X_{i1}	(3) Temperature X_{i2}	(4) x_{i1}	(5) x_{i2}	(6) x_{i1}^2	(7) x_{i2}^2	(8) $x_{i1} x_{i2}$
				Coded Values				
1	150	.6	10	−1	−1	1	1	1
2	86	1.0	10	0	−1	0	1	0
3	49	1.4	10	1	−1	1	1	−1
4	288	.6	20	−1	0	1	0	0
5	157	1.0	20	0	0	0	0	0
6	131	1.0	20	0	0	0	0	0
7	184	1.0	20	0	0	0	0	0
8	109	1.4	20	1	0	1	0	0
9	279	.6	30	−1	1	1	1	−1
10	235	1.0	30	0	1	0	1	0
11	224	1.4	30	1	1	1	1	1
		$\bar{X}_1 = 1.0$	$\bar{X}_2 = 20$					

Setting adapted from: S. M. Sidik, H. F. Leibecki, and J. M. Bozek, *Cycles Till Failure of Silver-Zinc Cells with Competing Failure Modes—Preliminary Data Analysis,* NASA Technical Memorandum 815–56, 1980.

Because of the balanced nature of the X_1 and X_2 levels studied, the researcher not only centered the variables X_1 and X_2 around their respective means but also scaled them in convenient units, as follows:

$$x_{i1} = \frac{X_{i1} - \bar{X}_1}{.4} = \frac{X_{i1} - 1.0}{.4}$$

$$x_{i2} = \frac{X_{i2} - \bar{X}_2}{10} = \frac{X_{i2} - 20}{10}$$

(8.15)

Here, the denominator used for each predictor variable is the absolute difference between adjacent levels of the variable. These centered and scaled variables are shown in columns 4 and 5 of Table 8.1. Note that the codings defined in (8.15) lead to simple coded values, -1, 0, and 1. The squared and cross-product terms are shown in columns 6–8 of Table 8.1.

Use of the coded variables x_1 and x_2 rather than the original variables X_1 and X_2 reduces the correlations between the first power and second power terms markedly here:

Correlation between		Correlation between	
X_1 and X_1^2:	.991	X_2 and X_2^2:	.986
x_1 and x_1^2:	0.0	x_2 and x_2^2:	0.0

The correlations for the coded variables are zero here because of the balance of the design of the experimental levels of the two explanatory variables. Similarly, the correlations between the cross-product term x_1x_2 and each of the terms x_1, x_1^2, x_2, x_2^2 are reduced to zero here from levels between .60 and .76 for the corresponding terms in the original variables. Low levels of multicollinearity can be helpful in avoiding computational inaccuracies.

The researcher was particularly interested in whether interaction effects and curvature effects are required in the model for the range of the X variables considered.

Fitting of Model.   Figure 8.4 contains the basic regression results for the fit of model (8.13) with the SAS regression package. Using the estimated regression coefficients (labeled Parameter Estimate), we see that the estimated regression function is as follows:

$$\hat{Y} = 162.84 - 55.83x_1 + 75.50x_2 + 27.39x_1^2 - 10.61x_2^2 + 11.50x_1x_2 \quad (8.16)$$

Residual Plots.   The researcher first investigated the appropriateness of regression model (8.13) for the data at hand. Plots of the residuals against $\hat{Y}$, x_1, and x_2 are shown in Figure 8.5, as is also a normal probability plot. None of these plots suggest any gross inadequacies of regression model (8.13). The coefficient of correlation between the ordered residuals and their expected values under normality is .974, which supports the assumption of normality of the error terms (see Table B.6).

Test of Fit.   Since there are three replications at $x_1 = 0$, $x_2 = 0$, another indication of the adequacy of regression model (8.13) can be obtained by the formal test in (6.68) of the goodness of fit of the regression function (8.14). The pure error sum of squares (3.16) is simple to obtain here, because there is only one combination of levels at which replications occur:

$$SSPE = (157 - 157.33)^2 + (131 - 157.33)^2 + (184 - 157.33)^2$$
$$= 1,404.67$$

FIGURE 8.4
SAS
Regression
Output for
Second-Order
Polynomial
Model
(8.13)—Power
Cells Example.

```
Model: MODEL1
Dependent Variable: Y

                          Analysis of Variance

                        Sum of          Mean
Source          DF      Squares        Square      F Value     Prob>F

Model            5    55365.56140   11073.11228     10.565      0.0109
Error            5     5240.43860    1048.08772
C Total         10    60606.00000

       Root MSE        32.37418     R-square      0.9135
       Dep Mean       172.00000     Adj R-sq      0.8271
       C.V.            18.82220

                         Parameter Estimates

                    Parameter     Standard    T for H0:
Variable      DF     Estimate       Error     Parameter=0    Prob > |T|

INTERCEP       1    162.842105   16.60760542      9.805        0.0002
X1             1    -55.833333   13.21670483     -4.224        0.0083
X2             1     75.500000   13.21670483      5.712        0.0023
X1SQ           1     27.394737   20.34007956      1.347        0.2359
X2SQ           1    -10.605263   20.34007956     -0.521        0.6244
X1X2           1     11.500000   16.18709146      0.710        0.5092

Variable      DF    Type I SS

INTERCEP       1       325424
X1             1        18704
X2             1        34202
X1SQ           1     1645.966667
X2SQ           1      284.928070
X1X2           1      529.000000
```

Since there are $c = 9$ distinct combinations of levels of the X variables here, there are $n - c = 11 - 9 = 2$ degrees of freedom associated with $SSPE$. Further, $SSE = 5,240.44$ according to Figure 8.4; hence the lack of fit sum of squares (3.24) is:

$$SSLF = SSE - SSPE = 5,240.44 - 1,404.67 = 3,835.77$$

with which $c - p = 9 - 6 = 3$ degrees of freedom are associated. (Remember that $p = 6$ regression coefficients in model (8.13) had to be estimated.) Hence, test statistic (6.68b) for testing the adequacy of the regression function (8.14) is:

$$F^* = \frac{SSLF}{c - p} \div \frac{SSPE}{n - c} = \frac{3,835.77}{3} \div \frac{1,404.67}{2} = 1.82$$

For $\alpha = .05$, we require $F(.95; 3, 2) = 19.2$. Since $F^* = 1.82 \leq 19.2$, we conclude according to decision rule (6.68c) that the second-order polynomial regression function (8.14) is a good fit.

Coefficient of Multiple Determination.   Figure 8.4 shows that the coefficient of multiple determination (labeled R-square) is $R^2 = .9135$. Thus, the variation in the lives of the power cells is reduced by about 91 percent when the first-order and second-order relations to the charge rate and ambient temperature are utilized. Note that the adjusted coefficient of multiple correlation (labeled Adj R-sq) is $R_a^2 = .8271$. This coefficient is considerably smaller here than the unadjusted coefficient because of the relatively large number of parameters in the polynomial regression function with two predictor variables.

FIGURE 8.5
Diagnostic
Residual
Plots—Power
Cells Example.

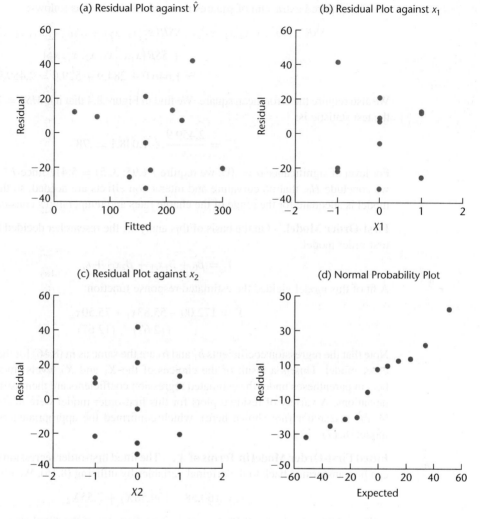

(a) Residual Plot against $\hat{Y}$

(b) Residual Plot against x_1

(c) Residual Plot against x_2

(d) Normal Probability Plot

Partial *F* Test.   The researcher now turned to consider whether a first-order model would be sufficient. The test alternatives are:

$$H_0: \beta_{11} = \beta_{22} = \beta_{12} = 0$$

$$H_a: \text{not all } \beta s \text{ in } H_0 \text{ equal zero}$$

The partial *F* test statistic (7.27) here is:

$$F^* = \frac{SSR\left(x_1^2, x_2^2, x_1 x_2 \mid x_1, x_2\right)}{3} \div MSE$$

In anticipation of this test, the researcher entered the X variables in the SAS regression program in the order $x_1, x_2, x_1^2, x_2^2, x_1 x_2$, as may be seen at the bottom of Figure 8.4. The extra sums of squares are labeled Type I SS. The first sum of squares shown is not relevant here. The second one is $SSR(x_1) = 18,704$, the third one is $SSR(x_2 \mid x_1) = 34,202$, and so on. The required extra sum of squares is therefore obtained as follows:

$$SSR(x_1^2, x_2^2, x_1x_2 | x_1, x_2) = SSR(x_1^2 | x_1, x_2) + SSR(x_2^2 | x_1, x_2, x_1^2)$$
$$+ SSR(x_1x_2 | x_1, x_2, x_1^2, x_2^2)$$
$$= 1,646.0 + 284.9 + 529.0 = 2,459.9$$

We also require the error mean square. We find in Figure 8.4 that it is $MSE = 1,048.1$. Hence the test statistic is:

$$F^* = \frac{2,459.9}{3} \div 1,048.1 = .78$$

For level of significance $\alpha = .05$, we require $F(.95; 3, 5) = 5.41$. Since $F^* = .78 \le 5.41$, we conclude H_0, that no curvature and interaction effects are needed, so that a first-order model is adequate for the range of the charge rates and temperatures considered.

First-Order Model. On the basis of this analysis, the researcher decided to consider the first-order model:

$$Y_i = \beta_0 + \beta_1 x_{i1} + \beta_2 x_{i2} + \varepsilon_i \qquad \textbf{(8.17)}$$

A fit of this model yielded the estimated response function:

$$\hat{Y} = 172.00 - 55.83x_1 + 75.50x_2 \qquad \textbf{(8.18)}$$
$$(12.67) \quad (12.67)$$

Note that the regression coefficients b_1 and b_2 are the same as in (8.16) for the fitted second-order model. This is a result of the choices of the X_1 and X_2 levels studied. The numbers in parentheses under the estimated regression coefficients are their estimated standard deviations. A variety of residual plots for this first-order model were made and analyzed by the researcher (not shown here), which confirmed the appropriateness of first-order model (8.17).

Fitted First-Order Model in Terms of X. The fitted first-order regression function (8.18) can be transformed back to the original variables by utilizing (8.15). We obtain:

$$\hat{Y} = 160.58 - 139.58X_1 + 7.55X_2 \qquad \textbf{(8.19)}$$

Figure 8.6 contains an S-Plus regression-scatter plot of the fitted response plane. The researcher used this fitted response surface for investigating the effects of charge rate and temperature on the life of this new type of power cell.

FIGURE 8.6
S-Plus Plot of
Fitted
Response Plane
(8.19)—Power
Cells Example.

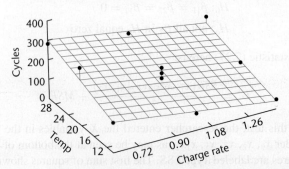

Estimation of Regression Coefficients.   The researcher wished to estimate the linear effects of the two predictor variables in the first-order model, with a 90 percent family confidence coefficient, by means of the Bonferroni method. Here, $g = 2$ statements are desired; hence, by (6.52a), we have:

$$B = t[1 - .10/2(2)] = t(.975; 8) = 2.306$$

The estimated standard deviations of b_1 and b_2 in (8.18) apply to the model in the coded variables. Since only first-order terms are involved in this fitted model, we obtain the estimated standard deviations of b_1' and b_2' for the fitted model (8.19) in the original variables as follows:

$$s\{b_1'\} = \left(\frac{1}{.4}\right)s\{b_1\} = \frac{12.67}{.4} = 31.68$$

$$s\{b_2'\} = \left(\frac{1}{10}\right)s\{b_2\} = \frac{12.67}{10} = 1.267$$

The Bonferroni confidence limits by (6.52) therefore are $-139.58 \pm 2.306(31.68)$ and $7.55 \pm 2.306(1.267)$, yielding the confidence limits:

$$-212.6 \le \beta_1 \le -66.5 \qquad 4.6 \le \beta_2 \le 10.5$$

With confidence .90, we conclude that the mean number of charge/discharge cycles before failure decreases by 66 to 213 cycles with a unit increase in the charge rate for given ambient temperature, and increases by 5 to 10 cycles with a unit increase of ambient temperature for given charge rate. The researcher was satisfied with the precision of these estimates for this initial small-scale study.

Some Further Comments on Polynomial Regression

1. The use of polynomial models is not without drawbacks. Such models can be more expensive in degrees of freedom than alternative nonlinear models or linear models with transformed variables. Another potential drawback is that serious multicollinearity may be present even when the predictor variables are centered.

2. An alternative to using centered variables in polynomial regression is to use *orthogonal polynomials*. Orthogonal polynomials are uncorrelated. Some computer packages use orthogonal polynomials in their polynomial regression routines and present the final fitted results in terms of both the orthogonal polynomials and the original polynomials. Orthogonal polynomials are discussed in specialized texts such as Reference 8.1.

3. Sometimes a quadratic response function is fitted for the purpose of establishing the linearity of the response function when repeat observations are not available for directly testing the linearity of the response function. Fitting the quadratic model:

$$Y_i = \beta_0 + \beta_1 x_i + \beta_{11} x_i^2 + \varepsilon_i \tag{8.20}$$

and testing whether $\beta_{11} = 0$ does not, however, necessarily establish that a linear response function is appropriate. Figure 8.2a provides an example. If sample data were obtained for the response function in Figure 8.2a, model (8.20) fitted, and a test on β_{11} made, it likely would lead to the conclusion that $\beta_{11} = 0$. Yet a linear response function clearly might not be appropriate. Examination of residuals would disclose this lack of fit and should always accompany formal testing of polynomial regression coefficients.

8.2 Interaction Regression Models

We have previously noted that regression models with cross-product interaction effects, such as regression model (6.15), are special cases of general linear regression model (6.7). We also encountered regression models with interaction effects briefly when we considered polynomial regression models, such as model (8.7). Now we consider in some detail regression models with interaction effects, including their interpretation and implementation.

Interaction Effects

A regression model with $p - 1$ predictor variables contains additive effects if the response function can be written in the form:

$$E\{Y\} = f_1(X_1) + f_2(X_2) + \cdots + f_{p-1}(X_{p-1}) \tag{8.21}$$

where $f_1, f_2, \ldots, f_{p-1}$ can be any functions, not necessarily simple ones. For instance, the following response function with two predictor variables can be expressed in the form of (8.21):

$$E\{Y\} = \underbrace{\beta_0 + \beta_1 X_1 + \beta_2 X_1^2}_{f_1(X_1)} + \underbrace{\beta_3 X_2}_{f_2(X_2)}$$

We say here that the effects of X_1 and X_2 on Y are additive.

In contrast, the following regression function:

$$E\{Y\} = \beta_0 + \beta_1 X_1 + \beta_2 X_2 + \beta_3 X_1 X_2$$

cannot be expressed in the form (8.21). Hence, this latter regression model is not additive, or, equivalently, it contains an interaction effect.

A simple and commonly used means of modeling the interaction effect of two predictor variables on the response variable is by a cross-product term, such as $\beta_3 X_1 X_2$ in the above response function. The cross-product term is called an *interaction term*. More specifically, it is sometimes called a *linear-by-linear* or a *bilinear* interaction term. When there are three predictor variables whose effects on the response variable are linear, but the effects on Y of X_1 and X_2 and of X_1 and X_3 are interacting, the response function would be modeled as follows using cross-product terms:

$$E\{Y\} = \beta_0 + \beta_1 X_1 + \beta_2 X_2 + \beta_3 X_3 + \beta_4 X_1 X_2 + \beta_5 X_1 X_3$$

Interpretation of Interaction Regression Models with Linear Effects

We shall explain the influence of interaction effects on the shape of the response function and on the interpretation of the regression coefficients by first considering the simple case of two quantitative predictor variables where each has a linear effect on the response variable.

Interpretation of Regression Coefficients. The regression model for two quantitative predictor variables with linear effects on Y and interacting effects of X_1 and X_2 on Y represented by a cross-product term is as follows:

$$Y_i = \beta_0 + \beta_1 X_{i1} + \beta_2 X_{i2} + \beta_3 X_{i1} X_{i2} + \varepsilon_i \tag{8.22}$$

The meaning of the regression coefficients β_1 and β_2 here is not the same as that given earlier because of the interaction term $\beta_3 X_{i1} X_{i2}$. The regression coefficients β_1 and β_2 no longer indicate the change in the mean response with a unit increase of the predictor variable, with the other predictor variable held constant at any given level. It can be shown that the change in the mean response with a unit increase in X_1 when X_2 is held constant is:

$$\beta_1 + \beta_3 X_2 \tag{8.23}$$

Similarly, the change in the mean response with a unit increase in X_2 when X_1 is held constant is:

$$\beta_2 + \beta_3 X_1 \tag{8.24}$$

Hence, in regression model (8.22) both the effect of X_1 for given level of X_2 and the effect of X_2 for given level of X_1 depend on the level of the other predictor variable.

We shall illustrate how the effect of one predictor variable depends on the level of the other predictor variable in regression model (8.22) by returning to the sales promotion response function shown in Figure 6.1 on page 215. The response function (6.3) for this example, relating locality sales (Y) to point-of-sale expenditures (X_1) and TV expenditures (X_2), is additive:

$$E\{Y\} = 10 + 2X_1 + 5X_2 \tag{8.25}$$

In Figure 8.7a, we show the response function $E\{Y\}$ as a function of X_1 when $X_2 = 1$ and when $X_2 = 3$. Note that the two response functions are parallel—that is, the mean sales response increases by the same amount $\beta_1 = 2$ with a unit increase of point-of-sale expenditures whether TV expenditures are $X_2 = 1$ or $X_2 = 3$. The plot in Figure 8.7a is called a *conditional effects plot* because it shows the effects of X_1 on the mean response conditional on different levels of the other predictor variable.

In Figure 8.7b, we consider the same response function but with the cross-product term $.5X_1 X_2$ added for interaction effect of the two types of promotional expenditures on sales:

$$E\{Y\} = 10 + 2X_1 + 5X_2 + .5X_1 X_2 \tag{8.26}$$

FIGURE 8.7   Illustration of Reinforcement and Interference Interaction Effects—Sales Promotion Example.

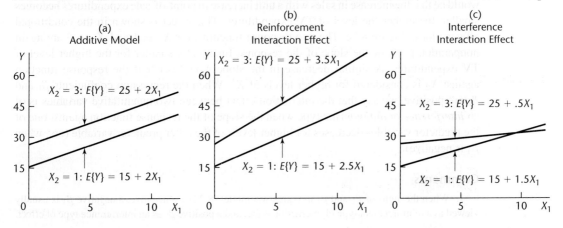

We again use a conditional effects plot to show the response function $E\{Y\}$ as a function of X_1 conditional on $X_2 = 1$ and on $X_2 = 3$. Note that the slopes of the response functions plotted against X_1 now differ for $X_2 = 1$ and $X_2 = 3$. The slope of the response function when $X_2 = 1$ is by (8.23):

$$\beta_1 + \beta_3 X_2 = 2 + .5(1) = 2.5$$

and when $X_2 = 3$, the slope is:

$$\beta_1 + \beta_3 X_2 = 2 + .5(3) = 3.5$$

Thus, a unit increase in point-of-sale expenditures has a larger effect on sales when TV expenditures are at a higher level than when they are at a lower level.

Hence, β_1 in regression model (8.22) containing a cross-product term for interaction effect no longer indicates the change in the mean response for a unit increase in X_1 for any given X_2 level. That effect in this model depends on the level of X_2. Although the mean response in regression model (8.22) when X_2 is constant is still a linear function of X_1, now both the intercept and the slope of the response function change as the level at which X_2 is held constant is varied. The same holds when the mean response is regarded as a function of X_2, with X_1 constant.

Note that as a result of the interaction effect in regression model (8.26), the increase in sales with a unit increase in point-of-sale expenditures is greater, the higher the level of TV expenditures, as shown by the larger slope of the response function when $X_2 = 3$ than when $X_2 = 1$. A similar increase in the slope occurs if the response function against X_2 is considered for higher levels of X_1. When the regression coefficients β_1 and β_2 are positive, we say that the interaction effect between the two quantitative variables is of a *reinforcement* or *synergistic* type when the slope of the response function against one of the predictor variables increases for higher levels of the other predictor variable (i.e., when β_3 is positive).

If the sign of β_3 in regression model (8.26) were negative:

$$E\{Y\} = 10 + 2X_1 + 5X_2 - .5X_1X_2 \tag{8.27}$$

the result of the interaction effect of the two types of promotional expenditures on sales would be that the increase in sales with a unit increase in point-of-sale expenditures becomes smaller, the higher the level of TV expenditures. This effect is shown in the conditional effects plot in Figure 8.7c. The two response functions for $X_2 = 1$ and $X_2 = 3$ are again nonparallel, but now the slope of the response function is smaller for the higher level of TV expenditures. A similar decrease in the slope would occur if the response function against X_2 is considered for higher levels of X_1. When the regression coefficients β_1 and β_2 are positive, we say that the interaction effect between two quantitative variables is of an *interference* or *antagonistic* type when the slope of the response function against one of the predictor variables decreases for higher levels of the other predictor variable (i.e., when β_3 is negative).

Comments

1. When the signs of β_1 and β_2 in regression model (8.22) are negative, a negative β_3 is usually viewed as a reinforcement type of interaction effect and a positive β_3 as an interference type of effect.

2. To derive (8.23) and (8.24), we differentiate:

$$E\{Y\} = \beta_0 + \beta_1 X_1 + \beta_2 X_2 + \beta_3 X_1 X_2$$

with respect to X_1 and X_2, respectively:

$$\frac{\partial E\{Y\}}{\partial X_1} = \beta_1 + \beta_3 X_2 \qquad \frac{\partial E\{Y\}}{\partial X_2} = \beta_2 + \beta_3 X_1$$

$\blacksquare$

Shape of Response Function.   Figure 8.8 shows for the sales promotion example the impact of the interaction effect on the shape of the response function. Figure 8.8a presents the additive response function in (8.25), and Figures 8.8b and 8.8c present the response functions with the reinforcement interaction effect in (8.26) and with the interference interaction effect in (8.27), respectively. Note that the additive response function is a plane, but that the two response functions with interaction effects are not. Also note in Figures 8.8b and 8.8c that the mean response as a function of X_1, for any given level of X_2, is no longer parallel to the same function at a different level of X_2, for either type of interaction effect.

We can also illustrate the difference in the shape of the response function when the two predictor variables do and do not interact by representing the response surface by means of a contour diagram. As we noted previously, such a diagram shows for different response levels the various combinations of levels of the two predictor variables that yield the same level of response. Figure 8.8d shows a contour diagram for the additive response surface in Figure 8.8a when the two predictor variables do not interact. Note that the contour curves are straight lines and that the contour lines are parallel and hence equally spaced. Figures 8.8e and 8.8f show contour diagrams for the response surfaces in Figures 8.8b and 8.8c, respectively, where the two predictor variables interact. Note that the contour curves are no longer straight lines and that the contour curves are not parallel here. For instance, in Figure 8.8e the vertical distance between the contours for $E\{Y\} = 200$ and $E\{Y\} = 400$ at $X_1 = 10$ is much larger than at $X_1 = 50$.

In general, additive or noninteracting predictor variables lead to parallel contour curves, whereas interacting predictor variables lead to nonparallel contour curves.

Interpretation of Interaction Regression Models with Curvilinear Effects

When one or more of the predictor variables in a regression model have curvilinear effects on the response variable, the presence of interaction effects again leads to response functions whose contour curves are not parallel. Figure 8.9a shows the response surface for a study of the volume of a quick bread:

$$E\{Y\} = 65 + 3X_1 + 4X_2 - 10X_1^2 - 15X_2^2 + 35X_1 X_2$$

Here, Y is the percentage increase in the volume of the quick bread from baking, X_1 is the amount of a leavening agent (coded), and X_2 is the oven temperature (coded). Figure 8.9b shows contour curves for this response function. Note the lack of parallelism in the contour curves, reflecting the interaction effect. Figure 8.10 presents a conditional effects plot to show in a simple fashion the nature of the interaction in the relation of oven temperature (X_2) to the mean volume when leavening agent amount (X_1) is held constant at different levels. Note that increasing oven temperature increases volume when leavening agent amount is high, and the opposite is true when leavening agent amount is low.

FIGURE 8.8
**Response
Surfaces and
Contour Plots
for Additive
and Interaction
Regression
Models—Sales
Promotion
Example.**

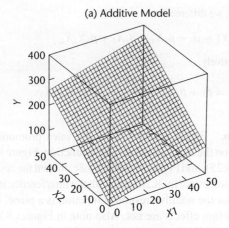

(a) Additive Model

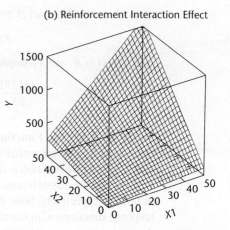

(b) Reinforcement Interaction Effect

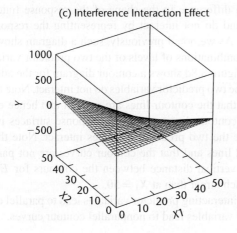

(c) Interference Interaction Effect

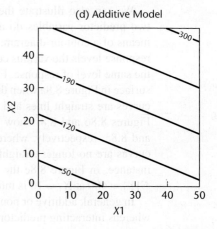

(d) Additive Model

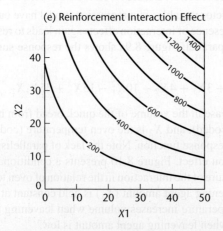

(e) Reinforcement Interaction Effect

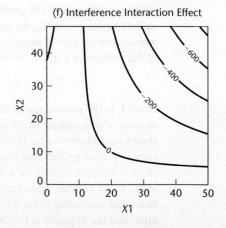

(f) Interference Interaction Effect

FIGURE 8.9   Response Surface and Contour Curves for Curvilinear Regression Model with Interaction Effect—Quick Bread Volume Example.

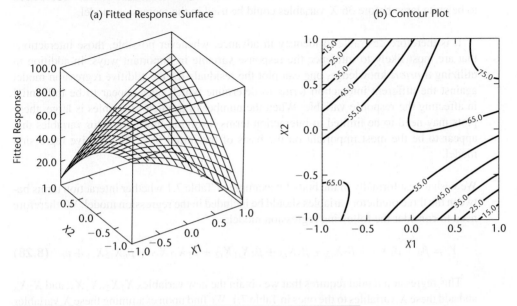

(a) Fitted Response Surface

(b) Contour Plot

FIGURE 8.10 Conditional Effects Plot for Curvilinear Regression Model with Interaction Effect—Quick Bread Volume Example.

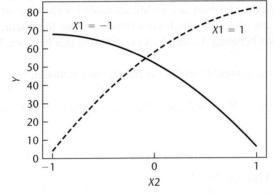

Implementation of Interaction Regression Models

The fitting of interaction regression models is routine, once the appropriate cross-product terms have been added to the data set. Two considerations need to be kept in mind when developing regression models with interaction effects.

1. When interaction terms are added to a regression model, high multicollinearities may exist between some of the predictor variables and some of the interaction terms, as well as among some of the interaction terms. A partial remedy to improve computational accuracy is to center the predictor variables; i.e., to use $x_{ik} = X_{ik} - \bar{X}_k$.

2. When the number of predictor variables in the regression model is large, the potential number of interaction terms can become very large. For example, if eight predictor

variables are present in the regression model in linear terms, there are potentially 28 pairwise interaction terms that could be added to the regression model. The data set would need to be quite large before 36 X variables could be used in the regression model.

It is therefore desirable to identify in advance, whenever possible, those interactions that are most likely to influence the response variable in important ways. In addition to utilizing *a priori* knowledge, one can plot the residuals for the additive regression model against the different interaction terms to determine which ones appear to be influential in affecting the response variable. When the number of predictor variables is large, these plots may need to be limited to interaction terms involving those predictor variables that appear to be the most important on the basis of the initial fit of the additive regression model.

Example

We wish to test formally in the body fat example of Table 7.1 whether interaction terms between the three predictor variables should be included in the regression model. We therefore need to consider the following regression model:

$$Y_i = \beta_0 + \beta_1 X_{i1} + \beta_2 X_{i2} + \beta_3 X_{i3} + \beta_4 X_{i1} X_{i2} + \beta_5 X_{i1} X_{i3} + \beta_6 X_{i2} X_{i3} + \varepsilon_i \quad \textbf{(8.28)}$$

This regression model requires that we obtain the new variables $X_1 X_2$, $X_1 X_3$, and $X_2 X_3$ and add these X variables to the ones in Table 7.1. We find upon examining these X variables that some of the predictor variables are highly correlated with some of the interaction terms, and that there are also some high correlations among the interaction terms. For example, the correlation between X_1 and $X_1 X_2$ is .989 and that between $X_1 X_3$ and $X_2 X_3$ is .998.

We shall therefore use centered variables in the regression model:

$$Y_i = \beta_0 + \beta_1 x_{i1} + \beta_2 x_{i2} + \beta_3 x_{i3} + \beta_4 x_{i1} x_{i2} + \beta_5 x_{i1} x_{i3} + \beta_6 x_{i2} x_{i3} + \varepsilon_i \quad \textbf{(8.29)}$$

where:

$$x_{i1} = X_{i1} - \bar{X}_1 = X_{i1} - 25.305$$
$$x_{i2} = X_{i2} - \bar{X}_2 = X_{i2} - 51.170$$
$$x_{i3} = X_{i3} - \bar{X}_3 = X_{i3} - 27.620$$

Upon obtaining the cross-product terms using the centered variables, we find that the intercorrelations involving the cross-product terms are now smaller. For example, the largest correlation, which was between $X_1 X_3$ and $X_2 X_3$, is reduced from .998 to .891. Other correlations are reduced in absolute magnitude even more.

Fitting regression model (8.29) yields the following estimated regression function, mean square error, and extra sums of squares:

$$\hat{Y} = 20.53 + 3.438 x_1 - 2.095 x_2 - 1.616 x_3 + .00888 x_1 x_2 - .08479 x_1 x_3 + .09042 x_2 x_3$$

$$MSE = 6.745$$

Variable	Extra Sum of Squares
x_1	$SSR(x_1) = 352.270$
x_2	$SSR(x_2|x_1) = 33.169$
x_3	$SSR(x_3|x_1, x_2) = 11.546$
$x_1 x_2$	$SSR(x_1 x_2|x_1, x_2, x_3) = 1.496$
$x_1 x_3$	$SSR(x_1 x_3|x_1, x_2, x_3, x_1 x_2) = 2.704$
$x_2 x_3$	$SSR(x_2 x_3|x_1, x_2, x_3, x_1 x_2, x_1 x_3) = 6.515$

We wish to test whether any interaction terms are needed:

$$H_0: \beta_4 = \beta_5 = \beta_6 = 0$$
$$H_a: \text{not all } \beta s \text{ in } H_0 \text{ equal zero}$$

The partial F test statistic (7.27) requires here the following extra sum of squares:

$$SSR(x_1 x_2, x_1 x_3, x_2 x_3|x_1, x_2, x_3) = 1.496 + 2.704 + 6.515 = 10.715$$

and the test statistic is:

$$F^* = \frac{SSR(x_1 x_2, x_1 x_3, x_2 x_3|x_1, x_2, x_3)}{3} \div MSE$$

$$= \frac{10.715}{3} \div 6.745 = .53$$

For level of significance $\alpha = .05$, we require $F(.95; 3, 13) = 3.41$. Since $F^* = .53 \leq 3.41$, we conclude H_0, that the interaction terms are not needed in the regression model. The P-value of this test is .67.

8.3 Qualitative Predictors

As mentioned in Chapter 6, qualitative, as well as quantitative, predictor variables can be used in regression models. Many predictor variables of interest in business, economics, and the social and biological sciences are qualitative. Examples of qualitative predictor variables are gender (male, female), purchase status (purchase, no purchase), and disability status (not disabled, partly disabled, fully disabled).

In a study of innovation in the insurance industry, an economist wished to relate the speed with which a particular insurance innovation is adopted (Y) to the size of the insurance firm (X_1) and the type of firm. The response variable is measured by the number of months elapsed between the time the first firm adopted the innovation and the time the given firm adopted the innovation. The first predictor variable, size of firm, is quantitative, and is measured by the amount of total assets of the firm. The second predictor variable, type of firm, is qualitative and is composed of two classes—stock companies and mutual companies. In order that such a qualitative variable can be used in a regression model, quantitative indicators for the classes of the qualitative variable must be employed.

Qualitative Predictor with Two Classes

There are many ways of quantitatively identifying the classes of a qualitative variable. We shall use indicator variables that take on the values 0 and 1. These indicator variables are easy to use and are widely employed, but they are by no means the only way to quantify a qualitative variable.

For the insurance innovation example, where the qualitative predictor variable has two classes, we might define two indicator variables X_2 and X_3 as follows:

$$X_2 = \begin{cases} 1 & \text{if stock company} \\ 0 & \text{otherwise} \end{cases}$$

$$X_3 = \begin{cases} 1 & \text{if mutual company} \\ 0 & \text{otherwise} \end{cases}$$

(8.30)

A first-order model then would be the following:

$$Y_i = \beta_0 + \beta_1 X_{i1} + \beta_2 X_{i2} + \beta_3 X_{i3} + \varepsilon_i$$

(8.31)

This intuitive approach of setting up an indicator variable for each class of the qualitative predictor variable unfortunately leads to computational difficulties. To see why, suppose we have $n = 4$ observations, the first two being stock firms (for which $X_2 = 1$ and $X_3 = 0$), and the second two being mutual firms (for which $X_2 = 0$ and $X_3 = 1$). The **X** matrix would then be:

$$\mathbf{X} = \begin{array}{ccc} X_1 & X_2 & X_3 \end{array} \\ \begin{bmatrix} 1 & X_{11} & 1 & 0 \\ 1 & X_{21} & 1 & 0 \\ 1 & X_{31} & 0 & 1 \\ 1 & X_{41} & 0 & 1 \end{bmatrix}$$

Note that the first column is equal to the sum of the X_2 and X_3 columns, so that the columns are linearly dependent according to definition (5.20). This has a serious effect on the $\mathbf{X'X}$ matrix:

$$\mathbf{X'X} = \begin{bmatrix} 1 & 1 & 1 & 1 \\ X_{11} & X_{21} & X_{31} & X_{41} \\ 1 & 1 & 0 & 0 \\ 0 & 0 & 1 & 1 \end{bmatrix} \begin{bmatrix} 1 & X_{11} & 1 & 0 \\ 1 & X_{21} & 1 & 0 \\ 1 & X_{31} & 0 & 1 \\ 1 & X_{41} & 0 & 1 \end{bmatrix}$$

$$= \begin{bmatrix} 4 & \sum_{i=1}^{4} X_{i1} & 2 & 2 \\ \sum_{i=1}^{4} X_{i1} & \sum_{i=1}^{4} X_{i1}^2 & \sum_{i=1}^{2} X_{i1} & \sum_{i=3}^{4} X_{i1} \\ 2 & \sum_{i=1}^{2} X_{i1} & 2 & 0 \\ 2 & \sum_{i=3}^{4} X_{i1} & 0 & 2 \end{bmatrix}$$

We see that the first column of the $\mathbf{X'X}$ matrix equals the sum of the last two columns, so that the columns are linearly dependent. Hence, the $\mathbf{X'X}$ matrix does not have an inverse, and no unique estimators of the regression coefficients can be found.

A simple way out of this difficulty is to drop one of the indicator variables. In our example, we might drop X_3. Dropping one indicator variable is not the only way out of the difficulty, but it leads to simple interpretations of the parameters. In general, therefore, we shall follow the principle:

> A qualitative variable with c classes will be represented by $c - 1$ indicator variables, each taking on the values 0 and 1. (8.32)

Comment

Indicator variables are frequently also called *dummy variables* or *binary variables*. The latter term has reference to the binary number system containing only 0 and 1. ∎

Interpretation of Regression Coefficients

Returning to the insurance innovation example, suppose that we drop the indicator variable X_3 from regression model (8.31) so that the model becomes:

$$Y_i = \beta_0 + \beta_1 X_{i1} + \beta_2 X_{i2} + \varepsilon_i \qquad (8.33)$$

where:

$$X_{i1} = \text{size of firm}$$

$$X_{i2} = \begin{cases} 1 & \text{if stock company} \\ 0 & \text{if mutual company} \end{cases}$$

The response function for this regression model is:

$$E\{Y\} = \beta_0 + \beta_1 X_1 + \beta_2 X_2 \qquad (8.34)$$

To understand the meaning of the regression coefficients in this model, consider first the case of a mutual firm. For such a firm, $X_2 = 0$ and response function (8.34) becomes:

$$E\{Y\} = \beta_0 + \beta_1 X_1 + \beta_2(0) = \beta_0 + \beta_1 X_1 \qquad \text{Mutual firms} \qquad (8.34a)$$

Thus, the response function for mutual firms is a straight line, with Y intercept β_0 and slope β_1. This response function is shown in Figure 8.11.

For a stock firm, $X_2 = 1$ and response function (8.34) becomes:

$$E\{Y\} = \beta_0 + \beta_1 X_1 + \beta_2(1) = (\beta_0 + \beta_2) + \beta_1 X_1 \qquad \text{Stock firms} \qquad (8.34b)$$

This also is a straight line, with the same slope β_1 but with Y intercept $\beta_0 + \beta_2$. This response function is also shown in Figure 8.11.

Let us consider now the meaning of the regression coefficients in response function (8.34) with specific reference to the insurance innovation example. We see that the mean time elapsed before the innovation is adopted, $E\{Y\}$, is a linear function of size of firm (X_1), with the same slope β_1 for both types of firms. β_2 indicates how much higher (lower) the response function for stock firms is than the one for mutual firms, for any given size of firm. Thus, β_2 measures the differential effect of type of firm. In general, β_2 shows how much higher (lower) the mean response line is for the class coded 1 than the line for the class coded 0, for any given level of X_1.

FIGURE 8.11
Illustration of Meaning of Regression Coefficients for Regression Model (8.33) with Indicator Variable X_2—Insurance Innovation Example.

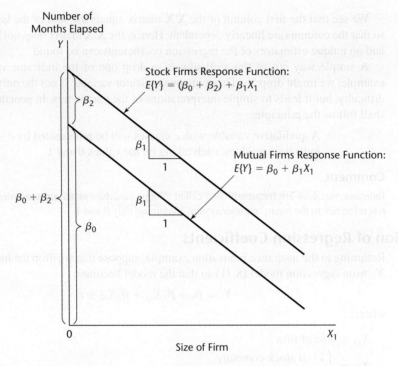

Example

In the insurance innovation example, the economist studied 10 mutual firms and 10 stock firms. The basic data are shown in Table 8.2, columns 1–3. The indicator coding for type of firm is shown in column 4. Note that $X_2 = 1$ for each stock firm and $X_2 = 0$ for each mutual firm.

The fitting of regression model (8.33) is now straightforward. Table 8.3 presents the key results from a computer run regressing Y on X_1 and X_2. The fitted response function is:

$$\hat{Y} = 33.87407 - .10174X_1 + 8.05547X_2$$

Figure 8.12 contains the fitted response function for each type of firm, together with the actual observations.

The economist was most interested in the effect of type of firm (X_2) on the elapsed time for the innovation to be adopted and wished to obtain a 95 percent confidence interval for β_2. We require $t(.975; 17) = 2.110$ and obtain from the results in Table 8.3 the confidence limits $8.05547 \pm 2.110(1.45911)$. The confidence interval for β_2 therefore is:

$$4.98 \leq \beta_2 \leq 11.13$$

Thus, with 95 percent confidence, we conclude that stock companies tend to adopt the innovation somewhere between 5 and 11 months later, on the average, than mutual companies, for any given size of firm.

A formal test of:

$$H_0: \beta_2 = 0$$
$$H_a: \beta_2 \neq 0$$

TABLE 8.2
Data and
Indicator
Coding—
Insurance
Innovation
Example.

Firm i	(1) Number of Months Elapsed Y_i	(2) Size of Firm (million dollars) X_{i1}	(3) Type of Firm	(4) Indicator Code X_{i2}	(5) $X_{i1}X_{i2}$
1	17	151	Mutual	0	0
2	26	92	Mutual	0	0
3	21	175	Mutual	0	0
4	30	31	Mutual	0	0
5	22	104	Mutual	0	0
6	0	277	Mutual	0	0
7	12	210	Mutual	0	0
8	19	120	Mutual	0	0
9	4	290	Mutual	0	0
10	16	238	Mutual	0	0
11	28	164	Stock	1	164
12	15	272	Stock	1	272
13	11	295	Stock	1	295
14	38	68	Stock	1	68
15	31	85	Stock	1	85
16	21	224	Stock	1	224
17	20	166	Stock	1	166
18	13	305	Stock	1	305
19	30	124	Stock	1	124
20	14	246	Stock	1	246

TABLE 8.3
Regression
Results for Fit
of Regression
Model (8.33)—
Insurance
Innovation
Example.

(a) Regression Coefficients

Regression Coefficient	Estimated Regression Coefficient	Estimated Standard Deviation	t^*
β_0	33.87407	1.81386	18.68
β_1	−.10174	.00889	−11.44
β_2	8.05547	1.45911	5.52

(b) Analysis of Variance

Source of Variation	SS	df	MS
Regression	1,504.41	2	752.20
Error	176.39	17	10.38
Total	1,680.80	19	

with level of significance .05 would lead to H_a, that type of firm has an effect, since the 95 percent confidence interval for β_2 does not include zero.

The economist also carried out other analyses, some of which will be described shortly.

Comment

The reader may wonder why we did not simply fit separate regressions for stock firms and mutual firms in our example, and instead adopted the approach of fitting one regression with an indicator

FIGURE 8.12
Fitted
Regression
Functions for
Regression
Model (8.33)—
Insurance
Innovation
Example.

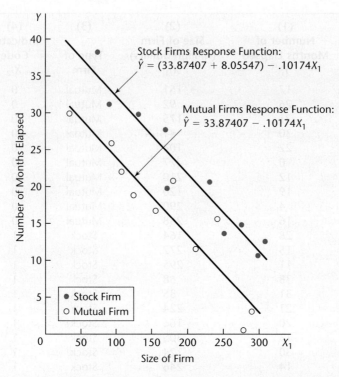

Stock Firms Response Function:
$\hat{Y} = (33.87407 + 8.05547) - .10174X_1$

Mutual Firms Response Function:
$\hat{Y} = 33.87407 - .10174X_1$

- ● Stock Firm
- ○ Mutual Firm

y-axis: Number of Months Elapsed

x-axis: Size of Firm, X_1

variable. There are two reasons for this. Since the model assumes equal slopes and the same constant error term variance for each type of firm, the common slope β_1 can best be estimated by pooling the two types of firms. Also, other inferences, such as for β_0 and β_2, can be made more precisely by working with one regression model containing an indicator variable since more degrees of freedom will then be associated with *MSE*. ∎

Qualitative Predictor with More than Two Classes

If a qualitative predictor variable has more than two classes, we require additional indicator variables in the regression model. Consider the regression of tool wear (Y) on tool speed (X_1) and tool model, where the latter is a qualitative variable with four classes (M1, M2, M3, M4). We therefore require three indicator variables. Let us define them as follows:

$$X_2 = \begin{cases} 1 & \text{if tool model M1} \\ 0 & \text{otherwise} \end{cases}$$

$$X_3 = \begin{cases} 1 & \text{if tool model M2} \\ 0 & \text{otherwise} \end{cases} \qquad \text{(8.35)}$$

$$X_4 = \begin{cases} 1 & \text{if tool model M3} \\ 0 & \text{otherwise} \end{cases}$$

First-Order Model.   A first-order regression model is:

$$Y_i = \beta_0 + \beta_1 X_{i1} + \beta_2 X_{i2} + \beta_3 X_{i3} + \beta_4 X_{i4} + \varepsilon_i \qquad \text{(8.36)}$$

For this model, the data input for the X variables would be as follows:

Tool Model	X_1	X_2	X_3	X_4
M1	X_{i1}	1	0	0
M2	X_{i1}	0	1	0
M3	X_{i1}	0	0	1
M4	X_{i1}	0	0	0

The response function for regression model (8.36) is:

$$E\{Y\} = \beta_0 + \beta_1 X_1 + \beta_2 X_2 + \beta_3 X_3 + \beta_4 X_4 \qquad \textbf{(8.37)}$$

To understand the meaning of the regression coefficients, consider first what response function (8.37) becomes for tool models M4 for which $X_2 = 0$, $X_3 = 0$, and $X_4 = 0$:

$$E\{Y\} = \beta_0 + \beta_1 X_1 \qquad \text{Tool models M4} \qquad \textbf{(8.37a)}$$

For tool models M1, $X_2 = 1$, $X_3 = 0$, and $X_4 = 0$, and response function (8.37) becomes:

$$E\{Y\} = (\beta_0 + \beta_2) + \beta_1 X_1 \qquad \text{Tool models M1} \qquad \textbf{(8.37b)}$$

Similarly, response functions (8.37) becomes for tool models M2 and M3:

$$E\{Y\} = (\beta_0 + \beta_3) + \beta_1 X_1 \qquad \text{Tool models M2} \qquad \textbf{(8.37c)}$$

$$E\{Y\} = (\beta_0 + \beta_4) + \beta_1 X_1 \qquad \text{Tool models M3} \qquad \textbf{(8.37d)}$$

Thus, response function (8.37) implies that the regression of tool wear on tool speed is linear, with the same slope for all four tool models. The coefficients β_2, β_3, and β_4 indicate, respectively, how much higher (lower) the response functions for tool models M1, M2, and M3 are than the one for tool models M4, for any given level of tool speed. Thus, β_2, β_3, and β_4 measure the differential effects of the qualitative variable classes on the height of the response function for any given level of X_1, always compared with the class for which $X_2 = X_3 = X_4 = 0$. Figure 8.13 illustrates a possible arrangement of the response functions.

When using regression model (8.36), we may wish to estimate differential effects other than against tool models M4. This can be done by estimating differences between regression coefficients. For instance, $\beta_4 - \beta_3$ measures how much higher (lower) the response function for tool models M3 is than the response function for tool models M2 for any given level of tool speed, as may be seen by comparing (8.37c) and (8.37d). The point estimator of this quantity is, of course, $b_4 - b_3$, and the estimated variance of this estimator is:

$$s^2\{b_4 - b_3\} = s^2\{b_4\} + s^2\{b_3\} - 2s\{b_4, b_3\} \qquad \textbf{(8.38)}$$

The needed variances and covariance can be readily obtained from the estimated variance-covariance matrix of the regression coefficients.

Time Series Applications

Economists and business analysts frequently use time series data in regression analysis. Indicator variables often are useful for time series regression models. For instance, savings (Y) may be regressed on income (X), where both the savings and income data are annual

FIGURE 8.13
Illustration of
Regression
Model (8.36)—
Tool Wear
Example.

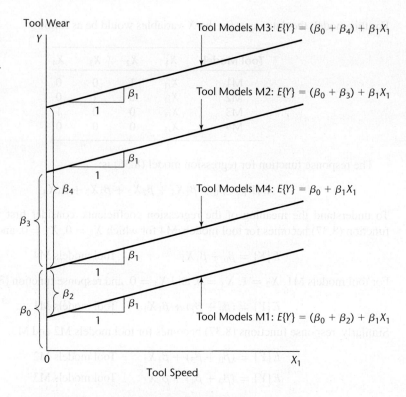

data for a number of years. The model employed might be:

$$Y_t = \beta_0 + \beta_1 X_t + \varepsilon_t \qquad t = 1, \dots, n \tag{8.39}$$

where Y_t and X_t are savings and income, respectively, for time period t. Suppose that the period covered includes both peacetime and wartime years, and that this factor should be recognized since savings in wartime years tend to be higher. The following model might then be appropriate:

$$Y_t = \beta_0 + \beta_1 X_{t1} + \beta_2 X_{t2} + \varepsilon_t \tag{8.40}$$

where:

$$X_{t1} = \text{income}$$
$$X_{t2} = \begin{cases} 1 & \text{if period } t \text{ peacetime} \\ 0 & \text{otherwise} \end{cases}$$

Note that regression model (8.40) assumes that the marginal propensity to save (β_1) is constant in both peacetime and wartime years, and that only the height of the response function is affected by this qualitative variable.

Another use of indicator variables in time series applications occurs when monthly or quarterly data are used. Suppose that quarterly sales (Y) are regressed on quarterly advertising expenditures (X_1) and quarterly disposable personal income (X_2). If seasonal effects also have an influence on quarterly sales, a first-order regression model incorporating seasonal effects would be:

$$Y_t = \beta_0 + \beta_1 X_{t1} + \beta_2 X_{t2} + \beta_3 X_{t3} + \beta_4 X_{t4} + \beta_5 X_{t5} + \varepsilon_t \qquad \text{(8.41)}$$

where:

$$X_{t1} = \text{quarterly advertising expenditures}$$

$$X_{t2} = \text{quarterly disposable personal income}$$

$$X_{t3} = \begin{cases} 1 & \text{if first quarter} \\ 0 & \text{otherwise} \end{cases}$$

$$X_{t4} = \begin{cases} 1 & \text{if second quarter} \\ 0 & \text{otherwise} \end{cases}$$

$$X_{t5} = \begin{cases} 1 & \text{if third quarter} \\ 0 & \text{otherwise} \end{cases}$$

Regression models for time series data are susceptible to correlated error terms. It is particularly important in these cases to examine whether the modeling of the time series components of the data is adequate to make the error terms uncorrelated. We discuss in Chapter 12 a test for correlated error terms and a regression model that is often useful when the error terms are correlated.

8.4   Some Considerations in Using Indicator Variables

Indicator Variables versus Allocated Codes

An alternative to the use of indicator variables for a qualitative predictor variable is to employ *allocated codes*. Consider, for instance, the predictor variable "frequency of product use" which has three classes: frequent user, occasional user, nonuser. With the allocated codes approach, a single X variable is employed and values are assigned to the classes; for instance:

Class	X_1
Frequent user	3
Occasional user	2
Nonuser	1

The allocated codes are, of course, arbitrary and could be other sets of numbers. The first-order model with allocated codes for our example, assuming no other predictor variables, would be:

$$Y_i = \beta_0 + \beta_1 X_{i1} + \varepsilon_i \qquad \text{(8.42)}$$

The basic difficulty with allocated codes is that they define a metric for the classes of the qualitative variable that may not be reasonable. To see this concretely, consider the mean responses with regression model (8.42) for the three classes of the qualitative variable:

Class	$E\{Y\}$
Frequent user	$E\{Y\} = \beta_0 + \beta_1(3) = \beta_0 + 3\beta_1$
Occasional user	$E\{Y\} = \beta_0 + \beta_1(2) = \beta_0 + 2\beta_1$
Nonuser	$E\{Y\} = \beta_0 + \beta_1(1) = \beta_0 + \beta_1$

Note the key implication:

$$E\{Y|\text{frequent user}\} - E\{Y|\text{occasional user}\} = E\{Y|\text{occasional user}\} - E\{Y|\text{nonuser}\} = \beta_1$$

Thus, the coding 1, 2, 3 implies that the mean response changes by the same amount when going from a nonuser to an occasional user as when going from an occasional user to a frequent user. This may not be in accord with reality and is the result of the coding 1, 2, 3, which assigns equal distances between the three user classes. Other allocated codes may, of course, imply different spacings of the classes of the qualitative variable, but these would ordinarily still be arbitrary.

Indicator variables, in contrast, make no assumptions about the spacing of the classes and rely on the data to show the differential effects that occur. If, for the same example, two indicator variables, say, X_1 and X_2, are employed to represent the qualitative variable, as follows:

Class	X_1	X_2
Frequent user	1	0
Occasional user	0	1
Nonuser	0	0

the first-order regression model would be:

$$Y_i = \beta_0 + \beta_1 X_{i1} + \beta_2 X_{i2} + \varepsilon_i \tag{8.43}$$

Here, β_1 measures the differential effect:

$$E\{Y|\text{frequent user}\} - E\{Y|\text{nonuser}\}$$

and β_2 measures the differential effect:

$$E\{Y|\text{occasional user}\} - E\{Y|\text{nonuser}\}$$

Thus, β_2 measures the differential effect between occasional user and nonuser, and $\beta_1 - \beta_2$ measures the differential effect between frequent user and occasional user. Notice that there are no arbitrary restrictions to be satisfied by these two differential effects. Also note that if $\beta_1 = 2\beta_2$, then equal spacing between the three classes would exist.

Indicator Variables versus Quantitative Variables

Indicator variables can be used even if the predictor variable is quantitative. For instance, the quantitative variable age may be transformed by grouping ages into classes such as under

21, 21–34, 35–49, etc. Indicator variables are then used for the classes of this new predictor variable. At first sight, this may seem to be a questionable approach because information about the actual ages is thrown away. Furthermore, additional parameters are placed into the model, which leads to a reduction of the degrees of freedom associated with *MSE*.

Nevertheless, there are occasions when replacement of a quantitative variable by indicator variables may be appropriate. Consider a large-scale survey in which the relation between liquid assets (Y) and age (X) of head of household is to be studied. Two thousand households were included in the study, so that the loss of 10 or 20 degrees of freedom is immaterial. The analyst is very much in doubt about the shape of the regression function, which could be highly complex, and hence may utilize the indicator variable approach in order to obtain information about the shape of the response function without making any assumptions about its functional form.

Thus, for large data sets use of indicator variables can serve as an alternative to lowess and other nonparametric fits of the response function.

Other Codings for Indicator Variables

As stated earlier, many different codings of indicator variables are possible. We now describe two alternatives to our 0, 1 coding for $c - 1$ indicator variables for a qualitative variable with c classes. We illustrate these alternative codings for the insurance innovation example, where Y is time to adopt an innovation, X_1 is size of insurance firm, and the second predictor variable is type of company (stock, mutual).

The first alternative coding is:

$$X_2 = \begin{cases} 1 & \text{if stock company} \\ -1 & \text{if mutual company} \end{cases} \tag{8.44}$$

For this coding, the first-order linear regression model:

$$Y_i = \beta_0 + \beta_1 X_{i1} + \beta_2 X_{i2} + \varepsilon_i \tag{8.45}$$

has the response function:

$$E\{Y\} = \beta_0 + \beta_1 X_1 + \beta_2 X_2 \tag{8.46}$$

This response function becomes for the two types of companies:

$$E\{Y\} = (\beta_0 + \beta_2) + \beta_1 X_1 \qquad \text{Stock firms} \tag{8.46a}$$

$$E\{Y\} = (\beta_0 - \beta_2) + \beta_1 X_1 \qquad \text{Mutual firms} \tag{8.46b}$$

Thus, β_0 here may be viewed as an "average" intercept of the regression line, from which the stock company and mutual company intercepts differ by β_2 in opposite directions. A test whether the regression lines are the same for both types of companies involves $H_0: \beta_2 = 0$, $H_a: \beta_2 \neq 0$.

A second alternative coding scheme is to use a 0, 1 indicator variable for each of the c classes of the qualitative variable and to drop the intercept term in the regression model. For the insurance innovation example, the model would be:

$$Y_i = \beta_1 X_{i1} + \beta_2 X_{i2} + \beta_3 X_{i3} + \varepsilon_i \tag{8.47}$$

where:

X_{i1} = size of firm

$$X_{i2} = \begin{cases} 1 & \text{if stock company} \\ 0 & \text{otherwise} \end{cases}$$

$$X_{i3} = \begin{cases} 1 & \text{if mutual company} \\ 0 & \text{otherwise} \end{cases}$$

Here, the two response functions are:

$$E\{Y\} = \beta_2 + \beta_1 X_1 \qquad \text{Stock firms} \tag{8.48a}$$

$$E\{Y\} = \beta_3 + \beta_1 X_1 \qquad \text{Mutual firms} \tag{8.48b}$$

A test of whether or not the two regression lines are the same would involve the alternatives $H_0: \beta_2 = \beta_3$, $H_a: \beta_2 \neq \beta_3$. This type of test, discussed in Section 7.3, cannot be conducted by using extra sums of squares and requires the fitting of both the full and reduced models.

8.5 Modeling Interactions between Quantitative and Qualitative Predictors

In the insurance innovation example, the economist actually did not begin the analysis with regression model (8.33) because of the possibility of interaction effects between size of firm and type of firm on the response variable. Even though one of the predictor variables in the regression model here is qualitative, interaction effects can still be introduced into the model in the usual manner, by including cross-product terms. A first-order regression model with an added interaction term for the insurance innovation example is:

$$Y_i = \beta_0 + \beta_1 X_{i1} + \beta_2 X_{i2} + \beta_3 X_{i1} X_{i2} + \varepsilon_i \tag{8.49}$$

where:

X_{i1} = size of firm

$$X_{i2} = \begin{cases} 1 & \text{if stock company} \\ 0 & \text{otherwise} \end{cases}$$

The response function for this regression model is:

$$E\{Y\} = \beta_0 + \beta_1 X_1 + \beta_2 X_2 + \beta_3 X_1 X_2 \tag{8.50}$$

Meaning of Regression Coefficients

The meaning of the regression coefficients in response function (8.50) can best be understood by examining the nature of this function for each type of firm. For a mutual firm, $X_2 = 0$ and hence $X_1 X_2 = 0$. Response function (8.50) therefore becomes for mutual firms:

$$E\{Y\} = \beta_0 + \beta_1 X_1 + \beta_2(0) + \beta_3(0) = \beta_0 + \beta_1 X_1 \qquad \text{Mutual firms} \tag{8.50a}$$

This response function is shown in Figure 8.14. Note that the Y intercept is β_0 and the slope is β_1 for the response function for mutual firms.

FIGURE 8.14
Illustration of
Meaning of
Regression
Coefficients for
Regression
Model (8.49)
with Indicator
Variable X_2
and Interaction
Term—
Insurance
Innovation
Example.

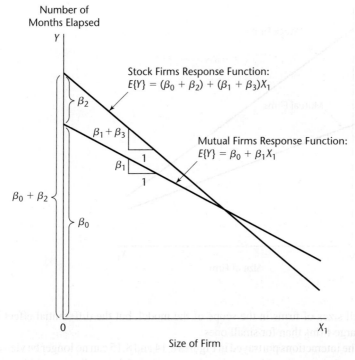

For stock firms, $X_2 = 1$ and hence $X_1 X_2 = X_1$. Response function (8.50) therefore becomes for stock firms:

$$E\{Y\} = \beta_0 + \beta_1 X_1 + \beta_2(1) + \beta_3 X_1$$

or:

$$E\{Y\} = (\beta_0 + \beta_2) + (\beta_1 + \beta_3)X_1 \qquad \text{Stock firms} \qquad \textbf{(8.50b)}$$

This response function is also shown in Figure 8.14. Note that the response function for stock firms has Y intercept $\beta_0 + \beta_2$ and slope $\beta_1 + \beta_3$.

We see that β_2 here indicates how much greater (smaller) is the Y intercept of the response function for the class coded 1 than that for the class coded 0. Similarly, β_3 indicates how much greater (smaller) is the slope of the response function for the class coded 1 than that for the class coded 0. Because both the intercept and the slope differ for the two classes in regression model (8.49), it is no longer true that β_2 indicates how much higher (lower) one response function is than the other for any given level of X_1. Figure 8.14 shows that the effect of type of firm with regression model (8.49) depends on X_1, the size of the firm. For smaller firms, according to Figure 8.14, mutual firms tend to innovate more quickly, but for larger firms stock firms tend to innovate more quickly. Thus, when interaction effects are present, the effect of the qualitative predictor variable can be studied only by comparing the regression functions within the scope of the model for the different classes of the qualitative variable.

Figure 8.15 illustrates another possible interaction pattern for the insurance innovation example. Here, mutual firms tend to introduce the innovation more quickly than stock firms

FIGURE 8.15
Another
Illustration of
Regression
Model (8.49)
with Indicator
Variable X_2
and Interaction
Term—
Insurance
Innovation
Example.

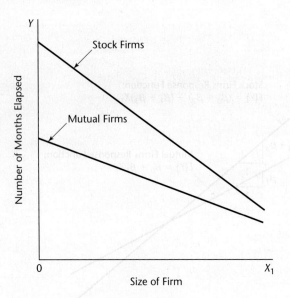

for all sizes of firms in the scope of the model, but the differential effect is much smaller for large firms than for small ones.

The interactions portrayed in Figures 8.14 and 8.15 can no longer be viewed as reinforcing or interfering types of interactions because one of the predictor variables here is qualitative. When one of the predictor variables is qualitative and the other quantitative, nonparallel response functions that do not intersect within the scope of the model (as in Figure 8.15) are sometimes said to represent an *ordinal interaction*. When the response functions intersect within the scope of the model (as in Figure 8.14), the interaction is then said to be a *disordinal interaction*.

Example

Since the economist was concerned that interaction effects between size and type of firm may be present, the initial regression model fitted was model (8.49):

$$Y_i = \beta_0 + \beta_1 X_{i1} + \beta_2 X_{i2} + \beta_3 X_{i1} X_{i2} + \varepsilon_i$$

The values for the interaction term $X_1 X_2$ for the insurance innovation example are shown in Table 8.2, column 5, on page 317. Note that this column contains 0 for mutual companies and X_{i1} for stock companies.

Again, the regression fit is routine. Basic results from a computer run regressing Y on X_1, X_2, and $X_1 X_2$ are shown in Table 8.4. To test for the presence of interaction effects:

$$H_0: \beta_3 = 0$$
$$H_a: \beta_3 \neq 0$$

the economist used the t^* statistic from Table 8.4a:

$$t^* = \frac{b_3}{s\{b_3\}} = \frac{-.0004171}{.01833} = -.02$$

TABLE 8.4
Regression
Results for Fit
of Regression
Model (8.49)
with
Interaction
Term—
Insurance
Innovation
Example.

(a) Regression Coefficients

Regression Coefficient	Estimated Regression Coefficient	Estimated Standard Deviation	t^*
β_0	33.83837	2.44065	13.86
β_1	−.10153	.01305	−7.78
β_2	8.13125	3.65405	2.23
β_3	−.0004171	.01833	−.02

(b) Analysis of Variance

Source of Variation	SS	df	MS
Regression	1,504.42	3	501.47
Error	176.38	16	11.02
Total	1,680.80	19	

For level of significance .05, we require $t(.975; 16) = 2.120$. Since $|t^*| = .02 \leq 2.120$, we conclude H_0, that $\beta_3 = 0$. The conclusion of no interaction effects is supported by the two-sided P-value for the test, which is very high, namely, .98. It was because of this result that the economist adopted regression model (8.33) with no interaction term, which we discussed earlier.

Comment

Fitting regression model (8.49) yields the same response functions as would fitting separate regressions for stock firms and mutual firms. An advantage of using model (8.49) with an indicator variable is that one regression run will yield both fitted regressions.

Another advantage is that tests for comparing the regression functions for the different classes of the qualitative variable can be clearly seen to involve tests of regression coefficients in a general linear model. For instance, Figure 8.14 for the insurance innovation example shows that a test of whether the two regression functions have the same slope involves:

$$H_0: \beta_3 = 0$$
$$H_a: \beta_3 \neq 0$$

Similarly, Figure 8.14 shows that a test of whether the two regression functions are identical involves:

$$H_0: \beta_2 = \beta_3 = 0$$
$$H_a: \text{not both } \beta_2 = 0 \text{ and } \beta_3 = 0$$

∎

8.6   More Complex Models

We now briefly consider more complex models involving quantitative and qualitative predictor variables.

More than One Qualitative Predictor Variable

Regression models can readily be constructed for cases where two or more of the predictor variables are qualitative. Consider the regression of advertising expenditures (Y) on sales (X_1), type of firm (incorporated, not incorporated), and quality of sales management (high, low). We may define:

$$X_2 = \begin{cases} 1 & \text{if firm incorporated} \\ 0 & \text{otherwise} \end{cases}$$

$$X_3 = \begin{cases} 1 & \text{if quality of sales management high} \\ 0 & \text{otherwise} \end{cases} \tag{8.51}$$

First-Order Model. A first-order regression model for the above example is:

$$Y_i = \beta_0 + \beta_1 X_{i1} + \beta_2 X_{i2} + \beta_3 X_{i3} + \varepsilon_i \tag{8.52}$$

This model implies that the response function of advertising expenditures on sales is linear, with the same slope for all "type of firm—quality of sales management" combinations, and β_2 and β_3 indicate the additive differential effects of type of firm and quality of sales management on the height of the regression line for any given levels of X_1 and the other predictor variable.

First-Order Model with Certain Interactions Added. A first-order regression model to which are added interaction effects between each pair of the predictor variables for the advertising example is:

$$Y_i = \beta_0 + \beta_1 X_{i1} + \beta_2 X_{i2} + \beta_3 X_{i3} + \beta_4 X_{i1} X_{i2} + \beta_5 X_{i1} X_{i3} + \beta_6 X_{i2} X_{i3} + \varepsilon_i \tag{8.53}$$

Note the implications of this model:

Type of Firm	Quality of Sales Management	Response Function
Incorporated	High	$E\{Y\} = (\beta_0 + \beta_2 + \beta_3 + \beta_6) + (\beta_1 + \beta_4 + \beta_5)X_1$
Not incorporated	High	$E\{Y\} = (\beta_0 + \beta_3) + (\beta_1 + \beta_5)X_1$
Incorporated	Low	$E\{Y\} = (\beta_0 + \beta_2) + (\beta_1 + \beta_4)X_1$
Not incorporated	Low	$E\{Y\} = \beta_0 + \beta_1 X_1$

Not only are all response functions different for the various "type of firm—quality of sales management" combinations, but the differential effects of one qualitative variable on the intercept depend on the particular class of the other qualitative variable. For instance, when we move from "not incorporated—low quality" to "incorporated—low quality," the intercept changes by β_2. But if we move from "not incorporated—high quality" to "incorporated—high quality," the intercept changes by $\beta_2 + \beta_6$.

Qualitative Predictor Variables Only

Regression models containing only qualitative predictor variables can also be constructed. With reference to our advertising example, we could regress advertising expenditures only on type of firm and quality of sales management. The first-order regression model then would be:

$$Y_i = \beta_0 + \beta_2 X_{i2} + \beta_3 X_{i3} + \varepsilon_i \tag{8.54}$$

where X_{i2} and X_{i3} are defined in (8.51).

Comments

1. Models in which all explanatory variables are qualitative are called *analysis of variance models*.

2. Models containing some quantitative and some qualitative explanatory variables, where the chief explanatory variables of interest are qualitative and the quantitative variables are introduced primarily to reduce the variance of the error terms, are called *analysis of covariance models*.

∎

8.7   Comparison of Two or More Regression Functions

Frequently we encounter regressions for two or more populations and wish to study their similarities and differences. We present three examples.

1. A company operates two production lines for making soap bars. For each line, the relation between the speed of the line and the amount of scrap for the day was studied. A scatter plot of the data for the two production lines suggests that the regression relation between production line speed and amount of scrap is linear but not the same for the two production lines. The slopes appear to be about the same, but the heights of the regression lines seem to differ. A formal test is desired to determine whether or not the two regression lines are identical. If it is found that the two regression lines are not the same, an investigation is to be made of why the difference in scrap yield exists.

2. An economist is studying the relation between amount of savings and level of income for middle-income families from urban and rural areas, based on independent samples from the two populations. Each of the two relations can be modeled by linear regression. The economist wishes to compare whether, at given income levels, urban and rural families tend to save the same amount—i.e., whether the two regression lines are the same. If they are not, the economist wishes to explore whether at least the amounts of savings out of an additional dollar of income are the same for the two groups—i.e., whether the slopes of the two regression lines are the same.

3. Two instruments were constructed for a company to identical specifications to measure pressure in an industrial process. A study was then made for each instrument of the relation between its gauge readings and actual pressures as determined by an almost exact but slow and costly method. If the two regression lines are the same, a single calibration schedule can be developed for the two instruments; otherwise, two different calibration schedules will be required.

When it is reasonable to assume that the error term variances in the regression models for the different populations are equal, we can use indicator variables to test the equality of the different regression functions. If the error variances are not equal, transformations of the response variable may equalize them at least approximately.

We have already seen how regression models with indicator variables that contain interaction terms permit testing of the equality of regression functions for the different classes of a qualitative variable. This methodology can be used directly for testing the equality of regression functions for different populations. We simply consider the different populations as classes of a predictor variable, define indicator variables for the different populations, and develop a regression model containing appropriate interaction terms. Since no new principles arise in the testing of the equality of regression functions for different populations, we immediately proceed with two of the earlier examples to illustrate the approach.

Soap Production Lines Example

The data on amount of scrap (Y) and line speed (X_1) for the soap production lines example are presented in Table 8.5. The variable X_2 is a code for the production line. A symbolic scatter plot of the data, using different symbols for the two production lines, is shown in Figure 8.16.

Tentative Model. On the basis of the symbolic scatter plot in Figure 8.16, the analyst decided to tentatively fit regression model (8.49). This model assumes that the regression relation between amount of scrap and line speed is linear for both production lines and that the variances of the error terms are the same, but permits the two regression lines to have different slopes and intercepts:

$$Y_i = \beta_0 + \beta_1 X_{i1} + \beta_2 X_{i2} + \beta_3 X_{i1} X_{i2} + \varepsilon_i \qquad (8.55)$$

	Production Line 1				Production Line 2		
Case *i*	Amount of Scrap Y_i	Line Speed X_{i1}	X_{i2}	Case *i*	Amount of Scrap Y_i	Line Speed X_{i1}	X_{i2}
1	218	100	1	16	140	105	0
2	248	125	1	17	277	215	0
3	360	220	1	18	384	270	0
4	351	205	1	19	341	255	0
5	470	300	1	20	215	175	0
6	394	255	1	21	180	135	0
7	332	225	1	22	260	200	0
8	321	175	1	23	361	275	0
9	410	270	1	24	252	155	0
10	260	170	1	25	422	320	0
11	241	155	1	26	273	190	0
12	331	190	1	27	410	295	0
13	275	140	1				
14	425	290	1				
15	367	265	1				

TABLE 8.5 Data—Soap Production Lines Example (all data are coded).

FIGURE 8.16
Symbolic
Scatter
Plot—Soap
Production
Lines Example.

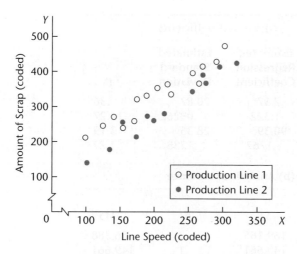

where:

$$X_{i1} = \text{line speed}$$

$$X_{i2} = \begin{cases} 1 & \text{if production line 1} \\ 0 & \text{if production line 2} \end{cases}$$

$$i = 1, 2, \ldots, 27$$

Note that for purposes of this model, the 15 cases for production line 1 and the 12 cases for production line 2 are combined into one group of 27 cases.

Diagnostics. A fit of regression model (8.55) to the data in Table 8.5 led to the results presented in Table 8.6 and the following fitted regression function:

$$\hat{Y} = 7.57 + 1.322X_1 + 90.39X_2 - .1767X_1X_2$$

Plots of the residuals against $\hat{Y}$ are shown in Figure 8.17 for each production line. Two plots are used in order to facilitate the diagnosis of possible differences between the two production lines. Both plots in Figure 8.17 are reasonably consistent with regression model (8.55). The splits between positive and negative residuals of 10 to 5 for production line 1 and 4 to 8 for production line 2 can be accounted for by randomness of the outcomes. Plots of the residuals against X_2 and a normal probability plot of the residuals (not shown) also support the appropriateness of the fitted model. For the latter plot, the coefficient of correlation between the ordered residuals and their expected values under normality is .990. This is sufficiently high according to Table B.6 to support the assumption of normality of the error terms.

Finally, the analyst desired to make a formal test of the equality of the variances of the error terms for the two production lines, using the Brown-Forsythe test described in Section 3.6. Separate linear regression models were fitted to the data for the two production lines, the residuals were obtained, and the absolute deviations d_{i1} and d_{i2} in (3.8) of the

TABLE 8.6
Regression
Results for Fit
of Regression
Model (8.55)—
Soap
Production
Lines Example.

	(a) Regression Coefficients		
Regression Coefficient	Estimated Regression Coefficient	Estimated Standard Deviation	t^*
β_0	7.57	20.87	.36
β_1	1.322	.09262	14.27
β_2	90.39	28.35	3.19
β_3	−.1767	.1288	−1.37

(b) Analysis of Variance			
Source of Variation	SS	df	MS
Regression	169,165	3	56,388
X_1	149,661	1	149,661
$X_2 \mid X_1$	18,694	1	18,694
$X_1 X_2 \mid X_1, X_2$	810	1	810
Error	9,904	23	430.6
Total	179,069	26	

FIGURE 8.17
Residual Plots
against
$\hat{Y}$—Soap
Production
Lines Example.

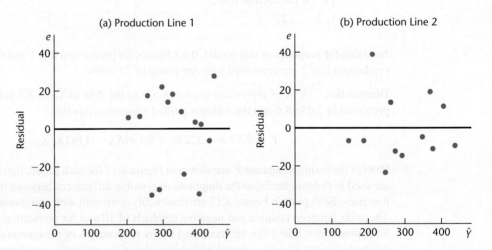

residuals around the median residual for each group were obtained for each production line. The results were as follows:

Production Line 1	Production Line 2
$\hat{Y} = 97.965 + 1.145 X_1$	$\hat{Y} = 7.574 + 1.322 X_1$
$\bar{d}_1 = 16.132$	$\bar{d}_2 = 12.648$
$\sum(d_{i1} - \bar{d}_1)^2 = 2,952.20$	$\sum(d_{i2} - \bar{d}_2)^2 = 2,045.82$

The pooled variance s^2 in (3.9a) therefore is:

$$s^2 = \frac{2{,}952.20 + 2{,}045.82}{27 - 2} = 199.921$$

Hence, the pooled standard deviation is $s = 14.139$, and the test statistic in (3.9) is:

$$t_{BF}^* = \frac{16.132 - 12.648}{14.139\sqrt{\dfrac{1}{15} + \dfrac{1}{12}}} = .636$$

For $\alpha = .05$, we require $t(.975; 25) = 2.060$. Since $|t_{BF}^*| = .636 \leq 2.060$, we conclude that the error term variances for the two production lines do not differ. The two-sided P-value for this test is .53.

At this point, the analyst was satisfied about the aptness of regression model (8.55) with normal error terms and was ready to proceed with comparing the regression relation between amount of scrap and line speed for the two production lines.

Inferences about Two Regression Lines. Identity of the regression functions for the two production lines is tested by considering the alternatives:

$$\begin{aligned} &H_0: \beta_2 = \beta_3 = 0 \\ &H_a: \text{not both } \beta_2 = 0 \text{ and } \beta_3 = 0 \end{aligned} \tag{8.56}$$

The appropriate test statistic is given by (7.27):

$$F^* = \frac{SSR(X_2, X_1X_2|X_1)}{2} \div \frac{SSE(X_1, X_2, X_1X_2)}{n - 4} \tag{8.56a}$$

where n represents the combined sample size for both populations. Using the regression results in Table 8.6, we find:

$$\begin{aligned} SSR(X_2, X_1X_2|X_1) &= SSR(X_2|X_1) + SSR(X_1X_2|X_1, X_2) \\ &= 18{,}694 + 810 = 19{,}504 \\ F^* &= \frac{19{,}504}{2} \div \frac{9{,}904}{23} = 22.65 \end{aligned}$$

To control α at level .01, we require $F(.99; 2, 23) = 5.67$. Since $F^* = 22.65 > 5.67$, we conclude H_a, that the regression functions for the two production lines are not identical.

Next, the analyst examined whether the slopes of the regression lines are the same. The alternatives here are:

$$\begin{aligned} &H_0: \beta_3 = 0 \\ &H_a: \beta_3 \neq 0 \end{aligned} \tag{8.57}$$

and the appropriate test statistic is either the t^* statistic (7.25) or the partial F test statistic (7.24):

$$F^* = \frac{SSR(X_1X_2|X_1, X_2)}{1} \div \frac{SSE(X_1, X_2, X_1X_2)}{n - 4} \tag{8.57a}$$

Using the regression results in Table 8.6 and the partial F test statistic, we obtain:

$$F^* = \frac{810}{1} \div \frac{9{,}904}{23} = 1.88$$

For $\alpha = .01$, we require $F(.99; 1, 23) = 7.88$. Since $F^* = 1.88 \leq 7.88$, we conclude H_0, that the slopes of the regression functions for the two production lines are the same.

Using the Bonferroni inequality (4.2), the analyst can therefore conclude at family significance level .02 that a given increase in line speed leads to the same amount of increase in expected scrap in each of the two production lines, but that the expected amount of scrap for any given line speed differs by a constant amount for the two production lines.

We can estimate this constant difference in the regression lines by obtaining a confidence interval for β_2. For a 95 percent confidence interval, we require $t(.975; 23) = 2.069$. Using the results in Table 8.6, we obtain the confidence limits $90.39 \pm 2.069(28.35)$. Hence, the confidence interval for β_2 is:

$$31.7 \leq \beta_2 \leq 149.0$$

We thus conclude, with 95 percent confidence, that the mean amount of scrap for production line 1, at any given line speed, exceeds that for production line 2 by somewhere between 32 and 149.

Instrument Calibration Study Example

The engineer making the calibration study believed that the regression functions relating gauge reading (Y) to actual pressure (X_1) for both instruments are second-order polynomials:

$$E\{Y\} = \beta_0 + \beta_1 X_1 + \beta_2 X_1^2$$

but that they might differ for the two instruments. Hence, the model employed (using a centered variable for X_1 to reduce multicollinearity problems—see Section 8.1) was:

$$Y_i = \beta_0 + \beta_1 x_{i1} + \beta_2 x_{i1}^2 + \beta_3 X_{i2} + \beta_4 x_{i1} X_{i2} + \beta_5 x_{i1}^2 X_{i2} + \varepsilon_i \qquad \textbf{(8.58)}$$

where:

$$x_{i1} = X_{i1} - \bar{X}_1 = \text{centered actual pressure}$$

$$X_{i2} = \begin{cases} 1 & \text{if instrument B} \\ 0 & \text{otherwise} \end{cases}$$

Note that for instrument A, where $X_2 = 0$, the response function is:

$$E\{Y\} = \beta_0 + \beta_1 x_1 + \beta_2 x_1^2 \qquad \text{Instrument A} \quad \textbf{(8.59a)}$$

and for instrument B, where $X_2 = 1$, the response function is:

$$E\{Y\} = (\beta_0 + \beta_3) + (\beta_1 + \beta_4)x_1 + (\beta_2 + \beta_5)x_1^2 \qquad \text{Instrument B} \quad \textbf{(8.59b)}$$

Hence, the test for equality of the two response functions involves the alternatives:

$$H_0: \beta_3 = \beta_4 = \beta_5 = 0$$
$$H_a: \text{not all } \beta_k \text{ in } H_0 \text{ equal zero} \qquad \textbf{(8.60)}$$

and the appropriate test statistic is (7.27):

$$F^* = \frac{SSR(X_2, x_1 X_2, x_1^2 X_2 | x_1, x_1^2)}{3} \div \frac{SSE(x_1, x_1^2, X_2, x_1 X_2, x_1^2 X_2)}{n - 6} \qquad \textbf{(8.60a)}$$

where n represents the combined sample size for both populations.

Comments

1. The approach just described is completely general. If three or more populations are involved, additional indicator variables are simply added to the model.

2. The use of indicator variables for testing whether two or more regression functions are the same is equivalent to the general linear test approach where fitting the full model involves fitting separate regressions to the data from each population, and fitting the reduced model involves fitting one regression to the combined data. ∎

Cited Reference

8.1. Draper, N. R., and H. Smith. *Applied Regression Analysis.* 3rd ed. New York: John Wiley & Sons, 1998.

Problems

8.1. Prepare a contour plot for the quadratic response surface $E\{Y\} = 140 + 4x_1^2 - 2x_2^2 + 5x_1x_2$. Describe the shape of the response surface.

8.2. Prepare a contour plot for the quadratic response surface $E\{Y\} = 124 - 3x_1^2 - 2x_2^2 - 6x_1x_2$. Describe the shape of the response surface.

8.3. A junior investment analyst used a polynomial regression model of relatively high order in a research seminar on municipal bonds and obtained an R^2 of .991 in the regression of net interest yield of bond (Y) on industrial diversity index of municipality (X) for seven bond issues. A classmate, unimpressed, said: "You overfitted. Your curve follows the random effects in the data."

   a. Comment on the criticism.

   b. Might R_a^2 defined in (6.42) be more appropriate than R^2 as a descriptive measure here?

*8.4. Refer to **Muscle mass** Problem 1.27. Second-order regression model (8.2) with independent normal error terms is expected to be appropriate.

   a. Fit regression model (8.2). Plot the fitted regression function and the data. Does the quadratic regression function appear to be a good fit here? Find R^2.

   b. Test whether or not there is a regression relation; use $\alpha = .05$. State the alternatives, decision rule, and conclusion.

   c. Estimate the mean muscle mass for women aged 48 years; use a 95 percent confidence interval. Interpret your interval.

   d. Predict the muscle mass for a woman whose age is 48 years; use a 95 percent prediction interval. Interpret your interval.

   e. Test whether the quadratic term can be dropped from the regression model; use $\alpha = .05$. State the alternatives, decision rule, and conclusion.

   f. Express the fitted regression function obtained in part (a) in terms of the original variable X.

   g. Calculate the coefficient of simple correlation between X and X^2 and between x and x^2. Is the use of a centered variable helpful here?

*8.5. Refer to **Muscle mass** Problems 1.27 and 8.4.

   a. Obtain the residuals from the fit in 8.4a and plot them against $\hat{Y}$ and against x on separate graphs. Also prepare a normal probability plot. Interpret your plots.

   b. Test formally for lack of fit of the quadratic regression function; use $\alpha = .05$. State the alternatives, decision rule, and conclusion. What assumptions did you make implicitly in this test?

c. Fit third-order model (8.6) and test whether or not $\beta_{111} = 0$; use $\alpha = .05$. State the alternatives, decision rule, and conclusion. Is your conclusion consistent with your finding in part (b)?

8.6. **Steroid level.** An endocrinologist was interested in exploring the relationship between the level of a steroid (Y) and age (X) in healthy female subjects whose ages ranged from 8 to 25 years. She collected a sample of 27 healthy females in this age range. The data are given below:

i:	1	2	3	$\ldots$	25	26	27
X_i:	23	19	25	$\ldots$	13	14	18
Y_i:	27.1	22.1	21.9	$\ldots$	12.8	20.8	20.6

a. Fit regression model (8.2). Plot the fitted regression function and the data. Does the quadratic regression function appear to be a good fit here? Find R^2.

b. Test whether or not there is a regression relation; use $\alpha = .01$. State the alternatives, decision rule, and conclusion. What is the P-value of the test?

c. Obtain joint interval estimates for the mean steroid level of females aged 10, 15, and 20, respectively. Use the most efficient simultaneous estimation procedure and a 99 percent family confidence coefficient. Interpret your intervals.

d. Predict the steroid levels of females aged 15 using a 99 percent prediction interval. Interpret your interval.

e. Test whether the quadratic term can be dropped from the model; use $\alpha = .01$. State the alternatives, decision rule, and conclusion.

f. Express the fitted regression function obtained in part (a) in terms of the original variable X.

8.7. Refer to **Steroid level** Problem 8.6.

a. Obtain the residuals and plot them against the fitted values and against x on separate graphs. Also prepare a normal probability plot. What do your plots show?

b. Test formally for lack of fit. Control the risk of a Type I error at .01. State the alternatives, decision rule, and conclusion. What assumptions did you make implicitly in this test?

8.8. Refer to **Commercial properties** Problems 6.18 and 7.7. The vacancy rate predictor (X_3) does not appear to be needed when property age (X_1), operating expenses and taxes (X_2), and total square footage (X_4) are included in the model as predictors of rental rates (Y).

a. The age of the property (X_1) appears to exhibit some curvature when plotted against the rental rates (Y). Fit a polynomial regression model with centered property age (x_1), the square of centered property age (x_1^2), operating expenses and taxes (X_2), and total square footage (X_4). Plot the Y observations against the fitted values. Does the response function provide a good fit?

b. Calculate R_a^2. What information does this measure provide?

c. Test whether or not the the square of centered property age (x_1^2) can be dropped from the model; use $\alpha = .05$. State the alternatives, decision rule, and conclusion. What is the P-value of the test?

d. Estimate the mean rental rate when $X_1 = 8$, $X_2 = 16$, and $X_4 = 250,000$; use a 95 percent confidence interval. Interpret your interval.

e. Express the fitted response function obtained in part (a) in the original X variables.

8.9. Consider the response function $E\{Y\} = 25 + 3X_1 + 4X_2 + 1.5X_1X_2$.

a. Prepare a conditional effects plot of the response function against X_1 when $X_2 = 3$ and when $X_2 = 6$. How is the interaction effect of X_1 and X_2 on Y apparent from this graph? Describe the nature of the interaction effect.

b. Plot a set of contour curves for the response surface. How is the interaction effect of X_1 and X_2 on Y apparent from this graph?

8.10. Consider the response function $E\{Y\} = 14 + 7X_1 + 5X_2 - 4X_1X_2$.

   a. Prepare a conditional effects plot of the response function against X_2 when $X_1 = 1$ and when $X_1 = 4$. How does the graph indicate that the effects of X_1 and X_2 on Y are not additive? What is the nature of the interaction effect?

   b. Plot a set of contour curves for the response surface. How does the graph indicate that the effects of X_1 and X_2 on Y are not additive?

8.11. Refer to **Brand preference** Problem 6.5.

   a. Fit regression model (8.22).

   b. Test whether or not the interaction term can be dropped from the model; use $\alpha = .05$. State the alternatives, decision rule, and conclusion.

8.12. A student who used a regression model that included indicator variables was upset when receiving only the following output on the multiple regression printout: XTRANSPOSE X SINGULAR. What is a likely source of the difficulty?

8.13. Refer to regression model (8.33). Portray graphically the response curves for this model if $\beta_0 = 25.3$, $\beta_1 = .20$, and $\beta_2 = -12.1$.

8.14. In a regression study of factors affecting learning time for a certain task (measured in minutes), gender of learner was included as a predictor variable (X_2) that was coded $X_2 = 1$ if male and 0 if female. It was found that $b_2 = 22.3$ and $s\{b_2\} = 3.8$. An observer questioned whether the coding scheme for gender is fair because it results in a positive coefficient, leading to longer learning times for males than females. Comment.

8.15. Refer to **Copier maintenance** Problem 1.20. The users of the copiers are either training institutions that use a small model, or business firms that use a large, commercial model. An analyst at Tri-City wishes to fit a regression model including both number of copiers serviced (X_1) and type of copier (X_2) as predictor variables and estimate the effect of copier model (S—small, L—large) on number of minutes spent on the service call. Records show that the models serviced in the 45 calls were:

i:	1	2	3	$\ldots$	43	44	45
X_{i2}:	S	L	L	$\ldots$	L	L	L

Assume that regression model (8.33) is appropriate, and let $X_2 = 1$ if small model and 0 if large, commercial model.

   a. Explain the meaning of all regression coefficients in the model.

   b. Fit the regression model and state the estimated regression function.

   c. Estimate the effect of copier model on mean service time with a 95 percent confidence interval. Interpret your interval estimate.

   d. Why would the analyst wish to include X_1, number of copiers, in the regression model when interest is in estimating the effect of type of copier model on service time?

   e. Obtain the residuals and plot them against X_1X_2. Is there any indication that an interaction term in the regression model would be helpful?

8.16. Refer to **Grade point average** Problem 1.19. An assistant to the director of admissions conjectured that the predictive power of the model could be improved by adding information on whether the student had chosen a major field of concentration at the time the application was submitted. Assume that regression model (8.33) is appropriate, where X_1 is entrance test score and $X_2 = 1$ if student had indicated a major field of concentration at the time of application and 0 if the major field was undecided. Data for X_2 were as follows:

i:	1	2	3	...	118	119	120
X_{i2}:	0	1	0	...	1	1	0

a. Explain how each regression coefficient in model (8.33) is interpreted here.

b. Fit the regression model and state the estimated regression function.

c. Test whether the X_2 variable can be dropped from the regression model; use $\alpha = .01$. State the alternatives, decision rule, and conclusion.

d. Obtain the residuals for regression model (8.33) and plot them against $X_1 X_2$. Is there any evidence in your plot that it would be helpful to include an interaction term in the model?

8.17. Refer to regression models (8.33) and (8.49). Would the conclusion that $\beta_2 = 0$ have the same implication for each of these models? Explain.

8.18. Refer to regression model (8.49). Portray graphically the response curves for this model if $\beta_0 = 25$, $\beta_1 = .30$, $\beta_2 = -12.5$, and $\beta_3 = .05$. Describe the nature of the interaction effect.

*8.19. Refer to **Copier maintenance** Problems 1.20 and 8.15.

a. Fit regression model (8.49) and state the estimated regression function.

b. Test whether the interaction term can be dropped from the model; control the α risk at .10. State the alternatives, decision rule, and conclusion. What is the P-value of the test? If the interaction term cannot be dropped from the model, describe the nature of the interaction effect.

8.20. Refer to **Grade point average** Problems 1.19 and 8.16.

a. Fit regression model (8.49) and state the estimated regression function.

b. Test whether the interaction term can be dropped from the model; use $\alpha = .05$. State the alternatives, decision rule, and conclusion. If the interaction term cannot be dropped from the model, describe the nature of the interaction effect.

8.21. In a regression analysis of on-the-job head injuries of warehouse laborers caused by falling objects, Y is a measure of severity of the injury, X_1 is an index reflecting both the weight of the object and the distance it fell, and X_2 and X_3 are indicator variables for nature of head protection worn at the time of the accident, coded as follows:

Type of Protection	X_2	X_3
Hard hat	1	0
Bump cap	0	1
None	0	0

The response function to be used in the study is $E\{Y\} = \beta_0 + \beta_1 X_1 + \beta_2 X_2 + \beta_3 X_3$.

a. Develop the response function for each type of protection category.

b. For each of the following questions, specify the alternatives H_0 and H_a for the appropriate test: (1) With X_1 fixed, does wearing a bump cap reduce the expected severity of injury as compared with wearing no protection? (2) With X_1 fixed, is the expected severity of injury the same when wearing a hard hat as when wearing a bump cap?

8.22. Refer to tool wear regression model (8.36). Suppose the indicator variables had been defined as follows: $X_2 = 1$ if tool model M2 and 0 otherwise, $X_3 = 1$ if tool model M3 and 0 otherwise, $X_4 = 1$ if tool model M4 and 0 otherwise. Indicate the meaning of each of the following: (1) β_3, (2) $\beta_4 - \beta_3$, (3) β_1.

8.23. A marketing research trainee in the national office of a chain of shoe stores used the following response function to study seasonal (winter, spring, summer, fall) effects on sales of a certain line of shoes: $E\{Y\} = \beta_0 + \beta_1 X_1 + \beta_2 X_2 + \beta_3 X_3$. The Xs are indicator variables defined as follows: $X_1 = 1$ if winter and 0 otherwise, $X_2 = 1$ if spring and 0 otherwise, $X_3 = 1$ if fall and 0 otherwise. After fitting the model, the trainee tested the regression coefficients β_k ($k = 0, \ldots, 3$) and came to the following set of conclusions at an .05 family level of significance: $\beta_0 \neq 0$, $\beta_1 = 0$, $\beta_2 \neq 0$, $\beta_3 \neq 0$. In the report the trainee then wrote: "Results of regression analysis show that climatic and other seasonal factors have no influence in determining sales of this shoe line in the winter. Seasonal influences do exist in the other seasons." Do you agree with this interpretation of the test results? Discuss.

8.24. **Assessed valuations.** A tax consultant studied the current relation between selling price and assessed valuation of one-family residential dwellings in a large tax district by obtaining data for a random sample of 16 recent "arm's-length" sales transactions of one-family dwellings located on corner lots and for a random sample of 48 recent sales of one-family dwellings not located on corner lots. In the data that follow, both selling price (Y) and assessed valuation (X_1) are expressed in thousand dollars, whereas lot location (X_2) is coded 1 for corner lots and 0 for non-corner lots.

i:	1	2	3	...	62	63	64
X_{i1}:	76.4	74.3	69.6	...	79.4	74.7	71.5
X_{i2}:	0	0	0	...	0	0	1
Y_i:	78.8	73.8	64.6	...	97.6	84.4	70.5

Assume that the error variances in the two populations are equal and that regression model (8.49) is appropriate.

a. Plot the sample data for the two populations as a symbolic scatter plot. Does the regression relation appear to be the same for the two populations?

b. Test for identity of the regression functions for dwellings on corner lots and dwellings in other locations; control the risk of Type I error at .05. State the alternatives, decision rule, and conclusion.

c. Plot the estimated regression functions for the two populations and describe the nature of the differences between them.

8.25. Refer to **Grocery retailer** Problems 6.9 and 7.4.

a. Fit regression model (8.58) using the number of cases shipped (X_1) and the binary variable (X_3) as predictors.

b. Test whether or not the interaction terms and the quadratic term can be dropped from the model; use $\alpha = .05$. State the alternatives, decision rule, and conclusion. What is the P-value of the test?

8.26. In time series analysis, the X variable representing time usually is defined to take on values 1, 2, etc., for the successive time periods. Does this represent an allocated code when the time periods are actually 1989, 1990, etc.?

8.27. An analyst wishes to include number of older siblings in family as a predictor variable in a regression analysis of factors affecting maturation in eighth graders. The number of older siblings in the sample observations ranges from 0 to 4. Discuss whether this variable should be placed in the model as an ordinary quantitative variable or by means of four 0, 1 indicator variables.

8.28. Refer to regression model (8.31) for the insurance innovation study. Suppose β_0 were dropped from the model to eliminate the linear dependence in the **X** matrix so that the model becomes $Y_i = \beta_1 X_{i1} + \beta_2 X_{i2} + \beta_3 X_{i3} + \varepsilon_i$. What is the meaning here of each of the regression coefficients β_1, β_2, and β_3?

Exercises   8.29. Consider the second-order regression model with one predictor variable in (8.2) and the following two sets of X values:

Set 1:	1.0	1.5	1.1	1.3	1.9	.8	1.2	1.4
Set 2:	12	1	123	17	415	71	283	38

For each set, calculate the coefficient of correlation between X and X^2, then between x and x^2. Also calculate the coefficients of correlation between X and X^3 and between x and x^3. What generalizations are suggested by your results?

8.30. (Calculus needed.) Refer to second-order response function (8.3). Explain precisely the meaning of the linear effect coefficient β_1 and the quadratic effect coefficient β_{11}.

8.31. a. Derive the expressions for b_0', b_1', and b_{11}' in (8.12).

   b. Using (5.46), obtain the variance-covariance matrix for the regression coefficients pertaining to the original X variable in terms of the variance-covariance matrix for the regression coefficients pertaining to the transformed x variable.

8.32. How are the normal equations (8.4) simplified if the X values are equally spaced, such as the time series representation $X_1 = 1$, $X_2 = 2, \ldots, X_n = n$?

8.33. Refer to the instrument calibration study example in Section 8.7. Suppose that three instruments (A, B, C) had been developed to identical specifications, that the regression functions relating gauge reading (Y) to actual pressure (X_1) are second-order polynomials for each instrument, that the error variances are the same, and that the polynomial coefficients may differ from one instrument to the next. Let X_3 denote a second indicator variable, where $X_3 = 1$ if instrument C and 0 otherwise.

   a. Expand regression model (8.58) to cover this situation.

   b. State the alternatives, define the test statistic, and give the decision rule for each of the following tests when the level of significance is .01: (1) test whether the second-order regression functions for the three instruments are identical, (2) test whether all three regression functions have the same intercept, (3) test whether both the linear and quadratic effects are the same in all three regression functions.

8.34. In a regression study, three types of banks were involved, namely, commercial, mutual savings, and savings and loan. Consider the following system of indicator variables for type of bank:

Type of Bank	X_2	X_3
Commercial	1	0
Mutual savings	0	1
Savings and loan	−1	−1

   a. Develop a first-order linear regression model for relating last year's profit or loss (Y) to size of bank (X_1) and type of bank (X_2, X_3).

   b. State the response functions for the three types of banks.

   c. Interpret each of the following quantities: (1) β_2, (2) β_3, (3) $-\beta_2 - \beta_3$.

8.35. Refer to regression model (8.54) and exclude variable X_3.

   a. Obtain the $\mathbf{X'X}$ matrix for this special case of a single qualitative predictor variable, for $i = 1, \ldots, n$ when n_1 firms are not incorporated.

   b. Using (6.25), find $\mathbf{b}$.

   c. Using (6.35) and (6.36), find SSE and SSR.

Projects

8.36. Refer to the **CDI** data set in Appendix C.2. It is desired to fit second-order regression model (8.2) for relating number of active physicians (Y) to total population (X).

    a. Fit the second-order regression model. Plot the residuals against the fitted values. How well does the second-order model appear to fit the data?

    b. Obtain R^2 for the second-order regression model. Also obtain the coefficient of simple determination for the first-order regression model. Has the addition of the quadratic term in the regression model substantially increased the coefficient of determination?

    c. Test whether the quadratic term can be dropped from the regression model; use $\alpha = .05$. State the alternatives, decision rule, and conclusion.

8.37. Refer to the **CDI** data set in Appendix C.2. A regression model relating serious crime rate (Y, total serious crimes divided by total population) to population density (X_1, total population divided by land area) and unemployment rate (X_3) is to be constructed.

    a. Fit second-order regression model (8.8). Plot the residuals against the fitted values. How well does the second-order model appear to fit the data? What is R^2?

    b. Test whether or not all quadratic and interaction terms can be dropped from the regression model; use $\alpha = .01$. State the alternatives, decision rule, and conclusion.

    c. Instead of the predictor variable population density, total population (X_1) and land area (X_2) are to be employed as separate predictor variables, in addition to unemployment rate (X_3). The regression model should contain linear and quadratic terms for total population, and linear terms only for land area and unemployment rate. (No interaction terms are to be included in this model.) Fit this regression model and obtain R^2. Is this coefficient of multiple determination substantially different from the one for the regression model in part (a)?

8.38. Refer to the **SENIC** data set in Appendix C.1. Second-order regression model (8.2) is to be fitted for relating number of nurses (Y) to available facilities and services (X).

    a. Fit the second-order regression model. Plot the residuals against the fitted values. How well does the second-order model appear to fit the data?

    b. Obtain R^2 for the second-order regression model. Also obtain the coefficient of simple determination for the first-order regression model. Has the addition of the quadratic term in the regression model substantially increased the coefficient of determination?

    c. Test whether the quadratic term can be dropped from the regression model; use $\alpha = .01$. State the alternatives, decision rule, and conclusion.

8.39. Refer to the **CDI** data set in Appendix C.2. The number of active physicians (Y) is to be regressed against total population (X_1), total personal income (X_2), and geographic region (X_3, X_4, X_5).

    a. Fit a first-order regression model. Let $X_3 = 1$ if NE and 0 otherwise, $X_4 = 1$ if NC and 0 otherwise, and $X_5 = 1$ if S and 0 otherwise.

    b. Examine whether the effect for the northeastern region on number of active physicians differs from the effect for the north central region by constructing an appropriate 90 percent confidence interval. Interpret your interval estimate.

    c. Test whether any geographic effects are present; use $\alpha = .10$. State the alternatives, decision rule, and conclusion. What is the P-value of the test?

8.40. Refer to the **SENIC** data set in Appendix C.1. Infection risk (Y) is to be regressed against length of stay (X_1), age (X_2), routine chest X-ray ratio (X_3), and medical school affiliation (X_4).

    a. Fit a first-order regression model. Let $X_4 = 1$ if hospital has medical school affiliation and 0 if not.

b. Estimate the effect of medical school affiliation on infection risk using a 98 percent confidence interval. Interpret your interval estimate.

c. It has been suggested that the effect of medical school affiliation on infection risk may interact with the effects of age and routine chest X-ray ratio. Add appropriate interaction terms to the regression model, fit the revised regression model, and test whether the interaction terms are helpful; use $\alpha = .10$. State the alternatives, decision rule, and conclusion.

8.41. Refer to the **SENIC** data set in Appendix C.1. Length of stay (Y) is to be regressed on age (X_1), routine culturing ratio (X_2), average daily census (X_3), available facilities and services (X_4), and region (X_5, X_6, X_7).

a. Fit a first-order regression model. Let $X_5 = 1$ if NE and 0 otherwise, $X_6 = 1$ if NC and 0 otherwise, and $X_7 = 1$ if S and 0 otherwise.

b. Test whether the routine culturing ratio can be dropped from the model; use a level of significance of .05. State the alternatives, decision rule, and conclusion.

c. Examine whether the effect on length of stay for hospitals located in the western region differs from that for hospitals located in the other three regions by constructing an appropriate confidence interval for each pairwise comparison. Use the Bonferroni procedure with a 95 percent family confidence coefficient. Summarize your findings.

8.42. Refer to **Market share** data set in Appendix C.3. Company executives want to be able to predict market share of their product (Y) based on merchandise price (X_1), the gross Nielsen rating points (X_2, an index of the amount of advertising exposure that the product received); the presence or absence of a wholesale pricing discount ($X_3 = 1$ if discount present; otherwise $X_3 = 0$); the presence or absence of a package promotion during the period ($X_4 = 1$ if promotion present; otherwise $X_4 = 0$); and year (X_5). Code year as a nominal level variable and use 2000 as the referent year.

a. Fit a first-order regression model. Plot the residuals against the fitted values. How well does the first-order model appear to fit the data?

b. Re-fit the model in part (a), after adding all second-order terms involving only the quantitative predictors. Test whether or not all quadratic and interaction terms can be dropped from the regression model; use $\alpha = .05$. State the alternatives, decision rule, and conclusion.

c. In part (a), test whether advertising index (X_2) and year (X_5) can be dropped from the model; use $\alpha = .05$. State the alternatives, decision rule, and conclusion.

Case Study

8.43. Refer to **University admissions** data set in Appendix C.4. The director of admissions at a state university wished to determine how accurately students' grade-point averages at the end of their freshman year (Y) can be predicted from the entrance examination (ACT) test score (X_2); the high school class rank (X_1, a percentile where 99 indicates student is at or near the top of his or her class and 1 indicates student is at or near the bottom of the class); and the academic year (X_3). The academic year variable covers the years 1996 through 2000. Develop a prediction model for the director of admissions. Justify your choice of model. Assess your model's ability to predict and discuss its use as a tool for admissions decisions.

Chapter 9

Building the Regression Model I: Model Selection and Validation

In earlier chapters, we considered how to fit simple and multiple regression models and how to make inferences from these models. In this chapter, we first present an overview of the model-building and model-validation process. Then we consider in more detail some special issues in the selection of the predictor variables for exploratory observational studies. We conclude the chapter with a detailed description of methods for validating regression models.

9.1 Overview of Model-Building Process

At the risk of oversimplifying, we present in Figure 9.1 a strategy for the building of a regression model. This strategy involves three or, sometimes, four phases:

1. Data collection and preparation
2. Reduction of explanatory or predictor variables (for exploratory observational studies)
3. Model refinement and selection
4. Model validation

We consider each of these phases in turn.

Data Collection

The data collection requirements for building a regression model vary with the nature of the study. It is useful to distinguish four types of studies.

Controlled Experiments. In a controlled experiment, the experimenter controls the levels of the explanatory variables and assigns a treatment, consisting of a combination of levels of the explanatory variables, to each experimental unit and observes the response. For example, an experimenter studied the effects of the size of a graphic presentation and the time allowed for analysis of the accuracy with which the analysis of the presentation is carried out. Here, the response variable is a measure of the accuracy of the analysis, and the explanatory variables are the size of the graphic presentation and the time allowed. Junior

FIGURE 9.1
Strategy for Building a Regression Model.

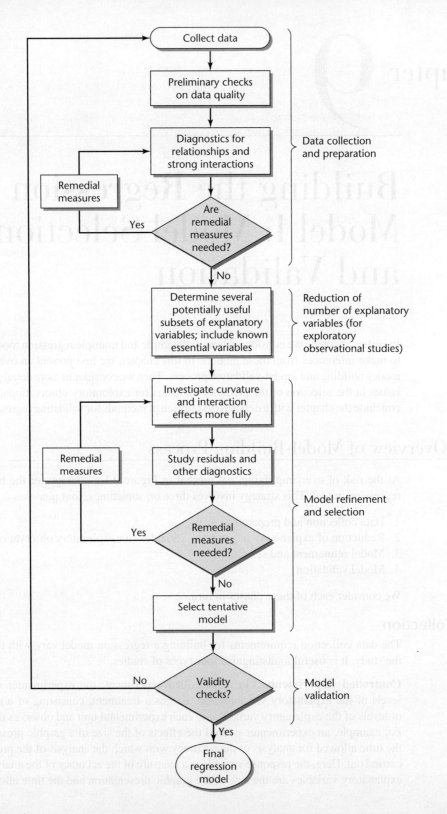

executives were used as the experimental units. A treatment consisted of a particular combination of size of presentation and length of time allowed. In controlled experiments, the explanatory variables are often called *factors* or *control variables*.

The data collection requirements for controlled experiments are straightforward, though not necessarily simple. Observations for each experimental unit are needed on the response variable and on the level of each of the control variables used for that experimental unit. There may be difficult measurement and scaling problems for the response variable that are unique to the area of application.

Controlled Experiments with Covariates. Statistical design of experiments uses supplemental information, such as characteristics of the experimental units, in designing the experiment so as to reduce the variance of the experimental error terms in the regression model. Sometimes, however, it is not possible to incorporate this supplemental information into the design of the experiment. Instead, it may be possible for the experimenter to incorporate this information into the regression model and thereby reduce the error variance by including *uncontrolled variables* or *covariates* in the model.

In our previous example involving the accuracy of analysis of graphic presentations, the experimenter suspected that gender and number of years of education could affect the accuracy responses in important ways. Because of time constraints, the experimenter was able to use only a completely randomized design, which does not incorporate any supplemental information into the design. The experimenter therefore also collected data on two uncontrolled variables (gender and number of years of education of the junior executives) in case that use of these covariates in the regression model would make the analysis of the effects of the explanatory variables (size of graphic presentation, time allowed) on the accuracy response more precise.

Confirmatory Observational Studies. These studies, based on observational, not experimental, data, are intended to test (i.e., to confirm or not to confirm) hypotheses derived from previous studies or from hunches. For these studies, data are collected for explanatory variables that previous studies have shown to affect the response variable, as well as for the new variable or variables involved in the hypothesis. In this context, the explanatory variable(s) involved in the hypothesis are sometimes called the *primary variables,* and the explanatory variables that are included to reflect existing knowledge are called the *control variables* (*known risk factors* in epidemiology). The control variables here are not controlled as in an experimental study, but they are used to account for known influences on the response variable. For example, in an observational study of the effect of vitamin E supplements on the occurrence of a certain type of cancer, known risk factors, such as age, gender, and race, would be included as control variables and the amount of vitamin E supplements taken daily would be the primary explanatory variable. The response variable would be the occurrence of the particular type of cancer during the period under consideration. (The use of qualitative response variables in a regression model will be considered in Chapter 14.)

Data collection for confirmatory observational studies involves obtaining observations on the response variable, the control variables, and the primary explanatory variable(s). Here, as in controlled experiments, there may be important and complex problems of measurement, such as how to obtain reliable data on the amount of vitamin supplements taken daily.

Exploratory Observational Studies. In the social, behavioral, and health sciences, management, and other fields, it is often not possible to conduct controlled experiments.

Furthermore, adequate knowledge for conducting confirmatory observational studies may be lacking. As a result, many studies in these fields are exploratory observational studies where investigators search for explanatory variables that might be related to the response variable. To complicate matters further, any available theoretical models may involve explanatory variables that are not directly measurable, such as a family's future earnings over the next 10 years. Under these conditions, investigators are often forced to prospect for explanatory variables that could conceivably be related to the response variable under study. Obviously, such a set of potentially useful explanatory variables can be large. For example, a company's sales of portable dishwashers in a district may be affected by population size, per capita income, percent of population in urban areas, percent of population under 50 years of age, percent of families with children at home, etc., etc.!

After a lengthy list of potentially useful explanatory variables has been compiled, some of these variables can be quickly screened out. An explanatory variable (1) may not be fundamental to the problem, (2) may be subject to large measurement errors, and/or (3) may effectively duplicate another explanatory variable in the list. Explanatory variables that cannot be measured may either be deleted or replaced by proxy variables that are highly correlated with them.

The number of cases to be collected for an exploratory observational regression study depends on the size of the pool of potentially useful explanatory variables available at this stage. More cases are required when the pool is large than when it is small. A general rule of thumb states that there should be at least 6 to 10 cases for every variable in the pool. The actual data collection for the pool of potentially useful explanatory variables and for the response variable again may involve important issues of measurement, just as for the other types of studies.

Data Preparation

Once the data have been collected, edit checks should be performed and plots prepared to identify gross data errors as well as extreme outliers. Difficulties with data errors are especially prevalent in large data sets and should be corrected or resolved before the model building begins. Whenever possible, the investigator should carefully monitor and control the data collection process to reduce the likelihood of data errors.

Preliminary Model Investigation

Once the data have been properly edited, the formal modeling process can begin. A variety of diagnostics should be employed to identify (1) the functional forms in which the explanatory variables should enter the regression model and (2) important interactions that should be included in the model. Scatter plots and residual plots are useful for determining relationships and their strengths. Selected explanatory variables can be fitted in regression functions to explore relationships, possible strong interactions, and the need for transformations. Whenever possible, of course, one should also rely on the investigator's prior knowledge and expertise to suggest appropriate transformations and interactions to investigate. This is particularly important when the number of potentially useful explanatory variables is large. In this case, it may be very difficult to investigate all possible pairwise interactions, and prior knowledge should be used to identify the important ones. The diagnostic procedures explained in previous chapters and in Chapter 10 should be used as resources in this phase of model building.

Reduction of Explanatory Variables

Controlled Experiments. The reduction of explanatory variables in the model-building phase is usually not an important issue for controlled experiments. The experimenter has chosen the explanatory variables for investigation, and a regression model is to be developed that will enable the investigator to study the effects of these variables on the response variable. After the model has been developed, including the use of appropriate functional forms for the variables and the inclusion of important interaction terms, the inferential procedures considered in previous chapters will be used to determine whether the explanatory variables have effects on the response variable and, if so, the nature and magnitude of the effects.

Controlled Experiments with Covariates. In studies of controlled experiments with covariates, some reduction of the covariates may take place because investigators often cannot be sure in advance that the selected covariates will be helpful in reducing the error variance. For instance, the investigator in our graphic presentation example may wish to examine at this stage of the model-building process whether gender and number of years of education are related to the accuracy response, as had been anticipated. If not, the investigator would wish to drop them as not being helpful in reducing the model error variance and, therefore, in the analysis of the effects of the explanatory variables on the response variable. The number of covariates considered in controlled experiments is usually small, so no special problems are encountered in determining whether some or all of the covariates should be dropped from the regression model.

Confirmatory Observational Studies. Generally, no reduction of explanatory variables should take place in confirmatory observational studies. The control variables were chosen on the basis of prior knowledge and should be retained for comparison with earlier studies even if some of the control variables turn out not to lead to any error variance reduction in the study at hand. The primary variables are the ones whose influence on the response variable is to be examined and therefore need to be present in the model.

Exploratory Observational Studies. In exploratory observational studies, the number of explanatory variables that remain after the initial screening typically is still large. Further, many of these variables frequently will be highly intercorrelated. Hence, the investigator usually will wish to reduce the number of explanatory variables to be used in the final model. There are several reasons for this. A regression model with numerous explanatory variables may be difficult to maintain. Further, regression models with a limited number of explanatory variables are easier to work with and understand. Finally, the presence of many highly intercorrelated explanatory variables may substantially increase the sampling variation of the regression coefficients, detract from the model's descriptive abilities, increase the problem of roundoff errors (as noted in Chapter 7), and not improve, or even worsen, the model's predictive ability. An actual worsening of the model's predictive ability can occur when explanatory variables are kept in the regression model that are not related to the response variable, given the other explanatory variables in the model. In that case, the variances of the fitted values $\sigma^2\{\hat{Y}_i\}$ tend to become larger with the inclusion of the useless additional explanatory variables.

Hence, once the investigator has tentatively decided upon the functional form of the regression relations (whether given variables are to appear in linear form, quadratic form, etc.) and whether any interaction terms are to be included, the next step in many exploratory observational studies is to identify a few "good" subsets of X variables for further intensive study. These subsets should include not only the potential explanatory variables in first-order form but also any needed quadratic and other curvature terms and any necessary interaction terms.

The identification of "good" subsets of potentially useful explanatory variables to be included in the final regression model and the determination of appropriate functional and interaction relations for these variables usually constitute some of the most difficult problems in regression analysis. Since the uses of regression models vary, no one subset of explanatory variables may always be "best." For instance, a descriptive use of a regression model typically will emphasize precise estimation of the regression coefficients, whereas a predictive use will focus on the prediction errors. Often, different subsets of the pool of potential explanatory variables will best serve these varying purposes. Even for a given purpose, it is often found that several subsets are about equally "good" according to a given criterion, and the choice among these "good" subsets needs to be made on the basis of additional considerations.

The choice of a few appropriate subsets of explanatory variables for final consideration in exploratory observational studies needs to be done with great care. Elimination of key explanatory variables can seriously damage the explanatory power of the model and lead to biased estimates of regression coefficients, mean responses, and predictions of new observations, as well as biased estimates of the error variance. The bias in these estimates is related to the fact that with observational data, the error terms in an underfitted regression model may reflect nonrandom effects of the explanatory variables not incorporated in the regression model. Important omitted explanatory variables are sometimes called *latent explanatory variables*.

On the other hand, if too many explanatory variables are included in the subset, then this overfitted model will often result in variances of estimated parameters that are larger than those for simpler models.

Another danger with observational data is that important explanatory variables may be observed only over narrow ranges. As a result, such important explanatory variables may be omitted just because they occur in the sample within a narrow range of values and therefore turn out to be statistically nonsignificant.

Another consideration in identifying subsets of explanatory variables is that these subsets need to be small enough so that maintenance costs are manageable and analysis is facilitated, yet large enough so that adequate description, control, or prediction is possible.

A variety of computerized approaches have been developed to assist the investigator in reducing the number of potential explanatory variables in an exploratory observational study when these variables are correlated among themselves. We present two of these approaches in this chapter. The first, which is practical for pools of explanatory variables that are small or moderate in size, considers all possible subsets of explanatory variables that can be developed from the pool of potential explanatory variables and identifies those subsets that are "good" according to a criterion specified by the investigator. The second approach employs automatic search procedures to arrive at a single subset of the explanatory variables. This approach is recommended primarily for reductions involving large pools of explanatory variables.

Even though computerized approaches can be very helpful in identifying appropriate subsets for detailed, final consideration, the process of developing a useful regression model must be pragmatic and needs to utilize large doses of subjective judgment. Explanatory variables that are considered essential should be included in the regression model before any computerized assistance is sought. Further, computerized approaches that identify only a single subset of explanatory variables as "best" need to be supplemented so that additional subsets are also considered before the final regression model is decided upon.

Comments

1. All too often, unwary investigators will screen a set of explanatory variables by fitting the regression model containing the entire set of potential X variables and then simply dropping those for which the t^* statistic (7.25):

$$t_k^* = \frac{b_k}{s\{b_k\}}$$

has a small absolute value. As we know from Chapter 7, this procedure can lead to the dropping of important intercorrelated explanatory variables. Clearly, a good search procedure must be able to handle important intercorrelated explanatory variables in such a way that not all of them will be dropped.

2. Controlled experiments can usually avoid many of the problems in exploratory observational studies. For example, the effects of latent predictor variables are minimized by using randomization. In addition, adequate ranges of the explanatory variables can be selected and correlations among the explanatory variables can be eliminated by appropriate choices of their levels. ∎

Model Refinement and Selection

At this stage in the model-building process, the tentative regression model, or the several "good" regression models in the case of exploratory observational studies, need to be checked in detail for curvature and interaction effects. Residual plots are helpful in deciding whether one model is to be preferred over another. In addition, the diagnostic checks to be described in Chapter 10 are useful for identifying influential outlying observations, multicollinearity, etc.

The selection of the ultimate regression model often depends greatly upon these diagnostic results. For example, one fitted model may be very much influenced by a single case, whereas another is not. Again, one fitted model may show correlations among the error terms, whereas another does not.

When repeat observations are available, formal tests for lack of fit can be made. In any case, a variety of residual plots and analyses can be employed to identify any lack of fit, outliers, and influential observations. For instance, residual plots against cross-product and/or power terms not included in the regression model can be useful in identifying ways in which the model fit can be improved further.

When an automatic selection procedure is utilized for an exploratory observational study and only a single model is identified as "best," other models should also be explored. One procedure is to use the number of explanatory variables in the model identified as "best" as an estimate of the number of explanatory variables needed in the regression model. Then the investigator explores and identifies other candidate models with approximately the same number of explanatory variables identified by the automatic procedure.

Eventually, after thorough checking and various remedial actions, such as transformations, the investigator narrows the number of competing models to one or just a few. At this point, it is good statistical practice to assess the validity of the remaining candidates through model validation studies. These methods can be used to help decide upon a final regression model, and to determine how well the model will perform in practice.

Model Validation

Model validity refers to the stability and reasonableness of the regression coefficients, the plausibility and usability of the regression function, and the ability to generalize inferences drawn from the regression analysis. Validation is a useful and necessary part of the model-building process. Several methods of assessing model validity will be described in Section 9.6.

9.2   Surgical Unit Example

With the completion of this overview of the model-building process for a regression study, we next present an example that will be used to illustrate all stages of this process as they are taken up in this and the following two chapters. A hospital surgical unit was interested in predicting survival in patients undergoing a particular type of liver operation. A random selection of 108 patients was available for analysis. From each patient record, the following information was extracted from the preoperation evaluation:

X_1 blood clotting score
X_2 prognostic index
X_3 enzyme function test score
X_4 liver function test score
X_5 age, in years
X_6 indicator variable for gender ($0 =$ male, $1 =$ female)
X_7 and X_8 indicator variables for history of alcohol use:

Alcohol Use	X_7	X_8
None	0	0
Moderate	1	0
Severe	0	1

These constitute the pool of potential explanatory or predictor variables for a predictive regression model. The response variable is survival time, which was ascertained in a follow-up study. A portion of the data on the potential predictor variables and the response variable is presented in Table 9.1. These data have already been screened and properly edited for errors.

TABLE 9.1   Potential Predictor Variables and Response Variable—Surgical Unit Example.

Case Number i	Blood-Clotting Score X_{i1}	Prognostic Index X_{i2}	Enzyme Test X_{i3}	Liver Test X_{i4}	Age X_{i5}	Gender X_{i6}	Alc. Use: Mod. X_{i7}	Alc. Use: Heavy X_{i8}	Survival Time Y_i	$Y_i' = \ln Y_i$
1	6.7	62	81	2.59	50	0	1	0	695	6.544
2	5.1	59	66	1.70	39	0	0	0	403	5.999
3	7.4	57	83	2.16	55	0	0	0	710	6.565
...	...	...	...	...	...	...	...	...	...	...
52	6.4	85	40	1.21	58	0	0	1	579	6.361
53	6.4	59	85	2.33	63	0	1	0	550	6.310
54	8.8	78	72	3.20	56	0	0	0	651	6.478

To illustrate the model-building procedures discussed in this and the next section, we will use only the first four explanatory variables. By limiting the number of potential explanatory variables, we can explain the procedures without overwhelming the reader with masses of computer printouts. We will also use only the first 54 of the 108 patients.

Since the pool of predictor variables is small, a reasonably full exploration of relationships and of possible strong interaction effects is possible at this stage of data preparation. Stem-and-leaf plots were prepared for each of the predictor variables (not shown). These highlighted several cases as outlying with respect to the explanatory variables. The investigator was thereby alerted to examine later the influence of these cases. A scatter plot matrix and the correlation matrix were also obtained (not shown).

A first-order regression model based on all predictor variables was fitted to serve as a starting point. A plot of residuals against predicted values for this fitted model is shown in Figure 9.2a. The plot suggests that both curvature and nonconstant error variance are apparent. In addition, some departure from normality is suggested by the normal probability plot of residuals in Figure 9.2b.

To make the distribution of the error terms more nearly normal and to see if the same transformation would also reduce the apparent curvature, the investigator examined the

FIGURE 9.2
Some Preliminary Residual Plots—Surgical Unit Example.

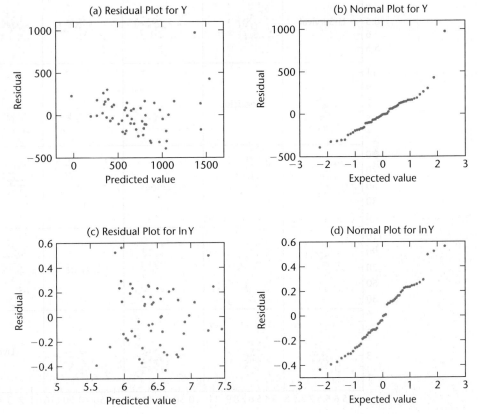

logarithmic transformation $Y' = \ln Y$. Data for the transformed response variable are also given in Table 9.1. Figure 9.2c shows a plot of residuals against fitted values when Y' is regressed on all four predictor variables in a first-order model; also the normal probability plot of residuals for the transformed data shows that the distribution of the error terms is more nearly normal.

The investigator also obtained a scatter plot matrix and the correlation matrix with the transformed Y variable; these are presented in Figure 9.3. In addition, various scatter and

FIGURE 9.3

JMP Scatter Plot Matrix and Correlation Matrix when Response Variable Is Y'—Surgical Unit Example.

Multivariate Correlations

	LnSurvival	Bloodclot	Progindex	Enzyme	Liver
LnSurvival	1.0000	0.2462	0.4699	0.6539	0.6493
Bloodclot	0.2462	1.0000	0.0901	−0.1496	0.5024
Progindex	0.4699	0.0901	1.0000	−0.0236	0.3690
Enzyme	0.6539	−0.1496	−0.0236	1.0000	0.4164
Liver	0.6493	0.5024	0.3690	0.4164	1.0000

Scatterplot Matrix

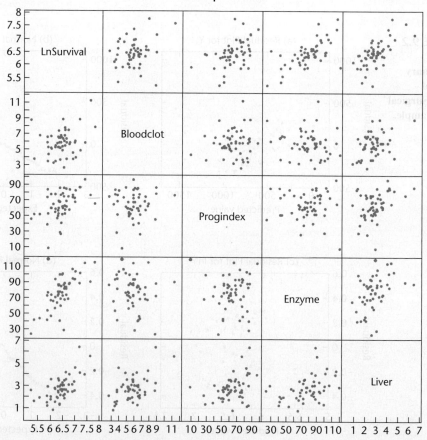

residual plots were obtained (not shown here). All of these plots indicate that each of the predictor variables is linearly associated with Y', with X_3 and X_4 showing the highest degrees of association and X_1 the lowest. The scatter plot matrix and the correlation matrix further show intercorrelations among the potential predictor variables. In particular, X_4 has moderately high pairwise correlations with X_1, X_2, and X_3.

On the basis of these analyses, the investigator concluded to use, at this stage of the model-building process, $Y' = \ln Y$ as the response variable, to represent the predictor variables in linear terms, and not to include any interaction terms. The next stage in the model-building process is to examine whether all of the potential predictor variables are needed or whether a subset of them is adequate. A number of useful measures have been developed to assess the adequacy of the various subsets. We now turn to a discussion of these measures.

9.3 Criteria for Model Selection

From any set of $p - 1$ predictors, 2^{p-1} alternative models can be constructed. This calculation is based on the fact that each predictor can be either included or excluded from the model. For example, the $2^4 = 16$ different possible subset models that can be formed from the pool of four X variables in the surgical unit example are listed in Table 9.2. First, there is the regression model with no X variables, i.e., the model $Y_i = \beta_0 + \varepsilon_i$. Then there are the regression models with one X variable (X_1, X_2, X_3, X_4), with two X variables (X_1 and X_2, X_1 and X_3, X_1 and X_4, X_2 and X_3, X_2 and X_4, X_3 and X_4), and so on.

TABLE 9.2 SSE_p, R_p^2, $R_{a,p}^2$, C_p, AIC_p, SBC_p, and $PRESS_p$ Values for All Possible Regression Models—Surgical Unit Example.

X Variables in Model	(1) p	(2) SSE_p	(3) R_p^2	(4) $R_{a,p}^2$	(5) C_p	(6) AIC_p	(7) SBC_p	(8) $PRESS_p$
None	1	12.808	0.000	0.000	151.498	−75.703	−73.714	13.296
X_1	2	12.031	0.061	0.043	141.164	−77.079	−73.101	13.512
X_2	2	9.979	0.221	0.206	108.556	−87.178	−83.200	10.744
X_3	2	7.332	0.428	0.417	66.489	−103.827	−99.849	8.327
X_4	2	7.409	0.422	0.410	67.715	−103.262	−99.284	8.025
X_1, X_2	3	9.443	0.263	0.234	102.031	−88.162	−82.195	11.062
X_1, X_3	3	5.781	0.549	0.531	43.852	−114.658	−108.691	6.988
X_1, X_4	3	7.299	0.430	0.408	67.972	−102.067	−96.100	8.472
X_2, X_3	3	4.312	0.663	0.650	20.520	−130.483	−124.516	5.065
X_2, X_4	3	6.622	0.483	0.463	57.215	−107.324	−101.357	7.476
X_3, X_4	3	5.130	0.599	0.584	33.504	−121.113	−115.146	6.121
X_1, X_2, X_3	4	3.109	0.757	0.743	3.391	−146.161	−138.205	3.914
X_1, X_2, X_4	4	6.570	0.487	0.456	58.392	−105.748	−97.792	7.903
X_1, X_3, X_4	4	4.968	0.612	0.589	32.932	−120.844	−112.888	6.207
X_2, X_3, X_4	4	3.614	0.718	0.701	11.424	−138.023	−130.067	4.597
X_1, X_2, X_3, X_4	5	3.084	0.759	0.740	5.000	−144.590	−134.645	4.069

In most circumstances, it will be impossible for an analyst to make a detailed examination of all possible regression models. For instance, when there are 10 potential X variables in the pool, there would be $2^{10} = 1,024$ possible regression models. With the availability of high-speed computers and efficient algorithms, running all possible regression models for 10 potential X variables is not time consuming. Still, the sheer volume of 1,024 alternative models to examine carefully would be an overwhelming task for a data analyst.

Model selection procedures, also known as subset selection or variables selection procedures, have been developed to identify a small group of regression models that are "good" according to a specified criterion. A detailed examination can then be made of a limited number of the more promising or "candidate" models, leading to the selection of the final regression model to be employed. This limited number might consist of three to six "good" subsets according to the criteria specified, so the investigator can then carefully study these regression models for choosing the final model.

While many criteria for comparing the regression models have been developed, we will focus on six: R_p^2, $R_{a,p}^2$, C_p, AIC_p, SBC_p, and $PRESS_p$. Before doing so, we will need to develop some notation. We shall denote the number of potential X variables in the pool by $P - 1$. We assume throughout this chapter that all regression models contain an intercept term β_0. Hence, the regression function containing all potential X variables contains P parameters, and the function with no X variables contains one parameter (β_0).

The number of X variables in a subset will be denoted by $p - 1$, as always, so that there are p parameters in the regression function for this subset of X variables. Thus, we have:

$$1 \leq p \leq P \tag{9.1}$$

We will assume that the number of observations exceeds the maximum number of potential parameters:

$$n > P \tag{9.2}$$

and, indeed, it is highly desirable that n be substantially larger than P, as we noted earlier, so that sound results can be obtained.

R_p^2 or SSE_p Criterion

The R_p^2 criterion calls for the use of the coefficient of multiple determination R^2, defined in (6.40), in order to identify several "good" subsets of X variables—in other words, subsets for which R^2 is high. We show the number of parameters in the regression model as a subscript of R^2. Thus R_p^2 indicates that there are p parameters, or $p - 1$ X variables, in the regression function on which R_p^2 is based.

The R_p^2 criterion is equivalent to using the error sum of squares SSE_p as the criterion (we again show the number of parameters in the regression model as a subscript). With the SSE_p criterion, subsets for which SSE_p is small are considered "good." The equivalence of the R_p^2 and SSE_p criteria follows from (6.40):

$$R_p^2 = 1 - \frac{SSE_p}{SSTO} \tag{9.3}$$

Since the denominator $SSTO$ is constant for all possible regression models, R_p^2 varies inversely with SSE_p.

The R_p^2 criterion is not intended to identify the subsets that maximize this criterion. We know that R_p^2 can never decrease as additional X variables are included in the model. Hence, R_p^2 will be a maximum when all $P - 1$ potential X variables are included in the regression model. The intent in using the R_p^2 criterion is to find the point where adding more X variables is not worthwhile because it leads to a very small increase in R_p^2. Often, this point is reached when only a limited number of X variables is included in the regression model. Clearly, the determination of where diminishing returns set in is a judgmental one.

Example

Table 9.2 for the surgical unit example shows in columns 1 and 2 the number of parameters in the regression function and the error sum of squares for each possible regression model. In column 3 are given the R_p^2 values. The results were obtained from a series of computer runs. For instance, when X_4 is the only X variable in the regression model, we obtain:

$$R_2^2 = 1 - \frac{SSE(X_4)}{SSTO} = 1 - \frac{7.409}{12.808} = .422$$

Note that $SSTO = SSE_1 = 12.808$.

Figure 9.4a contains a plot of the R_p^2 values against p, the number of parameters in the regression model. The maximum R_p^2 value for the possible subsets each consisting of $p - 1$ predictor variables, denoted by $\max(R_p^2)$, appears at the top of the graph for each p. These points are connected by solid lines to show the impact of adding additional X variables. Figure 9.4a makes it clear that little increase in $\max(R_p^2)$ takes place after three X variables are included in the model. Hence, consideration of the subsets (X_1, X_2, X_3) for which $R_4^2 = .757$ (as shown in column 3 of Table 9.2) and (X_2, X_3, X_4) for which $R_4^2 = .718$ appears to be reasonable according to the R_p^2 criterion.

Note that variables X_3 and X_4, correlate most highly with the response variable, yet this pair does not appear together in the $\max(R_p^2)$ model for $p = 4$. This suggests that X_1, X_2, and X_3 contain much of the information presented by X_4. Note also that the coefficient of multiple determination associated with subset (X_2, X_3, X_4), $R_4^2 = .718$, is somewhat smaller than $R_4^2 = .757$ for subset (X_1, X_2, X_3).

$R_{a,p}^2$ or MSE_p Criterion

Since R_p^2 does not take account of the number of parameters in the regression model and since $\max(R_p^2)$ can never decrease as p increases, the adjusted coefficient of multiple determination $R_{a,p}^2$ in (6.42) has been suggested as an alternative criterion:

$$R_{a,p}^2 = 1 - \left(\frac{n-1}{n-p}\right)\frac{SSE_p}{SSTO} = 1 - \frac{MSE_p}{\dfrac{SSTO}{n-1}} \tag{9.4}$$

This coefficient takes the number of parameters in the regression model into account through the degrees of freedom. It can be seen from (9.4) that $R_{a,p}^2$ increases if and only if MSE_p decreases since $SSTO/(n-1)$ is fixed for the given Y observations. Hence, $R_{a,p}^2$ and MSE_p provide equivalent information. We shall consider here the criterion $R_{a,p}^2$, again showing the number of parameters in the regression model as a subscript of the criterion. The largest $R_{a,p}^2$ for a given number of parameters in the model, $\max(R_{a,p}^2)$, can, indeed, decrease as p increases. This occurs when the increase in $\max(R_p^2)$ becomes so small that it is not

FIGURE 9.4   **Plot of Variables Selection Criteria—Surgical Unit Example.**

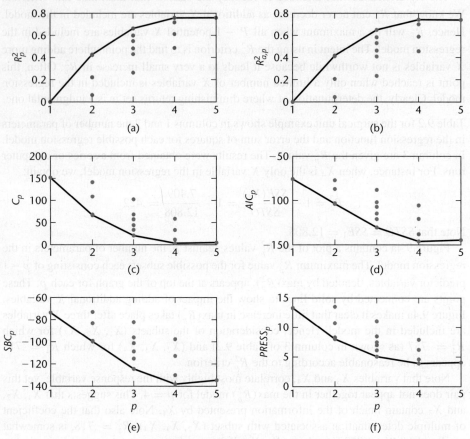

(a)

(b)

(c)

(d)

(e)

(f)

sufficient to offset the loss of an additional degree of freedom. Users of the $R^2_{a,p}$ criterion seek to find a few subsets for which $R^2_{a,p}$ is at the maximum or so close to the maximum that adding more variables is not worthwhile.

Example

The $R^2_{a,p}$ values for all possible regression models for the surgical unit example are shown in Table 9.2, column 4. For instance, we have for the regression model containing only X_4:

$$R^2_{a,2} = 1 - \left(\frac{n-1}{n-2}\right)\frac{SSE(X_4)}{SSTO} = 1 - \left(\frac{53}{52}\right)\frac{7.409}{12.808} = .410$$

Figure 9.4b contains the $R^2_{a,p}$ plot for the surgical unit example. We have again connected the $\max(R^2_{a,p})$ values by solid lines. The story told by the $R^2_{a,p}$ plot in Figure 9.4b is very similar to that told by the R^2_p plot in Figure 9.4a. Consideration of the subsets (X_1, X_2, X_3) and (X_2, X_3, X_4) appears to be reasonable according to the $R^2_{a,p}$ criterion. Notice that $R^2_{a,4} = .743$ is maximized for subset (X_1, X_2, X_3), and that adding X_4 to this subset—thus using all four predictors—decreases the criterion slightly: $R^2_{a,5} = .740$.

Mallows' C_p Criterion

This criterion is concerned with the *total mean squared error* of the n fitted values for each subset regression model. The mean squared error concept involves the total error in each fitted value:

$$\hat{Y}_i - \mu_i \tag{9.5}$$

where μ_i is the true mean response when the levels of the predictor variables X_k are those for the ith case. This total error is made up of a bias component and a random error component:

1. The bias component for the ith fitted value $\hat{Y}_i$, also called the model error component, is:

$$E\{\hat{Y}_i\} - \mu_i \tag{9.5a}$$

where $E\{\hat{Y}_i\}$ is the expectation of the ith fitted value for the given regression model. If the fitted model is not correct, $E\{\hat{Y}_i\}$ will differ from the true mean response μ_i and the difference represents the bias of the fitted model.

2. The random error component for $\hat{Y}_i$ is:

$$\hat{Y}_i - E\{\hat{Y}_i\} \tag{9.5b}$$

This component represents the deviation of the fitted value $\hat{Y}_i$ for the given sample from the expected value when the ith fitted value is obtained by fitting the same regression model to all possible samples.

The mean squared error for $\hat{Y}_i$ is defined as the expected value of the square of the total error in (9.5)—in other words, the expected value of:

$$(\hat{Y}_i - \mu_i)^2 = [(E\{\hat{Y}_i\} - \mu_i) + (\hat{Y}_i - E\{\hat{Y}_i\})]^2$$

It can be shown that this expected value is:

$$E\{\hat{Y}_i - \mu_i\}^2 = (E\{\hat{Y}_i\} - \mu_i)^2 + \sigma^2\{\hat{Y}_i\} \tag{9.6}$$

where $\sigma^2\{\hat{Y}_i\}$ is the variance of the fitted value $\hat{Y}_i$. We see from (9.6) that the mean squared error for the fitted value $\hat{Y}_i$ is the sum of the squared bias and the variance of $\hat{Y}_i$.

The total mean squared error for all n fitted values $\hat{Y}_i$ is the sum of the n individual mean squared errors in (9.6):

$$\sum_{i=1}^{n}[(E\{\hat{Y}_i\} - \mu_i)^2 + \sigma^2\{\hat{Y}_i\}] = \sum_{i=1}^{n}(E\{\hat{Y}_i\} - \mu_i)^2 + \sum_{i=1}^{n}\sigma^2\{\hat{Y}_i\} \tag{9.7}$$

The criterion measure, denoted by Γ_p, is simply the total mean squared error in (9.7) divided by σ^2, the true error variance:

$$\Gamma_p = \frac{1}{\sigma^2} \left[\sum_{i=1}^{n} (E\{\hat{Y}_i\} - \mu_i)^2 + \sum_{i=1}^{n} \sigma^2\{\hat{Y}_i\} \right] \tag{9.8}$$

The model which includes all $P - 1$ potential X variables is assumed to have been carefully chosen so that $MSE(X_1, \ldots, X_{P-1})$ is an unbiased estimator of σ^2. It can then be shown that an estimator of Γ_p is C_p:

$$C_p = \frac{SSE_p}{MSE(X_1, \ldots, X_{P-1})} - (n - 2p) \tag{9.9}$$

where SSE_p is the error sum of squares for the fitted subset regression model with p parameters (i.e., with $p - 1$ X variables).

When there is no bias in the regression model with $p - 1$ X variables so that $E\{\hat{Y}_i\} \equiv \mu_i$, the expected value of C_p is approximately p:

$$E\{C_p\} \approx p \qquad \text{when } E\{\hat{Y}_i\} \equiv \mu_i \tag{9.10}$$

Thus, when the C_p values for all possible regression models are plotted against p, those models with little bias will tend to fall near the line $C_p = p$. Models with substantial bias will tend to fall considerably above this line. C_p values below the line $C_p = p$ are interpreted as showing no bias, being below the line due to sampling error. The C_p value for the regression model containing all $P - 1$ X variables is, by definition, P. The C_p measure assumes that $MSE(X_1, \ldots, X_{P-1})$ is an unbiased estimator of σ^2, which is equivalent to assuming that this model contains no bias.

In using the C_p criterion, we seek to identify subsets of X variables for which (1) the C_p value is small and (2) the C_p value is near p. Subsets with small C_p values have a small total mean squared error, and when the C_p value is also near p, the bias of the regression model is small. It may sometimes occur that the regression model based on a subset of X variables with a small C_p value involves substantial bias. In that case, one may at times prefer a regression model based on a somewhat larger subset of X variables for which the C_p value is only slightly larger but which does not involve a substantial bias component. Reference 9.1 contains extended discussions of applications of the C_p criterion.

Example

Table 9.2, column 5, contains the C_p values for all possible regression models for the surgical unit example. For instance, when X_4 is the only X variable in the regression model, the C_p value is:

$$C_2 = \frac{SSE(X_4)}{\dfrac{SSE(X_1, X_2, X_3, X_4)}{n - 5}} - [n - 2(2)]$$

$$= \frac{7.409}{\dfrac{3.084}{49}} - [54 - 2(2)] = 67.715$$

The C_p values for all possible regression models are plotted in Figure 9.4c. We find that C_p is minimized for subset (X_1, X_2, X_3). Notice that $C_p = 3.391 < p = 4$ for this model, indicating little or no bias in the regression model.

Note that use of all potential X variables (X_1, X_2, X_3, X_4) results in a C_p value of exactly P, as expected; here, $C_5 = 5.00$. Also note that use of subset (X_2, X_3, X_4) with C_p value $C_4 = 11.424$ would be poor because of the substantial bias with this model. Thus, the C_p criterion suggests only one subset (X_1, X_2, X_3) for the surgical unit example.

Comments

1. Effective use of the C_p criterion requires careful development of the pool of $P - 1$ potential X variables, with the predictor variables expressed in appropriate form (linear, quadratic, transformed), and important interactions included, so that $MSE(X_1, \ldots, X_{P-1})$ provides an unbiased estimate of the error variance σ^2.

2. The C_p criterion places major emphasis on the fit of the subset model for the n sample observations. At times, a modification of the C_p criterion that emphasizes new observations to be predicted may be preferable.

3. To see why C_p as defined in (9.9) is an estimator of Γ_p, we need to utilize two results that we shall simply state. First, it can be shown that:

$$\sum_{i=1}^{n} \sigma^2\{\hat{Y}_i\} = p\sigma^2 \tag{9.11}$$

Thus, the total random error of the n fitted values $\hat{Y}_i$ increases as the number of variables in the regression model increases.

Further, it can be shown that:

$$E\{SSE_p\} = \sum (E\{\hat{Y}_i\} - \mu_i)^2 + (n - p)\sigma^2 \tag{9.12}$$

Hence, Γ_p in (9.8) can be expressed as follows:

$$\Gamma_p = \frac{1}{\sigma^2}[E\{SSE_p\} - (n - p)\sigma^2 + p\sigma^2]$$

$$= \frac{E\{SSE_p\}}{\sigma^2} - (n - 2p) \tag{9.13}$$

Replacing $E\{SSE_p\}$ by the estimator SSE_p and using $MSE(X_1, \ldots, X_{P-1})$ as an estimator of σ^2 yields C_p in (9.9).

4. To show that the C_p value for the regression model containing all $P - 1$ X variables is P, we substitute in (9.9), as follows:

$$C_p = \frac{SSE(X_1, \ldots, X_{P-1})}{\dfrac{SSE(X_1, \ldots, X_{P-1})}{n - P}} - (n - 2P)$$

$$= (n - P) - (n - 2P)$$

$$= P$$

∎

AIC_p and SBC_p Criteria

We have seen that both $R_{a,p}^2$ and C_p are model selection criteria that penalize models having large numbers of predictors. Two popular alternatives that also provide penalties for adding predictors are Akaike's information criterion (AIC_p) and Schwarz' Bayesian criterion (SBC_p). We search for models that have small values of AIC_p or SBC_p, where these criteria are given by:

$$AIC_p = n \ln SSE_p - n \ln n + 2p \qquad (9.14)$$

$$SBC_p = n \ln SSE_p - n \ln n + [\ln n]p \qquad (9.15)$$

Notice that for both of these measures, the first term is $n \ln SSE_p$, which decreases as p increases. The second term is fixed (for a given sample size n), and the third term increases with the number of parameters, p. Models with small SSE_p will do well by these criteria, as long as the penalties—$2p$ for AIC_p and $[\ln n]p$ for SBC_p—are not too large. If $n \geq 8$ the penalty for SBC_p is larger than that for AIC_p; hence the SBC_p criterion tends to favor more parsimonious models.

Example

Table 9.2, columns 6 and 7, contains the AIC_p and SBC_p values for all possible regression models for the surgical unit example. When X_4 is the only X variable in the regression model, the AIC_p value is:

$$AIC_2 = n \ln SSE_2 - n \ln n + 2p$$
$$= 54 \ln 7.409 - 54 \ln 54 + 2(2) = -103.262$$

Similarly, the SBC_p value is:

$$SBC_2 = n \ln SSE_2 - n \ln n + [\ln n]p$$
$$= 54 \ln 7.409 - 54 \ln 54 + [\ln 54](2) = -99.284$$

The AIC_p and SBC_p values for all possible regression models are plotted in Figures 9.4d and e. We find that both of these criteria are minimized for subset (X_1, X_2, X_3).

$PRESS_p$ Criterion

The $PRESS_p$ (prediction sum of squares) criterion is a measure of how well the use of the fitted values for a subset model can predict the observed responses Y_i. The error sum of squares, $SSE = \sum(Y_i - \hat{Y}_i)^2$, is also such a measure. The $PRESS$ measure differs from SSE in that each fitted value $\hat{Y}_i$ for the $PRESS$ criterion is obtained by deleting the ith case from the data set, estimating the regression function for the subset model from the remaining $n - 1$ cases, and then using the fitted regression function to obtain the predicted value $\hat{Y}_{i(i)}$ for the ith case. We use the notation $\hat{Y}_{i(i)}$ now for the fitted value to indicate, by the first subscript i, that it is a predicted value for the ith case and, by the second subscript (i), that the ith case was omitted when the regression function was fitted.

The $PRESS$ prediction error for the ith case then is:

$$Y_i - \hat{Y}_{i(i)} \qquad (9.16)$$

and the $PRESS_p$ criterion is the sum of the squared prediction errors over all n cases:

$$PRESS_p = \sum_{i=1}^{n}(Y_i - \hat{Y}_{i(i)})^2 \qquad (9.17)$$

Models with small $PRESS_p$ values are considered good candidate models. The reason is that when the prediction errors $Y_i - \hat{Y}_{i(i)}$ are small, so are the squared prediction errors and the sum of the squared prediction errors. Thus, models with small $PRESS_p$ values fit well in the sense of having small prediction errors.

$PRESS_p$ values can be calculated without requiring n separate regression runs, each time deleting one of the n cases. The relationship in (10.21) and (10.21a), to be explained in the next chapter, enables one to calculate all $\hat{Y}_{i(i)}$ values from a single regression run.

Example

Table 9.2, column 8, contains the $PRESS_p$ values for all possible regression models for the surgical unit example. The $PRESS_p$ values are plotted in Figure 9.4f. The message given by the $PRESS_p$ values in Table 9.2 and plot in Figure 9.4f is very similar to that told by the other criteria. We find that subsets (X_1, X_2, X_3) and (X_2, X_3, X_4) have small $PRESS$ values; in fact, the set of all X variables (X_1, X_2, X_3, X_4) involves a slightly larger $PRESS$ value than subset (X_1, X_2, X_3). The subset (X_2, X_3, X_4) involves a $PRESS$ value of 4.597, which is moderately larger than the $PRESS$ value of 3.914 for subset (X_1, X_2, X_3).

Comment

$PRESS$ values can also be useful for model validation, as will be explained in Section 9.6. ∎

9.4 Automatic Search Procedures for Model Selection

As noted in the previous section, the number of possible models, 2^{p-1}, grows rapidly with the number of predictors. Evaluating all of the possible alternatives can be a daunting endeavor. To simplify the task, a variety of automatic computer-search procedures have been developed. In this section, we will review the two most common approaches, namely "best" subsets regression and stepwise regression.

For the remainder of this chapter, we will employ the full set of eight predictors from the surgical unit data. Recall that these predictors are displayed in Table 9.1 on page 350 and described there as well.

"Best" Subsets Algorithms

Time-saving algorithms have been developed in which the best subsets according to a specified criterion are identified without requiring the fitting of all of the possible subset regression models. In fact, these algorithms require the calculation of only a small fraction of all possible regression models. For instance, if the C_p criterion is to be employed and the five best subsets according to this criterion are to be identified, these algorithms search for the five subsets of X variables with the smallest C_p values using much less computational effort than when all possible subsets are evaluated. These algorithms are called *"best" subsets algorithms*. Not only do these algorithms provide the best subsets according to the specified criterion, but they often also identify several "good" subsets for each possible number of X variables in the model to give the investigator additional helpful information in making the final selection of the subset of X variables to be employed in the regression model.

When the pool of potential X variables is very large, say greater than 30 or 40, even the "best" subset algorithms may require excessive computer time. Under these conditions, one of the stepwise regression procedures, described later in this section, may need to be employed to assist in the selection of X variables.

Example

For the eight predictors in the surgical unit example, we know there are $2^8 = 256$ possible models. Plots of the six model selection criteria discussed in this chapter are displayed in

FIGURE 9.5
Plot of Variable Selection Criteria with All Eight Predictors—Surgical Unit Example.

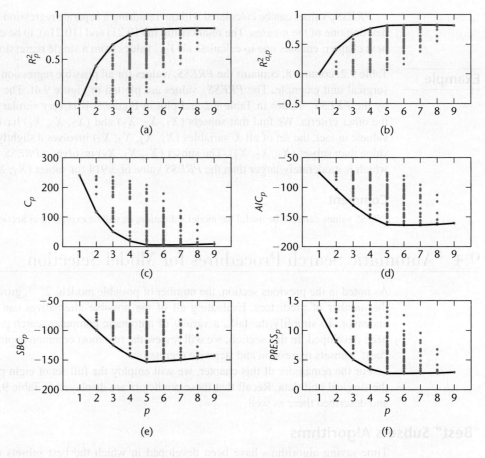

(a)

(b)

(c)

(d)

(e)

(f)

Figure 9.5. The best values of each criterion for each p have been connected with solid lines. These best values are also displayed in Table 9.3. The overall optimum criterion values have been underlined in each column of the table. Notice that the choice of a "best" model depends on the criterion. For example, a seven- or eight-parameter model is identified as best by the $R_{a,p}^2$ criterion (both have $\max(R_{a,p}^2) = .823$), a six-parameter model is identified by the C_p criterion ($\min(C_7) = 5.541$), and a seven-parameter model is identified by the AIC_p criterion ($\min(AIC_7) = -163.834$). As is frequently the case, the SBC_p criterion identifies a more parsimonious model as best. In this case both the SBC_p and $PRESS_p$ criteria point to five-parameter models ($\min(SBC_5) = -153.406$ and $\min(PRESS_5) = 2.738$). As previously emphasized, our objective at this stage is not to identify a single best model; we hope to identify a small set of promising models for further study.

Figure 9.6 contains, for the surgical unit example, MINITAB output for the "best" subsets algorithm. Here, we specified that the best two subsets be identified for each number of variables in the regression model. The MINITAB algorithm uses the R_p^2 criterion, but also shows for each of the "best" subsets the $R_{a,p}^2$, C_p, and $\sqrt{MSE_p}$ (labeled S) values. The right-most columns of the tabulation show the X variables in the subset. From the figure it is seen that the best subset, according to the $R_{a,p}^2$ criterion, is either the seven-parameter

TABLE 9.3
Best Variable-Selection Criterion Values—Surgical Unit Example.

p	(1) SSE_p	(2) R_p^2	(3) $R_{a,p}^2$	(4) C_p	(5) AIC_p	(6) SBC_p	(7) $PRESS_p$
1	12.808	0.000	0.000	240.452	−75.703	−73.714	13.296
2	7.332	0.428	0.417	117.409	−103.827	−99.849	8.025
3	4.312	0.663	0.650	50.472	−130.483	−124.516	5.065
4	2.843	0.778	0.765	18.914	−150.985	−143.029	3.469
5	2.179	0.830	0.816	5.751	−163.351	−153.406	2.738
6	2.082	0.837	0.821	5.541	−163.805	−151.871	2.739
7	2.005	0.843	0.823	5.787	−163.834	−149.911	2.772
8	1.972	0.846	0.823	7.029	−162.736	−146.824	2.809
9	1.971	0.846	0.819	9.000	−160.771	−142.870	2.931

FIGURE 9.6
MINITAB Output for "Best" Two Subsets for Each Subset Size—Surgical Unit Example.

```
Response is lnSurviv

                                            B P           H
                                            l r        H  i
                                            o o  E    G  i  s
                                            o g  n L  e  s  t
                                            d i  z i  n  t  h
                                            c n  y v  A  d  m  e
                                            l d  m e  g  e  o  a
Vars   R-Sq   R-Sq(adj)    C-p       S      o e  e r  e  r  d  v

  1    42.8     41.7     117.4    0.37549   X
  1    42.2     41.0     119.2    0.37746          X
  2    66.3     65.0      50.5    0.29079   X X
  2    59.9     58.4      69.1    0.31715     X X
  3    77.8     76.5      18.9    0.23845   X X           X
  3    75.7     74.3      25.0    0.24934   X X X
  4    83.0     81.6       5.8    0.21087   X X X         X
  4    81.4     79.9      10.3    0.22023   X X X         X
  5    83.7     82.1       5.5    0.20827   X X X    X    X
  5    83.6     81.9       6.0    0.20931   X X X  X      X
  6    84.3     82.3       5.8    0.20655   X X X  X X    X
  6    83.9     81.9       7.0    0.20934   X X X    X X  X
  7    84.6     82.3       7.0    0.20705   X X X  X X X  X
  7    84.4     82.0       7.7    0.20867   X X X X X    X
  8    84.6     81.9       9.0    0.20927   X X X X X X X X
```

model based on all predictors except Liver (X_4) and Histmod (history of moderate alcohol use—X_7), or the eight-parameter model based on all predictors except Liver (X_4). The $R_{a,p}^2$ criterion value for both of these models is .823.

The all-possible-regressions procedure leads to the identification of a small number of subsets that are "good" according to a specified criterion. In the surgical unit example, two of the four criteria—SBC_p and $PRESS_p$—pointed to models with 4 predictors, while the other criteria favored larger models. Consequently, one may wish at times to consider more than one criterion in evaluating possible subsets of X variables.

Once the investigator has identified a few "good" subsets for intensive examination, a final choice of the model variables must be made. This choice, as indicated by our model-building strategy in Figure 9.1, is aided by residual analyses (and other diagnostics to be covered in Chapter 10) and by the investigator's knowledge of the subject under study, and is finally confirmed through model validation studies.

Stepwise Regression Methods

In those occasional cases when the pool of potential X variables contains 30 to 40 or even more variables, use of a "best" subsets algorithm may not be feasible. An automatic search procedure that develops the "best" subset of X variables sequentially may then be helpful. The forward stepwise regression procedure is probably the most widely used of the automatic search methods. It was developed to economize on computational efforts, as compared with the various all-possible-regressions procedures. Essentially, this search method develops a sequence of regression models, at each step adding or deleting an X variable. The criterion for adding or deleting an X variable can be stated equivalently in terms of error sum of squares reduction, coefficient of partial correlation, t^* statistic, or F^* statistic.

An essential difference between stepwise procedures and the "best" subsets algorithm is that stepwise search procedures end with the identification of a *single* regression model as "best." With the "best" subsets algorithm, on the other hand, *several* regression models can be identified as "good" for final consideration. The identification of a single regression model as "best" by the stepwise procedures is a major weakness of these procedures. Experience has shown that each of the stepwise search procedures can sometimes err by identifying a suboptimal regression model as "best." In addition, the identification of a single regression model may hide the fact that several other regression models may also be "good." Finally, the "goodness" of a regression model can only be established by a thorough examination using a variety of diagnostics.

What then can we do on those occasions when the pool of potential X variables is very large and an automatic search procedure must be utilized? Basically, we should use the subset identified by the automatic search procedure as a starting point for searching for other "good" subsets. One possibility is to treat the number of X variables in the regression model identified by the automatic search procedure as being about the right subset size and then use the "best" subsets procedure for subsets of this and nearby sizes.

Forward Stepwise Regression

We shall describe the forward stepwise regression search algorithm in terms of the t^* statistics (2.17) and their associated P-values for the usual tests of regression parameters.

1. The stepwise regression routine first fits a simple linear regression model for each of the $P-1$ potential X variables. For each simple linear regression model, the t^* statistic (2.17) for testing whether or not the slope is zero is obtained:

$$t_k^* = \frac{b_k}{s\{b_k\}} \tag{9.18}$$

The X variable with the largest t^* value is the candidate for first addition. If this t^* value exceeds a predetermined level, or if the corresponding P-value is less than a predetermined α, the X variable is added. Otherwise, the program terminates with no X variable considered sufficiently helpful to enter the regression model. Since the degrees of freedom associated with *MSE* vary depending on the number of X variables in the model, and since repeated tests on the same data are undertaken, fixed t^* limits for adding or deleting a variable have no precise probabilistic meaning. For this reason, software programs often favor the use of predetermined α-limits.

2. Assume X_7 is the variable entered at step 1. The stepwise regression routine now fits all regression models with two X variables, where X_7 is one of the pair. For each such regression model, the t^* test statistic corresponding to the newly added predictor X_k is obtained. This is the statistic for testing whether or not $\beta_k = 0$ when X_7 and X_k are the variables in the model. The X variable with the largest t^* value—or equivalently, the smallest P-value—is the candidate for addition at the second stage. If this t^* value exceeds a predetermined level (i.e., the P-value falls below a predetermined level), the second X variable is added. Otherwise, the program terminates.

3. Suppose X_3 is added at the second stage. Now the stepwise regression routine examines whether any of the other X variables already in the model should be dropped. For our illustration, there is at this stage only one other X variable in the model, X_7, so that only one t^* test statistic is obtained:

$$t_7^* = \frac{b_7}{s\{b_7\}} \tag{9.19}$$

At later stages, there would be a number of these t^* statistics, one for each of the variables in the model besides the one last added. The variable for which this t^* value is smallest (or equivalently the variable for which the P-value is largest) is the candidate for deletion. If this t^* value falls below—or the P-value exceeds—a predetermined limit, the variable is dropped from the model; otherwise, it is retained.

4. Suppose X_7 is retained so that both X_3 and X_7 are now in the model. The stepwise regression routine now examines which X variable is the next candidate for addition, then examines whether any of the variables already in the model should now be dropped, and so on until no further X variables can either be added or deleted, at which point the search terminates.

Note that the stepwise regression algorithm allows an X variable, brought into the model at an earlier stage, to be dropped subsequently if it is no longer helpful in conjunction with variables added at later stages.

Example

Figure 9.7 shows MINITAB computer printout for the forward stepwise regression procedure for the surgical unit example. The maximum acceptable α limit for adding a variable is 0.10 and the minimum acceptable α limit for removing a variable is 0.15, as shown at the top of Figure 9.7.

We now follow through the steps.

1. At the start of the stepwise search, no X variable is in the model so that the model to be fitted is $Y_i = \beta_0 + \varepsilon_i$. In step 1, the t^* statistics (9.18) and corresponding P-values are calculated for each potential X variable, and the predictor having the smallest P-value (largest t^* value) is chosen to enter the equation. We see that Enzyme (X_3) had the largest

FIGURE 9.7
MINITAB
Forward
Stepwise
Regression
Output—
Surgical Unit
Example.

```
Alpha-to-Enter: 0.1  Alpha-to-Remove: 0.15

Response is lnSurviv on  8 predictors, with N = 54

   Step           1       2       3       4
   Constant     5.264   4.351   4.291   3.852

   Enzyme      0.0151  0.0154  0.0145  0.0155
   T-Value       6.23    8.19    9.33   11.07
   P-Value      0.000   0.000   0.000   0.000

   ProgInde             0.0141  0.0149  0.0142
   T-Value                5.98    7.68    8.20
   P-Value               0.000   0.000   0.000

   Histheav                     0.429   0.353
   T-Value                       5.08    4.57
   P-Value                      0.000   0.000

   Bloodclo                             0.073
   T-Value                               3.86
   P-Value                              0.000

   S           0.375   0.291   0.238   0.211
   R-Sq        42.76   66.33   77.80   82.99
   R-Sq(adj)   41.66   65.01   76.47   81.60
   C-p         117.4    50.5    18.9     5.8
```

test statistic:

$$t_3^* = \frac{b_3}{s\{b_3\}} = \frac{.015124}{.002427} = 6.23$$

The *P*-value for this test statistic is 0.000, which falls below the maximum acceptable α-to-enter value of 0.10; hence Enzyme (X_3) is added to the model.

2. At this stage, step 1 has been completed. The current regression model contains Enzyme (X_3), and the printout displays, near the top of the column labeled "Step 1," the regression coefficient for Enzyme (0.0151), the t^* value for this coefficient (6.23), and the corresponding *P*-value (0.000). At the bottom of column 1, a number of variables-selection criteria, including R_1^2 (42.76), $R_{a,1}^2$ (41.66), and C_1 (117.4) are also provided.

Next, all regression models containing X_3 and another X variable are fitted, and the t^* statistics calculated. They are now:

$$t_k^* = \sqrt{\frac{MSR(X_k|X_3)}{MSE(X_3, X_k)}}$$

Progindex (X_2) has the highest t^* value, and its *P*-value (0.000) falls below 0.10, so that X_2 now enters the model.

3. The column labeled Step 2 in Figure 9.7 summarizes the situation at this point. Enzyme and Progindex (X_3 and X_2) are now in the model, and information about this model is provided. At this point, a test whether Enzyme (X_3) should be dropped is undertaken, but because the P-value (0.000) corresponding to X_3 is not above 0.15, this variable is retained.

4. Next, all regression models containing X_2, X_3, and one of the remaining potential X variables are fitted. The appropriate t^* statistics now are:

$$t_k^* = \sqrt{\frac{MSR(X_k | X_2, X_3)}{MSE(X_2, X_3, X_k)}}$$

The predictor labeled Histheavy (X_8) had the largest t_k^* value (P-value $= 0.000$) and was next added to the model.

5. The column labeled Step 3 in Figure 9.7 summarizes the situation at this point. X_2, X_3, and X_8 are now in the model. Next, a test is undertaken to determine whether X_2 or X_3 should be dropped. Since both of the corresponding P-values are less than 0.15, neither predictor is dropped from the model.

6. At step 4 Bloodclot (X_1) is added, and no terms previously included were dropped. The right-most column of Figure 9.7 summarizes the addition of variable X_1 into the model containing variables X_2, X_3, and X_8. Next, a test is undertaken to determine whether either X_2, X_3, or X_8 should be dropped. Since all P-values are less than 0.15 (all are 0.000), all variables are retained.

7. Finally, the stepwise regression routine considers adding one of X_4, X_5, X_6, or X_7 to the model containing X_1, X_2, X_3, and X_8. In each case, the P-values are greater than 0.10 (not shown); therefore, no additional variables can be added to the model and the search process is terminated.

Thus, the stepwise search algorithm identifies (X_1, X_2, X_3, X_8) as the "best" subset of X variables. This model also happens to be the model identified by both the SBC_p and $PRESS_p$ criteria in our previous analyses based on an assessment of "best" subset selection.

Comments

1. The choice of α-to-enter and α-to-remove values essentially represents a balancing of opposing tendencies. Simulation studies have shown that for large pools of uncorrelated predictor variables that have been generated to be uncorrelated with the response variable, use of large or moderately large α-to-enter values as the entry criterion results in a procedure that is too liberal; that is, it allows too many predictor variables into the model. On the other hand, models produced by an automatic selection procedure with small α-to-enter values are often underspecified, resulting in σ^2 being badly overestimated and the procedure being too conservative (see, for example, References 9.2 and 9.3).

2. The maximum acceptable α-to-enter value should never be larger than the minimum acceptable α-to-remove value; otherwise, cycling is possible where a variable is continually entered and removed.

3. The order in which variables enter the regression model does not reflect their importance. At times, a variable may enter the model, only to be dropped at a later stage because it can be predicted well from the other predictors that have been subsequently added.   ■

Other Stepwise Procedures

Other stepwise procedures are available to find a "best" subset of predictor variables. We mention two of these.

Forward Selection. The forward selection search procedure is a simplified version of forward stepwise regression, omitting the test whether a variable once entered into the model should be dropped.

Backward Elimination. The backward elimination search procedure is the opposite of forward selection. It begins with the model containing all potential X variables and identifies the one with the largest P-value. If the maximum P-value is greater than a predetermined limit, that X variable is dropped. The model with the remaining $P - 2$ X variables is then fitted, and the next candidate for dropping is identified. This process continues until no further X variables can be dropped. A stepwise modification can also be adapted that allows variables eliminated earlier to be added later; this modification is called the backward stepwise regression procedure.

Comment

For small and moderate numbers of variables in the pool of potential X variables, some statisticians argue for backward stepwise search over forward stepwise search (see Reference 9.4). A potential disadvantage of the forward stepwise approach is that the *MSE*—and hence $s\{b_k\}$—will tend to be inflated during the initial steps, because important predictors have been omitted. This in turn leads to t_k^* test statistics (9.18) that are too small. For the backward stepwise procedure, *MSE* values tend to be more nearly unbiased because important predictors are retained at each step. An argument in favor of the backward stepwise procedure can also be made in situations where it is useful as a first step to look at each X variable in the regression function adjusted for all the other X variables in the pool. ∎

9.5 Some Final Comments on Automatic Model Selection Procedures

Our discussion of the major automatic selection procedures for identifying the "best" subset of X variables has focused on the main conceptual issues and not on options, variations, and refinements available with particular computer packages. It is essential that the specific features of the package employed be fully understood so that intelligent use of the package can be made. In some packages, there is an option for regression models through the origin. Some packages permit variables to be brought into the model and tested in pairs or other groupings instead of singly, to save computing time or for other reasons. Some packages, once a "best" regression model is identified, will fit all the possible regression models with the same number of variables and will develop information for each model so that a final choice can be made by the user. Some stepwise programs have options for forcing variables into the regression model; such variables are not removed even if their P-values become too large.

The diversity of these options and special features serves to emphasize a point made earlier: there is no unique way of searching for "good" subsets of X variables, and subjective elements must play an important role in the search process.

We have considered a number of important issues related to exploratory model building, but there are many others. (A good discussion of many of these issues may be found in Reference 9.5.) Most important for good model building is the recognition that no automatic search procedure will always find the "best" model, and that, indeed, there may exist several "good" regression models whose appropriateness for the purpose at hand needs to be investigated.

Judgment needs to play an important role in model building for exploratory studies. Some explanatory variables may be known to be more fundamental than others and therefore should be retained in the regression model if the primary purpose is to develop a good explanatory model. When a qualitative predictor variable is represented in the pool of potential X variables by a number of indicator variables (e.g., geographic region is represented by several indicator variables), it is often appropriate to keep these indicator variables together as a group to represent the qualitative variable, even if a subset containing only some of the indicator variables is "better" according to the criterion employed. Similarly, if second-order terms X_k^2 or interaction terms $X_k X_{k'}$ need to be present in a regression model, one would ordinarily wish to have the first-order terms in the model as representing the main effects.

The selection of a subset regression model for exploratory observational studies has been the subject of much recent research. Reference 9.5 provides information about many of these studies. New methods of identifying the "best" subset have been proposed, including methods based on deleting one case at a time and on bootstrapping. With the first method, the criterion is evaluated for identified subsets n times, each time with one case omitted, in order to select the "best" subset. With bootstrapping, repeated samples of cases are selected with replacement from the data set (alternatively, repeated samples of residuals from the model fitted to all X variables are selected with replacement to obtain observed Y values), and the criterion is evaluated for identified subsets in order to select the "best" subset. Research by Breiman and Spector (Ref. 9.7) has evaluated these methods from the standpoint of the closeness of the selected model to the true model and has found the two methods promising, the bootstrap method requiring larger data sets.

An important issue in exploratory model building that we have not yet considered is the bias in estimated regression coefficients and in estimated mean responses, as well as in their estimated standard deviations, that may result when the coefficients and error mean square for the finally selected regression model are estimated from the same data that were used for selecting the model. Sometimes, these biases may be substantial (see, for example, References 9.5 and 9.6). In the next section, we will show how one can examine whether the estimated regression coefficients and error mean square are biased to a substantial extent.

9.6 Model Validation

The final step in the model-building process is the validation of the selected regression models. Model validation usually involves checking a candidate model against independent data. Three basic ways of validating a regression model are:

1. Collection of new data to check the model and its predictive ability.
2. Comparison of results with theoretical expectations, earlier empirical results, and simulation results.
3. Use of a holdout sample to check the model and its predictive ability.

When a regression model is used in a controlled experiment, a repetition of the experiment and its analysis serves to validate the findings in the initial study if similar results for the regression coefficients, predictive ability, and the like are obtained. Similarly, findings in confirmatory observational studies are validated by a repetition of the study with other data.

As we noted in Section 9.1, there are generally no extensive problems in the selection of predictor variables in controlled experiments and confirmatory observational studies. In contrast, explanatory observational studies frequently involve large pools of explanatory variables and the selection of a subset of these for the final regression model. For these studies, validation of the regression model involves also the appropriateness of the variables selected, as well as the magnitudes of the regression coefficients, the predictive ability of the model, and the like. Our discussion of validation will focus primarily on issues that arise in validating regression models for exploratory observational studies. A good discussion of the need for replicating any study to establish the generalizability of the findings may be found in Reference 9.8. References 9.9 and 9.10 provide helpful presentations of issues arising in the validation of regression models.

Collection of New Data to Check Model

The best means of model validation is through the collection of new data. The purpose of collecting new data is to be able to examine whether the regression model developed from the earlier data is still applicable for the new data. If so, one has assurance about the applicability of the model to data beyond those on which the model is based.

Methods of Checking Validity.   There are a variety of methods of examining the validity of the regression model against the new data. One validation method is to reestimate the model form chosen earlier using the new data. The estimated regression coefficients and various characteristics of the fitted model are then compared for consistency to those of the regression model based on the earlier data. If the results are consistent, they provide strong support that the chosen regression model is applicable under broader circumstances than those related to the original data.

A second validation method is designed to calibrate the predictive capability of the selected regression model. When a regression model is developed from given data, it is inevitable that the selected model is chosen, at least in large part, because it fits well the data at hand. For a different set of random outcomes, one may likely have arrived at a different model in terms of the predictor variables selected and/or their functional forms and interaction terms present in the model. A result of this model development process is that the error mean square MSE will tend to understate the inherent variability in making future predictions from the selected model.

A means of measuring the actual predictive capability of the selected regression model is to use this model to predict each case in the new data set and then to calculate the mean of the squared prediction errors, to be denoted by $MSPR$, which stands for *mean squared prediction error*:

$$MSPR = \frac{\sum_{i=1}^{n^*}(Y_i - \hat{Y}_i)^2}{n^*} \tag{9.20}$$

where:

Y_i is the value of the response variable in the ith validation case

$\hat{Y}_i$ is the predicted value for the ith validation case based on the model-building data set

n^* is the number of cases in the validation data set

If the mean squared prediction error *MSPR* is fairly close to *MSE* based on the regression fit to the model-building data set, then the error mean square *MSE* for the selected regression model is not seriously biased and gives an appropriate indication of the predictive ability of the model. If the mean squared prediction error is much larger than *MSE*, one should rely on the mean squared prediction error as an indicator of how well the selected regression model will predict in the future.

Difficulties in Replicating a Study.   Difficulties often arise when new data are collected to validate a regression model, especially with observational studies. Even with controlled experiments, however, there may be difficulties in replicating an earlier study in identical fashion. For instance, the laboratory equipment for the new study to be conducted in a different laboratory may differ from that used in the initial study, resulting in somewhat different calibrations for the response measurements.

The difficulties in replicating a study are particularly acute in the social sciences where controlled experiments often are not feasible. Repetition of an observational study usually involves different conditions, the differences being related to changes in setting and/or time. For instance, a study investigating the relation between amount of delegation of authority by executives in a firm to the age of the executive was repeated in another firm which has a somewhat different management philosophy. As another example, a study relating consumer purchases of a product to special promotional incentives was repeated in another year when the business climate differed substantially from that during the initial study.

It may be thought that an inability to reproduce a study identically makes the replication study useless for validation purposes. This is not the case. No single study is fully useful until we know how much the results of the study can be generalized. If a replication study for which the conditions of the setting differ only slightly from those of the initial study yields substantially different regression results, then we learn that the results of the initial study cannot be readily generalized. On the other hand, if the conditions differ substantially and the regression results are still similar, we find that the regression results can be generalized to apply under substantially varying conditions. Still another possibility is that the regression results for the replication study differ substantially from those of the initial study, the differences being related to changes in the setting. This information may be useful for enriching the regression model by including new explanatory variables that make the model more widely applicable.

Comment

When the new data are collected under controlled conditions in an experiment, it is desirable to include data points of major interest to check out the model predictions. If the model is to be used for making predictions over the entire range of the *X* observations, a possibility is to include data points that are uniformly distributed over the *X* space.   ∎

Comparison with Theory, Empirical Evidence, or Simulation Results

In some cases, theory, simulation results, or previous empirical results may be helpful in determining whether the selected model is reasonable. Comparisons of regression coefficients and predictions with theoretical expectations, previous empirical results, or simulation results should be made. Unfortunately, there is often little theory that can be used to validate regression models.

Data Splitting

By far the preferred method to validate a regression model is through the collection of new data. Often, however, this is neither practical nor feasible. An alternative when the data set is large enough is to split the data into two sets. The first set, called the *model-building set* or the *training sample,* is used to develop the model. The second data set, called the *validation* or *prediction set,* is used to evaluate the reasonableness and predictive ability of the selected model. This validation procedure is often called *cross-validation*. Data splitting in effect is an attempt to simulate replication of the study.

The validation data set is used for validation in the same way as when new data are collected. The regression coefficients can be reestimated for the selected model and then compared for consistency with the coefficients obtained from the model-building data set. Also, predictions can be made for the data in the validation data set from the regression model developed from the model-building data set to calibrate the predictive ability of this regression model for the new data. When the calibration data set is large enough, one can also study how the "good" models considered in the model selection phase fare with the new data.

Data sets are often split equally into model-building and validation data sets. It is important, however, that the model-building data set be sufficiently large so that a reliable model can be developed. Recall in this connection that the number of cases should be at least 6 to 10 times the number of variables in the pool of predictor variables. Thus, when 10 variables are in the pool, the model-building data set should contain at least 60 to 100 cases. If the entire data set is not large enough under these circumstances for making an equal split, the validation data set will need to be smaller than the model-building data set.

Splits of the data can be made at random. Another possibility is to match cases in pairs and place one of each pair into one of the two split data sets. When data are collected sequentially in time, it is often useful to pick a point in time to divide the data. Generally, the earlier data are selected for the model-building set and the later data for the validation set. When seasonal or cyclical effects are present in the data (e.g., sales data), the split should be made at a point where the cycles are balanced.

Use of time or some other characteristic of the data to split the data set provides the opportunity to test the generalizability of the model since conditions may differ for the two data sets. Data in the validation set may have been created under different causal conditions than those of the model-building set. In some cases, data in the validation set may represent extrapolations with respect to the data in the model-building set (e.g., sales data collected over time may contain a strong trend component). Such differential conditions may lead to a lack of validity of the model based on the model-building data set and indicate a need to broaden the regression model so that it is applicable under a broader scope of conditions.

A possible drawback of data splitting is that the variances of the estimated regression coefficients developed from the model-building data set will usually be larger than those that would have been obtained from the fit to the entire data set. If the model-building data set is reasonably large, however, these variances generally will not be that much larger than those for the entire data set. In any case, once the model has been validated, it is customary practice to use the entire data set for estimating the final regression model.

Example

In the surgical unit example, three models were favored by the various model-selection criteria. The SBC_p and $PRESS_p$ criteria favored the four-predictor model:

$$Y_i' = \beta_0 + \beta_1 X_{i1} + \beta_2 X_{i2} + \beta_3 X_{i3} + \beta_8 X_{i8} + \varepsilon_i \qquad \text{Model 1} \qquad \textbf{(9.21)}$$

C_p was minimized by the five-predictor model:

$$Y_i' = \beta_0 + \beta_1 X_{i1} + \beta_2 X_{i2} + \beta_3 X_{i3} + \beta_5 X_{i5} + \beta_8 X_{i8} + \varepsilon_i \qquad \text{Model 2} \qquad \textbf{(9.22)}$$

while the $R_{a,p}^2$ and AIC_p criteria were optimized by the six-predictor model:

$$Y_i' = \beta_0 + \beta_1 X_{i1} + \beta_2 X_{i2} + \beta_3 X_{i3} + \beta_5 X_{i5} + \beta_6 X_{i6} + \beta_8 X_{i8} \qquad \text{Model 3} \qquad \textbf{(9.23)}$$

We wish to assess the validity of these three models, both internally and externally.

Some evidence of the internal validity of these fitted models can be obtained through an examination of the various model-selection criteria. Table 9.4 summarizes the fits of the three candidate models to the original (training) data set in columns (1), (3), and (5). We first consider the SSE_p, $PRESS_p$ and C_p criterion values. Recall that the $PRESS_p$ value is always larger than SSE_p because the regression fit for the ith case when this case is deleted in fitting can never be as good as that when the ith case is included. A $PRESS_p$

TABLE 9.4 **Regression Results for Candidate Models (9.21), (9.22), and (9.23) Based on Model-Building and Validation Data Sets—Surgical Unit Example.**

Statistic	(1) Model 1 Training Data Set	(2) Model 1 Validation Data Set	(3) Model 2 Training Data Set	(4) Model 2 Validation Data Set	(5) Model 3 Training Data Set	(6) Model 3 Validation Data Set
p	5	5	6	6	7	7
b_0	3.8524	3.6350	3.8671	3.6143	4.0540	3.4699
$s\{b_0\}$	0.1927	0.2894	0.1906	0.2907	0.2348	0.3468
b_1	0.0733	0.0958	0.0712	0.0999	0.0715	0.0987
$s\{b_1\}$	0.0190	0.0319	0.0188	0.0323	0.0186	0.0325
b_2	0.0142	0.0164	0.0139	0.0159	0.0138	0.0162
$s\{b_2\}$	0.0017	0.0023	0.0017	0.0024	0.0017	0.0024
b_3	0.0155	0.0156	0.0151	0.0154	0.0151	0.0156
$s\{b_3\}$	0.0014	0.0020	0.0014	0.0020	0.0014	0.0021
b_5	—	—	—	—	−0.0035	0.0025
$s\{b_5\}$	—	—	—	—	0.0026	0.0033
b_6	—	—	0.0869	0.0731	0.0873	0.0727
$s\{b_6\}$	—	—	0.0582	0.0792	0.0577	0.0795
b_8	0.3530	0.1860	0.3627	0.1886	0.3509	0.1931
$s\{b_8\}$	0.0772	0.0964	0.0765	0.0966	0.0764	0.0972
SSE_p	2.1788	3.7951	2.0820	3.7288	2.0052	3.6822
$PRESS_p$	2.7378	4.5219	2.7827	4.6536	2.7723	4.8981
C_p	5.7508	6.2094	5.5406	7.3331	5.7874	8.7166
MSE_p	0.0445	0.0775	0.0434	0.0777	0.0427	0.0783
$MSPR$	0.0773	—	0.0764	—	0.0794	—
$R_{a,p}^2$	0.8160	0.6824	0.8205	0.6815	0.8234	0.6787

TABLE 9.5   **Potential Predictor Variables and Response Variable—Surgical Unit Example.**

Case Number i	Blood-Clotting Score X_{i1}	Prognostic Index X_{i2}	Enzyme Test X_{i3}	Liver Test X_{i4}	Age X_{i5}	Gender X_{i6}	Alc. Use: Mod. X_{i7}	Alc. Use: Heavy X_{i8}	Survival Time Y_i	$Y_i' = \ln Y_i$
55	7.1	23	78	1.93	45	0	1	0	302	5.710
56	4.9	66	91	3.05	34	1	0	0	767	6.642
57	6.4	90	35	1.06	39	1	0	1	487	6.188
...	...	...	...	...	...	...	...	...	...	...
106	6.9	90	33	2.78	48	1	0	0	655	6.485
107	7.9	45	55	2.46	43	0	1	0	377	5.932
108	4.5	68	60	2.07	59	0	0	0	642	6.465

value reasonably close to SSE_p supports the validity of the fitted regression model and of MSE_p as an indicator of the predictive capability of this model. In this case, all three of the candidate models have $PRESS_p$ values that are reasonably close to SSE_p. For example, for Model 1, $PRESS_p = 2.7378$ and $SSE_p = 2.1788$. Recall also that if $C_p \approx p$, this suggests that there is little or no bias in the regression model. This is the case for the three models under consideration. The C_5, C_6, and C_7 values for the three models are, respectively, 5.7508, 5.5406, and 5.7874.

To validate the selected regression model externally, 54 additional cases had been held out for a validation data set. A portion of the data for these cases is shown in Table 9.5. The correlation matrix for these new data (not shown) is quite similar to the one in Figure 9.3 for the model-building data set. The estimated regression coefficients, their estimated standard deviations, and various model-selection criteria when regression models (9.21), (9.22), and (9.23) are fitted to the validation data set are shown in Table 9.4, columns 2, 4, and 6. Note the excellent agreement between the two sets of estimated regression coefficients, and the two sets of regression coefficient standard errors. For example, for Model 1 fit to the training data, $b_1 = .0733$; when fit to the validation data, we obtain $b_1 = .0958$. In view of the magnitude of the corresponding standard errors (.0190 and .0319), these values are reasonably close.

A review of Table 9.4 shows that most of the estimated coefficients agree quite closely. However, it is noteworthy that b_5 in Model 3—the coefficient of age—is negative for the training data ($b_5 = -0.0035$), and positive for the validation data ($b_5 = 0.0025$). This is certainly a cause for concern, and it raises doubts about the validity of Model 3.

To calibrate the predictive ability of the regression models fitted from the training data set, the mean squared prediction errors $MSPR$ in (9.20) were calculated for the 54 cases in the validation data set in Table 9.5 for each of the three candidate models; they are .0773, .0764, and .0794, respectively. The mean squared prediction error generally will be larger than MSE_p based on the training data set because entirely new data are involved in the validation data set. In this case, the relevant MSE_p values for the three models are .0445, .0434, and .0427. The fact that $MSPR$ here does not differ too greatly from MSE_p implies that the error mean square MSE_p based on the training data set is a reasonably valid indicator of the predictive ability of the fitted regression model. The closeness of the three $MSPR$

values suggest that the three candidate models perform comparably in terms of predictive accuracy.

As a consequence of the concerns noted earlier about Model 3, this model was eliminated from further consideration. The final selection was based on the principle of parsimony. While Models 1 and 2 performed comparably in the validation study, Model 1 achieves this level of performance with one fewer parameter. For this reason, Model 1 was ultimately chosen by the investigator as the final model.

Comments

1. Algorithms are available to split data so that the two data sets have similar statistical properties. The reader is referred to Reference 9.11 for a discussion of this and other issues associated with validation of regression models.

2. Refinements of data splitting have been proposed. With the *double cross-validation procedure,* for example, the model is built for each half of the split data and then tested on the other half of the data. Thus, two measures of consistency and predictive ability are obtained from the two fitted models. For smaller data sets, a procedure called *K-fold cross-validation* is often used. With this procedure, the data are first split into K roughly equal parts. For $k = 1, 2, \ldots, K$, we use the kth part as the validation set, fit the model using the other $k - 1$ parts, and obtain the predicted sum of squares for error. The K estimates of prediction error are then combined to produce a *K-fold cross-validation estimate.* Note that when $K = n$, the K-fold cross-validation estimate is the identical to the $PRESS_p$ statistic.

3. For small data sets where data splitting is impractical, the $PRESS$ criterion in (9.17), considered earlier for use in subset selection, can be employed as a form of data splitting to assess the precision of model predictions. Recall that with this procedure, each data point is predicted from the least squares fitted regression function developed from the remaining $n - 1$ data points. A fairly close agreement between $PRESS$ and SSE suggests that MSE may be a reasonably valid indicator of the selected model's predictive capability. Variations of $PRESS$ for validation have also been proposed, whereby m cases are held out for validation and the remaining $n - m$ cases are used to fit the model. Reference 9.11 discusses these procedures, as well as issues dealing with optimal splitting of data sets.

4. When regression models built on observational data do not predict well outside the range of the X observations in the data set, the usual reason is the existence of multicollinearity among the X variables. Chapter 11 introduces possible solutions for this difficulty including ridge regression or other biased estimation techniques.

5. If a data set for an exploratory observational study is very large, it can be divided into three parts. The first part is used for model training, the second part for cross-validation and model selection, and the third part for testing and calibrating the final model (Reference 9.10). This approach avoids any bias resulting from estimating the regression parameters from the same data set used for developing the model. A disadvantage of this procedure is that the parameter estimates are derived from a smaller data set and hence are more imprecise than if the original data set were divided into two parts for model building and validation. Consequently, the division of a data set into three parts is used in practice only when the available data set is very large. ∎

Cited References

9.1. Daniel, C., and F. S. Wood. *Fitting Equations to Data: Computer Analysis of Multifactor Data.* 2nd ed. New York: John Wiley & Sons, 1999.

9.2. Freedman, D. A. "A Note on Screening Regression Equations," *The American Statistician* 37 (1983), pp. 152–55.

9.3. Pope, P. T., and J. T. Webster. "The Use of an F-Statistic in Stepwise Regression," *Technometrics* 14 (1972), pp. 327–40.

9.4. Mantel, N. "Why Stepdown Procedures in Variable Selection," *Technometrics* 12 (1970), pp. 621–25.

9.5. Miller, A. J. *Subset Selection in Regression*. 2nd ed. London: Chapman and Hall, 2002.

9.6. Faraway, J. J. "On the Cost of Data Analysis," *Journal of Computational and Graphical Statistics* 1 (1992), pp. 213–29.

9.7. Breiman, L., and P. Spector. "Submodel Selection and Evaluation in Regression. The X-Random Case," *International Statistical Review* 60 (1992), pp. 291–319.

9.8. Lindsay, R. M., and A. S. C. Ehrenberg. "The Design of Replicated Studies," *The American Statistician* 47 (1993), pp. 217–28.

9.9. Snee, R. D. "Validation of Regression Models: Methods and Examples," *Technometrics* 19 (1977), pp. 415–28.

9.10. Hastie, T., Tibshirani, R., and J. Friedman. *The Elements of Statistical Learning: Data Mining, Inference, and Prediction*. New York: Springer-Verlag, 2001.

9.11. Stone, M. "Cross-validatory Choice and Assessment of Statistical Prediction," *Journal of the Royal Statistical Society B* 36 (1974), pp. 111–47.

Problems

9.1. A speaker stated: "In well-designed experiments involving quantitative explanatory variables, a procedure for reducing the number of explanatory variables after the data are obtained is not necessary." Discuss.

9.2. The dean of a graduate school wishes to predict the grade point average in graduate work for recent applicants. List a dozen variables that might be useful explanatory variables here.

9.3. Two researchers, investigating factors affecting summer attendance at privately operated beaches on Lake Ontario, collected information on attendance and 11 explanatory variables for 42 beaches. Two summers were studied, of relatively hot and relatively cool weather, respectively. A "best" subsets algorithm now is to be used to reduce the number of explanatory variables for the final regression model.

   a. Should the variables reduction be done for both summers combined, or should it be done separately for each summer? Explain the problems involved and how you might handle them.

   b. Will the "best" subsets selection procedure choose those explanatory variables that are most important in a causal sense for determining beach attendance?

9.4. In forward stepwise regression, what advantage is there in using a relatively small α-to-enter value for adding variables? What advantage is there in using a larger α-to-enter value?

9.5. In forward stepwise regression, why should the α-to-enter value for adding variables never exceed the α-to-remove value for deleting variables?

9.6. Prepare a flowchart of each of the following selection methods: (1) forward stepwise regression, (2) forward selection, (3) backward elimination.

9.7. An engineer has stated: "Reduction of the number of explanatory variables should always be done using the objective forward stepwise regression procedure." Discuss.

9.8. An attendee at a regression modeling short course stated: "I rarely see validation of regression models mentioned in published papers, so it must really not be an important component of model building." Comment.

*9.9. Refer to **Patient satisfaction** Problem 6.15. The hospital administrator wishes to determine the best subset of predictor variables for predicting patient satisfaction.

a. Indicate which subset of predictor variables you would recommend as best for predicting patient satisfaction according to each of the following criteria: (1) $R^2_{a,p}$, (2) AIC_p, (3) C_p, (4) $PRESS_p$. Support your recommendations with appropriate graphs.

b. Do the four criteria in part (a) identify the same best subset? Does this always happen?

c. Would forward stepwise regression have any advantages here as a screening procedure over the all-possible-regressions procedure?

*9.10. **Job proficiency.** A personnel officer in a governmental agency administered four newly developed aptitude tests to each of 25 applicants for entry-level clerical positions in the agency. For purpose of the study, all 25 applicants were accepted for positions irrespective of their test scores. After a probationary period, each applicant was rated for proficiency on the job. The scores on the four tests (X_1, X_2, X_3, X_4) and the job proficiency score (Y) for the 25 employees were as follows:

Subject	Test Score				Job Proficiency Score
i	X_{i1}	X_{i2}	X_{i3}	X_{i4}	Y_i
1	86	110	100	87	88
2	62	97	99	100	80
3	110	107	103	103	96
...	...	...	...	...	...
23	104	73	93	80	78
24	94	121	115	104	115
25	91	129	97	83	83

a. Prepare separate stem-and-leaf plots of the test scores for each of the four newly developed aptitude tests. Are there any noteworthy features in these plots? Comment.

b. Obtain the scatter plot matrix. Also obtain the correlation matrix of the X variables. What do the scatter plots suggest about the nature of the functional relationship between the response variable Y and each of the predictor variables? Are any serious multicollinearity problems evident? Explain.

c. Fit the multiple regression function containing all four predictor variables as first-order terms. Does it appear that all predictor variables should be retained?

*9.11. Refer to **Job proficiency** Problem 9.10.

a. Using only first-order terms for the predictor variables in the pool of potential X variables, find the four best subset regression models according to the $R^2_{a,p}$ criterion.

b. Since there is relatively little difference in $R^2_{a,p}$ for the four best subset models, what other criteria would you use to help in the selection of the best model? Discuss.

9.12. Refer to **Market share** data set in Appendix C.3 and Problem 8.42.

a. Using only first-order terms for predictor variables, find the three best subset regression models according to the SBC_p criterion.

b. Is your finding here in agreement with what you found in Problem 8.42 (b) and (c)?

9.13. **Lung pressure.** Increased arterial blood pressure in the lungs frequently leads to the development of heart failure in patients with chronic obstructive pulmonary disease (COPD). The standard method for determining arterial lung pressure is invasive, technically difficult, and involves some risk to the patient. Radionuclide imaging is a noninvasive, less risky method for estimating arterial pressure in the lungs. To investigate the predictive ability of this method, a cardiologist collected data on 19 mild-to-moderate COPD patients. The data that follow on the next page include the invasive measure of systolic pulmonary arterial pressure (Y) and three potential noninvasive predictor variables. Two were obtained by using radionuclide imaging—emptying rate of blood into the pumping chamber of the heart (X_1) and ejection rate of blood pumped out of the heart into the lungs (X_2)—and the third predictor variable measures a blood gas (X_3).

a. Prepare separate dot plots for each of the three predictor variables. Are there any noteworthy features in these plots? Comment.

b. Obtain the scatter plot matrix. Also obtain the correlation matrix of the X variables. What do the scatter plots suggest about the nature of the functional relationship between Y and each of the predictor variables? Are any serious multicollinearity problems evident? Explain.

c. Fit the multiple regression function containing the three predictor variables as first-order terms. Does it appear that all predictor variables should be retained?

Subject i	X_{i1}	X_{i2}	X_{i3}	Y_i
1	45	36	45	49
2	30	28	40	55
3	11	16	42	85
...	...	...	...	...
17	27	51	44	29
18	37	32	54	40
19	34	40	36	31

Adapted from A. T. Marmor et al., "Improved Radionuclide Method for Assessment of Pulmonary Artery Pressure in COPD," *Chest* 89 (1986), pp. 64–69.

9.14. Refer to **Lung pressure** Problem 9.13.

a. Using first-order and second-order terms for each of the three predictor variables (centered around the mean) in the pool of potential X variables (including cross products of the first-order terms), find the three best hierarchical subset regression models according to the $R^2_{a,p}$ criterion.

b. Is there much difference in $R^2_{a,p}$ for the three best subset models?

9.15. **Kidney function.** Creatinine clearance (Y) is an important measure of kidney function, but is difficult to obtain in a clinical office setting because it requires 24-hour urine collection. To determine whether this measure can be predicted from some data that are easily available, a kidney specialist obtained the data that follow for 33 male subjects. The predictor variables are serum creatinine concentration (X_1), age (X_2), and weight (X_3).

Subject i	X_{i1}	X_{i2}	X_{i3}	Y_i
1	.71	38	71	132
2	1.48	78	69	53
3	2.21	69	85	50
...	...	...	...	...
31	1.53	70	75	52
32	1.58	63	62	73
33	1.37	68	52	57

Adapted from W. J. Shih and S. Weisberg, "Assessing Influence in Multiple Linear Regression with Incomplete Data," *Technometrics* 28 (1986), pp. 231–40.

a. Prepare separate dot plots for each of the three predictor variables. Are there any noteworthy features in these plots? Comment.

b. Obtain the scatter plot matrix. Also obtain the correlation matrix of the X variables. What do the scatter plots suggest about the nature of the functional relationship between the response variable Y and each predictor variable? Discuss. Are any serious multicollinearity problems evident? Explain.

c. Fit the multiple regression function containing the three predictor variables as first-order terms. Does it appear that all predictor variables should be retained?

9.16. Refer to **Kidney function** Problem 9.15.

a. Using first-order and second-order terms for each of the three predictor variables (centered around the mean) in the pool of potential X variables (including cross products of the first-order terms), find the three best hierarchical subset regression models according to the C_p criterion.

b. Is there much difference in C_p for the three best subset models?

*9.17. Refer to **Patient satisfaction** Problems 6.15 and 9.9. The hospital administrator was interested to learn how the forward stepwise selection procedure and some of its variations would perform here.

a. Determine the subset of variables that is selected as best by the forward stepwise regression procedure, using F limits of 3.0 and 2.9 to add or delete a variable, respectively. Show your steps.

b. To what level of significance in any individual test is the F limit of 3.0 for adding a variable approximately equivalent here?

c. Determine the subset of variables that is selected as best by the forward selection procedure, using an F limit of 3.0 to add a variable. Show your steps.

d. Determine the subset of variables that is selected as best by the backward elimination procedure, using an F limit of 2.9 to delete a variable. Show your steps.

e. Compare the results of the three selection procedures. How consistent are these results? How do the results compare with those for all possible regressions in Problem 9.9?

*9.18. Refer to **Job proficiency** Problems 9.10 and 9.11.

a. Using forward stepwise regression, find the best subset of predictor variables to predict job proficiency. Use α limits of .05 and .10 for adding or deleting a variable, respectively.

b. How does the best subset according to forward stepwise regression compare with the best subset according to the $R^2_{a,p}$ criterion obtained in Problem 9.11a?

9.19. Refer to **Kidney function** Problems 9.15 and 9.16.

a. Using the same pool of potential X variables as in Problem 9.16a, find the best subset of variables according to forward stepwise regression with α limits of .10 and .15 to add or delete a variable, respectively.

b. How does the best subset according to forward stepwise regression compare with the best subset according to the $R^2_{a,p}$ criterion obtained in Problem 9.16a?

9.20. Refer to **Market share** data set in Appendix C.3 and Problems 8.42 and 9.12.

a. Using forward stepwise regression, find the best subset of predictor variables to predict market share of their product. Use α limits of .10 and .15 for adding or deleting a predictor, respectively.

b. How does the best subset according to forward stepwise regression compare with the best subset according to the SBC_p criterion used in 9.12a?

*9.21. Refer to **Job proficiency** Problems 9.10 and 9.18. To assess internally the predictive ability of the regression model identified in Problem 9.18, compute the *PRESS* statistic and compare it to *SSE*. What does this comparison suggest about the validity of *MSE* as an indicator of the predictive ability of the fitted model?

*9.22. Refer to **Job proficiency** Problems 9.10 and 9.18. To assess externally the validity of the regression model identified in Problem 9.18, 25 additional applicants for entry-level clerical positions in the agency were similarly tested and hired irrespective of their test scores. The data follow.

Subject	Test Score				Job Proficiency Score
i	X_{i1}	X_{i2}	X_{i3}	X_{i4}	Y_i
26	65	109	88	84	58
27	85	90	104	98	92
28	93	73	91	82	71
...	...	...	...	...	...
48	115	119	102	94	95
49	129	70	94	95	81
50	136	104	106	104	109

a. Obtain the correlation matrix of the X variables for the validation data set and compare it with that obtained in Problem 9.10b for the model-building data set. Are the two correlation matrices reasonably similar?

b. Fit the regression model identified in Problem 9.18a to the validation data set. Compare the estimated regression coefficients and their estimated standard deviations to those obtained in Problem 9.18a. Also compare the error mean squares and coefficients of multiple determination. Do the estimates for the validation data set appear to be reasonably similar to those obtained for the model-building data set?

c. Calculate the mean squared prediction error in (9.20) and compare it to *MSE* obtained from the model-building data set. Is there evidence of a substantial bias problem in *MSE* here? Is this conclusion consistent with your finding in Problem 9.21? Discuss.

d. Combine the model-building data set in Problem 9.10 with the validation data set and fit the selected regression model to the combined data. Are the estimated standard deviations of the estimated regression coefficients appreciably reduced now from those obtained for the model-building data set?

9.23. Refer to **Lung pressure** Problems 9.13 and 9.14. The validity of the regression model identified as best in Problem 9.14a is to be assessed internally.

a. Calculate the *PRESS* statistic and compare it to *SSE*. What does this comparison suggest about the validity of *MSE* as an indicator of the predictive ability of the fitted model?

b. Case 8 alone accounts for approximately one-half of the entire *PRESS* statistic. Would you recommend modification of the model because of the strong impact of this case? What are some corrective action options that would lessen the effect of case 8? Discuss.

Exercise

9.24 The true quadratic regression function is $E\{Y\} = 15 + 20X + 3X^2$. The fitted linear regression function is $\hat{Y} = 13 + 40X$, for which $E\{b_0\} = 10$ and $E\{b_1\} = 45$. What are the bias and sampling error components of the mean squared error for $X_i = 10$ and for $X_i = 20$?

Projects   9.25. Refer to the **SENIC** data set in Appendix C.1. Length of stay (Y) is to be predicted, and the pool of potential predictor variables includes all other variables in the data set except medical school affiliation and region. It is believed that a model with $\log_{10} Y$ as the response variable and the predictor variables in first-order terms with no interaction terms will be appropriate. Consider cases 57–113 to constitute the model-building data set to be used for the following analyses.

a. Prepare separate dot plots for each of the predictor variables. Are there any noteworthy features in these plots? Comment.

b. Obtain the scatter plot matrix. Also obtain the correlation matrix of the X variables. Is there evidence of strong linear pairwise associations among the predictor variables here?

c. Obtain the three best subsets according to the C_p criterion. Which of these subset models appears to have the smallest bias?

9.26. Refer to the **CDI** data set in Appendix C.2. A public safety official wishes to predict the rate of serious crimes in a CDI (Y, total number of serious crimes per 100,000 population). The pool of potential predictor variables includes all other variables in the data set except total population, total serious crimes, county, state, and region. It is believed that a model with predictor variables in first-order terms with no interaction terms will be appropriate. Consider the even-numbered cases to constitute the model-building data set to be used for the following analyses.

a. Prepare separate stem-and-leaf plots for each of the predictor variables. Are there any noteworthy features in these plots? Comment.

b. Obtain the scatter plot matrix. Also obtain the correlation matrix of the X variables. Is there evidence of strong linear pairwise associations among the predictor variables here?

c. Using the SBC_p criterion, obtain the three best subsets.

9.27. Refer to the **SENIC** data set in Appendix C.1 and Project 9.25. The regression model identified as best in Project 9.25 is to be validated by means of the validation data set consisting of cases 1–56.

a. Fit the regression model identified in Project 9.25 as best to the validation data set. Compare the estimated regression coefficients and their estimated standard deviations with those obtained in Project 9.25. Also compare the error mean squares and coefficients of multiple determination. Does the model fitted to the validation data set yield similar estimates as the model fitted to the model-building data set?

b. Calculate the mean squared prediction error in (9.20) and compare it to *MSE* obtained from the model-building data set. Is there evidence of a substantial bias problem in *MSE* here?

c. Combine the model-building and validation data sets and fit the selected regression model to the combined data. Are the estimated regression coefficients and their estimated standard deviations appreciably different from those for the model-building data set? Should you expect any differences in the estimates? Explain.

9.28. Refer to the **CDI** data set in Appendix C.2 and Project 9.26. The regression model identified as best in Project 9.26c is to be validated by means of the validation data set consisting of the odd-numbered CDIs.

a. Fit the regression model identified in Project 9.26 as best to the validation data set. Compare the estimated regression coefficients and their estimated standard deviations with those obtained in Project 9.26c. Also compare the error mean squares and coefficients of multiple determination. Does the model fitted to the validation data set yield similar estimates as the model fitted to the model-building data set?

b. Calculate the mean squared prediction error in (9.20) and compare it to *MSE* obtained from the model-building data set. Is there evidence of a substantial bias problem in *MSE* here?

c. Fit the selected regression model to the combined model-building and validation data sets. Are the estimated regression coefficients and their estimated standard deviations appreciably different from those for the model fitted to the model-building data set? Should you expect any differences in the estimates? Explain.

Case Studies

9.29. Refer to the **Website developer** data set in Appendix C.6. Management is interested in determining what variables have the greatest impact on production output in the release of new customer websites. Data on 13 three-person website development teams consisting of a project manager, a designer, and a developer are provided in the data set. Production data from January 2001 through August 2002 include four potential predictors: (1) the change in the website development process, (2) the size of the backlog of orders, (3) the team effect, and (4) the number of months experience of each team. Develop a best subset model for predicting production output. Justify your choice of model. Assess your model's ability to predict and discuss its use as a tool for management decisions.

9.30. Refer to the **Prostate cancer** data set in Appendix C.5. Serum prostate-specific antigen (PSA) was determined in 97 men with advanced prostate cancer. PSA is a well-established screening test for prostate cancer and the oncologists wanted to examine the correlation between level of PSA and a number of clinical measures for men who were about to undergo radical prostatectomy. The measures are cancer volume, prostate weight, patient age, the amount of benign prostatic hyperplasia, seminal vesicle invasion, capsular penetration, and Gleason score. Select a random sample of 65 observations to use as the model-building data set. Develop a best subset model for predicting PSA. Justify your choice of model. Assess your model's ability to predict and discuss its usefulness to the oncologists.

9.31. Refer to **Real estate sales** data set in Appendix C.7. Residential sales that occurred during the year 2002 were available from a city in the midwest. Data on 522 arms-length transactions include sales price, style, finished square feet, number of bedrooms, pool, lot size, year built, air conditioning, and whether or not the lot is adjacent to a highway. The city tax assessor was interested in predicting sales price based on the demographic variable information given above. Select a random sample of 300 observations to use in the model-building data set. Develop a best subset model for predicting sales price. Justify your choice of model. Assess your model's ability to predict and discuss its use as a tool for predicting sales price.

9.32. Refer to **Prostate cancer** Case Study 9.30. The regression model identified in Case Study 9.30 is to be validated by means of the validation data set consisting of those cases not selected for the model-building data set.

a. Fit the regression model identified in Case Study 9.30 to the validation data set. Compare the estimated regression coefficients and their estimated standard errors with those obtained in Case Study 9.30. Also compare the error mean square and coefficients of multiple determination. Does the model fitted to the validation data set yield similar estimates as the model fitted to the model-building data set?

b. Calculate the mean squared prediction error (9.20) and compare it to *MSE* obtained from the model-building data set. Is there evidence of a substantial bias problem in *MSE* here?

9.33. Refer to **Real estate sales** Case Study 9.31. The regression model identified in Case Study 9.31 is to be validated by means of the validation data set consisting of those cases not selected for the model building data set.

a. Fit the regression model identified in Case Study 9.31 to the validation data set. Compare the estimated regression coefficients and their estimated standard errors with those obtained in Case Study 9.31. Also compare the error mean square and coefficients of multiple determination. Does the model fitted to the validation data set yield similar estimates as the model fitted to the model-building data set?

b. Calculate the mean squared prediction error (9.20) and compare it to *MSE* obtained from the model-building data set. Is there evidence of a substantial bias problem in *MSE* here?

Chapter 10

Building the Regression Model II: Diagnostics

In this chapter we take up a number of refined diagnostics for checking the adequacy of a regression model. These include methods for detecting improper functional form for a predictor variable, outliers, influential observations, and multicollinearity. We conclude the chapter by illustrating the use of these diagnostic procedures in the surgical unit example. In the following chapter, we take up some remedial measures that are useful when the diagnostic procedures indicate model inadequacies.

10.1 Model Adequacy for a Predictor Variable—Added-Variable Plots

We discussed in Chapters 3 and 6 how a plot of residuals against a predictor variable in the regression model can be used to check whether a curvature effect for that variable is required in the model. We also described the plotting of residuals against predictor variables not yet in the regression model to determine whether it would be helpful to add one or more of these variables to the model.

A limitation of these residual plots is that they may not properly show the nature of the marginal effect of a predictor variable, given the other predictor variables in the model. *Added-variable plots,* also called *partial regression plots* and *adjusted variable plots,* are refined residual plots that provide graphic information about the marginal importance of a predictor variable X_k, given the other predictor variables already in the model. In addition, these plots can at times be useful for identifying the nature of the marginal relation for a predictor variable in the regression model.

Added-variable plots consider the marginal role of a predictor variable X_k, given that the other predictor variables under consideration are already in the model. In an added-variable plot, both the response variable Y and the predictor variable X_k under consideration are regressed against the other predictor variables in the regression model and the residuals are obtained for each. These residuals reflect the part of each variable that is not linearly associated with the other predictor variables already in the regression model. The plot of these residuals against each other (1) shows the marginal importance of this variable in reducing the residual variability and (2) may provide information about the nature of the marginal

FIGURE 10.1
Prototype Added-Variable Plots.

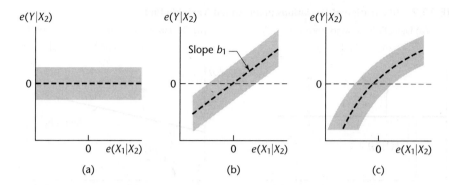

(a)　　　　　　　(b)　　　　　　　(c)

regression relation for the predictor variable X_k under consideration for possible inclusion in the regression model.

To make these ideas more specific, we consider a first-order multiple regression model with two predictor variables X_1 and X_2. The extension to more than two predictor variables is direct. Suppose we are concerned about the nature of the regression effect for X_1, given that X_2 is already in the model. We regress Y on X_2 and obtain the fitted values and residuals:

$$\hat{Y}_i(X_2) = b_0 + b_2 X_{i2} \tag{10.1a}$$

$$e_i(Y|X_2) = Y_i - \hat{Y}_i(X_2) \tag{10.1b}$$

The notation here indicates explicitly the response and predictor variables in the fitted model. We also regress X_1 on X_2 and obtain:

$$\hat{X}_{i1}(X_2) = b_0^* + b_2^* X_{i2} \tag{10.2a}$$

$$e_i(X_1|X_2) = X_{i1} - \hat{X}_{i1}(X_2) \tag{10.2b}$$

The added-variable plot for predictor variable X_1 consists of a plot of the Y residuals $e(Y|X_2)$ against the X_1 residuals $e(X_1|X_2)$.

Figure 10.1 contains several prototype added-variable plots for our example, where X_2 is already in the regression model and X_1 is under consideration to be added. Figure 10.1a shows a horizontal band, indicating that X_1 contains no additional information useful for predicting Y beyond that contained in X_2, so that it is not helpful to add X_1 to the regression model here.

Figure 10.1b shows a linear band with a nonzero slope. This plot indicates that a linear term in X_1 may be a helpful addition to the regression model already containing X_2. It can be shown that the slope of the least squares line through the origin fitted to the plotted residuals is b_1, the regression coefficient of X_1 if this variable were added to the regression model already containing X_2.

Figure 10.1c shows a curvilinear band, indicating that the addition of X_1 to the regression model may be helpful and suggesting the possible nature of the curvature effect by the pattern shown.

Added-variable plots, in addition to providing information about the possible nature of the marginal relationship for a predictor variable, given the other predictor variables already in the regression model, also provide information about the strength of this relationship. To see how this additional information is provided, consider Figure 10.2. Figure 10.2a illustrates

FIGURE 10.2   Illustration of Deviations in an Added-Variable Plot.

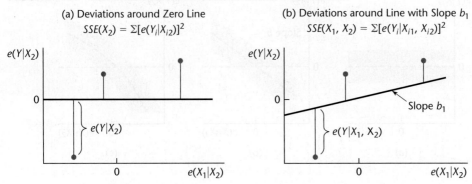

(a) Deviations around Zero Line
$$SSE(X_2) = \Sigma[e(Y_i|X_{i2})]^2$$

(b) Deviations around Line with Slope b_1
$$SSE(X_1, X_2) = \Sigma[e(Y_i|X_{i1}, X_{i2})]^2$$

an added-variable plot for X_1 when X_2 is already in the model, based on $n = 3$ cases. The vertical deviations of the plotted points around the horizontal line $e(Y|X_2) = 0$ shown in Figure 10.2a represent the Y residuals when X_2 alone is in the regression model. When these deviations are squared and summed, we obtain the error sum of squares $SSE(X_2)$. Figure 10.2b shows the same plotted points, but here the vertical deviations of these points are around the least squares line through the origin with slope b_1. These deviations are the residuals $e(Y|X_1, X_2)$ when both X_1 and X_2 are in the regression model. Hence, the sum of the squares of these deviations is the error sum of squares $SSE(X_1, X_2)$.

The difference between the two sums of squared deviations in Figures 10.2a and 10.2b according to (7.1a) is the extra sum of squares $SSR(X_1|X_2)$. Hence, the difference in the magnitudes of the two sets of deviations provides information about the marginal strength of the linear relation of X_1 to the response variable, given that X_2 is in the model. If the scatter of the points around the line through the origin with slope b_1 is much less than the scatter around the horizontal line, inclusion of the variable X_1 in the regression model will provide a substantial further reduction in the error sum of squares.

Added-variable plots are also useful for uncovering outlying data points that may have a strong influence in estimating the relationship of the predictor variable X_k to the response variable, given the other predictor variables already in the model.

Example 1

Table 10.1 shows a portion of the data on average annual income of managers during the past two years (X_1), a score measuring each manager's risk aversion (X_2), and the amount of life insurance carried (Y) for a sample of 18 managers in the 30–39 age group. Risk aversion was measured by a standard questionnaire administered to each manager: the higher the score, the greater the degree of risk aversion. Income and risk aversion are mildly correlated here, the coefficient of correlation being $r_{12} = .254$.

A fit of the first-order regression model yields:

$$\hat{Y} = -205.72 + 6.2880X_1 + 4.738X_2 \tag{10.3}$$

The residuals for this fitted model are plotted against X_1 in Figure 10.3a. This residual plot clearly suggests that a linear relation for X_1 is not appropriate in the model already containing X_2. To obtain more information about the nature of this relationship, we shall use an added-variable plot. We regress Y and X_1 each against X_2. When doing this, we

TABLE 10.1
Basic Data—Life Insurance Example.

Manager i	Average Annual Income (thousand dollars) X_{i1}	Risk Aversion Score X_{i2}	Amount of Life Insurance Carried (thousand dollars) Y_i
1	45.010	6	91
2	57.204	4	162
3	26.852	5	11
...	...	...	...
16	46.130	4	91
17	30.366	3	14
18	39.060	5	63

FIGURE 10.3   Residual Plot and Added-Variable Plot—Life Insurance Example.

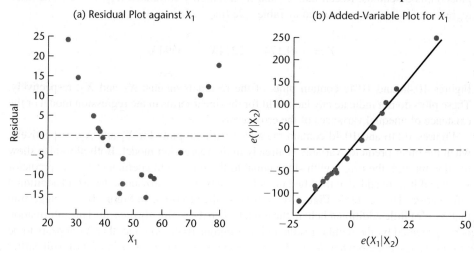

(a) Residual Plot against X_1

(b) Added-Variable Plot for X_1

obtain:

$$\hat{Y}(X_2) = 50.70 + 15.54X_2 \tag{10.4a}$$

$$\hat{X}_1(X_2) = 40.779 + 1.718X_2 \tag{10.4b}$$

The residuals from these two fitted models are plotted against each other in the added-variable plot in Figure 10.3b. This plot also contains the least squares line through the origin, which has slope $b_1 = 6.2880$. The added-variable plot suggests that the curvilinear relation between Y and X_1 when X_2 is already in the regression model is strongly positive, and that a slight concave upward shape may be present. The suggested concavity of the relationship is also evident from the vertical deviations around the line through the origin with slope b_1. These deviations are positive at the left, negative in the middle, and positive again at the right. Overall, the deviations from linearity appear to be modest in the range of the predictor variables.

Note also that the scatter of the points around the least squares line through the origin with slope $b_1 = 6.2880$ is much smaller than is the scatter around the horizontal line $e(Y|X_2) = 0$, indicating that adding X_1 to the regression model with a linear relation will substantially reduce the error sum of squares. In fact, the coefficient of partial determination for the linear effect of X_1 is $R^2_{Y1|2} = .984$. Incorporating a curvilinear effect for X_1 will lead to only a modest further reduction in the error sum of squares since the plotted points are already quite close to the linear relation through the origin with slope b_1.

Finally, the added-variable plot in Figure 10.3b shows one outlying case, in the upper right corner. The influence of this case needs to be investigated by procedures to be explained later in this chapter.

Example 2

For the body fat example in Table 7.1 (page 257), we consider here the regression of body fat (Y) only on triceps skinfold thickness (X_1) and thigh circumference (X_2). We omit the third predictor variable (X_3, midarm circumference) to focus the discussion of added-variable plots on its essentials. Recall that X_1 and X_2 are highly correlated ($r_{12} = .92$). The fitted regression function was obtained in Table 7.2c (page 258):

$$\hat{Y} = -19.174 + .2224X_1 + .6594X_2$$

Figures 10.4a and 10.4c contain plots of the residuals against X_1 and X_2, respectively. These plots do not indicate any lack of fit for the linear terms in the regression model or the existence of unequal variances of the error terms.

Figures 10.4b and 10.4d contain the added-variable plots for X_1 and X_2, respectively, when the other predictor variable is already in the regression model. Both plots also show the line through the origin with slope equal to the regression coefficient for the predictor variable if it were added to the fitted model. These two plots provide some useful additional information. The scatter in Figure 10.4b follows the prototype in Figure 10.1a, suggesting that X_1 is of little additional help in the model when X_2 is already present. This information is not provided by the regular residual plot in Figure 10.4a. The fact that X_1 appears to be of little marginal help when X_2 is already in the regression model is in accord with earlier findings in Chapter 7. We saw there that the coefficient of partial determination is only $R^2_{Y1|2} = .031$ and that the t^* statistic for b_1 is only .73.

The added-variable plot for X_2 in Figure 10.4d follows the prototype in Figure 10.1b, showing a linear scatter with positive slope. We also see in Figure 10.4d that there is somewhat less variability around the line with slope b_2 than around the horizontal line $e(Y|X_1) = 0$. This suggests that: (1) variable X_2 may be helpful in the regression model even when X_1 is already in the model, and (2) a linear term in X_2 appears to be adequate because no curvilinear relation is suggested by the scatter of points. Thus, the added-variable plot for X_2 in Figure 10.4d complements the regular residual plot in Figure 10.4c by indicating the potential usefulness of thigh circumference (X_2) in the regression model when triceps skinfold thickness (X_1) is already in the model. This information is consistent with the t^* statistic for b_2 of 2.26 in Table 7.2c and the moderate coefficient of partial determination of $R^2_{Y2|1} = .232$. Finally, the added-variable plot in Figure 10.4d reveals the presence of one potentially influential case (case 3) in the lower left corner. The influence of this case will be investigated in greater detail in Section 10.4.

FIGURE 10.4
**Residual Plots
and Added-
Variable
Plots—Body
Fat Example
with Two
Predictor
Variables.**

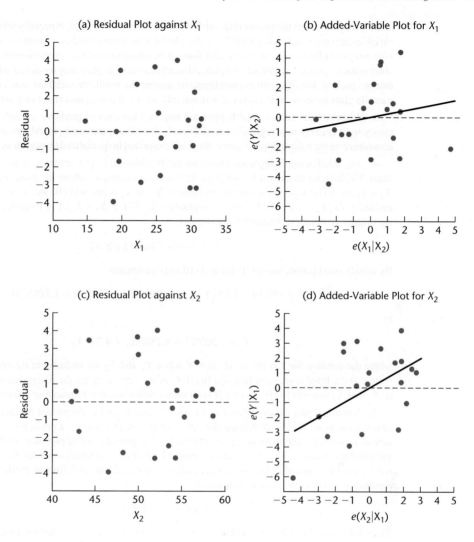

(a) Residual Plot against X_1

(b) Added-Variable Plot for X_1

(c) Residual Plot against X_2

(d) Added-Variable Plot for X_2

Comments

1. An added-variable plot only suggests the nature of the functional relation in which a predictor variable should be added to the regression model but does not provide an analytic expression of the relation. Furthermore, the relation shown is for X_k adjusted for the other predictor variables in the regression model, not for X_k directly. Hence, a variety of transformations or curvature effect terms may need to be investigated and additional residual plots utilized to identify the best transformation or curvature effect terms.

2. Added-variable plots need to be used with caution for identifying the nature of the marginal effect of a predictor variable. These plots may not show the proper form of the marginal effect of a predictor variable if the functional relations for some or all of the predictor variables already in the regression model are misspecified. For example, if X_2 and X_3 are related in a curvilinear fashion to the response variable but the regression model uses linear terms only, the added-variable plots for X_2

and X_3 may not show the proper relationships to the response variable, especially when the predictor variables are correlated. Since added-variable plots for the several predictor variables are all concerned with marginal effects only, they may therefore not be effective when the relations of the predictor variables to the response variable are complex. Also, added-variable plots may not detect interaction effects that are present. Finally, high multicollinearity among the predictor variables may cause the added-variable plots to show an improper functional relation for the marginal effect of a predictor variable.

3. When several added-variable plots are required for a set of predictor variables, it is not necessary to fit entirely new regression models each time. Computational procedures are available that economize on the calculations required; these are explained in specialized texts such as Reference 10.1.

4. Any fitted multiple regression function can be obtained from a sequence of fitted partial regressions. To illustrate this, consider again the life insurance example, where the fitted regression of Y on X_2 is given in (10.4a) and the fitted regression of X_1 on X_2 is given in (10.4b). If we now regress the residuals $e(Y|X_2) = Y - \hat{Y}(X_2)$ on the residuals $e(X_1|X_2) = X_1 - \hat{X}_1(X_2)$, using regression through the origin, we obtain (calculations not shown):

$$e(\widehat{Y|X_2}) = 6.2880[e(X_1|X_2)] \tag{10.5}$$

By simple substitution, using (10.4a) and (10.4b), we obtain:

$$[\hat{Y} - (50.70 + 15.54X_2)] = 6.2880[X_1 - (40.779 + 1.718X_2)]$$

or:

$$\hat{Y} = -205.72 + 6.2880X_1 + 4.737X_2 \tag{10.6}$$

where the solution for Y is the fitted value $\hat{Y}$ when X_1 and X_2 are included in the regression model. Note that the fitted regression function in (10.6) is the same as when the regression model was fitted to X_1 and X_2 directly in (10.3), except for a minor difference due to rounding effects.

5. A residual plot closely related to the added-variable plot is the *partial residual plot*. This plot also is used as an aid for identifying the nature of the relationship for a predictor variable X_k under consideration for addition to the regression model. The partial residual plot takes as the starting point the usual residuals $e_i = Y_i - \hat{Y}_i$ when the model including X_k is fitted, to which the regression effect for X_k is added. Specifically, the partial residuals for examining the effect of predictor variable X_k, denoted by $p_i(X_k)$, are defined as follows:

$$p_i(X_k) = e_i + b_k X_{ik} \tag{10.7}$$

Thus, for a partial residual, we add the effect of X_k, as reflected by the fitted model term $b_k X_{ik}$, back onto the residual. A plot of these partial residuals against X_k is referred to as a partial residual plot. The reader is referred to References 10.2 and 10.3 for more details on partial residual plots.   ■

10.2   Identifying Outlying Y Observations—Studentized Deleted Residuals

Outlying Cases

Frequently in regression analysis applications, the data set contains some cases that are outlying or extreme; that is, the observations for these cases are well separated from the remainder of the data. These outlying cases may involve large residuals and often have dramatic effects on the fitted least squares regression function. It is therefore important to

FIGURE 10.5
Scatter Plot for
Regression
with One
Predictor
Variable
Illustrating
Outlying
Cases.

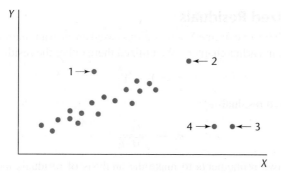

study the outlying cases carefully and decide whether they should be retained or eliminated, and if retained, whether their influence should be reduced in the fitting process and/or the regression model should be revised.

A case may be outlying or extreme with respect to its Y value, its X value(s), or both. Figure 10.5 illustrates this for the case of regression with a single predictor variable. In the scatter plot in Figure 10.5, case 1 is outlying with respect to its Y value, given X. Note that this point falls far outside the scatter, although its X value is near the middle of the range of observations on the predictor variable. Cases 2, 3, and 4 are outlying with respect to their X values since they have much larger X values than those for the other cases; cases 3 and 4 are also outlying with respect to their Y values, given X.

Not all outlying cases have a strong influence on the fitted regression function. Case 1 in Figure 10.5 may not be too influential because a number of other cases have similar X values that will keep the fitted regression function from being displaced too far by the outlying case. Likewise, case 2 may not be too influential because its Y value is consistent with the regression relation displayed by the nonextreme cases. Cases 3 and 4, on the other hand, are likely to be very influential in affecting the fit of the regression function. They are outlying with regard to their X values, and their Y values are not consistent with the regression relation for the other cases.

A basic step in any regression analysis is to determine if the regression model under consideration is heavily influenced by one or a few cases in the data set. For regression with one or two predictor variables, it is relatively simple to identify outlying cases with respect to their X or Y values by means of box plots, stem-and-leaf plots, scatter plots, and residual plots, and to study whether they are influential in affecting the fitted regression function. When more than two predictor variables are included in the regression model, however, the identification of outlying cases by simple graphic means becomes difficult because single-variable or two-variable examinations do not necessarily help find outliers relative to a multivariable regression model. Some univariate outliers may not be extreme in a multiple regression model, and, conversely, some multivariable outliers may not be detectable in single-variable or two-variable analyses.

We now discuss the use of some refined measures for identifying cases with outlying Y observations. In the following section we take up the identification of cases that are multivariable outliers with respect to their X values.

Residuals and Semistudentized Residuals

The detection of outlying or extreme Y observations based on an examination of the residuals has been considered in earlier chapters. We utilized there either the residual e_i:

$$e_i = Y_i - \hat{Y}_i \tag{10.8}$$

or the semistudentized residuals e_i^*:

$$e_i^* = \frac{e_i}{\sqrt{MSE}} \tag{10.9}$$

We introduce now two refinements to make the analysis of residuals more effective for identifying outlying Y observations. These refinements require the use of the hat matrix, which we encountered in Chapters 5 and 6.

Hat Matrix

The hat matrix was defined in (6.30a):

$$\underset{n \times n}{\mathbf{H}} = \mathbf{X}(\mathbf{X'X})^{-1}\mathbf{X'} \tag{10.10}$$

We noted in (6.30) that the fitted values $\hat{Y}_i$ can be expressed as linear combinations of the observations Y_i through the hat matrix:

$$\hat{\mathbf{Y}} = \mathbf{HY} \tag{10.11}$$

and similarly we noted in (6.31) that the residuals e_i can also be expressed as linear combinations of the observations Y_i by means of the hat matrix:

$$\mathbf{e} = (\mathbf{I} - \mathbf{H})\mathbf{Y} \tag{10.12}$$

Further, we noted in (6.32) that the variance-covariance matrix of the residuals involves the hat matrix:

$$\sigma^2\{\mathbf{e}\} = \sigma^2(\mathbf{I} - \mathbf{H}) \tag{10.13}$$

Therefore, the variance of residual e_i, denoted by $\sigma^2\{e_i\}$, is:

$$\sigma^2\{e_i\} = \sigma^2(1 - h_{ii}) \tag{10.14}$$

where h_{ii} is the ith element on the main diagonal of the hat matrix, and the covariance between residuals e_i and e_j $(i \neq j)$ is:

$$\sigma\{e_i, e_j\} = \sigma^2(0 - h_{ij}) = -h_{ij}\sigma^2 \qquad i \neq j \tag{10.15}$$

where h_{ij} is the element in the ith row and jth column of the hat matrix.

These variances and covariances are estimated by using MSE as the estimator of the error variance σ^2:

$$s^2\{e_i\} = MSE(1 - h_{ii}) \tag{10.16a}$$

$$s\{e_i, e_j\} = -h_{ij}(MSE) \qquad i \neq j \tag{10.16b}$$

We shall illustrate these different roles of the hat matrix by an example.

TABLE 10.2
Illustration of
Hat Matrix.

				(a) Data and Basic Results			
	(1)	(2)	(3)	(4)	(5)	(6)	(7)
i	X_{i1}	X_{i2}	Y_i	$\hat{Y}_i$	e_i	h_{ii}	$s^2\{e_i\}$
1	14	25	301	282.2	18.8	.3877	352.0
2	19	32	327	332.3	−5.3	.9513	28.0
3	12	22	246	260.0	−14.0	.6614	194.6
4	11	15	187	186.5	.5	.9996	.2

(b) H

$$\begin{bmatrix} .3877 & .1727 & .4553 & -.0157 \\ .1727 & .9513 & -.1284 & .0044 \\ .4553 & -.1284 & .6614 & .0117 \\ -.0157 & .0044 & .0117 & .9996 \end{bmatrix}$$

(c) $s^2\{e\}$

$$\begin{bmatrix} 352.0 & -99.3 & -261.8 & 9.0 \\ -99.3 & 28.0 & 73.8 & -2.5 \\ -261.8 & 73.8 & 194.6 & -6.7 \\ 9.0 & -2.5 & -6.7 & .2 \end{bmatrix}$$

Example

A small data set based on $n = 4$ cases for examining the regression relation between a response variable Y and two predictor variables X_1 and X_2 is shown in Table 10.2a, columns 1–3. The fitted first-order model and the error mean square are:

$$\hat{Y} = 80.93 - 5.84X_1 + 11.32X_2$$
$$MSE = 574.9 \tag{10.17}$$

The fitted values and the residuals for the four cases are shown in columns 4 and 5 of Table 10.2a.

The hat matrix for these data is shown in Table 10.2b. It was obtained by means of (10.10) for the **X** matrix:

$$\mathbf{X} = \begin{bmatrix} 1 & 14 & 25 \\ 1 & 19 & 32 \\ 1 & 12 & 22 \\ 1 & 11 & 15 \end{bmatrix}$$

Note from (10.10) that the hat matrix is solely a function of the predictor variable(s). Also note from Table 10.2b that the hat matrix is symmetric. The diagonal elements h_{ii} of the hat matrix are repeated in column 6 of Table 10.2a.

We illustrate that the fitted values are linear combinations of the Y values by calculating $\hat{Y}_1$ by means of (10.11):

$$\hat{Y}_1 = h_{11}Y_1 + h_{12}Y_2 + h_{13}Y_3 + h_{14}Y_4$$
$$= .3877(301) + .1727(327) + .4553(246) - .0157(187)$$
$$= 282.2$$

This is the same result, except for possible rounding effects, as obtained from the fitted regression function (10.17):

$$\hat{Y}_1 = 80.93 - 5.84(14) + 11.32(25) = 282.2$$

The estimated variance-covariance matrix of the residuals, $\mathbf{s}^2\{\mathbf{e}\} = MSE(\mathbf{I} - \mathbf{H})$, is shown in Table 10.2c. It was obtained by using $MSE = 574.9$. The estimated variances of the residuals are shown in the main diagonal of the variance-covariance matrix in Table 10.2c and are repeated in column 7 of Table 10.2a. We illustrate their direct calculation for case 1 by using (10.16a):

$$s^2\{e_1\} = 574.9(1 - .3877) = 352.0$$

We see from Table 10.2a, column 7, that the residuals do not have constant variance. In fact, the variances differ greatly here because the data set is so small. As we shall note in Section 10.3, residuals for cases that are outlying with respect to the X variables have smaller variances.

Note also that the covariances in the matrix in Table 10.2c are not zero; hence, pairs of residuals are correlated, some positively and some negatively. We noted this correlation in Chapter 3, but also pointed out there that the correlations become very small for larger data sets.

Comment

The diagonal element h_{ii} of the hat matrix can be obtained directly from:

$$h_{ii} = \mathbf{X}_i'(\mathbf{X}'\mathbf{X})^{-1}\mathbf{X}_i \tag{10.18}$$

where:

$$\mathbf{X}_i_{p \times 1} = \begin{bmatrix} 1 \\ X_{i,1} \\ \vdots \\ X_{i,p-1} \end{bmatrix} \tag{10.18a}$$

Note that $\mathbf{X}_i$ corresponds to the $\mathbf{X}_h$ vector in (6.53) except that $\mathbf{X}_i$ pertains to the ith case, and that $\mathbf{X}_i'$ is simply the ith row of the $\mathbf{X}$ matrix, pertaining to the ith case. ∎

Studentized Residuals

The first refinement in making residuals more effective for detecting outlying Y observations involves recognition of the fact that the residuals e_i may have substantially different variances $\sigma^2\{e_i\}$. It is therefore appropriate to consider the magnitude of each e_i relative to its estimated standard deviation to give recognition to differences in the sampling errors of the residuals. We see from (10.16a) that an estimator of the standard deviation of e_i is:

$$s\{e_i\} = \sqrt{MSE(1 - h_{ii})} \tag{10.19}$$

The ratio of e_i to $s\{e_i\}$ is called the *studentized residual* and will be denoted by r_i:

$$r_i = \frac{e_i}{s\{e_i\}} \tag{10.20}$$

While the residuals e_i will have substantially different sampling variations if their standard deviations differ markedly, the studentized residuals r_i have constant variance (when the model is appropriate). Studentized residuals often are called *internally studentized residuals*.

Deleted Residuals

The second refinement to make residuals more effective for detecting outlying Y observations is to measure the ith residual $e_i = Y_i - \hat{Y}_i$ when the fitted regression is based on all of the cases except the ith one. The reason for this refinement is that if Y_i is far outlying, the fitted least squares regression function based on all cases including the ith one may be influenced to come close to Y_i, yielding a fitted value $\hat{Y}_i$ near Y_i. In that event, the residual e_i will be small and will not disclose that Y_i is outlying. On the other hand, if the ith case is excluded before the regression function is fitted, the least squares fitted value $\hat{Y}_i$ is not influenced by the outlying Y_i observation, and the residual for the ith case will then tend to be larger and therefore more likely to disclose the outlying Y observation.

The procedure then is to delete the ith case, fit the regression function to the remaining $n - 1$ cases, and obtain the point estimate of the expected value when the X levels are those of the ith case, to be denoted by $\hat{Y}_{i(i)}$. The difference between the actual observed value Y_i and the estimated expected value $\hat{Y}_{i(i)}$ will be denoted by d_i:

$$d_i = Y_i - \hat{Y}_{i(i)} \tag{10.21}$$

The difference d_i is called the *deleted residual* for the ith case. We encountered this same difference in (9.16), where it was called the *PRESS* prediction error for the ith case.

An algebraically equivalent expression for d_i that does not require a recomputation of the fitted regression function omitting the ith case is:

$$d_i = \frac{e_i}{1 - h_{ii}} \tag{10.21a}$$

where e_i is the ordinary residual for the ith case and h_{ii} is the ith diagonal element in the hat matrix, as given in (10.18). Note that the larger is the value h_{ii}, the larger will be the deleted residual as compared to the ordinary residual.

Thus, deleted residuals will at times identify outlying Y observations when ordinary residuals would not identify these; at other times deleted residuals lead to the same identifications as ordinary residuals.

Note that a deleted residual also corresponds to the prediction error for a new observation in the numerator of (2.35). There, we are predicting a new $n + 1$ observation from the fitted regression function based on the earlier n cases. Modifying the earlier notation for the context of deleted residuals, where $n - 1$ cases are used for predicting the "new" nth case, we can restate the result in (6.63a) to obtain the estimated variance of d_i:

$$s^2\{d_i\} = MSE_{(i)}\left(1 + \mathbf{X}_i'\left(\mathbf{X}_{(i)}'\mathbf{X}_{(i)}\right)^{-1}\mathbf{X}_i\right) \tag{10.22}$$

where $\mathbf{X}_i$ is the X observations vector (10.18a) for the ith case, $MSE_{(i)}$ is the mean square error when the ith case is omitted in fitting the regression function, and $\mathbf{X}_{(i)}$ is the $\mathbf{X}$ matrix with the ith case deleted. An algebraically equivalent expression for $s^2\{d_i\}$ is:

$$s^2\{d_i\} = \frac{MSE_{(i)}}{1 - h_{ii}} \tag{10.22a}$$

It follows from (6.63) that:

$$\frac{d_i}{s\{d_i\}} \sim t(n - p - 1) \tag{10.23}$$

Remember that $n - 1$ cases are used here in predicting the ith observation; hence, the degrees of freedom are $(n - 1) - p = n - p - 1$.

Studentized Deleted Residuals

Combining the above two refinements, we utilize for diagnosis of outlying or extreme Y observations the deleted residual d_i in (10.21) and studentize it by dividing it by its estimated standard deviation given by (10.22). The *studentized deleted residual,* denoted by t_i, therefore is:

$$t_i = \frac{d_i}{s\{d_i\}} \tag{10.24}$$

It follows from (10.21a) and (10.22a) that an algebraically equivalent expression for t_i is:

$$t_i = \frac{e_i}{\sqrt{MSE_{(i)}(1 - h_{ii})}} \tag{10.24a}$$

The studentized deleted residual t_i in (10.24) is also called an *externally studentized residual,* in contrast to the internally studentized residual r_i in (10.20). We know from (10.23) that each studentized deleted residual t_i follows the t distribution with $n - p - 1$ degrees of freedom. The t_i, however, are not independent.

Fortunately, the studentized deleted residuals t_i in (10.24) can be calculated without having to fit new regression functions each time a different case is omitted. A simple relationship exists between MSE and $MSE_{(i)}$:

$$(n - p)MSE = (n - p - 1)MSE_{(i)} + \frac{e_i^2}{1 - h_{ii}} \tag{10.25}$$

Using this relationship in (10.24a) yields the following equivalent expression for t_i:

$$t_i = e_i \left[\frac{n - p - 1}{SSE(1 - h_{ii}) - e_i^2} \right]^{1/2} \tag{10.26}$$

Thus, the studentized deleted residuals t_i can be calculated from the residuals e_i, the error sum of squares SSE, and the hat matrix values h_{ii}, all for the fitted regression based on the n cases.

Test for Outliers.   We identify as outlying Y observations those cases whose studentized deleted residuals are large in absolute value. In addition, we can conduct a formal test by means of the Bonferroni test procedure of whether the case with the largest absolute studentized deleted residual is an outlier. Since we do not know in advance which case will have the largest absolute value $|t_i|$, we consider the family of tests to include n tests, one for each case. If the regression model is appropriate, so that no case is outlying because of a change in the model, then each studentized deleted residual will follow the t distribution with $n - p - 1$ degrees of freedom. The appropriate Bonferroni critical value therefore is $t(1 - \alpha/2n; n - p - 1)$. Note that the test is two-sided since we are not concerned with the direction of the residuals but only with their absolute values.

Example

For the body fat example with two predictor variables (X_1, X_2), we wish to examine whether there are outlying Y observations. Table 10.3 presents the residuals e_i in column 1,

TABLE 10.3
Residuals, Diagonal Elements of the Hat Matrix, and Studentized Deleted Residuals—Body Fat Example with Two Predictor Variables.

i	(1) e_i	(2) h_{ii}	(3) t_i
1	−1.683	.201	−.730
2	3.643	.059	1.534
3	−3.176	.372	−1.656
4	−3.158	.111	−1.348
5	.000	.248	.000
6	−.361	.129	−.148
7	.716	.156	.298
8	4.015	.096	1.760
9	2.655	.115	1.117
10	−2.475	.110	−1.034
11	.336	.120	.137
12	2.226	.109	.923
13	−3.947	.178	−1.825
14	3.447	.148	1.524
15	.571	.333	.267
16	.642	.095	.258
17	−.851	.106	.344
18	−.783	.197	.335
19	−2.857	.067	−1.176
20	1.040	.050	.409

the diagonal elements h_{ii} of the hat matrix in column 2, and the studentized deleted residuals t_i in column 3. We illustrate the calculation of the studentized deleted residual for the first case. The X values for this case, given in Table 7.1, are $X_{11} = 19.5$ and $X_{12} = 43.1$. Using the fitted regression function from Table 7.2c, we obtain:

$$\hat{Y}_1 = -19.174 + .2224(19.5) + .6594(43.1) = 13.583$$

Since $Y_1 = 11.9$, the residual for this case is $e_1 = 11.9 - 13.583 = -1.683$. We also know from Table 7.2c that $SSE = 109.95$ and from Table 10.3 that $h_{11} = .201$. Hence, by (10.26), we find:

$$t_1 = -1.683 \left[\frac{20 - 3 - 1}{109.95(1 - .201) - (-1.683)^2} \right]^{1/2} = -.730$$

Note from Table 10.3, column 3, that cases 3, 8, and 13 have the largest absolute studentized deleted residuals. Incidentally, consideration of the residuals e_i (shown in Table 10.3, column 1) here would have identified cases 2, 8, and 13 as the most outlying ones, but not case 3.

We would like to test whether case 13, which has the largest absolute studentized deleted residual, is an outlier resulting from a change in the model. We shall use the Bonferroni simultaneous test procedure with a family significance level of $\alpha = .10$. We therefore require:

$$t(1 - \alpha/2n; n - p - 1) = t(.9975; 16) = 3.252$$

Since $|t_{13}| = 1.825 \leq 3.252$, we conclude that case 13 is not an outlier. Still, we might wish to investigate whether case 13 and perhaps a few other outlying cases are influential in determining the fitted regression function because the Bonferroni procedure provides a very conservative test for the presence of an outlier.

10.3 Identifying Outlying X Observations—Hat Matrix Leverage Values

Use of Hat Matrix for Identifying Outlying X Observations

The hat matrix, as we saw, plays an important role in determining the magnitude of a studentized deleted residual and therefore in identifying outlying Y observations. The hat matrix also is helpful in directly identifying outlying X observations. In particular, the diagonal elements of the hat matrix are a useful indicator in a multivariable setting of whether or not a case is outlying with respect to its X values.

The diagonal elements h_{ii} of the hat matrix have some useful properties. In particular, their values are always between 0 and 1 and their sum is p:

$$0 \leq h_{ii} \leq 1 \qquad \sum_{i=1}^{n} h_{ii} = p \qquad (10.27)$$

where p is the number of regression parameters in the regression function including the intercept term. In addition, it can be shown that h_{ii} is a measure of the distance between the X values for the ith case and the means of the X values for all n cases. Thus, a large value h_{ii} indicates that the ith case is distant from the center of all X observations. The diagonal element h_{ii} in this context is called the *leverage* (in terms of the X values) of the ith case.

Figure 10.6 illustrates the role of the leverage values h_{ii} as distance measures for our earlier example in Table 10.2. Figure 10.6 shows a scatter plot of X_2 against X_1 for the four cases, and the center of the four cases located at $(\bar{X}_1, \bar{X}_2)$. This center is called the *centroid*. Here, the centroid is $(\bar{X}_1 = 14.0, \bar{X}_2 = 23.5)$. In addition, Figure 10.6 shows the leverage value for each case. Note that cases 1 and 3, which are closest to the centroid, have the smallest leverage values, while cases 2 and 4, which are farthest from the center, have the largest leverage values. Note also that the four leverage values sum to $p = 3$.

FIGURE 10.6
Illustration of Leverage Values as Distance Measures—Table 10.2 Example.

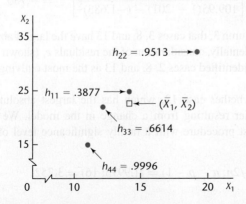

If the ith case is outlying in terms of its X observations and therefore has a large leverage value h_{ii}, it exercises substantial leverage in determining the fitted value $\hat{Y}_i$. This is so for the following reasons:

1. The fitted value $\hat{Y}_i$ is a linear combination of the observed Y values, as shown by (10.11), and h_{ii} is the weight of observation Y_i in determining this fitted value. Thus, the larger is h_{ii}, the more important is Y_i in determining $\hat{Y}_i$. Remember that h_{ii} is a function only of the X values, so h_{ii} measures the role of the X values in determining how important Y_i is in affecting the fitted value $\hat{Y}_i$.

2. The larger is h_{ii}, the smaller is the variance of the residual e_i, as we noted earlier from (10.14). Hence, the larger is h_{ii}, the closer the fitted value $\hat{Y}_i$ will tend to be to the observed value Y_i. In the extreme case where $h_{ii} = 1$, the variance $\sigma^2\{e_i\}$ equals 0, so the fitted value $\hat{Y}_i$ is then forced to equal the observed value Y_i.

A leverage value h_{ii} is usually considered to be large if it is more than twice as large as the mean leverage value, denoted by $\bar{h}$, which according to (10.27) is:

$$\bar{h} = \frac{\sum_{i=1}^n h_{ii}}{n} = \frac{p}{n} \qquad (10.28)$$

Hence, leverage values greater than $2p/n$ are considered by this rule to indicate outlying cases with regard to their X values. Another suggested guideline is that h_{ii} values exceeding .5 indicate very high leverage, whereas those between .2 and .5 indicate moderate leverage. Additional evidence of an outlying case is the existence of a gap between the leverage values for most of the cases and the unusually large leverage value(s).

The rules just mentioned for identifying cases that are outlying with respect to their X values are intended for data sets that are reasonably large, relative to the number of parameters in the regression function. They are not applicable, for instance, to the simple example in Table 10.2 where there are $n = 4$ cases and $p = 3$ parameters in the regression function. Here, the mean leverage value is $3/4 = .75$, and one cannot obtain a leverage value twice as large as the mean value since leverage values cannot exceed 1.0.

Example

We continue with the body fat example of Table 7.1. We again use only the two predictor variables triceps skinfold thickness (X_1) and thigh circumference (X_2) so that the results using the hat matrix can be compared to simple graphic plots. Figure 10.7 contains a scatter

FIGURE 10.7
Scatter Plot of Thigh Circumference against Triceps Skinfold Thickness— Body Fat Example with Two Predictor Variables.

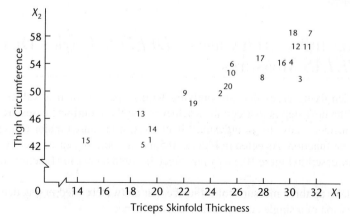

plot of X_2 against X_1, where the data points are identified by their case number. We note from Figure 10.7 that cases 15 and 3 appear to be outlying ones with respect to the pattern of the X values. Case 15 is outlying for X_1 and at the low end of the range for X_2, whereas case 3 is outlying in terms of the pattern of multicollinearity, though it is not outlying for either of the predictor variables separately. Cases 1 and 5 also appear to be somewhat extreme.

Table 10.3, column 2, contains the leverage values h_{ii} for the body fat example. Note that the two largest leverage values are $h_{33} = .372$ and $h_{15,15} = .333$. Both exceed the criterion of twice the mean leverage value, $2p/n = 2(3)/20 = .30$, and both are separated by a substantial gap from the next largest leverage values, $h_{55} = .248$ and $h_{11} = .201$. Having identified cases 3 and 15 as outlying in terms of their X values, we shall need to ascertain how influential these cases are in the fitting of the regression function.

Use of Hat Matrix to Identify Hidden Extrapolation

We have seen that the hat matrix is useful in the model-building stage for identifying cases that are outlying with respect to their X values and that, therefore, may be influential in affecting the fitted model. The hat matrix is also useful after the model has been selected and fitted for determining whether an inference for a mean response or a new observation involves a substantial extrapolation beyond the range of the data. When there are only two predictor variables, it is easy to see from a scatter plot of X_2 against X_1 whether an inference for a particular (X_1, X_2) set of values is outlying beyond the range of the data, such as from Figure 10.7. This simple graphic analysis is no longer available with larger numbers of predictor variables, where extrapolations may be hidden.

To spot hidden extrapolations, we can utilize the direct leverage calculation in (10.18) for the new set of X values for which inferences are to be made:

$$h_{\text{new,new}} = \mathbf{X}'_{\text{new}}(\mathbf{X}'\mathbf{X})^{-1}\mathbf{X}_{\text{new}} \tag{10.29}$$

where $\mathbf{X}_{\text{new}}$ is the vector containing the X values for which an inference about a mean response or a new observation is to be made, and the $\mathbf{X}$ matrix is the one based on the data set used for fitting the regression model. If $h_{\text{new,new}}$ is well within the range of leverage values h_{ii} for the cases in the data set, no extrapolation is involved. On the other hand, if $h_{\text{new,new}}$ is much larger than the leverage values for the cases in the data set, an extrapolation is indicated.

10.4 Identifying Influential Cases—*DFFITS*, Cook's Distance, and *DFBETAS* Measures

After identifying cases that are outlying with respect to their Y values and/or their X values, the next step is to ascertain whether or not these outlying cases are influential. We shall consider a case to be *influential* if its exclusion causes major changes in the fitted regression function. As noted in Figure 10.5, not all outlying cases need be influential. For example, case 1 in Figure 10.5 may not affect the fitted regression function to any substantial extent.

We take up three measures of influence that are widely used in practice, each based on the omission of a single case to measure its influence.

Influence on Single Fitted Value—*DFFITS*

A useful measure of the influence that case i has on the fitted value $\hat{Y}_i$ is given by:

$$(DFFITS)_i = \frac{\hat{Y}_i - \hat{Y}_{i(i)}}{\sqrt{MSE_{(i)}h_{ii}}} \qquad (10.30)$$

The letters *DF* stand for the difference between the fitted value $\hat{Y}_i$ for the ith case when all n cases are used in fitting the regression function and the predicted value $\hat{Y}_{i(i)}$ for the ith case obtained when the ith case is omitted in fitting the regression function. The denominator of (10.30) is the estimated standard deviation of $\hat{Y}_i$, but it uses the error mean square when the ith case is omitted in fitting the regression function for estimating the error variance σ^2. The denominator provides a standardization so that the value $(DFFITS)_i$ for the ith case represents the number of estimated standard deviations of $\hat{Y}_i$ that the fitted value $\hat{Y}_i$ increases or decreases with the inclusion of the ith case in fitting the regression model.

It can be shown that the *DFFITS* values can be computed by using only the results from fitting the entire data set, as follows:

$$(DFFITS)_i = e_i \left[\frac{n-p-1}{SSE(1-h_{ii})-e_i^2} \right]^{1/2} \left(\frac{h_{ii}}{1-h_{ii}} \right)^{1/2} = t_i \left(\frac{h_{ii}}{1-h_{ii}} \right)^{1/2} \qquad (10.30a)$$

Note from the last expression that the *DFFITS* value for the ith case is a studentized deleted residual, as given in (10.26), increased or decreased by a factor that is a function of the leverage value for this case. If case i is an X outlier and has a high leverage value, this factor will be greater than 1 and $(DFFITS)_i$ will tend to be large absolutely.

As a guideline for identifying influential cases, we suggest considering a case influential if the absolute value of *DFFITS* exceeds 1 for small to medium data sets and $2\sqrt{p/n}$ for large data sets.

Example

Table 10.4, column 1, lists the *DFFITS* values for the body fat example with two predictor variables. To illustrate the calculations, consider the *DFFITS* value for case 3, which was identified as outlying with respect to its X values. From Table 10.3, we know that the studentized deleted residual for this case is $t_3 = -1.656$ and the leverage value is $h_{33} = .372$. Hence, using (10.30a) we obtain:

$$(DFFITS)_3 = -1.656 \left(\frac{.372}{1-.372} \right)^{1/2} = -1.27$$

The only *DFFITS* value in Table 10.4 that exceeds our guideline for a medium-size data set is for case 3, where $|(DFFITS)_3| = 1.273$. This value is somewhat larger than our guideline of 1. However, the value is close enough to 1 that the case may not be influential enough to require remedial action.

Comment

The estimated variance of $\hat{Y}_i$ used in the denominator of (10.30) is developed from the relation $\hat{\mathbf{Y}} = \mathbf{HY}$ in (10.11). Using (5.46), we obtain:

$$\sigma^2\{\hat{\mathbf{Y}}\} = \mathbf{H}\sigma^2\{\mathbf{Y}\}\mathbf{H}' = \mathbf{H}(\sigma^2\mathbf{I})\mathbf{H}'$$

TABLE 10.4
DFFITS,
Cook's
Distances, and
DFBETAS—
Body Fat
Example with
Two Predictor
Variables.

	(1)	(2)	(3)	(4)	(5)
				DFBETAS	
i	$(DFFITS)_i$	D_i	b_0	b_1	b_2
1	$-.366$	.046	$-.305$	$-.132$	.232
2	.384	.046	.173	.115	$-.143$
3	-1.273	.490	$-.847$	-1.183	1.067
4	$-.476$	.072	$-.102$	$-.294$	.196
5	.000	.000	.000	.000	.000
6	$-.057$	.001	.040	.040	$-.044$
7	.128	.006	$-.078$	$-.016$	.054
8	.575	.098	.261	.391	$-.333$
9	.402	.053	$-.151$	$-.295$	.247
10	$-.364$	.044	.238	.245	$-.269$
11	.051	.001	$-.009$	.017	$-.003$
12	.323	.035	$-.131$	.023	.070
13	$-.851$	.212	.119	.592	$-.390$
14	.636	.125	.452	.113	$-.298$
15	.189	.013	$-.003$	$-.125$	.069
16	.084	.002	.009	.043	$-.025$
17	$-.118$	.005	.080	.055	$-.076$
18	$-.166$	.010	.132	.075	$-.116$
19	$-.315$	.032	$-.130$	$-.004$	.064
20	.094	.003	.010	.002	$-.003$

Since $\mathbf{H}$ is a symmetric matrix, so $\mathbf{H}' = \mathbf{H}$, and it is also idempotent, so $\mathbf{HH} = \mathbf{H}$, we obtain:

$$\sigma^2\{\hat{\mathbf{Y}}\} = \sigma^2 \mathbf{H} \tag{10.31}$$

Hence, the variance of $\hat{Y}_i$ is:

$$\sigma^2\{\hat{Y}_i\} = \sigma^2 h_{ii} \tag{10.32}$$

where h_{ii} is the ith diagonal element of the hat matrix. The error term variance σ^2 is estimated in (10.30) by the error mean square $MSE_{(i)}$ obtained when the ith case is omitted in fitting the regression model. ∎

Influence on All Fitted Values—Cook's Distance

In contrast to the *DFFITS* measure in (10.30), which considers the influence of the ith case on the fitted value $\hat{Y}_i$ for this case, Cook's distance measure considers the influence of the ith case on all n fitted values. Cook's distance measure, denoted by D_i, is an aggregate influence measure, showing the effect of the ith case on all n fitted values:

$$D_i = \frac{\sum_{j=1}^{n} \left(\hat{Y}_j - \hat{Y}_{j(i)}\right)^2}{pMSE} \tag{10.33}$$

Note that the numerator involves similar differences as in the *DFFITS* measure, but here each of the n fitted values $\hat{Y}_j$ is compared with the corresponding fitted value $\hat{Y}_{j(i)}$ when the ith case is deleted in fitting the regression model. These differences are then squared and summed, so that the aggregate influence of the ith case is measured without regard to the signs of the effects. Finally, the denominator serves as a standardizing measure. In matrix terms, Cook's distance measure can be expressed as follows:

$$D_i = \frac{\left(\hat{\mathbf{Y}} - \hat{\mathbf{Y}}_{(i)}\right)'\left(\hat{\mathbf{Y}} - \hat{\mathbf{Y}}_{(i)}\right)}{pMSE} \tag{10.33a}$$

Here, $\hat{\mathbf{Y}}$ as usual is the vector of the fitted values when all n cases are used for the regression fit and $\hat{\mathbf{Y}}_{(i)}$ is the vector of the fitted values when the ith case is deleted.

For interpreting Cook's distance measure, it has been found useful to relate D_i to the $F(p, n - p)$ distribution and ascertain the corresponding percentile value. If the percentile value is less than about 10 or 20 percent, the ith case has little apparent influence on the fitted values. If, on the other hand, the percentile value is near 50 percent or more, the fitted values obtained with and without the ith case should be considered to differ substantially, implying that the ith case has a major influence on the fit of the regression function.

Fortunately, Cook's distance measure D_i can be calculated without fitting a new regression function each time a different case is deleted. An algebraically equivalent expression is:

$$D_i = \frac{e_i^2}{pMSE}\left[\frac{h_{ii}}{(1 - h_{ii})^2}\right] \tag{10.33b}$$

Note from (10.33b) that D_i depends on two factors: (1) the size of the residual e_i and (2) the leverage value h_{ii}. The larger either e_i or h_{ii} is, the larger D_i is. Thus, the ith case can be influential: (1) by having a large residual e_i and only a moderate leverage value h_{ii}, or (2) by having a large leverage value h_{ii} with only a moderately sized residual e_i, or (3) by having both a large residual e_i and a large leverage value h_{ii}.

Example

For the body fat example with two predictor variables, Table 10.4, column 2, presents the D_i values. To illustrate the calculations, we consider again case 3, which is outlying with regard to its X values. We know from Table 10.3 that $e_3 = -3.176$ and $h_{33} = .372$. Further, $MSE = 6.47$ according to Table 7.2c and $p = 3$ for the model with two predictor variables. Hence, we obtain:

$$D_3 = \frac{(-3.176)^2}{3(6.47)}\left[\frac{.372}{(1 - .372)^2}\right] = .490$$

We note from Table 10.4, column 2 that case 3 clearly has the largest D_i value, with the next largest distance measure $D_{13} = .212$ being substantially smaller. Figure 10.8 presents the information provided by Cook's distance measure about the influence of each case in two different plots. Shown in Figure 10.8a is a proportional influence plot of the residuals e_i against the corresponding fitted values $\hat{Y}_i$, the size of the plotted points being proportional to Cook's distance measure D_i. Figure 10.8b presents the information about the Cook's distance measures in the form of an index influence plot, where Cook's distance measure D_i is plotted against the corresponding case index i. Both plots in Figure 10.8 clearly show that one case stands out as most influential (case 3) and that all the other cases are much less influential. The proportional influence plot in Figure 10.8a shows that the residual for the most influential case is large negative, but does not identify the case. The index influence plot in Figure 10.8b, on the other hand, identifies the most influential case as case 3 but does not provide any information about the magnitude of the residual for this case.

FIGURE 10.8 **Proportional Influence Plot (Points Porportional in Size to Cook's Distance Measure) and Index Influence Plot—Body Fat Example with Two Predictor Variables.**

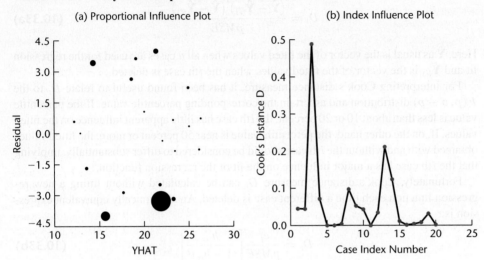

To assess the magnitude of the influence of case 3 ($D_3 = .490$), we refer to the corresponding F distribution, namely, $F(p, n - p) = F(3, 17)$. We find that .490 is the 30.6th percentile of this distribution. Hence, it appears that case 3 does influence the regression fit, but the extent of the influence may not be large enough to call for consideration of remedial measures.

Influence on the Regression Coefficients—*DFBETAS*

A measure of the influence of the ith case on each regression coefficient b_k ($k = 0, 1, \ldots, p - 1$) is the difference between the estimated regression coefficient b_k based on all n cases and the regression coefficient obtained when the ith case is omitted, to be denoted by $b_{k(i)}$. When this difference is divided by an estimate of the standard deviation of b_k, we obtain the measure *DFBETAS*:

$$(DFBETAS)_{k(i)} = \frac{b_k - b_{k(i)}}{\sqrt{MSE_{(i)}c_{kk}}} \qquad k = 0, 1, \ldots, p - 1 \qquad \textbf{(10.34)}$$

where c_{kk} is the kth diagonal element of $(\mathbf{X'X})^{-1}$. Recall from (6.46) that the variance-covariance matrix of the regression coefficients is given by $\sigma^2\{\mathbf{b}\} = \sigma^2(\mathbf{X'X})^{-1}$. Hence the variance of b_k is:

$$\sigma^2\{b_k\} = \sigma^2 c_{kk} \qquad \textbf{(10.35)}$$

The error term variance σ^2 here is estimated by $MSE_{(i)}$, the error mean square obtained when the ith case is deleted in fitting the regression model.

The *DFBETAS* value by its sign indicates whether inclusion of a case leads to an increase or a decrease in the estimated regression coefficient, and its absolute magnitude shows the size of the difference relative to the estimated standard deviation of the regression coefficient. A large absolute value of $(DFBETAS)_{k(i)}$ is indicative of a large impact of the

ith case on the kth regression coefficient. As a guideline for identifying influential cases, we recommend considering a case influential if the absolute value of *DFBETAS* exceeds 1 for small to medium data sets and $2/\sqrt{n}$ for large data sets.

Example

For the body fat example with two predictor variables, Table 10.4 lists the *DFBETAS* values in columns 3, 4, and 5. Note that case 3, which is outlying with respect to its X values, is the only case that exceeds our guideline of 1 for medium-size data sets for both b_1 and b_2. Thus, case 3 is again tagged as potentially influential. Again, however, the *DFBETAS* values do not exceed 1 by very much so that case 3 may not be so influential as to require remedial action.

Comment

Cook's distance measure of the aggregate influence of a case on the n fitted values, which was defined in (10.33), is algebraically equivalent to a measure of the aggregate influence of a case on the p regression coefficients. In fact, Cook's distance measure was originally derived from the concept of a confidence region for all p regression coefficients β_k $(k = 0, 1, \ldots, p - 1)$ simultaneously. It can be shown that the boundary of this joint confidence region for the normal error multiple regression model (6.19) is given by:

$$\frac{(\mathbf{b} - \boldsymbol{\beta})'\mathbf{X}'\mathbf{X}(\mathbf{b} - \boldsymbol{\beta})}{pMSE} = F(1 - \alpha; p, n - p) \tag{10.36}$$

Cook's distance measure D_i uses the same structure for measuring the combined impact of the ith case on the differences in the estimated regression coefficients:

$$D_i = \frac{\left(\mathbf{b} - \mathbf{b}_{(i)}\right)'\mathbf{X}'\mathbf{X}\left(\mathbf{b} - \mathbf{b}_{(i)}\right)}{pMSE} \tag{10.37}$$

where $\mathbf{b}_{(i)}$ is the vector of the estimated regression coefficients obtained when the ith case is omitted and $\mathbf{b}$, as usual, is the vector when all n cases are used. The expressions for Cook's distance measure in (10.33a) and (10.37) are algebraically identical.   ∎

Influence on Inferences

To round out the determination of influential cases, it is usually a good idea to examine in a direct fashion the inferences from the fitted regression model that would be made with and without the case(s) of concern. If the inferences are not essentially changed, there is little need to think of remedial actions for the cases diagnosed as influential. On the other hand, serious changes in the inferences drawn from the fitted model when a case is omitted will require consideration of remedial measures.

Example

In the body fat example with two predictor variables, cases 3 and 15 were identified as outlying X observations and cases 8 and 13 as outlying Y observations. All three influence measures (*DFFITS*, Cook's distance, and *DFBETAS*) identified only case 3 as influential, and, indeed, suggested that its influence may be of marginal importance so that remedial measures might not be required.

The analyst in the body fat example was primarily interested in the fit of the regression model because the model was intended to be used for making predictions within the range of the observations on the predictor variables in the data set. Hence, the analyst considered the fitted regression functions with and without case 3:

$$\text{With case 3: } \hat{Y} = -19.174 + .2224X_1 + .6594X_2$$
$$\text{Without case 3: } \hat{Y} = -12.428 + .5641X_1 + .3635X_2$$

Because of the high multicollinearity between X_1 and X_2, the analyst was not surprised by the shifts in the magnitudes of b_1 and b_2 when case 3 is omitted. Remember that the estimated standard deviations of the coefficients, given in Table 7.2c, are very large and that a single case can change the estimated coefficients substantially when the predictor variables are highly correlated.

To examine the effect of case 3 on inferences to be made from the fitted regression function in the range of the X observations in a direct fashion, the analyst calculated for each of the 20 cases the relative difference between the fitted value $\hat{Y}_i$ based on all 20 cases and the fitted value $\hat{Y}_{i(3)}$ obtained when case 3 is omitted. The measure of interest was the average absolute percent difference:

$$\frac{\sum_{i=1}^{n} \left| \frac{\hat{Y}_{i(3)} - \hat{Y}_i}{\hat{Y}_i} \right| 100}{n}$$

This mean difference is 3.1 percent; further, 17 of the 20 differences are less than 5 percent (calculations not shown). On the basis of this direct evidence about the effect of case 3 on the inferences to be made, the analyst was satisfied that case 3 does not exercise undue influence so that no remedial action is required for handling this case.

Some Final Comments

Analysis of outlying and influential cases is a necessary component of good regression analysis. However, it is neither automatic nor foolproof and requires good judgment by the analyst. The methods described often work well, but at times are ineffective. For example, if two influential outlying cases are nearly coincident, as depicted in Figure 10.5 by cases 3 and 4, an analysis that deletes one case at a time and estimates the change in fit will result in virtually no change for these two outlying cases. The reason is that the retained outlying case will mask the effect of the deleted outlying case. Extensions of the single-case diagnostic procedures described here have been developed that involve deleting two or more cases at a time. However, the computational requirements for these extensions are much more demanding than for the single-case diagnostics. Reference 10.4 describes some of these extensions.

Remedial measures for outlying cases that are determined to be highly influential by the diagnostic procedures will be discussed in the next chapter.

10.5   Multicollinearity Diagnostics—Variance Inflation Factor

When we discussed multicollinearity in Chapter 7, we noted some key problems that typically arise when the predictor variables being considered for the regression model are highly correlated among themselves:

1. Adding or deleting a predictor variable changes the regression coefficients.

2. The extra sum of squares associated with a predictor variable varies, depending upon which other predictor variables are already included in the model.

3. The estimated standard deviations of the regression coefficients become large when the predictor variables in the regression model are highly correlated with each other.

4. The estimated regression coefficients individually may not be statistically significant even though a definite statistical relation exists between the response variable and the set of predictor variables.

These problems can also arise without substantial multicollinearity being present, but only under unusual circumstances not likely to be found in practice.

We first consider some informal diagnostics for multicollinearity and then a highly useful formal diagnostic, the variance inflation factor.

Informal Diagnostics

Indications of the presence of serious multicollinearity are given by the following informal diagnostics:

1. Large changes in the estimated regression coefficients when a predictor variable is added or deleted, or when an observation is altered or deleted.
2. Nonsignificant results in individual tests on the regression coefficients for important predictor variables.
3. Estimated regression coefficients with an algebraic sign that is the opposite of that expected from theoretical considerations or prior experience.
4. Large coefficients of simple correlation between pairs of predictor variables in the correlation matrix $\mathbf{r}_{XX}$.
5. Wide confidence intervals for the regression coefficients representing important predictor variables.

Example

We consider again the body fat example of Table 7.1, this time with all three predictor variables—triceps skinfold thickness (X_1), thigh circumference (X_2), and midarm circumference (X_3). We noted in Chapter 7 that the predictor variables triceps skinfold thickness and thigh circumference are highly correlated with each other. We also noted large changes in the estimated regression coefficients and their estimated standard deviations when a variable was added, nonsignificant results in individual tests on anticipated important variables, and an estimated negative coefficient when a positive coefficient was expected. These are all informal indications that suggest serious multicollinearity among the predictor variables.

Comment

The informal methods just described have important limitations. They do not provide quantitative measurements of the impact of multicollinearity and they may not identify the nature of the multicollinearity. For instance, if predictor variables X_1, X_2, and X_3 have low pairwise correlations, then the examination of simple correlation coefficients may not disclose the existence of relations among groups of predictor variables, such as a high correlation between X_1 and a linear combination of X_2 and X_3.

Another limitation of the informal diagnostic methods is that sometimes the observed behavior may occur without multicollinearity being present. ∎

Variance Inflation Factor

A formal method of detecting the presence of multicollinearity that is widely accepted is use of variance inflation factors. These factors measure how much the variances of the estimated regression coefficients are inflated as compared to when the predictor variables are not linearly related.

To understand the significance of variance inflation factors, we begin with the precision of least squares estimated regression coefficients, which is measured by their variances. We know from (6.46) that the variance-covariance matrix of the estimated regression coefficients is:

$$\sigma^2\{\mathbf{b}\} = \sigma^2(\mathbf{X}'\mathbf{X})^{-1} \tag{10.38}$$

For purposes of measuring the impact of multicollinearity, it is useful to work with the standardized regression model (7.45), which is obtained by transforming the variables by means of the correlation transformation (7.44). When the standardized regression model is fitted, the estimated regression coefficients b_k^* are standardized coefficients that are related to the estimated regression coefficients for the untransformed variables according to (7.53). The variance-covariance matrix of the estimated standardized regression coefficients is obtained from (10.38) by using the result in (7.50), which states that the $\mathbf{X}'\mathbf{X}$ matrix for the transformed variables is the correlation matrix of the X variables $\mathbf{r}_{XX}$. Hence, we obtain:

$$\sigma^2\{\mathbf{b}^*\} = (\sigma^*)^2\mathbf{r}_{XX}^{-1} \tag{10.39}$$

where $\mathbf{r}_{XX}$ is the matrix of the pairwise simple correlation coefficients among the X variables, as defined in (7.47), and $(\sigma^*)^2$ is the error term variance for the transformed model.

Note from (10.39) that the variance of b_k^* ($k = 1, \ldots, p - 1$) is equal to the following, letting $(VIF)_k$ denote the kth diagonal element of the matrix $\mathbf{r}_{XX}^{-1}$:

$$\sigma^2\{b_k^*\} = (\sigma^*)^2(VIF)_k \tag{10.40}$$

The diagonal element $(VIF)_k$ is called the *variance inflation factor* (*VIF*) for b_k^*. It can be shown that this variance inflation factor is equal to:

$$(VIF)_k = (1 - R_k^2)^{-1} \qquad k = 1, 2, \ldots, p - 1 \tag{10.41}$$

where R_k^2 is the coefficient of multiple determination when X_k is regressed on the $p - 2$ other X variables in the model. Hence, we have:

$$\sigma^2\{b_k^*\} = \frac{(\sigma^*)^2}{1 - R_k^2} \tag{10.42}$$

We presented in (7.65) the special results for $\sigma^2\{b_k^*\}$ when $p - 1 = 2$, for which $R_k^2 = r_{12}^2$, the coefficient of simple determination between X_1 and X_2.

The variance inflation factor $(VIF)_k$ is equal to 1 when $R_k^2 = 0$, i.e., when X_k is not linearly related to the other X variables. When $R_k^2 \neq 0$, then $(VIF)_k$ is greater than 1, indicating an inflated variance for b_k^* as a result of the intercorrelations among the X variables. When X_k has a perfect linear association with the other X variables in the model so that $R_k^2 = 1$, then $(VIF)_k$ and $\sigma^2\{b_k^*\}$ are unbounded.

Diagnostic Uses.   The largest *VIF* value among all *X* variables is often used as an indicator of the severity of multicollinearity. A maximum *VIF* value in excess of 10 is frequently taken as an indication that multicollinearity may be unduly influencing the least squares estimates.

The mean of the *VIF* values also provides information about the severity of the multicollinearity in terms of how far the estimated standardized regression coefficients b_k^* are from the true values β_k^*. It can be shown that the expected value of the sum of these squared errors $(b_k^* - \beta_k^*)^2$ is given by:

$$E\left\{\sum_{k=1}^{p-1}(b_k^* - \beta_k^*)^2\right\} = (\sigma^*)^2 \sum_{k=1}^{p-1}(VIF)_k \tag{10.43}$$

Thus, large *VIF* values result, on the average, in larger differences between the estimated and true standardized regression coefficients.

When no *X* variable is linearly related to the others in the regression model, $R_k^2 \equiv 0$; hence, $(VIF)_k \equiv 1$, their sum is $p - 1$, and the expected value of the sum of the squared errors is:

$$E\left\{\sum_{k=1}^{p-1}(b_k^* - \beta_k^*)^2\right\} = (\sigma^*)^2(p - 1) \qquad \text{when } (VIF)_k \equiv 1 \tag{10.43a}$$

A ratio of the results in (10.43) and (10.43a) provides useful information about the effect of multicollinearity on the sum of the squared errors:

$$\frac{(\sigma^*)^2 \sum(VIF)_k}{(\sigma^*)^2(p - 1)} = \frac{\sum(VIF)_k}{p - 1}$$

Note that this ratio is simply the mean of the *VIF* values, to be denoted by $(\overline{VIF})$:

$$(\overline{VIF}) = \frac{\sum_{k=1}^{p-1}(VIF)_k}{p - 1} \tag{10.44}$$

Mean *VIF* values considerably larger than 1 are indicative of serious multicollinearity problems.

Example

Table 10.5 contains the estimated standardized regression coefficients and the *VIF* values for the body fat example with three predictor variables (calculations not shown). The maximum of the *VIF* values is 708.84 and their mean value is $(\overline{VIF}) = 459.26$. Thus, the expected sum of the squared errors in the least squares standardized regression coefficients is nearly 460 times as large as it would be if the *X* variables were uncorrelated. In addition, all three *VIF* values greatly exceed 10, which again indicates that serious multicollinearity problems exist.

TABLE 10.5
Variance Inflation Factors—Body Fat Example with Three Predictor Variables.

Variable	b_k^*	$(VIF)_k$
X_1	4.2637	708.84
X_2	-2.9287	564.34
X_3	-1.5614	104.61
Maximum $(VIF)_k = 708.84$		$(\overline{VIF}) = 459.26$

It is interesting to note that $(VIF)_3 = 105$ despite the fact that both r_{13}^2 and r_{23}^2 (see Figure 7.3b) are not large. Here is an instance where X_3 is strongly related to X_1 and X_2 together ($R_3^2 = .990$), even though the pairwise coefficients of simple determination are not large. Examination of the pairwise correlations does not disclose this multicollinearity.

Comments

1. Some computer regression programs use the reciprocal of the variance inflation factor to detect instances where an X variable should not be allowed into the fitted regression model because of excessively high interdependence between this variable and the other X variables in the model. Tolerance limits for $1/(VIF)_k = 1 - R_k^2$ frequently used are .01, .001, or .0001, below which the variable is not entered into the model.

2. A limitation of variance inflation factors for detecting multicollinearities is that they cannot distinguish between several simultaneous multicollinearities.

3. A number of other formal methods for detecting multicollinearity have been proposed. These are more complex than variance inflation factors and are discussed in specialized texts such as References 10.5 and 10.6. ∎

10.6   Surgical Unit Example—Continued

In Chapter 9 we developed a regression model for the surgical unit example (data in Table 9.1). Recall that validation studies in Section 9.6 led to the selection of model (9.21), the model containing variables X_1, X_2, X_3, and X_8. We will now utilize this regression model to demonstrate a more in-depth study of curvature, interaction effects, multicollinearity, and influential cases using residuals and other diagnostics.

To examine interaction effects further, a regression model containing first-order terms in X_1, X_2, X_3, and X_8 was fitted and added-variable plots for the six two-factor interaction terms, X_1X_2, X_1X_3, X_1X_8, X_2X_3, X_2X_8, and X_3X_8, were examined. These plots (not shown) did not suggest that any strong two-variable interactions are present and need to be included in the model. The absence of any strong interactions was also noted by fitting a regression model containing X_1, X_2, X_3, and X_8 in first-order terms and all two-variable interaction terms. The P-value of the formal F test statistic (7.19) for dropping all of the interaction terms from the model containing both the first-order effects and the interaction effects is .35, indicating that interaction effects are not present.

Figure 10.9 contains some of the additional diagnostic plots that were generated to check on the adequacy of the first-order model:

$$Y_i' = \beta_0 + \beta_1 X_{i1} + \beta_2 X_{i2} + \beta_3 X_{i3} + \beta_8 X_{i8} + \varepsilon_i \qquad \textbf{(10.45)}$$

where $Y_i' = \ln Y_i$. The following points are worth noting:

1. The residual plot against the fitted values in Figure 10.9a shows no evidence of serious departures from the model.

2. One of the three candidate models (9.23) subjected to validation studies in Section 9.6 contained X_5 (patient age) as a predictor. The regression coefficient for age (b_5) was negative in model (9.23), but when the same model was fit to the validation data, the sign of b_5 became positive. We will now use a residual plot and an added-variable plot to study graphically

FIGURE 10.9
Residual and Added-Variable Plots for Surgical Unit Example—Regression Model (10.45).

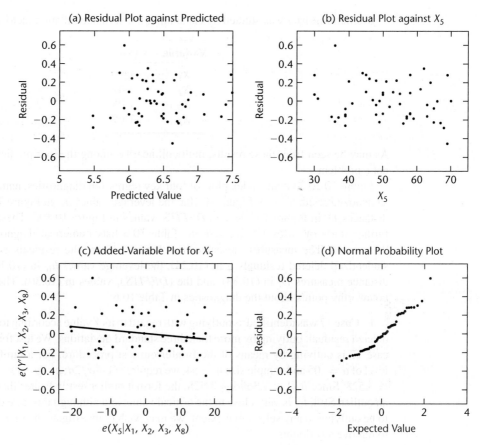

(a) Residual Plot against Predicted

(b) Residual Plot against X_5

(c) Added-Variable Plot for X_5

(d) Normal Probability Plot

the strength of the marginal relationship between X_5 and the response, when X_1, X_2, X_3, and X_8 are already in the model. Figure 10.9b shows the plot of the residuals for the model containing X_1, X_2, X_3, and X_8 against X_5, the predictor variable not in the model. This plot shows no need to include patient age (X_5) in the model to predict logarithm of survival time. A better view of this marginal relationship is provided by the added-variable plot in Figure 10.9c. The slope coefficient b_5 can be seen again to be slightly negative as depicted by the solid line in the added-variable plot. Overall, however, the marginal relationship between X_5 and Y' is weak. The P-value of the formal t test (9.18) for dropping X_5 from the model containing X_1, X_2, X_3, X_5 and X_8 is 0.194. In addition, the plot shows that the negative slope is driven largely by one or two outliers—one in the upper left region of the plot, and one in the lower right region. In this way the added-variable plot provides additional support for dropping X_5.

3. The normal probability plot of the residuals in Figure 10.9d shows little departure from linearity. The coefficient of correlation between the ordered residuals and their expected values under normality is .982, which is larger than the critical value for significance level .05 in Table B.6.

Multicollinearity was studied by calculating the variance inflation factors:

Variable	$(VIF)_k$
X_1	1.10
X_2	1.02
X_3	1.05
X_8	1.09

As may be seen from these results, multicollinearity among the four predictor variables is not a problem.

Figure 10.10 contains index plots of four key regression diagnostics, namely the deleted studentized residuals t_i in Figure 10.10a, the leverage values h_{ii} in Figure 10.10b, Cook's distances D_i in Figure 10.10c, and $DFFITS_i$ values in Figure 10.10d. These plots suggest further study of cases 17, 28, and 38. Table 10.6 lists numerical diagnostic values for these cases. The measures presented in columns 1–5 are the residuals e_i in (10.8), the studentized deleted residuals t_i in (10.24), the leverage values h_{ii} in (10.18), the Cook's distance measures D_i in (10.33), and the $(DFFITS)_i$ values in (10.30). The following are noteworthy points about the diagnostics in Table 10.6:

1. Case 17 was identified as outlying with regard to its Y value according to its studentized deleted residual, outlying by more than three standard deviations. We test formally whether case 17 is outlying by means of the Bonferroni test procedure. For a family significance level of $\alpha = .05$ and sample size $n = 54$, we require $t(1 - \alpha/2n; n - p - 1) = t(.99954; 49) = 3.528$. Since $|t_{17}| = 3.3696 \leq 3.528$, the formal outlier test indicates that case 22 is not an outlier. Still, t_{17} is very close to the critical value, and although this case does not appear to be outlying to any substantial extent, we may wish to investigate the influence of case 17 to remove any doubts.

2. With $2p/n = 2(5)/54 = .185$ as a guide for identifying outlying X observations, cases 23, 28, 32, 38, 42, and 52 were identified as outlying according to their leverage values. Incidentally, the univariate dot plots identify only cases 28 and 38 as outlying. Here we see the value of multivariable outlier identification.

3. To determine the influence of cases 17, 23, 28, 32, 38, 42, 32, and 52, we consider their Cook's distance and $DFFITS$ values. According to each of these measures, case 17 is the most influential, with Cook's distance $D_{17} = .3306$ and $(DFFITS)_{17} = 1.4151$. Referring to the F distribution with 5 and 49 degrees of freedom, we note that the Cook's value corresponds to the 11th percentile. It thus appears that the influence of case 38 is not large enough to warrant remedial measures, and consequently the other outlying cases also do not appear to be overly influential.

A direct check of the influence of case 17 on the inferences of interest was also conducted. Here, the inferences of primary interest are in the fit of the regression model because the model is intended to be used for making predictions in the range of the X observations. Hence, each fitted value $\hat{Y}_i$ based on all 54 observations was compared with the fitted value $\hat{Y}_{i(17)}$ when case 17 is deleted in fitting the regression model. The average of the absolute percent differences:

$$\left| \frac{\hat{Y}_{i(17)} - \hat{Y}_i}{\hat{Y}_i} \right| 100$$

FIGURE 10.10   Diagnostic Plots for Surgical Unit Example—Regression Model (10.45).

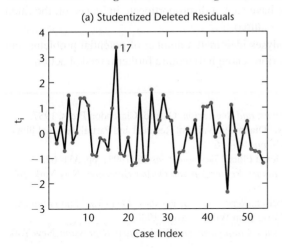

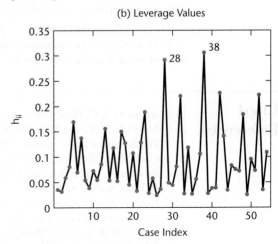

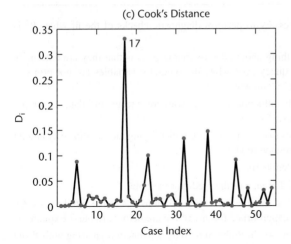

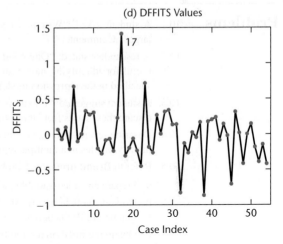

TABLE 10.6		(1)	(2)	(3)	(4)	(5)
Various Diagnostics for Outlying Cases— Surgical Unit Example, Regression Model (10.45).	**Case Number** i	e_i	t_i	h_{ii}	D_i	$(DFFITS)_i$
	17	0.5952	3.3696	0.1499	0.3306	1.4151
	23	0.2788	1.4854	0.1885	0.1001	0.7160
	28	0.0876	0.4896	0.2914	0.0200	0.3140
	32	−0.2861	−1.5585	0.2202	0.1333	−0.8283
	38	−0.2271	−1.3016	0.3059	0.1472	−0.8641
	42	−0.0303	−0.1620	0.2262	0.0016	−0.0876
	52	−0.1375	−0.7358	0.2221	0.0312	−0.3931

is only .42 percent, and the largest absolute percent difference (which is for case 17) is only 1.77 percent. Thus, case 17 does not have such a disproportionate influence on the fitted values that remedial action would be required.

4. In summary, the diagnostic analyses identified a number of potential problems, but none of these was considered to be serious enough to require further remedial action.

Cited References

10.1. Atkinson, A. C. *Plots, Transformations, and Regression*. Oxford: Clarendon Press, 1987.

10.2. Mansfield, E. R., and M. D. Conerly. "Diagnostic Value of Residual and Partial Residual Plots," *The American Statistician* 41 (1987), pp. 107–16.

10.3. Cook, R. D. "Exploring Partial Residual Plots," *Technometrics* 35 (1993), pp. 351–62.

10.4. Rousseeuw, P. J., and A. M. Leroy. *Robust Regression and Outlier Detection*. New York: John Wiley & Sons, 1987.

10.5. Belsley, D. A.; E. Kuh; and R. E. Welsch. *Regression Diagnostics: Identifying Influential Data and Sources of Collinearity*. New York: John Wiley & Sons, 1980.

10.6. Belsley, D. A. *Conditioning Diagnostics: Collinearity and Weak Data in Regression*. New York: John Wiley & Sons, 1991.

Problems

10.1. A student asked: "Why is it necessary to perform diagnostic checks of the fit when R^2 is large?" Comment.

10.2. A researcher stated: "One good thing about added-variable plots is that they are extremely useful for identifying model adequacy even when the predictor variables are not properly specified in the regression model." Comment.

10.3. A student suggested: "If extremely influential outlying cases are detected in a data set, simply discard these cases from the data set." Comment.

10.4. Describe several informal methods that can be helpful in identifying multicollinearity among the X variables in a multiple regression model.

10.5. Refer to **Brand preference** Problem 6.5b.

   a. Prepare an added-variable plot for each of the predictor variables.

   b. Do your plots in part (a) suggest that the regression relationships in the fitted regression function in Problem 6.5b are inappropriate for any of the predictor variables? Explain.

   c. Obtain the fitted regression function in Problem 6.5b by separately regressing both Y and X_2 on X_1, and then regressing the residuals in an appropriate fashion.

10.6. Refer to **Grocery retailer** Problem 6.9.

   a. Fit regression model (6.1) to the data using X_1 and X_2 only.

   b. Prepare an added-variable plot for each of the predictor variables X_1 and X_2.

   c. Do your plots in part (a) suggest that the regression relationships in the fitted regression function in part (a) are inappropriate for any of the predictor variables? Explain.

   d. Obtain the fitted regression function in part (a) by separately regressing both Y and X_2 on X_1, and then regressing the residuals in an appropriate fashion.

10.7. Refer to **Patient satisfaction** Problem 6.15c.

   a. Prepare an added-variable plot for each of the predictor variables.

   b. Do your plots in part (a) suggest that the regression relationships in the fitted regression function in Problem 6.15c are inappropriate for any of the predictor variables? Explain.

10.8. Refer to **Commercial properties** Problem 6.18c.

    a. Prepare an added-variable plot for each of the predictor variables.

    b. Do your plots in part (a) suggest that the regression relationships in the fitted regression function in Problem 6.18c are inappropriate for any of the predictor variables? Explain.

10.9. Refer to **Brand preference** Problem 6.5.

    a. Obtain the studentized deleted residuals and identify any outlying Y observations. Use the Bonferroni outlier test procedure with $\alpha = .10$. State the decision rule and conclusion.

    b. Obtain the diagonal elements of the hat matrix, and provide an explanation for the pattern in these elements.

    c. Are any of the observations outlying with regard to their X values according to the rule of thumb stated in the chapter?

    d. Management wishes to estimate the mean degree of brand liking for moisture content $X_1 = 10$ and sweetness $X_2 = 3$. Construct a scatter plot of X_2 against X_1 and determine visually whether this prediction involves an extrapolation beyond the range of the data. Also, use (10.29) to determine whether an extrapolation is involved. Do your conclusions from the two methods agree?

    e. The largest absolute studentized deleted residual is for case 14. Obtain the *DFFITS*, *DFBETAS*, and Cook's distance values for this case to assess the influence of this case. What do you conclude?

    f. Calculate the average absolute percent difference in the fitted values with and without case 14. What does this measure indicate about the influence of case 14?

    g. Calculate Cook's distance D_i for each case and prepare an index plot. Are any cases influential according to this measure?

*10.10. Refer to **Grocery retailer** Problems 6.9 and 6.10.

    a. Obtain the studentized deleted residuals and identify any outlying Y observations. Use the Bonferroni outlier test procedure with $\alpha = .05$. State the decision rule and conclusion.

    b. Obtain the diagonal element of the hat matrix. Identify any outlying X observations using the rule of thumb presented in the chapter.

    c. Management wishes to predict the total labor hours required to handle the next shipment containing $X_1 = 300,000$ cases whose indirect costs of the total hours is $X_2 = 7.2$ and $X_3 = 0$ (no holiday in week). Construct a scatter plot of X_2 against X_1 and determine visually whether this prediction involves an extrapolation beyond the range of the data. Also, use (10.29) to determine whether an extrapolation is involved. Do your conclusions from the two methods agree?

    d. Cases 16, 22, 43, and 48 appear to be outlying X observations, and cases 10, 32, 38, and 40 appear to be outlying Y observations. Obtain the *DFFITS*, *DFBETAS*, and Cook's distance values for each of these cases to assess their influence. What do you conclude?

    e. Calculate the average absolute percent difference in the fitted values with and without each of these cases. What does this measure indicate about the influence of each of the cases?

    f. Calculate Cook's distance D_i for each case and prepare an index plot. Are any cases influential according to this measure?

*10.11. Refer to **Patient satisfaction** Problem 6.15.

    a. Obtain the studentized deleted residuals and identify any outlying Y observations. Use the Bonferroni outlier test procedure with $\alpha = .10$. State the decision rule and conclusion.

    b. Obtain the diagonal elements of the hat matrix. Identify any outlying X observations.

c. Hospital management wishes to estimate mean patient satisfaction for patients who are $X_1 = 30$ years old, whose index of illness severity is $X_2 = 58$, and whose index of anxiety level is $X_3 = 2.0$. Use (10.29) to determine whether this estimate will involve a hidden extrapolation.

d. The three largest absolute studentized deleted residuals are for cases 11, 17, and 27. Obtain the *DFFITS*, *DFBETAS*, and Cook's distance values for this case to assess its influence. What do you conclude?

e. Calculate the average absolute percent difference in the fitted values with and without each of these cases. What does this measure indicate about the influence of each of these cases?

f. Calculate Cook's distance D_i for each case and prepare an index plot. Are any cases influential according to this measure?

10.12. Refer to **Commercial Properties** Problem 6.18.

a. Obtain the studentized deleted residuals and identify any outlying Y observations. Use the Bonferroni outlier test procedure with $\alpha = .01$. State the decision rule and conclusion.

b. Obtain the diagonal elements of the hat matrix. Identify any outlying X observations.

c. The researcher wishes to estimate the rental rates of a property whose age is 10 years, whose operating expenses and taxes are 12.00, whose ocupancy rate is 0.05, and whose square footage is 350,000. Use (10.29) to determine whether this estimate will involve a hidden extrapolation.

d. Cases 61, 8, 3, and 53 appear to be outlying X observations, and cases 6 and 62 appear to be outlying Y observations. Obtain the *DFFITS*, *DFBETAS*, and Cook's distance values for each case to assess its influence. What do you conclude?

e. Calculate the average absolute percent difference in the fitted values with and without each of the cases. What does this measure indicate about the influence of each case?

f. Calculate Cook's distance D_i for each case and prepare an index plot. Are any cases influential according to this measure?

10.13. **Cosmetics sales.** An assistant in the district sales office of a national cosmetics firm obtained data, shown below, on advertising expenditures and sales last year in the district's 44 territories. X_1 denotes expenditures for point-of-sale displays in beauty salons and department stores (in thousand dollars), and X_2 and X_3 represent the corresponding expenditures for local media advertising and prorated share of national media advertising, respectively. Y denotes sales (in thousand cases). The assistant was instructed to estimate the increase in expected sales when X_1 is increased by 1 thousand dollars and X_2 and X_3 are held constant, and was told to use an ordinary multiple regression model with linear terms for the predictor variables and with independent normal error terms.

i:	1	2	3	...	42	43	44
X_{i1}:	5.6	4.1	3.7	...	3.6	3.9	5.5
X_{i2}:	5.6	4.8	3.5	...	3.7	3.6	5.0
X_{i3}:	3.8	4.8	3.6	...	4.4	2.9	5.5
Y_i:	12.85	11.55	12.78	...	10.47	11.03	12.31

a. State the regression model to be employed and fit it to the data.

b. Test whether there is a regression relation between sales and the three predictor variables; use $\alpha = .05$. State the alternatives, decision rule, and conclusion.

c. Test for each of the regression coefficients β_k ($k = 1, 2, 3$) individually whether or not $\beta_k = 0$; use $\alpha = .05$ each time. Do the conclusions of these tests correspond to that obtained in part (b)?

    d. Obtain the correlation matrix of the X variables.

    e. What do the results in parts (b), (c), and (d) suggest about the suitability of the data for the research objective?

10.14. Refer to **Cosmetics sales** Problem 10.13.

    a. Obtain the three variance inflation factors. What do these suggest about the effects of multicollinearity here?

    b. The assistant eventually decided to drop variables X_2 and X_3 from the model "to clear up the picture." Fit the assistant's revised model. Is the assistant now in a better position to achieve the research objective?

    c. Why would an experiment here be more effective in providing suitable data to meet the research objective? How would you design such an experiment? What regression model would you employ?

10.15. Refer to **Brand preference** Problem 6.5a.

    a. What do the scatter plot matrix and the correlation matrix show about pairwise linear associations among the predictor variables?

    b. Find the two variance inflation factors. Why are they both equal to 1?

*10.16. Refer to **Grocery retailer** Problem 6.9c.

    a. What do the scatter plot matrix and the correlation matrix show about pairwise linear associations among the predictor variables?

    b. Find the three variance inflation factors. Do they indicate that a serious multicollinearity problem exists here?

*10.17. Refer to **Patient satisfaction** Problem 6.15b.

    a. What do the scatter plot matrix and the correlation matrix show about pairwise linear associations among the predictor variables?

    b. Obtain the three variance inflation factors. What do these results suggest about the effects of multicollinearity here? Are these results more revealing than those in part (a)?

10.18. Refer to **Commercial properties** Problem 6.18b.

    a. What do the scatter plot matrix and the correlation matrix show about pairwise linear associations among the predictor variables?

    b. Obtain the four variance inflation factors. Do they indicate that a serious multicollinearity problem exists here?

10.19. Refer to **Job proficiency** Problems 9.10 and 9.11. The subset model containing only first-order terms in X_1 and X_3 is to be evaluated in detail.

    a. Obtain the residuals and plot them separately against $\hat{Y}$, each of the four predictor variables, and the cross-product term X_1X_3. On the basis of these plots, should any modifications in the regression model be investigated?

    b. Prepare separate added-variable plots against $e(X_1|X_3)$ and $e(X_3|X_1)$. Do these plots suggest that any modifications in the model form are warranted?

    c. Prepare a normal probability plot of the residuals. Also obtain the coefficient of correlation between the ordered residuals and their expected values under normality. Test the reasonableness of the normality assumptions, using Table B.6 and $\alpha = .01$. What do you conclude?

    d. Obtain the studentized deleted residuals and identify any outlying Y observations. Use the Bonferroni outlier test procedure with $\alpha = .05$. State the decision rule and conclusion.

   e. Obtain the diagonal elements of the hat matrix. Using the rule of thumb in the text, identify any outlying X observations. Are your findings consistent with those in Problem 9.10a? Should they be? Comment.

   f. Cases 7 and 18 appear to be moderately outlying with respect to their X values, and case 16 is reasonably far outlying with respect to its Y value. Obtain *DFFITS*, *DFBETAS*, and Cook's distance values for these cases to assess their influence. What do you conclude?

   g. Obtain the variance inflation factors. What do they indicate?

10.20. Refer to **Lung pressure** Problems 9.13 and 9.14. The subset regression model containing first-order terms for X_1 and X_2 and the cross-product term $X_1 X_2$ is to be evaluated in detail.

   a. Obtain the residuals and plot them separately against $\hat{Y}$ and each of the three predictor variables. On the basis of these plots, should any further modifications of the regression model be attempted?

   b. Prepare a normal probability plot of the residuals. Also obtain the coefficient of correlation between the ordered residuals and their expected values under normality. Does the normality assumption appear to be reasonable here?

   c. Obtain the variance inflation factors. Are there any indications that serious multicollinearity problems are present? Explain.

   d. Obtain the studentized deleted residuals and identify any outlying Y observations. Use the Bonferroni outlier test procedure with $\alpha = .05$. State the decision rule and conclusion.

   e. Obtain the diagonal elements of the hat matrix. Using the rule of thumb in the text, identify any outlying X observations. Are your findings consistent with those in Problem 9.13a? Should they be? Discuss.

   f. Cases 3, 8, and 15 are moderately far outlying with respect to their X values, and case 7 is relatively far outlying with respect to its Y value. Obtain *DFFITS*, *DFBETAS*, and Cook's distance values for these cases to assess their influence. What do you conclude?

*10.21. Refer to **Kidney function** Problem 9.15 and the regression model fitted in part (c).

   a. Obtain the variance inflation factors. Are there indications that serious multicollinearity problems exist here? Explain.

   b. Obtain the residuals and plot them separately against $\hat{Y}$ and each of the predictor variables. Also prepare a normal probability plot of the residuals.

   c. Prepare separate added-variable plots against $e(X_1|X_2, X_3)$, $e(X_2|X_1, X_3)$, and $e(X_3|X_1, X_2)$.

   d. Do the plots in parts (b) and (c) suggest that the regression model should be modified?

*10.22. Refer to **Kidney function** Problems 9.15 and 10.21. Theoretical arguments suggest use of the following regression function:

$$E\{\ln Y\} = \beta_0 + \beta_1 \ln X_1 + \beta_2 \ln(140 - X_2) + \beta_3 \ln X_3$$

   a. Fit the regression function based on theoretical considerations.

   b. Obtain the residuals and plot them separately against $\hat{Y}$ and each predictor variable in the fitted model. Also prepare a normal probability plot of the residuals. Have the difficulties noted in Problem 10.21 now largely been eliminated?

   c. Obtain the variance inflation factors. Are there indications that serious multicollinearity problems exist here? Explain.

   d. Obtain the studentized deleted residuals and identify any outlying Y observations. Use the Bonferroni outlier test procedure with $\alpha = .10$. State the decision rule and conclusion.

e. Obtain the diagonal elements of the hat matrix. Using the rule of thumb in the text, identify any outlying X observations.

f. Cases 28 and 29 are relatively far outlying with respect to their Y values. Obtain *DFFITS*, *DFBETAS*, and Cook's distance values for these cases to assess their influence. What do you conclude?

Exercises

10.23. Show that (10.37) is algebraically equivalent to (10.33a).

10.24. If $n = p$ and the **X** matrix is invertible, use (5.34) and (5.37) to show that the hat matrix **H** is given by the $p \times p$ identity matrix. In this case, what are h_{ii} and $\hat{Y}_i$?

10.25. Show that (10.26) follows from (10.24a) and (10.25).

10.26. Prove (9.11), using (10.27) and Exercise 5.31.

Projects

10.27. Refer to the **SENIC** data set in Appendix C.1 and Project 9.25. The regression model containing age, routine chest X-ray ratio, and average daily census in first-order terms is to be evaluated in detail based on the model-building data set.

a. Obtain the residuals and plot them separately against $\hat{Y}$, each of the predictor variables in the model, and each of the related cross-product terms. On the basis of these plots, should any modifications of the model be made?

b. Prepare a normal probability plot of the residuals. Also obtain the coefficient of correlation between the ordered residuals and their expected values under normality. Test the reasonableness of the normality assumption, using Table B.6 and $\alpha = .05$. What do you conclude?

c. Obtain the scatter plot matrix, the correlation matrix of the X variables, and the variance inflation factors. Are there any indications that serious multicollinearity problems are present? Explain.

d. Obtain the studentized deleted residuals and prepare a dot plot of these residuals. Are any outliers present? Use the Bonferroni outlier test procedure with $\alpha = .01$. State the decision rule and conclusion.

e. Obtain the diagonal elements of the hat matrix. Using the rule of thumb in the text, identify any outlying X observations.

f. Cases 62, 75, 106, and 112 are moderately outlying with respect to their X values, and case 87 is reasonably far outlying with respect to its Y value. Obtain *DFFITS*, *DFBETAS*, and Cook's distance values for these cases to assess their influence. What do you conclude?

10.28. Refer to the **CDI** data set in Appendix C.2 and Project 9.26. The regression model containing variables 6, 8, 9, 13, 14, and 15 in first-order terms is to be evaluated in detail based on the model-building data set.

a. Obtain the residuals and plot them separately against $\hat{Y}$, each predictor variable in the model, and the related cross-product term. On the basis of these plots, should any modifications in the model be made?

b. Prepare a normal probability plot of the residuals. Also obtain the coefficient of correlation between the ordered residuals and their expected values under normality. Test the reasonableness of the normality assumption, using Table B.6 and $\alpha = .01$. What do you conclude?

    c. Obtain the scatter plot matrix, the correlation matrix of the X variables, and the variance inflation factors. Are there any indications that serious multicollinearity problems are present? Explain.

    d. Obtain the studentized deleted residuals and prepare a dot plot of these residuals. Are any outliers present? Use the Bonferroni outlier test procedure with $\alpha = .05$. State the decision rule and conclusion.

    e. Obtain the diagonal elements of the hat matrix. Using the rule of thumb in the text, identify any outlying X observations.

    f. Cases 2, 8, 48, 128, 206, and 404 are outlying with respect to their X values, and cases 2 and 6 are reasonably far outlying with respect to their Y values. Obtain *DFFITS*, *DFBETAS*, and Cook's distance values for these cases to assess their influence. What do you conclude?

Case Studies

10.29. Refer to the **Website developer** data set in Appendix C.6 and Case Study 9.29. For the best subset model developed in Case Study 9.29, perform appropriate diagnostic checks to evaluate outliers and assess their influence. Do any serious multicollinearity problems exist here?

10.30. Refer to the **Prostate cancer** data set in Appendix C.5 and Case Study 9.30. For the best subset model developed in Case Study 9.30, perform appropriate diagnostic checks to evaluate outliers and assess their influence. Do any serious multicollinearity problems exist here?

10.31. Refer to the **Real estate** data set in Appendix C.7 and Case Study 9.31. For the best subset model developed in Case Study 9.31, perform appropriate diagnostic checks to evaluate outliers and assess their influence. Do any serious multicollinearity problems exist here?

11

Building the Regression Model III: Remedial Measures

When the diagnostics indicate that a regression model is not appropriate or that one or several cases are very influential, remedial measures may need to be taken. In earlier chapters, we discussed some remedial measures, such as transformations to linearize the regression relation, to make the error distributions more nearly normal, or to make the variances of the error terms more nearly equal. In this chapter, we take up some additional remedial measures to deal with unequal error variances, a high degree of multicollinearity, and influential observations. We next consider two methods for nonparametric regression in detail, lowess and regression trees. Since these remedial measures and alternative approaches often involve relatively complex estimation procedures, we consider next a general approach, called bootstrapping, for evaluating the precision of these complex estimators. We conclude the chapter by presenting a case that illustrates some of the issues that arise in model building.

11.1 Unequal Error Variances Remedial Measures—Weighted Least Squares

We explained in Chapters 3 and 6 how transformations of Y may be helpful in reducing or eliminating unequal variances of the error terms. A difficulty with transformations of Y is that they may create an inappropriate regression relationship. When an appropriate regression relationship has been found but the variances of the error terms are unequal, an alternative to transformations is weighted least squares, a procedure based on a generalization of multiple regression model (6.7). We shall now denote the variance of the error term ε_i by σ_i^2 to recognize that different error terms may have different variances. The generalized multiple regression model can then be expressed as follows:

$$Y_i = \beta_0 + \beta_1 X_{i1} + \cdots + \beta_{p-1} X_{i,p-1} + \varepsilon_i \qquad \textbf{(11.1)}$$

where:

$\beta_0, \beta_1, \ldots, \beta_{p-1}$ are parameters

$X_{i1}, \ldots, X_{i,p-1}$ are known constants

ε_i are independent $N(0, \sigma_i^2)$

$i = 1, \ldots, n$

The variance-covariance matrix of the error terms for the generalized multiple regression model (11.1) is more complex than before:

$$
\underset{n \times n}{\sigma^2\{\boldsymbol{\varepsilon}\}} = \begin{bmatrix} \sigma_1^2 & 0 & \cdots & 0 \\ 0 & \sigma_2^2 & \cdots & 0 \\ \vdots & \vdots & & \vdots \\ 0 & 0 & \cdots & \sigma_n^2 \end{bmatrix} \tag{11.2}
$$

The estimation of the regression coefficients in generalized model (11.1) could be done by using the estimators in (6.25) for regression model (6.7) with equal error variances. These estimators are still unbiased and consistent for generalized regression model (11.1), but they no longer have minimum variance. To obtain unbiased estimators with minimum variance, we must take into account that the different Y observations for the n cases no longer have the same reliability. Observations with small variances provide more reliable information about the regression function than those with large variances. We shall first consider the estimation of the regression coefficients when the error variances σ_i^2 are known. This case is usually unrealistic, but it provides guidance as to how to proceed when the error variances are not known.

Error Variances Known

When the error variances σ_i^2 are known, we can use the method of maximum likelihood to obtain estimators of the regression coefficients in generalized regression model (11.1). The likelihood function in (6.26) for the case of equal error variances σ^2 is modified by replacing the σ^2 terms with the respective variances σ_i^2 and expressing the likelihood function in the first form of (1.26):

$$
L(\boldsymbol{\beta}) = \prod_{i=1}^{n} \frac{1}{\left(2\pi\sigma_i^2\right)^{1/2}} \exp\left[-\frac{1}{2\sigma_i^2}(Y_i - \beta_0 - \beta_1 X_{i1} - \cdots - \beta_{p-1} X_{i,p-1})^2\right] \tag{11.3}
$$

where $\boldsymbol{\beta}$ as usual denotes the vector of the regression coefficients. We define the reciprocal of the variance σ_i^2 as the *weight* w_i:

$$
w_i = \frac{1}{\sigma_i^2} \tag{11.4}
$$

We can then express the likelihood function (11.3) as follows, after making some simplifications:

$$
L(\boldsymbol{\beta}) = \left[\prod_{i=1}^{n}\left(\frac{w_i}{2\pi}\right)^{1/2}\right] \exp\left[-\frac{1}{2}\sum_{i=1}^{n} w_i(Y_i - \beta_0 - \beta_1 X_{i1} - \cdots - \beta_{p-1} X_{i,p-1})^2\right] \tag{11.5}
$$

We find the maximum likelihood estimators of the regression coefficients by *maximizing* $L(\boldsymbol{\beta})$ in (11.5) with respect to $\beta_0, \beta_1, \ldots, \beta_{p-1}$. Since the error variances σ_i^2 and hence the weights w_i are assumed to be known, maximizing $L(\boldsymbol{\beta})$ with respect to the regression coefficients is equivalent to *minimizing* the exponential term:

$$Q_w = \sum_{i=1}^{n} w_i (Y_i - \beta_0 - \beta_1 X_{i1} - \cdots - \beta_{p-1} X_{i,p-1})^2 \tag{11.6}$$

This term to be minimized for obtaining the maximum likelihood estimators is also the *weighted least squares criterion,* denoted by Q_w. Thus, the methods of maximum likelihood and weighted least squares lead to the same estimators for the generalized multiple regression model (11.1), as is also the case for the ordinary multiple regression model (6.7).

Note how the weighted least squares criterion (11.6) generalizes the ordinary least squares criterion in (6.22) by replacing equal weights of 1 by w_i. Since the weight w_i is inversely related to the variance σ_i^2, it reflects the amount of information contained in the observation Y_i. Thus, an observation Y_i that has a large variance receives less weight than another observation that has a smaller variance. Intuitively, this is reasonable. The more precise is Y_i (i.e., the smaller is σ_i^2), the more information Y_i provides about $E\{Y_i\}$ and therefore the more weight it should receive in fitting the regression function.

It is easiest to express the maximum likelihood and weighted least squares estimators of the regression coefficients for model (11.1) in matrix terms. Let the matrix $\mathbf{W}$ be a diagonal matrix containing the weights w_i:

$$\underset{n \times n}{\mathbf{W}} = \begin{bmatrix} w_1 & 0 & \cdots & 0 \\ 0 & w_2 & \cdots & 0 \\ \vdots & \vdots & & \vdots \\ 0 & 0 & \cdots & w_n \end{bmatrix} \tag{11.7}$$

The normal equations can then be expressed as follows:

$$(\mathbf{X'WX})\mathbf{b}_w = \mathbf{X'WY} \tag{11.8}$$

and the weighted least squares and maximum likelihood estimators of the regression coefficients are:

$$\underset{p \times 1}{\mathbf{b}_w} = (\mathbf{X'WX})^{-1}\mathbf{X'WY} \tag{11.9}$$

where $\mathbf{b}_w$ is the vector of the estimated regression coefficients obtained by weighted least squares. The variance-covariance matrix of the weighted least squares estimated regression coefficients is:

$$\underset{p \times p}{\sigma^2\{\mathbf{b}_w\}} = (\mathbf{X'WX})^{-1} \tag{11.10}$$

Note that this variance-covariance matrix is known since the variances σ_i^2 are assumed to be known.

The weighted least squares and maximum likelihood estimators of the regression coefficients in (11.9) are unbiased, consistent, and have minimum variance among unbiased linear estimators. Thus, when the weights are known, $\mathbf{b}_w$ generally exhibits less variability than the ordinary least squares estimator $\mathbf{b}$.

Many computer regression packages will provide the weighted least squares estimated regression coefficients. The user simply needs to provide the weights w_i.

Error Variances Known up to Proportionality Constant

We now relax the requirement that the variances σ_i^2 are known by considering the case where only the relative magnitudes of the variances are known. For instance, if we know that σ_2^2 is twice as large as σ_1^2, we might use the weights $w_1 = 1$, $w_2 = 1/2$. In that case, the relative weights w_i are a constant multiple of the unknown true weights $1/\sigma_i^2$:

$$w_i = k\left(\frac{1}{\sigma_i^2}\right) \tag{11.11}$$

where k is the proportionality constant. It can be shown that the weighted least squares and maximum likelihood estimators are unaffected by the unknown proportionality constant k and are still given by (11.9). The reason is that the proportionality constant k appears on both sides of the normal equations (11.8) and cancels out. The variance-covariance matrix of the weighted least squares regression coefficients is now as follows:

$$\underset{p \times p}{\sigma^2\{\mathbf{b}_w\}} = k(\mathbf{X'WX})^{-1} \tag{11.12}$$

This matrix is unknown because the proportionality constant k is not known. It can be estimated, however. The estimated variance-covariance matrix of the regression coefficients $\mathbf{b}_w$ is:

$$\underset{p \times p}{\mathbf{s}^2\{\mathbf{b}_w\}} = MSE_w(\mathbf{X'WX})^{-1} \tag{11.13}$$

where MSE_w is based on the weighted squared residuals:

$$MSE_w = \frac{\sum w_i(Y_i - \hat{Y}_i)^2}{n - p} = \frac{\sum w_i e_i^2}{n - p} \tag{11.13a}$$

Thus, MSE_w here is an estimator of the proportionality constant k.

Error Variances Unknown

If the variances σ_i^2 were known, or even known up to a proportionality constant, the use of weighted least squares with weights w_i would be straightforward. Unfortunately, one rarely has knowledge of the variances σ_i^2. We are then forced to use estimates of the variances. These can be obtained in a variety of ways. We discuss two methods of obtaining estimates of the variances σ_i^2.

Estimation of Variance Function or Standard Deviation Function.   The first method of obtaining estimates of the error term variances σ_i^2 is based on empirical findings that the magnitudes of σ_i^2 and σ_i often vary in a regular fashion with one or several predictor variables X_k or with the mean response $E\{Y_i\}$. Figure 3.4c, for example, shows a typical "megaphone" prototype residual plot where σ_i^2 increases as the predictor variable X becomes larger. Such a relationship between σ_i^2 and one or several predictor variables can be estimated because the squared residual e_i^2 obtained from an ordinary least squares regression fit is an estimate of σ_i^2, provided that the regression function is appropriate. We know from (A.15a) that the variance of the error term ε_i, denoted by σ_i^2, can be expressed as follows:

$$\sigma_i^2 = E\{\varepsilon_i^2\} - (E\{\varepsilon_i\})^2 \tag{11.14}$$

Since $E\{\varepsilon_i\} = 0$ according to the regression model, we obtain:

$$\sigma_i^2 = E\{\varepsilon_i^2\} \tag{11.15}$$

Hence, the squared residual e_i^2 is an estimator of σ_i^2. Furthermore, the absolute residual $|e_i|$ is an estimator of the standard deviation σ_i, since $\sigma_i = |\sqrt{\sigma_i^2}|$.

We can therefore estimate the variance function describing the relation of σ_i^2 to relevant predictor variables by first fitting the regression model using unweighted least squares and then regressing the squared residuals e_i^2 against the appropriate predictor variables. Alternatively, we can estimate the standard deviation function describing the relation of σ_i to relevant predictor variables by regressing the absolute residuals $|e_i|$ obtained from fitting the regression model using unweighted least squares against the appropriate predictor variables. If there are any outliers in the data, it is generally advisable to estimate the standard deviation function rather than the variance function, because regressing absolute residuals is less affected by outliers than regressing squared residuals. Reference 11.1 provides a detailed discussion of the issues encountered in estimating variance and standard deviation functions.

We illustrate the use of some possible variance and standard deviation functions:

1. A residual plot against X_1 exhibits a megaphone shape. Regress the absolute residuals against X_1.
2. A residual plot against $\hat{Y}$ exhibits a megaphone shape. Regress the absolute residuals against $\hat{Y}$.
3. A plot of the squared residuals against X_3 exhibits an upward tendency. Regress the squared residuals against X_3.
4. A plot of the residuals against X_2 suggests that the variance increases rapidly with increases in X_2 up to a point and then increases more slowly. Regress the absolute residuals against X_2 and X_2^2.

After the variance function or the standard deviation function is estimated, the fitted values from this function are used to obtain the estimated weights:

$$w_i = \frac{1}{(\hat{s}_i)^2} \quad \text{where } \hat{s}_i \text{ is fitted value from standard deviation function} \tag{11.16a}$$

$$w_i = \frac{1}{\hat{v}_i} \quad \text{where } \hat{v}_i \text{ is fitted value from variance function} \tag{11.16b}$$

The estimated weights are then placed in the weight matrix $\mathbf{W}$ in (11.7) and the estimated regression coefficients are obtained by (11.9), as follows:

$$\mathbf{b}_w = (\mathbf{X}'\mathbf{W}\mathbf{X})^{-1}\mathbf{X}'\mathbf{W}\mathbf{Y} \tag{11.17}$$

The weighted error mean square MSE_w may be viewed here as an estimator of the proportionality constant k in (11.11). If the modeling of the variance or standard deviation function is done well, the proportionality constant will be near 1 and MSE_w should then be near 1.

We summarize the estimation process:

1. Fit the regression model by unweighted least squares and analyze the residuals.
2. Estimate the variance function or the standard deviation function by regressing either the squared residuals or the absolute residuals on the appropriate predictor(s).
3. Use the fitted values from the estimated variance or standard deviation function to obtain the weights w_i.
4. Estimate the regression coefficients using these weights.

If the estimated coefficients differ substantially from the estimated regression coefficients obtained by ordinary least squares, it is usually advisable to iterate the weighted least squares process by using the residuals from the weighted least squares fit to reestimate the variance or standard deviation function and then obtain revised weights. Often one or two iterations are sufficient to stabilize the estimated regression coefficients. This iteration process is often called *iteratively reweighted least squares.*

Use of Replicates or Near Replicates. A second method of obtaining estimates of the error term variances σ_i^2 can be utilized in designed experiments where replicate observations are made at each combination of levels of the predictor variables. If the number of replications is large, the weights w_i may be obtained directly from the sample variances of the Y observations at each combination of levels of the X variables. Otherwise, the sample variances or sample standard deviations should first be regressed against appropriate predictor variables to estimate the variance or standard deviation function, from which the weights can then be obtained. Note that each case in a replicate group receives the same weight with this method.

In observational studies, replicate observations often are not present. Near replicates may then be used. For example, if the residual plot against X_1 shows a megaphone appearance, cases with similar X_1 values can be grouped together and the variance of the residuals in each group calculated. The reciprocals of these variances are then used as the weights w_i if the number of replications is large. Otherwise, a variance or standard deviation function may be estimated to obtain the weights. Again, all cases in a near-replicate group receive the same weight. If the estimated regression coefficients differ substantially from those obtained with ordinary least squares, the procedure may be iterated, as when an estimated variance or standard deviation function is used.

Inference Procedures when Weights Are Estimated. When the error variances σ_i^2 are unknown so that the weights w_i need to be estimated, which almost always is the case, the variance-covariance matrix of the estimated regression coefficients is usually estimated by means of (11.13), using the estimated weights, provided the sample size is not very small. Confidence intervals for regression coefficients are then obtained by means of (6.50), with the estimated standard deviation $s\{b_{wk}\}$ obtained from the matrix (11.13). Confidence intervals for mean responses are obtained by means of (6.59), using $\mathbf{s}^2\{\mathbf{b}_w\}$ from (11.13) in (6.58). These inference procedures are now only approximate, however, because the estimation of the variances σ_i^2 introduces another source of variability. The approximation is often quite good when the sample size is not too small. One means of determining whether the approximation is good is to use bootstrapping, a statistical procedure that will be explained in Section 11.5.

Use of Ordinary Least Squares with Unequal Error Variances. If one uses $\mathbf{b}$ (not $\mathbf{b}_w$) with unequal error variances, the ordinary least squares estimators of the regression coefficients are still unbiased and consistent, but they are no longer minimum variance estimators. Also, $\sigma^2\{\mathbf{b}\}$ is no longer given by $\sigma^2(\mathbf{X'X})^{-1}$. The correct variance-covariance matrix is:

$$\sigma^2\{\mathbf{b}\} = (\mathbf{X'X})^{-1}(\mathbf{X'}\sigma^2\{\boldsymbol{\varepsilon}\}\mathbf{X})(\mathbf{X'X})^{-1}$$

If error variances are unequal and unknown, an appropriate estimator of $\sigma^2\{\mathbf{b}\}$ can still be obtained using ordinary least squares. The *White estimator* (Ref. 11.2) is:

$$\mathbf{S}^2\{\mathbf{b}\} = (\mathbf{X'X})^{-1}(\mathbf{X'S}_0\mathbf{X})(\mathbf{X'X})^{-1}$$

where:

$$\mathbf{S}_0_{n \times n} = \begin{bmatrix} e_1^2 & 0 & \cdots & 0 \\ 0 & e_2^2 & \cdots & 0 \\ \vdots & \vdots & & \vdots \\ 0 & 0 & \cdots & e_n^2 \end{bmatrix}$$

and where $e_1, \ldots, e_n$ are the ordinary least squares estimators of the residuals. White's estimator is sometimes referred to as a robust covariance matrix, because it can be used to make appropriate inferences about the regression parameters based on ordinary least squares, without having to specify the form of the nonconstant error variance.

Example

A health researcher, interested in studying the relationship between diastolic blood pressure and age among healthy adult women 20 to 60 years old, collected data on 54 subjects. A portion of the data is presented in Table 11.1, columns 1 and 2. The scatter plot of the data in Figure 11.1a strongly suggests a linear relationship between diastolic blood pressure and age but also indicates that the error term variance increases with age. The researcher fitted a linear regression function by unweighted least squares to conduct some preliminary analyses of the residuals. The fitted regression function and the estimated standard deviations of b_0

TABLE 11.1
Weighted Least Squares— Blood Pressure Example.

Subject i	(1) Age X_i	(2) Diastolic Blood Pressure Y_i	(3) e_i	(4) $|e_i|$	(5) $\hat{s}_i$	(6) w_i
1	27	73	1.18	1.18	3.801	.06921
2	21	66	−2.34	2.34	2.612	.14656
3	22	63	−5.92	5.92	2.810	.12662
...	...	...	...	...	...	...
52	52	100	13.68	13.68	8.756	.01304
53	58	80	−9.80	9.80	9.944	.01011
54	57	109	19.78	19.78	9.746	.01053

FIGURE 11.1 Diagnostic Plots Detecting Unequal Error Variances—Blood Pressure Example.

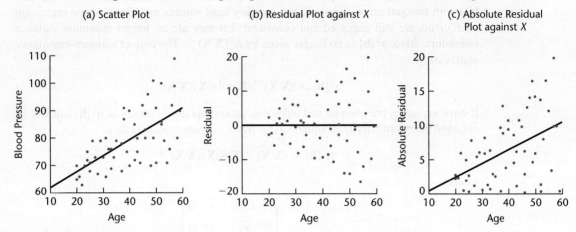

(a) Scatter Plot   (b) Residual Plot against X (c) Absolute Residual Plot against X

and b_1 are:

$$\hat{Y} = 56.157 + .58003X \tag{11.18}$$
$$(3.994) \quad (.09695)$$

The residuals are shown in Table 11.1, column 3, and the absolute residuals are presented in column 4. Figure 11.1a presents this estimated regression function. Figure 11.1b presents a plot of the residuals against X, which confirms the nonconstant error variance. A plot of the absolute residuals against X in Figure 11.1c suggests that a linear relation between the error standard deviation and X may be reasonable. The analyst therefore regressed the absolute residuals against X and obtained:

$$\hat{s} = -1.54946 + .198172X \tag{11.19}$$

Here, $\hat{s}$ denotes the estimated expected standard deviation. The estimated standard deviation function in (11.19) is shown in Figure 11.1c.

To obtain the weights w_i, the analyst obtained the fitted values from the standard deviation function in (11.19). For example, for case 1, for which $X_1 = 27$, the fitted value is:

$$\hat{s}_1 = -1.54946 + .198172(27) = 3.801$$

The fitted values are shown in Table 11.1, column 5. The weights are then obtained by using (11.16a). For case 1, we obtain:

$$w_1 = \frac{1}{(\hat{s}_1)^2} = \frac{1}{(3.801)^2} = .0692$$

The weights w_i are shown in Table 11.1, column 6.

Using these weights in a regression program that has weighted least squares capability, the analyst obtained the following estimated regression function:

$$\hat{Y} = 55.566 + .59634X \tag{11.20}$$

Note that the estimated regression coefficients are not much different from those in (11.18) obtained with unweighted least squares. Since the regression coefficients changed only a little, the analyst concluded that there was no need to reestimate the standard deviation function and the weights based on the residuals for the weighted regression in (11.20).

The analyst next obtained the estimated variance-covariance matrix of the estimated regression coefficients by means of (11.13) to find the approximate estimated standard deviation $s\{b_{w1}\} = .07924$. It is interesting to note that this standard deviation is somewhat smaller than the standard deviation of the estimate obtained by ordinary least squares in (11.18), .09695. The reduction of about 18 percent is the result of the recognition of unequal error variances when using weighted least squares.

To obtain an approximate 95 percent confidence interval for β_1, the analyst employed (6.50) and required $t(.975; 52) = 2.007$. The confidence limits then are $.59634 \pm 2.007$ $(.07924)$ and the approximate 95 percent confidence interval is:

$$.437 \leq \beta_1 \leq .755$$

We shall consider the appropriateness of this inference approximation in Section 11.5.

Comments

1. The condition of the error variance not being constant over all cases is called *heteroscedasticity*, in contrast to the condition of equal error variances, called *homoscedasticity*.

2. Heteroscedasticity is inherent when the response in regression analysis follows a distribution in which the variance is functionally related to the mean. (Significant nonnormality in Y is encountered as well in most such cases.) Consider, in this connection, a regression analysis where X is the speed of a machine which puts a plastic coating on cable and Y is the number of blemishes in the coating per thousand feet of cable. If Y is Poisson distributed with a mean which increases as X increases, the distributions of Y cannot have constant variance at all levels of X since the variance of a Poisson variable equals the mean, which is increasing with X.

3. Estimation of the weights by means of an estimated variance or standard deviation function or by means of groups of replicates or near replicates can be very helpful when there are major differences in the variances of the error terms. When the differences are only small or modest, however, weighted least squares with these approximate methods will not be particularly helpful.

4. The weighted least squares output of some multiple regression software packages includes R^2, the coefficient of multiple determination. Users of these packages need to treat this measure with caution, because R^2 does not have a clear-cut meaning for weighted least squares.

5. The weighted least squares estimators of the regression coefficients in (11.9) for the case of known error variances σ_i^2 can be derived readily. The derivation also shows that weighted least squares may be viewed as ordinary least squares of transformed variables. The generalized multiple regression model in (11.1) may be expressed as follows in matrix form:

$$\mathbf{Y} = \mathbf{X}\boldsymbol{\beta} + \boldsymbol{\varepsilon} \tag{11.21}$$

where:

$$\mathbf{E}\{\boldsymbol{\varepsilon}\} = \mathbf{0}$$
$$\sigma^2\{\boldsymbol{\varepsilon}\} = \mathbf{W}^{-1}$$

Note that the variance-covariance matrix of the error terms in (11.2) is the inverse of the weight matrix defined in (11.7).

We now define a diagonal matrix containing the square roots of the weights w_i and denote it by $\mathbf{W}^{1/2}$:

$$\underset{n \times n}{\mathbf{W}^{1/2}} = \begin{bmatrix} \sqrt{w_1} & 0 & \cdots & 0 \\ 0 & \sqrt{w_2} & \cdots & 0 \\ \vdots & \vdots & & \vdots \\ 0 & 0 & \cdots & \sqrt{w_n} \end{bmatrix} \qquad (11.22)$$

Note that $\mathbf{W}^{1/2}$ is symmetric and that $\mathbf{W}^{1/2}\mathbf{W}^{1/2} = \mathbf{W}$. The latter relation also holds for the corresponding inverse matrices: $\mathbf{W}^{-1/2}\mathbf{W}^{-1/2} = \mathbf{W}^{-1}$.

We premultiply the terms on both sides of regression model (11.21) by $\mathbf{W}^{1/2}$ and obtain:

$$\mathbf{W}^{1/2}\mathbf{Y} = \mathbf{W}^{1/2}\mathbf{X}\boldsymbol{\beta} + \mathbf{W}^{1/2}\boldsymbol{\varepsilon} \qquad (11.23)$$

which can be expressed as:

$$\mathbf{Y}_w = \mathbf{X}_w\boldsymbol{\beta} + \boldsymbol{\varepsilon}_w \qquad (11.23a)$$

where:

$$\mathbf{Y}_w = \mathbf{W}^{1/2}\mathbf{Y}$$
$$\mathbf{X}_w = \mathbf{W}^{1/2}\mathbf{X} \qquad (11.23b)$$
$$\boldsymbol{\varepsilon}_w = \mathbf{W}^{1/2}\boldsymbol{\varepsilon}$$

By (5.45) and (5.46), we obtain:

$$E\{\boldsymbol{\varepsilon}_w\} = \mathbf{W}^{1/2}E\{\boldsymbol{\varepsilon}\} = \mathbf{W}^{1/2}\mathbf{0} = \mathbf{0} \qquad (11.24a)$$

$$\sigma^2\{\boldsymbol{\varepsilon}_w\} = \mathbf{W}^{1/2}\sigma^2\{\boldsymbol{\varepsilon}\}\mathbf{W}^{1/2} = \mathbf{W}^{1/2}\mathbf{W}^{-1}\mathbf{W}^{1/2}$$
$$= \mathbf{W}^{1/2}\mathbf{W}^{-1/2}\mathbf{W}^{-1/2}\mathbf{W}^{1/2} = \mathbf{I} \qquad (11.24b)$$

Thus, regression model (11.23a) involves independent error terms with mean zero and constant variance $\sigma_i^2 \equiv 1$. We can therefore apply standard regression procedures to this transformed regression model.

For example, the ordinary least squares estimators of the regression coefficients in (6.25) here become:

$$\mathbf{b}_w = (\mathbf{X}_w'\mathbf{X}_w)^{-1}\mathbf{X}_w'\mathbf{Y}_w$$

Using the definitions in (11.23b), we obtain the result for weighted least squares given in (11.9):

$$\mathbf{b}_w = [(\mathbf{W}^{1/2}\mathbf{X})'\mathbf{W}^{1/2}\mathbf{X}]^{-1}(\mathbf{W}^{1/2}\mathbf{X})'\mathbf{W}^{1/2}\mathbf{Y}$$
$$= (\mathbf{X}'\mathbf{W}^{1/2}\mathbf{W}^{1/2}\mathbf{X})^{-1}\mathbf{X}'\mathbf{W}^{1/2}\mathbf{W}^{1/2}\mathbf{Y}$$
$$= (\mathbf{X}'\mathbf{W}\mathbf{X})^{-1}\mathbf{X}'\mathbf{W}\mathbf{Y}$$

6. Weighted least squares is a special case of *generalized least squares* where the error terms not only may have different variances but pairs of error terms may also be correlated.

7. For simple linear regression, the weighted least squares normal equations in (11.8) become:

$$\sum w_i Y_i = b_{w0} \sum w_i + b_{w1} \sum w_i X_i$$
$$\sum w_i X_i Y_i = b_{w0} \sum w_i X_i + b_{w1} \sum w_i X_i^2 \qquad (11.25)$$

and the weighted least squares estimators b_{w0} and b_{w1} in (11.9) are:

$$b_{w1} = \frac{\sum w_i X_i Y_i - \dfrac{\sum w_i X_i \sum w_i Y_i}{\sum w_i}}{\sum w_i X_i^2 - \dfrac{\left(\sum w_i X_i\right)^2}{\sum w_i}} \tag{11.26a}$$

$$b_{w0} = \frac{\sum w_i Y_i - b_1 \sum w_i X_i}{\sum w_i} \tag{11.26b}$$

Note that if all weights are equal so w_i is identically equal to a constant, the normal equations (11.25) for weighted least squares reduce to the ones for unweighted least squares in (1.9) and the weighted least squares estimators (11.26) reduce to the ones for unweighted least squares in (1.10). ∎

11.2 Multicollinearity Remedial Measures—Ridge Regression

We consider first some remedial measures for serious multicollinearity that can be implemented with ordinary least squares, and then take up ridge regression, a method of overcoming serious multicollinearity problems by modifying the method of least squares.

Some Remedial Measures

1. As we saw in Chapter 7, the presence of serious multicollinearity often does not affect the usefulness of the fitted model for estimating mean responses or making predictions, provided that the values of the predictor variables for which inferences are to be made follow the same multicollinearity pattern as the data on which the regression model is based. Hence, one remedial measure is to restrict the use of the fitted regression model to inferences for values of the predictor variables that follow the same pattern of multicollinearity.

2. In polynomial regression models, as we noted in Chapter 7, use of centered data for the predictor variable(s) serves to reduce the multicollinearity among the first-order, second-order, and higher-order terms for any given predictor variable.

3. One or several predictor variables may be dropped from the model in order to lessen the multicollinearity and thereby reduce the standard errors of the estimated regression coefficients of the predictor variables remaining in the model. This remedial measure has two important limitations. First, no direct information is obtained about the dropped predictor variables. Second, the magnitudes of the regression coefficients for the predictor variables remaining in the model are affected by the correlated predictor variables not included in the model.

4. Sometimes it is possible to add some cases that break the pattern of multicollinearity. Often, however, this option is not available. In business and economics, for instance, many predictor variables cannot be controlled, so that new cases will tend to show the same intercorrelation patterns as the earlier ones.

5. In some economic studies, it is possible to estimate the regression coefficients for different predictor variables from different sets of data and thereby avoid the problems of multicollinearity. Demand studies, for instance, may use both cross-section and time series data to this end. Suppose the predictor variables in a demand study are price and income,

and the relation to be estimated is:

$$Y_i = \beta_0 + \beta_1 X_{i1} + \beta_2 X_{i2} + \varepsilon_i \qquad (11.27)$$

where Y is demand, X_1 is income, and X_2 is price. The income coefficient β_1 may then be estimated from cross-section data. The demand variable Y is thereupon adjusted:

$$Y_i' = Y_i - b_1 X_{i1} \qquad (11.28)$$

Finally, the price coefficient β_2 is estimated by regressing the adjusted demand variable Y' on X_2.

6. Another remedial measure for multicollinearity that can be used with ordinary least squares is to form one or several composite indexes based on the highly correlated predictor variables, an index being a linear combination of the correlated predictor variables. The methodology of *principal components* provides composite indexes that are uncorrelated. Often, a few of these composite indexes capture much of the information contained in the predictor variables. These few uncorrelated composite indexes are then used in the regression analysis as predictor variables instead of the original highly correlated predictor variables. A limitation of principal components regression, also called latent root regression, is that it may be difficult to attach concrete meanings to the indexes.

More information about these remedial approaches as well as about Bayesian regression, where prior information about the regression coefficients is incorporated into the estimation procedure, may be obtained from specialized works such as Reference 11.3.

Ridge Regression

Biased Estimation.   Ridge regression is one of several methods that have been proposed to remedy multicollinearity problems by modifying the method of least squares to allow biased estimators of the regression coefficients. When an estimator has only a small bias and is substantially more precise than an unbiased estimator, it may well be the preferred estimator since it will have a larger probability of being close to the true parameter value. Figure 11.2 illustrates this situation. Estimator b is unbiased but imprecise, whereas estimator b^R is much more precise but has a small bias. The probability that b^R falls near the true value β is much greater than that for the unbiased estimator b.

FIGURE 11.2
Biased
Estimator with
Small Variance
May Be
Preferable to
Unbiased
Estimator with
Large
Variance.

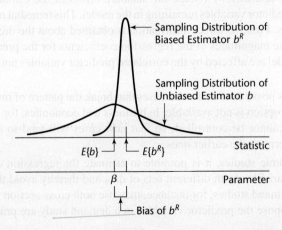

A measure of the combined effect of bias and sampling variation is the mean squared error, a concept that we encountered in Chapter 9 in connection with the C_p criterion. Here, the mean squared error is the expected value of the squared deviation of the biased estimator b^R from the true parameter β. As before, this expected value is the sum of the variance of the estimator and the squared bias:

$$E\{b^R - \beta\}^2 = \sigma^2\{b^R\} + (E\{b^R\} - \beta)^2 \tag{11.29}$$

Note that if the estimator is unbiased, the mean squared error is identical to the variance of the estimator.

Ridge Estimators.   For ordinary least squares, the normal equations are given by (6.24):

$$(\mathbf{X}'\mathbf{X})\mathbf{b} = \mathbf{X}'\mathbf{Y} \tag{11.30}$$

When all variables are transformed by the correlation transformation (7.44), the transformed regression model is given by (7.45):

$$Y_i^* = \beta_1^* X_{i1}^* + \beta_2^* X_{i2}^* + \cdots + \beta_{p-1}^* X_{i,p-1}^* + \varepsilon_i^* \tag{11.31}$$

and the least squares normal equations are given by (7.52a):

$$\mathbf{r}_{XX}\mathbf{b} = \mathbf{r}_{YX} \tag{11.32}$$

where $\mathbf{r}_{XX}$ is the correlation matrix of the X variables defined in (7.47) and $\mathbf{r}_{YX}$ is the vector of coefficients of simple correlation between Y and each X variable defined in (7.48).

The ridge standardized regression estimators are obtained by introducing into the least squares normal equations (11.32) a biasing constant $c \geq 0$, in the following form:

$$(\mathbf{r}_{XX} + c\mathbf{I})\mathbf{b}^R = \mathbf{r}_{YX} \tag{11.33}$$

where $\mathbf{b}^R$ is the vector of the standardized ridge regression coefficients b_k^R:

$$\underset{(p-1)\times 1}{\mathbf{b}^R} = \begin{bmatrix} b_1^R \\ b_2^R \\ \vdots \\ b_{p-1}^R \end{bmatrix} \tag{11.33a}$$

and $\mathbf{I}$ is the $(p-1) \times (p-1)$ identity matrix. Solution of the normal equations (11.33) yields the ridge standardized regression coefficients:

$$\mathbf{b}^R = (\mathbf{r}_{XX} + c\mathbf{I})^{-1}\mathbf{r}_{YX} \tag{11.34}$$

The constant c reflects the amount of bias in the estimators. When $c = 0$, (11.34) reduces to the ordinary least squares regression coefficients in standardized form, as given in (7.52b). When $c > 0$, the ridge regression coefficients are biased but tend to be more stable (i.e., less variable) than ordinary least squares estimators.

Choice of Biasing Constant c.   It can be shown that the bias component of the total mean squared error of the ridge regression estimator $\mathbf{b}^R$ increases as c gets larger (with all b_k^R tending toward zero) while the variance component becomes smaller. It can further be shown that there always exists some value c for which the ridge regression estimator $\mathbf{b}^R$ has a smaller total mean squared error than the ordinary least squares estimator **b**. The difficulty is that the optimum value of c varies from one application to another and is unknown.

A commonly used method of determining the biasing constant c is based on the *ridge trace* and the variance inflation factors $(VIF)_k$ in (10.41). The ridge trace is a simultaneous plot of the values of the $p - 1$ estimated ridge standardized regression coefficients for different values of c, usually between 0 and 1. Extensive experience has indicated that the estimated regression coefficients b_k^R may fluctuate widely as c is changed slightly from 0, and some may even change signs. Gradually, however, these wide fluctuations cease and the magnitudes of the regression coefficients tend to move slowly toward zero as c is increased further. At the same time, the values of $(VIF)_k$ tend to fall rapidly as c is changed from 0, and gradually the $(VIF)_k$ values also tend to change only moderately as c is increased further. One therefore examines the ridge trace and the VIF values and chooses the smallest value of c where it is deemed that the regression coefficients first become stable in the ridge trace and the VIF values have become sufficiently small. The choice is thus a judgmental one.

Example

In the body fat example with three predictor variables in Table 7.1, we noted previously several informal indications of severe multicollinearity in the data. Indeed, in the fitted model with three predictor variables (Table 7.2d), the estimated regression coefficient b_2 is negative even though it was expected that amount of body fat is positively related to thigh circumference. Ridge regression calculations were made for the body fat example data in Table 7.1 (calculations not shown). The ridge standardized regression coefficients for selected values of c are presented in Table 11.2, and the variance inflation factors are given in Table 11.3. The coefficients of multiple determination R^2 are also shown in the latter table. Figure 11.3 presents the ridge trace of the estimated standardized regression coefficients based on calculations for many more values of c than those shown in Table 11.2. To facilitate the analysis, the horizontal c scale in Figure 11.3 is logarithmic.

TABLE 11.2 Ridge Estimated Standardized Regression Coefficients for Different Biasing Constants c—Body Fat Example with Three Predictor Variables.

c	b_1^R	b_2^R	b_3^R
.000	4.264	−2.929	−1.561
.002	1.441	−.4113	−.4813
.004	1.006	−.0248	−.3149
.006	.8300	.1314	−.2472
.008	.7343	.2158	−.2103
.010	.6742	.2684	−.1870
.020	.5463	.3774	−.1369
.030	.5004	.4134	−.1181
.040	.4760	.4302	−.1076
.050	.4605	.4392	−.1005
.100	.4234	.4490	−.0812
.500	.3377	.3791	−.0295
1.000	.2798	.3101	−.0059

TABLE 11.3 *VIF* Values for Regression Coefficients and R^2 for Different Biasing Constants c—Body Fat Example with Three Predictor Variables.

c	$(VIF)_1$	$(VIF)_2$	$(VIF)_3$	R^2
.000	708.84	564.34	104.61	.8014
.002	50.56	40.45	8.28	.7901
.004	16.98	13.73	3.36	.7864
.006	8.50	6.98	2.19	.7847
.008	5.15	4.30	1.62	.7838
.010	3.49	2.98	1.38	.7832
.020	1.10	1.08	1.01	.7818
.030	.63	.70	.92	.7812
.040	.45	.56	.88	.7808
.050	.37	.49	.85	.7804
.100	.25	.37	.76	.7784
.500	.15	.21	.40	.7427
1.000	.11	.14	.23	.6818

FIGURE 11.3
Ridge Trace of
Estimated
Standardized
Regression
Coefficients—
Body Fat
Example with
Three
Predictor
Variables.

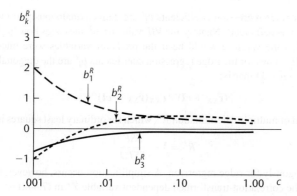

Note the instability in Figure 11.3 of the regression coefficients for very small values of c. The estimated regression coefficient b_2^R, in fact, changes signs. Also note the rapid decrease in the *VIF* values in Table 11.3. It was decided to employ $c = .02$ here because for this value of the biasing constant the ridge regression coefficients have *VIF* values near 1 and the estimated regression coefficients appear to have become reasonably stable. The resulting fitted model for $c = .02$ is:

$$\hat{Y}^* = .5463X_1^* + .3774X_2^* - .1369X_3^*$$

Transforming back to the original variables by (7.53), we obtain:

$$\hat{Y} = -7.3978 + .5553X_1 + .3681X_2 - .1917X_3$$

where $\bar{Y} = 20.195$, $\bar{X}_1 = 25.305$, $\bar{X}_2 = 51.170$, $\bar{X}_3 = 27.620$, $s_Y = 5.106$, $s_1 = 5.023$, $s_2 = 5.235$, and $s_3 = 3.647$.

The improper sign on the estimate for β_2 has now been eliminated, and the estimated regression coefficients are more in line with prior expectations. The sum of the squared residuals for the transformed variables, which increases with c, has only increased from .1986 at $c = 0$ to .2182 at $c = .02$ while R^2 decreased from .8014 to .7818. These changes are relatively modest. The estimated mean body fat when $X_{h1} = 25.0$, $X_{h2} = 50.0$, and $X_{h3} = 29.0$ is 19.33 for the ridge regression at $c = .02$ compared to 19.19 utilizing the ordinary least squares solution. Thus, the ridge solution at $c = .02$ appears to be quite satisfactory here and a reasonable alternative to the ordinary least squares solution.

Comments

1. The normal equations (11.33) for the ridge estimators are as follows:

$$(1 + c)b_1^R + r_{12}b_2^R + \cdots + r_{1,p-1}b_{p-1}^R = r_{Y1}$$
$$r_{21}b_1^R + (1 + c)b_2^R + \cdots + r_{2,p-1}b_{p-1}^R = r_{Y2}$$
$$\vdots$$
$$r_{p-1,1}b_1^R + r_{p-1,2}b_2^R + \cdots + (1 + c)b_{p-1}^R = r_{Y,p-1}$$

(11.35)

where r_{ij} is the coefficient of simple correlation between the ith and jth X variables and r_{Yj} is the coefficient of simple correlation between the response variable Y and the jth X variable.

2. *VIF* values for ridge regression coefficients b_k^R are defined analogously to those for ordinary least squares regression coefficients. Namely, the *VIF* value for b_k^R measures how large is the variance of b_k^R relative to what the variance would be if the predictor variables were uncorrelated. It can be shown that the *VIF* values for the ridge regression coefficients b_k^R are the diagonal elements of the following $(p-1) \times (p-1)$ matrix:

$$(\mathbf{r}_{XX} + c\mathbf{I})^{-1}\mathbf{r}_{XX}(\mathbf{r}_{XX} + c\mathbf{I})^{-1} \tag{11.36}$$

3. The coefficient of multiple determination R^2, which for ordinary least squares is given in (6.40):

$$R^2 = 1 - \frac{SSE}{SSTO} \tag{11.37}$$

can be defined analogously for ridge regression. A simplification occurs, however, because the total sum of squares for the correlation-transformed dependent variable Y^* in (7.44a) is:

$$SSTO_R = \sum (Y_i^* - \bar{Y}^*)^2 = 1 \tag{11.38}$$

The fitted values with ridge regression are:

$$\hat{Y}_i^* = b_1^R X_{i1}^* + \cdots + b_{p-1}^R X_{i,p-1}^* \tag{11.39}$$

where the X_{ik}^* are the X variables transformed according to the correlation transformation (7.44b). The error sum of squares, as usual, is:

$$SSE_R = \sum (Y_i^* - \hat{Y}_i^*)^2 \tag{11.40}$$

where $\hat{Y}_i^*$ is given in (11.39). R^2 for ridge regression then becomes:

$$R_R^2 = 1 - SSE_R \tag{11.41}$$

4. Ridge regression estimates can be obtained by the method of *penalized least squares*. The penalized least squares criterion combines the usual sum of squared errors with a penalty for large regression coefficients:

$$Q = \sum_{i=1}^{n} [Y_i^* - (\beta_1^* X_{i1}^* + \cdots + \beta_{p-1}^* X_{i,p-1}^*)]^2 + c\left[\sum_{j=1}^{p-1} (\beta_j^*)^2\right]$$

The penalty is a biasing constant, c, times the sum of squares of the regression coefficients. Large absolute regression parameters lead to a large penalty; thus, it can be seen that for $c > 0$ the "best" coefficients generally will be smaller in absolute magnitude than the ordinary least squares estimates. For this reason, ridge estimators are sometimes referred to as *shrinkage* estimators.

5. Ridge regression estimates tend to be stable in the sense that they are usually little affected by small changes in the data on which the fitted regression is based. In contrast, ordinary least squares estimates may be highly unstable under these conditions when the predictor variables are highly multicollinear. Predictions of new observations made from ridge estimated regression functions tend to be more precise than predictions made from ordinary least squares regression functions when the predictor variables are correlated and the new observations follow the same multicollinearity pattern (see, for instance, Reference 11.4). The prediction precision advantage with ridge regression is especially great when the intercorrelations among the predictor variables are high.

6. Ridge estimated regression functions at times will provide good estimates of mean responses or predictions of new observations for levels of the predictor variables outside the region of the observations on which the regression function is based. In contrast, estimated regression functions based on ordinary least squares may perform quite poorly in such circumstances. Of course, any estimation or prediction well outside the region of the observations should always be made with great caution.

7. A major limitation of ridge regression is that ordinary inference procedures are not applicable and exact distributional properties are not known. Bootstrapping, a computer-intensive procedure to be discussed in Section 11.5, can be employed to evaluate the precision of ridge regression coefficients. Another limitation of ridge regression is that the choice of the biasing constant c is a judgmental one. Although a variety of formal methods have been developed for making this choice, these have their own limitations.

8. The ridge regression procedures have been generalized to allow for differing biasing constants for the different estimated regression coefficients; see, for instance, Reference 11.3.

9. Ridge regression can be used to help in reducing the number of potential predictor variables in exploratory observational studies by analyzing the ridge trace. Variables whose ridge trace is unstable, with the coefficient tending toward the value of zero, are dropped with this approach. Also, variables whose ridge trace is stable but at a very small value are dropped. Finally, variables with unstable ridge traces that do not tend toward zero are considered as candidates for dropping. ∎

11.3   Remedial Measures for Influential Cases—Robust Regression

We noted in Chapter 10 that the hat matrix and studentized deleted residuals are valuable tools for identifying cases that are outlying with respect to the X and Y variables. In addition, we considered there how to measure the influence of these outlying cases on the fitted values and estimated regression coefficients by means of the *DFFITS*, Cook's distance, and *DFBETAS* measures. The reason for our concern with outlying cases is that the method of least squares is particularly susceptible to these cases, resulting sometimes in a seriously distorted fitted model for the remaining cases. A crucial question that arises now is how to handle highly influential cases.

A first step is to examine whether an outlying case is the result of a recording error, breakdown of a measurement instrument, or the like. For instance, in a study of the waiting time in a telephone reservation system, one waiting time was recorded as 1,000 rings. This observation was so extreme and unrealistic that it was clearly erroneous. If erroneous data can be corrected, this should be done. Often, however, erroneous data cannot be corrected later on and should be discarded. Many times, unfortunately, it is not possible after the data have been obtained to tell for certain whether the observations for an outlying case are erroneous. Such cases should usually not be discarded.

If an outlying influential case is not clearly erroneous, the next step should be to examine the adequacy of the model. Scientists frequently have primary interest in the outlying cases because they deviate from the currently accepted model. Examination of these outlying cases may provide important clues as to how the model needs to be modified. In a study of the yield of a process, a first-order model was fitted for the two important factors under consideration because previous studies had not found any interaction effects between these factors on the yield. One case in the current study was outlying and highly influential, with extremely high yield; it corresponded to unusually high levels of the two factors. The tentative conclusion drawn was that an interaction effect is present; this was subsequently confirmed in a follow-up study. The improved model, resulting from the outlying case, led to greatly improved process productivity.

Outlying cases may also lead to the finding of other types of model inadequacies, such as the omission of an important variable or the choice of an incorrect functional form (e.g., a quadratic function instead of an exponential function). The analysis of outlying influential cases can frequently lead to valuable insights for strengthening the model such that the outlying case is no longer an outlier but is accounted for by the model.

Discarding of outlying influential cases that are not clearly erroneous and that cannot be accounted for by model improvements should be done only rarely, such as when the model is not intended to cover the special circumstances related to the outlying cases. For example, a few cases in an industrial study were outlying and highly influential. These cases occurred early in the study, when the plant was in transition from one process to the new one under study. Discarding of these early cases was deemed to be reasonable since the model was intended for use after the new process had stabilized.

An alternative to discarding outlying cases that is less severe is to dampen the influence of these cases. That is the purpose of robust regression.

Robust Regression

Robust regression procedures dampen the influence of outlying cases, as compared to ordinary least squares estimation, in an effort to provide a better fit for the majority of cases. They are useful when a known, smooth regression function is to be fitted to data that are "noisy," with a number of outlying cases, so that the assumption of a normal distribution for the error terms is not appropriate. Robust regression procedures are also useful when automated regression analysis is required. For example, a complex measurement instrument used for internal medical examinations must be calibrated for each use. There is no time for a thorough identification of outlying cases and an analysis of their influence, nor for a careful consideration of remedial measures. Instead, an automated regression calibration must be used. Robust regression procedures will automatically guard against undue influence of outlying cases in this situation.

Numerous robust regression procedures have been developed. They are described in specialized texts, such as References 11.5 and 11.6. We mention briefly a few of these procedures and then describe in more detail one commonly used procedure based on iteratively reweighted least squares.

LAR or LAD Regression.   Least absolute residuals (LAR) or least absolute deviations (LAD) regression, also called *minimum L_1-norm regression,* is one of the most widely used robust regression procedures. It is insensitive to both outlying data values and inadequacies of the model employed. The method of least absolute residuals estimates the regression coefficients by minimizing the sum of the absolute deviations of the Y observations from their means. The criterion to be minimized, denoted by L_1, is:

$$L_1 = \sum_{i=1}^{n} |Y_i - (\beta_0 + \beta_1 X_{i1} + \cdots + \beta_{p-1} X_{i,p-1})| \tag{11.42}$$

Since absolute deviations rather than squared ones are involved here, the LAR method places less emphasis on outlying observations than does the method of least squares.

The estimated LAR regression coefficients can be obtained by linear programming techniques. Details about computational aspects may be found in specialized texts, such as Reference 11.7. The LAR fitted regression model differs from the least squares fitted model in that the residuals ordinarily will not sum to zero. Also, the solution for the estimated regression coefficients with the method of least absolute residuals may not be unique.

IRLS Robust Regression. Iteratively reweighted least squares (IRLS) robust regression uses the weighted least squares procedures discussed in Section 11.1 to dampen the influence of outlying observations. Instead of weights based on the error variances, IRLS robust regression uses weights based on how far outlying a case is, as measured by the residual for that case. The weights are revised with each iteration until a robust fit has been obtained. We shall discuss this procedure in more detail shortly.

LMS Regression. Least median of squares (LMS) regression replaces the sum of squared deviations in ordinary least squares by the median of the squared deviations, which is a robust estimator of location. The criterion for this procedure is to minimize the median squared deviation:

$$\text{median}\{[Y_i - (\beta_0 + \beta_1 X_{i1} + \cdots + \beta_{p-1} X_{i,p-1})]^2\} \tag{11.43}$$

with respect to the regression coefficients. Thus, this procedure leads to estimated regression coefficients $b_0, b_1, \ldots, b_{p-1}$ that minimize the median of the squared residuals.

Other Robust Regression Procedures. There are many other robust regression procedures. Some involve trimming one or several of the extreme squared deviations before applying the least squares criterion; others are based on ranks. Many of the robust regression procedures require extensive computing.

IRLS Robust Regression

Iteratively reweighted least squares was encountered in Section 11.1 as a remedial measure for unequal error variances in connection with the obtaining of weights from an estimated variance or standard deviation function. For robust regression, weighted least squares is used to reduce the influence of outlying cases by employing weights that vary inversely with the size of the residual. Outlying cases that have large residuals are thereby given smaller weights. The weights are revised as each iteration yields new residuals until the estimation process stabilizes. A summary of the steps follows:

1. Choose a weight function for weighting the cases.
2. Obtain starting weights for all cases.
3. Use the starting weights in weighted least squares and obtain the residuals from the fitted regression function.
4. Use the residuals in step 3 to obtain revised weights.
5. Continue the iterations until convergence is obtained.

We now discuss each of the steps in IRLS robust regression.

Weight Function. Many weight functions have been proposed for dampening the influence of outlying cases. Two widely used weight functions are the Huber and bisquare weight functions:

$$\text{Huber: } w = \begin{cases} 1 & |u| \leq 1.345 \\ \dfrac{1.345}{|u|} & |u| > 1.345 \end{cases} \tag{11.44}$$

$$\text{Bisquare: } w = \begin{cases} \left[1 - \left(\dfrac{u}{4.685}\right)^2\right]^2 & |u| \leq 4.685 \\ 0 & |u| > 4.685 \end{cases} \tag{11.45}$$

FIGURE 11.4
**Two Weight
Functions Used
in IRLS Robust
Regression.**

(a) Huber Weight Function

(b) Bisquare Weight Function

$$w = \begin{cases} 1 & |u| \leq 1.345 \\ 1.345/|u| & |u| > 1.345 \end{cases}$$

$$w = \begin{cases} [1 - (u/4.685)^2]^2 & |u| \leq 4.685 \\ 0 & |u| > 4.685 \end{cases}$$

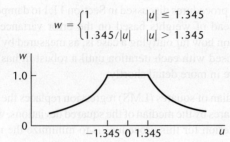

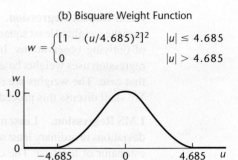

As before, w denotes the weight, and u denotes the scaled residual to be defined shortly. The constant 1.345 in the Huber weight function and the constant 4.685 in the bisquare weight function are called *tuning constants*. They were chosen to make the IRLS robust procedure 95 percent efficient for data generated by the normal error regression model (6.7). Figure 11.4 shows graphs of the two weight functions. Note how the weight w according to each weight function declines as the absolute scaled residual gets larger, and that each weight function is symmetric around $u = 0$. Also note that the Huber weight function does not reduce the weight of a case from 1.0 until the absolute scaled residual exceeds 1.345, and that all cases receive some positive weight, no matter how large the absolute scaled residual. In contrast, the bisquare weight function reduces the weights of all cases from 1.0 (unless the residual is zero). In addition, the bisquare weight function gives weight 0 to all cases whose absolute scaled residual exceeds 4.685, thereby entirely excluding these extreme cases.

Starting Values. Calculations with some of the weight functions are very sensitive to the starting values; with others, this is less of a problem. When the Huber weight function is employed, the initial residuals may be those obtained from an ordinary least squares fit. The bisquare function calculations, on the other hand, are more sensitive to the starting values. To obtain good starting values for the bisquare weight function, the Huber weight function is often used to obtain an initial robust regression fit, and the residuals for this fit are then employed as starting values for several iterations with the bisquare weight function. Alternatively, least absolute residuals regression in (11.42) may be used to obtain starting residuals when the bisquare weight function is used.

Scaled Residuals. The weight functions (11.44) and (11.45) are each designed to be used with scaled residuals. The semistudentized residuals in (3.5) are scaled residuals and could be employed. However, in the presence of outlying observations, $\sqrt{MSE}$ is not a resistant estimator of the error term standard deviation σ; the magnitude of $\sqrt{MSE}$ can be greatly influenced by one or several outlying observations. Also, $\sqrt{MSE}$ is not a robust estimator of σ when the distribution of the error terms is far from normal. Instead, the resistant and robust median absolute deviation (*MAD*) estimator is often employed:

$$MAD = \frac{1}{.6745} \text{median}\{|e_i - \text{median}\{e_i\}|\} \tag{11.46}$$

The constant .6745 provides an unbiased estimate of σ for independent observations from a normal distribution. Here, it serves to provide an estimate that is approximately unbiased.

The scaled residual u_i based on (11.46) then is:

$$u_i = \frac{e_i}{MAD} \tag{11.47}$$

Number of Iterations.   The iterative process of obtaining a new fit, new residuals and thereby new weights, and then refitting with the new weights continues until the process converges. Convergence can be measured by observing whether the weights change relatively little, whether the residuals change relatively little, whether the estimated regression coefficients change relatively little, or whether the fitted values change relatively little.

Example 1: Mathematics Proficiency with One Predictor

The Educational Testing Service Study *America's Smallest School: The Family* (Ref. 11.8) investigated the relation of educational achievement of students to their home environment. Although earlier studies examined the relation of educational achievement to family socioeconomic status (e.g., parents' education, family income, parents' occupation), this study employed more direct measures of the home environment. Specifically, the relation of educational achievement of eighth-grade students in mathematics to the following five explanatory variables was investigated:

PARENTS (X_1)—percentage of eighth-grade students with both parents living at home

HOMELIB (X_2)—percentage of eighth-grade students with three or more types of reading materials at home (books, encyclopedias, magazines, newspapers)

READING (X_3)—percentage of eighth-grade students who read more than 10 pages a day

TVWATCH (X_4)—percentage of eighth-grade students who watch TV for six hours or more per day

ABSENCES (X_5)—percentage of eighth-grade students absent three days or more last month

Data on average mathematics proficiency (MATHPROF) and the home environment variables were obtained from the 1990 National Assessment of Educational Progress for 37 states, the District of Columbia, Guam, and the Virgin Islands. A portion of the data is shown in Table 11.4.

Our first example of robust regression using iteratively reweighted least squares involves only one predictor, HOMELIB (X_2). In this way, simple plots can be used to present the data and the fitted regression function.

Figure 11.5a presents a scatter plot of the data, together with a plot of a first-order (simple linear) regression model fit by ordinary least squares and a lowess smooth. The lowess smooth suggests that the relationship between home reading resources and average mathematics proficiency is curvilinear—possibly second order—for the majority of states, but three points are clear outliers. The District of Columbia and the Virgin Islands are outliers with respect to mathematics proficiency (Y), and Guam appears to be an outlier with respect to both mathematics proficiency and available reading resources (X). Figure 11.5b presents a plot against X of the residuals obtained from the fitted first-order model in Figure 11.5a. This plot shows clearly the three outlying Y cases. Note also from the residual plot that there is a group of six states with low reading resources levels, between 68 and 73, whose average mathematics proficiency scores are all above the fitted regression line. This is another indication that a second-order polynomial model may be appropriate.

FIGURE 11.5
Comparison of Lowess, Ordinary Least Squares Fits, and Robust Quadratic Fits—Mathematics Proficiency Example.

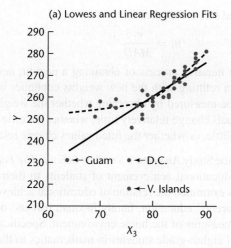

(a) Lowess and Linear Regression Fits

Guam, D.C., V. Islands

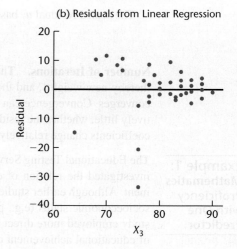

(b) Residuals from Linear Regression

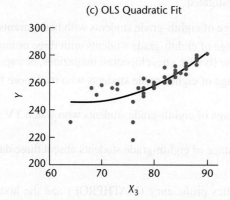

(c) OLS Quadratic Fit

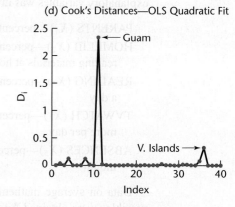

(d) Cook's Distances—OLS Quadratic Fit

Guam, V. Islands

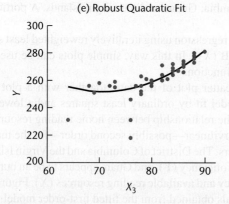

(e) Robust Quadratic Fit

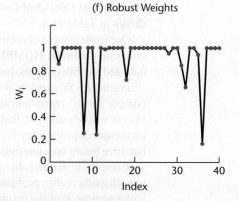

(f) Robust Weights

TABLE 11.4 Data Set—Mathematics Proficiency Example.

i	State	MATHPROF Y	PARENTS X_1	HOMELIB X_2	READING X_3	TVWATCH X_4	ABSENCES X_5
1	Alabama	252	75	78	34	18	18
2	Arizona	259	75	73	41	12	26
3	Arkansas	256	77	77	28	20	23
4	California	256	78	68	42	11	28
...	...	...	...	...	...	...	...
8	D.C.	231	47	76	24	33	37
...	...	...	...	...	...	...	...
11	Guam	231	81	64	32	20	28
...	...	...	...	...	...	...	...
35	Texas	258	77	70	34	15	18
36	Virgin_Islands	218	63	76	23	27	22
37	Virginia	264	78	82	33	16	24
38	West_Virginia	256	82	80	36	16	25
39	Wisconsin	274	81	86	38	8	21
40	Wyoming	272	85	86	43	7	23

Source: ETS Policy Information Center, *America's Smallest School: The Family* (Princeton, New Jersey: Educational Testing Service, 1992).

Second-order model (8.2):

$$Y_i = \beta_0 + \beta_2 x_{i2} + \beta_{22} x_{i2}^2 + \varepsilon_i \qquad (11.48)$$

was next fit, again using ordinary least squares. Recall that this model requires calculation of the centered predictor $x_{i2} = X_{i2} - \bar{X}_{i2}$ and its square, x_{i2}^2. A plot of the fit of the second-order model, superimposed on a scatter-plot of the data, is shown in Figure 11.5c. Though improved, the fit is again unsatisfactory: the six points that fell above the first-order fit are still above the fitted second-order model. The regression line is clearly being influenced by the three outliers identified above. The Cook's distance measures for the second-order fit are displayed in an index plot in Figure 11.5d. The plot confirms the influence of Guam and the Virgin Islands.

In an effort to dampen the effect of the three outliers, we shall fit second-order model (8.2) robustly, using iteratively reweighted least squares and the Huber weight function (11.44). We illustrate the calculations for case 1, Alabama. The regression model to be fitted is the first-order model. An ordinary least squares fit of this model yields:

$$\hat{Y} = 258.436 + 1.8327 x_2 + 0.06491 x_2^2 \qquad (11.49)$$

The residual for Alabama is $e_1 = -2.4109$. The residuals are shown in Column 1 of Table 11.5. The median of the 40 residuals is median$\{e_i\} = 0.7063$. Hence, $e_1 - $ median$\{e_i\} = -2.4109 - 0.7063 = -3.1172$, and the absolute deviation is $|e_1 - $ median$\{e_i\}| = 3.1172$. The median of the 40 absolute deviations is:

$$\text{median}\{|e_i - \text{median}\{e_i\}|\} = 3.1488$$

TABLE 11.5 **Iteratively Huber-Reweighted Least Squares Calculations—Mathematics Proficiency Example.**

	(1)	(2)	(3)	(4)	(5)	(6)	(7)	(8)
	Iteration 0		Iteration 1		Iteration 2		Iteration 7	
i	e_i	u_i	w_i	e_i	w_i	e_i	w_i	e_i
1	−2.4109	−0.51643	1.00000	−3.7542	1.00000	−4.0354	1.00000	−4.1269
2	10.5724	2.26466	0.59391	8.4297	0.71515	7.4848	0.86011	6.7698
3	3.0454	0.65234	1.00000	1.5411	1.00000	1.1559	1.00000	0.9731
4	10.3104	2.20853	0.60900	7.3822	0.81663	5.4138	1.00000	3.6583
...	...	...	...	...	...	...	...	...
8	−20.6282	−4.41866	0.30439	−22.2929	0.27042	−22.7964	0.25263	−23.0873
...	...	...	...	...	...	...	...	...
11	−14.8358	−3.17791	0.42323	−18.3824	0.32795	−21.4287	0.24019	−24.3167
...	...	...	...	...	...	...	...	...
36	−33.6282	−7.20333	0.18672	−35.2929	0.17081	−35.7964	0.16161	−36.0873
37	2.4659	0.52821	1.00000	1.7722	1.00000	1.7627	1.00000	1.8699
38	−1.7129	−0.36691	1.00000	−2.7325	1.00000	−2.8490	1.00000	−2.8079
39	3.2658	0.69954	1.00000	3.2305	1.00000	3.2624	1.00000	3.3014
40	1.2658	0.27113	1.00000	1.2305	1.00000	1.2624	1.00000	1.3014

so that the *MAD* estimator (11.46) is:

$$MAD = \frac{3.1488}{.6745} = 4.6683$$

Hence, the scaled residual (11.47) for Alabama is:

$$u_1 = \frac{-2.4109}{4.6683} = -.5164$$

The scaled residuals are shown in Table 11.5, column 2. Since $|u_1| = .5164 \leq 1.345$, the initial Huber weight for Alabama is $w_1 = 1.0$. The initial weights are shown in Table 11.5, column 3. To interpret these weights, remember that ordinary least squares may be viewed as a special case of weighted least squares with the weights for all cases being equal to 1. We note in column 3 that the initial weights for cases 8, 11, and 36 (District of Columbia, Guam, and Virgin Islands) are substantially reduced, and that the weights for some other states are reduced somewhat.

The first iteration of weighted least squares uses the initial weights in column 3, leading to the fitted regression model:

$$\hat{Y} = 259.390 + 1.6701x_2 + 0.06463x_2^2 \tag{11.50}$$

This fitted regression function differs considerably from the ordinary least squares fit in (11.49). The coefficient of x_2 has decreased from $b_2 = 1.8327$ to $b_2 = 1.6701$, while the curvature term $b_{22} = 0.06463$ changed little from its previous value of $b_{22} = 0.06491$. This has permitted the estimated regression function to increase for smaller values of X_2 and to therefore conform more closely to the six values that previously fell above the fitted line.

Iteration 2 uses the residuals in column 4 of Table 11.5, scales them, and obtains revised Huber weights, which are then used in iteration 2 of weighted least squares. The weights obtained for the eighth iteration differed relatively little from those for the seventh iteration; hence the iteration process was stopped with the seventh iteration. The final weights are shown in Table 11.5, column 7. Note that only minor changes in the weights occurred between iterations 2 and 7. Use of the weights in column 7 leads to the final fitted model:

$$\hat{Y} = 259.421 + 1.5649x_2 + 0.08016x_2^2 \tag{11.51}$$

The residuals for the final fit are shown in Table 11.5, column 8. Just as the weights changed only moderately between iterations 2 and 7, so the residuals changed only to a small extent after iteration 2. Note that the coefficient of the curvature term did change a bit more substantially—from $b_{22} = .06463$ to $b_{22} = .08016$.

Figure 11.5e shows the scatter plot and the IRLS fitted second-order regression function, and Figure 11.5f contains an index plot of the weights used in the final iteration. The robust fit now tracks the responses to the 37 states extremely well, and the fit to the six cases that were previously above the regression line is now satisfactory. The plot of the final weights in Figure 11.5f shows clearly the downweighting of the three outliers.

We conclude from the robust fit in Figure 11.5e that there is a clear upward-curving relationship between availability of reading resources in the home and average mathematics proficiency at the state level. This does not necessarily imply a causal relation, of course. The availability of reading resources may be positively correlated with other variables that are causally related to mathematics proficiency.

Example 2: Mathematics Proficiency with Five Predictors

We shall explore from a descriptive perspective the relationship between average mathematics proficiency and the five home environment variables. A MINITAB scatter plot matrix of the data is presented in Figure 11.6a and the correlation matrix is presented in Figure 11.6b. The scatter plot matrix also shows the lowess nonparametric regression fits, where $q = .9$ (the proportion defining a neighborhood) is used in the local fitting.

We see from the first row of the scatter plot matrix that average mathematics proficiency is related to each of the five explanatory variables and that there are three clear outliers. They are District of Columbia, Guam, and Virgin Islands, as noted earlier in this section. The lowess fits show positive relations for PARENTS, HOMELIB, and READING and a negative relation for ABSENCES. The lowess fit for TVWATCH is distorted because of the outliers. If these are ignored, the relation is negative. The correlation matrix shows fairly strong linear association with average mathematics proficiency for all explanatory variables except ABSENCES, where the degree of linear association is moderate.

The relationships with mathematics proficiency found in Figure 11.6a must be interpreted with caution. We see from the remainder of the scatter plot matrix and from the correlation matrix in Figure 11.6b that the explanatory variables are correlated with each other, some fairly strongly. Also, some of the explanatory variables are correlated with other important variables not considered in this study. For example, the percentage of students with both parents at home is related to family income.

For simplicity, we consider only first-order terms in this example. An initial fit of the first-order model to the data using ordinary least squares yields the following estimated regression function:

$$\hat{Y} = 155.03 + .3911X_1 + .8639X_2 + .3616X_3 - .8467X_4 + .1923X_5 \tag{11.52}$$

FIGURE 11.6
Scatter Plot Matrix with Lowess Smooths, and Correlation Matrix—Mathematics Proficiency Example.

(a) SYGRAPH Scatter Plot Matrix

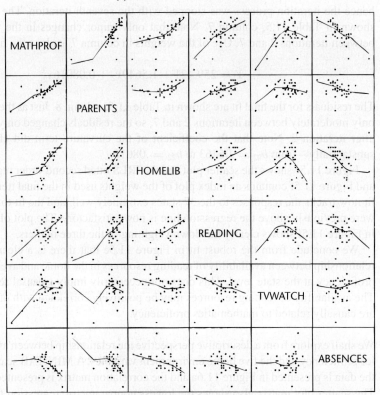

(b) Correlation Matrix

	MATHPROF	PARENTS	HOMELIB	READING	TVWATCH
PARENTS	0.741				
HOMELIB	0.745	0.395			
READING	0.717	0.693	0.377		
TVWATCH	−0.873	−0.831	−0.594	−0.792	
ABSENCES	−0.480	−0.565	−0.443	−0.357	0.512

The signs of the regression coefficients, except for b_5, are in the expected directions. The coefficient of multiple determination for this fitted model is $R^2 = .86$, suggesting that the explanatory variables are strongly related to average mathematics proficiency.

Table 11.6 presents some diagnostics for the fitted model in (11.52): leverage h_{ii}, studentized deleted residual t_i, and Cook's distance D_i. We see that the District of Columbia, Guam, Texas, and Virgin Islands have leverage values equal to or exceeding $2p/n = 12/40 = .30$.

TABLE 11.6
Diagnostics for First-Order Model with All Five Explanatory Variables—Mathematics Proficiency Example.

i	State	h_{ii}	t_i	D_i
1	Alabama	.16	−.05	.00
2	Arizona	.19	.40	.01
3	Arkansas	.16	1.41	.06
4	California	.29	.10	.00
...	...	...	...	...
8	D.C.	.69	1.41	.72
...	...	...	...	...
11	Guam	.34	−2.83	.57
...	...	...	...	...
35	Texas	.30	2.25	.33
36	Virgin_Islands	.32	−5.21	1.21
37	Virginia	.06	.90	.01
38	West_Virginia	.13	−.91	.02
39	Wisconsin	.08	.39	.00
40	Wyoming	.08	−.91	.01

We also see that the Virgin Islands is outlying with respect to its Y value; the absolute value of its studentized deleted residual $t_{36} = -5.21$ exceeds the Bonferroni critical value at $\alpha = .05$ of $t(1 - \alpha/2n; n - p - 1) = t(.99938; 33) = 3.53$. Of these outlying cases, the Virgin Islands is clearly influential according to Cook's distance measure, and District of Columbia and Guam are somewhat influential; the 50th percentile of the $F(6, 34)$ distribution is .91, and the 25th percentile is .57.

Residual plots against each of the explanatory variables and against $\hat{Y}$ (not shown here) presented no strong indication of nonconstancy of the error variance for the states aside from the outliers. Since the explanatory variables are correlated among themselves, the question arises whether a simpler model can be obtained with almost as much descriptive ability as the model containing all five explanatory variables. Figure 11.7 presents the MINITAB best subsets regression output, showing the two models with highest R^2 for each number of X variables. We see that the two best models for three variables ($p = 4$ parameters) contain relatively little bias according to the C_p criterion and have R^2 values almost as high as the model with all five variables.

We explore now one of these two models, the one containing HOMELIB, READING, and TVWATCH. In view of the outlying and influential cases, we employ IRLS robust regression with the Huber weight function (11.44). We find that after eight iterations, the weights change very little, so the iteration process is ended with the eighth iteration. The final robust fitted regression function is:

$$\hat{Y} = 207.83 + .7942X_2 + .1637X_3 - 1.1695X_4 \tag{11.53}$$

The signs of the regression coefficients agree with expectations. For comparison, the regression function fitted by ordinary least squares is:

$$\hat{Y} = 199.61 + .7804X_2 + .4012X_3 - 1.1565X_4 \tag{11.54}$$

FIGURE 11.7
MINITAB Best
Subsets
Regression—
Mathematics
Proficiency
Example.

Best Subsets Regression of MATHPROF

```
                                    A
                            P H R T B
                            A O E V S
                            R M A W E
                            E E D A N
                            N L I T C
                 Adj.       T I N C E
Vars   R-sq    R-sq    C-p      S      S B G H S

  1    76.3    75.7    22.0   6.5079          X
  1    55.5    54.3    72.8   8.9157      X
  2    84.2    83.4     4.6   5.3810      X   X
  2    79.2    78.1    16.8   6.1743    X X
  3    85.1    83.9     4.4   5.2939      X X X
  3    85.1    83.8     4.5   5.3062    X X   X
  4    85.9    84.3     4.5   5.2327    X X X X
  4    85.4    83.7     5.8   5.3285    X X   X X
  5    86.1    84.1     6.0   5.2680    X X X X X
```

Notice that the robust regression led to a deemphasis of X_3 (READING), with the other regression coefficients remaining almost the same.

To obtain an indication of how well the robust regression model (11.53) describes the relation between average mathematics proficiency of eighth-grade students and the three home environment variables, we have ranked the 40 states according to their average mathematics proficiency score and according to their corresponding fitted value. The Spearman rank correlation coefficient (2.97), is .945. This indicates a fairly good ability of the three explanatory variables to distinguish between states whose average mathematics proficiency is very high or very low.

The analysis of the mathematics proficiency data set in Table 11.4 presented here is by no means exhaustive. We have not analyzed higher-order effects, nor have we explored other subsets that might be reasonable to use. We have not recognized that the precision of the state data varies because the data are based on samples of different sizes, nor have we considered other explanatory variables that are related to mathematics proficiency, such as parents' education and family income. Furthermore, we have analyzed state averages, which may obscure important insights into relations between the variables at the family level.

Comments

1. Robust regression requires knowledge of the regression function. When the appropriate regression function is not clear, nonparametric regression may be useful. Nonparametric regression is discussed in Section 11.4.

2. Robust regression can be employed to identify outliers in situations where there are multiple outliers whose presence is masked with diagnostic measures that delete one case at a time. Cases whose final weights are relatively small are outlying.

3. As illustrated by the mathematics proficiency example, robust regression is often useful for confirming the reasonableness of ordinary least squares results. When robust regression yields similar results to ordinary least squares (for example, the residuals are similar), one obtains some reassurance that ordinary least squares is not unduly influenced by outlying cases.

4. A limitation of robust regression is that the evaluation of the precision of the estimated regression coefficients is more complex than for ordinary least squares. Some large-sample results have been obtained (see, for example, Reference 11.5), but they may not perform well in the presence of outliers. Bootstrapping (to be discussed in Section 11.5) may also be used for evaluating the precision of robust regression results.

5. When the Huber, bisquare, and other weight functions are based on the scaled residuals in (11.47), they primarily reduce the influence of cases that are outlying with respect to their Y values. To make the robust regression fit more sensitive to cases that are outlying with respect to their X values, studentized residuals in (10.20) or studentized deleted residuals in (10.24) may be used instead of the scaled residuals in (11.47). Again, $\sqrt{MSE}$ may be replaced by MAD in (11.46) for better resistance and robustness when calculating the studentized or studentized deleted residuals.

In addition, the weights w_i obtained from the weight function may be modified to reduce directly the influence of cases with large X leverage. One suggestion is to multiply the weight function weight w_i by $\sqrt{1 - h_{ii}}$, where h_{ii} is the leverage value of the ith case defined in (10.18).

Methods that reduce the influence of cases that are outlying with respect to their X values are called *bounded influence regression* methods. ∎

11.4 Nonparametric Regression: Lowess Method and Regression Trees

We considered nonparametric regression in Chapter 3 when there is one predictor variable in the regression model. We noted there that nonparametric regression fits are useful for exploring the nature of the response function, to confirm the nature of a particular response function that has been fitted to the data, and to obtain estimates of mean responses without specifying the nature of the response function.

Nonparametric regression can be extended to multiple regression when there are two or more predictor variables. Additional complexities are encountered, however, when making this extension. With more than two predictor variables, it is not possible to show the fitted response surface graphically, so one cannot see its appearance. Unlike parametric regression, no analytic expression for the response surface is provided by nonparametric regression. Also, as the number of predictor variables increases, there may be fewer and fewer cases in a neighborhood, leading to erratic smoothing. This latter problem is less serious when the predictor variables are highly correlated and interest in the response surface is confined to the region of the X observations.

Numerous procedures have been developed for fitting a response surface when there are two or more predictor variables without specifying the nature of the response function. Reference 11.9 discusses a number of these procedures. These include locally weighted regressions (Ref. 11.10), regression trees (Ref. 11.11), projection pursuit (Ref. 11.12), and smoothing splines (Ref. 11.13). We discuss the lowess method and regression trees in this section. We first extend the lowess method to multiple regression. In doing so, we will be able to describe it in far greater detail because we have established the necessary foundation of weighted least squares in Section 11.1.

Lowess Method

We described the lowess method briefly in Chapter 3 for regression with one predictor variable. The lowess method for multiple regression, developed by Cleveland and Devlin

(Ref. 11.10), assumes that the predictor variables have already been selected, that the response function is smooth, and that appropriate transformations have been made or other remedial steps taken so that the error terms are approximately normally distributed with constant variance. For any combination of X levels, the lowess method fits either a first-order model or a second-order model based on cases in the neighborhood, with more distant cases in the neighborhood receiving smaller weights. We shall explain the lowess method for the case of two predictor variables when we wish to obtain the fitted value at (X_{h1}, X_{h2}).

Distance Measure.   We need a distance measure showing how far each case is from (X_{h1}, X_{h2}). Usually, a Euclidean distance measure is employed. For the ith case, this measure is denoted by d_i and is defined:

$$d_i = [(X_{i1} - X_{h1})^2 + (X_{i2} - X_{h2})^2]^{1/2} \tag{11.55}$$

When the predictor variables are measured on different scales, each should be scaled by dividing it by its standard deviation. The median absolute deviation estimator in (11.46) can be used in place of the standard deviation if outliers are present.

Weight Function.   The neighborhood about the point (X_{h1}, X_{h2}) is defined in terms of the proportion q of cases that are nearest to the point. Let d_q denote the Euclidean distance of the furthest case in the neighborhood. The weight function used in the lowess method is the tricube weight function, which is defined as follows:

$$w_i = \begin{cases} [1 - (d_i/d_q)^3]^3 & d_i < d_q \\ 0 & d_i \geq d_q \end{cases} \tag{11.56}$$

Thus, cases outside the neighborhood receive weight zero and cases within the neighborhood receive weights between 0 and 1, the weight decreasing with greater distance. In this way, the mean response at (X_{h1}, X_{h2}) is estimated locally.

The choice of the proportion q defining the neighborhood requires a balancing of two opposing tendencies. The larger is q, the smoother will be the fit but at the same time the greater may be the bias in the fitted value. A choice of q between .4 and .6 may often be appropriate.

Local Fitting.   Given the weights for the n cases based on (11.55) and (11.56), weighted least squares is then used to fit either the first-order model (6.1) or the second-order model (6.16). The second-order model is helpful when the response surface has substantial curvature; moderate curvilinearities can be detected by using the first-order model. After the regression model is fitted by weighted least squares, the fitted value $\hat{Y}_h$ at (X_{h1}, X_{h2}) then serves as the nonparametric estimate of the mean response at these X levels. By recalculating the weights for different (X_{h1}, X_{h2}) levels, fitting the response function repeatedly, and each time obtaining the fitted value $\hat{Y}_h$, we obtain information about the response surface without making any assumptions about the nature of the response function.

Example

We shall fit a nonparametric regression function for the life insurance example in Chapter 10. A portion of the data for a second group of 18 managers is given in Table 11.7, columns 1–3. The relation between amount of life insurance carried (Y) and income (X_1) and risk aversion (X_2) is to be investigated, the data pertaining to managers in the 30–39 age group.

TABLE 11.7
Lowess
Calculations
for Non-
parametric
Regression Fit
at $X_{h1} = 30$,
$X_{h2} = 3$—Life
Insurance
Example.

i	(1) X_{i1}	(2) X_{i2}	(3) Y_i	(4) d_i	(5) w_i
1	66.290	7	240	3.013	0
2	40.964	5	73	1.143	.300
3	72.996	10	311	4.212	0
...	...	...	...	...	...
16	79.380	1	316	3.461	0
17	52.766	8	154	2.663	0
18	55.916	6	164	2.188	0

The local fitting will be done using the first-order model in (6.1) because the number of available cases is not too large. For the same reason, the proportion of cases defining the local neighborhoods is set at $q = .5$; in other words, each local neighborhood is to consist of half of the cases.

The exploration of the response surface begins at $X_{h1} = 30$, $X_{h2} = 3$. To obtain a locally fitted value at $X_{h1} = 30$, $X_{h2} = 3$, we need to obtain the Euclidean distances of each case from this point. We shall use the sample standard deviations of the two predictor variables to standardize the variables in obtaining the Euclidean distance since the two variables are measured on different scales. The sample standard deviations are $s_1 = 14.739$ and $s_2 = 2.3044$. For case 1, the Euclidean distance from $X_{h1} = 30$, $X_{h2} = 3$ is obtained as follows:

$$d_1 = \left[\left(\frac{66.290 - 30}{14.739} \right)^2 + \left(\frac{7 - 3}{2.3044} \right)^2 \right]^{1/2} = 3.013$$

The Euclidean distances are shown in Table 11.7, column 4. The Euclidean distance of the furthest case in the neighborhood of $X_{h1} = 30$, $X_{h2} = 3$ for $q = .5$ is for the ninth case when these are ordered according to their Euclidean distance. It is $d_q = 1.653$. Since $d_1 = 3.013 > 1.653$, the weight assigned for case 1 is $w_1 = 0$. For case 2, the Euclidean distance is $d_2 = 1.143$. Since this is less than 1.653, the weight for case 2 is:

$$w_2 = [1 - (1.143/1.653)^3]^3 = .300$$

The weights are shown in Table 11.7, column 5.

The fitted first-order regression function using these weights is:

$$\hat{Y} = -134.076 + 3.571X_1 + 10.532X_2$$

The fitted value for $X_{h1} = 30$, $X_{h2} = 3$ therefore is:

$$\hat{Y}_h = -134.076 + 3.571(30) + 10.532(3) = 4.65$$

In the same fashion, locally fitted values at other values of X_{h1} and X_{h2} are calculated. Figure 11.8a contains a contour plot of the fitted response surface. The surface clearly ascends as X_1 increases, but the effect of X_2 is more difficult to see from the contour plot. The effect of X_2 can be seen more easily by the conditional effects plots of Y against X_1 at low, middle, and high levels of X_2 in Figure 11.8b. The conditional effects plots in Figure 11.8b are also called *two-variable conditioning plots*. Note that the expected amount of life insurance carried increases with income (X_1) at all levels of risk aversion (X_2). The

FIGURE 11.8 **Contour and Conditioning Plots for Lowess Nonparametric Regression—Life Insurance Example.**

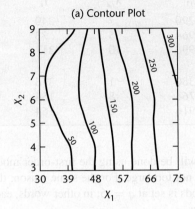

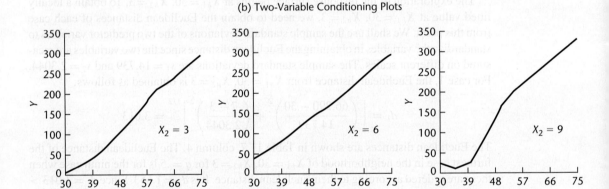

response functions for $X_2 = 3$ and $X_2 = 6$ appear to be approximately linear. The dip in the left part of the response function for $X_2 = 9$ may be the result of an interaction or of noisy data and inadequate smoothing. Note also from Figure 11.8b that the expected amount of life insurance carried at the higher income levels increases as the risk aversion becomes very high.

Comments

1. The fitted nonparametric response surface can be used, just as for simple regression, for examining the appropriateness of a fitted parametric regression model. If the fitted nonparametric response surface falls within the confidence band in (6.60) for the parametric regression function, the nonparametric fit supports the appropriateness of the parametric regression function.

2. Reference 11.10 discusses a procedure to assist in choosing the proportion q for defining a local neighborhood. It also describes how the precision of any fitted value $\hat{Y}_h$ obtained with lowess nonparametric multiple regression can be approximated.

3. The assumptions of normality and constant variance of the error terms required by the lowess nonparametric procedure can be checked in the usual fashion. The residuals are obtained by fitting the lowess nonparametric regression function for each case and calculating $e_i = Y_i - \hat{Y}_i$ as usual. These residuals will not have the least squares property of summing to zero, but can be examined for normality and constancy of variance. The residuals can also serve to identify outliers that might not be disclosed by standard diagnostic procedures.

4. A discussion of some of the advantages of the lowess smoothing procedure is presented in Reference 11.14. ∎

Regression Trees

Regression trees are a very powerful, yet conceptually simple, method of nonparametric regression. For the case of a single predictor, the range of the predictor is partitioned into segments and within each segment the estimated regression fit is given by the mean of the responses in the segment. For two or more predictors, the X space is partitioned into rectangular regions, and again, the estimated regression surface is given by the mean of the responses in each rectangle. Regression trees have become a popular alternative to multiple regression for exploratory studies, especially for extremely large data sets. Along with neural networks (see Chapter 13), regression trees are one of the standard methods used in the emerging field of data mining. Regression trees are easy to calculate, require virtually no assumptions, and are simple to interpret.

One Predictor Tree: Steroid Level Example.   Figure 1.3 on page 5 presents data on age and level of a steroid in plasma for 27 healthy females between 8 and 25 years of age. The data are shown in the first two columns of Table 11.8. A regression tree based on five regions is obtained by partitioning the range of X (age) into five segments or regions, and using the sample average of the Y responses in each region for the fitted regression surface. We will use R_{51} through R_{55} to denote the regions of a 5-region tree, and $\bar{Y}_{R_{51}}$ through $\bar{Y}_{R_{55}}$ to denote the corresponding sample averages. These values are shown for the steroid level example in columns 4–6 of Table 11.8. The fitted regression tree is shown in Figure 11.9a. Note that the regression tree is a step function that steps up rapidly for girls between the ages of 8 and 14, after which point steroid level is roughly constant.

A plot of residuals versus fitted values is shown in Figure 11.9b. Note that the variance of the residuals in each region seems roughly constant, an indication that further splitting may be unnecessary. We discuss the determination of appropriate tree size below.

TABLE 11.8
Data Set and 5-Region Regression Tree Fit— Steroid Level Example.

(1) Case i	(2) Steroid Level Y_i	(3) Age X_i	(4) Region Number k	(5) Region R_{5k}	(6) Fitted Value $\bar{Y}_{R_{5k}}$
1	27.1	23	1	$8 \leq X < 9$	3.550
2	22.1	19	2	$9 \leq X < 10$	8.133
3	21.9	25	3	$10 \leq X < 13$	13.675
⋯	⋯	⋯	4	$13 \leq X < 14$	16.950
25	12.8	13	5	$14 \leq X < 25$	22.200
26	20.8	14			
27	20.6	18			

FIGURE 11.9
Fitted
Regression
Tree, Residual
Plot, and
Regression
Tree
Diagram—
Steroid Level
Example.

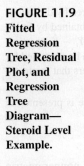

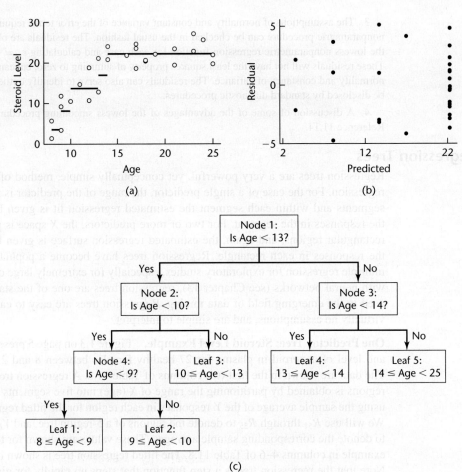

(a)

(b)

(c)

Determining the predicted value for a given X_h is accomplished with the help of a tree diagram, such as the one shown in Figure 11.9c. Suppose we wish to determine the predicted value at $X_h = 12.5$. Starting at node 1—the *root node*—we ask, "Is Age < 13?" Since $12.5 < 13$, we follow the left branch to node 2 where we ask, "Is Age < 10?" Since Age is not less than 10, we branch right to the terminal node labeled *Leaf 3*, where we find from Table 11.8 that $\bar{Y}_{R_{53}} = 13.675$. Tree diagrams such as that shown in Figure 11.9c are particularly helpful when more than a single predictor is present.

Growing a Regression Tree. To find a "best" regression tree, it is necessary to specify the number of regions, r, and the boundaries, or *split points,* between the regions. The process of determining a best value for r and the associated split points is referred to as *growing the tree.*

First consider the case of a single predictor, and assume that the range of X is to be divided into $r = 2$ regions, R_{21} and R_{22}. We need to find the split point X_s that optimally divides the data into two sets. The best point is chosen to minimize the error sum of squares

FIGURE 11.10
Growing the
Regression
Tree—Steroid
Level Example.

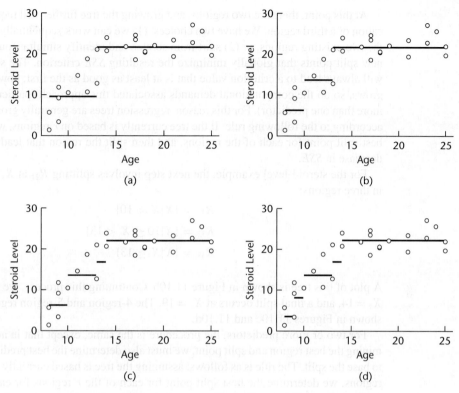

for the resulting regression tree:

$$SSE = SSE(R_{21}) + SSE(R_{22})$$

where $SSE(R_{rj})$ is the sum of squared residuals in region R_{rj}:

$$SSE(R_{rj}) = \sum (Y_i - \bar{Y}_{R_{jk}})^2$$

For the steroid level data, the best split point is shown in Figure 11.10a to be $X_s = 13.0$. For this tree, we have:

$$R_{21} = \{X | X < 13\}$$
$$R_{22} = \{X | X \geq 13\}$$

for which we obtain:

$$SSE = SSE(R_{21}) + SSE(R_{22}) = 238.55 + 167.79 = 406.35$$

From (2.72), the coefficient of determination for the regression tree is:

$$R^2 = 1 - \frac{SSE}{SSTO} = 1 - \frac{406.35}{1284.8} = .684$$

Also, $MSE = SSE/(n - r) = 406.35/(27 - 2) = 16.254.$

At this point, there are two regions, and growing the tree further will require the identification of a third region. We have two choices: (1) we can work sequentially and split one of the two existing regions, or (2) start from scratch and identify simultaneously two entirely new split points that globally minimize the resulting *SSE* criterion. The second approach will always lead to a criterion value that is at least as good as the first; however, as the tree grows, so do the computational demands associated this approach (particularly if there is more than one predictor). For this reason, regression trees are generally grown sequentially, according to the following rule: If the tree currently is based on r regions, we determine the best split point for each of the regions, and then split the region that leads to the greatest decrease in *SSE*.

For the steroid-level example, the next step involves splitting R_{21} at $X_s = 10$, resulting in three regions:

$$R_{21} = \{X|X < 10\}$$
$$R_{32} = \{X|10 \leq X < 13\}$$
$$R_{33} = \{X|X \geq 13\}$$

A plot of this tree is shown in Figure 11.10b. Continuing this process, we next split R_{33} at $X_s = 14$, and a final split occurs at $X_s = 19$. The 4-region and 5-region regression trees are shown in Figures 11.10c and 11.10d.

For two or more predictors, the procedure is the same, except that in addition to determining the best region and split point, we must also determine the best predictor upon which to base the split. The rule is as follows: assuming the tree is based currently on r rectangular regions, we determine the best split point for each of the r regions for each of the $p - 1$ predictors, and then implement a new split based on the region and predictor that leads to the largest decrease in *SSE*. Note that we are choosing the best predictor-and-split-point combination from $r(p - 1)$ possibilities.

This process is illustrated for two predictors in Figure 11.11. We first consider splitting the rectangular X space either on the basis of X_1 or X_2. We find the best split points X_{1s} and X_{2s} for X_1 and X_2 respectively, and then we base our next partition on the split point that leads to the greatest decrease in *SSE*. According to Figure 11.11a, the first split is based on X_1, resulting in two rectangular regions R_{21} and R_{22}. For each of these two regions, we determine the best predictor upon which to split and the associated split point, and choose the combination that leads to the largest decrease in *SSE*. Figure 11.11b indicates that region R_{22} was partitioned in this step on the basis of X_2. Finally, in the third split, region R_{31} is partitioned on the basis of X_1, resulting in a 4-region tree, as shown in Figure 11.11c.

FIGURE 11.11
Regression Tree Growth—Two-Predictor Example.

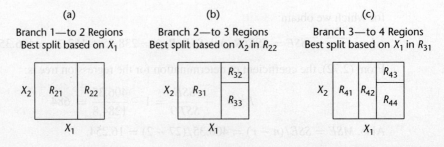

(a)
Branch 1—to 2 Regions
Best split based on X_1

(b)
Branch 2—to 3 Regions
Best split based on X_2 in R_{22}

(c)
Branch 3—to 4 Regions
Best split based on X_1 in R_{31}

Determining the Number of Regions, *r*.   If the tree-growing process is allowed to continue indefinitely, there will eventually be *n* regions, with each region containing a single observation, and further partitioning will be impossible. A "best" number of regions will generally fall between 1 and *n*, and is usually chosen through validation studies. For example, for each split we determine, in addition to *SSE*, the mean square for prediction error *MSPR* for data in a hold-out or validation sample. We then choose the tree that minimizes *MSPR*.

Example

We illustrate the use of regression trees with the University admissions data set in Appendix C.4. We fit GPA at the end of freshman year (Y) as a function of ACT entrance test score (X_1) and high school rank (X_2). The data consist of 705 cases, and a random sample of $n^* = 353$ records was selected for the validation set. Figure 11.12a provides a plot of *MSPR* versus the number of regions, or terminal nodes. The plot shows that the ability to predict improves as nodes are added until $r = 5$, for which $MSPR = .318$ (*MSE* for this

FIGURE 11.12   S-Plus Regression Tree Results—University Admissions Example.

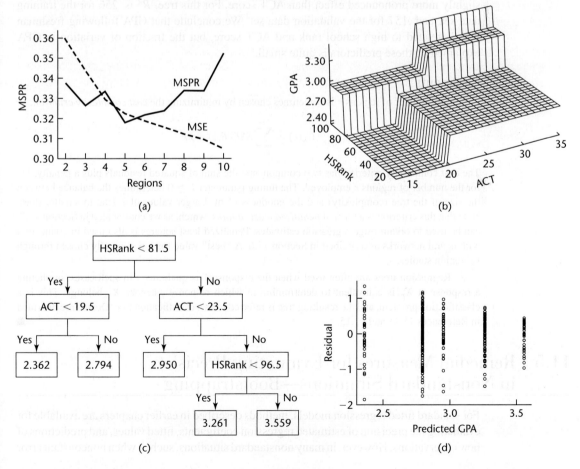

model is .322). For $r > 5$, the ability to predict responses in the validation set deteriorates as the number of regions increases. A plot of *MSE* is also included, and as expected, *MSE* decreases monotonically with the size of the tree. The fitted regression tree surface is shown in Figure 11.12b and the corresponding tree diagram is shown in Figure 11.12c.

A plot of residuals versus predicted values is shown for this tree in Figure 11.12d. Note that the variance of the residuals appears to be somewhat constant, and indication that further partitions may not be required.

It is instructive to compare qualitatively the fit of the regression tree to the fit obtained using standard regression methods. Using a full second-order model leads to the equation:

$$\hat{Y} = 1.77 - .0223X_1 + .0780X_2 + .000187X_1^2 - .00133X_2^2 + .000342X_1X_2$$

MSPR for the second-order regression model is .296, which is slightly better than the value obtained by the regression tree (.318). Interestingly the *MSE* value obtained by the second-order regression model (.333) is about the same as that obtained by the regression tree (.322).

In summary, the regression tree surface suggests as expected that college GPA increases with both ACT score and high school rank. Overall, high school rank seems to have a slightly more pronounced effect than ACT score. For this tree, R^2 is .256 for the training data set, and .157 for the validation data set. We conclude that GPA following freshman year is related to high school rank and ACT score, but the fraction of variation in GPA explained by these predictors is quite small.

Comments

1. The number of regions r is sometimes chosen by minimizing the *cost complexity criterion:*

$$C_\lambda(r) = \sum_{k=1}^{r} SSE(R_{rk}) + \lambda r$$

The cost complexity criterion has two components: the sum of squared residuals plus a penalty, λr, for the number of regions r employed. The tuning parameter $\lambda \geq 0$ determines the balance between the size of the tree (complexity) and the goodness of fit. Larger values of λ lead to smaller trees. Note that this criterion is a form of *penalized least squares,* which, as we commented in Section 11.2, can be used to obtain ridge regression estimates. Penalized least squares is also used in connection with neural networks as described in Section 13.6. A "best" value for λ is generally chosen through validation studies.

2. Regression trees are often used when the response Y is qualitative. In such cases, predicting a response at X_h is equivalent to determining to which response category X_h belongs. This is a classification problem, and the resulting tree is referred to as a classification tree. Details are provided in References 11.11 and 11.15. ∎

11.5 Remedial Measures for Evaluating Precision in Nonstandard Situations—Bootstrapping

For standard fitted regression models, methods described in earlier chapters are available for evaluating the precision of estimated regression coefficients, fitted values, and predictions of new observations. However, in many nonstandard situations, such as when nonconstant error variances are estimated by iteratively reweighted least squares or when robust regression estimation is used, standard methods for evaluating the precision may not be available or may only be approximately applicable when the sample size is large. Bootstrapping was developed by Efron (Ref. 11.16) to provide estimates of the precision of sample estimates for these complex cases. A number of bootstrap methods have now been developed. The bootstrap method that we shall explain is simple in principle and nonparametric in nature. Like all bootstrap methods, it requires extensive computer calculations.

General Procedure

We shall explain the bootstrap method in terms of evaluating the precision of an estimated regression coefficient. The explanation applies identically to any other estimate, such as a fitted value. Suppose that we have fitted a regression model (simple or multiple) by some procedure and obtained the estimated regression coefficient b_1; we now wish to evaluate the precision of this estimate by the bootstrap method. In essence, the bootstrap method calls for the selection from the observed sample data of a random sample of size n with replacement. Sampling with replacement implies that the bootstrap sample may contain some duplicate data from the original sample and omit some other data in the original sample. Next, the bootstrap method calculates the estimated regression coefficient from the bootstrap sample, using the same fitting procedure as employed for the original fitting. This leads to the first bootstrap estimate b_1^*. This process is repeated a large number of times; each time a bootstrap sample of size n is selected with replacement from the original sample and the estimated regression coefficient is obtained for the bootstrap sample. The estimated standard deviation of all of the bootstrap estimates b_1^*, denoted by $s^*\{b_1^*\}$, is an estimate of the variability of the sampling distribution of b_1 and therefore is a measure of the precision of b_1.

Bootstrap Sampling

Bootstrap sampling for regression can be done in two basic ways. When the regression function being fitted is a good model for the data, the error terms have constant variance, and the predictor variable(s) can be regarded as fixed, *fixed X sampling* is appropriate. Here the residuals e_i from the original fitting are regarded as the sample data to be sampled with replacement. After a bootstrap sample of the residuals of size n has been obtained, denoted by $e_1^*, \ldots, e_n^*$, the bootstrap sample residuals are added to the fitted values from the original fitting to obtain new bootstrap Y values, denoted by $Y_1^*, \ldots, Y_n^*$:

$$Y_i^* = \hat{Y}_i + e_i^* \tag{11.57}$$

These bootstrap Y^* values are then regressed on the original X variable(s) by the same procedure used initially to obtain the bootstrap estimate b_1^*.

When there is some doubt about the adequacy of the regression function being fitted, the error variances are not constant, and/or the predictor variables cannot be regarded as fixed, *random X sampling* is appropriate. For simple regression, the pairs of X and Y data in the original sample are considered to be the data to be sampled with replacement. Thus, this second procedure samples cases with replacement n times, yielding a bootstrap sample of n pairs of (X^*, Y^*) values. This bootstrap sample is then used for obtaining the bootstrap estimate b_1^*, as with fixed X sampling.

The number of bootstrap samples to be selected for evaluating the precision of an estimate depends on the special circumstances of each application. Sometimes, as few as 50 bootstrap samples are sufficient. Often, 200–500 bootstrap samples are adequate. One can observe the variability of the bootstrap estimates by calculating $s^*\{b_1^*\}$ as the number of bootstrap samples is increased. When $s^*\{b_1^*\}$ stabilizes fairly reasonably, bootstrapping can be terminated.

Bootstrap Confidence Intervals

Bootstrapping can also be used to arrive at approximate confidence intervals. Much research is ongoing on different procedures for obtaining bootstrap confidence intervals (see, for example, References 11.17 and 11.18). A relatively simple procedure for setting up a $1 - \alpha$ confidence interval is the *reflection method*. This procedure often produces a reasonable approximation, but not always. The reflection method confidence interval for β_1 is based on the $(\alpha/2)100$ and $(1 - \alpha/2)100$ percentiles of the bootstrap distribution of b_1^*. These percentiles are denoted by $b_1^*(\alpha/2)$ and $b_1^*(1 - \alpha/2)$, respectively. The distances of these percentiles from b_1, the estimate of β_1 from the original sample, are denoted by d_1 and d_2:

$$d_1 = b_1 - b_1^*(\alpha/2) \tag{11.58a}$$
$$d_2 = b_1^*(1 - \alpha/2) - b_1 \tag{11.58b}$$

The approximate $1 - \alpha$ confidence interval for β_1 then is:

$$b_1 - d_2 \le \beta_1 \le b_1 + d_1 \tag{11.59}$$

Bootstrap confidence intervals by the reflection method require a larger number of bootstrap samples than do bootstrap estimates of precision because tail percentiles are required. About 500 bootstrap samples may be a reasonable minimum number for reflection bootstrap confidence intervals.

Examples

We illustrate the bootstrap method by two examples. In the first one, standard analytical methods are available and bootstrapping is used simply to show that it produces similar results. In the second example, the estimation procedure is complex, and bootstrapping provides a means for assessing the precision of the estimate.

Example 1—Toluca Company

We use the Toluca Company example of Table 1.1 to illustrate how the bootstrap method approximates standard analytical results. We found in Chapter 2 that the estimate of the slope β_1 is $b_1 = 3.5702$, that the estimated precision of this estimate is $s\{b_1\} = .3470$, and that the 95 percent confidence interval for β_1 is $2.85 \le \beta_1 \le 4.29$.

To evaluate the precision of the estimate $b_1 = 3.5702$ by the bootstrap method, we shall use fixed X sampling. Here, the simple linear regression function fits the data well, the error variance appears to be constant, and it is reasonable to consider a repetition of the study with the same lot sizes. A portion of the data on lot size (X) and work hours (Y) is repeated in Table 11.9, columns 1 and 2. The fitted values and residuals obtained from the original sample are repeated from Table 1.2 in columns 3 and 4. Column 5 of Table 11.9 shows the first bootstrap sample of n residuals e_i^*, selected from column 4 with replacement. Finally, column 6 shows the first bootstrap sample Y_i^* observations. For example, by (11.57), we obtain $Y_1^* = \hat{Y}_1 + e_1^* = 347.98 - 19.88 = 328.1$.

When the Y_i^* values in column 6 are regressed against the X values in column 1, based on simple linear regression model (2.1), we obtain $b_1^* = 3.7564$. In the same way, 999 other bootstrap samples were selected and b_1^* obtained for each. Figure 11.13 contains a histogram

TABLE 11.9
Bootstrapping with Fixed X Sampling—Toluca Company Example.

	(1)	(2)	(3)	(4)	(5)	(6)
		Original Sample			Bootstrap Sample 1	
i	X_i	Y_i	$\hat{Y}_i$	e_i	e_i^*	Y_i^*
1	80	399	347.98	51.02	−19.88	328.1
2	30	121	169.47	−48.47	10.72	180.2
3	50	221	240.88	−19.88	−6.68	234.2
...	...	...	...	...	...	...
23	40	244	205.17	38.83	4.02	209.2
24	80	342	347.98	−5.98	−45.17	302.8
25	70	323	312.28	10.72	51.02	363.3

FIGURE 11.13
Histogram of Bootstrap Estimates b_1^*—Toluca Company Example.

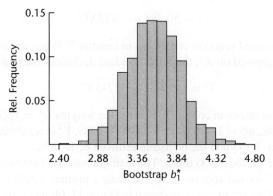

$b_1^*(.025) = 2.940 \qquad s^*\{b_1^*\} = .3251 \qquad b_1^*(.975) = 4.211$

of the 1,000 bootstrap b_1^* estimates. Note that this bootstrap sampling distribution is fairly symmetrical and appears to be close to a normal distribution. We also see in Figure 11.13 that the standard deviation of the 1,000 b_1^* estimates is $s^*\{b_1^*\} = .3251$, which is quite close to the analytical estimate $s\{b_1\} = .3470$.

To obtain an approximate 95 percent confidence interval for β_1 by the bootstrap reflection method, we note in Figure 11.13 that the 2.5th and 97.5th percentiles of the bootstrap sampling distribution are $b_1^*(.025) = 2.940$ and $b_1^*(.975) = 4.211$, respectively. Using (11.58), we obtain:

$$d_1 = 3.5702 - 2.940 = .630$$
$$d_2 = 4.211 - 3.5702 = .641$$

Finally, we use (11.59) to obtain the confidence limits $3.5702 + .630 = 4.20$ and $3.5702 - .641 = 2.93$ so that the approximate 95 percent confidence interval for β_1 is:

$$2.93 \leq \beta_1 \leq 4.20$$

Note that these limits are quite close to the confidence limits 2.85 and 4.29 obtained by analytical methods.

Example 2—
Blood
Pressure

For the blood pressure example in Table 11.1, the analyst used weighted least squares in order to recognize the unequal error variances and fitted a standard deviation function to estimate the unknown weights. The standard inference procedures employed by the analyst for estimating the precision of the estimated regression coefficient $b_{w1} = .59634$ and for obtaining a confidence interval for β_1 are therefore only approximate. To examine whether the approximation is good here, we shall evaluate the precision of the estimated regression coefficient in a way that recognizes the impreciseness of the weights by using bootstrapping. The X variable (age) probably should be regarded as random and the error variance varies with the level of X, so we shall use random X sampling. Table 11.10 repeats from Table 11.1 the original data for age (X) and diastolic blood pressure (Y) in columns 1 and 2. Columns 3 and 4 contain the (X_i^*, Y_i^*) observations for the first bootstrap sample selected with replacement from columns 1 and 2. When we now regress Y^* on X^* by ordinary least squares, we obtain the fitted regression function:

$$\hat{Y}^* = 50.384 + .7432X^*$$

The residuals for this fitted function are shown in column 5. When the absolute values of these residuals are regressed on X^*, the fitted standard deviation function obtained is:

$$\hat{s}^* = -5.409 + .32745X^*$$

The fitted values $\hat{s}_i^*$ are shown in column 6. Finally, the weights $w_i^* = 1/(\hat{s}_i^*)^2$ are shown in column 7. For example, $w_1^* = 1/(10.64)^2 = .0088$. Finally, Y^* is regressed on X^* by using the weights in column 7, to yield the bootstrap estimate $b_1^* = .838$.

This process was repeated 1,000 times. The histogram of the 1,000 bootstrap values b_1^* is shown in Figure 11.14 and appears to approximate a normal distribution. The standard deviation of the 1,000 bootstrap values is shown in Figure 11.14; it is $s^*\{b_1^*\} = .0825$. When we compare this precision with that obtained by the approximate use of (11.13), .0825 versus .07924, we see that recognition of the use of estimated weights has led here only to a small increase in the estimated standard deviation. Hence, the variability in b_{w1} associated with the use of estimated variances in the weights is not substantial and the standard inference procedures therefore provide a good approximation here.

A 95 percent bootstrap confidence interval for β_1 can be obtained from (11.59) by using the percentiles $b_1^*(.025) = .4375$ and $b_1^*(.975) = .7583$ shown in Figure 11.14. The

TABLE 11.10		(1)	(2)	(3)	(4)	(5)	(6)	(7)
Bootstrapping		**Original Sample**				**Bootstrap Sample 1**		
with Random								
X Sampling—	i	X_i	Y_i	X_i^*	Y_i^*	e_i^*	$\hat{s}_i^*$	w_i^*
Blood Pressure	1	27	73	49	101	14.20	10.64	.0088
Example.	2	21	66	34	73	−2.65	5.72	.0305
	3	22	63	49	101	14.20	10.64	.0088
	...	...	...	...	...	...	...	...
	52	52	100	46	89	4.43	9.65	.0107
	53	58	80	27	73	2.55	3.43	.0850
	54	57	109	40	70	−10.11	7.69	.0169

FIGURE 11.14
Histogram of
Bootstrap
Estimates
b_1^*—**Blood**
Pressure
Example.

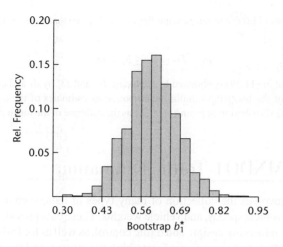

$b_1^*(.025) = .4375$ $s^*\{b_1^*\} = .0825$ $b_1^*(.975) = .7583$

approximate 95 percent confidence limits are [recall from (11.20) that $b_{w1} = .59634$]:

$$b_{w1} - d_2 = .59634 - (.7583 - .59634) = .4344$$
$$b_{w1} + d_1 = .59634 + (.59634 - .4375) = .7552$$

and the confidence interval for β_1 is:

$$.434 \leq \beta_1 \leq .755$$

Note that this confidence interval is almost the same as that obtained earlier by standard inference procedures ($.437 \leq \beta_1 \leq .755$). This again confirms that it is appropriate to use standard inference procedures here even though the weights were estimated.

Comment

The reason why d_1 is associated with the upper confidence limit in (11.59) and d_2 with the lower limit is that the upper $(1 - \alpha/2)100$ percentile in the sampling distribution of b_1 identifies the lower confidence limit for β_1, whereas the lower $(\alpha/2)100$ percentile identifies the upper confidence limit. To see this, consider the sampling distribution for b_1, for which we can state with probability $1 - \alpha$ that b_1 will fall between:

$$b_1(\alpha/2) \leq b_1 \leq b_1(1 - \alpha/2) \tag{11.60}$$

where $b_1(\alpha/2)$ and $b_1(1 - \alpha/2)$ denote the $(\alpha/2)100$ and $(1 - \alpha/2)100$ percentiles of the sampling distribution of b_1. We now express these percentiles in terms of distances from the mean of the sampling distribution, $E\{b_1\} = \beta_1$:

$$D_1 = \beta_1 - b_1(\alpha/2)$$
$$D_2 = b_1(1 - \alpha/2) - \beta_1 \tag{11.61}$$

and obtain:

$$b_1(\alpha/2) = \beta_1 - D_1$$
$$b_1(1 - \alpha/2) = \beta_1 + D_2 \tag{11.62}$$

Substituting (11.62) into (11.60) and rearranging the inequalities so that β_1 is in the middle leads to the limits:

$$b_1 - D_2 \leq \beta_1 \leq b_1 + D_1$$

The confidence interval in (11.59) is obtained by replacing D_1 and D_2 by d_1 and d_2, which involves using the percentiles of the bootstrap sampling distribution as estimates of the corresponding percentiles of the sampling distribution of b_1 and using b_1 as the estimate of the mean β_1 of the sampling distribution. ∎

11.6 Case Example—MNDOT Traffic Estimation

Traffic monitoring involves the collection of many types of data, such as traffic volume, traffic composition, vehicle speeds, and vehicle weights. These data provide information for highway planning, engineering design, and traffic control, as well as for legislative decisions concerning budget allocation, selection of state highway routes, and the setting of speed limits. One of the most important traffic monitoring variables is the average annual daily traffic (AADT) for a section of road or highway. AADT is defined as the average, over a year, of the number of vehicles that pass through a particular section of a road each day. Information on AADT is often collected by means of automatic traffic recorders (ATRs). Since it is not possible to install these recorders on all state road segments because of the expense involved, Cheng (Ref. 11.19) investigated the use of regression analysis for estimating AADT for road sections that are not monitored in the state of Minnesota.

The AADT Database

Seven potential predictors of traffic volume were chosen from the Minnesota Department of Transportation (MNDOT) road-log database, including type of road section, population density in the vicinity of road section, number of lanes in road section, and road section's width. Four of the seven variables were qualitative, requiring 19 indicator variables. Preliminary regression analysis indicated that the large number of levels of two of the qualitative variables was not helpful. Consequently, judgment and statistical information about marginal reductions in the error sum of squares were used to collapse the categories, so only 10 instead of 19 indicator variables remained in the AADT database.

The variables included in the initial analysis were as follows:

CTYPOP (X_1)—population of county in which road section is located (best proxy available for population density in immediate vicinity of road section)

LANES (X_2)—number of lanes in road section

WIDTH (X_3)—width of road section (in feet)

CONTROL (X_4)—two-category qualitative variable indicating whether or not there is control of access to road section (1 = access control; 2 = no access control)

CLASS (X_5, X_6, X_7)—four-category qualitative variable indicating road section function (1 = rural interstate; 2 = rural noninterstate; 3 = urban interstate, 4 = urban noninterstate)

TRUCK (X_8, X_9, X_{10}, X_{11})—five-category qualitative variable indicating availability status of road section to trucks (e.g., tonnage and time-of-year restrictions)

TABLE 11.11 Data—MNDOT Traffic Estimation Example.

Road Section *i*	AADT Y_i	County Population X_{i1}	Lanes X_{i2}	Width X_{i3}	Access Control Category X_{i4}	Function Class Category (X_{i5} to X_{i7})	Truck Route Category (X_{i8} to $X_{i,11}$)	Locale Category ($X_{i,12}$, $X_{i,13}$)
1	1,616	13,404	2	52	2	2	5	1
2	1,329	52,314	2	60	2	2	5	1
3	3,933	30,982	2	57	2	4	5	2
...	...	...	...	...	...	...	...	...
119	14,905	459,784	4	68	2	4	5	2
120	15,408	459,784	2	40	2	4	5	3
121	1,266	43,784	2	44	2	4	5	2

Source: C. Cheng, "Optimal Sampling for Traffic Volume Estimation," unpublished Ph.D. dissertation, University of Minnesota, Carlson School of Management, 1992.

LOCALE (X_{12}, X_{13})—three-category qualitative variable indicating type of locale (1 = rural; 2 = urban, population $\leq$ 50,000; 3 = urban, population $>$ 50,000)

A portion of the data is shown in Table 11.11. Altogether, complete records for 121 ATRs were available. For conciseness, only the category is shown for a qualitative variable and not the coding of the indicator variables.

Model Development

A SYSTAT scatter plot matrix of the data set, with lowess fits added, is presented in Figure 11.15. We see from the first row of the matrix that several of the predictor variables are related to AADT. The lowess fits suggest a potentially curvilinear relationship between LANES and AADT. Although the lowess fits of AADT to the qualitative categories designated 1, 2, 3, etc., are meaningless, they do highlight the average traffic volume for each category. For example, the lowess fit of AADT to CLASS shows that average AADT for the third category of CLASS is higher than for the other three categories. The scatter plot matrix also suggests that the variability of AADT may be increasing with some predictor variables, for instance, with CTYPOP.

An initial regression fit of a first-order model with ordinary least squares, using all predictor variables, indicated that CTYPOP and LANES are important variables. Regression diagnostics for this initial fit suggested two potential problems. First, the residual plot against predicted values revealed that the error variance might not be constant. Also, the maximum variance inflation factor (10.41) was 24.55, suggesting a severe degree of multicollinearity. The maximum Cook's distance measure (10.33) was .2076, indicating that none of the individual cases is particularly influential. Since many of the variables appeared to be unimportant, we next considered the use of subset selection procedures to identify promising, initial models.

The SAS all-possible-regressions procedure, PROC RSQUARE, was used for subset selection. To reduce the volume of computation, CTYPOP and LANES were forced to be included. The SAS output is given in Figure 11.16. The left column indicates the number of X variables in the model, i.e., $p - 1$. The names of the qualitative variables identify the

FIGURE 11.15   SYSTAT Scatter Plot Matrix—MNDOT Traffic Estimation Example.

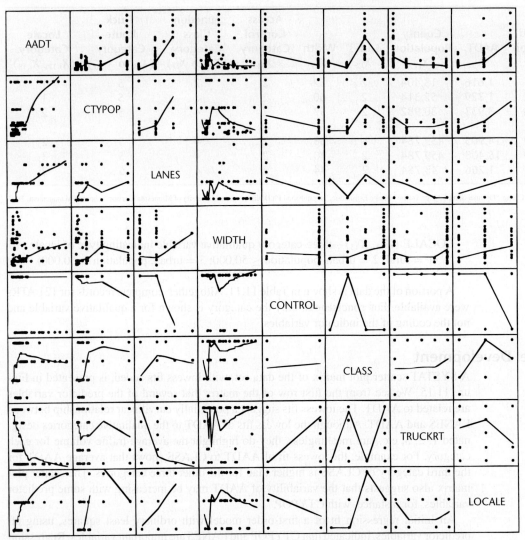

predictor variable and the category for which the indicator variable is coded 1. For example, CLASS1 refers to the first indicator variable for the predictor variable CLASS; i.e., it refers to X_5, which is coded 1 for category 1 (rural interstate). Two simple models look particularly promising. The three-variable model consisting of X_1 (CTYPOP), X_2 (LANES), and X_7 (CLASS = 3) stands out as the best three-variable model, with $R_p^2 = .805$ and $C_p = 5.23$. Since $p = 4$ for this model, the C_p statistic suggests that this model contains little bias. The best four-variable model includes X_1 (CTYPOP), X_2 (LANES), X_4 (CONTROL = 1), and X_5 (CLASS = 1). With this model, some improvements in the selection criteria are realized: $R_p^2 = .812$ and $C_p = 2.65$. On the basis of these results, it was decided to investigate

FIGURE 11.16
**SAS
All-Possible-
Regressions
Output—
MNDOT
Traffic
Estimation
Example.**

```
N = 121        Regression Models for Dependent Variable: AADT

          R-square    C(p)  Variables in Model
   In

    2     0.694589  69.7231  CTYPOP LANES

NOTE: The above variables are included in all models to follow.

-----------------------------------------
    3     0.804522   5.2315  CLASS3
    3     0.751353  37.3903  CONTROL1
    3     0.725755  52.8725  TRUCK1
    3     0.704495  65.7318  LOCALE2
    3     0.704250  65.8798  CLASS1
-----------------------------------------
    4     0.812099   2.6490  CONTROL1 CLASS1
    4     0.810364   3.6986  CLASS3 LOCALE2
    4     0.808001   5.1275  CLASS3 LOCALE1
    4     0.807122   5.6590  CLASS2 CLASS3
    4     0.806300   6.1562  CLASS3 TRUCK4
-----------------------------------------
    5     0.816245   2.1414  CONTROL1 CLASS1 LOCALE2
    5     0.815842   2.3848  CONTROL1 CLASS1 LOCALE1
    5     0.814362   3.2803  CONTROL1 CLASS1 CLASS2
    5     0.813901   3.5589  CONTROL1 CLASS1 TRUCK4
    5     0.812788   4.2321  CONTROL1 CLASS1 TRUCK2
-----------------------------------------
    6     0.818304   2.8958  WIDTH CONTROL1 CLASS1 LOCALE1
    6     0.817992   3.0845  CONTROL1 CLASS1 TRUCK4 LOCALE2
    6     0.817915   3.1309  CONTROL1 CLASS1 TRUCK2 LOCALE2
    6     0.817741   3.2367  CONTROL1 CLASS1 TRUCK2 LOCALE1
    6     0.817738   3.2383  WIDTH CONTROL1 CLASS1 LOCALE2
-----------------------------------------------------------------
    7     0.820443   3.6023  WIDTH CONTROL1 CLASS1 TRUCK4 LOCALE1
    7     0.819942   3.9050  WIDTH CONTROL1 CLASS1 TRUCK4 LOCALE2
    7     0.819473   4.1891  WIDTH CONTROL1 CLASS1 TRUCK2 LOCALE1
    7     0.819180   4.3663  CONTROL1 CLASS1 TRUCK2 TRUCK4 LOCALE2
    7     0.819007   4.4705  WIDTH CONTROL1 CLASS1 CLASS2 LOCALE1
-----------------------------------------------------------------
```

a model based on the five predictor variables included in these two models: X_1 (CTYPOP), X_2 (LANES), X_4 (CONTROL = 1), X_5 (CLASS = 1), and X_7 (CLASS = 3). Note that because X_6 (CLASS = 2) has been dropped from further consideration, the rural noninterstate (CLASS = 2) and urban noninterstate (CLASS = 4) categories of the CLASS variable have been collapsed into one category.

Figure 11.17a contains a plot of the studentized residuals against the fitted values for the five-variable model. The plot reveals two potential problems: (1) The residuals tend to be positive for small and large values of $\hat{Y}$ and negative for intermediate values, suggesting a curvilinearity in the response function. (2) The variability of the residuals tends to increase with increasing $\hat{Y}$, indicating nonconstancy of the error variance.

FIGURE 11.17 **Plots of Studentized Residuals versus Fitted Values—MNDOT Traffic Estimation Example.**

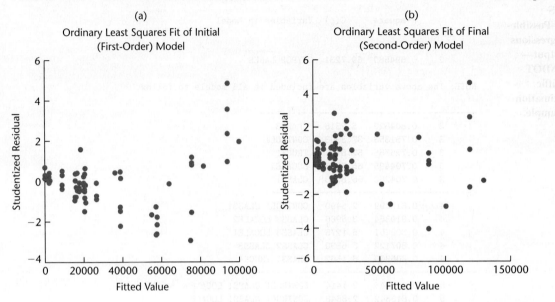

Curvilinearity was investigated next, together with possible interaction effects. A squared term for each of the two quantitative variables (CTYPOP and LANES) was added to the pool of potential X variables. To reduce potential multicollinearity problems, each of these variables was first centered. In addition, nine cross-product terms were added to the pool of potential X variables, consisting of the cross products of the X variables for the four predictor variables.

The SAS all-possible-regressions procedure was run again for this enlarged pool of potential X variables (output not shown). Analysis of the results suggested a model with five X variables: CTYPOP, LANES, LANES^2, CONTROL1, and CTYPOP $\times$ CONTROL1. For this model, R_p^2 is .925, and all P-values for the regression coefficients are 0+. Although this model does not have the largest R_p^2 value among five-term models, it is desirable because it is easy to interpret and does not differ substantially from other models favorably identified by the C_p or R_p^2 criteria. A plot of the studentized residuals against $\hat{Y}$, shown in Figure 11.17b, indicates that curvilinearity is no longer present. Also, neither Cook's distance measure (maximum = .47) nor the variance inflation factors (maximum = 2.5) revealed serious problems at this stage. Nonconstancy of the error term variance has persisted, however, as confirmed by the Breusch-Pagan test.

Weighted Least Squares Estimation

To remedy the problem with nonconstancy of the error term variance, weighted least squares was implemented by developing a standard deviation function. Residual plots indicated that the absolute residuals vary with CTYPOP and LANES. A fit of a first-order model where the absolute residuals are regressed on CTYPOP and LANES yielded an estimated standard deviation function for which $R^2 = .386$ and the P-values for the regression coefficients for CTYPOP and LANES are .001 and 0+. Note that, as is often the case, the R^2 value for

FIGURE 11.18
MINITAB
Weighted Least
Squares
Regression
Results—
MNDOT
Traffic
Estimation
Example.

```
The regression equation is
AADT = 9602 + 0.0146 CTYPOP + 6162 LANES + 16556 CONTROL1 + 2250 LANES2
         + 0.0637 POPXCTL1

Predictor      Coef      Stdev    t-ratio       p
Constant       9602       1432       6.71   0.000
CTYPOP     0.014567   0.003047       4.78   0.000
LANES        6161.8      933.9       6.60   0.000
CONTROL1      16556       2966       5.58   0.000
LANES2       2249.7      755.8       2.98   0.004
POPXCTL1   0.063696   0.008421       7.56   0.000


Analysis of Variance

SOURCE        DF        SS        MS       F       P
Regression     5    919.55    183.91   93.13   0.000
Error        115    227.10      1.97
Total        120   1146.65
```

the estimated standard deviation function (.386) is substantially smaller than that for the estimated response function (.925).

Using the weights obtained from the standard deviation function, weighted least squares estimates of the regression coefficients were obtained. Since some of the estimated regression coefficients differed substantially from those obtained with unweighted least squares, the residuals from the weighted least squares fit were used to reestimate the standard deviation function, and revised weights were obtained. Two more iterations of this iteratively reweighted least squares process led to stable estimated coefficients.

MINITAB regression results for the weighted least squares fit based on the final weights are shown in Figure 11.18. Note that the signs of the regression coefficients are all positive, as might be expected:

CTYPOP: Traffic increases with local population density

LANES: Traffic increases with number of lanes

CONTROL1: Traffic is highest for road sections under access control

LANES^2: An upward-curving parabola is consistent with the shape of the lowess fit of AADT to LANES in Figure 11.15

CTYPOP $\times$ CONTROL1: Traffic increase with access control is more pronounced for higher population density

Figure 11.19a contains a plot of the studentized residuals against the fitted values, and Figure 11.19b contains a normal probability plot of the studentized residuals. Notice that the variability of the studentized residuals is now approximately constant. While the normal probability plot in Figure 11.19b indicates some departure from normality (this was confirmed by the correlation test for normality), the departure does not appear to be serious, particularly in view of the large sample size.

To assess the usefulness of the model for estimating AADT, approximate 95 percent confidence intervals for mean traffic for typical rural, suburban, and urban road sections

FIGURE 11.19
Residual Plots for Final Weighted Least Squares Regression Fit—MNDOT Traffic Estimation Example.

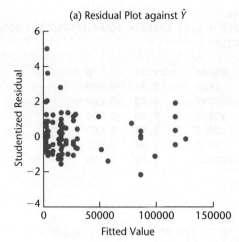

(a) Residual Plot against $\hat{Y}$

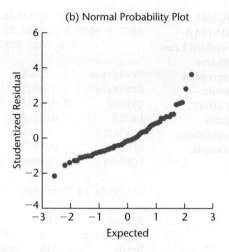

(b) Normal Probability Plot

TABLE 11.12 95 Percent Approximate Confidence Limits for Mean Responses—MNDOT Traffic Estimation Example.

	(1)	(2)	(3)	(4)	(5)	(6)	(7)
						Confidence Limits	
Road Section	CTYPOP	LANES	CONTROL1	$\hat{Y}_h$	$s\{\hat{Y}_h\}$	Lower	Upper
Rural	113,571	2	0	3,365	354	2,663	4,066
Suburban	222,229	4	0	16,379	1,827	12,758	19,999
Urban	941,411	6	1	116,024	6,597	102,953	129,095

were constructed. The levels of the predictor variables for these road sections are given in Table 11.12, columns 1–3. The estimated mean traffic is given in column 4. The approximate estimated standard deviations of the estimated mean responses for each of these road sections, shown in column 5, were obtained by using $s^2\{\mathbf{b}_w\}$ from (11.13) in (6.58):

$$s^2\{\hat{Y}_h\} = \mathbf{X}'_h s^2\{\mathbf{b}_w\}\mathbf{X}_h = MSE_w\mathbf{X}'_h(\mathbf{X}'\mathbf{WX})^{-1}\mathbf{X}_h \qquad (11.63)$$

where the vector $\mathbf{X}_h$ is defined in (6.53). Since the estimated standard deviations in column 5 are only approximations because the least squares weights were estimated by means of a standard deviation function, bootstrapping with random X sampling was employed to assess the precision of the fitted values. The standard deviations of the bootstrap sampling distributions were close to the estimated standard deviations in column 5. The consistency of the results shows that the iterative estimation of the weights by means of the standard deviation function did not have any substantial effect here on the precision of the fitted values.

The approximate 95 percent confidence limits for $E\{Y_h\}$, computed using (6.59), are presented in columns 6 and 7 of Table 11.12. The precision of these estimates was considered to be sufficient for planning purposes. However, because the suburban and rural road estimates have the poorest relative precision, it was recommended that better records be developed for population density in the immediate vicinity of a road section, since county population does not always reflect local population density. The improved information could lead to a better regression model, with more precise estimates for road sections in rural and suburban settings.

The approach for developing the regression model described here is not, of course, the only approach that can lead to a useful regression model, nor is the analysis complete as described. For example, the residual plot in Figure 11.19a suggests the presence of at least one outlier ($r_{92} = 5.02$). Possible remedial measures for this case should be considered. In addition, the departure from normality might be remedied by a transformation of the response variable. This transformation might also stabilize the variance of the error terms sufficiently so that weighted least squares would not be needed. In fact, subsequent analysis using the Box-Cox transformation approach found that a cube root transformation of the response is very effective in this instance. A final choice between the model fit obtained by weighted least squares and a model fit developed by an alternative approach can be made on the basis of model validation studies.

Cited References

11.1. Davidian, M., and R. J. Carroll. "Variance Function Estimation," *Journal of the American Statistical Association* 82 (1987), pp. 1079–91.

11.2. Greene, W. H. *Econometric Analysis,* 5th ed. Upper Saddle River, New Jersey: Prentice Hall, 2003.

11.3. Belsley, D. A. *Conditioning Diagnostics: Collinearity and Weak Data in Regression.* New York: John Wiley & Sons, 1991.

11.4. Frank, I. E., and J. H. Friedman. "A Statistical View of Some Chemometrics Regression Tools," *Technometrics* 35 (1993), pp. 109–35.

11.5. Hoaglin, D. C.; F. Mosteller; and J. W. Tukey. *Exploring Data Tables, Trends, and Shapes.* New York: John Wiley & Sons, 1985.

11.6. Rousseeuw, P. J., and A. M. Leroy. *Robust Regression and Outlier Detection.* New York: John Wiley & Sons, 1987.

11.7. Kennedy, W. J., Jr., and J. E. Gentle. *Statistical Computing.* New York: Marcel Dekker, 1980.

11.8. ETS Policy Information Center. *America's Smallest School: The Family.* Princeton, N.J.: Educational Testing Service, 1992.

11.9. Haerdle, W. *Applied Nonparametric Regression.* Cambridge: Cambridge University Press, 1992.

11.10. Cleveland, W. S., and S. J. Devlin. "Locally Weighted Regression: An Approach to Regression Analysis by Local Fitting," *Journal of the American Statistical Association* 83 (1988), pp. 596–610.

11.11. Breiman, L.; J. H. Friedman; R. A. Olshen; and C. J. Stone. *Classification and Regression Trees.* Belmont, Calif.: Wadsworth, 1984.

11.12. Friedman, J. H., and W. Stuetzle. "Projection Pursuit Regression," *Journal of the American Statistical Association* 76 (1981), pp. 817–23.

11.13. Eubank, R. L. *Spline Smoothing and Nonparametric Regression,* 2nd ed. New York: Marcel Dekker, 1999.

11.14. Hastie, T., and C. Loader. "Local Regression: Automatic Kernel Carpentry" (with discussion), *Statistical Science* 8 (1993), pp. 120–43.

11.15. Hastie, T., Tibshirani, R., and J. Friedman. *The Elements of Statistical Learning: Data Mining, Inference, and Prediction.* New York: Springer-Verlag, 2001.

11.16. Efron, B. *The Jackknife, The Bootstrap, and Other Resampling Plans.* Philadelphia, Penn.: Society for Industrial and Applied Mathematics, 1982.

11.17. Efron, B., and R. Tibshirani. "Bootstrap Methods for Standard Errors, Confidence Intervals, and Other Measures of Statistical Accuracy," *Statistical Science* 1 (1986), pp. 54–77.

11.18. Efron, B. "Better Bootstrap Confidence Intervals" (with discussion), *Journal of the American Statistical Association* 82 (1987), pp. 171–200.

11.19. Cheng, C. "Optimal Sampling for Traffic Volume Estimation," unpublished Ph.D. dissertation, University of Minnesota, Carlson School of Management, 1992.

Problems

11.1. One student remarked to another: "Your residuals show that nonconstancy of error variance is clearly present. Therefore, your regression results are completely invalid." Comment.

11.2. An analyst suggested: "One nice thing about robust regression is that you need not worry about outliers and influential observations." Comment.

11.3. Lowess smoothing becomes difficult when there are many predictors and the sample size is small. This is sometimes referred to as the "curse of dimensionality." Discuss the nature of this problem.

11.4. Regression trees become difficult to utilize when there are many predictors and the sample size is small. Discuss the nature of this problem.

11.5. Describe how bootstrapping might be used to obtain confidence intervals for regression coefficients when ridge regression is employed.

11.6. **Computer-assisted learning.** Data from a study of computer-assisted learning by 12 students, showing the total number of responses in completing a lesson (X) and the cost of computer time (Y, in cents), follow.

i:	1	2	3	4	5	6	7	8	9	10	11	12
X_i:	16	14	22	10	14	17	10	13	19	12	18	11
Y_i:	77	70	85	50	62	70	55	63	88	57	81	51

a. Fit a linear regression function by ordinary least squares, obtain the residuals, and plot the residuals against X. What does the residual plot suggest?

b. Divide the cases into two groups, placing the six cases with the smallest fitted values $\hat{Y}_i$ into group 1 and the other six cases into group 2. Conduct the Brown-Forsythe test for constancy of the error variance, using $\alpha = .05$. State the decision rule and conclusion.

c. Plot the absolute values of the residuals against X. What does this plot suggest about the relation between the standard deviation of the error term and X?

d. Estimate the standard deviation function by regressing the absolute values of the residuals against X, and then calculate the estimated weight for each case using (11.16a). Which case receives the largest weight? Which case receives the smallest weight?

e. Using the estimated weights, obtain the weighted least squares estimates of β_0 and β_1. Are these estimates similar to the ones obtained with ordinary least squares in part (a)?

f. Compare the estimated standard deviations of the weighted least squares estimates b_{w0} and b_{w1} in part (e) with those for the ordinary least squares estimates in part (a). What do you find?

g. Iterate the steps in parts (d) and (e) one more time. Is there a substantial change in the estimated regression coefficients? If so, what should you do?

*11.7. **Machine speed.** The number of defective items produced by a machine (Y) is known to be linearly related to the speed setting of the machine (X). The data below were collected from recent quality control records.

i:	1	2	3	4	5	6	7	8	9	10	11	12
X_i:	200	400	300	400	200	300	300	400	200	400	200	300
Y_i:	28	75	37	53	22	58	40	96	46	52	30	69

a. Fit a linear regression function by ordinary least squares, obtain the residuals, and plot the residuals against X. What does the residual plot suggest?

b. Conduct the Breusch-Pagan test for constancy of the error variance, assuming $\log_e \sigma_i^2 = \gamma_0 + \gamma_1 X_i$; use $\alpha = .10$. State the alternatives, decision rule, and conclusion.

c. Plot the squared residuals against X. What does the plot suggest about the relation between the variance of the error term and X?

d. Estimate the variance function by regressing the squared residuals against X, and then calculate the estimated weight for each case using (11.16b).

e. Using the estimated weights, obtain the weighted least squares estimates of β_0 and β_1. Are the weighted least squares estimates similar to the ones obtained with ordinary least squares in part (a)?

f. Compare the estimated standard deviations of the weighted least squares estimates b_{w0} and b_{w1} in part (e) with those for the ordinary least squares estimates in part (a). What do you find?

g. Iterate the steps in parts (d) and (e) one more time. Is there a substantial change in the estimated regression coefficients? If so, what should you do?

11.8. **Employee salaries.** A group of high-technology companies agreed to share employee salary information in an effort to establish salary ranges for technical positions in research and development. Data obtained for each employee included current salary (Y), a coded variable indicating highest academic degree obtained (1 = bachelor's degree, 2 = master's degree, 3 = doctoral degree), years of experience since last degree (X_3), and the number of persons currently supervised (X_4). The data follow.

Employee i	Y_{i1}	Degree	X_{i3}	X_{i4}
1	58.8	3	4.49	0
2	34.8	1	2.92	0
3	163.7	3	29.54	42
...	...	...	...	...
63	40.0	2	.44	0
64	60.5	3	2.10	0
65	104.8	3	19.81	24

a. Create two indicator variables for highest degree attained:

Degree	X_1	X_2
Bachelor's	0	0
Master's	1	0
Doctoral	0	1

b. Regress Y on X_1, X_2, X_3, and X_4, using a first-order model and ordinary least squares, obtain the residuals, and plot them against $\hat{Y}$. What does the residual plot suggest?

c. Divide the cases into two groups, placing the 33 cases with the smallest fitted values $\hat{Y}_i$ into group 1 and the other 32 cases into group 2. Conduct the Brown-Forsythe test for constancy of the error variance, using $\alpha = .01$. State the decision rule and conclusion.

d. Plot the absolute residuals against X_3 and against X_4. What do these plots suggest about the relation between the standard deviation of the error term and X_3 and X_4?

e. Estimate the standard deviation function by regressing the absolute residuals against X_3 and X_4 in first-order form, and then calculate the estimated weight for each case using (11.16a).

f. Using the estimated weights, obtain the weighted least squares fit of the regression model. Are the weighted least squares estimates of the regression coefficients similar to the ones obtained with ordinary least squares in part (b)?

g. Compare the estimated standard deviations of the weighted least squares coefficient estimates in part (f) with those for the ordinary least squares estimates in part (b). What do you find?

h. Iterate the steps in parts (e) and (f) one more time. Is there a substantial change in the estimated regression coefficients? If so, what should you do?

11.9. Refer to **Cosmetics sales** Problem 10.13. Given below are the estimated ridge standardized regression coefficients, the variance inflation factors, and R^2 for selected biasing constants c.

c:	.00	.01	.02	.04	.06	.08	.09	.10
b_1^R:	.490	.461	.443	.463	.410	.401	.398	.394
b_2^R:	.296	.322	.336	.349	.354	.356	.356	.356
b_3^R:	.169	.167	.167	.166	.165	.164	.164	.164
$(VIF)_1$:	20.07	10.36	6.37	3.20	1.98	1.38	1.20	1.05
$(VIF)_2$:	20.72	10.67	6.55	3.27	2.07	1.40	1.21	1.06
$(VIF)_3$:	1.22	1.17	1.14	1.08	1.02	.98	.95	.93
R^2:	.7417	.7416	.7145	.7412	.7409	.7045	.7402	.7399

a. Make a ridge trace plot for the given c values. Do the ridge regression coefficients exhibit substantial changes near $c = 0$?

b. Suggest a reasonable value for the biasing constant c based on the ridge trace, the VIF values, and R^2.

c. Transform the estimated standardized regression coefficients selected in part (b) back to the original variables and obtain the fitted values for the 44 cases. How similar are these fitted values to those obtained with the ordinary least squares fit in Problem 10.13a?

*11.10. **Chemical shipment.** The data to follow, taken on 20 incoming shipments of chemicals in drums arriving at a warehouse, show number of drums in shipment (X_1), total weight of shipment (X_2, in hundred pounds), and number of minutes required to handle shipment (Y).

i:	1	2	3	...	18	19	20
X_{i1}:	7	18	5	...	21	6	11
X_{i2}:	5.11	16.72	3.20	...	15.21	3.64	9.57
Y_i:	58	152	41	...	155	39	90

Given below are the estimated ridge standardized regression coefficients, the variance inflation factors, and R^2 for selected biasing constants c.

c:	.000	.005	.01	.05	.07	.09	.10	.20
b_1^R:	.451	.453	.455	.460	.460	.459	.458	.444
b_2^R:	.561	.556	.552	.526	.517	.508	.504	.473
$(VIF)_1 = (VIF)_2$:	7.03	6.20	5.51	2.65	2.03	1.61	1.46	.71
R^2:	.9869	.9869	.9869	.9862	.9856	.9852	.9844	.9780

a. Fit regression model (6.1) to the data and find the fitted values.

b. Make a ridge trace plot for the given c values. Do the ridge regression coefficients exhibit substantial changes near $c = 0$?

c. Why are the $(VIF)_1$ values the same as the $(VIF)_2$ values here?

d. Suggest a reasonable value for the biasing constant c based on the ridge trace, the VIF values, and R^2.

e. Transform the estimated standardized regression coefficients selected in part (c) back to the original variables and obtain the fitted values for the 20 cases. How similar are these fitted values to those obtained with the ordinary least squares fit in part (a)?

*11.11. Refer to **Copier maintenance** Problem 1.20. Two cases had been held out of the original data set because special circumstances led to unusually long service times:

Case i	X_i	Y_i
46	6	132
47	5	166

a. Using the enlarged (47-case) data set, fit a simple linear regression model using ordinary least squares and plot the data together with the fitted regression function. What is the effect of adding cases 46 and 47 on the fitted response function?

b. Obtain the scaled residuals in (11.47) and use the Huber weight function (11.44) to obtain the case weights for a first iteration of IRLS robust regression. Which cases receive the smallest Huber weights? Why?

c. Using the weights calculated in part (b), obtain the weighted least squares estimates of the regression coefficients. How do these estimates compare to those found in part (a) using ordinary least squares?

d. Continue the IRLS procedure for two more iterations. Which cases receive the smallest weights in the final iteration? How do the final IRLS robust regression estimates compare to the ordinary least squares estimates obtained in part (a)?

e. Plot the final IRLS estimated regression function, obtained in part (d), on the graph constructed in part (a). Does the robust fit differ substantially from the ordinary least squares fit? If so, which fit is preferred here?

11.12. **Weight and height.** The weights and heights of twenty male students in a freshman class are recorded in order to see how well weight (Y, in pounds) can be predicted from height (X, in inches). The data are given below. Assume that first-order regression (1.1) is appropriate.

i:	1	2	3	$\cdots$	18	19	20
X_i:	74	65	72	$\cdots$	69	68	67
Y_i:	185	195	216	$\cdots$	177	145	137

a. Fit a simple linear regression model using ordinary least squares, and plot the data together with the fitted regression function. Also, obtain an index plot of Cook's distance (10.33). What do these plots suggest?

b. Obtain the scaled residuals in (11.47) and use the Huber weight function (11.44) to obtain case weights for a first iteration of IRLS robust regression. Which cases receive the smallest Huber weights? Why?

c. Using the weights calculated in part (b), obtain the weighted least squares estimates of the regression coefficients. How do these estimates compare to those found in part (a) using ordinary least squares?

d. Continue the IRLS procedure for two more iterations. Which cases receive the smallest weights in the final iteration? How do the final IRLS robust regression estimates compare to the ordinary least squares estimates obtained in part (a)?

Exercises

11.13. (Calculus needed.) Derive the weighted least squares normal equations for fitting a simple linear regression function when $\sigma_i^2 = kX_i$, where k is a proportionality constant.

11.14. Express the weighted least squares estimator b_{w1} in (11.26a) in terms of the centered variables $Y_i - \bar{Y}_w$ and $X_i - \bar{X}_w$, where $\bar{Y}_w$ and $\bar{X}_w$ are the weighted means.

11.15. Refer to **Computer-assisted learning** Problem 11.6. Demonstrate numerically that the weighted least squares estimates obtained in part (e) are identical to those obtained using transformation (11.23) and ordinary least squares.

11.16. Refer to **Machine speed** Problem 11.7. Demonstrate numerically that the weighted least squares estimates obtained in part (e) are identical to those obtained when using transformation (11.23) and ordinary least squares.

11.17. Consider the weighted least squares criterion (11.6) with weights given by $w_i = .3/X_i$. Set up the variance-covariance matrix for the error terms when $i = 1, \ldots, 4$. Assume $\sigma\{\varepsilon_i, \varepsilon_j\} = 0$ for $i \neq j$.

11.18. Derive the variance-covariance matrix $\sigma^2\{\mathbf{b}_w\}$ in (11.10) for the weighted least squares estimators when the variance-covariance matrix of the observations Y_i is $k\mathbf{W}^{-1}$, where $\mathbf{W}$ is given in (11.7) and k is a proportionality constant.

11.19. Derive the mean squared error in (11.29).

11.20. Refer to the body fat example of Table 7.1. Employing least absolute residuals regression, the LAR estimates of the regression coefficients are $b_0 = -17.027$, $b_1 = .4173$, and $b_2 = .5203$.

a. Find the sum of the absolute residuals based on the LAR fit.

b. For the least squares estimated regression coefficients $b_0 = -19.174$, $b_1 = .2224$, and $b_2 = .6594$, find the sum of the absolute residuals. Is this sum larger than the sum obtained in part (a)? Is this to be expected?

Projects

11.21. Observations on Y are to be taken when $X = 10, 20, 30, 40$, and 50, respectively. The true regression function is $E\{Y\} = 20 + 10X$. The error terms are independent and normally distributed, with $E\{\varepsilon_i\} = 0$ and $\sigma^2\{\varepsilon_i\} = .8X_i$.

a. Generate a random Y observation for each X level and calculate both the ordinary and weighted least squares estimates of the regression coefficient β_1 in the simple linear regression function.

b. Repeat part (a) 200 times, generating new random numbers each time.

c. Calculate the mean and variance of the 200 ordinary least squares estimates of β_1 and do the same for the 200 weighted least squares estimates.

d. Do both the ordinary least squares and weighted least squares estimators appear to be unbiased? Explain. Which estimator appears to be more precise here? Comment.

11.22. Refer to **Patient satisfaction** Problem 6.15.

a. Obtain the estimated ridge standardized regression coefficients, variance inflation factors, and R^2 for the following biasing constants: $c = .000, .005, .01, .02, .03, .04, .05$.

b. Make a ridge trace plot for the given c values. Do the ridge regression coefficients exhibit substantial changes near $c = 0$?

c. Suggest a reasonable value for the biasing constant c based on the ridge trace, the *VIF* values, and R^2.

d. Transform the estimated standardized regression coefficients selected in part (c) back to the original variables and obtain the fitted values for the 46 cases. How similar are these fitted values to those obtained with the ordinary least squares fit in Problem 6.15c?

11.23. **Cement composition.** Data on the effect of composition of cement on heat evolved during hardening are given below. The variables collected were the amount of tricalcium aluminate (X_1), the amount of tricalcium silicate (X_2), the amount of tetracalcium alumino ferrite (X_3), the amount of dicalcium silicate (X_4), and the heat evolved in calories per gram of cement (Y).

i:	1	2	3	...	11	12	13
X_{i1}:	7	1	11	...	1	11	10
X_{i2}:	26	29	56	...	40	66	68
X_{i3}:	6	15	8	...	23	9	8
X_{i4}:	60	52	20	...	34	12	12
Y_i:	78.5	74.3	104.3	...	83.8	113.3	109.4

Adapted from H. Woods, H. H. Steinour, and H. R. Starke, "Effect of Composition of Portland Cement on Heat Evolved During Hardening," *Industrial and Engineering Chemistry*, 24, 1932, 1207–1214.

a. Fit regression model (6.5) for four predictor variables to the data. State the estimated regression function.

b. Obtain the estimated ridge standardized regression coefficients, variance inflation factors, and R^2 for the following biasing constants: $c = .000, .002, .004, .006, .008, .02, .04, .06, .08, .10$.

c. Make a ridge trace plot for the biasing constants listed in part (b). Do the ridge regression coefficients exhibit substantial changes near $c = 0$?

d. Suggest a reasonable value for the biasing constant c based on the ridge trace, *VIF* values, and R^2 values.

e. Transform the estimated standardized ridge regression coefficients selected in part (d) to the original variables and obtain the fitted values for the 13 cases. How similar are these fitted values to those obtained with the ordinary least squares fit in part (a)?

11.24. Refer to **Commercial properties** Problem 6.18.

a. Use least absolute residuals regression to obtain estimates of the parameters $\beta_0, \beta_1, \beta_2, \beta_3$, and β_4.

b. Find the sum of the absolute residuals based on the LAR fit in part (a).

c. For the least squares estimated regression function in Problem 6.18c, find the sum of the absolute residuals. Is this sum larger than the sum obtained in part (b)? Is this to be expected?

11.25. **Crop yield.** An agronomist studied the effects of moisture (X_1, in inches) and temperature (X_2, in °C) on the yield of a new hybrid tomato (Y). The experimental data follow.

i:	1	2	3	$\ldots$	23	24	25
X_{i1}:	6	6	6	$\ldots$	14	14	14
X_{i2}:	20	21	22	$\ldots$	22	23	24
Y_i:	49.2	48.1	48.0	$\ldots$	42.1	43.9	40.5

The agronomist expects that second-order polynomial regression model (8.7) with independent normal error terms is appropriate here.

a. Fit a second-order polynomial regression model omitting the interaction term and the quadratic effect term for temperature.

b. Construct a contour plot of the fitted surface obtained in part (a).

c. Use the lowess method to obtain a nonparametric estimate of the yield response surface as a function of moisture and temperature. Employ weight function (11.53), $q = 9/25$, and a Euclidean distance measure with unscaled variables. Obtain fitted values $\hat{Y}_h$ for the 9×9 rectangular grid of (X_{h1}, X_{h2}) values where $X_{h1} = 6, 7, \ldots, 13, 14$ and $X_{h2} = 20, 20.5, \ldots, 23.5, 24$, using a local first-order model.

d. Construct a contour plot of the resulting lowess surface. Are the lowess contours consistent with the contours in part (b) for the polynomial model? Discuss.

11.26. Refer to **Computer-assisted learning** Problem 11.6.

a. Based on the weighted least squares fit in Problem 11.6e, construct an approximate 95 percent confidence interval for β_1 by means of (6.50), using the estimated standard deviation $s\{b_{w1}\}$.

b. Using random X sampling, obtain 750 bootstrap samples of size 12. For each bootstrap sample, (1) use ordinary least squares to regress Y on X and obtain the residuals, (2) estimate the standard deviation function by regressing the absolute residuals on X and then use the fitted standard deviation function and (11.16a) to obtain weights, and (3) use weighted least squares to regress Y on X and obtain the bootstrap estimated regression coefficient b_1^*. (Note that for each bootstrap sample, only one iteration of the iteratively reweighted least squares procedure is to be used.)

c. Construct a histogram of the 750 bootstrap estimates b_1^*. Does the bootstrap sampling distribution of b_1^* appear to approximate a normal distribution?

d. Calculate the sample standard deviation of the 750 bootstrap estimates b_1^*. How does this value compare to the estimated standard deviation $s\{b_{w1}\}$ used in part (a)?

e. Construct a 95 percent bootstrap confidence interval for β_1 using reflection method (11.59). How does this confidence interval compare with that obtained in part (a)? Does the approximate interval in part (a) appear to be useful for this data set?

11.27. Refer to **Machine speed** Problem 11.7.

a. On the basis of the weighted least squares fit in Problem 11.7e, construct an approximate 90 percent confidence interval for β_1 by means of (6.50), using the estimated standard deviation $s\{b_{w1}\}$.

b. Using random X sampling, obtain 800 bootstrap samples of size 12. For each bootstrap sample, (1) use ordinary least squares to regress Y on X and obtain the residuals, (2) estimate the standard deviation function by regressing the absolute residuals on X and then use the fitted standard deviation function and (11.16a) to obtain weights, and (3) use weighted least squares to regress Y on X and obtain the bootstrap estimated regression coefficient b_1^*. (Note that for each bootstrap sample, only one iteration of the iteratively reweighted least squares procedure is to be used.)

c. Construct a histogram of the 800 bootstrap estimates b_1^*. Does the bootstrap sampling distribution of b_1^* appear to approximate a normal distribution?

d. Calculate the sample standard deviation of the 800 bootstrap estimates b_1^*. How does this value compare to the estimated standard deviation $s\{b_{w1}\}$ used in part (a)?

e. Construct a 90 percent bootstrap confidence interval for β_1 using reflection method (11.59). How does this confidence interval compare with that obtained in part (a)? Does the approximate interval in part (a) appear to be useful for this data set?

11.28. **Mileage study.** The effectiveness of a new experimental overdrive gear in reducing gasoline consumption was studied in 12 trials with a light truck equipped with this gear. In the data that follow, X_i denotes the constant speed (in miles per hour) on the test track in the ith trial and Y_i denotes miles per gallon obtained.

i:	1	2	3	4	5	6	7	8	9	10	11	12
X_i:	35	35	40	40	45	45	50	50	55	55	60	60
Y_i:	22	20	28	31	37	38	41	39	34	37	27	30

Second-order regression model (8.2) with independent normal error terms is expected to be appropriate.

a. Fit regression model (8.2). Plot the fitted regression function and the data. Does the quadratic regression function appear to be a good fit here?

b. Automotive engineers would like to estimate the speed X_{max} at which the average mileage $E\{Y\}$ is maximized. It can be shown for second-order model (8.2) that $X_{max} = \bar{X} - (.5\beta_1/\beta_{11})$, provided that β_{11} is negative. Estimate the speed X_{max} at which the average mileage is maximized, using $\hat{X}_{max} = \bar{X} - (.5b_1/b_{11})$. What is the estimated mean mileage at the estimated optimum speed?

c. Using fixed X sampling, obtain 1,000 bootstrap samples of size 12. For each bootstrap sample, fit regression model (8.2) and obtain the bootstrap estimate $\hat{X}_{max}^*$.

d. Construct a histogram of the 1,000 bootstrap estimates $\hat{X}_{max}^*$. Does the bootstrap sampling distribution of $\hat{X}_{max}^*$ appear to approximate a normal distribution?

e. Construct a 90 percent bootstrap confidence interval for X_{max} using reflection method (11.56). How precisely has X_{max} been estimated?

11.29. Refer to **Muscle mass** Problem 1.27.

a. Fit a two-region regression tree. What is the first split point based on age? What is SSE for this two-region tree?

b. Find the second split point given the two-region tree in part (a). What is SSE for the resulting three-region tree?

c. Find the third split point given the three-region tree in part (b). What is SSE for the resulting four-region tree?

d. Prepare a scatter plot of the data with the four-region tree in part (c) superimposed. How well does the tree fit the data? What does the tree suggest about the change in muscle mass with age?

e. Prepare a residual plot of e_i versus $\hat{Y}_i$ for the four-region tree in part (d). State your findings.

11.30. Refer to **Patient satisfaction** Problem 6.15. Consider only the first two predictors (patient's age, X_1, and severity of illness, X_2).

a. Fit a two-region regression tree. What is the first split point, and on which predictor is it based? What is *SSE* for the resulting two-region tree?

b. Find the second split point given the two-region tree in part (a). Is it based on X_1 or X_2? What is *SSE* for the resulting three-region tree?

c. Find the third split point given the three-region tree in part (b). Is it based on X_1 or X_2? What is *SSE* for the resulting four-region tree?

d. Find the fourth split point given the four-region tree in part (c). Is it based on X_1 or X_2? What is *SSE* for the resulting five-region tree?

e. Prepare a three-dimensional surface plot of the five-region tree obtained in part (d). What does this tree suggest about the relative importance of the two predictors?

f. Prepare a residual plot of e_i versus $\hat{Y}_i$ for the five-region tree in part (d). State your findings.

Case Studies

11.31. Refer to the **Prostate cancer** data set in Appendix C.5 and Case Study 9.30. Select a random sample of 65 observations to use as the model-building data set.

a. Develop a regression tree for predicting PSA. Justify your choice of number of regions (tree size), and interpret your regression tree.

b. Assess your model's ability to predict and discuss its usefulness to the oncologists.

c. Compare the performance of your regression tree model with that of the best regression model obtained in Case Study 9.30. Which model is more easily interpreted and why?

11.32. Refer to the **Real estate sales** data set in Appendix C.7 and Case Study 9.31. Select a random sample of 300 observations to use as the model-building data set.

a. Develop a regression tree for predicting sales price. Justify your choice of number of regions (tree size), and interpret your model.

b. Assess your model's ability to predict and discuss its usefulness as a tool for predicting sales prices.

c. Compare the performance of your regression tree model with that of the best regression model obtained in Case Study 9.31. Which model is more easily interpreted and why?

Chapter 12

Autocorrelation in Time Series Data

The basic regression models considered so far have assumed that the random error terms ε_i are either uncorrelated random variables or independent normal random variables. In business and economics, many regression applications involve time series data. For such data, the assumption of uncorrelated or independent error terms is often not appropriate; rather, the error terms are frequently correlated positively over time. Error terms correlated over time are said to be *autocorrelated* or *serially correlated*.

A major cause of positively autocorrelated error terms in business and economic regression applications involving time series data is the omission of one or several key variables from the model. When time-ordered effects of such "missing" key variables are positively correlated, the error terms in the regression model will tend to be positively autocorrelated since the error terms include effects of missing variables. Consider, for example, the regression of annual sales of a product against average yearly price of the product over a period of 30 years. If population size has an important effect on sales, its omission from the model may lead to the error terms being positively autocorrelated because the effect of population size on sales likely is positively correlated over time.

Another cause of positively autocorrelated error terms in economic data is the presence of systematic coverage errors in the response variable time series, which errors often tend to be positively correlated over time.

12.1 Problems of Autocorrelation

When the error terms in the regression model are positively autocorrelated, the use of ordinary least squares procedures has a number of important consequences. We summarize these first, and then discuss them in more detail:

1. The estimated regression coefficients are still unbiased, but they no longer have the minimum variance property and may be quite inefficient.
2. *MSE* may seriously underestimate the variance of the error terms.
3. $s\{b_k\}$ calculated according to ordinary least squares procedures may seriously underestimate the true standard deviation of the estimated regression coefficient.

4. Confidence intervals and tests using the t and F distributions, discussed earlier, are no longer strictly applicable.

To illustrate these problems intuitively, we consider the simple linear regression model with time series data:

$$Y_t = \beta_0 + \beta_1 X_t + \varepsilon_t$$

Here, Y_t and X_t are observations for period t. Let us assume that the error terms ε_t are positively autocorrelated as follows:

$$\varepsilon_t = \varepsilon_{t-1} + u_t$$

The u_t, called *disturbances*, are independent normal random variables. Thus, any error term ε_t is the sum of the previous error term ε_{t-1} and a new disturbance term u_t. We shall assume here that the u_t have mean 0 and variance 1.

In Table 12.1, column 1, we show 10 random observations on the normal variable u_t with mean 0 and variance 1, obtained from a standard normal random numbers generator. Suppose now that $\varepsilon_0 = 3.0$; we obtain then:

$$\varepsilon_1 = \varepsilon_0 + u_1 = 3.0 + .5 = 3.5$$
$$\varepsilon_2 = \varepsilon_1 + u_2 = 3.5 - .7 = 2.8$$

etc.

The error terms ε_t are shown in Table 12.1, column 2, and they are plotted in Figure 12.1. Note the systematic pattern in these error terms. Their positive relation over time is shown by the fact that adjacent error terms tend to be of the same sign and magnitude.

Suppose that X_t in the regression model represents time, such that $X_1 = 1$, $X_2 = 2$, etc. Further, suppose we know that $\beta_0 = 2$ and $\beta_1 = .5$ so that the true regression function is $E\{Y\} = 2 + .5X$. The observed Y values based on the error terms in column 2 of Table 12.1 are shown in column 3. For example, $Y_0 = 2 + .5(0) + 3.0 = 5.0$, and $Y_1 = 2 + .5(1) + 3.5 = 6.0$. Figure 12.2a on page 483 contains the true regression line $E\{Y\} = 2 + .5X$ and the observed Y values shown in Table 12.1, column 3. Figure 12.2b contains the estimated regression line, fitted by ordinary least squares methods, and repeats

TABLE 12.1
Example of Positively Autocorrelated Error Terms.

t	(1) u_t	(2) $\varepsilon_{t-1} + u_t = \varepsilon_t$	(3) $Y_t = 2 + .5X_t + \varepsilon_t$
0	—	3.0	5.0
1	.5	$3.0 + .5 = 3.5$	6.0
2	−.7	$3.5 - .7 = 2.8$	5.8
3	.3	$2.8 + .3 = 3.1$	6.6
4	0	$3.1 + 0 = 3.1$	7.1
5	−2.3	$3.1 - 2.3 = .8$	5.3
6	−1.9	$.8 - 1.9 = -1.1$	3.9
7	.2	$-1.1 + .2 = -.9$	4.6
8	−.3	$-.9 - .3 = -1.2$	4.8
9	.2	$-1.2 + .2 = -1.0$	5.5
10	−.1	$-1.0 - .1 = -1.1$	5.9

FIGURE 12.1
Example of Positively Autocorrelated Error Terms.

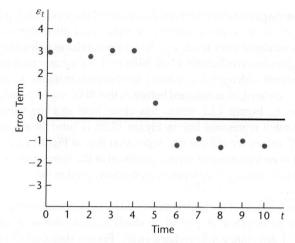

FIGURE 12.2   Regression with Positively Autocorrelated Error Terms.

(a) True Regression Line and Observation
when $\varepsilon_0 = 3$

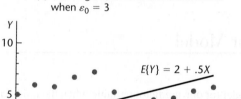

$$E\{Y\} = 2 + .5X$$

(b) Fitted Regression Line and Observations
when $\varepsilon_0 = 3$

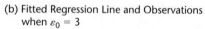

$$\hat{Y} = 5.85 - .070X$$

(c) Fitted Regression Line and Observations with
$\varepsilon_0 = -.2$ and Different Disturbances

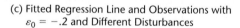

$$\hat{Y} = .200 + .779X$$

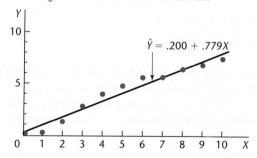

the observed Y values. Notice that the fitted regression line differs sharply from the true regression line because the initial ε_0 value was large and the succeeding positively autocorrelated error terms tended to be large for some time. This persistency pattern in the positively autocorrelated error terms leads to a fitted regression line far from the true one. Had the initial ε_0 value been small, say, $\varepsilon_0 = -.2$, and the disturbances different, a sharply different fitted regression line might have been obtained because of the persistency pattern, as shown in Figure 12.2c. This variation from sample to sample in the fitted regression lines due to the positively autocorrelated error terms may be so substantial as to lead to large variances of the estimated regression coefficients when ordinary least squares methods are used.

Another key problem with applying ordinary least squares methods when the error terms are positively autocorrelated, as mentioned before, is that *MSE* may seriously underestimate the variance of the ε_t. Figure 12.2 makes this clear. Note that the variability of the Y values around the fitted regression line in Figure 12.2b is substantially smaller than the variability of the Y values around the true regression line in Figure 12.2a. This is one of the factors leading to an indication of greater precision of the regression coefficients than is actually the case when ordinary least squares methods are used in the presence of positively autocorrelated errors.

In view of the seriousness of the problems created by autocorrelated errors, it is important that their presence be detected. A plot of residuals against time is an effective, though subjective, means of detecting autocorrelated errors. Formal statistical tests have also been developed. A widely used test is based on the first-order autoregressive error model, which we take up next. This model is a simple one, yet experience suggests that it is frequently applicable in business and economics when the error terms are serially correlated.

12.2   First-Order Autoregressive Error Model

Simple Linear Regression

The generalized simple linear regression model for one predictor variable when the random error terms follow a first-order autoregressive, or $AR(1)$, process is:

$$Y_t = \beta_0 + \beta_1 X_t + \varepsilon_t$$
$$\varepsilon_t = \rho \varepsilon_{t-1} + u_t$$

$$(12.1)$$

where:

ρ is a parameter such that $|\rho| < 1$
u_t are independent $N(0, \sigma^2)$

Note that generalized regression model (12.1) is identical to the simple linear regression model (2.1) except for the structure of the error terms. Each error term in model (12.1) consists of a fraction of the previous error term (when $\rho > 0$) plus a new disturbance term u_t. The parameter ρ is called the *autocorrelation parameter*.

Multiple Regression

The generalized multiple regression model when the random error terms follow a first-order autoregressive process is:

$$Y_t = \beta_0 + \beta_1 X_{t1} + \beta_2 X_{t2} + \cdots + \beta_{p-1} X_{t,p-1} + \varepsilon_t$$
$$\varepsilon_t = \rho \varepsilon_{t-1} + u_t$$

$$(12.2)$$

where:

$$|\rho| < 1$$

u_t are independent $N(0, \sigma^2)$

Thus, we see that generalized multiple regression model (12.2) is identical to the earlier multiple regression model (6.7) except for the structure of the error terms.

Properties of Error Terms

Regression models (12.1) and (12.2) are generalized regression models because the error terms ε_t in these models are correlated. However, the error terms still have mean zero and constant variance:

$$E\{\varepsilon_t\} = 0 \tag{12.3}$$

$$\sigma^2\{\varepsilon_t\} = \frac{\sigma^2}{1 - \rho^2} \tag{12.4}$$

Note that the variance of the error terms here is a function of the autocorrelation parameter ρ.

The covariance between adjacent error terms ε_t and ε_{t-1} is:

$$\sigma\{\varepsilon_t, \varepsilon_{t-1}\} = \rho\left(\frac{\sigma^2}{1 - \rho^2}\right) \tag{12.5}$$

The coefficient of correlation between ε_t and ε_{t-1}, denoted by $\rho\{\varepsilon_t, \varepsilon_{t-1}\}$, is defined as follows:

$$\rho\{\varepsilon_t, \varepsilon_{t-1}\} = \frac{\sigma\{\varepsilon_t, \varepsilon_{t-1}\}}{\sigma\{\varepsilon_t\}\sigma\{\varepsilon_{t-1}\}} \tag{12.6}$$

Since the variance of each error term according to (12.4) is $\sigma^2/(1 - \rho^2)$, the coefficient of correlation using (12.5) is:

$$\rho\{\varepsilon_t, \varepsilon_{t-1}\} = \frac{\rho\left(\dfrac{\sigma^2}{1 - \rho^2}\right)}{\sqrt{\dfrac{\sigma^2}{1 - \rho^2}}\sqrt{\dfrac{\sigma^2}{1 - \rho^2}}} = \rho \tag{12.6a}$$

Thus, the autocorrelation parameter ρ is the coefficient of correlation between adjacent error terms.

The covariance between error terms that are s periods apart can be shown to be:

$$\sigma\{\varepsilon_t, \varepsilon_{t-s}\} = \rho^s\left(\frac{\sigma^2}{1 - \rho^2}\right) \qquad s \neq 0 \tag{12.7}$$

and is called the *autocovariance function*. The coefficient of correlation between ε_t and ε_{t-s} therefore is:

$$\rho\{\varepsilon_t, \varepsilon_{t-s}\} = \rho^s \qquad s \neq 0 \tag{12.8}$$

Note that (12.8) is called the *autocorrelation function*. Thus, when ρ is positive, all error terms are correlated, but the further apart they are, the less is the correlation between them. The only time the error terms for the autoregressive error models (12.1) and (12.2) are uncorrelated is when $\rho = 0$.

From the results for the variances and covariances of the error terms in (12.4) and (12.7), we can now state the variance-covariance matrix of the error terms for the first-order autoregressive generalized regression models (12.1) and (12.2):

$$
\underset{n \times n}{\sigma^2\{\boldsymbol{\varepsilon}\}} =
\begin{bmatrix}
\kappa & \kappa\rho & \kappa\rho^2 & \cdots & \kappa\rho^{n-1} \\
\kappa\rho & \kappa & \kappa\rho & \cdots & \kappa\rho^{n-2} \\
\vdots & \vdots & \vdots & & \vdots \\
\kappa\rho^{n-1} & \kappa\rho^{n-2} & \kappa\rho^{n-3} & \cdots & \kappa
\end{bmatrix}
\tag{12.9}
$$

where:

$$
\kappa = \frac{\sigma^2}{1 - \rho^2}
\tag{12.9a}
$$

Note again that the variance-covariance matrix (12.9) reflects the generalized nature of regression models (12.1) and (12.2) by containing nonzero covariance terms.

Comments

1. It is instructive to expand the definition of the first-order autoregressive error term ε_t:

$$
\varepsilon_t = \rho\varepsilon_{t-1} + u_t
$$

Since this definition holds for all t, we have $\varepsilon_{t-1} = \rho\varepsilon_{t-2} + u_{t-1}$. When we substitute this expression above, we obtain:

$$
\varepsilon_t = \rho(\rho\varepsilon_{t-2} + u_{t-1}) + u_t = \rho^2\varepsilon_{t-2} + \rho u_{t-1} + u_t
$$

Replacing now ε_{t-2} by $\rho\varepsilon_{t-3} + u_{t-2}$, we obtain:

$$
\varepsilon_t = \rho^3\varepsilon_{t-3} + \rho^2 u_{t-2} + \rho u_{t-1} + u_t
$$

Continuing in this fashion, we find:

$$
\varepsilon_t = \sum_{s=0}^{\infty} \rho^s u_{t-s}
\tag{12.10}
$$

Thus, the error term ε_t in period t is a linear combination of the current and preceding disturbance terms. When $0 < \rho < 1$, (12.10) indicates that the further the period $t - s$ is in the past, the smaller is the weight of disturbance term u_{t-s} in determining ε_t.

2. The derivation of (12.3), that the error terms have expectation zero, follows directly from taking the expectation of ε_t in (12.10) and using the fact that $E\{u_t\} = 0$ for all t according to models (12.1) and (12.2).

3. To derive the variance of the error terms in (12.4), we utilize the assumption of models (12.1) and (12.2) that the u_t are independent with variance σ^2. It then follows from (12.10) that:

$$
\sigma^2\{\varepsilon_t\} = \sum_{s=0}^{\infty} \rho^{2s}\sigma^2\{u_{t-s}\} = \sigma^2 \sum_{s=0}^{\infty} \rho^{2s}
$$

Now for $|\rho| < 1$, it is known that:

$$
\sum_{s=0}^{\infty} \rho^{2s} = \frac{1}{1 - \rho^2}
$$

Hence, we have:

$$\sigma^2\{\varepsilon_t\} = \frac{\sigma^2}{1-\rho^2}$$

4. To derive the covariance of ε_t and ε_{t-1} in (12.5), we need to recognize that:

$$\sigma^2\{\varepsilon_t\} = E\{\varepsilon_t^2\}$$

$$\sigma\{\varepsilon_t, \varepsilon_{t-1}\} = E\{\varepsilon_t \varepsilon_{t-1}\}$$

These results follow from (A.15a) and (A.21a), respectively, since $E\{\varepsilon_t\} = 0$ by (12.3) for all t.
By (12.10), we have:

$$E\{\varepsilon_t \varepsilon_{t-1}\} = E\{(u_t + \rho u_{t-1} + \rho^2 u_{t-2} + \cdots)(u_{t-1} + \rho u_{t-2} + \rho^2 u_{t-3} + \cdots)\}$$

which can be rewritten:

$$E\{\varepsilon_t \varepsilon_{t-1}\} = E\{[u_t + \rho(u_{t-1} + \rho u_{t-2} + \cdots)][u_{t-1} + \rho u_{t-2} + \rho^2 u_{t-3} + \cdots]\}$$

$$= E\{u_t(u_{t-1} + \rho u_{t-2} + \rho^2 u_{t-3} + \cdots)\} + E\{\rho(u_{t-1} + \rho u_{t-2} + \rho^2 u_{t-3} + \cdots)^2\}$$

Since $E\{u_t u_{t-s}\} = 0$ for all $s \neq 0$ by the assumed independence of the u_t and the fact that $E\{u_t\} = 0$ for all t, the first term drops out and we obtain:

$$E\{\varepsilon_t \varepsilon_{t-1}\} = \rho E\{\varepsilon_{t-1}^2\} = \rho \sigma^2\{\varepsilon_{t-1}\}$$

Hence, by (12.4), which holds for all t, we have:

$$\sigma\{\varepsilon_t, \varepsilon_{t-1}\} = \rho\left(\frac{\sigma^2}{1-\rho^2}\right)$$

5. The first-order autoregressive error process in models (12.1) and (12.2) is the simplest kind. A second-order process would be:

$$\varepsilon_t = \rho_1 \varepsilon_{t-1} + \rho_2 \varepsilon_{t-2} + u_t \tag{12.11}$$

Still higher-order processes could be postulated. Specialized approaches have been developed for complex autoregressive error processes. These are discussed in treatments of time series procedures and forecasting, such as in Reference 12.1. ∎

12.3   Durbin-Watson Test for Autocorrelation

The Durbin-Watson test for autocorrelation assumes the first-order autoregressive error models (12.1) or (12.2), with the values of the predictor variable(s) fixed. The test consists of determining whether or not the autocorrelation parameter ρ in (12.1) or (12.2) is zero. Note that if $\rho = 0$, then $\varepsilon_t = u_t$. Hence, the error terms ε_t are independent when $\rho = 0$ since the disturbance terms u_t are independent.

Because correlated error terms in business and economic applications tend to show positive serial correlation, the usual test alternatives considered are:

$$H_0: \rho = 0$$
$$H_a: \rho > 0 \tag{12.12}$$

The Durbin-Watson test statistic D is obtained by using ordinary least squares to fit the regression function, calculating the ordinary residuals:

$$e_t = Y_t - \hat{Y}_t \tag{12.13}$$

and then calculating the statistic:

$$D = \frac{\sum_{t=2}^{n}(e_t - e_{t-1})^2}{\sum_{t=1}^{n} e_t^2} \tag{12.14}$$

where n is the number of cases.

Exact critical values are difficult to obtain, but Durbin and Watson have obtained lower and upper bounds d_L and d_U such that a value of D outside these bounds leads to a definite decision. The decision rule for testing between the alternatives in (12.12) is:

If $D > d_U$, conclude H_0

If $D < d_L$, conclude H_a $\qquad\qquad$ (12.15)

If $d_L \leq D \leq d_U$, the test is inconclusive

Small values of D lead to the conclusion that $\rho > 0$ because the adjacent error terms ε_t and ε_{t-1} tend to be of the same magnitude when they are positively autocorrelated. Hence, the differences in the residuals, $e_t - e_{t-1}$, would tend to be small when $\rho > 0$, leading to a small numerator in D and hence to a small test statistic D.

Table B.7 contains the bounds d_L and d_U for various sample sizes (n), for two levels of significance (.05 and .01), and for various numbers of X variables $(p-1)$ in the regression model.

Example

The Blaisdell Company wished to predict its sales by using industry sales as a predictor variable. (Accurate predictions of industry sales are available from the industry's trade association.) A portion of the seasonally adjusted quarterly data on company sales and industry sales for the period 1998–2002 is shown in Table 12.2, columns 1 and 2. A scatter plot (not shown) suggested that a linear regression model is appropriate. The market research analyst was, however, concerned whether or not the error terms are positively autocorrelated.

The results of using ordinary least squares to fit a regression line to the data in Table 12.2 are shown at the bottom of Table 12.2. The residuals e_t are shown in column 3 of Table 12.2 and are plotted against time in Figure 12.3. Note how the residuals consistently are above or below the zero line for extended periods. Positive autocorrelation in the error terms is suggested by such a pattern when an appropriate regression function has been employed.

The analyst wished to confirm this graphic diagnosis by using the Durbin-Watson test for the alternatives:

$$H_0: \rho = 0$$

$$H_a: \rho > 0$$

Columns 4, 5, and 6 of Table 12.2 contain the necessary calculations for the test statistic D. The analyst then obtained:

$$D = \frac{\sum_{t=2}^{20}(e_t - e_{t-1})^2}{\sum_{t=1}^{20} e_t^2} = \frac{.09794}{.13330} = .735$$

TABLE 12.2   **Data, Regression Results, and Durbin-Watson Test Calculations—Blaisdell Company Example (Company and Industry Sales Data Are Seasonally Adjusted).**

Year and Quarter	t	(1) Company Sales ($ millions) Y_t	(2) Industry Sales ($ millions) X_t	(3) Residual e_t	(4) $e_t - e_{t-1}$	(5) $(e_t - e_{t-1})^2$	(6) e_t^2
1998: 1	1	20.96	127.3	−.026052	—	—	.0006787
2	2	21.40	130.0	−.062015	−.035963	.0012933	.0038459
3	3	21.96	132.7	.022021	.084036	.0070620	.0004849
4	4	21.52	129.4	.163754	.141733	.0200882	.0268154
...	...	...	...	...	...	...	...
2002: 1	17	27.52	164.2	.029112	−.076990	.0059275	.0008475
2	18	27.78	165.6	.042316	.013204	.0001743	.0017906
3	19	28.24	168.7	−.044160	−.086476	.0074781	.0019501
4	20	28.78	171.7	−.033009	.011151	.0001243	.0010896
Total						.0979400	.1333018

$$\hat{Y} = -1.4548 + .17628X$$

$$s\{b_0\} = .21415 \qquad s\{b_1\} = .00144$$

$$MSE = .00741$$

FIGURE 12.3
Residuals Plotted against Time— Blaisdell Company Example.

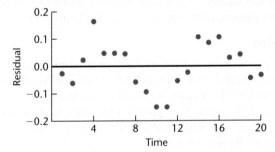

For level of significance of .01, we find in Table B.7 for $n = 20$ and $p - 1 = 1$:

$$d_L = .95 \qquad d_U = 1.15$$

Since $D = .735$ falls below $d_L = .95$, decision rule (12.15) indicates that the appropriate conclusion is H_a, namely, that the error terms are positively autocorrelated.

Comments

1. If a test for negative autocorrelation is required, the test statistic to be used is $4 - D$, where D is defined as above. The test is then conducted in the same manner described for testing for positive autocorrelation. That is, if the quantity $4 - D$ falls below d_L, we conclude $\rho < 0$, that negative autocorrelation exists, and so on.

2. A two-sided test for H_0: $\rho = 0$ versus H_a: $\rho \neq 0$ can be made by employing both one-sided tests separately. The Type I risk with the two-sided test is 2α, where α is the Type I risk for each one-sided test.

3. When the Durbin-Watson test employing the bounds d_L and d_U gives indeterminate results, in principle more cases are required. Of course, with time series data it may be impossible to obtain more cases, or additional cases may lie in the future and be obtainable only with great delay. Durbin and Watson (Ref. 12.2) do give an approximate test which may be used when the bounds test is indeterminate, but the degrees of freedom should be larger than about 40 before this approximate test will give more than a rough indication of whether autocorrelation exists.

A reasonable procedure is to treat indeterminate results as suggesting the presence of autocorrelated errors and employ one of the remedial actions to be discussed next. When remedial action does not lead to substantially different regression results as ordinary least squares, the assumption of uncorrelated error terms would appear to be satisfactory. When the remedial action does lead to substantially different regression results (such as larger estimated standard errors for the regression coefficients or the elimination of autocorrelated errors), the results obtained by means of the remedial action are probably the more useful ones.

4. The Durbin-Watson test is not robust against misspecifications of the model. For example, the Durbin-Watson test may not disclose the presence of autocorrelated errors that follow the second-order autoregressive pattern in (12.11).

5. The Durbin-Watson test is widely used; however, other tests for autocorrelation are available. One such test, due to Theil and Nagar, is found in Reference 12.3. ∎

12.4 Remedial Measures for Autocorrelation

The two principal remedial measures when autocorrelated error terms are present are to add one or more predictor variables to the regression model or to use transformed variables.

Addition of Predictor Variables

As noted earlier, one major cause of autocorrelated error terms is the omission from the model of one or more key predictor variables that have time-ordered effects on the response variable. When autocorrelated error terms are found to be present, the first remedial action should always be to search for missing key predictor variables. In an earlier illustration, we mentioned population size as a missing variable in a regression of annual sales of a product on average yearly price of the product during a 30-year period.

When the long-term persistent effects in a response variable cannot be captured by one or several predictor variables, a trend component can be added to the regression model, such as a linear trend or an exponential trend. Use of indicator variables for seasonal effects, as discussed on pages 319–321, can be helpful in eliminating or reducing autocorrelation in the error terms when the response variable is subject to seasonal effects (e.g., quarterly sales data).

Use of Transformed Variables

Only when use of additional predictor variables is not helpful in eliminating the problem of autocorrelated errors should a remedial action based on transformed variables be employed. A number of remedial procedures that rely on transformations of the variables have been developed. We shall explain three of these methods. Our explanation will be in terms of simple linear regression, but the extension to multiple regression is direct.

The three methods to be described are each based on an interesting property of the first-order autoregressive error term regression model (12.1). Consider the transformed dependent variable:

$$Y'_t = Y_t - \rho Y_{t-1}$$

Substituting in this expression for Y_t and Y_{t-1} according to regression model (12.1), we obtain:

$$Y'_t = (\beta_0 + \beta_1 X_t + \varepsilon_t) - \rho(\beta_0 + \beta_1 X_{t-1} + \varepsilon_{t-1})$$
$$= \beta_0(1 - \rho) + \beta_1(X_t - \rho X_{t-1}) + (\varepsilon_t - \rho \varepsilon_{t-1})$$

But, by (12.1), $\varepsilon_t - \rho \varepsilon_{t-1} = u_t$. Hence:

$$Y'_t = \beta_0(1 - \rho) + \beta_1(X_t - \rho X_{t-1}) + u_t \qquad \textbf{(12.16)}$$

where the u_t are the independent disturbance terms. Thus, when we use the transformed variable Y'_t, the regression model contains error terms that are independent. Further, model (12.16) is still a simple linear regression model with new X variable $X'_t = X_t - \rho X_{t-1}$, as may be seen by rewriting (12.16) as follows:

$$Y'_t = \beta'_0 + \beta'_1 X'_t + u_t \qquad \textbf{(12.17)}$$

where:

$$Y'_t = Y_t - \rho Y_{t-1}$$
$$X'_t = X_t - \rho X_{t-1}$$
$$\beta'_0 = \beta_0(1 - \rho)$$
$$\beta'_1 = \beta_1$$

Hence, by use of the transformed variables X'_t and Y'_t, we obtain a standard simple linear regression model with independent error terms. This means that ordinary least squares methods have their usual optimum properties with this model.

In order to be able to use the transformed model (12.17), one generally needs to estimate the autocorrelation parameter ρ since its value is usually unknown. The three methods to be described differ in how this is done. Often, however, the results obtained with the three methods are quite similar.

Once an estimate of ρ has been obtained, to be denoted by r, transformed variables are obtained using this estimate of ρ:

$$Y'_t = Y_t - r Y_{t-1} \qquad \textbf{(12.18a)}$$

$$X'_t = X_t - r X_{t-1} \qquad \textbf{(12.18b)}$$

Regression model (12.17) is then fitted to these transformed data, yielding an estimated regression function:

$$\hat{Y}' = b'_0 + b'_1 X' \qquad \textbf{(12.19)}$$

If this fitted regression function has eliminated the autocorrelation in the error terms, we can transform back to a fitted regression model in the original variables as follows:

$$\hat{Y} = b_0 + b_1 X \qquad \textbf{(12.20)}$$

where:

$$b_0 = \frac{b_0'}{1 - r} \qquad (12.20a)$$

$$b_1 = b_1' \qquad (12.20b)$$

The estimated standard deviations of the regression coefficients for the original variables can be obtained from those for the regression coefficients for the transformed variables as follows:

$$s\{b_0\} = \frac{s\{b_0'\}}{1 - r} \qquad (12.21a)$$

$$s\{b_1\} = s\{b_1'\} \qquad (12.21b)$$

Cochrane-Orcutt Procedure

The Cochrane-Orcutt procedure involves an iteration of three steps.

1. *Estimation of ρ.* This is accomplished by noting that the autoregressive error process assumed in model (12.1) can be viewed as a regression through the origin:

$$\varepsilon_t = \rho \varepsilon_{t-1} + u_t$$

where ε_t is the response variable, ε_{t-1} the predictor variable, u_t the error term, and ρ the slope of the line through the origin. Since the ε_t and ε_{t-1} are unknown, we use the residuals e_t and e_{t-1} obtained by ordinary least squares as the response and predictor variables, and estimate ρ by fitting a straight line through the origin. From our previous discussion of regression through the origin, we know by (4.14) that the estimate of the slope ρ, denoted by r, is:

$$r = \frac{\sum_{t=2}^{n} e_{t-1} e_t}{\sum_{t=2}^{n} e_{t-1}^2} \qquad (12.22)$$

2. *Fitting of transformed model (12.17).* Using the estimate r in (12.22), we next obtain the transformed variables Y_t' and X_t' in (12.18) and use ordinary least squares with these transformed variables to yield the fitted regression function (12.19).

3. *Test for need to iterate.* The Durbin-Watson test is then employed to test whether the error terms for the transformed model are uncorrelated. If the test indicates that they are uncorrelated, the procedure terminates. The fitted regression model in the original variables is then obtained by transforming the regression coefficients back according to (12.20).

If the Durbin-Watson test indicates that autocorrelation is still present after the first iteration, the parameter ρ is reestimated from the new residuals for the fitted regression model (12.20) with the original variables, which was derived from the fitted regression model (12.19) with the transformed variables. A new set of transformed variables is then obtained with the new r. This process may be continued for another iteration or two until the Durbin-Watson test suggests that the error terms in the transformed model are uncorrelated. If the process does not terminate after one or two iterations, a different procedure should be employed.

Example

For the Blaisdell Company example, the necessary calculations for estimating the autocorrelation parameter ρ, based on the residuals obtained with ordinary least squares applied to the original variables, are illustrated in Table 12.3. Column 1 repeats the residuals from

TABLE 12.3
Calculations for Estimating ρ with the Cochrane-Orcutt Procedure—Blaisdell Company Example.

t	(1) e_t	(2) e_{t-1}	(3) $e_{t-1}e_t$	(4) e_{t-1}^2
1	−.026052	—	—	—
2	−.062015	−.026052	.0016156	.0006787
3	.022021	−.062015	−.0013656	.0038459
4	.163754	.022021	.0036060	.0004849
...	...	...	...	...
17	.029112	.106102	.0030889	.0112576
18	.042316	.029112	.0012319	.0008475
19	−.044160	.042316	−.0018687	.0017906
20	−.033009	−.044160	.0014577	.0019501
Total			.0834478	.1322122

$$r = \frac{\sum e_{t-1}e_t}{\sum e_{t-1}^2} = \frac{.0834478}{.1322122} = .631166$$

TABLE 12.4
Transformed Variables and Regression Results for First Iteration with Cochrane-Orcutt Procedure—Blaisdell Company Example.

t	(1) Y_t	(2) X_t	(3) $Y_t' = Y_t - .631166Y_{t-1}$	(4) $X_t' = X_t - .631166X_{t-1}$
1	20.96	127.3	—	—
2	21.40	130.0	8.1708	49.653
3	21.96	132.7	8.4530	50.648
4	21.52	129.4	7.6596	45.644
...	...	...	...	...
17	27.52	164.2	10.4911	62.772
18	27.78	165.6	10.4103	61.963
19	28.24	168.7	10.7062	64.179
20	28.78	171.7	10.9559	65.222

$$\hat{Y}' = -.3941 + .17376X'$$

$$s\{b_0'\} = .1672 \qquad s\{b_1'\} = .002957$$

$$MSE = .00451$$

Table 12.2. Column 2 contains the residuals e_{t-1}, and columns 3 and 4 contain the necessary calculations. Hence, we estimate:

$$r = \frac{.0834478}{.1322122} = .631166$$

We now obtain the transformed variables Y_t' and X_t' in (12.18):

$$Y_t' = Y_t - .631166Y_{t-1}$$

$$X_t' = X_t - .631166X_{t-1}$$

These are found in Table 12.4. Columns 1 and 2 repeat the original variables Y_t and X_t, and columns 3 and 4 contain the transformed variables Y_t' and X_t'. Ordinary least squares fitting of linear regression is now used with these transformed variables based on the $n - 1$

cases remaining after the transformations. The fitted regression line and other regression results are shown at the bottom of Table 12.4. The fitted regression line in the transformed variables is:

$$\hat{Y}' = -.3941 + .17376X' \tag{12.23}$$

where:

$$Y'_t = Y_t - .631166Y_{t-1}$$
$$X'_t = X_t - .631166X_{t-1}$$

Since the random term in the transformed regression model (12.17) is the disturbance term u_t, $MSE = .00451$ is an estimate of the variance of this disturbance term; recall that $\sigma^2\{u_t\} = \sigma^2$.

From the fitted regression function for the transformed variables in (12.23), residuals were obtained and the Durbin-Watson statistic calculated. The result was (calculations not shown) $D = 1.65$. From Table B.7, we find for $\alpha = .01$, $p - 1 = 1$, and $n = 19$:

$$d_L = .93 \qquad d_U = 1.13$$

Since $D = 1.65 > d_U = 1.13$, we conclude that the autocorrelation coefficient for the error terms in the model with the transformed variables is zero.

Having successfully handled the problem of autocorrelated error terms, we now transform the fitted model in (12.23) back to the original variables, using (12.20):

$$b_0 = \frac{b'_0}{1 - r} = \frac{-.3941}{1 - .631166} = -1.0685$$
$$b_1 = b'_1 = .17376$$

leading to the fitted regression function in the original variables:

$$\hat{Y} = -1.0685 + .17376X \tag{12.24}$$

Finally, we obtain the estimated standard deviations of the regression coefficients for the original variables by using (12.21). From the results in Table 12.4, we find:

$$s\{b_0\} = \frac{s\{b'_0\}}{1 - r} = \frac{.1672}{1 - .631166} = .45332$$
$$s\{b_1\} = s\{b'_1\} = .002957$$

Comments

1. The Cochrane-Orcutt approach does not always work properly. A major reason is that when the error terms are positively autocorrelated, the estimate r in (12.22) tends to underestimate the autocorrelation parameter ρ. When this bias is serious, it can significantly reduce the effectiveness of the Cochrane-Orcutt approach.

2. There exists an approximate relation between the Durbin-Watson test statistic D in (12.14) and the estimated autocorrelation parameter r in (12.22):

$$D \approx 2(1 - r) \tag{12.25}$$

This relation indicates that the Durbin-Watson statistic ranges approximately between 0 and 4 since r takes on values between -1 and 1, and that D is approximately 2 when $r = 0$. Note that for the Blaisdell Company example ordinary least squares regression fit, $D = .735, r = .631$, and $2(1 - r) = .738$.

3. Under certain circumstances, it may be helpful to construct pseudotransformed values for period 1 so that the regression for the transformed variables is based on n, rather than $n - 1$, cases. Procedures for doing this are discussed in specialized texts such as Reference 12.4.

4. The least squares properties of the residuals, such as that the sum of the residuals is zero, apply to the residuals for the fitted regression function with the transformed variables, not to the residuals for the fitted regression function transformed back to the original variables. ∎

Hildreth-Lu Procedure

The Hildreth-Lu procedure for estimating the autocorrelation parameter ρ for use in the transformations (12.18) is analogous to the Box-Cox procedure for estimating the parameter λ in the power transformation of Y to improve the appropriateness of the standard regression model. The value of ρ chosen with the Hildreth-Lu procedure is the one that minimizes the error sum of squares for the transformed regression model (12.17):

$$SSE = \sum (Y_t' - \hat{Y}_t')^2 = \sum (Y_t' - b_0' - b_1' X_t')^2 \tag{12.26}$$

Computer programs are available to find the value of ρ that minimizes SSE. Alternatively, one can do a numerical search, running repeated regressions with different values of ρ for identifying the approximate magnitude of ρ that minimizes SSE. In the region of ρ that leads to minimum SSE, a finer search can be conducted to obtain a more precise value of ρ.

Once the value of ρ that minimizes SSE is found, the fitted regression function corresponding to that value of ρ is examined to see if the transformation has successfully eliminated the autocorrelation. If so, the fitted regression function in the original variables can then be obtained by means of (12.20).

Example

Table 12.5 contains the regression results for the Hildreth-Lu procedure when fitting the transformed regression model (12.17) to the Blaisdell Company data for different values of the autocorrelation parameter ρ. Note that SSE is minimized when ρ is near .96, so we shall let $r = .96$ be the estimate of ρ. The fitted regression function for the transformed variables corresponding to $r = .96$ and other regression results are given at the bottom of Table 12.5. The fitted regression function in the transformed variables is:

$$\hat{Y}' = .07117 + .16045X' \tag{12.27}$$

TABLE 12.5
Hildreth-Lu
Results—
Blaisdell
Company
Example.

ρ	SSE	ρ	SSE
.10	.1170	.94	.0718
.30	.0938	.95	.07171
.50	.0805	.96	.07167
.70	.0758	.97	.07175
.90	.0728	.98	.07197
.92	.0723		

For $\rho = .96$: $\hat{Y}' = .07117 + .16045X'$

$s\{b_0'\} = .05798$ $s\{b_1'\} = .006840$

$MSE = .00422$

where:

$$Y'_t = Y_t - .96Y_{t-1}$$
$$X'_t = X_t - .96X_{t-1}$$

The Durbin-Watson test statistic for this fitted model is $D = 1.73$. Since for $n = 19$, $p - 1 = 1$, and $\alpha = .01$ the upper critical value is $d_U = 1.13$, we conclude that no autocorrelation remains in the transformed model.

Therefore, we shall transform regression function (12.27) back to the original variables. Using (12.20), we obtain:

$$\hat{Y} = 1.7793 + .16045X \tag{12.28}$$

The estimated standard deviations of these regression coefficients are:

$$s\{b_0\} = 1.450 \qquad s\{b_1\} = .006840$$

Comments

1. The Hildreth-Lu procedure, unlike the Cochrane-Orcutt procedure, does not require any iterations once the estimate of the autocorrelation parameter ρ is obtained.

2. Note from Table 12.5 that SSE as a function of ρ is quite stable in a wide region around the minimum, as is often the case. It indicates that the numerical search for finding the best value of ρ need not be too fine unless there is particular interest in the intercept term β_0, since the estimate b_0 is sensitive to the value of r. ∎

First Differences Procedure

Since the autocorrelation parameter ρ is frequently large and SSE as a function of ρ often is quite flat for large values of ρ up to 1.0, as in the Blaisdell Company example, some economists and statisticians have suggested use of $\rho = 1.0$ in the transformed model (12.17). If $\rho = 1$, $\beta'_0 = \beta_0(1 - \rho) = 0$, and the transformed model (12.17) becomes:

$$Y'_t = \beta'_1 X'_t + u_t \tag{12.29}$$

where:

$$Y'_t = Y_t - Y_{t-1} \tag{12.29a}$$
$$X'_t = X_t - X_{t-1} \tag{12.29b}$$

Thus, again, the regression coefficient $\beta'_1 = \beta_1$ can be directly estimated by ordinary least squares methods, this time based on regression through the origin. Note that the transformed variables in (12.29a) and (12.29b) are ordinary first differences. It has been found that this first differences approach is effective in a variety of applications in reducing the autocorrelations of the error terms, and of course it is much simpler than the Cochrane-Orcutt and Hildreth-Lu procedures.

The fitted regression function in the transformed variables:

$$\hat{Y}' = b'_1 X' \tag{12.30}$$

can be transformed back to the original variables as follows:

$$\hat{Y} = b_0 + b_1 X \tag{12.31}$$

where:

$$b_0 = \bar{Y} - b_1' \bar{X} \tag{12.31a}$$

$$b_1 = b_1' \tag{12.31b}$$

Example

Table 12.6 illustrates the transformed variables Y_t' and X_t', based on the first differences transformations in (12.29a, b) for the Blaisdell Company example. Application of ordinary least squares for estimating a linear regression through the origin leads to the results shown at the bottom of Table 12.6. The fitted regression function in the transformed variables is:

$$\hat{Y}' = .16849X' \tag{12.32}$$

where:

$$Y_t' = Y_t - Y_{t-1}$$
$$X_t' = X_t - X_{t-1}$$

To examine whether the first differences procedure has removed the autocorrelations, we shall use the Durbin-Watson test. There are two points to note when using the Durbin-Watson test with the first differences procedure. Sometimes the first differences procedure can overcorrect, leading to negative autocorrelations in the error terms. Hence, it may be appropriate to use a two-sided Durbin-Watson test when testing for autocorrelation with first differences data. The second point is that the first differences model (12.29) has no intercept term, but the Durbin-Watson test requires a fitted regression with an intercept term. A valid test for autocorrelation in a no-intercept model can be carried out by fitting for this purpose a regression function with an intercept term. Of course, the fitted no-intercept model is still the model of basic interest.

In the Blaisdell Company example, the Durbin-Watson statistic for the fitted first differences regression model with an intercept term is $D = 1.75$. This indicates uncorrelated error terms for either a one-sided test (with $\alpha = .01$) or a two-sided test (with $\alpha = .02$).

With the first differences procedure successfully eliminating the autocorrelation, we return to a fitted model in the original variables by using (12.31):

$$\hat{Y} = -.30349 + .16849X \tag{12.33}$$

TABLE 12.6
First Differences and Regression Results with First Differences Procedure— Blaisdell Company Example.

		(1)	(2)	(3)	(4)
	t	Y_t	X_t	$Y_t' = Y_t - Y_{t-1}$	$X_t' = X_t - X_{t-1}$
	1	20.96	127.3	—	—
	2	21.40	130.0	.44	2.7
	3	21.96	132.7	.56	2.7
	4	21.52	129.4	−.44	−3.3
	...	...	...	...	...
	17	27.52	164.2	.54	3.5
	18	27.78	165.6	.26	1.4
	19	28.24	168.7	.46	3.1
	20	28.78	171.7	.54	3.0

$$\hat{Y}' = .16849X'$$

$$s\{b_1'\} = .005096 \qquad MSE = .00482$$

TABLE 12.7
Major
Regression
Results for
Three Trans-
formation
Procedures—
Blaisdell
Company
Example.

Procedure	b_1	$s\{b_1\}$	r	Estimate of σ^2 (MSE)
Cochrane-Orcutt	.1738	.0030	.63	.0045
Hildreth-Lu	.1605	.0068	.96	.0042
First differences	.1685	.0051	1.0	.0048
Ordinary least squares	.1763	.0014	—	—

where:

$$b_0 = 24.569 - .16849(147.62) = -.30349$$

We know from Table 12.6 that the estimated standard deviation of b_1 is $s\{b_1\} = .005096$
since $b_1 = b_1'$.

Comparison of Three Methods

Table 12.7 contains some of the main regression results for the three transformation methods
and also for the ordinary least squares regression fit to the original variables. A number of
key points stand out:

1. All of the estimates of β_1 are quite close to each other.
2. The estimated standard deviations of b_1 based on Hildreth-Lu and first differences transformation methods are quite close to each other; that with the Cochrane-Orcutt procedure is somewhat smaller. The estimated standard deviation of b_1 based on ordinary
   least squares regression with the original variables is still smaller. This is as expected,
   since we noted earlier that the estimated standard deviations $s\{b_k\}$ calculated according
   to ordinary least squares may seriously underestimate the true standard deviations $\sigma\{b_k\}$
   when positive autocorrelation is present.
3. All three transformation methods provide essentially the same estimate of σ^2, the variance of the disturbance terms u_t.

The three transformation methods do not always work equally well, as happens to be the
case here for the Blaisdell Company example. The Cochrane-Orcutt procedure may fail to
remove autocorrelation in one or two iterations, in which case the Hildreth-Lu or the first
differences procedures may be preferable. When several of the transformation methods are
effective in removing autocorrelation, then simplicity of calculations may be considered in
choosing from among these procedures.

Comment

Further discussions of the Cochrane-Orcutt, Hildreth-Lu, and first differences procedures, as well as
of other remedial procedures for autocorrelated errors, may be found in specialized texts, such as
Reference 12.4. ∎

12.5 Forecasting with Autocorrelated Error Terms

One important use of autoregressive error regression models is to make forecasts. With these models, information about the error term in the most recent period n can be incorporated into the forecast for period $n + 1$. This provides a more accurate forecast because, when autoregressive error regression models are appropriate, the error terms in successive periods are correlated. Thus, if sales in period n are above their expected value and successive error terms are positively correlated, it follows that sales in period $n + 1$ will likely be above their expected value also.

We shall explain the basic ideas underlying the development of forecasts using the presence of autocorrelated error terms by again employing the simple linear autoregressive error term regression model (12.1). The extension to multiple regression model (12.2) is direct. First, we consider forecasting when either the Cochrane-Orcutt or the Hildreth-Lu procedure has been utilized for estimating the regression parameters.

When we express regression model (12.1):

$$Y_t = \beta_0 + \beta_1 X_t + \varepsilon_t$$

by using the structure of the error terms:

$$\varepsilon_t = \rho \varepsilon_{t-1} + u_t$$

we obtain:

$$Y_t = \beta_0 + \beta_1 X_t + \rho \varepsilon_{t-1} + u_t$$

For period $n + 1$, we obtain:

$$Y_{n+1} = \beta_0 + \beta_1 X_{n+1} + \rho \varepsilon_n + u_{n+1} \tag{12.34}$$

Thus, Y_{n+1} is made up of three components:

1. The expected value $\beta_0 + \beta_1 X_{n+1}$.
2. A multiple ρ of the preceding error term ε_n.
3. An independent, random disturbance term with $E\{u_{n+1}\} = 0$.

The forecast for next period $n + 1$, to be denoted by F_{n+1}, is constructed by dealing with each of the three components in (12.34):

1. Given X_{n+1}, we estimate the expected value $\beta_0 + \beta_1 X_{n+1}$ as usual from the fitted regression function:

$$\hat{Y}_{n+1} = b_0 + b_1 X_{n+1}$$

where b_0 and b_1 are the estimated regression coefficients for the original variables obtained from b_0' and b_1' for the transformed variables according to (12.20).

2. ρ is estimated by r in (12.22), and ε_n is estimated by the residual e_n:

$$e_n = Y_n - (b_0 + b_1 X_n) = Y_n - \hat{Y}_n$$

Thus, $\rho \varepsilon_n$ is estimated by $r e_n$.

3. The disturbance term u_{n+1} has expected value zero and is independent of earlier information. Hence, we use its expected value of zero in the forecast.

Thus, the forecast for period $n + 1$ is:

$$F_{n+1} = \hat{Y}_{n+1} + r e_n \tag{12.35}$$

An approximate $1 - \alpha$ prediction interval for $Y_{n+1(\text{new})}$, the new observation on the response variable, may be obtained by employing the usual prediction limits for a new observation in (2.36), but based on the transformed observations. Thus, Y_i and X_i in formula (2.38a) for the estimated variance $s^2\{\text{pred}\}$ are replaced by Y'_t and X'_t as defined in (12.18).

The approximate $1 - \alpha$ prediction limits for $Y_{n+1(\text{new})}$ with simple linear regression therefore are:

$$F_{n+1} \pm t(1 - \alpha/2; n - 3)s\{\text{pred}\} \tag{12.36}$$

where $s\{\text{pred}\}$, defined in (2.38a), is here based on the transformed observations. Note the use of $n - 3$ degrees of freedom for the t multiple, since there are only $n - 1$ transformed cases and two degrees of freedom are lost for estimating the two parameters in the simple linear regression function.

When forecasts are based on the first differences procedure, the forecast in (12.35) is still applicable, but $r = 1$ now. The estimated standard deviation $s\{\text{pred}\}$ now is calculated according to formula (4.20) in Table 4.1 for one predictor variable, using the transformed variables. Finally, the degrees of freedom for the t multiple in (12.36) will be $n - 2$, since only one parameter has to be estimated in the no-intercept regression model (12.29).

Example

For the Blaisdell Company example, the trade association has projected that deseasonalized industry sales in the first quarter of 2003 (i.e., quarter 21) will be $X_{21} = \$175.3$ million. To forecast Blaisdell Company sales for quarter 21, we shall use the Cochrane-Orcutt fitted regression function (12.24):

$$\hat{Y} = -1.0685 + .17376X$$

First, we need to obtain the residual e_{20}:

$$e_{20} = Y_{20} - \hat{Y}_{20} = 28.78 - [-1.0685 + .17376(171.7)] = .0139$$

The fitted value when $X_{21} = 175.3$ is:

$$\hat{Y}_{21} = -1.0685 + .17376(175.3) = 29.392$$

The forecast for period 21 then is:

$$F_{21} = \hat{Y}_{21} + re_{20} = 29.392 + .631166(.0139) = 29.40$$

Note how the fact that company sales in quarter 20 were slightly above their estimated mean has a small positive influence on the forecast for company sales for quarter 21.

We wish to set up a 95 percent prediction interval for $Y_{21(\text{new})}$. Using the data for the transformed variables in Table 12.4, we calculate $s\{\text{pred}\}$ by (2.38) for:

$$X'_{n+1} = X_{n+1} - .631166X_n = 175.3 - .631166(171.7) = 66.929$$

We obtain $s\{\text{pred}\} = .0757$ (calculations not shown). We require $t(.975; 17) = 2.110$. We therefore obtain the prediction limits $29.40 \pm 2.110(.0757)$ and the prediction interval:

$$29.24 \leq Y_{21(\text{new})} \leq 29.56$$

Given quarter 20 seasonally adjusted company sales of \$28.78 million and other past sales, and given quarter 21 industry sales of \$175.3 million, we predict with approximately 95 percent confidence that seasonally adjusted Blaisdell Company sales in quarter 21 will be between \$29.24 and \$29.56 million.

To obtain a forecast of actual sales including seasonal effects in quarter 21, the Blaisdell Company still needs to incorporate the first quarter seasonal effect into the forecast of seasonally adjusted sales.

The forecasts with the other transformation procedures are very similar to the one with the Cochrane-Orcutt procedure. With the first differences estimated regression function (12.33), the forecast for quarter 21 is:

$$F_{21} = [-.30349 + .16849(175.3)] + 1.0[28.78 + .30349 - .16849(171.70)] = 29.39$$

The estimated standard deviation $s\{\text{pred}\}$ calculated according to (4.20) with the transformed data in Table 12.6 is $s\{\text{pred}\} = .0718$ (calculations not shown). For a 95 percent prediction interval, we require $t(.975; 18) = 2.101$. The prediction limits therefore are $29.39 \pm 2.101(.0718)$ and the approximate 95 percent prediction interval is:

$$29.24 \leq Y_{21(\text{new})} \leq 29.54$$

This forecast is practically the same as that with the Cochrane-Orcutt estimates.

The approximate 95 percent prediction interval with the estimated regression function (12.28) based on the Hildreth-Lu procedure is (calculations not shown):

$$29.24 \leq Y_{21(\text{new})} \leq 29.52$$

This forecast is practically the same as the other two.

Comments

1. Forecasts obtained with autoregressive error regression models (12.1) and (12.2) are conditional on the past observations Y_n, Y_{n-1}, etc. They are also conditional on X_{n+1}, which often has to be projected as in the Blaisdell Company example.

2. Forecasts for two or more periods ahead can also be developed, using the recursive relations of ε_t to earlier error terms developed in Section 12.2. For example, given X_{n+2} the forecast for period $n + 2$, based on either Cochrane-Orcutt or Hildreth-Lu estimates, is:

$$F_{n+2} = \hat{Y}_{n+2} + r^2 e_n \tag{12.37}$$

For the first differences estimates, the forecast in (12.37) is calculated with $r = 1$.

3. The approximate prediction limits (12.36) assume that the value of r used in the transformations (12.18) is the true value of ρ; that is, $r = \rho$. If that is the case, the standard regression assumptions apply since we are then dealing with the transformed model (12.17). To see that the prediction limits obtained from the transformed model are applicable to the forecast F_{n+1} in (12.35), recall that $\sigma^2\{\text{pred}\}$ in (2.37) is the variance of the difference $Y_{h(\text{new})} - \hat{Y}_h$. In terms of the situation here for the transformed variables, we have the following correspondences:

$$Y_{h(\text{new})} \text{ corresponds to } Y'_{n+1} = Y_{n+1} - rY_n$$

$$\hat{Y}_h \text{ corresponds to } \hat{Y}'_{n+1} = b'_0 + b'_1 X'_{n+1} = b_0(1 - r) + b_1(X_{n+1} - rX_n)$$

The difference $Y'_{n+1} - \hat{Y}'_{n+1}$ is:

$$\begin{aligned}
Y'_{n+1} - \hat{Y}'_{n+1} &= (Y_{n+1} - rY_n) - b_0(1 - r) - b_1(X_{n+1} - rX_n) \\
&= Y_{n+1} - (b_0 + b_1 X_{n+1}) - r(Y_n - b_0 - b_1 X_n) \\
&= Y_{n+1} - \hat{Y}_{n+1} - re_n \\
&= Y_{n+1} - F_{n+1}
\end{aligned}$$

Hence, Y_{n+1} plays the role of $Y_{h(\text{new})}$ and F_{n+1} plays the role of $\hat{Y}_h$ in (2.37). The prediction limits (12.36) are approximate because r is only an estimate of ρ. ∎

Cited References

12.1. Box, G. E. P., and G. M. Jenkins. *Time Series Analysis, Forecasting and Control.* Rev. ed. San Francisco: Holden-Day, 1976.

12.2. Durbin, J., and G. S. Watson. "Testing for Serial Correlation in Least Squares Regression. II," *Biometrika* 38 (1951), pp. 159–78.

12.3. Theil, H., and A. L. Nagar. "Testing the Independence of Regression Disturbances," *Journal of the American Statistical Association* 56 (1961), pp. 793–806.

12.4. Greene, W. H. *Econometric Analysis,* 5th ed. Upper Saddle River, New Jersey: Prentice Hall, 2003.

Problems

12.1. Refer to Table 12.1.

    a. Plot ε_t against ε_{t-1} for $t = 1, \ldots, 10$ on a graph. How is the positive first-order autocorrelation in the error terms shown by the plot?

    b. If you plotted u_t against ε_{t-1} for $t = 1, \ldots, 10$, what pattern would you expect?

12.2. Refer to **Plastic hardness** Problem 1.22. If the same test item were measured at 12 different points in time, would the error terms in the regression model likely be autocorrelated? Discuss.

12.3. A student stated that the first-order autoregressive error models (12.1) and (12.2) are too simple for business time series data because the error term in period t in such data is also influenced by random effects that occurred more than one period in the past. Comment.

12.4. A student writing a term paper used ordinary least squares in fitting a simple linear regression model to some time series data containing positively autocorrelated errors, and found that the 90 percent confidence interval for β_1 was too wide to be useful. The student then decided to employ regression model (12.1) to improve the precision of the estimate. Comment.

12.5. For each of the following tests concerning the autocorrelation parameter ρ in regression model (12.2) with three predictor variables, state the appropriate decision rule based on the Durbin-Watson test statistic for a sample of size 38: (1) $H_0: \rho = 0$, $H_a: \rho \neq 0$, $\alpha = .02$; (2) $H_0: \rho = 0$, $H_a: \rho < 0$, $\alpha = .05$; (3) $H_0: \rho = 0$, $H_a: \rho > 0$, $\alpha = .01$.

*12.6. Refer to **Copier maintenance** Problem 1.20. The observations are listed in time order. Assume that regression model (12.1) is appropriate. Test whether or not positive autocorrelation is present; use $\alpha = .01$. State the alternatives, decision rule, and conclusion.

12.7. Refer to **Grocery retailer** Problem 6.9. The observations are listed in time order. Assume that regression model (12.2) is appropriate. Test whether or not positive autocorrelation is present; use $\alpha = .05$. State the alternatives, decision rule, and conclusion.

12.8. Refer to **Crop yield** Problem 11.25. The observations are listed in time order. Assume that regression model (12.2) with first- and second-order terms for the two predictor variables and no interaction term is appropriate. Test whether or not positive autocorrelation is present; use $\alpha = .01$. State the alternatives, decision rule, and conclusion.

*12.9. **Microcomputer components.** A staff analyst for a manufacturer of microcomputer components has compiled monthly data for the past 16 months on the value of industry production of processing units that use these components (X, in million dollars) and the value of the firm's components used (Y, in thousand dollars). The analyst believes that a simple linear regression relation is appropriate but anticipates positive autocorrelation. The data follow:

t:	1	2	3	$\ldots$	14	15	16
X_t:	2.052	2.026	2.002	$\ldots$	2.080	2.102	2.150
Y_t:	102.9	101.5	100.8	$\ldots$	104.8	105.0	107.2

a. Fit a simple linear regression model by ordinary least squares and obtain the residuals. Also obtain $s\{b_0\}$ and $s\{b_1\}$.

b. Plot the residuals against time and explain whether you find any evidence of positive autocorrelation.

c. Conduct a formal test for positive autocorrelation using $\alpha = .05$. State the alternatives, decision rule, and conclusion. Is the residual analysis in part (b) in accord with the test result?

*12.10. Refer to **Microcomputer components** Problem 12.9. The analyst has decided to employ regression model (12.1) and use the Cochrane-Orcutt procedure to fit the model.

a. Obtain a point estimate of the autocorrelation parameter. How well does the approximate relationship (12.25) hold here between this point estimate and the Durbin-Watson test statistic?

b. Use one iteration to obtain the estimates b_0' and b_1' of the regression coefficients β_0' and β_1' in transformed model (12.17) and state the estimated regression function. Also obtain $s\{b_0'\}$ and $s\{b_1'\}$.

c. Test whether any positive autocorrelation remains after the first iteration using $\alpha = .05$. State the alternatives, decision rule, and conclusion.

d. Restate the estimated regression function obtained in part (b) in terms of the original variables. Also obtain $s\{b_0\}$ and $s\{b_1\}$. Compare the estimated regression coefficients obtained with the Cochrane-Orcutt procedure and their estimated standard deviations with those obtained with ordinary least squares in Problem 12.9a.

e. On the basis of the results in parts (c) and (d), does the Cochrane-Orcutt procedure appear to have been effective here?

f. The value of industry production in month 17 will be $2.210 million. Predict the value of the firm's components used in month 17; employ a 95 percent prediction interval. Interpret your interval.

g. Estimate β_1 with a 95 percent confidence interval. Interpret your interval.

*12.11. Refer to **Microcomputer components** Problem 12.9. Assume that regression model (12.1) is applicable.

a. Use the Hildreth-Lu procedure to obtain a point estimate of the autocorrelation parameter. Do a search at the values $\rho = .1, .2, \ldots, 1.0$ and select from these the value of ρ that minimizes *SSE*.

b. From your estimate in part (a), obtain an estimate of the transformed regression function (12.17). Also obtain $s\{b_0'\}$ and $s\{b_1'\}$.

c. Test whether any positive autocorrelation remains in the transformed regression model; use $\alpha = .05$. State the alternatives, decision rule, and conclusion.

d. Restate the estimated regression function obtained in part (b) in terms of the original variables. Also obtain $s\{b_0\}$ and $s\{b_1\}$. Compare the estimated regression coefficients obtained with the Hildreth-Lu procedure and their estimated standard deviations with those obtained with ordinary least squares in Problem 12.9a.

e. Based on the results in parts (c) and (d), has the Hildreth-Lu procedure been effective here?

f. The value of industry production in month 17 will be $2.210 million. Predict the value of the firm's components used in month 17; employ a 95 percent prediction interval. Interpret your interval.

g. Estimate β_1 with a 95 percent confidence interval. Interpret your interval.

*12.12. Refer to **Microcomputer components** Problem 12.9. Assume that regression model (12.1) is applicable and that the first differences procedure is to be employed.

   a. Estimate the regression coefficient β_1' in the transformed regression model (12.29), and obtain the estimated standard deviation of this estimate. State the estimated regression function.

   b. Test whether or not the error terms with the first differences procedure are autocorrelated, using a two-sided test and $\alpha = .10$. State the alternatives, decision rule, and conclusion. Why is a two-sided test meaningful here?

   c. Restate the estimated regression function obtained in part (a) in terms of the original variables. Also obtain $s\{b_1\}$. Compare the estimated regression coefficients obtained with the first differences procedure and the estimated standard deviation $s\{b_1\}$ with the results obtained with ordinary least squares in Problem 12.9a.

   d. On the basis of the results in parts (b) and (c), has the first differences procedure been effective here?

   e. The value of industry production in month 17 will be $2.210 million. Predict the value of the firm's components used in month 17; employ a 95 percent prediction interval. Interpret your interval.

   f. Estimate β_1 with a 95 percent confidence interval. Interpret your interval.

12.13. **Advertising agency.** The managing partner of an advertising agency is interested in the possibility of making accurate predictions of monthly billings. Monthly data on amount of billings (Y, in thousands of constant dollars) and on number of hours of staff time (X, in thousand hours) for the 20 most recent months follow. A simple linear regression model is believed to be appropriate, but positively autocorrelated error terms may be present.

t:	1	2	3	...	18	19	20
X_t:	2.521	2.171	2.234	...	3.117	3.623	3.618
Y_t:	220.4	203.9	207.2	...	252.4	278.6	278.5

   a. Fit a simple linear regression model by ordinary least squares and obtain the residuals. Also obtain $s\{b_0\}$ and $s\{b_1\}$.

   b. Plot the residuals against time and explain whether you find any evidence of positive autocorrelation.

   c. Conduct a formal test for positive autocorrelation using $\alpha = .01$. State the alternatives, decision rule, and conclusion. Is the residual analysis in part (b) in accord with the test result?

12.14. Refer to **Advertising agency** Problem 12.13. Assume that regression model (12.1) is applicable and that the Cochrane-Orcutt procedure is to be employed.

   a. Obtain a point estimate of the autocorrelation parameter. How well does the approximate relationship (12.25) hold here between the point estimate and the Durbin-Watson test statistic?

   b. Use one iteration to obtain the estimates b_0' and b_1' of the regression coefficients β_0' and β_1' in transformed model (12.17) and state the estimated regression function. Also obtain $s\{b_0'\}$ and $s\{b_1'\}$.

   c. Test whether any positive autocorrelation remains after the first iteration using $\alpha = .01$. State the alternatives, decision rule, and conclusion.

   d. Restate the estimated regression function obtained in part (b) in terms of the original variables. Also obtain $s\{b_0\}$ and $s\{b_1\}$. Compare the estimated regression coefficients obtained with the Cochrane-Orcutt procedure and their estimated standard deviations with those obtained with ordinary least squares in Problem 12.13a.

   e. Based on the results in parts (c) and (d), does the Cochrane-Orcutt procedure appear to have been effective here?

   f. Staff time in month 21 is expected to be 3.625 thousand hours. Predict the amount of billings in constant dollars for month 21, using a 99 percent prediction interval. Interpret your interval.

   g. Estimate β_1 with a 99 percent confidence interval. Interpret your interval.

12.15. Refer to **Advertising agency** Problem 12.13. Assume that regression model (12.1) is applicable.

   a. Use the Hildreth-Lu procedure to obtain a point estimate of the autocorrelation parameter. Do a search at the values $\rho = .1, .2, \ldots, 1.0$ and select from these the value of ρ that minimizes *SSE*.

   b. Based on your estimate in part (a), obtain an estimate of the transformed regression function (12.17). Also obtain $s\{b_0'\}$ and $s\{b_1'\}$.

   c. Test whether any positive autocorrelation remains in the transformed regression model; use $\alpha = .01$. State the alternatives, decision rule, and conclusion.

   d. Restate the estimated regression function obtained in part (b) in terms of the original variables. Also obtain $s\{b_0\}$ and $s\{b_1\}$. Compare the estimated regression coefficients obtained with the Hildreth-Lu procedure and their estimated standard deviations with those obtained with ordinary least squares in Problem 12.13a.

   e. Based on the results in parts (c) and (d), has the Hildreth-Lu procedure been effective here?

   f. Staff time in month 21 is expected to be 3.625 thousand hours. Predict the amount of billings in constant dollars for month 21, using a 99 percent prediction interval. Interpret your interval.

   g. Estimate β_1 with a 99 percent confidence interval. Interpret your interval.

12.16. Refer to **Advertising agency** Problem 12.13. Assume that regression model (12.1) is applicable and that the first differences procedure is to be employed.

   a. Estimate the regression coefficient β_1' in the transformed regression model (12.29) and obtain the estimated standard deviation of this estimate. State the estimated regression function.

   b. Test whether or not the error terms with the first differences procedure are autocorrelated, using a two-sided test and $\alpha = .02$. State the alternatives, decision rule, and conclusion. Why is a two-sided test meaningful here?

   c. Restate the estimated regression function obtained in part (a) in terms of the original variables. Also obtain $s\{b_1\}$. Compare the estimated regression coefficients obtained with the first differences procedure and the estimated standard deviation $s\{b_1\}$ with the results obtained with ordinary least squares in Problem 12.13a.

   d. Based on the results in parts (b) and (c), has the first differences procedure been effective here?

   e. Staff time in month 21 is expected to be 3.625 thousand hours. Predict the amount of billings in constant dollars for month 21, using a 99 percent prediction interval. Interpret your interval.

   f. Estimate β_1 with a 99 percent confidence interval. Interpret your interval.

12.17. **McGill Company sales.** The data below show seasonally adjusted quarterly sales for the McGill Company (Y, in million dollars) and for the entire industry (X, in million dollars) for the most recent 20 quarters.

t:	1	2	3	...	18	19	20
X_t:	127.3	130.0	132.7	...	165.6	168.7	172.0
Y_t:	20.96	21.40	21.96	...	27.78	28.24	28.78

a. Would you expect the autocorrelation parameter ρ to be positive, negative, or zero here?

b. Fit a simple linear regression model by ordinary least squares and obtain the residuals. Also obtain $s\{b_0\}$ and $s\{b_1\}$.

c. Plot the residuals against time and explain whether you find any evidence of positive autocorrelation.

d. Conduct a formal test for positive autocorrelation using $\alpha = .01$. State the alternatives, decision rule, and conclusion. Is the residual analysis in part (c) in accord with the test result?

12.18. Refer to **McGill Company sales** Problem 12.17. Assume that regression model (12.1) is applicable and that the Cochrane-Orcutt procedure is to be employed.

a. Obtain a point estimate of the autocorrelation parameter. How well does the approximate relationship (12.25) hold here between the point estimate and the Durbin-Watson test statistic?

b. Use one iteration to obtain the estimates b_0' and b_1' of the regression coefficients β_0' and β_1' in transformed model (12.17) and state the estimated regression function. Also obtain $s\{b_0'\}$ and $s\{b_1'\}$.

c. Test whether any positive autocorrelation remains after the first iteration; use $\alpha = .01$. State the alternatives, decision rule, and conclusion.

d. Restate the estimated regression function obtained in part (b) in terms of the original variables. Also obtain $s\{b_0\}$ and $s\{b_1\}$. Compare the estimated regression coefficients obtained with the Cochrane-Orcutt procedure and their estimated standard deviations with those obtained with ordinary least squares in Problem 12.17b.

e. On the basis of the results in parts (c) and (d), does the Cochrane-Orcutt procedure appear to have been effective here?

f. Industry sales for quarter 21 are expected to be $181.0 million. Predict the McGill Company sales for quarter 21, using a 90 percent prediction interval. Interpret your interval.

g. Estimate β_1 with a 90 percent confidence interval. Interpret your interval.

12.19. Refer to **McGill Company sales** Problem 12.17. Assume that regression model (12.1) is applicable.

a. Use the Hildreth-Lu procedure to obtain a point estimate of the autocorrelation parameter. Do a search at the values $\rho = .1, .2, \ldots, 1.0$ and select from these the value of ρ that minimizes SSE.

b. Based on your estimate in part (a), obtain an estimate of the transformed regression function (12.17). Also obtain $s\{b_0'\}$ and $s\{b_1'\}$.

c. Test whether any positive autocorrelation remains in the transformed regression model; use $\alpha = .01$. State the alternatives, decision rule, and conclusion.

d. Restate the estimated regression function obtained in part (b) in terms of the original variables. Also obtain $s\{b_0\}$ and $s\{b_1\}$. Compare the estimated regression coefficients obtained with the Hildreth-Lu procedure and their estimated standard deviations with those obtained with ordinary least squares in Problem 12.17b.

e. Based on the results in parts (c) and (d), has the Hildreth-Lu procedure been effective here?

f. Industry sales for quarter 21 are expected to be $181.0 million. Predict the McGill Company sales for quarter 21, using a 90 percent prediction interval. Interpret your interval.

g. Estimate β_1 with a 90 percent confidence interval. Interpret your interval.

12.20. Refer to **McGill Company sales** Problem 12.17. Assume that regression model (12.1) is applicable and that the first differences procedure is to be employed.

a. Estimate the regression coefficient β_1' in the transformed regression model (12.29) and obtain the estimated standard deviation of this estimate. State the estimated regression function.

b. Test whether or not the error terms with the first differences procedure are positively autocorrelated using $\alpha = .01$. State the alternatives, decision rule, and conclusion.

c. Restate the estimated regression function obtained in part (a) in terms of the original variables. Also obtain $s\{b_1\}$. Compare the estimated regression coefficients obtained with the first differences procedure and the estimated standard deviation $s\{b_1\}$ with the results obtained with ordinary least squares in Problem 12.17b.

d. On the basis of the results in parts (b) and (c), has the first differences procedure been effective here?

e. Industry sales for quarter 21 are expected to be $181.0 million. Predict the McGill Company sales for quarter 21, using a 90 percent prediction interval. Interpret your interval.

f. Estimate β_1 with a 90 percent confidence interval. Interpret your interval.

12.21. A student applying the first differences transformations in (12.29a, b) found that several X_t' values equaled zero but that the corresponding Y_t' values were nonzero. Does this signify that the first differences transformations are not appropriate for the data?

Exercises

12.22. Derive (12.7) for $s = 2$.

12.23. Refer to first-order autoregressive error model (12.1). Suppose Y_t is company's percent share of the market, X_t is company's selling price as a percent of average competitive selling price, $\beta_0 = 100$, $\beta_1 = -.35$, $\rho = .6$, $\sigma^2 = 1$, and $\varepsilon_0 = 2.403$. Let X_t and u_t be as follows for $t = 1, \ldots, 10$:

t:	1	2	3	4	5	6	7	8	9	10
X_t:	100	115	120	90	85	75	70	95	105	110
u_t:	.764	.509	−.242	−1.808	−.485	.501	−.539	.434	−.299	.030

a. Plot the true regression line. Generate the observations Y_t ($t = 1, \ldots, 10$), and plot these on the same graph. Fit a least squares regression line to the generated observations Y_t and plot it also on the same graph. How does your fitted regression line relate to the true line?

b. Repeat the steps in part (a) but this time let $\rho = 0$. In which of the two cases does the fitted regression line come closer to the true line? Is this the expected outcome?

c. Generate the observations Y_t for $\rho = -.7$. For each of the cases $\rho = .6$, $\rho = 0$, and $\rho = -.7$, obtain the successive error term differences $\varepsilon_t - \varepsilon_{t-1}$ ($t = 1, \ldots, 10$).

d. For which of the three cases in part (c) is $\sum (\varepsilon_t - \varepsilon_{t-1})^2$ smallest? For which is it largest? What generalization does this suggest?

12.24. For multiple regression model (12.2) with $p - 1 = 2$, derive the transformed model in which the random terms are uncorrelated.

12.25. Suppose the autoregressive error process for the model $Y_t = \beta_0 + \beta_1 X_t + \varepsilon_t$ is that given by (12.11).

    a. What would be the transformed variables Y_t' and X_t' for which the random terms in the regression model are uncorrelated?

    b. How would you estimate the parameters ρ_1 and ρ_2 for use with the Cochrane-Orcutt procedure?

    c. How would you estimate the parameters ρ_1 and ρ_2 with the Hildreth-Lu procedure?

12.26. Derive the forecast F_{n+1} for a simple linear regression model with the second-order autoregressive error process (12.11).

Projects

12.27. The true regression model is $Y_t = 10 + 24X_t + \varepsilon_t$, where $\varepsilon_t = .8\varepsilon_{t-1} + u_t$ and u_t are independent $N(0, 25)$.

    a. Generate 11 independent random numbers from $N(0, 25)$. Use the first random number as ε_0, obtain the 10 error terms $\varepsilon_1, \ldots, \varepsilon_{10}$, and then calculate the 10 observations $Y_1, \ldots, Y_{10}$ corresponding to $X_1 = 1, X_2 = 2, \ldots, X_{10} = 10$. Fit a linear regression function by ordinary least squares and calculate *MSE*.

    b. Repeat part (a) 100 times, using new random numbers each time.

    c. Calculate the mean of the 100 estimates of b_1. Does it appear that b_1 is an unbiased estimator of β_1 despite the presence of positive autocorrelation?

    d. Calculate the mean of the 100 estimates of *MSE*. Does it appear that *MSE* is a biased estimator of σ^2? If so, does the magnitude of the bias appear to be small or large?

Case Studies

12.28. Refer to the **Website developer** data set in Appendix C.6 and Case Study 9.29. The observations are listed in time order. Using the model developed in Case Study 9.29, test whether or not positive autocorrelation is present; use $\alpha = .01$. If autocorrelation is present, revise the model and analysis as needed.

12.29. Refer to the **Heating equipment** data set in Appendix C.8. The observations are listed in time order. Develop a reasonable predictor model for the monthly heating equipment orders. Potential predictors include new homes for sale, current monthly deviation of temperature from historical average temperature, the prime lending rate, current distributor inventory levels, the amount of distributor sell through, and the level of discounting being offered. Your analysis should determine whether or not autocorrelation is present using $\alpha = .05$. If autocorrelation is present, revise the model and analysis as needed.

Part III

Nonlinear Regression

13

Introduction to Nonlinear Regression and Neural Networks

The linear regression models considered up to this point are generally satisfactory approximations for most regression applications. There are occasions, however, when an empirically indicated or a theoretically justified nonlinear regression model is more appropriate. For example, growth from birth to maturity in human subjects typically is nonlinear in nature, characterized by rapid growth shortly after birth, pronounced growth during puberty, and a leveling off sometime before adulthood. In another example, dose-response relationships tend to be nonlinear with little or no change in response for low dose levels of a drug, followed by rapid S-shaped changes occurring in the more active dose region, and finally with dose response leveling off as it reaches a saturated level. We shall consider in this chapter and the next some nonlinear regression models, how to obtain estimates of the regression parameters in such models, and how to make inferences about these regression parameters.

In this chapter, we introduce exponential nonlinear regression models and present the basic methods of nonlinear regression. We also introduce neural network models, which are now widely used in data mining applications. In Chapter 14, we present logistic regression models and consider their uses when the response variable is binary or categorical with more than two levels.

13.1 Linear and Nonlinear Regression Models

Linear Regression Models

In previous chapters, we considered linear regression models, i.e., models that are linear in the parameters. Such models can be represented by the general linear regression model (6.7):

$$Y_i = \beta_0 + \beta_1 X_{i1} + \beta_2 X_{i2} + \cdots + \beta_{p-1} X_{i,p-1} + \varepsilon_i \tag{13.1}$$

Linear regression models, as we have seen, include not only first-order models in $p - 1$ predictor variables but also more complex models. For instance, a polynomial regression model in one or more predictor variables is linear in the parameters, such as the following model in two predictor variables with linear, quadratic, and interaction terms:

$$Y_i = \beta_0 + \beta_1 X_{i1} + \beta_2 X_{i1}^2 + \beta_3 X_{i2} + \beta_4 X_{i2}^2 + \beta_5 X_{i1} X_{i2} + \varepsilon_i \qquad \textbf{(13.2)}$$

Also, models with transformed variables that are linear in the parameters belong to the class of linear regression models, such as the following model:

$$\log_{10} Y_i = \beta_0 + \beta_1 \sqrt{X_{i1}} + \beta_2 \exp(X_{i2}) + \varepsilon_i \qquad \textbf{(13.3)}$$

In general, we can state a linear regression model in the form:

$$Y_i = f(\mathbf{X}_i, \boldsymbol{\beta}) + \varepsilon_i \qquad \textbf{(13.4)}$$

where $\mathbf{X}_i$ is the vector of the observations on the predictor variables for the ith case:

$$\mathbf{X}_i = \begin{bmatrix} 1 \\ X_{i1} \\ \vdots \\ X_{i,p-1} \end{bmatrix} \qquad \textbf{(13.4a)}$$

$\boldsymbol{\beta}$ is the vector of the regression coefficients in (6.18c), and $f(\mathbf{X}_i, \boldsymbol{\beta})$ represents the expected value $E\{Y_i\}$, which for linear regression models equals according to (6.54):

$$f(\mathbf{X}_i, \boldsymbol{\beta}) = \mathbf{X}_i'\boldsymbol{\beta} \qquad \textbf{(13.4b)}$$

Nonlinear Regression Models

Nonlinear regression models are of the same basic form as that in (13.4) for linear regression models:

$$Y_i = f(\mathbf{X}_i, \boldsymbol{\gamma}) + \varepsilon_i \qquad \textbf{(13.5)}$$

An observation Y_i is still the sum of a mean response $f(\mathbf{X}_i, \boldsymbol{\gamma})$ given by the nonlinear response function $f(\mathbf{X}, \boldsymbol{\gamma})$ and the error term ε_i. The error terms usually are assumed to have expectation zero, constant variance, and to be uncorrelated, just as for linear regression models. Often, a normal error model is utilized which assumes that the error terms are independent normal random variables with constant variance.

The parameter vector in the response function $f(\mathbf{X}, \boldsymbol{\gamma})$ is now denoted by $\boldsymbol{\gamma}$ rather than $\boldsymbol{\beta}$ as a reminder that the response function here is nonlinear in the parameters. We present now two examples of nonlinear regression models that are widely used in practice.

Exponential Regression Models. One widely used nonlinear regression model is the exponential regression model. When there is only a single predictor variable, one form of this regression model with normal error terms is:

$$Y_i = \gamma_0 \exp(\gamma_1 X_i) + \varepsilon_i \qquad \textbf{(13.6)}$$

where:

γ_0 and γ_1 are parameters

X_i are known constants

ε_i are independent $N(0, \sigma^2)$

The response function for this model is:

$$f(\mathbf{X}, \boldsymbol{\gamma}) = \gamma_0 \exp(\gamma_1 X) \tag{13.7}$$

Note that this model is not linear in the parameters γ_0 and γ_1.

A more general nonlinear exponential regression model in one predictor variable with normal error terms is:

$$Y_i = \gamma_0 + \gamma_1 \exp(\gamma_2 X_i) + \varepsilon_i \tag{13.8}$$

where the error terms are independent normal with constant variance σ^2. The response function for this regression model is:

$$f(\mathbf{X}, \boldsymbol{\gamma}) = \gamma_0 + \gamma_1 \exp(\gamma_2 X) \tag{13.9}$$

Exponential regression model (13.8) is commonly used in growth studies where the rate of growth at a given time X is proportional to the amount of growth remaining as time increases, with γ_0 representing the maximum growth value. Another use of this regression model is to relate the concentration of a substance (Y) to elapsed time (X). Figure 13.1a shows the response function (13.9) for parameter values $\gamma_0 = 100$, $\gamma_1 = -50$, and $\gamma_2 = -2$. We shall discuss exponential regression models (13.6) and (13.8) in more detail later in this chapter.

Logistic Regression Models. Another important nonlinear regression model is the *logistic regression model*. This model with one predictor variable and normal error terms is:

$$Y_i = \frac{\gamma_0}{1 + \gamma_1 \exp(\gamma_2 X_i)} + \varepsilon_i \tag{13.10}$$

where the error terms ε_i are independent normal with constant variance σ^2. The response

FIGURE 13.1
Plots of
Exponential
and Logistic
Response
Functions.

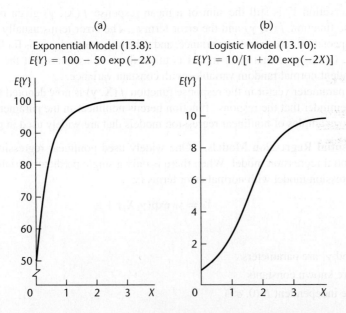

(a)

Exponential Model (13.8):
$E\{Y\} = 100 - 50 \exp(-2X)$

(b)

Logistic Model (13.10):
$E\{Y\} = 10/[1 + 20 \exp(-2X)]$

function here is:

$$f(\mathbf{X}, \boldsymbol{\gamma}) = \frac{\gamma_0}{1 + \gamma_1 \exp(\gamma_2 X)} \tag{13.11}$$

Note again that this response function is not linear in the parameters γ_0, γ_1, and γ_2.

This logistic regression model has been used in population studies to relate, for instance, number of species (Y) to time (X). Figure 13.1b shows the logistic response function (13.11) for parameter values $\gamma_0 = 10$, $\gamma_1 = 20$, and $\gamma_2 = -2$. Note that the parameter $\gamma_0 = 10$ represents the maximum growth value here.

Logistic regression model (13.10) is also widely used when the response variable is qualitative. An example of this use of the logistic regression model is predicting whether a household will purchase a new car this year (will, will not) on the basis of the predictor variables age of presently owned car, household income, and size of household. In this use of logistic regression models, the response variable (will, will not purchase car, in our example) is qualitative and will be represented by a 0, 1 indicator variable. Consequently, the error terms are not normally distributed here with constant variance. Logistic regression models and their use when the response variable is qualitative will be discussed in detail in Chapter 14.

General Form of Nonlinear Regression Models. As we have seen from the two examples of nonlinear regression models, these models are similar in general form to linear regression models. Each Y_i observation is postulated to be the sum of a mean response $f(\mathbf{X}_i, \boldsymbol{\gamma})$ based on the given nonlinear response function and a random error term ε_i. Furthermore, the error terms ε_i are often assumed to be independent normal random variables with constant variance.

An important difference of nonlinear regression models is that the number of regression parameters is not necessarily directly related to the number of X variables in the model. In linear regression models, if there are $p - 1$ X variables in the model, then there are p regression coefficients in the model. For the exponential regression model in (13.8), there is one X variable but three regression coefficients. The same is found for logistic regression model (13.10). Hence, we now denote the number of X variables in the nonlinear regression model by q, but we continue to denote the number of regression parameters in the response function by p. In the exponential regression model (13.6), for instance, there are $p = 2$ regression parameters and $q = 1$ X variable.

Also, we shall define the vector $\mathbf{X}_i$ of the observations on the X variables without the initial element 1. The general form of a nonlinear regression model is therefore expressed as follows:

$$Y_i = f(\mathbf{X}_i, \boldsymbol{\gamma}) + \varepsilon_i \tag{13.12}$$

where:

$$\underset{q \times 1}{\mathbf{X}_i} = \begin{bmatrix} X_{i1} \\ X_{i2} \\ \vdots \\ X_{iq} \end{bmatrix} \qquad \underset{p \times 1}{\boldsymbol{\gamma}} = \begin{bmatrix} \gamma_0 \\ \gamma_1 \\ \vdots \\ \gamma_{p-1} \end{bmatrix} \tag{13.12a}$$

Comment

Nonlinear response functions that can be linearized by a transformation are sometimes called *intrinsically linear* response functions. For example, the exponential response function:

$$f(\mathbf{X}, \boldsymbol{\gamma}) = \gamma_0[\exp(\gamma_1 X)]$$

is an intrinsically linear response function because it can be linearized by the logarithmic transformation:

$$\log_e f(\mathbf{X}, \boldsymbol{\gamma}) = \log_e \gamma_0 + \gamma_1 X$$

This transformed response function can be represented in the linear model form:

$$g(\mathbf{X}, \boldsymbol{\gamma}) = \beta_0 + \beta_1 X$$

where $g(\mathbf{X}, \boldsymbol{\gamma}) = \log_e f(\mathbf{X}, \boldsymbol{\gamma})$, $\beta_0 = \log_e \gamma_0$, and $\beta_1 = \gamma_1$.

Just because a nonlinear response function is intrinsically linear does not necessarily imply that linear regression is appropriate. The reason is that the transformation to linearize the response function will affect the error term in the model. For example, suppose that the following exponential regression model with normal error terms that have constant variance is appropriate:

$$Y_i = \gamma_0 \exp(\gamma_1 X_i) + \varepsilon_i$$

A logarithmic transformation of Y to linearize the response function will affect the normal error term ε_i so that the error term in the linearized model will no longer be normal with constant variance. Hence, it is important to study any nonlinear regression model that has been linearized for appropriateness; it may turn out that the nonlinear regression model is preferable to the linearized version. ∎

Estimation of Regression Parameters

Estimation of the parameters of a nonlinear regression model is usually carried out by the method of least squares or the method of maximum likelihood, just as for linear regression models. Also as in linear regression, both of these methods of estimation yield the same parameter estimates when the error terms in nonlinear regression model (13.12) are independent normal with constant variance.

Unlike linear regression, it is usually not possible to find analytical expressions for the least squares and maximum likelihood estimators for nonlinear regression models. Instead, numerical search procedures must be used with both of these estimation procedures, requiring intensive computations. The analysis of nonlinear regression models is therefore usually carried out by utilizing standard computer software programs.

Example

To illustrate the fitting and analysis of nonlinear regression models in a simple fashion, we shall use an example where the model has only two parameters and the sample size is reasonably small. In so doing, we shall be able to explain the concepts and procedures without overwhelming the reader with details.

A hospital administrator wished to develop a regression model for predicting the degree of long-term recovery after discharge from the hospital for severely injured patients. The predictor variable to be utilized is number of days of hospitalization (X), and the response variable is a prognostic index for long-term recovery (Y), with large values of the index reflecting a good prognosis. Data for 15 patients were studied and are presented in Table 13.1. A scatter plot of the data is shown in Figure 13.2. Related earlier studies reported in the literature found the relationship between the predictor variable and the response variable to be exponential. Hence, it was decided to investigate the appropriateness of the two-parameter nonlinear exponential regression model (13.6):

$$Y_i = \gamma_0 \exp(\gamma_1 X_i) + \varepsilon_i \tag{13.13}$$

TABLE 13.1
Data—Severely Injured Patients Example.

Patient i	Days Hospitalized X_i	Prognostic Index Y_i
1	2	54
2	5	50
3	7	45
4	10	37
5	14	35
6	19	25
7	26	20
8	31	16
9	34	18
10	38	13
11	45	8
12	52	11
13	53	8
14	60	4
15	65	6

FIGURE 13.2
Scatter Plot and Fitted Nonlinear Regression Function—Severely Injured Patients Example.

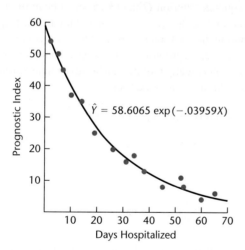

$\hat{Y} = 58.6065 \exp(-.03959X)$

where the ε_i are independent normal with constant variance. If this model is appropriate, it is desired to estimate the regression parameters γ_0 and γ_1.

13.2 Least Squares Estimation in Nonlinear Regression

We noted in Chapter 1 that the method of least squares for simple linear regression requires the minimization of the criterion Q in (1.8):

$$Q = \sum_{i=1}^{n} [Y_i - (\beta_0 + \beta_1 X_i)]^2 \qquad \textbf{(13.14)}$$

Those values of β_0 and β_1 that minimize Q for the given sample observations (X_i, Y_i) are the least squares estimates and are denoted by b_0 and b_1.

We also noted in Chapter 1 that one method for finding the least squares estimates is by use of a numerical search procedure. With this approach, Q in (13.14) is evaluated for different values of β_0 and β_1, varying β_0 and β_1 systematically until the minimum value of Q is found. The values of β_0 and β_1 that minimize Q are the least squares estimates b_0 and b_1.

A second method for finding the least squares estimates is by means of the least squares normal equations. Here, the least squares normal equations are found analytically by differentiating Q with respect to β_0 and β_1 and setting the derivatives equal to zero. The solution of the normal equations yields the least squares estimates.

As we saw in Chapter 6, these procedures extend directly to multiple linear regression, for which the least squares criterion is given in (6.22). The concepts of least squares estimation for linear regression also extend directly to nonlinear regression models. The least squares criterion again is:

$$Q = \sum_{i=1}^{n} [Y_i - f(\mathbf{X}_i, \boldsymbol{\gamma})]^2 \tag{13.15}$$

where $f(\mathbf{X}_i, \boldsymbol{\gamma})$ is the mean response for the ith case according to the nonlinear response function $f(\mathbf{X}, \boldsymbol{\gamma})$. The least squares criterion Q in (13.15) must be minimized with respect to the nonlinear regression parameters $\gamma_0, \gamma_1, \ldots, \gamma_{p-1}$ to obtain the least squares estimates. The same two methods for finding the least squares estimates—numerical search and normal equations—may be used in nonlinear regression. A difference from linear regression is that the solution of the normal equations usually requires an iterative numerical search procedure because analytical solutions generally cannot be found.

Example

The response function in the severely injured patients example is seen from (13.13) to be:

$$f(\mathbf{X}, \boldsymbol{\gamma}) = \gamma_0 \exp(\gamma_1 X)$$

Hence, the least squares criterion Q here is:

$$Q = \sum_{i=1}^{n} [Y_i - \gamma_0 \exp(\gamma_1 X_i)]^2$$

We can see that the method of maximum likelihood leads to the same criterion here when the error terms ε_i are independent normal with constant variance by considering the likelihood function:

$$L(\boldsymbol{\gamma}, \sigma^2) = \frac{1}{(2\pi\sigma^2)^{n/2}} \exp\left[-\frac{1}{2\sigma^2} \sum_{i=1}^{n} [Y_i - \gamma_0 \exp(\gamma_1 X_i)]^2\right]$$

Just as for linear regression, maximizing this likelihood function with respect to the regression parameters γ_0 and γ_1 is equivalent to minimizing the sum in the exponent, so that the maximum likelihood estimates are the same here as the least squares estimates.

We now discuss how to obtain the least squares estimates, first by use of the normal equations and then by direct numerical search procedures.

Solution of Normal Equations

To obtain the normal equations for a nonlinear regression model:

$$Y_i = f(\mathbf{X}_i, \boldsymbol{\gamma}) + \varepsilon_i$$

we need to minimize the least squares criterion Q:

$$Q = \sum_{i=1}^{n} [Y_i - f(\mathbf{X}_i, \boldsymbol{\gamma})]^2$$

with respect to $\gamma_0, \gamma_1, \ldots, \gamma_{p-1}$. The partial derivative of Q with respect to γ_k is:

$$\frac{\partial Q}{\partial \gamma_k} = \sum_{i=1}^{n} -2[Y_i - f(\mathbf{X}_i, \boldsymbol{\gamma})] \left[\frac{\partial f(\mathbf{X}_i, \boldsymbol{\gamma})}{\partial \gamma_k} \right] \tag{13.16}$$

When the p partial derivatives are each set equal to 0 and the parameters γ_k are replaced by the least squares estimates g_k, we obtain after some simplification the p normal equations:

$$\sum_{i=1}^{n} Y_i \left[\frac{\partial f(\mathbf{X}_i, \boldsymbol{\gamma})}{\partial \gamma_k} \right]_{\boldsymbol{\gamma}=\mathbf{g}} - \sum_{i=1}^{n} f(\mathbf{X}_i, \mathbf{g}) \left[\frac{\partial f(\mathbf{X}_i, \boldsymbol{\gamma})}{\partial \gamma_k} \right]_{\boldsymbol{\gamma}=\mathbf{g}} = 0 \qquad k = 0, 1, \ldots, p-1 \tag{13.17}$$

where $\mathbf{g}$ is the vector of the least squares estimates g_k:

$$\underset{p \times 1}{\mathbf{g}} = \begin{bmatrix} g_0 \\ g_1 \\ \vdots \\ g_{p-1} \end{bmatrix} \tag{13.18}$$

Note that the terms in brackets in (13.17) are the partial derivatives in (13.16) with the parameters γ_k replaced by the least squares estimates g_k.

The normal equations (13.17) for nonlinear regression models are nonlinear in the parameter estimates g_k and are usually difficult to solve, even in the simplest of cases. Hence, numerical search procedures are ordinarily required to obtain a solution of the normal equations iteratively. To make things still more difficult, multiple solutions may be possible.

Example

In the severely injured patients example, the mean response for the ith case is:

$$f(\mathbf{X}_i, \boldsymbol{\gamma}) = \gamma_0 \exp(\gamma_1 X_i) \tag{13.19}$$

Hence, the partial derivatives of $f(\mathbf{X}_i, \boldsymbol{\gamma})$ are:

$$\frac{\partial f(\mathbf{X}_i, \boldsymbol{\gamma})}{\partial \gamma_0} = \exp(\gamma_1 X_i) \tag{13.20a}$$

$$\frac{\partial f(\mathbf{X}_i, \boldsymbol{\gamma})}{\partial \gamma_1} = \gamma_0 X_i \exp(\gamma_1 X_i) \tag{13.20b}$$

Replacing γ_0 and γ_1 in (13.19), (13.20a), and (13.20b) by the respective least squares estimates g_0 and g_1, the normal equations (13.17) therefore are:

$$\sum Y_i \exp(g_1 X_i) - \sum g_0 \exp(g_1 X_i) \exp(g_1 X_i) \qquad = 0$$

$$\sum Y_i g_0 X_i \exp(g_1 X_i) - \sum g_0 \exp(g_1 X_i) g_0 X_i \exp(g_1 X_i) = 0$$

Upon simplification, the normal equations become:

$$\sum Y_i \exp(g_1 X_i) - g_0 \sum \exp(2g_1 X_i) \qquad = 0$$

$$\sum Y_i X_i \exp(g_1 X_i) - g_0 \sum X_i \exp(2g_1 X_i) = 0$$

These normal equations are not linear in g_0 and g_1, and no closed-form solution exists. Thus, numerical methods will be required to find the solution for the least squares estimates iteratively.

Direct Numerical Search—Gauss-Newton Method

In many nonlinear regression problems, it is more practical to find the least squares estimates by direct numerical search procedures rather than by first obtaining the normal equations and then using numerical methods to find the solution for these equations iteratively. The major statistical computer packages employ one or more direct numerical search procedures for solving nonlinear regression problems. We now explain one of these direct numerical search methods.

The *Gauss-Newton method,* also called the *linearization method,* uses a Taylor series expansion to approximate the nonlinear regression model with linear terms and then employs ordinary least squares to estimate the parameters. Iteration of these steps generally leads to a solution to the nonlinear regression problem.

The Gauss-Newton method begins with initial or starting values for the regression parameters $\gamma_0, \gamma_1, \ldots, \gamma_{p-1}$. We denote these by $g_0^{(0)}, g_1^{(0)}, \ldots, g_{p-1}^{(0)}$, where the superscript in parentheses denotes the iteration number. The starting values $g_k^{(0)}$ may be obtained from previous or related studies, theoretical expectations, or a preliminary search for parameter values that lead to a comparatively low criterion value Q in (13.15). We shall later discuss in more detail the choice of the starting values.

Once the starting values for the parameters have been obtained, we approximate the mean responses $f(\mathbf{X}_i, \boldsymbol{\gamma})$ for the n cases by the linear terms in the Taylor series expansion around the starting values $g_k^{(0)}$. We obtain for the ith case:

$$f(\mathbf{X}_i, \boldsymbol{\gamma}) \approx f(\mathbf{X}_i, \mathbf{g}^{(0)}) + \sum_{k=0}^{p-1} \left[\frac{\partial f(\mathbf{X}_i, \boldsymbol{\gamma})}{\partial \gamma_k} \right]_{\boldsymbol{\gamma}=\mathbf{g}^{(0)}} \left(\gamma_k - g_k^{(0)} \right) \qquad \textbf{(13.21)}$$

where:

$$\underset{p \times 1}{\mathbf{g}^{(0)}} = \begin{bmatrix} g_0^{(0)} \\ g_1^{(0)} \\ \vdots \\ g_{p-1}^{(0)} \end{bmatrix} \qquad \textbf{(13.21a)}$$

Note that $\mathbf{g}^{(0)}$ is the vector of the parameter starting values. The terms in brackets in (13.21) are the same partial derivatives of the regression function we encountered earlier in the normal equations (13.17), but here they are evaluated at $\gamma_k = g_k^{(0)}$ for $k = 0, 1, \ldots, p - 1$.

Let us now simplify the notation as follows:

$$f_i^{(0)} = f\left(\mathbf{X}_i, \mathbf{g}^{(0)}\right) \tag{13.22a}$$

$$\beta_k^{(0)} = \gamma_k - g_k^{(0)} \tag{13.22b}$$

$$D_{ik}^{(0)} = \left[\frac{\partial f(\mathbf{X}_i, \boldsymbol{\gamma})}{\partial \gamma_k}\right]_{\boldsymbol{\gamma}=\mathbf{g}^{(0)}} \tag{13.22c}$$

The Taylor approximation (13.21) for the mean response for the ith case then becomes in this notation:

$$f(\mathbf{X}_i, \boldsymbol{\gamma}) \approx f_i^{(0)} + \sum_{k=0}^{p-1} D_{ik}^{(0)} \beta_k^{(0)}$$

and an approximation to the nonlinear regression model (13.12):

$$Y_i = f(\mathbf{X}_i, \boldsymbol{\gamma}) + \varepsilon_i$$

is:

$$Y_i \approx f_i^{(0)} + \sum_{k=0}^{p-1} D_{ik}^{(0)} \beta_k^{(0)} + \varepsilon_i \tag{13.23}$$

When we shift the $f_i^{(0)}$ term to the left and denote the difference $Y_i - f_i^{(0)}$ by $Y_i^{(0)}$, we obtain the following linear regression model approximation:

$$Y_i^{(0)} \approx \sum_{k=0}^{p-1} D_{ik}^{(0)} \beta_k^{(0)} + \varepsilon_i \qquad i = 1, \ldots, n \tag{13.24}$$

where:

$$Y_i^{(0)} = Y_i - f_i^{(0)} \tag{13.24a}$$

Note that the linear regression model approximation (13.24) is of the form:

$$Y_i = \beta_0 X_{i0} + \beta_1 X_{i1} + \cdots + \beta_{p-1} X_{i,p-1} + \varepsilon_i$$

The responses $Y_i^{(0)}$ in (13.24) are residuals, namely, the deviations of the observations around the nonlinear regression function with the parameters replaced by the starting estimates. The X variables observations $D_{ik}^{(0)}$ are the partial derivatives of the mean response evaluated for each of the n cases with the parameters replaced by the starting estimates. Each regression coefficient $\beta_k^{(0)}$ represents the difference between the true regression parameter and the initial estimate of the parameter. Thus, the regression coefficients represent the adjustment amounts by which the initial regression coefficients must be corrected. The purpose of fitting the linear regression model approximation (13.24) is therefore to estimate the regression coefficients $\beta_k^{(0)}$ and use these estimates to adjust the initial starting estimates of the regression parameters. In fitting this linear regression approximation, note that there is no intercept term in the model. Use of a computer multiple regression package therefore requires a specification of no intercept.

We shall represent the linear regression model approximation (13.24) in matrix form as follows:

$$\mathbf{Y}^{(0)} \approx \mathbf{D}^{(0)}\boldsymbol{\beta}^{(0)} + \boldsymbol{\varepsilon} \tag{13.25}$$

where:

$$\textbf{(13.25a)} \quad \mathbf{Y}^{(0)}_{n \times 1} = \begin{bmatrix} Y_1 - f_1^{(0)} \\ \vdots \\ Y_n - f_n^{(0)} \end{bmatrix} \qquad \textbf{(13.25b)} \quad \mathbf{D}^{(0)}_{n \times p} = \begin{bmatrix} D_{10}^{(0)} & \cdots & D_{1,p-1}^{(0)} \\ \vdots & & \vdots \\ D_{n0}^{(0)} & \cdots & D_{n,p-1}^{(0)} \end{bmatrix}$$

$$\textbf{(13.25c)} \quad \boldsymbol{\beta}^{(0)}_{p \times 1} = \begin{bmatrix} \beta_0^{(0)} \\ \vdots \\ \beta_{p-1}^{(0)} \end{bmatrix} \qquad \textbf{(13.25d)} \quad \boldsymbol{\varepsilon}_{n \times 1} = \begin{bmatrix} \varepsilon_1 \\ \vdots \\ \varepsilon_n \end{bmatrix}$$

Note again that the approximation model (13.25) is precisely in the form of the general linear regression model (6.19), with the $\mathbf{D}$ matrix of partial derivatives now playing the role of the $\mathbf{X}$ matrix (but without a column of 1s for the intercept). We can therefore estimate the parameters $\boldsymbol{\beta}^{(0)}$ by ordinary least squares and obtain according to (6.25):

$$\mathbf{b}^{(0)} = \left(\mathbf{D}^{(0)\prime}\mathbf{D}^{(0)}\right)^{-1}\mathbf{D}^{(0)\prime}\mathbf{Y}^{(0)} \tag{13.26}$$

where $\mathbf{b}^{(0)}$ is the vector of the least squares estimated regression coefficients. As we noted earlier, an ordinary multiple regression computer program can be used to obtain the estimated regression coefficients $b_k^{(0)}$, with a specification of no intercept.

We then use these least squares estimates to obtain revised estimated regression coefficients $g_k^{(1)}$ by means of (13.22b):

$$g_k^{(1)} = g_k^{(0)} + b_k^{(0)}$$

where $g_k^{(1)}$ denotes the revised estimate of γ_k at the end of the first iteration. In matrix form, we represent the revision process as follows:

$$\mathbf{g}^{(1)} = \mathbf{g}^{(0)} + \mathbf{b}^{(0)} \tag{13.27}$$

At this point, we can examine whether the revised regression coefficients represent adjustments in the proper direction. We shall denote the least squares criterion measure Q in (13.15) evaluated for the starting regression coefficients $\mathbf{g}^{(0)}$ by $SSE^{(0)}$; it is:

$$SSE^{(0)} = \sum_{i=1}^{n} \left[Y_i - f\left(\mathbf{X}_i, \mathbf{g}^{(0)}\right)\right]^2 = \sum_{i=1}^{n} \left(Y_i - f_i^{(0)}\right)^2 \tag{13.28}$$

At the end of the first iteration, the revised estimated regression coefficients are $\mathbf{g}^{(1)}$, and the least squares criterion measure evaluated at this stage, now denoted by $SSE^{(1)}$, is:

$$SSE^{(1)} = \sum_{i=1}^{n} \left[Y_i - f\left(\mathbf{X}_i, \mathbf{g}^{(1)}\right)\right]^2 = \sum_{i=1}^{n} \left(Y_i - f_i^{(1)}\right)^2 \tag{13.29}$$

If the Gauss-Newton method is working effectively in the first iteration, $SSE^{(1)}$ should be smaller than $SSE^{(0)}$ since the revised estimated regression coefficients $\mathbf{g}^{(1)}$ should be better estimates.

Note that the nonlinear regression functions $f(\mathbf{X}_i, \mathbf{g}^{(0)})$ and $f(\mathbf{X}_i, \mathbf{g}^{(1)})$ are used in calculating $SSE^{(0)}$ and $SSE^{(1)}$, and not the linear approximations from the Taylor series expansion.

The revised regression coefficients $\mathbf{g}^{(1)}$ are not, of course, the least squares estimates for the nonlinear regression problem because the fitted model (13.25) is only an approximation of the nonlinear model. The Gauss-Newton method therefore repeats the procedure just described, with $\mathbf{g}^{(1)}$ now used for the new starting values. This produces a new set of revised estimates, denoted by $\mathbf{g}^{(2)}$, and a new least squares criterion measure $SSE^{(2)}$. The iterative process is continued until the differences between successive coefficient estimates $\mathbf{g}^{(s+1)} - \mathbf{g}^{(s)}$ and/or the difference between successive least squares criterion measures $SSE^{(s+1)} - SSE^{(s)}$ become negligible. We shall denote the final estimates of the regression coefficients simply by $\mathbf{g}$ and the final least squares criterion measure, which is the error sum of squares, by SSE.

The Gauss-Newton method works effectively in many nonlinear regression applications. In some instances, however, the method may require numerous iterations before converging, and in a few cases it may not converge at all.

Example

In the severely injured patients example, the initial values of the parameters γ_0 and γ_1 were obtained by noting that a logarithmic transformation of the response function linearizes it:

$$\log_e \gamma_0[\exp(\gamma_1 X)] = \log_e \gamma_0 + \gamma_1 X$$

Hence, a linear regression model with a transformed Y variable was fitted as an initial approximation to the exponential model:

$$Y_i' = \beta_0 + \beta_1 X_i + \varepsilon_i$$

where:

$$Y_i' = \log_e Y_i$$
$$\beta_0 = \log_e \gamma_0$$
$$\beta_1 = \gamma_1$$

This linear regression model was fitted by ordinary least squares and yielded the estimated regression coefficients $b_0 = 4.0371$ and $b_1 = -.03797$ (calculations not shown). Hence, the initial starting values are $g_0^{(0)} = \exp(b_0) = \exp(4.0371) = 56.6646$ and $g_1^{(0)} = b_1 = -.03797$.

The least squares criterion measure at this stage requires evaluation of the nonlinear regression function (13.7) for each case, utilizing the starting parameter values $g_0^{(0)}$ and $g_1^{(0)}$. For instance, for the first case, for which $X_1 = 2$, we obtain:

$$f(\mathbf{X}_1, \mathbf{g}^{(0)}) = f_1^{(0)} = g_0^{(0)} \exp(g_1^{(0)} X_1) = (56.6646) \exp[-.03797(2)] = 52.5208$$

TABLE 13.2
$\mathbf{Y}^{(0)}$ and $\mathbf{D}^{(0)}$
Matrices—
Severely
Injured
Patients
Example.

$$
\mathbf{Y}^{(0)}_{15 \times 1} =
\begin{bmatrix}
Y_1 - f_1^{(0)} \\
\cdot \\
\cdot \\
\cdot \\
Y_{15} - f_{15}^{(0)}
\end{bmatrix}
=
\begin{bmatrix}
Y_1 - g_0^{(0)} \exp(g_1^{(0)} X_1) \\
\cdot \\
\cdot \\
\cdot \\
Y_{15} - g_0^{(0)} \exp(g_1^{(0)} X_{15})
\end{bmatrix}
=
\begin{bmatrix}
1.4792 \\
3.1337 \\
1.5609 \\
-1.7624 \\
1.6996 \\
-2.5422 \\
-1.1139 \\
-1.4629 \\
2.4172 \\
-.3871 \\
-2.2625 \\
3.1327 \\
.4259 \\
-1.8063 \\
1.1977
\end{bmatrix}
$$

$$
\mathbf{D}^{(0)}_{15 \times 2} =
\begin{bmatrix}
\exp(g_1^{(0)} X_1) & g_0^{(0)} X_1 \exp(g_1^{(0)} X_1) \\
\cdot & \cdot \\
\cdot & \cdot \\
\cdot & \cdot \\
\exp(g_1^{(0)} X_{15}) & g_0^{(0)} X_{15} \exp(g_1^{(0)} X_{15})
\end{bmatrix}
=
\begin{bmatrix}
.92687 & 105.0416 \\
.82708 & 234.3317 \\
.76660 & 304.0736 \\
.68407 & 387.6236 \\
.58768 & 466.2057 \\
.48606 & 523.3020 \\
.37261 & 548.9603 \\
.30818 & 541.3505 \\
.27500 & 529.8162 \\
.23625 & 508.7088 \\
.18111 & 461.8140 \\
.13884 & 409.0975 \\
.13367 & 401.4294 \\
.10247 & 348.3801 \\
.08475 & 312.1510
\end{bmatrix}
$$

Since $Y_1 = 54$, the deviation from the mean response is:

$$
Y_1^{(0)} = Y_1 - f_1^{(0)} = 54 - 52.5208 = 1.4792
$$

Note again that the deviation $Y_1^{(0)}$ is the residual for case 1 at the initial fitting stage since $f_1^{(0)}$ is the estimated mean response when the initial estimates $\mathbf{g}^{(0)}$ of the parameters are employed. The stage 0 residuals for this and the other sample cases are presented in Table 13.2 and constitute the $\mathbf{Y}^{(0)}$ vector.

The least squares criterion measure at this initial stage then is simply the sum of the squared stage 0 residuals:

$$
SSE^{(0)} = \sum \left(Y_i - f_i^{(0)}\right)^2 = \sum \left(Y_i^{(0)}\right)^2
$$
$$
= (1.4792)^2 + \cdots + (1.1977)^2 = 56.0869
$$

To revise the initial estimates for the parameters, we require the $\mathbf{D}^{(0)}$ matrix and the $\mathbf{Y}^{(0)}$ vector. The latter was already obtained in the process of calculating the least squares criterion measure at stage 0. To obtain the $\mathbf{D}^{(0)}$ matrix, we need the partial derivatives of the regression function (13.19) evaluated at $\boldsymbol{\gamma} = \mathbf{g}^{(0)}$. The partial derivatives are given in (13.20). Table 13.2 shows the $\mathbf{D}^{(0)}$ matrix entries in symbolic form and also the numerical values. To illustrate the calculations for case 1, we know from Table 13.1 that $X_1 = 2$. Hence, evaluating the partial derivatives at $\mathbf{g}^{(0)}$, we find:

$$D_{10}^{(0)} = \left[\frac{\partial f(\mathbf{X}_1, \boldsymbol{\gamma})}{\partial \gamma_0} \right]_{\boldsymbol{\gamma}=\mathbf{g}^{(0)}} = \exp\left(g_1^{(0)} X_1\right) = \exp[-.03797(2)] = .92687$$

$$D_{11}^{(0)} = \left[\frac{\partial f(\mathbf{X}_1, \boldsymbol{\gamma})}{\partial \gamma_1} \right]_{\boldsymbol{\gamma}=\mathbf{g}^{(0)}} = g_0^{(0)} X_1 \exp\left(g_1^{(0)} X_1\right)$$

$$= 56.6646(2) \exp[-.03797(2)] = 105.0416$$

We are now ready to obtain the least squares estimates $\mathbf{b}^{(0)}$ by regressing the response variable $Y^{(0)}$ in Table 13.2 on the two X variables in $\mathbf{D}^{(0)}$ in Table 13.2, using regression with no intercept. A standard multiple regression computer program yielded $b_0^{(0)} = 1.8932$ and $b_1^{(0)} = -.001563$. Hence, the vector $\mathbf{b}^{(0)}$ of the estimated regression coefficients is:

$$\mathbf{b}^{(0)} = \left[\begin{array}{c} 1.8932 \\ -.001563 \end{array} \right]$$

By (13.27), we now obtain the revised least squares estimates $\mathbf{g}^{(1)}$:

$$\mathbf{g}^{(1)} = \mathbf{g}^{(0)} + \mathbf{b}^{(0)} = \left[\begin{array}{c} 56.6646 \\ -.03797 \end{array} \right] + \left[\begin{array}{c} 1.8932 \\ -.001563 \end{array} \right] = \left[\begin{array}{c} 58.5578 \\ -.03953 \end{array} \right]$$

Hence, $g_0^{(1)} = 58.5578$ and $g_1^{(1)} = -.03953$ are the revised parameter estimates at the end of the first iteration. Note that the estimated regression coefficients have been revised moderately from the initial values, as can be seen from Table 13.3a, which presents the estimated regression coefficients and the least squares criterion measures for the starting values and the first iteration. Note also that the least squares criterion measure has been reduced in the first iteration.

Iteration 2 requires that we now revise the residuals from the exponential regression function and the first partial derivatives, based on the revised parameter estimates $g_0^{(1)} = 58.5578$ and $g_1^{(1)} = -.03953$. For case 1, for which $Y_1 = 54$ and $X_1 = 2$, we obtain:

$$Y_1^{(1)} = Y_1 - f_1^{(1)} = 54 - (58.5578) \exp[-.03953(2)] = -.1065$$

$$D_{10}^{(1)} = \exp\left(g_1^{(1)} X_1\right) = \exp[-.03953(2)] = .92398$$

$$D_{11}^{(1)} = g_0^{(1)} X_1 \exp\left(g_1^{(1)} X_1\right) = 58.5578(2) \exp[-.03953(2)] = 108.2130$$

By comparing these results with the comparable stage 0 results for case 1 in Table 13.2, we see that the absolute magnitude of the residual for case 1 is substantially reduced as a result of the stage 1 revised fit and that the two partial derivatives are changed to a moderate extent. After the revised residuals $Y_i^{(1)}$ and the partial derivatives $D_{i0}^{(1)}$ and $D_{i1}^{(1)}$ have been

TABLE 13.3
Gauss-Newton
Method
Iterations
and Final
Nonlinear
Least Squares
Estimates—
Severely
Injured
Patients
Example.

(a) Estimates of Parameters and Least Squares Criterion Measure

Iteration	g_0	g_1	SSE
0	56.6646	−.03797	56.0869
1	58.5578	−.03953	49.4638
2	58.6065	−.03959	49.4593
3	58.6065	−.03959	49.4593

(b) Final Least Squares Estimates

k	g_k	$s\{g_k\}$	
0	58.6065	1.472	$MSE = \dfrac{49.4593}{13} = 3.80456$
1	−.03959	.00171	

(c) Estimated Approximate Variance-Covariance Matrix of Estimated Regression Coefficients

$$s^2\{\mathbf{g}\} = MSE(\mathbf{D'D})^{-1} = 3.80456 \begin{bmatrix} 5.696\text{E}{-}1 & -4.682\text{E}{-}4 \\ -4.682\text{E}{-}4 & 7.697\text{E}{-}7 \end{bmatrix}$$

$$= \begin{bmatrix} 2.1672 & -1.781\text{E}{-}3 \\ -1.781\text{E}{-}3 & 2.928\text{E}{-}6 \end{bmatrix}$$

obtained for all cases, the revised residuals are regressed on the revised partial derivatives, using a no-intercept regression fit, and the estimated regression parameters are again revised according to (13.27).

This process was carried out for three iterations. Table 13.3a contains the estimated regression coefficients and the least squares criterion measure for each iteration. We see that while iteration 1 led to moderate revisions in the estimated regression coefficients and a substantially better fit according to the least squares criterion, iteration 2 resulted only in minor revisions of the estimated regression coefficients and little improvement in the fit. Iteration 3 led to no change in either the estimates of the coefficients or the least squares criterion measure.

Hence, the search procedure was terminated after three iterations. The final regression coefficient estimates therefore are $g_0 = 58.6065$ and $g_1 = -.03959$, and the fitted regression function is:

$$\hat{Y} = (58.6065)\exp(-.03959X) \tag{13.30}$$

The error sum of squares for this fitted model is $SSE = 49.4593$. Figure 13.2 on page 515 shows a plot of this estimated regression function, together with a scatter plot of the data. The fit appears to be a good one.

Comments

1. The choice of initial starting values is very important with the Gauss-Newton method because a poor choice may result in slow convergence, convergence to a local minimum, or even divergence.

Good starting values will generally result in faster convergence, and if multiple minima exist, will lead to a solution that is the global minimum rather than a local minimum. Fast convergence, even if the initial estimates are far from the least squares solution, generally indicates that the linear approximation model (13.25) is a good approximation to the nonlinear regression model. Slow convergence, on the other hand, especially from initial estimates reasonably close to the least squares solution, usually indicates that the linear approximation model is not a good approximation to the nonlinear model.

2. A variety of methods are available for obtaining starting values for the regression parameters. Often, related earlier studies can be utilized to provide good starting values for the regression parameters. Another possibility is to select p representative observations, set the regression function $f(\mathbf{X}_i, \boldsymbol{\gamma})$ equal to Y_i for each of the p observations (thereby ignoring the random error), solve the p equations for the p parameters, and use the solutions as the starting values, provided they lead to reasonably good fits of the observed data. Still another possibility is to do a grid search in the parameter space by selecting in a grid fashion various trial choices of $\mathbf{g}$, evaluating the least squares criterion Q for each of these choices, and using as the starting values that $\mathbf{g}$ vector for which Q is smallest.

3. When using the Gauss-Newton or another direct search procedure, it is often desirable to try other sets of starting values after a solution has been obtained to make sure that the same solution will be found.

4. Some computer packages for nonlinear regression require that the user specify the starting values for the regression parameters. Others do a grid search to obtain starting values.

5. Most nonlinear computer programs have a library of commonly used regression functions. For nonlinear response functions not in the library and specified by the user, some computer programs using the Gauss-Newton method require the user to input also the partial derivatives of the regression function, while others numerically approximate partial derivatives from the regression function.

6. The Gauss-Newton method may produce iterations that oscillate widely or result in increases in the error sum of squares. Sometimes, these aberrations are only temporary, but occasionally serious convergence problems exist. Various modifications of the Gauss-Newton method have been suggested to improve its performance, such as the Hartley modification (Ref. 13.1).

7. Some properties that exist for linear regression least squares do not hold for nonlinear regression least squares. For example, the residuals do not necessarily sum to zero for nonlinear least squares. Additionally, the error sum of squares SSE and the regression sum of squares SSR do not necessarily sum to the total sum of squares $SSTO$. Consequently, the coefficient of multiple determination $R^2 = SSR/SSTO$ is not a meaningful descriptive statistic for nonlinear regression. ∎

Other Direct Search Procedures

Two other direct search procedures, besides the Gauss-Newton method, that are frequently used are the method of steepest descent and the Marquardt algorithm. The *method of steepest descent* searches for the minimum least squares criterion measure Q by iteratively determining the direction in which the regression coefficients $\mathbf{g}$ should be changed. The method of steepest descent is particularly effective when the starting values $\mathbf{g}^{(0)}$ are not good, being far from the final values $\mathbf{g}$.

The *Marquardt algorithm* seeks to utilize the best features of the Gauss-Newton method and the method of steepest descent, and occupies a middle ground between these two methods.

Additional information about direct search procedures can be found in specialized sources, such as References 13.2 and 13.3.

13.3   Model Building and Diagnostics

The model-building process for nonlinear regression models often differs somewhat from that for linear regression models. The reason is that the functional form of many nonlinear models is less suitable for adding or deleting predictor variables and curvature and interaction effects in the direct fashion that is feasible for linear regression models. Some types of nonlinear regression models do lend themselves to adding and deleting predictor variables in a direct fashion. We shall take up two such nonlinear regression models in Chapter 14, where we consider the logistic and Poisson multiple regression models.

Validation of the selected nonlinear regression model can be performed in the same fashion as for linear regression models.

Use of diagnostic tools to examine the appropriateness of a fitted model plays an important role in the process of building a nonlinear regression model. The appropriateness of a regression model must always be considered, whether the model is linear or nonlinear. Nonlinear regression models may not be appropriate for the same reasons as linear regression models. For example, when nonlinear growth models are used for time series data, there is the possibility that the error terms may be correlated. Also, unequal error variances are often present when nonlinear growth models with asymptotes are fitted, such as exponential models (13.6) and (13.8). Typically, the error variances for cases in the neighborhood of the asymptote(s) differ from the error variances for cases elsewhere.

When replicate observations are available and the sample size is reasonably large, the appropriateness of a nonlinear regression function can be tested formally by means of the lack of fit test for linear regression models in (6.68). This test will be an approximate one for nonlinear regression models, but the actual level of significance will be close to the specified level when the sample size is reasonably large. Thus, we calculate the pure error sum of squares by (3.16), obtain the lack of fit sum of squares by (3.24), and calculate test statistic (6.68b) in the usual fashion when performing a formal lack of fit test for a nonlinear response function.

Plots of residuals against time, against the fitted values, and against each of the predictor variables can be helpful in diagnosing departures from the assumed model, just as for linear regression models. In interpreting residual plots for nonlinear regression, one needs to remember that the residuals for nonlinear regression do not necessarily sum to zero.

If unequal error variances are found to be present, weighted least squares can be used in fitting the nonlinear regression model. Alternatively, transformations of the response variable can be investigated that may stabilize the variance of the error terms and also permit use of a linear regression model.

Example

In the severely injured patients example, the residuals were obtained by use of the fitted nonlinear regression function (13.30):

$$e_i = Y_i - (58.6065) \exp(-.03959 X_i)$$

A plot of the residuals against the fitted values is shown in Figure 13.3a, and a normal probability plot of the residuals is shown in Figure 13.3b. These plots do not suggest any serious departures from the model assumptions. The residual plot against the fitted values in Figure 13.3a does raise the question whether the error variance may be somewhat larger for cases with small fitted values near the asymptote. The Brown-Forsythe test (3.9) was

FIGURE 13.3
Diagnostic
Residual
Plots—
Severely
Injured
Patients
Example.

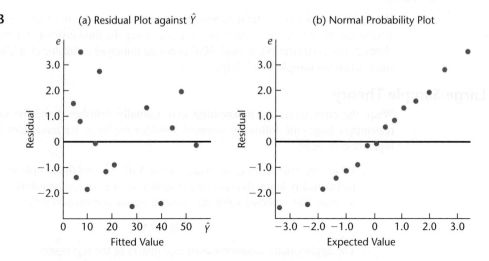

(a) Residual Plot against $\hat{Y}$

(b) Normal Probability Plot

conducted. Its P-value is .64, indicating that the residuals are consistent with constancy of the error variance.

On the basis of these, as well as some other diagnostics, it was concluded that exponential regression model (13.13) is appropriate for the data.

13.4 Inferences about Nonlinear Regression Parameters

Exact inference procedures about the regression parameters are available for linear regression models with normal error terms for any sample size. Unfortunately, this is not the case for nonlinear regression models with normal error terms, where the least squares and maximum likelihood estimators for any given sample size are not normally distributed, are not unbiased, and do not have minimum variance.

Consequently, inferences about the regression parameters in nonlinear regression are usually based on large-sample theory. This theory tells us that the least squares and maximum likelihood estimators for nonlinear regression models with normal error terms, when the sample size is large, are approximately normally distributed and almost unbiased, and have almost minimum variance. This large-sample theory also applies when the error terms are not normally distributed.

Before presenting details about large-sample inferences for nonlinear regression, we need to consider first how the error term variance σ^2 is estimated for nonlinear regression models.

Estimate of Error Term Variance

Inferences about nonlinear regression parameters require an estimate of the error term variance σ^2. This estimate is of the same form as for linear regression, the error sum of squares again being the sum of the squared residuals:

$$MSE = \frac{SSE}{n-p} = \frac{\sum(Y_i - \hat{Y}_i)^2}{n-p} = \frac{\sum[Y_i - f(\mathbf{X}_i, \mathbf{g})]^2}{n-p} \qquad \textbf{(13.31)}$$

Here **g** is the vector of the final parameter estimates, so that the residuals are the deviations around the fitted nonlinear regression function using the final estimated regression coefficients **g**. For nonlinear regression, *MSE* is not an unbiased estimator of σ^2, but the bias is small when the sample size is large.

Large-Sample Theory

When the error terms are independent and normally distributed and the sample size is reasonably large, the following theorem provides the basis for inferences for nonlinear regression models:

> When the error terms ε_i are independent $N(0, \sigma^2)$ and the sample size n
> is reasonably large, the sampling distribution of **g** is approximately $\qquad$ **(13.32)**
> normal. The expected value of the mean vector is approximately:

$$E\{g\} \approx \gamma \qquad \text{(13.32a)}$$

The approximate variance-covariance matrix of the regression coefficients is estimated by:

$$s^2\{g\} = MSE(D'D)^{-1} \qquad \text{(13.32b)}$$

Here **D** is the matrix of partial derivatives evaluated at the final least squares estimates **g**, just as $D^{(0)}$ in (13.25b) is the matrix of partial derivatives evaluated at $g^{(0)}$. Note that the estimated approximate variance-covariance matrix $s^2\{g\}$ is of exactly the same form as the one for linear regression in (6.48), with **D** again playing the role of the **X** matrix.

Thus, when the sample size is large and the error terms are independent normal with constant variance, the least squares estimators in **g** for nonlinear regression are approximately normally distributed and almost unbiased. They also have near minimum variance, since the variance-covariance matrix in (13.32b) estimates the minimum variances. We should add that theorem (13.32) holds even if the error terms are not normally distributed.

As a result of theorem (13.32), inferences for nonlinear regression parameters are carried out in the same fashion as for linear regression when the sample size is reasonably large. Thus, an interval estimate for a regression parameter is carried out by (6.50) and a test by (6.51). The needed estimated variance is obtained from the matrix $s^2\{g\}$ in (13.32b). These inference procedures when applied to nonlinear regression are only approximate, to be sure, but the approximation often is very good. For some nonlinear regression models, the sample size can be quite small for the large-sample approximation to be good. For other nonlinear regression models, however, the sample size may need to be quite large.

When Is Large-Sample Theory Applicable?

Ideally, we would like a rule that would tell us when the sample size in any given nonlinear regression application is large enough so that the large-sample inferences based on asymptotic theorem (13.32) are appropriate. Unfortunately, no simple rule exists that tells us when it is appropriate to use the large-sample inference methods and when it is not appropriate. However, a number of guidelines have been developed that are helpful in assessing the appropriateness of using the large-sample inference procedures in a given application.

1. Quick convergence of the iterative procedure in finding the estimates of the nonlinear regression parameters is often an indication that the linear approximation in (13.25) to

the nonlinear regression model is a good approximation and hence that the asymptotic properties of the regression estimates are applicable. Slow convergence suggests caution and consideration of other guidelines before large-sample inferences are employed.

2. Several measures have been developed for providing guidance about the appropriateness of the use of large-sample inference procedures. Bates and Watts (Ref. 13.4) developed curvature measures of nonlinearity. These indicate the extent to which the nonlinear regression function fitted to the data can be reasonably approximated by the linear approximation in (13.25). Box (Ref. 13.5) obtained a formula for estimating the bias of the estimated regression coefficients. A small bias supports the appropriateness of the large-sample inference procedures. Hougaard (Ref. 13.6) developed an estimate of the skewness of the sampling distributions of the estimated regression coefficients. An indication of little skewness supports the approximate normality of the sampling distributions and consequently the applicability of the large-sample inference procedures.

3. Bootstrap sampling described in Chapter 11 provides a direct means of examining whether the sampling distributions of the nonlinear regression parameter estimates are approximately normal, whether the variances of the sampling distributions are near the variances for the linear approximation model, and whether the bias in each of the parameter estimates is fairly small. If so, the sampling behavior of the nonlinear regression estimates is said to be *close-to-linear* and the large-sample inference procedures may appropriately be used. Nonlinear regression estimates whose sampling distributions are not close to normal, whose variances are much larger than the variances for the linear approximation model, and for which there is substantial bias are said to behave in a *far-from-linear* fashion and the large-sample inference procedures are then not appropriate.

Once many bootstrap samples have been obtained and the nonlinear regression parameter estimates calculated for each sample, the bootstrap sampling distribution for each parameter estimate can be examined to see if it is near normal. The variances of the bootstrap distributions of the estimated regression coefficients can be obtained next to see if they are close to the large-sample variance estimates obtained by (13.32b). Similarly, the bootstrap confidence intervals for the regression coefficients can be obtained and compared with the large-sample confidence intervals. Good agreement between these intervals again provides support for the appropriateness of the large-sample inference procedures. In addition, the difference between each final regression parameter estimate and the mean of its bootstrap sampling distribution is an estimate of the bias of the regression estimate. Small or negligible biases of the nonlinear regression estimates support the appropriateness of the large-sample inference procedures.

Remedial Measures. When the diagnostics suggest that large-sample inference procedures are not appropriate in a particular instance, remedial measures should be explored. One possibility is to reparameterize the nonlinear regression model. For example, studies have shown that for the nonlinear model:

$$Y_i = \gamma_0 X_i / (\gamma_1 + X_i) + \varepsilon_i$$

the use of large-sample inference procedures is often not appropriate. However, the following reparameterization:

$$Y_i = X_i / (\theta_1 X_i + \theta_2) + \varepsilon_i$$

where $\theta_1 = 1/\gamma_0$ and $\theta_2 = \gamma_1/\gamma_0$, yields identical fits and generally involves no problems in using large-sample inference procedures for moderate sample sizes (see Ref. 13.7 for details).

Another remedial measure is to use the bootstrap estimates of precision and confidence intervals instead of the large-sample inferences. However, when the linear approximation in (13.25) is not a close approximation to the nonlinear regression model, convergence may be very slow and bootstrap estimates of precision and confidence intervals may be difficult to obtain. Still another remedial measure that is sometimes available is to increase the sample size.

Example

For the severely injured patients example, we know from Table 13.3a on page 524 that the final error sum of squares is $SSE = 49.4593$. Since $p = 2$ parameters are present in the nonlinear response function (13.19), we obtain:

$$MSE = \frac{SSE}{n - p} = \frac{49.4593}{15 - 2} = 3.80456$$

Table 13.3b presents this mean square, and Table 13.3c contains the large-sample estimated variance-covariance matrix of the estimated regression coefficients. The matrix $(\mathbf{D'D})^{-1}$ is based on the final regression coefficient estimates $\mathbf{g}$ and is shown without computational details.

We see from Table 13.3c that $s^2\{g_0\} = 2.1672$ and $s^2\{g_1\} = .000002928$. The estimated standard deviations of the regression coefficients are given in Table 13.3b.

To check on the appropriateness of the large-sample variances of the estimated regression coefficients and on the applicability of large-sample inferences in general, we have generated 1,000 bootstrap samples of size 15. The fixed X sampling procedure was used since the exponential model appears to fit the data well and the error term variance appears to be fairly constant. Histograms of the resulting bootstrap sampling distributions of g_0^* and g_1^* are shown in Figure 13.4, together with some characteristics of these distributions. We see that the g_0^* distribution is close to normal. The g_1^* distribution suggests that the sampling distribution may be slightly skewed to the left, but the departure from normality does not appear to be great. The means of the distribution, denoted by $\bar{g}_0^*$ and $\bar{g}_1^*$, are very close to the final least squares estimates, indicating that the bias in the estimates is negligible:

$$\bar{g}_0^* = 58.67 \qquad \bar{g}_1^* = -.03936$$
$$g_0 = 58.61 \qquad g_1 = -.03959$$

Furthermore, the standard deviations of the bootstrap sampling distributions are very close to the large-sample standard deviations in Table 13.3b:

$$s^*\{g_0^*\} = 1.423 \qquad s^*\{g_1^*\} = .00142$$
$$s\{g_0\} = 1.472 \qquad s\{g_1\} = .00171$$

These indications all point to the appropriateness of large-sample inferences here, even though the sample size ($n = 15$) is not very large.

FIGURE 13.4   Bootstrap Sampling Distributions—Severely Injured Patients Example.

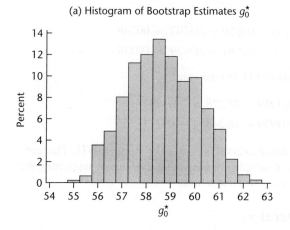

(a) Histogram of Bootstrap Estimates g_0^*

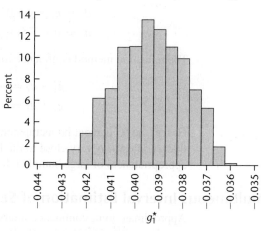

(b) Histogram of Bootstrap Estimates g_1^*

$$\bar{g}_0^* = 58.67$$
$$s^*\{g_0^*\} = 1.423$$
$$g_0^*(.025) = 56.044$$
$$g_0^*(.975) = 61.436$$

$$\bar{g}_1^* = -.03936$$
$$s^*\{g_1^*\} = .00142$$
$$g_1^*(.025) = -.04207$$
$$g_1^*(.975) = -.03681$$

Interval Estimation of a Single γ_k

Based on large-sample theorem (13.32), the following approximate result holds when the sample size is large and the error terms are normally distributed:

$$\frac{g_k - \gamma_k}{s\{g_k\}} \sim t(n - p) \qquad k = 0, 1, \ldots, p - 1 \qquad \textbf{(13.33)}$$

where $t(n - p)$ is a t variable with $n - p$ degrees of freedom. Hence, approximate $1 - \alpha$ confidence limits for any single γ_k are formed by means of (6.50):

$$g_k \pm t(1 - \alpha/2; n - p)s\{g_k\} \qquad \textbf{(13.34)}$$

where $t(1 - \alpha/2; n - p)$ is the $(1 - \alpha/2)100$ percentile of the t distribution with $n - p$ degrees of freedom.

Example

For the severely injured patients example, it is desired to estimate γ_1 with a 95 percent confidence interval. We require $t(.975; 13) = 2.160$, and find from Table 13.3b that $g_1 = -.03959$ and $s\{g_1\} = .00171$. Hence, the confidence limits are $-.03959 \pm 2.160(.00171)$, and the approximate 95 percent confidence interval for γ_1 is:

$$-.0433 \le \gamma_1 \le -.0359$$

Thus, we can conclude with approximate 95 percent confidence that γ_1 is between $-.0433$ and $-.0359$. To confirm the appropriateness of this large-sample confidence interval, we shall obtain the 95 percent bootstrap confidence interval for γ_1. Using (11.58) and the results in Figure 13.4b, we obtain:

$$d_1 = g_1 - g_1^*(.025) = -.03959 + .04207 = .00248$$
$$d_2 = g_1^*(.975) - g_1 = -.03681 + .03959 = .00278$$

The reflection method confidence limits by (11.59) then are:

$$g_1 - d_2 = -.03959 - .00278 = -.04237$$
$$g_1 + d_1 = -.03959 + .00248 = -.03711$$

Hence, the 95 percent bootstrap confidence interval is $-.0424 \leq \gamma_1 \leq -.0371$. This confidence interval is very close to the large-sample confidence interval, again supporting the appropriateness of large-sample inference procedures here.

Simultaneous Interval Estimation of Several γ_k

Approximate joint confidence intervals for several regression parameters in nonlinear regression can be developed by the Bonferroni procedure. If m parameters are to be estimated with approximate family confidence coefficient $1 - \alpha$, the joint Bonferroni confidence limits are:

$$g_k \pm Bs\{g_k\} \qquad (13.35)$$

where:

$$B = t(1 - \alpha/2m; n - p) \qquad (13.35a)$$

Example In the severely injured patients example, it is desired to obtain simultaneous interval estimates for γ_0 and γ_1 with an approximate 90 percent family confidence coefficient. With the Bonferroni procedure we therefore require separate confidence intervals for the two parameters, each with a 95 percent statement confidence coefficient. We have already obtained a confidence interval for γ_1 with a 95 percent statement confidence coefficient. The approximate 95 percent statement confidence limits for γ_0, using the results in Table 13.3b, are $58.6065 \pm 2.160(1.472)$ and the confidence interval for γ_0 is:

$$55.43 \leq \gamma_0 \leq 61.79$$

Hence, the joint confidence intervals with approximate family confidence coefficient of 90 percent are:

$$55.43 \leq \gamma_0 \leq 61.79$$
$$-.0433 \leq \gamma_1 \leq -.0359$$

Test Concerning a Single γ_k

A large-sample test concerning a single γ_k is set up in the usual fashion. To test:

$$H_0\text{: } \gamma_k = \gamma_{k0}$$
$$H_a\text{: } \gamma_k \neq \gamma_{k0} \qquad (13.36a)$$

where γ_{k0} is the specified value of γ_k, we may use the t^* test statistic based on (6.49) when n is reasonably large:

$$t^* = \frac{g_k - \gamma_{k0}}{s\{g_k\}} \tag{13.36b}$$

The decision rule for controlling the risk of making a Type I error at approximately α then is:

$$\text{If } |t^*| \leq t(1 - \alpha/2; n - p), \text{ conclude } H_0$$
$$\text{If } |t^*| > t(1 - \alpha/2; n - p), \text{ conclude } H_a \tag{13.36c}$$

Example   In the severely injured patients example, we wish to test:

$$H_0: \gamma_0 = 54$$
$$H_a: \gamma_0 \neq 54$$

The test statistic (13.36b) here is:

$$t^* = \frac{58.6065 - 54}{1.472} = 3.13$$

For $\alpha = .01$, we require $t(.995; 13) = 3.012$. Since $|t^*| = 3.13 > 3.012$, we conclude H_a, that $\gamma_0 \neq 54$. The approximate two-sided P-value of the test is .008.

Test Concerning Several γ_k

When a large-sample test concerning several γ_k simultaneously is desired, we use the same approach as for the general linear test, first fitting the full model and obtaining $SSE(F)$, then fitting the reduced model and obtaining $SSE(R)$, and finally calculating the same test statistic (2.70) as for linear regression:

$$F^* = \frac{SSE(R) - SSE(F)}{df_R - df_F} \div MSE(F) \tag{13.37}$$

For large n, this test statistic is distributed approximately as $F(df_R - df_F, df_F)$ when H_0 holds.

13.5   Learning Curve Example

We now present a second example, to provide an additional illustration of the nonlinear regression concepts developed in this chapter. An electronics products manufacturer undertook the production of a new product in two locations (location A: coded $X_1 = 1$, location B: coded $X_1 = 0$). Location B has more modern facilities and hence was expected to be more efficient than location A, even after the initial learning period. An industrial engineer calculated the expected unit production cost for a modern facility after learning has occurred. Weekly unit production costs for each location were then expressed as a fraction of this expected cost. The reciprocal of this fraction is a measure of relative efficiency, and this relative efficiency measure was utilized as the response variable (Y) in the study.

It is well known that efficiency increases over time when a new product is produced, and that the improvements eventually slow down and the process stabilizes. Hence, it was decided to employ an exponential model with an upper asymptote for expressing the relation between relative efficiency (Y) and time (X_2), and to incorporate a constant effect for the difference in the two production locations. The model decided on was:

$$Y_i = \gamma_0 + \gamma_1 X_{i1} + \gamma_3 \exp(\gamma_2 X_{i2}) + \varepsilon_i \qquad (13.38)$$

When γ_2 and γ_3 are negative, γ_0 is the upper asymptote for location B as X_2 gets large, and $\gamma_0 + \gamma_1$ is the upper asymptote for location A. The parameters γ_2 and γ_3 reflect the speed of learning, which was expected to be the same in the two locations.

While weekly data on relative production efficiency for each location were available, we shall only use observations for selected weeks during the first 90 weeks of production to simplify the presentation. A portion of the data on location, week, and relative efficiency is presented in Table 13.4; a plot of the data is shown in Figure 13.5. Note that learning was relatively rapid in both locations, and that the relative efficiency in location B toward the

TABLE 13.4
Data—
Learning
Curve
Example.

Observation i	Location X_{i1}	Week X_{i2}	Relative Efficiency Y_i
1	1	1	.483
2	1	2	.539
3	1	3	.618
...	...	...	...
13	1	70	.960
14	1	80	.967
15	1	90	.975
16	0	1	.517
17	0	2	.598
18	0	3	.635
...	...	...	...
28	0	70	1.028
29	0	80	1.017
30	0	90	1.023

FIGURE 13.5
Scatter Plot
and Fitted
Nonlinear
Regression
Functions—
Learning
Curve
Example.

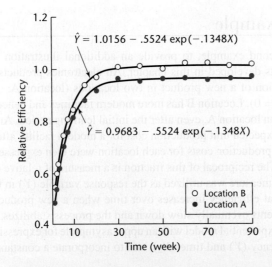

$\hat{Y} = 1.0156 - .5524 \exp(-.1348X)$

$\hat{Y} = 0.9683 - .5524 \exp(-.1348X)$

○ Location B
● Location A

end of the 90-week period even exceeded 1.0; i.e., the actual unit costs at this stage were lower than the industrial engineer's expected unit cost.

Regression model (13.38) is nonlinear in the parameters γ_2 and γ_3. Hence, a direct numerical search estimation procedure was to be employed, for which starting values for the parameters are needed. These were developed partly from past experience, partly from analysis of the data. Previous studies indicated that γ_3 should be in the neighborhood of $-.5$, so $g_3^{(0)} = -.5$ was used as the starting value. Since the difference in the relative efficiencies between locations A and B for a given week tended to average $-.0459$ during the 90-week period, a starting value $g_1^{(0)} = -.0459$ was specified. The largest observed relative efficiency for location B was 1.028, so that a starting value $g_0^{(0)} = 1.025$ was felt to be reasonable. Only a starting value for γ_2 remains to be found. This was chosen by selecting a typical relative efficiency observation in the middle of the time period, $Y_{24} = 1.012$, and equating it to the response function with $X_{24,1} = 0$, $X_{24,2} = 30$, and the starting values for the other regression coefficients (thus ignoring the error term):

$$1.012 = 1.025 - (.5) \exp(30\gamma_2)$$

Solving this equation for γ_2, the starting value $g_2^{(0)} = -.122$ was obtained. Tests for several other representative observations yielded similar starting values, and $g_2^{(0)} = -.122$ was therefore considered to be a reasonable initial value.

With the four starting values $g_0^{(0)} = 1.025$, $g_1^{(0)} = -.0459$, $g_2^{(0)} = -.122$, and $g_3^{(0)} = -.5$, a computer package direct numerical search program was utilized to obtain the least squares estimates. The least squares regression coefficients stabilized after five iterations. The final estimates, together with the large-sample estimated standard deviations of their sampling distributions, are presented in Table 13.5, columns 1 and 2. The fitted regression function is:

$$\hat{Y} = 1.0156 - .04727X_1 - (.5524) \exp(-.1348X_2) \tag{13.39}$$

The error sum of squares is $SSE = .00329$, with $30 - 4 = 26$ degrees of freedom. Figure 13.5 presents the fitted regression functions for the two locations, together with a plot of the data. The fit seems to be quite good, and residual plots (not shown) did not indicate any noticeable departures from the assumed model.

In order to explore the applicability of large-sample inference procedures here, bootstrap fixed X sampling was employed. One thousand bootstrap samples of size 30 were generated.

TABLE 13.5   **Nonlinear Least Squares Estimates and Standard Deviations and Bootstrap Results—Learning Curve Example.**

	(1)	(2)	(3)	(4)
	Nonlinear Least Squares		**Bootstrap**	
k	g_k	$s\{g_k\}$	$\bar{g}_k^*$	$s^*\{g_k^*\}$
0	1.0156	.003672	1.015605	.003374
1	$-.04727$	.004109	$-.04724$	.003702
2	$-.5524$	.008157	$-.55283$	.007275
3	$-.1348$	.004359	$-.13495$	.004102

FIGURE 13.6   MINITAB Histograms of Bootstrap Sampling Distributions—Learning Curve Example.

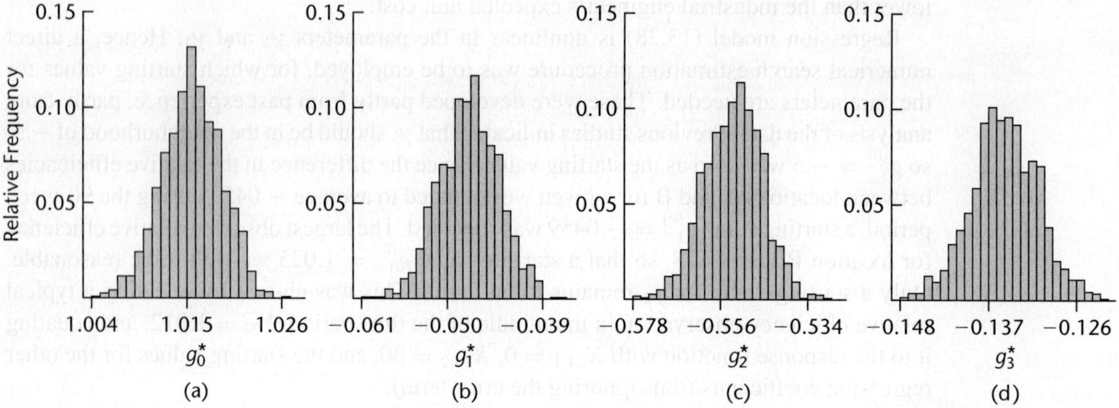

The estimated bootstrap means and standard deviations for each of the sampling distributions are presented in Table 13.5, columns 3 and 4. Note first that each least squares estimate g_k in column 1 of Table 13.5 is very close to the mean $\bar{g}_k^*$ of its respective bootstrap sampling distribution in column 3, indicating that the estimates have very little bias. Note also that each large-sample standard deviation $s\{g_k\}$ in column 2 of Table 13.5 is fairly close to the respective bootstrap standard deviation $s^*\{g_k^*\}$ in column 4, again supporting the applicability of large-sample inference procedures here. Finally, we present in Figure 13.6 MINITAB plots of the histograms of the four bootstrap sampling distributions. They appear to be consistent with approximately normal sampling distributions. These results all indicate that the sampling behavior of the nonlinear regression estimates is close to linear and therefore support the use of large-sample inferences here.

There was special interest in the parameter γ_1, which reflects the effect of location. An approximate 95 percent confidence interval is to be constructed. We require $t(.975;26) = 2.056$. The estimated standard deviation from Table 13.5 is $s\{g_1\} = .004109$. Hence, the approximate 95 percent confidence limits for γ_1 are $-.04727 \pm 2.056(.004109)$, and the confidence interval for γ_1 is:

$$-.0557 \leq \gamma_1 \leq -.0388$$

An approximate 95 percent confidence interval for γ_1 by the bootstrap reflection method was also obtained for comparative purposes using (11.59). It is:

$$-.0547 \leq \gamma_1 \leq -.0400$$

This is very close to that obtained by large-sample inference procedures. Since γ_1 is seen to be negative, these confidence intervals confirm that location A with its less modern facilities tends to be less efficient.

Comments

1. When learning curve models are fitted to data constituting repeated observations on the same unit, such as efficiency data for the same production unit at different points in time, the error terms may be correlated. Hence, in these situations it is important to ascertain whether or not a model assuming

uncorrelated error terms is reasonable. In the learning curve example, a plot of the residuals against time order did not suggest any serious correlations among the error terms.

2. With learning curve models, it is not uncommon to find that the error variances are unequal. Again, therefore, it is important to check whether the assumption of constancy of error variance is reasonable. In the learning curve example, plots of the residuals against the fitted values and time did not suggest any serious heteroscedasticity problem. ∎

13.6 Introduction to Neural Network Modeling

In recent years there has been an explosion in the amount of available data, made possible in part by the widespread availability of low-cost computer memory and automated data collection systems. The regression modeling techniques discussed to this point in this book typically were developed for use with data sets involving fewer than 1,000 observations and fewer than 50 predictors. Yet it is not uncommon now to be faced with data sets involving perhaps millions of observations and hundreds or thousands of predictors. Examples include point-of-sale data in marketing, credit card scoring data, on-line monitoring of production processes, optical character recognition, internet e-mail filtering data, microchip array data, and computerized medical record data. This exponential growth in available data has motivated researchers in the fields of statistics, artificial intelligence, and data mining to develop simple, flexible, powerful procedures for data modeling that can be applied to very large data sets. In this section we discuss one such technique, neural network modeling.

Neural Network Model

The basic idea behind the neural network approach is to model the response as a nonlinear function of various linear combinations of the predictors. Recall that our standard multiple regression model (6.7) involves just one linear combination of the predictors, namely $E\{Y_i\} = \beta_0 + \beta_1 X_{i1} + \cdots + \beta_{p-1} X_{i,p-1}$. Thus, as we will demonstrate, the neural network model is simply a nonlinear statistical model that contains many more parameters than the corresponding linear statistical model. One result of this is that the models will typically be overparameterized, resulting in parameters that are uninterpretable, which is a major shortcoming of neural network modeling. An advantage of the neural network approach is that the resulting model will often perform better in predicting future responses than a standard regression model. Such models require large data sets, and are evaluated solely on their ability to predict responses in hold-out (validation) data sets.

In this section we describe the simplest, but most widely used, neural network model, the *single-hidden-layer, feedforward neural network*. This network is sometimes referred to as a *single-layer perceptron*. In a neural network model the ith response Y_i is modeled as a nonlinear function g_Y of m *derived predictor values*, $H_{i0}, H_{i1}, \ldots, H_{i,m-1}$:

$$Y_i = g_Y(\beta_0 H_{i0} + \beta_1 H_{i1} + \cdots + \beta_{i,m-1} H_{i,m-1}) + \varepsilon_i = g_Y(\mathbf{H}_i'\boldsymbol{\beta}) + \varepsilon_i \quad \textbf{(13.40)}$$

where:

$$\underset{m \times 1}{\boldsymbol{\beta}} = \begin{bmatrix} \beta_0 \\ \beta_1 \\ \vdots \\ \beta_{m-1} \end{bmatrix} \qquad \underset{m \times 1}{\mathbf{H}_i} = \begin{bmatrix} H_{i0} \\ H_{i1} \\ \vdots \\ H_{i,m-1} \end{bmatrix} \qquad \textbf{(13.40a)}$$

We take H_{i0} equal to 1 and for $j = 1, \ldots, p - 1$, the jth derived predictor value for the ith observation, H_{ij}, is a nonlinear function g_j of a linear combination of the original predictors:

$$H_{ij} = g_j(\mathbf{X}'_i \boldsymbol{\alpha}_j) \qquad j = 1, \ldots, m - 1 \qquad \textbf{(13.41)}$$

where:

$$\boldsymbol{\alpha}_j = \begin{bmatrix} \alpha_{j0} \\ \alpha_{j1} \\ \vdots \\ \alpha_{j,p-1} \end{bmatrix} \qquad \mathbf{X}_i = \begin{bmatrix} X_{i0} \\ X_{i1} \\ \vdots \\ X_{i,p-1} \end{bmatrix} \qquad \textbf{(13.41a)}$$

and where $X_{i0} = 1$. Note that $\mathbf{X}'_i$ is the ith row of the $\mathbf{X}$ matrix. Equations (13.40) and (13.41) together form the neural network model:

$$Y_i = g_Y(\mathbf{H}'_i \boldsymbol{\beta}) + \varepsilon_i = g_Y \left[\beta_0 + \sum_{j=1}^{m-1} \beta_j g_j(\mathbf{X}'_i \boldsymbol{\alpha}_j) \right] + \varepsilon_i \qquad \textbf{(13.42)}$$

The m functions $g_Y, g_1, \ldots, g_{m-1}$ are called *activation functions* in the neural networks literature. To completely specify the neural network model, it is necessary to identify the m activation functions. A common choice for each of these functions is the logistic function:

$$g(Z) = \frac{1}{1 + e^{-Z}} = [1 + e^{-Z}]^{-1} \qquad \textbf{(13.43)}$$

This function is flexible and can be adapted to a variety of circumstances.

As a simple example, consider the case of a single predictor, X_1. Then from (13.41), the jth derived predictor for the ith observation is:

$$g_j(\mathbf{X}'_i \boldsymbol{\alpha}_j) = [1 + \exp(-\alpha_{j0} - \alpha_{j1} X_{i1})]^{-1} \qquad \textbf{(13.44)}$$

(Note that (13.44) is a reparameterization of (13.11), with $\gamma_0 = 1$, $\gamma_1 = e^{-\alpha_{j0}}$, and $\gamma_2 = -\alpha_{j1}$.) This function is shown in Figure 13.7 for various choices of α_{j0} and α_{j1}. In Figure 13.7a, the logistic function is plotted for fixed $\alpha_{j0} = 0$, and $\alpha_{j1} = .1$, 1, and 10. When $\alpha_{j1} = .1$, the logistic function is approximately linear over a wide range; when $\alpha_{j1} = 10$, the function is highly nonlinear in the center of the plot. Generally, relatively larger parameters (in absolute value) are required for highly nonlinear responses, and relatively smaller parameters result for approximately linear responses. Changing the sign of α_{j1} reverses the orientation of the logistic function, as shown in Figure 13.7b. Finally, for a given value of α_{j1}, the position of the logistic function along the X_1-axis is controlled by α_{j0}. In Figure 13.7c, the logistic function is plotted for fixed $\alpha_{j1} = 1$ and $\alpha_{j0} = -5$, 0, and 5. Note that all of the plots in Figure 13.7 reflect a characteristic S- or *sigmoidal*-shape, and the fact that the logistic function has a maximum of 1 and a minimum of 0.

Substitution of g in (13.43) for each of $g_Y, g_1, \ldots, g_{m-1}$ in (13.42) yields the specific neural network model to be discussed in this section:

$$
\begin{aligned}
Y_i &= [1 + \exp(-\mathbf{H}'_i \boldsymbol{\beta})]^{-1} + \varepsilon_i \\
&= \left[1 + \exp\left[-\beta_0 - \sum_{j=1}^{m-1} \beta_j [1 + \exp(-\mathbf{X}'_i \boldsymbol{\alpha}_j)]^{-1} \right] \right]^{-1} + \varepsilon_i \\
&= f(\mathbf{X}_i, \boldsymbol{\alpha}_1, \ldots, \boldsymbol{\alpha}_{m-1}, \boldsymbol{\beta}) + \varepsilon_i \qquad \textbf{(13.45)}
\end{aligned}
$$

FIGURE 13.7   **Various Logistic Activation Functions for Single Predictor.**

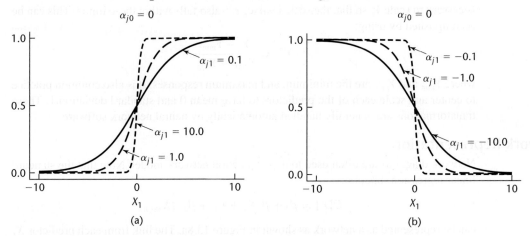

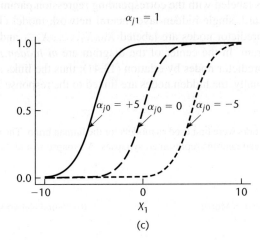

where:

$\boldsymbol{\beta}, \boldsymbol{\alpha}_1, \ldots, \boldsymbol{\alpha}_{m-1}$ are unknown parameter vectors

$\mathbf{X}_i$ is a vector of known constants

ε_i are residuals

Neural network model (13.45) is a special case of (13.12) and is therefore a nonlinear regression model. In principle, all of the methods discussed in this chapter for estimation, testing, and prediction with nonlinear models are applicable. Indeed, any nonlinear regression package can be used to estimate the unknown coefficients. Recall, however, that these models are generally overparameterized, and use of standard estimation methods will result in fitted models that have poor predictive ability. This is analogous to leaving too many unimportant predictors in a linear regression model. Special procedures for fitting model (13.45) that lead to better prediction will be considered later in this section.

Note that because the logistic activation function is bounded between 0 and 1, it is necessary to scale Y_i so that the scaled value, Y_i^{sc} also falls within these limits. This can be accomplished by using:

$$Y_i^{sc} = \frac{Y_i - Y_{\min}}{Y_{\max} - Y_{\min}}$$

where $Y_{\min}$ and $Y_{\max}$ are the minimum and maximum responses. It is also common practice to center and scale each of the predictors to have mean 0 and standard deviation 1. These transformations are generally handled automatically by neural network software.

Network Representation

Network diagrams are often used to depict a neural network model. Note that the standard linear regression function:

$$E\{Y\} = \beta_0 + \beta_1 X_1 + \cdots + \beta_{p-1} X_{p-1}$$

can be represented as a network as shown in Figure 13.8a. The link from each predictor X_i to the response is labeled with the corresponding regression parameter, β_i.

The feedforward, single-hidden-layer neural network model (13.45) is shown in Figure 13.8b. The predictor nodes are labeled $X_0, X_1, \ldots, X_{p-1}$ and are located on the left side of the diagram. In the center of the diagram are *m hidden nodes*. These nodes are linked to the p predictor nodes by relation (13.41); thus the links are labeled by using the α parameters. Finally, the hidden nodes are linked to the response Y by the β parameters.

Comments

1. Neural networks were first used as models for the human brain. The nodes represented neurons and the links between neurons represented synapses. A synapse would "fire" if the signal surpassed

FIGURE 13.8
Network Representations of Linear Regression and Neural Network Models.

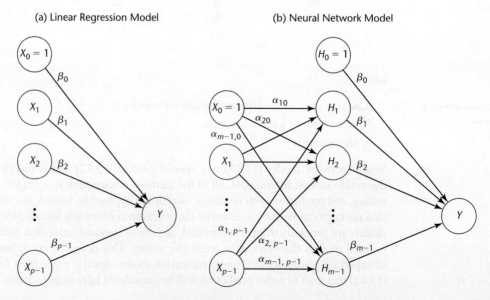

(a) Linear Regression Model

(b) Neural Network Model

a threshold. This suggested the use of step functions for the activation function, which were later replaced by smooth functions such as the logistic function.

2. The logistic activation function is sometimes replaced by a *radial basis function,* which is an n-dimensional normal probability density function. Details are provided in Reference 13.8. ∎

Neural Network as Generalization of Linear Regression

It is easy to see that the standard multiple regression model is a special case of neural network model (13.45). If we choose for each of the activation functions $g_Y, g_1, \ldots, g_{m-1}$ the identity activation:

$$g(Z) = Z$$

we have:

$$E\{Y_i\} = \beta_0 + \beta_1 H_{i1} + \cdots + \beta_{m-1} H_{i,m-1} \tag{13.46a}$$

and:

$$H_{ij} = \alpha_{j0} + \alpha_{j1} X_{i1} + \cdots + \alpha_{j,p-1} X_{i,p-1} \tag{13.46b}$$

Substitution of (13.46b) into (13.46a) and rearranging yields:

$$
E\{Y_i\} = \left[\beta_0 + \sum_{j=1}^{m-1} \beta_j \alpha_{j0} \right] + \left[\sum_{j=1}^{m-1} \beta_j \alpha_{j1} \right] X_{i1} + \cdots + \left[\sum_{j=1}^{m-1} \beta_j \alpha_{j,p-1} \right] X_{i,p-1}
$$
$$
= \beta_0^* + \beta_1^* X_{i1} + \cdots + \beta_{p-1}^* X_{i,p-1} \tag{13.47}
$$

where:

$$\beta_0^* = \beta_0 + \sum_{j=1}^{m-1} \beta_j \alpha_{j0}$$

$$\beta_k^* = \sum_{j=1}^{m-1} \beta_j \alpha_{jk} \qquad \text{for } k = 1, \ldots, p-1 \tag{13.47a}$$

The neural network with identity activation functions thus reduces to the standard linear regression model.

There is a problem, however, with the interpretation of the neural network regression coefficients. If the regression function is given by $E\{Y_i\} = \beta_0^* + \beta_1^* X_{i1} + \cdots + \beta_p^* X_{i,p-1}$ as indicated in (13.47), then *any* set of neural network parameters satisfying the p equations in (13.47a) gives the correct model. Since there are many more neural network parameters than there are equations (or equivalently, β^* parameters) there are infinitely many sets of neural network parameters that lead to the correct model. Thus, any particular set of neural network parameters will have no intrinsic meaning in this case.

This overparameterization problem is somewhat reduced with the use of the logistic activation function in place of the identity function. Generally, however, if the number of hidden nodes is more than just a few, overparameterization will be present, and will lead to a fitted model with low predictive ability unless this issue is explicitly considered when the parameters are estimated. We now take up such estimation procedures.

Parameter Estimation: Penalized Least Squares

In Chapter 9 we considered model selection and validation. There, we observed that while R^2 never decreases with the addition of a new predictor, our ability to predict holdout responses in the validation stage can deteriorate if too many predictors are incorporated. Various model selection criteria, such as $R_{a,p}^2$, SBC_p, and AIC_p, have been adopted that contain penalties for the addition of predictors. We commented in Section 11.2 that ridge regression estimates can be obtained by the method of penalized least squares, which directly incorporates a penalty for the sum of squares of the regression coefficients. In order to control the level of overfitting, penalized least squares is frequently used for parameter estimation with neural networks.

The penalized least squares criterion is given by:

$$Q = \sum_{i=1}^{n} [Y_i - f(\mathbf{X}_i, \boldsymbol{\beta}, \boldsymbol{\alpha}_1, \ldots, \boldsymbol{\alpha}_{m-1}]^2 + p_\lambda(\boldsymbol{\beta}, \boldsymbol{\alpha}_1, \ldots, \boldsymbol{\alpha}_{m-1}) \qquad \textbf{(13.48)}$$

where the overfit penalty is:

$$p_\lambda(\boldsymbol{\beta}, \boldsymbol{\alpha}_1, \ldots, \boldsymbol{\alpha}_{m-1}) = \lambda \left[\sum_{i=0}^{m-1} \beta_i^2 + \sum_{i=1}^{m-1} \sum_{j=0}^{p-1} \alpha_{ij}^2 \right] \qquad \textbf{(13.48a)}$$

Thus, the penalty is a positive constant, λ, times the sum of squares of the nonlinear regression coefficients. Note that the penalty is imposed not on the number of parameters $m + mp$, but on the total magnitude of the parameters. The *penalty weight* λ assigned to the regression coefficients governs the trade-off between overfitting and underfitting. If λ is large, the parameters estimates will be relatively small in absolute magnitude; if λ is small, the estimates will be relatively large. A "best" value for λ is generally between .001 and .1 and is chosen by cross-validation. For example, we may fit the model for a range of λ-values between .001 and .1, and choose the value that minimizes the total prediction error of the hold-out sample. The resulting parameter estimates are called shrinkage estimates because use of $\lambda > 0$ leads to reductions in their absolute magnitudes.

In Section 13.3 we described various search procedures, such as the Gauss-Newton method for finding nonlinear least squares estimates. Such methods can also be used with neural networks and penalized least squares criterion (13.48). We observed in Comment 1 on page 524, that the choice of starting values is important. Poor choice of starting values may lead to convergence to a local minimum (rather than the global minimum) when multiple minima exist. The problem of multiple minima is especially prevalent when fitting neural networks, due to the typically large numbers of parameters and the functional form of model (13.48). For this reason, it is common practice to fit the model many times (typically between 10 and 50 times) using different sets of randomly chosen starting values for each fit. The set of parameter estimates that leads to the lowest value of criterion function (13.48)—i.e., the best of the best—is chosen for further study. In the neural networks literature, finding a set of parameter values that minimize criterion (13.48) is referred to as *training the network*. The number of searches conducted before arriving at the final estimates is referred to as the number of *tours*.

Comment

Neural networks are often trained by a procedure called *back-propagation*. Back propagation is in fact the method of steepest descent, which can be very slow. Recommended methods include the *conjugate gradient* and *variable metric* methods. Reference 13.8 provides further details concerning back-propagation and other search procedures. ∎

Example: Ischemic Heart Disease

We illustrate the use of neural network model (13.44) and the penalized least squares fitting procedure using the Ischemic heart disease data set in Appendix C.9. These data were collected by a health insurance plan and provide information concerning 788 subscribers who made claims resulting from coronary heart disease. The response (Y) is the natural logarithm of the total cost of services provided and the predictors to be studied here are:

Predictor	Description
X_1:	Number of interventions, or procedures, carried out
X_2:	Number of tracked drugs used
X_3:	Number of comorbidities—other conditions present that complicate the treatment
X_4:	Number of complications—other conditions that arose during treatment due to heart disease

The first 400 observations are used to fit model (13.45) and the last $n^* = 388$ observations were held out for validation. (Note that the observations were originally sorted in a random order, so that the hold-out data set is a random sample.) We used JMP to fit and evaluate the neural network model.

Shown in Figure 13.9 is the JMP control panel, which allows the user to specify the various characteristics of the model and the fitting procedure. Here, we have chosen 5 hidden nodes, and we are using $\lambda = .05$ as the penalty weight. Also, we have chosen the default values for the number of tours (20), the maximum number of iterations for the search procedure

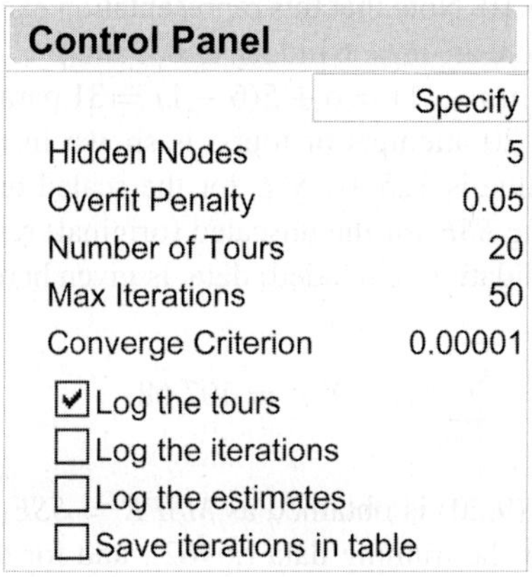

FIGURE 13.9
JMP Control Panel for Neural Network Fit—Ischemic Heart Disease Example.

Control Panel	
	Specify
Hidden Nodes	5
Overfit Penalty	0.05
Number of Tours	20
Max Iterations	50
Converge Criterion	0.00001

☑ Log the tours
☐ Log the iterations
☐ Log the estimates
☐ Save iterations in table

FIGURE 13.10
JMP Neural Network Diagram—Ischemic Heart Disease Example.

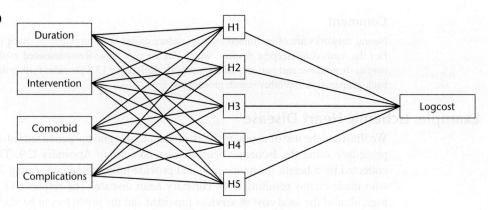

FIGURE 13.11
JMP Results for Neural Network Fit—Ischemic Heart Disease Example.

Results

Objective	
SSE	120.90315177
Penalty	4.4087731663
Total	125.31192493

17 Converged At Best
2 Converged Worse Than Best
0 Stuck on Flat
0 Failed to Improve
1 Reached Max Iter

Y	SSE	SSE Scaled	SSE Excluded	RMSE	RSquare	RSquare Excluded
logCost	441.3037691	120.90315177	407.68215505	0.55465449	0.6962	0.7024

(50) and the convergence criterion (.00001). By checking the "log the tours" box, we will be keeping a record of the results of each of the 20 tours. A JMP network representation of model (13.45) is shown in Figure 13.10. Note that this representation excludes the constant nodes X_0 and H_0. In our notation, there are $m = 6$ hidden nodes and $p = 5$ predictor nodes, and it is necessary to estimate $m + p(m - 1) = 6 + 5(6 - 1) = 31$ parameters.

The results of the best fit, after 20 attempts or tours, is shown in Figure 13.11. The penalized least squares criterion value is 125.31. *SSE* for the scaled response is 120.90. JMP indicates that the corresponding *SSE* for the unscaled (original) responses is 441.30. The total prediction error for the validation (excluded) data, is given here by:

$$SSE_{VAL} = \sum_{i=401}^{788} (Y_i - \hat{Y}_i)^2 = 407.68$$

The mean squared prediction error (9.20) is obtained as $MSPR = SSE_{VAL}/n^* = 407.68/388 = 1.05$. JMP also gives R^2 for the training data (.6962), and for the validation data

FIGURE 13.12
JMP
Parameter
Estimates for
Neural
Network
Fit—Ischemic
Heart Disease
Example.

Parameter Estimates	
Parameter	Estimate
H1:Intercept	0.3216346311
H2:Intercept	1.2553122156
H3:Intercept	2.5829942469
H4:Intercept	-1.505357347
H5:Intercept	-1.832118976
H1:Duration	-0.410405493
H1:Interventions	2.7694118008
H1:Comorbids	1.3823080642
H1:Complications	0.4148583852
H2:Duration	0.1040924583
H2:Interventions	0.983043751
H2:Comorbids	2.3589628016
H2:Complications	-0.201333282
H3:Duration	1.5025299752
H3:Interventions	1.0761596691
H3:Comorbids	-0.414620124
H3:Complications	0.0543940406
H4:Duration	1.2332218124
H4:Interventions	-4.887856867
H4:Comorbids	-1.576610999
H4:Complications	-1.068032684
H5:Duration	-0.159788267
H5:Interventions	1.2562445429
H5:Comorbids	0.1951585824
H5:Complications	0.3717883109
logCost:Intercept	-0.443318204
logCost:H1	-2.165884717
logCost:H2	1.4877032149
logCost:H3	1.5396831425
logCost:H4	-2.285420806
logCost:H5	1.662288417

(.7024). This latter diagnostic was obtained using:

$$R_{VAL}^2 = 1 - \frac{SSE_{VAL}}{SST_{VAL}}$$

where SST_{VAL} is the total sum of squares for the validation data. Because these R^2 values are approximately equal, we conclude that the use of weight penalty $\lambda = .05$ led to a good balance between underfitting and overfitting.

Figure 13.12 shows the 31 parameter estimates produced by JMP and the corresponding parameters. We display these values only for completeness–we make no attempt at interpretation. As noted earlier, our interest is centered on the prediction of future responses.

For comparison, two least squares regressions of Y on the four predictors X_1, X_2, X_3, and X_4 were also carried out. The first was based on a first-order model consisting of the four predictors and an intercept term; the second was based on a full second-order model consisting of an intercept plus the four linear terms, the four quadratic terms, and the six cross-products among the four predictors. The results for these two multiple regression models and the neural network model are summarized in the Table 13.6.

From the results, we see that the neural network model's ability to predict holdout responses is superior to the first-order multiple regression and slightly better that the second-order multiple regression model. *MSPR* for the neural network is 1.05, whereas this statistic for the first and second-order multiple regression models is 1.28 and 1.09, respectively.

TABLE 13.6
Comparisons of Results for Neural Network Model with Multiple Linear Regression Model— Ischemic Heart Disease Example.

	Neural Network	Multiple Linear Regression	
		First-Order	Second-Order
Number of Parameters	31	5	15
MSE	1.20	1.74	1.34
MSPR	1.05	1.28	1.09

FIGURE 13.13
Conditional Effects Plot—Ischemic Heart Disease Example.

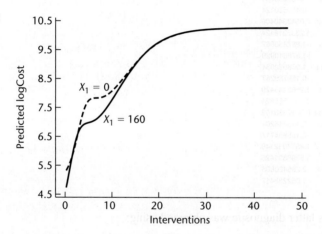

Model Interpretation and Prediction

While individual parameters and derived predictors are usually not interpretable, some understanding of the effects of individual predictors can be realized through the use of conditional effects plots. For example, Figure 13.13 shows for the ischemic heart data example, plots of predicted response as a function the number of interventions (X_2) for duration (X_1) equal to 0 and 160. The remaining predictors, comorbidities ($X_3 = 3.55$) and complications ($X_4 = 0.05$), are fixed at their averages for values in the training set. The plot indicates that the natural logarithm of cost increases rapidly as the number of interventions increases from 0 to 25, and then reaches a plateau and is stable as the number of interventions increases from 25 to 50. The duration variable seems to have very little effect, except possibly when interventions are between 5 and 10.

We have noted that neural network models can be very effective tools for prediction when large data sets are available. As always, it is important that the uncertainty in any prediction be quantified. Methods for producing approximate confidence intervals for estimation and prediction have been developed and some packages such as JMP now provide these intervals. Details are provided in Reference 13.9.

Some Final Comments on Neural Network Modeling

In recent years, neural networks have found widespread application in many fields. Indeed, they have become one of the standard tools in the field of data mining, and their use continues to grow. This is due largely to the widespread availability of powerful computers that permit the fitting of complex models having dozens, hundreds, and even thousands, of parameters.

A vocabulary has developed that is unique to the field of neural networks. The table below (adapted from Ref. 13.10) lists a number of terms that are commonly used by statisticians and their neural network equivalents:

Statistical Term	Neural Network Term
coefficient	weight
predictor	input
response	output
observation	exemplar
parameter estimation	training or learning
steepest descent	back-propagation
intercept	bias term
derived predictor	hidden node
penalty function	weight decay

There are a number of advantages to the neural network modeling approach. These include:

1. Model (13.45) is extremely flexible, and can be used to represent a wide range of response surface shapes. For example, with sufficient data, curvatures, interactions, plateaus, and step functions can be effectively modeled.
2. Standard regression assumptions, such as the requirements that the true residuals are mutually independent, normally distributed, and have constant variance, are not required for neural network modeling.
3. Outliers in the response and predictors can still have a detrimental effect on the fit of the model, but the use of the bounded logistic activation function tends to limit the influence of individual cases in comparison with standard regression approaches.

Of course, there are disadvantages associated with the use of neural networks. Model parameters are generally uninterpretable, and the method depends on the availability of large data sets. Diagnostics, such as lack of fit tests, identification of influential observations and outliers, and significance testing for the effects of the various predictors, are currently not generally available.

Cited References

13.1. Hartley, H. O. "The Modified Gauss-Newton Method for the Fitting of Non-linear Regression Functions by Least Squares," *Technometrics* 3 (1961), pp. 269–80.

13.2. Gallant, A. R. *Nonlinear Statistical Models.* New York: John Wiley & Sons, 1987.

13.3. Kennedy, W. J., Jr., and J. E. Gentle. *Statistical Computing.* New York: Marcel Dekker, 1980.

13.4. Bates, D. M., and D. G. Watts. *Nonlinear Regression Analysis and Its Applications.* New York: John Wiley & Sons, 1988.

13.5. Box, M. J. "Bias in Nonlinear Estimation," *Journal of the Royal Statistical Society B* 33 (1971), pp. 171–201.

13.6. Hougaard, P. "The Appropriateness of the Asymptotic Distribution in a Nonlinear Regression Model in Relation to Curvature," *Journal of the Royal Statistical Society B* 47 (1985), pp. 103–14.

13.7. Ratkowsky, D. A. *Nonlinear Regression Modeling.* New York: Marcel Dekker, 1983.

13.8. Hastie, T., Tibshirani, R., and J. Friedman. *The Elements of Statistical Learning: Data Mining, Inference, and Prediction.* New York: Springer, 2001.

13.9. DeVeaux, R. D., Schumi, J., Schweinsberg, J., and L. H. Ungar. "Prediction Intervals for Neural Networks via Nonlinear Regression," *Technometrics* 40 (1998), pp. 273–82.

13.10. DeVeaux, R. D., and L. H. Ungar. "A Brief Introduction to Neural Networks," www.williams.edu/mathematics/rdeveaux/pubs.html (1996).

Problems

*13.1. For each of the following response functions, indicate whether it is a linear response function, an intrinsically linear response function, or a nonlinear response function. In the case of an intrinsically linear response function, state how it can be linearized by a suitable transformation:

a. $f(\mathbf{X}, \boldsymbol{\gamma}) = \exp(\gamma_0 + \gamma_1 X)$

b. $f(\mathbf{X}, \boldsymbol{\gamma}) = \gamma_0 + \gamma_1(\gamma_2)^{X_1} - \gamma_3 X_2$

c. $f(\mathbf{X}, \boldsymbol{\gamma}) = \gamma_0 + \dfrac{\gamma_1}{\gamma_0} X$

13.2. For each of the following response functions, indicate whether it is a linear response function, an intrinsically linear response function, or a nonlinear response function. In the case of an intrinsically linear response function, state how it can be linearized by a suitable transformation:

a. $f(\mathbf{X}, \boldsymbol{\gamma}) = \exp(\gamma_0 + \gamma_1 \log_e X)$

b. $f(\mathbf{X}, \boldsymbol{\gamma}) = \gamma_0 (X_1)^{\gamma_1} (X_2)^{\gamma_2}$

c. $f(\mathbf{X}, \boldsymbol{\gamma}) = \gamma_0 - \gamma_1(\gamma_2)^{X}$

*13.3. a. Plot the logistic response function:

$$f(\mathbf{X}, \boldsymbol{\gamma}) = \frac{300}{1 + (30)\exp(-1.5X)} \qquad X \geq 0$$

b. What is the asymptote of this response function? For what value of X does the response function reach 90 percent of its asymptote?

13.4. a. Plot the exponential response function:

$$f(\mathbf{X}, \boldsymbol{\gamma}) = 49 - (30)\exp(-1.1X) \qquad X \geq 0$$

b. What is the asymptote of this response function? For what value of X does the response function reach 95 percent of its asymptote?

*13.5. **Home computers.** A computer manufacturer hired a market research firm to investigate the relationship between the likelihood a family will purchase a home computer and the price of the home computer. The data that follow are based on replicate surveys done in two similar cities. One thousand heads of households in each city were randomly selected and asked if they would be likely to purchase a home computer at a given price. Eight prices (X, in dollars) were studied, and 100 heads of households in each city were randomly assigned to a given price. The proportion likely to purchase at a given price is denoted by Y.

City A

i:	1	2	3	4	5	6	7	8
X_i:	200	400	800	1200	1600	2000	3000	4000
Y_i:	.65	.46	.34	.26	.17	.15	.06	.04

City B

i:	9	10	11	12	13	14	15	16
X_i:	200	400	800	1200	1600	2000	3000	4000
Y_i:	.63	.50	.30	.24	.19	.12	.08	.05

No location effect is expected and the data are to be treated as independent replicates at each of the 8 prices. The following exponential model with independent normal error terms is deemed to be appropriate:

$$Y_i = \gamma_0 + \gamma_2 \exp(-\gamma_1 X_i) + \varepsilon_i$$

a. To obtain initial estimates of γ_0, γ_1, and γ_2, note that $f(\mathbf{X}, \boldsymbol{\gamma})$ approaches a lower asymptote γ_0 as X increases without bound. Hence, let $g_0^{(0)} = 0$ and observe that when we ignore the error term, a logarithmic transformation then yields $Y_i' = \beta_0 + \beta_1 X_i$, where $Y_i' = \log_e Y_i$, $\beta_0 = \log_e \gamma_2$, and $\beta_1 = -\gamma_1$. Therefore, fit a linear regression function based on the transformed data and use as initial estimates $g_0^{(0)} = 0$, $g_1^{(0)} = -b_1$, and $g_2^{(0)} = \exp(b_0)$.

b. Using the starting values obtained in part (a), find the least squares estimates of the parameters γ_0, γ_1, and γ_2.

*13.6. Refer to **Home computers** Problem 13.5.

a. Plot the estimated nonlinear regression function and the data. Does the fit appear to be adequate?

b. Obtain the residuals and plot them against the fitted values and against X on separate graphs. Also obtain a normal probability plot. Does the model appear to be adequate?

*13.7. Refer to **Home computers** Problem 13.5. Assume that large-sample inferences are appropriate here. Conduct a formal approximate test for lack of fit of the nonlinear regression function; use $\alpha = .01$. State the alternatives, decision rule, and conclusion.

*13.8. Refer to **Home computers** Problem 13.5. Assume that the fitted model is appropriate and that large-sample inferences can be employed. Obtain approximate joint confidence intervals for the parameters γ_0, γ_1, and γ_2, using the Bonferroni procedure and a 90 percent family confidence coefficient.

*13.9. Refer to **Home computers** Problem 13.5. A question has been raised whether the two cities are similar enough so that the data can be considered to be replicates. Adding a location effect parameter analogous to (13.38) to the model proposed in Problem 13.5 yields the four-parameter nonlinear regression model:

$$Y_i = \gamma_0 + \gamma_3 X_{i2} + \gamma_2 \exp(-\gamma_1 X_{i1}) + \varepsilon_i$$

where:

$$X_2 = \begin{cases} 0 & \text{if city A} \\ 1 & \text{if city B} \end{cases}$$

a. Using the same starting values as those obtained in Problem 13.5a and $g_3^{(0)} = 0$, find the least squares estimates of the parameters γ_0, γ_1, γ_2, and γ_3.

b. Assume that large-sample inferences can be employed reasonably here. Obtain an approximate 95 percent confidence interval for γ_3. What does this interval indicate about city differences? Is this result consistent with your conclusion in Problem 13.7? Does it have to be? Discuss.

13.10. **Enzyme kinetics.** In an enzyme kinetics study the velocity of a reaction (Y) is expected to be related to the concentration (X) as follows:

$$Y_i = \frac{\gamma_0 X_i}{\gamma_1 + X_i} + \varepsilon_i$$

Eighteen concentrations have been studied and the results follow:

i:	1	2	3	...	16	17	18
X_i:	1	1.5	2	...	30	35	40
Y_i:	2.1	2.5	4.9	...	19.7	21.3	21.6

a. To obtain starting values for γ_0 and γ_1, observe that when the error term is ignored we have $Y_i' = \beta_0 + \beta_1 X_i'$, where $Y_i' = 1/Y_i$, $\beta_0 = 1/\gamma_0$, $\beta_1 = \gamma_1/\gamma_0$, and $X_i' = 1/X_i$. Therefore fit a linear regression function to the transformed data to obtain initial estimates $g_0^{(0)} = 1/b_0$ and $g_1^{(0)} = b_1/b_0$.

b. Using the starting values obtained in part (a), find the least squares estimates of the parameters γ_0 and γ_1.

13.11. Refer to **Enzyme kinetics** Problem 13.10.

a. Plot the estimated nonlinear regression function and the data. Does the fit appear to be adequate?

b. Obtain the residuals and plot them against the fitted values and against X on separate graphs. Also obtain a normal probability plot. What do your plots show?

c. Can you conduct an approximate formal lack of fit test here? Explain.

d. Given that only 18 trials can be made, what are some advantages and disadvantages of considering fewer concentration levels but with some replications, as compared to considering 18 different concentration levels as was done here?

13.12. Refer to **Enzyme kinetics** Problem 13.10. Assume that the fitted model is appropriate and that large-sample inferences can be employed here. (1) Obtain an approximate 95 percent confidence interval for γ_0. (2) Test whether or not $\gamma_1 = 20$; use $\alpha = .05$. State the alternatives, decision rule, and conclusion.

*13.13. **Drug responsiveness.** A pharmacologist modeled the responsiveness to a drug using the following nonlinear regression model:

$$Y_i = \gamma_0 - \frac{\gamma_0}{1 + \left(\dfrac{X_i}{\gamma_2}\right)^{\gamma_1}} + \varepsilon_i$$

X denotes the dose level, in coded form, and Y the responsiveness expressed as a percent of the maximum possible responsiveness. In the model, γ_0 is the expected response at saturation, γ_2 is the concentration that produces a half-maximal response, and γ_1 is related to the slope. The data for 19 cases at 13 dose levels follow:

i:	1	2	3	...	17	18	19
X_i:	1	2	3	...	7	8	9
Y_i:	.5	2.3	3.4	...	94.8	96.2	96.4

Obtain least squares estimates of the parameters γ_0, γ_1, and γ_2, using starting values $g_0^{(0)} = 100$, $g_1^{(0)} = 5$, and $g_2^{(0)} = 4.8$.

*13.14. Refer to **Drug responsiveness** Problem 13.13.

a. Plot the estimated nonlinear regression function and the data. Does the fit appear to be adequate?

b. Obtain the residuals and plot them against the fitted values and against X on separate graphs. Also obtain a normal probability plot. What do your plots show about the adequacy of the regression model?

*13.15. Refer to **Drug responsiveness** Problem 13.13. Assume that large-sample inferences are appropriate here. Conduct a formal approximate test for lack of fit of the nonlinear regression function; use $\alpha = .01$. State the alternatives, decision rule, and conclusion.

*13.16. Refer to **Drug responsiveness** Problem 13.13. Assume that the fitted model is appropriate and that large-sample inferences can be employed here. Obtain approximate joint confidence intervals for the parameters γ_0, γ_1, and γ_2 using the Bonferroni procedure with a 91 percent family confidence coefficient. Interpret your results.

13.17. **Process yield.** The yield (Y) of a chemical process depends on the temperature (X_1) and pressure (X_2). The following nonlinear regression model is expected to be applicable:

$$Y_i = \gamma_0 (X_{i1})^{\gamma_1} (X_{i2})^{\gamma_2} + \varepsilon_i$$

Prior to beginning full-scale production, 18 tests were undertaken to study the process yield for various temperature and pressure combinations. The results follow.

i:	1	2	3	...	16	17	18
X_{i1}:	1	10	100	...	1	10	100
X_{i2}:	1	1	1	...	100	100	100
Y_i:	12	32	103	...	43	128	398

a. To obtain starting values for γ_0, γ_1, and γ_2, note that when we ignore the random error term, a logarithmic transformation yields $Y_i' = \beta_0 + \beta_1 X_{i1}' + \beta_1 X_{i2}'$, where $Y_i' = \log_{10} Y_i$, $\beta_0 = \log_{10} \gamma_0$, $\beta_1 = \gamma_1$, $X_{i1}' = \log_{10} X_{i1}$, $\beta_2 = \gamma_2$, and $X_{i2}' = \log_{10} X_{i2}$. Fit a first-order multiple regression model to the transformed data, and use as starting values $g_0^{(0)} = \text{antilog}_{10} b_0$, $g_1^{(0)} = b_1$, and $g_2^{(0)} = b_2$.

b. Using the starting values obtained in part (a), find the least squares estimates of the parameters γ_0, γ_1, and γ_2.

13.18. Refer to **Process yield** Problem 13.17.

a. Plot the estimated nonlinear regression function and the data. Does the fit appear to be adequate?

b. Obtain the residuals and plot them against $\hat{Y}$, X_1, and X_2 on separate graphs. Also obtain a normal probability plot. What do your plots show about the adequacy of the model?

13.19. Refer to **Process yield** Problem 13.17. Assume that large-sample inferences are appropriate here. Conduct a formal approximate test for lack of fit of the nonlinear regression function; use $\alpha = .05$. State the alternatives, decision rule, and conclusion.

13.20. Refer to **Process yield** Problem 13.17. Assume that the fitted model is appropriate and that large-sample inferences are applicable here.

a. Test the hypotheses $H_0: \gamma_1 = \gamma_2$ against $H_a: \gamma_1 \neq \gamma_2$ using $\alpha = .05$. State the alternatives, decision rule, and conclusion.

b. Obtain approximate joint confidence intervals for the parameters γ_1 and γ_2, using the Bonferroni procedure and a 95 percent family confidence coefficient.

c. What do you conclude about the parameters γ_1 and γ_2 based on the results in parts (a) and (b)?

Exercises

13.21. (Calculus needed.) Refer to **Home computers** Problem 13.5.

a. Obtain the least squares normal equations and show that they are nonlinear in the estimated regression coefficients g_0, g_1, and g_2.

b. State the likelihood function for the nonlinear regression model, assuming that the error terms are independent $N(0, \sigma^2)$.

13.22. (Calculus needed.) Refer to **Enzyme kinetics** Problem 13.10.

a. Obtain the least squares normal equations and show that they are nonlinear in the estimated regression coefficients g_0 and g_1.

b. State the likelihood function for the nonlinear regression model, assuming that the error terms are independent $N(0, \sigma^2)$.

13.23. (Calculus needed.) Refer to **Process yield** Problem 13.17.

a. Obtain the least squares normal equations and show that they are nonlinear in the estimated regression coefficients g_0, g_1, and g_2.

b. State the likelihood function for the nonlinear regression model, assuming that the error terms are independent $N(0, \sigma^2)$.

13.24. Refer to **Drug responsiveness** Problem 13.13.

a. Assuming that $E\{\varepsilon_i\} = 0$, show that:

$$E\{Y\} = \gamma_0 \left(\frac{A}{1 + A} \right)$$

where:

$$A = \exp[\gamma_1 (\log_e X - \log_e \gamma_2)] = \exp(\beta_0 + \beta_1 X')$$

and $\beta_0 = -\gamma_1 \log_e \gamma_2$, $\beta_1 = \gamma_1$, and $X' = \log_e X$.

b. Assuming γ_0 is known, show that:

$$\frac{E\{Y'\}}{1 - E\{Y'\}} = \exp(\beta_0 + \beta_1 X')$$

where $Y' = Y/\gamma_0$.

c. What transformation do these results suggest for obtaining a simple linear regression function in the transformed variables?

d. How can starting values for finding the least squares estimates of the nonlinear regression parameters be obtained from the estimates of the linear regression coefficients?

Projects

13.25. Refer to **Enzyme kinetics** Problem 13.10. Starting values for finding the least squares estimates of the nonlinear regression model parameters are to be obtained by a grid search. The following bounds for the two parameters have been specified:

$$5 \leq \gamma_0 \leq 65$$
$$5 \leq \gamma_1 \leq 65$$

Obtain 49 grid points by using all possible combinations of the boundary values and five other equally spaced points for each parameter range. Evaluate the least squares criterion (13.15) for each grid point and identify the point providing the best fit. Does this point give reasonable starting values here?

13.26. Refer to **Process yield** Problem 13.17. Starting values for finding the least squares estimates of the nonlinear regression model parameters are to be obtained by a grid search. The following bounds for the parameters have been postulated:

$$1 \leq \gamma_0 \leq 21$$
$$.2 \leq \gamma_1 \leq .8$$
$$.1 \leq \gamma_2 \leq .7$$

Obtain 27 grid points by using all possible combinations of the boundary values and the midpoint for each of the parameter ranges. Evaluate the least squares criterion (13.15) for each grid point and identify the point providing the best fit. Does this point give reasonable starting values here?

13.27. Refer to **Home computers** Problem 13.5.

a. To check on the appropriateness of large-sample inferences here, generate 1,000 bootstrap samples of size 16 using the fixed X sampling procedure. For each bootstrap sample, obtain the least squares estimates g_0^*, g_1^*, and g_2^*.

b. Plot histograms of the bootstrap sampling distributions of g_0^*, g_1^*, and g_2^*. Do these distributions appear to be approximately normal?

c. Compute the means and standard deviations of the bootstrap sampling distributions for g_0^*, g_1^*, and g_2^*. Are the bootstrap means and standard deviations close to the final least squares estimates?

d. Obtain a confidence interval for γ_1 using the reflection method in (11.59) and confidence coefficient .9667. How does this interval compare with the one obtained in Problem 13.8 by the large-sample inference method?

e. What are the implications of your findings in parts (b), (c), and (d) about the appropriateness of large-sample inferences here? Discuss.

13.28. Refer to **Enzyme kinetics** Problem 13.10.

a. To check on the appropriateness of large-sample inferences here, generate 1,000 bootstrap samples of size 18 using the fixed X sampling procedure. For each bootstrap sample, obtain the least squares estimates g_0^* and g_1^*.

b. Plot histograms of the bootstrap sampling distributions of g_0^* and g_1^*. Do these distributions appear to be approximately normal?

c. Compute the means and standard deviations of the bootstrap sampling distributions for g_0^* and g_1^*. Are the bootstrap means and standard deviations close to the final least squares estimates?

d. Obtain a confidence interval for γ_0 using the reflection method in (11.59) and confidence coefficient .95. How does this interval compare with the one obtained in Problem 13.12 by the large-sample inference method?

e. What are the implications of your findings in parts (b), (c), and (d) about the appropriateness of large-sample inferences here? Discuss.

13.29. Refer to **Drug responsiveness** Problem 13.13.

a. To check on the appropriateness of large-sample inferences here, generate 1,000 bootstrap samples of size 19 using the fixed X sampling procedure. For each bootstrap sample, obtain the least squares estimates g_0^*, g_1^*, and g_2^*.

b. Plot histograms of the bootstrap sampling distributions of g_0^*, g_1^*, and g_2^*. Do these distributions appear to be approximately normal?

c. Compute the means and standard deviations of the bootstrap sampling distributions for g_0^*, g_1^*, and g_2^*. Are the bootstrap means and standard deviations close to the final least squares estimates?

d. Obtain a confidence interval for γ_2 using the reflection method in (11.59) and confidence coefficient .97. How does this interval compare with the one obtained in Problem 13.16 by the large-sample inference method?

e. What are the implications of your findings in parts (b), (c), and (d) about the appropriateness of large-sample inferences here? Discuss.

13.30. Refer to **Process yield** Problem 13.17.

a. To check on the appropriateness of large-sample inferences here, generate 1,000 bootstrap samples of size 18 using the fixed X sampling procedure. For each bootstrap sample, obtain the least squares estimates g_0^*, g_1^*, and g_2^*.

b. Plot histograms of the bootstrap sampling distributions of g_0^*, g_1^*, and g_2^*. Do these distributions appear to be approximately normal?

c. Compute the means and standard deviations of the bootstrap sampling distributions for g_0^*, g_1^*, and g_2^*. Are the bootstrap means and standard deviations close to the final least squares estimates?

d. Obtain a confidence interval for γ_1 using the reflection method in (11.59) and confidence coefficient .975. How does this interval compare with the one obtained in Problem 13.20b by the large-sample inference method?

e. What are the implications of your findings in parts (b), (c), and (d) about the appropriateness of large-sample inferences here? Discuss.

Case Studies

13.31. Refer to the **Prostate cancer** data set in Appendix C.5 and Case Study 9.30. Select a random sample of 65 observations to use as the model-building data set.

a. Develop a neural network model for predicting PSA. Justify your choice of number of hidden nodes and penalty function weight and interpret your model.

b. Assess your model's ability to predict and discuss its usefulness to the oncologists.

c. Compare the performance of your neural network model with that of the best regression model obtained in Case Study 9.30. Which model is more easily interpreted and why?

13.32. Refer to the **Real estate sales** data set in Appendix C.7 and Case Study 9.31. Select a random sample of 300 observations to use as the model-building data set.

a. Develop a neural network model for predicting sales price. Justify your choice of number of hidden nodes and penalty function weight and interpret your model.

b. Assess your model's ability to predict and discuss its usefulness as a tool for predicting sales prices.

c. Compare the performance of your neural network model with that of the best regression model obtained in Case Study 9.31. Which model is more easily interpreted and why?

Chapter 14

Logistic Regression, Poisson Regression, and Generalized Linear Models

In Chapter 13 we considered nonlinear regression models where the error terms are normally distributed. In this chapter, we take up nonlinear regression models for two important cases where the response outcomes are discrete and the error terms are not normally distributed. First, we consider the logistic nonlinear regression model for use when the response variable is qualitative with two possible outcomes, such as financial status of firm (sound status, headed toward insolvency) or blood pressure status (high blood pressure, not high blood pressure). We then extend this model so that it can be applied when the response variable is a qualitative variable having more than two possible outcomes; for instance, blood pressure status might be classified as high, normal, or low.

Next we take up the Poisson regression model for use when the response variable is a count where large counts are rare events, such as the number of tornadoes in an upper Midwest locality during a year. Finally, we explain that nearly all of the nonlinear regression models discussed in Chapter 13 and in this chapter, as well as the normal error linear models discussed earlier, belong to a family of regression models called generalized linear models.

The nonlinear regression models presented in this chapter are appropriate for analyzing data arising from either observational studies or from experimental studies.

14.1 Regression Models with Binary Response Variable

In a variety of regression applications, the response variable of interest has only two possible qualitative outcomes, and therefore can be represented by a binary indicator variable taking on values 0 and 1.

1. In an analysis of whether or not business firms have an industrial relations department, according to size of firm, the response variable was defined to have the two possible

outcomes: firm has industrial relations department, firm does not have industrial relations department. These outcomes may be coded 1 and 0, respectively (or vice versa).

   2. In a study of labor force participation of married women, as a function of age, number of children, and husband's income, the response variable Y was defined to have the two possible outcomes: married woman in labor force, married woman not in labor force. Again, these outcomes may be coded 1 and 0, respectively.

   3. In a study of liability insurance possession, according to age of head of household, amount of liquid assets, and type of occupation of head of household, the response variable Y was defined to have the two possible outcomes: household has liability insurance, household does not have liability insurance. These outcomes again may be coded 1 and 0, respectively.

   4. In a longitudinal study of coronary heart disease as a function of age, gender, smoking history, cholesterol level, percent of ideal body weight, and blood pressure, the response variable Y was defined to have the two possible outcomes: person developed heart disease during the study, person did not develop heart disease during the study. These outcomes again may be coded 1 and 0, respectively.

   These examples show the wide range of applications in which the response variable is binary and hence may be represented by an indicator variable. A binary response variable, taking on the values 0 and 1, is said to involve *binary responses* or *dichotomous responses*. We consider first the meaning of the response function when the outcome variable is binary, and then we take up some special problems that arise with this type of response variable.

Meaning of Response Function when Outcome Variable Is Binary

Consider the simple linear regression model:

$$Y_i = \beta_0 + \beta_1 X_i + \varepsilon_i \qquad Y_i = 0, 1 \tag{14.1}$$

where the outcome Y_i is binary, taking on the value of either 0 or 1. The expected response $E\{Y_i\}$ has a special meaning in this case. Since $E\{\varepsilon_i\} = 0$ we have:

$$E\{Y_i\} = \beta_0 + \beta_1 X_i \tag{14.2}$$

Consider Y_i to be a Bernoulli random variable for which we can state the probability distribution as follows:

Y_i	Probability
1	$P(Y_i = 1) = \pi_i$
0	$P(Y_i = 0) = 1 - \pi_i$

Thus, π_i is the probability that $Y_i = 1$, and $1 - \pi_i$ is the probability that $Y_i = 0$. By the definition of expected value of a random variable in (A.12), we obtain:

$$E\{Y_i\} = 1(\pi_i) + 0(1 - \pi_i) = \pi_i = P(Y_i = 1) \tag{14.3}$$

Equating (14.2) and (14.3), we thus find:

$$E\{Y_i\} = \beta_0 + \beta_1 X_i = \pi_i \tag{14.4}$$

FIGURE 14.1
Illustration of Response Function when Response Variable Is Binary— Industrial Relations Department Example.

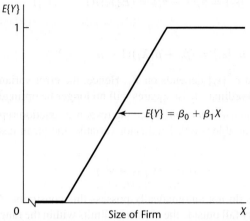

Probability That Firm Has Industrial Relations Department

The mean response $E\{Y_i\} = \beta_0 + \beta_1 X_i$ as given by the response function is therefore simply the probability that $Y_i = 1$ when the level of the predictor variable is X_i. This interpretation of the mean response applies whether the response function is a simple linear one, as here, or a complex multiple regression one. The mean response, when the outcome variable is a 0, 1 indicator variable, always represents the probability that $Y = 1$ for the given levels of the predictor variables. Figure 14.1 illustrates a simple linear response function for an indicator outcome variable. Here, the indicator variable Y refers to whether or not a firm has an industrial relations department, and the predictor variable X is size of firm. The response function in Figure 14.1 shows the probability that firms of given size have an industrial relations department.

Special Problems when Response Variable Is Binary

Special problems arise, unfortunately, when the response variable is an indicator variable. We consider three of these now, using a simple linear regression model as an illustration.

1. *Nonnormal Error Terms.* For a binary 0, 1 response variable, each error term $\varepsilon_i = Y_i - (\beta_0 + \beta_1 X_i)$ can take on only two values:

$$\text{When } Y_i = 1: \quad \varepsilon_i = 1 - \beta_0 - \beta_1 X_i \tag{14.5a}$$

$$\text{When } Y_i = 0: \quad \varepsilon_i = -\beta_0 - \beta_1 X_i \tag{14.5b}$$

Clearly, normal error regression model (2.1), which assumes that the ε_i are normally distributed, is not appropriate.

2. *Nonconstant Error Variance.* Another problem with the error terms ε_i is that they do not have equal variances when the response variable is an indicator variable. To see this, we shall obtain $\sigma^2\{Y_i\}$ for the simple linear regression model (14.1), utilizing (A.15):

$$\sigma^2\{Y_i\} = E\{(Y_i - E\{Y_i\})^2\} = (1 - \pi_i)^2 \pi_i + (0 - \pi_i)^2 (1 - \pi_i)$$

or:

$$\sigma^2\{Y_i\} = \pi_i(1 - \pi_i) = (E\{Y_i\})(1 - E\{Y_i\}) \tag{14.6}$$

The variance of ε_i is the same as that of Y_i because $\varepsilon_i = Y_i - \pi_i$ and π_i is a constant:

$$\sigma^2\{\varepsilon_i\} = \pi_i(1 - \pi_i) = (E\{Y_i\})(1 - E\{Y_i\}) \tag{14.7}$$

or:

$$\sigma^2\{\varepsilon_i\} = (\beta_0 + \beta_1 X_i)(1 - \beta_0 - \beta_1 X_i) \tag{14.7a}$$

Note from (14.7a) that $\sigma^2\{\varepsilon_i\}$ depends on X_i. Hence, the error variances will differ at different levels of X, and ordinary least squares will no longer be optimal.

3. *Constraints on Response Function.* Since the response function represents probabilities when the outcome variable is a 0, 1 indicator variable, the mean responses should be constrained as follows:

$$0 \le E\{Y\} = \pi \le 1 \tag{14.8}$$

Many response functions do not automatically possess this constraint. A linear response function, for instance, may fall outside the constraint limits within the range of the predictor variable in the scope of the model.

FIGURE 14.2 **Examples of Probit and Logistic Mean Response Functions.**

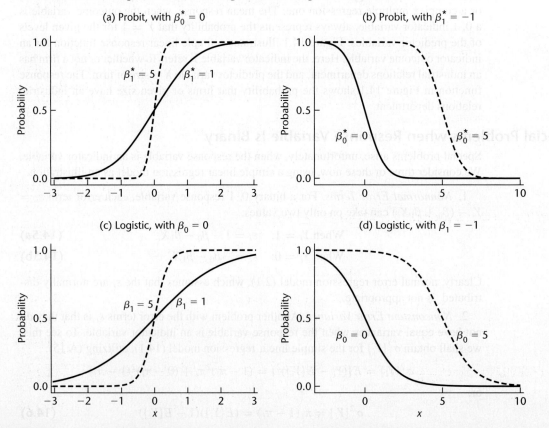

The difficulties created by the need for the restriction in (14.8) on the response function are the most serious. One could use weighted least squares to handle the problem of unequal error variances. In addition, with large sample sizes the method of least squares provides estimators that are asymptotically normal under quite general conditions, even if the distribution of the error terms is far from normal. However, the constraint on the mean responses to fall between 0 and 1 frequently will rule out a linear response function. In the industrial relations department example, for instance, use of a linear response function subject to the constraints on the mean response might require a probability of 0 for the mean response for all small firms and a probability of 1 for the mean response for all large firms, as illustrated in Figure 14.1. Such a model would often be considered unreasonable. Instead, a model where the probabilities 0 and 1 are reached asymptotically, as illustrated by each of the S-shaped curves in Figure 14.2, would usually be more appropriate.

14.2   Sigmoidal Response Functions for Binary Responses

In this section, we introduce three response functions for modeling binary responses. These functions are bounded between 0 and 1, have a characteristic *sigmoidal-* or *S*-shape, and approach 0 and 1 asymptotically. These functions arise naturally when the binary response variable results from a zero-one recoding (or dichotomization) of an underlying continuous response variable, and they are often appropriate for discrete binary responses as well.

Probit Mean Response Function

Consider a health researcher studying the effect of a mother's use of alcohol (X—an index of degree of alcohol use during pregnancy) on the duration of her pregnancy (Y^c). Here we use the superscript c to emphasize that the response variable, pregnancy duration, is a continuous response. This can be represented by a simple linear regression model:

$$Y_i^c = \beta_0^c + \beta_1^c X_i + \varepsilon_i^c \tag{14.9}$$

and we will assume that ε_i^c is normally distributed with mean zero and variance σ_c^2.

If the continuous response variable, pregnancy duration, were available, we might proceed with the usual simple linear regression analysis. However, in this instance, researchers coded each pregnancy duration as preterm or full term using the following rule:

$$Y_i = \begin{cases} 1 & \text{if } Y_i^c \leq 38 \text{ weeks (preterm)} \\ 0 & \text{if } Y_i^c > 38 \text{ weeks (full term)} \end{cases}$$

It follows from (14.3) and (14.9) that:

$$P(Y_i = 1) = \pi_i = P\left(Y_i^c \leq 38\right) \tag{14.10a}$$

$$= P\left(\beta_0^c + \beta_1^c X_i + \varepsilon_i^c \leq 38\right) \tag{14.10b}$$

$$= P\left(\varepsilon_i^c \leq 38 - \beta_0^c - \beta_1^c X_i\right) \tag{14.10c}$$

$$= P\left(\frac{\varepsilon_i^c}{\sigma_c} \leq \frac{38 - \beta_0^c}{\sigma_c} - \frac{\beta_1^c}{\sigma_c} X_i\right) \tag{14.10d}$$

$$= P(Z \leq \beta_0^* + \beta_1^* X_i) \tag{14.10e}$$

where $\beta_0^* = (38 - \beta_0^c)/\sigma_c$, $\beta_1^* = -\beta_1^c/\sigma_c$, and $Z = \varepsilon_i^c/\sigma_c$ follows a standard normal distribution. If we let $P(Z \leq z) = \Phi(z)$, we have, from (14.10a–e):

$$P(Y_i = 1) = \Phi(\beta_0^* + \beta_1^* X_i) \tag{14.11}$$

Equations (14.3) and (14.11) together yield the nonlinear regression function known as the *probit mean response function:*

$$E\{Y_i\} = \pi_i = \Phi(\beta_0^* + \beta_1^* X_i) \tag{14.12}$$

The inverse function, Φ^{-1}, of the standard normal cumulative distribution function Φ, is sometimes called the probit transformation. We solve for the linear predictor, $\beta_0^* + \beta_1^* X_i$ in (14.12) by applying the probit transformation to both sides of the expression, obtaining:

$$\Phi^{-1}(\pi_i) = \pi_i' = \beta_0^* + \beta_1^* X_i \tag{14.13}$$

The resulting expression, $\pi_i' = \beta_0^* + \beta_1^* X_i$, is called the *probit response function,* or more generally, the *linear predictor.*

Plots of the probit mean response function (14.12) for various values of β_0^* and β_1^* are shown in Figures 14.2a and 14.2b. Some characteristics of this response function are:

1. The probit mean response function is bounded between 0 and 1, and it approaches these limits asymptotically.
2. As β_1^* increases (for $\beta_1^* > 0$), the mean function becomes more *S*-shaped, changing more rapidly in the center. Figure 14.2a shows two probit mean response functions, where both intercept coefficients are 0, and the slope coefficients are 1 and 5. Notice that the curve has a more pronounced *S*-shape with $\beta_1^* = 5$.
3. Changing the sign of β_1^* from positive to negative changes the mean response function from a monotone increasing function to a monotone decreasing function. The probit mean response functions plotted in Figure 14.2a have positive slope coefficients while those in Figure 14.2b have negative slope coefficients.
4. Increasing or decreasing the intercept β_0^* shifts the mean response function horizontally. (The direction of the shift depends on the signs of both β_0^* and β_1^*.) Figure 14.2b shows two probit mean response functions, where both slope coefficients are -1, and the intercept coefficients are 0 and 5. Notice that the curve has shifted to the right as β_0^* changes from 0 to 5.
5. Finally, we note the following *symmetry property* of the probit response function. If the response variable is recoded using $Y_i' = 1 - Y_i$, that is, by changing the 1s to 0s and the 0s to 1s—the signs of all of the coefficients are reversed. This follows easily from the symmetry of the standard normal distribution: since $\Phi(Z) = 1 - \Phi(-Z)$, it follows that $P(Y_i' = 1) = P(Y_i = 0) = 1 - \Phi(\beta_0^* + \beta_1^* X_i) = \Phi(-\beta_0^* - \beta_1^* X_i)$.

Logistic Mean Response Function

We have seen that the assumption of normally distributed errors for the underlying continuous response variable in (14.9) led to the use of the standard normal cumulative distribution function, Φ, to model π_i. An alternative error distribution that is very similar to the normal distribution is the logistic distribution. Figure 14.3 presents plots of the standard normal density function and the logistic density function, each with mean zero and variance one. The plots are nearly indistinguishable, although the logistic distribution has slightly heavier

FIGURE 14.3
Plots of Normal
Density
(dashed line)
and Logistic
Density (solid
line), Each
Having Mean 0
and Variance 1.

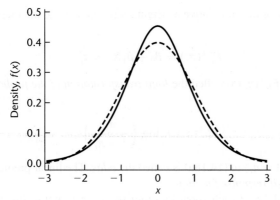

tails. The density of a logistic random variable ε_L having mean zero and standard deviation $\sigma = \pi/\sqrt{3}$ has a simple form:

$$f_L(\varepsilon_L) = \frac{\exp(\varepsilon_L)}{[1 + \exp(\varepsilon_L)]^2} \qquad (14.14a)$$

Its cumulative distribution function is:

$$F_L(\varepsilon_L) = \frac{\exp(\varepsilon_L)}{1 + \exp(\varepsilon_L)} \qquad (14.14b)$$

Suppose now that ε_i^c in (14.9) has a logistic distribution with mean zero and standard deviation σ_c. Then, from (14.10d) we have:

$$P(Y_i = 1) = P\left(\frac{\varepsilon_i^c}{\sigma_c} \le \beta_0^* + \beta_1^* X_i\right)$$

where ε_i^c/σ_c follows a logistic distribution with mean zero and standard deviation one. Multiplying both sides of the inequality inside the probability statement on the right by $\pi/\sqrt{3}$ does not change the probability; therefore:

$$P(Y_i = 1) = \pi_i = P\left(\frac{\pi}{\sqrt{3}}\frac{\varepsilon_i^c}{\sigma_c} \le \frac{\pi}{\sqrt{3}}\beta_0^* + \frac{\pi}{\sqrt{3}}\beta_1^* X_i\right) \qquad (14.15a)$$

$$= P(\varepsilon_L \le \beta_0 + \beta_1 X_i) \qquad (14.15b)$$

$$= F_L(\beta_0 + \beta_1 X_i) \qquad (14.15c)$$

$$= \frac{\exp(\beta_0 + \beta_1 X_i)}{1 + \exp(\beta_0 + \beta_1 X_i)} \qquad (14.15d)$$

where $\beta_0 = (\pi/\sqrt{3})\beta_0^*$ and $\beta_1 = (\pi/\sqrt{3})\beta_1^*$ denote the logistic regression parameters. To summarize, the *logistic mean response function* is:

$$E\{Y_i\} = \pi_i = F_L(\beta_0 + \beta_1 X_i) = \frac{\exp(\beta_0 + \beta_1 X_i)}{1 + \exp(\beta_0 + \beta_1 X_i)} \qquad (14.16)$$

Straightforward algebra shows that an equivalent form of (14.16) is given by:

$$E\{Y_i\} = \pi_i = [1 + \exp(-\beta_0 - \beta_1 X_i)]^{-1} \qquad (14.17)$$

Applying the inverse of the cumulative distribution function F_L to the two middle terms in (14.16) yields:

$$F_L^{-1}(\pi_i) = \beta_0 + \beta_1 X_i = \pi_i' \qquad (14.18)$$

The transformation $F_L^{-1}(\pi_i)$ is called the *logit transformation of the probability* π_i, and is given by:

$$F_L^{-1}(\pi_i) = \log_e\left(\frac{\pi_i}{1 - \pi_i}\right) \qquad (14.18a)$$

where the ratio $\pi_i/(1 - \pi_i)$ in (14.18a) is called the *odds*. The linear predictor in (14.18) is referred to as the *logit response function*.

Figures 14.2c and 14.2d each show two logistic mean response functions, where the parameters correspond to those in Figures 14.2a and 14.2b for the probit mean response function. It is clear from the plots that these logistic mean response functions are qualitatively similar to the corresponding probit mean response functions. The five properties of the probit mean response function, listed earlier, are also true for the logistic mean response function. The observed differences in logistic and probit mean response functions are largely due to the differences in the scaling of the parameters mentioned previously. Note that the symmetry property for the probit mean response function also holds for the logistic mean response function.

Complementary Log-Log Response Function

A third mean response function is sometimes used when the error distribution of ε^c is not symmetric. The density function $f_G(\varepsilon)$ of the *extreme value* or *Gumbel* probability distribution having mean zero and variance one is shown in Figure 14.4, along with the comparable standard normal and logistic densities discussed earlier. Notice that this density is skewed to the right and clearly distinct from the standard normal and logistic densities. It can be shown that use of the Gumbel error distribution for ε^c in (14.9) leads to the mean response function:

$$\pi_i = 1 - \exp\left(-\exp\left(\beta_0^G + \beta_1^G X_i\right)\right) \qquad (14.19)$$

FIGURE 14.4
Plots of Gumbel (dashed line), Normal (black line), and Logistic (gray line) Density Functions, Each Having Mean 0 and Variance 1.

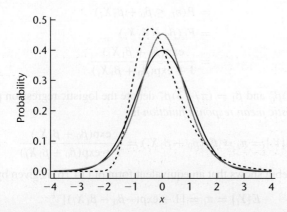

Solving for the linear predictor $\beta_0^G + \beta_1^G X_i$, we obtain the *complementary log-log* response model:

$$\pi_i' = \log[-\log(1 - \pi(X_i))] = \beta_0^G + \beta_1^G X_i \qquad \textbf{(14.19a)}$$

The symmetry property discussed on page 560 for the logit and probit models does not hold for (14.19).

For the remainder of this chapter, we focus on the use of the logistic mean response function. This is currently the most widely used model for two reasons: (1) we shall see that the regression parameters have relatively simple and useful interpretations, and (2) statistical software is widely available for analysis of logistic regression models. In the next two sections we consider in detail the fitting of simple and multiple logistic regression models to binary data.

Comment

Our development of the logistic and probit mean response functions assumed that the binary response Y_i was obtained from an explicit dichotomization of an observed continuous response Y_i^c, but this is not required. These response functions often work well for binary responses that do not arise from such a dichotomization. In addition, binary responses frequently can be interpreted as having arisen from a dichotomization of an unobserved, or latent, continuous response. ∎

14.3   Simple Logistic Regression

We shall use the method of maximum likelihood to estimate the parameters of the logistic response function. This method is well suited to deal with the problems associated with the responses Y_i being binary. As explained in Section 1.8, we first need to develop the joint probability function of the sample observations. Instead of using the normal distribution for the Y observations as was done earlier in (1.26), we now need to utilize the Bernoulli distribution for a binary random variable.

Simple Logistic Regression Model

First, we require a formal statement of the simple logistic regression model. Recall that when the response variable is binary, taking on the values 1 and 0 with probabilities π and $1 - \pi$, respectively, Y is a Bernoulli random variable with parameter $E\{Y\} = \pi$. We could state the simple logistic regression model in the usual form:

$$Y_i = E\{Y_i\} + \varepsilon_i$$

Since the distribution of the error term ε_i depends on the Bernoulli distribution of the response Y_i, it is preferable to state the simple logistic regression model in the following fashion:

Y_i are independent Bernoulli random variables with expected values $E\{Y_i\} = \pi_i$, where:

$$E\{Y_i\} = \pi_i = \frac{\exp(\beta_0 + \beta_1 X_i)}{1 + \exp(\beta_0 + \beta_1 X_i)} \qquad \textbf{(14.20)}$$

The X observations are assumed to be known constants. Alternatively, if the X observations are random, $E\{Y_i\}$ is viewed as a conditional mean, given the value of X_i.

Likelihood Function

Since each Y_i observation is an ordinary Bernoulli random variable, where:

$$P(Y_i = 1) = \pi_i$$
$$P(Y_i = 0) = 1 - \pi_i$$

we can represent its probability distribution as follows:

$$f_i(Y_i) = \pi_i^{Y_i}(1 - \pi_i)^{1-Y_i} \qquad Y_i = 0, 1; \quad i = 1, \ldots, n \tag{14.21}$$

Note that $f_i(1) = \pi_i$ and $f_i(0) = 1 - \pi_i$. Hence, $f_i(Y_i)$ simply represents the probability that $Y_i = 1$ or 0.

Since the Y_i observations are independent, their joint probability function is:

$$g(Y_1, \ldots, Y_n) = \prod_{i=1}^{n} f_i(Y_i) = \prod_{i=1}^{n} \pi_i^{Y_i}(1 - \pi_i)^{1-Y_i} \tag{14.22}$$

Again, it will be easier to find the maximum likelihood estimates by working with the logarithm of the joint probability function:

$$\log_e g(Y_1, \ldots, Y_n) = \log_e \prod_{i=1}^{n} \pi_i^{Y_i}(1 - \pi_i)^{1-Y_i}$$

$$= \sum_{i=1}^{n}[Y_i \log_e \pi_i + (1 - Y_i) \log_e(1 - \pi_i)]$$

$$= \sum_{i=1}^{n}\left[Y_i \log_e\left(\frac{\pi_i}{1 - \pi_i}\right)\right] + \sum_{i=1}^{n} \log_e(1 - \pi_i) \tag{14.23}$$

Since $E\{Y_i\} = \pi_i$ for a binary variable, it follows from (14.16) that:

$$1 - \pi_i = [1 + \exp(\beta_0 + \beta_1 X_i)]^{-1} \tag{14.24}$$

Furthermore, from (14.18a), we obtain:

$$\log_e\left(\frac{\pi_i}{1 - \pi_i}\right) = \beta_0 + \beta_1 X_i \tag{14.25}$$

Hence, (14.23) can be expressed as follows:

$$\log_e L(\beta_0, \beta_1) = \sum_{i=1}^{n} Y_i(\beta_0 + \beta_1 X_i) - \sum_{i=1}^{n} \log_e[1 + \exp(\beta_0 + \beta_1 X_i)] \tag{14.26}$$

where $L(\beta_0, \beta_1)$ replaces $g(Y_1, \ldots, Y_n)$ to show explicitly that we now view this function as the likelihood function of the parameters to be estimated, given the sample observations.

Maximum Likelihood Estimation

The maximum likelihood estimates of β_0 and β_1 in the simple logistic regression model are those values of β_0 and β_1 that maximize the log-likelihood function in (14.26). No closed-form solution exists for the values of β_0 and β_1 in (14.26) that maximize the log-likelihood function. Computer-intensive numerical search procedures are therefore required to find the maximum likelihood estimates b_0 and b_1. There are several widely used numerical search procedures; one of these employs iteratively reweighted least squares, which we shall explain in Section 14.4. Reference 14.1 provides a discussion of several numerical search procedures for finding maximum likelihood estimates. We shall rely on standard statistical software programs specifically designed for logistic regression to obtain the maximum likelihood estimates b_0 and b_1.

Once the maximum likelihood estimates b_0 and b_1 are found, we substitute these values into the response function in (14.20) to obtain the fitted response function. We shall use $\hat{\pi}_i$ to denote the fitted value for the ith case:

$$\hat{\pi}_i = \frac{\exp(b_0 + b_1 X_i)}{1 + \exp(b_0 + b_1 X_i)} \tag{14.27}$$

The fitted logistic response function is as follows:

$$\hat{\pi} = \frac{\exp(b_0 + b_1 X)}{1 + \exp(b_0 + b_1 X)} \tag{14.28}$$

If we utilize the logit transformation in (14.18), we can express the fitted response function in (14.28) as follows:

$$\hat{\pi}' = b_0 + b_1 X \tag{14.29}$$

where:

$$\hat{\pi}' = \log_e\left(\frac{\hat{\pi}}{1 - \hat{\pi}}\right) \tag{14.29a}$$

We call (14.29) the *fitted logit response function.*

Once the fitted logistic response function has been obtained, the usual next steps are to examine the appropriateness of the fitted response function and, if the fit is good, to make a variety of inferences and predictions. We shall postpone a discussion of how to examine the goodness of fit of a logistic response function and how to make inferences and predictions until we have considered the multiple logistic regression model with a number of predictor variables.

Example

A systems analyst studied the effect of computer programming experience on ability to complete within a specified time a complex programming task, including debugging. Twenty-five persons were selected for the study. They had varying amounts of programming experience (measured in months of experience), as shown in Table 14.1a, column 1. All persons were given the same programming task, and the results of their success in the task are shown in column 2. The results are coded in binary fashion: $Y = 1$ if the task was completed successfully in the allotted time, and $Y = 0$ if the task was not completed successfully. Figure 14.5 contains a scatter plot of the data. This plot is not too informative because of the nature of the response variable, other than to indicate that ability to complete the task successfully appears to increase with amount of experience. A lowess nonparametric response curve was fitted to the data and is also shown in Figure 14.5. A sigmoidal S-shaped response function is clearly suggested by the nonparametric lowess fit. It was therefore decided to fit the logistic regression model (14.20).

A standard logistic regression package was run on the data. The results are contained in Table 14.1b. Since $b_0 = -3.0597$ and $b_1 = .1615$, the estimated logistic regression

TABLE 14.1
Data and Maximum Likelihood Estimates—Programming Task Example.

(a) Data				
	(1)	(2)	(3)	(4)
	Months of	Task	Fitted	Deviance
Person	Experience	Success	Value	Residual
i	X_i	Y_i	$\hat{\pi}_i$	dev_i
1	14	0	.310	−.862
2	29	0	.835	−1.899
3	6	0	.110	−.483
...	...	...	...	...
23	28	1	.812	.646
24	22	1	.621	.976
25	8	1	.146	1.962

(b) Maximum Likelihood Estimates			
Regression Coefficient	Estimated Regression Coefficient	Estimated Standard Deviation	Estimated Odds Ratio
β_0	−3.0597	1.259	—
β_1	.1615	.0650	1.175

FIGURE 14.5
Scatter Plot, Lowess Curve (dashed line), and Estimated Logistic Mean Response Function (solid line)—Programming Task Example.

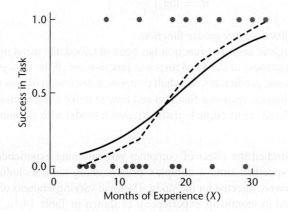

function (14.28) is:

$$\hat{\pi} = \frac{\exp(-3.0597 + .1615X)}{1 + \exp(-3.0597 + .1615X)} \qquad (14.30)$$

The fitted values are given in Table 14.1a, column 3. For instance, the estimated mean response for $i = 1$, where $X_1 = 14$, is:

$$\hat{\pi}_1 = \frac{\exp[-3.0597 + .1615(14)]}{1 + \exp[-3.0597 + .1615(14)]} = .310$$

This fitted value is the estimated probability that a person with 14 months experience will successfully complete the programming task. In addition to the lowess fit, Figure 14.5 also contains a plot of the fitted logistic response function, $\hat{\pi}(x)$.

Interpretation of b_1

The interpretation of the estimated regression coefficient b_1 in the fitted logistic response function (14.30) is not the straightforward interpretation of the slope in a linear regression model. The reason is that the effect of a unit increase in X varies for the logistic regression model according to the location of the starting point on the X scale. An interpretation of b_1 is found in the property of the fitted logistic function that the estimated odds $\hat{\pi}/(1 - \hat{\pi})$ are multiplied by $\exp(b_1)$ for any unit increase in X.

To see this, we consider the value of the fitted logit response function (14.29) at $X = X_j$:

$$\hat{\pi}'(X_j) = b_0 + b_1 X_j$$

The notation $\hat{\pi}'(X_j)$ indicates specifically the X level associated with the fitted value. We also consider the value of the fitted logit response function at $X = X_j + 1$:

$$\hat{\pi}'(X_j + 1) = b_0 + b_1(X_j + 1)$$

The difference between the two fitted values is simply:

$$\hat{\pi}'(X_j + 1) - \hat{\pi}'(X_j) = b_1$$

Now according to (14.29a), $\hat{\pi}'(X_j)$ is the logarithm of the estimated odds when $X = X_j$; we shall denote it by $\log_e(\text{odds}_1)$. Similarly, $\hat{\pi}'(X_j + 1)$ is the logarithm of the estimated odds when $X = X_j + 1$; we shall denote it by $\log_e(\text{odds}_2)$. Hence, the difference between the two fitted logit response values can be expressed as follows:

$$\log_e(\text{odds}_2) - \log_e(\text{odds}_1) = \log_e\left(\frac{\text{odds}_2}{\text{odds}_1}\right) = b_1$$

Taking antilogs of each side, we see that the estimated ratio of the odds, called the *odds ratio* and denoted by $\widehat{OR}$, equals $\exp(b_1)$:

$$\widehat{OR} = \frac{\text{odds}_2}{\text{odds}_1} = \exp(b_1) \tag{14.31}$$

Example

For the programming task example, we see from Figure 14.5 that the probability of success increases sharply with experience. Specifically, Table 14.1b shows that the odds ratio is $\widehat{OR} = \exp(b_1) = \exp(.1615) = 1.175$, so that the odds of completing the task increase by 17.5 percent with each additional month of experience.

Since a unit increase of one month is quite small, the estimated odds ratio of 1.175 may not adequately show the change in odds for a longer difference in time. In general, the estimated odds ratio when there is a difference of c units of X is $\exp(cb_1)$. For example, should we wish to compare individuals with relatively little experience to those with extensive experience, say 10 months versus 25 months so that $c = 15$, then the odds ratio would be estimated to be $\exp[15(.1615)] = 11.3$. This indicates that the odds of completing the task increase over 11-fold for experienced persons compared to relatively inexperienced persons.

FIGURE 14.6
Logistic (solid line), Probit (dashed line), and Complementary Log-Log (gray line) Fits—Programming Task Example.

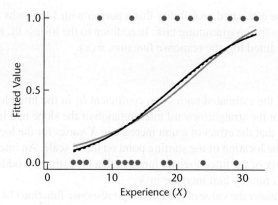

Comment

The odds ratio interpretation of the estimated regression coefficient b_1 makes the logistic regression model especially attractive for modeling and interpreting epidemiologic studies. ∎

Use of Probit and Complementary Log-Log Response Functions

As we discussed earlier in Section 14.2, alternative sigmoidal shaped response functions, such as the probit or complementary log-log functions, can be utilized as well. For example, it is interesting to fit the programming task data in Table 14.1 to these alternative response functions. Figure 14.6 shows the scatter plot of the data and the fitted logistic, probit, and complementary log-log mean response functions. The logistic and probit fits are very similar, whereas the complementary log-log fit differs slightly, having a less pronounced S-shape.

Repeat Observations—Binomial Outcomes

In some cases, particularly for designed experiments, a number of repeat observations are obtained at several levels of the predictor variable X. For instance, a pricing experiment involved showing a new product to 1,000 consumers, providing information about it, and then asking each consumer whether he or she would buy the product at a given price. Five prices were studied, and 200 persons were randomly selected for each price level. The response variable here is binary (would purchase, would not purchase); the predictor variable is price and has five levels.

When repeat observations are present, the log-likelihood function in (14.26) can be simplified. We shall adopt the notation used for replicate observations in our discussion of the F test for lack of fit in Section 3.7. We denote the X levels at which repeat observations are obtained by $X_1, \ldots, X_c$ and we assume that there are n_j binary responses at level X_j. Then the observed value of the ith binary response at X_j is denoted by Y_{ij}, where $i = 1, \ldots, n_j$, and $j = 1, \ldots, c$. The number of 1s at level X_j is denoted by $Y_{.j}$:

$$Y_{.j} = \sum_{i=1}^{n_j} Y_{ij} \tag{14.32a}$$

and the proportion of 1s at level X_j is denoted by p_j:

$$p_j = \frac{Y_{.j}}{n_j} \tag{14.32b}$$

The random variable $Y_{.j}$ has a *binomial distribution* given by:

$$f(Y_{.j}) = \binom{n_j}{Y_{.j}} \pi_j^{Y_{.j}} (1 - \pi_j)^{n_j - Y_{.j}} \tag{14.33}$$

where:

$$\binom{n_j}{Y_{.j}} = \frac{n_j!}{(Y_{.j})!(n_j - Y_{.j})!}$$

and the factorial notation $a!$ represents $a(a-1)(a-2)\cdots 1$. The binomial random variable $Y_{.j}$ has mean $n_j \pi_j$ and variance $n_j \pi_j (1 - \pi_j)$. The log-likelihood function then can be stated as follows:

$$\log_e L(\beta_0, \beta_1) = \sum_{j=1}^{c} \left\{ \log_e \binom{n_j}{Y_{.j}} + Y_{.j}(\beta_0 + \beta_1 X_j) - n_j \log_e[1 + \exp(\beta_0 + \beta_1 X_j)] \right\} \tag{14.34}$$

Example

In a study of the effectiveness of coupons offering a price reduction on a given product, 1,000 homes were selected at random. A packet containing advertising material and a coupon for the product were mailed to each home. The coupons offered different price reductions (5, 10, 15, 20, and 30 dollars), and 200 homes were assigned at random to each of the price reduction categories. The predictor variable X in this study is the amount of price reduction, and the response variable Y is a binary variable indicating whether or not the coupon was redeemed within a six-month period.

Table 14.2 contains the data for this study. X_j denotes the price reduction offered by a coupon, n_j the number of households that received a coupon with price reduction X_j, $Y_{.j}$ the number of these households that redeemed the coupon, and p_j the proportion of households receiving a coupon with price reduction X_j that redeemed the coupon. The logistic regression model (14.20) was fitted by a logistic regression package and the fitted

TABLE 14.2
Data—Coupon Effectiveness Example.

Level j	(1) Price Reduction X_j	(2) Number of Households n_j	(3) Number of Coupons Redeemed $Y_{.j}$	(4) Proportion of Coupons Redeemed p_j	(5) Model-Based Estimate $\hat{\pi}_j$
1	5	200	30	.150	.1736
2	10	200	55	.275	.2543
3	15	200	70	.350	.3562
4	20	200	100	.500	.4731
5	30	200	137	.685	.7028

FIGURE 14.7
Plot of
Proportions
of Coupons
Redeemed and
Fitted Logistic
Response
Function—
Coupon
Effectiveness
Example.

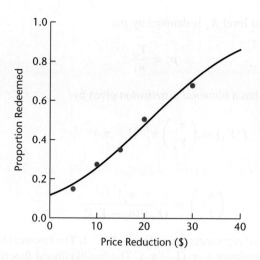

response function was found to be:

$$\hat{\pi} = \frac{\exp(-2.04435 + .096834X)}{1 + \exp(-2.04435 + .096834X)} \tag{14.35}$$

Fitted values are given in column 5 of Table 14.2. Figure 14.7 shows the fitted response function, as well as the proportions of coupons redeemed at each of the X_j levels. The logistic response function appears to provide a very good fit. The odds ratio here is:

$$\widehat{OR} = \exp(b_1) = \exp(.096834) = 1.102$$

Hence, the odds of a coupon being redeemed are estimated to increase by 10.2 percent with each one dollar increase in the coupon value, that is, with each one dollar reduction in price.

14.4 Multiple Logistic Regression

Multiple Logistic Regression Model

The simple logistic regression model (14.20) is easily extended to more than one predictor variable. In fact, several predictor variables are usually required with logistic regression to obtain adequate description and useful predictions.

In extending the simple logistic regression model, we simply replace $\beta_0 + \beta_1 X$ in (14.16) by $\beta_0 + \beta_1 X_1 + \cdots + \beta_{p-1} X_{p-1}$. To simplify the formulas, we shall use matrix notation and the following three vectors:

$$\underset{p \times 1}{\boldsymbol{\beta}} = \begin{bmatrix} \beta_0 \\ \beta_1 \\ \vdots \\ \beta_{p-1} \end{bmatrix} \qquad \underset{p \times 1}{\mathbf{X}} = \begin{bmatrix} 1 \\ X_1 \\ X_2 \\ \vdots \\ X_{p-1} \end{bmatrix} \qquad \underset{p \times 1}{\mathbf{X}_i} = \begin{bmatrix} 1 \\ X_{i1} \\ X_{i2} \\ \vdots \\ X_{i,p-1} \end{bmatrix} \tag{14.36}$$

We then have:

$$\mathbf{X}'\boldsymbol{\beta} = \beta_0 + \beta_1 X_1 + \cdots + \beta_{p-1} X_{p-1} \tag{14.37a}$$

$$\mathbf{X}_i'\boldsymbol{\beta} = \beta_0 + \beta_1 X_{i1} + \cdots + \beta_{p-1} X_{i,p-1} \tag{14.37b}$$

With this notation, the simple logistic response function (14.20) extends to the multiple logistic response function as follows:

$$E\{Y\} = \frac{\exp(\mathbf{X}'\boldsymbol{\beta})}{1 + \exp(\mathbf{X}'\boldsymbol{\beta})} \tag{14.38}$$

and the equivalent simple logistic response form (14.17) extends to:

$$E\{Y\} = [1 + \exp(-\mathbf{X}'\boldsymbol{\beta})]^{-1} \tag{14.38a}$$

Similarly, the logit transformation (14.18a):

$$\pi' = \log_e\left(\frac{\pi}{1 - \pi}\right) \tag{14.39}$$

now leads to the logit response function, or linear predictor:

$$\pi' = \mathbf{X}'\boldsymbol{\beta} \tag{14.40}$$

The multiple logistic regression model can therefore be stated as follows:

Y_i are independent Bernoulli random variables with expected values $E\{Y_i\} = \pi_i$, where:

$$E\{Y_i\} = \pi_i = \frac{\exp(\mathbf{X}_i'\boldsymbol{\beta})}{1 + \exp(\mathbf{X}_i'\boldsymbol{\beta})} \tag{14.41}$$

Again, the X observations are considered to be known constants. Alternatively, if the X variables are random, $E\{Y_i\}$ is viewed as a conditional mean, given the values of $X_{i1}, \ldots, X_{i,p-1}$.

Like the simple logistic response function (14.16), the multiple logistic response function (14.41) is monotonic and sigmoidal in shape with respect to $\mathbf{X}'\boldsymbol{\beta}$ and is almost linear when π is between .2 and .8. The X variables may be different predictor variables, or some may represent curvature and/or interaction effects. Also, the predictor variables may be quantitative, or they may be qualitative and represented by indicator variables. This flexibility makes the multiple logistic regression model very attractive.

Comment

When the logistic regression model contains only qualitative variables, it is often referred to as a log-linear model. See Reference 14.2 for an in-depth discussion of the analysis of log-linear models. ∎

Fitting of Model

Again, we shall utilize the method of maximum likelihood to estimate the parameters of the multiple logistic response function (14.41). The log-likelihood function for simple logistic regression in (14.26) extends directly for multiple logistic regression:

$$\log_e L(\boldsymbol{\beta}) = \sum_{i=1}^{n} Y_i(\mathbf{X}_i'\boldsymbol{\beta}) - \sum_{i=1}^{n} \log_e[1 + \exp(\mathbf{X}_i'\boldsymbol{\beta})] \tag{14.42}$$

Numerical search procedures are used to find the values of $\beta_0, \beta_1, \ldots, \beta_{p-1}$ that maximize $\log_e L(\boldsymbol{\beta})$. These maximum likelihood estimates will be denoted by $b_0, b_1, \ldots, b_{p-1}$. Let $\mathbf{b}$ denote the vector of the maximum likelihood estimates:

$$
\underset{p \times 1}{\mathbf{b}} = \begin{bmatrix} b_0 \\ b_1 \\ \vdots \\ b_{p-1} \end{bmatrix} \tag{14.43}
$$

The fitted logistic response function and fitted values can then be expressed as follows:

$$
\hat{\pi} = \frac{\exp(\mathbf{X'b})}{1 + \exp(\mathbf{X'b})} = [1 + \exp(-\mathbf{X'b})]^{-1} \tag{14.44a}
$$

$$
\hat{\pi}_i = \frac{\exp(\mathbf{X'_i b})}{1 + \exp(\mathbf{X'_i b})} = [1 + \exp(-\mathbf{X'_i b})]^{-1} \tag{14.44b}
$$

where:

$$
\mathbf{X'b} = b_0 + b_1 X_1 + \cdots + b_{p-1} X_{p-1} \tag{14.44c}
$$

$$
\mathbf{X'_i b} = b_0 + b_1 X_{i1} + \cdots + b_{p-1} X_{i,p-1} \tag{14.44d}
$$

Geometric interpretation. Recall that when fitting a standard multiple regression model with two predictors, the estimated regression surface is a plane in three-dimensional space, as shown in Figure 6.7 on page 240 for the Dwaine Studios example. A multiple logistic regression fit based on two continuous predictors can also be represented by a surface in three-dimensional space, but the surface follows the characteristic S-shape that we saw for simple logistic models. For example, Figure 14.8 displays a three-dimensional plot of a logistic response function that depicts the relationship between the development of coronary disease (Y, the binary outcome) and two continuous predictors, cholesterol level (X_1) and age (X_2). This surface increases in an approximately linear fashion for larger values of

FIGURE 14.8
Three-Dimensional Fitted Logistic Response Surface—Coronary Heart Disease Example.

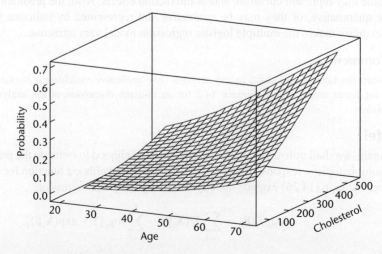

cholesterol level and age, but levels off and is nearly horizontal for small values of these predictors.

We shall rely on standard statistical packages for logistic regression to conduct the numerical search procedures for obtaining the maximum likelihood estimates. We therefore proceed directly to an example to illustrate the fitting and interpretation of a multiple logistic regression model.

Example

In a health study to investigate an epidemic outbreak of a disease that is spread by mosquitoes, individuals were randomly sampled within two sectors in a city to determine if the person had recently contracted the disease under study. This was ascertained by the interviewer, who asked pertinent questions to assess whether certain specific symptoms associated with the disease were present during the specified period. The response variable Y was coded 1 if this disease was determined to have been present, and 0 if not.

Three predictor variables were included in the study, representing known or potential risk factors. They are age, socioeconomic status of household, and sector within city. Age (X_1) is a quantitative variable. Socioeconomic status is a categorical variable with three levels. It is represented by two indicator variables $(X_2$ and $X_3)$, as follows:

Class	X_2	X_3
Upper	0	0
Middle	1	0
Lower	0	1

City sector is also a categorical variable. Since there were only two sectors in the study, one indicator variable (X_4) was used, defined so that $X_4 = 0$ for sector 1 and $X_4 = 1$ for sector 2.

The reason why the upper socioeconomic class was chosen as the reference class (i.e., the class for which the indicator variables X_2 and X_3 are coded 0) is that it was expected that this class would have the lowest disease rate among the socioeconomic classes. By making this class the reference class, the odds ratios associated with regression coefficients β_2 and β_3 would then be expected to be greater than 1, facilitating their interpretation. For the same reason, sector 1, where the epidemic was less severe, was chosen as the reference class for the sector indicator variable X_4.

The data for 196 individuals in the sample are given in the disease outbreak data set in Appendix C.10. The first 98 cases were selected for fitting the model. The remaining 98 cases were saved to serve as a validation data set. Table 14.3 in columns 1–5 contains the data for a portion of the 98 cases used for fitting the model. Note the use of the indicator variables as just explained for the two categorical variables. The primary purpose of the study was to assess the strength of the association between each of the predictor variables and the probability of a person having contracted the disease.

A first-order multiple logistic regression model with the three predictor variables was considered *a priori* to be reasonable:

$$E\{Y\} = [1 + \exp(-\mathbf{X}'\boldsymbol{\beta})]^{-1} \tag{14.45}$$

TABLE 14.3
Portion of Model-Building Data Set—Disease Outbreak Example.

		(1)	(2) Socioeconomic Status	(3)	(4)	(5)	(6)
	Case *i*	Age X_{i1}	X_{i2}	X_{i3}	City Sector X_{i4}	Disease Status Y_i	Fitted Value $\hat{\pi}_i$
(Coded)	1	33	0	0	0	0	.209
	2	35	0	0	0	0	.219
	3	6	0	0	0	0	.106
	4	60	0	0	0	0	.371
	5	18	0	1	0	1	.111
	6	26	0	1	0	0	.136
	...	...	...	...	...	...	...
	98	35	0	1	0	0	.171

TABLE 14.4
Maximum Likelihood Estimates of Logistic Regression Function (14.45)— Disease Outbreak Example.

(a) Estimated Coefficients, Standard Deviations, and Odds Ratios

Regression Coefficient	Estimated Regression Coefficient	Estimated Standard Deviation	Estimated Odds Ratio
β_0	−3.8877	.9955	—
β_1	.02975	.01350	1.030
β_2	.4088	.5990	1.505
β_3	−.30525	.6041	.737
β_4	1.5747	.5016	4.829

(b) Estimated Approximate Variance-Covariance Matrix

	b_0	b_1	b_2	b_3	b_4
	.4129	−.0057	−.1836	−.2010	−.1632
	−.0057	.00018	.00115	.00073	.00034
$s^2\{b\} =$	−.1836	.00115	.3588	.1482	.0129
	−.2010	.00073	.1482	.3650	.0623
	−.1632	.00034	.0129	.0623	.2516

where:

$$\mathbf{X}'\boldsymbol{\beta} = \beta_0 + \beta_1 X_1 + \beta_2 X_2 + \beta_3 X_3 + \beta_4 X_4 \qquad (14.45a)$$

This model was fitted by the method of maximum likelihood to the data for the 98 cases. The results are summarized in Table 14.4a. The estimated logistic response function is:

$$\hat{\pi} = [1 + \exp(3.8877 - .02975X_1 - .4088X_2 + .30525X_3 - 1.5747X_4]^{-1} \qquad (14.46)$$

The interpretation of the estimated regression coefficients in the fitted first-order multiple logistic response function parallels that for the simple logistic response function: $\exp(b_k)$ is the estimated odds ratio for predictor variable X_k. The only difference in interpretation for multiple logistic regression is that the estimated odds ratio for predictor variable X_k

assumes that all other predictor variables are held constant. The levels at which they are held constant does not matter in a first-order model. We see from Table 14.4a, for instance, that the odds of a person having contracted the disease increase by about 3.0 percent with each additional year of age (X_1), for given socioeconomic status and city sector location. Also, the odds of a person in sector 2 (X_4) having contracted the disease are almost five times as great as for a person in sector 1, for given age and socioeconomic status. These are point estimates, to be sure, and we shall need to consider how precise these estimates are.

Table 14.3, column 6, contains the fitted values $\hat{\pi}_i$. These are calculated as usual. For instance, the estimated mean response for case $i = 1$, where $X_{11} = 33$, $X_{12} = 0$, $X_{13} = 0$, $X_{14} = 0$, is:

$$\hat{\pi}_1 = \{1 + \exp[2.3129 - .02975(33) - .4088(0) + .30525(0) - 1.5747(0)]\}^{-1} = .209$$

Polynomial Logistic Regression

Occasionally, the first-order logistic model may not provide an adequate fit to the data and a more complicated model may be needed. One such model is the kth-order polynomial logistic regression model, with logit response function:

$$\pi'(x) = \beta_0 + \beta_{11}x + \beta_{22}x^2 + \cdots + \beta_{kk}x^k \tag{14.47}$$

where x denotes the centered predictor, $X - \bar{X}$. This model for the logit is still linear in the β parameters. For simplicity, we will use a second-order polynomial:

$$\pi'(x) = \beta_0 + \beta_{11}x + \beta_{22}x^2$$

to demonstrate the procedure.

Example

A study of 482 initial public offering companies (IPOs) was conducted to determine the characteristics of companies that attract venture capital. Here, the response of interest is whether or not the company was financed by venture capital funds. Several potential predictors are: the face value of the company; the number of shares offered; and whether or not the company was a leveraged buyout. The IPO data set is listed in Appendix C.11. In this example we consider just one predictor, the face value of the company.

Figure 14.9a contains a plot of venture capital involvement (Y) versus the the natural logarithm of the face value of the company (X) with a lowess smooth and the fitted

FIGURE 14.9
First- and Second-order Logistic Regression Fits (Solid Lines), with Lowess Smooths (Dashed Lines)—IPO Example.

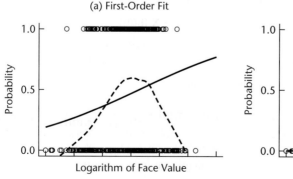

(a) First-Order Fit

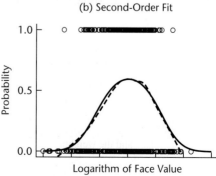

(b) Second-Order Fit

TABLE 14.5
Logistic
Regression
Output for
Second-Order
Model—IPO
Example.

Predictor	Estimated Coefficient	Estimated Standard Error	z^*	P-value
Constant	$b_0 = 0.3005$	0.1240	2.42	0.015
x	$b_{11} = 0.5516$	0.1385	3.98	0.000
x^2	$b_{22} = -0.8615$	0.1404	-6.14	0.000

first-order logistic regression fit superimposed. (Here we chose to analyze the natural logarithm of face value because face value ranges over several orders of magnitude, with a highly skewed distribution.) The lowess smooth clearly suggests a mound-shaped relationship: for small and large companies, the likelihood of venture capital involvement is near zero, but for midsized companies it is over .5. The first-order logistic regression fit is unable to capture the characteristic mound shape of the mean response function and is clearly inadequate. Table 14.5 shows the fitted second-order response function:

$$\hat{\pi}' = .3005 + .5516x - .8615x^2$$

where $x = X - \bar{X}$. Also shown in Table 14.5 are three quantities to be discussed in Section 14.5, namely, the estimated standard error of each coefficient, a statistic, z^*, for testing the hypothesis that the coefficient is zero, and the resulting P-value. We simply note for now that the P-value for b_{22} is .000, confirming the need for a second-order term. Figure 14.9b plots the data, the lowess smooth, and the second-order polynomial logistic regression fit. Note that the second-order polynomial fit tracks the lowess smooth closely.

The above example demonstrated the use of polynomial regression for a single predictor. For multiple logistic regression, higher order polynomial terms and cross-products may be added to improve the fit of a model, as discussed in Section 8.1 in the context of multiple linear regression models.

Comments

1. The maximum likelihood estimates of the parameters $\boldsymbol{\beta}$ for the logistic regression model can be obtained by iteratively reweighted least squares. The procedure is straightforward, although it involves intensive use of a computer.

   a. Obtain starting values for the regression parameters, to be denoted by $\mathbf{b}(0)$. Often, reasonable starting values can be obtained by ordinary least squares regression of Y on the predictor variables $X_1, \ldots, X_{p-1}$, using a first-order linear model.

   b. Using these starting values, obtain:

$$\hat{\pi}_i'(0) = \mathbf{X}_i'[\mathbf{b}(0)] \tag{14.48a}$$

$$\hat{\pi}_i(0) = \frac{\exp[\hat{\pi}_i'(0)]}{1 + \exp[\hat{\pi}_i'(0)]} \tag{14.48b}$$

   c. Calculate the new response variable:

$$Y_i'(0) = \hat{\pi}_i'(0) + \frac{Y_i - \hat{\pi}_i(0)}{\hat{\pi}_i(0)[1 - \hat{\pi}_i(0)]} \tag{14.49a}$$

and the weights:

$$w_i(0) = \hat{\pi}_i(0)[1 - \hat{\pi}_i(0)] \tag{14.49b}$$

d. Regress $Y'(0)$ in (14.49a) on the predictor variables $X_1, \ldots, X_{p-1}$ using a first-order linear model with weights in (14.49b) to obtain revised estimated regression coefficients, denoted by $\mathbf{b}(1)$.

e. Repeat steps b through d, making revisions in (14.48) and (14.49) by using the latest revised estimated regression coefficients until there is little if any change in the estimated coefficients. Often three or four iterations are sufficient to obtain convergence.

2. When the multiple logistic regression model is not a first-order model and contains quadratic or higher-power terms for the predictor variables and/or cross-product terms for interaction effects, the estimated regression coefficients b_k no longer have a simple interpretation.

3. When the assumptions of a monotonic sigmoidal relation between π and $\mathbf{X}'\boldsymbol{\beta}$, required for the multiple logistic regression model, are not appropriate, an alternative is to convert all predictor variables to categorical variables and employ a log-linear model. In the disease outbreak example, for instance, age could be converted into a categorical variable with three classes 0–18, 19–50, and 51–75. Reference 14.2 describes the use of log-linear models for binary response variables when the predictor variables are categorical.

4. Convergence difficulties in the numerical search procedures for finding the maximum likelihood estimates of the multiple logistic regression function may be encountered when the predictor variables are highly correlated or when there is a large number of predictor variables. Another instance that causes convergence problems occurs when a collection of the predictors either completely or nearly perfectly separates the outcome groups. Indication of this problem often can be detected by noting large estimated parameters and large estimated standard errors, similar to what occurs with multicollinearity problems. When convergence problems occur, it may be necessary to reduce the number of predictor variables in order to obtain convergence. ■

14.5   Inferences about Regression Parameters

The same types of inferences are of interest in logistic regression as for linear regression models—inferences about the regression coefficients, estimation of mean responses, and predictions of new observations.

The inference procedures that we shall present rely on large sample sizes. For large samples, under generally applicable conditions, maximum likelihood estimators for logistic regression are approximately normally distributed, with little or no bias, and with approximate variances and covariances that are functions of the second-order partial derivatives of the logarithm of the likelihood function.

Specifically, let $\mathbf{G}$ denote the matrix of second-order partial derivatives of the log-likelihood function in (14.42), the derivatives being taken with regard to the parameters $\beta_0, \beta_1, \ldots, \beta_{p-1}$:

$$\underset{p \times p}{\mathbf{G}} = [g_{ij}] \qquad i = 0, 1, \ldots, p-1; \; j = 0, 1, \ldots, p-1 \qquad \textbf{(14.50)}$$

where:

$$g_{00} = \frac{\partial^2 \log_e L(\boldsymbol{\beta})}{\partial \beta_0^2}$$

$$g_{01} = \frac{\partial^2 \log_e L(\boldsymbol{\beta})}{\partial \beta_0 \partial \beta_1}$$

etc.

This matrix is called the *Hessian* matrix. When the second-order partial derivatives in the Hessian matrix are evaluated at $\beta = b$, that is, at the maximum likelihood estimates, the estimated approximate variance-covariance matrix of the estimated regression coefficients for logistic regression can be obtained as follows:

$$\mathbf{s}^2\{\mathbf{b}\} = ([-g_{ij}]_{\beta=b})^{-1} \tag{14.51}$$

The estimated approximate variances and covariances in (14.51) are routinely provided by most logistic regression computer packages.

Inferences about the regression coefficients for the simple logistic regression model (14.20) or the multiple logistic regression model (14.41) are based on the following approximate result when the sample size is large:

$$\frac{b_k - \beta_k}{s\{b_k\}} \sim z \qquad k = 0, 1, \dots, p-1 \tag{14.52}$$

where z is a standard normal random variable and $s\{b_k\}$ is the estimated approximate standard deviation of b_k obtained from (14.51).

Test Concerning a Single β_k: Wald Test

A large-sample test of a single regression parameter can be constructed based on (14.52). For the alternatives:

$$H_0: \beta_k = 0$$
$$H_a: \beta_k \neq 0 \tag{14.53a}$$

an appropriate test statistic is:

$$z^* = \frac{b_k}{s\{b_k\}} \tag{14.53b}$$

and the decision rule is:

If $|z^*| \leq z(1 - \alpha/2)$, conclude H_0
If $|z^*| > z(1 - \alpha/2)$, conclude H_a $\qquad$ (14.53c)

One-sided alternatives will involve a one-sided decision rule. The testing procedure in (14.53) is commonly referred to as the Wald test. On occasion, the square of z^* is used instead, and the test is then based on a chi-square distribution with 1 degree of freedom. This is also referred to as the Wald test.

Example

In the programming task example, β_1 was expected to be positive. The alternatives of interest therefore are:

$$H_0: \beta_1 \leq 0$$
$$H_a: \beta_1 > 0$$

Test statistic (14.53b), using the results in Table 14.1b, is:

$$z^* = \frac{.1615}{.0650} = 2.485$$

For $\alpha = .05$, we require $z(.95) = 1.645$. The decision rule therefore is:

$$\text{If } z^* \leq 1.645, \text{ conclude } H_0$$
$$\text{If } z^* > 1.645, \text{ conclude } H_a$$

Since $z^* = 2.485 > 1.645$, we conclude H_a, that β_1 is positive, as expected. The one-sided P-value of this test is .0065.

Interval Estimation of a Single β_k

From (14.52), we obtain directly the approximate $1 - \alpha$ confidence limits for β_k:

$$b_k \pm z(1 - \alpha/2)s\{b_k\} \tag{14.54}$$

where $z(1 - \alpha/2)$ is the $(1 - \alpha/2)100$ percentile of the standard normal distribution.

The corresponding confidence limits for the odds ratio $\exp(\beta_k)$ are:

$$\exp[b_k \pm z(1 - \alpha/2)s\{b_k\}] \tag{14.55}$$

Example

For the programming task example, it is desired to estimate β_1 with an approximate 95 percent confidence interval. We require $z(.975) = 1.960$, as well as the estimates $b_1 = .1615$ and $s\{b_1\} = .0650$ which are given in Table 14.1b. Hence, the confidence limits are $.1615 \pm 1.960(.0650)$, and the approximate 95 percent confidence interval for β_1 is:

$$.0341 \leq \beta_1 \leq .2889$$

Thus, we can conclude with approximately 95 percent confidence that β_1 is between .0341 and .2889. The corresponding 95 percent confidence limits for the odds ratio are $\exp(.0341) = 1.03$ and $\exp(.2889) = 1.33$.

To examine whether the large-sample inference procedures are applicable here when $n = 25$, bootstrap sampling can be employed, as described in Chapter 13. Alternatively, estimation procedures have been developed for logistic regression that do not depend on any large-sample approximations. LogXact (Reference 14.3) was run on the data and produced 95 percent confidence limits for β_1 of .041 and .296. The large-sample limits of .034 and .289 are reasonably close to the LogXact limits, confirming the applicability of large-sample theory here.

If we wish to consider the odds ratio for persons whose experience differs by, say, five months, the point estimate of this odds ratio would be $\exp(5b_1) = \exp[5(.1615)] = 2.242$, and the 95 percent confidence limits would be obtained from the confidence limits for b_1 as follows: $\exp[5(.0341)] = 1.186$ and $\exp[5(.2889)] = 4.240$. Thus, with 95 percent confidence we estimate that the odds of success increase by between 19 percent and 324 percent with an additional five months of experience.

Comments

1. If the large-sample conditions for inferences are not met, the bootstrap procedure can be employed to obtain confidence limits for the regression coefficients. The bootstrap here requires generating Bernoulli random variables as discussed in Section 14.8 for the construction of simulated envelopes.

2. We are using the z approximation here for large-sample inferences rather than the t approximation used in Chapter 13 for nonlinear regression. This choice is conventional for logistic regression.

For large sample sizes, there is little difference between the t distribution and the standard normal distribution.

3. Approximate joint confidence intervals for several logistic regression parameters can be developed by the Bonferroni procedure. If g parameters are to be estimated with family confidence coefficient of approximately $1 - \alpha$, the joint Bonferroni confidence limits are:

$$b_k \pm Bs\{b_k\} \tag{14.56}$$

where:

$$B = z(1 - \alpha/2g) \tag{14.56a}$$

4. For power and sample size considerations in logistic regression modeling, see Reference 14.4.

∎

Test whether Several $\beta_k = 0$: Likelihood Ratio Test

Frequently there is interest in determining whether a subset of the X variables in a multiple logistic regression model can be dropped, that is, in testing whether the associated regression coefficients β_k equal zero. The test procedure we shall employ is a general one for use with maximum likelihood estimation, and is analogous to the general linear test procedure for linear models. The test is called the *likelihood ratio test,* and, like the general linear test, is based on a comparison of full and reduced models. The test is valid for large sample sizes.

We begin with the full logistic model with response function:

$$\pi = [1 + \exp(-\mathbf{X}'\boldsymbol{\beta}_F)]^{-1} \qquad \text{Full model} \tag{14.57}$$

where:

$$\mathbf{X}'\boldsymbol{\beta}_F = \beta_0 + \beta_1 X_1 + \cdots + \beta_{p-1} X_{p-1}$$

We then find the maximum likelihood estimates for the full model, now denoted by $\mathbf{b}_F$, and evaluate the likelihood function $L(\boldsymbol{\beta})$ when $\boldsymbol{\beta}_F = \mathbf{b}_F$. We shall denote this value of the likelihood function for the full model by $L(F)$.

The hypothesis we wish to test is:

$$
\begin{aligned}
H_0\!: \beta_q &= \beta_{q+1} = \cdots = \beta_{p-1} = 0 \\
H_a\!: &\text{ not all of the } \beta_k \text{ in } H_0 \text{ equal zero}
\end{aligned}
\tag{14.58}
$$

where, for convenience, we arrange the model so that the last $p - q$ coefficients are those tested. The reduced logistic model therefore has the response function:

$$\pi = [1 + \exp(-\mathbf{X}'\boldsymbol{\beta}_R)]^{-1} \qquad \text{Reduced model} \tag{14.59}$$

where:

$$\mathbf{X}'\boldsymbol{\beta}_R = \beta_0 + \beta_1 X_1 + \cdots + \beta_{q-1} X_{q-1}$$

Now we obtain the maximum likelihood estimates $\mathbf{b}_R$ for the reduced model and evaluate the likelihood function for the reduced model containing q parameters when $\boldsymbol{\beta}_R = \mathbf{b}_R$. We shall denote this value of the likelihood function for the reduced model by $L(R)$. It can be shown that $L(R)$ cannot exceed $L(F)$ since one cannot obtain a larger maximum for the likelihood function using a subset of the parameters.

The actual test statistic for the likelihood ratio test, denoted by G^2, is:

$$G^2 = -2 \log_e \left[\frac{L(R)}{L(F)} \right] = -2[\log_e L(R) - \log_e L(F)] \tag{14.60}$$

Note that if the ratio $L(R)/L(F)$ is small, indicating H_a is the appropriate conclusion, then G^2 is large. Thus, large values of G^2 lead to conclusion H_a.

Large-sample theory states that when n is large, G^2 is distributed approximately as $\chi^2(p - q)$ when H_0 in (14.58) holds. The degrees of freedom correspond to $df_R - df_F = (n - q) - (n - p) = p - q$. The appropriate decision rule therefore is:

$$
\begin{aligned}
&\text{If } G^2 \leq \chi^2(1 - \alpha; p - q), \text{ conclude } H_0 \\
&\text{If } G^2 > \chi^2(1 - \alpha; p - q), \text{ conclude } H_a
\end{aligned}
\tag{14.61}
$$

Example

In the disease outbreak example, the model building began with the three predictor variables that were considered *a priori* to be key explanatory variables—age, socioeconomic status, and city sector. A logistic regression model was fitted containing these three predictor variables and the log-likelihood for this model was obtained. Then tests were conducted to see whether a variable could be dropped from the model. First, age (X_1) was dropped from the logistic model and the log-likelihood for this reduced model was obtained. The results were:

$$L(F) = L(b_0, b_1, b_2, b_3, b_4) = -50.527 \qquad L(R) = L(b_0, b_2, b_3, b_4) = -53.102$$

Hence the required test statistic is:

$$G^2 = -2[\log_e L(R) - \log_e L(F)] = -2[-53.102 - (-50.527)] = 5.150$$

For $\alpha = .05$, we require $\chi^2(.95; 1) = 3.84$. Hence to test $H_0: \beta_1 = 0$, $H_a: \beta_1 \neq 0$, the appropriate decision rule is:

$$
\begin{aligned}
&\text{If } G^2 \leq 3.84, \text{ conclude } H_0 \\
&\text{If } G^2 > 3.84, \text{ conclude } H_a
\end{aligned}
$$

Since $G^2 = 5.15 \geq 3.84$, we conclude H_a, that X_1 should not be dropped from the model. The P-value of this test is .023.

Similar tests for socioeconomic status (X_2, X_3) and city sector (X_4) led to P-values of .55 and .001. The P-value for socioeconomic status suggests that it can be dropped from the model containing the other two predictor variables. However, since this variable was considered *a priori* to be important, additional analyses were conducted. When socioeconomic status is the only predictor in the logistic regression model, the P-value for the test whether this predictor variable is helpful is .16, suggesting marginal importance for this variable. In addition, the estimated regression coefficients for age and city sector and their estimated standard deviations are not appreciably affected by whether or not socioeconomic status is in the regression model. Hence, it was decided to keep socioeconomic status in the logistic regression model in view of its *a priori* importance.

The next question of concern was whether any two-factor interaction terms are required in the model. The full model now includes all possible two-factor interactions, in addition to the main effects, so that $\mathbf{X}'\boldsymbol{\beta}_F$ for this model is as follows:

$$\mathbf{X}'\boldsymbol{\beta}_F = \beta_0 + \beta_1 X_1 + \beta_2 X_2 + \beta_3 X_3 + \beta_4 X_4 + \beta_5 X_1 X_2 + \beta_6 X_1 X_3$$
$$+ \beta_7 X_1 X_4 + \beta_8 X_2 X_4 + \beta_9 X_3 X_4 \qquad\qquad \text{Full model}$$

We wish to test:

$$H_0: \beta_5 = \beta_6 = \beta_7 = \beta_8 = \beta_9 = 0$$
$$H_a: \text{not all } \beta_k \text{ in } H_0 \text{ equal zero}$$

so that $\mathbf{X}'\boldsymbol{\beta}_R$ for the reduced model is:

$$\mathbf{X}'\boldsymbol{\beta}_R = \beta_0 + \beta_1 X_1 + \beta_2 X_2 + \beta_3 X_3 + \beta_4 X_4 \qquad\qquad \text{Reduced model}$$

A computer run of a multiple logistic regression package yielded:

$$L(F) = -46.998$$
$$L(R) = -50.527$$
$$G^2 = -2[\log_e(R) - \log_e(F)] = 7.058$$

If H_0 holds, G^2 follows approximately the chi-square distribution with 5 degrees of freedom. For $\alpha = .05$, we require $\chi^2(.95; 5) = 11.07$. Since $G^2 = 7.058 < 11.07$, we conclude H_0, that the two-factor interactions are not needed in the logistic regression model. The P-value of this test is .22. We note again that a logistic regression model without interaction terms is desirable, because otherwise $\exp(\beta_k)$ no longer can be interpreted as the odds ratio.

Thus, the fitted logistic regression model (14.46) was accepted as the model to be checked diagnostically and, finally, to be validated.

Comment

The Wald test for a single regression parameter in (14.53) is more versatile than the likelihood ratio test in (14.60). The latter can only be used to test $H_0: \beta_k = 0$, whereas the former can be used also for one-sided tests and for testing whether β_k equals some specified value other than zero. When testing $H_0: \beta_k = 0$, the two tests are not identical and may occasionally lead to different conclusions. For example, the Wald test P-value for dropping age when socioeconomic status and sector are in the model for the disease data set example is .0275; the P-value for the likelihood ratio test is .023. ∎

14.6   Automatic Model Selection Methods

Several automatic model selection methods are available for building logistic regression models. These include all-possible-regressions and stepwise procedures. We begin with a discussion of criteria for model selection.

Model Selection Criteria

In the context of multiple linear regression models, we discussed the use of the following model selection criteria in Chapter 9: R_p^2, $R_{a,p}^2$, C_p, AIC_p, SBC_p, and $PRESS_p$. For logistic regression modeling, the AIC_p and SBC_p criteria are easily adapted and are generally available in commercial software. For these reasons we will focus on the use of these two criteria. The modifications are as follows:

$$AIC_p = -2\log_e L(\mathbf{b}) + 2p \tag{14.62}$$

$$SBC_p = -2\log_e L(\mathbf{b}) + p\log_e(n) \tag{14.63}$$

where $\log_e L(\mathbf{b})$ is the log-likelihood expression in (14.42). Promising models will yield relatively small values for these criteria. A third criterion that is frequently provided by software packages is -2 times the log-likelihood, or $-2\log_e L(\mathbf{b})$. For this criterion, we also seek models giving small values. A drawback of this third criterion is that $-2\log_e L(\mathbf{b})$ will never increase as terms are added to the model, because there is no penalty for adding predictors. This is analogous to the use of SSE_p or R_p^2 in multiple linear regression. It is easily seen from (14.62) and (14.63) that AIC_p and SBC_p also involve $-2\log_e L(\mathbf{b})$, but penalties are added based on the number of terms p. This penalty is $2p$ for AIC_p and $p\log_e(n)$ for SBC_p.

Best Subsets Procedures

"Best" subsets procedures were discussed in Section 9.4 in the context of multiple linear regression. Recall that these procedures identify a group of subset models that give the best values of a specified criterion. As long as the number of parameters is not too large (typically less than 30 or 40) these procedures can be useful. As we noted in Section 9.4, time-saving algorithms have been developed that can identify the most promising models, without having to evaluate all 2^{p-1} candidates. These procedures are similarly applicable in the context of logistic regression. We now illustrate the use of the the best subsets procedure based on the AIC_p and SBC_p criteria.

Example

For the disease outbreak example, there are four predictors, age (X_1), socioeconomic status (X_2 and X_3) and city sector (X_4). Normally, it is advantageous to tie the two indicators for the qualitative predictor socioeconomic status together; that is, a model should either have both predictors, or neither. Since very few statistical software packages follow this convention, we will allow them to be independently included. This leads to the $2^4 = 16$ possible regression models listed in columns 2–5 of Table 14.6a. The AIC_p, SBC_p, and $-2\log_e L(\mathbf{b})$ criterion values for each of the 16 models are listed in columns 6–8 of Table 14.6a and are plotted against p in Figures 14.10a–c, respectively.

As shown in Figures 14.10a and 14.10b, both AIC_p and SBC_p are minimized for $p = 3$. Inspection of Table 14.6b reveals that the best two-predictor model for both criteria is based on X_1 (age) and X_4 (city sector). Other models that appear promising on the basis of the AIC_p criterion are the three-predictor subsets based on X_1, X_2, and X_4 and X_1, X_3, and X_4, and the full model based on all four predictors. SBC_p also identifies the two three-predictor subset models just noted, as well as the one-predictor model based on X_4. The tendency of SBC_p to favor smaller models is evident in this example.

The plot of $-2\log_e L(\mathbf{b})$ in Figure 14.10c also points to a two- or three-predictor subset. The additional reduction in $-2\log_e L(\mathbf{b})$ from moving from the best two-predictor model to the best three-predictor model are small, and the returns continue to diminish as we move from three predictors to the full, four-predictor model.

Stepwise Model Selection

As we noted in Chapter 9 in the context of model selection for multiple linear regression, when the number of predictors is large (i.e., 40 or more) the use of all-possible-regression

TABLE 14.6 Best Subsets Results—Disease Outbreak Example.

(a) Results for All Possible Models ($X_{ij} = 1$ if X_j in model i; $X_{ij} = 0$ otherwise)								
	(1)	(2)	(3)	(4)	(5)	(6)	(7)	(8)
			Socioeconomic Status		City Sector			
Model i	Parameters p	Age X_{i1}	X_{i2}	X_{i3}	X_{i4}	AIC_p	SBC_p	$-2\log_e L$ (b)
1	1	0	0	0	0	124.318	126.903	122.318
2	2	1	0	0	0	118.913	124.083	114.913
3	2	0	1	0	0	124.882	130.052	120.882
4	2	0	0	1	0	122.229	127.399	118.229
5	2	0	0	0	1	111.534	116.704	107.534
6	3	1	1	0	0	119.109	126.864	113.109
7	3	1	0	1	0	117.968	125.723	111.968
8	3	1	0	0	1	108.259	116.014	102.259
9	3	0	1	1	0	124.085	131.840	118.085
10	3	0	1	0	1	112.881	120.636	106.881
11	3	0	0	1	1	112.371	120.126	106.371
12	4	1	1	1	0	119.502	129.842	111.502
13	4	1	1	0	1	109.310	119.650	101.310
14	4	1	0	1	1	109.521	119.861	101.521
15	4	0	1	1	1	114.204	124.543	106.204
16	5	1	1	1	1	111.054	123.979	101.054

(b) Best Four Models for Each Criterion				
	AIC_p Criterion		SBC_p Criterion	
Rank	Predictors	AIC_p	Predictors	SBC_p
1	X_1, X_4	108.259	X_1, X_4	116.014
2	X_1, X_2, X_4	109.310	X_4	116.704
3	X_1, X_3, X_4	109.521	X_1, X_2, X_4	119.650
4	X_1, X_2, X_3, X_4	111.054	X_1, X_3, X_4	119.861

procedures for model selection may not be feasible. In such cases, stepwise selection procedures are generally employed. The stepwise procedures discussed in Section 9.4 for multiple linear regression are easily adapted for use in logistic regression. The only change required concerns the decision rule for adding or deleting a predictor. For multiple linear regression, this decision is based on t_k, the t-value associated with b_k, and its P-value. For logistic regression, we obtain an analogous procedure by basing the decision on the Wald statistic z^* in (14.53b) for the kth estimated regression parameter, and its P-value. With this change, implementation of the various stepwise variants, such as the forward stepwise, forward selection, and backward elimination algorithms is straightforward. We illustrate the use of forward stepwise selection for the disease outbreak data.

Example

Figure 14.11 provides partial output from the SPSS forward stepwise selection procedure for the disease outbreak example. This routine will add a predictor only if the P-value associated with its Wald test statistic is less than 0.05. In step one, city sector (X_4) is

FIGURE 14.10   **Plots of AIC_p, SBC_p, and $-2\log_e L(\mathbf{b})$—Disease Outbreak Example.**

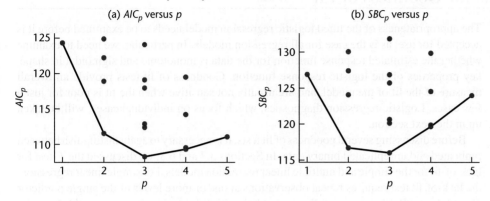

(a) AIC_p versus p

(b) SBC_p versus p

(c) $-2\log_e(\mathbf{b})$ versus p

FIGURE 14.11
**Partial Output
from SPSS
Logistic
Stepwise
Selection
Procedure—
Disease
Outbreak
Example.**

Logistic Regression

Block 1: Method = Forward Stepwise (Wald)

Variables in the Equation

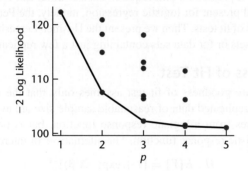

		B	S.E.	Wald	df	Sig.	Exp(B)
Step 1[a]	SECTOR	1.743	.473	13.593	1	.000	5.716
	Constant	−3.332	.765	18.990	1	.000	.036
Step 2[b]	AGE	.029	.013	4.946	1	.026	1.030
	SECTOR	1.673	.487	11.791	1	.001	5.331
	Constant	−4.009	.873	21.060	1	.000	.018

a. Variable(s) entered on step 1: SECTOR.

b. Variable(s) entered on step 2: AGE.

entered; its P-value .000. In Step 2, age (X_1) is entered, with a P-value of 0.026. At this
point the procedure terminates, because no further predictors can be added with resulting
P-values less than 0.05. Thus, the forward stepwise selection procedure has identified the
same model favored by AIC_p and SBC_p. Notice that SPSS also prints the square of the Wald
test statistics z^* from (14.53b) in the column labeled "Wald." As noted earlier, when $(z^*)^2$
is used, P-values are obtained from a chi-square distribution with 1 degree of freedom.

14.7 Tests for Goodness of Fit

The appropriateness of the fitted logistic regression model needs to be examined before it is accepted for use, as is the case for all regression models. In particular, we need to examine whether the estimated response function for the data is monotonic and sigmoidal in shape, key properties of the logistic response function. Goodness of fit tests provide an overall measure of the fit of the model, and are usually not sensitive when the fit is poor for just a few cases. Logistic regression diagnostics, which focus on individual cases, will be taken up in the next section.

Before discussing several goodness of fit tests, it is necessary to again distinguish between replicated and unreplicated binary data. In Sections 3.7 and 6.8, we discussed the F test for lack-of-fit for the simple and multiple linear regression models. For simple linear regression, the lack-of-fit test requires repeat observations at one or more levels of the single predictor X, and, for multiple regression, there must be multiple or repeat observations that have the same values for all of the predictors. This requirement also holds true for two of the goodness of fit tests that we will present for logistic regression, namely, the Pearson chi-square and the deviance goodness of fit tests. Then we present the Hosmer-Lemeshow test that is useful for unreplicated data sets or for data sets containing just a few replicated observations.

Pearson Chi-Square Goodness of Fit Test

The Pearson chi-square goodness of fit test assumes only that the Y_{ij} observations are independent and that replicated data of reasonable sample size are available. The test can detect major departures from a logistic response function, but is not sensitive to small departures from a logistic response function. The alternatives of interest are:

$$H_0: E\{Y\} = [1 + \exp(-\mathbf{X}'\boldsymbol{\beta})]^{-1}$$
$$H_a: E\{Y\} \neq [1 + \exp(-\mathbf{X}'\boldsymbol{\beta})]^{-1} \tag{14.64}$$

As was the case with tests for lack-of-fit in simple and multiple linear regression, we shall denote the number of distinct combinations of the predictor variables by c, the ith binary response at predictor combination $\mathbf{X}_j$ by Y_{ij}, and the number of cases in the jth class ($j = 1, \ldots, c$) will be denoted by n_j. Recall from (14.32a) that:

$$\sum_{i=1}^{n_j} Y_{ij} = Y_{.j} \tag{14.65}$$

The number of cases in the jth class with outcome 1 will be denoted O_{j1} and the number of cases in the jth class with outcome 0 will be denoted by O_{j0}. Because the response variable Y_{ij} is a Bernoulli variable whose outcomes are 1 and 0, the number of cases O_{j1} and O_{j2} are given as follows:

$$O_{j1} = \sum_{i=1}^{n_j} Y_{ij} = Y_{.j} \tag{14.66a}$$

$$O_{j0} = \sum_{i=1}^{n_j} (1 - Y_{ij}) = n_j - Y_{.j} = n_j - O_{j1} \tag{14.66b}$$

for $j = 1, \ldots, c$.

If the logistic response function is appropriate, the expected value of Y_{ij} is given by:

$$E\{Y_{ij}\} = \pi_j = [1 + \exp(-\mathbf{X}_j'\boldsymbol{\beta})]^{-1} \qquad (14.67)$$

and is estimated by the fitted value $\hat{\pi}_j$:

$$\hat{\pi}_j = [1 + \exp(-\mathbf{X}_j'\mathbf{b})]^{-1} \qquad (14.68)$$

Consequently, if the logistic response function is appropriate, the expected numbers of cases with $Y_{ij} = 1$ and $Y_{ij} = 0$ for the jth class are estimated to be:

$$E_{j1} = n_j\hat{\pi}_j \qquad (14.69a)$$

$$E_{j0} = n_j(1 - \hat{\pi}_j) = n_j - E_{j1} \qquad (14.69b)$$

where E_{j1} denotes the estimated expected number of 1s in the jth class, and E_{j0} denotes the estimated expected number of 0s in the jth class.

The test statistic is the usual chi-square goodness of fit test statistic:

$$X^2 = \sum_{j=1}^{c} \sum_{k=0}^{1} \frac{(O_{jk} - E_{jk})^2}{E_{jk}} \qquad (14.70)$$

If the logistic response function is appropriate, X^2 follows approximately a χ^2 distribution with $c - p$ degrees of freedom when n_j is large and $p < c$. As with other chi-square goodness of fit tests, it is advisable that most expected frequencies E_{jk} be moderately large, say 5 or greater, and none smaller than 1.

Large values of the test statistic X^2 indicate that the logistic response function is not appropriate. The decision rule for testing the alternatives in (14.64), when controlling the level of significance at α, therefore is:

$$\text{If } X^2 \leq \chi^2(1 - \alpha; c - p), \text{ conclude } H_0$$
$$\text{If } X^2 > \chi^2(1 - \alpha; c - p), \text{ conclude } H_a \qquad (14.71)$$

Example

For the coupon effectiveness example, we have five classes. Table 14.7 provides for each class j: n_j, the number of binary outcomes; $\hat{\pi}_j$, the model-based estimate of π_j; p_j, the observed proportion of 1s; O_{j0} and O_{j1}, the number of cases with $Y_{ij} = 0$ and $Y_{ij} = 1$ for each class; and finally, the estimated expected frequencies E_{j0} and E_{j1}, if the logistic regression model (14.35) is appropriate (calculations not shown).

TABLE 14.7
Goodness of Fit Test for Logistic Regression Function— Coupon Effectiveness Example.

| Class | | | | Number of Coupons Not Redeemed | | Number of Coupons Redeemed | |
| | | | | Observed | Expected | Observed | Expected |
j	n_j	$\hat{\pi}_j$	p_j	O_{j0}	E_{j0}	O_{j1}	E_{j1}
1	200	.1736	.150	170	165.3	30	34.7
2	200	.2543	.275	145	149.1	55	50.9
3	200	.3562	.350	130	128.8	70	71.2
4	200	.4731	.500	100	105.4	100	94.6
5	200	.7028	.685	63	59.4	137	140.6

Test statistic (14.76) is calculated as follows:

$$X^2 = \frac{(170 - 165.3)^2}{165.3} + \frac{(30 - 34.7)^2}{34.7} + \cdots + \frac{(137 - 140.6)^2}{140.6}$$

$$= 2.15$$

For $\alpha = 0.05$ and $c - p = 5 - 2 = 3$, we require $\chi^2(.95; 3) = 7.81$. Since $X^2 = 2.15 \le 7.81$, we conclude H_0, that the logistic response function is appropriate. The P-value of the test is .54.

Deviance Goodness of Fit Test

The *deviance goodness of fit test* for logistic regression models is completely analogous to the F test for lack of fit for simple and multiple linear regression models. Like the F test for lack of fit and the Pearson chi-square goodness of fit test, we assume there are c unique combinations of the predictors denoted $X_1, \ldots, X_c$, the number of repeat binary observations at X_j is n_j, and the ith binary response at predictor combination X_j is denoted Y_{ij}.

The lack of fit test for standard regression was based on the general linear test of the reduced model $E\{Y_{ij}\} = \mathbf{X}'_j\boldsymbol{\beta}$ against the full model $E\{Y_{ij}\} = \mu_i$. In similar fashion, the deviance goodness of fit test is based on a likelihood ratio test of the reduced model:

$$E\{Y_{ij}\} = [1 + \exp(-\mathbf{X}'_j\boldsymbol{\beta})]^{-1} \qquad \text{Reduced model} \qquad (14.72)$$

against the full model:

$$E\{Y_{ij}\} = \pi_j \qquad j = 1, \ldots, c \qquad \text{Full model} \qquad (14.73)$$

where π_j are parameters, $j = 1, \ldots, c$. In the lack of fit test for standard regression, the full model allowed for a unique mean for each unique combination of the predictors, X_j. Similarly, the full model for the deviance goodness of fit test allows for a unique probability π_j for each predictor combination. This full model in the logistic regression case is usually referred to as the *saturated model*.

To carry out the likelihood ratio test in (14.60), we must obtain the values of the maximized likelihoods for the full and reduced models, namely $L(F)$ and $L(R)$. $L(R)$ is obtained by fitting the reduced model, and the maximum likelihood estimates of the c parameters in the full model are given by the sample proportions in (14.32b):

$$p_j = \frac{Y_{.j}}{n_j} \qquad j = 1, 2, \ldots, c \qquad (14.74)$$

Letting $\hat{\pi}_j$ denote the reduced model estimate of π_j at X_j, $j = 1, \ldots, c$, it can be shown that likelihood ratio test statistic (14.60) is given by:

$$G^2 = -2[\log_e L(R) - \log_e L(F)]$$

$$= -2\sum_{j=1}^{c}\left[Y_{.j}\log_e\left(\frac{\hat{\pi}_j}{p_j}\right) + (n_j - Y_{.j})\log_e\left(\frac{1 - \hat{\pi}_j}{1 - p_j}\right)\right]$$

$$= DEV(X_0, X_1, \ldots, X_{p-1}) \qquad (14.75)$$

The likelihood ratio test statistic in (14.75) is called the *deviance,* and we use $DEV(X_0, X_1, \ldots, X_{p-1})$ to denote the deviance for a logistic regression model based on predictors $X_0, X_1, \ldots, X_{p-1}$. The deviance measures the deviation, in terms of $-2 \log_e L$, between the saturated model and the fitted reduced logistic regression model based on $X_0, X_1, \ldots, X_{p-1}$.

If the logistic response function is the correct response function and the sample sizes n_j are large, then the deviance will follow approximately a chi-square distribution with $c - p$ degrees of freedom. Large values of the deviance indicate that the fitted logistic model is not correct. Hence, to test the alternatives:

$$H_0: E\{Y\} = [1 + \exp(-\mathbf{X}'\boldsymbol{\beta})]^{-1}$$
$$H_a: E\{Y\} \neq [1 + \exp(-\mathbf{X}'\boldsymbol{\beta})]^{-1} \tag{14.76}$$

the appropriate decision rule is:

$$\text{If } DEV(X_0, X_1, \ldots, X_{p-1}) \leq \chi^2(1 - \alpha; c - p), \text{ conclude } H_0$$
$$\text{If } DEV(X_0, X_1, \ldots, X_{p-1}) > \chi^2(1 - \alpha; c - p), \text{ conclude } H_a \tag{14.77}$$

Example

For the coupon effectiveness example, we use the results in Table 14.2 to calculate the deviance in (14.75) directly:

$$DEV(X_0, X_1) = -2\left[30 \log_e\left(\frac{.1736}{.150}\right) + (200 - 30) \log_e\left(\frac{.8264}{.850}\right)\right.$$
$$\left. + \cdots + 137 \log_e\left(\frac{.7028}{.685}\right) + (200 - 137) \log_e\left(\frac{.2972}{.315}\right)\right]$$
$$= 2.16$$

For $\alpha = .05$ and $c - p = 3$, we require $\chi^2(.95; 3) = 7.81$. Since $DEV(X_0, X_1) = 2.16 \leq 7.81$, we conclude H_0, that the logistic model is a satisfactory fit. The P-value of this test is approximately .54, the same as that obtained earlier for the Pearson chi-square goodness of fit test.

Comment

If $p_j = 0$ for some j in the first term in (14.75), then $Y_{.j} = 0$ and:

$$Y_{.j} \log_e\left(\frac{\hat{\pi}_j}{p_j}\right) = 0$$

Similarly, if $p_j = 1$ for some j in the second term in (14.75), then $Y_{.j} = n_j$ and:

$$(n_j - Y_{.j}) \log_e\left(\frac{1 - \hat{\pi}_j}{1 - p_j}\right) = 0$$

∎

Hosmer-Lemeshow Goodness of Fit Test

Hosmer and Lemeshow (Reference 14.4) proposed, for either unreplicated data sets or data sets with few replicates, the grouping of cases based on the values of the estimated probabilities. Suppose there are no replicates, i.e., $n_j = 1$ for all j. The procedure consists of grouping the data into classes with similar fitted values $\hat{\pi}_i$, with approximately the same

TABLE 14.8 Hosmer-Lemeshow Goodness of Fit Test for Logistic Regression Function—Disease Outbreak Example.

Class j	$\hat{\pi}'_i$ Interval	n_j	Number of Persons without Disease		Number of Persons with Disease	
			Observed O_{j0}	Expected E_{j0}	Observed O_{j1}	Expected E_{j1}
1	−2.60—under −2.08	20	19	18.196	1	1.804
2	−2.08—under −1.43	20	17	17.093	3	2.907
3	−1.43—under −.70	20	14	14.707	6	5.293
4	−.70—under .16	19	9	10.887	10	8.113
5	.16—under 1.70	19	8	6.297	11	12.703
	Total	98	67	67.180	31	30.820

number of cases in each class. The grouping may be accomplished equivalently by using the fitted logit values $\hat{\pi}'_i = \mathbf{X}'_i\mathbf{b}$ since the logit values $\hat{\pi}'_i$ are monotonically related to the fitted mean responses $\hat{\pi}_i$. We shall do the grouping according to the fitted logit values $\hat{\pi}'_i$. Use of from 5 to 10 classes is common, depending on the total number of cases. Once the groups are formed, then the Hosmer-Lemeshow goodness of fit statistic is calculated by using the Pearson chi-square test statistic (14.70) from the $c \times 2$ table of observed and expected frequencies as described earlier. Hosmer and Lemeshow showed, using an extensive simulation study, that the test statistic (14.70) is well approximated by the chi-square distribution with $c - 2$ degrees of freedom.

Example

For the disease outbreak example, we shall use five classes. Table 14.8 shows the class intervals for the logit fitted values $\hat{\pi}'_i$ and the number of cases n_j in each class. It also gives O_{j0} and O_{j1}, the number of cases with $Y_i = 0$ and $Y_i = 1$ for each class. Finally, Table 14.8 contains the estimated expected frequencies E_{j0} and E_{j1} based on logistic regression model (14.46) (calculations not shown).

Test statistic (14.70) is calculated as follows:

$$X^2 = \frac{(19 - 18.196)^2}{18.196} + \frac{(1 - 1.804)^2}{1.804} + \cdots + \frac{(8 - 6.297)^2}{6.297} + \frac{(11 - 12.703)^2}{12.703}$$

$$= 1.98$$

Since all of the n_j are approximately 20 and only two expected frequencies are less than 5 and both are greater than 1, the chi-square test is appropriate here. For $\alpha = .05$ and $c - 2 = 3$, we require $\chi^2(.95; 3) = 7.81$. Since $X^2 = 1.98 \leq 7.81$, we conclude H_0, that the logistic response function is appropriate. The P-value of the test is .58.

Comment

We have noted that the Pearson chi-square and deviance goodness of fit tests are only appropriate when there are repeat observations and when the number of replicates at each X category is sufficiently large. Care must be taken in interpreting logistic regression output since some packages will provide these statistics and the associated P-values whether or not sufficient numbers of replicate observations are present. ∎

14.8 Logistic Regression Diagnostics

In this section we take up the analysis of residuals and the identification of influential cases for logistic regression. We shall first introduce various residuals that have been defined for logistic regression and some associated plots. We then turn to the identification of influential observations. Throughout, we shall assume that the responses are binary; i.e., we focus on the ungrouped case.

Logistic Regression Residuals

Residual analysis for logistic regression is more difficult than for linear regression models because the responses Y_i take on only the values 0 and 1. Consequently, the ith ordinary residual, e_i will assume one of two values:

$$e_i = \begin{cases} 1 - \hat{\pi}_i & \text{if } Y_i = 1 \\ -\hat{\pi}_i & \text{if } Y_i = 0 \end{cases} \tag{14.78}$$

The ordinary residuals will not be normally distributed and, indeed, their distribution under the assumption that the fitted model is correct is unknown. Plots of ordinary residuals against fitted values or predictor variables will generally be uninformative.

Pearson Residuals. The ordinary residuals can be made more comparable by dividing them by the estimated standard error of Y_i, namely, $\sqrt{\hat{\pi}_i(1 - \hat{\pi}_i)}$. The resulting *Pearson residuals* are given by:

$$r_{P_i} = \frac{Y_i - \hat{\pi}_i}{\sqrt{\hat{\pi}_i(1 - \hat{\pi}_i)}} \tag{14.79}$$

The Pearson residuals are directly related to Pearson chi-square goodness of fit statistic (14.70). To see this we first expand (14.70) as follows:

$$X^2 = \sum_{j=1}^{c} \sum_{k=0}^{1} \frac{(O_{jk} - E_{jk})^2}{E_{jk}} = \sum_{j=1}^{c} \frac{(O_{j0} - E_{j0})^2}{E_{j0}} + \sum_{j=1}^{c} \frac{(O_{j1} - E_{j1})^2}{E_{j1}} \tag{14.79a}$$

For binary outcome data, we set $j = i$, $c = n$, $O_{j1} = Y_i$, $O_{j0} = 1 - Y_i$, $E_{j1} = \hat{\pi}_i$, $E_{j0} = 1 - \hat{\pi}_i$, and (14.79a) becomes:

$$X^2 = \sum_{i=1}^{n} \frac{[(1 - Y_i) - (1 - \hat{\pi}_i)]^2}{1 - \hat{\pi}_i} + \sum_{i=1}^{n} \frac{(Y_i - \hat{\pi}_i)^2}{\hat{\pi}_i}$$

$$= \sum_{i=1}^{n} \frac{(Y_i - \hat{\pi}_i)^2}{1 - \hat{\pi}_i} + \sum_{i=1}^{n} \frac{(Y_i - \hat{\pi}_i)^2}{\hat{\pi}_i}$$

$$= \sum_{i=1}^{n} \frac{(Y_i - \hat{\pi}_i)^2}{\hat{\pi}_i(1 - \hat{\pi}_i)} \tag{14.79b}$$

Hence, we see that the sum of the squares of the Pearson residuals (14.79) is numerically equal to the Pearson chi-square test statistic (14.79a). Therefore the square of each Pearson residual measures the contribution of each binary response to the Pearson chi-square test statistic. Note that test statistic (14.79b) does not follow an approximate chi-square distribution for binary data without replicates.

Studentized Pearson Residuals. The Pearson residuals do not have unit variance since no allowance has been made for the inherent variation in the fitted value $\hat{\pi}_i$. A better procedure is to divide the ordinary residuals by their estimated standard deviation. This value is approximated by $\sqrt{\hat{\pi}_i(1-\hat{\pi}_i)(1-h_{ii})}$, where h_{ii} is the ith diagonal element of the $n \times n$ estimated hat matrix for logistic regression:

$$\mathbf{H} = \widehat{\mathbf{W}}^{\frac{1}{2}} \mathbf{X}(\mathbf{X}'\widehat{\mathbf{W}}\mathbf{X})^{-1}\mathbf{X}'\widehat{\mathbf{W}}^{\frac{1}{2}} \tag{14.80}$$

Here, $\widehat{\mathbf{W}}$ is the $n \times n$ diagonal matrix with elements $\hat{\pi}_i(1-\hat{\pi}_i)$, $\mathbf{X}$ is the usual $n \times p$ design matrix (6.18b), and $\widehat{\mathbf{W}}^{\frac{1}{2}}$ is a diagonal matrix with diagonal elements equal to the square roots of those in $\widehat{\mathbf{W}}$. The resulting *studentized Pearson residuals* are defined as:

$$r_{SP_i} = \frac{r_{P_i}}{\sqrt{1-h_{ii}}} \tag{14.81}$$

Recall that for multiple linear regression, the hat matrix satisfies the matrix expression $\hat{\mathbf{Y}} = \mathbf{HY}$. The hat matrix for logistic regression is developed in analogous fashion; it satisfies approximately the expression $\hat{\boldsymbol{\pi}}' = \mathbf{HY}$, where $\hat{\boldsymbol{\pi}}'$ is the $(n \times 1)$ vector of linear predictors.

Deviance Residuals. The model deviance (14.75) was obtained by carrying out the likelihood ratio test where the reduced model is the logistic regression model and the full model is the saturated model for grouped outcome data. For binary outcome data, we take the number of X categories to be $c = n$, $n_j = 1$, $j = i$, $Y_{\cdot j} = Y_i$, $p_j = Y_{\cdot j}/n_j = Y_i$, and (14.75) becomes:

$$G^2 = -2\sum_{i=1}^{n}\left[Y_i \log_e\left(\frac{\hat{\pi}_i}{Y_i}\right) + (1-Y_i)\log_e\left(\frac{1-\hat{\pi}_i}{1-Y_i}\right)\right]$$

$$= -2\sum_{i=1}^{n}[Y_i \log_e(\hat{\pi}_i) + (1-Y_i)\log_e(1-\hat{\pi}_i) - Y_i\log_e(Y_i) - (1-Y_i)\log_e(1-Y_i)]$$

$$= -2\sum_{i=1}^{n}[Y_i \log_e(\hat{\pi}_i) + (1-Y_i)\log_e(1-\hat{\pi}_i)] \tag{14.82}$$

since $Y_i \log_e(Y_i) = (1-Y_i)\log_e(1-Y_i) = 0$ for $Y_i = 0$ or $Y_i = 1$. Thus for binary data the model deviance in (14.75) is:

$$DEV(X_0, \ldots, X_{p-1}) = -2\sum_{i=1}^{n}[Y_i \log_e(\hat{\pi}_i) + (1-Y_i)\log_e(1-\hat{\pi}_i)] \tag{14.82a}$$

The deviance residual for case i, denoted by dev_i, is defined as the signed square root of the contribution of the ith case to the model deviance DEV in (14.82a):

$$dev_i = sign(Y_i - \hat{\pi}_i)\sqrt{-2[Y_i \log_e(\hat{\pi}_i) + (1-Y_i)\log_e(1-\hat{\pi}_i)]} \tag{14.83}$$

where the sign is positive when $Y_i \geq \hat{\pi}_i$ and negative when $Y_i < \hat{\pi}_i$. Thus the sum of the squared deviance residuals equals the model deviance in (14.82a):

$$\sum_{i=1}^{n}(dev_i)^2 = DEV(X_0, X_1, \ldots, X_{p-1})$$

TABLE 14.9
Logistic
Regression
Residuals and
Hat Matrix
Diagonal
Elements—
Disease
Outbreak
Example.

	(1)	(2)	(3)	(4)	(5)	(6)	(7)
i	Y_i	$\hat{\pi}_i$	e_i	r_{P_i}	r_{SP_i}	dev_i	h_{ii}
1	0	0.209	−0.209	−0.514	−0.524	−0.685	.039
2	0	0.219	−0.219	−0.529	−0.541	−0.703	.040
3	0	0.106	−0.106	−0.344	−0.350	−0.473	.033
...	...	...	...	...	...	...	...
96	0	0.114	−0.114	−0.358	−0.363	−0.491	.025
97	0	0.092	−0.092	−0.318	−0.322	−0.439	.024
98	0	0.171	−0.171	−0.455	−0.463	−0.613	.036

Therefore the square of each deviance residual measures the contribution of each binary response to the deviance goodness of fit test statistic (14.82a). Note that test statistic (14.82a) does not follow an approximate chi-square distribution for binary data without replicates.

Example

Table 14.9 lists in columns 1–7, for a portion of the disease outbreak example, the response Y_i, the predicted mean response $\hat{\pi}_i$, the ordinary residual e_i, the Pearson residual r_{P_i}, the studentized Pearson residual r_{SP_i}, the deviance residual dev_i, and the hat matrix diagonal elements h_{ii}. We illustrate the calculations needed to obtain these residuals for the first case. The ordinary residual for the first case is from (14.78):

$$e_1 = Y_1 - \hat{\pi}_1 = 0 - .209 = -.209$$

The first Pearson residual (14.79) is:

$$r_{P_1} = \frac{e_1}{\sqrt{\hat{\pi}_1(1 - \hat{\pi}_1)}} = \frac{-.209}{\sqrt{.209(1 - .209)}} = -.514$$

Substitution of r_{P_1} and the leverage value h_{11} from column 7 of Table 14.9 into (14.81) yields the studentized Pearson residual:

$$r_{SP_1} = \frac{r_{P_1}}{\sqrt{1 - h_{11}}} = \frac{-.514}{\sqrt{1 - .039}} = -.524$$

Finally, the first deviance residual is obtained from (14.83):

$$dev_1 = sign(Y_1 - \hat{\pi}_1)\sqrt{-2[Y_1 \log_e(\hat{\pi}_1) + (1 - Y_1)\log_e(1 - \hat{\pi}_1)]}$$

$$= sign(-.209)\sqrt{-2[0\log_e(.209) + (1 - 0)\log_e(1 - .209)]}$$

$$= -\sqrt{-2\log_e(.791)} = -.685$$

The various residuals are plotted against the predicted mean response in Figure 14.12, although we emphasize that such plots are not particularly informative. Consider, for example, the ordinary residuals in Figure 14.12a. Here we see two trends of decreasing residuals with slope equal to −1. These two linear trends result from the fact, noted above, that the residuals take on just one of two values at a point X_i, $1 - \hat{\pi}_i$ or $0 - \hat{\pi}_i$. Plotting these values against $\hat{\pi}_i$ will always result in two linear trends with slope −1. The remaining plots lead to similar patterns.

FIGURE 14.12 **Selected Residuals Plotted against Predicted Mean Response—Disease Outbreak Example.**

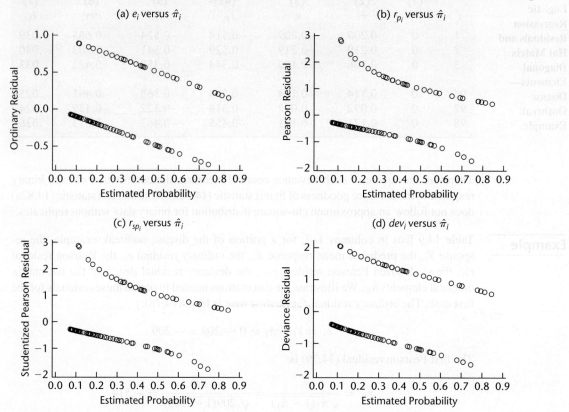

(a) e_i versus $\hat{\pi}_i$

(b) r_{p_i} versus $\hat{\pi}_i$

(c) r_{sp_i} versus $\hat{\pi}_i$

(d) dev_i versus $\hat{\pi}_i$

Diagnostic Residual Plots

In this section we consider two useful residual plots that provide some information about the adequacy of the logistic regression fit. Recall that in ordinary regression, residual plots are useful for diagnosing model inadequacy, nonconstant variance, and the presence of response outliers. In logistic regression, we generally focus only on the detection of model inadequacy. As we discussed in Section 14.1, nonconstant variance is always present in the logistic regression setting, and the form that it takes is known. Moreover, response outliers in binary logistic regression are difficult to diagnose and may only be evident if all responses in a particular region of the X space have the same response value except one or two. Thus we focus here on model adequacy.

Residuals versus Predicted Probabilities with Lowess Smooth. If the logistic regression model is correct, then $E\{Y_i\} = \pi_i$ and it follows asymptotically that:

$$E\{Y_i - \hat{\pi}_i\} = E\{e_i\} = 0$$

This suggests that if the model is correct, a lowess smooth of the plot of the residuals against the estimated probability $\hat{\pi}_i$ (or against the linear predictor $\hat{\pi}_i'$) should result approximately in a horizontal line with zero intercept. Any significant departure from this

FIGURE 14.13   **Residual Plots with Lowess Smooth—Disease Outbreak Example.**

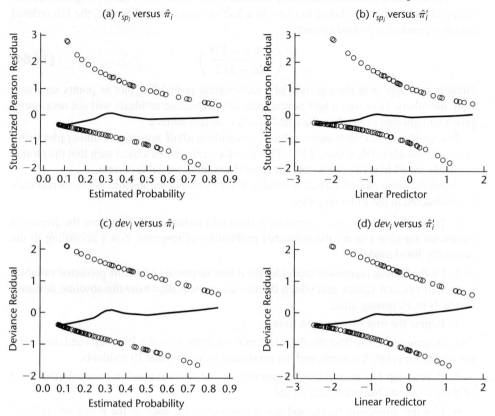

(a) r_{sp_i} versus $\hat{\pi}_i$

(b) r_{sp_i} versus $\hat{\pi}_i'$

(c) dev_i versus $\hat{\pi}_i$

(d) dev_i versus $\hat{\pi}_i'$

suggests that the model may be inadequate. In practice, the lowess smooth of the ordinary residuals, the Pearson residuals, or the studentized Pearson residuals can be employed. (Further details regarding the plotting of logistic regression residuals can be found in Reference 14.5.)

Example

Shown in Figures 14.13a–d are residual plots for the disease outbreak example, each with the suggested lowess smooth superimposed. (We used the MINITAB lowess option with degree of smoothing equal to .7 and number of steps equal to 0 to produce these plots.) In Figures 14.13a and 14.13b, the studentized Pearson residuals are plotted respectively against the estimated probability and the linear predictor. Figures 14.13c and 14.13d provide similar plots for the deviance residuals. In all cases, the lowess smooth approximates a line having zero slope and intercept, and we conclude that no significant model inadequacy is apparent.

Half-Normal Probability Plot with Simulated Envelope.   A half-normal probability plot of the deviance residuals with a simulated envelope is useful both for examining the adequacy of the linear part of the logistic regression model and for identifying deviance residuals that are outlying. A half-normal probability plot helps to highlight outlying deviance residuals even though the residuals are not normally distributed. In a normal probability plot, the *k*th ordered residual is plotted against the percentile $z[(k - .375)/(n + .25)]$ or against $\sqrt{MSE}$ times this percentile, as shown in (3.6). In a half-normal probability plot, the kth ordered *absolute* residual is plotted against:

$$z\left(\frac{k + n - 1/8}{2n + 1/2}\right) \tag{14.84}$$

Outliers will appear at the top right of a half-normal probability plot as points separated from the others. However, a half-normal plot of the absolute residuals will not necessarily give a straight line even when the fitted model is in fact correct.

To identify outlying deviance residuals, we combine a half-normal probability plot with a *simulated envelope* (Reference 14.6). This envelope constitutes a band such that the plotted residuals are all likely to fall within the band if the fitted model is correct.

A simulated envelope for a half-normal probability plot of the absolute deviance residuals is constructed in the following way:

1. For each of the n cases, generate a Bernoulli outcome (0, 1), where the Bernoulli parameter for case i is $\hat{\pi}_i$, the estimated probability of response $Y_i = 1$ according to the originally fitted model.

2. Fit the logistic regression model for the n new responses where the predictor variables keep their original values, and obtain the deviance residuals. Order the absolute deviance residuals in ascending order.

3. Repeat the first two steps 18 times.

4. Assemble the smallest absolute deviance residuals from the 19 groups and determine the minimum value, the mean, and the maximum value of these 19 residuals.

5. Repeat step 4 by assembling the group of second smallest absolute residuals, the group of third smallest absolute residuals, etc.

6. Plot the minimum, mean, and maximum values for each of the n ordered residual groups against the corresponding expected value in (14.84) on the half-normal probability plot for the original data and connect the points by straight lines.

By using 19 simulations, there is one chance in 20, or 5 percent, that the largest absolute deviance residual from the original data set lies outside the simulated envelope when the fitted model is correct. Large deviations of points from the means of the simulated values or the occurrence of points near to or outside the simulated envelope, are indications that the fitted model is not appropriate.

Example

Table 14.10a repeats a portion of the data for the disease outbreak example, as well as the fitted values for the logistic regression model. It also contains a portion of the simulated responses for the 19 simulation samples. For instance, the simulated responses for case 1 were obtained by generating Bernoulli random outcomes with probability $\hat{\pi}_1 = .209$.

Table 14.10b shows some of the ordered absolute deviance residuals for the 19 simulation samples. Finally, Table 14.10c presents the minimum, mean, and maximum for the 19 simulation samples for some of the rank order positions, the ordered absolute deviance for the original sample for these rank order positions, and corresponding z percentiles. The results in Table 14.10c are plotted in Figure 14.14. We see clearly from this figure that the largest deviance residuals (which here correspond to cases 5 and 14) are farthest to the right and are somewhat separated from the other cases. However, they fall well within the

TABLE 14.10
Results for
Simulated
Envelope for
Half-Normal
Probability
Plot—Disease
Outbreak
Example.

(a) Simulated Bernoulli Outcomes

			Simulation Sample		
i	Y_i	$\hat{\pi}_i$	(1)	$\cdots$	(19)
1	0	.209	0	$\cdots$	0
2	0	.219	0	$\cdots$	0
$\cdots$	$\cdots$	$\cdots$	$\cdots$	$\cdots$	$\cdots$
97	0	.092	0	$\cdots$	0
98	0	.171	1	$\cdots$	0

(b) Ordered Absolute Deviance Residuals for Simulation Samples

Order Position k	Simulation Sample		
	(1)	$\cdots$	(19)
1	.468	$\cdots$	.368
2	.468	$\cdots$	.368
$\cdots$	$\cdots$	$\cdots$	$\cdots$
97	1.849	$\cdots$	2.085
98	1.919	$\cdots$	2.228

(c) Minimum, Mean, and Maximum of Ordered Absolute Deviance Residuals for Simulation Samples

Order Position k	Simulation Samples			Original Data	$z\left(\dfrac{k+97.875}{196.5}\right)$
	Minimum	Mean	Maximum		
1	.046	.289	.491	.386	.008
2	.060	.296	.491	.386	.021
$\cdots$	$\cdots$	$\cdots$	$\cdots$	$\cdots$	$\cdots$
97	1.804	2.273	3.194	2.082	2.397
98	1.869	2.387	3.391	2.098	2.729

FIGURE 14.14
Half-Normal
Probability
Plot and
Simulated
Envelope—
Disease
Outbreak
Example.

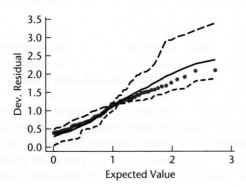

simulated envelope so that remedial measures do not appear to be required. Figure 14.10 also shows that most of the absolute deviance residuals fall near the simulation means, suggesting that the logistic regression model is appropriate here.

Detection of Influential Observations

In this section we introduce three measures that can be used to identify influential observations. We consider the influence of individual binary cases on three aspects of the analysis:

1. The Pearson chi-square statistic (14.79b).
2. The deviance statistic (14.82a).
3. The fitted linear predictor, $\hat{\pi}_i'$.

As was the case in standard regression situations, we will employ case-deletion diagnostics to assess the effect of individual cases on the results of the analysis.

Influence on Pearson Chi-Square and the Deviance Statistics.   Let X^2 and DEV denote the Pearson and deviance statistics (14.79b) and (14.82a) based on the full data set, and let $X^2_{(i)}$ and $DEV_{(i)}$ denote the values of these test statistics when case i is deleted. The ith *delta chi-square statistic* is defined as the change in the Pearson statistic when the ith case is deleted:

$$\Delta X_i^2 = X^2 - X^2_{(i)}$$

Similarly, the ith *delta deviance statistic* is defined as the change in the deviance statistic when the ith case is deleted:

$$\Delta dev_i = DEV - DEV_{(i)}$$

Determination of the n delta chi-square statistics or the n delta deviance statistics requires n maximizations of the likelihood, which can be time consuming. For faster computing, the following one-step approximations have been developed:

$$\Delta X_i^2 = r_{SP_i}^2 \tag{14.85}$$

$$\Delta dev_i = h_{ii} r_{SP_i}^2 + dev_i^2 \tag{14.86}$$

In summary, ΔX_i^2 and Δdev_i give the change in the Pearson chi-square and deviance statistics, respectively, when the ith case is deleted. They therefore provide measures of the influence of the ith case on these summary statistics.

Interpretation of the delta chi-square and delta deviance statistics is not always a simple matter. In standard regression situations, we employ various rules of thumb for judging the magnitude of a regression diagnostic. An example of this is the Bonferroni outlier test (Section 10.2) that is used in conjunction with the studentized deleted residual (10.26). Another is the use of various percentiles of the F distribution for interpretation of Cook's distance (Section 10.4). Guidelines such as these are generally not available for logistic regression, as the distribution of the delta statistics is unknown except under certain restrictive assumptions. The judgment as to whether or not a case is outlying or overly influential is typically made on the basis of a subjective visual assessment of an appropriate graphic. Usually, the delta chi-square and delta deviance statistics are plotted against case number i, against $\hat{\pi}_i$,

TABLE 14.11 Pearson Residuals, Studentized Pearson Residuals, Hat Diagonals, Deviance Residuals, Delta Chi-Square and Delta Deviance Statistics, and Cook's Distance—Disease Outbreak Example.

	(1)	(2)	(3)	(4)	(5)	(6)	(7)
i	r_{P_i}	r_{SP_i}	h_{ii}	dev_i	ΔX_i^2	Δdev_i	D_i
1	−0.514	−0.524	.039	−0.685	0.275	0.479	0.002
2	−0.529	−0.541	.040	−0.703	0.292	0.506	0.002
3	−0.344	−0.350	.033	−0.473	0.122	0.228	0.001
...	...	...	...	...	...	...	...
96	−0.358	−0.363	.025	−0.491	0.132	0.245	0.001
97	−0 318	−0.322	.024	−0.439	0.104	0.195	0.001
98	−0.455	−0.463	.036	−0.613	0.214	0.383	0.002

or against $\hat{\pi}_i'$. Extreme values appear as spikes when plotted against case number, or as outliers in the upper corners of the plot when plotted against $\hat{\pi}_i$ or $\hat{\pi}_i'$.

Example

Table 14.11 lists in columns 1–6 for a portion of the disease outbreak data the Pearson residuals r_{P_i}, the studentized Pearson residuals r_{SP_i}, the hat matrix diagonal elements h_{ii}, the deviance residuals, dev_i, the delta chi-square statistics ΔX_i^2, and the delta deviance residuals Δdev_i. We illustrate the calculations needed to obtain ΔX_i^2, and Δdev_i, for the first case. As noted in (14.85) the first delta chi-square statistic is given by the square of the first studentized Pearson residual:

$$\Delta X_1^2 = r_{SP_1}^2 = (-.524)^2 = .275$$

Using (14.86) with $h_{11} = .039$ and $dev_1 = -.685$ from columns 3 and 4 of Table 14.11, the first delta deviance statistic is:

$$\Delta dev_1 = h_{11} r_{SP_1}^2 + dev_1^2 = .039(-.524)^2 + (-.685)^2 = .479$$

Figures 14.15a and 14.15b provide index plots of the delta chi-square and delta deviance statistics for the disease outbreak example. The two spikes corresponding to cases 5 and 14 indicate clearly that these cases have the largest values of the delta deviance and delta chi-square statistics. Shown just below each of these in Figures 14.15c and 14.15d are plots of the delta chi-square and delta deviance statistics against the model-estimated probabilities. Note that cases 5 and 14 again stand out—this time in the upper left corner of the plot. The results suggest that cases 5 and 14 may substantively affect the conclusions. The cases were therefore flagged for potential remedial action at a later stage of the analysis.

Influence on the Fitted Linear Predictor: Cook's Distance. In Chapter 10, we introduced Cook's distance statistic, D_i, for the identification of influential observations. We noted that for the standard regression case D_i measures the standardized change in the fitted response vector $\hat{\mathbf{Y}}$ when the ith case is deleted. Similarly, Cook's distance for logistic regression measures the standardized change in the linear predictor $\hat{\pi}_i$ when the ith case is deleted. Like the delta statistics described above, obtaining these values exactly requires n maximizations of the likelihood. Instead, the following one-step approximation is used

FIGURE 14.15   Delta Chi-Square and Delta Deviance Plots—Disease Outbreak Example.

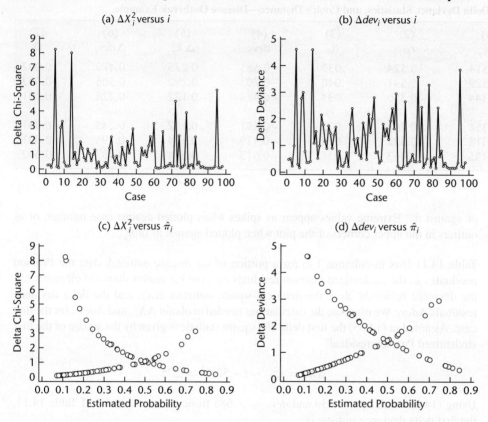

(a) ΔX_i^2 versus i

(b) Δdev_i versus i

(c) ΔX_i^2 versus $\hat{\pi}_i$

(d) Δdev_i versus $\hat{\pi}_i$

(Reference 14.5):

$$D_i = \frac{r_{P_i}^2 h_{ii}}{p(1 - h_{ii})^2} \tag{14.87}$$

Index plots of leverage values h_{ii} are useful for identifying outliers in the X space, and index plots of D_i can be used to identify cases that have a large effect on the fitted linear predictor. As was the case with the delta chi-square and delta deviance statistics, rules of thumb for judging the magnitudes of these diagnostics are not available, and we must rely on a visual assessment of an appropriate graphic. Note that influence on both the deviance (or Pearson chi-square) statistic and the linear predictor can be assessed simultaneously using a *proportional influence* or *bubble* plot of the delta deviance (or delta chi-square) statistics, in which the area of the plot symbol is proportional to D_i.

Example   Cook's distances are listed in column 7 of Table 14.11 for a portion of the disease outbreak example. To illustrate the calculation of Cook's distance we again focus on the first case. We require $h_{11} = .039$, $r_{P_1} = -.514$ from columns 1 and 3 of Table 14.11. Then, we have

FIGURE 14.16 **Index Plots of Leverage Values, Cook's Distances, and Proportional-Influence Plot of Delta Deviance Statistic—Disease Outbreak Example.**

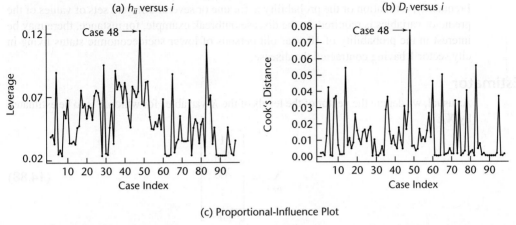

(a) h_{ii} versus i

(b) D_i versus i

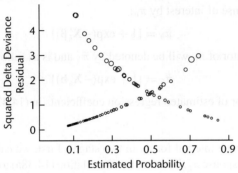

(c) Proportional-Influence Plot

from (14.87) with $p = 5$:

$$D_1 = \frac{r_{P_i}^2 h_{ii}}{p(1 - h_{ii})^2} = \frac{(-.514)^2(.039)}{5(1 - .039)^2} = .0022$$

Figures 14.16a–c display an index plot of h_{ii}, an index plot of D_i, and a proportional-influence plot of the delta deviance statistics. The leverage plot identifies case 48 as being somewhat outlying in the X space—and therefore potentially influential—and the plot of Cook's distances indicates that case 48 is indeed the most influential in terms of effect on the linear predictor. Note that cases 5 and 14—previously identified as most influential in terms of their effect on the Pearson chi-square and deviance statistics—have relatively less influence on the linear predictor. This is shown also by the proportional-influence plot in Figure 14.16c. These two cases, which have the largest delta deviance values, are located in the upper left region of the plot. The plot symbols for these cases are not overly large, indicating that these cases are not particularly influential in terms of the fitted linear predictor values. Case 48 was temporarily deleted and the logistic regression fit was obtained (not shown). The results were not appreciably different from those obtained from the full data set, and the case was retained.

14.9   Inferences about Mean Response

Frequently, estimation of the probability π for one or several different sets of values of the predictor variables is required. In the disease outbreak example, for instance, there may be interest in the probability of 10-year-old persons of lower socioeconomic status living in city sector 1 having contracted the disease.

Point Estimator

As usual, we denote the vector of the levels of the X variables for which π is to be estimated by $\mathbf{X}_h$:

$$\underset{p \times 1}{\mathbf{X}_h} = \begin{bmatrix} 1 \\ X_{h1} \\ X_{h2} \\ \vdots \\ X_{h,p-1} \end{bmatrix} \tag{14.88}$$

and the mean response of interest by π_h:

$$\pi_h = [1 + \exp(-\mathbf{X}_h'\boldsymbol{\beta})]^{-1} \tag{14.89}$$

The point estimator of π_h will be denoted by $\hat{\pi}_h$ and is as follows:

$$\hat{\pi}_h = [1 + \exp(-\mathbf{X}_h'\mathbf{b})]^{-1} \tag{14.90}$$

where $\mathbf{b}$ is the vector of estimated regression coefficients in (14.43).

Interval Estimation

We obtain a confidence interval for π_h in two stages. First, we calculate confidence limits for the logit mean response π_h'. Then we use the relation (14.38a) to obtain confidence limits for the mean response π_h. To see this clearly, we consider (14.38a) for $\mathbf{X} = \mathbf{X}_h$:

$$E\{Y_h\} = [1 + \exp(-\mathbf{X}_h'\boldsymbol{\beta})]^{-1}$$

and restate the expression by using the fact that $E\{Y_h\} = \pi_h$ and $\mathbf{X}_h'\boldsymbol{\beta} = \pi_h'$:

$$\pi_h = [1 + \exp(-\pi_h')]^{-1} \tag{14.91}$$

It is this relation in (14.91) that we utilize to convert confidence limits for π_h' into confidence limits for π_h.

The point estimator of the logit mean response $\pi_h' = \mathbf{X}_h'\boldsymbol{\beta}$ is $\hat{\pi}_h' = \mathbf{X}_h'\mathbf{b}$. The estimated approximate variance of $\hat{\pi}_h' = \mathbf{X}_h'\mathbf{b}$ according to (5.46) is:

$$s^2\{\hat{\pi}_h'\} = s^2\{\mathbf{X}_h'\mathbf{b}\} = \mathbf{X}_h's^2\{\mathbf{b}\}\mathbf{X}_h \tag{14.92}$$

where $s^2\{\mathbf{b}\}$ is the estimated approximate variance-covariance matrix of the regression coefficients in (14.51) when n is large.

Approximate $1 - \alpha$ large-sample confidence limits for the logit mean response π_h' are then obtained in the usual fashion:

$$L = \hat{\pi}_h' - z(1 - \alpha/2)s\{\hat{\pi}_h'\} \tag{14.93a}$$

$$U = \hat{\pi}_h' + z(1 - \alpha/2)s\{\hat{\pi}_h'\} \tag{14.93b}$$

Here, L and U are, respectively, the lower and upper confidence limits for π_h'.

Finally, we use the monotonic relation between π_h and π_h' in (14.91) to convert the confidence limits L and U for π_h' into approximate $1 - \alpha$ confidence limits L^* and U^* for the mean response π_h:

$$L^* = [1 + \exp(-L)]^{-1} \tag{14.94a}$$

$$U^* = [1 + \exp(-U)]^{-1} \tag{14.94b}$$

Simultaneous Confidence Intervals for Several Mean Responses

When it is desired to estimate several mean responses π_h corresponding to different $\mathbf{X}_h$ vectors with family confidence coefficient $1 - \alpha$, Bonferroni simultaneous confidence intervals may be used. The procedure for g confidence intervals is the same as that for a single confidence interval except that $z(1 - \alpha/2)$ in (14.93) is replaced by $z(1 - \alpha/2g)$.

Example

In the disease outbreak example of Table 14.3, it is desired to find an approximate 95 percent confidence interval for the probability π_h that persons 10 years old who are of lower socioeconomic status and live in sector 1 have contracted the disease. The vector $\mathbf{X}_h$ in (14.88) here is:

$$\mathbf{X}_h = \begin{bmatrix} 1 \\ 10 \\ 0 \\ 1 \\ 0 \end{bmatrix}$$

Using the results in Table 14.4a, we obtain the point estimate of the logit mean response:

$$\hat{\pi}_h' = \mathbf{X}_h'\mathbf{b} = -2.3129(1) + .02975(10) + .4088(0) - .30525(1) + 1.5747(0)$$
$$= -2.32065$$

The estimated variance of $\hat{\pi}_h'$ is obtained by using (14.92) (calculations not shown):

$$s^2\{\hat{\pi}_h'\} = .2945$$

so that $s\{\hat{\pi}_h'\} = .54268$. For $1 - \alpha = .95$, we require $z(.975) = 1.960$. Hence, the confidence limits for the logit mean response π_h' are according to (14.93):

$$L = -2.32065 - 1.960(.54268) = -3.38430$$
$$U = -2.32065 + 1.960(.54268) = -1.25700$$

Finally, we use (14.94) to obtain the confidence limits for the mean response π_h:

$$L^* = [1 + \exp(3.38430)]^{-1} = .033$$
$$U^* = [1 + \exp(1.25700)]^{-1} = .22$$

Thus, the approximate 95 percent confidence interval for the mean response π_h is:

$$.033 \leq \pi_h \leq .22$$

We therefore find, with approximate 95 percent confidence, that the probability is between .033 and .22 that 10-year-old persons of lower socioeconomic status who live in sector 1 have contracted the disease. This confidence interval is useful for indicating that persons with the specified characteristics are not subject to a very high probability of having contracted the disease, but the confidence interval is quite wide and thus not precise.

Comment

The confidence limits for π_h in (14.94) are not symmetric around the point estimate. In the disease outbreak example, for instance, the point estimate is:

$$\hat{\pi}_h = [1 + \exp(2.32065)]^{-1} = .089$$

while the confidence limits are .033 and .22. The reason for the asymmetry is that $\hat{\pi}_h$ is not a linear function of $\hat{\pi}_h'$. ∎

14.10 Prediction of a New Observation

Multiple logistic regression is frequently employed for making predictions for new observations. In one application, for example, health personnel wished to predict whether a certain surgical procedure will ameliorate a new patient's condition, given the patient's age, gender, and various symptoms. In another application, marketing officials of a computer firm wished to predict whether a retail chain will purchase a new computer, on the basis of the age of the company's current computer, the company's current workload, and other factors.

Choice of Prediction Rule

Forecasting a binary outcome for given levels $\mathbf{X}_h$ of the X variables is simple in the sense that the outcome 1 will be predicted if the estimated value $\hat{\pi}_h$ is large, and the outcome 0 will be predicted if $\hat{\pi}_h$ is small. The difficulty in making predictions of a binary outcome is in determining the cutoff point, below which the outcome 0 is predicted and above which the outcome 1 is predicted. A variety of approaches are possible to determine where this cutoff point is to be located. We consider three approaches.

1. *Use .5 as the cutoff.* With this approach, the prediction rule is:

If $\hat{\pi}_h$ exceeds .5, predict 1; otherwise predict 0.

This approach is reasonable when (a) it is equally likely in the population of interest that outcomes 0 and 1 will occur; and (b) the costs of incorrectly predicting 0 and 1 are approximately the same.

2. *Find the best cutoff for the data set on which the multiple logistic regression model is based.* This approach involves evaluating different cutoffs. For each cutoff, the rule is employed on the n cases in the model-building data set and the proportion of cases incorrectly predicted is ascertained. The cutoff for which the proportion of incorrect predictions is lowest is the one to be employed.

This approach is reasonable when (a) the data set is a random sample from the relevant population, and thus reflects the proper proportions of 0s and 1s in the population, and (b) the costs of incorrectly predicting 0 and 1 are approximately the same. The proportion of incorrect predictions observed for the optimal cutoff is likely to be an overstatement of the ability of the cutoff to correctly predict new observations, especially if the model-building data set is not large. The reason is that the cutoff is chosen with reference to the same data set from which the logistic model was fitted and thus is best for these data only. Consequently, as we explained in Chapter 9, it is important that a validation data set be employed to indicate whether the observed predictive ability for a fitted regression model is a valid indicator for predicting new observations.

3. *Use prior probabilities and costs of incorrect predictions in determining the cutoff.* When prior information is available about the likelihood of 1s and 0s in the population and the data set is not a random sample from the population, the prior information can be used in finding an optimal cutoff. In addition, when the cost of incorrectly predicting outcome 1 differs substantially from the cost of incorrectly predicting outcome 0, these costs of incorrect consequences can be incorporated into the determination of the cutoff so that the expected cost of incorrect predictions will be minimized. Specialized references, such as Reference 14.7, discuss the use of prior information and costs of incorrect predictions for determining the optimal cutoff.

Example

We shall use the disease outbreak example of Table 14.3 to illustrate how to obtain the cutoff point for predicting a new observation, even though the main purpose of that study was to determine whether age, socioeconomic status, and city sector are important risk factors. We assume that the cost of incorrectly predicting that a person has contracted the disease is about the same as the cost of incorrectly predicting that a person has not contracted the disease. The estimated logistic response function is given in (14.46).

Since a random sample of individuals was selected in the two city sectors, the 98 cases in the study constitute a cross section of the relevant population. Consequently, information is provided in the sample about the proportion of persons who have contracted the disease in the population. Of the 98 persons in the study, 31 had contracted the disease (see the disease outbreak data set in Appendix C.10); hence the estimated proportion of persons who had contracted the disease is $31/98 = .316$. This proportion can be used as the starting point in the search for the best cutoff in the prediction rule.

Thus, the first rule investigated was:

$$\text{Predict 1 if } \hat{\pi}_h \geq .316; \text{ predict 0 if } \hat{\pi}_h < .316 \tag{14.95}$$

Note from Table 14.3, column 6, that $\hat{\pi}_1 = .209$ for case 1; hence prediction rule (14.95) calls for a prediction that the person has not contracted the disease. This would be a correct prediction. Similarly, prediction rule (14.95) would correctly predict cases 2 and 3 not to have contracted the disease. However, the prediction with rule (14.95) for case 4 (person has contracted the disease because $\hat{\pi}_4 = .371 \geq .316$) would be incorrect. Similarly, the prediction for case 5 (person has not contracted the disease because $\hat{\pi}_5 = .111 < .316$) would be incorrect. Table 14.12a provides a summary of the number of correct and incorrect classifications based on prediction rule (14.95). Of the 67 persons without the disease, 20 would be incorrectly predicted to have contracted the disease, or an error rate of 29.9 percent.

TABLE 14.12   **Classification Based on Logistic Response Function (14.46) and Prediction Rules (14.95) and (14.96)—Disease Outbreak Example.**

True Classification	(a) Rule (14.95)			(b) Rule (14.96)		
	$\hat{Y} = 0$	$\hat{Y} = 1$	Total	$\hat{Y} = 0$	$\hat{Y} = 1$	Total
$Y = 0$	47	20	67	50	17	67
$Y = 1$	8	23	31	9	22	31
Total	55	43	98	59	39	98

Of the 31 persons with the disease, eight would be incorrectly predicted with rule (14.95) not to have contracted the disease, or 25.8 percent. Altogether, $20 + 8 = 28$ of the 98 predictions would be incorrect, so that the prediction error rate for rule (14.95) is $28/98 = .286$ or 28.6 percent.

Similar analyses were made for other cutoff points and it appears that among the cutoffs considered, use of the following rule may be best:

$$\text{Predict 1 if } \hat{\pi}_h \geq .325; \text{ predict 0 if } \hat{\pi}_h < .325 \tag{14.96}$$

Table 14.12b provides a summary of the correct and incorrect classifications based on prediction rule (14.96). The prediction error rate for this rule is $(9 + 17)/98 = .265$ or 26.5 percent. Note also that for this rule, the error rates for persons with and without the disease $(9/31$ and $17/67)$ are quite close to each other. Thus, the risks of incorrect predictions for the two groups are fairly balanced, which is often desirable. Note also that the error rates for persons with and without the disease are much less balanced as the cutoff is shifted further away from the optimal one in either direction.

An effective way to display this information graphically is through the *receiver operating characteristic* (ROC) *curve,* which plots $P(\hat{Y} = 1 | Y = 1)$ (also called *sensitivity*) as a function of $1 - P(\hat{Y} = 0 | Y = 0)$ (also called $1-$*specificity*) for the possible cutpoints $\hat{\pi}_h$. Figure 14.17 exhibits the ROC curve for model (14.46) for all possible cutpoints between 0 and 1. (See A.7a for the definition of conditional probability.)

To see how a single point on the ROC curve in Figure 14.17 is determined, we consider rule (14.95), for which the cutoff is .316. From Table 14.12a, the *sensitivity* is:

$$P(\hat{Y} = 1 | Y = 1) = \frac{23}{31} = .74$$

FIGURE 14.17
JMP ROC Curve—Disease Outbreak Example.

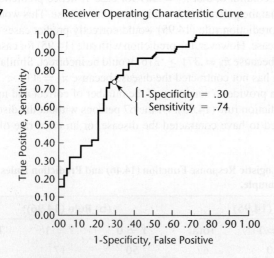

Receiver Operating Characteristic Curve

1-Specificity = .30
Sensitivity = .74

True Positive, Sensitivity

1-Specificity, False Positive

Using $Y = '1'$ to be the positive level
Area Under Curve = 0.77684

Also, $1-specificity$ here is:

$$1 - P(\hat{Y} = 0|Y = 0) = 1 - \frac{47}{67} = .30$$

This point is highlighted on the ROC curve in Figure 14.17.

The area under the ROC curve is a useful summary measure of the model's predictive power and is identical to the *concordance index*. Consider any pair of observations (i, j) such that $Y_i = 1$ and $Y_j = 0$. Since $Y_i > Y_j$, this pair is said to be concordant if $\hat{\pi}_i > \hat{\pi}_j$. The concordance index estimates the probability that the predictions and the outcomes are concordant (Reference 14.2). A value of 0.5 means that the predictions were no better than random guessing. For the disease outbreak model (14.96), the ROC area is 0.777.

A validation study will now be required to determine whether the observed prediction error rate for the optimal cutoff properly indicates the risks of incorrect predictions for new observations, or whether it seriously understates them. In any case, it appears already that fitted logistic regression model (14.96) may not be too useful as a predictive model because of the relatively high risks of making incorrect predictions.

Comment

A limitation of the prediction rule approach is that it dichotomizes a continuous predictor $\hat{\pi}$ where the choice of cutpoint $\hat{\pi}_h$ is arbitrary and is highly dependent upon the relative frequencies of 1s and 0s observed in the sample.   ∎

Validation of Prediction Error Rate

The reliability of the prediction error rate observed in the model-building data set is examined by applying the chosen prediction rule to a validation data set. If the new prediction error rate is about the same as that for the model-building data set, then the latter gives a reliable indication of the predictive ability of the fitted logistic regression model and the chosen prediction rule. If the new data lead to a considerably higher prediction error rate, then the fitted logistic regression model and the chosen prediction rule do not predict new observations as well as originally indicated.

Example

In the disease outbreak example, the fitted logistic regression function (14.46) based on the model-building data set:

$$\hat{\pi} = [1 + \exp(-3.8877 - .02975X_1 - .4088X_2 + .30525X_3 - 1.5747X_4)]^{-1}$$

was used to calculate estimated probabilities $\hat{\pi}_h$ for cases 99-196 in the disease outbreak data set in Appendix C.10. These cases constitute the validation data set. The chosen prediction rule (14.96):

Predict 1 if $\hat{\pi}_h \geq .325$; predict 0 if $\hat{\pi}_h < .325$

was then applied to these estimated probabilities. The percent prediction error rates were as follows:

	Disease Status		
	With Disease	Without Disease	Total
	46.2	38.9	40.8

Note that the total prediction error rate of 40.8 percent is considerably higher than the 26.5 percent error rate based on the model-building data set. The latter therefore is not a reliable indicator of the predictive capability of the fitted logistic regression model and the chosen prediction rule.

We should mention again that making predictions was not the primary objective in the disease outbreak study. Rather, the main purpose was to identify key explanatory variables. Still, the prediction error rate for the validation data set shows that there must be other key explanatory variables affecting whether a person has contracted the disease that have not yet been identified for inclusion in the logistic regression model.

Comment

An alternative to multiple logistic regression for predicting a binary response variable when the predictor variables are continuous is *discriminant analysis*. This approach assumes that the predictor variables follow a joint multivariate normal distribution. Discriminant analysis can also be used when this condition is not met, but the approach is not optimal then and logistic regression frequently is preferable. The reader is referred to Reference 14.8 for an in-depth discussion of discriminant analysis. ∎

14.11 Polytomous Logistic Regression for Nominal Response

Logistic regression is most frequently used to model the relationship between a dichotomous response variable and a set of predictor variables. On occasion, however, the response variable may have more than two levels. Logistic regression can still be employed by means of a *polytomous*—or *multicategory*—logistic regression model. Polytomous logistic regression models are used in many fields. In business, for instance, a market researcher may wish to relate a consumer's choice of product (product A, product B, product C) to the consumer's age, gender, geographic location, and several other potential explanatory variables. This is an example of *nominal* polytomous regression, because the response categories are purely qualitative and not ordered in any way. *Ordinal* response categories can also be modeled using polytomous regression. For example, the relation between severity of disease measured on an ordinal scale (mild, moderate, severe) and age of patient, gender of patient, and some other explanatory variables may be of interest. We consider ordinal polytomous logistic regression in detail in Section 14.12.

In this section we discuss the use of polytomous logistic regression for nominal multi-category responses. Throughout, we will use the pregnancy duration example, introduced in Section 14.2 in the context of binary logistic regression, to illustrate concepts. This time, however, the response will have more than two categories.

Pregnancy Duration Data with Polytomous Response

A study was undertaken to determine the strength of association between several risk factors and the duration of pregnancies. The risk factors considered were mother's age, nutritional status, history of tobacco use, and history of alcohol use. The response of interest, pregnancy duration, is a three-category variable that was coded as follows:

Y_i	Pregnancy Duration Category
1	Preterm (less than 36 weeks)
2	Intermediate term (36 to 37 weeks)
3	Full term (38 weeks or greater)

Relevant data for 102 women who had recently given birth at a large metropolitan hospital were obtained. A portion of these data is displayed in Table 14.13. The polytomous response, pregnancy duration (Y), is shown in column 1. Nutritional status (X_1), shown in column 5, is an index of nutritional status (higher score denotes better nutritional status). The predictor variable age was categorized into three groups: less than 20 years of age (coded 1), from 21 to 30 years of age (coded 2), and greater than 30 years of age (coded 3). It is represented by two indicator variables $(X_2$ and $X_3)$, shown in columns 6 and 7 of Table 14.13, as follows:

Class	X_2	X_3
Less than or equal to 20 years of age	1	0
21 to 30 years of age	0	0
Greater than 30 years of age	0	1

(The researchers chose the middle category—21 to 30 years of age—as the referent category for this qualitative predictor because mothers in this age group tend to have the lowest risk of preterm deliveries. This leads to positive regression coefficients for these predictors, and a slightly simpler interpretation.) Alcohol and smoking history were also qualitative predictors; the categories were "Yes" (coded 1) and "No" (coded 0). Alcohol use history (X_4), and smoking history (X_5) are listed in columns 8 and 9 of Table 14.13.

TABLE 14.13   Data—Pregnancy Duration Example with Polytomous Response.

	(1)	(2)	(3)	(4)	(5)	(6)	(7)	(8)	(9)
	Duration	Response Category			Nutritional Status	Age-Category		Alcohol Use History	Smoking History
Case									
i	Y_i	Y_{i1}	Y_{i2}	Y_{i3}	X_{i1}	X_{i2}	X_{i3}	X_{i4}	X_{i5}
1	1	1	0	0	150	0	0	0	1
2	1	1	0	0	124	1	0	0	0
3	1	1	0	0	128	0	0	0	1
...	...	...	...	...	...	...	...	...	...
100	3	0	0	1	117	0	0	1	1
101	3	0	0	1	165	0	0	1	1
102	3	0	0	1	134	0	0	1	1

Because pregnancy duration is a qualitative variable with three categories, we will create three binary response variables, one for each response category as follows:

$$Y_{i1} = \begin{cases} 1 & \text{if case } i \text{ response is category 1} \\ 0 & \text{otherwise} \end{cases}$$

$$Y_{i2} = \begin{cases} 1 & \text{if case } i \text{ response is category 2} \\ 0 & \text{otherwise} \end{cases}$$

$$Y_{i3} = \begin{cases} 1 & \text{if case } i \text{ response is category 3} \\ 0 & \text{otherwise} \end{cases}$$

These three coded variables are also included in Table 14.13 in columns 2, 3, and 4. Note that because $Y_{i1} + Y_{i2} + Y_{i3} = 1$, the value of any one of these three binary variables can be determined from the other two. For example, $Y_{i3} = 1 - Y_{i1} - Y_{i2}$.

We first treat pregnancy duration as a nominal response, ignoring the time-based ordering of the categories; later we will show how a more parsimonious model results when we treat pregnancy duration as an ordinal response.

J − 1 Baseline-Category Logits for Nominal Response

In general, we will assume there are J response categories. Then for the ith observation, there will be J binary response variables, $Y_{i1}, \ldots, Y_{iJ}$, where:

$$Y_{ij} = \begin{cases} 1 & \text{if case } i \text{ response is category } j \\ 0 & \text{otherwise} \end{cases}$$

Since only one category can be selected for response i, we have:

$$\sum_{j=1}^{J} Y_{ij} = 1$$

We will require some additional notation for the multicategory case. First, let π_{ij} denote the probability that category j is selected for the ith response. Then:

$$\pi_{ij} = P(Y_{ij} = 1)$$

In the binary case, $J = 2$. Suppose that we code $Y_i = 1$ if the ith response is category 1, and we code $Y_i = 0$ if the ith response is category 2. Then:

$$\pi_i = \pi_{i1} \quad \text{and} \quad 1 - \pi_i = \pi_{i2}$$

For binary logistic regression, we model the logit of π_i using the linear predictor. Since there are only two categories in binary logistic regression, the logit in fact compares the probability of a category-1 response to the probability of a category-2 response:

$$\pi_i' = \log_e \left[\frac{\pi_i}{1 - \pi_i} \right] = \log_e \left[\frac{\pi_{i1}}{\pi_{i2}} \right] = \pi_{i12}' = \mathbf{X}_i' \boldsymbol{\beta}_{12}$$

Note that we have used π_{i12}' and $\boldsymbol{\beta}_{12}$ to emphasize that the linear predictor is modeling the logarithm of the ratio of the probabilities for categories 1 and 2.

Now for the J polytomous categories, there are $J(J - 1)/2$ pairs of categories, and therefore $J(J - 1)/2$ linear predictors. For example, for the pregnancy duration data,

$J = 3$ and we have $3(3 - 1)/2 = 3$ comparisons:

$$\pi'_{i12} = \log_e \left[\frac{\pi_{i1}}{\pi_{i2}} \right] = \mathbf{X}'_i \boldsymbol{\beta}_{12}$$

$$\pi'_{i13} = \log_e \left[\frac{\pi_{i1}}{\pi_{i3}} \right] = \mathbf{X}'_i \boldsymbol{\beta}_{13}$$

$$\pi'_{i23} = \log_e \left[\frac{\pi_{i2}}{\pi_{i3}} \right] = \mathbf{X}'_i \boldsymbol{\beta}_{23}$$

Fortunately, it is not necessary to develop all $J(J - 1)/2$ logistic regression models. One category will be chosen as the *baseline* or *referent* category, and then all other categories will be compared to it. The choice of baseline or referent category is arbitrary. Frequently the last category is chosen and, indeed, this is usually the default choice for statistical software programs. One exception to this may be found in epidemiological studies, where the category having the lowest risk is often used as the referent category.

Using category J to denote the baseline category, we need consider only the $J - 1$ comparisons to this referent category. The logit for the jth such comparison is:

$$\pi'_{ijJ} = \log_e \left[\frac{\pi_{ij}}{\pi_{iJ}} \right] = \mathbf{X}'_i \boldsymbol{\beta}_{jJ} \qquad j = 1, 2, \ldots, J - 1 \qquad \textbf{(14.97a)}$$

Since it is understood that comparisons are always made to category J, we let $\pi'_{ij} = \pi'_{ijJ}$ and $\boldsymbol{\beta}_j = \boldsymbol{\beta}_{jJ}$ in (14.97a), giving:

$$\pi'_{ij} = \log_e \left[\frac{\pi_{ij}}{\pi_{iJ}} \right] = \mathbf{X}'_i \boldsymbol{\beta}_j \qquad j = 1, 2, \ldots, J - 1 \qquad \textbf{(14.97b)}$$

The reason that we need to consider only these $J - 1$ logits is that the logits for any other comparisons can be obtained from them. To see this, suppose $J = 4$, and we wish to compare categories 1 and 2. Then:

$$\log_e \left[\frac{\pi_{i1}}{\pi_{i2}} \right] = \log_e \left[\frac{\pi_{i1}}{\pi_{i4}} \times \frac{\pi_{i4}}{\pi_{i2}} \right]$$

$$= \log_e \left[\frac{\pi_{i1}}{\pi_{i4}} \right] - \log_e \left[\frac{\pi_{i2}}{\pi_{i4}} \right]$$

$$= \mathbf{X}'_i \boldsymbol{\beta}_1 - \mathbf{X}'_i \boldsymbol{\beta}_2$$

In general, to compare categories k and l, we have:

$$\log_e \left[\frac{\pi_{ik}}{\pi_{il}} \right] = \mathbf{X}'_i (\boldsymbol{\beta}_k - \boldsymbol{\beta}_l) \qquad \textbf{(14.98)}$$

Given the $J - 1$ logit expressions in (14.98) it is possible (algebra not shown) to obtain the $J - 1$ direct expressions for the category probabilities in terms of the $J - 1$ linear predictors, $\mathbf{X}' \boldsymbol{\beta}_j$. The resulting expressions are:

$$\pi_{ij} = \frac{\exp(\mathbf{X}'_i \boldsymbol{\beta}_j)}{1 + \sum_{k=1}^{J-1} \exp(\mathbf{X}'_i \boldsymbol{\beta}_k)} \qquad j = 1, 2, \ldots, J - 1 \qquad \textbf{(14.99)}$$

We next consider methods for obtaining estimates of the $J - 1$ parameter vectors $\boldsymbol{\beta}_1$, $\boldsymbol{\beta}_2, \ldots, \boldsymbol{\beta}_{J-1}$.

Maximum Likelihood Estimation

There are two approaches commonly used for obtaining estimates of the parameter vectors, $\boldsymbol{\beta}_1, \ldots, \boldsymbol{\beta}_{J-1}$; both employ maximum likelihood estimation. With the first approach, separate binary logistic regressions are carried out for each of the $J - 1$ comparisons to the baseline category. For example, to estimate $\boldsymbol{\beta}_1$, we drop from the data set all cases except those for which either $Y_{i1} = 1$ or $Y_{iJ} = 1$. Since only two categories are then present, we can apply binary logistic regression directly. This approach is particularly useful when statistical software is not available for multicategory logistic regression (Reference 14.9).

A more effective approach from a statistical viewpoint is to obtain estimates of the $J - 1$ logits simultaneously. To do so, we require the likelihood for the full data set. To fix ideas, suppose that there are $J = 4$ categories and that the third category is selected for the ith response. That is, for case i we have:

$$Y_{i1} = 0 \qquad Y_{i2} = 0 \qquad Y_{i3} = 1 \qquad Y_{i4} = 0$$

The probability of this response is:

$$P(Y_i = 3) = \pi_{i3}$$
$$= [\pi_{i1}]^0 \times [\pi_{i2}]^0 \times [\pi_{i3}]^1 \times [\pi_{i4}]^0$$
$$= \prod_{j=1}^{4} [\pi_{ij}]^{Y_{ij}}$$

For n independent observations and J categories, it is easily seen that the likelihood is:

$$P(Y_1, \ldots, Y_n) = \prod_{i=1}^{n} P(Y_i) = \prod_{i=1}^{n} \left[\prod_{j=1}^{J} [\pi_{ij}]^{Y_{ij}} \right] \qquad \textbf{(14.100)}$$

It can be shown that the log likelihood is given by:

$$\log_e[P(Y_1, \ldots, Y_n)] = \sum_{i=1}^{n} \left(\sum_{j=1}^{J-1} (Y_{ij} \mathbf{X}_i' \boldsymbol{\beta}_j) - \log_e \left[1 + \sum_{j=1}^{J-1} \exp(\mathbf{X}_i' \boldsymbol{\beta}_j) \right] \right) \qquad \textbf{(14.101)}$$

The maximum likelihood estimates of $\boldsymbol{\beta}_1, \ldots, \boldsymbol{\beta}_{J-1}$ are those values, $\mathbf{b}_1, \ldots, \mathbf{b}_{J-1}$, that maximize (14.101). As usual, we will rely on standard statistical software programs to obtain these estimates.

As was the case for binary logistic regression, the $J - 1$ fitted response functions may be obtained by substituting the maximum likelihood estimates of the $J - 1$ parameter vectors into the expression in (14.99):

$$\hat{\pi}_{ij} = \frac{\exp(\mathbf{X}_i' \mathbf{b}_j)}{1 + \sum_{k=1}^{J-1} \exp(\mathbf{X}_i' \mathbf{b}_k)} \qquad \textbf{(14.102)}$$

We turn now to an example to illustrate the analysis and interpretation of a nominal-level polytomous logistic regression model.

Example

For the pregnancy duration data in Table 14.13, a set of $J - 1 = 2$ first-order linear predictors was initially proposed:

$$\log_e \left[\frac{\pi_{ij}}{\pi_{i3}} \right] = \mathbf{X}'_i \boldsymbol{\beta}_j \qquad \text{for } j = 1, 2$$

MINITAB's nominal logistic regression output is displayed in Figure 14.18. It first indicates that the response had three levels, 1, 2, and 3, and that the referent response event is $Y_i = 3$. Following this summary is the logistic regression table, which contains the estimated regression coefficients, estimated approximate standard errors, the Wald test statistics and P-values, the estimated odds ratios for the two estimated linear predictors, and the 95 percent confidence intervals for the odds ratios. The maximum likelihood estimates of $\boldsymbol{\beta}_1$ and $\boldsymbol{\beta}_2$ are:

$$\mathbf{b}_1 = \begin{bmatrix} 3.958 \\ -0.0464 \\ 2.9135 \\ 1.8875 \\ 1.0670 \\ 2.2305 \end{bmatrix} \qquad \mathbf{b}_2 = \begin{bmatrix} 5.475 \\ -0.0654 \\ 2.9570 \\ 2.0597 \\ 2.0429 \\ 2.4524 \end{bmatrix}$$

Before using the fitted model to make inferences, various regression diagnostics similar to those already discussed for binary logistic regression should be examined. In polytomous logistic regression, the multiple outcome categories make this a more difficult problem

FIGURE 14.18
MINITAB
Nominal
Logistic
Regression
Output—
Pregnancy
Duration
Example.

```
                              Polytomous Nominal MTB Output
Response Information

Variable   Value    Count
preterm    3           41    (Reference Event)
           2           35
           1           26
           Total      102

Logistic Regression Table
```

					Odds	95% CI	
Predictor	Coef	SE Coef	Z	P	Ratio	Lower	Upper
Logit 1:	(2/3)						
Constant	3.958	1.941	2.04	0.041			
nutritio	-0.04645	0.01489	-3.12	0.002	0.95	0.93	0.98
agecat1	2.9135	0.8575	3.40	0.001	18.42	3.43	98.91
agecat3	1.8875	0.8088	2.33	0.020	6.60	1.35	32.23
alcohol	1.0670	0.6495	1.64	0.100	2.91	0.81	10.38
smoking	2.2305	0.6682	3.34	0.001	9.30	2.51	34.47
Logit 2:	(1/3)						
Constant	5.475	2.272	2.41	0.016			
nutritio	-0.06542	0.01824	-3.59	0.000	0.94	0.90	0.97
agecat1	2.9570	0.9645	3.07	0.002	19.24	2.91	127.41
agecat3	2.0597	0.8947	2.30	0.021	7.84	1.36	45.30
alcohol	2.0429	0.7097	2.88	0.004	7.71	1.92	31.00
smoking	2.4524	0.7315	3.35	0.001	11.62	2.77	48.72

```
Log-likelihood = -84.338
Test that all slopes are zero: G = 52.011, DF = 10, P-Value = 0.000
```

than was the case for binary logistic regression. We thus recommend assessing the fit and monitoring logistic regression diagnostics using the $J - 1$ individual binary logistic regressions, as described in the first paragraph on page 612. Hence, we would assess the fit of the two logistic regression models separately, and then make a statement about the fit of the polytomous logistic model descriptively. Diagnostics, including the Hosmer-Lemeshow test for goodness of fit, simulated envelopes for deviance residuals, and plots of influence statistics were examined for the pregnancy duration data, and no serious departures were found (results not shown). We turn now to model interpretation and inference.

As indicated in Figure 14.18, all Wald test P-values are less than .05—with the exception of alcohol in the first linear predictor—indicating that all of the predictors should be retained. In all cases, the direction of the association between the predictors and the estimated logits, as indicated by the signs of the estimated regression coefficients, were as expected.

For teenagers, the estimated odds of delivering preterm compared to full term are 18.42 times the estimated odds for women 20–30 years of age; the 95% confidence interval for this odds ratio has a lower limit of 3.43 and an upper limit of 98.91. Thus while the age effect is estimated to be very large, there is considerable uncertainty in the estimate. Similarly, the estimated odds for teenagers of delivering intermediate term compared to full term are 19.24; the lower 95% confidence limit is 2.91 and the upper limit is 127.41. History of smoking, history of alcohol use, and being in the 30-and-over age category also increase the estimated odds of delivering preterm or intermediate term compared to full term, though less dramatically. The negative estimated coefficients for nutritional status indicate that a lower nutritional status is associated with increased odds of delivering preterm or intermediate term compared to full term.

Comment

To derive expression (14.101) for the log likelihood, we first obtain the logarithm of (14.100) and let $\pi_{iJ} = 1 - \sum_{j=1}^{J-1} \pi_{ij}$ and $Y_{iJ} = 1 - \sum_{j=1}^{J-1} Y_{ij}$. It follows that:

$$\log_e P(Y_1, \ldots, Y_n) = \sum_{i=1}^{n} \left(\sum_{j=1}^{J-1} Y_{ij} \log_e [\pi_{ij}] + \left(1 - \sum_{j=1}^{J-1} Y_{ij} \right) \log_e \left[1 - \sum_{j=1}^{J-1} \pi_{ij} \right] \right)$$

$$= \sum_{i=1}^{n} \left(\sum_{j=1}^{J-1} Y_{ij} \log_e [\pi_{ij}] + \log_e \left[1 - \sum_{j=1}^{J-1} \pi_{ij} \right] - \sum_{j=1}^{J-1} Y_{ij} \log_e \left[1 - \sum_{j=1}^{J-1} \pi_{ij} \right] \right)$$

$$= \sum_{i=1}^{n} \left(\sum_{j=1}^{J-1} Y_{ij} \log_e \left[\frac{\pi_{ij}}{\pi_{iJ}} \right] + \log_e \left[1 - \sum_{j=1}^{J-1} \pi_{ij} \right] \right)$$

Substitution of the expressions in (14.97b) for $\log_e[\pi_{ij}/\pi_{iJ}]$ and in (14.99) for π_{ij} in the second term leads to the desired log likelihood in (14.101). ∎

14.12 Polytomous Logistic Regression for Ordinal Response

Up to this point, we have considered polytomous logistic regression models for unordered categories. Categories, however, are frequently ordered. Consider the following response variables:

1. A food product is rated by consumers on a 1–10 hedonic scale.

2. In an economic study, persons are classified as either not employed, employed part time, or employed full time.
3. The quality of sheet metal produced is rated on a 1–5 scale, depending on the clarity and reflectivity of the surface.
4. Employees are asked to rate working conditions using a 7-point scale (unacceptable, poor, fair, acceptable, good, excellent, outstanding).
5. The severity of cancer is rated by stages on a 1–4 basis.

Such responses can be analyzed by using the techniques for nominal logistic regression described in Section 14.11, but a more effective strategy, yielding a more parsimonious and more easily interpreted model, results if the ordering of the categories is taken into account explicitly. The model that is usually employed is called the *proportional odds model.*

To motivate this model, we revisit the pregnancy duration example. We will assume that pregnancy duration is a continuous response denoted by Y_i^c. For ease of exposition, we will also assume that there is just one (quantitiative) predictor, nutrition index, X_{i1}. Assume that Y_i^c can be represented by the simple linear regression model:

$$Y_i^c = \beta_0^* + \beta_1^* X_{i1} + k\varepsilon_L$$

where ε_L follows the standard logistic distribution (14.14) with mean zero and standard deviation $\pi/\sqrt{3}$, and k is a constant that satisfies:

$$\sigma\{Y_i^c\} = k\sigma\{\varepsilon_L\} = k\frac{\pi}{\sqrt{3}}$$

Researchers were interested in specific categories of pregnancy delivery time and therefore discretized pregnancy duration Y_i^c using the following upperbounds or cutpoints for each category:

Y_i	Category	Y_i^c	Cutpoint T
1	Preterm	$0 \leq Y_i^c < 36$ weeks	$T_1 = 36$ weeks
2	Intermediate term	36 weeks $\leq Y_i^c < 38$ weeks	$T_2 = 38$ weeks
3	Full term	38 weeks $\leq Y_i^c < \infty$	$T_3 = \infty$

The proportional odds model for ordinal logistic regression models the cumulative probabilities $P(Y_i \leq j)$ rather than the specific category probabilities $P(Y_i = j)$ as was the case for nominal logistic regression. We now develop the required expressions for the cumulative probabilities.

For $j = 1$ we have:

$$P(Y_i \leq 1) = P\left(Y_i^c \leq T_1\right) \tag{14.103a}$$

$$= P(\beta_0^* + \beta_1^* X_i + k\varepsilon_L \leq T_1) \tag{14.103b}$$

$$= P(k\varepsilon_L \leq T_1 - \beta_0^* - \beta_1^* X_i) \tag{14.103c}$$

$$= P\left(\varepsilon_L \leq \frac{T_1 - \beta_0^*}{k} - \frac{\beta_1^*}{k}X_i\right) \tag{14.103d}$$

$$= P(\varepsilon_L \leq \alpha_1 + \beta_1 X_i) \tag{14.103e}$$

where $\alpha_1 = (T_1 - \beta_0^*)/k$ and $\beta_1 = -\beta_1^*/k$. Since ε_L follows a standard logistic distribution, the cumulative probability in (14.103e) is obtained by using the cumulative distribution function (14.14b):

$$P(Y_i \leq 1) = \pi_{i1} = \frac{\exp(\alpha_1 + \beta_1 X_i)}{1 + \exp(\alpha_1 + \beta_1 X_i)} \qquad \textbf{(14.103f)}$$

For $j = 2$, following the development in (14.103), we have:

$$P(Y_i \leq 2) = P(Y_i^c \leq T_2) \qquad \textbf{(14.104a)}$$

$$= P(\beta_0^* + \beta_1^* X_i + k\varepsilon_L \leq T_2) \qquad \textbf{(14.104b)}$$

$$= P(k\varepsilon_L \leq T_2 - \beta_0^* - \beta_1^* X_i) \qquad \textbf{(14.104c)}$$

$$= P\left(\varepsilon_L \leq \frac{T_2 - \beta_0^*}{k} - \frac{\beta_1^*}{k} X_i\right) \qquad \textbf{(14.104d)}$$

$$= P(\varepsilon_L \leq \alpha_2 + \beta_1 X_i) \qquad \textbf{(14.104e)}$$

$$= \frac{\exp(\alpha_2 + \beta_1 X_i)}{1 + \exp(\alpha_2 + \beta_1 X_i)} \qquad \textbf{(14.104f)}$$

Notice that the only difference between (14.103f) and (14.104f) involves the intercept terms α_1 and α_2. The slopes β_1 are the same in both expressions. For the multiple regression case involving J ordered categories, we let:

$$\mathbf{X}_i = \begin{bmatrix} X_{i1} \\ X_{i2} \\ \cdots \\ X_{i,p-1} \end{bmatrix} \qquad \boldsymbol{\beta} = \begin{bmatrix} \beta_1 \\ \beta_2 \\ \cdots \\ \beta_{p-1} \end{bmatrix}$$

Equations (14.103f) and (14.104f) become for category j:

$$P(Y_i \leq j) = \frac{\exp(\alpha_j + \mathbf{X}_i' \boldsymbol{\beta})}{1 + \exp(\alpha_j + \mathbf{X}_i' \boldsymbol{\beta})} \qquad \text{for } j = 1, 2, \ldots, J-1 \qquad \textbf{(14.105)}$$

Model (14.105) is often referred to as the *proportional odds model*. Taking the logit transformation of both sides yields the $J - 1$ *cumulative logits*:

$$\log_e\left[\frac{P(Y_i \leq j)}{1 - P(Y_i \leq j)}\right] = \alpha_j + \mathbf{X}_i' \boldsymbol{\beta} \qquad \text{for } j = 1, \ldots, J-1 \qquad \textbf{(14.106)}$$

The difference between the ordinal logits in (14.106) and the nominal logits in (14.97b) should now be clear. In the nominal case, each of the $J - 1$ parameter vectors $\boldsymbol{\beta}_j$ is unique. For ordinal responses, the slope coefficient vectors $\boldsymbol{\beta}$ are identical for each of the $J - 1$ cumulative logits, but the intercepts differ.

As in the binary logistic regression case, each slope parameter can again be interpreted as the change in the logarithm of an odds ratio—this time the cumulative odds ratio—for a unit change in its associated predictor. In general, (14.106) satisfies, for $j = 1, \ldots, J-1$:

$$\log_e\left[\frac{P(Y_i \leq k)}{P(Y_i > k)} \div \frac{P(Y_j \leq k)}{P(Y_j > k)}\right] = (\mathbf{X}_i - \mathbf{X}_j)' \boldsymbol{\beta} \qquad \textbf{(14.107)}$$

We now briefly discuss estimation methods before returning to the pregnancy duration example.

Maximum Likelihood Estimation.   As was the case for nominal logistic regression, separate binary logistic regressions can be used to obtain estimates of the $J - 1$ linear predictors in (14.106). For $j = 1, \ldots, J - 1$, we construct the binary outcome variable:

$$Y_i^{(j)} = \begin{cases} 1 & \text{if } Y_i \leq j \\ 0 & \text{if } Y_i > j \end{cases}$$

and carry out a logistic regression analysis based on $Y_i^{(j)}$. Note that this approach leads to $J - 1$ separate estimates of the slope parameter vector $\boldsymbol{\beta}$.

A better approach, if the required software is available, is to estimate $\alpha_1, \ldots, \alpha_{J-1}$ and $\boldsymbol{\beta}$ simultaneously using maximum likelihood estimation. From (14.100), the likelihood is given by:

$$P(Y_1, \ldots, Y_n) = \prod_{i=1}^{n} \left(\prod_{j=1}^{J} [\pi_{ij}]^{Y_{ij}} \right)$$

$$= \prod_{i=1}^{n} \left(\prod_{j=1}^{J} [P(Y_i \leq j) - P(Y_i \leq j - 1)]^{Y_{ij}} \right) \qquad \textbf{(14.108)}$$

Substitution of $P(Y_i \leq J) = 1$, $P(Y_i \leq 0) = 0$, and the expression for $P(Y_i \leq j)$, $j = 1, \ldots, J - 1$, in (14.105) yields the required expression for the likelihood in terms of $\alpha_1, \ldots, \alpha_{J-1}$, and $\boldsymbol{\beta}$. The maximum likelihood estimates are those values of $\alpha_1, \ldots, \alpha_{J-1}$ and $\boldsymbol{\beta}$, namely, $a_1, \ldots, a_{J-1}$ and $\mathbf{b}$ that maximize (14.108). As always, we shall rely on standard statistical software to carry out the maximization. We now return to the pregnancy duration example.

Example

We continue the analysis of the pregnancy duration data, this time under the assumption that the response is ordinal, rather than nominal. Recall that $Y_i = 1$ indicates preterm delivery, $Y_i = 2$ indicates intermediate-term delivery, and $Y_i = 3$ indicates full-term delivery. MINITAB ordinal logistic regression output is shown in Figure 14.19. As required with $J = 3$, the program provides estimates for two intercepts, $a_1 = 2.930$ and $a_2 = 5.025$, and $p - 1 = 5$ slope coefficients, $b_1 = -.04887$, $b_2 = 1.9760$, $b_3 = 1.3635$, $b_4 = 1.5915$, and $b_5 = 1.6699$. The Wald P-values indicate that all of the regression coefficients are statistically significant at the .05 level.

As noted above, the coefficients can be interpreted as the change in the cumulative odds ratio for a unit change in the predictor. For example, the results indicate that the logarithm of the odds of a pre- or intermediate-term delivery ($Y_i \leq 2$) for smokers ($X_5 = 1$) is estimated to be $b_4 = 1.5915$ times the logarithm of the odds for nonsmokers ($X_5 = 0$). The estimated cumulative odds ratio is given by $\exp(1.519) = 4.91$ and a 95% confidence interval for the true cumulative odds ratio has a lower limit of 2.02 and an upper limit of 11.92. The remaining slope parameters can be interpreted in a similar fashion.

Notice again that the interpretation of the ordinal logistic regression model is much simpler than that for the nominal logistic regression model, because only a single slope vector $\boldsymbol{\beta}$ is estimated.

FIGURE 14.19
MINITAB
Ordinal
Logistic
Regression
Output—
Pregnancy
Duration
Example.

```
Link Function: Logit

Response Information

Variable   Value    Count
preterm      1         26
             2         35
             3         41
           Total      102

Logistic Regression Table
                                                     Odds          95% CI
Predictor      Coef     SE Coef      Z      P      Ratio    Lower    Upper
Const(1)      2.930      1.465     2.00  0.045
Const(2)      5.025      1.521     3.30  0.001
nutritio     -0.04887    0.01168  -4.18  0.000    0.95     0.93     0.97
agecat1       1.9760     0.5875    3.36  0.001    7.21     2.28    22.82
agecat3       1.3635     0.5547    2.46  0.014    3.91     1.32    11.60
smoking       1.5915     0.4525    3.52  0.000    4.91     2.02    11.92
alcohol       1.6699     0.4727    3.53  0.000    5.31     2.10    13.42

Log-likelihood = -86.756
Test that all slopes are zero: G = 47.174, DF = 5, P-Value = 0.000
```

Comment

Our development of the proportional odds model assumed that the ordinal response Y_i was obtained from an explicit discretization of an observed continuous response Y_i^c, but this is not required. This model often works well for ordinal responses that do not arise from such a discretization. ∎

14.13 Poisson Regression

We consider now another nonlinear regression model where the response outcomes are discrete. Poisson regression is useful when the outcome is a count, with large-count outcomes being rare events. For instance, the number of times a household shops at a particular supermarket in a week is a count, with a large number of shopping trips to the store during the week being a rare event. A researcher may wish to study the relation between a family's number of shopping trips to the store during a particular week and the family's income, number of children, distance from the store, and some other explanatory variables. As another example, the relation between the number of hospitalizations of a member of a health maintenance organization during the past year and the member's age, income, and previous health status may be of interest.

Poisson Distribution

The Poisson distribution can be utilized for outcomes that are counts ($Y_i = 0, 1, 2, \ldots$), with a large count or frequency being a rare event. The Poisson probability distribution is as follows:

$$f(Y) = \frac{\mu^Y \exp(-\mu)}{Y!} \qquad Y = 0, 1, 2, \ldots \tag{14.109}$$

where $f(Y)$ denotes the probability that the outcome is Y and $Y! = Y(Y-1)\cdots 3 \cdot 2 \cdot 1$. The mean and variance of the Poisson probability distribution are:

$$E\{Y\} = \mu \tag{14.110a}$$

$$\sigma^2\{Y\} = \mu \tag{14.110b}$$

Note that the variance is the same as the mean. Hence, if the number of store trips follows the Poisson distribution and the mean number of store trips for a family with three children is larger than the mean number of trips for a family with no children, the variances of the distributions of outcomes for the two families will also differ.

Comment

At times, the count responses Y will pertain to different units of time or space. For instance, in a survey intended to obtain the total number of store trips during a particular month, some of the counts pertained only to the last week of the month. In such cases, let μ denote the mean response for Y for a unit of time or space (e.g., one month), and let t denote the number of units of time or space to which Y corresponds. For instance, $t = 7/30$ if Y is the number of store trips during one week where the unit time is one month; $t = 1$ if Y is the number of store trips during the month. The Poisson probability distribution is then expressed as follows:

$$f(Y) = \frac{(t\mu)^Y \exp(-t\mu)}{Y!} \qquad Y = 0, 1, 2, \ldots \tag{14.111}$$

Our discussion throughout this section assumes that all responses Y_i pertain to the same unit of time or space. ∎

Poisson Regression Model

The Poisson regression model, like any nonlinear regression model, can be stated as follows:

$$Y_i = E\{Y_i\} + \varepsilon_i \qquad i = 1, 2, \ldots, n$$

The mean response for the ith case, to be denoted now by μ_i for simplicity, is assumed as always to be a function of the set of predictor variables, $X_1, \ldots, X_{p-1}$. We use the notation $\mu(\mathbf{X}_i, \boldsymbol{\beta})$ to denote the function that relates the mean response μ_i to $\mathbf{X}_i$, the values of the predictor variables for case i, and $\boldsymbol{\beta}$, the values of the regression coefficients. Some commonly used functions for Poisson regression are:

$$\mu_i = \mu(\mathbf{X}_i, \boldsymbol{\beta}) = \mathbf{X}_i'\boldsymbol{\beta} \tag{14.112a}$$

$$\mu_i = \mu(\mathbf{X}_i, \boldsymbol{\beta}) = \exp(\mathbf{X}_i'\boldsymbol{\beta}) \tag{14.112b}$$

$$\mu_i = \mu(\mathbf{X}_i, \boldsymbol{\beta}) = \log_e(\mathbf{X}_i'\boldsymbol{\beta}) \tag{14.112c}$$

In all three cases, the mean responses μ_i must be nonnegative.

Since the distribution of the error terms ε_i for Poisson regression is a function of the distribution of the response Y_i, which is Poisson, it is easiest to state the Poisson regression model in the following form:

> Y_i are independent Poisson random variables with expected values μ_i, where: $\qquad\qquad$ **(14.113)**

$$\mu_i = \mu(\mathbf{X}_i, \boldsymbol{\beta})$$

The most commonly used response function is $\mu_i = \exp(\mathbf{X}'\boldsymbol{\beta})$.

Maximum Likelihood Estimation

For Poisson regression model (14.113), the likelihood function is as follows:

$$L(\boldsymbol{\beta}) = \prod_{i=1}^{n} f_i(Y_i) = \prod_{i=1}^{n} \frac{[\mu(\mathbf{X}_i, \boldsymbol{\beta})]^{Y_i} \exp[-\mu(\mathbf{X}_i, \boldsymbol{\beta})]}{Y_i!}$$

$$= \frac{\left\{ \prod_{i=1}^{n} [\mu(\mathbf{X}_i, \boldsymbol{\beta})]^{Y_i} \right\} \exp\left[-\sum_{i=1}^{n} \mu(\mathbf{X}_i, \boldsymbol{\beta}) \right]}{\prod_{i=1}^{n} Y_i!} \qquad \textbf{(14.114)}$$

Once the functional form of $\mu(\mathbf{X}_i, \boldsymbol{\beta})$ is chosen, the maximization of (14.114) produces the maximum likelihood estimates of the regression coefficients $\boldsymbol{\beta}$. As before, it is easier to work with the logarithm of the likelihood function:

$$\log_e L(\boldsymbol{\beta}) = \sum_{i=1}^{n} Y_i \log_e [\mu(\mathbf{X}_i, \boldsymbol{\beta})] - \sum_{i=1}^{n} \mu(\mathbf{X}_i, \boldsymbol{\beta}) - \sum_{i=1}^{n} \log_e (Y_i!) \qquad \textbf{(14.115)}$$

Numerical search procedures are used to find the maximum likelihood estimates $b_0, b_1, \ldots,$ b_{p-1}. Iteratively reweighted least squares can again be used to obtain these estimates. We shall rely on standard statistical software packages specifically designed to handle Poisson regression to obtain the maximum likelihood estimates.

After the maximum likelihood estimates have been found, we can obtain the fitted response function and the fitted values:

$$\hat{\mu} = \mu(\mathbf{X}, \mathbf{b}) \qquad\qquad \textbf{(14.116a)}$$

$$\hat{\mu}_i = \mu(\mathbf{X}_i, \mathbf{b}) \qquad\qquad \textbf{(14.116b)}$$

For the three functions in (14.112), the fitted response functions and fitted values are:

$$\mu = \mathbf{X}'\boldsymbol{\beta}: \qquad \hat{\mu} = \mathbf{X}'\mathbf{b} \qquad \hat{\mu}_i = \mathbf{X}_i'\mathbf{b} \qquad \textbf{(14.116c)}$$

$$\mu = \exp(\mathbf{X}'\boldsymbol{\beta}): \qquad \hat{\mu} = \exp(\mathbf{X}'\mathbf{b}) \qquad \hat{\mu}_i = \exp(\mathbf{X}_i'\mathbf{b}) \qquad \textbf{(14.116d)}$$

$$\mu = \log_e(\mathbf{X}'\boldsymbol{\beta}): \qquad \hat{\mu} = \log_e(\mathbf{X}'\mathbf{b}) \qquad \hat{\mu}_i = \log_e(\mathbf{X}_i'\mathbf{b}) \qquad \textbf{(14.116e)}$$

Model Development

Model development for a Poisson regression model is carried out in a similar fashion to that for logistic regression, conducting tests for individual coefficients or groups of coefficients based on the likelihood ratio test statistic G^2 in (14.60). For Poisson regression model (14.113), the model deviance is as follows:

$$DEV(X_0, X_1, \ldots, X_{p-1}) = -2\left[\sum_{i=1}^{n} Y_i \log_e\left(\frac{\hat{\mu}_i}{Y_i}\right) + \sum_{i=1}^{n}(Y_i - \hat{\mu}_i)\right] \qquad \textbf{(14.117)}$$

where $\hat{\mu}_i$ is the fitted value for the ith case according to (14.116b). The deviance residual for the ith case is:

$$dev_i = \pm\left[-2Y_i \log_e\left(\frac{\hat{\mu}_i}{Y_i}\right) - 2(Y_i - \hat{\mu}_i)\right]^{1/2} \qquad \textbf{(14.118)}$$

The sign of the deviance residual is selected according to whether $Y_i - \hat{\mu}_i$ is positive or negative. Index plots of the deviance residuals and half-normal probability plots with simulated envelopes are useful for identifying outliers and checking the model fit.

Comment

If $Y_i = 0$, the term $[Y_i \log_e(\hat{\mu}_i/Y_i)]$ in (14.117) and (14.118) equals 0.   ■

Inferences

Inferences for a Poisson regression model are carried out in the same way as for logistic regression. For instance, there is often interest in estimating the mean response for predictor variables $\mathbf{X}_h$. This estimate is obtained by substituting $\mathbf{X}_h$ into (14.116).

In Poisson regression analysis, there is sometimes also interest in estimating probabilities of certain outcomes for given levels of the predictor variables, for instance, $P(Y = 0 \mid \mathbf{X}_h)$. Such an estimated probability can be obtained readily by substituting $\hat{\mu}_h$ into (14.109).

Interval estimation of individual regression coefficients can be carried out by use of the large-sample estimated standard deviations furnished by regression programs with Poisson regression capabilities.

Example

The Miller Lumber Company is a large retailer of lumber and paint, as well as of plumbing, electrical, and other household supplies. During a representative two-week period, in-store surveys were conducted and addresses of customers were obtained. The addresses were then used to identify the metropolitan area census tracts in which the customers reside. At the end of the survey period, the total number of customers who visited the store from each census tract within a 10-mile radius was determined and relevant demographic information for each tract (average income, number of housing units, etc.) was obtained. Several other variables expected to be related to customer counts were constructed from maps, including distance from census tract to nearest competitor and distance to store.

Initial screening of the potential predictor variables was conducted which led to the retention of five predictor variables:

X_1: Number of housing units

X_2: Average income, in dollars

X_3: Average housing unit age, in years

X_4: Distance to nearest competitor, in miles

X_5: Distance to store, in miles

Y_i: Number of customers who visited store from census tract

TABLE 14.14
Data—Miller
Lumber
Company
Example.

Census Tract i	Housing Units X_1	Average Income X_2	Average Age X_3	Competitor Distance X_4	Store Distance X_5	Number of Customers Y
1	606	41,393	3	3.04	6.32	9
2	641	23,635	18	1.95	8.89	6
3	505	55,475	27	6.54	2.05	28
...	...	...	...	...	...	...
108	817	54,429	47	1.90	9.90	6
109	268	34,022	54	1.20	9.51	4
110	519	52,850	43	2.92	8.62	6

TABLE 14.15
Fitted Poisson
Response
Function and
Related
Results—
Miller Lumber
Company
Example.

(a) Fitted Poisson Response Function

$$\hat{\mu} = \exp[2.942 + .000606X_1 - .0000117X_2 - .00373X_3 + .168X_4 - .129X_5]$$
$$DEV(X_0, X_1, X_2, X_3, X_4, X_5) = 114.985$$

(b) Estimated Coefficients, Standard Deviations, and G^2 Test Statistics

Regression Coefficient	Estimated Regression Coefficient	Estimated Standard Deviation	G^2	P-value
β_0	2.9424	.207		
β_1	.0006058	.00014	18.21	.000
β_2	−.00001169	.0000021	31.80	.000
β_3	−.003726	.0018	4.38	.036
β_4	.1684	.026	41.66	.000
β_5	−.1288	.016	67.50	.000

Data for a portion of the $n = 110$ census tracts are shown in Table 14.14.

Poisson regression model (14.113) with response function:

$$\mu(\mathbf{X}, \boldsymbol{\beta}) = \exp(\mathbf{X}'\boldsymbol{\beta})$$

was fitted to the data, using LISP-STAT (Reference 14.10). Some principal results are presented in Table 14.15. Note that the deviance for this model is 114.985.

Likelihood ratio test statistics (14.60) were calculated for each of the individual regression coefficients. These G^2 test statistics are shown in Table 14.15b, together with their associated P-values, each based on the chi-square distribution with one degree of freedom. We note from the P-values that each predictor variable makes a marginal contribution to the fit of the regression model and consequently should be retained in the model.

A portion of the deviance residuals dev_i is shown in Table 14.16, together with the responses Y_i and the fitted values $\hat{\mu}_i$. Analysis of the deviance residuals did not disclose any major problems. Figure 14.20 contains an index plot of the deviance residuals. We note a few large negative deviance residuals; these are for census tracts where $Y = 0$; i.e.,

TABLE 14.16
Responses,
Fitted Values,
and Deviance
Residuals—
Miller Lumber
Company
Example.

Census Tract			
i	Y_i	$\hat{\mu}_i$	dev_i
1	9	12.3	−.999
2	6	8.8	−.992
3	28	28.1	−.024
...	...	...	...
108	6	5.3	.289
109	4	4.4	−.197
110	6	6.4	−.171

FIGURE 14.20
Index Plot of
Deviance
Residuals—
Miller Lumber
Company
Example.

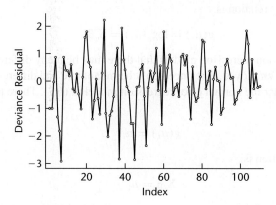

there were no customers from these areas. These may be difficult cases to fit with a Poisson regression model.

14.14   Generalized Linear Models

We conclude this chapter and the regression portion of this book by noting that all of the regression models considered, linear and nonlinear, belong to a family of models called *generalized linear models*. This family was first introduced by Nelder and Wedderburn (Reference 14.11) and encompasses normal error linear regression models and the nonlinear exponential, logistic, and Poisson regression models, as well as many other models, such as log-linear models for categorical data.

The class of generalized linear models can be described as follows:

1. $Y_1, \ldots, Y_n$ are n independent responses that follow a probability distribution belonging to the *exponential family* of probability distributions, with expected value $E\{Y_i\} = \mu_i$.

2. A *linear predictor* based on the predictor variables $X_{i1}, \ldots, X_{i,p-1}$ is utilized, denoted by $\mathbf{X}_i'\boldsymbol{\beta}$:

$$\mathbf{X}_i'\boldsymbol{\beta} = \beta_0 + \beta_1 X_{i1} + \cdots + \beta_{p-1} X_{i,p-1}$$

3. The *link function* g relates the linear predictor to the mean response:

$$\mathbf{X}_i'\boldsymbol{\beta} = g(\mu_i)$$

Generalized linear models may have nonconstant variances σ_i^2 for the responses Y_i, but the variance σ_i^2 must be a function of the predictor variables through the mean response μ_i.

To illustrate the concept of the link function, consider first logistic regression model (14.41). There, the logit transformation $F_L^{-1}(\pi_i)$ in (14.18a) serves to link the linear predictor $\mathbf{X}_i'\boldsymbol{\beta}$ to the mean response $\mu_i = \pi_i$:

$$g(\mu_i) = g(\pi_i) = \log_e\left(\frac{\pi_i}{1-\pi_i}\right) = \mathbf{X}_i'\boldsymbol{\beta}$$

As a second example, consider Poisson regression model (14.113). There we considered several response functions in (14.112). For the response function $\mu_i = \exp(\mathbf{X}_i'\boldsymbol{\beta})$ in (14.112b), the linking relation is:

$$g(\mu_i) = \log_e(\mu_i) = \mathbf{X}_i'\boldsymbol{\beta}$$

We see from the Poisson regression models that there may be many different possible link functions that can be employed. They need only be monotonic and differentiable.

Finally, we consider the normal error regression model in (6.7). There the link function is simply:

$$g(\mu_i) = \mu_i$$

since the linking relation is:

$$\mathbf{X}_i'\boldsymbol{\beta} = \mu_i$$

The link function $g(\mu_i)$ for the normal error case is called the identity or unity link function.

Any regression model that belongs to the family of generalized linear models can be analyzed in a unified fashion. The maximum likelihood estimates of the regression parameters can be obtained by iteratively reweighted least squares [by ordinary least squares for normal error linear regression models (6.7)]. Tests for model development to determine whether some predictor variables may be dropped from the model can be conducted using likelihood ratio tests. Reference 14.12 provides further details about generalized linear models and their analysis.

Cited References

14.1. Kennedy, W. J., Jr., and J. E. Gentle. *Statistical Computing*. New York: Marcel Dekker, 1980.

14.2. Agresti, A. *Categorical Data Analysis*. 2nd ed. New York: John Wiley & Sons, 2002.

14.3. *LogXact 5*. Cytel Software Corporation. Cambridge, Massachusetts, 2003.

14.4. Hosmer, D. W., and S. Lemeshow. *Applied Logistic Regression*. 2nd ed. New York: John Wiley & Sons, 2000.

14.5. Cook, R. D., and S. Weisberg. *Applied Regression Including Computing and Graphics*. New York: John Wiley & Sons, 1999.

14.6. Atkinson, A. C. "Two Graphical Displays for Outlying and Influential Observations in Regression," *Biometrika* 68 (1981), pp. 13–20.

14.7. Johnson, R. A., and D. W. Wichern. *Applied Multivariate Statistical Analysis*. 5th ed. Englewood Cliffs, N.J.: Prentice Hall, 2001.

14.8. Lachenbruch, P. A. *Discriminant Analysis*. New York: Hafner Press, 1975.

14.9. Begg, C. B., and R. Gray. "Calculation of Polytomous Logistic Regression Parameters Using Individualized Regressions," *Biometrika* 71 (1984), pp. 11–18.

14.10. Tierney, L. *LISP-STAT: An Object-Oriented Environment for Statistical Computing and Dynamic Graphics*. New York: John Wiley & Sons, 1990.

14.11. Nelder, J. A., and R. W. M. Wedderburn. "Generalized Linear Models," *Journal of the Royal Statistical Society A* 135 (1972), pp. 370–84.

14.12. McCullagh, P., and J. A. Nelder. *Generalized Linear Models*. 2nd ed. London: Chapman and Hall, 1999.

Problems

14.1. A student stated: "I fail to see why the response function needs to be constrained between 0 and 1 when the response variable is binary and has a Bernoulli distribution. The fit to 0, 1 data will take care of this problem for any response function." Comment.

14.2. Since the logit transformation (14.18) linearizes the logistic response function, why can't this transformation be used on the individual responses Y_i and a linear response function then fitted? Explain.

14.3. If the true response function is J-shaped when the response variable is binary, would the use of the logistic response function be appropriate? Explain.

14.4. a. Plot the logistic mean response function (14.16) when $\beta_0 = -25$ and $\beta_1 = .2$.

    b. For what value of X is the mean response equal to .5?

    c. Find the odds when $X = 150$, when $X = 151$, and the ratio of the odds when $X = 151$ to the odds when $X = 150$. Is this odds ratio equal to $\exp(\beta_1)$ as it should be?

*14.5. a. Plot the logistic mean response function (14.16) when $\beta_0 = 20$ and $\beta_1 = -.2$.

    b. For what value of X is the mean response equal to .5?

    c. Find the odds when $X = 125$, when $X = 126$, and the ratio of the odds when $X = 126$ to the odds when $X = 125$. Is the odds ratio equal to $\exp(\beta_1)$ as it should be?

14.6. a. Plot the probit mean response function (14.12) for $\beta_0^* = -25$ and $\beta_1^* = .2$. How does this function compare to the logistic mean response function in part (a) of Problem 14.4?

    b. For what value of X is the mean response equal to .5?

*14.7. **Annual dues.** The board of directors of a professional association conducted a random sample survey of 30 members to assess the effects of several possible amounts of dues increase. The sample results follow. X denotes the dollar increase in annual dues posited in the survey interview, and $Y = 1$ if the interviewee indicated that the membership will not be renewed at that amount of dues increase and 0 if the membership will be renewed.

i:	1	2	3	...	28	29	30
X_i:	30	30	30	...	49	50	50
Y_i:	0	1	0	...	0	1	1

Logistic regression model (14.20) is assumed to be appropriate.

a. Find the maximum likelihood estimates of β_0 and β_1. State the fitted response function.

b. Obtain a scatter plot of the data with both the fitted logistic response function from part (a) and a lowess smooth superimposed. Does the fitted logistic response function appear to fit well?

c. Obtain $\exp(b_1)$ and interpret this number.

d. What is the estimated probability that association members will not renew their membership if the dues are increased by $40?

e. Estimate the amount of dues increase for which 75 percent of the members are expected not to renew their association membership.

14.8. Refer to **Annual dues** Problem 14.7.

   a. Fit a probit mean response function (14.12) to the data. Qualitatively compare the fit here with the logistic fit obtained in part (a) of Problem 14.7. What do you conclude?

   b. Fit a complimentary log-log mean response function (14.19) to the data. Qualitatively compare the fit here with the logistic fit obtained in part (a) of Problem 14.7. What do you conclude?

14.9. **Performance ability.** A psychologist conducted a study to examine the nature of the relation, if any, between an employee's emotional stability (X) and the employee's ability to perform in a task group (Y). Emotional stability was measured by a written test for which the higher the score, the greater is the emotional stability. Ability to perform in a task group $(Y = 1$ if able, $Y = 0$ if unable) was evaluated by the supervisor. The results for 27 employees were:

i:	1	2	3	$\ldots$	25	26	27
X_i:	474	432	453	$\ldots$	562	506	600
Y_i:	0	0	0	$\ldots$	1	0	1

Logistic regression model (14.20) is assumed to be appropriate.

   a. Find the maximum likelihood estimates of β_0 and β_1. State the fitted response function.

   b. Obtain a scatter plot of the data with both the fitted logistic response function from part (a) and a lowess smooth superimposed. Does the fitted logistic response function appear to fit well?

   c. Obtain $\exp(b_1)$ and interpret this number.

   d. What is the estimated probability that employees with an emotional stability test score of 550 will be able to perform in a task group?

   e. Estimate the emotional stability test score for which 70 percent of the employees with this test score are expected to be able to perform in a task group.

14.10. Refer to **Performance ability** Problem 14.9.

   a. Fit a probit mean response function (14.12) to the data. Qualitatively compare the fit here with the logistic fit obtained in part (a) of Problem 14.9. What do you conclude?

   b. Fit a complementary log-log mean response function (14.19) to the data. Qualitatively compare the fit here with the logistic fit obtained in part (a) of Problem 14.9. What do you conclude?

*14.11. **Bottle return.** A carefully controlled experiment was conducted to study the effect of the size of the deposit level on the likelihood that a returnable one-liter soft-drink bottle will be returned. A bottle return was scored 1, and no return was scored 0. The data to follow show the number of bottles that were returned $(Y_{.j})$ out of 500 sold (n_j) at each of six deposit levels $(X_j,$ in cents):

j:	1	2	3	4	5	6
Deposit level X_j:	2	5	10	20	25	30
Number sold n_j:	500	500	500	500	500	500
Number returned $Y_{.j}$:	72	103	170	296	406	449

An analyst believes that logistic regression model (14.20) is appropriate for studying the relation between size of deposit and the probability a bottle will be returned.

   a. Plot the estimated proportions $p_j = Y_{.j}/n_j$ against X_j. Does the plot support the analyst's belief that the logistic response function is appropriate?

   b. Find the maximum likelihood estimates of β_0 and β_1. State the fitted response function.

c. Obtain a scatter plot of the data with the estimated proportions from part (a), and super-impose the fitted logistic response function from part (b). Does the fitted logistic response function appear to fit well?

d. Obtain $\exp(b_1)$ and interpret this number.

e. What is the estimated probability that a bottle will be returned when the deposit is 15 cents?

f. Estimate the amount of deposit for which 75 percent of the bottles are expected to be returned.

14.12. **Toxicity experiment.** In an experiment testing the effect of a toxic substance, 1,500 experimental insects were divided at random into six groups of 250 each. The insects in each group were exposed to a fixed dose of the toxic substance. A day later, each insect was observed. Death from exposure was scored 1, and survival was scored 0. The results are shown below; X_j denotes the dose level (on a logarithmic scale) administered to the insects in group j and $Y_{.j}$ denotes the number of insects that died out of the 250 (n_j) in the group.

j:	1	2	3	4	5	6
X_j:	1	2	3	4	5	6
n_j:	250	250	250	250	250	250
$Y_{.j}$:	28	53	93	126	172	197

Logistic regression model (14.20) is assumed to be appropriate.

a. Plot the estimated proportions $p_j = Y_{.j}/n_j$ against X_j. Does the plot support the analyst's belief that the logistic response function is appropriate?

b. Find the maximum likelihood estimates of β_0 and β_1. State the fitted response function.

c. Obtain a scatter plot of the data with the estimated proportions from part (a), and super-impose the fitted logistic response function from part (b). Does the fitted logistic response function appear to fit well?

d. Obtain $\exp(b_1)$ and interpret this number.

e. What is the estimated probability that an insect dies when the dose level is $X = 3.5$?

f. What is the estimated median lethal dose—that is, the dose for which 50 percent of the experimental insects are expected to die?

14.13. **Car purchase.** A marketing research firm was engaged by an automobile manufacturer to conduct a pilot study to examine the feasibility of using logistic regression for ascertaining the likelihood that a family will purchase a new car during the next year. A random sample of 33 suburban families was selected. Data on annual family income (X_1, in thousand dollars) and the current age of the oldest family automobile (X_2, in years) were obtained. A follow-up interview conducted 12 months later was used to determine whether the family actually purchased a new car ($Y = 1$) or did not purchase a new car ($Y = 0$) during the year.

i:	1	2	3	...	31	32	33
X_{i1}:	32	45	60	...	21	32	17
X_{i2}:	3	2	2	...	3	5	1
Y_i:	0	0	1	...	0	1	0

Multiple logistic regression model (14.41) with two predictor variables in first-order terms is assumed to be appropriate.

a. Find the maximum likelihood estimates of β_0, β_1, and β_2. State the fitted response function.

b. Obtain $\exp(b_1)$ and $\exp(b_2)$ and interpret these numbers.

c. What is the estimated probability that a family with annual income of $50 thousand and an oldest car of 3 years will purchase a new car next year?

*14.14. **Flu shots.** A local health clinic sent fliers to its clients to encourage everyone, but especially older persons at high risk of complications, to get a flu shot in time for protection against an expected flu epidemic. In a pilot follow-up study, 159 clients were randomly selected and asked whether they actually received a flu shot. A client who received a flu shot was coded $Y = 1$, and a client who did not receive a flu shot was coded $Y = 0$. In addition, data were collected on their age (X_1) and their health awareness. The latter data were combined into a health awareness index (X_2), for which higher values indicate greater awareness. Also included in the data was client gender, where males were coded $X_3 = 1$ and females were coded $X_3 = 0$.

i:	1	2	3	...	157	158	159
X_{i1}:	59	61	82	...	76	68	73
X_{i2}:	52	55	51	...	22	32	56
X_{i3}:	0	1	0	...	1	0	1
Y_i:	0	0	1	...	1	1	1

Multiple logistic regression model (14.41) with three predictor variables in first-order terms is assumed to be appropriate.

a. Find the maximum likelihood estimates of β_0, β_1, β_2, and β_3. State the fitted response function.

b. Obtain $\exp(b_1)$, $\exp(b_2)$, and $\exp(b_3)$. Interpret these numbers.

c. What is the estimated probability that male clients aged 55 with a health awareness index of 60 will receive a flu shot?

*14.15. Refer to **Annual dues** Problem 14.7. Assume that the fitted model is appropriate and that large-sample inferences are applicable.

a. Obtain an approximate 90 percent confidence interval for $\exp(\beta_1)$. Interpret your interval.

b. Conduct a Wald test to determine whether dollar increase in dues (X) is related to the probability of membership renewal; use $\alpha = .10$. State the alternatives, decision rule, and conclusion. What is the approximate P-value of the test?

c. Conduct a likelihood ratio test to determine whether dollar increase in dues (X) is related to the probability of membership renewal; use $\alpha = .10$. State the full and reduced models, decision rule, and conclusion. What is the approximate P-value of the test? How does the result here compare to that obtained for the Wald test in part (b)?

14.16. Refer to **Performance ability** Problem 14.9. Assume that the fitted model is appropriate and that large-sample inferences are applicable.

a. Obtain an approximate 95 percent confidence interval for $\exp(\beta_1)$. Interpret your interval.

b. Conduct a Wald test to determine whether employee's emotional stability (X) is related to the probability that the employee will be able to perform in a task group; use $\alpha = .05$. State the alternatives, decision rule, and conclusion. What is the approximate P-value of the test?

c. Conduct a likelihood ratio test to determine whether employee's emotional stability (X) is related to the probability that the employee will be able to perform in a task group; use $\alpha = .05$. State the full and reduced models, decision rule, and conclusion. What is the approximate P-value of the test? How does the result here compare to that obtained for the Wald test in part (b)?

*14.17. Refer to **Bottle return** Problem 14.11. Assume that the fitted model is appropriate and that large-sample inferences are applicable.

a. Obtain an approximate 95 percent confidence interval for β_1. Convert this confidence interval into one for the odds ratio. Interpret this latter interval.

b. Conduct a Wald test to determine whether deposit level (X) is related to the probability that a bottle is returned; use $\alpha = .05$. State the alternatives, decision rule, and conclusion. What is the approximate P-value of the test?

c. Conduct a likelihood ratio test to determine whether deposit level (X) is related to the probability that a bottle is returned; use $\alpha = .05$. State the full and reduced models, decision rule, and conclusion. What is the approximate P-value of the test? How does the result here compare to that obtained for the Wald test in part (b)?

14.18. Refer to **Toxicity experiment** Problem 14.12. Assume that the fitted model is appropriate and that large-sample inferences are applicable.

a. Obtain an approximate 99 percent confidence interval for β_1. Convert this confidence interval into one for the odds ratio. Interpret this latter interval.

b. Conduct a Wald test to determine whether dose level (X) is related to the probability that an insect dies; use $\alpha = .01$. State the alternatives, decision rule, and conclusion. What is the approximate P-value of the test?

c. Conduct a likelihood ratio test to determine whether dose level (X) is related to the probability that an insect dies; use $\alpha = .01$. State the full and reduced models, decision rule, and conclusion. What is the approximate P-value of the test? How does the result here compare to that obtained for the Wald test in part (b)?

14.19. Refer to **Car purchase** Problem 14.13. Assume that the fitted model is appropriate and that large-sample inferences are applicable.

a. Obtain joint confidence intervals for the family income odds ratio $\exp(20\beta_1)$ for families whose incomes differ by 20 thousand dollars and for the age of the oldest family automobile odds ratio $\exp(2\beta_2)$ for families whose oldest automobiles differ in age by 2 years, with family confidence coefficient of approximately .90. Interpret your intervals.

b. Use the Wald test to determine whether X_2, age of oldest family automobile, can be dropped from the regression model; use $\alpha = .05$. State the alternatives, decision rule, and conclusion. What is the approximate P-value of the test?

c. Use the likelihood ratio test to determine whether X_2, age of oldest family automobile, can be dropped from the regression model; use $\alpha = .05$. State the full and reduced models, decision rule, and conclusion. What is the approximate P-value of the test? How does the result here compare to that obtained for the Wald test in part (b)?

d. Use the likelihood ratio test to determine whether the following three second-order terms, the square of annual family income, the square of age of oldest automobile, and the two-factor interaction effect between annual family income and age of oldest automobile, should be added simultaneously to the regression model containing family income and age of oldest automobile as first-order terms; use $\alpha = .05$. State the full and reduced models, decision rule, and conclusion. What is the approximate P-value of the test?

*14.20. Refer to **Flu shots** Problem 14.14.

a. Obtain joint confidence intervals for the age odds ratio $\exp(30\beta_1)$ for male clients whose ages differ by 30 years and for the health awareness index odds ratio $\exp(25\beta_2)$ for male clients whose health awareness index differs by 25, with family confidence coefficient of approximately .90. Interpret your intervals.

b. Use the Wald test to determine whether X_3, client gender, can be dropped from the regression model; use $\alpha = .05$. State the alternatives, decision rule, and conclusion. What is the approximate P-value of the test?

c. Use the likelihood ratio test to determine whether X_3, client gender, can be dropped from the regression model; use $\alpha = .05$. State the full and reduced models, decision rule, and conclusion. What is the approximate P-value of the test? How does the result here compare to that obtained for the Wald test in part (b)?

d. Use the likelihood ratio test to determine whether the following three second-order terms, the square of age, the square of health awareness index, and the two-factor interaction effect between age and health awareness index, should be added simultaneously to the regression model containing age and health awareness index as first-order terms; use $\alpha = .05$. State the alternatives, full and reduced models, decision rule, and conclusion. What is the approximate P-value of the test?

14.21. Refer to **Car purchase** Problem 14.13 where the pool of predictors consists of all first-order terms and all second-order terms in annual family income and age of oldest family automobile.

a. Use forward selection to decide which predictor variables enter into the regression model. Control the α risk at .10 at each stage. Which variables are entered into the regression model?

b. Use backward elimination to decide which predictor variables can be dropped from the regression model. Control the α risk at .10 at each stage. Which variables are retained? How does this compare to your results in part (a)?

c. Find the best model according to the AIC_p criterion. How does this compare to your results in parts (a) and (b)?

d. Find the best model according to the SBC_p criterion. How does this compare to your results in parts (a), (b) and (c)?

*14.22. Refer to **Flu shots** Problem 14.14 where the pool of predictors consists of all first-order terms and all second-order terms in age and health awareness index.

a. Use forward selection to decide which predictor variables enter into the regression model. Control the α risk at .10 at each stage. Which variables are entered into the regression model?

b. Use backward elimination to decide which predictor variables can be dropped from the regression model. Control the α risk at .10 at each stage. Which variables are retained? How does this compare to your results in part (a)?

c. Find the best model according to the AIC_p criterion. How does this compare to your results in parts (a) and (b)?

d. Find the best model according to the SBC_p criterion. How does this compare to your results in parts (a), (b) and (c)?

*14.23. Refer to **Bottle return** Problem 14.11. Use the groups given there to conduct a chi-square goodness of fit test of the appropriateness of logistic regression model (14.20). Control the risk of a Type I error at .01. State the alternatives, decision rule, and conclusion.

14.24. Refer to **Toxicity experiment** Problem 14.12. Use the groups given there to conduct a deviance goodness of fit test of the appropriateness of logistic regression model (14.20). Control the risk of a Type I error at .01. State the alternatives, decision rule, and conclusion.

*14.25. Refer to **Annual dues** Problem 14.7.

a. To assess the appropriateness of the logistic regression function, form three groups of 10 cases each according to their fitted logit values $\hat{\pi}'$. Plot the estimated proportions p_j against the midpoints of the $\hat{\pi}'$ intervals. Is the plot consistent with a response function of monotonic sigmoidal shape? Explain.

b. Obtain the studentized Pearson residuals (14.81) and plot them against the estimated model probabilities with a lowess smooth superimposed. What does the plot suggest about the adequacy of the fit of the logistic regression model?

14.26. Refer to **Performance ability** Problem 14.9.

a. To assess the appropriateness of the logistic regression function, form three groups of nine cases each according to their fitted logit values $\hat{\pi}'$. Plot the estimated proportions p_j

against the midpoints of the $\hat{\pi}'$ intervals. Is the plot consistent with a response function of monotonic sigmoidal shape? Explain.

b. Obtain the deviance residuals (14.83) and plot them against the estimated model probabilities with a lowess smooth superimposed. What does the plot suggest about the adequacy of the fit of the logistic regression model?

14.27. Refer to **Car purchase** Problems 14.13 and 14.21.

a. To assess the appropriateness of the logistic regression model obtained in part (d) of Problem 14.21, form three groups of 11 cases each according to their fitted logit values $\hat{\pi}'$. Plot the estimated proportions p_j against the midpoints of the $\hat{\pi}'$ intervals. Is the plot consistent with a response function of monotonic sigmoidal shape? Explain.

b. Obtain the studentized Pearson residuals (14.81) and plot them against the estimated model probabilities with a lowess smooth superimposed. What does the plot suggest about the adequacy of the fit of the logistic regression model?

*14.28. Refer to **Flu shots** Problems 14.14 and 14.22.

a. To assess the appropriateness of the logistic regression model obtained in part (d) of Problem 14.22, form 8 groups of approximately 20 cases each according to their fitted logit values $\hat{\pi}'$. Plot the estimated proportions p_j against the midpoints of the $\hat{\pi}'$ intervals. Is the plot consistent with a response function of monotonic sigmoidal shape? Explain.

b. Using the groups formed in part (a), conduct a Hosmer-Lemeshow goodness of fit test for the appropriateness of the logistic regression function; use $\alpha = .05$. State the alternatives, decision rule, and conclusions. What is the P-value of the test?

c. Obtain the deviance residuals (14.83) and plot them against the estimated model probabilities with a lowess smooth superimposed. What does the plot suggest about the adequacy of the fit of the logistic regression model?

*14.29. Refer to **Annual dues** Problem 14.7.

a. For the logistic regression model fit in Problem 14.7a, prepare an index plot of the diagonal elements of the estimated hat matrix (14.80). Use the plot to identify any outlying X observations.

b. To assess the influence of individual observations, obtain the delta chi-square statistic (14.85), the delta deviance statistic (14.86), and Cook's distance (14.87) for each observation. Plot each of these in separate index plots and identify any influential observations. Summarize your findings.

14.30. Refer to **Performance ability** Problem 14.9.

a. For the logistic regression fit in Problem 14.9a, prepare an index plot of the diagonal elements of the estimated hat matrix (14.80). Use the plot to identify any outlying X observations.

b. To assess the influence of individual observations, obtain the delta chi-square statistic (14.85), the delta deviance statistic (14.86), and Cook's distance (14.87) for each observation. Plot each of these in separate index plots and identify any influential observations. Summarize your findings.

14.31. Refer to **Car Purchase** Problems 14.13 and 14.21.

a. For the logistic regression model obtained in part (d) of Problem 14.21, prepare an index plot of the diagonal elements of the estimated hat matrix (14.80). Use the plot to identify any outlying X observations.

b. To assess the influence of individual observations, obtain the delta chi-square statistic (14.85), the delta deviance statistic (14.86), and Cook's distance (14.87) for each observation. Plot each of these in separate index plots and identify any influential observations. Summarize your findings.

*14.32. Refer to **Flu shots** Problem 14.14.

a. For the logistic regression fit in Problem 14.14a, prepare an index plot of the diagonal elements of the estimated hat matrix (14.80). Use the plot to identify any outlying X observations.

b. To assess the influence of individual observations, obtain the delta chi-square statistic (14.85), the delta deviance statistic (14.86), and Cook's distance (14.87) for each observation. Plot each of these in separate index plots and identify any influential observations. Summarize your findings.

*14.33. Refer to **Annual dues** Problem 14.7.

a. Based on the fitted regression function in Problem 14.7a, obtain an approximate 90 percent confidence interval for the mean response π_h for a dues increase of $X_h = \$40$.

b. A prediction rule is to be developed, based on the fitted regression function in Problem 14.7a. Based on the sample cases, find the total error rate, the error rate for renewers, and the error rate for nonrenewers for the following cutoffs: .40, .45, .50, .55, .60.

c. Based on your results in part (b), which cutoff minimizes the total error rate? Are the error rates for renewers and nonrenewers fairly balanced at this cutoff? Obtain the area under the ROC curve to assess the model's predictive power here. What do you conclude?

d. How can you establish whether the observed total error rate for the best cutoff in part (b) is a reliable indicator of the predictive ability of the fitted regression function and the chosen cutoff?

14.34. Refer to **Performance ability** Problem 14.9.

a. Using the fitted regression function in Problem 14.9a, obtain joint confidence intervals for the mean response π_h for persons with emotional stability test scores $X_h = 550$ and 625, respectively, with an approximate 90 percent family confidence coefficient. Interpret your intervals.

b. A prediction rule, based on the fitted regression function in Problem 14.9a, is to be developed. For the sample cases, find the total error rate, the error rate for employees able to perform in a task group, and the error rate for employees not able to perform for the following cutoffs: .325, .425, .525, .625.

c. On the basis of your results in part (b), which cutoff minimizes the total error rate? Are the error rates for employees able to perform in a task group and for employees not able to perform fairly balanced at this cutoff? Obtain the area under the ROC curve to assess the model's predictive power here. What do you conclude?

d. How can you establish whether the observed total error rate for the best cutoff in part (c) is a reliable indicator of the predictive ability of the fitted regression function and the chosen cutoff?

14.35. Refer to **Bottle return** Problem 14.11.

a. For the fitted regression function in Problem 14.11a, obtain an approximate 95 percent confidence interval for the probability of a purchase for deposit $X_h = 15$ cents. Interpret your interval.

b. A prediction rule is to be developed, based on the fitted regression function in Problem 14.11a. For the sample cases, find the total error rate, the error rate for purchasers, and the error rate for nonpurchasers for the following cutoffs: .150, .300, .450, .600, .750.

c. According to your results in part (b), which cutoff minimizes the total error rate? Are the error rates for purchasers and nonpurchasers fairly balanced at this cutoff? Obtain the area under the ROC curve to assess the model's predictive power here. What do you conclude?

d. How can you establish whether the observed total error rate for the best cutoff in part (c) is a reliable indicator of the predictive ability of the fitted regression function and the chosen cutoff?

*14.36. Refer to **Flu shots** Problem 14.14.

a. On the basis of the fitted regression function in Problem 14.14a, obtain a confidence interval for the mean response π_h for a female whose age is 65 and whose health awareness index is 50, with an approximate 90 percent family confidence coefficient. Interpret your intervals.

b. A prediction rule is to be based on the fitted regression function in Problem 14.14a. For the sample cases, find the total error rate, the error rate for clients receiving the flu shot, and the error rate for clients not receiving the flu shot for the following cutoffs: .05, .10, .15, .20.

c. Based on your results in part (b), which cutoff minimizes the total error rate? Are the error rates for clients receiving the flu shot and for clients not receiving the flu shot fairly balanced at this cutoff? Obtain the area under the ROC curve to assess the model's predictive power here. What do you conclude?

d. How can you establish whether the observed total error rate for the best cutoff in part (c) is a reliable indicator of the predictive ability of the fitted regression function and the chosen cutoff?

14.37. Polytomous logistic regression extends the binary response outcome to a multicategory response outcome for either nominal level or ordinal level data. Discuss the advantages and disadvantages of treating multicategory ordinal level outcomes as a series of binary logistic regression models, as a nominal level polytomous regression model, or as a proportional odds model.

*14.38. Refer to **Airfreight breakage** Problem 1.21.

a. Fit the Poisson regression model (14.113) with the response function $\mu(\mathbf{X}, \boldsymbol{\beta}) = \exp(\beta_0 + \beta_1 X)$. State the estimated regression coefficients, their estimated standard deviations, and the estimated response function.

b. Obtain the deviance residuals and present them in an index plot. Do there appear to be any outlying cases?

c. Estimate the mean number of ampules broken when $X = 0, 1, 2, 3$. Compare these estimates with those obtained by means of the fitted linear regression function in Problem 1.21a.

d. Plot the Poisson and linear regression functions, together with the data. Which regression function appears to be a better fit here? Discuss.

e. Management wishes to estimate the probability that 10 or fewer ampules are broken when there is no transfer of the shipment. Use the fitted Poisson regression function to obtain this estimate.

f. Obtain an approximate 95 percent confidence interval for β_1. Interpret your interval estimate.

14.39. **Geriatric study.** A researcher in geriatrics designed a prospective study to investigate the effects of two interventions on the frequency of falls. One hundred subjects were randomly assigned to one of the two interventions: education only ($X_1 = 0$) and education plus aerobic exercise training ($X_1 = 1$). Subjects were at least 65 years of age and in reasonably good health.

Three variables considered to be important as control variables were gender (X_2: $0 =$ female; $1 =$ male), a balance index (X_3), and a strength index (X_4). The higher the balance index, the more stable is the subject; and the higher the strength index, the stronger is the subject. Each subject kept a diary recording the number of falls (Y) during the six months of the study. The data follow:

Subject i	Number of Falls Y_i	Intervention X_{i1}	Gender X_{i2}	Balance Index X_{i3}	Strength Index X_{i4}
1	1	1	0	45	70
2	1	1	0	62	66
3	2	1	1	43	64
...	...	...			...
98	4	0	0	69	48
99	4	0	1	50	52
100	2	0	0	37	56

a. Fit the Poisson regression model (14.113) with the response function $\mu(\mathbf{X}, \boldsymbol{\beta}) = \exp(\beta_0 + \beta_1 X_1 + \beta_2 X_2 + \beta_3 X_3 + \beta_4 X_4)$. State the estimated regression coefficients, their estimated standard deviations, and the estimated response function.

b. Obtain the deviance residuals and present them in an index plot. Do there appear to be any outlying cases?

c. Assuming that the fitted model is appropriate, use the likelihood ratio test to determine whether gender (X_2) can be dropped from the model; control α at .05. State the full and reduced models, decision rule, and conclusion. What is the P-value of the test.

d. For the fitted model containing only X_1, X_3, and X_4 in first-order terms, obtain an approximate 95 percent confidence interval for β_1. Interpret your confidence interval. Does aerobic exercise reduce the frequency of falls when controlling for balance and strength?

Exercises

14.40. Show the equivalence of (14.16) and (14.17).

14.41. Derive (14.34) from (14.26).

14.42. Derive (14.18a), using (14.16) and (14.18).

14.43. (Calculus needed.) Maximum likelihood estimation theory states that the estimated large-sample variance-covariance matrix for maximum likelihood estimators is given by the inverse of the information matrix, the elements of which are the negatives of the expected values of the second-order partial derivatives of the logarithm of the likelihood function evaluated at $\boldsymbol{\beta} = \mathbf{b}$:

$$\left[-E\left\{ \frac{\partial^2 \log_e L(\boldsymbol{\beta})}{\partial \beta_i \, \partial \beta_j} \right\}_{\boldsymbol{\beta}=\mathbf{b}} \right]^{-1}$$

Show that this matrix simplifies to (14.51) for logistic regression. Consider the case where $p - 1 = 1$.

14.44. (Calculus needed.) Estimate the approximate variance-covariance matrix of the estimated regression coefficients for the programming task example in Table 14.1a, using (14.51), and verify the estimated standard deviations in Table 14.1b.

14.45. Show that the logistic response function (13.10) reduces to the response function in (14.20) when the Y_i are independent Bernoulli random variables with $E\{Y_i\} = \pi_i$.

14.46. Consider the multiple logistic regression model with $\mathbf{X}'\boldsymbol{\beta} = \beta_0 + \beta_1 X_1 + \beta_2 X_2 + \beta_3 X_1 X_2$. Derive an expression for the odds ratio for X_1. Does $\exp(\beta_1)$ have the same meaning here as for a regression model containing no interaction term?

14.47. A Bernoulli response Y_i has expected value:

$$E\{Y_i\} = \pi_i = 1 - \exp\left[-\exp\left(\frac{X_i - \gamma_0}{\gamma_1}\right)\right]$$

Show that the link function here is the complementary log-log transformation of π_i, namely, $\log_e[-\log_e(1 - \pi_i)]$.

Projects

14.48. Refer to the **Disease outbreak** data set in Appendix C.10. Savings account status is the response variable and age, socioeconomic status, and city sector are the predictor variables. Cases 1–98 are to be utilized for developing the logistic regression model.

    a. Fit logistic regression model (14.41) containing the predictor variables in first-order terms and interaction terms for all pairs of predictor variables. State the fitted response function.

    b. Use the likelihood ratio test to determine whether all interaction terms can be dropped from the regression model; use $\alpha = .01$. State the alternatives, full and reduced models, decision rule, and conclusion. What is the approximate P-value of the test?

    c. For logistic regression model in part (a), use backward elimination to decide which predictor variables can be dropped from the regression model. Control the α risk at .05 at each stage. Which variables are retained in the regression model?

14.49. Refer to the **Disease outbreak** data set in Appendix C.10 and Project 14.48. Logistic regression model (14.41) with predictor variables age and socioeconomic status in first-order terms is to be further evaluated.

    a. Conduct the Hosmer-Lemeshow goodness of fit test for the appropriateness of the logistic regression function by forming five groups of approximately 20 cases each; use $\alpha = .05$. State the alternatives, decision rule, and conclusion. What is the approximate P-value of the test?

    b. Obtain the deviance residuals and plot them against the estimated probabilities with a lowess smooth superimposed. What does the plot suggest about the adequacy of the fit of the logistic regression model?

    c. Prepare an index plot of the diagonal elements of the estimated hat matrix (14.80). Use the plot to identify any outlying X observations.

    d. To assess the influence of individual observations, obtain the delta chi-square statistic (14.85), the delta deviance statistic (14.86), and Cook's distance (14.87) for each observation. Plot each of these in separate index plots and identify any influential observations. Summarize your findings.

    e. Construct a half-normal probability plot of the absolute deviance residuals and superimpose a simulated envelope. Are any cases outlying? Does the logistic model appear to be a good fit? Discuss.

    f. To predict savings account status, you must identify the optimal cutoff. On the basis of the sample cases, find the total error rate, the error rate for persons with a savings account, and the error rate for persons with no savings account for the following cutoffs: .45, .50, .55, .60. Which of the cutoffs minimizes the total error rate? Are the two error rates for persons with and without savings accounts fairly balanced at this cutoff? Obtain the area under the ROC curve to assess the model's predictive power here. What do you conclude?

14.50. Refer to the **Disease outbreak** data set in Appendix C.10 and Project 14.49. The regression model identified in Project 14.49 is to be validated using cases 99–196.

a. Use the rule obtained in Project 14.49f to make a prediction for each of the holdout validation cases. What are the total and the two component prediction error rates for the validation data set? How do these error rates compare with those for the model-building data set in Project 14.49f?

b. Combine the model-building and validation data sets and fit the model identified in Project 14.49 to the combined data. Are the estimated coefficients and their estimated standard deviations similar to those obtained for the model-building data set? Should they be? Comment.

c. Based on the fitted regression model in part (b), obtain joint 90 percent confidence intervals for the odds ratios for age and socioeconomic status. Interpret your intervals.

14.51. Refer to the **SENIC** data set in Appendix C.1. Medical school affiliation is the response variable, to be coded $Y = 1$ if medical school affiliation and $Y = 0$ if no medical school affiliation. The pool of potential predictor variables includes age, routine chest X-ray ratio, average daily census, and number of nurses. All 113 cases are to be used in developing the logistic regression model.

a. Fit logistic regression model (14.41) containing all predictor variables in the pool in first-order terms and interaction terms for all pairs of predictor variables. State the fitted response function.

b. Test whether all interaction terms can be dropped from the regression model; use $\alpha = .05$. State the full and reduced models, decision rule, and conclusion. What is the approximate P-value of the test?

c. For logistic regression model (14.41) containing the predictor variables in first-order terms only, use forward stepwise regression to decide which predictor variables can be retained in the regression model. Control the α risk at .10 at each stage. Which variables should be retained in the regression model?

d. For logistic regression model (14.41) containing the predictor variables in first-order terms only, identify the best subset models using the AIC_p criterion and the SBC_p criterion. Does the use of these two criteria lead to the same model? Are either of the models identified the same as that found in part (c)?

14.52. Refer to the **SENIC** data set in Appendix C.1 and Project 14.51. Logistic regression model (14.41) with predictor variables age and average daily census in first-order terms is to be further evaluated.

a. Conduct Hosmer-Lemshow goodness of fit test for the appropriateness of the logistic regression function by forming five groups of approximately 23 cases each; use $\alpha = .05$. State the alternatives, decision rule, and conclusion. What is the approximate P-value of the test?

b. Obtain the deviance residuals and plot them against the estimated probabilities with a lowess smooth superimposed. What does the plot suggest about the adequacy of the fit of the logistic regression model?

c. Construct a half-normal probability plot of the absolute deviance residuals and superimpose a simulated envelope. Are any cases outlying? Does the logistic model appear to be a good fit? Discuss.

d. Prepare an index plot of the diagonal elements of the estimated hat matrix (14.80). Use the plot to identify any outlying X observations.

e. To assess the influence of individual observations, obtain the delta chi-square statistic (14.85), the delta deviance statistic (14.86), and Cook's distance (14.87) for each observation. Plot each of these in separate index plots and identify any influential observations. Summarize your findings.

   f. To predict medical school affiliation, you must identify the optimal cutoff. For the sample cases, find the total error rate, the error rate for hospitals with medical school affiliation, and the error rate for hospitals without medical school affiliation for the following cutoffs: .30, .40, .50, .60. Which of the cutoffs minimizes the total error rate? Are the two error rates for hospitals with and without medical school affiliation fairly balanced at this cutoff? Obtain the area under the ROC curve to assess the model's predictive power here. What do you conclude?

   g. Estimate by means of an approximate 90 percent confidence interval the odds of a hospital having medical school affiliation for hospitals with average age of patients of 55 years and average daily census of 500 patients.

14.53. Refer to **Annual dues** Problem 14.7. Obtain a simulated envelope and superimpose it on the half-normal probability plot of the absolute deviance residuals. Are there any indications that the fitted model is not appropriate? Are there any outlying cases? Discuss.

14.54. Refer to **Annual dues** Problem 14.7. In order to assess the appropriateness of large-sample inferences here, employ the following parametric bootstrap procedure: For each of the 30 cases, generate a Bernoulli outcome (0, 1), using the estimated probability $\hat{\pi}_i$ for the original X_i level according to the fitted model. Fit the logistic regression model to the bootstrap sample and obtain the bootstrap estimates b_0^* and b_1^*. Repeat this procedure 500 times. Compute the mean and standard deviation of the 500 bootstrap estimates b_0^*, and do the same for b_1^*. Plot separate histograms of the bootstrap distributions of b_0^* and b_1^*. Are these distributions approximately normal? Compare the point estimates b_0 and b_1 and their estimated standard deviations obtained in the original fit to the means and standard deviations of the bootstrap distributions. What do you conclude about the appropriateness of large-sample inferences here? Discuss.

14.55. Refer to **Car purchase** Problem 14.13. Obtain a simulated envelope and superimpose it on the half-normal probability plot of the absolute deviance residuals. Are there any indications that the fitted model is not appropriate? Are there any outlying cases? Discuss.

14.56. Refer to **Car purchase** Problem 14.13. In order to assess the appropriateness of large-sample inferences here, employ the following parametric bootstrapping procedure: For each of the 33 cases, generate a Bernoulli outcome (0, 1), using the estimated probability $\hat{\pi}_i$ for the original levels of the predictor variables according to the fitted model. Fit the logistic regression model to the bootstrap sample. Repeat this procedure 500 times. Compute the mean and standard deviation of the 500 bootstrap estimates b_1^*, and do the same for b_2^*. Plot separate histograms of the bootstrap distributions of b_1^* and b_2^*. Are these distributions approximately normal? Compare the point estimates b_1 and b_2 and their estimated standard deviations obtained in the original fit to the means and standard deviations of the bootstrap distributions. What do you conclude about the appropriateness of large-sample inferences here? Discuss.

14.57. Refer to the **SENIC** data set in Appendix C.1. Region is the nominal level response variable coded $1 = \text{NE}, 2 = \text{NC}, 3 = \text{S}$, and $4 = \text{W}$. The pool of potential predictor variables includes age, routine chest X-ray ratio, number of beds, medical school affiliation, average daily census, number of nurses, and available facilities and services. All 113 hospitals are to be used in developing the polytomous logistic regression model.

   a. Fit polytomous regression model (14.99) using response variable region with $1 = \text{NE}$ as the referent category. Which predictors appear to be most important? Interpret the results.

   b. Conduct a likelihood ratio test to determine if the three parameters corresponding to age can be dropped from the nominal logistic regression model. Control α at .05. State the full and reduced models, decision rule, and conclusion. What is the approximate P-value of the test?

c. Conduct a likelihood ratio test to determine if all parameters corresponding to age and available facilities and services can be dropped from the nominal logistic regression model. Control α at .05. State the full and reduced models, decision rule, and conclusion. What is the approximate P-value of the test?

d. For the full model in part (a), carry out separate binary logistic regressions for each of the three comparisons with the referent category, as described at the top of page 612. How do the slope coefficients compare to those obtained in part (a).

e. For each of the separate binary logistic regressions carried out in part (d), obtain the deviance residuals and plot them against the estimated probabilities with a lowess smooth superimposed. What do the plots suggest about the adequacy of the fit of the binary logistic regression models?

f. For each of the separate binary logistic regressions carried out in part (d), obtain the delta chi-square statistic (14.85), the delta deviance statistic (14.86), and Cook's distance (14.87) for each observation. Plot each of these in separate index plots and identify any influential observations. Summarize your findings.

14.58. Refer to the **CDI** data set in Appendix C.2. Region is the nominal level response variable coded $1 = NE, 2 = NC, 3 = S$, and $4 = W$. The pool of potential predictor variables includes population density (total population/land area), percent of population aged 18–34, percent of population aged 65 or older, serious crimes per capita (total serious crimes/total population), percent high school graduates, percent bachelor's degrees, percent below poverty level, percent unemployment, and per capita income. The even-numbered cases are to be used in developing the polytomous logistic regression model.

a. Fit polytomous regression model (14.99) using response variable region with $1 = NE$ as the referent category. Which predictors appear to be most important? Interpret the results.

b. Conduct a series of likelihood ratio tests to determine which predictors, if any, can be dropped from the nominal logistic regression model. Control α at .01 for each test. State the alternatives, decision rules, and conclusions.

c. For the full model in part (a), carry out separate binary logistic regressions for each of the three comparisons with the referent category, as described at the top of page 612. How do the slope coefficients compare to those obtained in part (a).

d. For each of the separate binary logistic regressions carried out in part (c), obtain the deviance residuals and plot them against the estimated probabilities with a lowess smooth superimposed. What do the plots suggest about the adequacy of the fit of the binary logistic regression models?

e. For each of the separate binary logistic regressions carried out in part (d), obtain the delta chi-square statistic (14.85), the delta deviance statistic (14.86), and Cook's distance (14.87) for each observation. Plot each of these in separate index plots and identify any influential observations. Summarize your findings.

14.59. Refer to the **Prostate cancer** data set in Appendix C.5. Gleason score (variable 9) is the ordinal level response variable, and the pool of potential predictor variables includes PSA level, cancer volume, weight, age, benign prostatic hyperplasia, seminal vesicle invasion, and capsular penetration (variables 2 through 8).

a. Fit the proportional odds model (14.105). Which predictors appear to be most important? Interpret the results.

b. Conduct a series of Wald tests to determine which predictors, if any, can be dropped from the nominal logistic regression model. Control α at .05 for each test. State the alternatives, decision rule, and conclusion. What is the approximate P-value of the test?

c. Starting with the full model of part (a), use backward elimination to decide which predictor variables can be dropped from the ordinal regression model. Control the α risk at .05 at each stage. Which variables should be retained?

d. For the model in part (c), carry out separate binary logistic regressions for each of the two binary variables $Y_i^{(1)}$ and $Y_i^{(2)}$, as described at the top of page 617. How do the estimated coefficients compare to those obtained in part (c)?

e. For each of the separate binary logistic regressions carried out in part (d), obtain the deviance residuals and plot them against the estimated probabilities with a lowess smooth superimposed. What do the plots suggest about the adequacy of the fit of the binary logistic regression models?

f. For each of the separate binary logistic regressions carried out in part (d), obtain the delta chi-square statistic (14.85), the delta deviance statistic (14.86), and Cook's distance (14.87) for each observation. Plot each of these in separate index plots and identify any influential observations. Summarize your findings.

14.60. Refer to the **Real estate sales** data set in Appendix C.7. Quality of construction (variable 10) is the ordinal level response variable, and the pool of potential predictor variables includes sales price, finished square feet, number of bedrooms, number of bathrooms, air conditioning, garage size, pool, year built, lot size, and adjacent to highway (variables 2 through 9 and 12 through 13).

a. Fit the proportional odds model (14.105). Which predictors appear to be most important? Interpret the results.

b. Conduct a series of Wald tests to determine which predictors, if any, can be dropped from the nominal logistic regression model. Control α at .01 for each test. State the alternatives, decision rules, and conclusions. Which predictors should be retained?

c. Starting with the full model of part (a), use backward elimination to decide which predictor variables can be dropped from the ordinal regression model. Control the α risk at .05 at each stage. Which variables should be retained?

d. For the model obtained in part (c), carry out separate binary logistic regressions for each of the two binary variables $Y_i^{(1)}$ and $Y_i^{(2)}$, as described at the top of page 617. How do the estimated coefficients compare to those obtained in part (a)?

e. For each of the separate binary logistic regressions carried out in part (d), obtain the deviance residuals and plot them against the estimated probabilities with a lowess smooth superimposed. What do the plots suggest about the adequacy of the fit of the binary logistic regression models?

f. For each of the separate binary logistic regressions carried out in part (d), obtain the delta chi-square statistic (14.85), the delta deviance statistic (14.86), and Cook's distance (14.87) for each observation. Plot each of these in separate index plots and identify any influential observations. Summarize your findings.

14.61. Refer to the **Ischemic heart disease** data set in Appendix C.9. The response is the number of emergency room visits (variable 7) and the pool of potential predictor variables includes total cost, age, gender, number of interventions, number of drugs, number of complications, number of comorbidities, and duration (variables 2 through 6 and 8 through 10).

a. Obtain the fitted the Poisson regression model (14.113) with the response function $\mu(\mathbf{X}, \boldsymbol{\beta}) = \exp(\mathbf{X}'\boldsymbol{\beta})$. State the estimated regression coefficients, their estimated standard deviations, and the estimated response function.

b. Obtain the deviance residuals (14.118) and plot them against the estimated model probabilities with a lowess smooth superimposed. What does the plot suggest about the adequacy of the fit of the Poisson regression model?

c. Conduct a series of Wald tests to determine which predictors, if any, can be dropped from the nominal logistic regression model. Control α at .01 for each test. State the alternatives, decision rules, and conclusions.

d. Assuming that the fitted model in part (a) is appropriate, use the likelihood ratio test to determine whether duration, coomplications, and comorbidities can be dropped from the model; control α at .05. State the full and reduced models, decision rule, and conclusion.

e. Use backward elimination to decide which predictor variables can be dropped from the regression model. Control the α risk at .10 at each stage. Which variables are retained?

Case Studies

14.62. Refer to the **IPO** data set in Appendix C.11. Carry out a complete analysis of this data set, where the response of interest is venture capital funding, and the pool of predictors includes face value of the company, number of shares offered, and whether or not the company underwent a leveraged buyout. The analysis should consider transformations of predictors, inclusion of second-order predictors, analysis of residuals and influential observations, model selection, goodness of fit evaluation, and the development of an ROC curve. Model validation should also be employed. Document the steps taken in your analysis, and assess the strengths and weaknesses of your final model.

14.63. Refer to the **Real estate sales** data set in Appendix C.7. Create a new binary response variable Y, called high quality construction, by letting $Y = 1$ if quality (variable 10) equals 1, and $Y = 0$ otherwise (i.e., if quality equals 2 or 3). Carry out a complete logistic regression analysis, where the response of interest is high quality construction (Y), and the pool of predictors includes sales price, finished square feet, number of bedrooms, number of bathrooms, air conditioning, garage size, pool, year built, style, lot size, and adjacent to highway (variables 2 through 9 and 11 through 13). The analysis should consider transformations of predictors, inclusion of second-order predictors, analysis of residuals and influential observations, model selection, goodness of fit evaluation, and the development of an ROC curve. Develop a prediction rule for determining whether the quality of construction is predicted to be of high quality or not. Model validation should also be employed. Document the steps taken in your analysis, and assess the strengths and weaknesses of your final model.

14.64. Refer to the **Prostate cancer** data set in Appendix C.5. Create a new binary response variable Y, called high-grade cancer, by letting $Y = 1$ if Gleason score (variable 9) equals 8, and $Y = 0$ otherwise (i.e., if Gleason score equals 6 or 7). Carry out a complete logistic regression analysis, where the response of interest is high-grade cancer (Y), and the pool of predictors includes PSA level, cancer volume, weight, age, benign prostatic hyperplasia, seminal vesicle invasion, and capsular penetration (variables 2 through 8). The analysis should consider transformations of predictors, inclusion of second-order predictors, analysis of residuals and influential observations, model selection, goodness of fit evaluation, and the development of an ROC curve. Develop a prediction rule for determining whether the grade of disease is predicted to be high grade or not. Model validation should also be employed. Document the steps taken in your analysis, and assess the strengths and weaknesses of your final model.

Appendix

Some Basic Results in Probability and Statistics

This appendix contains some basic results in probability and statistics. It is intended as a reference to which you may refer as you read the book.

A.1 Summation and Product Operators

Summation Operator

The summation operator $\sum$ is defined as follows:

$$\sum_{i=1}^{n} Y_i = Y_1 + Y_2 + \cdots + Y_n \tag{A.1}$$

Some important properties of this operator are:

$$\sum_{i=1}^{n} k = nk \qquad \text{where } k \text{ is a constant} \tag{A.2a}$$

$$\sum_{i=1}^{n} (Y_i + Z_i) = \sum_{i=1}^{n} Y_i + \sum_{i=1}^{n} Z_i \tag{A.2b}$$

$$\sum_{i=1}^{n} (a + cY_i) = na + c \sum_{i=1}^{n} Y_i \qquad \text{where } a \text{ and } c \text{ are constants} \tag{A.2c}$$

The double summation operator $\sum \sum$ is defined as follows:

$$\sum_{i=1}^{n} \sum_{j=1}^{m} Y_{ij} = \sum_{i=1}^{n} (Y_{i1} + \cdots + Y_{im})$$

$$= Y_{11} + \cdots + Y_{1m} + Y_{21} + \cdots + Y_{2m} + \cdots + Y_{nm} \tag{A.3}$$

An important property of the double summation operator is:

$$\sum_{i=1}^{n} \sum_{j=1}^{m} Y_{ij} = \sum_{j=1}^{m} \sum_{i=1}^{n} Y_{ij} \tag{A.4}$$

Product Operator

The product operator $\prod$ is defined as follows:

$$\prod_{i=1}^{n} Y_i = Y_1 \cdot Y_2 \cdot Y_3 \cdots Y_n \tag{A.5}$$

A.2   Probability

Addition Theorem

Let A_i and A_j be two events defined on a sample space. Then:

$$P(A_i \cup A_j) = P(A_i) + P(A_j) - P(A_i \cap A_j) \tag{A.6}$$

where $P(A_i \cup A_j)$ denotes the probability of either A_i or A_j or both occurring; $P(A_i)$ and $P(A_j)$ denote, respectively, the probability of A_i and the probability of A_j; and $P(A_i \cap A_j)$ denotes the probability of both A_i and A_j occurring.

Multiplication Theorem

Let $P(A_i|A_j)$ denote the conditional probability of A_i occurring, given that A_j has occurred, and let $P(A_j|A_i)$ denote the conditional probability of A_j occurring, given that A_i has occurred. These conditional probabilities are defined as follows:

$$P(A_i|A_j) = \frac{P(A_i \cap A_j)}{P(A_j)} \qquad P(A_j) \neq 0 \tag{A.7a}$$

$$P(A_j|A_i) = \frac{P(A_i \cap A_j)}{P(A_i)} \qquad P(A_i) \neq 0 \tag{A.7b}$$

The multiplication theorem states:

$$P(A_i \cap A_j) = P(A_i)P(A_j|A_i) = P(A_j)P(A_i|A_j) \tag{A.8}$$

Complementary Events

The complementary event of A_i is denoted by $\bar{A}_i$. The following results for complementary events are useful:

$$P(\bar{A}_i) = 1 - P(A_i) \tag{A.9}$$

$$P(\overline{A_i \cup A_j}) = P(\bar{A}_i \cap \bar{A}_j) \tag{A.10}$$

A.3   Random Variables

Throughout this section, except as noted, we assume that the random variable Y assumes a finite number of outcomes.

Expected Value

Let the random variable Y assume the outcomes $Y_1, \ldots, Y_k$ with probabilities given by the probability function:

$$f(Y_s) = P(Y = Y_s) \qquad s = 1, \ldots, k \tag{A.11}$$

The expected value of Y, denoted by $E\{Y\}$, is defined by:

$$E\{Y\} = \sum_{s=1}^{k} Y_s f(Y_s) \tag{A.12}$$

$E\{\ \}$ is called the *expectation operator*.

An important property of the expectation operator is:

$$E\{a + cY\} = a + cE\{Y\} \qquad \text{where } a \text{ and } c \text{ are constants} \tag{A.13}$$

Special cases of this are:

$$E\{a\} = a \tag{A.13a}$$

$$E\{cY\} = cE\{Y\} \tag{A.13b}$$

$$E\{a + Y\} = a + E\{Y\} \tag{A.13c}$$

Comment

If the random variable Y is continuous, with density function $f(Y)$, $E\{Y\}$ is defined as follows:

$$E\{Y\} = \int_{-\infty}^{\infty} Y f(Y)\, dY \tag{A.14}$$

∎

Variance

The variance of the random variable Y is denoted by $\sigma^2\{Y\}$ and is defined as follows:

$$\sigma^2\{Y\} = E\{(Y - E\{Y\})^2\} \tag{A.15}$$

An equivalent expression is:

$$\sigma^2\{Y\} = E\{Y^2\} - (E\{Y\})^2 \tag{A.15a}$$

$\sigma^2\{\ \}$ is called the *variance operator*.

The variance of a linear function of Y is frequently encountered. We denote the variance of $a + cY$ by $\sigma^2\{a + cY\}$ and have:

$$\sigma^2\{a + cY\} = c^2\sigma^2\{Y\} \qquad \text{where } a \text{ and } c \text{ are constants} \tag{A.16}$$

Special cases of this result are:

$$\sigma^2\{a + Y\} = \sigma^2\{Y\} \tag{A.16a}$$

$$\sigma^2\{cY\} = c^2\sigma^2\{Y\} \tag{A.16b}$$

Comment

If Y is continuous, $\sigma^2\{Y\}$ is defined as follows:

$$\sigma^2\{Y\} = \int_{-\infty}^{\infty} (Y - E\{Y\})^2 f(Y)\, dY \tag{A.17}$$

∎

Joint, Marginal, and Conditional Probability Distributions

Let the joint probability function for the two random variables Y and Z be denoted by $g(Y, Z)$:

$$g(Y_s, Z_t) = P(Y = Y_s \cap Z = Z_t) \qquad s = 1, \ldots, k; t = 1, \ldots, m \qquad \textbf{(A.18)}$$

The marginal probability function of Y, denoted by $f(Y)$, is:

$$f(Y_s) = \sum_{t=1}^{m} g(Y_s, Z_t) \qquad s = 1, \ldots, k \qquad \textbf{(A.19a)}$$

and the marginal probability function of Z, denoted by $h(Z)$, is:

$$h(Z_t) = \sum_{s=1}^{k} g(Y_s, Z_t) \qquad t = 1, \ldots, m \qquad \textbf{(A.19b)}$$

The conditional probability function of Y, given $Z = Z_t$, is:

$$f(Y_s | Z_t) = \frac{g(Y_s, Z_t)}{h(Z_t)} \qquad h(Z_t) \neq 0; s = 1, \ldots, k \qquad \textbf{(A.20a)}$$

and the conditional probability function of Z, given $Y = Y_s$, is:

$$h(Z_t | Y_s) = \frac{g(Y_s, Z_t)}{f(Y_s)} \qquad f(Y_s) \neq 0; t = 1, \ldots, m \qquad \textbf{(A.20b)}$$

Covariance

The covariance of Y and Z is denoted by $\sigma\{Y, Z\}$ and is defined by:

$$\sigma\{Y, Z\} = E\{(Y - E\{Y\})(Z - E\{Z\})\} \qquad \textbf{(A.21)}$$

An equivalent expression is:

$$\sigma\{Y, Z\} = E\{YZ\} - (E\{Y\})(E\{Z\}) \qquad \textbf{(A.21a)}$$

$\sigma\{ \ , \ \}$ is called the *covariance operator*.

The covariance of $a_1 + c_1 Y$ and $a_2 + c_2 Z$ is denoted by $\sigma\{a_1 + c_1 Y, a_2 + c_2 Z\}$, and we have:

$$\sigma\{a_1 + c_1 Y, a_2 + c_2 Z\} = c_1 c_2 \sigma\{Y, Z\} \qquad \text{where } a_1, a_2, c_1, c_2 \text{ are constants} \qquad \textbf{(A.22)}$$

Special cases of this are:

$$\sigma\{c_1 Y, c_2 Z\} = c_1 c_2 \sigma\{Y, Z\} \qquad \textbf{(A.22a)}$$

$$\sigma\{a_1 + Y, a_2 + Z\} = \sigma\{Y, Z\} \qquad \textbf{(A.22b)}$$

By definition, we have:

$$\sigma\{Y, Y\} = \sigma^2\{Y\} \qquad \textbf{(A.23)}$$

where $\sigma^2\{Y\}$ is the variance of Y.

Coefficient of Correlation

The standardized form of a random variable Y, whose mean and variance are $E\{Y\}$ and $\sigma^2\{Y\}$, respectively, is as follows:

$$Y' = \frac{Y - E\{Y\}}{\sigma\{Y\}} \tag{A.24}$$

where Y' denotes the *standardized random variable* form of random variable Y.

The coefficient of correlation between random variables Y and Z, denoted by $\rho\{Y, Z\}$, is the covariance between the standardized variables Y' and Z':

$$\rho\{Y, Z\} = \sigma\{Y', Z'\} \tag{A.25}$$

Equivalently, the coefficient of correlation can be expressed as follows:

$$\rho\{Y, Z\} = \frac{\sigma\{Y, Z\}}{\sigma\{Y\}\sigma\{Z\}} \tag{A.25a}$$

$\rho\{\ ,\ \}$ is called the *correlation operator*.

The coefficient of correlation can take on values between -1 and 1:

$$-1 \le \rho\{Y, Z\} \le 1 \tag{A.26}$$

When $\sigma\{Y, Z\} = 0$, it follows from (A.25a) that $\rho\{Y, Z\} = 0$ and Y and Z are said to be uncorrelated.

Independent Random Variables

The independence of two discrete random variables is defined as follows:

Random variables Y and Z are independent if and only if:

$$g(Y_s, Z_t) = f(Y_s)h(Z_t) \qquad s = 1, \ldots, k; t = 1, \ldots, m \tag{A.27}$$

If Y and Z are independent random variables:

$$\sigma\{Y, Z\} = 0 \text{ and } \rho\{Y, Z\} = 0 \qquad \text{when } Y \text{ and } Z \text{ are independent} \tag{A.28}$$

(In the special case where Y and Z are jointly normally distributed, $\sigma\{Y, Z\} = 0$ implies that Y and Z are independent.)

Functions of Random Variables

Let $Y_1, \ldots, Y_n$ be n random variables. Consider the function $\sum a_i Y_i$, where the a_i are constants. We then have:

$$E\left\{\sum_{i=1}^{n} a_i Y_i\right\} = \sum_{i=1}^{n} a_i E\{Y_i\} \qquad \text{where the } a_i \text{ are constants} \tag{A.29a}$$

$$\sigma^2\left\{\sum_{i=1}^{n} a_i Y_i\right\} = \sum_{i=1}^{n}\sum_{j=1}^{n} a_i a_j \sigma\{Y_i, Y_j\} \qquad \text{where the } a_i \text{ are constants} \tag{A.29b}$$

Specifically, we have for $n = 2$:

$$E\{a_1 Y_1 + a_2 Y_2\} = a_1 E\{Y_1\} + a_2 E\{Y_2\} \quad\quad\quad \text{(A.30a)}$$
$$\sigma^2\{a_1 Y_1 + a_2 Y_2\} = a_1^2 \sigma^2\{Y_1\} + a_2^2 \sigma^2\{Y_2\} + 2a_1 a_2 \sigma\{Y_1, Y_2\} \quad \text{(A.30b)}$$

If the random variables Y_i are independent, we have:

$$\sigma^2 \left\{ \sum_{i=1}^{n} a_i Y_i \right\} = \sum_{i=1}^{n} a_i^2 \sigma^2 \{Y_i\} \quad\quad \text{when the } Y_i \text{ are independent} \quad \text{(A.31)}$$

Special cases of this are:

$$\sigma^2\{Y_1 + Y_2\} = \sigma^2\{Y_1\} + \sigma^2\{Y_2\} \quad\quad \text{when } Y_1 \text{ and } Y_2 \text{ are independent} \quad \text{(A.31a)}$$
$$\sigma^2\{Y_1 - Y_2\} = \sigma^2\{Y_1\} + \sigma^2\{Y_2\} \quad\quad \text{when } Y_1 \text{ and } Y_2 \text{ are independent} \quad \text{(A.31b)}$$

When the Y_i are independent random variables, the covariance of two linear functions $\sum a_i Y_i$ and $\sum c_i Y_i$ is:

$$\sigma \left\{ \sum_{i=1}^{n} a_i Y_i, \sum_{i=1}^{n} c_i Y_i \right\} = \sum_{i=1}^{n} a_i c_i \sigma^2 \{Y_i\} \quad\quad \text{when the } Y_i \text{ are independent} \quad \text{(A.32)}$$

Central Limit Theorem

The central limit theorem is basic for much of statistical inference.

If $Y_1, \ldots, Y_n$ are independent random observations from a population with probability function $f(Y)$ for which $\sigma^2\{Y\}$ is finite, the sample mean $\bar{Y}$:

$$\bar{Y} = \frac{\sum_{i=1}^{n} Y_i}{n} \quad\quad\quad\quad \text{(A.33)}$$

is approximately normally distributed when the sample size n is reasonably large, with mean $E\{Y\}$ and variance $\sigma^2\{Y\}/n$.

A.4 Normal Probability Distribution and Related Distributions

Normal Probability Distribution

The density function for a normal random variable Y is:

$$f(Y) = \frac{1}{\sqrt{2\pi}\sigma} \exp\left[-\frac{1}{2} \left(\frac{Y - \mu}{\sigma} \right)^2 \right] \quad\quad -\infty < Y < \infty \quad \text{(A.34)}$$

where μ and σ are the two parameters of the normal distribution and $\exp(a)$ denotes e^a. The mean and variance of a normal random variable Y are:

$$E\{Y\} = \mu \quad\quad\quad\quad \text{(A.35a)}$$
$$\sigma^2\{Y\} = \sigma^2 \quad\quad\quad\quad \text{(A.35b)}$$

Linear Function of Normal Random Variable. A linear function of a normal random variable Y has the following property:

If Y is a normal random variable, the transformed variable $Y' = a + cY$ (a and c are constants) is normally distributed, with mean $a + cE\{Y\}$ and variance $c^2\sigma^2\{Y\}$. (A.36)

Standard Normal Random Variable. The standard normal random variable

$$z = \frac{Y - \mu}{\sigma} \quad \text{where } Y \text{ is a normal random variable} \tag{A.37}$$

is normally distributed, with mean 0 and variance 1. We denote this as follows:

$$z \sim N(0, 1) \tag{A.38}$$
$$\nearrow \quad \nwarrow$$
$$\text{Mean} \quad \text{Variance}$$

Table B.1 in Appendix B contains the cumulative probabilities A for percentiles $z(A)$ where:

$$P\{z \leq z(A)\} = A \tag{A.39}$$

For instance, when $z(A) = 2.00$, $A = .9772$. Because the normal distribution is symmetrical about 0, when $z(A) = -2.00$, $A = 1 - .9772 = .0228$.

Linear Combination of Independent Normal Random Variables. Let $Y_1, \ldots, Y_n$ be independent normal random variables. We then have:

When $Y_1, \ldots, Y_n$ are independent normal random variables, the linear combination $a_1Y_1 + a_2Y_2 + \cdots + a_nY_n$ is normally distributed, with mean $\sum a_i E\{Y_i\}$ and variance $\sum a_i^2\sigma^2\{Y_i\}$. (A.40)

χ^2 Distribution

Let $z_1, \ldots, z_\nu$ be ν independent standard normal random variables. We then define a chi-square random variable as follows:

$$\chi^2(\nu) = z_1^2 + z_2^2 + \cdots + z_\nu^2 \quad \text{where the } z_i \text{ are independent} \tag{A.41}$$

The χ^2 distribution has one parameter, ν, which is called the *degrees of freedom* (*df*). The mean of the χ^2 distribution with ν degrees of freedom is:

$$E\{\chi^2(\nu)\} = \nu \tag{A.42}$$

Table B.3 in Appendix B contains percentiles of various χ^2 distributions. We define $\chi^2(A; \nu)$ as follows:

$$P\{\chi^2(\nu) \leq \chi^2(A; \nu)\} = A \tag{A.43}$$

Suppose $\nu = 5$. The 90th percentile of the χ^2 distribution with 5 degrees of freedom is $\chi^2(.90; 5) = 9.24$.

t Distribution

Let z and $\chi^2(v)$ be independent random variables (standard normal and χ^2, respectively). We then define a t random variable as follows:

$$t(v) = \frac{z}{\left[\frac{\chi^2(v)}{v}\right]^{1/2}} \qquad \text{where } z \text{ and } \chi^2(v) \text{ are independent} \qquad \textbf{(A.44)}$$

The t distribution has one parameter, the *degrees of freedom* v. The mean of the t distribution with v degrees of freedom is:

$$E\{t(v)\} = 0 \qquad \textbf{(A.45)}$$

Table B.2 in Appendix B contains percentiles of various t distributions. We define $t(A; v)$ as follows:

$$P\{t(v) \le t(A; v)\} = A \qquad \textbf{(A.46)}$$

Suppose $v = 10$. The 90th percentile of the t distribution with 10 degrees of freedom is $t(.90; 10) = 1.372$. Because the t distribution is symmetrical about 0, we have $t(.10; 10) = -1.372$.

F Distribution

Let $\chi^2(v_1)$ and $\chi^2(v_2)$ be two independent χ^2 random variables. We then define an F random variable as follows:

$$F(v_1, v_2) = \underset{\underset{\substack{df}}{\nwarrow}}{\frac{\chi^2(v_1)}{v_1}} \div \underset{\underset{\substack{df}}{\searrow}}{\frac{\chi^2(v_2)}{v_2}} \qquad \text{where } \chi^2(v_1) \text{ and } \chi^2(v_2) \text{ are independent} \qquad \textbf{(A.47)}$$

Numerator Denominator
df   df

The F distribution has two parameters, the *numerator degrees of freedom* and the *denominator degrees of freedom,* here v_1 and v_2, respectively.

Table B.4 in Appendix B contains percentiles of various F distributions. We define $F(A; v_1, v_2)$ as follows:

$$P\{F(v_1, v_2) \le F(A; v_1, v_2)\} = A \qquad \textbf{(A.48)}$$

Suppose $v_1 = 2$, $v_2 = 3$. The 90th percentile of the F distribution with 2 and 3 degrees of freedom, respectively, in the numerator and denominator is $F(.90; 2, 3) = 5.46$. Percentiles below 50 percent can be obtained by utilizing the relation:

$$F(A; v_1, v_2) = \frac{1}{F(1 - A; v_2, v_1)} \qquad \textbf{(A.49)}$$

Thus, $F(.10; 3, 2) = 1/F(.90; 2, 3) = 1/5.46 = .183$.

The following relation exists between the t and F random variables:

$$[t(v)]^2 = F(1, v) \qquad \textbf{(A.50a)}$$

and the percentiles of the t and F distributions are related as follows:

$$[t(.5 + A/2; v)]^2 = F(A; 1, v) \qquad \textbf{(A.50b)}$$

Comment

Throughout this text, we consider $z(A)$, $\chi^2(A; \nu)$, $t(A; \nu)$, and $F(A; \nu_1, \nu_2)$ as $A(100)$ percentiles. Equivalently, they can be considered as A fractiles. ∎

A.5 Statistical Estimation

Properties of Estimators

Four important properties of estimators are as follows:

An estimator $\hat{\theta}$ of the parameter θ is *unbiased* if:

$$E\{\hat{\theta}\} = \theta$$

(A.51)

An estimator $\hat{\theta}$ is a *consistent estimator* of θ if:

$$\lim_{n \to \infty} P(|\hat{\theta} - \theta| \geq \varepsilon) = 0 \qquad \text{for any } \varepsilon > 0$$

(A.52)

An estimator $\hat{\theta}$ is a *sufficient estimator* of θ if the conditional joint probability function of the sample observations, given $\hat{\theta}$, does not depend on the parameter θ.

(A.53)

An estimator $\hat{\theta}$ is a *minimum variance estimator* of θ if for any other estimator $\hat{\theta}^*$:

$$\sigma^2\{\hat{\theta}\} \leq \sigma^2\{\hat{\theta}^*\} \text{ for all } \hat{\theta}^*$$

(A.54)

Maximum Likelihood Estimators

The method of maximum likelihood is a general method of finding estimators. Suppose we are sampling a population whose probability function $f(Y; \theta)$ involves one parameter, θ. Given independent observations $Y_1, \ldots, Y_n$, the joint probability function of the sample observations is:

$$g(Y_1, \ldots, Y_n) = \prod_{i=1}^{n} f(Y_i; \theta)$$

(A.55a)

When this joint probability function is viewed as a function of θ, with the observations given, it is called the *likelihood function* $L(\theta)$:

$$L(\theta) = \prod_{i=1}^{n} f(Y_i; \theta)$$

(A.55b)

Maximizing $L(\theta)$ with respect to θ yields the maximum likelihood estimator of θ. Under quite general conditions, maximum likelihood estimators are consistent and sufficient.

Least Squares Estimators

The method of least squares is another general method of finding estimators. The sample observations are assumed to be of the form (for the case of a single parameter θ):

$$Y_i = f_i(\theta) + \varepsilon_i \qquad i = 1, \ldots, n$$

(A.56)

where $f_i(\theta)$ is a known function of the parameter θ and the ε_i are random variables, usually assumed to have expectation $E\{\varepsilon_i\} = 0$.

With the method of least squares, for the given sample observations, the sum of squares:

$$Q = \sum_{i=1}^{n} [Y_i - f_i(\theta)]^2 \tag{A.57}$$

is considered as a function of θ. The least squares estimator of θ is obtained by minimizing Q with respect to θ. In many instances, least squares estimators are unbiased and consistent.

A.6   Inferences about Population Mean—Normal Population

We have a random sample of n observations $Y_1, \ldots, Y_n$ from a normal population with mean μ and standard deviation σ. The sample mean and sample standard deviation are:

$$\bar{Y} = \frac{\sum_i Y_i}{n} \tag{A.58a}$$

$$s = \left[\frac{\sum_i (Y_i - \bar{Y})^2}{n - 1} \right]^{1/2} \tag{A.58b}$$

and the estimated standard deviation of the sampling distribution of $\bar{Y}$, denoted by $s\{\bar{Y}\}$, is:

$$s\{\bar{Y}\} = \frac{s}{\sqrt{n}} \tag{A.58c}$$

We then have:

$$\frac{\bar{Y} - \mu}{s\{\bar{Y}\}} \text{ is distributed as } t \text{ with } n - 1 \text{ degrees of freedom} \tag{A.59}$$
$$\text{when the random sample is from a normal population.}$$

Interval Estimation

The confidence limits for μ with confidence coefficient $1 - \alpha$ are obtained by means of (A.59):

$$\bar{Y} \pm t(1 - \alpha/2; n - 1)s\{\bar{Y}\} \tag{A.60}$$

Example 1

Obtain a 95 percent confidence interval for μ when:

$$n = 10 \qquad \bar{Y} = 20 \qquad s = 4$$

We require:

$$s\{\bar{Y}\} = \frac{4}{\sqrt{10}} = 1.265 \qquad t(.975; 9) = 2.262$$

The 95 percent confidence limits therefore are $20 \pm 2.262(1.265)$ and the 95 percent confidence interval for μ is:

$$17.1 \leq \mu \leq 22.9$$

TABLE A.1
Decision Rules
for Tests
Concerning
Mean μ of
Normal
Population.

Alternatives	Decision Rule
	(a)
$H_0: \mu = \mu_0$	If $|t^*| \leq t(1 - \alpha/2; n - 1)$, conclude H_0
$H_a: \mu \neq \mu_0$	If $|t^*| > t(1 - \alpha/2; n - 1)$, conclude H_a
	where:
	$t^* = \dfrac{\bar{Y} - \mu_0}{s\{\bar{Y}\}}$
	(b)
$H_0: \mu \geq \mu_0$	If $t^* \geq t(\alpha; n - 1)$, conclude H_0
$H_a: \mu < \mu_0$	If $t^* < t(\alpha; n - 1)$, conclude H_a
	(c)
$H_0: \mu \leq \mu_0$	If $t^* \leq t(1 - \alpha; n - 1)$, conclude H_0
$H_a: \mu > \mu_0$	If $t^* > t(1 - \alpha; n - 1)$, conclude H_a

Tests

One-sided and two-sided tests concerning the population mean μ are constructed by means of (A.59), based on the test statistic:

$$t^* = \frac{\bar{Y} - \mu_0}{s\{\bar{Y}\}} \tag{A.61}$$

Table A.1 contains the decision rules for three possible cases, with the risk of making a Type I error controlled at α.

Example 2   Choose between the alternatives:

$$H_0: \mu \leq 20$$
$$H_a: \mu > 20$$

when α is to be controlled at .05 and:

$$n = 15 \qquad \bar{Y} = 24 \qquad s = 6$$

We require:

$$s\{\bar{Y}\} = \frac{6}{\sqrt{15}} = 1.549$$

$$t(.95; 14) = 1.761$$

The decision rule is:

$$\text{If } t^* \leq 1.761, \text{ conclude } H_0$$
$$\text{If } t^* > 1.761, \text{ conclude } H_a$$

Since $t^* = (24 - 20)/1.549 = 2.58 > 1.761$, we conclude H_a.

Example 3

Choose between the alternatives:

$$H_0: \mu = 10$$
$$H_a: \mu \neq 10$$

when α is to be controlled at .02 and:

$$n = 25 \qquad \bar{Y} = 5.7 \qquad s = 8$$

We require:

$$s\{\bar{Y}\} = \frac{8}{\sqrt{25}} = 1.6$$
$$t(.99; 24) = 2.492$$

The decision rule is:

If $|t^*| \leq 2.492$, conclude H_0

If $|t^*| > 2.492$, conclude H_a

where the symbol | | stands for the absolute value. Since $|t^*| = |(5.7 - 10)/1.6| = |-2.69| = 2.69 > 2.492$, we conclude H_a.

***P*-Value for Sample Outcome.**   The *P*-value for a sample outcome is the probability that the sample outcome could have been more extreme than the observed one when $\mu = \mu_0$. Large *P*-values support H_0 while small *P*-values support H_a. A test can be carried out by comparing the *P*-value with the specified α risk. If the *P*-value equals or is greater than the specified α, H_0 is concluded. If the *P*-value is less than α, H_a is concluded.

Example 4

In Example 2, $t^* = 2.58$. The *P*-value for this sample outcome is the probability $P\{t(14) > 2.58\}$. From Table B.2, we find $t(.985; 14) = 2.415$ and $t(.990; 14) = 2.624$. Hence, the *P*-value is between .010 and .015. The exact *P*-value can be found from many statistical calculators or statistical computer packages; it is .0109. Thus, for $\alpha = .05$, H_a is concluded.

Example 5

In Example 3, $t^* = -2.69$. We find from Table B.2 that the one-sided *P*-value, $P\{t(24) < -2.69\}$, is between .005 and .0075. The exact one-sided *P*-value is .0064. Because the test is two-sided and the t distribution is symmetrical, the two-sided *P*-value is twice the one-sided value, or $2(.0064) = .013$. Hence, for $\alpha = .02$, we conclude H_a.

Relation between Tests and Confidence Intervals.   There is a direct relation between tests and confidence intervals. For example, the two-sided confidence limits (A.60) can be used for testing:

$$H_0: \mu = \mu_0$$
$$H_a: \mu \neq \mu_0$$

If μ_0 is contained within the $1 - \alpha$ confidence interval, then the two-sided decision rule in Table A.1a, with level of significance α, will lead to conclusion H_0, and vice versa. If μ_0 is not contained within the confidence interval, the decision rule will lead to H_a, and vice versa.

There are similar correspondences between one-sided confidence intervals and one-sided decision rules.

A.7 Comparisons of Two Population Means—Normal Populations

Independent Samples

There are two normal populations, with means μ_1 and μ_2, respectively, and with the same standard deviation σ. The means μ_1 and μ_2 are to be compared on the basis of independent samples for each of the two populations:

$$\text{Sample 1: } Y_1, \ldots, Y_{n_1}$$
$$\text{Sample 2: } Z_1, \ldots, Z_{n_2}$$

Estimators of the two population means are the sample means:

$$\bar{Y} = \frac{\sum_i Y_i}{n_1} \tag{A.62a}$$

$$\bar{Z} = \frac{\sum_i Z_i}{n_2} \tag{A.62b}$$

and an estimator of $\mu_1 - \mu_2$ is $\bar{Y} - \bar{Z}$.

An estimator of the common variance σ^2 is:

$$s^2 = \frac{\sum_i (Y_i - \bar{Y})^2 + \sum_i (Z_i - \bar{Z})^2}{n_1 + n_2 - 2} \tag{A.63}$$

and an estimator of $\sigma^2\{\bar{Y} - \bar{Z}\}$, the variance of the sampling distribution of $\bar{Y} - \bar{Z}$, is:

$$s^2\{\bar{Y} - \bar{Z}\} = s^2 \left(\frac{1}{n_1} + \frac{1}{n_2} \right) \tag{A.64}$$

We have:

$$\frac{(\bar{Y} - \bar{Z}) - (\mu_1 - \mu_2)}{s\{\bar{Y} - \bar{Z}\}} \text{ is distributed as } t \text{ with } n_1 + n_2 - 2 \text{ degrees of}$$

freedom when the two independent samples come from normal populations with the same standard deviation. $\tag{A.65}$

Interval Estimation. The confidence limits for $\mu_1 - \mu_2$ with confidence coefficient $1 - \alpha$ are obtained by means of (A.65):

$$(\bar{Y} - \bar{Z}) \pm t(1 - \alpha/2; n_1 + n_2 - 2)s\{\bar{Y} - \bar{Z}\} \tag{A.66}$$

Example 6

Obtain a 95 percent confidence interval for $\mu_1 - \mu_2$ when:

$$n_1 = 10 \qquad \bar{Y} = 14 \qquad \sum (Y_i - \bar{Y})^2 = 105$$

$$n_2 = 20 \qquad \bar{Z} = 8 \qquad \sum (Z_i - \bar{Z})^2 = 224$$

TABLE A.2
Decision Rules for Tests Concerning Means μ_1 and μ_2 of Two Normal Populations $(\sigma_1 = \sigma_2 = \sigma)$— Independent Samples.

Alternatives	Decision Rule
	(a)
$H_0: \mu_1 = \mu_2$	If $|t^*| \leq t(1 - \alpha/2; n_1 + n_2 - 2)$, conclude H_0
$H_a: \mu_1 \neq \mu_2$	If $|t^*| > t(1 - \alpha/2; n_1 + n_2 - 2)$, conclude H_a
	where:
	$$t^* = \frac{\bar{Y} - \bar{Z}}{s\{\bar{Y} - \bar{Z}\}}$$
	(b)
$H_0: \mu_1 \geq \mu_2$	If $t^* \geq t(\alpha; n_1 + n_2 - 2)$, conclude H_0
$H_a: \mu_1 < \mu_2$	If $t^* < t(\alpha; n_1 + n_2 - 2)$, conclude H_a
	(c)
$H_0: \mu_1 \leq \mu_2$	If $t^* \leq t(1 - \alpha; n_1 + n_2 - 2)$, conclude H_0
$H_a: \mu_1 > \mu_2$	If $t^* > t(1 - \alpha; n_1 + n_2 - 2)$, conclude H_a

We require:

$$s^2 = \frac{105 + 224}{10 + 20 - 2} = 11.75 \qquad s\{\bar{Y} - \bar{Z}\} = 1.328$$

$$s^2\{\bar{Y} - \bar{Z}\} = 11.75\left(\frac{1}{10} + \frac{1}{20}\right) = 1.7625 \qquad t(.975; 28) = 2.048$$

Hence, the 95 percent confidence interval for $\mu_1 - \mu_2$ is:

$$3.3 = (14 - 8) - 2.048(1.328) \leq \mu_1 - \mu_2 \leq (14 - 8) + 2.048(1.328) = 8.7$$

Tests. One-sided and two-sided tests concerning $\mu_1 - \mu_2$ are constructed by means of (A.65). Table A.2 contains the decision rules for three possible cases, based on the test statistic:

$$t^* = \frac{\bar{Y} - \bar{Z}}{s\{\bar{Y} - \bar{Z}\}} \qquad\qquad \text{(A.67)}$$

with the risk of making a Type I error controlled at α.

Example 7

Choose between the alternatives:

$$H_0: \mu_1 = \mu_2$$
$$H_a: \mu_1 \neq \mu_2$$

when α is to be controlled at .10 and the data are those of Example 6. We require $t(.95; 28) = 1.701$, so that the decision rule is:

$$\text{If } |t^*| \leq 1.701, \text{ conclude } H_0$$
$$\text{If } |t^*| > 1.701, \text{ conclude } H_a$$

Since $|t^*| = |(14 - 8)/1.328| = |4.52| = 4.52 > 1.701$, we conclude H_a.

The one-sided P-value here is the probability $P\{t(28) > 4.52\}$. We see from Table B.2 that this P-value is less than .0005; the exact one-sided P-value is .00005. Hence, the two-sided P-value is .0001. For $\alpha = .10$, the appropriate conclusion therefore is H_a.

Paired Observations

When the observations in the two samples are paired (e.g., attitude scores Y_i and Z_i for the ith sample employee before and after a year's experience on the job), we use the differences:

$$W_i = Y_i - Z_i \qquad i = 1, \ldots, n \tag{A.68}$$

in the fashion of a sample from a single population. Thus, when the W_i can be treated as observations from a normal population, we have:

$$\frac{\bar{W} - (\mu_1 - \mu_2)}{s\{\bar{W}\}} \text{ is distributed as } t \text{ with } n - 1 \text{ degrees of freedom when}$$

the differences W_i can be considered to be observations from a normal population and: $\tag{A.69}$

$$\bar{W} = \frac{\sum_i W_i}{n} \qquad s^2\{\bar{W}\} = \left(\frac{\sum_i (W_i - \bar{W})^2}{n - 1}\right) \div n$$

A.8   Inferences about Population Variance—Normal Population

When sampling from a normal population, the following holds for the sample variance s^2, where s is defined in (A.58b):

$$\frac{(n - 1)s^2}{\sigma^2} \text{ is distributed as } \chi^2 \text{ with } n - 1 \text{ degrees of freedom when the}$$

random sample is from a normal population. $\tag{A.70}$

Interval Estimation

The lower confidence limit L and the upper confidence limit U in a confidence interval for the population variance σ^2 with confidence coefficient $1 - \alpha$ are obtained by means of (A.70):

$$L = \frac{(n - 1)s^2}{\chi^2(1 - \alpha/2; n - 1)} \qquad U = \frac{(n - 1)s^2}{\chi^2(\alpha/2; n - 1)} \tag{A.71}$$

Example 8

Obtain a 98 percent confidence interval for σ^2, using the data of Example 1 ($n = 10$, $s = 4$). We require:

$$s^2 = 16 \qquad \chi^2(.01; 9) = 2.09 \qquad \chi^2(.99; 9) = 21.67$$

The 98 percent confidence interval for σ^2 therefore is:

$$6.6 = \frac{9(16)}{21.67} \leq \sigma^2 \leq \frac{9(16)}{2.09} = 68.9$$

Tests

One-sided and two-sided tests concerning the population variance σ^2 are constructed by means of (A.70). Table A.3 contains the decision rules for three possible cases, with the risk of making a Type I error controlled at α.

Comment

The inference procedures about the population variance described here are very sensitive to the assumption of a normal population, and the procedures are not robust to departures from normality. ∎

TABLE A.3
Decision Rules
for Tests
Concerning
Variance σ^2
of Normal
Populations.

Alternatives	Decision Rule
	(a)
$H_0: \sigma^2 = \sigma_0^2$	If $\chi^2(\alpha/2; n-1) \leq \dfrac{(n-1)s^2}{\sigma_0^2} \leq \chi^2(1-\alpha/2; n-1)$,
$H_a: \sigma^2 \neq \sigma_0^2$	conclude H_0
	Otherwise conclude H_a
	(b)
$H_0: \sigma^2 \geq \sigma_0^2$	If $\dfrac{(n-1)s^2}{\sigma_0^2} \geq \chi^2(\alpha; n-1)$, conclude H_0
$H_a: \sigma^2 < \sigma_0^2$	If $\dfrac{(n-1)s^2}{\sigma_0^2} < \chi^2(\alpha; n-1)$, conclude H_a
	(c)
$H_0: \sigma^2 \leq \sigma_0^2$	If $\dfrac{(n-1)s^2}{\sigma_0^2} \leq \chi^2(1-\alpha; n-1)$, conclude H_0
$H_a: \sigma^2 > \sigma_0^2$	If $\dfrac{(n-1)s^2}{\sigma_0^2} > \chi^2(1-\alpha; n-1)$, conclude H_a

A.9 Comparisons of Two Population Variances—Normal Populations

Independent samples are selected from two normal populations, with means and variances μ_1 and σ_1^2 and μ_2 and σ_2^2, respectively. Using the notation of Section A.7, the two sample variances are:

$$s_1^2 = \frac{\sum_i (Y_i - \bar{Y})^2}{n_1 - 1} \tag{A.72a}$$

$$s_2^2 = \frac{\sum_i (Z_i - \bar{Z})^2}{n_2 - 1} \tag{A.72b}$$

We have:

$$\frac{s_1^2}{\sigma_1^2} \div \frac{s_2^2}{\sigma_2^2} \text{ is distributed as } F(n_1 - 1, n_2 - 1) \text{ when the two independent} \tag{A.73}$$

samples come from normal populations.

Interval Estimation

The lower and upper confidence limits L and U for σ_1^2/σ_2^2 with confidence coefficient $1 - \alpha$ are obtained by means of (A.73):

$$L = \frac{s_1^2}{s_2^2} \left[\frac{1}{F(1 - \alpha/2; n_1 - 1, n_2 - 1)} \right]$$

$$\tag{A.74}$$

$$U = \frac{s_1^2}{s_2^2} \left[\frac{1}{F(\alpha/2; n_1 - 1, n_2 - 1)} \right]$$

Example 9 Obtain a 90 percent confidence interval for σ_1^2/σ_2^2 when the data are:

$$n_1 = 16 \qquad n_2 = 21 \qquad s_1^2 = 54.2 \qquad s_2^2 = 17.8$$

TABLE A.4
Decision Rules for Tests Concerning Variances σ_1^2 and σ_2^2 of Two Normal Populations—Independent Samples.

Alternatives	Decision Rule
	(a)
$H_0: \sigma_1^2 = \sigma_2^2$	If $F(\alpha/2; n_1 - 1, n_2 - 1) \leq \dfrac{s_1^2}{s_2^2}$
$H_a: \sigma_1^2 \neq \sigma_2^2$	$\leq F(1 - \alpha/2; n_1 - 1, n_2 - 1)$, conclude H_0
	Otherwise conclude H_a
	(b)
$H_0: \sigma_1^2 \geq \sigma_2^2$	If $\dfrac{s_1^2}{s_2^2} \geq F(\alpha; n_1 - 1, n_2 - 1)$, conclude H_0
$H_a: \sigma_1^2 < \sigma_2^2$	If $\dfrac{s_1^2}{s_2^2} < F(\alpha; n_1 - 1, n_2 - 1)$, conclude H_a
	(c)
$H_0: \sigma_1^2 \leq \sigma_2^2$	If $\dfrac{s_1^2}{s_2^2} \leq F(1 - \alpha; n_1 - 1, n_2 - 1)$, conclude H_0
$H_a: \sigma_1^2 > \sigma_2^2$	If $\dfrac{s_1^2}{s_2^2} > F(1 - \alpha; n_1 - 1, n_2 - 1)$, conclude H_a

We require:

$$F(.05; 15, 20) = 1/F(.95; 20, 15) = 1/2.33 = .429$$
$$F(.95; 15, 20) = 2.20$$

The 90 percent confidence interval for σ_1^2/σ_2^2 therefore is:

$$1.4 = \frac{54.2}{17.8}\left(\frac{1}{2.20}\right) \leq \frac{\sigma_1^2}{\sigma_2^2} \leq \frac{54.2}{17.8}\left(\frac{1}{.429}\right) = 7.1$$

Tests

One-sided and two-sided tests concerning σ_1^2/σ_2^2 are constructed by means of (A.73). Table A.4 contains the decision rules for three possible cases, with the risk of making a Type I error controlled at α.

Example 10

Choose between the alternatives:

$$H_0: \sigma_1^2 = \sigma_2^2 \qquad H_a: \sigma_1^2 \neq \sigma_2^2$$

when α is to be controlled at .02 and the data are those of Example 9.
We require:

$$F(.01; 15, 20) = 1/F(.99; 20, 15) = 1/3.37 = .297$$
$$F(.99; 15, 20) = 3.09$$

The decision rule is:

$$\text{If } .297 \leq \frac{s_1^2}{s_2^2} \leq 3.09, \text{ conclude } H_0$$

Otherwise conclude H_a

Since $s_1^2/s_2^2 = 54.2/17.8 = 3.04$, we conclude H_0.

Comment

The inference procedures about the ratio of two population variances described here are very sensitive to the assumption of normal populations, and the procedures are not robust to departures from normality. ∎

Appendix B

Tables

TABLE B.1   Cumulative Probabilities of the Standard Normal Distribution.

Entry is area A under the standard normal curve from $-\infty$ to $z(A)$

z	.00	.01	.02	.03	.04	.05	.06	.07	.08	.09
.0	.5000	.5040	.5080	.5120	.5160	.5199	.5239	.5279	.5319	.5359
.1	.5398	.5438	.5478	.5517	.5557	.5596	.5636	.5675	.5714	.5753
.2	.5793	.5832	.5871	.5910	.5948	.5987	.6026	.6064	.6103	.6141
.3	.6179	.6217	.6255	.6293	.6331	.6368	.6406	.6443	.6480	.6517
.4	.6554	.6591	.6628	.6664	.6700	.6736	.6772	.6808	.6844	.6879
.5	.6915	.6950	.6985	.7019	.7054	.7088	.7123	.7157	.7190	.7224
.6	.7257	.7291	.7324	.7357	.7389	.7422	.7454	.7486	.7517	.7549
.7	.7580	.7611	.7642	.7673	.7704	.7734	.7764	.7794	.7823	.7852
.8	.7881	.7910	.7939	.7967	.7995	.8023	.8051	.8078	.8106	.8133
.9	.8159	.8186	.8212	.8238	.8264	.8289	.8315	.8340	.8365	.8389
1.0	.8413	.8438	.8461	.8485	.8508	.8531	.8554	.8577	.8599	.8621
1.1	.8643	.8665	.8686	.8708	.8729	.8749	.8770	.8790	.8810	.8830
1.2	.8849	.8869	.8888	.8907	.8925	.8944	.8962	.8980	.8997	.9015
1.3	.9032	.9049	.9066	.9082	.9099	.9115	.9131	.9147	.9162	.9177
1.4	.9192	.9207	.9222	.9236	.9251	.9265	.9279	.9292	.9306	.9319
1.5	.9332	.9345	.9357	.9370	.9382	.9394	.9406	.9418	.9429	.9441
1.6	.9452	.9463	.9474	.9484	.9495	.9505	.9515	.9525	.9535	.9545
1.7	.9554	.9564	.9573	.9582	.9591	.9599	.9608	.9616	.9625	.9633
1.8	.9641	.9649	.9656	.9664	.9671	.9678	.9686	.9693	.9699	.9706
1.9	.9713	.9719	.9726	.9732	.9738	.9744	.9750	.9756	.9761	.9767
2.0	.9772	.9778	.9783	.9788	.9793	.9798	.9803	.9808	.9812	.9817
2.1	.9821	.9826	.9830	.9834	.9838	.9842	.9846	.9850	.9854	.9857
2.2	.9861	.9864	.9868	.9871	.9875	.9878	.9881	.9884	.9887	.9890
2.3	.9893	.9896	.9898	.9901	.9904	.9906	.9909	.9911	.9913	.9916
2.4	.9918	.9920	.9922	.9925	.9927	.9929	.9931	.9932	.9934	.9936
2.5	.9938	.9940	.9941	.9943	.9945	.9946	.9948	.9949	.9951	.9952
2.6	.9953	.9955	.9956	.9957	.9959	.9960	.9961	.9962	.9963	.9964
2.7	.9965	.9966	.9967	.9968	.9969	.9970	.9971	.9972	.9973	.9974
2.8	.9974	.9975	.9976	.9977	.9977	.9978	.9979	.9979	.9980	.9981
2.9	.9981	.9982	.9982	.9983	.9984	.9984	.9985	.9985	.9986	.9986
3.0	.9987	.9987	.9987	.9988	.9988	.9989	.9989	.9989	.9990	.9990
3.1	.9990	.9991	.9991	.9991	.9992	.9992	.9992	.9992	.9993	.9993
3.2	.9993	.9993	.9994	.9994	.9994	.9994	.9994	.9995	.9995	.9995
3.3	.9995	.9995	.9995	.9996	.9996	.9996	.9996	.9996	.9996	.9997
3.4	.9997	.9997	.9997	.9997	.9997	.9997	.9997	.9997	.9997	.9998

Selected Percentiles

Cumulative probability A:	.90	.95	.975	.98	.99	.995	.999
$z(A)$:	1.282	1.645	1.960	2.054	2.326	2.576	3.090

TABLE B.2
Percentiles
of the *t*
Distribution.

Entry is $t(A; \nu)$ where $P\{t(\nu) \leq t(A; \nu)\} = A$

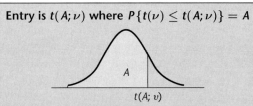

$t(A; \nu)$

				A			
ν	.60	.70	.80	.85	.90	.95	.975
1	0.325	0.727	1.376	1.963	3.078	6.314	12.706
2	0.289	0.617	1.061	1.386	1.886	2.920	4.303
3	0.277	0.584	0.978	1.250	1.638	2.353	3.182
4	0.271	0.569	0.941	1.190	1.533	2.132	2.776
5	0.267	0.559	0.920	1.156	1.476	2.015	2.571
6	0.265	0.553	0.906	1.134	1.440	1.943	2.447
7	0.263	0.549	0.896	1.119	1.415	1.895	2.365
8	0.262	0.546	0.889	1.108	1.397	1.860	2.306
9	0.261	0.543	0.883	1.100	1.383	1.833	2.262
10	0.260	0.542	0.879	1.093	1.372	1.812	2.228
11	0.260	0.540	0.876	1.088	1.363	1.796	2.201
12	0.259	0.539	0.873	1.083	1.356	1.782	2.179
13	0.259	0.537	0.870	1.079	1.350	1.771	2.160
14	0.258	0.537	0.868	1.076	1.345	1.761	2.145
15	0.258	0.536	0.866	1.074	1.341	1.753	2.131
16	0.258	0.535	0.865	1.071	1.337	1.746	2.120
17	0.257	0.534	0.863	1.069	1.333	1.740	2.110
18	0.257	0.534	0.862	1.067	1.330	1.734	2.101
19	0.257	0.533	0.861	1.066	1.328	1.729	2.093
20	0.257	0.533	0.860	1.064	1.325	1.725	2.086
21	0.257	0.532	0.859	1.063	1.323	1.721	2.080
22	0.256	0.532	0.858	1.061	1.321	1.717	2.074
23	0.256	0.532	0.858	1.060	1.319	1.714	2.069
24	0.256	0.531	0.857	1.059	1.318	1.711	2.064
25	0.256	0.531	0.856	1.058	1.316	1.708	2.060
26	0.256	0.531	0.856	1.058	1.315	1.706	2.056
27	0.256	0.531	0.855	1.057	1.314	1.703	2.052
28	0.256	0.530	0.855	1.056	1.313	1.701	2.048
29	0.256	0.530	0.854	1.055	1.311	1.699	2.045
30	0.256	0.530	0.854	1.055	1.310	1.697	2.042
40	0.255	0.529	0.851	1.050	1.303	1.684	2.021
60	0.254	0.527	0.848	1.045	1.296	1.671	2.000
120	0.254	0.526	0.845	1.041	1.289	1.658	1.980
∞	0.253	0.524	0.842	1.036	1.282	1.645	1.960

TABLE B.2
(*concluded*)
**Percentiles
of the *t*
Distribution.**

				A			
ν	.98	.985	.99	.9925	.995	.9975	.9995
1	15.895	21.205	31.821	42.434	63.657	127.322	636.590
2	4.849	5.643	6.965	8.073	9.925	14.089	31.598
3	3.482	3.896	4.541	5.047	5.841	7.453	12.924
4	2.999	3.298	3.747	4.088	4.604	5.598	8.610
5	2.757	3.003	3.365	3.634	4.032	4.773	6.869
6	2.612	2.829	3.143	3.372	3.707	4.317	5.959
7	2.517	2.715	2.998	3.203	3.499	4.029	5.408
8	2.449	2.634	2.896	3.085	3.355	3.833	5.041
9	2.398	2.574	2.821	2.998	3.250	3.690	4.781
10	2.359	2.527	2.764	2.932	3.169	3.581	4.587
11	2.328	2.491	2.718	2.879	3.106	3.497	4.437
12	2.303	2.461	2.681	2.836	3.055	3.428	4.318
13	2.282	2.436	2.650	2.801	3.012	3.372	4.221
14	2.264	2.415	2.624	2.771	2.977	3.326	4.140
15	2.249	2.397	2.602	2.746	2.947	3.286	4.073
16	2.235	2.382	2.583	2.724	2.921	3.252	4.015
17	2.224	2.368	2.567	2.706	2.898	3.222	3.965
18	2.214	2.356	2.552	2.689	2.878	3.197	3.922
19	2.205	2.346	2.539	2.674	2.861	3.174	3.883
20	2.197	2.336	2.528	2.661	2.845	3.153	3.849
21	2.189	2.328	2.518	2.649	2.831	3.135	3.819
22	2.183	2.320	2.508	2.639	2.819	3.119	3.792
23	2.177	2.313	2.500	2.629	2.807	3.104	3.768
24	2.172	2.307	2.492	2.620	2.797	3.091	3.745
25	2.167	2.301	2.485	2.612	2.787	3.078	3.725
26	2.162	2.296	2.479	2.605	2.779	3.067	3.707
27	2.158	2.291	2.473	2.598	2.771	3.057	3.690
28	2.154	2.286	2.467	2.592	2.763	3.047	3.674
29	2.150	2.282	2.462	2.586	2.756	3.038	3.659
30	2.147	2.278	2.457	2.581	2.750	3.030	3.646
40	2.123	2.250	2.423	2.542	2.704	2.971	3.551
60	2.099	2.223	2.390	2.504	2.660	2.915	3.460
120	2.076	2.196	2.358	2.468	2.617	2.860	3.373
∞	2.054	2.170	2.326	2.432	2.576	2.807	3.291

TABLE B.3 Percentiles of the χ^2 Distribution.

Entry is $\chi^2(A; \nu)$ where $P\{\chi^2(\nu) \leq \chi^2(A; \nu)\} = A$

ν	.005	.010	.025	.050	.100	.900	.950	.975	.990	.995
1	0.0^4393	0.0^3157	0.0^3982	0.0^2393	0.0158	2.71	3.84	5.02	6.63	7.88
2	0.0100	0.0201	0.0506	0.103	0.211	4.61	5.99	7.38	9.21	10.60
3	0.072	0.115	0.216	0.352	0.584	6.25	7.81	9.35	11.34	12.84
4	0.207	0.297	0.484	0.711	1.064	7.78	9.49	11.14	13.28	14.86
5	0.412	0.554	0.831	1.145	1.61	9.24	11.07	12.83	15.09	16.75
6	0.676	0.872	1.24	1.64	2.20	10.64	12.59	14.45	16.81	18.55
7	0.989	1.24	1.69	2.17	2.83	12.02	14.07	16.01	18.48	20.28
8	1.34	1.65	2.18	2.73	3.49	13.36	15.51	17.53	20.09	21.96
9	1.73	2.09	2.70	3.33	4.17	14.68	16.92	19.02	21.67	23.59
10	2.16	2.56	3.25	3.94	4.87	15.99	18.31	20.48	23.21	25.19
11	2.60	3.05	3.82	4.57	5.58	17.28	19.68	21.92	24.73	26.76
12	3.07	3.57	4.40	5.23	6.30	18.55	21.03	23.34	26.22	28.30
13	3.57	4.11	5.01	5.89	7.04	19.81	22.36	24.74	27.69	29.82
14	4.07	4.66	5.63	6.57	7.79	21.06	23.68	26.12	29.14	31.32
15	4.60	5.23	6.26	7.26	8.55	22.31	25.00	27.49	30.58	32.80
16	5.14	5.81	6.91	7.96	9.31	23.54	26.30	28.85	32.00	34.27
17	5.70	6.41	7.56	8.67	10.09	24.77	27.59	30.19	33.41	35.72
18	6.26	7.01	8.23	9.39	10.86	25.99	28.87	31.53	34.81	37.16
19	6.84	7.63	8.91	10.12	11.65	27.20	30.14	32.85	36.19	38.58
20	7.43	8.26	9.59	10.85	12.44	28.41	31.41	34.17	37.57	40.00
21	8.03	8.90	10.28	11.59	13.24	29.62	32.67	35.48	38.93	41.40
22	8.64	9.54	10.98	12.34	14.04	30.81	33.92	36.78	40.29	42.80
23	9.26	10.20	11.69	13.09	14.85	32.01	35.17	38.08	41.64	44.18
24	9.89	10.86	12.40	13.85	15.66	33.20	36.42	39.36	42.98	45.56
25	10.52	11.52	13.12	14.61	16.47	34.38	37.65	40.65	44.31	46.93
26	11.16	12.20	13.84	15.38	17.29	35.56	38.89	41.92	45.64	48.29
27	11.81	12.88	14.57	16.15	18.11	36.74	40.11	43.19	46.96	49.64
28	12.46	13.56	15.31	16.93	18.94	37.92	41.34	44.46	48.28	50.99
29	13.12	14.26	16.05	17.71	19.77	39.09	42.56	45.72	49.59	52.34
30	13.79	14.95	16.79	18.49	20.60	40.26	43.77	46.98	50.89	53.67
40	20.71	22.16	24.43	26.51	29.05	51.81	55.76	59.34	63.69	66.77
50	27.99	29.71	32.36	34.76	37.69	63.17	67.50	71.42	76.15	79.49
60	35.53	37.48	40.48	43.19	46.46	74.40	79.08	83.30	88.38	91.95
70	43.28	45.44	48.76	51.74	55.33	85.53	90.53	95.02	100.4	104.2
80	51.17	53.54	57.15	60.39	64.28	96.58	101.9	106.6	112.3	116.3
90	59.20	61.75	65.65	69.13	73.29	107.6	113.1	118.1	124.1	128.3
100	67.33	70.06	74.22	77.93	82.36	118.5	124.3	129.6	135.8	140.2

Source: Reprinted, with permission, from C. M. Thompson, "Table of Percentage Points of the Chi-Square Distribution," *Biometrika* 32 (1941), pp. 188–89.

TABLE B.4   Percentiles of the F Distribution.

Entry is $F(A; \nu_1, \nu_2)$ where $P\{F(\nu_1, \nu_2) \le F(A; \nu_1, \nu_2)\} = A$

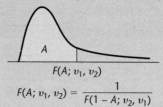

$$F(A; \nu_1, \nu_2)$$

$$F(A; \nu_1, \nu_2) = \frac{1}{F(1 - A; \nu_2, \nu_1)}$$

TABLE B.4 (*continued*) **Percentiles of the *F* Distribution.**

Den. df	A	\multicolumn{9}{c}{Numerator df}
		1	2	3	4	5	6	7	8	9
1	.50	1.00	1.50	1.71	1.82	1.89	1.94	1.98	2.00	2.03
	.90	39.9	49.5	53.6	55.8	57.2	58.2	58.9	59.4	59.9
	.95	161	200	216	225	230	234	237	239	241
	.975	648	800	864	900	922	937	948	957	963
	.99	4,052	5,000	5,403	5,625	5,764	5,859	5,928	5,981	6,022
	.995	16,211	20,000	21,615	22,500	23,056	23,437	23,715	23,925	24,091
	.999	405,280	500,000	540,380	562,500	576,400	585,940	592,870	598,140	602,280
2	.50	0.667	1.00	1.13	1.21	1.25	1.28	1.30	1.32	1.33
	.90	8.53	9.00	9.16	9.24	9.29	9.33	9.35	9.37	9.38
	.95	18.5	19.0	19.2	19.2	19.3	19.3	19.4	19.4	19.4
	.975	38.5	39.0	39.2	39.2	39.3	39.3	39.4	39.4	39.4
	.99	98.5	99.0	99.2	99.2	99.3	99.3	99.4	99.4	99.4
	.995	199	199	199	199	199	199	199	199	199
	.999	998.5	999.0	999.2	999.2	999.3	999.3	999.4	999.4	999.4
3	.50	0.585	0.881	1.00	1.06	1.10	1.13	1.15	1.16	1.17
	.90	5.54	5.46	5.39	5.34	5.31	5.28	5.27	5.25	5.24
	.95	10.1	9.55	9.28	9.12	9.01	8.94	8.89	8.85	8.81
	.975	17.4	16.0	15.4	15.1	14.9	14.7	14.6	14.5	14.5
	.99	34.1	30.8	29.5	28.7	28.2	27.9	27.7	27.5	27.3
	.995	55.6	49.8	47.5	46.2	45.4	44.8	44.4	44.1	43.9
	.999	167.0	148.5	141.1	137.1	134.6	132.8	131.6	130.6	129.9
4	.50	0.549	0.828	0.941	1.00	1.04	1.06	1.08	1.09	1.10
	.90	4.54	4.32	4.19	4.11	4.05	4.01	3.98	3.95	3.94
	.95	7.71	6.94	6.59	6.39	6.26	6.16	6.09	6.04	6.00
	.975	12.2	10.6	9.98	9.60	9.36	9.20	9.07	8.98	8.90
	.99	21.2	18.0	16.7	16.0	15.5	15.2	15.0	14.8	14.7
	.995	31.3	26.3	24.3	23.2	22.5	22.0	21.6	21.4	21.1
	.999	74.1	61.2	56.2	53.4	51.7	50.5	49.7	49.0	48.5
5	.50	0.528	0.799	0.907	0.965	1.00	1.02	1.04	1.05	1.06
	.90	4.06	3.78	3.62	3.52	3.45	3.40	3.37	3.34	3.32
	.95	6.61	5.79	5.41	5.19	5.05	4.95	4.88	4.82	4.77
	.975	10.0	8.43	7.76	7.39	7.15	6.98	6.85	6.76	6.68
	.99	16.3	13.3	12.1	11.4	11.0	10.7	10.5	10.3	10.2
	.995	22.8	18.3	16.5	15.6	14.9	14.5	14.2	14.0	13.8
	.999	47.2	37.1	33.2	31.1	29.8	28.8	28.2	27.6	27.2
6	.50	0.515	0.780	0.886	0.942	0.977	1.00	1.02	1.03	1.04
	.90	3.78	3.46	3.29	3.18	3.11	3.05	3.01	2.98	2.96
	.95	5.99	5.14	4.76	4.53	4.39	4.28	4.21	4.15	4.10
	.975	8.81	7.26	6.60	6.23	5.99	5.82	5.70	5.60	5.52
	.99	13.7	10.9	9.78	9.15	8.75	8.47	8.26	8.10	7.98
	.995	18.6	14.5	12.9	12.0	11.5	11.1	10.8	10.6	10.4
	.999	35.5	27.0	23.7	21.9	20.8	20.0	19.5	19.0	18.7
7	.50	0.506	0.767	0.871	0.926	0.960	0.983	1.00	1.01	1.02
	.90	3.59	3.26	3.07	2.96	2.88	2.83	2.78	2.75	2.72
	.95	5.59	4.74	4.35	4.12	3.97	3.87	3.79	3.73	3.68
	.975	8.07	6.54	5.89	5.52	5.29	5.12	4.99	4.90	4.82
	.99	12.2	9.55	8.45	7.85	7.46	7.19	6.99	6.84	6.72
	.995	16.2	12.4	10.9	10.1	9.52	9.16	8.89	8.68	8.51
	.999	29.2	21.7	18.8	17.2	16.2	15.5	15.0	14.6	14.3

TABLE B.4 (*continued*) **Percentiles of the *F* Distribution.**

Den. df	A	\multicolumn{9}{c}{Numerator df}
		10	12	15	20	24	30	60	120	∞
1	.50	2.04	2.07	2.09	2.12	2.13	2.15	2.17	2.18	2.20
	.90	60.2	60.7	61.2	61.7	62.0	62.3	62.8	63.1	63.3
	.95	242	244	246	248	249	250	252	253	254
	.975	969	977	985	993	997	1,001	1,010	1,014	1,018
	.99	6,056	6,106	6,157	6,209	6,235	6,261	6,313	6,339	6,366
	.995	24,224	24,426	24,630	24,836	24,940	25,044	25,253	25,359	25,464
	.999	605,620	610,670	615,760	620,910	623,500	626,100	631,340	633,970	636,620
2	.50	1.34	1.36	1.38	1.39	1.40	1.41	1.43	1.43	1.44
	.90	9.39	9.41	9.42	9.44	9.45	9.46	9.47	9.48	9.49
	.95	19.4	19.4	19.4	19.4	19.5	19.5	19.5	19.5	19.5
	.975	39.4	39.4	39.4	39.4	39.5	39.5	39.5	39.5	39.5
	.99	99.4	99.4	99.4	99.4	99.5	99.5	99.5	99.5	99.5
	.995	199	199	199	199	199	199	199	199	200
	.999	999.4	999.4	999.4	999.4	999.5	999.5	999.5	999.5	999.5
3	.50	1.18	1.20	1.21	1.23	1.23	1.24	1.25	1.26	1.27
	.90	5.23	5.22	5.20	5.18	5.18	5.17	5.15	5.14	5.13
	.95	8.79	8.74	8.70	8.66	8.64	8.62	8.57	8.55	8.53
	.975	14.4	14.3	14.3	14.2	14.1	14.1	14.0	13.9	13.9
	.99	27.2	27.1	26.9	26.7	26.6	26.5	26.3	26.2	26.1
	.995	43.7	43.4	43.1	42.8	42.6	42.5	42.1	42.0	41.8
	.999	129.2	128.3	127.4	126.4	125.9	125.4	124.5	124.0	123.5
4	.50	1.11	1.13	1.14	1.15	1.16	1.16	1.18	1.18	1.19
	.90	3.92	3.90	3.87	3.84	3.83	3.82	3.79	3.78	3.76
	.95	5.96	5.91	5.86	5.80	5.77	5.75	5.69	5.66	5.63
	.975	8.84	8.75	8.66	8.56	8.51	8.46	8.36	8.31	8.26
	.99	14.5	14.4	14.2	14.0	13.9	13.8	13.7	13.6	13.5
	.995	21.0	20.7	20.4	20.2	20.0	19.9	19.6	19.5	19.3
	.999	48.1	47.4	46.8	46.1	45.8	45.4	44.7	44.4	44.1
5	.50	1.07	1.09	1.10	1.11	1.12	1.12	1.14	1.14	1.15
	.90	3.30	3.27	3.24	3.21	3.19	3.17	3.14	3.12	3.11
	.95	4.74	4.68	4.62	4.56	4.53	4.50	4.43	4.40	4.37
	.975	6.62	6.52	6.43	6.33	6.28	6.23	6.12	6.07	6.02
	.99	10.1	9.89	9.72	9.55	9.47	9.38	9.20	9.11	9.02
	.995	13.6	13.4	13.1	12.9	12.8	12.7	12.4	12.3	12.1
	.999	26.9	26.4	25.9	25.4	25.1	24.9	24.3	24.1	23.8
6	.50	1.05	1.06	1.07	1.08	1.09	1.10	1.11	1.12	1.12
	.90	2.94	2.90	2.87	2.84	2.82	2.80	2.76	2.74	2.72
	.95	4.06	4.00	3.94	3.87	3.84	3.81	3.74	3.70	3.67
	.975	5.46	5.37	5.27	5.17	5.12	5.07	4.96	4.90	4.85
	.99	7.87	7.72	7.56	7.40	7.31	7.23	7.06	6.97	6.88
	.995	10.2	10.0	9.81	9.59	9.47	9.36	9.12	9.00	8.88
	.999	18.4	18.0	17.6	17.1	16.9	16.7	16.2	16.0	15.7
7	.50	1.03	1.04	1.05	1.07	1.07	1.08	1.09	1.10	1.10
	.90	2.70	2.67	2.63	2.59	2.58	2.56	2.51	2.49	2.47
	.95	3.64	3.57	3.51	3.44	3.41	3.38	3.30	3.27	3.23
	.975	4.76	4.67	4.57	4.47	4.42	4.36	4.25	4.20	4.14
	.99	6.62	6.47	6.31	6.16	6.07	5.99	5.82	5.74	5.65
	.995	8.38	8.18	7.97	7.75	7.65	7.53	7.31	7.19	7.08
	.999	14.1	13.7	13.3	12.9	12.7	12.5	12.1	11.9	11.7

TABLE B.4   (*continued*) **Percentiles of the *F* Distribution.**

Den. df	A	Numerator df 1	2	3	4	5	6	7	8	9
8	.50	0.499	0.757	0.860	0.915	0.948	0.971	0.988	1.00	1.01
	.90	3.46	3.11	2.92	2.81	2.73	2.67	2.62	2.59	2.56
	.95	5.32	4.46	4.07	3.84	3.69	3.58	3.50	3.44	3.39
	.975	7.57	6.06	5.42	5.05	4.82	4.65	4.53	4.43	4.36
	.99	11.3	8.65	7.59	7.01	6.63	6.37	6.18	6.03	5.91
	.995	14.7	11.0	9.60	8.81	8.30	7.95	7.69	7.50	7.34
	.999	25.4	18.5	15.8	14.4	13.5	12.9	12.4	12.0	11.8
9	.50	0.494	0.749	0.852	0.906	0.939	0.962	0.978	0.990	1.00
	.90	3.36	3.01	2.81	2.69	2.61	2.55	2.51	2.47	2.44
	.95	5.12	4.26	3.86	3.63	3.48	3.37	3.29	3.23	3.18
	.975	7.21	5.71	5.08	4.72	4.48	4.32	4.20	4.10	4.03
	.99	10.6	8.02	6.99	6.42	6.06	5.80	5.61	5.47	5.35
	.995	13.6	10.1	8.72	7.96	7.47	7.13	6.88	6.69	6.54
	.999	22.9	16.4	13.9	12.6	11.7	11.1	10.7	10.4	10.1
10	.50	0.490	0.743	0.845	0.899	0.932	0.954	0.971	0.983	0.992
	.90	3.29	2.92	2.73	2.61	2.52	2.46	2.41	2.38	2.35
	.95	4.96	4.10	3.71	3.48	3.33	3.22	3.14	3.07	3.02
	.975	6.94	5.46	4.83	4.47	4.24	4.07	3.95	3.85	3.78
	.99	10.0	7.56	6.55	5.99	5.64	5.39	5.20	5.06	4.94
	.995	12.8	9.43	8.08	7.34	6.87	6.54	6.30	6.12	5.97
	.999	21.0	14.9	12.6	11.3	10.5	9.93	9.52	9.20	8.96
12	.50	0.484	0.735	0.835	0.888	0.921	0.943	0.959	0.972	0.981
	.90	3.18	2.81	2.61	2.48	2.39	2.33	2.28	2.24	2.21
	.95	4.75	3.89	3.49	3.26	3.11	3.00	2.91	2.85	2.80
	.975	6.55	5.10	4.47	4.12	3.89	3.73	3.61	3.51	3.44
	.99	9.33	6.93	5.95	5.41	5.06	4.82	4.64	4.50	4.39
	.995	11.8	8.51	7.23	6.52	6.07	5.76	5.52	5.35	5.20
	.999	18.6	13.0	10.8	9.63	8.89	8.38	8.00	7.71	7.48
15	.50	0.478	0.726	0.826	0.878	0.911	0.933	0.949	0.960	0.970
	.90	3.07	2.70	2.49	2.36	2.27	2.21	2.16	2.12	2.09
	.95	4.54	3.68	3.29	3.06	2.90	2.79	2.71	2.64	2.59
	.975	6.20	4.77	4.15	3.80	3.58	3.41	3.29	3.20	3.12
	.99	8.68	6.36	5.42	4.89	4.56	4.32	4.14	4.00	3.89
	.995	10.8	7.70	6.48	5.80	5.37	5.07	4.85	4.67	4.54
	.999	16.6	11.3	9.34	8.25	7.57	7.09	6.74	6.47	6.26
20	.50	0.472	0.718	0.816	0.868	0.900	0.922	0.938	0.950	0.959
	.90	2.97	2.59	2.38	2.25	2.16	2.09	2.04	2.00	1.96
	.95	4.35	3.49	3.10	2.87	2.71	2.60	2.51	2.45	2.39
	.975	5.87	4.46	3.86	3.51	3.29	3.13	3.01	2.91	2.84
	.99	8.10	5.85	4.94	4.43	4.10	3.87	3.70	3.56	3.46
	.995	9.94	6.99	5.82	5.17	4.76	4.47	4.26	4.09	3.96
	.999	14.8	9.95	8.10	7.10	6.46	6.02	5.69	5.44	5.24
24	.50	0.469	0.714	0.812	0.863	0.895	0.917	0.932	0.944	0.953
	.90	2.93	2.54	2.33	2.19	2.10	2.04	1.98	1.94	1.91
	.95	4.26	3.40	3.01	2.78	2.62	2.51	2.42	2.36	2.30
	.975	5.72	4.32	3.72	3.38	3.15	2.99	2.87	2.78	2.70
	.99	7.82	5.61	4.72	4.22	3.90	3.67	3.50	3.36	3.26
	.995	9.55	6.66	5.52	4.89	4.49	4.20	3.99	3.83	3.69
	.999	14.0	9.34	7.55	6.59	5.98	5.55	5.23	4.99	4.80

TABLE B.4 *(continued)* **Percentiles of the *F* Distribution.**

Den. df	A	Numerator df								
		10	**12**	**15**	**20**	**24**	**30**	**60**	**120**	**∞**
8	.50	1.02	1.03	1.04	1.05	1.06	1.07	1.08	1.08	1.09
	.90	2.54	2.50	2.46	2.42	2.40	2.38	2.34	2.32	2.29
	.95	3.35	3.28	3.22	3.15	3.12	3.08	3.01	2.97	2.93
	.975	4.30	4.20	4.10	4.00	3.95	3.89	3.78	3.73	3.67
	.99	5.81	5.67	5.52	5.36	5.28	5.20	5.03	4.95	4.86
	.995	7.21	7.01	6.81	6.61	6.50	6.40	6.18	6.06	5.95
	.999	11.5	11.2	10.8	10.5	10.3	10.1	9.73	9.53	9.33
9	.50	1.01	1.02	1.03	1.04	1.05	1.05	1.07	1.07	1.08
	.90	2.42	2.38	2.34	2.30	2.28	2.25	2.21	2.18	2.16
	.95	3.14	3.07	3.01	2.94	2.90	2.86	2.79	2.75	2.71
	.975	3.96	3.87	3.77	3.67	3.61	3.56	3.45	3.39	3.33
	.99	5.26	5.11	4.96	4.81	4.73	4.65	4.48	4.40	4.31
	.995	6.42	6.23	6.03	5.83	5.73	5.62	5.41	5.30	5.19
	.999	9.89	9.57	9.24	8.90	8.72	8.55	8.19	8.00	7.81
10	.50	1.00	1.01	1.02	1.03	1.04	1.05	1.06	1.06	1.07
	.90	2.32	2.28	2.24	2.20	2.18	2.16	2.11	2.08	2.06
	.95	2.98	2.91	2.84	2.77	2.74	2.70	2.62	2.58	2.54
	.975	3.72	3.62	3.52	3.42	3.37	3.31	3.20	3.14	3.08
	.99	4.85	4.71	4.56	4.41	4.33	4.25	4.08	4.00	3.91
	.995	5.85	5.66	5.47	5.27	5.17	5.07	4.86	4.75	4.64
	.999	8.75	8.45	8.13	7.80	7.64	7.47	7.12	6.94	6.76
12	.50	0.989	1.00	1.01	1.02	1.03	1.03	1.05	1.05	1.06
	.90	2.19	2.15	2.10	2.06	2.04	2.01	1.96	1.93	1.90
	.95	2.75	2.69	2.62	2.54	2.51	2.47	2.38	2.34	2.30
	.975	3.37	3.28	3.18	3.07	3.02	2.96	2.85	2.79	2.72
	.99	4.30	4.16	4.01	3.86	3.78	3.70	3.54	3.45	3.36
	.995	5.09	4.91	4.72	4.53	4.43	4.33	4.12	4.01	3.90
	.999	7.29	7.00	6.71	6.40	6.25	6.09	5.76	5.59	5.42
15	.50	0.977	0.989	1.00	1.01	1.02	1.02	1.03	1.04	1.05
	.90	2.06	2.02	1.97	1.92	1.90	1.87	1.82	1.79	1.76
	.95	2.54	2.48	2.40	2.33	2.29	2.25	2.16	2.11	2.07
	.975	3.06	2.96	2.86	2.76	2.70	2.64	2.52	2.46	2.40
	.99	3.80	3.67	3.52	3.37	3.29	3.21	3.05	2.96	2.87
	.995	4.42	4.25	4.07	3.88	3.79	3.69	3.48	3.37	3.26
	.999	6.08	5.81	5.54	5.25	5.10	4.95	4.64	4.48	4.31
20	.50	0.966	0.977	0.989	1.00	1.01	1.01	1.02	1.03	1.03
	.90	1.94	1.89	1.84	1.79	1.77	1.74	1.68	1.64	1.61
	.95	2.35	2.28	2.20	2.12	2.08	2.04	1.95	1.90	1.84
	.975	2.77	2.68	2.57	2.46	2.41	2.35	2.22	2.16	2.09
	.99	3.37	3.23	3.09	2.94	2.86	2.78	2.61	2.52	2.42
	.995	3.85	3.68	3.50	3.32	3.22	3.12	2.92	2.81	2.69
	.999	5.08	4.82	4.56	4.29	4.15	4.00	3.70	3.54	3.38
24	.50	0.961	0.972	0.983	0.994	1.00	1.01	1.02	1.02	1.03
	.90	1.88	1.83	1.78	1.73	1.70	1.67	1.61	1.57	1.53
	.95	2.25	2.18	2.11	2.03	1.98	1.94	1.84	1.79	1.73
	.975	2.64	2.54	2.44	2.33	2.27	2.21	2.08	2.01	1.94
	.99	3.17	3.03	2.89	2.74	2.66	2.58	2.40	2.31	2.21
	.995	3.59	3.42	3.25	3.06	2.97	2.87	2.66	2.55	2.43
	.999	4.64	4.39	4.14	3.87	3.74	3.59	3.29	3.14	2.97

TABLE B.4 (*continued*) **Percentiles of the *F* Distribution.**

Den. df	A	\multicolumn{9}{c}{Numerator df}								
		1	2	3	4	5	6	7	8	9
30	.50	0.466	0.709	0.807	0.858	0.890	0.912	0.927	0.939	0.948
	.90	2.88	2.49	2.28	2.14	2.05	1.98	1.93	1.88	1.85
	.95	4.17	3.32	2.92	2.69	2.53	2.42	2.33	2.27	2.21
	.975	5.57	4.18	3.59	3.25	3.03	2.87	2.75	2.65	2.57
	.99	7.56	5.39	4.51	4.02	3.70	3.47	3.30	3.17	3.07
	.995	9.18	6.35	5.24	4.62	4.23	3.95	3.74	3.58	3.45
	.999	13.3	8.77	7.05	6.12	5.53	5.12	4.82	4.58	4.39
60	.50	0.461	0.701	0.798	0.849	0.880	0.901	0.917	0.928	0.937
	.90	2.79	2.39	2.18	2.04	1.95	1.87	1.82	1.77	1.74
	.95	4.00	3.15	2.76	2.53	2.37	2.25	2.17	2.10	2.04
	.975	5.29	3.93	3.34	3.01	2.79	2.63	2.51	2.41	2.33
	.99	7.08	4.98	4.13	3.65	3.34	3.12	2.95	2.82	2.72
	.995	8.49	5.80	4.73	4.14	3.76	3.49	3.29	3.13	3.01
	.999	12.0	7.77	6.17	5.31	4.76	4.37	4.09	3.86	3.69
120	.50	0.458	0.697	0.793	0.844	0.875	0.896	0.912	0.923	0.932
	.90	2.75	2.35	2.13	1.99	1.90	1.82	1.77	1.72	1.68
	.95	3.92	3.07	2.68	2.45	2.29	2.18	2.09	2.02	1.96
	.975	5.15	3.80	3.23	2.89	2.67	2.52	2.39	2.30	2.22
	.99	6.85	4.79	3.95	3.48	3.17	2.96	2.79	2.66	2.56
	.995	8.18	5.54	4.50	3.92	3.55	3.28	3.09	2.93	2.81
	.999	11.4	7.32	5.78	4.95	4.42	4.04	3.77	3.55	3.38
∞	.50	0.455	0.693	0.789	0.839	0.870	0.891	0.907	0.918	0.927
	.90	2.71	2.30	2.08	1.94	1.85	1.77	1.72	1.67	1.63
	.95	3.84	3.00	2.60	2.37	2.21	2.10	2.01	1.94	1.88
	.975	5.02	3.69	3.12	2.79	2.57	2.41	2.29	2.19	2.11
	.99	6.63	4.61	3.78	3.32	3.02	2.80	2.64	2.51	2.41
	.995	7.88	5.30	4.28	3.72	3.35	3.09	2.90	2.74	2.62
	.999	10.8	6.91	5.42	4.62	4.10	3.74	3.47	3.27	3.10

TABLE B.4 *(concluded)* **Percentiles of the *F* Distribution.**

Den. df	A	\multicolumn{9}{c}{Numerator df}								
		10	12	15	20	24	30	60	120	∞
30	.50	0.955	0.966	0.978	0.989	0.994	1.00	1.01	1.02	1.02
	.90	1.82	1.77	1.72	1.67	1.64	1.61	1.54	1.50	1.46
	.95	2.16	2.09	2.01	1.93	1.89	1.84	1.74	1.68	1.62
	.975	2.51	2.41	2.31	2.20	2.14	2.07	1.94	1.87	1.79
	.99	2.98	2.84	2.70	2.55	2.47	2.39	2.21	2.11	2.01
	.995	3.34	3.18	3.01	2.82	2.73	2.63	2.42	2.30	2.18
	.999	4.24	4.00	3.75	3.49	3.36	3.22	2.92	2.76	2.59
60	.50	0.945	0.956	0.967	0.978	0.983	0.989	1.00	1.01	1.01
	.90	1.71	1.66	1.60	1.54	1.51	1.48	1.40	1.35	1.29
	.95	1.99	1.92	1.84	1.75	1.70	1.65	1.53	1.47	1.39
	.975	2.27	2.17	2.06	1.94	1.88	1.82	1.67	1.58	1.48
	.99	2.63	2.50	2.35	2.20	2.12	2.03	1.84	1.73	1.60
	.995	2.90	2.74	2.57	2.39	2.29	2.19	1.96	1.83	1.69
	.999	3.54	3.32	3.08	2.83	2.69	2.55	2.25	2.08	1.89
120	.50	0.939	0.950	0.961	0.972	0.978	0.983	0.994	1.00	1.01
	.90	1.65	1.60	1.55	1.48	1.45	1.41	1.32	1.26	1.19
	.95	1.91	1.83	1.75	1.66	1.61	1.55	1.43	1.35	1.25
	.975	2.16	2.05	1.95	1.82	1.76	1.69	1.53	1.43	1.31
	.99	2.47	2.34	2.19	2.03	1.95	1.86	1.66	1.53	1.38
	.995	2.71	2.54	2.37	2.19	2.09	1.98	1.75	1.61	1.43
	.999	3.24	3.02	2.78	2.53	2.40	2.26	1.95	1.77	1.54
∞	.50	0.934	0.945	0.956	0.967	0.972	0.978	0.989	0.994	1.00
	.90	1.60	1.55	1.49	1.42	1.38	1.34	1.24	1.17	1.00
	.95	1.83	1.75	1.67	1.57	1.52	1.46	1.32	1.22	1.00
	.975	2.05	1.94	1.83	1.71	1.64	1.57	1.39	1.27	1.00
	.99	2.32	2.18	2.04	1.88	1.79	1.70	1.47	1.32	1.00
	.995	2.52	2.36	2.19	2.00	1.90	1.79	1.53	1.36	1.00
	.999	2.96	2.74	2.51	2.27	2.13	1.99	1.66	1.45	1.00

Source: Reprinted from Table 5 of Pearson and Hartley, *Biometrika Tables for Statisticians,* Volume 2, 1972, published by the Cambridge University Press, on behalf of The Biometrika Society, by permission of the authors and publishers.

TABLE B.5
Power Values
for Two-Sided
t **Test.**

	$\alpha = .05$								
	δ								
df	1.0	2.0	3.0	4.0	5.0	6.0	7.0	8.0	9.0
1	.07	.13	.19	.25	.31	.36	.42	.47	.52
2	.10	.22	.39	.56	.72	.84	.91	.96	.98
3	.11	.29	.53	.75	.90	.97	.99	1.00	1.00
4	.12	.34	.62	.84	.95	.99	1.00	1.00	1.00
5	.13	.37	.67	.89	.98	1.00	1.00	1.00	1.00
6	.14	.39	.71	.91	.98	1.00	1.00	1.00	1.00
7	.14	.41	.73	.93	.99	1.00	1.00	1.00	1.00
8	.14	.42	.75	.94	.99	1.00	1.00	1.00	1.00
9	.15	.43	.76	.94	.99	1.00	1.00	1.00	1.00
10	.15	.44	.77	.95	.99	1.00	1.00	1.00	1.00
11	.15	.45	.78	.95	.99	1.00	1.00	1.00	1.00
12	.15	.45	.79	.96	1.00	1.00	1.00	1.00	1.00
13	.15	.46	.79	.96	1.00	1.00	1.00	1.00	1.00
14	.15	.46	.80	.96	1.00	1.00	1.00	1.00	1.00
15	.16	.46	.80	.96	1.00	1.00	1.00	1.00	1.00
16	.16	.47	.80	.96	1.00	1.00	1.00	1.00	1.00
17	.16	.47	.81	.96	1.00	1.00	1.00	1.00	1.00
18	.16	.47	.81	.97	1.00	1.00	1.00	1.00	1.00
19	.16	.48	.81	.97	1.00	1.00	1.00	1.00	1.00
20	.16	.48	.81	.97	1.00	1.00	1.00	1.00	1.00
21	.16	.48	.82	.97	1.00	1.00	1.00	1.00	1.00
22	.16	.48	.82	.97	1.00	1.00	1.00	1.00	1.00
23	.16	.48	.82	.97	1.00	1.00	1.00	1.00	1.00
24	.16	.48	.82	.97	1.00	1.00	1.00	1.00	1.00
25	.16	.49	.82	.97	1.00	1.00	1.00	1.00	1.00
26	.16	.49	.82	.97	1.00	1.00	1.00	1.00	1.00
27	.16	.49	.82	.97	1.00	1.00	1.00	1.00	1.00
28	.16	.49	.83	.97	1.00	1.00	1.00	1.00	1.00
29	.16	.49	.83	.97	1.00	1.00	1.00	1.00	1.00
30	.16	.49	.83	.97	1.00	1.00	1.00	1.00	1.00
40	.16	.50	.83	.97	1.00	1.00	1.00	1.00	1.00
50	.17	.50	.84	.98	1.00	1.00	1.00	1.00	1.00
60	.17	.50	.84	.98	1.00	1.00	1.00	1.00	1.00
100	.17	.51	.84	.98	1.00	1.00	1.00	1.00	1.00
120	.17	.51	.85	.98	1.00	1.00	1.00	1.00	1.00
∞	.17	.52	.85	.98	1.00	1.00	1.00	1.00	1.00

TABLE B.5
(*concluded*)
**Power Values
for Two-Sided
t Test.**

					$\alpha = .01$				
					δ				
df	1.0	2.0	3.0	4.0	5.0	6.0	7.0	8.0	9.0
1	.01	.03	.04	.05	.06	.08	.09	.10	.11
2	.02	.05	.09	.16	.23	.31	.39	.48	.56
3	.02	.08	.17	.31	.47	.62	.75	.85	.92
4	.03	.10	.25	.45	.65	.82	.92	.97	.99
5	.03	.12	.31	.55	.77	.91	.97	.99	1.00
6	.04	.14	.36	.63	.84	.95	.99	1.00	1.00
7	.04	.16	.40	.68	.88	.97	1.00	1.00	1.00
8	.04	.17	.43	.72	.91	.98	1.00	1.00	1.00
9	.04	.18	.45	.75	.93	.99	1.00	1.00	1.00
10	.04	.19	.47	.77	.94	.99	1.00	1.00	1.00
11	.04	.19	.49	.79	.95	.99	1.00	1.00	1.00
12	.04	.20	.50	.80	.96	.99	1.00	1.00	1.00
13	.05	.21	.52	.82	.96	1.00	1.00	1.00	1.00
14	.05	.21	.53	.83	.96	1.00	1.00	1.00	1.00
15	.05	.21	.54	.83	.97	1.00	1.00	1.00	1.00
16	.05	.22	.55	.84	.97	1.00	1.00	1.00	1.00
17	.05	.22	.55	.85	.97	1.00	1.00	1.00	1.00
18	.05	.22	.56	.85	.97	1.00	1.00	1.00	1.00
19	.05	.23	.56	.86	.98	1.00	1.00	1.00	1.00
20	.05	.23	.57	.86	.98	1.00	1.00	1.00	1.00
21	.05	.23	.57	.86	.98	1.00	1.00	1.00	1.00
22	.05	.23	.58	.87	.98	1.00	1.00	1.00	1.00
23	.05	.24	.58	.87	.98	1.00	1.00	1.00	1.00
24	.05	.24	.59	.87	.98	1.00	1.00	1.00	1.00
25	.05	.24	.59	.88	.98	1.00	1.00	1.00	1.00
26	.05	.24	.59	.88	.98	1.00	1.00	1.00	1.00
27	.05	.24	.59	.88	.98	1.00	1.00	1.00	1.00
28	.05	.24	.60	.88	.98	1.00	1.00	1.00	1.00
29	.05	.25	.60	.88	.98	1.00	1.00	1.00	1.00
30	.05	.25	.60	.88	.98	1.00	1.00	1.00	1.00
40	.05	.26	.62	.90	.99	1.00	1.00	1.00	1.00
50	.05	.26	.63	.90	.99	1.00	1.00	1.00	1.00
60	.05	.26	.63	.91	.99	1.00	1.00	1.00	1.00
100	.06	.27	.65	.91	.99	1.00	1.00	1.00	1.00
120	.06	.27	.65	.91	.99	1.00	1.00	1.00	1.00
∞	.06	.28	.66	.92	.99	1.00	1.00	1.00	1.00

TABLE B.6
Critical Values
for Coefficient
of Correlation
between
Ordered
Residuals and
Expected
Values under
Normality
when
Distribution of
Error Terms
Is Normal.

| | | Level of Significance α | | | |
n	.10	.05	.025	.01	.005
5	.903	.880	.865	.826	.807
6	.910	.888	.866	.838	.820
7	.918	.898	.877	.850	.828
8	.924	.906	.887	.861	.840
9	.930	.912	.894	.871	.854
10	.934	.918	.901	.879	.862
12	.942	.928	.912	.892	.876
14	.948	.935	.923	.905	.890
16	.953	.941	.929	.913	.899
18	.957	.946	.935	.920	.908
20	.960	.951	.940	.926	.916
22	.963	.954	.945	.933	.923
24	.965	.957	.949	.937	.927
26	.967	.960	.952	.941	.932
28	.969	.962	.955	.944	.936
30	.971	.964	.957	.947	.939
40	.977	.972	.966	.959	.953
50	.981	.977	.972	.966	.961
60	.984	.980	.976	.971	.967
70	.986	.983	.979	.975	.971
80	.987	.985	.982	.978	.975
90	.988	.986	.984	.980	.977
100	.989	.987	.985	.982	.979

Source: Reprinted, with permission, from S. W. Looney and T. R. Gulledge, Jr., "Use of the Correlation Coefficient with Normal Probability Plots," *The American Statistician* 39 (1985), pp. 75–79.

TABLE B.7
Durbin-Watson
Test Bounds.

	Level of Significance $\alpha = .05$									
	$p-1=1$		$p-1=2$		$p-1=3$		$p-1=4$		$p-1=5$	
n	d_L	d_U	d_L	d_U	d_L	d_U	d_L	d_U	d_L	d_U
15	1.08	1.36	0.95	1.54	0.82	1.75	0.69	1.97	0.56	2.21
16	1.10	1.37	0.98	1.54	0.86	1.73	0.74	1.93	0.62	2.15
17	1.13	1.38	1.02	1.54	0.90	1.71	0.78	1.90	0.67	2.10
18	1.16	1.39	1.05	1.53	0.93	1.69	0.82	1.87	0.71	2.06
19	1.18	1.40	1.08	1.53	0.97	1.68	0.86	1.85	0.75	2.02
20	1.20	1.41	1.10	1.54	1.00	1.68	0.90	1.83	0.79	1.99
21	1.22	1.42	1.13	1.54	1.03	1.67	0.93	1.81	0.83	1.96
22	1.24	1.43	1.15	1.54	1.05	1.66	0.96	1.80	0.86	1.94
23	1.26	1.44	1.17	1.54	1.08	1.66	0.99	1.79	0.90	1.92
24	1.27	1.45	1.19	1.55	1.10	1.66	1.01	1.78	0.93	1.90
25	1.29	1.45	1.21	1.55	1.12	1.66	1.04	1.77	0.95	1.89
26	1.30	1.46	1.22	1.55	1.14	1.65	1.06	1.76	0.98	1.88
27	1.32	1.47	1.24	1.56	1.16	1.65	1.08	1.76	1.01	1.86
28	1.33	1.48	1.26	1.56	1.18	1.65	1.10	1.75	1.03	1.85
29	1.34	1.48	1.27	1.56	1.20	1.65	1.12	1.74	1.05	1.84
30	1.35	1.49	1.28	1.57	1.21	1.65	1.14	1.74	1.07	1.83
31	1.36	1.50	1.30	1.57	1.23	1.65	1.16	1.74	1.09	1.83
32	1.37	1.50	1.31	1.57	1.24	1.65	1.18	1.73	1.11	1.82
33	1.38	1.51	1.32	1.58	1.26	1.65	1.19	1.73	1.13	1.81
34	1.39	1.51	1.33	1.58	1.27	1.65	1.21	1.73	1.15	1.81
35	1.40	1.52	1.34	1.58	1.28	1.65	1.22	1.73	1.16	1.80
36	1.41	1.52	1.35	1.59	1.29	1.65	1.24	1.73	1.18	1.80
37	1.42	1.53	1.36	1.59	1.31	1.66	1.25	1.72	1.19	1.80
38	1.43	1.54	1.37	1.59	1.32	1.66	1.26	1.72	1.21	1.79
39	1.43	1.54	1.38	1.60	1.33	1.66	1.27	1.72	1.22	1.79
40	1.44	1.54	1.39	1.60	1.34	1.66	1.29	1.72	1.23	1.79
45	1.48	1.57	1.43	1.62	1.38	1.67	1.34	1.72	1.29	1.78
50	1.50	1.59	1.46	1.63	1.42	1.67	1.38	1.72	1.34	1.77
55	1.53	1.60	1.49	1.64	1.45	1.68	1.41	1.72	1.38	1.77
60	1.55	1.62	1.51	1.65	1.48	1.69	1.44	1.73	1.41	1.77
65	1.57	1.63	1.54	1.66	1.50	1.70	1.47	1.73	1.44	1.77
70	1.58	1.64	1.55	1.67	1.52	1.70	1.49	1.74	1.46	1.77
75	1.60	1.65	1.57	1.68	1.54	1.71	1.51	1.74	1.49	1.77
80	1.61	1.66	1.59	1.69	1.56	1.72	1.53	1.74	1.51	1.77
85	1.62	1.67	1.60	1.70	1.57	1.72	1.55	1.75	1.52	1.77
90	1.63	1.68	1.61	1.70	1.59	1.73	1.57	1.75	1.54	1.78
95	1.64	1.69	1.62	1.71	1.60	1.73	1.58	1.75	1.56	1.78
100	1.65	1.69	1.63	1.72	1.61	1.74	1.59	1.76	1.57	1.78

TABLE B.7
(*concluded*)
**Durbin-Watson
Test Bounds.**

	Level of Significance $\alpha = .01$									
	$p-1=1$		$p-1=2$		$p-1=3$		$p-1=4$		$p-1=5$	
n	d_L	d_U	d_L	d_U	d_L	d_U	d_L	d_U	d_L	d_U
15	0.81	1.07	0.70	1.25	0.59	1.46	0.49	1.70	0.39	1.96
16	0.84	1.09	0.74	1.25	0.63	1.44	0.53	1.66	0.44	1.90
17	0.87	1.10	0.77	1.25	0.67	1.43	0.57	1.63	0.48	1.85
18	0.90	1.12	0.80	1.26	0.71	1.42	0.61	1.60	0.52	1.80
19	0.93	1.13	0.83	1.26	0.74	1.41	0.65	1.58	0.56	1.77
20	0.95	1.15	0.86	1.27	0.77	1.41	0.68	1.57	0.60	1.74
21	0.97	1.16	0.89	1.27	0.80	1.41	0.72	1.55	0.63	1.71
22	1.00	1.17	0.91	1.28	0.83	1.40	0.75	1.54	0.66	1.69
23	1.02	1.19	0.94	1.29	0.86	1.40	0.77	1.53	0.70	1.67
24	1.04	1.20	0.96	1.30	0.88	1.41	0.80	1.53	0.72	1.66
25	1.05	1.21	0.98	1.30	0.90	1.41	0.83	1.52	0.75	1.65
26	1.07	1.22	1.00	1.31	0.93	1.41	0.85	1.52	0.78	1.64
27	1.09	1.23	1.02	1.32	0.95	1.41	0.88	1.51	0.81	1.63
28	1.10	1.24	1.04	1.32	0.97	1.41	0.90	1.51	0.83	1.62
29	1.12	1.25	1.05	1.33	0.99	1.42	0.92	1.51	0.85	1.61
30	1.13	1.26	1.07	1.34	1.01	1.42	0.94	1.51	0.88	1.61
31	1.15	1.27	1.08	1.34	1.02	1.42	0.96	1.51	0.90	1.60
32	1.16	1.28	1.10	1.35	1.04	1.43	0.98	1.51	0.92	1.60
33	1.17	1.29	1.11	1.36	1.05	1.43	1.00	1.51	0.94	1.59
34	1.18	1.30	1.13	1.36	1.07	1.43	1.01	1.51	0.95	1.59
35	1.19	1.31	1.14	1.37	1.08	1.44	1.03	1.51	0.97	1.59
36	1.21	1.32	1.15	1.38	1.10	1.44	1.04	1.51	0.99	1.59
37	1.22	1.32	1.16	1.38	1.11	1.45	1.06	1.51	1.00	1.59
38	1.23	1.33	1.18	1.39	1.12	1.45	1.07	1.52	1.02	1.58
39	1.24	1.34	1.19	1.39	1.14	1.45	1.09	1.52	1.03	1.58
40	1.25	1.34	1.20	1.40	1.15	1.46	1.10	1.52	1.05	1.58
45	1.29	1.38	1.24	1.42	1.20	1.48	1.16	1.53	1.11	1.58
50	1.32	1.40	1.28	1.45	1.24	1.49	1.20	1.54	1.16	1.59
55	1.36	1.43	1.32	1.47	1.28	1.51	1.25	1.55	1.21	1.59
60	1.38	1.45	1.35	1.48	1.32	1.52	1.28	1.56	1.25	1.60
65	1.41	1.47	1.38	1.50	1.35	1.53	1.31	1.57	1.28	1.61
70	1.43	1.49	1.40	1.52	1.37	1.55	1.34	1.58	1.31	1.61
75	1.45	1.50	1.42	1.53	1.39	1.56	1.37	1.59	1.34	1.62
80	1.47	1.52	1.44	1.54	1.42	1.57	1.39	1.60	1.36	1.62
85	1.48	1.53	1.46	1.55	1.43	1.58	1.41	1.60	1.39	1.63
90	1.50	1.54	1.47	1.56	1.45	1.59	1.43	1.61	1.41	1.64
95	1.51	1.55	1.49	1.57	1.47	1.60	1.45	1.62	1.42	1.64
100	1.52	1.56	1.50	1.58	1.48	1.60	1.46	1.63	1.44	1.65

Source: Reprinted, with permission, from J. Durbin and G. S. Watson, "Testing for Serial Correlation in Least Squares Regression. II," *Biometrika* 38 (1951), pp. 159–78.

TABLE B.8
Table of z'
Transformation of
Correlation
Coefficient.

r ρ	z' ζ	r ρ	z' ζ	r ρ	z' ζ	r ρ	z' ζ
.00	.0000	.25	.2554	.50	.5493	.75	.973
.01	.0100	.26	.2661	.51	.5627	.76	.996
.02	.0200	.27	.2769	.52	.5763	.77	1.020
.03	.0300	.28	.2877	.53	.5901	.78	1.045
.04	.0400	.29	.2986	.54	.6042	.79	1.071
.05	.0500	.30	.3095	.55	.6184	.80	1.099
.06	.0601	.31	.3205	.56	.6328	.81	1.127
.07	.0701	.32	.3316	.57	.6475	.82	1.157
.08	.0802	.33	.3428	.58	.6625	.83	1.188
.09	.0902	.34	.3541	.59	.6777	.84	1.221
.10	.1003	.35	.3654	.60	.6931	.85	1.256
.11	.1104	.36	.3769	.61	.7089	.86	1.293
.12	.1206	.37	.3884	.62	.7250	.87	1.333
.13	.1307	.38	.4001	.63	.7414	.88	1.376
.14	.1409	.39	.4118	.64	.7582	.89	1.422
.15	.1511	.40	.4236	.65	.7753	.90	1.472
.16	.1614	.41	.4356	.66	.7928	.91	1.528
.17	.1717	.42	.4477	.67	.8107	.92	1.589
.18	.1820	.43	.4599	.68	.8291	.93	1.658
.19	.1923	.44	.4722	.69	.8480	.94	1.738
.20	.2027	.45	.4847	.70	.8673	.95	1.832
.21	.2132	.46	.4973	.71	.8872	.96	1.946
.22	.2237	.47	.5101	.72	.9076	.97	2.092
.23	.2342	.48	.5230	.73	.9287	.98	2.298
.24	.2448	.49	.5361	.74	.9505	.99	2.647

Source: Abridged from Table 14 of Pearson and Hartley, *Biometrika Tables for Statisticians,* Volume 1, 1966, published by the Cambridge University Press, on behalf of The Biometrika Society, by permission of the authors and publishers.

Appendix C

Data Sets

Data Set C.1   SENIC

The primary objective of the Study on the Efficacy of Nosocomial Infection Control (**SENIC** Project) was to determine whether infection surveillance and control programs have reduced the rates of nosocomial (hospital-acquired) infection in United States hospitals. This data set consists of a random sample of 113 hospitals selected from the original 338 hospitals surveyed.

Each line of the data set has an identification number and provides information on 11 other variables for a single hospital. The data presented here are for the 1975–76 study period. The 12 variables are:

Variable Number	Variable Name	Description
1	Identification number	1–113
2	Length of stay	Average length of stay of all patients in hospital (in days)
3	Age	Average age of patients (in years)
4	Infection risk	Average estimated probability of acquiring infection in hospital (in percent)
5	Routine culturing ratio	Ratio of number of cultures performed to number of patients without signs or symptoms of hospital-acquired infection, times 100
6	Routine chest X-ray ratio	Ratio of number of X-rays performed to number of patients without signs or symptoms of pneumonia, times 100
7	Number of beds	Average number of beds in hospital during study period
8	Medical school affiliation	1 = Yes, 2 = No
9	Region	Geographic region, where: 1 = NE, 2 = NC, 3 = S, 4 = W
10	Average daily census	Average number of patients in hospital per day during study period
11	Number of nurses	Average number of full-time equivalent registered and licensed practical nurses during study period (number full time plus one half the number part time)
12	Available facilities and services	Percent of 35 potential facilities and services that are provided by the hospital

Reference: Special Issue, "The SENIC Project," *American Journal of Epidemiology* 111 (1980), pp. 465–653. Data obtained from Robert W. Haley, M.D., Hospital Infections Program, Center for Infectious Diseases, Centers for Disease Control, Atlanta, Georgia 30333.

	1	2	3	4	5	6	7	8	9	10	11	12
	1	7.13	55.7	4.1	9.0	39.6	279	2	4	207	241	60.0
	2	8.82	58.2	1.6	3.8	51.7	80	2	2	51	52	40.0
	3	8.34	56.9	2.7	8.1	74.0	107	2	3	82	54	20.0
	...	...	...	...	...	...	...	...	...	...	...	...
	111	7.70	56.9	4.4	12.2	67.9	129	2	4	85	136	62.9
	112	17.94	56.2	5.9	26.4	91.8	835	1	1	791	407	62.9
	113	9.41	59.5	3.1	20.6	91.7	29	2	3	20	22	22.9

Data Set C.2   CDI

This data set provides selected county demographic information (CDI) for 440 of the most populous counties in the United States. Each line of the data set has an identification number with a county name and state abbreviation and provides information on 14 variables for a single county. Counties with missing data were deleted from the data set. The information generally pertains to the years 1990 and 1992. The 17 variables are:

Variable Number	Variable Name	Description
1	Identification number	1–440
2	County	County name
3	State	Two-letter state abbreviation
4	Land area	Land area (square miles)
5	Total population	Estimated 1990 population
6	Percent of population aged 18–34	Percent of 1990 CDI population aged 18–34
7	Percent of population 65 or older	Percent of 1990 CDI population aged 65 years old or older
8	Number of active physicians	Number of professionally active nonfederal physicians during 1990
9	Number of hospital beds	Total number of beds, cribs, and bassinets during 1990
10	Total serious crimes	Total number of serious crimes in 1990, including murder, rape, robbery, aggravated assault, burglary, larceny-theft, and motor vehicle theft, as reported by law enforcement agencies
11	Percent high school graduates	Percent of adult population (persons 25 years old or older) who completed 12 or more years of school
12	Percent bachelor's degrees	Percent of adult population (persons 25 years old or older) with bachelor's degree
13	Percent below poverty level	Percent of 1990 CDI population with income below poverty level
14	Percent unemployment	Percent of 1990 CDI labor force that is unemployed
15	Per capita income	Per capita income of 1990 CDI population (dollars)
16	Total personal income	Total personal income of 1990 CDI population (in millions of dollars)
17	Geographic region	Geographic region classification is that used by the U.S. Bureau of the Census, where: 1 = NE, 2 = NC, 3 = S, 4 = W

Source: Geospatial and Statistical Data Center, University of Virginia.

1	2	3	4	5	6	7	8	9	10
1	Los_Angeles	CA	4060	8863164	32.1	9.7	23677	27700	688936
2	Cook	IL	946	5105067	29.2	12.4	15153	21550	436936
3	Harris	TX	1729	2818199	31.3	7.1	7553	12449	253526
...	...	...	...	...	...	...	...	...	...
438	Montgomery	TN	539	100498	35.7	7.9	87	188	6537
439	Maui	HI	1159	100374	26.2	11.3	192	182	7130
440	Morgan	AL	582	100043	26.3	11.7	122	464	4693

11	12	13	14	15	16	17
70.0	22.3	11.6	8.0	20786	184230	4
73.4	22.8	11.1	7.2	21729	110928	2
74.9	25.4	12.5	5.7	19517	55003	3
...	...	...	...	...	...	...
77.9	16.5	10.8	8.0	13169	1323	3
77.0	17.8	5.7	3.2	18504	1857	4
69.4	15.5	9.4	7.1	16458	1647	3

Data Set C.3   Market Share

Company executives from a large packaged foods manufacturer wished to determine which factors influence the market share of one of its products. Data were collected from a national database (Nielsen) for 36 consecutive months. Each line of the data set has an identification number and provides information on 6 other variables for each month. The data presented here are for September, 1999, through August, 2002. The variables are:

Variable Number	Variable Name	Description
1	Identification number	1–36
2	Market share	Average monthly market share for product (percent)
3	Price	Average monthly price of product (dollars)
4	Gross Nielsen rating points	An index of the amount of advertising exposure that the product received
5	Discount price	Presence or absence of discount price during period: 1 if discount, 0 otherwise
6	Package promotion	Presence or absence of package promotion during period: 1 if promotion present, 0 otherwise
7	Month	Month (Jan–Dec)
8	Year	Year (1999–2002)

1	2	3	4	5	6	7	8
1	3.15	2.198	498	1	1	Sep	1999
2	2.52	2.186	510	0	0	Oct	1999
3	2.64	2.293	422	1	1	Nov	1999
...	...	...	...	...	...	...	...
34	2.80	2.518	270	1	0	Jun	2002
35	2.48	2.497	322	0	1	Jul	2002
36	2.85	2.781	317	1	1	Aug	2002

Data Set C.4 University Admissions

The director of admissions at a state university wanted to determine how accurately students' grade-point averages at the end of their freshman year could be predicted by entrance test scores and high school class rank. The academic years cover 1996 through 2000. Each line of the data set has an identification number and information on 4 other variables for each student. The 5 variables are:

Variable Number	Variable Name	Description
1	Identification number	1–705
2	GPA	Grade-point average following freshman year
3	High school class rank	High school class rank as percentile: lower percentiles imply higher class ranks
4	ACT score	ACT entrance examination score
5	Academic year	Calendar year that freshman entered university

1	2	3	4	5
1	0.980	61	20	1996
2	1.130	84	20	1996
3	1.250	74	19	1996
...	...	...	...	...
703	4.000	97	29	2000
704	4.000	97	29	2000
705	4.000	99	32	2000

Data Set C.5 Prostate Cancer

A university medical center urology group was interested in the association between prostate-specific antigen (PSA) and a number of prognostic clinical measurements in men with advanced prostate cancer. Data were collected on 97 men who were about to undergo radical prostectomies. Each line of the data set has an identification number and provides information on 8 other variables for each person. The 9 variables are:

Variable Number	Variable Name	Description
1	Identification number	1–97
2	PSA level	Serum prostate-specific antigen level (mg/ml)
3	Cancer volume	Estimate of prostate cancer volume (cc)
4	Weight	Prostate weight (gm)
5	Age	Age of patient (years)
6	Benign prostatic hyperplasia	Amount of benign prostatic hyperplasia (cm^2)
7	Seminal vesicle invasion	Presence or absence of seminal vesicle invasion: 1 if yes; 0 otherwise
8	Capsular penetration	Degree of capsular penetration (cm)
9	Gleason score	Pathologically determined grade of disease using total score of two patterns (summed scores were either 6, 7, or 8 with higher scores indicating worse prognosis)

1	2	3	4	5	6	7	8	9
1	0.651	0.5599	15.959	50	0	0	0	6
2	0.852	0.3716	27.660	58	0	0	0	7
3	0.852	0.6005	14.732	74	0	0	0	7
...	...	...	...	...	...	...	...	...
95	170.716	18.3568	29.964	52	0	1	11.7048	8
96	239.847	17.8143	43.380	68	4.7588	1	4.7588	8
97	265.072	32.1367	52.985	68	1.5527	1	18.1741	8

Adapted in part from: Hastie, T. J.; R. J. Tibshirani; and J. Friedman. *The Elements of Statistical Learning: Data Mining, Inference, and Prediction.* New York: Springer-Verlag, 2001.

Data Set C.6   Website Developer

Management of a company that develops websites was interested in determining which variables have the greatest impact on the number of websites developed and delivered to customers per quarter. Data were collected on website production output for 13 three-person website development teams, from January 2001 through August 2002. Each line of the data set has an identification number and provides information on 6 other variables for thirteen teams over time. The 8 variables are:

Variable Number	Variable Name	Description
1	Identification number	1–73
2	Websites delivered	Number of websites completed and delivered to customers during the quarter
3	Backlog of orders	Number of website orders in backlog at the close of the quarter
4	Team number	1–13
5	Team experience	Number of months team has been together
6	Process change	A change in the website development process occurred during the second quarter of 2002: 1 if quarter 2 or 3, 2002; 0 otherwise
7	Year	2001 or 2002
8	Quarter	1, 2, 3, or 4

1	2	3	4	5	6	7	8
1	1	12	1	3	0	2001	1
2	2	18	1	6	0	2001	2
3	7	26	1	9	0	2001	3
...	...	...	...	...	...	...	...
71	7	36	13	14	0	2002	1
72	19	37	13	17	1	2002	2
73	12	26	13	20	1	2002	3

Data Set C.7   Real Estate Sales

The city tax assessor was interested in predicting residential home sales prices in a midwestern city as a function of various characteristics of the home and surrounding property. Data on 522 arms-length transactions were obtained for home sales during the year 2002. Each line of the data set has an identification number and provides information on 12 other variables. The 13 variables are:

Variable Number	Variable Name	Description
1	Identification number	1–522
2	Sales price	Sales price of residence (dollars)
3	Finished square feet	Finished area of residence (square feet)
4	Number of bedrooms	Total number of bedrooms in residence
5	Number of bathrooms	Total number of bathrooms in residence
6	Air conditioning	Presence or absence of air conditioning: 1 if yes; 0 otherwise
7	Garage size	Number of cars that garage will hold
8	Pool	Presence or absence of swimming pool: 1 if yes; 0 otherwise
9	Year built	Year property was originally constructed
10	Quality	Index for quality of construction: 1 indicates high quality; 2 indicates medium quality; 3 indicates low quality
11	Style	Qualitative indicator of architectural style
12	Lot size	Lot size (square feet)
13	Adjacent to highway	Presence or absence of adjacency to highway: 1 if yes; 0 otherwise

1	2	3	4	5	6	7	8	9	10	11	12	13
1	360000	3032	4	4	1	2	0	1972	2	1	22221	0
2	340000	2058	4	2	1	2	0	1976	2	1	22912	0
3	250000	1780	4	3	1	2	0	1980	2	1	21345	0
...	...	...	...	...	...	...	...	...	...	...	...	...
520	133500	1922	3	1	0	2	0	1950	3	1	14805	0
521	124000	1480	3	2	1	2	0	1953	3	1	28351	0
522	95500	1184	2	1	0	1	0	1951	3	1	14786	0

Data Set C.8   Heating Equipment

A manufacturer of heating equipment was interested in forecasting the volume of monthly orders as a function of various economic indicators, supply-chain factors, and weather in a particular sales region. Data by month over a four-year period (1999–2002) for this region were available for analysis. Each line of the data set has an identification number and provides information on 9 other variables. The 10 variables are:

Variable Number	Variable Name	Description
1	Identification number	1–43
2	Number of orders	Number of heating equipment orders during month
3	Interest rate	Prime rate in effect during month
4	New homes	Number of new homes completed and for sale in sales region during month
5	Discount	Percent discount (0–5) offered to distributors during month; value is usually 0, indicating no discount
6	Inventories	Distributor inventories in warehouses during month
7	Sell through	Number of units sold by distributor to contractors in previous month
8	Temperature deviation	Difference between average temperature for month and 30-year average for that month
9	Year	1999, 2000, 2001, or 2002
10	Month	Coded 1–12

	1	2	3	4	5	6	7	8	9	10
	1	121	0.0750	64	0	3536	615	2.22	1999	1
	2	227	0.0750	64	0	3042	813	0.28	1999	2
	3	446	0.0750	65	0	2456	704	0.79	1999	3
	…	…	…	…	…	…	…	…	…	…
	41	754	0.0475	64	0	1417	927	0.81	2002	6
	42	1098	0.0475	65	0	1244	877	0.28	2002	7
	43	1158	0.0475	65	0	1465	809	0.50	2002	8

Data Set C.9   Ischemic Heart Disease

A health insurance company collected information on 788 of its subscribers who had made claims resulting from ischemic (coronary) heart disease. Data were obtained on total costs of services provided for these 788 subscribers and the nature of the various services for the period of January 1, 1998 through December 31, 1999. Each line in the data set has an identification number and provides information on 9 other variables for each subscriber. The 10 variables are:

Variable Number	Variable Name	Description
1	Identification number	1–788
2	Total cost	Total cost of claims by subscriber (dollars)
3	Age	Age of subscriber (years)
4	Gender	Gender of subscriber: 1 if male; 0 otherwise
5	Interventions	Total number of interventions or procedures carried out
6	Drugs	Number of tracked drugs prescribed
7	Emergency room visits	Number of emergency room visits
8	Complications	Number of other complications that arose during heart disease treatment
9	Comorbidities	Number of other diseases that the subscriber had during period
10	Duration	Number of days of duration of treatment condition

1	2	3	4	5	6	7	8	9	10
1	179.1	63	0	2	1	4	0	3	300
2	319.0	59	0	2	0	6	0	0	120
3	9310.7	62	0	17	0	2	0	5	353
...	...	...	...	...	...	...	...	...	...
786	2677.7	68	0	3	2	6	0	10	303
787	1282.2	58	0	7	2	2	0	7	244
788	586.0	56	0	4	4	6	0	3	336

Data Set C.10   Disease Outbreak

This data set provides information from a study based on 196 persons selected in a probability sample within two sectors in a city. Each line of the data set has an identification number and provides information on 5 other variables for a single person. The 6 variables are:

Variable Number	Variable Name	Description
1	Identification number	1–196
2	Age	Age of person (in years)
3	Socioeconomic status	1 = upper, 2 = middle, 3 = lower
4	Sector	Sector within city, where: 1 = sector 1, 2 = sector 2
5	Disease status	1 = with disease, 0 = without disease
6	Savings account status	1 = has savings account, 0 = does not have savings account

Adapted in part from H. G. Dantes, J. S. Koopman, C. L. Addy, et al., "Dengue Epidemics on the Pacific Coast of Mexico," *International Journal of Epidemiology* 17 (1988), pp. 178–86.

1	2	3	4	5	6
1	33	1	1	0	1
2	35	1	1	0	1
3	6	1	1	0	0
...	...	...	...	...	...
194	31	3	1	0	0
195	85	3	1	0	1
196	24	2	1	0	0

Data Set C.11   IPO

Private companies often go public by issuing shares of stock referred to as initial public offerings (IPOs). A study of 482 IPOs was conducted to determine what are the characteristics of companies that attract venture capital funding. The response of interest is whether or not a company was financed with venture capital funds. Potential predictors include the face value of the company, the number of shares offered, and whether or not the company underwent a leveraged buyout. Each line of the data set has an identification number and provides information on 4 other variables for a single person. The 5 variables are:

Variable Number	Variable Name	Description
1	Identification number	1–482
2	Venture capital funding	Presence or absence of venture capital funding: 1 if yes; 0 otherwise
3	Face value of company	Estimated face value of company from prospectus (in dollars)
4	Number of shares offered	Total number of shares offered
5	Leveraged buyout	Presence or absence of leveraged buyout: 1 if yes; 0 otherwise

1	2	3	4	5
1	0	1,200,000	3,000,000	0
2	0	1,454,000	1,454,000	1
3	0	1,500,000	300,000	0
. . .	. . .	. . .	. . .	. . .
480	0	159,500,000	7,250,000	0
481	0	165,000,000	11,000,000	0
482	0	234,600,000	9,200,000	0

Appendix D

Selected Bibliography

The selected references are grouped into the following categories:

1. General regression books
2. General linear models books
3. Diagnostics and model building
4. Statistical computing
5. Nonlinear regression
6. Miscellaneous regression topics

1. General Regression Books

Allison, P. D. *Multiple Regression: A Primer*. Thousand Oaks, Calif.: Sage Publications, 1999.

Bowerman, B. L., and R. T. O'Connell. *Linear Statistical Models: An Applied Approach*. 2nd ed. Boston: Duxbury Press, 1990.

Chatterjee, S.; A. S. Hadi; and B. Price. *Regression Analysis by Example*. 3rd. ed. New York: John Wiley & Sons, 1999.

Cohen, J.; P. Cohen; S. G. West; and L. S. Aiken. *Applied Multiple Regression/ Correlation Analysis for the Behavioral Sciences*. 3rd ed. Hillsdale, NJ: Lawrence Erlbaum Associates, 2003.

Cook, R. D., and S. Weisberg. *Applied Regression Including Computing and Graphics*. New York: John Wiley & Sons, 1999.

Daniel, C., and F. S. Wood. *Fitting Equations to Data: Computer Analysis of Multifactor Data*. 2nd ed. New York: John Wiley & Sons, 1999.

Draper, N. R., and H. Smith. *Applied Regression Analysis*. 3rd ed. New York: John Wiley & Sons, 1998.

Freund, R. J., and R. C. Littell. *SAS System for Regression*. 3rd ed. New York: John Wiley & Sons, 2000.

Graybill, F. A., and H. Iyer. *Regression Analysis: Concepts and Applications*. Belmont, Calif.: Duxbury Press, 1994.

Hamilton, L. C. *Regression with Graphics: A Second Course in Applied Statistics*. Pacific Grove, Calif.: Brooks/Cole Publishing, 1992.

Kleinbaum, D. G.; L. L. Kupper; K. E. Muller; and A. Nizam. *Applied Regression Analysis and Other Multivariate Methods*. 3rd ed. Belmont, Calif.: Duxbury Press, 1998.

Mendenhall, W., and T. Sincich. *A Second Course in Business Statistics: Regression Analysis*. 5th ed. Upper Saddle River, New Jersey: Prentice Hall, 1996.

Muller, K. E., and B. A. Fetterman. *Regression and ANOVA: An Integrated Approach Using SAS Software*. New York: John Wiley & Sons, 2003.

Myers, R. H. *Classical and Modern Regression with Applications*. 2nd ed. Boston: Duxbury Press, 1990.

Pedhazur, E. J. *Multiple Regression in Behavioral Research*. 3rd ed. Belmont, Calif.: Duxbury Press, 1997.

Rawlings, J. O.; S. G. Pantula; and D. A. Dickey. *Applied Regression Analysis: A Research Tool*. New York: Springer-Verlag, 1998.

Ryan, T. P. *Modern Regression Methods*. New York: John Wiley & Sons, 1997.

Seber, G. A. F., and A. S. Lee. *Linear Regression Analysis*. 2nd ed. New York: John Wiley & Sons, 2003.

Sen, A., and M. Srivastava. *Regression Analysis: Theory, Methods, and Applications*. 4th ed. New York: Springer-Verlag, 1997.

2. General Linear Models Books

Graybill, F. A. *Theory and Application of the Linear Model*. Boston: Duxbury Press, 1976.

Hocking, R. R. *Methods and Applications of Linear Models: Regression and the Analysis of Variance*. 2nd ed. New York: John Wiley & Sons, 2003.

Littell, R. C.; W. W. Stroup; and R. J. Freund. *SAS System for Linear Models*. 4th ed. New York: John Wiley & Sons, 2002.

Searle, S. R. *Linear Models*. New York: John Wiley & Sons, 1997.

Searle, S. R. *Linear Models for Unbalanced Data*. New York: John Wiley & Sons, 1987.

3. Diagnostics and Model Building

Allen, D. M. "Mean Square Error of Prediction as a Criterion for Selecting Variables." *Technometrics* 13 (1971), pp. 469–75.

Anscombe, F. J., and J. W. Tukey. "The Examination and Analysis of Residuals." *Technometrics* 5 (1963), pp. 141–60.

Atkinson, A. C. "Two Graphical Displays for Outlying and Influential Observations in Regression." *Biometrika* 68 (1981), pp. 13–20.

Atkinson, A. C. *Plots, Transformations, and Regression*. Oxford: Clarendon Press, 1987.

Barnett, V., and T. Lewis. *Outliers in Statistical Data*. 3rd ed. New York: John Wiley & Sons, 1994.

Belsley, D. A. *Conditioning Diagnostics: Collinearity and Weak Data in Regression*. New York: John Wiley & Sons, 1991.

Belsley, D. A.; E. Kuh; and R. E. Welsch. *Regression Diagnostics: Identifying Influential Data and Sources of Collinearity*. New York: John Wiley & Sons, 1980.

Box, G. E. P., and D. R. Cox. "An Analysis of Transformations." *Journal of the Royal Statistical Society B* 26 (1964), pp. 211–43.

Box, G. E. P., and N. R. Draper. *Empirical Model-Building and Response Surfaces*. New York: John Wiley & Sons, 1987.

Box, G. E. P., and P. W. Tidwell. "Transformations of the Independent Variables." *Technometrics* 4 (1962), pp. 531–50.

Breiman, L., and P. Spector. "Submodel Selection and Evaluation in Regression: The *X*-Random Case." *International Statistical Review* 60 (1992), pp. 291–319.

Breusch, T. S., and A. R. Pagan. "A Simple Test for Heteroscedasticity and Random Coefficient Variation." *Econometrica* 47 (1979), pp. 1287–94.

Brown, M. B., and A. B. Forsythe. "Robust Tests for Equality of Variances." *Journal of the American Statistical Association* 69 (1974), pp. 364–67.

Carroll, R. J., and D. Ruppert. *Transformation and Weighting in Regression*. New York: Chapman & Hall, 1988.

Chatterjee, S., and A. S. Hadi. *Sensitivity Analysis in Linear Regression*. New York: John Wiley & Sons, 1988.

Conover, W. J.; M. E. Johnson; and M. M. Johnson. "A Comparative Study of Tests for Homogeneity of Variances, with Applications to the Outer Continental Shelf Bidding Data." *Technometrics* 23 (1981), pp. 351–61.

Cook, R. D. "Exploring Partial Residual Plots." *Technometrics* 35 (1993), pp. 351–62.

Cook, R. D., and S. Weisberg. "Diagnostics for Heteroscedasticity in Regression." *Biometrika* 70 (1983), pp. 1–10.

Cox, D. R. *Planning of Experiments*. New York: John Wiley & Sons, 1958.

Davidian, M., and R. J. Carroll. "Variance Function Estimation." *Journal of the American Statistical Association* 82 (1987), pp. 1079–91.

Durbin, J., and G. S. Watson. "Testing for Serial Correlation in Least Squares Regression. II." *Biometrika* 38 (1951), pp. 159–78.

Faraway, J. J. "On the Cost of Data Analysis." *Journal of Computational and Graphical Statistics* 1 (1992), pp. 213–29.

Flack, V. F., and P. C. Chang. "Frequency of Selecting Noise Variables in Subset-Regression Analysis: A Simulation Study." *The American Statistician* 41 (1987), pp. 84–86.

Freedman, D. A. "A Note on Screening Regression Equations." *The American Statistician* 37 (1983), pp. 152–55.

Hoaglin, D. C.; F. Mosteller; and J. W. Tukey. *Exploring Data Tables, Trends, and Shapes*. New York: John Wiley & Sons, 1985.

Hoaglin, D. C., and R. Welsch. "The Hat Matrix in Regression and ANOVA." *The American Statistician* 32 (1978), pp. 17–22.

Hocking, R. R. "The Analysis and Selection of Variables in Linear Regression." *Biometrics* 32 (1976), pp. 1–49.

Hoerl, A. E., and R. W. Kennard. "Ridge Regression: Applications to Nonorthogonal Problems." *Technometrics* 12 (1970), pp. 69–82.

Joglekar, G.; J. H. Schuenemeyer; and V. LaRiccia. "Lack-of-Fit Testing When Replicates Are Not Available." *The American Statistician* 43 (1989), pp. 135–43.

Levene, H. "Robust Tests for Equality of Variances," in *Contributions to Probability and Statistics,* ed. I. Olkin. Palo Alto, Calif.: Stanford University Press, 1960, pp. 278–92.

Lindsay, R. M., and A. S. C. Ehrenberg. "The Design of Replicated Studies." *The American Statistician* 47 (1993), pp. 217–28.

Looney, S. W., and T. R. Gulledge, Jr. "Use of the Correlation Coefficient with Normal Probability Plots." *The American Statistician* 39 (1985), pp. 75–79.

Mallows, C. L. "Some Comments on C_p." *Technometrics* 15 (1973), pp. 661–75.

Mansfield, E. R., and M. D. Conerly. "Diagnostic Value of Residual and Partial Residual Plots." *The American Statistician* 41 (1987), pp. 107–16.

Mantel, N. "Why Stepdown Procedures in Variable Selection." *Technometrics* 12 (1970), pp. 621–25.

Miller, A. J. *Subset Selection in Regression.* 2nd ed. London: Chapman & Hall, 2002.

Pope, P. T., and J. T. Webster. "The Use of an F-Statistic in Stepwise Regression Procedures." *Technometrics* 14 (1972), pp. 327–40.

Rousseeuw, P. J., and A. M. Leroy. *Robust Regression and Outlier Detection.* New York: John Wiley & Sons, 1987.

Shapiro, S. S., and M. B. Wilk. "An Analysis of Variance Test for Normality (Complete Samples)." *Biometrika* 52 (1965), pp. 591–611.

Snee, R. D. "Validation of Regression Models: Methods and Examples." *Technometrics* 19 (1977), pp. 415–28.

Stone, M. "Cross-Validatory Choice and Assessment of Statistical Prediction." *Journal of the Royal Statistical Society B* 36 (1974), pp. 111–47.

Velleman, P. F., and D. C. Hoaglin. *Applications, Basics, and Computing of Exploratory Data Analysis.* Boston: Duxbury Press, 1981.

4. Statistical Computing

BMDP New System 2.0. Statistical Solutions, Inc.

JMP Version 5. SAS Institute Inc.

Kennedy, W. J., and J. E. Gentle. *Statistical Computing.* New York: Marcel Dekker, 1980.

LogXact 5. Cytel Software Corporation. Cambridge, Massachusetts, 2003.

MATLAB 6.5. The MathWorks, Inc.

MINITAB Release 13. Minitab Inc.

S-Plus 6 for Windows. Insightful Corporation

SAS/STAT Release 8.2. SAS Institute, Inc.

SPSS 11.5 for Windows. SPSS Inc.

SYSTAT 10.2. SYSTAT Software Inc.

Tierney, L. *LISP-STAT: An Object-Oriented Environment for Statistical Computing and Dynamic Graphics.* New York: John Wiley & Sons, 1990.

5. Nonlinear Regression

Allison, P. D. *Logistic Regression Using the SAS System: Theory and Applications*. New York: John Wiley & Sons, 1999.

Bates, D. M., and D. G. Watts. *Nonlinear Regression Analysis and Its Applications*. New York: John Wiley & Sons, 1988.

Begg, C. B., and R. Gray. "Calculation of Polytomous Logistic Regression Parameters Using Individualized Regressions." *Biometrika* 71 (1984), pp. 11–18.

Box, M. J. "Bias in Nonlinear Estimation." *Journal of the Royal Statistical Society B* 33 (1971), pp. 171–201.

DeVeaux, R. D., Schumi, J., Schweinsberg, J., and L. H. Ungar. "Prediction Intervals for Neural Networks via Nonlinear Regression." *Technometrics* 40 (1998), pp. 273–82.

DeVeaux, R. D., and L. H. Ungar. "A Brief Introduction to Neural Networks," http://www.williams.edu/Mathematics/rdeveaux/pubs.html (1996).

Gallant, A. R. "Nonlinear Regression." *The American Statistician* 29 (1975), pp. 73–81.

Gallant, A. R. *Nonlinear Statistical Models*. New York: John Wiley & Sons, 1987.

Halperin, M.; W. C. Blackwelder; and J. I. Verter. "Estimation of the Multivariate Logistic Risk Function: A Comparison of Discriminant Function and Maximum Likelihood Approaches." *Journal of Chronic Diseases* 24 (1971), pp. 125–58.

Hartley, H. O. "The Modified Gauss-Newton Method for the Fitting of Non-linear Regression Functions by Least Squares." *Technometrics* 3 (1961), pp. 269–80.

Hosmer, D. W., and S. Lemeshow. "Goodness of Fit Tests for the Multiple Logistic Regression Model." *Communications in Statistics A* 9 (1980), pp. 1043–69.

Hosmer, D. W., and S. Lemeshow. *Applied Logistic Regression*. 2nd ed. New York: John Wiley & Sons, 2000.

Hougaard, P. "The Appropriateness of the Asymptotic Distribution in a Nonlinear Regression Model in Relation to Curvature." *Journal of the Royal Statistical Society B* 47 (1985), pp. 103–14.

Kleinbaum, D. G.; L. L. Kupper; and L. E. Chambless. "Logistic Regression Analysis of Epidemiologic Data: Theory and Practice." *Communications in Statistics A* 11 (1982), pp. 485–547.

Landwehr, J. M.; D. Pregibon; and A. C. Shoemaker. "Graphical Methods for Assessing Logistic Regression Models (with discussion)." *Journal of the American Statistical Association* 79 (1984), pp. 61–83.

Marquardt, D. W. "An Algorithm for Least Squares Estimation of Non-linear Parameters." *Journal of the Society of Industrial and Applied Mathematics* 11 (1963), pp. 431–41.

Menard, S. *Applied Logistic Regression Analysis*. Thousand Oaks, Calif.: Sage Publications, 1995.

Pregibon, D. "Logistic Regression Diagnostics." *Annals of Statistics* 9 (1981), pp. 705–24.

Prentice, R. L. "Use of the Logistic Model in Retrospective Studies." *Biometrics* 32 (1976), pp. 599–606.

Ratkowsky, D. A. *Nonlinear Regression Modeling*. New York: Marcel Dekker, 1983.

Truett, J.; J. Cornfield; and W. Kannel. "A Multivariate Analysis of the Risk of Coronary Heart Disease in Framingham." *Journal of Chronic Diseases* 20 (1967), pp. 511–24.

6. Miscellaneous Regression Topics

Agresti, A. *Categorical Data Analysis*. 2nd ed. New York: John Wiley & Sons, 2002.

Altman, N. S. "An Introduction to Kernel and Nearest-Neighbor Nonparametric Regression." *The American Statistician* 46 (1992), pp. 175–85.

Berkson, J. "Are There Two Regressions?" *Journal of the American Statistical Association* 45 (1950), pp. 164–80.

Bishop, Y. M. M.; S. E. Fienberg; and P. W. Holland. *Discrete Multivariate Analysis: Theory and Practice*. Cambridge, Mass.: MIT Press, 1975.

Box, G. E. P. "Use and Abuse of Regression." *Technometrics* 8 (1966), pp. 625–29.

Box, G. E. P., and G. M. Jenkins. *Time Series Analysis, Forecasting and Control*. 3rd ed. San Francisco: Holden-Day, 1994.

Breiman, L.; J. H. Friedman; R. A. Olshen; and C. J. Stone. *Classification and Regression Trees*. New York: Chapman & Hall, 1993.

Christensen, R. *Log-Linear Models and Logistic Regression*. 2nd ed. New York: Springer-Verlag, 1997.

Cleveland, W. S. "Robust Locally Weighted Regression and Smoothing Scatterplots." *Journal of the American Statistical Association* 74 (1979), pp. 829–36.

Cleveland, W. S., and S. J. Devlin. "Locally Weighted Regression: An Approach to Regression Analysis by Local Fitting." *Journal of the American Statistical Association* 83 (1988), pp. 596–610.

Collett, D. *Modelling Binary Data*. 2nd ed. London: Chapman & Hall, 2002.

Cox, D. R. "Notes on Some Aspects of Regression Analysis." *Journal of the Royal Statistical Society A* 131 (1968), pp. 265–79.

Cox, D. R. *The Analysis of Binary Data*. 2nd ed. London: Chapman & Hall, 1989.

Efron, B. *The Jackknife, The Bootstrap, and Other Resampling Plans*. Philadelphia: Society for Industrial and Applied Mathematics, 1982.

Efron, B. "Better Bootstrap Confidence Intervals" (with discussion). *Journal of the American Statistical Association* 82 (1987), pp. 171–200.

Efron, B., and R. Tibshirani. "Bootstrap Methods for Standard Errors, Confidence Intervals, and Other Measures of Statistical Accuracy." *Statistical Science* 1 (1986), pp. 54–77.

Efron, B., and R. J. Tibshirani. *An Introduction to the Bootstrap*. New York: Chapman & Hall, 1993.

Eubank, R. L. *Nonparametric Regression and Spline Smoothing*. 2nd ed. New York: Marcel Dekker, 1999.

Finney, D. J. *Probit Analysis*. 3rd ed. Cambridge, England: Cambridge University Press, 1971.

Frank, I. E., and J. H. Friedman. "A Statistical View of Some Chemometrics Regression Tools." *Technometrics* 35 (1993), pp. 109–35.

Friedman, J. H., and W. Stuetzle. "Projection Pursuit Regression." *Journal of the American Statistical Association* 76 (1981), pp. 817–23.

Fuller, W. A. *Measurement Error Models*. New York: John Wiley & Sons, 1987.

Gibbons, J. D. *Nonparametric Methods for Quantitative Analysis*. 2nd ed. Columbus, Ohio: American Sciences Press, 1985.

Graybill, F. A. *Matrices with Applications in Statistics*. 2nd ed. Belmont, Calif.: Duxbury Press, 2001.

Greene, W. H. *Econometric Analysis*. 5th ed. Upper Saddle River, NJ: Prentice Hall, 2003.

Haerdle, W. *Applied Nonparametric Regression*. Cambridge, England: Cambridge University Press, 1990.

Harrell, F. E. *Regression Modeling Strategies: With Application to Linear Models, Logistic Regression, and Survival Analysis*. New York: Springer-Verlag, 2001.

Hastie, T., and C. Loader. "Local Regression: Automatic Kernel Carpentry" (with discussion). *Statistical Science* 8 (1993), pp. 120–43.

Hastie, T. J., and R. J. Tibshirani. *Generalized Additive Models*. New York: Chapman & Hall, 1990.

Hastie, T. J.; R. J. Tibshirani; and J. Friedman. *The Elements of Statistical Learning: Data Mining, Inference, and Prediction*. New York: Springer-Verlag, 2001.

Hochberg, Y., and A. C. Tamhane. *Multiple Comparison Procedures*. John Wiley & Sons, 1987.

Hogg, R. V. "Statistical Robustness: One View of Its Use in Applications Today." *The American Statistician* 33 (1979), pp. 108–15.

Johnson, R. A., and D. W. Wichern. *Applied Multivariate Statistical Analysis*. 5th ed. Englewood Cliffs, NJ: Prentice-Hall, 2002.

Kendall, M. G., and J. D. Gibbons. *Rank Correlation Methods*. 5th ed. London: Oxford University Press, 1990.

Lachenbruch, P. A. *Discriminant Analysis*. New York: Hafner Press, 1975.

McCulloch, P., and J. A. Nelder. *Generalized Linear Models*. 2nd ed. New York: Chapman & Hall, 1989.

Miller, R. G., Jr. *Simultaneous Statistical Inference*. 2nd ed. New York: Springer-Verlag, 1991.

Nelder, J. A., and R. W. M. Wedderburn. "Generalized Linear Models." *Journal of the Royal Statistical Society A* 135 (1972), pp. 370–84.

Pindyck, R. S., and D. L. Rubinfeld. *Econometric Models and Economic Forecasts*. 4th ed. New York: McGraw-Hill, 1997.

Satterthwaite, F. E. "An Approximate Distribution of Estimates of Variance Components." *Biometrics Bulletin* 2 (1946), pp. 110–14.

Searle, S. R. *Matrix Algebra Useful for Statistics*. New York: John Wiley & Sons, 1982.

Snedecor, G. W., and W. G. Cochran. *Statistical Methods*. 8th ed. Ames, Iowa: Iowa State University Press, 1989.

Theil, H., and A. L. Nagar. "Testing the Independence of Regression Disturbances." *Journal of the American Statistical Association* 56 (1961), pp. 793–806.

Index

Description of CD Contents

This compact disc contains the Student Solutions Manual in Adobe portable document (pdf) format and data files in ASCII format for the book:

Applied Linear Regression Models, 4/E by Kutner, Nachtsheim, and Neter, McGraw-Hill/Irwin c 2004.

All files on the compact disc can also be downloaded from the book's website:

http://www.mhhe.com/kutnerALRM4e

The Student Solutions Manual is in the file named STUSOLNS.pdf. The Student Solutions Manual provides intermediate and final numerical results for easy self-checking of solutions for selected problems. We use an asterisk (*) in front of the problem number to designate the problems for which the solutions appear in the Student Solutions Manual.

The compact disc also includes the data set files for all text examples, the data sets for the problems, exercises, projects, and case studies at the end of chapters, and the data sets in Appendix C. The data in a data set are arranged in columns that are separated by spaces. The ordering of the columns (variables) can be readily ascertained from the tabular display of the data set in the text since the text always provides the data for at least the initial and final cases.

Data sets have names in one of the following formats, depending on whether the data pertain to a problem, a table, a figure, or an appendix (xx denotes the number):

CHxxPRxx   For data sets from end-of-chapter problems, exercises, and projects.
         Example: CH04PR12 denotes the data set for Problem 4.12 in Chapter 4.

ChxxTAxx   For data sets from text tables.
         Example: CH12TA02 denotes the data set for Table 12.2 in Chapter 12.

ChxxFIxx   For data sets from text figures.
         Example: CH06FI05 denotes the data set for Figure 6.5 in Chapter 6.

APPENCxx   For data sets from Appendix C.
         Example: APPENC09 denotes the data set in Appendix C.9.

All data set file names are followed by the extension .TXT, indicating that the file is a text file.

These directions are also provided in the file README.TXT, which is included on the compact disc.